U1065289

中国植物分类学者

CHINESE PLANT TAXONOMISTS

主编
杜诚　马金双

Editors in Chief
DU Cheng & MA Jin Shuang

高等教育出版社·北京

This Book is Sponsored by

Shanghai Chenshan Botanical Garden

上海辰山植物园

Shanghai Chenshan Plant Science Research Center, Chinese Academy of Sciences

中国科学院上海辰山植物科学研究中心

Special Fund for Scientific Research of Shanghai Landscaping & City Appearance Administrative Bureau (G182416, G182415)

上海市绿化和市容管理局科研专项
(G182416，G182415)

Abstract

This book in two parts and with four appendices contains systematic data on Chinese plant taxonomists, updates an earlier account published since 1916. It includes the names of 2,862 authors who published new names of vascular plants and 2,669 plant collectors and members of the staff of herbaria.

Part Ⅰ contains information on the 2,862 authors, including standard form of the name, accepted transliterated name into the Western alphabet, other forms of romanization, accepted Chinese name, standard pinyin form, other Chinese names, year of birth and death (when known), year of first publication, employment history, research interest, published taxa, author's institution, location of author's collections, geographic region, and other ancillary information.

Part Ⅱ provides information on 2,669 Chinese plant collectors, collection teams and staff of herbaria, excluding those in Part I. Some collectors who published the names of mosses, algae and fungi are also in this section along with relevant detailed information.

Appendix Ⅰ is an account of institutional name changes.

Appendix Ⅱ provides the name, history and international acronym of the Chinese herbaria.

Appendix Ⅲ is an index to detailed information based on the standard form or other abbreviations of a person's name.

Appendix Ⅳ is an index to detailed information based on the Romanized spelling of the person's name.

To aid as a reference, this book attempts to present a standardized spelling for the names of all Chinese authors who have proposed new taxa of vascular plants.

内容简介

本书系统的整理了自 1916 年首篇中国植物命名相关文章发表以来几乎所有的植物分类学者的完整资料，其中命名过维管植物的中国学者 2 862 人，中国植物采集人或植物标本馆工作人员 2 669 人。

本书由正文分为 2 个部分。第一部分是 2 862 位命名过中国维管植物的学者信息，包括标准拼写形式、公认的罗马化名称、其他罗马化形式、中文姓名、标准拼音形式、中文姓名其他形式、生卒年份、首次出版年份、所隶属的研究机构（根据出版物给出）、研究兴趣领域、已发表的分类群、隶属的标本馆、标本的保藏地、研究类群的地理区域、其他缩写形式等。第二部分是除了上述发表过维管植物类群的其他 2 669 名中国植物采集人、采集团队和标本馆工作人员的信息。其中有些学者是苔藓、藻类和真菌的命名人，这些命名人详细信息的排版方式与第一部分一致。

本书包含 4 个附录。分别是中国的植物学研究机构及名称沿革，中国植物标本馆，中国植物分类学者标准拼写索引，中国植物分类学者名称罗马拼写索引。

本书一方面可用于在植物学名中对中国学者的引证提供标准拼写建议；另一方面便于后来学者在使用自己姓名时，查阅是否有重名现象的存在，从源头上避免重名。

Editors

Editors in Chief

DU Cheng & MA Jin Shuang

Vice Editors in Chief

LIU Jun, LIAO Shuai, LIU Bing, LI Li & CHEN Jian Ping

编写者

主编

杜诚　马金双

副主编

刘军　廖帅　刘冰　李莉　陈建平

Preface

Author citations should be included where precision is needed and confusion is to be avoided, or, to quote the International Code of Nomenclature for algae, fungi, and plants, "In publications, particularly those dealing with taxonomy and nomenclature, it may be desirable, even when no bibliographic reference to the protologue is made, to cite the author(s) of the name concerned" (Art. 46.1). It is also recommended by the Code, "When it is a well-established custom to abridge a name in another manner, it is advisable to conform to custom." (Rec. 46A.4.) There are also some detailed recommendations for the romanization of an author's names (Rec. 46B.1, 46B.2), and it is recommended to establish a standard form of an author's names according to Authors of plant names (1992) (Rec. 46A.4. note 1). Therefore, in publications dealing with classification and nomenclature, the Latin names of plants are always closely related to the Romanized transliterated name of the author(s).

Chinese botanists have been formally associated with plant names since Sung Shu Chien published the first modern taxonomic paper in China in 1916. At that time, Romanization of Chinese names was mainly based on the Wade–Giles system of Romanization mixed with the pronunciation customs of various regions, particularly in the pronunciation of Wu and Canton languages. Such non-standard Romanizations of the name of Chinese plant taxonomists are quite different from the current Chinese phonetic form.

The Scheme of the Chinese Phonetic Alphabet has been in use since 1958, and by the end of the 1970s, it has become the standard Romanized form of Chinese names and is recognized internationally. However, in Taiwan and Hong Kong, this system has been only partially adopted, while other scholars continued to use the Tongyong Pinyin system or other local Chinese romanization systems. The Romanized names of older scholars of mainland China are also maintained in their original style to avoid confusion. The Chinese phonetic alphabet spelling rules for Chinese names (GB/T 28039-2011) was implemented in 2012. It regulates the use of the Western alphabet to transliterate Chinese names in standard form. In particular, it stipulates that the family name is placed first followed by the given name(s) in the Scheme of the Chinese Phonetic Alphabet. However, the standard also allows for the romanization of Chinese names in biological sciences to be modified.

In recent years, many young scholars have discovered and named plant species. Although most young scholars have adopted the national standard spelling system, the short syllable characteristics of Chinese characters and the popularity of two-character given names have caused duplication among contemporary plant taxonomists. To resolve the problem of duplicate names, the names of Chinese authors have been standardized in the International

Plant Names Index (IPNI). However, understanding Chinese characters, documents and customs by non-Chinese is still limited. Chinese scholars have independently established a standard form of Romanization for their names.

For this reason, we have compiled this book, Chinese Plant Taxonomists, under the premise that the standard spelling in internationally accepted IPNI is accepted so that the spelling of the 2,862 Chinese authors of vascular plant names is uniform.

The principles are:

1. In accordance with tradition, in Romanized spelling of Chinese names, the given name(s) comes first followed by the family name.
2. On the premise that there is no duplicate name, abbreviate each Chinese character of the given name. If an abbreviated name results in the duplication of an earlier name, the name of the later author will spelled in full. If a duplication remains after the first character is spelled out, the second character is transliterated in full.
3. If a duplicate name still exists after all names are transliterated, the IUPAC (International Union of Pure and Applied Chemistry) numerical suffix will be used at the end of the name as a distinction based on the order of publication (such as the second occurrence, bis, the third, tris, and the fourth, tetrakis and so on.)
4. The romanization method used in IPNI should be maintained as far as possible. Although a few spellings do not fully comply with the above three principles, duplicate names will be distinguished according to the aforementioned method, and significant misspellings or misuses will be changed as necessary.
5. The judgment of the duplicate names covers all taxa defined by the ICN, although only the Chinese authors of vascular plants involved in this book.

To avoid confusion, the names of collectors and herbarium staff should be transliterated in full, with given names first followed by family name. Given names should be not hyphenated or merged as a single name, such as Jin Shuang Ma instead of Jinshuang Ma.

This book is a compilation of data on most plant taxonomists who have published since the establishment of Chinese plant taxonomy in 1916 for use in databases of plant names, floras and monographs to provide a standard form for the authors of plant names. It also shows duplicate names to avoid confusing different authors. Although the International Code of Nomenclature for algae, fungi, and plants does not stipulate s standard transliteration for accuracy and clear distinction, it is recommended that an author's name be in strict accordance with the form provided in this book, especially in databases so that queries can be applied correctly.

User's Guide

Finding an author's name in Part I

Part I contains 2,862 authors of Chinese vascular plant names, arranged alphabetically by family name then given name(s) according to the pinyin transliteration. Each entry contains the following details:

- Standard Form The standard form of the name of authors of Chinese vascular plants, in accordance with the IPNI system. However, fixing the obvious spelling errors, duplicate names, multiple forms and other issues, and supplement the standard forms of vascular plants authors were not included in IPNI.
- Romanized Name is used to create a standard form, with the family name cited first and the given name second, separated by a comma.
- Other Forms of Romanization based on different rules for transliteration.
- Accepted Chinese Name is the correct form of the Chinese name as provided by the author.
- Standard Pinyin Form is the Chinese pinyin form established according to Chinese national standards GB/T 28039-2011. In information processing, all letters of the family name can be in upper case and accented letters indicating tone can be omitted.
- Other Chinese names include widely used Chinese forms that are not accepted by the author, traditional Chinese characters of early mainland authors, as well as the simplified Chinese characters for authors in Taiwan and Hong Kong.
- Year of Birth and Death The author's birth and death years are separated by a hyphen; uncertain years are indicated by a question mark.
- Year of First Publication is the year of first publication related to nomenclature by the author, used to judge the priority of the abbreviated form.
- Employment is the name of the institution of the author when (s)he published the article related to nomenclature.
- Research Interest are families of taxa published by the author of the names of vascular plants and the families claimed by the author, sometimes including information on other research areas, such as floristics, geographic areas and other branches of botany.
- Group of Research Interest is the main group of study by the author: [A] for algae, [B] for bryophytes, [M] for microorganisms, [P] for pteridophytes, [S] for seed plants.
- Published Taxa, the genus/genera of the taxa published by the author of vascular plant names.
- Author's Institution: the name of the institution where the author worked, indicated by the Herbarium Acronym.

- Location of Author's Collections: the herbaria where specimens collected by the author can be located, recorded by the Herbarium Acronym.
- Geographic Region: distribution of taxa published by the author.
- Notes: additional information that does not fit in the above categories.

(1) **C. H. An**
(2) **An, Cheng Hsi**; An, Chêng Hsi; An, Zheng Xi; (12)
(3) 安争夕；Ān Zhēngxī; 安争皙 (13)
(4) **1928-** **First publication: 1981** (14)
(5) • Employment: Xinjiang Bayi Agricultural College (15)
（新疆八一农学院）
(6) • Research interest: Asteraceae, Brassicaceae, Papaveraceae [S] (16)
(7) • Published taxa: *Ajania, Alliaria, Alyssum, Aphragmus, Arabidopsis, Arabis, Aster, Berteroa, Bidens, Brachyactis, Brassica, Braya, Camelina, Chorispora, Christolea, Crepis, Dicranostigma, Doronicum, Draba, Erigeron, Erysimum, Eutrema, Galatella, Hedinia, Helichrysum, Hypecoum, Inula, Lactuca, Lepidium, Ligularia, Malcolmia, Microsisymbrium, Mulgedium, Neotorularia, Scorzonera, Senecio, Sisymbriopsis, Sisymbrium, Solms-laubachia, Synstemon, Taphrospermum, Taraxacum, Torularia, Tragopogon, Yinshania*
(8) • Affiliation: XJA
(9) • Location of specimens: XJA
(10) • Region: CHINA (Xinjiang)
(11) • Also as: Z. X. An

1 Standard Form
2 Accepted Romanized Name
3 Accepted Chinese Name
4 Year of Birth and Death
5 Employment
6 Research Interest
7 Published Taxa (Genus)
8 Author's Institution
9 Location of Author's Collections
10 Geographic Region
11 Notes
12 Other Forms of Romanization
13 Other Chinese Names
14 Year of First Publication
15 Standard Pinyin Form
16 Group of Research Interest

Finding a name of Chinese collectors and herbarium staff in Part II

Part II is 2,669 Chinese plant collectors and herbarium staff, arranged in the pinyin order of Chinese characters. Since the author of the vascular plants has been included in Part I, it will not be included here. Some authors who have published in other plant groups and authors of taxonomic monographs also exist in standard forms accepted by IPNI. For the author who has a standard form, it will give detailed information which is similar to Part I, and other scholars who have no standard forms, and it will give relatively simple information.

- Romanized Name is used to create a standard form, with the family name cited first and the given name second, separated by a comma.
- Other Forms of Romanization based on different rules for transliteration.
- Accepted Chinese Name is the correct form of the Chinese name as provided by the author.
- Standard Pinyin Form is the Chinese pinyin form established according to Chinese national standards GB/T 28039-2011. In information processing, all letters of the family name can be in upper case and accented letters indicating tone can be omitted.
- Other Chinese names include widely used Chinese forms that are not accepted by the author, traditional Chinese characters of early mainland authors, as well as the simplified

Chinese characters for authors in Taiwan and Hong Kong.

- Year of Birth and Death The author's birth and death years are separated by a hyphen; uncertain years are indicated by a question mark.
- Year of First Publication is the year of first publication related to nomenclature by the author, used to judge the priority of the abbreviated form.
- Employment is the name of the institution of the author when (s)he published the article related to nomenclature.
- Research Interest are families of taxa published by the author of the names of vascular plants and the families claimed by the author, sometimes including information on other research areas, such as floristics, geographic areas and other branches of botany.
- Notes mainly record the monograph published by the author and other related information

(1) **Abudula, Abas**; 阿布都拉 • 阿巴斯 ; Ābùdūlā Ābāsī (8)
(1951-)
(2) • Research interest: Fungi
(3) • Affiliation: XJU
(4) • Location of specimens: XJU

Altay Exped.; 阿勒泰队 ; Ālètài Duì (9)
• Location of specimens: XTNM. Collection Team

Ai, Xi Zhi; 艾喜芝 ; Ài Xǐzhī (1948-)
• Research interest: Medicinal Plants
• Affiliation: ECM

(5) **L. J. Bi**
Bi, Lie Jue; Bi, Lie Jiu; 毕列爵 ; Bì Lièjué; 畢列爵 (10)
(6) (1917-2004) (11)
(7) • Employment: Department of Biology, Hubei University（湖北大学生物系）
• Research interest: Algae
• Affiliation: EU
• Location of specimens: EU

1 Accepted Romanized Name
2 Research Interest
3 Author's Institution
4 Location of Author's Collections
5 Standard Form
6 Year of Birth and Death
7 Employment
8 Accepted Chinese Name
9 Standard Pinyin Form
10 Other Chinese Names
11 Other Forms of Romanization

Finding the name of the research institution

Research institutions listed in Part I and Part II are according to when the article was published. The names of many institutions have changed for various reasons. Changes in names of institutions are summarized in Appendix I. The institutions are arranged alphabetically by the province where they are located. For easy access, the Chinese Academy of Sciences and various professional academies and institutions established before 1949 and foreign institutions are arranged separately. The names of those institutions are in brackets following the current name.

Finding the herbarium according to the herbarium acronym

The herbaria mentioned in Part I and Part II are cited by an acronym. Readers can find the current name, previous name and status of the herbaria in Appendix II according to the acronym.

Finding information about Chinese plant taxonomists according to the standard form of their name

The standard spelling of an author's name, the Chinese name and page number are indexed in Appendix III. Incorrect or unacceptable spellings are also included here, but they are in italics to distinguish them.

1	**Abdulla**	阿布都拉·吐尔逊阿依	3	3
	Ai	艾铁民	3	
	C. H. An	安争夕	3	
	L. Z. An	安黎哲	3	
	M. T. An	安明态	3	
	Q. F. An	安庆富	3	
2	***Z. X. An***	安争夕	3	
	Aur	敖志文	325	
		4		

1 Standard Form
2 Incorrect or Unacceptable Form
3 Page Number
4 Accepted Chinese Name

Finding information about Chinese plant taxonomists according to the Romanized spelling forms

According to the author's various Romanized spelling forms, the Chinese name and page number of the corresponding author can be indexed in Appendix IV.

	236-6 Exped.	236-6 队	325	2
	75 Exped.	75 考察队	325	
1	**Abdulla,Tursunay**	阿布都拉·吐尔逊阿依	3	
	Abudula, Abas	阿布都拉·阿巴斯	325	
	Ai, Tie Min	艾铁民	3	
		3		

1 Romanized Name
2 Page Number
3 Accepted Chinese Name

Acknowledgments

We are very grateful for the following institutions and individuals for providing literature and help!

Chinese Virtual Herbarium (CVH) 中国数字植物标本馆
Duocet Wiki of Plants 多识植物百科
Harvard University Herbaria & Libraries
Index Herbariorum: A Global Directory of Public Herbaria and Associated Staff
Library of Arnold Arboretum, Harvard University
National Specimen Information Infrastructure (NSII) 中国国家标本平台
The International Plant Names Index (IPNI)
Tropicos® Missouri Botanical Garden's Electronic Databases

Anhui : MIN Yun Jiang 闵运江 , SHAO Jian Wen 邵剑文

Beijing : CHEN Zhi Duan 陈之端 , CHU Fu Xiang 储富祥 , GU Lei 顾垒 , JING Xin Ming 景新明 , LI Ai Li 李爱莉 , LIU Quan Ru 刘全儒 , LIN Qin Wen 林秦文 , LONG Chun Lin 龙春林 , MA Xin Tang 马欣堂 , MENG Shi Yong 孟世勇 , QI Yao Dong 齐耀东 , WANG Qiang 王强 , WANG Yu Fei 王宇飞 , WANG Mei Zhi 汪梅芝 , WANG Yuan 汪远 , XIANG Xiao Guo 向小果 , XIAO Cui 肖翠 , YANG Yong 杨永 , YU Ning Ning 于宁宁 , ZHANG Xian Chun 张宪春 , ZHANG Yu 张毓 , ZHANG Zhi Yun 张志耘 , ZHANG Zhong Shuai 张中帅 , ZHAO Peng 赵鹏 , ZHAO Xin Lei 赵鑫磊 , ZHU Xiang Yun 朱相云

Chongqing : DENG Hong Ping 邓洪平 , ZHANG Jun 张军 , ZUO You Wei 左有为

Fujian : CAI Bang Ping 蔡邦平 , CHEN Heng Bin 陈恒彬 , CHEN Shi Pin 陈世品 , LI Zhen Ji 李振基 , ZHAI Jun Wen 翟俊文

Gansu : DU Wei Bo 杜维波 , FENG Hu Yuan 冯虎元 , SUN Kun 孙坤 , SUN Xue Gang 孙学刚

Guizhou : DENG Chao Yi 邓朝义 , HAN Guo Ying 韩国营 , SUN Qing Wen 孙庆文 , WANG Zhi Wei 王志威 , XU Zong Qiang 许宗强 , ZHANG Ren Bo 张仁波

Guangdong : BAI Lin 白琳 , CHEN Zhong He 陈忠和 , CUI Da Fang 崔大方 , DENG Yun Fei 邓云飞 , DUAN Lei 段磊 , HU Chi Ming 胡启明, HUANG Rui Lan 黄瑞兰, LI Ping Tao 李秉滔, LIAO Wen Bo 廖文波, LIU Ying 刘莹, REN Chen 任琛, SONG Zhu Qiu 宋柱秋, TONG Yi 童毅, TONG Yi Hua 童毅华, WANG Rui Jiang 王瑞江, XIA Nian He 夏念和 , YANG Qin Er 杨亲二 , YE Wen 叶文 , ZHANG Shou Zhou 张寿洲 , ZHOU Xin Xin 周欣欣

Guangxi : HAN Meng Qi 韩孟奇 , LIU Yan 刘演 , MA Zhong Hui 马仲辉 , TANG Sai Chun 唐赛春 , WEN Fang 温放 , ZHANG Zi Bin 张自斌

Hainan : TANG Huan 汤欢

Heilongjiang : CHEN Yong Sheng 陈永生 , HUANG Hui Na 黄慧娜 , HUANG Pu Hua 黄普华 , LIU Bao Dong 刘保东 , MAO Zi Jun 毛子军 , WANG Hong Feng 王洪峰 , WANG Zheng Quan 王政权 , ZHENG Bao Jiang 郑宝江

Hebei : SHI Shuo 石硕

Henan : LI Jia Mei 李家美 , LIU Ling 刘玲 , ZHU Xin Xin 朱鑫鑫

Hong Kong : BUT Pui Hay Paul 毕培曦 , CHEN Hu Biao 陈虎彪 , LAU Yuen Yung 刘苑容 , WU Jia Lin 邬家林

Hubei : AI Xun Ru 艾训儒 , GUO You Hao 郭友好 , LI Jian Qiang 李建强 , LI Xin Wei 李新伟 , LIANG Qiong 梁琼 , LIU Hong 刘虹 , LIU Yan Jun 刘燕君 , LIU Xing 刘星 , QIN Rui 覃瑞 , WANG Xiao Fan 汪小凡 , XU Wen Bin 徐文斌

Hunan : CHEN Gong Xi 陈功锡 , LI Wei Ping 黎维平 , PENG Chun Liang 彭春良 , WANG Min Qiu 王敏求 , WU Lei 吴磊 , YU Xun Lin 喻勋林 , ZHOU Jian Jun 周建军

Jiangsu : CHEN Geng Yu 陈耕宇 , HANG Yue Yu 杭悦宇 , HAO Jian Hua 郝建华 , HE Shan An 贺善安 , LIU Xing Jian 刘兴剑 , TIAN Xing Jun 田兴军

Jiangxi : HU Zong Gang 胡宗刚 , LI Bo 李波 , ZHAN Xuan Huai 詹选怀

Jilin : LI Yu 李玉 , LIN Hong Mei 林红梅 , SUN Ming Zhou 孙明洲 , ZHANG Bo 张波

Liaoning : CAO Wei 曹伟 , QI Shu Yan 齐淑艳 , XU Liang 许亮 , YU De Lin 于德林 , ZHANG Shu Mei 张淑梅

Nei Mongol : GAO Gui Ying 高桂英 , LIU Lei 刘磊 , MA Ping 马平 , ZHANG Chong Ling 张重岭 , ZHAO Li Qing 赵利清

Ningxia : LI Xiao Yong 李小勇

Qinghai : CHEN Shi Long 陈世龙 , WU Yu Hu 吴玉虎

Shaanxi : LIU Pei Liang 刘培亮 , LU Yuan 卢元 , JIANG Zai Min 姜在民 , SU Qi Zhen 苏其珍 , WU Zhen Hai 吴振海 , YUE Ming 岳明

Shandong : HOU Yuan Tong 侯元同 , LI Jian Xiu 李建秀 , WANG Fei 王斐

Shanghai : CAO Tong 曹同 , GONG Ji Ming 龚继明 , GE Bin Jie 葛斌杰 , GUO Shui Liang 郭水良 , HU Chao 胡超 , LI Hui Ru 李惠茹 , LI Hong Qing 李宏庆 , LI Li 李莉 , JIA Min 贾敏 , QIN Xiang Kun 秦祥堃 , SHANG Kan Kan 商侃侃 , SHAO Wen 邵文 , SHI Rui Ping 师瑞萍 , WANG You Fang 王幼芳 , WANG Zhang Hua 王樟华 , WEI Yu Kun 魏宇昆 , WU Guang Chao 吴广超 , XIAO Yue E 肖月娥 , XU Lei 徐蕾 , XU Shan 徐珊珊 , YAN Jing 严靖 , YAN Xiao Ling 闫小玲 , ZHANG Qing Fei 张庆费 , ZHANG Zhi Yu 张芝玉

Shanxi : KONG Dong Mei 孔冬梅

Sichuan : HE Xing Jin 何兴金 , LI Ce Hong 李策宏 , LIU Jing 刘静 , LIU Jun 刘君 , LIU Xiao Li 刘晓莉 , PENG Yu Lan 彭玉兰 , ZHU Da Hai 朱大海

Tianjin : LI Yong 李勇

Xinjiang : LI Wen Jun 李文军 , PAN Bo Rong 潘伯荣 , YANG Zong Zong 杨宗宗

Yunnan : CAI Jie 蔡杰 , DENG Tao 邓涛 , DUAN Bao Zhong 段宝忠 , FANG Zhen Dong 方振东 , LI De Zhu 李德铢 , LI Heng 李恒 , LI Jie 李捷 , LIU Cheng 刘成 , LIU Fang Yuan 刘芳媛 , MENG Jing 孟静 , MO Hai Bo 莫海波 , PAN Bo 潘勃 , SUN Wei Bang 孙卫邦 , TAN Yun Hong 谭运洪 , WANG Huan Chong 王焕冲 , XU Bo 徐波 , YANG Bin 杨斌 , YANG Xi 杨玺 , YANG Zhu Liang 杨祝良 , YUE Ji Pei 乐霁培 , ZHU Wei Dong 朱卫东 , ZHANG Da Cai 张大才 , ZHANG Jian Wen 张建文 , ZHANG Yong Hong 张永洪 , ZUO Yun Juan 左云娟

Zhejiang : CHEN Chuan 陈川 , CHEN Zheng Hai 陈征海 , DING Bing Yang 丁炳扬 , FU Cheng Xin 傅承新 , JIANG Kai Wen 蒋凯文 , JIN Xiao Feng 金孝锋 , LAI Jin Peng 来金朋 , LI Pan 李攀 , WU Yu Huan 吴玉环 , ZHAO Yun Peng 赵云鹏 , ZHOU Zhuang 周庄

Overseas : BOUFFORD David E. 鲍棣伟 , CUI Xian Ju 崔现举 , GAO Fang You 高仿优 , GUO Qing Fing 郭勤峰 , LI Shi You 李世友 , LIU Wu Sheng 刘武生 , MA Zheng Xu 马政旭 , QIAN Hong 钱宏 , WANG Hui 王卉 , WANG Jian 王健 , ZHUGE Ren 诸葛仁

Contents

目录

Part I

Chinese Authors of Plant Names

第一部分

植物学名中的中国作者

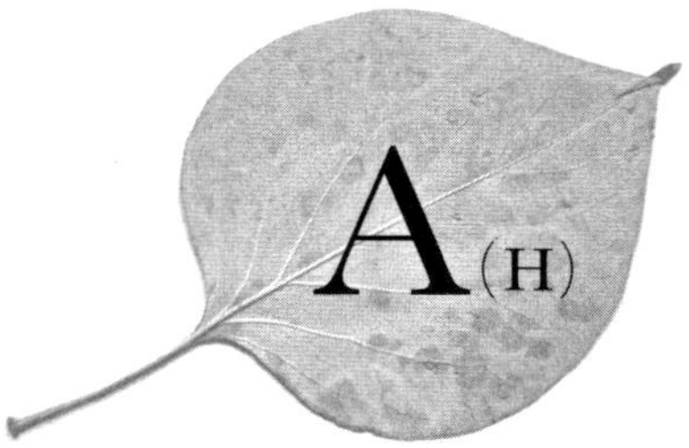

Abdulla

Abdulla, Tursunay; 阿布都拉·吐尔逊阿依；Ābùdūlā Tǔěrxùnāyī

First publication: 1991

- Employment: Xinjiang Institute of Biology, Pedology and Desert Research, Chinese Academy of Sciences（中国科学院新疆生物土壤沙漠研究所）
- Research interest: Caprifoliaceae [S]
- Published taxa: *Dipsacus*
- Region: CHINA (Xinjiang)

Hazit

Hazit, Yasin; 阿孜提·亚森；Āzītí Yàsēn

First publication: 1982

- Employment: Xinjiang Bayi Agricultural College（新疆八一农学院）
- Research interest: Caprifoliaceae [S]
- Published taxa: *Cerastium, Scabiosa*
- Region: CHINA (Xinjiang)

Ai

Ai, Tie Min; 艾铁民；Ài Tiěmín; 艾鐵民

1946- **First publication: 1985**

- Employment: Institute of Chinese Materia Medica, China Academy of Chinese Medical Sciences; School of Pharmacy, Beijing Medical University（中国中医研究院中药研究所；北京医科大学药学院）
- Research interest: Caprifoliaceae, Dipsacaceae, Orobanchaceae [S]
- Published taxa: *Chingyungia, Dipsacus*
- Affiliation: PEM
- Location of specimens: PEM, CMMI
- Region: CHINA

L. Z. An

An, Li Zhe; 安黎哲；Ān Lízhé

1963- **First publication: 2009**

- Employment: School of Life Sciences, Lanzhou University（兰州大学生命科学学院）
- Research interest: Papaveraceae [S]
- Published taxa: *Meconopsis*
- Region: CHINA (Gansu)

M. T. An

An, Ming Tai; 安明态；Ān Míngtài

1975- **First publication: 2008**

- Employment: College of Forestry, Guizhou University（贵州大学林学院）
- Research interest: Araceae, Asparagaceae, Berberidaceae, Brassicaceae, Caprifoliaceae, Urticaceae; Woody Plants [S]
- Published taxa: *Abelia, Arisaema, Berberis, Cardamine, Elatostema, Polygonatum*
- Affiliation: GZAC
- Location of specimens: GZAC
- Region: CHINA (Guizhou)

Q. F. An

An, Qing Fu; 安庆富；Ān Qìngfù; 安慶富

1940-2015 **First publication: 1986**

- Employment: Dongfanghong Forest Farm, Tailai, Heilongjiang（黑龙江泰来东方红林场）
- Research interest: Pinaceae [S]
- Published taxa: *Pinus*
- Region: CHINA (Heilongjiang, Nei Mongol)

C. H. An

An, Cheng Hsi; An, Chêng Hsi; An, Zheng Xi; 安争夕；Ān Zhēngxī; 安争晳

1928- **First publication: 1981**

- Employment: Xinjiang Bayi Agricultural College（新疆八一农学院）
- Research interest: Asteraceae, Brassicaceae, Papaveraceae [S]
- Published taxa: *Ajania, Alliaria, Alyssum, Aphragmus, Arabidopsis, Arabis, Aster, Berteroa, Bidens, Brachyactis, Brassica, Braya, Camelina, Chorispora, Christolea, Crepis, Dicranostigma, Doronicum, Draba, Erigeron, Erysimum, Eutrema, Galatella, Hedinia, Helichrysum, Hypecoum, Inula, Lactuca, Lepidium, Ligularia, Malcolmia, Microsisymbrium, Mulgedium, Neotorularia, Scorzonera, Senecio, Sisymbriopsis, Sisymbrium, Solms-laubachia, Synstemon, Taphrospermum, Taraxacum, Torularia, Tragopogon, Yinshania*
- Affiliation: XJA
- Location of specimens: XJA
- Region: CHINA (Xinjiang)
- Also as: Z. X. An

B (P)

C. G. Bai

Bai, Chang Guo; 白长国 ; Bái Chángguó

1961- **First publication: 1995**

- Employment: Huanggangliang Forest Farm of Keshiketeng Banner, Inner Mongolia（内蒙古克什克腾旗黄岗梁林场）
- Research interest: Pinaceae [S]
- Published taxa: *Picea*
- Region: CHINA (Nei Mongol)

H. F. Bai

Bai, Hong Feng; 白宏锋 ; Bái Hóngfēng

1970- **First publication: 2008**

- Employment: Huzhou University（湖州师范学院）
- Research interest: Brassicaceae [S]
- Published taxa: *Cardamine*
- Region: CHINA (Hunan)

H. Q. Bai

Bai, Hong Qing; 白洪青 ; Bái Hóngqīng

1974- **First publication: 2017**

- Employment: Deqing Forestry Bureau, Zhejiang（浙江省德清县林业局）
- Research interest: Rosaceae [S]
- Published taxa: *Cerasus*
- Region: CHINA (Zhejiang)

L. Bai

Bai, Lin; 白琳 ; Bái Lín

1989- **First publication: 2015**

- Employment: South China Botanical Garden, Chinese Academy of Sciences; Kunming Institute of Botany, Chinese Academy of Sciences（中国科学院华南植物园 ; 中国科学院昆明植物研究所）
- Research interest: Apocynaceae, Fabaceae, Zingiberaceae [S]
- Published taxa: *Amomum, Hoya, Senegalia, Zingiber*
- Region: CHINA

P. Y. Pai

Pai, Pei Yu; Pai, P'ei Yü; Bai, Pei Yu; 白佩瑜 ; Bái Pèiyú

1938- **First publication: 1978**

- Employment: Kunming Institute of Botany, Chinese Academy of Sciences（中国科学院昆明植物研究所）
- Research interest: Diapensiaceae, Gentianaceae, Lauraceae, Myrtaceae, Oleaceae, Pyrolaceae [S]
- Published taxa: *Fraxinus, Jasminum, Ligustrum, Litsea, Osmanthus, Syringa, Syzygium*
- Location of specimens: KUN
- Region: CHINA

Y. Y. Pai

Pai, Yin Yüan; Pai, Yin Yuan; 白荫元 ; Bái Yīnyuán; 白蔭元

1905-1967 **First publication: 1933**

- Employment: Institute of Botany, National Academy of Peiping（国立北平研究院植物学研究所）
- Research interest: Caprifoliaceae, Phrymaceae [S]
- Published taxa: *Mimulus, Morina*
- Location of specimens: PE, WUK
- Region: CHINA (Gansu, Sichuan)

D. Q. Bai

Bai, Da Quan; 柏大全 ; Bǎi Dàquán

1982- **First publication: 2011**

- Employment: College of Life Sciences, Sichuan Agricultural University（四川农业大学生命科学学院）
- Research interest: Polygonaceae [S]
- Published taxa: *Fagopyrum*
- Region: CHINA (Sichuan)

Q. Ban

Ban, Qin; 班勤 ; Bān Qín

1965- **First publication: 2003**

- Employment: Institute of Botany, Chinese Academy of Sciences（中国科学院植物研究所）
- Research interest: Caryophyllaceae [S]
- Published taxa: *Arenaria*
- Affiliation: PE
- Region: CHINA (Sichuan)

B. J. Bao

Bao, Bo Jian; 包伯坚 ; Bāo Bójiān

1959- **First publication: 2010**

- Employment: Institute of Botany, Chinese Academy of Sciences（中国科学院植物研究所）
- Research interest: Fabaceae, Polygonaceae; Digitization of specimens [S]
- Published taxa: *Polygonum, Sophora, Vicia*
- Affiliation: PE
- Region: CHINA

H. Y. Bao

Bao, Hai Ying; 包海鹰 ; Bāo Hǎiyīng

First publication: 1996

- Employment: Jilin Agricultural University（吉林农业大学）
- Research interest: Ranunculaceae [S]

- Published taxa: *Aconitum*
- Region: CHINA (Nei Mongol)

S. Y. Bao

Bao, Shih Ying; Pao, Shih Ying; Bao, Shi Ying; 包士英；Bāo Shìyīng

1935-2013 **First publication: 1977**

- Employment: Kunming Institute of Botany, Chinese Academy of Sciences（中国科学院昆明植物研究所）
- Research interest: Berberidaceae, Celastraceae, Juncaceae, Oleaceae, Passifloraceae, Salicaceae, Scrophulariaceae [S]
- Published taxa: *Berberis, Buddleja, Casearia, Dysosma, Epimedium, Jasminum, Juncus, Loeseneriella, Mahonia, Nandina, Passiflora, Salacia*
- Affiliation: KUN
- Location of specimens: HSIB, KUN
- Region: CHINA
- Also as: S. Y. Pao

Z. R. Bao

Bao, Zhuo Ran; 暴卓然；Bào Zhuórán

1938- **First publication: 1984**

- Employment: Yunnan Agricultural University（云南农业大学）
- Research interest: Rutaceae [S]
- Published taxa: *Poncirus*
- Region: CHINA (Yunnan)

H. Y. Bi

Bi, Hai Yan; 毕海燕；Bì Hǎiyàn

1978- **First publication: 2009**

- Employment: Institute of Botany, Chinese Academy of Sciences（中国科学院植物研究所）
- Research interest: Balsaminaceae, Cyperaceae, Schisandraceae [S]
- Published taxa: *Cyperus, Impatiens, Schoenoplectus*
- Affiliation: BJM
- Location of specimens: BJM
- Region: CHINA

But

But, Pui Hay, Paul; 畢培曦；Bì Péixī; 毕培曦

1948- **First publication: 1982**

- Employment: Department of Biology, the Chinese University of Hong Kong（香港中文大学生物学系）
- Research interest: Poaceae, Rubiaceae, Rutaceae; Medicinal Plants [S]
- Published taxa: *Arundinaria, Bambusa, Dendrocalamus, Lophochlaena, Murraya, Pleuropogon, Tovarochloa, Tsiangia*
- Affiliation: CUHK
- Location of specimens: CUHK
- Region: CHINA

Y. K. Bi

Bi, Yu Ke; 毕玉科；Bì Yùkē

1989- **First publication: 2013**

- Employment: School of Life Sciences, East China Normal University（华东师范大学生命科学学院）
- Research interest: Burmanniaceae [S]
- Published taxa: *Thismia*
- Region: CHINA (Yunnan)

F. H. Bian

Bian, Fu Hua; 卞福花；Biàn Fúhuā

1973- **First publication: 2002**

- Employment: Kunming Institute of Botany, Chinese Academy of Sciences（中国科学院昆明植物研究所）
- Research interest: Araceae [S]
- Published taxa: *Typhonium*
- Region: CHINA (Yunnan)

B. P. Cai

Cai, Bang Ping; 蔡邦平；Cài Bāngpíng

1969- **First publication: 2018**

- Employment: Xiamen Botanical Garden（厦门市园林植物园）
- Research interest: Staphyleaceae; Biodiversity [S]
- Published taxa: *Euscaphis*
- Affiliation: XMBG
- Location of specimens: XMBG
- Region: CHINA (Fujian)

J. Cai

Cai, Jie; 蔡杰；Cài Jié

1979- **First publication: 2005**

- Employment: Kunming Institute of Botany, Chinese Academy of Sciences（中国科学院昆明植物研究所）
- Research interest: Gesneriaceae, Phrymaceae [S]
- Published taxa: *Didymocarpus, Mimulicalyx*
- Region: CHINA (Yunnan)

J. L. Tsai

Tsai, Jinn Lai; Tsai, Jenn Lai; Ts'ai, Ching Lai; 蔡進來；Cài Jìnlái; 蔡进来

First publication: 1987

- Employment: Department of Life Sciences, Chung Hsing University（中兴大学生命科学系）

- Research interest: Linderniaceae, Thelypteridaceae;
- Pteridophytes [P]
- Published taxa: *Cyclosorus, Lindernia, Pronephrium, Thelypteris, Torenia*
- Affiliation: TCB
- Location of specimens: TCB
- Region: CHINA (Taiwan)

Lei Cai

Cai, Lei; 蔡磊 ; Cài Lěi

1986- **First publication: 2006**

- Employment: Kunming Institute of Botany, Chinese Academy of Sciences（中国科学院昆明植物研究所）
- Research interest: Asparagaceae, Ericaceae, Gesneriaceae [S]
- Published taxa: *Aspidistra, Didymocarpus, Henckelia, Loxostigma, Oreocharis, Rhododendron*
- Region: CHINA

L. B. Cai

Cai, Lian Bing; 蔡联炳 ; Cài Liánbǐng; 蔡聯炳

1948- **First publication: 1993**

- Employment: Northwest Plateau Institute of Biology, Chinese Academy of Sciences（中国科学院西北高原生物研究所）
- Research interest: Poaceae [S]
- Published taxa: *Capillipedium, Elymus, Hordeum, Kengyilia, Leymus, Orinus, Ptilagrostis, Roegneria, Tripogon, Triticum*
- Affiliation: HNWP
- Region: CHINA

C. C. Tsai

Tsai, Chi Chu; 蔡奇助 ; Cài Qízhù

First publication: 2009

- Employment: Kaohsiung District Agricultural Research and Extension Station, Council of Agriculture, "Executive Yuan"（"行政院"农业委员会高雄区农业改良场）
- Research interest: Orchidaceae, Rhizophoraceae [S]
- Published taxa: *× Amenopsis, × Chenara, × Chenlanara, × Chouara, × Jungara, × Linara, × Rongwuara, × Tsaiara, Ceriops*
- Region: CHINA (Taiwan)

S. L. Tsai

Tsai, Shao Lan; 蔡少兰 ; Cài Shàolán; 蔡少蘭

1931- **First publication: 1956**

- Employment: Department of Biology, Sun Yat-sen University（中山大学生物系）
- Research interest: Thymelaeaceae [S]
- Published taxa: *Wikstroemia*
- Location of specimens: SYS
- Region: CHINA (Guangdong)

S. Q. Cai

Cai, Shao Qing; 蔡少青 ; Cài Shàoqīng

1960- **First publication: 2003**

- Employment: Department of natural medicines, School of Pharmaceutical Sciences, Peking University（北京大学药学院天然药物学系）
- Research interest: Araliaceae [S]
- Published taxa: *Panax*
- Region: CHINA (Yunnan)

C. Q. Cai

Cai, Chu Qin; Cai, Shu Qin; **蔡淑琴 ; Cài Shūqín**

1940-2017 **First publication: 1995**

- Employment: Institute of Botany, Chinese Academy of Sciences（中国科学院植物研究所）
- Research interest: Asteraceae; Scientific Illustrator [S]
- Published taxa: *Youngia*
- Affiliation: PE
- Region: CHINA (Xizang)

H. T. Tsai

Tsai, Hse Tao; Ts'ai, Hsi T'ao; Tsai, Hsi Tao; **蔡希陶 ; Cài Xītáo**

1911-1981 **First publication: 1936**

- Employment: Fan Memorial Institute of Biology; Xishuangbanna Tropical Botanical Garden, Chinese Academy of Sciences; Yunnan Institute of Tropical Botany, Chinese Academy of Sciences（静生生物调查所；中国科学院西双版纳热带植物园；中国科学院云南热带植物研究所）
- Research interest: Fabaceae, Malvaceae, Rosaceae, Theaceae, Zingiberaceae; Plants of Yunnan [S]
- Published taxa: *Amomum, Astragalus, Camellia, Erythrina, Sorbus, Sterculia*
- Affiliation: HITBC
- Location of specimens: HITBC, LBG, KUN, NAS, PE
- Region: CHINA (Yunnan)

X. A. Cai

Cai, Xi An; 蔡锡安 ; Cài Xī'ān

1968- **First publication: 2019**

- Employment: South China Botanical Garden, Chinese Academy of Sciences（中国科学院华南植物园）
- Research interest: Lowiaceae [S]
- Published taxa: *Orchidantha*
- Region: CHINA (Guangxi)

X. Cai

Cai, Xin; 蔡鑫 ; Cài Xīn

1994- **First publication: 2019**

- Employment: College of Life and Environmental Sciences, Hangzhou Normal University（杭州师范大学生命与环境科学学院）

- Research interest: Asteraceae [S]
- Published taxa: *Youngia*
- Region: CHINA (Zhejiang)

X. Z. Cai

Cai, Xiu Zhen; 蔡秀珍；Cài Xiùzhēn

1979- **First publication: 2006**

- Employment: College of Life Sciences, Hunan Normal University（湖南师范大学生命科学学院）
- Research interest: Araceae, Balsaminaceae, Gesneriaceae [S]
- Published taxa: *Colocasia, Impatiens, Primulina*
- Affiliation: HNNU
- Location of specimens: HNNU
- Region: CHINA

F. Cao

Cao, Feng; 曹峰；Cáo Fēng

1981- **First publication: 2020**

- Employment: Xinyang Normal University（信阳师范学院）
- Research interest: Aristolochiaceae [S]
- Published taxa: *Isotrema*
- Region: CHINA

H. F. Cao

Cao, Hai Feng; 曹海峰；Cáo Hǎifēng

1985- **First publication: 2019**

- Employment: Shanghai University of Traditional Chinese Medicine（上海中医药大学）
- Research interest: Gentianaceae [S]
- Published taxa: *Gentianella*
- Region: CHINA (Xinjiang)

J. Y. Chao

Chao, Jiang Ying; Cao, Jiang Ying; 曹江营；Cáo Jiāngyíng

First publication: 1989

- Employment: Department of Biology, Inner Mongolia University（内蒙古大学生物系）
- Research interest: Amaryllidaceae [S]
- Published taxa: *Allium*
- Region: CHINA (Nei Mongol)

L. M. Cao

Cao, Li Min; 曹利民；Cáo Lìmín

1965- **First publication: 2003**

- Employment: Kunming Institute of Botany, Chinese Academy of Sciences; Gannan Normal University（中国科学院昆明植物研究所；赣南师范学院）
- Research interest: Araceae, Ericaceae [S]
- Published taxa: *Colocasia, Rhododendron*
- Region: CHINA (Jiangxi, Yunnan)

R. Cao

Cao, Rui; 曹瑞；Cáo Ruì

1958- **First publication: 1996**

- Employment: School of Life Sciences, Inner Mongolia University（内蒙古大学生命科学学院）
- Research interest: Cistaceae, Fabaceae, Orobanchaceae; Plants of Nei Mongol [S]
- Published taxa: *Cistanche, Hedysarum, Helianthemum*
- Affiliation: HIMC
- Location of specimens: HIMC
- Region: CHINA (Nei Mongol)

T. R. Cao

Cao, Tie Ru; 曹铁如；Cáo Tiěrú; 曹鐵如

1938- **First publication: 1988**

- Employment: Central South College of Forestry（中南林学院）
- Research interest: Araliaceae, Styracaceae; Economic Plants [S]
- Published taxa: *Hunaniopanax, Sinojackia*
- Affiliation: CSFI
- Location of specimens: CSFI
- Region: CHINA (Hunan)

W. Cao

Cao, Wei; 曹伟；Cáo Wěi

1962- **First publication: 1996**

- Employment: Institute of Applied Ecology, Chinese Academy of Sciences（中国科学院沈阳应用生态研究所）
- Research interest: Aceraceae, Fagaceae, Sapindaceae [S]
- Published taxa: *Acer*
- Affiliation: IFP
- Location of specimens: IFP
- Region: CHINA (Jilin)

Y. L. Cao

Cao, Ya Ling; 曹亚玲；Cáo Yàlíng; 曹亞玲

1937- **First publication: 1983**

- Employment: Chengdu Institute of Biology, Chinese Academy of Sciences（中国科学院成都生物研究所）
- Research interest: Stachyuraceae, Vitaceae [S]
- Published taxa: *Stachyurus, Vitis*
- Affiliation: CDBI
- Location of specimens: CDBI
- Region: CHINA

Z. Y. Cao

Cao, Zi Yu; Csao, Z. Y.; 曹子余；Cáo Zǐyú; 曹子餘

1935- **First publication: 1991**

- Employment: Institute of Botany, Chinese Academy of Sciences（中国科学院植物研究所）
- Research interest: Moraceae, Vitaceae [S]

- Published taxa: *Morus, Tetrastigma*
- Affiliation: PE
- Location of specimens: PE
- Region: CHINA

H. F. Cen

Cen, Hua Fei; 岑华飞 ; Cén Huáfēi

1987- **First publication: 2017**

- Employment: Guangxi Institute of Botany, Chinese Academy of Sciences（广西壮族自治区中国科学院广西植物研究所）
- Research interest: Gesneriaceae [S]
- Published taxa: *Petrocodon*
- Region: CHINA (Hunan)

J. M. Cen

Cen, Jia Meng; 岑佳梦 ; Cén Jiāmèng

1994- **First publication: 2015**

- Employment: College of Life and Environmental Sciences, Hangzhou Normal University（杭州师范大学生命与环境科学学院）
- Research interest: Cyperaceae [S]
- Published taxa: *Carex*
- Region: CHINA (Yunnan)

Q. Y. Cen

Cen, Qing Ya; 岑庆雅 ; Cén Qìngyǎ

1957- **First publication: 1996**

- Employment: Department of Biology, Xijiang University（西江大学生物系）
- Research interest: Orobanchaceae [S]
- Published taxa: *Lindenbergia*
- Region: CHINA (Guangdong)

B. L. Chai

Chai, Ben Li; 柴本立 ; Chái Běnlì

First publication: 1991

- Employment: Department of Biology, Sichuan University（四川大学生物系）
- Research interest: Celastraceae [S]
- Published taxa: *Parnassia*
- Region: CHINA (Sichuan)

S. F. Chai

Chai, Sheng Feng; 柴胜丰 ; Chái Shèngfēng

1980- **First publication: 2020**

- Employment: Guangxi Institute of Botany, Chinese Academy of Sciences（广西壮族自治区中国科学院广西植物研究所）
- Research interest: Theaceae [S]
- Published taxa: *Camellia*
- Region: CHINA (Guangxi)

X. L. Chang

Chang, Xiao Lin; 常效琳 ; Cháng Xiàolín

First publication: 1990

- Employment: Shandong Institute for Drug Control（山东省药检所）
- Research interest: Cyperaceae [S]
- Published taxa: *Scirpus*
- Region: CHINA (Shandong)

Y. Fen Chang

Chang, Yan Fen; 常艳芬 ; Cháng Yànfēn

1980- **First publication: 2018**

- Employment: College of Life Sciences and Environment, Hengyang Normal University; Xishuangbanna Tropical Botanical Garden, Chinese Academy of Sciences（衡阳师范学院生命科学与环境学院；中国科学院西双版纳热带植物园）
- Research interest: Aspleniaceae; Pteridophytes [P]
- Published taxa: *Asplenium, Hymenasplenium*
- Affiliation: HITBC
- Location of specimens: HITBC
- Region: CHINA

Zhao Y. Chang

Chang, Zhao Yang; 常朝阳 ; Cháng Zhāoyáng

1965- **First publication: 2005**

- Employment: College of Life Sciences, Northwest A&F University（西北农林科技大学生命科学学院）
- Research interest: Fabaceae [S]
- Published taxa: *Astragalus, Caragana, Chesneya, Chesniella, Hedysarum, Oxytropis*
- Affiliation: WUK
- Location of specimens: WUK
- Region: CHINA

Z. Chao

Chao, Zhi; 晁志 ; Cháo Zhì

1971- **First publication: 2020**

- Employment: School of Chinese Medicine, Southern Medical University（南方医科大学中医药学院）
- Research interest: Crassulaceae [S]
- Published taxa: *Phedicmus*
- Region: CHINA (Guangdong)

P. H. Chen

Chen, Po Hao; 陳柏豪 ; Chén Bǎiháo; 陈柏豪

First publication: 2015

- Employment: Department of Forestry, Pingtung University of Science and Technology（屏东科技大学森林系）
- Research interest: Convolvulaceae, Orobanchaceae [S]
- Published taxa: *Argyreia, Striga*
- Region: CHINA (Taiwan)

P. Y. Chen

Chen, Pang Yu; Ch'ên, Pang Yü; 陈邦余；Chén Bāngyú; 陳邦餘

1936- **First publication: 1981**

- Employment: South China Institute of Botany, Chinese Academy of Sciences; South China Botanical Garden, Chinese Academy of Sciences（中国科学院华南植物研究所；中国科学院华南植物园）
- Research interest: Aquifoliaceae, Fabaceae, Juglandaceae, Meliaceae, Rosaceae, Simaroubaceae; Plants of Guangdong [S]
- Published taxa: *Derris, Dysoxylum, Engelhardia, Ilex, Ormosia, Picrasma, Rosa, Toona*
- Affiliation: IBSC
- Region: CHINA

B. L. Chen

Chen, Bao Liang; 陈宝樑；Chén Bǎoliáng; 陳寶樑，陈宝梁

1942-1991 **First publication: 1987**

- Employment: Department of Biology, Sun Yat-sen University（中山大学生物系）
- Research interest: Magnoliaceae [S]
- Published taxa: *Magnolia, Manglietia, Michelia*
- Region: CHINA

B. Chen

Chen, Bin; 陈彬；Chén Bīn

1980- **First publication: 2005**

- Employment: School of Life Sciences, Nanjing University（南京大学生命科学学院）
- Research interest: Ranunculaceae; Biodiversity [S]
- Published taxa: *Thalictrum*
- Affiliation: CSH
- Location of specimens: CSH
- Region: CHINA (Jiangsu)

B. Hua Chen

Chen, Bing Hua; 陈炳华；Chén Bǐnghuá

1970- **First publication: 2016**

- Employment: College of Life Sciences, Fujian Normal University（福建师范大学生命科学学院）
- Research interest: Gentianaceae, Orchidaceae [S]
- Published taxa: *Platanthera, Swertia*
- Affiliation: FNU
- Region: CHINA (Fujian)
- IPNI as: B. H. Chen

B. H. Chen

Chen, Bing Huan; 陈炳环；Chén Bǐnghuán; 陳炳環

1929-2017 **First publication: 1983**

- Employment: Tea Research Institute, Chinese Academy of Agricultural Sciences（中国农业科学院茶叶研究所）
- Research interest: Theaceae [S]
- Published taxa: *Camellia*
- Region: CHINA

Chong G. Chen

Chen, Chong Gui; 陈崇贵；Chén Chóngguì; 陳崇貴

1943- **First publication: 1991**

- Employment: Forestry Bureau of Huaying City, Sichuan（四川省华蓥市林业局）
- Research interest: Poaceae [S]
- Published taxa: *Phyllostachys*
- Region: CHINA (Sichuan)

C. G. Chen

Chen, Chun Gen; 陈存根；Chén Cúngēn

1952- **First publication: 1981**

- Employment: Shaanxi Institute of Forestry（陕西省林业科学研究所）
- Research interest: Cupressaceae [S]
- Published taxa: *Sabina*
- Location of specimens: YL
- Region: CHINA (Shaanxi)

D. L. Chen

Chen, De Liang; 陈德良；Chén Déliáng

1962- **First publication: 2019**

- Employment: Administration of Zhejiang Fengyangshan-Baishanzu National Nature Reserve, Zhejiang（浙江凤阳山 - 百山祖国家级自然保护区管理局）
- Research interest: Primulaceae [S]
- Published taxa: *Stimpsonia*
- Region: CHINA (Zhejiang)

D. M. Chen

Chen, De Mao; Ch'ên, Tê Mao; Chen, Dao Men; 陈德懋；Chén Démào; 陳德懋

1941- **First publication: 1983**

- Employment: Department of Biology, Central China Normal University; School of Life Sciences, Central China Normal University（华中师范大学生物系；华中师范大学生命科学学院）
- Research interest: Poaceae, Woodsiaceae [PS]
- Published taxa: *Arundinella, Woodsia*
- Affiliation: CCNU
- Location of specimens: CCNU
- Region: CHINA (Hubei)

D. Y. Chen

Chen, De Yuan; 陈德媛；Chén Déyuàn; 陳德媛

1939- **First publication: 1981**

- Employment: Herbarium, School of Pharmacy, Guiyang College of Traditional Chinese Medicine（贵阳中医学院药学院标本室）

• Research interest: Aristolochiaceae, Gesneriaceae, Lamiaceae [S]
• Published taxa: *Aristolochia, Chirita*
• Affiliation: GZTM
• Location of specimens: GZTM
• Region: CHINA (Guizhou)

T. C. Chen

Chen, Te Chao; Ch'ên, Tê Chao; Chen, De Zhao; 陈德昭; Chén Dézhāo; 陳德昭
1926- **First publication: 1955**
• Employment: South China Institute of Botany, Chinese Academy of Sciences; South China Botanical Garden, Chinese Academy of Sciences（中国科学院华南植物研究所；中国科学院华南植物园）
• Research interest: Fabaceae, Lardizabalaceae, Meliaceae, Putranjivaceae, Sapindaceae [S]
• Published taxa: *Aganope, Aglaia, Amphicarpaea, Aphanamixis, Archakebia, Bauhinia, Boniodendron, Christia, Crotalaria, Dalbergia, Drypetes, Dysoxylum, Heynea, Holboellia, Indigofera, Koelreuteria, Millettia, Munronia, Paraderris, Senna, Sophora, Spatholobus, Stauntonia*
• Affiliation: IBSC
• Region: CHINA
• Also as: T. Chen

D. Z. Chen

Chen, De Zhong; 陈德忠; Chén Dézhōng; 陳德忠
1942- **First publication: 1998**
• Employment: Yuzhong Heping Peony Garden, Gansu（甘肃省榆中和平牡丹园）
• Research interest: Paeoniaceae [S]
• Published taxa: *Paeonia*
• Region: CHINA (Gansu)

D. Chen

Chen, Di; Chen, Ti; Ch'ên, Ti; 陈蒂; Chén Dì; 陳蒂
1936- **First publication: 1988**
• Employment: Shenyang Agricultural University（沈阳农业大学）
• Research interest: Aceraceae, Anacardiaceae, Betulaceae, Commelinaceae [S]
• Published taxa: *Alnus, Commelina, Corylus*
• Affiliation: SYAUF
• Location of specimens: SYAUF
• Region: CHINA (Liaoning)
Also as: T. Chen; Ti Chen

E. Y. Chen

Chen, Er Ying; 陈二英; Chén Èryīng
First publication: 1985
• Employment: Forestry Department of Hainan Province（海南省林业局）
• Research interest: Lythraceae [S]
• Published taxa: *Sonneratia*
• Region: CHINA (Hainan)

F. P. Chen

Chen, Fei Pong; 陈飞鹏; Chén Fēipéng
1962- **First publication: 1987**
• Employment: Department of Biology, Sun Yat-sen University; Department of Agricultural Biology, South China Agricultural University（中山大学生物系；华南农业大学农业生物系）
• Research interest: Primulaceae, Theaceae; Plant Ecology [S]
• Published taxa: *Camellia, Lysimachia*
• Affiliation: SCAUB
• Location of specimens: SCAUB
• Region: CHINA (Guangxi)

F. L. Chen

Chen, Feng Lin; 陈丰林; Chén Fēnglín
1987- **First publication: 2019**
• Employment: South China Botanical Garden, Chinese Academy of Sciences（中国科学院华南植物园）
• Research interest: Acanthaceae, Apiaceae [S]
• Published taxa: *Peucedanum, Strobilanthes*
• Region: CHINA

F. H. Chen

Chen, Feng Hwai; Chen, Feng Huai; Ch'ên, Fêng Huai; Chen, Feng Huei; 陈封怀; Chén Fēnghuái; 陳封懷
1900-1993 **First publication: 1935**
• Employment: Lushan Forestry Garden; South China Institute of Botany, Chinese Academy of Sciences（庐山森林植物园；中国科学院华南植物研究所）
• Research interest: Araliaceae, Asteraceae, Celastraceae, Euphorbiaceae, Fagaceae, Malvaceae, Primulaceae, Ranunculaceae, Rhamnaceae, Rutaceae, Symplocaceae [S]
• Published taxa: *Aconitum, Anaphalis, Androsace, Artemisia, Aster, Carduus, Carpesium, Coptis, Delphinium, Euodia, Euonymus, Hovenia, Ligularia, Lithocarpus, Lysimachia, Mallotus, Panax, Primula, Saussurea, Symplocos, Tilia, Ziziphus*
• Affiliation: IBSC
• Region: CHINA
• IPNI as: Chen

F. Chen

Chen, Feng; 陈锋; Chén Fēng
1978- **First publication: 2019**
• Employment: Forest Resources Monitoring Center of Zhejiang Province（浙江省森林资源监测中心）
• Research interest: Cucurbitaceae, Rosaceae, Vitaceae

[S]
- Published taxa: *Rubus, Trichosanthes, Vitis*
- Region: CHINA (Zhejiang)

G. Chen

Chen, Gao; 陈高 ; Chén Gāo

1978- **First publication: 2019**

- Employment: Kunming Institute of Botany, Chinese Academy of Sciences（中国科学院昆明植物研究所）
- Research interest: Chloranthaceae [S]
- Published taxa: *Chloranthus*
- Region: CHINA (Guangxi)

G. R. Chen

Chen, Gen Rong; 陈根荣 ; Chén Gēnróng

1930-2008 **First publication: 1989**

- Employment: Zhejiang Forestry School（浙江林业学校）
- Research interest: Ericaceae [S]
- Published taxa: *Rhododendron*
- Region: CHINA (Zhejiang)

G. X. Chen

Chen, Gong Xi; 陈功锡 ; Chén Gōngxī

1966- **First publication: 2006**

- Employment: College of Resources and Planning Sciences, Jishou University（吉首大学城乡资源与规划学院）
- Research interest: Asparagaceae, Asteraceae; Pteridophytes [S]
- Published taxa: *Aster, Heteropolygonatum*
- Affiliation: JIU
- Location of specimens: JIU
- Region: CHINA (Hunan)

G. H. Chen

Chen, Guang Hou; 陈光后 ; Chén Guānghòu

1937- **First publication: 1996**

- Employment: Chengdu Second Institute for Drug Control, Sichuan（四川省成都市第二药品检验所）
- Research interest: Asteraceae, Brassicaceae, Ranunculaceae [S]
- Published taxa: *Aconitum, Cardamine, Delphinium, Ligularia*
- Region: CHINA (Sichuan)

G. Y. Chen

Chen, Guang Yan; 陈光焰 ; Chén Guāngyàn

1955- **First publication: 1985**

- Employment: Institute of Hubei Traditional Chinese Medicine Company（湖北省中药材公司科学研究所）
- Research interest: Liliaceae [S]
- Published taxa: *Fritillaria*
- Region: CHINA (Hubei)

G. Z. Chen

Chen, Gui Zhen; 陈桂珍 ; Chén Guìzhēn

1989- **First publication: 2017**

- Employment: The Orchid Conservation & Research Center of Shenzhen, Guangdong（广东省深圳市兰科植物保护研究中心）
- Research interest: Orchidaceae [S]
- Published taxa: *Bletilla, Cymbidium*
- Region: CHINA (Guizhou)

G. B. Chen

Chen, Guo Ben; 陈国本 ; Chén Guóběn; 陳國本

1934-2017 **First publication: 1990**

- Employment: Hunan Agricultural College（湖南农学院）
- Research interest: Theaceae [S]
- Published taxa: *Camellia*
- Region: CHINA (Yunnan)

H. S. Chen

Chen, Hai Shan; 陈海山 ; Chén Hǎishān

1965- **First publication: 2001**

- Employment: South China Institute of Botany, Chinese Academy of Sciences; South China Botanical Garden, Chinese Academy of Sciences（中国科学院华南植物研究所；中国科学院华南植物园）
- Research interest: Aquifoliaceae, Symplocaceae [S]
- Published taxa: *Ilex, Symplocos*
- Location of specimens: IBSC
- Region: CHINA (Guangdong)

Heng B. Chen

Chen, Heng Bin; 陈恒彬 ; Chén Héngbīn

1960- **First publication: 1987**

- Employment: Fujian Institute of Subtropical Botany; Xiamen Botanical Garden（福建省亚热带植物研究所；厦门市园林植物园）
- Research interest: Acanthaceae, Lamiaceae; Plants of Fujian [S]
- Published taxa: *Acanthus, Keiskea, Paraphlomis, Stachys*
- Affiliation: XMBG
- Location of specimens: FJSI, XMBG
- Region: CHINA (Fujian, Guangdong)

H. F. Chen

Chen, Hong Feng; 陈红锋 ; Chén Hóngfēng

1974- **First publication: 2005**

- Employment: South China Botanical Garden, Chinese Academy of Sciences（中国科学院华南植物园）
- Research interest: Magnoliaceae, Putranjivaceae [S]
- Published taxa: *Drypetes, Magnolia*

• Region: CHINA (Guangxi)

H. L. Chen

Chen, Hong Liang; 陈洪梁 ; Chén Hóngliáng
1988- **First publication: 2014**

- Employment: Kunming Institute of Botany, Chinese Academy of Sciences（中国科学院昆明植物研究所）
- Research interest: Brassicaceae [S]
- Published taxa: *Draba, Solms-laubachia*
- Region: CHINA (Yunnan)

H. B. Chen

Chen, Hu Biao; 陈虎彪 ; Chén Hǔbiāo
1962- **First publication: 1990**

- Employment: School of Pharmacy, Beijing Medical University（北京医科大学药学院）
- Research interest: Caprifoliaceae, Dipsacaceae, Valerianaceae [S]
- Published taxa: *Dipsacus, Morina, Valeriana*
- Affiliation: PEM
- Location of specimens: PEM
- Region: CHINA

H. Q. Chen

Chen, Huan Qiang; 陈焕强 ; Chén Huànqiáng
1962- **First publication: 2011**

- Employment: Jianfengling National Nature Reserve Administration, Hainan（海南尖峰岭国家级自然保护区管理局）
- Research interest: Aristolochiaceae, Triuridaceae [S]
- Published taxa: *Aristolochia, Sciaphila*
- Region: CHINA (Hainan)

W. Y. Chen

Chen, Wan Yong; Chen, Huan Xiong; **陈焕雄 ; Chén Huànxióng**
First publication: 1985

- Employment: Forestry Department of Hainan Province（海南省林业局）
- Research interest: Lythraceae [S]
- Published taxa: *Sonneratia*
- Region: CHINA (Hainan)

Chun

Chun, Woon Young; Chun, Woon Yung; Chen, Huan Yung; Chen, Huan Yong; Ch'ên, Huan Yung; **陈焕镛 ; Chén Huànyōng; 陳煥鏞**
1890-1971 **First publication: 1925**

- Employment: Botanical Institute, College of Agriculture, National Sun Yat-sen University; South China Institute of Botany, Chinese Academy of Sciences（国立中山大学农林植物研究所；中国科学院华南植物研究所）
- Research interest: Acanthaceae, Adoxaceae, Altingiaceae, Annonaceae, Apocynaceae, Aquifoliaceae, Araliaceae, Arecaceae, Aristolochiaceae, Asparagaceae, Begoniaceae, Berberidaceae, Betulaceae, Boraginaceae, Buxaceae, Cannabaceae, Capparaceae, Celastraceae, Chloranthaceae, Convolvulaceae, Cornaceae, Cucurbitaceae, Cyperaceae, Dichapetalaceae, Dilleniaceae, Dipterocarpaceae, Ebenaceae, Elaeocarpaceae, Ericaceae, Euphorbiaceae, Fabaceae, Fagaceae, Garryaceae, Gentianaceae, Gesneriaceae, Hamamelidaceae, Hydrangeaceae, Iteaceae, Lamiaceae, Lardizabalaceae, Lauraceae, Linderniaceae, Loganiaceae, Lythraceae, Magnoliaceae, Malvaceae, Melastomataceae, Meliaceae, Menyanthaceae, Metteniusaceae, Moraceae, Myrtaceae, Nyssaceae, Oleaceae, Pentaphragmataceae, Pentaphylacaceae, Petrosaviaceae, Phyllanthaceae, Pinaceae, Pittosporaceae, Poaceae, Polygalaceae, Primulaceae, Proteaceae, Putranjivaceae, Rhamnaceae, Rosaceae, Rubiaceae, Rutaceae, Sabiaceae, Salicaceae, Sapindaceae, Schisandraceae, Solanaceae, Staphyleaceae, Styracaceae, Taxaceae, Theaceae, Thymelaeaceae, Urticaceae, Vitaceae [PS]
- Published taxa: *Acalypha, Acanthopanax, Actephila, Adinandra, Allophylus, Alphonsea, Alseodaphne, Alstonia, Altingia, Alyxia, Andrachne, Antidesma, Apama, Ardisia, Aristolochia, Artabotrys, Arundinaria, Aucuba, Bauhinia, Begonia, Betula, Bredia, Briggsia, Buxus, Callicarpa, Camellia, Campylandra, Canthium, Capparis, Carex, Castanopsis, Cathaya, Cathayanthe, Cayratia, Cenesmon, Ceratoscyphus, Cercis, Chonemorpha, Clausena, Cornus, Crawfurdia, Cyclobalanopsis, Dalbergia, Dasymaschalon, Dendrobenthamia, Dendropanax, Derris, Desmodium, Desmos, Dichapetalum, Didymocarpus, Diospyros, Drypetes, Elaeocarpus, Eriobotrya, Erycibe, Eugenia, Euonymus, Eurya, Ficus, Fissistigma, Gilibertia, Goniothalamus, Gymnosporia, Halesia, Hartia, Hedyosmum, Hedyotis, Helicia, Hibiscus, Holboellia, Homalium, Hopea, Hovenia, Hydrangea, Ilex, Illicium, Itea, Ixora, Lagerstroemia, Lasianthus, Lauro-cerasus, Lindernia, Linociera, Lithocarpus, Litsea, Lyonia, Lysionotus, Maesa, Mahonia, Mallotus, Mastixia, Medinilla, Meliosma, Memecylon, Merrillanthus, Michelia, Microcos, Miliusa, Millettia, Nauclea, Neolitsea, Nymphoides, Oldenlandia, Ophiopogon, Oreocharis, Oreocnide, Ormosia, Osbeckia, Ostrya, Paedicalyx, Parthenocissus, Pasania, Pentaphragma, Pentaphylax, Petrocosmea, Petrosavia, Photinia, Phyllagathis, Phyllanthus, Phyllodium, Pieris, Pinus,*

Pittosporum, Platea, Pleomele, Polyalthia, Polygala, Premna, Quercus, Randia, Raphiocarpus, Reevesia, Rhamnus, Rhododendron, Rhodoleia, Rubus, Sauropus, Schefflera, Schizophragma, Sinoboea, Slackia, Sloanea, Solanum, Sonerila, Sophora, Stauntonia, Staurogyne, Sterculia, Strychnos, Styrax, Tarrietia, Tengia, Ternstroemia, Thea, Tilia, Torreya, Tournefortia, Trachelospermum, Tragia, Trema, Trichosanthes, Trigonostemon, Triticum, Tsoongiodendron, Turpinia, Tutcheria, Urophyllum, Vanieria, Ventilago, Viburnum, Wikstroemia, Xanthophytopsis, Zenia

- Affiliation: IBSC
- Location of specimens: IBSC, N, NAS, PE
- Region: CHINA

J. J. Chen

Chen, Ji Jun; 陈纪军 ; Chén Jìjūn

1965- **First publication: 1997**

- Employment: Kunming Institute of Botany, Chinese Academy of Sciences（中国科学院昆明植物研究所）
- Research interest: Apocynaceae [S]
- Published taxa: *Sinomarsdenia*
- Region: CHINA (Yunnan)

J. K. Chen

Chen, Jia Kuan; 陈家宽 ; Chén Jiākuān; 陳家寬

1947- **First publication: 1983**

- Employment: Department of Biology, Wuhan University; Institute of Biodiversity Science, Fudan University（武汉大学生物系；复旦大学生物多样性科学研究所）
- Research interest: Alismataceae [S]
- Published taxa: *Alisma, Sagittaria*
- Affiliation: WH
- Region: CHINA (Hubei)

C. J. Chen

Chen, Chia Jui; Chen, Chia Jue; Chen, Jia Rui; 陈家瑞 ; Chén Jiāruì; 陳家瑞

1935- **First publication: 1979**

- Employment: Institute of Botany, Chinese Academy of Sciences（中国科学院植物研究所）
- Research interest: Cannabaceae, Cycadaceae, Fabaceae, Onagraceae, Urticaceae [S]
- Published taxa: *Aphananthe, Archiboehmeria, Astragalus, Boehmeria, Campylotropis, Chamabainia, Cycas, Debregeasia, Epilobium, Girardinia, Laportea, Lecanthus, Lespedeza, Oreocnide, Pilea, Pouzolzia, Sphaerotylos, Thermopsis, Trema, Urtica*
- Affiliation: PE
- Region: CHINA

Jian B. Chen

Chen, Jian Bing; 陈建兵 ; Chén Jiànbīng

1964- **First publication: 2019**

- Employment: The Orchid Conservation & Research Center of Shenzhen, Guangdong（广东省深圳市兰科植物保护研究中心）
- Research interest: Orchidaceae [S]
- Published taxa: *Cheirostylis*
- Region: CHINA (Yunnan)
- IPNI as: J. B. Chen

Chien F. Chen

Chen, Chien Fan; 陳建帆 ; Chén Jiànfān; 陈建帆

First publication: 2008

- Employment: Department of Forestry, Pingtung University of Science and Technology（屏东科技大学森林系）
- Research interest: Gentianaceae, Magnoliaceae, Melastomataceae, Orobanchaceae; Plants of Taiwan [S]
- Published taxa: *Magnolia, Phyllagathis, Sonerila, Striga, Swertia*
- Affiliation: TAIF
- Region: CHINA (Taiwan)
- IPNI as: C. F. Chen

Jian Y. Chen

Chen, Jian Ye; 陈建业 ; Chén Jiànyè

First publication: 1990

- Employment: Xuchang Institute of Forestry Science, Henan（河南省许昌林业科学技术研究所）
- Research interest: Simaroubaceae [S]
- Published taxa: *Ailanthus*
- Region: CHINA (Henan)

C. Chen

Chen, Chieh; Chen, Jie; Chen, Cheih; 陈介 ; Chén Jiè 陳介

1928-2011 **First publication: 1964**

- Employment: Kunming Institute of Botany, Chinese Academy of Sciences（中国科学院昆明植物研究所）
- Research interest: Aquifoliaceae, Combretaceae, Cycadaceae, Cyperaceae, Elaeocarpaceae, Fabaceae, Lamiaceae, Melastomataceae, Myrtaceae, Primulaceae, Smilacaceae, Solanaceae, Symplocaceae [S]
- Published taxa: *Abarema, Acacia, Ajuga, Allomorphia, Anisodus, Ardisia, Astragalus, Blastus, Bredia, Combretum, Crotalaria, Cycas, Cylindrokelupha, Desmodium, Elaeocarpus, Embelia, Entada, Euchresta, Fordiophyton, Glechoma, Ilex, Isodon, Lysimachia, Maesa, Medinilla, Memecylon, Myrsine, Osbeckia, Phyllagathis, Plagiopetalum, Podocarpium, Rapanea, Sarcopyramis, Schnabelia,*

Schoenus, Scopolia, Scorpiothyrsus, Scutellaria, Smilax, Sonerila, Sporoxeia, Stapfiophyton, Symplocos, Syzygium, Terminalia, Tigridiopalma
- Affiliation: KUN
- Region: CHINA

Jin Y. Chen

Chen, Jin Yong; 陈进勇 ; Chén Jìnyǒng

1971- First publication: 2007

- Employment: Institute of Botany, Chinese Academy of Sciences; Beijing Botanical Garden（中国科学院植物研究所；北京植物园）
- Research interest: Oleaceae [S]
- Published taxa: *Syringa*
- Region: CHINA
- IPNI as: J. Y. Chen

J. F. Chen

Chen, Jing Fong; Chen, Jin Feng; **陈劲枫 ; Chén Jìnfēng**

First publication: 1984

- Employment: Department of Horticulture, Southwest Agricultural College; College of Horticulture, Nanjing Agricultural University（西南农学院园艺系；南京农业大学园艺学院）
- Research interest: Araceae, Cucurbitaceae [S]
- Published taxa: *Amorphophallus, Cucumis*
- Region: CHINA (Sichuan)
- Also as: Jin F. Chen

Juan Chen

Chen, Juan; 陈娟 ; Chén Juān

1986- First publication: 2008

- Employment: South China Botanical Garden, Chinese Academy of Sciences（中国科学院华南植物园）
- Research interest: Zingiberaceae [S]
- Published taxa: *Curcuma, Zingiber*
- Affiliation: IBSC
- Region: CHINA

J. T. Chen

Chen, Jun Tong; 陈俊通 ; Chén Jùntōng

1993- First publication: 2018

- Employment: School of Landscape Architecture, Beijing Forestry University（北京林业大学园林学院）
- Research interest: Asteraceae [S]
- Published taxa: *Chrysanthemum*
- Region: CHINA (Shandong)

Jun Y. Chen

Chen, Jun Yu; Chen, Chun Yu; Chen, Chün Yü; Ch'ên, Chün Yü; **陈俊愉 ; Chén Jùnyú; 陳俊愉**

1917-2012 First publication: 1987

- Employment: Beijing Forestry University; Beijing Forestry University Forest Science Co., Ltd.（北京林业大学；北京林大林业科技股份有限公司）
- Research interest: Asteraceae, Theaceae [S]
- Published taxa: *Camellia, Chrysanthemum*
- Region: CHINA (Guangxi, Henan, Hubei)
- IPNI as: J. Y. Chen

K. Chen

Chen, Kun; 陈堃 ; Chén Kūn

1989- First publication: 2013

- Employment: Department of Horticulture, Jinling Institute of Technology（金陵科技学院园艺系）
- Research interest: Ericaceae [S]
- Published taxa: *Rhododendron*
- Region: CHINA (Zhejiang)

K. L. Chen

Chen, Ku Lin; 陳堃霖 ; Chén Kūnlín; 陈堃霖

First publication: 1988

- Employment: College of Agriculture, Chung Hsing University（中兴大学农学院）
- Research interest: Loranthaceae [S]
- Published taxa: *Scurrula*
- Region: CHINA (Taiwan)

Li Chen

Chen, Li; 陈丽 ; Chén Lì

1984- First publication: 2009

- Employment: Wuhan Botanical Garden, Chinese Academy of Sciences（中国科学院武汉植物园）
- Research interest: Fagaceae [S]
- Published taxa: *Castanopsis, Lithocarpus*
- Affiliation: HIB
- Region: CHINA (Guangxi, Yunnan)

L. Y. Chen

Chen, Li Yun; 陈丽云 ; Chén Lìyún

1964- First publication: 1995

- Employment: Fujian Institute of Subtropical Botany（福建省亚热带植物研究所）
- Research interest: Rosaceae; Plants of Fujian [S]
- Published taxa: *Rubus*
- Affiliation: FJSI
- Location of specimens: FJSI
- Region: CHINA (Fujian)

L. J. Chen

Chen, Li Jun; 陈利君 ; Chén Lìjūn

1980- First publication: 2008

- Employment: The Orchid Conservation & Research Center of Shenzhen, Guangdong（广东省深圳市兰科植物保护研究中心）
- Research interest: Hypoxidaceae, Orchidaceae [S]
- Published taxa: *Apostasia, Bulbophyllum, Calanthe, Cheirostylis, Chenorchis, Chroniochilus, Coelogyne,*

Cymbidium, Cypripedium, Dendrobium, Gastrochilus, Gunnaria, Holcoglossum, Neuwiedia, Paphiopedilum, Paraholcoglossum, Pendulorchis, Platanthera, Pleione, Singchia, Sinocurculigo, Tsiorchis, Ypsilorchis
- Affiliation: NOCC
- Location of specimens: NOCC
- Region: CHINA

L. Chen

Chen, Lian; 陈琏；Chén Liǎn; 陳璉
1947- **First publication: 2007**
- Employment: Panzhihua Municipal Gardening Institute, Sichuan（四川省攀枝花市园林绿化处）
- Research interest: Urticaceae [S]
- Published taxa: *Pilea*
- Region: CHINA (Sichuan)

L. B. Chen

Chen, Liang Bi; 陈良碧；Chén Liángbì
1955- **First publication: 2008**
- Employment: College of Life Sciences, Hunan Normal University（湖南师范大学生命科学学院）
- Research interest: Brassicaceae [S]
- Published taxa: *Cardamine*
- Region: CHINA (Hunan)

Lin Chen

Chen, Lin; 陈林；Chén Lín
1982- **First publication: 2011**
- Employment: South China Botanical Garden, Chinese Academy of Sciences（中国科学院华南植物园）
- Research interest: Celastraceae, Oleaceae, Zingiberaceae; Plants of S. China [S]
- Published taxa: *Microtropis, Zingiber*
- Affiliation: NF
- Region: CHINA (Guangdong)

Ling Chen

Chen, Ling; 陈玲；Chén Líng; 胡喻陈；陳玲
1937- **First publication: 1991**
- Employment: Nanjing University（南京大学）
- Research interest: Poaceae [S]
- Published taxa: *Polyanthus*
- Region: CHINA (Hunan)
- IPNI as: Y. C. Hu

M. Chen

Chen, Max; Chen, Lung Hui; 陳隆輝；Chén Lónghuī; 陈隆辉
1948- **First publication: 2003**
- Employment: Jumbo Orchids, Taiwan（台湾珍宝兰园）
- Research interest: Orchidaceae [S]
- Published taxa: *× Catamangis, × Catasellia, × Cycnophyllum, × Cymbidimangis, × Cymbisellia, × Eulophyllum, × Eulosellia, × Grammatomangis, × Mormosellia*
- Region: CHINA (Taiwan)

P. S. Chen

Chen, Pei Shan; 陈佩珊；Chén Pèishān; 陳佩珊
1938- **First publication: 1979**
- Employment: Kunming Institute of Botany, Chinese Academy of Sciences（中国科学院昆明植物研究所）
- Research interest: Begoniaceae, Piperaceae, Zingiberaceae; Plants of Yunnan [S]
- Published taxa: *Amomum, Peperomia, Piper*
- Affiliation: HITBC, KUNE
- Region: CHINA (Yunnan)

Chi C. Chen

Chen, Chi Chuan; 陳綺娟；Chén Qǐjuān; 陈绮娟
First publication: 2020
- Employment: University of Helsinki, Finland; Xishuangbanna Tropical Botanical Garden, Chinese Academy of Sciences（芬兰赫尔辛基大学；中国科学院西双版纳热带植物园）
- Research interest: Polypodiaceae [P]
- Published taxa: *Goniophlebieae, Lecanoptereae, Thylacoptereae*
- Region: [ASIA]

Q. H. Chen

Chen, Qian Hai; 陈谦海；Chén Qiānhǎi; 陳謙海
1940- **First publication: 1987**
- Employment: Institute of Biology, Guizhou Academy of Sciences（贵州省科学院生物研究所）
- Research interest: Acanthaceae, Anacardiaceae, Asparagaceae, Brassicaceae, Celastraceae, Euphorbiaceae, Lardizabalaceae, Orchidaceae, Rhamnaceae, Rosaceae, Sabiaceae; Plants of Guizhou [S]
- Published taxa: *Cardamine, Celastrus, Cremastra, Croton, Euonymus, Holboellia, Justicia, Leptostachya, Maytenus, Microtropis, Prunus, Rhamnus, Rubus, Sabia, Tetragoga, Toxicodendron, Tupistra*
- Affiliation: HGAS
- Location of specimens: HGAS
- Region: CHINA (Guizhou)

Q. L. Chen

Chen, Qing Lian; 陈清莲；Chén Qīnglián; 陳清蓮，陈青莲
1912-2005 **First publication: 1982**
- Employment: Hunan Normal University（湖南师范大学）
- Research interest: Asteraceae, Berberidaceae [S]
- Published taxa: *Berberis, Epimedium*
- Affiliation: HNNU

• Region: CHINA (Hunan)

Q. F. Chen

Chen, Qing Fu; 陈庆富 ; Chén Qìngfù
1966- **First publication: 1999**

- Employment: Department of Biology, Guizhou Normal University (贵州师范大学生物系)
- Research interest: Polygonaceae [S]
- Published taxa: *Fagopyrum*
- Region: CHINA (Guizhou, Sichuan, Xizang)

R. S. Chen

Chen, Rong Sheng; 陈榕生 ; Chén Róngshēng; 陳榕生
1933- **First publication: 2013**

- Employment: Xiamen Botanical Garden (厦门市园林植物园)
- Research interest: Poaceae [S]
- Published taxa: *Dendrocalamus*
- Region: CHINA (Fujian)

San Y. Chen

Chen, San Yang; 陈三阳 ; Chén Sānyáng; 陳三陽
1937-2008 **First publication: 1989**

- Employment: Kunming Institute of Botany, Chinese Academy of Sciences (中国科学院昆明植物研究所)
- Research interest: Arecaceae [S]
- Published taxa: *Calamus*
- Affiliation: KUN
- Region: CHINA

Shan Chen

Chen, Shan; 陈山 ; Chén Shān; 陳山
1935- **First publication: 1979**

- Employment: Institute of Grassland Research, Chinese Academy of Agricultural Sciences (中国农业科学院草原研究所)
- Research interest: Amaryllidaceae, Lamiaceae, Poaceae [S]
- Published taxa: *Allium, Dracocephalum, Poa, Roegneria*
- Affiliation: NMTC
- Location of specimens: FGC, NMTC
- Region: CHINA (Nei Mongol)

Shan Yong Chen

Chen, Shan Yong; 陈善墉 ; Chén Shànyōng; 陳善墉
1915-2005 **First publication: 1980**

- Employment: Sichuan Institute of Chinese Materia Medica (四川省中药研究所)
- Research interest: Violaceae; Plants of Sichuan [S]
- Published taxa: *Viola*
- Affiliation: SM
- Location of specimens: SM
- Region: CHINA (Sichuan, Xizang)
- Also as: S. Y. Chun

Shao F. Chen

Chen, Shao Feng; 陈少风 ; Chén Shàofēng
1958- **First publication: 2008**

- Employment: School of Life Sciences, Nanchang University (南昌大学生命科学学院)
- Research interest: Polygonaceae; Plants of Jiangxi [S]
- Published taxa: *Persicaria, Polygonum*
- Affiliation: JXU
- Region: CHINA
- IPNI as: S. F. Chen

S. H. Chun

Chun, Shao Hing; Chun, Siu Hing; 陈少卿 ; Chén Shàoqīng; 陳少卿
1911-1997 **First publication: 2001**

- Employment: South China Institute of Botany, Chinese Academy of Sciences (中国科学院华南植物研究所)
- Research interest: Pentaphylacaceae; Plants of S. China [S]
- Published taxa: *Cleyera*
- Affiliation: IBSC
- Location of specimens: IBK, IBSC, PE
- Region: CHINA (Hainan)

S. T. Chen

Chen, Shao Tian; 陈绍田 ; Chén Shàotián
1976- **First publication: 2006**

- Employment: Kunming Institute of Botany, Chinese Academy of Sciences (中国科学院昆明植物研究所)
- Research interest: Bignoniaceae, Boraginaceae [S]
- Published taxa: *Incarvillea, Microula*
- Region: CHINA (Sichuan)

S. Y. Chen

Chen, Shao Yun; 陈绍云 ; Chén Shàoyún; 陳紹雲
1935- **First publication: 1980**

- Employment: Hangzhou Botanical Garden (杭州植物园)
- Research interest: Gesneriaceae, Poaceae [S]
- Published taxa: *Briggsia, Phyllostachys, Pleioblastus, Sinobambusa*
- Affiliation: HHBG
- Region: CHINA

S.J. Chen

Chen, Sen Jen; Chen, Sheng Zhen; 陈升振 ; Chén Shēngzhèn; 陳昇振
1931-2009 **First publication: 1976**

- Employment: South China Institute of Botany, Chinese Academy of Sciences; South China Botanical Garden, Chinese Academy of Sciences (中国科学院华南植物研究所 ; 中国科学院华南植物园)

- Research interest: Costaceae, Marantaceae, Zingiberaceae [S]
- Published taxa: *Achasma, Alpinia, Amomum, Costus, Curcuma, Hedychium, Hornstedtia, Monolophus, Phrynium, Plagiostachys, Zingiber*
- Affiliation: IBSC
- Region: CHINA

S. X. Chen

Chen, Shi Xia; 陈时夏 ; Chén Shíxià; 陳時夏

1935- **First publication: 1987**

- Employment: Sichuan School of Chinese Materia Medica（四川省中药学校）
- Research interest: Zingiberaceae [S]
- Published taxa: *Zingiber*
- Region: CHINA (Sichuan)

Shi Chen

Chen, Shi; 陈实 ; Chén Shí

1926- **First publication: 1982**

- Employment: Qinghai Forestry Bureau（青海省林业局）
- Research interest: Pinaceae [S]
- Published taxa: *Picea*
- Region: CHINA (Qinghai)

Shi C. Chen

Chen, Shi Chiang; Chen, Shi Qiang; 陈士强 ; Chén Shìqiáng

1956- **First publication: 1984**

- Employment: Wucheng Science and Technology Bureau, Jinhua, Zhejiang（浙江省金华市婺城区科技局）
- Research interest: Poaceae [S]
- Published taxa: *Pseudosasa*
- Region: CHINA (Zhejiang)
- IPNI as: S. C. Chen

Shih H. Chen

Chen, Shih Huei; 陳世輝 ; Chén Shìhuī; 陈世辉

First publication: 1999

- Employment: Graduate Institute of Biological Resource and Technology, Hualien University of Education（花莲教育大学生物资源与科技研究所）
- Research interest: Asteraceae, Nyctaginaceae [S]
- Published taxa: *Boerhavia, Centratherum*
- Region: CHINA (Taiwan)

Shi L. Chen

Chen, Shi Long; 陈世龙 ; Chén Shìlóng

1967- **First publication: 2001**

- Employment: Northwest Plateau Institute of Biology, Chinese Academy of Sciences（中国科学院西北高原生物研究所）
- Research interest: Caryophyllaceae, Gentianaceae, Saxifragaceae [S]
- Published taxa: *Metagentiana, Stellaria, Swertia*
- Affiliation: HNWP
- Location of specimens: HNWP
- Region: CHINA

S. P. Chen

Chen, Shi Pin; 陈世品 ; Chén Shìpǐn

1968- **First publication: 2014**

- Employment: Forestry College, Fujian Agriculture and Forestry University（福建农林大学林学院）
- Research interest: Fagaceae, Gesneriaceae, Lauraceae, Orchidaceae, Poaceae [S]
- Published taxa: *Bulbophyllum, Dendrobium, Gastrodia, Goodyera, Primulina*
- Affiliation: FJFC
- Region: CHINA

S. L. Chen

Chen, Shou Liang; 陈守良 ; Chén Shǒuliáng; 陳守良

1921-2013 **First publication: 1963**

- Employment: Nanjing Institute of Botany, Chinese Academy of Sciences; Institute of Botany, Jiangsu Province; Institute of Botany, Jiangsu Province and Chinese Academy of Sciences（中国科学院南京植物研究所；江苏省植物研究所；江苏省中国科学院植物研究所）
- Research interest: Lamiaceae, Poaceae [S]
- Published taxa: *Aeluropus, Ampelocalamus, Apocopis, Arthraxon, Arundinella, Brachiaria, Brachystachyum, Callicarpa, Caryopteris, Cleistogenes, Clerodendrum, Cymbopogon, Digitaria, Dimeria, Echinochloa, Elymus, Eulalia, Garnotia, Imperata, Isachne, Kengyilia, Leymus, Microstegium, Miscanthus, Mnesithea, Oplismenus, Ottochloa, Panicum, Pennisetum, Phacelurus, Phyllostachys, Pleioblastus, Poa, Pogonatherum, Polytrias, Premna, Psathyrostachys, Pseudanthistiria, Pseudopogonatherum, Pseudoraphis, Pseudosasa, Puccinellia, Roegneria, Saccharum, Sacciolepis, Setaria, Setiacis, Spodiopogon, Themeda, Tripogon, Triticum, Urochloa, Vitex, Zizania*
- Affiliation: NAS
- Location of specimens: NAS
- Region: CHINA

S. K. Chen

Chen, Shu Kun; 陈书坤 ; Chénshūkūn; 陳書坤

1936-2018 **First publication: 1977**

- Employment: Kunming Institute of Botany, Chinese Academy of Sciences（中国科学院昆明植物研究所）
- Research interest: Actinidiaceae, Aquifoliaceae, Begoniaceae, Cucurbitaceae, Malpighiaceae, Polygalaceae, Rhamnaceae, Sabiaceae,

Stachyuraceae [S]
• Published taxa: *Actinidia, Aspidopterys, Begonia, Gynostemma, Hiptage, Ilex, Meliosma, Polygala, Sabia, Sageretia, Saurauia, Stachyurus, Trichosanthes, Zehneria*
• Affiliation: KUN
• Region: CHINA

Shu Y. Chen

Chen, Shu Yan; 陈书燕 ; Chén Shūyān
1978- **First publication: 2009**
• Employment: School of Life Sciences, Lanzhou University（兰州大学生命科学学院）
• Research interest: Papaveraceae [S]
• Published taxa: *Meconopsis*
• Region: CHINA (Gansu)

S. R. Chen

Chen, Shu Rong; 陈淑荣 ; Chén Shūróng
1962- **First publication: 2000**
• Employment: Institute of Botany, Chinese Academy of Sciences（中国科学院植物研究所）
• Research interest: Asteraceae, Ranunculaceae [S]
• Published taxa: *Eupatorium, Ranunculus*
• Affiliation: PE
• Region: CHINA

F. Chun

Chun, Faith; Chun, Shu Chen; Ch'ên, Shu Chên; Chun, Shu Chên; **陳淑珍 ; Chén Shūzhēn; 陈淑珍**
1905-? **First publication: 1939**
• Employment: Botanical Institute, College of Sciences, National Sun Yat-sen University; Botanical Institute, National Kwangsi Univertsity（国立中山大学理学院植物学研究所；国立广西大学经济植物研究所）
• Research interest: Actinidiaceae, Begoniaceae, Berberidaceae, Capparaceae, Pentaphragmataceae, Primulaceae, Sapindaceae, Styracaceae [S]
• Published taxa: *Acer, Actinidia, Begonia, Capparis, Halesia, Lysimachia, Mahonia, Pentaphragma, Styrax*
• Location of specimens: IBSC
• Region: CHINA

S. G. Chen

Chen, Shu Gang; 陈树钢 ; Chén Shùgāng
1989- **First publication: 2013**
• Employment: South China Botanical Garden, Chinese Academy of Sciences（中国科学院华南植物园）
• Research interest: Magnoliaceae [S]
• Published taxa: *Magnolia*
• Region: CHINA (Yunnan)

S. S. Chen

Chen, Shu Sen; 陈树森 ; Chén Shùsēn
1957- **First publication: 2010**
• Employment: Wuhan Botanical Garden, Chinese Academy of Sciences（中国科学院武汉植物园）
• Research interest: Magnoliaceae [S]
• Published taxa: *Yulania*
• Region: CHINA (Hubei)

Shu Yang Chen

Chen, Shu Yang; 陈漱阳 ; Chén Shùyáng; 陳漱陽
1930-2018 **First publication: 1990**
• Employment: Northwest China Institute of Botany, Chinese Academy of Sciences and Shaanxi Province（陕西省中国科学院西北植物研究所）
• Research interest: Poaceae [S]
• Published taxa: × *Tritihaynaldia*
• Region: [cult.]
• IPNI as: S. Y. Chen

S. H. Chen

Chen, Song He; 陈松河 ; Chén Sōnghé
1968- **First publication: 2007**
• Employment: Xiamen Botanical Garden（厦门市园林植物园）
• Research interest: Poaceae [S]
• Published taxa: *Bambusa, Dendrocalamus, Drepanostachyum, Pseudosasa, Schizostachyum*
• Region: CHINA

Su F. Chen

Chen, Su Fang; 陈素芳 ; Chén Sùfāng
1979- **First publication: 2020**
• Employment: School of Life Sciences, Sun Yat-sen University（中山大学生命科学学院）
• Research interest: Rosaceae [S]
• Published taxa: *Eriobotrya*
• Region: CHINA (Yunnan)

Tao Chen

Chen, Tao; 陈涛 ; Chén Tāo
First publication: 1986
• Employment: Tahe Forestry Bureau, Heilongjiang（黑龙江省塔河林业局）
• Research interest: Celastraceae [S]
• Published taxa: *Euonymus*
• Region: CHINA (Heilongjiang)

Tao Chen bis

Chen, Tao; Chen, Tao, Carl; **陈涛 ; Chén Tāo**
1963- **First publication: 1990**
• Employment: Department of Biology, Anhui Normal University; Department of Biology, Sun Yat-sen University; South China Institute of

Botany, Chinese Academy of Sciences; South China Botanical Garden, Chinese Academy of Sciences; Fairy Lake Botanical Garden, Shenzhen & Chinese Academy of Sciences（安徽师范大学生物系；中山大学生物系；中国科学院华南植物研究所；中国科学院华南植物园；深圳市中国科学院仙湖植物园）
- Research interest: Lamiaceae, Orchidaceae, Rubiaceae, Styracaceae; Plants of S. China [S]
- Published taxa: *Changiostyrax, Hedyotis, Ixora, Leptodermis, Meehania, Mussaenda, Mycetia, Phaius, Pseudopyxis, Sinojackia, Tarenna*
- Affiliation: IBSC, SZG
- Location of specimens: SZG
- Region: CHINA
- IPNI as: Tao Chen; T. Chen; C. T. Chen

T. G. Chen

Chen, Tian Guo; 陈天国; Chén Tiānguó
1968- **First publication: 2013**
- Employment: Changzhou Special Bamboo Breeding Farm, Jiangsu（江苏省常州市特种竹繁育场）
- Research interest: Poaceae [S]
- Published taxa: *Phyllostachys*
- Region: CHINA (Jiangsu)

T. Y. Chen

Chen, Tian Yun; 陈天云; Chén Tiānyún
1957- **First publication: 2012**
- Employment: Ningxia Agriculture Environmental Monitoring Station（宁夏农业环境保护监测站）
- Research interest: Solanaceae [S]
- Published taxa: *Lycium*
- Region: CHINA (Ningxia)

Tien T. Chen

Chen, Tien Tsai; 陳添財; Chén Tiāncái; 陈添财
First publication: 2008
- Employment: Institute of Natural Resources Management, Dong Hwa University, Taiwan（台湾东华大学自然资源管理研究所）
- Research interest: Plantaginaceae [S]
- Published taxa: *Veronicastrum*
- Region: CHINA (Taiwan)

Tong Chen

Chen, Tong; 陈彤; Chén Tóng
1961- **First publication: 1985**
- Employment: Guangxi Forestry Research Institute（广西林业科学研究所）
- Research interest: Poaceae [S]
- Published taxa: *Gelidocalamus*
- Region: CHINA (Guangxi)
- IPNI as: T. Chen

W. J. Chen

Chen, Wei Jie; 陈伟杰; Chén Wěijié
1989- **First publication: 2013**
- Employment: College of Life and Environmental Sciences, Hangzhou Normal University（杭州师范大学生命与环境科学学院）
- Research interest: Cyperaceae, Iridaceae, Rosaceae, Zingiberaceae [S]
- Published taxa: *Carex, Prunus*
- Affiliation: HTC
- Location of specimens: HTC
- Region: CHINA (Zhejiang)

W. C. Chen

Chen, Wei Chiu; Chen, Wei Qiu; 陈伟球; Chén Wěiqiú; 陳偉球
1934- **First publication: 1983**
- Employment: South China Institute of Botany, Chinese Academy of Sciences（中国科学院华南植物研究所）
- Research interest: Apocynaceae, Bretschneideraceae, Moringaceae, Rosaceae, Resedaceae, Rubiaceae [S]
- Published taxa: *Aidia, Beaumontia, Brachytome, Galium, Hedyotis, Hymenopogon, Luculia, Oxyceros, Porterandia, Prunus, Psychotria, Randia, Tarenna, Wendlandia*
- Affiliation: IBSC
- Region: CHINA

W. H. Chen

Chen, Wen Hong; 陈文红；Chén Wénhóng
1975- **First publication: 2002**
- Employment: Kunming Institute of Botany, Chinese Academy of Sciences（中国科学院昆明植物研究所）
- Research interest: Acanthaceae, Asparagaceae, Balsaminaceae, Begoniaceae, Celastraceae, Gesneriaceae, Magnoliaceae, Melanthiaceae, Melastomataceae, Orchidaceae, Polygalaceae, Rubiaceae [S]
- Published taxa: *Amitostigma, Ancylostemon, Anoectochilus, Begonia, Glabrella, Hemiboea, Impatiens, Litostigma, Manglietia, Microtropis, Oreocharis, Oxyspora, Paraboea, Pararuellia, Peliosanthes, Petrocodon, Polygala, Raphiocarpus, Rothmannia, Thrixspermum, Tremacron, Ypsilandra*
- Affiliation: KUN
- Region: CHINA (Yunnan)

W. L. Chen

Chen, Wen Li; 陈文俐；Chén Wénlì
1972- **First publication: 2001**
- Employment: Institute of Botany, Chinese Academy of Sciences（中国科学院植物研究所）

- Research interest: Poaceae [S]
- Published taxa: *Achnatherum, Deyeuxia, Poa, Ptilagrostis*
- Affiliation: PE
- Region: CHINA

W. N. Chen

Chen, Wen Na; 陈文娜 ; Chén Wénnà

1984- **First publication: 2014**

- Employment: South China Botanical Garden, Chinese Academy of Sciences（中国科学院华南植物园）
- Research interest: Musaceae [S]
- Published taxa: *Musa*
- Region: CHINA (Yunnan)

Wen Y. Chen

Chen, Wen Yun; 陈文允 ; Chén Wényǔn

1974- **First publication: 2012**

- Employment: Kunming Institute of Botany, Chinese Academy of Sciences（中国科学院昆明植物研究所）
- Research interest: Lamiaceae [S]
- Published taxa: *Elsholtzia*
- Region: CHINA (Sichuan)
- IPNI as: W. Y. Chen

X. C. Chen

Chen, Xi Cang; 陈西仓 ; Chén Xīcāng

1965- **First publication: 2002**

- Employment: Gansu Forestry Technological College（甘肃林业职业技术学院）
- Research interest: Apocynaceae, Salicaceae; Plants of Gansu [S]
- Published taxa: *Periploca, Populus*
- Affiliation: GSFS
- Location of specimens: GSFS
- Region: CHINA (Gansu)

H. H. Chen

Chen, H. H.; Chen, Hsi Tsun; **陳西村 ; Chén Xīcūn; 陈西村**

First publication: 2011

- Employment: Kinmen County Forestry Bureau（金门县林务所）
- Research interest: Isoetaceae [P]
- Published taxa: *Isoetes*
- Region: CHINA (Taiwan)

X. D. Chen

Chen, Xi Dian; 陈锡典 ; Chén Xīdiǎn; 陳錫典

1935- **First publication: 1984**

- Employment: Shandong Forestry School（山东省林业学校）
- Research interest: Crassulaceae, Cyperaceae, Rosaceae, Rubiaceae; Plants of Shandong [S]
- Published taxa: *Borreria, Carex, Orostachys, Sedum, Sorbus*
- Affiliation: SDFS
- Location of specimens: SDFS
- Region: CHINA (Shandong)

X. M. Chen

Chen, Xi Mu; 陈锡沐 ; Chén Xīmù; 陳錫沐

1949- **First publication: 1984**

- Employment: South China Agricultural University（华南农业大学）
- Research interest: Fagaceae, Meliaceae [S]
- Published taxa: *Aglaia, Amoora, Castanopsis, Chisocheton, Dysoxylum, Munronia, Reinwardtiodendron, Toona, Trichilia, Turraea*
- Affiliation: CANT
- Location of specimens: CANT
- Region: CHINA

X. H. Chen

Chen, Xian Hui; 陈先晖 ; Chén Xiānhuī

1973- **First publication: 1999**

- Employment: Department of Biology, Anhui Normal University（安徽师范大学生物系）
- Research interest: Crassulaceae [S]
- Published taxa: *Sedum*
- Region: CHINA (Anhui)

Xian X. Chen

Chen, Xian Xi; 陈贤喜 ; Chén Xiánxǐ

First publication: 2014

- Employment: Chen Bamboo Garden, Anji, Zhejiang（浙江省安吉陈氏竹园）
- Research interest: Poaceae [S]
- Published taxa: *Phyllostachys*
- Region: CHINA (Zhejiang)

Xiang Chen

Chen, Xiang; 陈翔 ; Chén Xiáng

1972- **First publication: 2003**

- Employment: South China Botanical Garden, Chinese Academy of Sciences; Institute of Biology, Guizhou Academy of Sciences（中国科学院华南植物园；贵州省科学院生物研究所）
- Research interest: Ericaceae, Poaceae [S]
- Published taxa: *Festuca, Rhododendron*
- Affiliation: HGAS
- Region: CHINA (Guizhou)

Xiao Q. Chen

Chen, Xiao Qing; 陈晓庆 ; Chén Xiǎoqìng

1982- **First publication: 2012**

- Employment: Institute of Botany, Chinese Academy

of Sciences（中国科学院植物研究所）
- Research interest: Dennstaedtiaceae [P]
- Published taxa: *Pteridium*
- Region: CHINA

X. Y. Chen

Chen, Xiao Ya; 陈晓亚；Chén Xiǎoyà
1955- **First publication: 1989**
- Employment: Department of Biology, Nanjing University; Institute of Plant Physiology and Ecology, Chinese Academy of Sciences（南京大学生物系；中国科学院上海植物生理生态研究所）
- Research interest: Apiaceae, Poaceae [S]
- Published taxa: *Acidosasa, Prangos*
- Affiliation: N
- Location of specimens: N
- Region: CHINA

S. C. Chen

Chen, Sing Chi; Chen, Xin Qi; Chen, Shing Chi; Chen, H. C.; 陈心启；Chén Xīnqǐ; 陳心啟
1931-2021 **First publication: 1966**
- Employment: Institute of Botany, Chinese Academy of Sciences（中国科学院植物研究所）
- Research interest: Araceae, Asparagaceae, Burmanniaceae, Hypoxidaceae, Liliaceae, Melanthiaceae, Nartheciaceae, Orchidaceae, Poaceae, Smilacaceae, Vitaceae [S]
- Published taxa: *Aletris, Apostasia, Arachnis, Archineottia, Arisaema, Asparagus, Bulbophyllum, Burmannia, Calanthe, Callostylis, Campanulorchis, Cephalanthera, Cheirostylis, Coelogyne, Conchidium, Cremastra, Crepidium, Cryptochilus, Curculigo, Cylindrolobus, Cymbidium, Cypripedium, Dendrobium, Dendrolirium, Didymoplexiella, Diplandrorchis, Dracaena, Epipactis, Eria, Eulophia, Flickingeria, Frigidorchis, Fritillaria, Galearis, Gastrochilus, Gastrodia, Gelidocalamus, Goodyera, Gunnaria, Hemipiliopsis, Heteropolygonatum, Hippeophyllum, Holcoglossum, Holopogon, Liparis, Listera, Luisia, Maianthemum, Malaxis, Mycaranthes, Neofinetia, Neottia, Neottianthe, Oberonia, Odontochilus, Ophiopogon, Pachystoma, Panisea, Paphiopedilum, Paraholcoglossum, Paris, Pennilabium, Peristylus, Phaius, Phalaenopsis, Pholidota, Pinalia, Platanthera, Pleione, Polygonatum, Ponerorchis, Renanthera, Sinorchis, Smilax, Tainia, Tangtsinia, Tipularia, Tsiorchis, Tupistra, Vanilla, Vitis, Ypsilorchis, Yushania*
- Affiliation: PE
- Region: CHINA
- Also as: H. C. Chen

Xin Chen

Chen, Xin; 陈昕；Chén Xīn
1968- **First publication: 2012**
- Employment: College of Biology and the Environment, Nanjing Forestry University（南京林业大学生物与环境学院）
- Research interest: Anisophylleaceae, Rosaceae; Plants of E. China [S]
- Published taxa: *Anisophyllea, Sorbus*
- Affiliation: NF
- Region: [WORLD]

X. L. Chen

Chen, Xin Lu; 陈新露；Chén Xīnlù
1963- **First publication: 1989**
- Employment: Northwest Agricultural University（西北农业大学）
- Research interest: Oleaceae [S]
- Published taxa: *Syringa*
- Location of specimens: SHM
- Region: CHINA

Xin Y. Chen

Chen, Xin Yan; 陈新艳；Chén Xīnyàn
1982- **First publication: 2019**
- Employment: Sanming Garden Center, Sanming, Fujian（福建省三明市园林中心）
- Research interest: Orchidaceae [S]
- Published taxa: *Bulbophyllum, Gastrodia*
- Region: CHINA (Fujian)

Xing Y. Chen

Chen, Xing Yan; 陈兴琰；Chén Xīngyǎn; 陳興琰
1911-2001 **First publication: 1990**
- Employment: Hunan Agricultural College（湖南农学院）
- Research interest: Theaceae [S]
- Published taxa: *Camellia*
- Region: CHINA (Yunnan)
- IPNI as: X. Y. Chen

X. X. Chen

Chen, Xiu Xiang; Chen, Hsiu Siang; 陈秀香；Chén Xiùxiāng; 陳秀香
1937- **First publication: 1978**
- Employment: Guangxi Institute of Ethnic Medicine（广西民族医药研究所）
- Research interest: Apocynaceae, Asparagaceae, Begoniaceae, Celastraceae, Cucurbitaceae, Euphorbiaceae, Fabaceae, Gentianaceae, Gesneriaceae, Phyllanthaceae, Rubiaceae, Sabiaceae, Salicaceae, Zingiberaceae; Medicinal Plants [S]
- Published taxa: *Alpinia, Alstonia, Amomum,*

Aspidistra, Begonia, Bennettiodendron, Blachia, Canscora, Chirita, Curcuma, Dunbaria, Gueldenstaedtia, Gynostemma, Hemsleya, Leptopus, Maytenus, Plagiopteron, Sabia, Spiradiclis
- Affiliation: GXEM
- Location of specimens: GXEM, GXMI
- Region: CHINA (Guangxi)

H. Y. Chen

Chen, Hsiu Ying; Ch'en, Hsiu Ying; Chen, Luetta; 陳秀英 ; Chén Xiùyīng; 陈秀英

1910-1949 First publication: 1935

- Employment: Lingnan Natural History Survey and Museum, Lingnan University; Arnold Arboretum, Harvard University, U.S.A.（岭南自然历史考察与博物馆 ; 美国哈佛大学阿诺德树木园）
- Research interest: Ebenaceae, Fabaceae, Sabiaceae [S]
- Published taxa: *Bauhinia, Diospyros, Ormosia, Sabia*
- Region: CHINA
- Also as: L. Chen

X. B. Chen

Chen, Xu Bo; 陈旭波 ; Chén Xùbō

1982- First publication: 2018

- Employment: Faculty of Ecology, Lishui Universtiy（丽水学院生态学院）
- Research interest: Primulaceae [S]
- Published taxa: *Primula*
- Region: CHINA (Zhejiang)

Xue L. Chen

Chen, Xue Lin; 陈学林 ; Chén Xuélín

1963- First publication: 1994

- Employment: Department of Biology, Northwest Normal University（西北师范大学生物系）
- Research interest: Araliaceae, Elaeagnaceae, Rosaceae [S]
- Published taxa: *Acanthopanax, Amygdalus, Hippophae, Prunus*
- Affiliation: NWTC
- Region: CHINA (Gansu)

X. Chen

Chen, Xun; 陈训 ; Chén Xùn

1956- First publication: 1987

- Employment: Institute of Biology, Guizhou Academy of Sciences（贵州省科学院生物研究所）
- Research interest: Cornaceae, Ericaceae [S]
- Published taxa: *Dendrobenthamia, Rhododendron*
- Region: CHINA (Guizhou)

Y. P. Chen

Chen, Ya Ping; 陈亚萍 ; Chén Yàpíng

1990- First publication: 2014

- Employment: Kunming Institute of Botany, Chinese Academy of Sciences（中国科学院昆明植物研究所）
- Research interest: Lamiaceae [S]
- Published taxa: *Isodon, Siphocranion*
- Region: CHINA (Yunnan)

Yen J. Chen

Chen, Yen Jui; 陳彥儒 ; Chén Yànrú; 陈彦儒

First publication: 2017

- Employment: Luodong Forest District Office, Forestry Bureau, Council of Agriculture, "Executive Yuan"（"行政院"农业委员会林务局罗东林区管理处）
- Research interest: Phyllanthaceae [S]
- Published taxa: *Phyllanthus*
- Region: CHINA (Taiwan)
- IPNI as: Y. J. Chen

Y. Q. Chen

Chen, Yan Qiong; 陈燕琼 ; Chén Yànqióng

1991- First publication: 2020

- Employment: College of Landscape Architecture, Fujian Agriculture and Forestry University（福建农林大学园林学院）
- Research interest: Orchidaceae [S]
- Published taxa: *Calanthe*
- Region: CHINA (Yunnan)

Y. D. Chen

Chen, Yao Dong; 陈耀东 ; Chén Yàodōng; 陳耀東

1934-2006 First publication: 1981

- Employment: Institute of Botany, Chinese Academy of Sciences（中国科学院植物研究所）
- Research interest: Cyperaceae, Potamogetonaceae, Typhaceae; Aquatic Plants [S]
- Published taxa: *Eleocharis, Potamogeton, Sparganium, Zannichellia*
- Affiliation: PE
- Region: CHINA

Y. L. Chen

Chen, Yi Ling; Chen, Yi Lin; 陈艺林 ; Chén Yìlín; 陳藝林

1930- First publication: 1965

- Employment: Institute of Botany, Chinese Academy of Sciences（中国科学院植物研究所）
- Research interest: Asteraceae, Balsaminaceae, Rhamnaceae [S]
- Published taxa: *Anaphalis, Asterothamnus, Aster, Berchemia, Berchemiella, Cissampelopsis, Conyza, Cremanthodium, Dicercoclados, Dolomiaea, Doronicum, Erigeron, Faberiopsis, Galatella, Heteropappus, Heteroplexis, Hovenia, Impatiens, Leontopodium, Ligularia, Ligulariopsis, Miyamayomena, Nannoglottis, Nemosenecio,*

Parasenecio, Psychrogeton, Rhamnus, Sageretia, Saussurea, Senecio, Sinacalia, Sinoleontopodium, Sinosenecio, Synotis, Tephroseris, Ventilago, Vernonia, Ziziphus
- Affiliation: PE
- Location of specimens: HSIB, PE
- Region: CHINA

A. Chen

Chen, Andy; Chen, I Sheng; **陳易聖 ; Chén Yìshèng; 陈易圣**

First publication: 2008

- Employment: Jumbo Orchids, Taiwan（台湾珍宝兰园）
- Research interest: Orchidaceae [S]
- Published taxa: *× Cycgalenodes, × Cymbidilophia, × Cyrtogramcymbidium, × Geoclades, × Gramcymbimangis, × Gramcymbiphia, × Longhueiara, × Zygomatophyllum*
- Region: CHINA (Taiwan)

I. S. Chen

Chen, Ih Sheng; 陳益昇 ; Chén Yìshēng; 陈益升

First publication: 1972

- Employment: College of Medicine, Kaohsiung Medical University（高雄医学大学医学院）
- Research interest: Rosaceae, Rutaceae [S]
- Published taxa: *Spiraea, Zanthoxylum*
- Region: CHINA (Taiwan)

Y. K. Chen

Chen, Yung Kuang; 陳永寬 ; Chén Yǒngkuān; 陈永宽

First publication: 1988

- Employment: Biodiversity Research Center, "Academia Sinica"（中研院生物多样性研究中心）
- Research interest: Begoniaceae [S]
- Published taxa: *Begonia*
- Region: CHINA (Taiwan)

Y. M. Chen

Chen, You Min; 陈有民 ; **Chén Yǒumín**; 陳有民

1926- **First publication: 1988**

- Employment: Department of Landscape, Beijing Forestry University（北京林业大学园林系）
- Research interest: Pinaceae; Woody Plants [S]
- Published taxa: *Larix*
- Affiliation: BJFC
- Location of specimens: BJFC
- Region: CHINA (Hebei)

Yo J. Chen

Chen, Yo Jiun; 陳又君 ; Chén Yòujūn; 陈又君

First publication: 2000

- Employment: Department of Life Science, Taiwan Normal University（台湾师范大学生命科学系）
- Research interest: Commelinaceae [S]
- Published taxa: *Belosynapsis*
- Region: CHINA (Taiwan)

Y. S. Chen

Chen, You Sheng; 陈又生 ; Chén Yòushēng

1972- **First publication: 2003**

- Employment: Institute of Botany, Chinese Academy of Sciences; South China Botanical Garden, Chinese Academy of Sciences（中国科学院植物研究所；中国科学院华南植物园）
- Research interest: Asteraceae, Sapindaceae, Violaceae [S]
- Published taxa: *Acer, Cremanthodium, Dolomiaea, Faberia, Gamochaeta, Himalaiella, Leontopodium, Ligularia, Nabalus, Parasenecio, Pseudognaphalium, Saussurea, Viola, Youngia*
- Affiliation: IBSC, PE
- Region: CHINA

Y. A. Chen

Chen, Yu An; 陈佑安 ; Chén Yòu'ān 陳佑安

1933-1990 **First publication: 1986**

- Employment: Institute of Forestry and Soil Sciences, Chinese Academy of Sciences; Institute of Applied Ecology, Chinese Academy of Sciences（中国科学院林业土壤研究所；中国科学院沈阳应用生态研究所）
- Research interest: Fabaceae, Iridaceae, Juncaceae, Lamiaceae [S]
- Published taxa: *Astragalus, Glycine, Iris, Luzula, Medicago, Melilotoides, Melissitus, Oxytropis, Pocockia, Trifolium, Vicia*
- Affiliation: IFP
- Region: CHINA (Liaoning)

Yu Chen

Chen, Yu; Cheng, Yu; **陈渝 ; Chén Yú**

1967- **First publication: 1983**

- Employment: Yunnan Institute of Tropical Botany, Chinese Academy of Sciences（中国科学院云南热带植物研究所）
- Research interest: Asparagaceae [S]
- Published taxa: *Smilacina*
- Region: CHINA (Yunnan)

Y. H. Chen

Chen, Yu Heng; 陈毓亨 ; Chén Yùhēng; 陳毓亨

1934- **First publication: 1981**

- Employment: Institute of Materia Medica, Chinese Academy of Medical Sciences（中国医学科学院药物研究所）
- Research interest: Taxaceae, Zingiberaceae [S]

- Published taxa: *Curcuma*
- Affiliation: IMM
- Region: CHINA

Y. T. Chen

Chen, Yun Tsao; 陳運造 ; Chén Yùnzào; 陈运造

1943- **First publication: 2011**

- Employment: Miaoli District Agricultural Research and Extension Station,Council of Agriculture, "Executive Yuan"（"行政院"农业委员会苗栗区改良场）
- Research interest: Buxaceae, Cannabaceae, Ebenaceae, Melastomataceae, Rosaceae, Salicaceae, Styracaceae [S]
- Published taxa: *Buxus, Celtis, Maba, Memecylon, Rubus, Salix, Sarcococca, Styrax*
- Region: CHINA (Taiwan)

Z. K. Chen

Chen, Zhan Kuan; 陈占宽 ; Chén Zhànkuān; 陳占寬

1946- **First publication: 1992**

- Employment: Henan Academy of Agricultural Sciences（河南省农业科学院）
- Research interest: Orchidaceae [S]
- Published taxa: *Dendrobium*
- Location of specimens: HEAC
- Region: CHINA (Henan)

Z. C. Chen

Chen, Zhao Chou; Chun, Chao Chou; Chun, Zhao Chou; 陈照宙 ; Chén Zhàozhòu

First publication: 1985

- Employment: Guangxi Institute of Botany, Chinese Academy of Sciences（广西壮族自治区中国科学院广西植物研究所）
- Research interest: Betulaceae [S]
- Published taxa: *Carpinus*
- Affiliation: IBK
- Location of specimens: IBK
- Region: CHINA (Guangxi)

Z. F. Chen

Chen, Zhen Feng; 陈振峰 ; Chén Zhènfēng

1962- **First publication: 1988**

- Employment: Northwest Forestry College; Xi' an Institute of Lacquer, Ministry of Commerce（西北林学院；商业部西安生漆研究所）
- Research interest: Anacardiaceae, Salicaceae [S]
- Published taxa: *Populus, Toxicodendron*
- Affiliation: LAC
- Location of specimens: LAC
- Region: CHINA

Zhen R. Chen

Chen, Zhen Ren; 陈镇仁 ; Chén Zhènrén

1952- **First publication: 2018**

- Employment: Wuping County Science and Technology Association, Fujian（福建省武平县科学技术协会）
- Research interest: Staphyleaceae [S]
- Published taxa: *Euscaphis*
- Region: CHINA (Fujian)
- IPNI as: Z. R. Chen

Z. H. Chen

Chen, Zheng Hai; Cheng, Zheng Hai; 陈征海 ; Chén Zhēnghǎi

1963- **First publication: 1989**

- Employment: Zhejiang Forestry Surveying and Designing Institute; Forest Resources Monitoring Center of Zhejiang Province（浙江省林业勘察设计院；浙江省森林资源监测中心）
- Research interest: Balsaminaceae, Betulaceae, Fagaceae, Lamiaceae, Liliaceae, Magnoliaceae, Rosaceae, Rubiaceae, Zingiberaceae; Plants of Zhejiang [S]
- Published taxa: *Alnus, Cerasus, Cyclobalanopsis, Globba, Impatiens, Magnolia, Paraphlomis, Rubus, Salvia, Scleromitrion, Scutellaria, Tricyrtis*
- Affiliation: ZJFC
- Location of specimens: ZJFC
- Region: CHINA (Zhejiang)
- Also as: Z. H. Cheng

Zheng R. Chen

Chen, Zheng Ren; 陈正仁 ; Chén Zhèngrén

First publication: 2003

- Employment: Mayanghe National Nature Reserve Administration Bureau, Guizhou（贵州麻阳河国家级自然保护区管理局）
- Research interest: Ericaceae [S]
- Published taxa: *Rhododendron*
- Region: CHINA (Guizhou)

C. W. Chen

Chen, Cheng Wei; 陳正為 ; Chén Zhèngwéi; 陈正为

1984- **First publication: 2014**

- Employment: Taiwan Forestry Research Institute, Council of Agriculture, "Executive Yuan"; Institute of Molecular & Cellular Biology, Tsing Hua University, Taiwan（"行政院"农业委员会林业试验所；台湾清华大学院分子与细胞生物研究所）
- Research interest: Aspleniaceae, Davalliaceae, Polypodiaceae, Pteridaceae, Pteridryaceae, Saccolomataceae, Tectariaceae, Thelypteridaceae [P]
- Published taxa: *Amblovenatum, Antrophyum, Asplenium, Davallia, Haplopteris, Hymenasplenium,*

Polydictyum, Pyrrosia, Saccoloma, Stegnogramma, Tectaria
- Region: CHINA (Taiwan)

Z. D. Chen
Chen, Zhi Duan; 陈之端; Chén Zhīduān
1964- **First publication: 1994**
- Employment: Institute of Botany, Chinese Academy of Sciences (中国科学院植物研究所)
- Research interest: Betulaceae, Borthwickiaceae, Ranunculaceae, Vitaceae; Plant Systematics [S]
- Published taxa: *Betula,* Borthwickiaceae, *Cayratia, Gymnaconitum, Pseudocayratia*
- Affiliation: PE
- Region: CHINA

Z. Chen
Chen, Zhi Lin; Chen, Z. L.; **陈之林; Chén Zhī Lín**
1974- **First publication: 2005**
- Employment: South China Botanical Garden, Chinese Academy of Sciences (中国科学院华南植物园)
- Research interest: Orchidaceae [S]
- Published taxa: *Dendrobium, × Haraenopsis*
- Region: CHINA (Guangdong)
- Also as: Z. L. Chen

C. Hui Chen
Chen, Chih Hui; 陳志輝; Chén Zhìhuī; 陈志辉
1966- **First publication: 2009**
- Employment: Endemic Species Research Institute, Council of Agriculture, "Executive Yuan" ("行政院"农业委员会特有生物研究保育中心)
- Research interest: Poaceae [S]
- Published taxa: *Leptatherum, Microstegium*
- Location of specimens: NCKU
- Region: CHINA (Taiwan)

Chih H. Chen
Chen, Chih Hsiung; 陳志雄; Chén Zhìxióng; 陈志雄
First publication: 1999
- Employment: Museum of Natural Science (自然科学博物馆)
- Research interest: Apiaceae, Gentianaceae, Linderniaceae [S]
- Published taxa: *Gentiana, Lindernia, Lomatogonium, Oreomyrrhis, Swertia, Tripterospermum*
- Region: CHINA (Taiwan)

Zhi X. Chen
Chen, Zhi Xiu; 陈志秀; Chén Zhìxiù; 陳志秀
1936- **First publication: 1985**
- Employment: Henan Agricultural University (河南农业大学)
- Research interest: Calycanthaceae, Ginkgoaceae, Magnoliaceae, Orchidaceae, Podocarpaceae, Rosaceae, Salicaceae [S]
- Published taxa: *Chimonanthus, Dendrobium, Ginkgo, Magnolia, Podocarpus, Populus, Pyracantha, Yulania*
- Location of specimens: HEAC
- Region: CHINA (Henan)
- Also as: Z. S. Chun;
- IPNI as: Z. X. Chen

Z. R. Chen
Chen, Zhi Rong; 陈治蓉; Chén Zhìróng; 陳治蓉
1939- **First publication: 1983**
- Employment: Sichuan School of Chinese Materia Medica (四川省中药学校)
- Research interest: Asparagaceae [S]
- Published taxa: *Reineckea*
- Region: CHINA (Sichuan)

Jr J. Chen
Chen, Jr Jen; 陳智真; Chén Zhìzhēn; 陈智真
First publication: 2000
- Employment: Institute of Forestry, Taiwan University (台湾大学森林学研究所)
- Research interest: Orchidaceae [S]
- Published taxa: *Ponerorchis*
- Region: CHINA (Taiwan)

Z. Y. Chen
Chen, Zhong Yi; Chen, Chong Yi; **陈忠毅; Chén Zhōngyì; 陳忠毅**
1943- **First publication: 1976**
- Employment: South China Institute of Botany, Chinese Academy of Sciences (中国科学院华南植物研究所)
- Research interest: Fabaceae, Magnoliaceae, Rubiaceae, Zingiberaceae [S]
- Published taxa: *Alpinia, Caesalpinia, Morinda*
- Affiliation: IBSC
- Region: CHINA
- Also as: C. Y. Chen

T. T. Chen
Chen, Tzu Tsung; 陳子聰; Chén Zǐcōng; 陈子聪
First publication: 1983
- Employment: Faculty of Science, Tohoku University, Japan (日本东北大学理学部)
- Research interest: Fabaceae, Lamiaceae [S]
- Published taxa: *Callicarpa, Desmodium*
- Region: CHINA (Taiwan)

Zi L. Chen
Chen, Zi Li; 陈子林; Chén Zǐlín

1970- First publication: 2013

- Employment: Administration of Dapanshan National Natural Reserve, Zhejiang（浙江省大盘山国家级自然保护区管理局）
- Research interest: Rosaceae [S]
- Published taxa: *Prunus*
- Region: CHINA (Zhejiang)
- IPNI as: Z. L. Chen

Zi X. Chen

Chen, Zi Xuan; 陳子玄 ; Chén Zǐxuán; 陈子玄

First publication: 2018

- Employment: Department of Forestry, Pingtung University of Science and Technology（屏东科技大学森林系）
- Research interest: Orobanchaceae [S]
- Published taxa: *Striga*
- Region: CHINA (Taiwan)

Z. L. Chen

Chen, Zong Lian; Chen, Chung Lien; 陈宗莲 ; Chén Zōnglián; 陳宗蓮

1937- First publication: 1985

- Employment: Kunming Institute of Botany, Chinese Academy of Sciences（中国科学院昆明植物研究所）
- Research interest: Cucurbitaceae [S]
- Published taxa: *Hemsleya*
- Affiliation: KUN
- Region: CHINA (Yunnan)

K. W. Cheng

Cheng, Ke Wu; 成克武 ; Chéng Kèwǔ

1970- First publication: 2006

- Employment: Beijing Forestry University（北京林业大学）
- Research interest: Boraginaceae [S]
- Published taxa: *Eritrichium*
- Region: CHINA (Beijing)

M. H. Cheng

Cheng, Ming Hao; 成明昊 ; Chéng Mínghào

1935- First publication: 1983

- Employment: Department of Horticulture, Southwest Agricultural University（西南农业大学园艺系）
- Research interest: Rosaceae [S]
- Published taxa: *Malus*
- Affiliation: SWAU
- Location of specimens: SWAU
- Region: CHINA (Sichuan)

X. Cheng

Cheng, Xiao; 成晓 ; Chéng Xiǎo

1957- First publication: 1985

- Employment: Kunming Institute of Botany, Chinese Academy of Sciences（中国科学院昆明植物研究所）
- Research interest: Aspleniaceae, Lycopodiaceae, Polypodiaceae; Pteridophytes [P]
- Published taxa: *Crypsinus, Huperzia, Hymenasplenium*
- Affiliation: KUN
- Region: CHINA (Yunnan)

C. Y. Cheng

Cheng, Ching Yung; Chang, Jing Rong; Cheng, Jing Rong; 诚静容 ; Chéng Jìngróng; 誠靜容

1913-2012 First publication: 1962

- Employment: Department of Pharmacy, Beijing Medical College; School of Pharmacy, Beijing Medical University（北京医学院药学系；北京医科大学药学院）
- Research interest: Araliaceae, Aristolochiaceae, Caprifoliaceae, Celastraceae, Crassulaceae, Cucurbitaceae, Cycadaceae, Dipentodontaceae, Ephedraceae, Gnetaceae, Pinaceae, Polygonaceae, Rhamnaceae, Taxaceae [S]
- Published taxa: *Aristolochia, Asarum, Bryophyllum, Celastrus, Cephalotaxus, Cycas, Dipentodon, Dipsacus, Ephedra, Euonymus, Glyptopetalum, Gnetum, Larix, Maytenus, Microtropis, Morina, Panax, Pinus, Rheum, Trichosanthes, Valeriana, Ziziphus*
- Affiliation: PEM
- Location of specimens: PEM
- Region: CHINA

J. F. Cheng

Cheng, Jing Fu; Cheng, Jian Fu; 程景福 ; Chéng Jǐngfú

1927-1999 First publication: 1987

- Employment: Department of Biology, Jiangxi University（江西大学生物系）
- Research interest: Dryopteridaceae, Lycopodiaceae, Plagiogyriaceae, Thelypteridaceae, Vittariaceae; Pteridophytes [PS]
- Published taxa: *Cyclosorus, Dryopteris, Huperzia, Parathelypteris, Plagiogyria, Polystichum, Pseudocyclosorus, Thelypteris, Thelypteris, Vittaria*
- Affiliation: JXU
- Location of specimens: JXU
- Region: CHINA (Jiangxi)

M. E. Cheng

Cheng, Ming En; 程铭恩 ; Chéng Míng'ēn

1976- First publication: 2019

- Employment: College of Pharmacy, Anhui University of Chinese Medicine（安徽中医药大学药学院）
- Research interest: Commelinaceae, Violaceae [S]

• Published taxa: *Commelina, Viola*
• Location of specimens: ACM
• Region: CHINA (Anhui)

S. Z. Cheng

Cheng, Shu Zhi; 程树志 ; Chéng Shùzhì; 程樹志
1940- First publication: 1981
• Employment: Institute of Botany, Chinese Academy of Sciences (中国科学院植物研究所)
• Research interest: Cycadaceae [S]
• Published taxa: *Cycas*
• Location of specimens: PE
• Region: CHINA (Sichuan)

S. J. Cheng

Cheng, Shi Jun; Cheng, Sek Kuan; 程式君 ; Chéng Shìjūn
1934-2012 First publication: 1980
• Employment: South China Institute of Botany, Chinese Academy of Sciences (中国科学院华南植物研究所)
• Research interest: Orchidaceae [S]
• Published taxa: *Dendrobium*
• Region: CHINA (Hainan)

Y. C. Tseng

Tseng, Yung Chien; Tseng, Yong Qian; Cheng, Yong Qian; 程用谦 ; Chéng Yòngqiān; 程用謙
1930-1999 First publication: 1974
• Employment: South China Institute of Botany, Chinese Academy of Sciences (中国科学院华南植物研究所)
• Research interest: Asteraceae, Euphorbiaceae, Piperaceae, Rubiaceae [S]
• Published taxa: *Ainsliaea, Gerbera, Inula, Lactuca, Ophiorrhiza, Pertya, Piper, Sapium, Senecio*
• Affiliation: IBSC
• Region: CHINA
• Also as: Y. Q. Tseng

Z. L. Cheng

Cheng, Zeng Lin; 程增林 ; Chéng Zēnglín
1955- First publication: 1991
• Employment: Tiantangzhai Nature Reserve of Anhui (安徽省天堂寨自然保护区)
• Research interest: Rosaceae [S]
• Published taxa: *Rosa, Rubus*
• Location of specimens: NAS
• Region: CHINA (Anhui)

Tiang

Tiang, Choon Lin; 程章麟 ; Chéng Zhānglín
First publication: 2007
• Employment: Biodiversity Research Center, "Academia Sinica" (中研院生物多样性研究中心)
• Research interest: Liliaceae [S]
• Published taxa: *Tricyrtis*
• Location of specimens: HAST
• Region: CHINA (Taiwan)

T. P. Chen

Chen, Tsi Pai; Cheng, Zi Bai; Chen, Zi Bai; 程子白 ; Chéng Zǐbái; 陈子白
1934- First publication: 1975
• Employment: Department of Biology, Sichuan University (四川大学生物系)
• Research interest: Nyssaceae [S]
• Published taxa: *Nyssa*
• Location of specimens: SZ
• Region: CHINA (Sichuan)
• IPNI as: Z. B. Chen

S. S. Chu

Chu, Shan Shan; 储姗姗 ; Chǔ Shānshān
First publication: 2020
• Employment: College of Pharmacy, Anhui University of Chinese Medicine (安徽中医药大学药学院)
• Research interest: Apiaceae [S]
• Published taxa: *Peucedanum*
• Region: CHINA (Anhui)

X. D. Cong

Cong, Xiao Dong; 丛晓东 ; Cóng Xiǎodōng
First publication: 1990
• Employment: China Pharmaceutical University (中国药科大学)
• Research interest: Lamiaceae [S]
• Published taxa: *Caryopteris*
• Region: CHINA (Yunnan)

Y. Y. Cong

Cong, Yi Yan; 丛义艳 ; Cóng Yìyàn
1977- First publication: 2008
• Employment: College of Life Sciences, Hunan Normal University (湖南师范大学生命科学学院)
• Research interest: Balsaminaceae [S]
• Published taxa: *Impatiens*
• Affiliation: HNNU
• Location of specimens: HNNU
• Region: CHINA

D. F. Cui

Cui, Da Fang; 崔大方 ; Cuī Dàfāng
1964- First publication: 1987
• Employment: Department of Biology, Xinjiang Normal University; College of Forestry and Landscape Architecture, South China Agricultural

University（新疆师范大学生物系；华南农业大学林学与风景园林学院）
- Research interest: Alismataceae, Asparagaceae, Fabaceae, Poaceae, Rosaceae, Tamaricaceae [S]
- Published taxa: *Agropyron, Alisma, Calamagrostis, Elymus, Eriobotrya, Kengyilia, Leymus, Medicago, Poa, Polygonatum, Puccinellia, Reaumuria, Stipa*
- Affiliation: CANT, XJNU
- Location of specimens: XJNU
- Region: CHINA

D. L. Cui

Cui, Da Lian; 崔大练；Cuī Dàliàn

1970- First publication: 2012

- Employment: College of Marine Science, Zhejiang Ocean University（浙江海洋学院海洋科学学院）
- Research interest: Caryophyllaceae [S]
- Published taxa: *Spergularia*
- Region: CHINA (Zhejiang)

H. P. Tsui

Tsui, Hung Pin; Ts'ui, Hung Pin; Cui, Hong Bing; Cui, Hong Bin; 崔鸿宾；Cuī Hóngbīn; 崔鴻賓

1928-1994 First publication: 1978

- Employment: Institute of Botany, Chinese Academy of Sciences（中国科学院植物研究所）
- Research interest: Acanthaceae, Fabaceae, Lauraceae [S]
- Published taxa: *Actinodaphne, Adenacanthus, Alseodaphne, Barleria, Beilschmiedia, Calophanoides, Diflugossa, Eranthemum, Goldfussia, Gueldenstaedtia, Lathyrus, Lindera, Litsea, Neolitsea, Paragutzlaffia, Pararuellia, Pteracanthus, Semnostachya, Thunbergia, Tibetia*
- Affiliation: PE
- Region: CHINA

N. R. Cui

Cui, Nai Ran; 崔乃然；Cuī Nǎirán

1935-2017 First publication: 1982

- Employment: Department of Biology, Xinjiang Normal University（新疆师范大学生物系）
- Research interest: Caprifoliaceae, Crassulaceae, Cyperaceae, Poaceae, Rosaceae [S]
- Published taxa: *Carex, Elymus, Elytrigia, Festuca, Leymus, Poa, Prunus, Rhodiola, Roegneria, Scabiosa, Scirpus*
- Affiliation: XJNU
- Location of specimens: XJA, XJNU
- Region: CHINA (Xinjiang)

T. C. Cui

Cui, Tie Cheng; 崔铁成；Cuī Tiěchéng

1956- First publication: 1987

- Employment: Xi' an Botanical Garden, Shaanxi（陕西省西安植物园）
- Research interest: Asparagaceae, Magnoliaceae, Oleaceae, Rosaceae; Plants of Shaanxi [S]
- Published taxa: *Crataegus, Diuranthera, Fraxinus, Magnolia*
- Affiliation: XBGH
- Location of specimens: XBGH
- Region: CHINA (Shaanxi)

X. J. Cui

Cui, Xian Ju; 崔现举；Cuī Xiànjǔ

1960- First publication: 1987

- Employment: Institute of Forestry and Soil Sciences, Chinese Academy of Sciences（中国科学院林业土壤研究所）
- Research interest: Fabaceae [S]
- Published taxa: *Desmodium, Podocarpium*
- Region: CHINA (Yunnan)

S. C. Cui

Cui, Shun Chang; Cui, Xiang Dong; 崔向东；Cuī Xiàngdōng; 崔向東，崔顺昌，崔順昌

1934- First publication: 1980

- Employment: Northwest China Institute of Botany, Chinese Academy of Sciences and Shaanxi Province; Shanxi Institute of Forestry Science（陕西省中国科学院西北植物研究所；山西省林业科学研究所）
- Research interest: Asteraceae, Brassicaceae, Sapindaceae; Economic Plants [S]
- Published taxa: *Acer, Ajania, Artemisia, Dendranthema, Rorippa*
- Affiliation: TYF
- Location of specimens: TYF, WUK
- Region: CHINA (Shaanxi, Shanxi)
- Also as: X. D. Cui

Tsui

Tsui, You Wen; Tsui, Yu Wen; Tsueh, Yu Wan; Ts'ui, You Wên; 崔友文；Cuī Yǒuwén

1907-1980 First publication: 1949

- Employment: Botanical Survey of North-Western China, National Academy of Peiping; Institute of Botany, Chinese Academy of Sciences; Northwest China Institute of Botany, Chinese Academy of Sciences and Shaanxi Province（国立北平研究院西北植物调查所；中国科学院植物研究所；陕西省中国科学院西北植物研究所）
- Research interest: Asparagaceae, Caryophyllaceae [S]
- Published taxa: *Arenaria, Gypsophila, Melandrium, Polygonatum, Stellaria*
- Affiliation: WUK

- Location of specimens: PE, WUK
- Region: CHINA
- Also as: Y. W. Tsui; • IPNI as: T. W. Tsui

Z. J. Cui

Cui, Zhi Jia; 崔治家 ; Cuī Zhìjiā

1980- **First publication: 2005**

- Employment: College of Life Sciences, Northwest Normal University（西北师范大学生命科学学院）
- Research interest: Papaveraceae [S]
- Published taxa: *Meconopsis*
- Region: CHINA (Gansu)

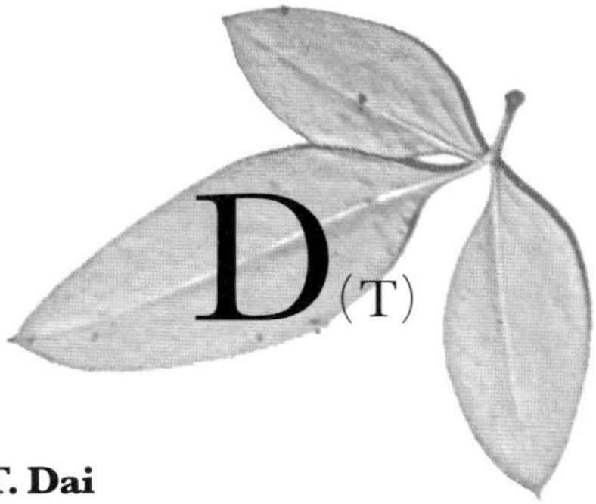

H. T. Dai

Dai, Hui Tang; 戴惠堂 ; Dài Huìtáng

1962- **First publication: 2007**

- Employment: Jigong Mountain National Nature Reserve Administration, Henan（河南鸡公山国家级自然保护区管理局）
- Research interest: Magnoliaceae [S]
- Published taxa: *Magnolia, Yulania*
- Region: CHINA (Henan)

J. H. Dai

Dai, Jin Hong; 戴金宏 ; Dài Jīnhóng

1997- **First publication: 2019**

- Employment: School of Life Sciences, Sun Yat-sen University（中山大学生命科学学院）
- Research interest: Melastomataceae [S]
- Published taxa: *Fordiophyton*
- Region: CHINA (Yunnan)

K. M. Dai

Dai, Ke Min; 戴克敏 ; Dài Kèmǐn

1930- **First publication: 1981**

- Employment: Shanghai First Medical College; Shanghai Medical University（上海第一医学院；上海医科大学）
- Research interest: Lamiaceae, Paeoniaceae [S]
- Published taxa: *Mentha, Paeonia*
- Location of specimens: SHMU
- Region: CHINA (Shanghai, Xinjiang)

L. K. Dai

Dai, Lun Kai; 戴伦凯 ; Dài Lúnkǎi; 戴倫凱

1930- **First publication: 1963**

- Employment: Institute of Botany, Chinese Academy of Sciences（中国科学院植物研究所）
- Research interest: Asparagaceae, Cyperaceae, Euphorbiaceae, Liliaceae [S]
- Published taxa: *Carex, Cyperus, Mariscus, Ophiopogon, Pycreus, Schoenoplectus, Scirpus, Trigonostemon*
- Affiliation: PE
- Region: CHINA

Q. H. Dai

Dai, Qi Hui; 戴启惠 ; Dài Qǐhuì

1937-2010 **First publication: 1985**

- Employment: Guangxi Forestry Research Institute（广西壮族自治区林业科学研究院）
- Research interest: Poaceae [S]
- Published taxa: *Acidosasa, Arundinaria, Bambusa, Chimonobambusa, Dendrocalamopsis, Gelidocalamus, Indocalamus, Indosasa, Lingnania, Neosinocalamus, Phyllostachys, Pseudosasa, Schizostachyum, Sinocalamus*
- Affiliation: GXFI
- Region: CHINA

S. L. Dai

Dai, Shui Lian; 戴水连 ;Dài Shuǐlián; 戴水連

1942- **First publication: 1986**

- Employment: Guangzhou Traditional Chinese Medicine College（广州中医学院）
- Research interest: Poaceae [S]
- Published taxa: *Echinochloa*
- Region: CHINA

X. K. Dai

Dai, Xiao Kang; 戴小康 ; Dài Xiǎokāng

1992- **First publication: 2019**

- Employment: College of Life Sciences, Wuhan University（武汉大学生命科学学院）
- Research interest: Isoetaceae [P]
- Published taxa: *Isoetes*
- Region: CHINA (Yunnan)

X. Y. Dai

Dai, Xiao Yong; 戴晓勇 ; Dài Xiǎoyǒng

1971- **First publication: 2012**

- Employment: Guizhou Academy of Forestry（贵州省林业科学研究院）
- Research interest: Amaryllidaceae [S]
- Published taxa: *Lycoris*
- Region: CHINA (Guizhou)

Y. Y. Dai

Dai, Yi Yuan; 戴益源 ; Dài Yìyuán
1964- **First publication: 1987**
- Employment: Southwest Forestry College（西南林学院）
- Research interest: Apocynaceae, Lauraceae, Poaceae, Rosaceae [S]
- Published taxa: *Sinarundinaria*
- Affiliation: YAF
- Region: CHINA (Yunnan)

Zhen L. Dai

Dai, Zhen Lun; 戴振伦 ; Dài Zhènlún; 戴振倫
1935- **First publication: 1997**
- Employment: Baokang County Forestry Bureau, Hubei（湖北省保康县林业局）
- Research interest: Paeoniaceae [S]
- Published taxa: *Paeonia*
- Region: CHINA (Hubei)
- IPNI as: Z. L. Dai

Z. L. Dai

Dai, Zong Lei; 戴宗垒 ; Dài Zōnglěi
1961- **First publication: 1986**
- Employment: Fujian Forestry College（福建林学院）
- Research interest: Poaceae [S]
- Published taxa: *Gelidocalamus, Indocalamus*
- Region: CHINA (Fujian)
- IPNI as: C. D. Dai

G. D. Dang

Dang, Gao Di; 党高弟 ; Dǎng Gāodì
1961- **First publication: 2003**
- Employment: Foping Natural Reserve Administrative Bureau, Shaanxi（陕西佛坪国家级自然保护区管理局）
- Research interest: Poaceae [S]
- Published taxa: *Bashania*
- Region: CHINA (Shaanxi)

R. L. Dang

Dang, Rong Li; 党荣理 ; Dǎng Rónglǐ
1965- **First publication: 1995**
- Employment: Military Institute of Medical Research, Xinjiang Military Region Logistics Department（新疆军区后勤部军事医学研究所）
- Research interest: Caryophyllaceae [S]
- Published taxa: *Cerastium*
- Region: CHINA (Xinjiang)

Z. L. Dao

Dao, Zhi Ling; 刀志灵 ; Dāo Zhìlíng
1965- **First publication: 2003**
- Employment: Kunming Institute of Botany, Chinese Academy of Sciences（中国科学院昆明植物研究所）
- Research interest: Araceae, Elaeocarpaceae, Gesneriaceae, Hydrocharitaceae, Orchidaceae, Papaveraceae [S]
- Published taxa: *Amorphophallus, Calanthe, Coelogyne, Cymbidium, Elaeocarpus, Henckelia, Loxostigma, Meconopsis, Ottelia, Typhonium*
- Region: CHINA (Sichuan, Yunnan)

C. Y. Deng

Deng, Chao Yi; Deng, Cao Yi; Deng, Zhao Yi; 邓朝义 ; Dèng Cháoyì
1960- **First publication: 1986**
- Employment: Forest Institute of Southwestern Guizhou（贵州黔西南州林业科学研究所）
- Research interest: Cycadaceae, Magnoliaceae, Theaceae; Plants of S. W. Guizhou [S]
- Published taxa: *Camellia, Cycas, Magnolia*
- Affiliation: XIN
- Location of specimens: XIN
- Region: CHINA (Guizhou)

C. Z. Deng

Deng, Chao Zuo; 邓朝佐 ; Dèng Cháozuǒ; 鄧朝佐
1938- **First publication: 1991**
- Employment: Nanning Arboretum, Guangxi Zhuang Autonomous Region（广西壮族自治区南宁树木园）
- Research interest: Theaceae [S]
- Published taxa: *Camellia*
- Region: CHINA (Guangxi)

D. S. Deng

Deng, De Shan; 邓德山 ; Dèng Déshān
1968- **First publication: 1996**
- Employment: Guangxi Institute of Botany, Chinese Academy of Sciences（广西壮族自治区中国科学院广西植物研究所）
- Research interest: Cyperaceae, Orchidaceae [S]
- Published taxa: *Blysmocarex, Peristylus*
- Region: CHINA (Qinghai)

H. P. Deng

Deng, Hong Ping; 邓洪平 ; Dèng Hóngpíng
1970- **First publication: 2016**
- Employment: College of Life Sciences, Southwest University（西南大学生命科学学院）
- Research interest: Balsaminaceae, Lamiaceae, Orchidaceae, Ranunculaceae, Rosaceae, Theaceae [S]
- Published taxa: *Calanthe, Clematis, Impatiens*
- Affiliation: SWCTU
- Location of specimens: SWCTU
- Region: CHINA

Hua Deng

Deng, Hua; 邓华 ; Dèng Huá

1979- **First publication: 2015**

- Employment: Chinese Academy of Forestry（中国林业科学研究院）
- Research interest: Orchidaceae [S]
- Published taxa: *Phalaenopsis*
- Region: CHINA (Guangxi, Hunan)

J. Q. Deng

Deng, Jia Qi; 邓家祺 ; Dèng Jiāqí; 鄧家祺

1930- **First publication: 1987**

- Employment: Jin County Agricultural Technology Extension Center, Liaoning（辽宁省金县农业技术推广中心）
- Research interest: Rosaceae [S]
- Published taxa: *Malus*
- Region: CHINA (Liaoning)

J. P. Deng

Deng, Jian Ping; 邓建平 ; Dèng Jiànpíng

First publication: 2018

- Employment: Xishuangbanna Tropical Botanical Garden, Chinese Academy of Sciences（中国科学院西双版纳热带植物园）
- Research interest: Orchidaceae [S]
- Published taxa: *Bulbophyllum*
- Region: CHINA (Yunnan)

L. L. Deng

Deng, Li Lan; 邓莉兰 ; Dèng Lìlán

1962- **First publication: 1995**

- Employment: Southwest Forestry College（西南林学院）
- Research interest: Araliaceae, Pteridaceae, Rhamnaceae, Sapindaceae, Theaceae; Woody Plants [S]
- Published taxa: *Acer, Aralia, Gordonia, Pteris, Rhamnus, Sageretia*
- Affiliation: SWFC
- Location of specimens: GZAC, SWFC
- Region: CHINA (Yunnan)

M. B. Deng

Deng, Mao Bin; Deng, Mao Pin; 邓懋彬 ; Dèng Màobīn; 鄧懋彬

1932-2016 **First publication: 1987**

- Employment: Institute of Botany, Jiangsu Province（江苏省植物研究所）
- Research interest: Aquifoliaceae, Elaeagnaceae, Hamamelidaceae, Helwingiaceae, Liliaceae, Rosaceae, Rubiaceae [S]
- Published taxa: *Damnacanthus, Elaeagnus, Fritillaria, Hamamelis, Helwingia, Ilex, Photinia, Shaniodendron*
- Location of specimens: NAS
- Region: CHINA
- Also as: M. P. Deng

M. J. Deng

Deng, Mei Jih; Deng, Mei Zhi; 鄧美智 ; Dèng Měizhì; 邓美智

First publication: 1993

- Employment: Institute of Biology, Taiwan Normal University（台湾师范大学生物学研究所）
- Research interest: Phyllanthaceae [S]
- Published taxa: *Breynia, Breynia*
- Region: CHINA (Taiwan)

M. Deng

Deng, Min; 邓敏 ; Dèng Mǐn

1977- **First publication: 2006**

- Employment: Kunming Institute of Botany, Chinese Academy of Sciences; Shanghai Chenshan Botanical Garden（中国科学院昆明植物研究所 ; 上海辰山植物园）
- Research interest: Fagaceae [S]
- Published taxa: *Cyclobalanopsis*
- Affiliation: CSH
- Location of specimens: CSH
- Region: CHINA

S. J. Deng

Deng, Shi Jin; 邓士谨 ; Dèng Shìjǐn

First publication: 1982

- Employment: Department of Biology, Northwest University（辽宁大学生物系）
- Research interest: Lamiaceae [S]
- Published taxa: *Scutellaria*
- Region: CHINA (Nei Mongol)

Shu J. Deng

Deng, Shu Jun; 邓淑君 ; Dèng Shūjūn

1988- **First publication: 2012**

- Employment: South China Botanical Garden, Chinese Academy of Sciences（中国科学院华南植物园）
- Research interest: Rubiaceae [S]
- Published taxa: *Hedyotis*
- Region: CHINA (Guangdong)
- IPNI as: S. J. Deng

Tan Deng

Deng, Tan; 邓坦 ; Dèng Tǎn

1972- **First publication: 2019**

- Employment: Department of Biology, Zunyi Normal College（遵义师范学院生物系）
- Research interest: Crassulaceae, Lamiaceae; Bryophyte, Pteridophytes [BS]

• Published taxa: *Paraphlomis, Sedum*
• Affiliation: ZY
• Location of specimens: ZY
• Region: CHINA (Guizhou)
• IPNI as: D. Tan

T. Deng

Deng, Tao; 邓涛 ; Dèng Tāo
1985- **First publication: 2013**
• Employment: Kunming Institute of Botany, Chinese Academy of Sciences; Shanghai Chenshan Botanical Garden (中国科学院昆明植物研究所)
• Research interest: Asteraceae, Berberidaceae, Brassicaceae, Caryophyllaceae, Cornaceae, Mazaceae, Oxalidaceae, Rosaceae, Urticaceae; Plants of Yunnan [S]
• Published taxa: *Carpesium, Cornus, Draba, Epimedium, Mazus, Oxalis, Prunus, Silene, Youngia, Zhengyia*
• Affiliation: KUN
• Location of specimens: KUN
• Region: CHINA (Yunnan)

W. S. Deng

Deng, Wei Sheng; 邓伟胜 ; Dèng Wěishèng
1968- **First publication: 2019**
• Employment: Zhoutian Town Government, Renhua County, Guangdong (广东仁化县周田镇镇政府)
• Research interest: Ranunculaceae [S]
• Published taxa: *Semiaquilegia*
• Region: CHINA (Guangdong)

X. F. Deng

Deng, Xiao Fang; 邓小芳 ; Dèng Xiǎofāng
1971- **First publication: 2004**
• Employment: South China Botanical Garden, Chinese Academy of Sciences (中国科学院华南植物园)
• Research interest: Rubiaceae [S]
• Published taxa: *Mussaenda, Schizomussaenda*
• Region: CHINA (Guangdong, Yunnan)

Y. B. Deng

Deng, Yan Bin; 邓彦斌 ; Dèng Yànbīn
1957- **First publication: 1999**
• Employment: Department of Biology, Xinjiang University (新疆大学生物系)
• Research interest: Fabaceae [S]
• Published taxa: *Oxytropis*
• Location of specimens: XJU
• Region: CHINA (Xinjiang)

Y. C. Teng

Deng, Yu Cheng; 邓玉诚 ; Dèng Yùchéng
1930- **First publication: 1977**
• Employment: Institute of Forestry and Soil Sciences, Chinese Academy of Sciences (中国科学院林业土壤研究所)
• Research interest: Violaceae [S]
• Published taxa: *Viola*
• Region: CHINA

Y. F. Deng

Deng, Yun Fei; 邓云飞 ; Dèng Yúnfēi
1970- **First publication: 2001**
• Employment: Kunming Institute of Botany, Chinese Academy of Sciences; South China Botanical Garden, Chinese Academy of Sciences (中国科学院昆明植物研究所；中国科学院华南植物园)
• Research interest: Acanthaceae, Apiaceae, Araliaceae, Aristolochiaceae, Asparagaceae, Aspleniaceae, Campanulaceae, Celastraceae, Cyperaceae, Fabaceae, Gesneriaceae, Lamiaceae, Lauraceae, Melastomataceae, Myrtaceae, Oleaceae, Pittosporaceae, Poaceae, Primulaceae, Rhamnaceae, Rosaceae, Rubiaceae, Vitaceae [PS]
• Published taxa: *Acanthus, Afgekia, Ampelocalamus, Aralia, Aristolochia, Asplenium, Beilschmiedia, Brassaiopsis, Campanula, Carex, Chimonocalamus, Cystacanthus, Dendropanax, Eleutherococcus, Eranthemum, Fimbristylis, Fleroya, Fordiophyton, Haplanthus, Heteropanax, Hygrophila, Hylodesmum, Justicia, Ligustrum, Lysimachia, Mackaya, Microtropis, Ophiorrhiza, Ophiorrhiziphyllon, Osmanthus, Parthenocissus, Pentapanax, Peristrophe, Pertusadina, Peucedanum, Phlogacanthus, Pittosporum, Pogostemon, Primulina, Pseudopogonatherum, Pycreus, Rhamnus, Rohdea, Rubovietnamia, Rubus, Rungia, Sadiria, Sorbus, Strobilanthes, Syndiclis, Syzygium, Wuacanthuss*
• Affiliation: IBSC
• Region: CHINA

W. Z. Di

Di, Wei Zhong; 狄维忠 ; Dí Wéizhōng; 狄維忠
1934-2015 **First publication: 1985**
• Employment: Department of Biology, Northwest University (西北大学生物系)
• Research interest: Adoxaceae, Amaranthaceae, Caryophyllaceae, Cyperaceae, Lamiaceae, Sapindaceae, Urticaceae; Plants of N. W. China [S]
• Published taxa: *Acer, Chenopodium, Kobresia, Lagochilus, Pseudostellaria, Stellaria, Urtica, Viburnum*
• Affiliation: WNU
• Location of specimens: WNU
• Region: CHINA (Gansu, Ningxia, Shaanxi)

Z. S. Diao

Diao, Zheng Su; 刁正俗 ; Diāo Zhèngsú

1914-1998 **First publication: 1988**

- Employment: Department of Biology, Yuzhou University, Chongqing（渝州大学生物系）
- Research interest: Poaceae, Potamogetonaceae, Trapaceae; Aquatic Plants. [AS]
- Published taxa: *Echinochloa, Potamogeton, Trapa*
- Affiliation: YZU
- Location of specimens: YZU
- Region: CHINA

B. C. Ding

Ding, Bao Chang; Ding, Bao Zhang; 丁宝章 ; Dīng Bǎozhāng; 丁寶章

1924-1995 **First publication: 1980**

- Employment: Henan Agricultural College（河南农学院）
- Research interest: Euphorbiaceae, Fagaceae, Magnoliaceae, Phyllanthaceae, Rosaceae, Salicaceae, Simaroubaceae, Staphyleaceae; Plants of Henan [S]
- Published taxa: *Ailanthus, Magnolia, Potentilla, Quercus, Salix, Sapium, Securinega, Staphylea*
- Affiliation: HEAC
- Location of specimens: HEAC
- Region: CHINA (Henan)

B. Y. Ding

Ding, Bing Yang; 丁炳扬 ; Dīng Bǐngyáng

1953- **First publication: 1987**

- Employment: Department of Biology, Hangzhou University; College of Life Sciences, Zhejiang University; College of Life Sciences, Wenzhou University; Zhejiang Academy of Forestry（杭州大学生物系；浙江大学生命科学学院；温州大学生命科学学院；浙江省林业科学研究院）
- Research interest: Balsaminaceae, Caryophyllaceae, Crassulaceae, Cyperaceae, Ericaceae, Gleicheniaceae, Lamiaceae, Melastomataceae [S]
- Published taxa: *Bredia, Callicarpa, Carex, Dicranopteris, Impatiens, Meehania, Paraphlomis, Pseudostellaria, Rhododendron, Salvia, Scutellaria, Sedum*
- Affiliation: HZU
- Location of specimens: HTC, HZU, ZM, ZNU
- Region: CHINA (Zhejiang)

B. Ding

Ding, Bo; 丁博 ; Dīng Bó

1986- **First publication: 2014**

- Employment: College of Life Science and Engineering,Chongqing Three Gorges University（重庆三峡学院生命科学与工程学院）
- Research interest: Begoniaceae [S]
- Published taxa: *Begonia*
- Region: CHINA (Chongqing)

C. S. Ding

Ding, Chen Sen; 丁陈森 ; Dīng Chénsēn; 丁陳森

1933-2012 **First publication: 1979**

- Employment: Zhejiang Forestry College（浙江林学院）
- Research interest: Calycanthaceae, Ulmaceae; Woody Plants [S]
- Published taxa: *Chimonanthus, Ulmus*
- Affiliation: ZJFC
- Location of specimens: ZJFC
- Region: CHINA

K. C. Ting

Ting, Kwang Chi; Ting, Kuang Chi; Ting, Kuang Ch'i; Ding, Guang Qi; 丁广奇 ; Dīng Guǎngqí; 丁廣奇

1930-1990 **First publication: 1963**

- Employment: South China Institute of Botany, Chinese Academy of Sciences（中国科学院华南植物研究所）
- Research interest: Elaeocarpaceae; Plants of S. China [S]
- Published taxa: *Sloanea*
- Affiliation: IBSD
- Location of specimens: ATCH, IBSC, IBSD
- Region: CHINA (Hainan)

H. B. Ding

Ding, Hong Bo; 丁洪波 ; Dīng Hóngbō

1988- **First publication: 2019**

- Employment: Xishuangbanna Tropical Botanical Garden, Chinese Academy of Sciences（中国科学院西双版纳热带植物园）
- Research interest: Gesneriaceae [S]
- Published taxa: *Petrocosmea*
- Region: CHINA (Yunnan)

J. N. Ding

Ding, Jian Nan; 丁建南 ; Dīng Jiànnán

1955- **First publication: 1990**

- Employment: Jiangxi Academy of Sciences（江西省科学院）
- Research interest: Cucurbitaceae [S]
- Published taxa: *Gynostemma*
- Location of specimens: N
- Region: CHINA (Anhui)

M. Y. Ding

Ding, Ming Yan; 丁明艳 ; Dīng Míngyàn

1981- **First publication: 2015**

- Employment: School of Life Sciences, Sun Yat-sen University（中山大学生命科学学院）

• Research interest: Rosaceae [S]
• Published taxa: *Eriobotrya*
• Region: CHINA (Sichuan)

Q. L. Ding

Ding, Qiao Ling; 丁巧玲 ; Dīng Qiǎolíng
1986- **First publication: 2018**
• Employment: School of Life Sciences, Sun Yat-sen University（中山大学生命科学学院）
• Research interest: Begoniaceae [S]
• Published taxa: *Begonia*
• Region: CHINA (Guangdong)

S. Q. Ding

Ding, Su Qin; 丁素琴 ; Dīng Sùqín
1930-1999 **First publication: 1976**
• Employment: Horticultural Research Institute, Yunnan Academy of Agricultural Sciences（云南省农业科学院园艺作物研究所）
• Research interest: Rutaceae [S]
• Published taxa: *Citrus*
• Region: CHINA (Yunnan)

T. Y. Ding

Ding, Tuo Ya; 丁托娅 ; Dīng Tuōyà
1955- **First publication: 1993**
• Employment: Institute of Applied Ecology, Chinese Academy of Sciences（中国科学院沈阳应用生态研究所）
• Research interest: Salicaceae [S]
• Published taxa: *Salix*
• Affiliation: KUN
• Region: CHINA (Qinghai, Sichuan)

Y. L. Ding

Ding, Yu Long; 丁雨龙 ; Dīng Yǔlóng
1958- **First publication: 2002**
• Employment: Bamboo Research Institute, Nanjing Forestry University（南京林业大学竹类研究所）
• Research interest: Poaceae [S]
• Published taxa: *Phyllostachys*
• Region: CHINA (Jiangsu)

C. T. Ting

Ting, Chih Tsun; Ting, Chih Chi; Ding, Zhi Zun; 丁志遵 ; Dīng Zhìzūn
1926- **First publication: 1976**
• Employment: Institute of Botany, Jiangsu Province（江苏省植物研究所）
• Research interest: Apiaceae, Dioscoreaceae, Ranunculaceae [S]
• Published taxa: *Clematis, Dioscorea, Notopterygium, Schizocapsa, Tacca*
• Affiliation: NAS
• Location of specimens: NAS
• Region: CHINA
• Also as: C. C. Ting;
• IPNI as: Ting

Z. C. Ding

Ding, Zuo Chao; 丁作超 ; Dīng Zuòchāo
1935- **First publication: 1988**
• Employment: Shandong College of Traditional Chinese Medicine（山东中医学院）
• Research interest: Athyriaceae; Medicinal Plants [PS]
• Published taxa: *Athyriopsis*
• Affiliation: SDCM
• Location of specimens: SDCM
• Region: CHINA (Shandong)

A. Q. Dong

Dong, An Qiang; 董安强 ; Dǒng Ānqiáng
1982- **First publication: 2009**
• Employment: College of Life Sciences, Zhongkai University of Agriculture and Engineering（仲恺农业工程学院生命科学学院）
• Research interest: Balsaminaceae, Gesneriaceae, Magnoliaceae, Violaceae, Zingiberaceae [S]
• Published taxa: *Impatiens, Manglietia, Primulina, Viola, Zingiber*
• Region: CHINA (Guangdong)

K. Y. Tong

Tong, Koe Yang; Tung, Koe Yang; Tung, Kwei Yang; Tung, Shuang Chiu; Tung, Shuang Ch'iu; Dong, Shuang Qiu; 董桂阳 ; Dǒng Guìyáng; 董爽秋
1897-1980 **First publication: 1930**
• Employment: Department of Biology, National Sun Yat-sen University（国立中山大学生物学系）
• Research interest: Hamamelidaceae [S]
• Published taxa: *Loropetalum, Rhodoleia*
• Region: CHINA (Yunnan, Xizang)

H. J. Dong

Dong, Hong Jin; 董洪进 ; Dǒng Hóngjìn
1985- **First publication: 2010**
• Employment: Kunming Institute of Botany, Chinese Academy of Sciences; South China Botanical Garden, Chinese Academy of Sciences（中国科学院昆明植物研究所）
• Research interest: Asteraceae, Lamiaceae, Salicaceae [S]
• Published taxa: *Flacourtia, Ligularia, Nepeta*
• Region: CHINA (Yunnan)

H. D. Dong

Dong, Hou De; 董厚德 ; Dǒng Hòudé

1935- **First publication: 1997**
• Employment: Liaoning University（辽宁大学）
• Research interest: Poaceae [S]
• Published taxa: *Zoysia*
• Region: CHINA (Liaoning)

H. Dong

Dong, Hui; 董辉; Dǒng Huī
First publication: 1993
• Employment: School of Traditional Chinese Pharmacy, China Pharmaceutical University（中国药科大学中药学院）
• Research interest: Zingiberaceae [S]
• Published taxa: *Alpinia, Hedychium*
• Region: CHINA (Hainan, Yunnan)

J. Z. Dong

Dong, Jing Zhou; 董静洲; Dǒng Jìngzhōu
1974- **First publication: 2011**
• Employment: Hubei Minzu University; South China Botanical Garden, Chinese Academy of Sciences（湖北民族大学；中国科学院华南植物园）
• Research interest: Asparagaceae, Rosaceae [S]
• Published taxa: *Duchesnea, Potentilla, Reineckea*
• Region: CHINA (Hubei, Guangxi)

L. N. Dong

Dong, Li Na; 董莉娜; Dǒng Lìnà
1979- **First publication: 2011**
• Employment: Kunming Institute of Botany, Chinese Academy of Sciences; Guangxi Institute of Botany, Chinese Academy of Sciences（中国科学院昆明植物研究所；广西壮族自治区中国科学院广西植物研究所）
• Research interest: Begoniaceae, Orobanchaceae, Primulaceae, Scrophulariaceae [S]
• Published taxa: *Lysimachia, Pterygiella*
• Affiliation: IBK
• Region: CHINA (Guangxi, Yunnan)

L. X. Dong

Dong, Lian Xin; 董连新; Dǒng Liánxīn
1963- **First publication: 2008**
• Employment: College of Forest Resources and Environment, Nanjing Forestry University; College of Forestry, Xinjiang Agricultural University（南京林业大学森林资源与环境学院；新疆农业大学林学院）
• Research interest: Caryophyllaceae [S]
• Published taxa: *Dianthus*
• Region: CHINA (Xinjiang)

Q. Z. Dong

Dong, Quan Zhong; 董全忠; Dǒng Quánzhōng
1944- **First publication: 1983**
• Employment: Yunnan Forestry College（云南林学院）
• Research interest: Fagaceae; Economic Plants [S]
• Published taxa: *Cyclobalanopsis, Lithocarpus*
• Affiliation: SWFC
• Location of specimens: SWFC
• Region: CHINA (Yunnan)

S. L. Tung

Tung, Shi Lin; 董世林; Dǒng Shìlín
1936-2010 **First publication: 1979**
• Employment: Northeast Forestry Institute（东北林学院）
• Research interest: Betulaceae, Caprifoliaceae, Ericaceae, Fabaceae, Pinaceae, Rosaceae, Salicaceae, Sapindaceae [S]
• Published taxa: *Acer, Alnus, Betula, Carpinus, Corylus, Crataegus, Ledum, Lespedeza, Lonicera, Picea, Populus, Rhododendron, Salix, Sorbus*
• Affiliation: NEFI
• Location of specimens: NEFI
• Region: CHINA

S. Y. Dong

Dong, Shi Yong; 董仕勇; Dǒng Shìyǒng
1970- **First publication: 2001**
• Employment: Department of Environmental Science, Yunnan University; South China Botanical Garden, Chinese Academy of Sciences; Institute of Botany, Chinese Academy of Sciences（云南大学环境科学系；中国科学院华南植物园；中国科学院植物研究所）
• Research interest: Aspleniaceae, Cyatheaceae, Dryopteridaceae, Lindsaeaceae, Pteridryaceae, Tectariaceae; Pteridophytes [P]
• Published taxa: *Asplenium, Bolbitis, Ctenitis, Dryopsis, Dryopteris, Gymnosphaera, Hymenasplenium, Lindsaea, Pleocnemia, Polydictyum, Tectaria, Teratophyllum*
• Affiliation: IBSC
• Region: CHINA

S. P. Dong

Dong, Shu Peng; 董书鹏; Dǒng Shūpéng
First publication: 2020
• Employment: College of Horticulture and Landscape Architecture, Hainan University（海南大学园艺园林学院）
• Research interest: Malpighiaceae [S]
• Published taxa: *Hiptage*
• Region: CHINA (Yunnan)

X. D. Dong

Dong, Xiao Dong; 董晓东; Dǒng Xiǎodōng
1964- **First publication: 1997**
• Employment: Department of Biology, Dali Teachers'

College; Department of Life Science and Chemistry, Dali University（大理师范高等专科学校生物系；大理学院生命科学与化学系）
- Research interest: Araceae, Asteraceae, Boraginaceae, Iridaceae, Mazaceae, Ranunculaceae, Rosaceae, Zingiberaceae [S]
- Published taxa: *Anemone, Arisaema, Cynoglossum, Erigeron, Iris, Mazus, Rosa, Roscoea*
- Region: CHINA (Xizang, Yunnan)

Y. Dong

Dong, Yang; 董阳 ; Dǒng Yáng

1986- **First publication: 2011**

- Employment: Institute of Botany, Chinese Academy of Sciences（中国科学院植物研究所）
- Research interest: Gesneriaceae [S]
- Published taxa: *Primulina*
- Region: CHINA

C. Du

Du, Cheng; 杜诚 ; Dù Chéng

1984- **First publication: 2009**

- Employment: College of Life Sciences, Northwest A&F University; Shanghai Chenshan Botanical Garden（西北农林科技大学生命科学学院；上海辰山植物园）
- Research interest: Athyriaceae, Celastraceae, Lamiaceae, Ranunculaceae [PS]
- Published taxa: *Deparia, Teucrium, Trollius*
- Affiliation: CSH
- Location of specimens: CSH
- Region: CHINA (Shaanxi)

D. Q. Du

Du, Duo Qing; 杜多青 ; Dù Duōqīng

First publication: 2010

- Employment: Louxing District Agriculture Bureau, Loudi City, Hunan Province（湖南省娄底市娄星区农业局）
- Research interest: Aquifoliaceae [S]
- Published taxa: *Ilex*
- Region: CHINA (Hunan)

F. Du

Du, Fan; 杜凡 ; Dù Fán

1957- **First publication: 2010**

- Employment: College of Forestry, Southwest Forestry University（西南林业大学林学院）
- Research interest: Apocynaceae, Crassulaceae, Ebenaceae, Euphorbiaceae [S]
- Published taxa: *Cynanchum, Diospyros, Sinocrassula, Trigonostemon*
- Region: CHINA (Yunnan)

G. Z. Du

Du, Guo Zhen; 杜国祯 ; Dù Guózhēn

1955- **First publication: 2007**

- Employment: Key Laboratory of Arid and Grassland Ecology with the Ministry of Education, Lanzhou University（兰州大学干旱与草地农业生态教育部重点实验室）
- Research interest: Asteraceae, Orobanchaceae [S]
- Published taxa: *Euphrasia, Saussurea*
- Region: CHINA (Gansu)

W. Du

Du, Wei; 杜巍 ; Dù Wēi

1981- **First publication: 2016**

- Employment: College of Life Sciences, Wuhan University（武汉大学生命科学学院）
- Research interest: Papaveraceae, Polygonaceae [S]
- Published taxa: *Hylomecon, Koenigia*
- Region: CHINA (Hubei)

W. Y. Du

Du, Wen Yan; 杜文妍 ; Dù Wényán

First publication: 2019

- Employment: Nanyue College of Hengyang Normal University（衡阳师范学院南岳学院）
- Research interest: Araceae [S]
- Published taxa: *Arisaema*
- Region: CHINA (Guangdong)

X. C. Du

Du, Xi Chun; 杜喜春 ; Dù Xǐchūn

1970- **First publication: 2005**

- Employment: College of Life Sciences, Shaanxi Normal University（陕西师范大学生命科学学院）
- Research interest: Araliaceae, Hypericaceae [S]
- Published taxa: *Hydrocotyle, Hypericum*
- Region: CHINA (Shaanxi)

Y. F. Du

Du, Yu Fen; 杜玉芬 ; Dù Yùfēn

1962- **First publication: 2000**

- Employment: Institute of Botany, Chinese Academy of Sciences（中国科学院植物研究所）
- Research interest: Fabaceae [S]
- Published taxa: *Butea, Codariocalyx, Crotalaria, Medicago, Oxytropis*
- Affiliation: PE
- Region: CHINA

Duanmu

Duanmu, Shing; Duanmu, Xin; 端木炘 ; Duānmù Xīn; 端木忻

1929-2017 **First publication: 1963**

- Employment: Chinese Academy of Forestry（中国林

业科学研究院）
• Research interest: Fagaceae [S]
• Published taxa: *Castanopsis*
• Region: CHINA

B. Z. Duan

Duan, Bao Zhong; 段宝忠；Duàn Bǎozhōng
1983- **First publication: 2017**
• Employment: College of Pharmacy, Dali University （大理大学药学院）
• Research interest: Melanthiaceae [S]
• Published taxa: *Paris*
• Region: CHINA (Yunnan)

D. X. Duan

Duan, Dai Xiang; 段代祥；Duàn Dàixiáng
1977- **First publication: 2015**
• Employment: Binzhou University（滨州学院）
• Research interest: Malvaceae [S]
• Published taxa: *Malva*
• Region: CHINA (Xizang)

J. K. Duan

Duan, Jian Kun; 段剑坤；Duàn Jiànkūn
1969- **First publication: 1998**
• Employment: Southwest Forestry College（西南林学院）
• Research interest: Poaceae [S]
• Published taxa: *Fargesia*
• Region: CHINA (Yunan)

J. A. Duan

Duan, Jing Ao; 段金廒；Duàn Jīn'áo
1956- **First publication: 1993**
• Employment: Ningxia Institute for Food and Drug Control（宁夏药品检验研究所）
• Research interest: Orobanchaceae [S]
• Published taxa: *Cistanche*
• Region: CHINA (Ningxia)

J. Duan

Duan, Jun; 段俊；Duàn Jùn
1964- **First publication: 2010**
• Employment: South China Botanical Garden, Chinese Academy of Sciences（中国科学院华南植物园）
• Research interest: Orchidaceae [S]
• Published taxa: *Dendrobium*
• Region: CHINA (Guangdong)

L. Duan

Duan, Lei; 段磊；Duàn Lěi
1985- **First publication: 2016**
• Employment: College of Life Sciences, Northwest A&F University; South China Botanical Garden, Chinese Academy of Sciences（西北农林科技大学生命科学学院；中国科学院华南植物园）
• Research interest: Fabaceae [S]
• Published taxa: *Caragana, Chesneya, Chesniella, Styphnolobium*
• Affiliation: IBSC
• Region: CHINA

L. D. Duan

Duan, Lin Dong; 段林东；Duàn Líndōng
1960- **First publication: 2003**
• Employment: Shaoyang University; Institute of Botany, Chinese Academy of Sciences（邵阳学院；中国科学院植物研究所）
• Research interest: Rubiaceae, Urticaceae [S]
• Published taxa: *Elatostema, Ophiorrhiza*
• Location of specimens: HUST, PE
• Region: CHINA

P. C. Tuan

Tuan, Pei Chin; Duan, Pei Qin; **段佩琴**；Duàn Pèiqín
1933- **First publication: 1978**
• Employment: Sichuan University（四川大学）
• Research interest: Elaeocarpaceae. [AS]
• Published taxa: *Elaeocarpus, Sloanea*
• Location of specimens: SZ
• Region: CHINA (Sichuan)

T. T. Duan

Duan, Ting Ting; 段婷婷；Duàn Tíngtíng
1987- **First publication: 2016**
• Employment: South China Botanical Garden, Chinese Academy of Sciences; College of Agriculture, Guangdong Ocean University（中国科学院华南植物园；广东海洋大学农学院）
• Research interest: Rubiaceae [S]
• Published taxa: *Mussaenda*
• Region: CHINA (Yunnan)

X. Z. Duan

Duan, Xian Zhen; 段咸珍；Duàn Xiánzhēn
1933- **First publication: 1987**
• Employment: Yumin County Fritillaria Test Station, Xinjiang（新疆裕民县贝母试验站）
• Research interest: Liliaceae [S]
• Published taxa: *Fritillaria*
• Region: CHINA (Xinjiang)

Yi F. Duan

Duan, Yi Fan; 段一凡；Duàn Yīfán
1984- **First publication: 2014**
• Employment: College of Biology and the Environment, Nanjing Forestry University（南京林业大学生物与环境学院）

- Research interest: Boraginaceae, Dryopteridaceae, Lamiaceae, Oleaceae, Phyllanthaceae, Solanaceae, Tectariaceae, Ulmaceae [PS]
- Published taxa: *Bischofia, Callicarpa, Chengiodendron, Ctenitis, Eritrichium, Lycianthes, Megalastrum, Polystichum, Premna, Solanum, Tectaria, Ulmus*
- Affiliation: NF
- Region: CHINA

F

Q. Fan

Fan, Qiang; 凡强 ; Fán Qiáng

1978- **First publication: 2007**

- Employment: School of Life Sciences, Sun Yat-sen University（中山大学生命科学学院）
- Research interest: Aquifoliaceae, Rosaceae, Violaceae; Plants of S. China [S]
- Published taxa: *Eriobotrya, Ilex, Pyrus, Rhaphiolepis, Viola*
- Affiliation: SYS
- Location of specimens: SYS
- Region: CHINA

G. S. Fan

Fan, Guo Sheng; 樊国盛 ; Fán Guóshèng

1963- **First publication: 1988**

- Employment: Southwest Forestry College（西南林学院）
- Research interest: Berberidaceae, Cannabaceae, Celastraceae, Fabaceae, Fagaceae, Flacourtiaceae, Hamamelidaceae, Rhamnaceae, Salicaceae, Sapindaceae, Styracaceae, Theaceae [S]
- Published taxa: *Acer, Bennettiodendron, Berberis, Camellia, Celtis, Cladrastis, Cyclobalanopsis, Glyptopetalum, Gordonia, Homalium, Idesia, Itoa, Neostyrax, Rhamnus, Rhodoleia, Sageretia, Ventilago*
- Affiliation: SWFC
- Location of specimens: SWFC
- Region: CHINA (Yunnan)

J. H. Fan

Fan, Jian Hua; 樊建华 ; Fán Jiànhuá

1956- **First publication: 2011**

- Employment: Xinjiang Agricultural University（新疆农业大学）
- Research interest: Papaveraceae, Zygophyllaceae [S]
- Published taxa: *Zygophyllum*
- Affiliation: XJA
- Location of specimens: XJA
- Region: CHINA (Xinjiang)

S. J. Fan

Fan, Shou Jin; 樊守金 ; Fán Shǒujīn

1965- **First publication: 1993**

- Employment: Department of Biology, Shandong Normal University（山东师范大学生物系）
- Research interest: Cyperaceae, Polygonaceae; Plants of Shandong [S]
- Published taxa: *Carex, Polygonum*
- Affiliation: SDNU
- Location of specimens: SDNU
- Region: CHINA (Shandong, Sichuan)

G. J. Fan

Fan, Guang Jin; 范广进 ; Fàn Guǎngjìn

First publication: 1974

- Employment: Shanghai Institute of Materia Medica, Chinese Academy of Sciences（中国科学院上海药物研究所）
- Research interest: Amaryllidaceae [S]
- Published taxa: *Lycoris*
- Location of specimens: PE
- Region: CHINA

J. C. Fan

Fan, Ji Cai; 范继才 ; Fàn Jìcái

1955- **First publication: 2009**

- Employment: Sichuan Agricultural University（四川农业大学）
- Research interest: Magnoliaceae [S]
- Published taxa: *Michelia*
- Region: CHINA (Sichuan)

S. T. Fan

Fan, Shang Tan; 范尚坦 ; Fàn Shàngtǎn

First publication: 1988

- Employment: Department of Pharmacy, Second Military Medical University（第二军医大学药学系）
- Research interest: Piperaceae [S]
- Published taxa: *Piper*
- Region: CHINA (Fujian)

S. M. Fan

Fan, Shi Ming; 范世明 ; Fàn Shìmíng

1964- **First publication: 2017**

- Employment: College of Pharmacy, Fujian University of Traditional Chinese Medicine（福建中医药大学药学院）

- Research interest: Orchidaceae [S]
- Published taxa: *Liparis*
- Region: CHINA (Fujian)

S. W. Fan

Fan, Si Wei; 范思伟; Fàn Sīwěi

First publication: 1966

- Employment: Department of Biology, Fudan University（复旦大学生物系）
- Research interest: Adoxaceae [S]
- Published taxa: *Viburnum*
- Region: CHINA

W. T. Fan

Fan, Wen Tao; 范文涛; Fàn Wéntāo; 範文濤

1936- **First publication: 1987**

- Employment: Zhejiang Agricultural University（浙江农业大学）
- Research interest: Apiaceae, Chenopodiaceae, Malvaceae, Phytolaceaceae, Polygonaceae [S]
- Published taxa: *Ligusticum, Phytolacca*
- Affiliation: HZU, ZAU
- Location of specimens: HZU, PE, ZAU
- Region: CHINA (Hebei, Zhejiang)

D. Fang

Fang, Ding; 方鼎; Fāng Dǐng

1926-2017 **First publication: 1977**

- Employment: Guangxi Institute of Traditional Medical and Pharmaceutical Sciences（广西中医药研究所）
- Research interest: Acanthaceae, Apocynaceae, Asparagaceae, Balanophoraceae, Begoniaceae, Betulaceae, Commelinaceae, Cucurbitaceae, Elaeagnaceae, Ericaceae, Gentianaceae, Gesneriaceae, Hypoxidaceae, Icacinaceae, Lamiaceae, Lauraceae, Loganiaceae, Lowiaceae, Marantaceae, Moraceae, Oleaceae, Pentaphylacaceae, Primulaceae, Rhamnaceae, Rubiaceae, Theaceae, Thymelaeaceae, Zingiberaceae [S]
- Published taxa: *Adinandra, Agapetes, Alpinia, Alstonia, Amomum, Ardisia, Aspidistra, Balanophora, Begonia, Berchemia, Camellia, Chionanthus, Chirita, Chiritopsis, Cosmianthemum, Curculigo, Daphne, Didymocarpus, Didymostigma, Dolicholoma, Echinacanthus, Elaeagnus, Elettariopsis, Ficus, Gaultheria, Hedychium, Hygrophila, Justicia, Lagarosolen, Leptostachya, Litsea, Loxostigma, Lysimachia, Machilus, Mappianthus, Mitreola, Murdannia, Mussaenda, Ophiopogon, Ophiorrhiza, Orchidantha, Oreocharis, Ostrya, Paraboea, Paraphlomis, Periploca, Peristrophe, Phrynium, Primula, Rungia, Siraitia, Spiradiclis, Strobilanthes, Trachelospermum, Tripterospermum, Wentsaiboea, Zingiber*
- Affiliation: GXMI
- Location of specimens: GXMI
- Region: CHINA

M. Y. Fang

Fang, Ming Yuan; 方明渊; Fāng Míngyuān; 方明淵

1935- **First publication: 1984**

- Employment: Department of Biology, Sichuan University（四川大学生物系）
- Research interest: Ericaceae, Papaveraceae, Ranunculaceae, Sapindaceae, Symplocaceae [S]
- Published taxa: *Acer, Clematis, Enkianthus, Rhododendron, Symplocos*
- Affiliation: SZ
- Location of specimens: JSPC, SZ
- Region: CHINA

M. M. Fang

Fang, Min Man; 方铭满; Fāng Míngmǎn

First publication: 1987

- Employment: Anhui Institute for Drug Control（安徽省药品检验所）
- Research interest: Liliaceae [S]
- Published taxa: *Fritillaria*
- Region: CHINA (Anhui)

Q. Fang

Fang, Qiong; 方琼; Fāng Qióng

1995- **First publication: 2020**

- Employment: College of Life and Environmental Sciences, Minzu University of China（中央民族大学生命与环境科学学院）
- Research interest: Araceae [S]
- Published taxa: *Alocasia*
- Region: CHINA (Yunnan)

R. C. Fang

Fang, Rhui Cheng; Fang, Rui Zheng; **方瑞征; Fāng Ruìzhēng; 方瑞徵**

1932- **First publication: 1979**

- Employment: Kunming Institute of Botany, Chinese Academy of Sciences（中国科学院昆明植物研究所）
- Research interest: Brassicaceae, Convolvulaceae, Ericaceae, Lamiaceae, Primulaceae [S]
- Published taxa: *Agapetes, Aniseia, Cardamine, Cassiope, Clerodendrum, Cuscuta, Enkianthus, Gaultheria, Ipomoea, Loxostemon, Merremia, Omphalogramma, Pharbitis, Primula, Rhododendron, Vaccinium*
- Affiliation: KUN
- Region: CHINA

S. T. Fang

Fang, Shang Tu; 方尚土 ; Fāng Shàngtǔ

1945-2016 First publication: 1983

- Employment: Department of Pharmacy, Zhejiang Medical University（浙江医科大学药学系）
- Research interest: Araliaceae [S]
- Published taxa: *Acanthopanax*
- Region: CHINA (Zhejiang)

S. Z. Fang

Fang, Si Zhao; 方嗣昭 ; Fāng Sìzhāo

1940- First publication: 1984

- Employment: Department of Geography, Guiyang Normal College（贵阳师范学院地理系）
- Research interest: Pinaceae [S]
- Published taxa: *Abies*
- Region: CHINA (Guizhou)

S. Q. Fang

Fang, Su Qin; 方素琴 ; Fāng Sùqín

First publication: 2020

- Employment: School of Life Sciences, Sun Yat-sen University（中山大学生命科学学院）
- Research interest: Burmanniaceae [S]
- Published taxa: *Thismia*
- Region: CHINA (Hainan)

W. P. Fang

Fang, Wen Pei; Fang, Wên P'ei; 方文培 ; Fāng Wénpéi

1899-1983 First publication: 1932

- Employment: Department of Biology, National Sichuan University; Department of Biology, Sichuan University（国立四川大学生物系；四川大学生物系）
- Research interest: Aceraceae, Aquifoliaceae, Celastraceae, Combretaceae, Cornaceae, Ericaceae, Garryaceae, Helwingiaceae, Hydrangeaceae, Lauraceae, Nyssaceae, Primulaceae, Rhamnaceae, Sapindaceae [S]
- Published taxa: *Acer, Aesculus, Alangium, Aucuba, Berchemia, Cornus, Dendrobenthamia, Deutzia, Euonymus, Helwingia, Ilex, Lindera, Macrocarpium, Mastixia, Philadelphus, Primula, Rhododendron, Terminalia, Vaccinium*
- Affiliation: SZ
- Location of specimens: CQNM, HWA, NAS, PE, SHM, SZ
- Region: CHINA

W. Z. Fang

Fang, Wen Zhe; 方文哲 ; Fāng Wénzhé

1929-2007 First publication: 1979

- Employment: Institute of Botany, Jiangsu Province and Chinese Academy of Sciences（江苏省中国科学院植物研究所）
- Research interest: Lamiaceae, Poaceae, Primulaceae [S]
- Published taxa: *Ardisia, Bothriochloa, Callicarpa, Isachne*
- Affiliation: NAS
- Location of specimens: NAS
- Region: CHINA

X. M. Fang

Fang, Xiang Ming; 方向明 ; Fāng Xiàngmíng

1965- First publication: 2009

- Employment: Department of Biology, Anhui University（安徽大学生物系）
- Research interest: Cyperaceae [S]
- Published taxa: *Carex*
- Region: CHINA (Anhui)

X. P. Fang

Fang, Xin Ping; 方忻平 ; Fāng Xīnpíng

1955- First publication: 1987

- Employment: College of Pharmacy, West China University of Medical Sciences（华西医科大学药学院）
- Research interest: Araliaceae [S]
- Published taxa: *Acanthopanax*
- Region: CHINA (Sichuan)

Y. Y. Fang

Fang, Yun Yi; Fang, Y. I; 方云亿 ; Fāng Yúnyì; 方雲億

1921-2003 First publication: 1983

- Employment: Department of Biology, Hangzhou University（杭州大学生物系）
- Research interest: Boraginaceae, Ericaceae, Fabaceae, Gentianaceae, Polygonaceae, Primulaceae [S]
- Published taxa: *Indigofera, Lysimachia, Omphalotrigonotis, Polygonum, Rhododendron, Swertia*
- Affiliation: HZU
- Location of specimens: HZU
- Region: CHINA

C. F. Fang

Fang, Cheng Fu; Fang, Zhen Fu; Fang, Chen Fu ; 方振富 ; Fāng Zhènfù

1925- First publication: 1979

- Employment: Institute of Applied Ecology, Chinese Academy of Sciences（中国科学院沈阳应用生态研究所）
- Research interest: Caprifoliaceae, Ericaceae, Polygonaceae, Salicaceae, Typhaceae [S]
- Published taxa: *Abelia, Lonicera, Polygonum, Populus, Reynoutria, Rhododendron, Salix, Typha, Weigela*
- Affiliation: IFP
- Location of specimens: IFP

• Region: CHINA

Z. D. Fang

Fang, Zheng Dong; 方震东; Fāng Zhèndōng

1964- **First publication: 1990**

• Employment: The Science and Technology Commission of Diqing Tibetan Autonomous Prefecture, Yunnan（云南省迪庆藏族自治州科学技术委员会）

• Research interest: Primulaceae, Ranunculaceae; Plants of Yunnan [S]

• Published taxa: *Aconitum, Primula*

• Affiliation: SABG

• Location of specimens: SABG

• Region: CHINA (Yunnan)

Z. J. Fang

Fang, Zhi Jian; 房志坚; Fáng Zhìjiān

1956- **First publication: 2011**

• Employment: School of Traditional Chinese Medicine, Guangdong Pharmaceutical University（广东药科大学中药学院）

• Research interest: Polygonaceae; Medicinal Plants [S]

• Published taxa: *Fallopia*

• Affiliation: GDMP

• Region: CHINA (Guangxi)

W. Q. Fei

Fei, Wen Qun; 费文群; Fèi Wénqún

1992- **First publication: 2019**

• Employment: South China Botanical Garden, Chinese Academy of Sciences（中国科学院华南植物园）

• Research interest: Asteraceae [S]

• Published taxa: *Cremanthodium, Ligularia*

• Region: [ASIA]

Y. Fei

Fei, Yong; 费勇; Fèi Yǒng

1960-2001 **First publication: 1997**

• Employment: Kunming Institute of Botany, Chinese Academy of Sciences（中国科学院昆明植物研究所）

• Research interest: Ranunculaceae [S]

• Published taxa: *Naravelia*

• Affiliation: KUN

• Location of specimens: PE

• Region: CHINA (Yunan)

Y. J. Fei

Fei, Yong Jun; 费永俊; Fèi Yǒngjùn

1965- **First publication: 1999**

• Employment: Department of Horticulture, Hubei Agricultural College; College of Horticulture and Gardening, Yangtze University（湖北农学院园艺系；长江大学园艺园林学院）

• Research interest: Lauraceae, Poaceae, Taxaceae [S]

• Published taxa: *Lolium, Phoebe, Taxus*

• Region: CHINA (Hubei)

B. Y. Feng

Feng, Bao Yuan; 冯宝元; Féng Bǎoyuán

1950- **First publication: 1997**

• Employment: Xi County Agricultural Experiment Station, Shanxi Academy of Agricultural Sciences（山西省农业科学院隰县农业试验站）

• Research interest: Rosaceae [S]

• Published taxa: *Cerasus*

• Region: CHINA (Shanxi)

C. L. Feng

Feng, Chang Lin; 冯昌林; Féng Chānglín

First publication: 2010

• Employment: Experimental Center of Tropical Forestry, Chinese Academy of Forestry（中国林业科学研究院热带林业实验中心）

• Research interest: Orchidaceae [S]

• Published taxa: *Liparis*

• Region: CHINA (Guangxi)

C. X. Feng

Feng, Chang Xue; 冯昌学; Féng Chāngxué

First publication: 1987

• Employment: Zhouqu County Science and Technology Commission（舟曲县科委）

• Research interest: Liliaceae [S]

• Published taxa: *Fritillaria*

• Region: CHINA (Gansu)

D. C. Feng

Feng, De Cheng; 冯德诚; Féng Déchéng; 馮德誠

1934- **First publication: 1993**

• Employment: Department of Biology and Basic Courses, Shihezi Agricultural College（石河子农学院生物基础部）

• Research interest: Fabaceae [S]

• Published taxa: *Glycyrrhiza*

• Region: CHINA (Xinjiang)

G. H. Feng

Feng, Gui Hua; 冯桂华; Féng Guìhuá; 馮桂華

1937-2006 **First publication: 1984**

• Employment: Kunming Institute of Botany, Chinese Academy of Sciences（中国科学院昆明植物研究所）

• Research interest: Orchidaceae [S]

• Published taxa: *Cymbidium, Pleione*

• Region: CHINA (Yunnan)

K. M. Feng

Feng, Kuo Mei; Fêng, Kuo Mei; Feng, Guo Mei; 冯国楣; Féng Guóméi; 馮國楣

1917-2007 **First publication: 1951**

- Employment: Kunming Institute of Botany, Chinese Academy of Sciences（中国科学院昆明植物研究所）
- Research interest: Anacardiaceae, Araliaceae, Elaeocarpaceae, Ericaceae, Hamamelidaceae, Malvaceae, Oleaceae, Orchidaceae, Papaveraceae, Pentaphylacaceae, Pittosporaceae, Rutaceae, Staphyleaceae, Styracaceae, Taxaceae, Theaceae [S]
- Published taxa: *Abelmoschus, Abutilon, Acanthopanax, Aralia, Brassaiopsis, Camellia, Cephalotaxus, Cymbidium, Dendropanax, Eurya, Eustigma, Fortunella, Fraxinus, Hibiscus, Macropanax, Meconopsis, Nothopanax, Panax, Parastyrax, Pentapanax, Pittosporum, Rehderodendron, Rhododendron, Schefflera, Sida, Sloanea, Spondias, Staphylea, Urena*
- Affiliation: KUN
- Location of specimens: KUN, PE
- Region: CHINA (Yunnan)

H. Y. Feng

Feng, Hu Yuan; 冯虎元; Féng Hǔyuán

1967- **First publication: 1999**

- Employment: Department of Biology, Lanzhou University（兰州大学生物系）
- Research interest: Orobanchaceae; Plants of Gansu [S]
- Published taxa: *Pedicularis*
- Affiliation: LZU
- Region: CHINA (Gansu)

T. Feng

Feng, Tao; 冯涛; Féng Tāo

1986- **First publication: 2014**

- Employment: Wuhan Botanical Garden, Chinese Academy of Sciences（中国科学院武汉植物园）
- Research interest: Rosaceae [S]
- Published taxa: *Argentina*
- Region: CHINA (Xizang)

T. J. Feng

Feng, Tian Jie; 冯天杰; Féng Tiānjié

1954- **First publication: 1991**

- Employment: Hebei Forestry College（河北林学院）
- Research interest: Euphorbiaceae, Lamiaceae, Primulaceae, Ranunculaceae, Rosaceae [S]
- Published taxa: *Crataegus, Delphinium, Euphorbia, Primula, Schizonepeta*
- Location of specimens: HBFC
- Region: CHINA (Hebei)

H. L. Fung

Fung, Hok Lam; Feng, Xue Lin; 冯学琳; Féng Xuélín; 馮學琳

1923-2019 **First publication: 1988**

- Employment: South China Institute of Botany, Chinese Academy of Sciences; South China Botanical Garden, Chinese Academy of Sciences（中国科学院华南植物研究所；中国科学院华南植物园）
- Research interest: Poaceae [S]
- Published taxa: *Bambusa, Dendrocalamus, Leptocanna, Monocladus*
- Affiliation: IBSC
- Location of specimens: CUHK, IBSC
- Region: CHINA
- Also as: X. L. Feng

X. F. Feng

Feng, Xue Feng; 冯雪峰; Féng Xuěfēng

1955- **First publication: 1995**

- Employment: Institute of Chinese Materia Medica, China Academy of Chinese Medical Sciences（中国中医研究院中药研究所）
- Research interest: Asteraceae, Caprifoliaceae [S]
- Published taxa: *Atractylodes, Dipsacus*
- Region: CHINA

X. Z. Feng

Feng, Xue Zhou; 冯雪舟; Féng Xuězhōu; 冯燮舟

1942- **First publication: 1988**

- Employment: Shanghai Botanical Garden（上海植物园）
- Research interest: Juglandaceae; Woody Plants [S]
- Published taxa: *Cyclocarya*
- Affiliation: SG
- Location of specimens: SG
- Region: CHINA (Anhui, Zhejiang)

Y. Feng

Feng, Ying; 冯缨; Féng Yīng

1963- **First publication: 2011**

- Employment: Xinjiang Institute of Ecology and Geography, Chinese Academy of Sciences（中国科学院新疆生态与地理研究所）
- Research interest: Rosaceae, Tamaricaceae, Zygophyllaceae [S]
- Published taxa: *Zygophyllum*
- Affiliation: XJBI
- Region: CHINA (Xinjiang)

Z. J. Feng

Feng, Zhi Jian; 冯志坚; Féng Zhìjiān; 馮志堅

1932- **First publication: 1980**

- Employment: Department of Biology, Shanghai Normal University; Department of Biology, East

China Normal University (上海师范大学生物系；华东师范大学生物系)
- Research interest: Apocynaceae, Lamiaceae, Plantaginaceae [S]
- Published taxa: *Biondia, Callicarpa, Veronicastrum*
- Affiliation: HSNU
- Location of specimens: HSNU
- Region: CHINA

Zhi J. Feng

Feng, Zhi Jian; 冯志坚；Féng Zhìjiān

1962- **First publication: 1990**

- Employment: College of Forestry, South China Agricultural University (华南农业大学林学院)
- Research interest: Ericaceae, Poaceae; Plants of Guangdong [S]
- Published taxa: *Acidosasa, Arundinaria, Bambusa, Gelidocalamus, Indosasa, Lingnania, Oligostachyum, Phyllostachys, Pleioblastus, Pseudosasa, Rhododendron, Sasa, Sinobambusa*
- Affiliation: CANT
- Location of specimens: CANT
- Region: CHINA
- IPNI as: Z. J. Feng

Z. C. Feng

Feng, Zi Cheng; 冯自诚；Féng Zìchéng; 馮自誠

1935- **First publication: 1990**

- Employment: College of Forestry, Gansu Agricultural University (甘肃农业大学林学院)
- Research interest: Ericaceae, Salicaceae; Plants of Gansu [S]
- Published taxa: *Populus, Rhododendron*
- Affiliation: GAUF
- Location of specimens: GAUF
- Region: CHINA (Gansu)

Y. X. Feng

Feng, Yu Xing; 俸宇星；Fèng Yǔxīng

1970- **First publication: 1998**

- Employment: Institute of Botany, Chinese Academy of Sciences (中国科学院植物研究所)
- Research interest: Aquifoliaceae [S]
- Published taxa: *Ilex*
- Region: CHINA

G. A. Fu

Fu, Guo Ai; 符国瑗；Fú Guó'ài; 符國瑗

1936- **First publication: 1982**

- Employment: Forestry Bureau of Hainan Administrative Region; Forestry Department of Hainan Province (海南行政区林业局；海南省林业局)
- Research interest: Cupressaceae, Cycadaceae, Dipterocarpaceae, Fabaceae, Fagaceae, Hamamelidaceae, Lauraceae, Magnoliaceae, Moraceae, Pinaceae, Poaceae, Rosaceae, Rubiaceae, Theaceae; Plants of Hainan [S]
- Published taxa: *Adenanthera, Bambusa, Calocedrus, Camellia, Canthium, Castanopsis, Cerasus, Cycas, Cyclobalanopsis, Dalbergia, Ficus, Keteleeria, Lingnania, Machilus, Magnolia, Michelia, Prunus, Pseudosasa, Quercus, Rhodoleia, Vatica*
- Affiliation: HFB
- Location of specimens: HFB
- Region: CHINA (Hainan)

L. F. Fu

Fu, Long Fei; 符龙飞；Fú Lóngfēi

1988- **First publication: 2012**

- Employment: Guangxi Institute of Botany, Chinese Academy of Sciences (广西壮族自治区中国科学院广西植物研究所)
- Research interest: Gesneriaceae, Urticaceae [S]
- Published taxa: *Elatostema, Petrocodon, Pilea, Primulina*
- Region: CHINA (Guangxi)

Y. C. Fu

Fu, Yu Chin; Fu, Yu Qin; 符毓秦；Fú Yùqín

1937- **First publication: 1975**

- Employment: Shaanxi Institute of Forestry (陕西省林业科学研究所)
- Research interest: Salicaceae [S]
- Published taxa: *Populus*
- Region: CHINA (Shaanxi)

A. L. Fu

Fu, Ai Liang; 付爱良；Fù Àiliáng

1954- **First publication: 2008**

- Employment: Institute of Grassland, Xinjiang Academy of Animal Sciences (新疆畜牧科学院草原研究所)
- Research interest: Amaranthaceae [S]
- Published taxa: *Krascheninnikovia*
- Region: CHINA (Xinjiang)

C. X. Fu

Fu, Cheng Xin; 傅承新；Fù Chéngxīn

1954- **First publication: 1986**

- Employment: Department of Biology, Harbin Normal University; Faculty of Botany, Zhejiang Agricultural University; College of Life Sciences, Zhejiang University (哈尔滨师范大学生物系；浙江农业大学植物教研室；浙江大学生命科学学院)
- Research interest: Campanulaceae, Smilacaceae [S]
- Published taxa: *Adenophora, Smilax*
- Affiliation: HZU, ZAU
- Location of specimens: HZU, ZAU

- Region: [WORLD]

D. L. Fu

Fu, Da Li; 傅大立；Fù Dàlì

1965- **First publication: 2001**

- Employment: Henan Agricultural University; Beijing Forestry University; Non-timber Forestry Research and Development Center, Chinese Academy of Forestry（河南农业大学；北京林业大学；中国林业科学研究院经济林研究开发中心）
- Research interest: Magnoliaceae, Rosaceae [S]
- Published taxa: *Armeniaca, Magnolia, Yulania*
- Region: CHINA

D. Z. Fu

Fu, De Zhi; 傅德志；Fù Dézhì

1952- **First publication: 1988**

- Employment: Institute of Botany, Chinese Academy of Sciences（中国科学院植物研究所）
- Research interest: Cupressaceae, Ephedraceae, Nageiaceae, Poaceae, Podocarpaceae, Ranunculaceae; Gymnospermae [S]
- Published taxa: *Cupressus, Dichocarpum, Ephedra, Fargesia,* Nageiaceae
- Affiliation: PE
- Location of specimens: PE, WCSBG
- Region: CHINA

G. X. Fu

Fu, Guo Xun; 傅国勋；Fù Guóxūn; 傅國勳

1932- **First publication: 1979**

- Employment: Institute of Botany, Chinese Academy of Sciences（中国科学院植物研究所）
- Research interest: Asteraceae; Plants of N. China [S]
- Published taxa: *Tripleurospermum, Waldheimia*
- Affiliation: PE
- Location of specimens: PE
- Region: CHINA

J. Fu

Fu, Jie; 傅杰；Fù Jié

1943- **First publication: 1990**

- Employment: Northwest China Institute of Botany, Chinese Academy of Sciences and Shaanxi Province（陕西省中国科学院西北植物研究所）
- Research interest: Poaceae [S]
- Published taxa: × *Tritihaynaldia*
- Region: [cult.]

J. Q. Fu

Fu, Jing Qiu; Fu, Ching Chu; Fu, Jing Qiou; 傅竞秋；Fù Jìngqiū; 傅競秋

1934-2014 **First publication: 1981**

- Employment: Northwest China Institute of Botany, Chinese Academy of Sciences and Shaanxi Province（陕西省中国科学院西北植物研究所）
- Research interest: Amaranthaceae, Asteraceae, Cannabaceae, Ericaceae, Lamiaceae, Malvaceae, Polygonaceae, Ranunculaceae, Sapindaceae [S]
- Published taxa: *Acer, Anaphalis, Anemone, Aster, Carpesium, Chenopodium, Clematis, Gymnaster, Heteropappus, Hibiscus, Humulus, Inula, Kalimeris, Miyamayomena, Phlomis, Polygonum, Ranunculus, Rhododendron, Rumex*
- Affiliation: WUK
- Location of specimens: WUK
- Region: CHINA
- Also as: C. C. Fu

K. T. Fu

Fu, Kun Tsun; Fu, Kun Jun; 傅坤俊；Fù Kūnjùn; 付坤俊

1912-2010 **First publication: 1974**

- Employment: Northwest China Institute of Botany, Chinese Academy of Sciences and Shaanxi Province（陕西省中国科学院西北植物研究所）
- Research interest: Apiaceae, Convolvulaceae, Crassulaceae, Cyperaceae, Fabaceae, Lamiaceae, Malvaceae, Papaveraceae [S]
- Published taxa: *Angelica, Astragalus, Calystegia, Campylotropis, Carex, Cnidium, Corydalis, Hedysarum, Heracleum, Hibiscus, Hylotelephium, Kungia, Libanotis, Ligusticum, Peucedanum, Phedimus, Phlomis, Pimpinella, Pleurospermum, Pternopetalum, Rhodiola, Sanicula, Sedum, Seseli, Sinocrassula, Tillaea, Tongoloa, Vicia*
- Affiliation: WUK
- Location of specimens: WUK, PE
- Region: CHINA

L. K. Fu

Fu, Li Kuo; Fu, Li Guo; 傅立国；Fù Lìguó; 傅立國

1932- **First publication: 1975**

- Employment: Institute of Botany, Chinese Academy of Sciences（中国科学院植物研究所）
- Research interest: Berberidaceae, Cupressaceae, Cycadaceae, Ephedraceae, Gnetaceae, Pinaceae, Taxaceae, Ulmaceae; Gymnospermae [S]
- Published taxa: *Abies, Calocedrus, Cephalotaxus, Cupressus, Cycas, Dysosma, Ephedra, Gnetum, Juniperus, Keteleeria, Larix, Picea, Pinus, Pseudotsuga, Sabina, Taxus, Torreya, Tsuga, Ulmus*
- Affiliation: PE
- Region: CHINA

L. Fu

Fu, Lin; 傅琳；Fù Lín

1981- **First publication: 2012**

- Employment: South China Botanical Garden, Chinese Academy of Sciences（中国科学院华南植物园）
- Research interest: Dennstaedtiaceae, Magnoliaceae, Malvaceae, Marantaceae [PS]
- Published taxa: *Magnolia, Malva, Manglietia, Microlepia, Phrynium*
- Location of specimens: IBSC
- Region: CHINA

P. Y. Fu

Fu, Pei Yun; Fuh, Pei Yun; 傅沛云；Fù Pèiyún; 傅沛雲
1926-2017 **First publication: 1974**

- Employment: Institute of Forestry and Soil Sciences, Chinese Academy of Sciences（中国科学院林业土壤研究所）
- Research interest: Amaranthaceae, Asparagaceae, Brassicaceae, Campanulaceae, Fabaceae, Iridaceae, Juncaceae, Lamiaceae, Liliaceae, Orchidaceae, Papaveraceae, Salicaceae, Violaceae [S]
- Published taxa: *Adenophora, Astragalus, Campylotropis, Cardamine, Chenopodium, Corispermum, Corydalis, Elsholtzia, Erythronium, Glycine, Hosta, Iris, Luzula, Melissitus, Neottianthe, Oxytropis, Papaver, Pocockia, Populus, Salix, Trifolium, Vicia, Viola*
- Affiliation: IFP
- Location of specimens: IFP
- Region: CHINA

Q. Fu

Fu, Qiong; 傅琼；Fù Qióng
1990- **First publication: 2019**

- Employment: School of Life Sciences, South China Normal University（华南师范大学生命科学学院）
- Research interest: Gesneriaceae [S]
- Published taxa: *Oreocharis*
- Region: CHINA (Guizhou)

S. M. Fu

Fu, Shi Min; 傅世敏；Fù Shìmǐn
First publication: 1989

- Employment: Institute of Grassland Research, Chinese Academy of Agricultural Sciences（中国农业科学院草原研究所）
- Research interest: Fabaceae [S]
- Published taxa: *Vicia*
- Region: CHINA (Nei Mongol)

S. H. Fu

Fu, Shu Hsia; Fu, Shu Xia; 傅书遐；Fù Shūxiá; 傅書遐
1916-1986 **First publication: 1956**

- Employment: Wuhan Botanical Garden, Chinese Academy of Sciences（中国科学院武汉植物园）
- Research interest: Aspleniaceae, Crassulaceae, Fagaceae, Garryaceae, Lamiaceae, Polypodiaceae; Pteridophytes [PS]
- Published taxa: *Aucuba, Ceterachopsis, Hylotelephium, Lemmaphyllum, Phlomis, Quercus, Rhodiola, Sedum, Sinocrassula*
- Affiliation: HIB
- Region: CHINA

Y. S. Fu

Fu, Yun Sheng; 傅运生；Fù Yùnshēng; 付运生
1950-2008 **First publication: 1993**

- Employment: Department of Biology, Hubei University（湖北大学生物系）
- Research interest: Araliaceae, Onagraceae [S]
- Published taxa: *Aralia, Epilobium*
- Location of specimens: EU
- Region: CHINA (Hubei)

H. C. Fu

Fu, Hiang Chian; Fu, Xiang Qian; 富象乾；Fù Xiàngqián
1926-2016 **First publication: 1978**

- Employment: Inner Mongolia College of Agriculture and Animal Husbandry（内蒙古农牧学院）
- Research interest: Amaranthaceae, Asteraceae, Fabaceae, Lamiaceae, Polygonaceae, Rubiaceae [S]
- Published taxa: *Ajania, Artemisia, Astragalus, Atraphaxis, Atriplex, Caragana, Ceratoides, Chesneya, Cirsium, Corispermum, Dendranthema, Dracocephalum, Elachanthemum, Hedysarum, Heteropappus, Ixeris, Kalidium, Leptodermis, Melilotoides, Melissitus, Oxytropis, Pocockia, Polygonum, Pterocypsela, Salsola, Saussurea, Schizonepeta, Serratula, Stilpnolepis, Suaeda, Taraxacum, Youngia*
- Affiliation: NMAC
- Location of specimens: NMAC
- Region: CHINA (Nei Mongol)

C. F. Gan

Gan, Chang Fei; 甘长飞；Gān Chángfēi
1957- **First publication: 1983**

- Employment: Qingyuan Institute of Agricultural Science, Zhejiang（浙江省庆元县农科所）
- Research interest: Actinidiaceae [S]

• Published taxa: *Actinidia*
• Region: CHINA (Zhejiang)

Q. L. Gan

Gan, Qi Liang; 甘启良 ; Gān Qǐliáng
1952- **First publication: 2011**
• Employment: Zhuxi Radio Station, Hubei; Shennong Wudang Institute of Traditional Chinese Medicine, Shiyan, Hubei; Zhuxi Qiliang Institute of Biology, Hubei (湖北竹溪广播电台；湖北省十堰神农武当中医药研究所；竹溪县启良生物研究所)
• Research interest: Asteraceae, Balsaminaceae, Brassicaceae, Caryophyllaceae, Ranunculaceae [S]
• Published taxa: *Delphinium, Eutrema, Impatiens, Ligularia, Saussurea, Stellaria*
• Region: CHINA (Hubei)

P. C. Kao

Kao, Pao Chun; Kao, Pao Chung; Gao, Bao Chun; 高宝莼 ; Gāo Bǎochún; 高寶蒓
1935- **First publication: 1980**
• Employment: Chengdu Institute of Biology, Chinese Academy of Sciences (中国科学院成都生物研究所)
• Research interest: Araceae, Combretaceae, Velloziaceae; Monocotyledons [S]
• Published taxa: *Acanthochlamys, Arisaema, Terminalia*
• Affiliation: CDBI
• Region: CHINA (Sichuan)

C. Z. Gao

Gao, Cheng Zhi; 高成芝 ; Gāo Chéngzhī
1939- **First publication: 1981**
• Employment: Guangxi Institute of Traditional Medical and Pharmaceutical Sciences (广西中医药研究所)
• Research interest: Apocynaceae, Asparagaceae, Celastraceae, Fabaceae, Gentianaceae, Gesneriaceae, Grossulariaceae, Menispermaceae, Primulaceae, Rhamnaceae, Saxifragaceae; Medicinal Plants [S]
• Published taxa: *Aganosma, Berchemia, Buxiphyllum, Desmodium, Lysimachia, Paliurus, Parnassia, Polygonatum, Ribes, Sageretia, Saxifraga, Swertia, Tinospora*
• Affiliation: GXMI
• Location of specimens: GXMI
• Region: CHINA (Guangxi)

C. M. Gao

Gao, Chun Ming; 高春明 ; Gāo Chūnmíng
1982- **First publication: 2007**
• Employment: South China Botanical Garden, Chinese Academy of Sciences (中国科学院华南植物园)
• Research interest: Acanthaceae [S]
• Published taxa: *Justicia, Rungia*
• Region: CHINA

D. F. Gao

Gao, Dong Fan; 高东藩 ; Gāo Dōngfān
?-2019 **First publication: 1980**
• Employment: Wenjiang Institute for Drug Control, Sichuan (四川省温江药检所)
• Research interest: Cucurbitaceae [S]
• Published taxa: *Trichosanthes*
• Location of specimens: GZTM
• Region: CHINA (Sichuan)

F. Y. Gao

Gao, Fang You; 高仿优 ; Gāo Fǎngyōu
1964- **First publication: 1998**
• Employment: Beijing University of Agriculture (北京农学院)
• Research interest: Rosaceae, Ulmaceae [S]
• Published taxa: *Exochorda, Ulmus*
• Location of specimens: PE
• Region: CHINA

H. S. Gao

Gao, Hai Shan; 高海山 ; Gāo Hǎishān
1979- **First publication: 2008**
• Employment: Enshi Polytechnic (恩施职业技术学院)
• Research interest: Gesneriaceae [S]
• Published taxa: *Chiritopsis, Lagarosolen*
• Region: CHINA (Guangxi)

C. C. Kao

Kao, Chi Ching; 高紀清 ; Gāo Jìqīng; 高纪清
First publication: 2009
• Employment: Ching Hua Orchids, Taiwan (台湾清华兰园)
• Research interest: Orchidaceae [S]
• Published taxa: ×*Chrisnetia*
• Region: CHINA (Taiwan)

C. Y. Kao

Kao, Chien Yuan; 高建元 ; Gāo Jiànyuán
First publication: 2006
• Employment: Ilan University (宜兰大学)
• Research interest: Orchidaceae [S]
• Published taxa: ×*Kingistylis*, ×*Tubecentron*
• Region: CHINA (Taiwan)

J. Y. Gao

Gao, Jiang Yun; 高江云 ; Gāo Jiāngyún
1970- **First publication: 2018**
• Employment: Yunnan University (云南大学)
• Research interest: Orchidaceae [S]
• Published taxa: *Gastrochilus*

• Region: CHINA (Yunnan)

J. T. Gao

Gao, Ju Tang; 高聚堂 ; Gāo Jùtáng
1938- **First publication: 1983**

- Employment: Nanzhao County Forestry Bureau, Henan (河南省南召县林业局)
- Research interest: Magnoliaceae [S]
- Published taxa: *Magnolia*
- Region: CHINA (Henan)

L. X. Gao

Gao, Li Xian; 高立献 ; Gāo Lìxiàn
1968- **First publication: 1990**

- Employment: Henan Laojieling Nature Reserve (河南省西峡老界岭自然保护区)
- Research interest: Orchidaceae [S]
- Published taxa: *Dendrobium*
- Region: CHINA (Henan)

L. M. Gao

Gao, Lian Ming; 高连明 ; Gāo Liánmíng
1972- **First publication: 2001**

- Employment: Kunming Institute of Botany, Chinese Academy of Sciences (中国科学院昆明植物研究所)
- Research interest: Cephalotaxaceae, Ericaceae, Poaceae, Taxaceae [S]
- Published taxa: *Amentotaxus, Pseudosasa, Rhododendron, Taxus*
- Affiliation: KUN
- Region: CHINA (Yunnan)

L. Z. Gao

Gao, Lian Zhong; 高连仲 ; Gāo Liánzhòng
First publication: 1987

- Employment: Institute of Forest Plant, Southwest Forestry College (西南林学院森林植物研究所)
- Research interest: Poaceae [S]
- Published taxa: *Chimonobambusa*
- Region: CHINA (Yunnan)

M. T. Kao

Kao, Muh Tsuen; Gao, Mu Cun; 高木村 ; Gāo Mùcūn
1925-2006 **First publication: 1978**

- Employment: Herbarium of Taiwan University (台湾大学植物标本馆)
- Research interest: Gesneriaceae, Juncaceae; Plants of Taiwan [S]
- Published taxa: *Epithema, Juncus*
- Affiliation: TAI
- Location of specimens: TAI
- Region: CHINA (Taiwan)

M. M. Gao

Gao, Mu Mu; 高木木 ; Gāo Mùmù
1982- **First publication: 2008**

- Employment: College of Life Sciences, Shihezi University (石河子大学生命科学学院)
- Research interest: Fabaceae [S]
- Published taxa: *Oxytropis*
- Region: CHINA (Xinjiang)

Q. Gao

Gao, Qi; 高乞 ; Gāo Qǐ
1981- **First publication: 2009**

- Employment: Institute of Botany, Chinese Academy of Sciences (中国科学院植物研究所)
- Research interest: Asparagaceae, Ranunculaceae [S]
- Published taxa: *Aconitum, Aspidistra*
- Affiliation: IBK
- Location of specimens: IBK
- Region: CHINA

R. Q. Gao

Gao, Run Qing; 高润清 ; Gāo Rùnqīng; 高潤清
1943- **First publication: 1984**

- Employment: Beijing Forestry College (北京林学院)
- Research interest: Fagaceae, Salicaceae [S]
- Published taxa: *Quercus, Salix*
- Region: CHINA

T. G. Gao

Gao, Tian Gang; 高天刚 ; Gāo Tiāngāng
1973- **First publication: 2004**

- Employment: Kunming Institute of Botany, Chinese Academy of Sciences; Institute of Botany, Chinese Academy of Sciences (中国科学院昆明植物研究所；中国科学院植物研究所)
- Research interest: Asteraceae [S]
- Published taxa: *Ainsliaea, Artemisia, Aster, Gerbera, Nannoglottis, Oreoseris, Pertya*
- Affiliation: PE
- Location of specimens: PE
- Region: CHINA

W. H. Gao

Gao, Wei Heng; 高维衡 ; Gāo Wéihéng; 高維衡
1930-2015 **First publication: 1987**

- Employment: Pingliang Normal School, Gansu (甘肃平凉师范学校)
- Research interest: Hydrangeaceae [S]
- Published taxa: *Hydrangea*
- Region: CHINA (Gansu)

X. F. Gao

Gao, Xin Fen; 高信芬 ; Gāo Xìnfēn
1965- **First publication: 1998**

- Employment: Chengdu Institute of Biology, Chinese Academy of Sciences（中国科学院成都生物研究所）
- Research interest: Asteraceae, Dryopteridaceae, Ericaceae, Fabaceae, Papaveraceae, Primulaceae, Pteridaceae, Rosaceae, Woodsiaceae, Zingiberaceae [PS]
- Published taxa: *Alysicarpus, Arachniodes, Corydalis, Desmodium, Eriobotrya, Flemingia, Hylodesmum, Indigofera, Lespedeza, Polystichum, Primula, Pteris, Rhododendron, Roscoea, Rubus, Sorbus, Woodsia, Youngia*
- Affiliation: CDBI
- Location of specimens: CDBI
- Region: CHINA

Y. D. Gao

Gao, Yun Dong; 高云东；Gāo Yúndōng

1985- **First publication: 2012**

- Employment: College of Life Sciences, Sichuan University; Chengdu Institute of Biology, Chinese Academy of Sciences（四川大学生命科学学院；中国科学院成都生物研究所）
- Research interest: Asteraceae, Liliaceae, Rosaceae [S]
- Published taxa: *Lilium, Nomocharis, Youngia*
- Affiliation: CDBI
- Location of specimens: CDBI
- Region: CHINA

W. C. Ko

Ko, Wan Chang; Ko, Wan Cheung; Kao, Yün Chang; Gao, Yun Zhang; 高蕴璋；Gāo Yùnzhāng; 高蘊璋

1917-2005 **First publication: 1958**

- Employment: South China Institute of Botany, Chinese Academy of Sciences（中国科学院华南植物研究所）
- Research interest: Fagaceae, Lythraceae, Melastomataceae, Moraceae, Pentaphylacaceae, Rhizophoraceae, Rubiaceae, Salicaceae, Sonneratiaceae [S]
- Published taxa: *Adinandra, Bruguiera, Carallia, Casearia, Cephaëlis, Hedyotis, Homalium, Ixora, Mussaenda, Neanotis, Phyllagathis, Quercus, Sonneratia, Taxotrophis*
- Affiliation: IBSC
- Location of specimens: IBSC
- Region: CHINA

Z. Y. Gao

Gao, Zeng Yi; 高增义；Gāo Zēngyì; 高增義

1930- **First publication: 1984**

- Employment: Henan Institute of Biology（河南生物研究所）
- Research interest: Lamiaceae, Liliaceae, Magnoliaceae; Plants of Henan [S]
- Published taxa: *Fritillaria, Magnolia, Rabdosia*
- Affiliation: HEBI
- Location of specimens: HEBI
- Region: CHINA (Henan)

Z. H. Gao

Gao, Zhi Hai; 高志海；Gāo Zhìhǎi

1963- **First publication: 1989**

- Employment: Gansu Desert Control Research Institute（甘肃省治沙研究所）
- Research interest: Fabaceae; Woody Plants [S]
- Published taxa: *Caragana*
- Affiliation: MQ
- Location of specimens: MQ
- Region: CHINA (Gansu)

T. C. Kao

Kao, Tso Ching; Gao, Zuo Jing; 高作经；Gāo Zuòjīng; 高作經

1924-1995 **First publication: 1975**

- Employment: Department of Pharmacy, Beijing Medical College; School of Pharmacy, Beijing Medical University（北京医学院药学系；北京医科大学药学院）
- Research interest: Celastraceae, Polygonaceae [S]
- Published taxa: *Celastrus, Microtropis, Rheum*
- Affiliation: PEM
- Location of specimens: PEM
- Region: CHINA

Gesang

Gesang Suolang; Gesan Suolang; Kelsang Sonam; 格桑索朗；Gésāng Suǒlǎng

1949- **First publication: 1985**

- Employment: Xizang Institute for Drug Control（西藏药检所）
- Research interest: Liliaceae; Medicinal Plants [S]
- Published taxa: *Fritillaria*
- Affiliation: XZDC
- Location of specimens: XZDC
- Region: CHINA (Xizang)

J. W. Ge

Ge, Ji Wen; 葛继稳；Gě Jìwěn

1965- **First publication: 2007**

- Employment: School of Environment, China University of Geosciences（中国地质大学环境学院）
- Research interest: Styracaceae; Plants of Hubei [S]
- Published taxa: *Sinojackia*
- Affiliation: EBF
- Location of specimens: EBF
- Region: CHINA (Hubei)

S. Ge

Ge, Song; 葛颂; Gě Sòng

1961- **First publication: 1999**

- Employment: Institute of Botany, Chinese Academy of Sciences (中国科学院植物研究所)
- Research interest: Campanulaceae [S]
- Published taxa: *Adenophora*
- Affiliation: PE
- Region: CHINA

X. J. Ge

Ge, Xue Jun; 葛学军; Gě Xuéjūn

1965- **First publication: 1991**

- Employment: Xinjiang Institute of Biology, Pedology and Desert Research, Chinese Academy of Sciences; South China Institute of Botany, Chinese Academy of Sciences (中国科学院新疆生物土壤沙漠研究所; 中国科学院华南植物研究所)
- Research interest: Asteraceae, Balsaminaceae, Lamiaceae, Musaceae, Papaveraceae, Rhizophoraceae, Scrophulariaceae [S]
- Published taxa: *Bruguiera, Impatiens, Musa, Papaver, Pogostemon, Taraxacum*
- Affiliation: XJBI
- Location of specimens: XJBI
- Region: CHINA

Y. Z. Ge

Ge, Yu Zhen; 葛玉珍; Gě Yùzhēn

1982- **First publication: 2015**

- Employment: Guangxi Institute of Botany, Chinese Academy of Sciences (广西壮族自治区中国科学院广西植物研究所)
- Research interest: Gesneriaceae [S]
- Published taxa: *Primulina*
- Region: CHINA (Guangxi)

Keng f.

Keng, Pai Chieh; Kêng, Pai Chieh; Keng, Kwan Hou; Geng, Bao Jie; Geng, Bo Jie; 耿伯介; Gěng Bójiè; 耿宽厚

1917-1997 **First publication: 1945**

- Employment: Department of Biology, National Central University; Department of Biology, Nanjing University (国立中央大学生物系; 南京大学生物系)
- Research interest: Fabaceae, Plantaginaceae, Poaceae [S]
- Published taxa: *Achnatherum, Acidosasa, Agrostis, Arundinaria, Bambusa, Bashania, Brachypodium, Bromus, Burmabambus, Butania, Calamagrostis, Cercis, Chimonobambusa, Clavinodum, Cleistogenes, Coelorachis, Dendrocalamopsis, Drepanostachyum, Duthiea, Eccoilopus, Elymus, Eragrostiella, Eulalia, Fargesia, Festuca, Gelidocalamus, Gigantochloa, Glyceria, Helictotrichon, Himalayacalamus, Indocalamus, Isachne, Kokonoria, Lingnania, Neobambus, Neomicrocalamus, Neosinocalamus, Orinus, Oxytenanthera, Panicum, Phyllostachys, Pleioblastus, Poa, Pseudopogonatherum, Pseudosasa, Ptilagrostis, Racemobambos, Sasa, Sclerodactylon, Setaria, Sinarundinaria, Sinocalamus, Sporobolus, Thamnocalamus, Tripogon, Yushania*
- Affiliation: N
- Location of specimens: N
- Region: CHINA

L. B. Geng

Geng, Lian Bo; 耿涟波; Gěng Liánbō; 耿漣波

1924-1998 **First publication: 1987**

- Employment: Jian' ou Wanmulin Nature Reserve Administrative Bureau, Fujian (福建建瓯万木林自然保护区管理局)
- Research interest: Mazaceae [S]
- Published taxa: *Mazus*
- Region: CHINA (Fujian)

S. L. Keng

Keng, Shi Lei; Geng, Shi Lei; 耿世磊; Gěng Shìlěi

1965- **First publication: 1995**

- Employment: Environmental and Resource Branch, Xinjiang Bayi Agricultural College (新疆八一农学院环境资源分院)
- Research interest: Asteraceae, Brassicaceae [S]
- Published taxa: *Ligularia*
- Affiliation: SCAUB, XJA
- Location of specimens: XJA
- Region: CHINA (Xinjiang)

H. Keng

Keng, Hsüan; Keng Hsiuan; Keng, Hsuan; Geng, Xuan; 耿煊; Gěng Xuān

1923-2009 **First publication: 1951**

- Employment: Department of Botany, Taiwan University; Department of Botany, National University of Singapore (台湾大学植物学系; 新加坡国立大学植物系)
- Research interest: Daphniphyllaceae, Ericaceae, Euphorbiaceae, Lamiaceae, Magnoliaceae, Melastomataceae, Pentaphylacaceae, Phyllanthaceae, Pinaceae, Podocarpaceae, Putranjivaceae, Theaceae [S]
- Published taxa: *Acalypha, Agyneia, Cheilotheca, Cleyera, Daphniphyllum, Elsholtzia, Euphorbia, Eurya, Godonia, Gomphostemma, Gordonia, Liodendron, Magnolia, Medinilla, Micheliopsis, Nosema, Phyllocladus, Plectranthus, Pogostemon, Pyrenaria, Ternstroemia, Tsuga*
- Region: CHINA (Taiwan)

Keng

Keng, Yi Li; Keng, I Li; Geng, Yi Li; 耿以礼；Gěng Yǐlǐ; 耿以禮

1897-1975 **First publication: 1931**

- Employment: Department of Biology, National Central University; Department of Biology, Nanjing University（国立中央大学生物系；南京大学生物系）
- Research interest: Poaceae [S]
- Published taxa: *Achnatherum, Agropyron, Anthoxanthum, Arundinaria, Arundinella, Bambusa, Bothriochloa, Brachypodium, Bromus, Chloris, Cleistogenes, Clinelymus, Deyeuxia, Duthiea, Elymus, Enteropogon, Eulalia, Glyceria, Harpachne, Helictotrichon, Miscanthus, Orinus, Orthoraphium, Oryzopsis, Poa, Puccinellia, Roegneria*
- Affiliation: N
- Location of specimens: N, NAS
- Region: CHINA

Y. Y. Geng

Geng, Yu Ying; 耿玉英；Gěng Yùyīng

1956- **First publication: 2003**

- Employment: West China Subalpine Botanical Garden, Institute of Botany, Chinese Academy of Sciences（中国科学院植物研究所华西亚高山植物园）
- Research interest: Ericaceae, Primulaceae [S]
- Published taxa: *Primula, Rhododendron*
- Affiliation: WCSBG
- Region: CHINA (Sichuan)

L. J. Gong

Gong, Li Jun; 宫莉君；Gōng Lìjūn

1935- **First publication: 1997**

- Employment: Liaoning College of Traditional Chinese Medicine（辽宁中医学院）
- Research interest: Poaceae [S]
- Published taxa: *Zoysia*
- Region: CHINA (Liaoning)

G. T. Gong

Gong, Gu Tang; 龚固堂；Gōng Gùtáng

1965- **First publication: 1994**

- Employment: Sichuan Academy of Forestry（四川省林业科学研究院）
- Research interest: Lauraceae, Moraceae, Myrtaceae, Salicaceae [S]
- Published taxa: *Balsamiflua, Litsea, Pleiarina, Salix*
- Affiliation: SCFI
- Location of specimens: SCFI
- Region: CHINA (Sichuan)

K. N. Kung

Kung, Kuan Ning; 龔冠寧；Gōng Guānníng; 龚冠宁

First publication: 2020

- Employment: Department of Forestry and Natural Resources, Chiayi University; Lioukuei Research Center, Taiwan Forestry Research Institute, Council of Agriculture, "Executive Yuan"（嘉义大学森林暨自然资源学系暨研究所；"行政院"农业委员会林业试验所六龟研究中心）
- Research interest: Piperaceae [S]
- Published taxa: *Piper*
- Region: CHINA (Taiwan)

Q. B. Gong

Gong, Qiang Bang; 龚强帮；Gōng Qiángbāng

1987- **First publication: 2018**

- Employment: Yunnan Tongbiguan Provincial Nature Reserve Administrative Bureau（云南铜壁关省级自然保护区管护局）
- Research interest: Aristolochiaceae [S]
- Published taxa: *Aristolochia*
- Region: CHINA (Yunnan)

T. Gong

Gong, Tong; 龚彤；Gōng Tóng

First publication: 1976

- Employment: Henan Institute of Forestry Science（河南省林业科学研究所）
- Research interest: Paulowniaceae [S]
- Published taxa: *Paulownia*
- Region: CHINA

X. Gong

Gong, Xun; 龚洵；Gōng Xún

1965- **First publication: 2008**

- Employment: Kunming Institute of Botany, Chinese Academy of Sciences（中国科学院昆明植物研究所）
- Research interest: Asteraceae [S]
- Published taxa: *Ligularia*
- Region: CHINA (Yunnan)

G. Q. Gou

Gou, Guang Qian; 苟光前；Gǒu Guāngqián

1960- **First publication: 2015**

- Employment: College of Life Sciences, Guizhou University（贵州大学生命科学学院）
- Research interest: Amaryllidaceae, Caprifoliaceae, Gesneriaceae, Poaceae, Rubiaceae, Selaginellaceae; Pteridophytes [PS]
- Published taxa: *Abelia, Allium, Ophiorrhiza, Petrocosmea, Selaginella*
- Affiliation: GACP, GZAC
- Location of specimens: GACP, GZAC
- Region: CHINA (Guizhou)

W. Gou

Gou, Wei; 苟巍；Gǒu Wēi

First publication: 2020

- Employment: College of Life Sciences, Sichuan University (四川大学生命科学学院)
- Research interest: Apioideae [S]
- Published taxa: *Meeboldia*
- Region: CHINA (Xizang)

S. M. Ku

Ku, Shin Ming; 古訓銘; Gǔ Xùnmíng; 古训铭

First publication: 2004

- Employment: Biodiversity Research Center, "Academia Sinica"; Department of Life Sciences, "National" Cheng Kung University (中研院生物多样性研究中心;"国立"成功大学生命科学系)
- Research interest: Begoniaceae, Gentianaceae [S]
- Published taxa: *Begonia, Gentiana*
- Region: CHINA

A. G. Gu

Gu, An Gen; 谷安根; Gǔ Āngēn

1924-2016 First publication: 1988

- Employment: Jilin Agricultural University (吉林农业大学)
- Research interest: Caprifoliaceae, Pinaceae [S]
- Published taxa: *Metalonicera, Pinus*
- Location of specimens: NEFI
- Region: CHINA (Jilin)

T. C. Ku

Ku, Tsue Chih; Gu, Cui Zhi; 谷粹芝; Gǔ Cuìzhī

1931- First publication: 1975

- Employment: Institute of Botany, Chinese Academy of Sciences (中国科学院植物研究所)
- Research interest: Begoniaceae, Celastraceae, Grossulariaceae, Hydrangeaceae, Linderniaceae, Rosaceae, Saxifragaceae [S]
- Published taxa: *Begonia, Cerasus, Chrysosplenium, Coluria, Crataegus, Lindernia, Maddenia, Malus, Neillia, Padus, Parnassia, Philadelphus, Photinia, Ribes, Rosa, Saniculiphyllum, Saxifraga, Sorbus, Stranvaesia*
- Affiliation: PE
- Region: CHINA

S. F. Gu

Gu, Shu Fen; 谷淑芬; Gǔ Shūfēn

1959- First publication: 1993

- Employment: Forest Botanical Garden of Heilongjiang Province (黑龙江省森林植物园)
- Research interest: Araliaceae [S]
- Published taxa: *Acanthopanax*
- Region: CHINA (Heilongjiang)

B. J. Gu

Gu, Bo Jian; 顾伯健; Gù Bójiàn

1990- First publication: 2017

- Employment: Xishuangbanna Tropical Botanical Garden, Chinese Academy of Sciences (中国科学院西双版纳热带植物园)
- Research interest: Euphorbiaceae [S]
- Published taxa: *Tsaiodendron*
- Region: CHINA (Yunnan)

C. H. Gu

Gu, Cui Hua; 顾翠花; Gù Cuìhuā

1981- First publication: 2012

- Employment: School of Landscape Architecture, Zhejiang A&F University (浙江农林大学园林学院)
- Research interest: Lythraceae [S]
- Published taxa: *Lagerstroemia*
- Region: CHINA (Guangxi, Yunnan)

D. X. Gu

Gu, De Xing; 顾德兴; Gù Déxīng; 顧德興

1941- First publication: 1983

- Employment: Nanjing Agricultural College (南京农学院)
- Research interest: Fabaceae; Plants of E. China [S]
- Published taxa: *Lespedeza*
- Affiliation: NAU
- Location of specimens: NAU
- Region: CHINA

H. Y. Gu

Gu, Hong Ya; 顾红雅; Gù Hóngyǎ

1960- First publication: 1991

- Employment: School of Life Sciences, Peking University (北京大学生命科学学院)
- Research interest: Asteraceae, Onagraceae [S]
- Published taxa: *Kalimeris, Ludwigia*
- Region: CHINA

Y. Gu

Gu, Yin; 顾姻; Gù Yīn; 顧姻

1932- First publication: 2000

- Employment: Institute of Botany, Jiangsu Province and Chinese Academy of Sciences (江苏省中国科学院植物研究所)
- Research interest: Rosaceae [S]
- Published taxa: *Rubus*
- Region: CHINA

Z. M. Gu

Gu, Zhe Ming; 顾哲明; Gù Zhémíng

1953- First publication: 1991

- Employment: Chengdu College of Traditional Chinese Medicine (成都中医学院)

- Research interest: Celastraceae [S]
- Published taxa: *Euonymus*
- Location of specimens: PEM
- Region: CHINA (Sichuan)

K. C. Kuan

Kuan, Ke Chien; Kuan, K'o Chien; Guan, Ke Jian; 关克俭 ; Guān Kèjiǎn; 關克儉

1913-1982 First publication: 1963

- Employment: Institute of Botany, Chinese Academy of Sciences（中国科学院植物研究所）
- Research interest: Amaranthaceae, Brassicaceae, Ceratophyllaceae, Rosaceae; Plants of N. China [S]
- Published taxa: *Arabidopsis, Ceratophyllum, Cheiranthus, Christolea, Cladostachys, Cochlearia, Cotoneaster, Cyathula, Eriobotrya, Erysimum, Eutrema, Goldbachia, Isatis, Photinia, Sterigmostemum, Torularia*
- Affiliation: PE
- Location of specimens: PE, HSIB
- Region: CHINA

Q. X. Guan

Guan, Qiu Xiang; 官秋香 ; Guān Qiūxiāng

1990- First publication: 2014

- Employment: College of Landscape Architecture, Fujian Agriculture and Forestry University（福建农林大学园林学院）
- Research interest: Orchidaceae [S]
- Published taxa: *Goodyera*
- Region: CHINA (Yunnan)

S. F. Guan

Guan, Shao Fei; 官少飞 ; Guān Shàofēi

1958- First publication: 1987

- Employment: Institute of Biological Resources, Jiangxi Academy of Sciences（江西省科学院生物资源研究所）
- Research interest: Hydrocharitaceae, Lythraceae [S]
- Published taxa: *Najas, Trapa*
- Region: CHINA (Jiangxi)

K. Y. Guan

Guan, Kai Yun; 管开云 ; Guǎn Kāiyún

1953- First publication: 1993

- Employment: Kunming Institute of Botany, Chinese Academy of Sciences（中国科学院昆明植物研究所）
- Research interest: Begoniaceae, Bignoniaceae, Dioscoreaceae, Iridaceae, Ranunculaceae, Scrophulariaceae, Smilacaceae, Theaceae [S]
- Published taxa: *Begonia, Dioscorea, Heterosmilax, Incarvillea, Iris, Junopsis, Smilax*
- Affiliation: TURP
- Region: CHINA (Yunnan)

C. T. Kuan

Kuan, Chung Tian; Guan, Zhong Tian; 管中天 ; Guǎn Zhōngtiān

1925- First publication: 1983

- Employment: Sichuan Forestry Exploration and Design Institute（四川省林业勘察设计研究院）
- Research interest: Cupressaceae, Cycadaceae, Pinaceae, Taxaceae [S]
- Published taxa: *Abies, Cupressus, Cycas, Picea, Pinus, Pseudotsuga, Taxus*
- Location of specimens: PE, SCFI
- Region: CHINA
- Also as: Z. T. Guan

K. I. B

Kwangsi Institute of Botany; Guangxi Institute of Botany, Chinese Academy of Sciences; K. I. B. 广西植物研究所 ; Guǎngxī Zhíwù Yánjiūsuǒ

First publication: 1977

- Employment: Guangxi Institute of Botany, Chinese Academy of Sciences（广西壮族自治区中国科学院广西植物研究所）
- Research interest: Schisandraceae [S]
- Published taxa: *Illicium*
- Region: CHINA (Guangxi)
- Organization

K. I. M

Kwangsi Institute of Medicine; Guangxi Institute of Chinese Medicine & Pharmaceutical Science; K. I. M. 广西中医药研究所 ; Guǎngxī Zhōngyīyào Yánjiūsuǒ

First publication: 1977

- Employment: Guangxi Institute of Traditional Medical and Pharmaceutical Sciences（广西中医药研究所）
- Research interest: Schisandraceae [S]
- Published taxa: *Illicium*
- Region: CHINA (Guangxi)
- Organization

L. J. Gui

Gui, Ling Jian; 桂凌健 ; Guì Língjiàn

1988- First publication: 2020

- Employment: College of Life Sciences, Sichuan University（四川大学生命科学学院）
- Research interest: Apioideae [S]
- Published taxa: *Tongoloa*
- Region: CHINA (Sichuan)

B. L. Guo

Guo, Bao Lin; 郭宝林 ; Guō Bǎolín

1966- First publication: 1993

- Employment: Institute of Medicinal Plant Development, Chinese Academy of Medical Sciences

（中国医学科学院药用植物资源开发研究所）
• Research interest: Berberidaceae [S]
• Published taxa: *Epimedium*
• Affiliation: IMD
• Region: CHINA

P. C. Kuo

Kuo, Pung Chao; Kuo, Pen Chao; Guo, Ben Zhao; 郭本兆; Guō Běnzhào
1920-1993 **First publication: 1980**
• Employment: Northwest China Institute of Botany, Chinese Academy of Sciences and Shaanxi Province; Northwest Plateau Institute of Biology, Chinese Academy of Sciences（陕西省中国科学院西北植物研究所；中国科学院西北高原生物研究所）
• Research interest: Betulaceae, Eupteleaceae, Lardizabalaceae, Liliaceae, Poaceae [S]
• Published taxa: *Achnatherum, Betula, Calamagrostis, Carpinus, Deschampsia, Deyeuxia, Euptelea, Holboellia, Hordeum, Koeleria, Lloydia, Oryzopsis, Stephanachne, Stipa, Trikeraia, Trisetum, Triticum*
• Affiliation: HNWP
• Location of specimens: HNWP, PE, WUK
• Region: CHINA

Kuoh

Kuoh, Chang Sheng; Guo, Chang Sheng; 郭長生; Guō Chángshēng; 郭长生
1946- **First publication: 1999**
• Employment: Department of Life Sciences, Cheng Kung University（成功大学生命科学系）
• Research interest: Cyperaceae, Poaceae [S]
• Published taxa: *Leptatherum, Microstegium*
• Affiliation: NCKU
• Location of specimens: NCKU
• Region: CHINA (Taiwan)

C. Z. Guo

Guo, Cheng Ze; 郭承则; Guō Chéngzé; 郭承則
1929- **First publication: 1988**
• Employment: Nanyue Arboretum, Hunan（湖南省南岳树木园）
• Research interest: Ericaceae [S]
• Published taxa: *Rhododendron*
• Location of specimens: NYA
• Region: CHINA (Hunan)

C. M. Kuo

Kuo, Chen Meng; Kuo, Cheng Meng; Guo, Cheng Meng; 郭城孟; Guō Chéngmèng
1948- **First publication: 1975**
• Employment: Department of Botany, Taiwan University（台湾大学植物学系）
• Research interest: Aspleniaceae, Athyriaceae, Blechnaceae, Cibotiaceae, Dennstaedtiaceae, Dryopteridaceae, Gleicheniaceae, Lycopodiaceae, Orchidaceae, Polypodiaceae, Pteridaceae, Tectariaceae, Thelypteridaceae; Pteridophytes. [BP]
• Published taxa: *Allantodia, Asplenium, Blechnum, Bolbitis, Cheilanthes, Cibotium, Cyclosorus, Dicranopteris, Gastrodia, Huperzia, Lepisorus, Lycopodium, Microlepia, Microsorum, Nervilia, Polystichum, Pronephrium, Pteris, Pyrrosia, Tectaria, Thelypteris*
• Affiliation: TAI
• Region: CHINA (Taiwan)

C. L. Guo

Guo, Chun Lan; 郭春兰; Guō Chūnlán; 郭春蘭
1941- **First publication: 1992**
• Employment: Institute of Hubei Traditional Chinese Medicine Company（湖北省中药材公司科学研究所）
• Research interest: Magnoliaceae [S]
• Published taxa: *Magnolia*
• Region: CHINA (Hubei)

F. T. Kuo

Kuo, Fang Tuan; 郭方端; Guō Fāngduān
First publication: 1968
• Employment: Department of Biology, Taiwan Normal University（台湾师范大学生物系）
• Research interest: Lentibulariaceae [S]
• Published taxa: *Utricularia*
• Region: CHINA (Taiwan)

Han S. Guo

Guo, Han Shen; 郭汉身; Guō Hànshēn; 郭漢身
1938- **First publication: 1993**
• Employment: Zhejiang Medical University（浙江医科大学）
• Research interest: Orchidaceae; Pteridophytes [S]
• Published taxa: *Platanthera*
• Affiliation: ZMU
• Location of specimens: ZMU
• Region: CHINA (Zhejiang)

H. J. Guo

Guo, Hui Jun; 郭辉军; Guō Huījūn
1963- **First publication: 2006**
• Employment: Xishuangbanna Tropical Botanical Garden, Chinese Academy of Sciences（中国科学院西双版纳热带植物园）
• Research interest: Asparagaceae [S]
• Published taxa: *Dracaena*
• Region: CHINA (Yunnan)

H. Z. Guo

Guo, Hui Zhu; 郭惠珠 ; Guō Huìzhū

1982- **First publication: 2011**

- Employment: Xiamen Botanical Garden (厦门市园林植物园)
- Research interest: Poaceae [S]
- Published taxa: *Pseudosasa, Schizostachyum*
- Affiliation: XMBG
- Location of specimens: XMBG
- Region: CHINA (Fujian)

C. F. Kuo

Kuo, Chi Fan; Guo, Ji Fan; 郭紀凡 ; Guō Jìfán; 郭纪凡

First publication: 2016

- Employment: Department of Biological Sciences, Sun Yat-sen University Taiwan (台湾中山大学生物科学系)
- Research interest: Polygonaceae [S]
- Published taxa: *Persicaria*
- Region: CHINA (Taiwan)

J. X. Guo

Guo, Ji Xian; 郭济贤 ; Guō Jìxián

1936- **First publication: 1993**

- Employment: School of Pharmacy, Shanghai Medical University (上海医科大学药学院)
- Research interest: Apiaceae [S]
- Published taxa: *Bupleurum*
- Region: CHINA (Qinghai)

J. H. Guo

Guo, Jian Hua; 郭建华 ; Guō Jiànhuá; 郭建華

1939-2007 **First publication: 1988**

- Employment: Xilingol League Institute of Forestry Sciences, Inner Mongolia (内蒙古锡林郭勒盟林业科学研究所)
- Research interest: Ulmaceae [S]
- Published taxa: *Ulmus*
- Region: CHINA (Nei Mongol)

J. L. Guo

Guo, Jian Lin; 郭建林 ; Guō Jiànlín

First publication: 1990

- Employment: Baishuijiang Natural Reserve Administrative Bureau, Gansu (甘肃白水江自然保护区管理局)
- Research interest: Salicaceae [S]
- Published taxa: *Populus*
- Region: CHINA (Gansu)

J. Guo

Guo, Jing; 郭婧 ; Guō Jìng

1990- **First publication: 2016**

- Employment: Guangxi Institute of Botany, Chinese Academy of Sciences (广西壮族自治区中国科学院广西植物研究所)
- Research interest: Gesneriaceae [S]
- Published taxa: *Petrocodon*
- Region: CHINA (Guangxi)

K. Guo

Guo, Ke; 郭柯 ; Guō Kē

1961- **First publication: 2011**

- Employment: Institute of Botany, Chinese Academy of Sciences (中国科学院植物研究所)
- Research interest: Poaceae [S]
- Published taxa: *Stipa*
- Region: CHINA (Nei Mongol)

L. B. Guo

Guo, Lan Bin; 郭兰斌 ; Guō Lánbīn

1959- **First publication: 1989**

- Employment: Inner Mongolia Forestry College (内蒙古林学院)
- Research interest: Lamiaceae, Saxifragaceae [S]
- Published taxa: *Vitex*
- Affiliation: NMAC, NMFC
- Location of specimens: NMAC, NMFC
- Region: CHINA (Shanxi)

L. Y. Kuo

Kuo, Li Yaung; 郭立園 ; Guō Lìyuán; 郭立园

1986- **First publication: 2016**

- Employment: Taiwan University; Tsing Hua University, Taiwan (台湾大学 ; 台湾清华大学)
- Research interest: Aspleniaceae, Athyriaceae, Dryopteridaceae [P]
- Published taxa: *Asplenium, Deparia, Diplazium, Dryopteris*
- Region: CHINA (Taiwan)

L. X. Guo

Guo, Li Xiu; 郭丽秀 ; Guō Lìxiù

1964- **First publication: 2007**

- Employment: South China Botanical Garden, Chinese Academy of Sciences (中国科学院华南植物园)
- Research interest: Arecaceae [S]
- Published taxa: *Calamus, Licuala*
- Affiliation: IBSC
- Region: CHINA

L. F. Guo

Guo, Lun Fa; 郭伦发 ; Guō Lúnfā

1973- **First publication: 2013**

- Employment: Guangxi Institute of Botany, Chinese Academy of Sciences (广西壮族自治区中国科学院广西植物研究所)
- Research interest: Asparagaceae [S]
- Published taxa: *Aspidistra*

• Region: CHINA (Guangxi)

M. Guo

Guo, Ming; 郭明 ; Guō Míng

1970- **First publication: 2017**

- Employment: Taibai Mountain Natural Reserve Administrative Bureau, Shaanxi (陕西太白山国家级自然保护区管理局)
- Research interest: Orchidaceae [S]
- Published taxa: *Calanthe*
- Region: CHINA (Shaanxi)

P. Guo

Guo, Ping; 郭平 ; Guō Píng

First publication: 1990

- Employment: Department of Chinese Medicine, Chengdu College of Traditional Chinese Medicine (成都中医学院中药系)
- Research interest: Ranunculaceae [S]
- Published taxa: *Aconitum*
- Location of specimens: PE
- Region: CHINA (Sichuan)

Q. F. Guo

Guo, Qing Fing; Guo, Qin Feng; **郭勤峰 ; Guō Qínfēng**

1962- **First publication: 1987**

- Employment: Kunming Institute of Botany, Chinese Academy of Sciences (中国科学院昆明植物研究所)
- Research interest: Araceae [S]
- Published taxa: *Remusatia*
- Region: CHINA (Yunnan)

Chiu C. Kuo

Kuo, Chiu Chen; Guo, Qiu Cheng; **郭秋成 ; Guō Qiūchéng**

1933- **First publication: 1974**

- Employment: Taiwan University (台湾大学)
- Research interest: Gentianaceae [S]
- Published taxa: *Gentiana, Tripterospermum*
- Location of specimens: NTUF
- Region: CHINA (Taiwan)

R. F. Guo

Guo, Rong Fa; 郭荣发 ; Guō Róngfā

First publication: 2002

- Employment: Shenzhen City Landscape Group Co., Ltd. (深圳市园林(集团)有限公司)
- Research interest: Orchidaceae [S]
- Published taxa: *Paphiopedilum*
- Region: VETNAM

R. L. Guo

Guo, Rong Lin; 郭荣麟 ; Guō Rónglín; 郭榮麟

1935- **First publication: 1980**

- Employment: Institute of Botany, Jiangsu Province (江苏省植物研究所)
- Research interest: Brassicaceae, Lamiaceae [S]
- Published taxa: *Caryopteris, Dimorphostemon, Pegaeophyton*
- Affiliation: NAS
- Region: CHINA

T. C. Guo

Guo, Tian Chi; 郭天池 ; Guō Tiānchí

1939- **First publication: 1997**

- Employment: Citrus Research Institute, Chinese Academy of Agricultural Sciences (中国农业科学院柑橘研究所)
- Research interest: Rutaceae [S]
- Published taxa: *Citrus*
- Affiliation: CIT
- Location of specimens: CIT
- Region: CHINA (Guangxi)

W. Guo

Guo, Wei; 郭微 ; Guō Wēi

1982- **First publication: 2010**

- Employment: School of Life Sciences, Sun Yat-sen University (中山大学生命科学学院)
- Research interest: Rosaceae [S]
- Published taxa: *Photinia, Sorbus*
- Region: CHINA (Guangdong, Guangxi)

Wei Guo

Guo, Wei; 郭伟 ; Guō Wěi

First publication: 2015

- Employment: Amateur (业余爱好者)
- Research interest: Orchidaceae [S]
- Published taxa: *Habenaria*
- Region: CHINA (Guangxi)
- IPNI as: W. Guo

W. Y. Guo

Guo, Wen Yuan; 郭文源 ; Guō Wényuán

1938-1994 **First publication: 1993**

- Employment: Department of Biology, Hubei University; Department of Biology, Wuhan Teachers' College (湖北大学生物系 ; 武汉师范学院生物学系)
- Research interest: Araliaceae, Onagraceae; Plants of Hubei [S]
- Published taxa: *Aralia, Epilobium*
- Affiliation: EU
- Location of specimens: EU
- Region: CHINA (Hubei)

X. L. Guo

Guo, Xian Lin; 郭先林 ; Guō Xiānlín

1991- First publication: 2017
- Employment: College of Life Sciences, Sichuan University（四川大学生命科学学院）
- Research interest: Apiaceae [S]
- Published taxa: *Chamaesium*
- Region: CHINA (Sichuan)

X. S. Guo

Guo, Xiao Si; 郭晓思；Guō Xiǎosī

1962- First publication: 1995
- Employment: Northwest China Institute of Botany, Chinese Academy of Sciences and Shaanxi Province; College of Life Sciences, Northwest A&F University（陕西省中国科学院西北植物研究所；西北农林科技大学生命科学学院）
- Research interest: Athyriaceae, Dennstaedtiaceae, Dryopteridaceae, Pteridaceae, Selaginellaceae, Woodsiaceae; Pteridophytes [P]
- Published taxa: *Aleuritopteris, Cheilanthopsis, Coniogramme, Deparia, Dryopteris, Lycopodioides, Microlepia, Woodsia*
- Affiliation: WUK
- Location of specimens: WUK
- Region: CHINA (Shaanxi)

X. H. Guo

Guo, Xin Hu; 郭新弧；Guō Xīnhú

1933- First publication: 1988
- Employment: Department of Biology, Anhui Normal University（安徽师范大学生物系）
- Research interest: Araceae, Caryophyllaceae, Crassulaceae, Gesneriaceae, Lamiaceae, Linderniaceae, Lythraceae, Mazaceae, Melastomataceae, Orobanchaceae, Polypodiaceae, Primulaceae, Ranunculaceae, Santalaceae, Saxifragaceae, Scrophulariaceae, Solanaceae [BS]
- Published taxa: *Boea, Buckleya, Caltha, Chiritopsis, Chrysosplenium, Keiskea, Lagerstroemia, Lindernia, Lysimachia, Mazus, Melampyrum, Mentha, Orostachys, Paraphlomis, Physaliastrum, Pinellia, Pogonanthera, Pseudocerastium, Pyrrosia, Scutellaria, Sedum, Silene*
- Affiliation: ANUB
- Location of specimens: ANUB
- Region: CHINA (Anhui)

X. Guo

Guo, Xing; 郭兴；Guō Xīng

1985- First publication: 2011
- Employment: South China Botanical Garden, Chinese Academy of Sciences; School of Biological Sciences, The University of Hong Kong（中国科学院华南植物园；香港大学生物科学学院）
- Research interest: Annonaceae, Rubiaceae [S]
- Published taxa: *Afroguatteria, Hedyotis, Sphaerocoryne, Wangia*
- Region: CHINA

Y. P. Guo

Guo, Yan Ping; 郭延平；Guō Yánpíng

1964- First publication: 2005
- Employment: Universität Wien, Österreich; College of Life Sciences, Beijing Normal University（奥地利维也纳大学；北京师范大学生命科学学院）
- Research interest: Asteraceae; Plant Systematics [S]
- Published taxa: *Achillea*
- Affiliation: BNU
- Location of specimens: KAI
- Region: [WORLD]

Y. L. Kuo

Kuo, Yau Lung; Kuo, Yau Lun; 郭耀綸；Guō Yàolún; 郭耀纶

First publication: 1976
- Employment: Department of Forestry, Taiwan University; Department of Forestry, Pingtung University of Science and Technology（台湾大学森林学系；屏东科技大学森林系）
- Research interest: Lauraceae [S]
- Published taxa: *Cinnamomum*
- Region: CHINA (Taiwan)

Y. Guo

Guo, Ying; 郭应；Guō Yìng

First publication: 2019
- Employment: Liupanshui Niangniangshan National Wetland Park, Guizhou（贵州六盘水娘娘山国家湿地公园）
- Research interest: Gesneriaceae [S]
- Published taxa: *Oreocharis*
- Region: CHINA (Guizhou)

Y. B. Guo

Guo, Yong Bing; 郭永兵；Guō Yǒngbīng

1972- First publication: 2010
- Employment: South China Botanical Garden, Chinese Academy of Sciences（中国科学院华南植物园）
- Research interest: Poaceae [S]
- Published taxa: *Dendrocalamus*
- Region: CHINA (Yunnan)

Y. J. Guo

Guo, Yong Jie; 郭永杰；Guō Yǒngjié

1983- First publication: 2019
- Employment: Kunming Institute of Botany, Chinese Academy of Sciences（中国科学院昆明植物研究所）
- Research interest: Orchidaceae [S]
- Published taxa: *Bulbophyllum*

- Region: CHINA (Xizang)

Y. H. Guo

Guo, You Hao; 郭友好 ; Guō Yǒuhǎo

1952- **First publication: 1983**

- Employment: Department of Biology, Wuhan University（武汉大学生物系）
- Research interest: Asteraceae, Potamogetonaceae [S]
- Published taxa: *Cacalia, Parasenecio, Potamogeton, Senecio*
- Affiliation: WH
- Location of specimens: WUK
- Region: CHINA (Gansu, Shaanxi)

Y. W. Kuo

Kuo, Yu Wen; 郭育奻 ; Guō Yùwèn

First publication: 2008

- Employment: Department of Forestry and Natural Resources, Chiayi University（嘉义大学森林暨自然资源学系暨研究所）
- Research interest: Zingiberaceae [S]
- Published taxa: *Alpinia*
- Region: CHINA (Taiwan)

Yuan H. Guo

Guo, Yuan Hua; 郭院华 ; Guō Yuànhuá

1965- **First publication: 1995**

- Employment: Suchuan County Forestry Bureau, Jiangxi（江西遂川县林业局）
- Research interest: Poaceae [S]
- Published taxa: *Indocalamus*
- Region: CHINA (Jiangxi)
- IPNI as: Y. H. Guo

Z. H. Guo

Guo, Zhen Hua; 郭振华 ; Guō Zhènhuá

1975- **First publication: 2001**

- Employment: Kunming Institute of Botany, Chinese Academy of Sciences（中国科学院昆明植物研究所）
- Research interest: Poaceae [S]
- Published taxa: *Melocalamus, Yushania*
- Region: CHINA (Yunnan)

Z. Y. Guo

Guo, Zhi You; 郭治友 ; Guō Zhìyǒu

1973- **First publication: 2018**

- Employment: College of Biological Science and Agriculture, Qiannan Normal University for Nationalities; College of Life Sciences, Guizhou University（黔南民族师范学院生物科学与农学院；贵州大学生命科学学院）
- Research interest: Gesneriaceae; Pteridophytes [S]
- Published taxa: *Hemiboea, Oreocharis*
- Affiliation: QNUN
- Location of specimens: QNUN
- Region: CHINA (Guizhou)

H(W)

B. X. Han

Han, Bang Xing; 韩邦兴 ; Hán Bāngxīng

1978- **First publication: 2014**

- Employment: College of Biological and Pharmaceutical Engineering, West Anhui University（皖西学院生物与制药工程学院）
- Research interest: Liliaceae [S]
- Published taxa: *Amana*
- Region: CHINA (Anhui, Jiangsu)

M. Q. Han

Han, Meng Qi; 韩孟奇 ; Hán Mèngqí

1991- **First publication: 2013**

- Employment: Guangxi Institute of Botany, Chinese Academy of Sciences; Guangxi Normal University（广西壮族自治区中国科学院广西植物研究所；广西师范大学）
- Research interest: Dryopteridaceae, Gesneriaceae, Lauraceae [PS]
- Published taxa: *Litsea, Oreocharis, Paraboea, Petrocosmea, Polystichum*
- Region: CHINA

Q. Z. Han

Han, Quan Zhong; 韩全忠 ; Hán Quánzhōng; 韓全忠

1936-? **First publication: 1980**

- Employment: Dalian Natural History Museum（大连自然博物馆）
- Research interest: Asteraceae, Caryophyllaceae, Fabaceae, Plumbaginaceae; Plants of N. E. China [S]
- Published taxa: *Cerastium, Indigofera, Limonium, Saussurea*
- Affiliation: DNHM
- Location of specimens: DNHM
- Region: CHINA (Liaoning)

R. L. Han

Han, Rong Lan; 韩荣兰 ; Hán Rónglán

1970- **First publication: 2006**

- Employment: South China Botanical Garden, Chinese Academy of Sciences（中国科学院华南植物园）
- Research interest: Santalaceae [S]
- Published taxa: *Viscum*
- Region: CHINA (Hainan, Yunnan)

R. G. Han

Han, Ru Gang; 韩如刚；Hán Rúgāng

1978- **First publication: 2018**

- Employment: Chongqing Institute of Medical Plant Cultivation（重庆市药物种植研究所）
- Research interest: Cyperaceae [S]
- Published taxa: *Carex*
- Region: CHINA (Chongqing)

W. D. Han

Han, Wei Dong; 韩维栋；Hán Wéidòng

1963- **First publication: 1989**

- Employment: Institute of Botany, Jiangsu Province; College of Agriculture, Guangdong Ocean University（江苏省植物研究所；广东海洋大学农学院）
- Research interest: Hydrangeaceae, Lauraceae, Pentaphylacaceae, Pittosporaceae, Rosaceae [S]
- Published taxa: *Eurya, Hydrangea, Lauro-cerasus, Lindera, Pittosporum*
- Region: CHINA

Y. L. Han

Han, Ying Lan; 韩英兰；Hán Yīnglán

1936- **First publication: 1982**

- Employment: Tianjin Agricultural University（天津农学院）
- Research interest: Grossulariaceae, Polygonaceae, Rosaceae [S]
- Published taxa: *Atraphaxis, Padus, Pentaphylloides, Ribes, Rosa, Sorbus*
- Location of specimens: PE
- Region: CHINA (Xinjiang)

Y. Y. Hang

Hang, Yue Yu; 杭悦宇；Háng Yuèyǔ

1961- **First publication: 2008**

- Employment: Institute of Botany, Jiangsu Province and Chinese Academy of Sciences（江苏省中国科学院植物研究所）
- Research interest: Dioscoreaceae [S]
- Published taxa: *Dioscorea*
- Region: CHINA (Yunnan)

C. Y. Hao

Hao, Chao Yun; 郝朝运；Hǎo Cháoyùn

1979- **First publication: 2015**

- Employment: Spice and Beverage Research Institute, Chinese Academy of Tropical Agricultural Sciences（中国热带农业科学院香料饮料研究所）
- Research interest: Piperaceae [S]
- Published taxa: *Piper*
- Region: CHINA (Hainan)

G. Hao

Hao, Gang; 郝刚；Hǎo Gāng

1966- **First publication: 2005**

- Employment: South China Botanical Garden, Chinese Academy of Sciences; College of Life Sciences, South China Agricultural University（中国科学院华南植物园；华南农业大学生命科学学院）
- Research interest: Asteraceae, Hydrangeaceae, Oleaceae, Primulaceae; Plant Systematics [S]
- Published taxa: *Ardisia, Cartrema, Dichroa, Lysimachia, Osmanthus, Primula, Saussurea, Stimpsonia*
- Affiliation: SCAUB
- Location of specimens: SCAUB
- Region: CHINA

G. Q. Hao

Hao, Guo Qian; 郝国歉；Hǎo Guóqiàn

1986- **First publication: 2015**

- Employment: Management Committee of Scenic Area of Emeishan, Sichuan（四川省峨眉山风景名胜区管理委员会）
- Research interest: Brassicaceae [S]
- Published taxa: *Aphragmus, Eutrema*
- Region: CHINA

K. S. Hao

Hao, Kin Shen; Ho, Ching Shêng; Hao, Ching Sheng; 郝景盛；Hǎo Jǐngshèng

1903-1955 **First publication: 1932**

- Employment: Institute of Botany, National Academy of Peiping; Institute of Systematic Botany, Academia Sinica（国立北平研究院植物学研究所；中国科学院植物分类研究所）
- Research interest: Berberidaceae, Boraginaceae, Caprifoliaceae, Clethraceae, Crassulaceae, Cucurbitaceae, Ephedraceae, Grossulariaceae, Hernandiaceae, Orobanchaceae, Plumbaginaceae, Poaceae, Polygalaceae, Polygonaceae, Ranunculaceae, Rosaceae, Salicaceae, Sapindaceae, Saxifragaceae; Gymnospermae [S]
- Published taxa: *Acer, Calligonum, Cistanche, Cleistogenes, Clethra, Cymbaria, Diarrhena, Ephedra, Epimedium, Hystrix, Illigera, Leersia, Lonicera, Morina, Plumbago, Poa, Podophyllum, Ranunculus, Ribes, Rosa, Rubus, Salix, Saxifraga, Securidaca, Sedum, Sibiraea, Stipa, Trichosanthes, Trigonotis*
- Affiliation: PE

- Location of specimens: PE
- Region: CHINA

R. M. Hao

Hao, Ri Ming; 郝日明 ; Hǎo Rìmíng

1959- **First publication: 1998**

- Employment: Institute of Botany, Jiangsu Province and Chinese Academy of Sciences（江苏省中国科学院植物研究所）
- Research interest: Hamamelidaceae [S]
- Published taxa: *Parrotia*
- Region: CHINA (Anhui, Jiangsu)

S. J. Hao

Hao, Si Jun; 郝思军 ; Hǎo Sījūn

1965- **First publication: 1993**

- Employment: Shanghai Natural History Museum (Branch of Shanghai Science & Technology Museum)（上海自然博物馆(上海科技馆分馆)）
- Research interest: Oleaceae; Plants of Shanghai [S]
- Published taxa: *Ligustrum*
- Affiliation: SHM
- Region: CHINA

Y. Q. Hao

Hao, Yun Qing; 郝云庆 ; Hǎo Yúnqìng

1976- **First publication: 2016**

- Employment: Chengdu University of Information Technology（成都信息技术大学）
- Research interest: Ranunculaceae [S]
- Published taxa: *Caltha*
- Region: CHINA (Sichuan)

Z. P. Hao

Hao, Zhen Ping; 郝振萍 ; Hǎo Zhènpíng

First publication: 2008

- Employment: School of Horticulture, Jinling Vocational College（金陵职业学院园艺学院）
- Research interest: Acanthaceae [S]
- Published taxa: *Justicia, Peristrophe*
- Region: CHINA

C. X. He

He, Cheng Xin; 何成新 ; Hé Chéngxīn

1965- **First publication: 2012**

- Employment: Guangxi Institute of Botany, Chinese Academy of Sciences（广西壮族自治区中国科学院广西植物研究所）
- Research interest: Urticaceae [S]
- Published taxa: *Elatostema*
- Region: CHINA (Guangxi)

C. M. He

He, Chun Mei; 何春梅 ; Hé Chūnméi

1986- **First publication: 2020**

- Employment: Guangdong Academy of Forestry（广东省林业科学研究院）
- Research interest: Melanthiaceae, Melastomataceae [S]
- Published taxa: *Bredia, Chamaelirium*
- Region: CHINA (Guangdong)

C. N. Ho

Ho, Chun Nien; Ho, Ch'un Nien; He, Chun Nian; 何椿年 ; Hé Chūnnián

1906-1968 **First publication: 1952**

- Employment: Institute of Agriculture and Forestry, Sun Yat-Sen University（中山大学植物研究所）
- Research interest: Araliaceae, Rhizophoraceae, Sapindaceae [S]
- Published taxa: *Aralia, Brassaiopsis, Carallia, Dendropanax, Dimocarpus, Koelreuteria, Pseudonephelium, Sapindopsis, Schefflera*
- Affiliation: IBSC
- Region: CHINA

D. M. He

He, De Ming; 何德明 ; Hé Démíng

1983- **First publication: 2020**

- Employment: Wenshan Administration of National Nature Reserves, Yunnan（云南省文山市国家级自然保护区管护分局）
- Research interest: Aristolochiaceae [S]
- Published taxa: *Aristolochia*
- Region: CHINA (Yunnan)

T. C. Ho

Ho, Tung Chi; 何東輯 ; Hé Dōngjí; 何东辑

First publication: 2007

- Employment: Endemic Species Research Institute, Council of Agriculture, "Executive Yuan"（"行政院"农业委员会特有生物研究保育中心）
- Research interest: Rutaceae [S]
- Published taxa: *Glycosmis, Skimmia*
- Region: CHINA (Taiwan)

F. C. Ho

Ho, Feng Chi; He, Feng Ji; 何豐吉 ; Hé Fēngjí; 何丰吉

First publication: 1979

- Employment: Hengchun Tropical Botanic Garden, Taiwan Forestry Research Institute, Council of Agriculture, "Executive Yuan"（"行政院"农业委员会林业试验所恒春热带植物园）
- Research interest: Apocynaceae, Euphorbiaceae, Fabaceae, Malvaceae, Moraceae, Rubiaceae [S]
- Published taxa: *Asclepias, Chamaesyce, Dichrophyllum, Entada, Ficus, Gardenia, Meximalva, Poinsettia*
- Region: CHINA (Taiwan)

F. S. Ho

Ho, Fu Shun; 何富顺；Hé Fùshùn; 何富順

First publication: 1986

- Employment: Wild Orchid, Taiwan（台湾山野兰花）
- Research interest: Orchidaceae [S]
- Published taxa: *Cymbidium*
- Region: CHINA (Taiwan)

G. S. He

He, Guo Sheng; Hoo, Guo Sheng; 何国生；Hé Guóshēng

1954- First publication: 1990

- Employment: Fujian Forestry School（福建林业学校）
- Research interest: Ericaceae, Primulaceae; Plants of Fujian [S]
- Published taxa: *Cassiope, Primula*
- Affiliation: FFVTC
- Location of specimens: FFVTC, FJSI
- Region: CHINA (Fujian)
- Also as: G. S. Hoo

H. He

He, Hai; 何海；Hé Hǎi

1967- First publication: 1996

- Employment: Chongqing Normal University（重庆师范大学）
- Research interest: Anisophylleaceae, Aspleniaceae, Dryopteridaceae, Lycopodiaceae, Orchidaceae, Pteridaceae, Selaginellaceae; Pteridophytes [P]
- Published taxa: *Anisophyllea, Arachniodes, Cymbidium, Dryopteris, Hymenasplenium, Polystichum, Pteris, Selaginella, Spinulum*
- Affiliation: CTC
- Location of specimens: CTC
- Region: CHINA

H. W. He

He, Heng Wei; 何恒巍；Hé Héngwēi

First publication: 2010

- Employment: Amateur（业余爱好者）
- Research interest: Araceae [S]
- Published taxa: *Cryptocoryne*
- Region: CHINA (Guangxi)

J. Q. He

He, Jia Qing; 何家庆；Hé Jiāqìng; 何家慶

1949-2019 First publication: 1984

- Employment: Department of Biology, Anhui University（安徽大学生物系）
- Research interest: Cyperaceae, Fabaceae, Lamiaceae; Plants of Anhui [S]
- Published taxa: *Salvia, Scirpus, Teucrium, Vicia*
- Affiliation: ANU
- Location of specimens: ANU
- Region: CHINA (Anhui)

G. Hoo

Hoo, Gin; Ho, Ching; Ho, Chin; He, Jing; 何景；Hé Jǐng

1912-1978 First publication: 1951

- Employment: Department of Biology, Xiamen University（厦门大学生物系）
- Research interest: Araliaceae, Caprifoliaceae, Hydrangeaceae, Polygonaceae, Rosaceae, Salicaceae [S]
- Published taxa: *Abelia, Acanthopanax, Aralia, Brassaiopsis, Dendropanax, Euaraliopsis, Heteropanax, Hydrangea, Macropanax, Panax, Pentapanax, Polygonum, Rhaphiolepis, Salix, Schefflera, Tetrapanax*
- Location of specimens: AU, FJFC, FNU
- Region: CHINA
- Also as: C. Ho

J. B. He

He, Jing Biao; 何景彪；Hé Jǐngbiāo

1959- First publication: 1988

- Employment: Department of Biology, Wuhan University（武汉大学生物系）
- Research interest: Hydrocharitaceae, Potamogetonaceae; Aquatic Plants [S]
- Published taxa: *Najas, Potamogeton*
- Affiliation: WH
- Region: CHINA (Hubei)

Ju He

He, Ju; 何菊；Hé Jú

1976- First publication: 2010

- Employment: Department of Forestry Resources, Southwest Forestry College（西南林学院森林资源系）
- Research interest: Euphorbiaceae [S]
- Published taxa: *Trigonostemon*
- Region: CHINA (Yunnan)

Jun He

He, Jun; 何俊；Hé Jùn

1982- First publication: 2018

- Employment: Kunming Institute of Botany, Chinese Academy of Sciences（中国科学院昆明植物研究所）
- Research interest: Ranunculaceae [S]
- Published taxa: *Aconitum*
- Region: CHINA (Yunnan)
- IPNI as: J. He

K. J. He

He, Kai Jia; 何开家；Hé Kāijiā

1956- First publication: 2007

- Employment: Guangxi Institute of Traditional Medical and Pharmaceutical Sciences（广西中医药研究所）
- Research interest: Acanthaceae [S]

- Published taxa: *Strobilanthes*
- Region: CHINA (Guangxi)

L. He

He, Li; 何理 ; Hé Lǐ

1986- **First publication: 2014**

- Employment: School of Nature Conservation, Beijing Forestry University; Forestry College, Fujian Agriculture and Forestry University（北京林业大学自然保护区学院；福建农林大学林学院）
- Research interest: Lauraceae, Salicaceae [S]
- Published taxa: *Salix*
- Affiliation: FJFC
- Location of specimens: BJFC
- Region: CHINA (Xizang)

L. J. He

He, Li Juan; 何丽娟 ; Hé Lìjuān

1985- **First publication: 2012**

- Employment: Institute of Botany, Chinese Academy of Sciences（中国科学院植物研究所）
- Research interest: Polypodiaceae, Thelypteridaceae [P]
- Published taxa: *Coryphopteris, Cyclosorus, Parathelypteris, Selliguea, Stegnogramma*
- Region: CHINA

M. Y. He

He, Ming You; 何明友 ; Hé Míngyǒu

1938- **First publication: 1985**

- Employment: Department of Biology, Sichuan University; Department of Biology, Sichuan Union University（四川大学生物系；四川联合大学生物系）
- Research interest: Cornaceae, Ericaceae [S]
- Published taxa: *Alangium, Rhododendron*
- Affiliation: SZ
- Location of specimens: SZ
- Region: CHINA (Sichuan)

P. X. He

He, Pi Xu; 何丕绪 ; Hé Pīxù

1925-2003 **First publication: 1983**

- Employment: Yunnan Forestry College（云南林学院）
- Research interest: Fagaceae, Pentaphylacaceae, Salicaceae [S]
- Published taxa: *Eurya, Lithocarpus, Populus, Salix*
- Location of specimens: SWFC
- Region: CHINA (Yunnan)
- Also as: P. S. Ho

P. He

He, Ping; 何平 ; Hé Píng

1963- **First publication: 1990**

- Employment: Department of Biology, Southwest Normal University（西南师范大学生物系）
- Research interest: Annonaceae, Hydrangeaceae [S]
- Published taxa: *Deutzia, Duguetia*
- Affiliation: SWCTU
- Location of specimens: SZ
- Region: CHINA

S. B. Ho

Ho, Shan Bao; 何善宝 ; Hé Shànbǎo; 何善寶

1930-2020 **First publication: 1981**

- Employment: Northwest China Institute of Botany, Chinese Academy of Sciences and Shaanxi Province（陕西省中国科学院西北植物研究所）
- Research interest: Euphorbiaceae, Fabaceae, Phyllanthaceae [S]
- Published taxa: *Astragalus, Euphorbia, Leptopus, Sapium*
- Affiliation: WUK
- Location of specimens: WUK
- Region: CHINA

Shao Y. He

He, Shao Yun; 何少云 ; Hé Shàoyún

1957- **First publication: 2009**

- Employment: College of Horticulture, South China Agricultural University（华南农业大学园艺学院）
- Research interest: Apocynaceae [S]
- Published taxa: *Hoya*
- Region: CHINA (Hainan, Yunnan)

S. Q. He

He, Shun Qing; 何顺清 ; Hé Shùnqīng

First publication: 1989

- Employment: Guangxi Institute of Botany（广西植物研究所）
- Research interest: Theaceae [S]
- Published taxa: *Camellia*
- Affiliation: IBK
- Location of specimens: IBK
- Region: CHINA (Guangxi)

S. Z. He

He, Shun Zhi; 何顺志 ; Hé Shùnzhì

1954- **First publication: 1992**

- Employment: Department of Chinese Materia Medica, Guiyang College of Traditional Chinese Medicine（贵阳中医学院药学系）
- Research interest: Araceae, Asteraceae, Asparagaceae, Berberidaceae, Convallariaceae, Gesneriaceae, Melanthiaceae, Rosaceae [S]
- Published taxa: *Aspidistra, Parasenecio, Paris, Rubus, Tengia, Tremacron, Typhonium*
- Affiliation: GZTM
- Location of specimens: GZTM

- Region: CHINA (Chongqing, Guangxi, Guizhou, Sichuan, Yunnan)

T. N. Ho

Ho, Ting Nung; Ho, Ting Nong; He, Ting Nong; 何廷农 ; Hé Tíngnóng; 何廷農

1938-2011 **First publication: 1976**

- Employment: Northwest Plateau Institute of Biology, Chinese Academy of Sciences（中国科学院西北高原生物研究所）
- Research interest: Asteraceae, Caprifoliaceae, Elaeagnaceae, Gentianaceae [S]
- Published taxa: *Anagallidium, Chaetoseris, Comastoma, Cremanthodium, Gentiana, Gentianella, Gentianopsis, Hippophae, Jaeschkea, Kingdon-wardia, Ligularia, Lomatogoniopsis, Lomatogonium, Lonicera, Metagentiana, Mulgedium, Saussurea, Sinoswertia, Swertia, Youngia*
- Affiliation: HNWP
- Location of specimens: HNWP
- Region: CHINA

X. R. He

He, Xi Rong; 何锡荣 ; Hé Xīróng

1968- **First publication: 1993**

- Employment: Administrative Bureau of Nature Reserve of Changbai Mountain, Jilin（吉林省长白山自然保护区管理局）
- Research interest: Fabaceae [S]
- Published taxa: *Oxytropis*
- Region: CHINA (Jilin)

X. J. He

He, Xing Jin; 何兴金 ; Hé Xīngjīn

1962- **First publication: 1993**

- Employment: Department of Biology, Sichuan Union University; College of Life Sciences, Sichuan University（四川联合大学生物系 ; 四川大学生命科学学院）
- Research interest: Amaryllidaceae, Apiaceae, Asparagaceae, Liliaceae, Rosaceae [S]
- Published taxa: *Allium, Angelica, Bupleurum, Chamaesium, Heracleum, Lilium, Nomocharis, Polygonatum, Pternopetalum, Semenovia, Spiraea, Spuriopimpinella, Tetrataenium*
- Affiliation: SITC, SZ
- Location of specimens: SITC, SZ
- Region: CHINA (Sichuan)

Y. C. Ho

Ho, Ye Chi; Hou, Yeh Chi; He, Ye Qi; 何业祺 ; Hé Yèqí; 何業祺

1933- **First publication: 1979**

- Employment: Northwest China Institute of Botany, Chinese Academy of Sciences and Shaanxi Province; Department of Biology, Hangzhou Normal College（陕西省中国科学院西北植物研究所 ; 杭州师范学院生物系）
- Research interest: Apiaceae, Celastraceae, Cornaceae, Crassulaceae, Fabaceae [S]
- Published taxa: *Alangium, Astragalus, Celastrus, Pleurospermum, Sedum*
- Affiliation: HTC
- Location of specimens: HTC, PE, WUK
- Region: CHINA

Yi He

He, Yi; 何毅 ; Hé Yì

1991- **First publication: 2018**

- Employment: College of Life Sciences, Beijing Normal University（北京师范大学生命科学学院）
- Research interest: Boraginaceae [S]
- Published taxa: *Onosma*
- Region: CHINA (Xizang)
- IPNI as: Y. He

Y. M. He

He, Yong Ming; 何永明 ; Hé Yǒngmíng

1968- **First publication: 1999**

- Employment: Daweishan Nature Reserve Administration Office, Pingbian, Yunnan（云南屏边县大围山自然保护区管理所）
- Research interest: Cyatheaceae [P]
- Published taxa: *Alsophila*
- Region: CHINA (Yunnan)

Y. He

He, Yue; 何跃 ; Hé Yuè

1958- **First publication: 1989**

- Employment: Liaoning Institute of Pomology（辽宁省果树科学研究所）
- Research interest: Rosaceae [S]
- Published taxa: *Armeniaca, Prunus*
- Region: CHINA (Liaoning)

Y. H. He

He, Yun He; 何云核 ; Hé Yúnhé

1960- **First publication: 1988**

- Employment: Department of Forestry, Anhui Agricultural College; Faculty of Forest Utilization, Anhui Agricultural University（安徽农学院林学系 ; 安徽农业大学森林利用学院）
- Research interest: Aquifoliaceae, Celastraceae, Staphyleaceae, Vitaceae [S]
- Published taxa: *Euonymus, Ilex, Staphylea, Vitis*
- Affiliation: AAUF
- Region: CHINA (Anhui, Shaanxi)

Chu Ho

Ho, Chu; He, Zhu; **何铸 ; Hé Zhù; 何鑄**

1924-1991 **First publication: 1979**

- Employment: Sichuan Institute of Chinese Materia Medica（四川省中药研究所）
- Research interest: Gentianaceae, Illiciaceae, Schisandraceae, Violaceae [S]
- Published taxa: *Rinorea*
- Affiliation: HWA
- Location of specimens: HWA, SHM, SM, SZ
- Region: CHINA (Sichuan)

J. J. He

He, Ji Jian; 和积鉴 ; Hé Jījiàn; 和積鑑

1933- **First publication: 1981**

- Employment: Yunnan University（云南大学）
- Research interest: Athyriaceae, Plagiogyriaceae; Pteridophytes [P]
- Published taxa: *Allantodia, Plagiogyria*
- Affiliation: PYU, YUYU
- Location of specimens: PYU, YUYU
- Region: CHINA (Yunnan)

Z. R. He

He, Zhao Rong; 和兆荣 ; Hé Zhàoróng

1970- **First publication: 1998**

- Employment: Institute of Ecology and Geobotany, Yunnan University（云南大学生态学与地植物学研究所）
- Research interest: Apiaceae, Athyriaceae, Dryopteridaceae, Gesneriaceae, Gleicheniaceae, Marattiaceae, Ophioglossaceae, Polypodiaceae, Pteridaceae, Rosaceae, Selaginellaceae; Pteridophytes [P]
- Published taxa: *Allantodia, Angiopteris, Athyriopsis, Athyrium, Botrypus, Bupleurum, Deparia, Diplazium, Diplopterygium, Lastreopsis, Microsorum, Monomelangium, Ophioglossum, Petrocosmea, Polystichum, Potentilla, Pteris, Rubus, Selaginella*
- Affiliation: YUKU
- Region: CHINA (Yunnan)

J. R. He

He, Jia Ren; 贺家仁 ; Hè Jiārén

1953-2012 **First publication: 1991**

- Employment: Sichuan Academy of Forestry（四川省林业科学研究院）
- Research interest: Rosaceae, Salicaceae [S]
- Published taxa: *Populus, Prunus*
- Region: CHINA (Sichuan)

P. C. He

He, Pu Chao; 贺普超 ; Hè Pǔchāo; 賀普超

1926-2006 **First publication: 1995**

- Employment: Department of Horticulture, Northwest Agricultural University（西北农业大学园艺系）
- Research interest: Vitaceae [S]
- Published taxa: *Vitis*
- Region: CHINA (Shaanxi)

Rong He

He, Rong; 贺蓉 ; Hè Róng

1964- **First publication: 1994**

- Employment: Department of Fisheries, Sichuan College of Husbandry and Veterinary Medicine（四川畜牧兽医学院水产系）
- Research interest: Fabaceae [S]
- Published taxa: *Vicia*
- Region: CHINA
- IPNI as: He Rong

S. W. He

He, Shan Wen; 贺善文 ; Hè Shànwén; 賀善文

1923-1991 **First publication: 1990**

- Employment: Horticulture Institute, Hunan Academy of Agricultural Sciences（湖南省农业科学院园艺研究所）
- Research interest: Rutaceae [S]
- Published taxa: *Citrus*
- Region: CHINA (Hunan)

S. Y. He

He, Shi Yuan; Ho, Shih Yuen; **贺士元 ; Hè Shìyuán; 賀士元**

1927-2015 **First publication: 1984**

- Employment: College of Life Sciences, Beijing Normal University; Department of Biology, Beijing Normal University（北京师范大学生命科学学院；北京师范大学生物系）
- Research interest: Apiaceae, Apocynaceae, Caprifoliaceae, Caryophyllaceae, Fabaceae, Orobanchaceae, Papaveraceae, Saxifragaceae; Plants of N. China [S]
- Published taxa: *Corydalis, Hedysarum, Heterostemma, Ligusticum, Pedicularis, Saxifraga, Scabiosa, Silene*
- Affiliation: BNU
- Location of specimens: BNU
- Region: CHINA (Beijing, Hebei, Shanxi)

Xue L. He

He, Xue Li; 贺学礼 ; Hè Xuélǐ

1963- **First publication: 1996**

- Employment: Department of Basic Courses, Northwest Agricultural University（西北农业大学基础课部）
- Research interest: Asteraceae, Brassicaceae; Plant

Ecology [S]
- Published taxa: *Hedinia, Scorzonera*
- Affiliation: HBU
- Location of specimens: HBU
- Region: CHINA (Xinjiang, Xizang)

L. M. Heng

Heng, La Mei; 衡腊梅 ; Héng Làméi

1992- **First publication: 2018**

- Employment: School of Life Sciences, Lanzhou University（兰州大学生命科学学院）
- Research interest: Asteraceae [S]
- Published taxa: *Soroseris*
- Region: CHINA

D. Y. Hong

Hong, De Yuan; Hong, De Yuang; 洪德元 ; Hóng Déyuán

1937- **First publication: 1974**

- Employment: Institute of Botany, Chinese Academy of Sciences（中国科学院植物研究所）
- Research interest: Aquifoliaceae, Campanulaceae, Caprifoliaceae, Colchicaceae, Commelinaceae, Goodeniaceae, Liliaceae, Linderniaceae, Mazaceae, Oleaceae, Orobanchaceae, Paeoniaceae, Paulowniaceae, Plantaginaceae, Rosaceae, Scrophulariaceae [S]
- Published taxa: *Acanthocalyx, Adenophora, Amana, Amischotolype, Asyneuma, Campanula, Campanumoea, Cochlidiosperma, Codonopsis, Craterocapsa, Cyananthus, Cyclocodon, Dictyospermum, Disporum, Echinocodon, Euphrasia, Floscopa, Goodenia, Himalacodon, Homocodon, Ilex, Kashmiria, Leptocodon, Linaria, Lobelia, Mazus, Melampyrum, Morina, Murdannia, Neopicrorhiza, Oligospermum, Orthocarpus, Paeonia, Pankycodon, Paulownia, Pedicularis, Pollia, Porandra, Pourthiaea, Pseudobartsia, Pseudocodon, Pseudolysimachion, Pterygiella, Scrophularia, Sinobacopa, Streptolirion, Striga, Syringa, Theilera, Torenia, Tricarpelema, Triphysaria, Valeriana, Veronica, Veronicastrum, Wulfeniopsis, Xizangia*
- Affiliation: PE
- Region: [WORLD]

J. Y. Hong

Hong, Jian Yuan; 洪建元 ; Hóng Jiànyuán

1925-2003 **First publication: 1987**

- Employment: Shenyang Agricultural College（沈阳农学院）
- Research interest: Rosaceae [S]
- Published taxa: *Malus*
- Region: CHINA (Liaoning)

T. Hong

Hong, Tao; 洪涛 ; Hóng Tāo; 洪濤

1923-2018 **First publication: 1963**

- Employment: Chinese Academy of Forestry（中国林业科学研究院）
- Research interest: Cannabaceae, Fagaceae, Paeoniaceae, Salicaceae; Woody Plants [S]
- Published taxa: *Celtis, Cyclobalanopsis, Paeonia, Populus*
- Affiliation: CAF
- Location of specimens: CAF
- Region: CHINA

X. J. Hong

Hong, Xiao Jiang; 洪小江 ; Hóng Xiǎojiāng

1973- **First publication: 2004**

- Employment: Hainan Jianfengling Forestry Bureau（海南省尖峰岭林业局）
- Research interest: Fagaceae, Lauraceae [S]
- Published taxa: *Cyclobalanopsis, Machilus*
- Region: CHINA (Hainan)

Xin Hong

Hong, Xin; 洪欣 ; Hóng Xīn

1990- **First publication: 2012**

- Employment: Guangxi Institute of Botany, Chinese Academy of Sciences（广西壮族自治区中国科学院广西植物研究所）
- Research interest: Gesneriaceae [S]
- Published taxa: *Didymocarpus, Hemiboea, Paraboea, Petrocodon, Primulina*
- Region: CHINA (Guangxi)
- IPNI as: X. Hong

H. C. Hung

Hung, Hsin Chieh; 洪信介 ; Hóng Xìnjiè

First publication: 2018

- Employment: Dr. Cecilia Koo Botanic Conservation Center（辜严倬云植物保种中心）
- Research interest: Orchidaceae [S]
- Published taxa: *Gastrochilus*
- Region: CHINA (Taiwan)

Ding Hou

Hou, Ding; Hou, Ting; 侯定 ; Hóu Dìng

1921-2008 **First publication: 1958**

- Employment: National Herbarium Nederland（荷兰国家植物标本馆）
- Research interest: Anacardiaceae, Anisophylleaceae, Aristolochiaceae, Celastraceae, Centroplacaceae, Rhizophoraceae, Thymelaeaceae. [MS]
- Published taxa: *Anisophyllea, Aquilaria, Aristolochia, Bhesa, Blepharistemma, Bruguiera, Carallia, Cassine,*

Ceriops, Crossostylis, Drimycarpus, Euonymus, Gluta, Glyptopetalum, Gyrinops, Kokoona, Loeseneriella, Lophopetalum, Mangifera, Maytenus, Melanochyla, Microtropis, Nothopegia, Reissantia, Salacia, Sarawakodendron, Semecarpus, Siphonodon, Swintonia, Thottea,
- Region: [ASIA]

H. G. Hou

Hou, Hai Gong; 侯海宫 ; Hóu Hǎigōng
1969- **First publication: 2000**
- Employment: Baiyin Institute for Drug Control, Gansu（甘肃省白银市药品检验所）
- Research interest: Asteraceae [S]
- Published taxa: *Xanthium*
- Region: CHINA (Gansu)

F. C. How

How, Foon Chew; Hou, Kuan Chao; Hou, K'uan Chao; Hou, Kuan Zhao; 侯宽昭 ; Hóu Kuānzhāo; 侯寬昭
1908-1959 **First publication: 1939**
- Employment: Botanical Institute, College of Agriculture, National Sun Yat-sen University; South China Institute of Botany, Chinese Academy of Sciences（国立中山大学农林植物研究所 ; 中国科学院华南植物研究所）
- Research interest: Akaniaceae, Amaranthaceae, Annonaceae, Aristolochiaceae, Asparagaceae, Bignoniaceae, Cardiopteridaceae, Celastraceae, Clusiaceae, Convolvulaceae, Cyperaceae, Elaeocarpaceae, Euphorbiaceae, Fabaceae, Fagaceae, Garryaceae, Icacinaceae, Lamiaceae, Linaceae, Lythraceae, Malvaceae, Melastomataceae, Meliaceae, Moraceae, Pentaphylacaceae, Polygalaceae, Portulacaceae, Ranunculaceae, Rhamnaceae, Rhizophoraceae, Rubiaceae, Rutaceae, Sabiaceae, Salicaceae, Sapindaceae, Sapotaceae, Saxifragaceae, Stemonuraceae, Styracaceae, Theaceae, Vitaceae [S]
- Published taxa: *Adinandra, Adina, Aerva, Aglaia, Albizia, Alniphyllum, Alphonsea, Aphanamixis, Argostemma, Aristolochia, Aspidistra, Aucuba, Bretschneidera, Burretiodendron, Caesalpinia, Camellia, Carallia, Carex, Casearia, Cephaëlis, Cladium, Clematis, Derris, Dysoxylum, Elaeocarpus, Erycibe, Euonymus, Garcinia, Gleditsia, Gomphandra, Gonocaryum, Grewia, Gymnosporia, Hedyotis, Heynea, Homalium, Hymenopogon, Iodes, Ixora, Koelreuteria, Lagerstroemia, Lithocarpus, Madhuca, Mariscus, Medinilla, Meliosma, Morinda, Munronia, Muricococcum, Mycetia, Neanotis, Ophiorrhiza, Paedicalyx, Pavetta, Pithecellobium, Polygala, Porana, Portulaca, Pouteria, Premna, Pseudonephelium, Pycreus, Radermachera, Rhamnus, Rubia, Salacia, Sapindopsis, Saxifraga, Scleria, Sindora, Sloanea, Sonerila, Sphenodesme, Styrax, Tarenna, Tetrastigma, Tirpitzia, Uncaria, Urophyllum, Wendlandia, Xanthophytopsis, Zanthoxylum, Ziziphus*
- Affiliation: IBSC
- Location of specimens: IBSC
- Region: CHINA

M. F. Hou

Hou, Man Fu; 侯满福 ; Hóu Mǎnfú
1976- **First publication: 2009**
- Employment: Institute of Botany, Chinese Academy of Sciences（中国科学院植物研究所）
- Research interest: Asparagaceae [S]
- Published taxa: *Aspidistra*
- Region: CHINA (Guangxi)

W. H. Hou

Hou, Wen Hu; 侯文虎 ; Hóu Wénhǔ
1937-1989 **First publication: 1986**
- Employment: Xinjiang Academy of Forestry Sciences（新疆林业科学院）
- Research interest: Ranunculaceae; Woody Plants [S]
- Published taxa: *Clematis*
- Affiliation: XJFA
- Location of specimens: XJFA
- Region: CHINA (Xinjiang)

X. Hou

Hou, Xin; 侯鑫 ; Hóu Xīn
1976- **First publication: 2003**
- Employment: Institute of Botany, Chinese Academy of Sciences（中国科学院植物研究所）
- Research interest: Aspleniaceae [P]
- Published taxa: *Asplenium*
- Region: CHINA

X. L. Hou

Hou, Xue Liang; 侯学良 ; Hóu Xuéliáng
1969- **First publication: 2003**
- Employment: School of Life Sciences, Xiamen University; College of Forestry, South China Agricultural University（厦门大学生命科学学院 ; 华南农业大学林学院）
- Research interest: Annonaceae, Euphorbiaceae [S]
- Published taxa: *Dasymaschalon, Goniothalamus, Miliusa, Polyalthia, Wuodendron*
- Affiliation: AU
- Location of specimens: AU
- Region: CHINA (Yunnan)

Y. T. Hou

Hou, Yuan Tong; 侯元同 ; Hóu Yuántóng
1964- **First publication: 2006**

- Employment: Key Laboratory of Plant Stress, Shandong Normal University; College of Life Science, Qufu Normal University（山东师范大学逆境植物重点实验室；曲阜师范大学生命科学学院）
- Research interest: Asteraceae, Balsaminaceae, Polygonaceae; Plants of Shandong [S]
- Published taxa: *Chrysanthemum, Impatiens, Polygonum*
- Affiliation: QFNU
- Location of specimens: QFNU
- Region: CHINA

Y. S. Hou

Hou, Yue Shin; Hou, Yue Xin; 侯月欣；Hóu Yuèxīn

1940- **First publication: 1986**

- Employment: Xinjiang Academy of Forestry Sciences（新疆林业科学院）
- Research interest: Ranunculaceae; Woody Plants [S]
- Published taxa: *Clematis*
- Affiliation: XJFA
- Location of specimens: XJFA
- Region: CHINA (Xinjiang)

A. Q. Hu

Hu, Ai Qun; 胡爱群；Hú Àiqún; 胡爱群

1980- **First publication: 2009**

- Employment: School of Biological Sciences, The University of Hong Kong; Kadoorie Farm and Botanic Garden（香港大学生物科学学院；嘉道理农场暨植物园）
- Research interest: Orchidaceae [S]
- Published taxa: *Bulbophyllum, Cephalanthera, Gastrodia, Leptogastrodia, Liparis, Malaxis*
- Region: CHINA

Cheng H. Hu

Hu, Cheng Hua; 胡成华；Hú Chénghuá; 胡喻陈，胡成華

1933- **First publication: 1981**

- Employment: Nanjing University（南京大学）
- Research interest: Poaceae [S]
- Published taxa: *Indocalamus, Phyllostachys, Polyanthus, Sasamorpha, Sasa*
- Affiliation: N
- Location of specimens: N
- Region: CHINA
- IPNI as: C. H. Hu; Y. C. Hu

T. W. Hu

Hu, Ta Wei; Hu, Da Wei; 胡大維；Hú Dàwéi; 胡大维

1921-2005 **First publication: 1975**

- Employment: Taiwan Forestry Research Institute, Taiwan Provincial Administrative Office（台湾省政府农林厅林业试验所）
- Research interest: Orchidaceae, Paulowniaceae [S]
- Published taxa: *Habenaria, Paulownia, Tulotis*
- Region: CHINA (Taiwan)

D. H. Hu

Hu, Deng He; 胡登荷；Hú Dēnghé

1941- **First publication: 1995**

- Employment: Ji'an Institute of Forestry Science, Jiangxi（江西吉安地区林业科学研究所）
- Research interest: Poaceae [S]
- Published taxa: *Pseudosasa*
- Region: CHINA (Jiangxi)

G. W. Hu

Hu, Guang Wan; 胡光万；Hú Guāngwàn

1974- **First publication: 2007**

- Employment: Kunming Institute of Botany, Chinese Academy of Sciences; Wuhan Botanical Garden, Chinese Academy of Sciences（中国科学院昆明植物研究所；中国科学院武汉植物园）
- Research interest: Adoxaceae, Araceae, Asparagaceae, Balsaminaceae, Berberidaceae, Campanulaceae, Crassulaceae, Cucurbitaceae, Lentibulariaceae, Liliaceae, Melanthiaceae, Menyanthaceae, Orchidaceae, Passifloraceae [S]
- Published taxa: *Adenia, Arisaema, Aspidistra, Cremastra, Dendrobium, Epimedium, Gastrodia, Habenaria, Impatiens, Lobelia, Nymphoides, Paris, Polygonatum, Polystachya, Sambucus, Sedum, Tupistra, Utricularia, Zehneria*
- Affiliation: HIB
- Location of specimens: HIB
- Region: CHINA; [AFRICA]

G. X. Hu

Hu, Guo Xiong; 胡国雄；Hú Guóxióng

1987- **First publication: 2013**

- Employment: Kunming Institute of Botany, Chinese Academy of Sciences（中国科学院昆明植物研究所）
- Research interest: Lamiaceae, Zingiberaceae [S]
- Published taxa: *Salvia, Zingiber*
- Region: CHINA (Yunnan)

H. Y. Hu

Hu, Hao Yu; Hu, Hao You; 胡灏禹；Hú Hàoyǔ

1989- **First publication: 2016**

- Employment: College of Life Sciences, Sichuan University（四川大学生命科学学院）
- Research interest: Rosaceae [S]
- Published taxa: *Spiraea*
- Region: CHINA (Sichuan)

Huan Hu

Hu, Huan; 胡欢；Hú Huān

1990- **First publication: 2018**
- Employment: College of Life Sciences, Sichuan University（四川大学生命科学学院）
- Research interest: Brassicaceae [S]
- Published taxa: *Orychophragmus*
- Region: CHINA

C. C. Hu

Hu, Chia Chi; Hu, Jia Qi; 胡嘉琪；Hú Jiāqí
1932- **First publication: 2002**
- Employment: Institute of Biodiversity Science, Fudan University（复旦大学生物多样性科学研究所）
- Research interest: Acanthaceae, Caprifoliaceae, Fabaceae [S]
- Published taxa: *Acanthus, Calophanoides, Championella, Diflugossa, Goldfussia, Hymenochlaena, Mananthes, Perilepta, Pseuderanthemum, Pteracanthus, Pyrrothrix, Rostellularia, Tetraglochidium*
- Affiliation: FUS
- Location of specimens: FUS
- Region: CHINA

C. Y. Hu

Hu, Chia Ying; Hu, Jia Ying; 胡嘉穎；Hú Jiāyǐng; 胡嘉颖
First publication: 2000
- Employment: Biodiversity Research Center, "Academia Sinica"（中研院生物多样性研究中心）
- Research interest: Orchidaceae [S]
- Published taxa: *Listera*
- Location of specimens: HAST
- Region: CHINA (Taiwan)

C. H. Hu

Hu, Chün Hung; Hu, Chun Hung; 胡俊鋐；Hú Jùnhóng
First publication: 1966
- Employment: Nanjing Institute of Materia Medica（南京药物研究所）
- Research interest: Lamiaceae, Poaceae [S]
- Published taxa: *Ajuga, Dysophylla, Elsholtzia, Orthodon, Orthosiphon, Phlomis, Plectranthus, Pogostemon, Scutellaria, Shibataea, Teucrium*
- Region: CHINA
- IPNI as: C. Y. Hu

L. C. Hu

Hu, Lin Cheng; Hu, Ling Cheng; Hu, Lin Zheng; Hu Lin Zhen; 胡琳祯；Hú Línzhēn; 胡琳珍；胡琳贞；胡琳禎
1925-1994 **First publication: 1966**
- Employment: Department of Biology, Sichuan University（四川大学生物系）
- Research interest: Clethraceae, Ericaceae, Hydrangeaceae, Sapindaceae [S]
- Published taxa: *Acer, Clethra, Deutzia, Rhododendron*
- Affiliation: SZ
- Region: CHINA

C. M. Hu

Hu, Chi Ming; Hu, Qi Ming; 胡启明；Hú Qǐmíng; 胡啟明
1935- **First publication: 1974**
- Employment: South China Institute of Botany, Chinese Academy of Sciences; South China Botanical Garden, Chinese Academy of Sciences（中国科学院华南植物研究所；中国科学院华南植物园）
- Research interest: Asteraceae, Begoniaceae, Berberidaceae, Corsiaceae, Myrsinaceae, Primulaceae, Rubiaceae [S]
- Published taxa: *Androsace, Ardisia, Begonia, Berberis, Carpesium, Corsiopsis, Embelia, Fittingia, Lysimachia, Maesa, Mahonia, Pertusadina, Primula, Rapanea, Sadiria*
- Affiliation: IBSC
- Location of specimens: LBG, PE
- Region: CHINA

R. C. Hu

Hu, Ren Chuan; 胡仁传；Hú Rénchuán
1988- **First publication: 2014**
- Employment: Guangxi Institute of Chinese Medicine & Pharmaceutical Science; Guangxi Institute of Botany, Chinese Academy of Sciences（广西中医药研究院；广西壮族自治区中国科学院广西植物研究所）
- Research interest: Asparagaceae, Colchicaceae, Theaceae [S]
- Published taxa: *Aspidistra, Camellia, Disporum*
- Region: CHINA (Guangxi)

S. L. Hu

Hu, Shi Lin; 胡世林；Hú Shìlín
1942- **First publication: 1984**
- Employment: Institute of Chinese Materia Medica, China Academy of Chinese Medical Sciences; School of Chinese Medicine, Hong Kong Baptist University（中国中医研究院中药研究所；香港浸会大学中医药学院）
- Research interest: Araceae, Asteraceae [S]
- Published taxa: *Atractylodes, Pinellia*
- Affiliation: CMMI
- Location of specimens: CMMI
- Region: CHINA

S. H. Hu

Hu, Song Hua; 胡松华；Hú Sōnghuá
1954- **First publication: 1995**
- Employment: Guangzhou Flower Research Center

(广州花卉研究中心)
- Research interest: Orchidaceae [S]
- Published taxa: *Paphiopedilum*
- Region: [cult.]
- IPNI as: H. S. Hua

W. K. Hu

Hu, Wen Kwang; Hu, Wên Kwang; Hu, Wen Guang; Hu, Wen Kuang; 胡文光; Hú Wénguāng
1914-1992 **First publication: 1966**
- Employment: Department of Biology, Sichuan University (四川大学生物系)
- Research interest: Betulaceae, Cornaceae, Elaeagnaceae, Ericaceae, Garryaceae, Sapindaceae [S]
- Published taxa: *Acer, Aucuba, Cornus, Dendrobenthamia, Elaeagnus, Macrocarpium, Ostrya, Rhododendron, Swida*
- Affiliation: SZ
- Location of specimens: SHM, SZ
- Region: CHINA

Hu

Hu, Hsen Hsu; Hu, Hsien Su; Hu, Xian Su; 胡先骕; Hú Xiānsù; 胡先驌
1894-1968 **First publication: 1922**
- Employment: National Southeast University; Fan Memorial Institute of Biology; Biological Laboratory of Science Society of China; Institute of Systematic Botany, Academia Sinica; Institute of Botany, Chinese Academy of Sciences (国立东南大学;静生生物调查所;中国科学社生物研究所;中国科学院植物分类研究所;中国科学院植物研究所)
- Research interest: Anacardiaceae, Annonaceae, Apocynaceae, Betulaceae, Calycanthaceae, Cupressaceae, Dilleniaceae, Elaeocarpaceae, Fabaceae, Fagaceae, Hydrangeaceae, Iteaceae, Magnoliaceae, Malpighiaceae, Malvaceae, Meliaceae, Myrtaceae, Orchidaceae, Pentaphylacaceae, Pinaceae, Polygalaceae, Primulaceae, Rhamnaceae, Rosaceae, Rubiaceae, Rutaceae, Salicaceae, Sapindaceae, Stemonuraceae, Styracaceae, Theaceae, Torricelliaceae, Urticaceae, Vitaceae; Woody Plants. [APS]
- Published taxa: *Acer, Alnus, Aromadendron, Aspidopterys, Berchemiella, Betula, Carpinus, Corylus, Cyathostemma, Cyclobalanopsis, Deutzia, Elaeocarpus, Eriolaena, Eurya, Fagara, Gilibertia, Hartia, Hovenia, Itea, Maesa, Magnolia, Manglietia, Meratia, Metaplexis, Metasequoia, Michelia, Neofinetia, Nothotsuga, Ostrya, Parakmeria, Paramanglietia, Paramichelia, Pasania, Polychroa, Polyspora, Populus, Quercus, Rubus, Sloanea, Spatholobus, Stemonurus, Styrax, Syzygium, Tabernaemontana, Tapirira,* Torricelliaceae, *Tricalysia, Tylophora, Vanieria, Vitis, Xanthophyllum, Ziziphus*
- Affiliation: PE
- Location of specimens: CQNM, JXU, PE
- Region: CHINA

X. M. Hu

Hu, Xiao Min; 胡晓敏; Hú Xiǎomǐn
1985- **First publication: 2011**
- Employment: South China Botanical Garden, Chinese Academy of Sciences (中国科学院华南植物园)
- Research interest: Magnoliaceae [S]
- Published taxa: *Magnolia, Manglietia*
- Region: CHINA (Yunnan)

X. H. Hu

Hu, Xiao Hong; 胡孝纮; Hú Xiàohóng; 胡孝宏
1938- **First publication: 1984**
- Employment: Chengdu Institute of Biology, Chinese Academy of Sciences (中国科学院成都生物研究所)
- Research interest: Asparagaceae [S]
- Published taxa: *Polygonatum*
- Location of specimens: CDBI
- Region: CHINA (Sichuan)

X. W. Hu

Hu, Xin Wen; 胡新文; Hú Xīnwén
1963- **First publication: 2006**
- Employment: College of Agriculture, South China University of Tropical Agriculture (华南热带农业大学农学院)
- Research interest: Brassicaceae [S]
- Published taxa: *Neomartinella*
- Region: CHINA (Hubei)

X. Hu

Hu, Xiu; 胡秀; Hú Xiù
1976- **First publication: 2010**
- Employment: Zhongkai University of Agriculture and Engineering; South China Botanical Garden, Chinese Academy of Sciences (仲恺农业工程学院;中国科学院华南植物园)
- Research interest: Zingiberaceae [S]
- Published taxa: *Hedychium*
- Region: CHINA (Yunnan)

S. Y. Hu

Hu, Shiu Ying; Hu, Hsiu Ying; Hu, Xiu Ying; 胡秀英; Hú Xiùyīng
1908-2012 **First publication: 1945**
- Employment: Arnold Arboretum, Harvard University, U.S.A. (美国哈佛大学阿诺德树木园)

- Research interest: Acoraceae, Aquifoliaceae, Araceae, Araliaceae, Asphodelaceae, Asteraceae, Balanophoraceae, Bignoniaceae, Calycanthaceae, Campanulaceae, Clethraceae, Cornaceae, Cupressaceae, Ericaceae, Fabaceae, Gesneriaceae, Hydrangeaceae, Lamiaceae, Lauraceae, Malvaceae, Melastomataceae, Menispermaceae, Oleaceae, Orchidaceae, Paulowniaceae, Phyllanthaceae, Podocarpaceae, Ranunculaceae, Rosaceae, Rubiaceae, Rutaceae, Sapindaceae, Taxaceae, Theaceae [S]
- Published taxa: *Abelmoschus, Abutilon, Acer, Acorus, Alangium, Ania, Anoectochilus, Arisaema, Arundina, Aster, Atractylis, Balanophora, Blastus, Boenninghausenia, Bulbophyllum, Calanthe, Camellia, Catalpa, Cephalantheropsis, Cheirostylis, Chimonanthus, Chrysanthemum, Cirrhopetalum, Clematis, Clethra, Coelogyne, Craibiodendron, Cryptocoryne, Cupressus, Cymbidium, Cyphotheca, Dendrobium, Dichroa, Didymocarpus, Disperis, Eleutherococcus, Epipactis, Eulophia, Evodiopanax, Fordiophyton, Fraxinus, Gastrochilus, Goodyera, Gossypium, Habenaria, Hemerocallis, Hibiscus, Ilex, Ixeris, Kalimeris, Lactuca, Leonurus, Leucaena, Ligustrum, Lindera, Liparis, Lobelia, Luculia, Malaxis, Manniella, Medinilla, Microcos, Morinda, Neolitsea, Nothopanax, Pachycentria, Paulownia, Peristylus, Phaius, Philadelphus, Phyllagathis, Plagiopetalum, Podocarpus, Prunus, Pseudodracontium, Pycnospatha, Saccolabium, Sauropus, Saussurea, Sida, Sonchus, Spiranthes, Stapfiophyton, Styrophyton, Taxus, Thespesia, Thomsonia, Thrixspermum, Tinospora, Typhonium, Vicia, Youngia*
- Affiliation: CUHK
- Location of specimens: A, CUHK, GH, PE, SZ
- Region: CHINA

Y. M. Hu

Hu, Yi Min; 胡一民 ; Hú Yīmín

1958- **First publication: 2015**

- Employment: Anhui Academy of Forestry（安徽省林业科学研究院）
- Research interest: Orchidaceae [S]
- Published taxa: *Bulbophyllum*
- Region: CHINA (Anhui)

Y. F. Hu

Hu, Yong Fu; 胡永富 ; Hú Yǒngfù

First publication: 1994

- Employment: Saihanba Mechanized Forest Farm, Hebei（河北省塞罕坝机械林场）
- Research interest: Primulaceae [S]
- Published taxa: *Primula*
- Region: CHINA (Hebei)

Y. H. Hu

Hu, Yu Hua; 胡玉华 ; Hú Yùhuá; 胡玉華

1936- **First publication: 1980**

- Employment: Henan Institute of Forestry Science（河南省林业科学研究所）
- Research interest: Vitaceae [S]
- Published taxa: *Vitis*
- Region: CHINA (Henan)

Cheng H. Hu, F. G. Yu & Ling Chen

Hu, Cheng Hua, Yu, Fu Gen & Chen, Ling; Hu, Yu Chen; Hu, Cheng Hua; Yu, Fu Gen; Chen, Ling; **胡喻陈 ; Hú Yùchén; 胡成华，喻富根，陈玲**

First publication: 1991

- Employment: Nanjing University（南京大学）
- Research interest: Poaceae [S]
- Published taxa: *Polyanthus*
- Region: CHINA (Hunan)
- Also as: Y. C. Hu
  Cheng H. Hu 1933, F. G. Yu 1965 & Ling Chen 1937 Collectively

J. M. Hu

Hu, Jer Ming; 胡哲明 ; Hú Zhémíng

1968- **First publication: 2014**

- Employment: Institute of Ecology and Evolutionary Biology, Taiwan University（台湾大学生态学与演化生物学研究所）
- Research interest: Urticaceae; Plants of Taiwan [S]
- Published taxa: *Elatostematoides, Elatostema*
- Affiliation: TAI
- Location of specimens: TAI
- Region: CHINA (Taiwan)

Z. B. Hu

Hu, Zhi Bi; 胡之壁 ; Hú Zhībì

1934- **First publication: 1981**

- Employment: Shanghai Institute of Materia Medica, Chinese Academy of Sciences（中国科学院上海药物研究所）
- Research interest: Amaryllidaceae, Crassulaceae [S]
- Published taxa: *Lycoris, Sedum*
- Region: CHINA

Z. H. Hu

Hu, Zhi Hao; 胡志浩 ; Hú Zhìhào

1937- **First publication: 1980**

- Employment: Department of Biology, Yunnan University（云南大学生物系）
- Research interest: Poaceae [S]
- Published taxa: *Arundinella, Chloris, Microchloa, Phacelurus, Urochloa*

- Affiliation: YUKU
- Location of specimens: YUKU
- Region: CHINA (Yunnan)

G. J. Hua

Hua, Guo Jun; 华国军 ; Huà Guójūn

1982- **First publication: 2012**

- Employment: Amateur（业余爱好者）
- Research interest: Gesneriaceae [S]
- Published taxa: *Primulina*
- Region: CHINA (Zhejiang)

X. Q. Hua

Hua, Xi Qi; 华锡奇 ; Huà Xīqí

1954- **First publication: 2013**

- Employment: Zhejiang Academy of Forestry（浙江省林业科学研究院）
- Research interest: Poaceae [S]
- Published taxa: *Phyllostachys*
- Affiliation: ZJFI
- Location of specimens: ZJFI
- Region: CHINA (Zhejiang)

A. Huang

Huang, An; 黄安 ; Huáng Ān

1965- **First publication: 1990**

- Employment: South China Institute of Botany, Chinese Academy of Sciences（中国科学院华南植物研究所）
- Research interest: Piperaceae [S]
- Published taxa: *Piper*
- Location of specimens: IBSC
- Region: CHINA (Hainan)

B. G. Huang

Huang, Bo Gao; 黄伯高 ; Huáng Bógāo

1969- **First publication: 2016**

- Employment: Yachang Wild Orchids National Nature Reserve Administration, Guangxi（广西雅长兰科植物国家级自然保护区管理局）
- Research interest: Orchidaceae [S]
- Published taxa: *Oreorchis*
- Region: CHINA (Guangxi)

C. F. Huang

Huang, Cai Fen; 黄才芬 ; Huáng Cáifēn

1953- **First publication: 1981**

- Employment: Guangxi Forestry Research Institute（广西林业科学研究所）
- Research interest: Poaceae [S]
- Published taxa: *Acidosasa, Indocalamus, Indosasa, Sinocalamus*
- Region: CHINA (Guangxi)

Chang C. Huang

Huang, Chang Chun; 黄长春 ; Huáng Chángchūn

First publication: 1987

- Employment: Guangxi Botanical Garden of Medicinal Plants（广西药用植物园）
- Research interest: Convallariaceae, Gesneriaceae, Rubiaceae [S]
- Published taxa: *Aspidistra, Chirita, Spiradiclis*
- Location of specimens: GXEM, GXMG, GXSP
- Region: CHINA (Guangxi)
- IPNI as: C. C. Huang

C. C. Huang

Huang, Cheng Chiu; Huang, Ch'êng Chiu; Huang, Cheng Chieu; Huang, Cheng Jiu; 黄成就 ; Huáng Chéngjiù

1922-2002 **First publication: 1951**

- Employment: Institute of Botany, Chinese Academy of Sciences; South China Institute of Botany, Chinese Academy of Sciences（中国科学院植物研究所；中国科学院华南植物研究所）
- Research interest: Anacardiaceae, Asparagaceae, Combretaceae, Daphniphyllaceae, Fabaceae, Fagaceae, Iteaceae, Oxalidaceae, Polygonaceae, Rutaceae, Staphyleaceae [S]
- Published taxa: *Atalantia, Castanopsis, Citrus, Clausena, Combretum, Crotalaria, Damnacanthus, Daphniphyllum, Euodia, Fagus, Fortunella, Geranium, Glycosmis, Itea, Lithocarpus, Melicope, Murraya, Ophiopogon, Oxalis, Polygonum, Quercus, Skimmia, Toxicodendron, Turpinia, Zanthoxylum*
- Affiliation: IBSC
- Region: CHINA

C. L. Huang

Huang, Cheng Lin; 黄成林 ; Huáng Chénglín

1962- **First publication: 1996**

- Employment: Faculty of Forest Utilization, Anhui Agricultural University（安徽农业大学森林利用学院）
- Research interest: Poaceae; Plants of Anhui [S]
- Published taxa: *Pleioblastus*
- Affiliation: AAUF
- Location of specimens: AAUF
- Region: CHINA (Anhui)

C. Q. Huang

Huang, Cheng Qian; 黄程前 ; Huáng Chéngqián

1965- **First publication: 2001**

- Employment: Hunan Forest Botanical Garden（湖南省森林植物园）
- Research interest: Hamamelidaceae [S]
- Published taxa: *Loropetalum*
- Region: CHINA (Hunan)

C. Huang

Huang, Chi; 黄驰 ; Huáng Chí

First publication: 1987

- Employment: Department of Pharmacognosy, China Pharmaceutical University（中国药科大学生药教研室）
- Research interest: Ranunculaceae [S]
- Published taxa: *Cimicifuga*
- Region: CHINA (Sichuan)

C. Y. Huang

Huang, Cui Ying; 黄翠莹 ; Huáng Cuìyíng

First publication: 2020

- Employment: School of Life Sciences, Sun Yat-sen University（中山大学生命科学学院）
- Research interest: Gesneriaceae [S]
- Published taxa: *Primulina*
- Region: CHINA (Guangdong)

D. M. Huang

Huang, Da Ming; 黄大明 ; Huáng Dàmíng

First publication: 2017

- Employment: Amateur（业余爱好者）
- Research interest: Orchidaceae [S]
- Published taxa: *Habenaria, Neottia*
- Region: CHINA (Taiwan)

D. Y. Huang

Huang, Da Yong; 黄大勇 ; Huáng Dàyǒng

1968- **First publication: 1995**

- Employment: Guangxi Forestry Research Institute（广西壮族自治区林业科学研究院）
- Research interest: Poaceae [S]
- Published taxa: *Bambusa, Dendrocalamus, Schizostachyum*
- Region: CHINA (Guangxi)

D. Q. Huang

Huang, De Qing; 黄德青 ; Huáng Déqīng

1980- **First publication: 2013**

- Employment: College of Life Sciences, Sichuan University（四川大学生命科学学院）
- Research interest: Amaryllidaceae [S]
- Published taxa: *Allium*
- Region: CHINA

T. S. Hwang

Hwang, Tung Sheng; 黄东昇; Huáng Dōngshēng; 黄東昇

1929- **First publication: 1982**

- Employment: Research Institute of Forestry, Chinese Academy of Forestry（中国林业科学研究院林业研究所）
- Research interest: Salicaceae [S]
- Published taxa: *Populus*
- Region: CHINA (Beijing)

E. F. Huang

Huang, Er Feng; 黄尔峰 ; Huáng Ěrfēng

1981- **First publication: 2020**

- Employment: Guangxi Nanning Roy Garden Co., Ltd.（广西睿玺园林有限公司）
- Research interest: Apocynaceae [S]
- Published taxa: *Hoya*
- Region: CHINA (Yunnan)

G. H. Huang

Huang, Ge Han; 黄戈晗 ; Huáng Gēhán

1992- **First publication: 2017**

- Employment: College of Life Sciences, South China Agricultural University; Suzhou Entry-Exit Inspection and Quarantine Bureau, Jiangsu（华南农业大学生命科学学院；江苏省苏州出入境检验检疫局）
- Research interest: Hydrangeaceae, Primulaceae [S]
- Published taxa: *Ardisia, Dichroa, Stimpsonia*
- Region: CHINA (Guangdong, Hainan)

G. Q. Huang

Huang, Gui Qin; 黄桂芹 ; Huáng Guìqín

First publication: 1987

- Employment: Harbin Institute of Landscape Architecture（哈尔滨市园林研究所）
- Research interest: Ulmaceae [S]
- Published taxa: *Ulmus*
- Region: CHINA (Heilongjiang)

H. L. Huang

Huang, Hua Li; 黄华梨 ; Huáng Huálí

1963- **First publication: 1996**

- Employment: Baishuijiang Natural Reserve Administrative Bureau, Gansu（甘肃白水江自然保护区管理局）
- Research interest: Brassicaceae [S]
- Published taxa: *Cardamine*
- Region: CHINA (Gansu)

H. X. Huang

Huang, Hui Xia; 黄慧霞 ; Huáng Huìxiá

First publication: 2018

- Employment: China National Orchid Conservation Center（全国兰科植物种质资源保护中心）
- Research interest: Orchidaceae [S]
- Published taxa: *Liparis*
- Region: CHINA (Yunnan)

Jia Y. Huang

Huang, Jia Yong; 黄家勇 ; Huáng Jiāyǒng

1962- **First publication: 2010**

- Employment: Research Division, Management

Committee for Nature Reserve of Azalea Forest （贵州百里杜鹃管理委员会科研所）
- Research interest: Ericaceae [S]
- Published taxa: *Rhododendron*
- Region: CHINA (Guizhou)

Jie Huang

Huang, Jie; 黄洁 ; Huáng Jié

First publication: 2013

- Employment: Amateur（业余爱好者）
- Research interest: Gesneriaceae [S]
- Published taxa: *Didymocarpus*
- Region: CHINA (Fujian)

Jie Huang bis

Huang, Jie; 黄洁 ; Huáng Jié

1987- **First publication: 2017**

- Employment: Guangxi Institute of Botany, Chinese Academy of Sciences（广西壮族自治区中国科学院广西植物研究所）
- Research interest: Gesneriaceae [S]
- Published taxa: *Hemiboea*
- Region: CHINA (Guangxi)

Jie Huang tris

Huang, Jie; 黄捷 ; Huáng Jié

1987- **First publication: 2019**

- Employment: The Orchid Conservation & Research Center of Shenzhen, Guangdong（广东省深圳市兰科植物保护研究中心）
- Research interest: Orchidaceae [S]
- Published taxa: *Bletilla*
- Region: CHINA (Guizhou)

J. X. Huang

Huang, Jin Xiang; 黄金祥 ; Huáng Jīnxiáng

1954- **First publication: 1986**

- Employment: Hebei Agricultural University（河北农业大学）
- Research interest: Betulaceae, Euphorbiaceae, Grossulariaceae, Lamiaceae, Ranunculaceae, Rosaceae, Salicaceae [S]
- Published taxa: *Betula, Crataegus, Delphinium, Euphorbia, Populus, Ribes, Schizonepeta*
- Location of specimens: HBFC
- Region: CHINA (Hebei)

J. L. Huang

Huang, Jin Ling; 黄锦岭 ; Huáng Jǐnlǐng

1964- **First publication: 1996**

- Employment: Institute of Botany, Chinese Academy of Sciences; Kunming Institute of Botany, Chinese Academy of Sciences（中国科学院植物研究所；中国科学院昆明植物研究所）
- Research interest: Asparagaceae, Colchicaceae [S]
- Published taxa: *Disporum, Maianthemum, Tupistra*
- Region: CHINA (Yunnan)

J. P. Huang

Huang, Jin Pei; 黄锦培 ; Huáng Jǐnpéi

First publication: 1985

- Employment: Department of Biology, Guangxi Normal University（广西师范大学生物系）
- Research interest: Corylaceae [S]
- Published taxa: *Carpinus*
- Location of specimens: GUN
- Region: CHINA (Guangxi)

J. Y. Huang

Huang, Jing Yi; 黄敬怡 ; Huáng Jìngyí

1963- **First publication: 1993**

- Employment: Nanjing Forestry University（南京林业大学）
- Research interest: Araliaceae, Ericaceae [S]
- Published taxa: *Chengiopanax, Eleutherococcus, Evodiopanax*
- Affiliation: GAFS
- Location of specimens: GAFS
- Region: CHINA

Jiu X. Huang

Huang, Jiu Xiang; 黄久香 ; Huáng Jiǔxiāng

1975- **First publication: 2014**

- Employment: College of Forestry, South China Agricultural University（华南农业大学林学院）
- Research interest: Apocynaceae, Orchidaceae [S]
- Published taxa: *Bulbophyllum, Vanda*
- Affiliation: CANT
- Location of specimens: CANT
- Region: CHINA (Yunnan)

J. H. Huang

Huang, Jun Hua; 黄俊华 ; Huáng Jùnhuá

1973- **First publication: 2001**

- Employment: College of Forestry, Xinjiang Agricultural University（新疆农业大学林学院）
- Research interest: Amaryllidaceae [S]
- Published taxa: *Allium*
- Region: CHINA (Xinjiang)

K. X. Huang

Huang, Kai Xiang; 黄开响 ; Huáng Kāixiǎng

First publication: 1990

- Employment: Yachang State-owend and Affiliated Forest Farm of Guangxi（国营广西壮族自治区直属雅长林场）
- Research interest: Pinaceae [S]
- Published taxa: *Pinus*

• Affiliation: IBK, KUN
• Region: CHINA (Guangxi)

K. F. Huang

Huang, Ke Fu; 黄克福 ; Huáng Kèfú; 黄克福
1936- **First publication: 1982**
• Employment: Fujian Forestry College; Xiamen Botanical Garden（福建林学院；厦门市园林植物园）
• Research interest: Poaceae [S]
• Published taxa: *Dendrocalamus, Gelidocalamus, Indocalamus, Oligostachyum, Pleioblastus, Pseudosasa, Schizostachyum, Shibataea, Yushania*
• Affiliation: FJFC, XMBG
• Location of specimens: FJFC, XMBG
• Region: CHINA (Fujian)

K. M. Wong

Wong, Khoon Meng; 黄昆明 ; Huáng Kūnmíng
1954- **First publication: 1982**
• Employment: Herbarium, Singapore Botanic Gardens, National Parks Board（新加坡植物园植物标本馆）
• Research interest: Actinidiaceae, Annonaceae, Apocynaceae, Araceae, Arecaceae, Cornaceae, Crypteroniaceae, Gentianaceae, Gesneriaceae, Goodeniaceae, Lecythidaceae, Malvaceae, Melastomataceae, Orchidaceae, Poaceae, Rosaceae, Rubiaceae, Selaginellaceae [PS]
• Published taxa: × *Gigantocalamus, Acranthera, Adonidia, Aidia, Alangium, Alocasia, Alstonia, Bambusa, Barringtonia, Bungarimba, Canthium, Canthiumera, Ceriscoides, Chassalia, Crypteronia, Cymbidium, Cyrtophyllum, Dibridsonia, Eriobotrya, Fagerlindia, Fagraea, Gardenia, Gentingia, Gigantochloa, Gynochthodes, Holttumochloa, Hydnophytum, Hypobathrum, Ixora, Jarandersonia, Kinabaluchloa, Kochummenia, Limahlania, Livistona, Maclurochloa, Melastoma, Morinda, Mullerochloa, Neonauclea, Oxyceros, Paraboea, Picrophloeus, Polyalthia, Porterandia, Psydrax, Racemobambos, Rennellia, Ridsdalea, Rothmannia, Ruhooglandia, Saurauia, Scaevola, Schizostachyum, Selaginella, Singaporandia, Soejatmia, Tarenna, Temburongia, Timonius, Urophyllum, Utania, Widjajachloa*
• Region: [ASIA]

L. L. Huang

Huang, Lei Lei; 黄蕾蕾 ; Huáng Lěilěi
1957- **First publication: 1992**
• Employment: Institute of Hubei Traditional Chinese Medicine Company（湖北省中药材公司科学研究所）
• Research interest: Magnoliaceae [S]
• Published taxa: *Magnolia*
• Region: CHINA (Hubei)

Kuo Huang

Kuo Huang, Ling Lung; Huang, Ling Lung, Kuo; Huang, Ling Lung; 黄玲瓏 ; Huáng Línglóng; 郭黄玲瓏，郭黄玲珑，黄玲珑
1955- **First publication: 2005**
• Employment: Institute of Ecology and Evolutionary Biology, Taiwan University（台湾大学生态学与演化生物学研究所）
• Research interest: Orchidaceae; Plant Anatomy [S]
• Published taxa: *Bulbophyllum, Dendrobium, Eulophia, Flickingeria, Saccolabiopsis, Tropidia*
• Affiliation: TAI
• Region: CHINA (Taiwan)

Lu Q. Huang

Huang, Lu Qi; Huang, Lu Gi; 黄璐琦 ; Huáng Lùqí
1968- **First publication: 1997**
• Employment: Institute of Chinese Materia Medica, China Academy of Chinese Medical Sciences（中国中医研究院中药研究所）
• Research interest: Apiaceae, Crassulaceae, Cucurbitaceae, Liliaceae, Orchidaceae, Papaveraceae, Phytolaccaceae, Ranunculaceae, Solanaceae [S]
• Published taxa: *Amana, Clematis, Corydalis, Herminium, Hsenhsua, Lycium, Peucedanum, Phytolacca, Platanthera, Sedum, Shizhenia, Trichosanthes*
• Affiliation: CMMI
• Location of specimens: CMMI
• Region: CHINA
• Also as: L. Q. Huang

M. S. Huang

Huang, Mao Sien; Huang, Mao Xian; 黄茂先 ; Huáng Màoxiān; 黄茂先
1932- **First publication: 1976**
• Employment: South China Institute of Botany, Chinese Academy of Sciences（中国科学院华南植物研究所）
• Research interest: Cleomaceae, Meliaceae, Rubiaceae [S]
• Published taxa: *Morinda*
• Affiliation: IBSC
• Region: CHINA (Guangdong)

M. Z. Huang

Huang, Ming Zhong; 黄明忠 ; Huáng Míngzhōng
1983- **First publication: 2012**
• Employment: Tropical Crops Genetic Resources Institute, Chinese Academy of Tropical Agricultural Sciences（中国热带农业科学院热带作物品种资源研

究所）
- Research interest: Orchidaceae [S]
- Published taxa: *Cleisostoma, Cymbidium, Gastrochilus, Panisea*
- Affiliation: ATCH
- Location of specimens: ATCH
- Region: CHINA (Hainan)

P. C. Huang

Huang, Peng Cheng; 黄鹏成；Huáng Péngchéng; 黃鵬成
1932- **First publication: 1980**
- Employment: Nanjing Forestry University（南京林业大学）
- Research interest: Bignoniaceae, Ericaceae, Fabaceae, Magnoliaceae, Rosaceae, Theaceae [S]
- Published taxa: *Albizia, Camellia, Catalpa, Enkianthus, Gymnocladus, Pyrus, Rhaphiolepis, Sorbus*
- Affiliation: NF
- Region: CHINA

P. H. Huang

Huang, Pu Hwa; Huang, Pu Hua; **黄普华；Huáng Pǔhuá; 黃普華**
1932- **First publication: 1978**
- Employment: Northeast Forestry Institute; Northeast Forestry University（东北林学院；东北林业大学）
- Research interest: Adoxaceae, Asteraceae, Fabaceae, Lauraceae, Polemoniaceae, Primulaceae, Rosaceae, Schisandraceae, Ulmaceae; Woody Plants [S]
- Published taxa: *Actinodaphne, Alysicarpus, Christia, Desmodium, Erigeron, Geum, Lespedeza, Litsea, Neolitsea, Oxytropis, Podocarpium, Polemonium, Primula, Sambucus, Schisandra, Tadehagi, Ulmus, Uraria, Urariopsis*
- Affiliation: NEFI
- Location of specimens: NEFI
- Region: CHINA

Q. Huang

Huang, Quan; 黄全；Huáng Quán; 黃全
1929-? **First publication: 1985**
- Employment: Research Institute of Tropical Forestry, Chinese Academy of Forestry（中国林业科学研究院热带林业研究所）
- Research interest: Passifloraceae [S]
- Published taxa: *Passiflora*
- Region: CHINA (Hainan)

R. H. Huang

Huang, Ren Huang; 黄仁煌；Huáng Rénhuáng; 黃仁煌
1937- **First publication: 1982**
- Employment: Wuhan Institute of Botany, Chinese Academy of Sciences（中国科学院武汉植物研究所）
- Research interest: Actinidiaceae [S]
- Published taxa: *Actinidia*
- Location of specimens: HIB
- Region: CHINA (Hubei)

R. F. Huang

Huang, Rong Fu; Huang, Jong Fu; Huang, Yong Fu; **黄荣福；Huáng Róngfú; 黃榮福**
1940- **First publication: 1985**
- Employment: Northwest Plateau Institute of Biology, Chinese Academy of Sciences（中国科学院西北高原生物研究所）
- Research interest: Adoxaceae, Amaranthaceae, Brassicaceae, Caprifoliaceae, Caryophyllaceae, Cyperaceae, Fabaceae, Gentianaceae, Primulaceae [S]
- Published taxa: *Androsace, Arabidopsis, Arenaria, Astragalus, Carex, Christolea, Corispermum, Gentiana, Kobresia, Leycesteria, Lonicera, Neotorularia, Rorippa, Sinadoxa, Solms-laubachia, Torularia, Viburnum*
- Affiliation: HNWP
- Location of specimens: HNWP
- Region: CHINA
- Also as: J. F. Huang; Y. F. Huang

R. Z. Huang

Huang, Rui Zhou; 黄锐洲；Huáng Ruìzhōu
1994- **First publication: 2020**
- Employment: College of Forestry and Landscape Architecture, South China Agricultural University（华南农业大学林学与风景园林学院）
- Research interest: Primulaceae [S]
- Published taxa: *Lysimachia*
- Region: CHINA (Guangdong)

Shao F. Huang

Huang, Shao Fu; 黄少甫；Huáng Shàofǔ
1938-2007 **First publication: 1989**
- Employment: Research Institute of Subtropical Forestry, Chinese Academy of Forestry（中国林业科学研究院亚热带林业研究所）
- Research interest: Ericaceae [S]
- Published taxa: *Vaccinium*
- Region: CHINA (Jiangxi)
- IPNI as: S. F. Huang

S. Huang

Huang, Sheng; 黄升；Huáng Shēng
1972- **First publication: 2015**
- Employment: College of Forestry and Horticulture, Hubei University for Nationalities（湖北民族学院林

学与园艺学院)
- Research interest: Zingiberaceae [S]
- Published taxa: *Zingiber*
- Location of specimens: ENS
- Region: CHINA (Hubei)

S. H. Hwang

Hwang, Shi Hua; 黄世华; Huáng Shìhuá; 黃世華
1937- **First publication: 1991**
- Employment: Anhui College of Traditional Chinese Medicine(安徽中医学院)
- Research interest: Aristolochiaceae [S]
- Published taxa: *Asarum*
- Location of specimens: ACM
- Region: CHINA (Anhui)

S. L. Huang

Huang, Shi Lian; 黄石连; Huáng Shílián
1989- **First publication: 2014**
- Employment: College of Life Sciences, Guangxi Normal University; Guangxi Institute of Botany, Chinese Academy of Sciences(广西师范大学生命科学学院;广西壮族自治区中国科学院广西植物研究所)
- Research interest: Gesneriaceae [S]
- Published taxa: *Primulina*
- Region: CHINA (Guangxi)

S. X. Huang

Huang, Shi Xun; 黄仕训; Huáng Shìxùn
1966- **First publication: 2010**
- Employment: Guangxi Institute of Botany, Chinese Academy of Sciences(广西壮族自治区中国科学院广西植物研究所)
- Research interest: Gesneriaceae [S]
- Published taxa: *Chirita, Primulina*
- Region: CHINA (Guangxi)

S. M. Hwang

Hwang, Shu Mei; Huang, Shu Mei; 黄淑美; Huáng Shūměi; 黃淑美
1933-2019 **First publication: 1975**
- Employment: South China Institute of Botany, Chinese Academy of Sciences(中国科学院华南植物研究所)
- Research interest: Aristolochiaceae, Cyperaceae, Euphorbiaceae, Hydrangeaceae, Passifloraceae, Styracaceae [S]
- Published taxa: *Aristolochia, Asarum, Carex, Cyperus, Deutzia, Dichroa, Fimbristylis, Huodendron, Mallotus, Mariscus, Passiflora, Philadelphus, Pileostegia, Pycreus, Scirpus, Speranskia, Styrax*
- Affiliation: IBSC
- Location of specimens: IBSC
- Region: CHINA
- Also as: S. M. Huang

S. C. Huang

Huang, Shu Chung; Huang, Shu Qiong; 黄蜀琼; Huáng Shǔqióng; 黃蜀瓊
1921-2000 **First publication: 1974**
- Employment: Kunming Institute of Botany, Chinese Academy of Sciences(中国科学院昆明植物研究所)
- Research interest: Aquifoliaceae, Combretaceae, Iteaceae, Lamiaceae, Pittosporaceae, Solanaceae, Thymelaeaceae [S]
- Published taxa: *Aquilaria, Combretum, Daphne, Edgeworthia, Elsholtzia, Ilex, Itea, Lycianthes, Pittosporum, Rhamnoneuron, Solanum, Stellera, Vitex, Wikstroemia*
- Affiliation: KUN
- Region: CHINA (Yunnan)

S. H. Huang

Huang, Shu Hua; Huang, Su Hua; 黄素华; Huáng Sùhuá; 黃素華
1938- **First publication: 1979**
- Employment: Department of Biology, Yunnan University(云南大学生物系)
- Research interest: Balsaminaceae, Begoniaceae, Campanulaceae, Convolvulaceae, Ericaceae, Fabaceae, Lardizabalaceae, Violaceae [S]
- Published taxa: *Agapetes, Aniseia, Argyreia, Begonia, Codonopsis, Cuscuta, Cyananthus, Evolvulus, Holboellia, Impatiens, Ipomoea, Jacquemontia, Lyonia, Porana, Rhododendron, Stauntonia, Viola*
- Affiliation: YUKU
- Location of specimens: YUKU
- Region: CHINA (Sichuan, Xizang, Yunnan)

W. L. Huang

Huang, Wei Lian; 黄威廉; Huáng Wēilián; 黃威廉
1925- **First publication: 1984**
- Employment: Department of Geography, Guiyang Normal College(贵阳师范学院地理系)
- Research interest: Melastomataceae, Myrsinaceae, Pinaceae, Sapindaceae [S]
- Published taxa: *Abies*
- Affiliation: GNUG
- Location of specimens: GNUG
- Region: CHINA (Guizhou)

W. J. Huang

Huang, Wei Jie; 黄瑋傑; Huáng Wěijié; 黄玮杰
First publication: 2020
- Employment: Taiwan Forestry Research Institute, Council of Agriculture, "Executive Yuan"("行政院"农业委员会林业试验所)
- Research interest: Asteraceae [S]
- Published taxa: *Aster*

- Region: CHINA (Taiwan)

W. C. Huang

Huang, Wei Chang; 黄卫昌 ; Huáng Wèichāng
1971- **First publication: 2013**
- Employment: Shanghai Chenshan Botanical Garden (上海辰山植物园)
- Research interest: Orchidaceae [S]
- Published taxa: *Gastrodia, Malleola, Polystachya, Robiquetia*
- Region: [ASIA]

W. X. Huang

Huang, Wen Xian; 黄文先 ; Huáng Wénxiān
1954- **First publication: 1990**
- Employment: Anji Forestry Bureau, Zhejiang (浙江省安吉县林业局)
- Research interest: Poaceae [S]
- Published taxa: *Phyllostachys*
- Region: CHINA (Zhejiang)

X. T. Huang

Huang, Xiang Tong; 黄祥童 ; Huáng Xiángtóng
1963- **First publication: 1997**
- Employment: Changbai Mountain National Nature Reserve Administration, Jilin (吉林长白山国家级自然保护区管理局)
- Research interest: Amaryllidaceae, Apiaceae, Brassicaceae, Caprifoliaceae, Iridaceae, Rosaceae, Typhaceae [S]
- Published taxa: *Allium*
- Affiliation: ANTU
- Location of specimens: ANTU
- Region: CHINA (Jilin)

S. Z. Huang

Huang, Se Zei; Huang, Xie Cai; **黄燮才 ; Huáng Xiècái; 黄燮才**
1936- **First publication: 1979**
- Employment: Guangxi Institute for Drug Control (广西药品检验所)
- Research interest: Acanthaceae, Annonaceae, Apocynaceae, Asparagaceae, Euphorbiaceae, Fabaceae, Gesneriaceae, Hernandiaceae, Rosaceae, Theaceae; Medicinal Plants [S]
- Published taxa: *Aspidistra, Camellia, Chirita, Croton, Eranthemum, Hoya, Illigera, Malus, Orophea, Oxystelma, Rauvolfia, Sophora, Strobilanthes*
- Affiliation: GXDC, GXMG
- Location of specimens: GXDC, GXMG
- Region: CHINA (Guangxi)
- Also as: X. C. Huang

X. Y. Huang

Huang, Xin Yi; 黄歆怡 ; Huáng Xīnyí
1988- **First publication: 2015**
- Employment: Guangxi Institute of Botany, Chinese Academy of Sciences; College of Life Sciences, Guangxi Normal University (广西壮族自治区中国科学院广西植物研究所；广西师范大学生命科学学院)
- Research interest: Orchidaceae [S]
- Published taxa: *Gastrodia*
- Region: CHINA (Guangxi)

S. F. Huang

Huang, Shing Fan; Huang, Xing Fan; **黄星凡 ; Huáng Xīngfán; 黄星凡**
First publication: 1987
- Employment: Department of Botany, Taiwan University (台湾大学植物学系)
- Research interest: Aristolochiaceae, Brassicaceae, Ericaceae, Euphorbiaceae, Fabaceae, Melastomataceae, Menispermaceae, Oxalidaceae, Rubiaceae [BS]
- Published taxa: *Acalypha, Arabis, Asarum, Bredia, Cyclea, Hedyotis, Ormosia, Oxalis, Sarcopyramis, Strongylodon, Vaccinium*
- Region: CHINA (Taiwan)

X. L. Huang

Huang, Xiu Lan; 黄秀兰 ; Huáng Xiùlán; 黄秀蘭
1932- **First publication: 1981**
- Employment: Shanghai Institute of Materia Medica, Chinese Academy of Sciences (中国科学院上海药物研究所)
- Research interest: Amaryllidaceae, Asteraceae, Lamiaceae [S]
- Published taxa: *Lycoris, Salvia*
- Affiliation: SHMI
- Location of specimens: SHMI
- Region: CHINA

Xue Y. Huang

Huang, Xue Yan; 黄雪彦 ; Huáng Xuěyàn
1978- **First publication: 2018**
- Employment: Guangxi Botanical Garden of Medicinal Plants (广西药用植物园)
- Research interest: Asparagaceae [S]
- Published taxa: *Aspidistra*
- Location of specimens: GXMG
- Region: [ASIA]
- IPNI as: X. Y. Huang

Yan B. Huang

Huang, Yan Bo; 黄艳波 ; Huáng Yànbō
1989- **First publication: 2019**
- Employment: Shanghai Chenshan Botanical Garden

（上海辰山植物园）
- Research interest: Lamiaceae [S]
- Published taxa: *Salvia*
- Region: CHINA (Hunan)
- IPNI as: Y. B. Huang

Y. L. Huang

Huang, Ye Lin; Huang, Yelin; **黄椰林；Huáng Yēlín**

1974- **First publication: 2003**

- Employment: School of Life Sciences, Sun Yat-sen University（中山大学生命科学学院）
- Research interest: Styracaceae [S]
- Published taxa: *Styrax*
- Region: CHINA

Y. Z. Huang

Huang, Yi Zhong; 黄以钟；Huáng Yǐzhōng

1965- **First publication: 1995**

- Employment: Department of Biology, Fujian Normal University（福建师范大学生物系）
- Research interest: Cyperaceae [S]
- Published taxa: *Carex*
- Region: CHINA (Fujian)

Yi Jun Huang

Huang, Yi Jun; 黄义钧；Huáng Yìjūn

1985- **First publication: 2018**

- Employment: Fairy Lake Botanical Garden, Shenzhen & Chinese Academy of Sciences（深圳市中国科学院仙湖植物园）
- Research interest: Araceae; Plants of S. China [S]
- Published taxa: *Arisaema*
- Affiliation: SZG
- Location of specimens: SZG
- Region: CHINA (Guangdong)

Yi Huang

Huang, Yi; 黄易；Huáng Yì

1990- **First publication: 2019**

- Employment: Guangxi Institute of Botany, Chinese Academy of Sciences（广西壮族自治区中国科学院广西植物研究所）
- Research interest: Gesneriaceae [S]
- Published taxa: *Primulina*
- Region: CHINA (Guangxi)

Yi L. Huang

Huang, Yi Lang; 黄逸朗；Huáng Yìlǎng

1993- **First publication: 2015**

- Employment: College of Forestry and Landscape Architecture, South China Agricultural University; The Orchid Conservation & Research Center of Shenzhen, Guangdong（华南农业大学林学与风景园林学院；广东省深圳市兰科植物保护研究中心）
- Research interest: Orchidaceae [S]
- Published taxa: *Liparis*
- Region: CHINA (Yunnan)
- IPNI as: Y. L. Huang

Y. Huang

Huang, Yi; 黄毅；Huáng Yì

1958- **First publication: 1990**

- Employment: Yunnan Agricultural University（云南农业大学）
- Research interest: Theaceae [S]
- Published taxa: *Camellia*
- Region: CHINA (Yunnan)

Y. Q. Huang

Huang, Yin Qin; 黄应钦；Huáng Yīngqīn

1955- **First publication: 1989**

- Employment: Guangxi Forestry Research Institute（广西林业科学研究所）
- Research interest: Sapindaceae; Scientific Illustrator [S]
- Published taxa: *Acer*
- Affiliation: GXFI
- Location of specimens: GXFI
- Region: CHINA (Guangxi)

Y. C. Huang

Huang, Yong Chin; Huang, Yong Qin; **黄咏琴；Huáng Yǒngqín**

First publication: 1965

- Employment: Kunming Branch Institute, Institute of Botany, Chinese Academy of Sciences; Kunming Institute of Botany, Chinese Academy of Sciences（中国科学院植物研究所昆明分所；中国科学院昆明植物研究所）
- Research interest: Lamiaceae, Melastomataceae, Salicaceae [S]
- Published taxa: *Blastus, Casearia, Coleus, Fordiophyton, Lophanthus, Melissa, Nepeta, Plectranthus, Pogostemon, Salvia, Sporoxeia, Thymus*
- Affiliation: KUN
- Region: CHINA (Yunnan)

Yong Huang

Huang, Yong; 黄勇；Huáng Yǒng

1964- **First publication: 1997**

- Employment: Department of Biology, Liaocheng Normal College（聊城师范学院生物系）
- Research interest: Plumbaginaceae [S]
- Published taxa: *Limonium*
- Region: CHINA (Shandong)
- IPNI as: Y. Huang

Yu F. Huang

Huang, Yu Fang; 黄于芳 ; Huáng Yúfāng; 黄于芳
First publication: 2019

- Employment: Department of Biological Sciences, Sun Yat-sen University,Taiwan（中山大学生物科学系）
- Research interest: Dryopteridaceae [P]
- Published taxa: *Bolbitis*
- Region: CHINA (Taiwan)
- IPNI as: Y. F. Huang

Y. S. Huang

Huang, Yu Song; 黄俞淞 ; Huáng Yúsōng
1983- **First publication: 2010**

- Employment: Guangxi Institute of Botany, Chinese Academy of Sciences; College of Life Sciences, Guangxi Normal University（广西壮族自治区中国科学院广西植物研究所；广西师范大学生命科学学院）
- Research interest: Acanthaceae, Aristolochiaceae, Asparagaceae, Capparaceae, Ebenaceae, Gesneriaceae, Lauraceae, Malvaceae, Orchidaceae, Ranunculaceae [S]
- Published taxa: *Aristolochia, Aspidistra, Calanthe, Capparis, Chirita, Diospyros, Firmiana, Hemiboea, Justicia, Liparis, Litsea, Primulina, Semiaquilegia*
- Affiliation: GXMG, IBK
- Location of specimens: GXMG, IBK
- Region: CHINA (Guangxi)

Y. B. Huang

Huang, Yu Bi; 黄玉碧 ; Huáng Yùbì
1963- **First publication: 2017**

- Employment: Maize Research Institute, Sichuan Agricultural University（四川农业大学玉米研究所）
- Research interest: Orchidaceae [S]
- Published taxa: *Dendrobium*
- Region: CHINA (Yunnan)

Yu L. Huang

Huang, Yu Ling; 黄玉玲 ; Huáng Yùlíng
1987- **First publication: 2017**

- Employment: Kunming Institute of Botany, Chinese Academy of Sciences（中国科学院昆明植物研究所）
- Research interest: Melanthiaceae [S]
- Published taxa: *Paris*
- Region: CHINA (Yunnan)

Y. Y. Huang

Huang, Yu Yuan; 黄玉源 ; Huáng Yùyuán
1959- **First publication: 1996**

- Employment: Guangxi Agricultural University; School of Life Sciences, Sun Yat-sen University（广西农业大学；中山大学生命科学学院）
- Research interest: Arthropteridaceae, Cycadaceae [PS]
- Published taxa: *Arthropteris, Cycas*
- Location of specimens: GAUA
- Region: CHINA
- IPNI as: Y. Yuan Huang

Yu Q. Huang

Huang, Yu Qian; 黄钰倩 ; Huáng Yùqiàn
1991- **First publication: 2019**

- Employment: College of Life Sciences, Wuhan University（武汉大学生命科学学院）
- Research interest: Isoetaceae [P]
- Published taxa: *Isoetes*
- Region: CHINA (Yunnan)

Yuan Huang

Huang, Yuan; 黄媛 ; Huáng Yuán
1978- **First publication: 2019**

- Employment: School of Life Science, Yunnan Normal University（云南师范大学生命科学学院）
- Research interest: Primulaceae [S]
- Published taxa: *Primula*
- Region: CHINA (Yunnan)

Y. Feng Huang

Huang, Yun Feng; 黄云峰 ; Huáng Yúnfēng
1980- **First publication: 2011**

- Employment: Guangxi Institute of Chinese Medicine & Pharmaceutical Science（广西中医药研究院）
- Research interest: Aquifoliaceae, Asparagaceae, Colchicaceae, Dryopteridaceae, Melanthiaceae, Orchidaceae, Primulaceae, Rubiaceae; Medicinal Plants [PS]
- Published taxa: *Anoectochilus, Aspidistra, Bolbitis, Chamaelirium, Chionographis, Disporum, Ilex, Lysimachia, Odontochilus, Ophiorrhiza*
- Affiliation: GXMI
- Location of specimens: GXMG, GXMI
- Region: CHINA (Guangxi)
- IPNI as: Y. F. Huang

Y. H. Huang

Huang, Yun Huei; Huang, Yun Hui; 黄云晖 ; Huáng Yúnhuī; 黄雲暉
1936- **First publication: 1975**

- Employment: Department of Biology, Sun Yat-sen University（中山大学生物系）
- Research interest: Apiaceae, Crassulaceae, Fabaceae, Primulaceae, Ranunculaceae; Plants of N. E. China [S]
- Published taxa: *Aconitum, Actaea, Albizia, Androsace, Aquilegia, Bupleurum, Caltha, Clematis, Halerpestes, Kitagawia, Ostericum, Peucedanum, Phedimus, Pulsatilla, Ranunculus, Sedum*

- Affiliation: SYS
- Region: CHINA

T. C. Huang

Huang, Tseng Chieng; Huang, Tseng Chuan; Huang, Zeng Quan; 黄增泉 ; Huáng Zēngquán; 黃增泉

1931- **First publication: 1960**

- Employment: Department of Botany, Taiwan University（台湾大学植物学系）
- Research interest: Acanthaceae, Araceae, Aristolochiaceae, Balsaminaceae, Blechnaceae, Coriariaceae, Daphniphyllaceae, Diapensiaceae, Dioscoreaceae, Dryopteridaceae, Elaeagnaceae, Euphorbiaceae, Fabaceae, Hymenophyllaceae, Lamiaceae, Melanthiaceae, Melastomataceae, Menispermaceae, Orobanchaceae, Oxalidaceae, Ranunculaceae, Salicaceae, Theaceae, Violaceae, Zygophyllaceae; Plants of Taiwan. [MPS]
- Published taxa: *Acalypha, Aconitum, Arisaema, Asarum, Bredia, Camellia, Cephalomanes, Clematis, Clinopodium, Coriaria, Cyclea, Daiswa, Daphniphyllum, Dioscorea, Diploblechnum, Egenolfia, Elaeagnus, Entada, Euphrasia, Goldfussia, Hymenophyllum, Impatiens, Indigofera, Justicia, Ormosia, Oxalis, Parachampionella, Paraphlomis, Paris, Salix, Salvia, Sarcopyramis, Schismatoglottis, Scutellaria, Semnostachya, Shortia, Teucrium, Triaenacanthus, Tribulus, Vigna, Viola*
- Affiliation: TAI
- Location of specimens: TAI
- Region: CHINA (Taiwan)

Z. R. Huang

Huang, Zeng Ren; 黄增任 ; Huáng Zēngrèn; 黃增任

1936-2012 **First publication: 1990**

- Employment: Guangxi School of Pharmacy（广西药科学校）
- Research interest: Rosaceae; Medicinal Plants [S]
- Published taxa: *Rosa*
- Affiliation: GXSP
- Location of specimens: GXSP
- Region: CHINA (Guangxi)

Z. P. Huang

Huang, Zhang Ping; 黄章平 ; Huáng Zhāngpíng

First publication: 2020

- Employment: Guangxi Institute of Botany, Chinese Academy of Sciences（广西壮族自治区中国科学院广西植物研究所）
- Research interest: Gesneriaceae [S]
- Published taxa: *Hemiboea*
- Region: CHINA (Guangxi)

Z. Y. Huang

Huang, Zhao Yu; 黄肇宇 ; Huáng Zhàoyǔ

1959- **First publication: 2005**

- Employment: Yulin Normal University, Guangxi（广西玉林师范学院）
- Research interest: Lamiaceae, Malvaceae [S]
- Published taxa: *Grewia, Vitex*
- Region: CHINA (Guangxi)

Z. S. Huang

Huang, Zhi Sen; 黄志森 ; Huáng Zhìsēn

1966- **First publication: 2008**

- Employment: Administrative Bureau of Daiyunshan National Nature Reserve, Fujian（福建省戴云山国家级自然保护区管理局）
- Research interest: Celastraceae [S]
- Published taxa: *Microtropis*
- Region: CHINA (Fujian)

Wong Sui

Wong Sui, Tak Ping; 黄蕭德萍 ; Huáng-Xiāo Dépíng; 黃蕭德萍

First publication: 1990

- Employment: Hong Kong Herbarium, Agriculture and Fisheries Department（香港渔农处香港植物标本室）
- Research interest: Aristolochiaceae [S]
- Published taxa: *Asarum*
- Affiliation: HK
- Region: CHINA (Hong Kong)

C. M. Hui

Hui, Chao Mao; 辉朝茂 ; Huī Cháomào

1962- **First publication: 1992**

- Employment: Southwest Forestry College（西南林学院）
- Research interest: Poaceae [S]
- Published taxa: *Cephalostachyum, Dendrocalamus, Fargesia, Melocalamus*
- Affiliation: SWFC
- Location of specimens: SWFC
- Region: CHINA

S. H. Hao

Hao, Shu Hwa; Huo, Shu Hwa; Huo, Shu Hua; 火树华 ; Huǒ Shùhuá; 火樹華

1931-2002 **First publication: 1981**

- Employment: Beijing Forestry College（北京林学院）
- Research interest: Pinaceae; Woody Plants [S]
- Published taxa: *Keteleeria*
- Affiliation: BJFC
- Location of specimens: BJFC
- Region: CHINA (Yunnan)

J. X. Ji

Ji, Jin Xiang; 吉金祥 ; Jí Jīnxiáng
1942- **First publication: 1989**
- Employment: Changchun College of Tridational Chinese Medicine（长春中医学院）
- Research interest: Ranunculaceae [S]
- Published taxa: *Pulsatilla*
- Location of specimens: CCM
- Region: CHINA (Jilin)

Z. H. Tsi

Tsi, Zhan Huo; Ji, Zhan He; 吉占和 ; Jí Zhànhé; 吉佔和
1937-2001 **First publication: 1980**
- Employment: Institute of Botany, Chinese Academy of Sciences（中国科学院植物研究所）
- Research interest: Liliaceae, Melanthiaceae, Orchidaceae, Rosaceae, Sabiaceae [S]
- Published taxa: *Anoectochilus, Bulbophyllum, Calanthe, Callostylis, Ceratostylis, Chiloschista, Cleisostoma, Coelogyne, Dendrobium, Epigeneium, Eria, Flickingeria, Gastrochilus, Gastrodia, Holcoglossum, Hygrochilus, Luisia, Nothodoritis, Oberonia, Ornithochilus, Panisea, Paphiopedilum, Phaius, Pholidota, Pleione, Rubus, Sabia, Sarcoglyphis, Sunipia, Tainia, Veratrum*
- Affiliation: PE
- Location of specimens: PE
- Region: CHINA

G. Q. Ji

Ji, Guo Qin; 计国琴 ; Jì Guóqín; 計國琴
1948- **First publication: 1985**
- Employment: Institute of Hubei Traditional Chinese Medicine Company（湖北省中药材公司科学研究所）
- Research interest: Liliaceae [S]
- Published taxa: *Fritillaria*
- Region: CHINA (Hubei)

W. T. Ji

Ji, Wei Tao; 纪伟涛 ; Jǐ Wěitāo
1963- **First publication: 1991**
- Employment: Wuyishan Nature Reserve Management Office, Jiangxi（江西省武夷山自然保护区管理处）
- Research interest: Rosaceae [S]
- Published taxa: *Rubus*
- Region: CHINA (Jiangxi)

Y. H. Ji

Ji, Yun Heng; 纪运恒 ; Jǐ Yùnhéng
1972- **First publication: 2004**
- Employment: Kunming Institute of Botany, Chinese Academy of Sciences（中国科学院昆明植物研究所）
- Research interest: Araceae, Hydrocharitaceae, Melanthiaceae, Trilliaceae [S]
- Published taxa: *Arisaema, Paris*
- Affiliation: KUN
- Location of specimens: KUN
- Region: CHINA (Yunnan)

C. F. Ji

Ji, Chun Feng; 季春峰 ; Jì Chūnfēng
1977- **First publication: 2001**
- Employment: College of Forest Resources and Environment, Nanjing Forestry University（南京林业大学森林资源与环境学院）
- Research interest: Araliaceae, Lauraceae, Oleaceae [S]
- Published taxa: *Cinnamomum, Macropanax, Osmanthus, Pentapanax, Phoebe*
- Affiliation: JXAU
- Location of specimens: JXAU
- Region: CHINA

M. C. Ji

Ji, Meng Cheng; 季梦成 ; Jì Mèngchéng
1966- **First publication: 2005**
- Employment: School of Landscape Architecture, Zhejiang A&F University（浙江农林大学园林学院）
- Research interest: Lythraceae [BS]
- Published taxa: *Lagerstroemia*
- Region: CHINA (Yunnan)

L. C. Chia

Chia, Liang Chi; Chia, Liang Zhi; 贾良智 ; Jiǎ Liángzhì; 賈良智
1921-2004 **First publication: 1952**
- Employment: South China Institute of Botany, Chinese Academy of Sciences（中国科学院华南植物研究所）
- Research interest: Oleaceae, Poaceae [S]
- Published taxa: *Acroceras, Arundinaria, Bambusa, Dendrocalamus, Digitaria, Eragrostis, Garnotia, Jasminum, Leptocanna, Monocladus, Myxopyrum, Olea, Oplismenus, Pennisetum, Pseudoraphis*
- Affiliation: IBSC

- Location of specimens: CUHK, IBSC
- Region: CHINA

M. R. Jia

Jia, Min Ru; 贾敏如 ; Jiǎ Mǐnrú; 賈敏如

1934- **First publication: 1992**

- Employment: Chengdu College of Traditional Chinese Medicine（成都中医学院）
- Research interest: Magnoliaceae, Ranunculaceae [S]
- Published taxa: *Aconitum, Cimicifuga, Magnolia*
- Affiliation: CDCM
- Location of specimens: CDCM
- Region: CHINA (Sichuan)

C. P. Tsien

Tsien, Cho Po; Jien, Zhuo Po; Jian, Zhuo Po; 简焯坡 ; Jiǎn Zhuōpō; 簡焯坡

1916-2003 **First publication: 1963**

- Employment: Institute of Botany, Chinese Academy of Sciences（中国科学院植物研究所）
- Research interest: Amaranthaceae, Aristolochiaceae, Celastraceae, Chenopodiaceae, Oleaceae, Saxifragaceae [S]
- Published taxa: *Aristolochia, Ceratoides, Corispermum, Cornulaca, Parnassia, Syringa*
- Affiliation: PE
- Location of specimens: HGAS, PE
- Region: CHINA
- Also as: Z. P. Jien

S. G. Jian

Jian, Shu Guang; 简曙光 ; Jiǎn Shǔguāng

1972- **First publication: 2007**

- Employment: South China Botanical Garden, Chinese Academy of Sciences（中国科学院华南植物园）
- Research interest: Magnoliaceae [S]
- Published taxa: *Michelia*
- Region: CHINA (Yunnan)

P. Y. Jiang

Jiang, Po Yi; Chiang, Po Yi; 江柏毅 ; Jiāng Bǎiyì

First publication: 2011

- Employment: Department of Life Sciences, University of Tainan（台南大学生命科学系）
- Research interest: Burmanniaceae [S]
- Published taxa: *Thismia*
- Region: CHINA (Taiwan)

G. B. Jiang

Jiang, Guo Bin; 江国彬 ; Jiāng Guóbīn

1995- **First publication: 2019**

- Employment: South China Institute of Botany, Chinese Academy of Sciences（中国科学院华南植物园）
- Research interest: Rubiaceae [S]
- Published taxa: *Hedyotis*
- Region: CHINA (Hainan)

H. E. Chiang

Chiang, Hoai En; 江懷恩 ; Jiāng Huái'ēn; 江怀恩

First publication: 1989

- Employment: Institute of Forestry, Taiwan University（台湾大学森林学研究所）
- Research interest: Aquifoliaceae [S]
- Published taxa: *Ilex*
- Region: CHINA (Taiwan)

M. T. Jiang

Jiang, Ming Tao; 江鸣涛 ; Jiāng Míngtāo

1990- **First publication: 2018**

- Employment: College of Landscape Architecture, Fujian Agriculture and Forestry University; The Orchid Conservation & Research Center of Shenzhen, Guangdong（福建农林大学园林学院；广东省深圳市兰科植物保护研究中心）
- Research interest: Orchidaceae [S]
- Published taxa: *Pleione*
- Region: CHINA (Zhejiang)

Nan Jiang

Jiang, Nan; 江南 ; Jiāng Nán

1981- **First publication: 2015**

- Employment: Institute of Subtropical Crops, Zhejiang Academy of Agricultural Sciences（浙江省农业科学院亚热带作物研究所）
- Research interest: Ranunculaceae [S]
- Published taxa: *Anemone*
- Region: CHINA

N. G. Jiang

Jiang, Ning Gong; 江宁拱 ; Jiāng Nínggǒng; 江寧拱

1936- **First publication: 1983**

- Employment: Department of Horticulture, Southwest Agricultural College（西南农学院园艺系）
- Research interest: Rosaceae [S]
- Published taxa: *Malus*
- Affiliation: SWAU
- Region: CHINA (Sichuan)

X. P. Jiang

Jiang, Xian Pu; Jiang, Xian Fu; 江先甫 ; Jiāng Xiānfǔ

1932- **First publication: 1984**

- Employment: Department of Biology, Beijing Normal University（北京师范大学生物系）
- Research interest: Fabaceae [S]
- Published taxa: *Melissitus*
- Affiliation: LYAC
- Location of specimens: LYAC

• Region: CHINA (Beijing)

Xin Jiang

Jiang, Xin; 江心 ; Jiāng Xīn

1931-2013 **First publication: 1984**

• Employment: Department of Forestry, Sichuan Agricultural College（四川农学院林学系）
• Research interest: Poaceae [S]
• Published taxa: *Dendrocalamus, Lingnania, Phyllostachys*
• Region: CHINA (Sichuan)
• IPNI as: X. Jiang

Z. P. Jiang

Jiang, Ze Ping; 江泽平 ; Jiāng Zépíng

1966- **First publication: 1997**

• Employment: Research Institute of Forestry, Chinese Academy of Forestry（中国林业科学研究院林业研究所）
• Research interest: Cupressaceae [S]
• Published taxa: *Widdringtonia*
• Region: [WORLD]

D. H. Jiang

Jiang, De Hu; 姜德互 ; Jiāng Déhù

First publication: 1987

• Employment: Pingwu County Institute of Chinese Materia Medica, Sichuan（四川省平武县中药研究所）
• Research interest: Liliaceae [S]
• Published taxa: *Fritillaria*
• Region: CHINA (Sichuan)

H. Y. Jiang

Jiang, Hai Yan; 姜海燕 ; Jiāng Hǎiyàn

1964- **First publication: 2003**

• Employment: Technology Promotion Station of Forest Management Bureau of Great Khingan（大兴安岭林业管理局森林经营局技术推广站）
• Research interest: Salicaceae [S]
• Published taxa: *Populus*
• Region: CHINA (Heilongjiang)

H. M. Jiang

Jiang, Huei Ming; 姜惠明 ; Jiāng Huìmíng

First publication: 1989

• Employment: Hebei Forestry College（河北林学院）
• Research interest: Salicaceae [S]
• Published taxa: *Populus*
• Region: CHINA (Hebei)

Li J. Jiang

Jiang, Li Ju; 姜立举 ; Jiāng Lìjǔ

1990- **First publication: 2020**

• Employment: Xishuangbanna Tropical Botanical Garden, Chinese Academy of Sciences（中国科学院西双版纳热带植物园）
• Research interest: Begoniaceae [S]
• Published taxa: *Begonia*
• Region: CHINA (Yunnan)

Y. C. Jiang

Jiang, Yan Cheng; 姜彦成 ; Jiāng Yànchéng

1965- **First publication: 2004**

• Employment: College of Life Science and Technology, Xinjiang University（新疆大学生命科学技术学院）
• Research interest: Fabaceae [S]
• Published taxa: *Crotalaria*
• Affiliation: XJU
• Location of specimens: XJU
• Region: CHINA (Zhejiang)
• IPNI as: Yan C. Jiang

Y. T. Jiang

Jiang, Yu Ting; 姜玉婷 ; Jiāng Yùtíng

First publication: 2020

• Employment: Forestry College, Fujian Agriculture and Forestry University（福建农林大学林学院）
• Research interest: Orchidaceae [S]
• Published taxa: *Cymbidium*
• Region: CHINA (Yunnan)

D. S. Jiang

Jiang, Dao Song; 蒋道松 ; Jiǎng Dàosōng

1963- **First publication: 2000**

• Employment: College of Science, Hunan Agricultural University（湖南农业大学理学院）
• Research interest: Dryopteridaceae, Woodsiaceae [P]
• Published taxa: *Woodsia, Polystichum*
• Region: CHINA (Hubei)

H. Jiang

Jiang, Hong; 蒋宏 ; Jiǎng Hóng

1974- **First publication: 2003**

• Employment: Yunnan Academy of Forestry（云南省林业科学院）
• Research interest: Cycadaceae, Gesneriaceae, Magnoliaceae, Orchidaceae [S]
• Published taxa: *Anoectochilus, Ascocentrum, Bulbophyllum, Chirita, Coelogyne, Cremastra, Cryptochilus, Dendrolirium, Gastrochilus, Luisia, Magnolia, Michelia, Petrocosmea, Stereochilus, Thunia*
• Affiliation: YCP
• Location of specimens: YCP
• Region: CHINA (Yunnan)

H. R. Jiang

Jiang, Hua Ren; 蒋华仁 ; Jiǎng Huárén; 蔣華仁

1940- **First publication: 1986**

- Employment: Sichuan Agricultural University（四川农业大学）
- Research interest: Poaceae [S]
- Published taxa: *Triticum*
- Region: [cult.]

H. Z. Jiang

Jiang, Hua Zeng; 蒋华曾 ; Jiǎng Huázēng

First publication: 1995

- Employment: Citrus Research Institute, Chinese Academy of Agricultural Sciences（中国农业科学院柑橘研究所）
- Research interest: Actinidiaceae [S]
- Published taxa: *Actinidia*
- Region: CHINA (Yunnan)

K. W. Jiang

Jiang, Kai Wen; 蒋凯文 ; Jiǎng Kǎiwén

1999- **First publication: 2020**

- Employment: College of Forestry, Southwest Forestry University（西南林业大学林学院）
- Research interest: Fabaceae [S]
- Published taxa: *Mucuna*
- Region: CHINA (Guangxi)

Lei Jiang

Jiang, Lei; 蒋蕾 ; Jiāng Lěi

First publication: 2020

- Employment: Guangzhou Linfang Eco-Technology Co., Ltd.（广州林芳生态科技有限公司）
- Research interest: Aquifoliaceae [S]
- Published taxa: *Ilex*
- Region: CHINA (Guangdong)

L. Jiang

Jiang, Lin; 蒋林 ; Jiǎng Lín

1963- **First publication: 1992**

- Employment: South China Institute of Botany, Chinese Academy of Sciences（中国科学院华南植物研究所）
- Research interest: Asteraceae [S]
- Published taxa: *Artemisia*
- Affiliation: IBSC
- Region: CHINA

N. Jiang

Jiang, Neng; 蒋能 ; Jiǎng Néng

1973- **First publication: 2013**

- Employment: Guangxi Institute of Botany, Chinese Academy of Sciences（广西壮族自治区中国科学院广西植物研究所）
- Research interest: Gesneriaceae [S]
- Published taxa: *Primulina*
- Region: CHINA (Guangxi)

Q. Q. Jiang

Jiang, Qing Qing; 蒋庆庆 ; Jiǎng Qìngqìng

1993- **First publication: 2017**

- Employment: College of Life Sciences, Southwest University（西南大学生命科学学院）
- Research interest: Ranunculaceae [S]
- Published taxa: *Clematis*
- Region: CHINA (Chongqing)

R. H. Jiang

Jiang, Ri Hong; 蒋日红 ; Jiǎng Rìhóng

1983- **First publication: 2011**

- Employment: Guangxi Institute of Botany, Chinese Academy of Sciences; Guangxi Forestry Group（广西壮族自治区中国科学院广西植物研究所；广西林业集团）
- Research interest: Asparagaceae, Aspleniaceae, Dryopteridaceae, Melanthiaceae, Polypodiaceae [P]
- Published taxa: *Asplenium, Chionographis, Colysis, Ophiopogon, Polystichum*
- Location of specimens: IBK
- Region: CHINA (Guangxi)

S. Y. Jiang

Jiang, Shun Yuan; 蒋舜媛 ; Jiǎng Shùnyuàn

1973- **First publication: 1998**

- Employment: Chengdu Institute of Biology, Chinese Academy of Sciences（中国科学院成都生物研究所）
- Research interest: Rosaceae [S]
- Published taxa: *Armeniaca, Cerasus*
- Region: CHINA

W. Jiang

Jiang, Wei; 蒋伟 ; Jiǎng Wěi

1983- **First publication: 2010**

- Employment: Kunming Institute of Botany, Chinese Academy of Sciences（中国科学院昆明植物研究所）
- Research interest: Cucurbitaceae [S]
- Published taxa: *Thladiantha*
- Region: CHINA

Xu L. Jiang

Jiang, Xu Liang; 蒋旭亮 ; Jiǎng Xùliàng

1972- **First publication: 2011**

- Employment: Ningxia Agriculture Environmental Monitoring Station（宁夏农业环境保护监测站）
- Research interest: Solanaceae [S]
- Published taxa: *Lycium*
- Region: CHINA (Ningxia)

Tsiang

Tsiang, Ying; Ch'iang, Ying; Tsiang, Chi Ying; Jiang, Ying; 蒋英 ; Jiǎng Yīng; 蒋积英

1898-1982 **First publication: 1934**

- Employment: Botanical Institute, College of Agriculture, National Sun Yat-sen University; Department of Forestry, South China Agricultural College; South China Institute of Botany, Chinese Academy of Sciences（国立中山大学农林植物研究所；华南农学院林学系；中国科学院华南植物研究所）
- Research interest: Adoxaceae, Annonaceae, Apocynaceae, Aristolochiaceae, Euphorbiaceae, Fabaceae, Fagaceae, Malvaceae, Pinaceae, Primulaceae, Rhamnaceae [S]
- Published taxa: *Absolmsia, Adelostemma, Aganosma, Alstonia, Alyxia, Amalocalyx, Amsonia, Anodendron, Ardisia, Asarum, Beaumontia, Belostemma, Biondia, Carissa, Ceropegia, Chieniodendron, Chonemorpha, Chunechites, Cosmostigma, Cyathella, Cynanchum, Dischidanthus, Dischidia, Dolichopetalum, Dregea, Ecdysanthera, Epigynum, Ervatamia, Fissistigma, Friesodielsia, Genianthus, Goniostemma, Gymnema, Heterostemma, Hibiscus, Hovenia, Hoya, Huthamnus, Ichnocarpus, Keteleeria, Kopsia, Lithocarpus, Marsdenia, Melodinus, Merrillanthus, Micrechites, Ormosia, Parabarium, Paravallaris, Parepigynum, Parsonsia, Periploca, Pinus, Pottsia, Quercus, Rauvolfia, Rhynchodia, Saccopetalum, Secamone, Sindechites, Sinopimelodendron, Stephanotis, Strophanthus, Toxocarpus, Trachelospermum, Tylophora, Vallaris, Viburnum, Wattakaka, Wrightia*
- Affiliation: CANT
- Location of specimens: CANT, IBSC, NAS, PE, SCAUB, WUK
- Region: CHINA

Y. Q. Jiang

Jiang, You Quan; Jiang, You Chuan; Tsiang, Y. C.; 蒋尤泉 ; Jiǎng Yóuquán; 蔣尤泉

1939- **First publication: 1978**

- Employment: Institute of Grassland Research, Chinese Academy of Agricultural Sciences（中国农业科学院草原研究所）
- Research interest: Fabaceae, Poaceae [S]
- Published taxa: *Bromus, Melilotoides, Melissitus, Pocockia, Vicia*
- Affiliation: FGC
- Location of specimens: FGC
- Region: CHINA (Nei Mongol)

Y. S. Jiang

Jiang, Yun Sheng; 蒋运生 ; Jiǎng Yùnshēng

1966- **First publication: 2011**

- Employment: Guangxi Institute of Botany, Chinese Academy of Sciences（广西壮族自治区中国科学院广西植物研究所）
- Research interest: Gesneriaceae [S]
- Published taxa: *Petrocodon*
- Region: CHINA (Guangxi)

Z. Jiang

Jiang, Zheng; 蒋政 ; Jiǎng Zhèng

1991- **First publication: 2019**

- Employment: College of Biology and the Environment, Nanjing Forestry University（南京林业大学生物与环境学院）
- Research interest: Lythraceae [S]
- Published taxa: *Trapa*
- Region: CHINA (Jiangsu)

Z. G. Jiang

Jiang, Zhi Gang; 蒋志刚 ; Jiǎng Zhìgāng

1964- **First publication: 1991**

- Employment: Hebei Normal University（河北师范大学）
- Research interest: Fabaceae [S]
- Published taxa: *Astragalus*
- Affiliation: HBNU
- Location of specimens: HBNU
- Region: CHINA

Z. T. Jiang

Jiang, Zhu Tan; 蒋柱檀 ; Jiǎng Zhùtán

1980- **First publication: 2005**

- Employment: Kunming Institute of Botany, Chinese Academy of Sciences（中国科学院昆明植物研究所）
- Research interest: Hydrocharitaceae [S]
- Published taxa: *Ottelia*
- Region: CHINA (Yunnan)

B. H. Jiao

Jiao, Bo Han; 焦伯晗 ; Jiāo Bóhán

1994- **First publication: 2016**

- Employment: Institute of Botany, Chinese Academy of Sciences（中国科学院植物研究所）
- Research interest: Asteraceae [S]
- Published taxa: *Artemisia*
- Region: CHINA

C. Y. Chiao

Chiao, Chi Yuen; Chiao, Chi Yuan; Chiao, Ch'i Yüan; Jiao, Chi Yuan; Jiao, Qi Yuan; 焦启源 ; Jiāo Qǐyuán; 焦啟源

1901-1968 **First publication: 1932**

- Employment: University of Nanking; Fudan University（金陵大学；复旦大学）
- Research interest: Fabaceae; Bryophyte [BS]
- Published taxa: *Ormosia*

- Affiliation: N
- Location of specimens: N, NF
- Region: CHINA
- Also as: C. Y. Jao

C. Y. King

King, Chuang Yin; 金春英 ; Jīn Chūnyīng
1934-2012 **First publication: 1974**
- Employment: Department of Forestry, Northeast Forestry Institute（东北林学院林学系）
- Research interest: Salicaceae [S]
- Published taxa: *Salix*
- Region: CHINA (Heilongjiang)

T. L. Chin

Chin, Tsen Li; Jin, Cun Li; 金存礼 ; Jīn Cúnlǐ; 金存禮
1929- **First publication: 1979**
- Employment: Shanghai Institute of Education; School of Life Sciences, East China Normal University（上海教育学院；华东师范大学生命科学学院）
- Research interest: Euphorbiaceae, Linderniaceae, Orobanchaceae, Phyllanthaceae, Plantaginaceae [S]
- Published taxa: *Adenosma, Baliospermum, Glochidion, Phyllanthus, Rehmannia, Torenia, Veronicastrum*
- Location of specimens: HSNU
- Region: CHINA

L. Y. Jin

Jin, Lie Yi; 金烈谊 ; Jīn Lièyì
First publication: 1990
- Employment: Xuchang Institute of Forestry Science, Henan（河南省许昌林业科学技术研究所）
- Research interest: Simaroubaceae [S]
- Published taxa: *Ailanthus*
- Region: CHINA (Henan)

J. H. Jin

Jin, Jian Hua; 金建华 ; Jīn Jiànhuá
1966- **First publication: 2007**
- Employment: The Museum of Biology, Sun Yat-sen University（中山大学生物博物馆）
- Research interest: Asparagaceae, Saxifragaceae; Plant Systematics [S]
- Published taxa: *Ophiopogon, Saxifraga*
- Affiliation: SYS
- Region: CHINA (Guangdong, Guangxi)

J. Y. Chin

Chin, Jian Yung; Jin, Jian Rong; 金剑荣 ; Jīn Jiànróng
1957- **First publication: 1982**
- Employment: Jinhua Forestry Bureau, Zhejiang（浙江省金华市林业局）
- Research interest: Poaceae [S]
- Published taxa: *Schizostachyum*
- Region: CHINA (Jiangxi)

Q. Jin

Jin, Qiang; 金强 ; Jīn Qiáng
First publication: 1992
- Employment: Aba Institute of Forestry, Sichuan（四川省阿坝州林业科学技术研究所）
- Research interest: Roaceae [S]
- Published taxa: *Malus*
- Region: CHINA (Sichuan)

S. H. Jin

Jin, Shui Hu; 金水虎 ; Jīn Shuǐhǔ
1965- **First publication: 2010**
- Employment: School of Forestry and Biotechnology, Zhejiang A&F University（浙江农林大学林业与生物技术学院）
- Research interest: Crassulaceae, Cyperaceae, Lamiaceae, Rosaceae, Verbenaceae; Plants of Zhejiang [S]
- Published taxa: *Carex, Caryopteris, Photinia, Sedum, Verbena*
- Affiliation: ZJFC
- Location of specimens: ZJFC
- Region: CHINA (Zhejiang)

W. T. Jin

Jin, Wei Tao; 金伟涛 ; Jīn Wěitāo
1985- **First publication: 2014**
- Employment: Institute of Botany, Chinese Academy of Sciences（中国科学院植物研究所）
- Research interest: Orchidaceae [S]
- Published taxa: *Bulbophyllum, Galearis, Hemipilia, Hsenhsua, Peristylus, Platanthera, Ponerorchis, Shizhenia, Tsaiorchis*
- Region: CHINA

W. Y. Jin

Jin, Wei Yin; 金维胤 ; Jīn Wéiyìn
First publication: 2020
- Employment: Institute of Botany, Chinese Academy of Sciences（中国科学院植物研究所）
- Research interest: Lauraceae [S]
- Published taxa: *Phoebe*
- Region: CHINA (Yunnan)

X. F. Jin

Jin, Xiao Feng; 金孝锋 ; Jīn Xiàofēng
1978- **First publication: 2002**
- Employment: College of Life Sciences, Zhejiang University; College of Life and Environmental Sciences, Hangzhou Normal University（浙江大学生

命科学学院；杭州师范大学生命与环境科学学院）
- Research interest: Asteraceae, Balsaminaceae, Brassicaceae, Cannabaceae, Caryophyllaceae, Crassulaceae, Cyperaceae, Ericaceae, Gentianaceae, Gleicheniaceae, Lamiaceae, Polygonaceae, Rhamnaceae, Rosaceae, Urticaceae [S]
- Published taxa: *Aster, Berchemia, Carex, Celtis, Cerastium, Cerasus, Dicranopteris, Fimbristylis, Impatiens, Meehania, Nanocnide, Orychophragmus, Persicaria, Polygonum, Prunus, Pseudostellaria, Rhododendron, Rosa, Rubus, Scirpus, Scutellaria, Sedum, Sinalliaria, Tripterospermum, Youngia*
- Affiliation: HTC, HZU
- Location of specimens: HTC, HZU, ZM
- Region: CHINA

X. H. Jin

Jin, Xiao Hua; 金效华；Jīn Xiàohuá

1975- **First publication: 2001**

- Employment: Institute of Botany, Chinese Academy of Sciences（中国科学院植物研究所）
- Research interest: Begoniaceae, Orchidaceae, Violaceae [S]
- Published taxa: *Anoectochilus, Begonia, Bulbophyllum, Calanthe, Cephalanthera, Cheirostylis, Coelogyne, Cylindrolobus, Dendrobium, Didymoplexiella, Galearis, Gastrochilus, Gastrodia, Gennaria, Goodyera, Hemipilia, Herminium, Holcoglossum, Hsenhsua, Leptogastrodia, Liparis, Listera, Malleola, Micropera, Neottia, Nujiangia, Odontochilus, Paraholcoglossum, Peristylus, Platanthera, Ponerorchis, Robiquetia, Shizhenia, Trichotosia, Tsaiorchis, Viola*
- Affiliation: PE
- Location of specimens: PE
- Region: CHINA

Y. X. Jin

Jin, Yue Xing; Jing, Yue Xing; Chin, Yu Xing; 金岳杏；Jīn Yuèxìng

1937- **First publication: 1984**

- Employment: Institute of Botany, Jiangsu Province（江苏省植物研究所）
- Research interest: Poaceae [PS]
- Published taxa: *Arthraxon, Brachiaria, Cenchrus, Echinochloa, Elymus, Oplismenus, Pennisetum, Setiacis, Urochloa*
- Affiliation: NAS
- Location of specimens: NAS
- Region: CHINA

L. Jin

Jin, Ling; 晋玲；Jìn Líng

1974- **First publication: 2002**

- Employment: Department of Chinese Materia Medica, Gansu College of Traditional Chinese Medicine（甘肃中医学院中药系）
- Research interest: Caprifoliaceae [S]
- Published taxa: *Patrinia*
- Region: CHINA (Gansu)

S. Y. Jin

Jin, Shu Ying; 靳淑英；Jìn Shūyīng

1935- **First publication: 1983**

- Employment: Institute of Botany, Chinese Academy of Sciences（中国科学院植物研究所）
- Research interest: Asteraceae, Iteaceae; Plant Bibliography [S]
- Published taxa: *Dendranthema, Eupatorium, Itea, Jurinea, Vladimiria*
- Affiliation: PE
- Region: CHINA

H. J. Jing

Jing, Hui Juan; 景慧娟；Jǐng Huìjuān

1987- **First publication: 2016**

- Employment: School of Life Sciences, Sun Yat-sen University（中山大学生命科学学院）
- Research interest: Rosaceae [S]
- Published taxa: *Sorbus*
- Region: CHINA (Yunnan)

W. B. Ju

Ju, Wen Bin; 鞠文彬；Jū Wénbīn

1987- **First publication: 2015**

- Employment: Chengdu Institute of Biology, Chinese Academy of Sciences（中国科学院成都生物研究所）
- Research interest: Asteraceae, Primulaceae, Rosaceae; Biodiversity [S]
- Published taxa: *Primula, Rubus, Youngia*
- Affiliation: CDBI
- Location of specimens: CDBI
- Region: CHINA (Sichuan)

K

M. Kang

Kang, Ming; 康明；Kāng Míng

1973- **First publication: 2015**

- Employment: South China Botanical Garden, Chinese Academy of Sciences（中国科学院华南植物园）
- Research interest: Gesneriaceae [S]
- Published taxa: *Oreocharis, Primulina*
- Region: CHINA

M. S. Kang

Kang, Mu Sheng; 康木生 ; Kāng Mùshēng

1929- **First publication: 1993**

- Employment: Beijing Forestry University（北京林业大学）
- Research interest: Vitaceae; Woody Plants [S]
- Published taxa: *Vitis*
- Affiliation: BJFC
- Location of specimens: BJFC
- Region: CHINA (Beijing)

N. Kang

Kang, Ning; 康宁 ; Kāng Níng

1966- **First publication: 1995**

- Employment: Institute of Botany, Chinese Academy of Sciences（中国科学院植物研究所）
- Research interest: Taxaceae [S]
- Published taxa: *Torreya*
- Region: CHINA

Yun Kang

Kang, Yun; 康云 ; Kāng Yún

1976- **First publication: 2017**

- Employment: School of Pharmacy, Fudan University（复旦大学药学院）
- Research interest: Fabaceae [S]
- Published taxa: *Phyllolobium*
- Affiliation: SHMU
- Region: CHINA (Gansu, Qinghai)
- IPNI as: Y. Kang

D. F. Ke

Ke, Dong Fan; 柯洞凡 ; Kē Dòngfán

1924-1989 **First publication: 1995**

- Employment: Zhongtiaoshan Forest Administration, Shanxi（山西省中条山林业局）
- Research interest: Fagaceae [S]
- Published taxa: *Quercus*
- Region: CHINA (Shanxi)

P. Ke

Ke, Ping; 柯平 ; Kē Píng

1925- **First publication: 1983**

- Employment: Northwest China Institute of Botany, Chinese Academy of Sciences and Shaanxi Province（陕西省中国科学院西北植物研究所）
- Research interest: Caryophyllaceae [S]
- Published taxa: *Melandrium, Stellaria*
- Affiliation: WUK
- Location of specimens: WUK
- Region: CHINA

R. Ke

Ke, Rui; 柯芮 ; Kē Ruì

1993- **First publication: 2016**

- Employment: Institute of Botany, Chinese Academy of Sciences（中国科学院植物研究所）
- Research interest: Asteraceae [S]
- Published taxa: *Nabalus, Youngia*
- Region: CHINA (Sichuan, Yunnan)

D. M. Kong

Kong, De Min; 孔德敏 ; Kǒng Démǐn

1985- **First publication: 2019**

- Employment: China National Orchid Conservation Center（全国兰科植物种质资源保护中心）
- Research interest: Orchidaceae [S]
- Published taxa: *Holcoglossum*
- Region: CHINA (Yunnan)

H. H. Kong

Kong, Hang Hui; 孔航辉 ; Kǒng Hánghuī

1977- **First publication: 2018**

- Employment: South China Botanical Garden, Chinese Academy of Sciences（中国科学院华南植物园）
- Research interest: Apocynaceae, Gesneriaceae [S]
- Published taxa: *Primulina, Vincetoxicum*
- Region: CHINA

H. Kong

Kong, Hong; 孔红 ; Kǒng Hóng

1964- **First publication: 1996**

- Employment: Department of Biology, Tianshui Teachers' College, Gansu（甘肃天水师范高等专科学校生物系）
- Research interest: Asphodelaceae [S]
- Published taxa: *Hemerocallis*
- Region: CHINA (Gansu)

L. J. Kong

Kong, Ling Jie; 孔令杰 ; Kǒng Lìngjié

1986- **First publication: 2011**

- Employment: School of Life Science and Food Engineering, Nanchang University（南昌大学生命科学与食品工程学院）
- Research interest: Orchidaceae [S]
- Published taxa: *Calanthe*
- Region: CHINA (Jiangxi)

W. Y. Kong

Kong, Wen Yan; 孔文彦 ; Kǒng Wényàn; 孔文彥

1934- **First publication: 1988**

- Employment: Chongqing Traditional Chinese Medicine Company（重庆中药材公司）
- Research interest: Ranunculaceae [S]
- Published taxa: *Coptis*
- Region: CHINA (Sichuan)

H. W. Kung

Kung, Hsien Wu; K'ung, Hsien Wu; Kong, Xian Wu; 孔宪武 ; Kǒng Xiànwǔ; 孔憲武

1897-1984 **First publication: 1934**

- Employment: Institute of Botany, National Academy of Peiping; Northwest Agricultural College; Northwest Normal College（国立北平研究院植物学研究所；西北农学院；西北师范学院）
- Research interest: Amaranthaceae, Asteraceae, Fabaceae, Polygonaceae [S]
- Published taxa: *Baolia, Chenopodium, Polygonum, Suaeda, Tanacetum, Vicia*
- Affiliation: NWTC
- Location of specimens: LZU, NWTC, PE
- Region: CHINA

H. S. Kung

Kung, Hsian Shiu; Kong, Xian Xu; 孔宪需 ; Kǒng Xiànxū; 孔憲需

1930-2001 **First publication: 1978**

- Employment: Chengdu Institute of Biology, Chinese Academy of Sciences（中国科学院成都生物研究所）
- Research interest: Aspleniaceae, Athyriaceae, Dryopteridaceae, Gleicheniaceae, Hymenophyllaceae, Lauraceae, Lycopodiaceae, Ophioglossaceae, Poaceae, Pteridaceae, Selaginellaceae, Thelypteridaceae, Woodsiaceae; Pteridophytes [PS]
- Published taxa: *Aleuritopteris, Asplenium, Athyrium, Botrypus, Coniogramme, Cyclosorus, Cyrtomium, Diplopterygium, Dryopteris, Huperzia, Lindera, Litsea, Lycopodioides, Lycopodium, Mecodium, Palhinhaea, Phlegmariurus, Polystichum, Pteris, Sceptridium, Selaginella, Triticum, Woodsia*
- Affiliation: CDBI
- Location of specimens: CDBI, SCFI
- Region: CHINA

Kuang

Kuang, Ko Zen; Kuang, Ko Rjên; K'uang, K'o Jên; Kuang, Ke Ren; 匡可任 ; Kuāng Kěrèn

1914-1977 **First publication: 1941**

- Employment: Yunnan Provincial Institute of Agricultural and Forestry Botany; Institute of Systematic Botany, Academia Sinica; Institute of Botany, Chinese Academy of Sciences（云南农林植物研究所；中国科学院植物分类研究所；中国科学院植物研究所）
- Research interest: Cucurbitaceae, Fabaceae, Garryaceae, Juglandaceae, Pinaceae, Solanaceae [S]
- Published taxa: *Archiphysalis, Aucuba, Caragana, Carya, Cathaya, Hemsleya, Lycium, Mandragora, Physaliastrum, Physochlaina, Rhamphocarya, Withania*
- Affiliation: PE
- Region: [ASIA]

Y. F. Kuang

Kuang, Yan Feng; 匡延凤 ; Kuāng Yánfèng

1981- **First publication: 2019**

- Employment: South China Botanical Garden, Chinese Academy of Sciences（中国科学院华南植物园）
- Research interest: Apocynaceae [S]
- Published taxa: *Hoya*
- Region: CHINA (Yunnan)

L

B. D. Lai

Lai, Bi Dan; 赖碧丹 ; Lài Bìdān

1983- **First publication: 2015**

- Employment: Guangxi Vocational and Technical College of Agriculture（广西农业职业技术学院）
- Research interest: Gesneriaceae [S]
- Published taxa: *Primulina*
- Region: CHINA (Guangxi)

G. H. Lai

Lai, Guang Hui; 赖广辉 ; Lài Guǎnghuī

First publication: 1995

- Employment: Guangde Forestry Bureau of Anhui Province（安徽省广德县林业局）
- Research interest: Poaceae [S]
- Published taxa: *Brachystachyum, Phyllostachys, Pseudosasa, Semiarundinaria*
- Region: CHINA (Anhui, Zhejiang)

M. X. Lai

Lai, Mao Xiang; 赖茂祥 ; Lài Màoxiáng

1953- **First publication: 2014**

- Employment: Guangxi Institute of Chinese Medicine & Pharmaceutical Science（广西中医药

研究院）
- Research interest: Aquifoliaceae; Medicinal Plants [S]
- Published taxa: *Ilex*
- Affiliation: GXMI
- Location of specimens: GXMI
- Region: CHINA (Guangxi)

M. J. Lai

Lai, Ming Jou; Lai, Ming Chou; Lai, Ming Zhou; 賴明洲；Lài Míngzhōu; 赖明洲

1949-2007 **First publication: 1976**

- Employment: Department of Landscape Architecture, Tunghai University（东海大学景观学系）
- Research interest: Amaranthaceae, Aristolochiaceae, Begoniaceae, Polygonaceae. [BMPS]
- Published taxa: *Alternanthera, Aristolochia, Begonia, Polygonum*
- Region: CHINA (Taiwan)

Q. R. Lai

Lai, Qi Rui; 赖其瑞；Lài Qíruì

1962- **First publication: 1989**

- Employment: Guangxi Institute of Traditional Medical and Pharmaceutical Sciences（广西中医药研究所）
- Research interest: Fabaceae [S]
- Published taxa: *Desmodium*
- Location of specimens: GXMI, PE
- Region: CHINA (Guangxi)

S. S. Lai

Lai, Shu Shen; Lai, Shu Sheng; 赖书绅；Lài Shūshēn; 賴書紳

1931- **First publication: 1994**

- Employment: Lushan Botanical Garden, Chinese Academy of Sciences（中国科学院庐山植物园）
- Research interest: Caryophyllaceae, Crassulaceae, Flacourtiaceae, Polygonaceae, Salicaceae; Plants of Jiangxi [S]
- Published taxa: *Bennettiodendron, Casearia, Cerastium, Homalium, Idesia, Poliothyrsis, Polygonum, Sedum, Xylosma*
- Affiliation: LBG
- Location of specimens: LBG, PE, SHM
- Region: CHINA

Y. J. Lai

Lai, Yang Jun; 赖阳均；Lài Yángjūn

1987- **First publication: 2012**

- Employment: Institute of Botany, Chinese Academy of Sciences; Nanjing Institute of Geology and Palaeontology, Chinese Academy of Sciences（中国科学院植物研究所；中国科学院南京地质古生物研究所）
- Research interest: Orchidaceae, Ranunculaceae [S]
- Published taxa: *Caltha, Micropera*
- Region: CHINA (Sichuan, Xizang)

S. R. Lan

Lan, Si Ren; 兰思仁；Lán Sīrén

1963- **First publication: 2013**

- Employment: College of Landscape Architecture, Fujian Agriculture and Forestry University（福建农林大学园林学院）
- Research interest: Orchidaceae [S]
- Published taxa: *Bulbophyllum, Calanthe, Cymbidium, Hygrochilus, Paphiopedilum, Pleione*
- Region: CHINA

X. Z. Lan

Lan, Xiao Zhong; 兰小中；Lán Xiǎozhōng

1973- **First publication: 2020**

- Employment: Xizang Agriculture and Animal Husbandry College（西藏农牧学院）
- Research interest: Crassulaceae [S]
- Published taxa: *Rhodiola*
- Region: CHINA (Xizang)

C. Y. Lan

Lan, Chong Yu; 蓝崇钰；Lán Chóngyù; 藍崇鈺

1947- **First publication: 2003**

- Employment: School of Life Sciences, Sun Yat-sen University（中山大学生命科学学院）
- Research interest: Violaceae [S]
- Published taxa: *Viola*
- Region: CHINA (Hunan)

K. M. Lan

Lan, Kai Min; 蓝开敏；Lán Kāimǐn; 藍開敏

1935- **First publication: 1983**

- Employment: Department of Forestry, Guizhou University; Department of Forestry, Guizhou Agricultural College（贵州大学林学系；贵州农学院林学系）
- Research interest: Cycadaceae, Ericaceae, Fabaceae, Lauraceae, Poaceae, Taxaceae, Theaceae [S]
- Published taxa: *Amentotaxus, Arundinaria, Bambusa, Camellia, Chimonobambusa, Cinnamomum, Cycas, Indosasa, Machilus, Ormosia, Rhododendron, Sinarundinaria*
- Affiliation: GZAC
- Location of specimens: FAN, GZAC
- Region: CHINA (Guizhou)

S. F. Lan

Lan, Sheng Fang; 蓝盛芳；Lán Shèngfāng; 藍盛芳

1943- **First publication: 1983**
- Employment: South China Agricultural College（华南农学院）
- Research interest: Schisandraceae [S]
- Published taxa: *Kadsura*
- Region: CHINA

Y. Z. Lan

Lan, Yong Zhen; Lan, Young Zhen; Lan, Young Chen; 蓝永珍 ; Lán Yǒngzhēn; 藍永珍
1932-2009 **First publication: 1977**
- Employment: Institute of Botany, Jiangsu Province（江苏省植物研究所）
- Research interest: Brassicaceae, Dryopteridaceae, Hypodematiaceae [PS]
- Published taxa: *Arabidopsis, Arabis, Arachniodes, Brassica, Cyrtomium, Dryopteris, Hypodematium, Loxostemon, Neomartinella, Solms-laubachia*
- Affiliation: NAS
- Location of specimens: NAS
- Region: CHINA
- Also as: Y. C. Lan

K. Y. Lang

Lang, Kai Yung; Lang, Kai Yong; 郎楷永 ; Láng Kǎiyǒng
1937- **First publication: 1978**
- Employment: Institute of Botany, Chinese Academy of Sciences（中国科学院植物研究所）
- Research interest: Asparagaceae, Lilicaceae, Orchidaceae [S]
- Published taxa: *Amitostigma, Androcorys, Anoectochilus, Apostasia, Aspidistra, Bulbophyllum, Calanthe, Cephalanthera, Cheirostylis, Coelogyne, Cypripedium, Diphylax, Diuranthera, Goodyera, Gymnadenia, Habenaria, Hemipilia, Hippeophyllum, Liparis, Mischobulbum, Myrmechis, Neottianthe, Neottia, Orchis, Peristylus, Platanthera, Tropidia*
- Affiliation: PE
- Location of specimens: PE
- Region: CHINA

Q. Lang

Lang, Qing; 郎青 ; Láng Qīng
1962- **First publication: 1987**
- Employment: Institute of Biological Resources, Jiangxi Academy of Sciences（江西省科学院生物资源研究所）
- Research interest: Hydrocharitaceae, Lythraceae [S]
- Published taxa: *Najas, Trapa*
- Region: CHINA (Jiangxi)

X. D. Lang

Lang, Xue Dong; 郎学东 ; Láng Xuédōng
1969- **First publication: 2013**
- Employment: Research Institute of Resource Insects, Chinese Academy of Forestry; School of Life Sciences, Yunnan University（中国林业科学研究院资源昆虫研究所 ; 云南大学生命科学学院）
- Research interest: Taxaceae [S]
- Published taxa: *Cephalotaxus*
- Region: CHINA (Yunnan)

L. G. Lei

Lei, Li Gong; 雷立公 ; Léi Lìgōng
1964- **First publication: 2008**
- Employment: Kunming Institute of Botany, Chinese Academy of Sciences（中国科学院昆明植物研究所）
- Research interest: Aquifoliaceae, Melanthiaceae, Saxifragaceae [S]
- Published taxa: *Ilex, Paris*
- Affiliation: KUN
- Location of specimens: KUN
- Region: CHINA (Yunnan)

S. P. Lei

Lei, Si Peng; 雷嗣鹏 ; Léi Sìpéng
1954- **First publication: 2002**
- Employment: Shenzhen City Wutongshan Nurseries, Guangdong; The Orchid Conservation & Research Center of Shenzhen, Guangdong（广东省深圳市梧桐山苗圃总场 ; 广东省深圳市兰科植物保护研究中心）
- Research interest: Orchidaceae [S]
- Published taxa: *Arachnis, Bulbophyllum, Cymbidium, Paphiopedilum*
- Region: CHINA

Z. P. Lei

Lei, Zu Pei; 雷祖培 ; Léi Zǔpéi
1967- **First publication: 2013**
- Employment: Administration of Zhejiang Wuyanling National Natural Reserve（浙江乌岩岭国家级自然保护区管理局）
- Research interest: Rubiaceae [S]
- Published taxa: *Rubia*
- Region: CHINA (Zhejiang)

Bin Li

Li, Bin; 黎斌 ; Lí Bīn
1973- **First publication: 2006**
- Employment: Northwest A&F University; Xi' an Botanical Garden, Shaanxi; Shaanxi Institute of Botany（西北农林科技大学 ; 陕西省西安植物园 ; 陕西省植物研究所）
- Research interest: Dennstaedtiaceae, Pteridaceae; Plants of Qinling [S]
- Published taxa: *Coniogramme, Microlepia*
- Affiliation: XBGH

- Location of specimens: XBGH
- Region: CHINA (Shaanxi)

C. X. Li

Li, Cheng Xiang; 黎承湘 ; Lí Chéngxiāng

1937-2009 **First publication: 1995**

- Employment: Liaoning Institute of Sand Fixation and Forestation（辽宁省固沙造林研究所）
- Research interest: Pinaceae [S]
- Published taxa: *Pinus*
- Region: CHINA (Liaoning)

Hua Li

Li, Hua; 黎桦 ; Lí Huà

1962- **First publication: 1993**

- Employment: Guangxi Agricultural College（广西农学院）
- Research interest: Dryopteridaceae, Polypodiaceae; Pteridophytes [P]
- Published taxa: *Colysis, Polystichum*
- Affiliation: GAUA
- Location of specimens: GAUA
- Region: CHINA (Guangxi)

Ming Li

Li, Ming; 黎明 ; Lí Míng

1990- **First publication: 2014**

- Employment: College of Forestry, Central South University of Forestry and Technology（中南林业科技大学林学院）
- Research interest: Gesneriaceae [S]
- Published taxa: *Petrocodon, Primulina*
- Region: CHINA (Hunan)

Q. K. Li

Li, Qian Kun; 黎乾坤 ; Lí Qiánkūn

1986- **First publication: 2015**

- Employment: College of Chemistry and Bioengineering, Guilin University of Technology（桂林理工大学化学与生物工程学院）
- Research interest: Gesneriaceae [S]
- Published taxa: *Primulina*
- Region: CHINA (Guangxi)

S. Li

Li, Shu; 黎舒 ; Lí Shū

1988- **First publication: 2019**

- Employment: Guangxi Institute of Botany, Chinese Academy of Sciences（广西壮族自治区中国科学院广西植物研究所）
- Research interest: Gesneriaceae [S]
- Published taxa: *Primulina*
- Region: CHINA (Guangxi)

W. P. Li

Li, Wei Ping; 黎维平 ; Lí Wéipíng

1959- **First publication: 1992**

- Employment: College of Life Sciences, Hunan Normal University（湖南师范大学生命科学学院）
- Research interest: Asteraceae [S]
- Published taxa: *Aster, Bidens, Blumea*
- Affiliation: HNNU
- Location of specimens: HNNU
- Region: CHINA (Hubei, Hunan)

Z. J. Li

Li, Zhang Ju; 黎章矩 ; Lí Zhāngjǔ

1935- **First publication: 1984**

- Employment: Zhejiang Forestry College（浙江林学院）
- Research interest: Juglandaceae [S]
- Published taxa: *Carya*
- Region: CHINA (Anhui)

A. M. Li

Li, An Ming; 李安明 ; Lǐ Ānmíng

First publication: 1983

- Employment: Yunnan Institute of Tropical Botany, Chinese Academy of Sciences（中国科学院云南热带植物研究所）
- Research interest: Araceae [S]
- Published taxa: *Arisaema*
- Region: CHINA (Yunnan)

A. J. Li

Li, An Jen; Lee, An Jen; Lee, An Jên; Li, An Jên; Li, An Ren; 李安仁 ; Lǐ Ānrén

1927- **First publication: 1981**

- Employment: Institute of Botany, Chinese Academy of Sciences（中国科学院植物研究所）
- Research interest: Amaranthaceae, Caryophyllaceae, Chenopodiaceae, Polygonaceae [S]
- Published taxa: *Antenoron, Arenaria, Chenopodium, Fagopyrum, Fallopia, Kalidium, Parapteropyrum, Polygonum, Rheum, Rumex, Salsola*
- Affiliation: PE
- Location of specimens: PE
- Region: CHINA

B. L. Li

Li, Ben Liang; 李本良 ; Lǐ Běnliáng

1929-2009 **First publication: 1989**

- Employment: Department of Biology, Shanxi University（山西大学生物系）
- Research interest: Aceraceae, Ranunculaceae; Plants of Shanxi [S]
- Published taxa: *Acer, Anemone*
- Affiliation: SXU

- Location of specimens: SXU
- Region: CHINA (Shanxi)

Ben X. Li

Li, Ben Xiang; 李本祥 ; Lǐ Běnxiáng

First publication: 2015

- Employment: Changning County Shiji Bamboo Garden, Sichuan (四川省长宁县世纪竹园)
- Research interest: Poaceae [S]
- Published taxa: *Bambusa*
- Region: CHINA (Sichuan)
- IPNI as: B. X. Li

B. K. Lee

Lee, Bing Kwe; Li, Bing Gui; 李丙贵 ; Lǐ Bǐngguì; 李丙貴

1921-2009 **First publication: 1981**

- Employment: Department of Biology, Hunan Normal University (湖南师范大学生物系)
- Research interest: Berberidaceae, Fabaceae, Rosaceae, Theaceae; Gymnospermae [S]
- Published taxa: *Camellia, Epimedium, Gleditsia*
- Affiliation: HNNU
- Location of specimens: HNNU
- Region: CHINA (Hunan)
- Also as: B. G. Li

P. T. Li

Li, Ping Tao; Li, Ping T'ao; Li, Bing Tao; 李秉滔 ; Lǐ Bǐngtāo

1936- **First publication: 1964**

- Employment: Department of Forestry, South China Agricultural College; College of Forestry, South China Agricultural University (华南农学院林学系 ; 华南农业大学林学院)
- Research interest: Annonaceae, Apocynaceae, Asclepiadaceae, Calycanthaceae, Euphorbiaceae, Fabaceae, Lauraceae, Loganiaceae, Malvaceae, Meliaceae, Pentaphylacaceae, Phyllanthaceae, Putranjivaceae, Rubiaceae [S]
- Published taxa: *Aglaia, Alphonsea, Alyxia, Amsonia, Anodendron, Antiostelma, Archileptopus, Belostemma, Bidaria, Biondia, Blachia, Bridelia, Calotropis, Calycanthus, Carissa, Centrostemma, Ceropegia, Chieniodendron, Chisocheton, Chonemorpha, Cleghornia, Croton, Cynanchum, Dasymaschalon, Desmos, Dischidia, Dregea, Drypetes, Dysoxylum, Ecdysanthera, Epigynum, Ervatamia, Eurya, Excoecaria, Fissistigma, Friesodielsia, Gardneria, Glochidion, Gongronema, Goniostemma, Goniothalamus, Gonolobus, Heterostemma, Hoya, Jasminanthes, Kopsia, Leptopus, Mallotus, Marsdenia, Meiogyne, Melodinus, Micrechites, Miliusa, Mitreola, Neoshirakia, Oncodostigma, Orophea, Oxystelma, Paravallaris, Parepigynum, Pentastelma, Periploca, Phoebe, Phyllanthodendron, Phyllanthus, Polyalthia, Pottsia, Rauvolfia, Richella, Sapium, Sauropus, Secamone, Sichuania, Sinomarsdenia, Sophora, Stephanotis, Sterculia, Tabernaemontana, Trachelospermum, Trichilia, Tsiangia, Turraea, Tylophora, Uvaria, Vallaris, Vietnamia, Vincetoxicum*
- Affiliation: CANT
- Region: CHINA

B. R. Li

Li, Bing Ren; 李炳仁 ; Lǐ Bǐngrén

First publication: 2010

- Employment: Northern Kernel-Apricot Research Society (北方仁用杏研究会)
- Research interest: Rosaceae [S]
- Published taxa: *Armeniaca*
- Region: CHINA (Hebei)

Bo Li

Li, Bo; 李波 ; Lǐ Bō

1984- **First publication: 2008**

- Employment: Jiangxi Agricultural University; South China Botanical Garden, Chinese Academy of Sciences (江西农业大学 ; 中国科学院华南植物园)
- Research interest: Lamiaceae, Orchidaceae, Polygonaceae, Wightiaceae [S]
- Published taxa: *Calanthe, Danxiaorchis, Koenigia, Persicaria, Polygonum, Premna, Tipularia,* Wightiaceae
- Region: [ASIA]

Ce H. Li

Li, Ce Hong; 李策宏 ; Lǐ Cèhóng

1964- **First publication: 2015**

- Employment: Sichuan Provincial Academy of Natural Resource Sciencs (四川省自然资源科学研究院)
- Research interest: Apiaceae, Begoniaceae; Plant of Emeishan [S]
- Published taxa: *Begonia*, *Pternopetalum*
- Location of specimens: AU, IBSC, KUN, NAS, PE
- Region: CHINA (Sichuan)
- IPNI as: C. H. Li

C. L. Li

Li, Chao Luang; Li, Chao Luan; 李朝銮 ; Lǐ Cháoluán; 李朝鑾

1938-1998 **First publication: 1979**

- Employment: Chengdu Institute of Biology, Chinese Academy of Sciences (中国科学院成都生物研究所)
- Research interest: Rosaceae, Vitaceae [S]
- Published taxa: *Acomastylis, Ampelocissus, Ampelopsis, Armeniaca, Cayratia, Cerasus, Cissus,*

Leea, Malus, Parthenocissus, Photinia, Potentilla, Prunus, Sanguisorba, Sibbaldia, Taihangia, Tetrastigma, Vitis, Waldsteinia, Yua
- Affiliation: CDBI
- Region: CHINA (Sichuan)

C. Q. Li

Li, Chao Qun; 李超群 ; Lǐ Chāoqún

First publication: 2019

- Employment: Institute of Botany, Chinese Academy of Sciences（中国科学院植物研究所）
- Research interest: Gesneriaceae [S]
- Published taxa: *Petrocosmea*
- Region: CHINA

C. H. Li

Li, Cheng Hu; 李承祜 ; Lǐ Chénghù

1905-1995 **First publication: 1993**

- Employment: College of Pharmacy, Second Military Medical University（第二军医大学药学院）
- Research interest: Poaceae [S]
- Published taxa: *Cymbopogon*
- Location of specimens: SMMU-BH
- Region: CHINA (Sichuan, Yunnan)

Chun Li

Li, Chun; 李春 ; Lǐ Chūn

1986- **First publication: 2016**

- Employment: Shanghai Chenshan Botanical Garden（上海辰山植物园）
- Research interest: Begoniaceae; Plants of Sichuan [S]
- Published taxa: *Begonia*
- Region: CHINA (Guangxi)

Chun L. Li

Li, Chun Lu; 李春鲁 ; Lǐ Chūnlǔ ; 李春魯

1933- **First publication: 2004**

- Employment: Jiangxi Agricultural University（江西农业大学）
- Research interest: Brassicaceae [S]
- Published taxa: *Cardamine, Cochlearia, Rorippa*
- Region: CHINA (Jiangxi)

Chun X. Li

Li, Chun Xiang; 李春香 ; Lǐ Chūnxiāng

1969- **First publication: 2005**

- Employment: Nanjing Institute of Geology and Palaeontology, Chinese Academy of Sciences（中国科学院南京地质古生物研究所）
- Research interest: Cyatheaceae, Dryopteridaceae [P]
- Published taxa: *Gymnosphaera, Polystichum*
- Region: CHINA (Guizhou, Yunnan)

Cong R. Li

Li, Cong Rui; 李从瑞 ; Lǐ Cóngruì

1981- **First publication: 2019**

- Employment: Guizhou Academy of Forestry（贵州省林业科学研究院）
- Research interest: Gesneriaceae [S]
- Published taxa: *Petrocodon*
- Region: CHINA (Guizhou)

Da X. Li

Li, Da Xiao; 李达孝 ; Lǐ Dáxiào; 李達孝

1941- **First publication: 2004**

- Employment: Yunnan Academy of Forestry; Yunnan Introduction & Propagation Center for Rare & Endangered Plants（云南省林业科学院；云南省珍稀濒危植物引种繁育中心）
- Research interest: Magnoliaceae [S]
- Published taxa: *Manglietia*
- Region: CHINA (Yunnan)
- IPNI as: D. X. Li

Da M. Li

Li, Da Ming; 李大明 ; Lǐ Dàmíng

1981- **First publication: 2007**

- Employment: Beijing Forestry University（北京林业大学）
- Research interest: Orchidaceae [S]
- Published taxa: *Gastrodia*
- Region: CHINA (Fujian)
- IPNI as: D. M. Li

D. X. Li

Li, Dao Xin; 李道新 ; Lǐ Dàoxīn

1971- **First publication: 2000**

- Employment: Dalaoling National Forest Park, Yichang（宜昌大老岭国家森林公园）
- Research interest: Primulaceae [S]
- Published taxa: *Lysimachia*
- Region: CHINA (Hubei)

D. Z. Li

Li, De Zhu; 李德铢 ; Lǐ Dézhū

1963- **First publication: 1987**

- Employment: Southwest Forestry College; Kunming Institute of Botany, Chinese Academy of Sciences（西南林学院；中国科学院昆明植物研究所）
- Research interest: Apocynaceae, Celastraceae, Cucurbitaceae, Ericaceae, Musaceae, Opiliaceae, Orchidaceae, Orobanchaceae, Phrymaceae, Pinaceae, Poaceae, Zingiberaceae [S]
- Published taxa: *Acidosasa, Ampelocalamus, Arundinaria, Bambusa, Bonia, Cephalostachyum, Chimonobambusa, Chimonocalamus, Cyathella, Dendrocalamus, Drepanostachyum, Fargesia,*

Gaoligongshania, Gennaria, Gymnosporia, Hemsleya, Holttumochloa, Hsuehochloa, Melocalamus, Mimulicalyx, Musa, Nujiangia, Oldeania, Pedicularis, Pinus, Pseudobartsia, Pseudosasa, Qiongzhuea, Rhododendron, Rhodostegiella, Sinarundinaria, Vincetoxicum, Yunnanopilia, Yushania, Zingiber
- Affiliation: KUN
- Location of specimens: KUN, SWFC
- Region: CHINA

Dian M. Li

Li, Dian Ming; 李殿明 ; Lǐ Diànmíng
1959- **First publication: 2000**
- Employment: Forestry Bureau, Heilongjiang Farms & Land Reclamation Administration（黑龙江省农垦总局林业局）
- Research interest: Salicaceae [S]
- Published taxa: *Salix*
- Region: CHINA (Heilongjiang)
- IPNI as: D. M. Li

F. Z. Li

Li, Fa Zeng; 李法曾 ; Lǐ Fǎzēng
1941- **First publication: 1982**
- Employment: Shandong Forestry School（山东省林业学校）
- Research interest: Amaranthaceae, Amaryllidaceae, Asparagaceae, Athyriaceae, Brassicaceae, Crassulaceae, Cyperaceae, Dryopteridaceae, Eriocaulaceae, Fabaceae, Geraniaceae, Lamiaceae, Linderniaceae, Poaceae, Polygonaceae, Pteridaceae, Rosaceae, Rubiaceae, Woodsiaceae; Plants of Shandong [PS]
- Published taxa: *Agrostis, Aleuritopteris, Allium, Amaranthus, Borreria, Carex, Cleistogenes, Crataegus, Cyperus, Dryopteris, Eriocaulon, Festuca, Geranium, Gueldenstaedtia, Lepidium, Lindernia, Liriope, Lunathyrium, Orostachys, Polygonum, Potentilla, Scirpus, Sisymbrium, Sorbus, Stachys, Woodsia*
- Affiliation: SDNU
- Location of specimens: SDFS, SDNU
- Region: CHINA (Shandong)

F. W. Li

Li, Fang Wen; 李芳文 ; Lǐ Fāngwén
1968- **First publication: 2010**
- Employment: Chengdu Botanical Garden（成都市植物园）
- Research interest: Magnoliaceae [S]
- Published taxa: *Yulania*
- Region: CHINA (Sichuan)

F. F. Li

Li, Fei Fei; 李飞飞 ; Lǐ Fēifēi
1983- **First publication: 2012**
- Employment: School of Life Sciences, Sun Yat-sen University（中山大学生命科学学院）
- Research interest: Rosaceae [S]
- Published taxa: *Eriobotrya*
- Region: CHINA (Guangdong)

Fay W. Li

Li, Fay Wei; 李飞苇 ; Lǐ Fēiwěi
First publication: 2012
- Employment: University Herbarium and Department of Integrative Biology, University of California, Berkeley, U.S.A.; Department of Biology, Duke University, U.S.A.（美国加州大学伯克利分校标本室和整合生物学系；美国杜克大学生物系）
- Research interest: Aspleniaceae, Pteridaceae [P]
- Published taxa: *Aleuritopteris, Asplenium, Gaga, Hemionitis*
- Region: [WORLD]
- IPNI as: F. W. Li

F. Li

Li, Feng; 李峰 ; Lǐ Fēng
1957- **First publication: 1988**
- Employment: Shandong College of Traditional Chinese Medicine（山东中医学院）
- Research interest: Dryopteridaceae [P]
- Published taxa: *Dryopteris*
- Region: CHINA (Shandong)

F. X. Li

Li, Fu Xiu; 李福秀 ; Lǐ Fúxiù
1954- **First publication: 1990**
- Employment: Faculty of Natural Resources, Southwest Forestry University（西南林学院资源学院）
- Research interest: Liliaceae [S]
- Published taxa: *Lilium*
- Region: CHINA (Yunnan)

C. Li

Li, Chien; Li, Qian; **李乾 ; Lǐ Qián**
1929-2019 **First publication: 1984**
- Employment: Sichuan Ya' an Middle School（四川省雅安中学）
- Research interest: Poaceae [S]
- Published taxa: *Chimonobambusa, Dendrocalamus, Lingnania, Phyllostachys*
- Location of specimens: IFP
- Region: CHINA (Sichuan)
- Also as: Q. Li

G. Y. Li

Li, Gen You; 李根有 ; Lǐ Gēnyǒu

1956- **First publication: 1998**

- Employment: Department of Forestry, Zhejiang Forestry College; School of Forestry and Biotechnology, Zhejiang A&F University; Jiyang College of Zhejiang A&F University（浙江林学院林学系；浙江农林大学林业与生物技术学院；浙江农林大学暨阳学院）
- Research interest: Apiaceae, Asparagaceae, Asteraceae, Berberidaceae, Betulaceae, Caryophyllaceae, Lamiaceae, Liliaceae, Orobanchaceae, Primulaceae, Rosaceae, Styracaceae, Zingiberaceae; Plants of Zhejiang [S]
- Published taxa: *Alnus, Ardisia, Cerasus, Cirsium, Epimedium, Globba, Lauro-cerasus, Liriope, Ostericum, Pseudostellaria, Rehmannia, Rubus, Salvia, Sinojackia, Tricyrtis*
- Affiliation: ZJFC
- Location of specimens: ZJFC
- Region: CHINA (Yunnan, Zhejiang)

G. Z. Li

Li, Guang Zhao; 李光照；Lǐ Guāngzhào

1940- **First publication: 1983**

- Employment: Guangxi Institute of Botany, Chinese Academy of Sciences（广西壮族自治区中国科学院广西植物研究所）
- Research interest: Asparagaceae, Celastraceae, Ericaceae, Fabaceae, Hydrangeaceae, Orchidaceae, Primulaceae, Saxifragaceae, Scrophulariaceae, Zingiberaceae [S]
- Published taxa: *Aspidistra, Hedychium, Lysimachia, Mucuna, Parnassia, Phaius, Rhododendron, Saxifraga*
- Affiliation: IBK
- Region: CHINA (Guangxi)

G. F. Li

Li, Guo Feng; 李国锋；Lǐ Guófēng

1983- **First publication: 2011**

- Employment: Kunming Institute of Botany, Chinese Academy of Sciences（中国科学院昆明植物研究所）
- Research interest: Balsaminaceae [S]
- Published taxa: *Impatiens*
- Region: CHINA (Yunnan)

G. P. Li

Li, Guo Ping; 李国平；Lǐ Guópíng

1966- **First publication: 1995**

- Employment: Putian College, Fujian（福建莆田高等专科学校）
- Research interest: Cyperaceae [S]
- Published taxa: *Scleria*
- Region: CHINA (Fujian)

H. M. Li

Li, He Min; 李贺敏；Lǐ Hèmǐn

1972- **First publication: 2002**

- Employment: Henan Agricultural University（河南农业大学）
- Research interest: Caryophyllaceae [S]
- Published taxa: *Stellaria*
- Region: CHINA (Henan)

H. Li

Li, Heng; Li, Hen; **李恒**；**Lǐ Héng**; **李恆**

1929- **First publication: 1977**

- Employment: Kunming Institute of Botany, Chinese Academy of Sciences（中国科学院昆明植物研究所）
- Research interest: Alismataceae, Apiaceae, Araceae, Araliaceae, Asparagaceae, Berberidaceae, Betulaceae, Brassicaceae, Burmanniaceae, Campanulaceae, Caprifoliaceae, Colchicaceae, Dennstaedtiaceae, Dioscoreaceae, Dipteridaceae, Elaeocarpaceae, Ericaceae, Fagaceae, Gesneriaceae, Hydrangeaceae, Hydrocharitaceae, Lamiaceae, Liliaceae, Marantaceae, Melanthiaceae, Meliaceae, Onagraceae, Ophioglossaceae, Orchidaceae, Rosaceae, Rubiaceae, Salicaceae, Smilacaceae, Solanaceae, Staphyleaceae, Thelypteridaceae, Zingiberaceae; Monocotyledons [S]
- Published taxa: *Agapetes, Amomum, Amoora, Amorphophallus, Amydrium, Arisaema, Aspidistra, Asyneuma, Briggsia, Bulbophyllum, Burmannia, Calanthe, Cardamine, Carpinus, Caryopteris, Circaea, Clintonia, Coelogyne, Colocasia, Cryptocoryne, Cyclobalanopsis, Cymbidium, Dendrobium, Dichroa, Dioscorea, Disporum, Dysoxylum, Elaeocarpus, Epilobium, Epipremnopsis, Galium, Gaultheria, Gonatanthus, Hapaline, Homalomena, Hydrocotyle, Hypolepis, Ligusticum, Lithocarpus, Lloydia, Lonicera, Lycianthes, Mahonia, Maianthemum, Metapanax, Metathelypteris, Mussaenda, Ophioglossum, Ophiopogon, Ophiorrhiza, Ottelia, Paederia, Parathelypteris, Paris, Peliosanthes, Photinia, Phymatodes, Pinellia, Pleione, Pleurospermum, Pothos, Remusatia, Rhaphidophora, Rubia, Sagittaria, Salix, Sauromatum, Schismatoglottis, Sloanea, Smilacina, Smilax, Stachyphrynium, Sunipia, Tupistra, Turpinia, Typhonium, Vaccinium, Walsura, Whytockia*
- Affiliation: KUN
- Location of specimens: KUN
- Region: CHINA

Hong Qing Li

Li, Hong Qing; 李宏庆；Lǐ Hóngqìng

1966- **First publication: 2013**

- Employment: School of Life Sciences, East China Normal University（华东师范大学生命科学学院）

• Research interest: Asteraceae, Burmanniaceae, Moraceae [S]
• Published taxa: *Ainsliaea, Ficus, Thismia*
• Affiliation: HSNU
• Location of specimens: HSNU
• Region: CHINA
• Also as: H. Q. Li

Hong Z. Li

Li, Hong Zhe; 李宏哲 ; Lǐ Hóngzhé
1972- **First publication: 2006**
• Employment: Kunming Institute of Botany, Chinese Academy of Sciences; School of Chinese Materia Medica, Yunnan University of Traditional Chinese Medicine（中国科学院昆明植物研究所；云南中医药大学中药学院）
• Research interest: Begoniaceae, Lamiaceae [S]
• Published taxa: *Begonia*
• Affiliation: YNTCM
• Region: CHINA (Yunnan)
• IPNI as: H. Z. Li

Hong Li

Li, Hong; 李虹 ; Lǐ Hóng
1974- **First publication: 2013**
• Employment: Guangxi Institute of Botany, Chinese Academy of Sciences（广西壮族自治区中国科学院广西植物研究所）
• Research interest: Gesneriaceae [S]
• Published taxa: *Primulina*
• Region: CHINA (Guangxi)

H. T. Li

Li, Hong Tao; 李洪涛 ; Lǐ Hóngtāo
1971- **First publication: 2007**
• Employment: Kunming Institute of Botany, Chinese Academy of Sciences（中国科学院昆明植物研究所）
• Research interest: Cucurbitaceae [S]
• Published taxa: *Hemsleya*
• Region: CHINA (Yunnan)

H. L. Li

Li, Hui Lin; 李惠林 ; Lǐ Huìlín
1911-2002 **First publication: 1942**
• Employment: Taiwan University; University of Pennsylvania, U.S.A.（台湾大学；美国宾夕法尼亚大学）
• Research interest: Achariaceae, Actinidiaceae, Adoxaceae, Anacardiaceae, Annonaceae, Aquifoliaceae, Araliaceae, Begoniaceae, Berberidaceae, Celastraceae, Clethraceae, Clusiaceae, Combretaceae, Cornaceae, Cupressaceae, Diapensiaceae, Ebenaceae, Elaeagnaceae, Elaeocarpaceae, Fabaceae, Fagaceae, Hamamelidaceae, Hydrangeaceae, Hypericaceae, Iteaceae, Lamiaceae, Lauraceae, Loranthaceae, Malvaceae, Mazaceae, Melastomataceae, Meliaceae, Menispermaceae, Olacaceae, Oleaceae, Orobanchaceae, Passifloraceae, Pentaphylacaceae, Pinaceae, Plantaginaceae, Polygonaceae, Proteaceae, Rosaceae, Rubiaceae, Salicaceae, Sapindaceae, Sapotaceae, Scrophulariaceae, Simaroubaceae, Styracaceae, Symplocaceae, Taxaceae, Theaceae, Thymelaeaceae, Urticaceae, Vitaceae [PS]
• Published taxa: *Acanthopanax, Acer, Actinidia, Adinandra, Adina, Aglaia, Alangium, Albertisia, Allomorphia, Amentotaxus, Anneslea, Aralia, Begonia, Bennettiodendron, Berberis, Berneuxia, Blastus, Botryopleuron, Brandisia, Brassaiopsis, Bredia, Brucea, Cardiandra, Cedrela, Centranthera, Cephalotaxus, Cercis, Chamaecyparis, Chionanthus, Clerodendrum, Clethra, Combretum, Cornus, Corylopsis, Dendropanax, Deutzia, Diospyros, Diphylleia, Dracontomelon, Dunnia, Dysoxylum, Elaeagnus, Embolanthera, Euphrasia, Fissistigma, Fordiophyton, Genitia, Geophila, Goniothalamus, Gordonia, Hartia, Helicia, Heteropanax, Heyderia, Huodendron, Hydnocarpus, Hymenopogon, Hypericum, Ilex, Itea, Ixora, Lagotis, Lasianthus, Linociera, Loranthus, Macropanax, Madhuca, Mahonia, Maughania, Mazus, Medinilla, Memecylon, Merrilliopanax, Mischocarpus, Mussaenda, Neillia, Ochrocarpos, Olax, Olea, Ophiorrhiza, Oxyspora, Paederia, Panax, Papuacedrus, Pasania, Passiflora, Pedicularis, Persea, Photinia, Phyllagathis, Plagiopetalum, Pouzolzia, Psychotria, Pygeum, Pyracantha, Randia, Reevesia, Rehderodendron, Rehmannia, Rosa, Rubus, Sarcopyramis, Schefflera, Schizomussaenda, Scorpiothyrsus, Scrophularia, Shortia, Sibbaldia, Sinopanax, Sloanea, Sonerila, Spiraea, Stapfiophyton, Stewartia, Styrax, Sycopsis, Symplocos, Taxus, Tetrastigma, Tovara, Tsuga, Tutcheria, Verbascum, Veronica, Viburnum, Wikstroemia*
• Affiliation: TAI
• Location of specimens: TAI
• Region: [ASIA]

J. N. Li

Li, Ji Ning; 李吉宁 ; Lǐ Jíníng
1964- **First publication: 1988**
• Employment: Key Laboratory for Restoration and Reconstruction of Degraded Ecosystem in North-western China of Ministry of Education,Ningxia University（宁夏大学西北退化生态系统恢复与重建教育部重点实验室）
• Research interest: Poaceae, Solanaceae [S]
• Published taxa: *Agrostis, Calamagrostis, Lycium*
• Region: CHINA (Ningxia)

Ji H. Li

Li, Ji Hong; 李继红; Lǐ Jìhóng

1960- **First publication: 2003**

- Employment: Department of Life Science and Chemistry, Dali University (大理学院生命科学与化学系)
- Research interest: Asteraceae, Zingiberaceae [S]
- Published taxa: *Erigeron, Roscoea*
- Region: CHINA (Yunnan)

C. Y. Li

Li, Chi Yun; Li, Ji Yun; **李冀云; Lǐ Jìyún; 李冀雲**

1933- **First publication: 1976**

- Employment: Institute of Forestry and Soil Sciences, Chinese Academy of Sciences (中国科学院林业土壤研究所)
- Research interest: Apocynaceae, Asteraceae, Campanulaceae, Lamiaceae, Rosaceae [S]
- Published taxa: *Adenophora, Agrimonia, Artemisia, Aruncus, Cacalia, Chrysanthemum, Cirsium, Cynanchum, Echinops, Filipendula, Fragaria, Inula, Ixeris, Leonurus, Malus, Potentilla, Sanguisorba, Saussurea, Stachys, Taraxacum, Tephroseris, Thymus*
- Affiliation: IFP
- Location of specimens: IFP
- Region: CHINA (Heilongjiang, Jilin, Liaoning)

J. Z. Li

Li, Jia Zheng; 李佳政; Lǐ Jiāzhèng

1936- **First publication: 1992**

- Employment: Xinjiang Uygur Autonomous Region Institute of Chinese & Ethnic Materia Medica (新疆维吾尔自治区中药民族药研究所)
- Research interest: Campanulaceae, Orobanchaceae, Tamaricaceae [S]
- Published taxa: *Campanula*
- Affiliation: XTNM
- Location of specimens: XTNM
- Region: CHINA (Xinjiang)

J. M. Li

Li, Jia Mei; 李家美; Lǐ Jiāměi

1969- **First publication: 2008**

- Employment: College of Life Sciences, Henan Agricultural University (河南农业大学生命科学学院)
- Research interest: Gesneriaceae [S]
- Published taxa: *Chirita, Didymocarpus, Microchirita, Oreocharis, Petrocodon, Primulina*
- Affiliation: HEAC
- Location of specimens: HEAC
- Region: CHINA

Jia X. Li

Li, Jia Xiang; 李家湘; Lǐ Jiāxiāng

1979- **First publication: 2014**

- Employment: College of Forestry, Central South University of Forestry and Technology (中南林业科技大学林学院)
- Research interest: Fabaceae, Gentianaceae; Plants of Hunan [S]
- Published taxa: *Astragalus, Swertia*
- Affiliation: CSFI
- Location of specimens: CSFI
- Region: CHINA (Hunan)

J. J. Li

Li, Jia Jue; 李嘉珏; Lǐ Jiājué

1938- **First publication: 1992**

- Employment: Forestry Science Institute of Gansu Province (甘肃省林业科学研究所)
- Research interest: Paeoniaceae [S]
- Published taxa: *Paeonia*
- Region: CHINA (Gansu)

J. Hong Li

Li, Jian Hong; 李建宏; Lǐ Jiànhóng

First publication: 2010

- Employment: Northern Kernel-Apricot Research Society (北方仁用杏研究会)
- Research interest: Rosaceae [S]
- Published taxa: *Armeniaca*
- Region: CHINA (Hebei)

Jian Hua Li

Li, Jian Hua; 李建华; Lǐ Jiànhuá

1962- **First publication: 2001**

- Employment: Arnold Arboretum, Harvard University, U.S.A. (美国哈佛大学阿诺德树木园)
- Research interest: Betulaceae [S]
- Published taxa: *Betula*
- Region: CHINA (Fujian)
- IPNI as: J. H. Li

J. Q. Li

Li, Jian Qiang; 李建强; Lǐ Jiànqiáng

1954- **First publication: 1988**

- Employment: Department of Biology, Hubei University; Wuhan Institute of Botany, Chinese Academy of Sciences; Wuhan Botanical Garden, Chinese Academy of Sciences (湖北大学生物系; 中国科学院武汉植物研究所; 中国科学院武汉植物园)
- Research interest: Actinidiaceae, Berberidaceae, Cucurbitaceae, Fabaceae, Fagaceae, Hamamelidaceae, Orobanchaceae, Ranunculaceae [S]
- Published taxa: *Actinidia, Baijiania, Castanopsis,*

Crotalaria, Epimedium, Fagus, Hepatica, Lithocarpus, Microlagenaria, Quercus, Saurauia, Siraitia, Thladiantha, Triaenophora
- Affiliation: EU, HIB
- Region: CHINA

Jian X. Li

Li, Jian Xiu; 李建秀 ; Lǐ Jiànxiù

1937- **First publication: 1983**

- Employment: Shandong University of Traditional Chinese Medicine（山东中医药大学）
- Research interest: Athyriaceae, Caryophyllaceae, Dryopteridaceae, Equisetaceae, Hypodematiaceae, Polygonaceae, Polypodiaceae; Medicinal Plants [PS]
- Published taxa: *Athyriopsis, Cyrtomium, Deparia, Dianthus, Dryopteris, Hippochaete, Hypodematium, Lunathyrium, Phymatopsis, Polygonum, Polystichum*
- Affiliation: SDCM
- Location of specimens: SDCM
- Region: CHINA (Shandong)
- IPNI as: J. X. Li

Jian Y. Li

Li, Jian Yi; 李建仪 ; Lǐ Jiànyí

First publication: 1986

- Employment: Liaoning Saline-alkali Land Improvement and Research Institute（辽宁省盐碱地土壤改良研究所）
- Research interest: Vitaceae [S]
- Published taxa: *Vitis*
- Region: CHINA (Liaoning)
- IPNI as: J. Y. Li

Jian W. Li

Li, Jian Wu; 李剑武 ; Lǐ Jiànwǔ

1983- **First publication: 2013**

- Employment: Xishuangbanna Tropical Botanical Garden, Chinese Academy of Sciences（中国科学院西双版纳热带植物园）
- Research interest: Aristolochiaceae, Begoniaceae, Gesneriaceae, Orchidaceae [S]
- Published taxa: *Aristolochia, Begonia, Bulbophyllum, Dendrobium, Nervilia, Oreocharis, Petrocosmea*
- Affiliation: HITBC
- Location of specimens: HITBC
- Region: CHINA (Yunnan)
- IPNI as: J. W. Li

Jian Li

Li, Jian; 李健 ; Lǐ Jiàn

1974- **First publication: 2014**

- Employment: College of Life Sciences, Zhejiang University; School of Landscape Architecture, Zhejiang A&F University（浙江大学生命科学学院；浙江农林大学园林学院）
- Research interest: Gesneriaceae [S]
- Published taxa: *Primulina*
- Region: CHINA (Fujian, Guangxi)

Jian H. Li

Li, Jian Hua; 李健华 ; Lǐ Jiànhuá; 李健華

1942- **First publication: 1984**

- Employment: Northwest Plateau Institute of Biology, Chinese Academy of Sciences（中国科学院西北高原生物研究所）
- Research interest: Gentianaceae [S]
- Published taxa: *Gentiana*
- Region: CHINA (Qinghai)

J. W. Li

Li, Jie Wei; 李洁维 ; Lǐ Jiéwéi

1962- **First publication: 2002**

- Employment: Guangxi Institute of Botany, Chinese Academy of Sciences（广西壮族自治区中国科学院广西植物研究所）
- Research interest: Actinidiaceae [S]
- Published taxa: *Actinidia*
- Region: CHINA (Guangxi)

J. Li

Li, Jie; 李捷 ; Lǐ Jié

1967- **First publication: 1996**

- Employment: Xishuangbanna Tropical Botanical Garden, Chinese Academy of Sciences（中国科学院西双版纳热带植物园）
- Research interest: Cupressaceae, Lamiaceae, Lauraceae, Theaceae [S]
- Published taxa: *Actinodaphne, Alseodaphnopsis, Cinnamomum, Cupressus, Isodon, Litsea, Machilus, Sinopora, Stewartia*
- Affiliation: HITBC, KUN
- Location of specimens: HITBC, KUN
- Region: CHINA

Jin Y. Li

Li, Jin Yu; 李进宇 ; Lǐ Jìnyǔ

1981- **First publication: 2015**

- Employment: Beijing Forestry University（北京林业大学）
- Research interest: Ranunculaceae [S]
- Published taxa: *Thalictrum*
- Location of specimens: BJFC
- Region: CHINA (Xizang)
- IPNI as: J. Y. Li

J. H. Li

Li, Jing Hua; 李晶华 ; Lǐ Jīnghuá; 李晶華

1947- **First publication: 1988**

- Employment: Xilingol League Institute of Forestry Sciences, Inner Mongolia（内蒙古锡林郭勒盟林业科学研究所）
- Research interest: Ulmaceae [S]
- Published taxa: *Ulmus*
- Region: CHINA (Nei Mongol)

J. F. Li

Li, Jing Fu; 李景富 ; Lǐ Jǐngfù

1934- **First publication: 1979**

- Employment: Institute of Natural Resources, Heilongjiang Academy of Sciences（黑龙江省科学院自然资源研究所）
- Research interest: Asparagaceae, Orobanchaceae; Plants of N. E. China [S]
- Published taxa: *Convallaria, Rehmannia*
- Affiliation: HNR
- Location of specimens: HNR
- Region: CHINA (Liaoning, Heilongjiang)

J. X. Li

Li, Jing Xi; 李景熹 ; Lǐ Jǐngxī

First publication: 1981

- Employment: Department of Forestry, Sichuan Agricultural College（四川农学院林学系）
- Research interest: Cupressaceae [S]
- Published taxa: *Cunninghamia*
- Region: CHINA (Sichuan)

J. S. Li

Li, Jun Shan; 李君山 ; Lǐ Jūnshān

First publication: 1997

- Employment: School of Pharmacy, Beijing Medical University（北京医科大学药学院）
- Research interest: Asteraceae [S]
- Published taxa: *Saussurea*
- Region: CHINA (Xinjiang)

K. M. Li

Li, Kuang Ming; 李矿明 ; Lǐ Kuàngmíng

First publication: 1989

- Employment: Central South Forestry Industry Survey and Design Research Institute, Department of Forestry（林业部中南林业调查规划设计院）
- Research interest: Ericaceae, Lauraceae, Rhamnaceae, Rosaceae [S]
- Published taxa: *Enkianthus, Lindera, Rhamnus, Rhaphiolepis*
- Region: CHINA (Fujian)

Lang Li

Li, Lang; 李朗 ; Lǐ Lǐng

1981- **First publication: 2011**

- Employment: Xishuangbanna Tropical Botanical Garden, Chinese Academy of Sciences（中国科学院西双版纳热带植物园）
- Research interest: Lauraceae [S]
- Published taxa: *Machilus*
- Affiliation: HITBC
- Location of specimens: HITBC
- Region: CHINA (Yunnan)
- IPNI as: L. Li

L. B. Li

Li, Li Bo; 李丽波 ; Lǐ Lìbō

1963- **First publication: 1993**

- Employment: Institute of Botany, Jiangsu Province（江苏省植物研究所）
- Research interest: Apiaceae [S]
- Published taxa: *Selinum*
- Region: CHINA

Li Q. Li

Li, Li Qiang; 李利强 ; Lǐ Lìqiáng

1977- **First publication: 2007**

- Employment: The Orchid Conservation & Research Center of Shenzhen, Guangdong（广东省深圳市兰科植物保护研究中心）
- Research interest: Orchidaceae [S]
- Published taxa: *Cymbidium*
- Region: CHINA (Yunnan)

L. Q. Li

Li, Liang Qian; Li, Liang Ching; **李良千 ; Lǐ Liángqiān**

1953- **First publication: 1986**

- Employment: Institute of Botany, Chinese Academy of Sciences（中国科学院植物研究所）
- Research interest: Lamiaceae, Ranunculaceae [S]
- Published taxa: *Aconitum, Callicarpa, Clematis, Thalictrum*
- Affiliation: PE
- Location of specimens: PE
- Region: CHINA

L. Chu Li

Li, Lin Chu; 李林初 ; Lǐ Línchū

1943- **First publication: 1982**

- Employment: Department of Biology, Fudan University（复旦大学生物系）
- Research interest: Asparagaceae, Fabaceae, Rosaceae; Gymnospermae [S]
- Published taxa: *Gleditsia, Lespedeza, Liriope, Photinia*
- Affiliation: FUS
- Location of specimens: FUS
- Region: CHINA

L. Li

Li, Lin; 李琳 ; Lǐ Lín

1974- **First publication: 2008**
- Employment: South China Botanical Garden, Chinese Academy of Sciences（中国科学院华南植物园）
- Research interest: Orchidaceae [S]
- Published taxa: *Anoectochilus, Bulbophyllum, Hetaeria, Liparis, Thuniopsis, Zeuxine*
- Affiliation: IBSC
- Location of specimens: IBSC
- Region: CHINA

Lu Li

Li, Lu; 李璐 ; Lǐ Lù
1974- **First publication: 2018**
- Employment: Yunnan Academy of Biodiversity, Southwest Forestry University（西南林业大学云南生物多样性研究院）
- Research interest: Ranunculaceae [S]
- Published taxa: *Aquilegia*
- Region: CHINA (Yunnan)

M. F. Li

Li, Man Fei; 李满飞 ; Lǐ Mǎnfēi
1957- **First publication: 1989**
- Employment: Department of Pharmacognosy, China Pharmaceutical University（中国药科大学生药教研室）
- Research interest: Orchidaceae [S]
- Published taxa: *Dendrobium*
- Affiliation: TIPR
- Location of specimens: TIPR
- Region: CHINA (Guangxi)

Meng Li

Li, Meng; 李蒙 ; Lǐ Méng
1989- **First publication: 2015**
- Employment: Chengdu Institute of Biology, Chinese Academy of Sciences（中国科学院成都生物研究所）
- Research interest: Rosaceae [S]
- Published taxa: *Sorbus*
- Region: CHINA (Yunnan)

Min H. Li

Li, Min Hui; 李旻辉 ; Lǐ Mínhuī
1978- **First publication: 2016**
- Employment: Baotou Medical College（包头医学院）
- Research interest: Lamiaceae, Orobanchaceae [S]
- Published taxa: *Rehmannia*
- Affiliation: CMMI
- Region: CHINA (Nei Mongol)
- IPNI as: M. H. Li

M. J. Li

Li, Min Jie; 李敏洁 ; Lǐ Mǎnjié
1988- **First publication: 2019**
- Employment: College of Life Sciences, Sichuan University（四川大学生命科学学院）
- Research interest: Amaryllidaceae [S]
- Published taxa: *Allium*
- Region: CHINA (Qinghai, Sichuan)

Ming F. Li

Li, Ming Fei; 李名非 ; Lǐ Míngfēi
1947- **First publication: 1994**
- Employment: Anhui Institute of Biology（安徽省生物研究所）
- Research interest: Poaceae [S]
- Published taxa: *Bromus, Deyeuxia, Stipa*
- Region: CHINA (Xizang)
- IPNI as: M. F. Li

Ming H. Li

Li, Ming He; 李明河 ; Lǐ Mínghé
1985- **First publication: 2014**
- Employment: Forestry College, Fujian Agriculture and Forestry University（福建农林大学林学院）
- Research interest: Orchidaceae [S]
- Published taxa: *Bulbophyllum, Dendrobium, Hygrochilus, Liparis, Phalaenopsis, Platanthera, Yoania, Yunorchis*
- Region: CHINA
- IPNI as: M. H. Li; also as: M. He Li

M. R. Li

Li, Ming Rui; 李明瑞 ; Lǐ Míngruì
First publication: 1992
- Employment: Wanhuashan Management Office, Yan' an, Shaanxi（陕西省延安万花山管理处）
- Research interest: Paeoniaceae [S]
- Published taxa: *Paeonia*
- Region: CHINA (Shaanxi)

M. S. Li

Li, Ming Sheng; 李明生 ; Lǐ Míngshēng
First publication: 1989
- Employment: Yangkou Hospital of Shunchang County, Fujian（福建省顺昌县洋口卫生院）
- Research interest: Lamiaceae [S]
- Published taxa: *Paraphlomis*
- Location of specimens: AU, FJSI, IBSC
- Region: CHINA (Fujian)

M. Li

Li, Ming; 李鸣 ; Lǐ Míng
1959- **First publication: 1994**
- Employment: Institute of Medicinal Plant Development, Chinese Academy of Medical Sciences（中国医学科学院药用植物资源开发研究所）

- Research interest: Ranunculaceae [S]
- Published taxa: *Aconitum*
- Region: CHINA (Sichuan)

Nan Li

Li, Nan; 李楠 ; Lǐ Nán

1963- **First publication: 1992**

- Employment: Xinjiang Bayi Agricultural College; Institute of Botany, Chinese Academy of Sciences; Fairy Lake Botanical Garden, Shenzhen & Chinese Academy of Sciences（新疆八一农学院；中国科学院植物研究所；深圳市中国科学院仙湖植物园）
- Research interest: Fabaceae, Pinaceae, Taxaceae; Gymnospermae [S]
- Published taxa: *Abies, Cephalotaxus, Hedysarum, Keteleeria, Larix, Picea, Pinus, Pseudotsuga, Taxus, Tsuga*
- Affiliation: SZG
- Location of specimens: SZG
- Region: CHINA

N. H. Li

Li, Ning Hon; 李甯漢 ; Lǐ Nínghàn; 李宁汉

1933- **First publication: 2003**

- Employment: Chinese Medical Research Institute（香港中国医学研究所）
- Research interest: Balanophoraceae [S]
- Published taxa: *Balanophora*
- Region: CHINA (Hong Kong)

N. Li

Li, Nong; 李秾 ; Lǐ Nóng; 李穠

1921-2016 **First publication: 1994**

- Employment: Department of Forestry, Anhui Agricultural University（安徽农业大学林学系）
- Research interest: Elaeagnaceae, Staphyleaceae [S]
- Published taxa: *Elaeagnus, Staphylea*
- Region: CHINA (Anhui)

Pan Li

Li, Pan; 李攀 ; Lǐ Pān

1984- **First publication: 2011**

- Employment: College of Life Sciences, Zhejiang University（浙江大学生命科学学院）
- Research interest: Lamiaceae, Liliaceae, Scrophulariaceae, Smilacaceae [S]
- Published taxa: *Scrophularia, Smilax*
- Affiliation: HZU
- Location of specimens: HZU
- Region: CHINA
- IPNI as: P. Li

P. Y. Li

Li, Pei Yuan; 李培元 ; Lǐ Péiyuán

First publication: 1987

- Employment: Northwest Institute of Soil and Water Conservation, Biology and Soil, Chinese Academy of Sciences（中国科学院西北水土保持生物土壤研究所）
- Research interest: Asparagaceae, Berberidaceae, Liliaceae [S]
- Published taxa: *Berberis, Fritillaria, Polygonatum*
- Location of specimens: KUN, PE, WUK
- Region: CHINA (Shaanxi)

P. H. Li

Li, Pei Hua; 李佩华 ; Lǐ Pèihuá

First publication: 1985

- Employment: The Institute of Vegetables, Chinese Academy of Agricultural Sciences（中国农业科学院蔬菜研究所）
- Research interest: Solanaceae [S]
- Published taxa: *Capsicum, Solanum*
- Affiliation: IVF
- Location of specimens: IVF
- Region: CHINA (Yunnan)

P. C. Li

Li, Pei Chun; Li, Pei Qiong; 李沛琼 ; Lǐ Pèiqióng; 李沛瓊

1934- **First publication: 1981**

- Employment: Institute of Botany, Chinese Academy of Sciences; Fairy Lake Botanical Garden, Shenzhen; Fairy Lake Botanical Garden, Shenzhen & Chinese Academy of Sciences（中国科学院植物研究所；深圳市仙湖植物园；深圳市中国科学院仙湖植物园）
- Research interest: Betulaceae, Cornaceae, Cyperaceae, Fabaceae [S]
- Published taxa: *Astragalus, Betula, Campylotropis, Carex, Carpinus, Chesneya, Chesniella, Cornus, Corylus, Crotalaria, Desmodium, Eleocharis, Glycyrrhiza, Gueldenstaedtia, Hedysarum, Indigofera, Kobresia, Oxytropis, Piptanthus, Pueraria, Schoenoplectus, Scleria, Thermopsis, Tibetia, Vicia*
- Affiliation: SZG
- Location of specimens: SZG
- Region: CHINA

P. F. Li

Li, Peng Fei; Lei, Paang Fei; 李鹏飞 ; Lǐ Péngfēi; 李鵬飛

First publication: 1946

- Employment: Lingnan University, Canton（岭南大学）
- Research interest: Poaceae [S]
- Published taxa: *Sinocalamus*
- Region: CHINA (Guangdong)

P. Li

Li, Ping; 李萍 ; Lǐ Píng

1960- **First publication: 1985**

- Employment: Department of Pharmacognosy, Nanjing Pharmaceutical College（南京药学院生药学教研室）
- Research interest: Liliaceae [S]
- Published taxa: *Fritillaria*
- Region: CHINA (Hubei)

C. T. Lee

Lee, Chi Te; 李祈德 ; Lǐ Qídé

First publication: 2013

- Employment: Nantou Forest District Office, Forestry Bureau, Council of Agriculture, "Executive Yuan"（"行政院"农业委员会林务局南投林区管理处）
- Research interest: Orchidaceae [S]
- Published taxa: *Aphyllorchis*
- Region: CHINA (Taiwan)

Q. S. Li

Li, Qian Sheng; 李谦盛 ; Lǐ Qiānshèng

1975- **First publication: 2018**

- Employment: Shanghai Chenshan Botanical Garden; Shanghai Institute of Technology（上海辰山植物园；上海应用技术大学）
- Research interest: Fagaceae [S]
- Published taxa: *Quercus*
- Region: CHINA (Guangdong)

Q. Y. Li

Li, Qin Yi; 李清义 ; Lǐ Qīngyì; 李清義

1927- **First publication: 1992**

- Employment: Department of Biology, Wuhan University（武汉大学生物系）
- Research interest: Acoraceae, Potamogetonaceae, Triuridaceae [S]
- Published taxa: *Potamogeton*
- Affiliation: WH
- Region: CHINA (Qinghai)

Q. J. Li

Li, Qing Jun; 李庆军 ; Lǐ Qìngjūn

1965- **First publication: 2008**

- Employment: Xishuangbanna Tropical Botanical Garden, Chinese Academy of Sciences（中国科学院西双版纳热带植物园）
- Research interest: Dioscoreaceae [S]
- Published taxa: *Tacca*
- Location of specimens: HITBC, KUN, PE
- Region: CHINA (Yunnan)

Ren Li

Li, Ren; 李仁 ; Lǐ Rén

1988- **First publication: 2020**

- Employment: Xishuangbanna Tropical Botanical Garden, Chinese Academy of Sciences（中国科学院西双版纳热带植物园）
- Research interest: Zingiberaceae [S]
- Published taxa: *Zingiber*
- Region: CHINA (MYANMAR)

R. Li

Li, Rong; 李嵘 ; Lǐ Róng

1975- **First publication: 2002**

- Employment: Kunming Institute of Botany, Chinese Academy of Sciences（中国科学院昆明植物研究所）
- Research interest: Apiaceae, Araceae, Araliaceae, Asparagaceae, Liliaceae, Nartheciaceae, Orchidaceae, Papaveraceae, Primulaceae, Rubiaceae [S]
- Published taxa: *Aletris, Arisaema, Calanthe, Coelogyne, Hydrocotyle, Ligusticum, Lloydia, Maianthemum, Meconopsis, Pholidota, Pleurospermum, Primula, Rubia*
- Affiliation: KUN
- Location of specimens: KUN
- Region: CHINA

R. T. Li

Li, Rong Tao; 李榕涛 ; Lǐ Róngtāo

1997- **First publication: 2019**

- Employment: Hainan Branch, Institute of Medicinal Plant Development, Chinese Academy of Medical Sciences（中国医学科学院药用植物研究所海南分所）
- Research interest: Aristolochiaceae [S]
- Published taxa: *Isotrema*
- Region: CHINA (Hainan)

R. G. Li

Li, Rui Gao; 李瑞高 ; Lǐ Ruìgāo

1941- **First publication: 1989**

- Employment: Guangxi Institute of Botany; Guangxi Institute of Botany, Chinese Academy of Sciences（广西植物研究所；广西壮族自治区中国科学院广西植物研究所）
- Research interest: Actinidiaceae, Theaceae [S]
- Published taxa: *Actinidia, Camellia*
- Location of specimens: IBK
- Region: CHINA (Guangxi)

Sheng Feng Li

Li, Sheng Feng; 李升峰 ; Lǐ Shēngfēng

1964- **First publication: 1995**

- Employment: Nanjing University（南京大学）
- Research interest: Poaceae [S]
- Published taxa: *Chimonocalamus*

• Location of specimens: N
• Region: CHINA (Yunnan)

S. L. Lee

Lee, Shih Lin; 李士林 ; Lǐ Shìlín
First publication: 1989
• Employment: Dr. Cecilia Koo Botanic Conservation Center (辜严倬云植物保种中心)
• Research interest: Theaceae [S]
• Published taxa: *Camellia*
• Region: CHINA

Shi J. Li

Li, Shi Jin; 李世晋 ; Lǐ Shìjìn
1973- **First publication: 2003**
• Employment: College of Life Sciences, South China Agricultural University; South China Botanical Garden, Chinese Academy of Sciences (华南农业大学生命科学学院 ; 中国科学院华南植物园)
• Research interest: Annonaceae, Fabaceae, Gesneriaceae, Orchidaceae [S]
• Published taxa: *Caesalpinia, Cladrastis, Didymocarpus, Liparis, Polyalthia, Thuniopsis, Zeuxine*
• Affiliation: IBSC
• Location of specimens: IBSC
• Region: CHINA

S. Y. Li

Li, Shi You; 李世友 ; Lǐ Shìyǒu
1963- **First publication: 1987**
• Employment: Botanical Laboratory, Northeast Forestry University (东北林业大学植物研究室)
• Research interest: Adoxaceae, Nyssaceae, Penthoraceae, Pinaceae, Polemoniaceae, Rhamnaceae [S]
• Published taxa: *Adoxa, Camptotheca, Penthorum, Pinus, Polemonium, Rhamnus*
• Region: CHINA

S. C. Li

Li, Shu Chun; 李书春 ; Lǐ Shūchūn; 李書春
1920- **First publication: 1981**
• Employment: Department of Forestry, Anhui Agricultural University (安徽农业大学林学系)
• Research interest: Araliaceae, Lardizabalaceae, Pinaceae, Poaceae, Rhamnaceae, Theaceae; Plants of Anhui, Plants of Shanxi [S]
• Published taxa: *Acanthopanax, Phyllostachys, Pinus, Pleioblastus, Rhamnus, Sargentodoxa, Stewartia*
• Affiliation: AAUF
• Location of specimens: AAUF
• Region: CHINA (Anhui)

S. X. Li

Li, Shu Xin; Li, Shu Hsin; 李书馨 ; Lǐ Shūxīn; 李書馨 , 李書心 , 李书心
1926-2007 **First publication: 1959**
• Employment: Institute of Forestry and Soil Sciences, Chinese Academy of Sciences (中国科学院林业土壤研究所)
• Research interest: Athyriaceae, Caprifoliaceae, Equisetaceae, Orobanchaceae, Plantaginaceae, Polygonaceae, Ranunculaceae; Pteridophytes [S]
• Published taxa: *Aconitum, Hippochaete, Neoathyrium, Pedicularis, Plantago, Polygonum, Ranunculus, Valeriana*
• Affiliation: IFP
• Location of specimens: IFP
• Region: CHINA (Liaoning)
• Also as: S. H. Li

S. J. Li

Li, Shu Jiu; 李淑久 ; Lǐ Shūjiǔ
1935- **First publication: 1988**
• Employment: Department of Forestry, Guizhou Agricultural College (贵州农学院)
• Research interest: Cucurbitaceae, Rosaceae [S]
• Published taxa: *Trichosanthes*
• Affiliation: GACP
• Location of specimens: GACP
• Region: CHINA (Guizhou)

S. H. Lee

Lee, Shu Hsien; Li, Shu Hsien; Li, Shu Suan; Li, Shu Xuan; 李曙轩 ; Lǐ Shǔ xuān; 李曙軒
1917-1990 **First publication: 1936**
• Employment: Department of Horticulture, College of Agriculture, National Central University (国立中央大学农学院园艺系)
• Research interest: Brassicaceae, Malvaceae [S]
• Published taxa: *Brassica, Corchorus*
• Region: CHINA

S. W. Li

Li, Shu Wan; 李述万 ; Lǐ Shùwàn
1990- **First publication: 2018**
• Employment: Guangxi Institute of Botany, Chinese Academy of Sciences (广西壮族自治区中国科学院广西植物研究所)
• Research interest: Gesneriaceae [S]
• Published taxa: *Hemiboea*
• Region: CHINA (Guizhou)

S. K. Lee

Lee, Shu Kang; Li, Shu Gang; Lee, Shu Gang; Li, Shu Kang; 李树刚 ; Lǐ Shùgāng; 李樹剛
1915-1998 **First publication: 1956**

- Employment: Guangxi Institute of Botany, Chinese Academy of Sciences（广西壮族自治区中国科学院广西植物研究所）
- Research interest: Arecaceae, Ebenaceae, Euphorbiaceae, Fabaceae, Fagaceae, Lauraceae, Lythraceae, Oleaceae, Rosaceae [S]
- Published taxa: *Amphicarpaea, Atylosia, Beilschmiedia, Cajanus, Cinnamomum, Cryptocarya, Cyclobalanopsis, Diospyros, Dumasia, Endiandra, Erythrina, Euchresta, Excoecaria, Flemingia, Fraxinus, Guihaia, Lagerstroemia, Lindera, Litsea, Machilus, Neocinnamomum, Phoebe, Rhynchosia, Rubus, Sapium, Syndiclis, Trachycarpus*
- Affiliation: IBK
- Location of specimens: GAC, IBK
- Region: CHINA
- Also as: S. G. Lee; S. Lee

S. C. Lee

Lee, Shun Ching; Li, Shun Ching; Lee, Shun Ch'ing; Li, Shun Ch'ing; Li, Shun Qing; 李顺卿；Lǐ Shùnqīng; 李顺卿

1894-1972 **First publication: 1935**

- Employment: College of Sciences, Provincial Anhui University（省立安徽大学理学院）
- Research interest: Cannabaceae, Lauraceae [S]
- Published taxa: *Homoioceltis, Machilus*
- Region: CHINA

Si Feng Li

Li, Si Feng; 李思锋；Lǐ Sīfēng

1960- **First publication: 1990**

- Employment: Northwest China Institute of Botany, Chinese Academy of Sciences and Shaanxi Province（陕西省中国科学院西北植物研究所）
- Research interest: Fabaceae, Rosaceae; Plants of Shaanxi [S]
- Published taxa: *Oxytropis, Potentilla*
- Affiliation: WUK, XBGH
- Location of specimens: WUK, XBGH
- Region: CHINA (Shaanxi, Xizang)

S. M. Li

Li, Sz Ming; 李思明；Lǐ Sīmíng

First publication: 1999

- Employment: Kou-Fu Elementary School, Hualien（花莲县国福国民小学）
- Research interest: Asteraceae [S]
- Published taxa: *Centratherum*
- Region: CHINA (Taiwan)

S. P. Li

Li, Sung Po; Li, Song Bo; Li, Song Bai; 李松柏；Lǐ Sōngbǎi

1966- **First publication: 2002**

- Employment: Long-Hai Elementary School, Taichung County（台中县龙海国民小学）
- Research interest: Menyanthaceae [S]
- Published taxa: *Nymphoides*
- Location of specimens: HAST
- Region: CHINA (Taiwan)

T. Li

Li, Tao; 李涛；Lǐ Tāo

1971- **First publication: 2010**

- Employment: West China School of Pharmacy, Sichuan Univerisity（四川大学华西药学院）
- Research interest: Crassulaceae, Orchidaceae [S]
- Published taxa: *Rhodiola*
- Affiliation: WCU
- Location of specimens: WCU
- Region: CHINA (Sichuan)
- Also as: Tao Li

T. L. Li

Li, Te Ling; 李特灵；Lǐ Tèlíng

1982- **First publication: 2007**

- Employment: School of Resources and Environment, Central South University of Forestry and Technology（中南林业科技大学资源与环境学院）
- Research interest: Acanthaceae [S]
- Published taxa: *Eranthemum*
- Region: CHINA

T. Z. Li

Li, Ti Zhi; 李体智；Lǐ Tǐzhì

1954- **First publication: 1989**

- Employment: Liaoning Institute of Pomology（辽宁省果树科学研究所）
- Research interest: Rosaceae [S]
- Published taxa: *Armeniaca*
- Region: CHINA (Liaoning)

W. C. Li

Li, Wan Cheng; 李万成；Lǐ Wànchéng

1952- **First publication: 1981**

- Employment: Qiaoduan Forest Farm, Nanzhao County, Henan（河南省南召县乔端林场）
- Research interest: Fagaceae, Salicaceae [S]
- Published taxa: *Populus, Quercus*
- Region: CHINA (Henan)

W. L. Li

Li, Wei Lin; 李维林；Lǐ Wéilín

1966- **First publication: 2000**

- Employment: Institute of Botany, Jiangsu Province and Chinese Academy of Sciences（江苏省中国科学院植物研究所）

- Research interest: Rosaceae [S]
- Published taxa: *Rubus*
- Region: CHINA

W. D. Li

Li, Wen De; 李文德；Lǐ Wéndé

1937- **First publication: 1985**

- Employment: Guizhou Research Institute of Forestry（贵州省林业科学研究所）
- Research interest: Poaceae [S]
- Published taxa: *Ampelocalamus, Chimonobambusa, Drepanostachyum*
- Region: CHINA (Guizhou)

W. H. Li

Li, Wen Hua; 李文华；Lǐ Wénhuá

1951- **First publication: 2006**

- Employment: Boltala Mongolia Autonomous Prefecture Forestry Bureau, Xinjiang（新疆博尔塔拉蒙古自治州林业局）
- Research interest: Betulaceae [S]
- Published taxa: *Betula*
- Location of specimens: PE
- Region: CHINA (Xinjiang)

Wen H. Li

Li, Wen Hui; 李文卉；Lǐ Wénhuì

1991- **First publication: 2017**

- Employment: College of Life Sciences, Nanjing Agricultural University（南京农业大学生命科学学院）
- Research interest: Berberidaceae [S]
- Published taxa: *Berberis*
- Region: CHINA (Sichuan)
- IPNI as: W. H. Li

Wen L. Li

Li, Wen Lan; 李文兰；Lǐ Wénlán

First publication: 2015

- Employment: College of Chemistry and Bioengineering, Guilin University of Technology; College of Life Science and Technology, Guangxi University（桂林理工大学化学与生物工程学院；广西大学生命科学与技术学院）
- Research interest: Gesneriaceae [S]
- Published taxa: *Primulina*
- Region: CHINA (Guangxi)
- IPNI as: W. L. Li

W. Z. Li

Li, Wen Zheng; 李文政；Lǐ Wénzhèng

1937- **First publication: 1983**

- Employment: Yunnan Forestry College（云南林学院）
- Research interest: Fagaceae, Opiliaceae, Salicaceae [S]
- Published taxa: *Cyclobalanopsis, Melientha, Salix*
- Location of specimens: SWFC
- Region: CHINA (Yunnan)

H. W. Li

Li, Hsi Wen; Li, Xi Wen; **李锡文；Lǐ Xīwén; 李錫文**

1931-2021 **First publication: 1965**

- Employment: Kunming Institute of Botany, Chinese Academy of Sciences（中国科学院昆明植物研究所）
- Research interest: Acanthaceae, Adoxaceae, Aquifoliaceae, Asparagaceae, Brassicaceae, Caprifoliaceae, Carlemanniaceae, Celastraceae, Ebenaceae, Gentianaceae, Geraniaceae, Gesneriaceae, Lamiaceae, Lauraceae, Malpighiaceae, Melastomataceae, Musaceae, Oleaceae, Sabiaceae, Solanaceae, Thymelaeaceae, Urticaceae [S]
- Published taxa: *Aeschynanthus, Alseodaphne, Alseodaphnopsis, Ancylostemon, Aspidopterys, Beccarinda, Beilschmiedia, Boeicopsis, Calcareoboea, Chelonopsis, Chirita, Cinnamomum, Clinopodium, Comanthosphace, Comastoma, Cryptocarya, Daphne, Didissandra, Didymocarpus, Diospyros, Dysophylla, Elatostema, Elsholtzia, Gentiana, Gentianopsis, Geranium, Girardinia, Goldfussia, Hanceola, Haplanthoides, Hemiboea, Hilliella, Hyssopus, Ilex, Isodon, Iteadaphne, Keiskea, Kinostemon, Lamium, Lecanthus, Leonurus, Lindera, Litsea, Lomatogonium, Loxostigma, Lycopus, Lysionotus, Machilus, Marmoritis, Meliosma, Mentha, Metastachydium, Microtoena, Mosla, Musella, Neolitsea, Nepeta, Notochaete, Ophiopogon, Oreocharis, Ornithoboea, Osmanthus, Panzeria, Panzerina, Paraphlomis, Pellionia, Perilla, Petrocosmea, Phlomis, Phoebe, Pilea, Pogonanthera, Pogostemon, Pteracanthus, Rabdosia, Salacia, Salvia, Scutellaria, Silvianthus, Sinopogonanthera, Sinopora, Sinosassafras, Skapanthus, Syndiclis, Tremacron, Tumidinodus, Viburnum*
- Affiliation: KUN
- Location of specimens: KUN
- Region: CHINA

Xian Y. Li

Li, Xian Yuan; 李先源；Lǐ Xiānyuán

1965- **First publication: 2019**

- Employment: College of Horticulture and Landscape Architecture, Southwest University（西南大学园艺园林学院）
- Research interest: Arecaceae; Economic Plants [S]
- Published taxa: *Guihaia*
- Affiliation: HWA
- Location of specimens: HWA

• Region: CHINA (Chongqing)

Y. T. Lee

Lee, Yin Tse; 李賢祉 ; Lǐ Xiánzhǐ; 李贤祉

First publication: 1973

• Employment: Northeastern University, U.S.A. (美国东北大学)
• Research interest: Fabaceae [S]
• Published taxa: *Gleditsia, Hymenaea*
• Region: [AMERICA]

Xiang W. Li

Li, Xiang Wang; 李乡旺 ; Lǐ Xiāngwàng; 李鄉旺

1944- **First publication: 1990**

• Employment: Institute of Forest Plant, Southwest Forestry College (西南林学院森林植物研究所)
• Research interest: Berberidaceae, Cannabaceae, Pinaceae, Sapindaceae [S]
• Published taxa: *Aesculus, Berberis, Pinus, Celtis*
• Affiliation: SWFC
• Location of specimens: SWFC
• Region: CHINA (Yunnan)

X. P. Li

Li, Xiang Ping; 李湘萍 ; Lǐ Xiāngpíng

1964- **First publication: 1990**

• Employment: Department of Forestry, Nanjing Forestry University (南京林业大学林学系)
• Research interest: Araliaceae, Pinaceae; Gymnospermae [S]
• Published taxa: *Aralia, Pentapanax, Pinus*
• Affiliation: NF
• Location of specimens: NF
• Region: CHINA

Xiang Li

Li, Xiang; 李想 ; Lǐ Xiǎng

1991- **First publication: 2019**

• Employment: College of Life Sciences, Wuhan University (武汉大学生命科学学院)
• Research interest: Isoetaceae [P]
• Published taxa: *Isoetes*
• Region: CHINA (Yunnan)

Xiao Q. Li

Li, Xiao Qian; 李小倩 ; Lǐ Xiǎoqiàn

1996- **First publication: 2019**

• Employment: Institute of Botany, Chinese Academy of Sciences (中国科学院植物研究所)
• Research interest: Gesneriaceae [S]
• Published taxa: *Hemiboea*
• Region: CHINA (Guangdong)
• IPNI as: X. Q. Li

X. Jie Li

Li, Xiao Jie; 李小杰 ; Lǐ Xiǎojié

1986- **First publication: 2020**

• Employment: Sichuan Provincial Academy of Natural Resource Sciencs (四川省自然资源科学研究院)
• Research interest: Apiaceae; Plants of Emei Shan [S]
• Published taxa: *Pternopetalum*
• Region: CHINA (Sichuan)

Xiao D. Li

Li, Xiao Dong; 李晓东 ; Lǐ Xiǎodōng

1967- **First publication: 2005**

• Employment: Wuhan Botanical Garden, Chinese Academy of Sciences (中国科学院武汉植物园)
• Research interest: Asteraceae, Orobanchaceae, Ranunculaceae; Plants of Hubei [S]
• Published taxa: *Hepatica, Triaenophora*
• Affiliation: HIB
• Location of specimens: HIB
• Region: CHINA (Hubei)
• IPNI as: Xi. D. Li

X. Jiang Li

Li, Xiao Jiang; 李晓江 ; Lǐ Xiǎojiāng

First publication: 2012

• Employment: Xichang University (西昌学院)
• Research interest: Polygonaceae [S]
• Published taxa: *Fagopyrum*
• Region: CHINA (Sichuan)
• IPNI as: X. J. Li

Xiao J. Li

Li, Xiao Juan; 李晓娟 ; Lǐ Xiǎojuān

1985- **First publication: 2012**

• Employment: Shandong University of Traditional Chinese Medicine (山东中医药大学)
• Research interest: Dryopteridaceae, Hypodematiaceae [P]
• Published taxa: *Cyrtomium, Hypodematium*
• Region: CHINA (Shandong)
• IPNI as: X. J. Li

Xiao Juan Li

Li, Xiao Juan; 李晓娟 ; Lǐ Xiǎojuān

First publication: 2020

• Employment: South China Botanical Garden, Chinese Academy of Sciences (中国科学院华南植物园)
• Research interest: Burmanniaceae [S]
• Published taxa: *Burmannia*
• Region: CHINA (Guangdong)

X. Q. Li

Li, Xiao Qing; 李晓青 ; ǐ Xiǎoqīng

1968- First publication: 1994
- Employment: Department of Biology, Fujian Normal University（福建师范大学生物系）
- Research interest: Malvaceae [S]
- Published taxa: *Urena*
- Region: CHINA (Fujian)

X. Z. Li

Li, Xin Zheng; 李心正；Lǐ Xīnzhèng
1982- First publication: 2007
- Employment: Institute of Botany, Chinese Academy of Sciences（中国科学院植物研究所）
- Research interest: Colchicaceae [S]
- Published taxa: *Disporum*
- Region: CHINA (Chongqing)

X. H. Li

Li, Xin Hua; 李新华；Lǐ Xīnhuá
1968- First publication: 1996
- Employment: College of Life Sciences, Nanjing Agricultural University; Institute of Botany, Jiangsu Province and Chinese Academy of Sciences（南京农业大学生命科学学院；江苏省中国科学院植物研究所）
- Research interest: Apiaceae, Berberidaceae [S]
- Published taxa: *Berberis, Ostericum*
- Location of specimens: NAU
- Region: CHINA

Xin W. Li

Li, Xin Wei; 李新伟；Lǐ Xīnwěi
1973- First publication: 2016
- Employment: Wuhan Botanical Garden, Chinese Academy of Sciences（中国科学院武汉植物园）
- Research interest: Actinidiaceae, Balsaminaceae [S]
- Published taxa: *Impatiens*
- Affiliation: HIB
- Location of specimens: HIB
- Region: CHINA (Hubei)
- IPNI as: X. W. Li

X. X. Lee

Lee, Xin Xian; Lee, X. S.; 李信贤；Lǐ Xìnxián; 李信賢
1939-2016 First publication: 1982
- Employment: Guangxi Agricultural College（广西农学院）
- Research interest: Capparaceae, Sapindaceae; Woody Plants [S]
- Published taxa: *Capparis, Lepisanthes*
- Affiliation: GAC
- Location of specimens: GAC
- Region: CHINA (Guangxi)
- Also as: X. S. Lee

X. W. Li

Li, Xing Wen; 李兴文；Lǐ Xīngwén; 李興文
1932- First publication: 1986
- Employment: Shandong Forestry School（山东省林业学校）
- Research interest: Fagaceae, Rosaceae, Salicaceae; Woody Plants [S]
- Published taxa: *Malus, Populus, Quercus, Salix, Spiraea*
- Affiliation: SDFS
- Location of specimens: SDFS
- Region: CHINA (Shandong)

Xiong Li

Li, Xiong; 李雄；Lǐ Xióng
1995- First publication: 2019
- Employment: College of Forestry, Central South University of Forestry and Technology（中南林业科技大学林学院）
- Research interest: Rubiaceae [S]
- Published taxa: *Spiradiclis*
- Region: CHINA (Yunnan)
- IPNI as: X. Li

Xiu P. Li

Li, Xiu Peng; 李修鹏；Lǐ Xiūpéng
1970- First publication: 2014
- Employment: Ningbo Technology Extension Center for Forestry and Specialty Forest Products, Zhejiang（浙江省宁波市林特科技推广中心）
- Research interest: Orchidaceae [S]
- Published taxa: *Bulbophyllum*
- Region: CHINA (Zhejiang)
- IPNI as: X. P. Li

Xui J. Li

Li, Xiu Jie; 李秀杰；Lǐ Xiùjié
1955- First publication: 1989
- Employment: Liaoning Institute of Pomology（辽宁省果树科学研究所）
- Research interest: Rosaceae [S]
- Published taxa: *Armeniaca*
- Region: CHINA (Liaoning)
- IPNI as: X. J. Li

X. De Li

Li, Xue De; 李学德；Lǐ Xuédé
First publication: 1996
- Employment: Zhengzhou Teachers' School（郑州师范学校）
- Research interest: Amaranthaceae [S]
- Published taxa: *Chenopodium*
- Region: CHINA (Henan)

X. D. Li

Li, Xue Dong; 李学东 ; Lǐ Xuédōng

1968- First publication: 1995

- Employment: Kunming Institute of Botany, Chinese Academy of Sciences（中国科学院昆明植物研究所）
- Research interest: Phrymaceae [S]
- Published taxa: *Cyrtandromoea*
- Region: CHINA (Yunnan)

X. Y. Li

Li, Xue Yu; 李学禹 ; Lǐ Xuéyǔ ; 李學禹

1932- First publication: 1983

- Employment: Department of Biology and Basic Courses, Shihezi Agricultural College（石河子农学院生物基础部）
- Research interest: Fabaceae [S]
- Published taxa: *Glycyrrhiza, Lespedeza*
- Affiliation: SHI
- Location of specimens: SHI
- Region: CHINA (Xinjiang)

Y. R. Li

Li, Ya Ru; 李雅茹 ; Lǐ Yǎrú

1935- First publication: 1979

- Employment: Kunming Institute of Botany, Chinese Academy of Sciences（中国科学院昆明植物研究所）
- Research interest: Aquifoliaceae, Araliaceae, Celastraceae, Hernandiaceae, Lamiaceae [S]
- Published taxa: *Acanthopanax, Brassaiopsis, Celastrus, Dendropanax, Eleutherococcus, Euonymus, Ilex, Illigera, Macropanax, Pentapanax, Rabdosia, Schefflera*
- Affiliation: HEBI
- Location of specimens: HEBI
- Region: CHINA (Yunnan, Xizang)

Y. H. Li

Li, Yan Hui; 李延辉 ; Lǐ Yánhuī; 李延輝

1930-2016 First publication: 1981

- Employment: Yunnan Institute of Tropical Botany, Chinese Academy of Sciences; Kunming Institute of Botany, Chinese Academy of Sciences（中国科学院云南热带植物研究所；中国科学院昆明植物研究所）
- Research interest: Amaranthaceae, Apocynaceae, Araliaceae, Celastraceae, Clusiaceae, Dioscoreaceae, Euphorbiaceae, Myristicaceae, Vitaceae [S]
- Published taxa: *Achyranthes, Cissus, Dioscorea, Excoecaria, Garcinia, Heterostemma, Hydrocotyle, Knema, Marsdenia, Maytenus*
- Affiliation: KUN
- Location of specimens: HITBC, KUN
- Region: CHINA (Yunnan)

Yan B. Li

Li, Yan Bo; 李彦波 ; Lǐ Yànbō

1992- First publication: 2018

- Employment: Kunming Institute of Botany, Chinese Academy of Sciences（中国科学院昆明植物研究所）
- Research interest: Asteraceae [S]
- Published taxa: *Carpesium*
- Region: CHINA (Yunnan)
- IPNI as: Y. B. Li

Yan J. Li

Li, Yan Jun; 李艳君 ; Lǐ Yànjūn

1963- First publication: 2000

- Employment: Fengcheng Garden Management Office, Liaoning（辽宁省凤城市园林管理处）
- Research interest: Liliaceae [S]
- Published taxa: *Lilium*
- Region: CHINA (Liaoning)
- IPNI as: Y. J. Li

Yi F. Li

Li, Yi Fan; 李一凡 ; Lǐ Yīfán

1994- First publication: 2020

- Employment: Bazi Art Collection & Botanical Garden, Mengzi, Yunnan（云南蒙自八子花园）
- Research interest: Araceae [S]
- Published taxa: *Alocasia*
- Region: CHINA (Yunnan)
- IPNI as: Yifan Li

Y. D. Li

Li, Yi De; 李意德 ; Lǐ Yìdé

1961- First publication: 2011

- Employment: Research Institute of Tropical Forestry, Chinese Academy of Forestry（中国林业科学研究院热带林业研究所）
- Research interest: Aristolochiaceae, Orchidaceae, Triuridaceae [S]
- Published taxa: *Aristolochia, Sciaphila, Zeuxine*
- Region: CHINA (Hainan)

Yin K. Li

Li, Yin Kun; 李荫昆 ; Lǐ Yīnkūn; 李蔭昆

1935- First publication: 1985

- Employment: Guangxi Institute of Botany（广西植物研究所）
- Research interest: Acoraceae [S]
- Published taxa: *Acorus*
- Location of specimens: IBK
- Region: CHINA (Guangxi, Hunan)
- IPNI as: Y. K. Li

Yin Li

Li, Yin; Li, Ying; 李颖 ; Lǐ Yǐng

1929- **First publication: 1974**

- Employment: Shanghai First Medical College; School of Pharmacy, Shanghai Medical University（上海第一医学院；上海医科大学药学院）
- Research interest: Apiaceae [S]
- Published taxa: *Bupleurum*
- Location of specimens: SHMU
- Region: CHINA

Y. K. Li

Li, Yong Kang; 李永康；Lǐ Yǒngkāng

1918-2006 **First publication: 1980**

- Employment: Institute of Biology, Guizhou Academy of Sciences（贵州省科学院生物研究所）
- Research interest: Altingiaceae, Aquifoliaceae, Betulaceae, Fagaceae, Hamamelidaceae, Iteaceae, Lauraceae, Magnoliaceae, Pentaphylacaceae, Rosaceae, Sapindaceae, Theaceae; Woody Plants [S]
- Published taxa: *Acer, Beilschmiedia, Camellia, Carpinus, Cinnamomum, Cyclobalanopsis, Distylium, Eurya, Ilex, Itea, Lindera, Machilus, Michelia, Phoebe, Photinia, Semiliquidambar, Tutcheria*
- Affiliation: GZAC
- Location of specimens: GZAC, HGAS
- Region: CHINA (Guizhou)

Y. I Lee

Lee, Yung I; 李勇毅；Lǐ Yǒngyì

First publication: 2013

- Employment: Biology Department, Museum of Natural Science（自然科学博物馆生物学组）
- Research interest: Orchidaceae [S]
- Published taxa: *Calanthe, Cypripedium, Paphiopedilum*
- Region: CHINA (Taiwan)

Yong F. Li

Li, Yong Fu; 李涌福；Lǐ Yǒngfú

1994- **First publication: 2020**

- Employment: College of Biology and the Environment, Nanjing Forestry University（南京林业大学生物与环境学院）
- Research interest: Oleaceae [S]
- Published taxa: *Chengiodendron*
- Region: CHINA

Y. F. Li

Li, Yu Feng; 李玉峰；Lǐ Yùfēng

1987- **First publication: 2018**

- Employment: Zijin Baixi Provincial Nature Reserve Management Office, Guangdong（广东紫金白溪省级自然保护区管理处）
- Research interest: Orchidaceae [S]
- Published taxa: *Platanthera*
- Region: CHINA (Guangdong)

Yu L. Li

Li, Yu Ling; 李玉玲；Lǐ Yùlíng

1987- **First publication: 2020**

- Employment: College of Forestry and Landscape Architecture, South China Agricultural University; South China Botanical Garden, Chinese Academy of Sciences（华南农业大学林学与风景园林学院；中国科学院华南植物园）
- Research interest: Begoniaceae, Orchidaceae [S]
- Published taxa: *Begonia, Oberonia*
- Region: CHINA (Guangxi, Yunnan)

Y. P. Li

Li, Yu Ping; 李玉萍；Lǐ Yùpíng

1976- **First publication: 2013**

- Employment: Department of Horticulture, Jinling Institute of Technology（金陵科技学院园艺系）
- Research interest: Ericaceae [S]
- Published taxa: *Rhododendron*
- Region: CHINA (Zhejiang)

Y. S. Li

Li, Yu Shan; 李玉珊；Lǐ Yùshān

1935-2018 **First publication: 1988**

- Employment: Xilingol League Institute of Forestry Sciences, Inner Mongolia（内蒙古锡林郭勒盟林业科学研究所）
- Research interest: Ulmaceae [S]
- Published taxa: *Ulmus*
- Region: CHINA (Nei Mongol)

Yuan B. Li

Li, Yuan Bo; 李渊博；Lǐ Yuānbó

1982- **First publication: 2006**

- Employment: Institute of Botany, Chinese Academy of Sciences（中国科学院植物研究所）
- Research interest: Gesneriaceae [S]
- Published taxa: *Chirita*
- Region: CHINA (Guangxi)
- IPNI as: Y. B. Li

Y. Q. Li

Li, Yuan Qiu; 李远球；Lǐ Yuǎnqiú

First publication: 2020

- Employment: Administration Bureau of Shimentai National Natural Reserve, Guangdong（广东石门台国家级自然保护区管理局）
- Research interest: Melanthiaceae [S]
- Published taxa: *Chamaelirium*
- Region: CHINA (Guangdong)

Yun Li

Li, Yun; 李云 ; Lǐ Yún

1977- **First publication: 2003**

- Employment: College of Life Sciences, Northwest University（西北大学生命科学学院）
- Research interest: Poaceae [S]
- Published taxa: *Bashania*
- Region: CHINA (Shaanxi)
- IPNI as: Y. Li

Ze X. Li

Li, Ze Xian; 李泽贤 ; Lǐ Zéxián; 李澤賢

1936- **First publication: 1986**

- Employment: South China Botanical Garden, Chinese Academy of Sciences（中国科学院华南植物研究所）
- Research interest: Balanophoraceae, Berberidaceae, Boraginaceae, Dioscoreaceae, Euphorbiaceae, Fagaceae, Gesneriaceae, Menispermaceae, Polygalaceae, Primulaceae, Saxifragaceae; Plants of S. China [S]
- Published taxa: *Ardisia, Balanophora, Blachia, Chrysosplenium, Cyclobalanopsis, Dioscorea, Ehretia, Mahonia, Paraboea, Polygala, Quercus, Tinospora*
- Affiliation: IBSC
- Location of specimens: IBSC
- Region: CHINA (Guangdong, Hainan)

Zhen Q. Li

Li, Zhen Qing; 李振卿 ; Lǐ Zhènqīng

1953- **First publication: 1989**

- Employment: Xuchang Institute of Forestry Science, Henan（河南省许昌林业科学技术研究所）
- Research interest: Calycanthaceae, Podocarpaceae [S]
- Published taxa: *Chimonanthus, Podocarpus*
- Region: CHINA (Henan)

Z. Yu Li

Li, Zhen Yu; Li, Zheng Yu; 李振宇 ; Lǐ Zhènyǔ

1952- **First publication: 1983**

- Employment: Institute of Botany, Chinese Academy of Sciences（中国科学院植物研究所）
- Research interest: Asteraceae, Brassicaceae, Cactaceae, Campanulaceae, Caryophyllaceae, Cornaceae, Gesneriaceae, Haloragaceae, Hamamelidaceae, Hypericaceae, Lamiaceae, Lentibulariaceae, Plantaginaceae, Poaceae, Podostemaceae, Salicaceae [S]
- Published taxa: *Alangium, Campanula, Chirita, Cladopus, Deinostigma, Distylium, Epithema, Fargesia, Gelidocalamus, Hemiboea, Hilliella, Hypericum, Ligularia, Myriophyllum, Oligostachyum, Opithandra, Opuntia, Oreocharis, Paraphlomis, Plantago, Pleioblastus, Primulina, Salix, Stellaria, Terniopsis, Utricularia, Whytockia*
- Affiliation: PE
- Location of specimens: PE,WCSBG
- Region: CHINA
- IPNI as: Z. Y. Li

Zheng H. Li

Li, Zheng Hong; 李正红 ; Lǐ Zhènghóng

1964- **First publication: 2011**

- Employment: Research Institute of Resource Insects, Chinese Academy of Forestry（中国林业科学研究院资源昆虫研究所）
- Research interest: Musaceae [S]
- Published taxa: *Musella*
- Region: CHINA (Yunnan)
- IPNI as: Z. H. Li

Zhi Li

Li, Zhi; 李志 ; Lǐ Zhì

1989- **First publication: 2017**

- Employment: Hunan Normal University; College of Forestry, Guizhou University（湖南师范大学；贵州大学林学院）
- Research interest: Asteraceae [S]
- Published taxa: *Aster*
- Region: CHINA (Guizhou, Hunan)
- IPNI as: Z. Li

Zhi M. Li

Li, Zhi Min; 李志敏 ; Lǐ Zhìmǐn

1963- **First publication: 2009**

- Employment: School of Life Science, Yunnan Normal University（云南师范大学生命科学学院）
- Research interest: Cornaceae, Fabaceae, Gesneriaceae, Lamiaceae [S]
- Published taxa: *Cornus, Eriophyton, Oreocharis, Salweenia*
- Affiliation: YNUB
- Region: CHINA (Sichuan, Yunnan, Xizang)
- IPNI as: Z. M. Li

Zhi Yong Li

Li, Zhi Yong; 李志勇 ; Lǐ Zhìyǒng

1965- **First publication: 2020**

- Employment: Institute of Grassland Research, Chinese Academy of Agricultural Sciences（中国农业科学院草原研究所）
- Research interest: Fabaceae [S]
- Published taxa: *Astragalus*
- Region: CHINA (Nei Mongol)

Zhi Y. Li

Li, Zhi Yun; 李志云 ; Lǐ Zhìyún; 李志雲

1934- **First publication: 1995**

- Employment: Suichang Institute of Forestry, Zhejiang (浙江省遂昌县林业科学研究所)
- Research interest: Taxaceae [S]
- Published taxa: *Torreya*
- Region: CHINA (Zhejiang)

Zhi Z. Li

Li, Zhi Zhong; 李治中; Lǐ Zhìzhōng

1992- **First publication: 2018**

- Employment: Wuhan Botanical Garden, Chinese Academy of Sciences (中国科学院武汉植物园)
- Research interest: Hydrocharitaceae [S]
- Published taxa: *Ottelia*
- Region: CHINA (Guangxi)
- IPNI as: Z. Z. Li

Zhu Li bis

Li, Zhu; 李柱; Lǐ Zhù

1957- **First publication: 2008**

- Employment: Institute of Grassland, Xinjiang Academy of Animal Sciences (新疆畜牧科学院草原研究所)
- Research interest: Amaranthaceae [S]
- Published taxa: *Krascheninnikovia*
- Region: CHINA (Xinjiang)

W. Y. Lien

Lien, Wen Yen; Lian, Wen Yen; Lian, Wen Yan; 连文琰; Lián Wényǎn; 連文琰

1929- **First publication: 1975**

- Employment: Institute of Materia Medica, Chinese Academy of Medical Sciences (中国医学科学院药物研究所)
- Research interest: Fabaceae, Menispermaceae [S]
- Published taxa: *Cyclea*
- Affiliation: IMD
- Location of specimens: IMD
- Region: CHINA

Y. S. Lian

Lian, Yong Shan; Lian, Yung Shan; 廉永善; Lián Yǒngshàn

1939- **First publication: 1979**

- Employment: College of Life Sciences, Northwest Normal University (西北师范大学生命科学学院)
- Research interest: Araliaceae, Asteraceae, Boraginaceae, Campanulaceae, Caprifoliaceae, Caryophyllaceae, Elaeagnaceae, Orobanchaceae, Papaveraceae, Pittosporaceae, Rosaceae, Saxifragaceae, Thymelaeaceae [S]
- Published taxa: *Acanthopanax, Amygdalus, Cyananthus, Dipelta, Eritrichium, Euphrasia, Hippophae, Lobelia, Meconopsis, Melandrium, Pittosporum, Pratia, Pseudostellaria, Saussurea, Saxifraga, Stellaria, Wikstroemia*
- Affiliation: NWTC, NWUB
- Location of specimens: NWTC, NWUB
- Region: CHINA

P. H. Liang

Liang, Pao Han; Liang, Bao Han; 梁宝汉; Liáng Bǎohàn; 梁寶漢

1911-1988 **First publication: 1982**

- Employment: Department of Forestry, South China Agricultural College (华南农学院林学系)
- Research interest: Moraceae; Plants of S. China [S]
- Published taxa: *Broussonetia*
- Affiliation: CANT
- Location of specimens: CANT, SCAUB
- Region: CHINA (Guangdong)

C. F. Liang

Liang, Chou Fen; Liang, Chou Feng; 梁畴芬; Liáng Chóufēn; 梁疇芬

1921-1998 **First publication: 1975**

- Employment: Guangxi Institute of Botany, Chinese Academy of Sciences (广西壮族自治区中国科学院广西植物研究所)
- Research interest: Actinidiaceae, Aquifoliaceae, Aristolochiaceae, Malvaceae, Primulaceae, Rutaceae, Sapindaceae, Styracaceae, Theaceae, Zingiberaceae [S]
- Published taxa: *Actinidia, Alpinia, Amomum, Aristolochia, Asarum, Camellia, Clausena, Clematoclethra, Curcuma, Firmiana, Huodendron, Ilex, Isotrema, Lepisanthes, Lysimachia, Saurauia, Wurfbainia*
- Affiliation: IBK
- Location of specimens: GAC, IBK
- Region: CHINA (Guangxi)

C. Z. Liang

Liang, Cun Zhu; 梁存柱; Liáng Cúnzhù

1964- **First publication: 2003**

- Employment: Department of Ecology and Environmental Science, Inner Mongolia University (内蒙古大学生态与环境科学系)
- Research interest: Asteraceae; Plants of C. Asia [S]
- Published taxa: *Elachanthemum*
- Affiliation: HIMC
- Location of specimens: HIMC
- Region: CHINA (Gansu)

D. R. Liang

Liang, Ding Ren; 梁定仁; Liáng Dìngrén

1962- **First publication: 1991**

- Employment: Guangxi Institute of Ethnic Medicine (广西民族医药研究所)

- Research interest: Begoniaceae, Cucurbitaceae, Elaeagnaceae, Sabiaceae; Medicinal Plants [S]
- Published taxa: *Begonia, Elaeagnus, Gynostemma, Hemsleya, Sabia*
- Affiliation: GXEM
- Location of specimens: GXEM
- Region: CHINA (Guangxi)

G. J. Liang

Liang, Gui Juan; 梁桂娟 ; Liáng Guìjuān

1973- **First publication: 1999**

- Employment: Guangxi Forestry Research Institute (广西壮族自治区林业科学研究院)
- Research interest: Juglandaceae [S]
- Published taxa: *Platycarya*
- Region: CHINA (Guangxi)

G. Y. Liang

Liang, Gui You; 梁桂友 ; Liáng Guìyǒu

1975- **First publication: 2013**

- Employment: Guangxi Institute of Botany, Chinese Academy of Sciences (广西壮族自治区中国科学院广西植物研究所)
- Research interest: Gesneriaceae [S]
- Published taxa: *Hemiboea*
- Region: CHINA (Guangxi)

H. R. Liang

Liang, Hai Rui; 梁海锐 ; Liáng Hǎiruì

1970- **First publication: 1990**

- Employment: Faculty of Chinese Pharmacy, Beijing College of Traditional Chinese Medicine (北京中医学院中药鉴定室)
- Research interest: Berberidaceae [S]
- Published taxa: *Epimedium*
- Region: CHINA

H. P. Liang

Liang, Hong Ping; 梁红平 ; Liáng Hóngpíng

1963- **First publication: 1993**

- Employment: College of Forestry Resources, Beijing Forestry University (北京林业大学林业资源学院)
- Research interest: Vitaceae; Woody Plants [S]
- Published taxa: *Vitis*
- Affiliation: BJFC
- Region: CHINA (Hebei)

H. L. Liang

Liang, Hui Ling; 梁惠凌 ; Liáng Huìlíng

1973- **First publication: 2013**

- Employment: Guangxi Institute of Botany, Chinese Academy of Sciences (广西壮族自治区中国科学院广西植物研究所)
- Research interest: Gesneriaceae [S]
- Published taxa: *Primulina*
- Region: CHINA (Guangxi)

W. C. Leong

Leong, Wai Chao; Liang, Hui Zhou; **梁慧舟 ; Liáng Huìzhōu**

First publication: 2005

- Employment: Herbarium, Biodiversity Research Center, "Academia Sinica" (中研院生物多样性研究中心植物标本馆)
- Research interest: Begoniaceae [S]
- Published taxa: *Begonia*
- Affiliation: HAST
- Region: CHINA (Taiwan)

J. S. Liang

Liang, Jia Sheng; 梁嘉声 ; Liáng Jiāshēng

1975- **First publication: 2006**

- Employment: School of Life Sciences, Sun Yat-sen University (中山大学生命科学学院)
- Research interest: Sapindaceae [S]
- Published taxa: *Acer*
- Region: CHINA (Guangdong)

J. Y. Liang

Liang, Jian Ying; Liang, Jiang Ying; **梁健英 ; Liáng Jiànyīng**

1942- **First publication: 1983**

- Employment: Guangxi Institute of Botany (广西植物研究所)
- Research interest: Anacardiaceae, Asteraceae, Betulaceae, Cycadaceae, Euphorbiaceae, Magnoliaceae, Polygalaceae, Theaceae [S]
- Published taxa: *Camellia, Carpinus, Cycas, Heteroplexis, Mangifera, Trigonostemon*
- Affiliation: IBK
- Location of specimens: IBK
- Region: CHINA (Guangxi)

M. Q. Liang

Liang, Min Qing; 梁明清 ; Liáng Míngqīng

1936- **First publication: 1976**

- Employment: Yunnan Agricultural University (云南农业大学)
- Research interest: Rutaceae [S]
- Published taxa: *Citrus, Poncirus*
- Region: CHINA (Yunnan)

M. Y. Liang

Liang, Mu Yuan; 梁木源 ; Liáng Mùyuán

1937- **First publication: 2002**

- Employment: Guangxi Institute of Botany, Chinese Academy of Sciences (广西壮族自治区中国科学院广西植物研究所)

- Research interest: Actinidiaceae [S]
- Published taxa: *Actinidia*
- Region: CHINA (Guangxi)

N. K. Liang

Liang, Nai Kuan; 梁乃宽 ; Liáng Nǎikuān

First publication: 1977

- Employment: Guangxi Institute of Chinese Medicine & Pharmaceutical Science（广西中医药研究院）
- Research interest: Ericaceae [S]
- Published taxa: *Gaultheria*
- Location of specimens: GXMI
- Region: CHINA (Guangxi)

S. Ye Liang

Liang, Sheng Ye; Liang, Sheng Yeh; **梁盛业 ; Liáng Shèngyè; 梁盛業**

1933-2014 First publication: 1979

- Employment: Guangxi Forestry Research Institute（广西壮族自治区林业科学研究院）
- Research interest: Iteaceae, Juglandaceae, Sapindaceae, Styracaceae, Theaceae [S]
- Published taxa: *Acer, Camellia, Kurrimia, Platycarya, Styrax, Tutcheria*
- Affiliation: GXFI
- Location of specimens: EBF, GXFI
- Region: CHINA (Guangxi)

S. B. Liang

Liang, Shu Bin; 梁书宾 ; Liáng Shūbīn; 梁書賓 , 梁书滨

1924-? First publication: 1982

- Employment: Shandong Forestry School（山东省林业学校）
- Research interest: Anacardiaceae, Betulaceae, Lauraceae, Malvaceae, Phyllanthaceae, Rosaceae, Salicaceae; Woody Plants [S]
- Published taxa: *Betula, Carpinus, Lindera, Populus, Rhus, Salix, Securinega, Sorbus, Tilia*
- Affiliation: SDFS
- Location of specimens: SDFI
- Region: CHINA (Shandong)

S. Q. Liang

Liang, Si Qi; 梁思琪 ; Liáng Sīqí

1995- First publication: 2019

- Employment: Institute of Botany, Chinese Academy of Sciences（中国科学院植物研究所）
- Research interest: Aspleniaceae [P]
- Published taxa: *Asplenium*
- Region: CHINA (Yunnan)

S. Yun Liang

Liang, Sung Yun; Liang, Song Jun; **梁松筠 ; Liáng Sōngyún**

1935- First publication: 1978

- Employment: Institute of Botany, Chinese Academy of Sciences（中国科学院植物研究所）
- Research interest: Asparagaceae, Asteraceae, Cyperaceae, Liliaceae, Melanthiaceae [S]
- Published taxa: *Aster, Campylandra, Carex, Heteropappus, Lilium, Lloydia, Nomocharis, Paris, Polygonatum, Saussurea, Schoenoplectus, Senecio, Smilacina, Trichophorum, Tupistra*
- Affiliation: PE
- Location of specimens: PE
- Region: CHINA

T. J. Liang

Liang, Tong Jun; 梁同军 ; Liáng Tóngjūn

1975- First publication: 2014

- Employment: Lushan Botanical Garden, Chinese Academy of Sciences（中国科学院庐山植物园）
- Research interest: Polygonaceae; Plants of Jiangxi [S]
- Published taxa: *Persicaria*
- Affiliation: LBG
- Region: CHINA (Guangdong)

W. J. Liang

Liang, Wei Jian; 梁维坚 ; Liáng Wéijiān; 梁維堅

1941- First publication: 1988

- Employment: Institute of Economic Forestry, Liaoning（辽宁省经济林研究所）
- Research interest: Betulaceae [S]
- Published taxa: *Corylus*
- Affiliation: LEF
- Location of specimens: LEF
- Region: CHINA (Jiangxi)

Y. Liang

Liang, Yan; 梁彦 ; Liáng Yàn; 梁彥

1938-2000 First publication: 1982

- Employment: Research Institute of Forestry, Chinese Academy of Forestry（中国林业科学研究院林业研究所）
- Research interest: Salicaceae [S]
- Published taxa: *Populus*
- Region: CHINA (Beijing, Jilin, Nei Mongol)

Y. C. Liang

Liang, Yi Chi; 梁一池 ; Liáng Yīchí

1952- First publication: 2016

- Employment: College of Landscape Architecture, Fujian Agriculture and Forestry University; College of Pharmacy, Fujian University of Traditional Chinese Medicine（福建农林大学园林学院；福建中医药大学药学院）

• Research interest: Orchidaceae [S]
• Published taxa: *Bulbophyllum*
• Region: CHINA (Fujian)

Y. S. Liang

Liang, Yi Shou; 梁珆碩 ; Liáng Yíshuò; 梁珆硕
1982- **First publication: 2011**
• Employment: Department of Life Science, Taiwan Normal University（台湾师范大学生命科学系）
• Research interest: Acanthaceae, Linderniaceae [S]
• Published taxa: *Bonnaya, Craterostigma, Lepidagathis, Lindernia, Torenia, Vandellia, Yamazakia*
• Region: CHINA (Fujian, Taiwan)

Y. X. Liang

Liang, Yong Xi; 梁永禧 ; Liáng Yǒngxǐ
First publication: 1996
• Employment: College of Forestry, South China Agricultural University（华南农业大学林学院）
• Research interest: Clusiaceae [S]
• Published taxa: *Garcinia*
• Region: CHINA (Guangxi)

Y. Y. Liang

Liang, Yong Yan; 梁永延 ; Liáng Yǒngyán
1982- **First publication: 2009**
• Employment: Guangxi Institute of Botany, Chinese Academy of Sciences（广西壮族自治区中国科学院广西植物研究所）
• Research interest: Asparagaceae; Woody Plants [S]
• Published taxa: *Aspidistra*
• Affiliation: GXF
• Location of specimens: GXF
• Region: CHINA (Guangxi)

Z. L. Liang

Liang, Zhen Long; 梁振龙 ; Liáng Zhènlóng
First publication: 2020
• Employment: Chengdu Institute of Biology, Chinese Academy of Sciences（中国科学院成都生物研究所）
• Research interest: Polypodiaceae [P]
• Published taxa: *Leptochilus*
• Region: CHINA (Yunnan)

B. R. Liao

Liao, Bo Ru; 廖博儒 ; Liào Bórú
First publication: 1997
• Employment: Yongding Institute of Forestry Science, Zhangjiajie（张家界市永定区林业科学研究所）
• Research interest: Malvaceae [S]
• Published taxa: *Tilia*
• Region: CHINA (Hunan)

C. Y. Liao

Liao, Chen Yang; 廖晨阳 ; Liào Chényáng
1982- **First publication: 2012**
• Employment: College of Architecture & Environment, Sichuan University（四川大学建筑与环境学院）
• Research interest: Apiaceae [S]
• Published taxa: *Angelica, Ferula*
• Region: CHINA (Shaanxi, Sichuan)

G. L. Liao

Liao, Guang Lu; 廖光庐 ; Liào Guānglú
First publication: 1991
• Employment: Jiangxi Institute of Forestry Science（江西省林业科学研究所）
• Research interest: Poaceae [S]
• Published taxa: *Sasa*
• Region: CHINA (Jiangxi)

J. P. Liao

Liao, Jing Ping; 廖景平 ; Liào Jǐngpíng
1964- **First publication: 2000**
• Employment: South China Institute of Botany, Chinese Academy of Sciences（中国科学院华南植物研究所）
• Research interest: Violaceae, Zingiberaceae [S]
• Published taxa: *Alpinia, Amomum, Viola*
• Region: CHINA (Guangdong, Hainan)

C. K. Liao

Liao, Chun Kuei; 廖俊奎 ; Liào Jùnkuí
First publication: 2013
• Employment: Department of Biological Sciences, Sun Yat-sen University, Taiwan（台湾中山大学生物科学系）
• Research interest: Orchidaceae [S]
• Published taxa: *Tropidia*
• Region: CHINA (Taiwan)

L. Liao

Liao, Liang; 廖亮 ; Liào Liàng
1958- **First publication: 1992**
• Employment: Institute of Biology, Jiujiang Teachers' College, Jiangxi; School of Pharmacy and Life Science, Jiujiang University（江西九江师范专科学校生物研究所；九江学院药学与生命科学学院）
• Research interest: Lardizabalaceae, Ranunculaceae, Urticaceae [S]
• Published taxa: *Ranunculus*
• Affiliation: JJT
• Location of specimens: JJT
• Region: CHINA

M. Liao

Liao, Min; 廖敏 ; Liào Mǐn

First publication: 2020

- Employment: Chengdu Institute of Biology, Chinese Academy of Sciences（中国科学院成都生物研究所）
- Research interest: Fabaceae [S]
- Published taxa: *Campylotropis*
- Region: CHINA (Yunnan)

P. C. Liao

Liao, Pei Chun; 廖培鈞 ; Liào Péijūn; 廖培钧

First publication: 2019

- Employment: School of Life Science, Taiwan Normal University（台湾师范大学生命科学专业学院）
- Research interest: Orchidaceae [S]
- Published taxa: *Cypripedium*
- Region: CHINA (Taiwan)

Q. Liao

Liao, Qi; 廖琦 ; Liào Qí

1990- First publication: 2014

- Employment: South China Botanical Garden, Chinese Academy of Sciences（中国科学院华南植物园）
- Research interest: Solanaceae [S]
- Published taxa: *Lycium*
- Region: CHINA (Ningxia)

J. C. Liao

Liao, Jih Ching; Liao, Ri Jing; **廖日京 ; Liào Rìjīng**

1929-2013 First publication: 1971

- Employment: Department of Forestry, Taiwan University（台湾大学森林学系）
- Research interest: Fagaceae, Garryaceae, Lauraceae, Moraceae, Oleaceae, Rubiaceae, Rutaceae; Woody Plants [S]
- Published taxa: *Actinodaphne, Aucuba, Cinnamomum, Cyclobalanopsis, Damnacanthus, Ficus, Ligustrum, Lindera, Litsea, Machilus, Melicope, Neolitsea, Osmanthus, Pasania, Quercus*
- Affiliation: NTUF
- Location of specimens: NTUF
- Region: CHINA (Taiwan)

R. G. Liao

Liao, Rong Gui; 廖荣贵 ; Liào Róngguì; 廖榮貴

1938- First publication: 1988

- Employment: Mianyang Institute for Drug Control, Sichuan（四川省绵阳市药品检验所）
- Research interest: Cucurbitaceae, Phytolaccaceae, Piperaceae [S]
- Published taxa: *Trichosanthes*
- Affiliation: MYDC
- Location of specimens: MYDC
- Region: CHINA (Sichuan)

R. L. Liao

Liao, Rong Li; 廖荣丽 ; Liào Rónglì

1990- First publication: 2015

- Employment: Kunming Institute of Botany, Chinese Academy of Sciences（中国科学院昆明植物研究所）
- Research interest: Ericaceae [S]
- Published taxa: *Rhododendron*
- Region: CHINA (Yunnan)

S. Liao

Liao, Shuai; 廖帅 ; Liào Shuài

1990- First publication: 2016

- Employment: School of Nature Conservation, Beijing Forestry University; Shanghai Chenshan Botanical Garden; School of Life Sciences, East China Normal University（北京林业大学自然保护区学院；上海辰山植物园；华东师范大学生命科学学院）
- Research interest: Aristolochiaceae, Salicaceae, Thymelaeaceae [S]
- Published taxa: *Dianyuea, Isotrema, Wikstroemia*
- Region: CHINA

W. B. Liao

Liao, Wen Bo; 廖文波 ; Liào Wénbō

1963- First publication: 1999

- Employment: School of Life Sciences, Sun Yat-sen University（中山大学生命科学学院）
- Research interest: Adoxaceae, Aquifoliaceae, Asparagaceae, Aspleniaceae, Begoniaceae, Boraginaceae, Gesneriaceae, Melanthiaceae, Melastomataceae, Rosaceae, Saxifragaceae, Styracaceae, Violaceae; Plants of S. China [PS]
- Published taxa: *Asplenium, Begonia, Bredia, Chamaelirium, Chiritopsis, Eriobotrya, Hymenasplenium, Ilex, Ophiopogon, Photinia, Primulina, Rehderodendron, Rhaphiolepis, Saxifraga, Sinojohnstonia, Sorbus, Viburnum, Viola*
- Affiliation: SYS
- Location of specimens: SYS
- Region: CHINA

W. F. Liao

Liao, Wen Fang; 廖文芳 ; Liào Wénfāng

1974- First publication: 2009

- Employment: South China Botanical Garden, Chinese Academy of Sciences（中国科学院华南植物园）
- Research interest: Magnoliaceae [S]
- Published taxa: *Manglietia*
- Region: CHINA (Yunnan)

X. Y. Liao

Liao, Xing Yu; 廖星宇 ; Liào Xīngyǔ

1996- First publication: 2019

- Employment: Forestry College, Fujian Agriculture

and Forestry University (福建农林大学林学院)
- Research interest: Orchidaceae [S]
- Published taxa: *Cymbidium, Paphiopedilum*
- Region: CHINA (Yunnan)

B. N. Lin

Lin, Bing Nan; 林秉南 ; Lín Bǐngnán

First publication: 1994

- Employment: Greening Company of Lianyungang Economic and Technological Development Zone (连云港经济技术开发区绿化公司)
- Research interest: Lamiaceae [S]
- Published taxa: *Vitex*
- Region: CHINA (Jiangsu)

Chun C. Lin

Lin, Chun Chi; 林春吉 ; Lín Chūnjí

1966- First publication: 2002

- Employment: Long-Hai Elementary School, Taichung County (台中县龙海国民小学)
- Research interest: Menyanthaceae [S]
- Published taxa: *Nymphoides*
- Region: CHINA (Taiwan)

C. R. Lin

Lin, Chun Rui; 林春蕊 ; Lín Chūnruǐ

1973- First publication: 2009

- Employment: Guangxi Institute of Botany, Chinese Academy of Sciences (广西壮族自治区中国科学院广西植物研究所)
- Research interest: Aristolochiaceae, Asparagaceae [S]
- Published taxa: *Aristolochia, Aspidistra*
- Affiliation: IBK
- Location of specimens: IBK
- Region: CHINA

H. L. Lin

Lin, Hai Lun; 林海伦 ; Lín Hǎilún

1966- First publication: 2014

- Employment: Ningbo Institute for Drug Control, Zhejiang (浙江省宁波市药品检验所)
- Research interest: Orchidaceae [S]
- Published taxa: *Bulbophyllum*
- Region: CHINA (Zhejiang)

H. H. Lin

Lin, Hong Hui; 林宏辉 ; Lín Hónghuī

1968- First publication: 2007

- Employment: College of Life Sciences, Sichuan University (四川大学生命科学学院)
- Research interest: Zingiberaceae [S]
- Published taxa: *Roscoea*
- Region: CHINA (Yunnan)

H. W. Lin

Lin, Hung Wen; 林鴻文 ; Lín Hóngwén; 林鸿文

First publication: 2013

- Employment: School of Life Science, Taiwan Normal University (台湾师范大学生命科学学院)
- Research interest: Crassulaceae [S]
- Published taxa: *Sedum*
- Region: CHINA (Taiwan)

J. Y. Lin

Lin, Jia Yi; 林家怡 ; Lín Jiāyí

1964- First publication: 1988

- Employment: South China Agricultural University (华南农业大学)
- Research interest: Apocynaceae, Cannabaceae, Poaceae [S]
- Published taxa: *Bambusa, Heterostemma, Sasa, Trema*
- Region: CHINA (Guangdong)

J. Z. Lin

Lin, Jin Zhen; 林巾箴 ; Lín Jīnzhēn

1940-2019 First publication: 1994

- Employment: Hangzhou Botanical Garden (杭州植物园)
- Research interest: Amaryllidaceae [S]
- Published taxa: *Lycoris*
- Region: CHINA (Gansu, Hubei)

L. K. Ling

Ling, Lai Kuan; Lin, Lai Guan; 林来官 ; Lín Láiguān; 林來官

1925-2014 First publication: 1966

- Employment: Department of Biology, Fujian Teachers' College (福建师范学院生物系)
- Research interest: Brassicaceae, Cyperaceae, Ericaceae, Fagaceae, Pentaphylacaceae, Theaceae [S]
- Published taxa: *Adinandra, Anneslea, Camellia, Carex, Cassiope, Cleyera, Eurya, Quercus, Rhododendron, Sisymbrium, Ternstroemia*
- Affiliation: FNU
- Location of specimens: FNU, PE
- Region: CHINA

M. J. Lin

Lin, Mong Jia; 林蒙嘉 ; Lín Méngjiā

1931- First publication: 1984

- Employment: Meitan Tea Research Institute of Guizhou Province (贵州湄潭茶叶科学研究所)
- Research interest: Theaceae [S]
- Published taxa: *Camellia*
- Region: CHINA (Guizhou)

M. M. Lin

Lin, Mu Mu; 林木木 ; Lín Mùmù

1943- **First publication: 1987**

- Employment: Changting County Forestry Bureau, Fujian（福建省长汀县林业局）
- Research interest: Aquifoliaceae, Lauraceae, Magnoliaceae, Poaceae, Pteridaceae [PS]
- Published taxa: *Coniogramme, Ilex, Machilus, Michelia, Oligostachyum, Pleioblastus*
- Region: CHINA (Fujian)

N. Lin

Lin, Nan; 林楠 ; Lín Nán

1993- **First publication: 2019**

- Employment: Kunming Institute of Botany, Chinese Academy of Sciences; Wuhan Botanical Garden, Chinese Academy of Sciences（中国科学院昆明植物研究所；中国科学院武汉植物园）
- Research interest: Caryophyllaceae [S]
- Published taxa: *Silene*
- Region: CHINA (Hubei)

Q. Lin

Lin, Qi; 林祁 ; Lín Qí

1957- **First publication: 1987**

- Employment: South China Institute of Botany, Chinese Academy of Sciences; Institute of Botany, Chinese Academy of Sciences（中国科学院华南植物研究所；中国科学院植物研究所）
- Research interest: Araceae, Brassicaceae, Betulaceae, Elaeagnaceae, Magnoliaceae, Poaceae, Rubiaceae, Schisandraceae, Smilacaceae, Urticaceae [S]
- Published taxa: *Arisaema, Betula, Elaeagnus, Elatostema, Illicium, Kmeria, Leptodermis, Miscanthus, Schisandra, Smilax*
- Affiliation: IBSC, PE
- Region: CHINA

Q. Z. Lin

Lin, Qin Zhong; Lin, Qing Zhong; 林亲众 ; Lín Qīnzhòng

1950-2007 **First publication: 1986**

- Employment: Central South College of Forestry（中南林学院）
- Research interest: Aquifoliaceae, Betulaceae, Elaeagnaceae, Ericaceae, Fagaceae, Oleaceae, Pinaceae; Woody Plants [S]
- Published taxa: *Carpinus, Cyclobalanopsis, Elaeagnus, Ilex, Linociera, Pinus, Vaccinium*
- Affiliation: CSFI
- Region: CHINA (Hunan)

Q. W. Lin

Lin, Qin Wen; 林秦文 ; Lín Qínwén

1983- **First publication: 2009**

- Employment: College of Biological Sciences and Technology, Beijing Forestry University; Beijing Botanical Garden, Institute of Botany, Chinese Academy of Sciences（北京林业大学生物科学与技术学院；中国科学院植物研究所北京植物园）
- Research interest: Boraginaceae, Celastraceae, Podostemaceae [S]
- Published taxa: *Bothriospermum, Cladopus, Glyptopetalum, Microtropis, Terniopsis*
- Location of specimens: BJFC
- Region: CHINA

Qin W. Lin

Lin, Qin Wen; 林沁文 ; Lín Qìnwén

1974- **First publication: 2015**

- Employment: Fujian Guilong Mountain Provincial Nature Reserve; Fujian Tingjiangyuan National Nature Reserve Administration（福建圭龙山省级自然保护区；福建汀江源国家级自然保护区管理局）
- Research interest: Gesneriaceae, Melastomataceae, Poaceae [S]
- Published taxa: *Beccarinda, Oligostachyum, Sonerila*
- Region: CHINA (Fujian)
- IPNI as: Q. W. Lin

C. Ling

Ling, Chuan; Ling, Chüan; Lin, Chuan; Lin, Quan; 林泉 ; Lín Quán

1937-2020 **First publication: 1975**

- Employment: Zhejiang Institutes for Drug Control（浙江省药检所）
- Research interest: Acanthaceae, Asteraceae, Ericaceae, Liliaceae, Poaceae, Vitaceae, Zingiberaceae [S]
- Published taxa: *Aster, Championella, Cheilotheca, Curcuma, Fritillaria, Poa, Vitis*
- Affiliation: ZDC
- Location of specimens: ZDC
- Region: CHINA (Zhejiang)
- Also as: C. Lin

Y. Ling

Ling, Yong; Ling, Yuang; Ling, Young; Ling, Yung; Lin, Jung; Lin, Rong; 林镕 ; Lín Róng; 林鎔

1903-1981 **First publication: 1934**

- Employment: Institute of Botany, National Academy of Peiping; Institute of Zoology and Botany, Fujian Provincial Academy; Institute of Botany, Chinese Academy of Sciences（国立北平研究院植物学研究所；福建省研究院动植物研究所；中国科学院植物研究所）

• Research interest: Araliaceae, Asteraceae, Ebenaceae, Gentianaceae, Malvaceae, Pentaphylacaceae, Sapindaceae, Symplocaceae; Plants of S. China. [MS]
• Published taxa: *Acer, Ajania, Anaphalis, Artemisia, Aster, Blumea, Cacalia, Cancrinia, Carpesium, Chrysanthemum, Cirsium, Cremanthodium, Dendranthema, Dendropanax, Diospyros, Diplazoptilon, Dolomiaea, Elachanthemum, Erigeron, Eupatorium, Eurya, Galatella, Gentiana, Gnaphalium, Gymnaster, Heteropappus, Inula, Kalimeris, Leontopodium, Ligularia, Mycelis, Myriactis, Nannoglottis, Pentanema, Pertya, Psychrogeton, Pulicaria, Reevesia, Saussurea, Senecio, Sigesbeckia, Symplocos, Syncalathium, Ternstroemia, Tilia, Tugarinovia, Vladimiria*
• Affiliation: PE
• Location of specimens: AU, FNU, PE
• Region: CHINA
• Also as: Ling

R. S. Lin

Lin, Ru Shun; 林汝顺 ; Lín Rǔ shùn
1955- **First publication: 2008**
• Employment: South China Botanical Garden, Chinese Academy of Sciences（中国科学院华南植物园）
• Research interest: Poaceae [S]
• Published taxa: *Bambusa, Dendrocalamus, Gigantochloa, Schizostachyum*
• Region: CHINA

C. Q. Lin

Lin, Cheng Qiu; 林盛秋 ; Lín Shèngqiū
1937-2016 **First publication: 1988**
• Employment: Guangxi Institute of Botany（广西植物研究所）
• Research interest: Lauraceae [S]
• Published taxa: *Machilus*
• Region: CHINA (Guangxi)

S. S. Lin

Lin, Shi Shi; 林石狮 ; Lín Shíshī
1984- **First publication: 2010**
• Employment: School of Life Sciences, Sun Yat-sen University（中山大学生命科学学院）
• Research interest: Gesneriaceae [S]
• Published taxa: *Chiritopsis*
• Region: CHINA (Guangdong)

S. C. Lin

Lin, Shu Chien; Lin, Shu Qian; **林叔芊 ; Lín Shūqiān**
First publication: 1991
• Employment: Herbarium, Institute of Botany, "Academia Sinica"（中研院植物研究所）
• Research interest: Euphorbiaceae [S]
• Published taxa: *Chamaesyce*
• Region: CHINA (Taiwan)

S. J. Lin

Lin, Su Juan; 林蘇娟 ; Lín Sūjuān; 林苏娟
1957- **First publication: 1994**
• Employment: Botanical Gardens, Graduate School of Science, The University of Tokyo, Japan; Department of Biological Science, Shimane University, Japan（日本东京大学理学系研究科附属植物园；日本岛根大学生物科学系）
• Research interest: Lindsaeaceae, Thelypteridaceae [P]
• Published taxa: *Odontosoria, Sphaerostephanos*
• Region: CHINA, JAPAN

T. H. Lin

Lin, Tai Hong; 林太宏 ; Lín Tàihóng
First publication: 1991
• Employment: Guangdong Academy of Agricultural Sciences（广东省农业科学院）
• Research interest: Actinidiaceae [S]
• Published taxa: *Actinidia*
• Location of specimens: IBK
• Region: CHINA (Hunan)

W. T. Lin

Lin, Wan Tao; Lin, Wan T'ao; **林万涛 ; Lín Wàntāo; 林萬濤**
1927-2006 **First publication: 1978**
• Employment: South China Agricultural University（华南农业大学）
• Research interest: Dipterocarpaceae, Gesneriaceae, Poaceae, Sellulocalamus; Plants of S. China [S]
• Published taxa: *Acidosasa, Arundinaria, Bambusa, Dendrocalamopsis, Drepanostachyum, Gelidocalamus, Hopea, Indocalamus, Indosasa, Lingnania, Melocalamus, Metasasa, Monocladus, Monospatha, Neosinocalamus, Oligostachyum, Patellocalamus, Phyllostachys, Pleioblastus, Pseudosasa, Qiongzhuea, Sasa, Sellulocalamus, Sinarundinaria, Sinobambusa, Sinocalamus, Titanotrichum*
• Affiliation: CANT
• Location of specimens: CANT
• Region: CHINA

W. M. Lin

Lin, Wei Min; 林維明 ; Lín Wéimíng; 林维明
1959- **First publication: 2006**
• Employment: Amateur（业余爱好者）
• Research interest: Orchidaceae [S]
• Published taxa: *Brachycorythis, Bulbophyllum, Cheirostylis, Corybas, Erythrodes, Eulophia, Lecanorchis, Liparis, Listera, Malaxis, Nervilia, Oberonia, Saccolabiopsis, Spiranthes, Tainia,*

Tropidia
- Region: CHINA (Taiwan)

W. C. Lin

Lin, Wei Chih; Lin, Wei Ch'ih; Lin, Wei Zhi; 林維治；Lín Wéizhì; 林维治
1915-1995 **First publication: 1970**
- Employment: Taiwan Forestry Research Institute, Taiwan Provincial Administrative Office（台湾省政府农林厅林业试验所）
- Research interest: Poaceae [S]
- Published taxa: *Arthrostylidium, Bambusa, Chimonobambusa, Yushania*
- Region: CHINA (Taiwan)

W. F. Lin

Lin, Wei Fang; 林渭訪；Lín Wèifǎng; 林渭访
1896-1974 **First publication: 1967**
- Employment: Taiwan Forestry Research Institute, Taiwan Provincial Administrative Office; Department of Forestry, Taiwan University（台湾省政府农林厅林业试验所；台湾大学森林学系）
- Research interest: Lamiaceae [S]
- Published taxa: *Callicarpa*
- Region: CHINA (Taiwan)
- Also as: Lin

X. Z. Lin

Lin, Xia Zhen; 林夏珍；Lín Xiàzhēn
1965- **First publication: 2007**
- Employment: Zhejiang Forestry College（浙江林学院）
- Research interest: Lauraceae [S]
- Published taxa: *Machilus*
- Region: CHINA (Zhejiang)

X. Lin

Lin, Xiang; 林湘；Lín Xiāng
First publication: 1992
- Employment: Shuangyashan Coal Mine Teachers Training College（双鸭山煤矿教师进修学院）
- Research interest: Rosaceae [S]
- Published taxa: *Rosa*
- Region: CHINA (Heilongjiang)

Y. Y. Lin

Lin, Yan Yun; 林彦云；Lín Yànyún; 林彥云
1944- **First publication: 2008**
- Employment: Quanzhou City Forestry Bureau, Fujian（福建泉州市林业局）
- Research interest: Celastraceae [S]
- Published taxa: *Microtropis*
- Region: CHINA (Fujian)

Y. S. Lin

Lin, Yang San; Lin, Yang Saun; 林仰三；Lín Yǎngsān
1931- **First publication: 1988**
- Employment: Forestry Administration of Guangdong（广东省林业厅）
- Research interest: Rosaceae; Plants of Hainan [S]
- Published taxa: *Cerasus*
- Affiliation: HFB
- Location of specimens: HFB
- Region: CHINA (Hainan)

Y. M. Lin

Lin, Yi Ming; 林益明；Lín Yìmíng
1967-2011 **First publication: 1995**
- Employment: Department of Biology, Xiamen University（厦门大学生物系）
- Research interest: Poaceae [S]
- Published taxa: *Bambusa, Dendrocalamopsis, Oligostachyum, Phyllostachys*
- Region: CHINA (Fujian)

Y. X. Lin

Lin, You Xing; Ling, You Xing; Lin, You Xin; 林尤兴；Lín Yóuxīng; 林尤興
1934- **First publication: 1980**
- Employment: Institute of Botany, Chinese Academy of Sciences（中国科学院植物研究所）
- Research interest: Aspleniaceae, Athyriaceae, Dennstaedtiaceae, Dryopteridaceae, Lindsaeaceae, Lycopodiaceae, Marattiaceae, Ophioglossaceae, Polypodiaceae, Pteridaceae, Salviniaceae, Thelypteridaceae; Pteridophytes [P]
- Published taxa: *Adiantum, Allantodia, Angiopteris, Arthromeris, Asplenium, Azolla, Botrypus, Glaphyropteridopsis, Huperzia, Lepisorus, Leptogramma, Microlepia, Platygyria, Polypodiodes, Polystichum, Pronephrium, Pseudocyclosorus, Sceptridium, Sphenomeris, Stegnogramma, Thelypteris, Tricholepidium*
- Affiliation: PE
- Location of specimens: PE
- Region: CHINA

Y. R. Ling

Ling, Yeou Ruenn; Lin, You Run 林有润；Lín Yǒurùn; 林有潤
1937- **First publication: 1977**
- Employment: South China Institute of Botany, Chinese Academy of Sciences（中国科学院华南植物研究所）
- Research interest: Araliaceae, Asteraceae, Combretaceae, Olacaceae, Schoepfiaceae [S]
- Published taxa: *Anaphalis, Artemisia, Combretum, Elachanthemum, Eleutherococcus, Euaraliopsis, Neotaraxacum, Neopallasia, Olax, Prenanthes, Schoepfia,*

Seriphidium, Taraxacum
- Affiliation: IBSC
- Location of specimens: IBSC
- Region: CHINA

Y. L. Lin

Lin, Yu Li; 林玉立 ; Lín Yùlì

First publication: 1992

- Employment: Shuangyashan Coal Mine Teachers Training College（双鸭山煤矿教师进修学院）
- Research interest: Rosaceae [S]
- Published taxa: *Rosa*
- Region: CHINA (Heilongjiang)

Yuan C. Lin

Lin, Yuan Chien; 林元千 ; Lín Yuánqiān

First publication: 2020

- Employment: Department of Forestry, Chung Hsing University（中兴大学森林学系）
- Research interest: Zingiberaceae [S]
- Published taxa: *Zingiber*
- Region: CHINA (Taiwan)

Yun Lin

Lin, Yun; 林云 ; Lín Yún

1987- **First publication: 2013**

- Employment: Hunan Medical Technical School; Hunan Food and Drug Vocational College（湖南省医药技工学校；湖南食品药品职业学院）
- Research interest: Asparagaceae, Brassicaceae, Rubiaceae, Urticaceae [S]
- Published taxa: *Cardamine, Elatostema, Ophiorrhiza, Polygonatum*
- Region: [ASIA]
- IPNI as: Y. Lin

T. P. Lin

Lin, Tsan Piao; Lin, Zan Biao; **林讚標 ; Lín Zànbiāo; 林赞标**

1948- **First publication: 1975**

- Employment: Institute of Plant Biology, Taiwan University（台湾大学植物科学研究所）
- Research interest: Orchidaceae; Plant Systematics [S]
- Published taxa: *Aphyllorchis, Appendicula, Bletilla, Brachycorythis, Bulbophyllum, Calanthe, Cephalantheropsis, Cheirostylis, Corybas, Crepidium, Cymbidium, Dendrobium, Dienia, Epipactis, Epipogium, Erythrodes, Eulophia, Flickingeria, Gastrochilus, Gastrodia, Goodyera, Habenaria, Hayata, Hippeophyllum, Hylophila, Lecanorchis, Liparis, Luisia, Malaxis, Neottia, Nervilia, Oberonia, Odontochilus, Peristylus, Phaius, Pinalia, Platanthera, Saccolabiopsis, Spiranthes, Styloglossum, Sunipia, Tainia, Thrixspermum, Tropidia, Tulotis*
- Affiliation: TAI
- Region: CHINA (Taiwan)

T. T. Lin

Lin, Tzer Tong; Lin, Ze Tong; **林則桐 ; Lín Zétóng; 林则桐**

First publication: 1995

- Employment: Fushan Branch, Taiwan Forestry Research Institute, Taiwan Provincial Administrative Office（台湾省政府农林厅林业试验所福山分所）
- Research interest: Piperaceae [S]
- Published taxa: *Peperomia, Piper*
- Region: CHINA (Taiwan)

Z. L. Lin

Lin, Zhe Li; 林哲丽 ; Lín Zhélì

1988- **First publication: 2017**

- Employment: South China Botanical Garden, Chinese Academy of Sciences（中国科学院华南植物园）
- Research interest: Acanthaceae [S]
- Published taxa: *Rungia*
- Region: CHINA (Yunnan)

C. W. Lin

Lin, Che Wei; 林哲緯 ; Lín Zhéwěi; 林哲纬

First publication: 2014

- Employment: Herbarium of Taiwan Forest Research Instiitute, Council of Agriculture, "Executive Yuan"（"行政院"农业委员会林业试验所植物标本馆）
- Research interest: Asphodelaceae, Begoniaceae, Melastomataceae, Pentaphragmataceae [S]
- Published taxa: *Begonia, Driessenia, Pentaphragma, Phyllagathis, Sonerila, Trachyandra*
- Affiliation: TAIF
- Region: CHINA (Taiwan)

C. C. Lin

Lin, Chih Chao; 林志超 ; Lín Zhìchāo

First publication: 1976

- Employment: Department of Forestry, Taiwan University（台湾大学森林学系）
- Research interest: Lauraceae [S]
- Published taxa: *Cinnamomum*
- Region: CHINA (Taiwan)

Z. H. Lin

Lin, Zhi Hua; 林志华 ; Lín Zhìhuá; 林志華

1933- **First publication: 1987**

- Employment: Zhejiang Institute of Experimental Medicine & Hygiene（浙江卫生实验院）
- Research interest: Liliaceae [S]

- Published taxa: *Fritillaria*
- Region: CHINA (Zhejiang)

Lin Chi

Chingtianshu Research Group; Lin Ye Zhi Wu Yan Jiu Zu; Lin Chi; 林植 ; Lín Zhí

First publication: 1977

- Employment: Chingtianshu Research Group (Forestry Plant Research Group) (擎天树研究组 (林业植物研究组))
- Research interest: Dipterocarpaceae [S]
- Published taxa: *Parashorea*
- Region: CHINA (Guangxi)
- Organization

H. Z. Ling

Ling, Hui Zhu; 凌惠珠 ; Líng Huìzhū

1954- First publication: 1994

- Employment: Guangxi Institute of Traditional Medical and Pharmaceutical Sciences (广西中医药研究所)
- Research interest: Apocynaceae [S]
- Published taxa: *Periploca*
- Affiliation: GXMI
- Region: CHINA (Guangxi)

P. P. Ling

Ling, Ping Ping; 凌萍萍 ; Líng Píngpíng

1934- First publication: 1980

- Employment: Institute of Botany, Jiangsu Province and Chinese Academy of Sciences (江苏省中国科学院植物研究所)
- Research interest: Dioscoreaceae, Liliaceae, Ranunculaceae [BS]
- Published taxa: *Clematis, Dioscorea, Fritillaria, Schizocapsa, Tacca*
- Affiliation: NAS
- Location of specimens: NAS
- Region: CHINA

S. J. Ling

Ling, Shao Jun; 凌少军 ; Líng Shàojūn

First publication: 2020

- Employment: College of Ecology and Environment, Hainan University (海南大学生态与环境学院)
- Research interest: Gesneriaceae [S]
- Published taxa: *Oreocharis*
- Region: CHINA (Hainan)

A. T. Liu

Liu, Ai Tang; 刘霭堂 ; Liú Ǎitáng

1939- First publication: 1980

- Employment: Department of Biology, Nanjing Normal University (南京师范大学生物系)
- Research interest: Poaceae [S]
- Published taxa: *Pennisetum, Phyllostachys*
- Region: CHINA

A. Z. Liu

Liu, Ai Zhong; 刘爱忠 ; Liú Àizhōng

1969- First publication: 2002

- Employment: Kunming Institute of Botany, Chinese Academy of Sciences (中国科学院昆明植物研究所)
- Research interest: Musaceae [S]
- Published taxa: *Musa*
- Region: CHINA

B. B. Liu

Liu, Bin Bin; 刘彬彬 ; Liú Bīnbīn

1987- First publication: 2017

- Employment: Institute of Botany, Chinese Academy of Sciences (中国科学院植物研究所)
- Research interest: Rosaceae [S]
- Published taxa: *Pourthiaea*
- Region: CHINA

Bin Liu bis

Liu, Bin; 刘斌 ; Liú Bīn

1995- First publication: 1995

- Employment: Forestry College, Fujian Agriculture and Forestry University (福建农林大学林学院)
- Research interest: Orchidaceae [S]
- Published taxa: *Paphiopedilum*
- Region: CHINA (Yunnan)
- IPNI as: B. Liu

Bing Liu

Liu, Bing; 刘冰 ; Liú Bīng

1984- First publication: 2008

- Employment: Institute of Botany, Chinese Academy of Sciences (中国科学院植物研究所)
- Research interest: Boraginaceae, Fabaceae, Lauraceae, Orchidaceae, Ranunculaceae, Wightiaceae [S]
- Published taxa: *Anemone, Beilschmiedia, Bothriospermum, Caltha, Caryodaphnopsis, Holopogon, Phoebe, Pueraria,* Wightiaceae
- Affiliation: PE
- Location of specimens: PE
- Region: [ASIA]

B. W. Liu

Liu, Bing Wen; 刘秉温 ; Liú Bǐngwēn; 劉秉溫

1929-1989 First publication: 1981

- Employment: Fujian Longxi District Traditional Chinese Medicine Hospital (福建龙溪地区中医院)
- Research interest: Aquifoliaceae [S]
- Published taxa: *Ilex*

• Region: CHINA (Guangxi, Jiangxi)

C. Liu

Liu, Cheng; 刘成 ; Liú Chéng

1986- **First publication: 2019**

- Employment: Kunming Institute of Botany, Chinese Academy of Sciences (中国科学院昆明植物研究所)
- Research interest: Apocynaceae, Orchidaceae [S]
- Published taxa: *Bulbophyllum, Marsdenia*
- Region: CHINA (Xizang)

C. D. Liu

Liu, Chu Dian; 刘初钿 ; Liú Chūdiàn; 劉初鈿

1942- **First publication: 2007**

- Employment: Administrative Bureau of Wuyishan National Nature Reserve, Fujian (福建省武夷山国家级自然保护区管理局)
- Research interest: Orchidaceae [S]
- Published taxa: *Gastrodia*
- Region: CHINA (Fujian)

D. J. Liu

Liu, Da Ji; Liou, Da Ji; 刘大济 ; Liú Dàjì; 劉大濟

1940- **First publication: 1988**

- Employment: Institute of Biology, Guizhou Academy of Sciences (贵州省科学院生物研究所)
- Research interest: Asteraceae, Oleaceae [S]
- Published taxa: *Aster, Ligustrum, Osmanthus, Paraprenanthes*
- Affiliation: HGAS
- Location of specimens: HGAS
- Region: CHINA (Guizhou)
- Also as: D. J. Liou

D. M. Liu

Liu, Dai Ming; 刘代明 ; Liú Dàimíng; 劉代明

1936- **First publication: 1986**

- Employment: Department of Chinese Medicine, Chengdu College of Traditional Chinese Medicine (成都中医学院中药系)
- Research interest: Asparagaceae [S]
- Published taxa: *Polygonatum, Smilacina*
- Affiliation: CDCM
- Location of specimens: CDCM
- Region: CHINA (Sichuan)

D. Q. Liu

Liu, Dao Qing; 刘道庆 ; Liú Dàoqìng; 劉道慶

1948- **First publication: 1984**

- Employment: Liangshan Prefecture Institute for Drug Control, Sichuan (四川省凉山州药品检验所)
- Research interest: Asparagaceae; Medicinal Plants [S]
- Published taxa: *Asparagus, Polygonatum*
- Affiliation: LSDC
- Region: CHINA (Sichuan)

D. T. Liu

Liu, De Tuan; 刘德团 ; Liú Détuán

1984- **First publication: 2019**

- Employment: Kunming Institute of Botany, Chinese Academy of Sciences (中国科学院昆明植物研究所)
- Research interest: Apocynaceae, Chloranthaceae [S]
- Published taxa: *Ceropegia, Chloranthus*
- Region: CHINA (Guangxi, Yunnan)

D. Y. Liu

Liu, Deng Yi; 刘登义 ; Liú Dēngyì

1958- **First publication: 1986**

- Employment: College of Life Sciences, Anhui Normal University (安徽师范大学生命科学学院)
- Research interest: Cyperaceae, Hydrangeaceae, Orchidaceae, Phyllanthaceae [S]
- Published taxa: *Carex, Deutzia, Phyllanthus*
- Affiliation: ANUB
- Location of specimens: ANUB
- Region: CHINA (Anhui)

D. K. Liu

Liu, Ding Kun; 刘定坤 ; Liú Dìngkūn

First publication: 2020

- Employment: Forestry College, Fujian Agriculture and
- Forestry University (福建农林大学林学院)
- Research interest: Orchidaceae [S]
- Published taxa: *Cleisostoma, Cymbilabia*
- Region: CHINA (Xizang, Yunnan)

Dong M. Liu

Liu, Dong Ming; 刘东明 ; Liú Dōngmíng

1971- **First publication: 2009**

- Employment: South China Botanical Garden, Chinese Academy of Sciences (中国科学院华南植物园)
- Research interest: Magnoliaceae [S]
- Published taxa: *Magnolia*
- Region: CHINA (Hainan)
- IPNI as: D. M. Liu

E. D. Liu

Liu, En De; 刘恩德 ; Liú Ēndé

1975- **First publication: 2004**

- Employment: Kunming Institute of Botany, Chinese Academy of Sciences (中国科学院昆明植物研究所)
- Research interest: Lamiaceae, Magnoliaceae, Poaceae, Primulaceae, Ranunculaceae, Scrophulariaceae; Plants of Yunnan [S]
- Published taxa: *Aconitum, Buddleja, Elsholtzia, Isodon, Lysimachia, Magnolia, Michelia, Paraphlomis, Salvia, Yushania*

• Affiliation: KUN
• Location of specimens: KUN
• Region: CHINA (Yunnan)

F. Y. Liu

Liu, Fang Yuan; 刘芳媛 ; Liú Fāngyuàn; 劉芳媛 ; 刘方媛
1936- **First publication: 1983**
• Employment: Kunming Institute of Botany, Chinese Academy of Sciences（中国科学院昆明植物研究所）
• Research interest: Orchidaceae [S]
• Published taxa: *Cymbidium, Gastrodia, Paphiopedilum, Phaius, Phalaenopsis*
• Location of specimens: KUN
• Region: CHINA (Yunnan)

G. F. Liu

Liu, Geng Feng; 刘庚峰 ; Liú Gēngfēng; 劉庚峰
1940- **First publication: 1990**
• Employment: Horticulture Institute, Hunan Academy of Agricultural Sciences（湖南省农业科学院园艺研究所）
• Research interest: Rutaceae [S]
• Published taxa: *Citrus*
• Region: CHINA (Hunan)

G. Z. Liu

Liu, Guang Zheng; 刘光正 ; Liú Guāngzhèng
1962- **First publication: 1991**
• Employment: Jiangxi Agricultural University（江西农业大学）
• Research interest: Rosaceae [S]
• Published taxa: *Rosa*
• Region: CHINA (Jiangxi)

G. S. Liu

Liu, Gui Sen; 刘桂森 ; Liú Guìsēn; 劉桂森
1932- **First publication: 1989**
• Employment: Hebei Agrotechnical Teachers' College; Department of Horticulture and Landscape Architecture, Hebei Normal University Of Science & Technology（河北农业技术师范学院；河北科技师范学院园艺园林系）
• Research interest: Rosaceae [S]
• Published taxa: *Armeniaca*
• Region: CHINA (Hebei)

G. D. Liu

Liu, Guo Dao; 刘国道 ; Liú Guódào
1963- **First publication: 2014**
• Employment: Tropical Crops Genetic Resources Institute, Chinese Academy of Tropical Agricultural Sciences（中国热带农业科学院热带作物品种资源研究所）
• Research interest: Cyperaceae, Fabaceae, Poaceae [S]
• Published taxa: *Carex*
• Affiliation: ATCH
• Region: CHINA (Hainan)

G. J. Liu

Liu, Guo Jun; 刘国钧 ; Liú Guójūn; 劉國鈞
1936-2009 **First publication: 1985**
• Employment: Xinjiang Institute of Biology, Pedology and Desert Research, Chinese Academy of Sciences（中国科学院新疆生物土壤沙漠研究所）
• Research interest: Caprifoliaceae, Lamiaceae, Liliaceae [S]
• Published taxa: *Dracocephalum, Fritillaria, Lagochilus, Mentha, Salvia, Scabiosa*
• Affiliation: XJBI
• Location of specimens: XJBI
• Region: CHINA (Xinjiang)

G. H. Liu

Liu, Guo Hou; 刘果厚 ; Liú Guǒhòu
1956- **First publication: 1989**
• Employment: Department of Biology, Inner Mongolia University（内蒙古大学生物系）
• Research interest: Berberidaceae, Betulaceae, Euphorbiaceae, Polemoniaceae, Rubiaceae [S]
• Published taxa: *Berberis, Betula, Euphorbia, Polemonium, Rubia*
• Affiliation: NMAC, NMFC
• Location of specimens: NMAC, NMFC
• Region: CHINA (Nei Mongol)

H. L. Liu

Liu, Huo Lin; 刘和林 ; Liú Hélín; 劉和林
1938- **First publication: 1982**
• Employment: Sichuan Institute of Forest Science（四川省林业科学研究所）
• Research interest: Cupressaceae [S]
• Published taxa: *Cunninghamia*
• Region: CHINA (Sichuan)

H. Y. Liu

Liu, Ho Yih; Liu, He Yi; 劉和義 ; Liú Héyì; 刘和义
1952- **First publication: 1989**
• Employment: Department of Biological Sciences, Sun Yat-sen University, Taiwan（中山大学生物科学系）
• Research interest: Athyriaceae, Boraginaceae, Crassulaceae, Cucurbitaceae, Cyperaceae, Dryopteridaceae, Helwingiaceae, Melastomataceae, Plantaginaceae, Pteridaceae, Rhizophoraceae, Rosaceae [PS]
• Published taxa: *Aeonium, Athyrium, Bolbitis, Ceriops, Cordia, Fimbristylis, Heliotropium, Helwingia, Kandelia, Medinilla, Melastoma, Pteris, Rhaphiolepis,*

Veronicastrum, Zehneria
- Region: CHINA (Taiwan)

H. S. Liu

Liu, Heng Shen; 刘恒生 ; Liú Héngshēng
?-1992 First publication: 1991
- Employment: Forestry Bureau of Dukou Municipal, Sichuan（四川省渡口市林业局）
- Research interest: Theaceae [S]
- Published taxa: *Camellia*
- Region: CHINA (Sichuan)

Hong Liu

Liu, Hong; 刘红 ; Liú Hóng
First publication: 1985
- Employment: The Institute of Vegetables, Chinese Academy of Agricultural Sciences（中国农业科学院蔬菜研究所）
- Research interest: Solanaceae [S]
- Published taxa: *Capsicum, Solanum*
- Affiliation: IVF
- Location of specimens: IVF
- Region: CHINA (Yunnan)

Hong M. Liu

Liu, Hong Mei; 刘红梅 ; Liú Hóngméi
1979- First publication: 2013
- Employment: Fairy Lake Botanical Garden, Shenzhen & Chinese Academy of Sciences（深圳市中国科学院仙湖植物园）
- Research interest: Arthropteridaceae, Dryopteridaceae; Pteridophytes [PS]
- Published taxa: *Arthropteris, Dryopteris*
- Affiliation: SZG
- Location of specimens: SZG
- Region: CHINA
- IPNI as: H. M. Liu

Hong Liu bis

Liu, Hong; 刘虹 ; Liú Hóng
1977- First publication: 2005
- Employment: College of Life Sciences, Wuhan University; South-Central Minzu University（武汉大学生命科学学院 ; 中南民族大学）
- Research interest: Isoetaceae, Saxifragaceae [PS]
- Published taxa: *Chrysosplenium, Isoetes*
- Region: CHINA (Hubei, Zhejiang)
- IPNI as: Hong Liu

H. X. Liu

Liu, Hong Xian; 刘洪先 ; Liú Hóngxiān; 劉洪先
1940-2019 First publication: 1984
- Employment: Sichuan Institute of Grassland（四川省草原研究所）
- Research interest: Poaceae [S]
- Published taxa: *Aristida, Dactylis*
- Region: CHINA (Sichuan)

H. Liu

Liu, Ho; Liou, Ho; Liou, Hou; Liu, Hou; 刘厚 ; Liú Hòu; 劉厚
1894-1984 First publication: 1932
- Employment: Faculté des sciences, Université de Paris, France; Institut Franco-Chinois de Lyon, France; Institute of Botany, National Academy of Peiping（法国巴黎大学理学院 ; 法国里昂中法大学 ; 国立北平研究院植物学研究所）
- Research interest: Lauraceae [S]
- Published taxa: *Actinodaphne, Alseodaphne, Beilschmiedia, Cryptocarya, Haasia, Lindera, Litsea, Machilus, Neocinnamomum, Neolitsea, Nothaphoebe, Phoebe*
- Location of specimens: PE
- Region: [ASIA]

Hui L. Liu

Liu, Hui Lan; 刘惠兰 ; Liú Huìlán; 劉惠蘭
1935-2018 First publication: 1990
- Employment: Ningxia Agricultural College（宁夏农学院）
- Research interest: Adoxaceae, Lamiaceae, Melanthiaceae [S]
- Published taxa: *Paris, Thymus, Viburnum*
- Region: CHINA (Ningxia)
- IPNI as: H. L. Liu

J. N. Liu

Liu, Ji Nan; 刘基男 ; Liú Jīnán
1992- First publication: 2018
- Employment: Amateur（业余爱好者）
- Research interest: Aristolochiaceae [S]
- Published taxa: *Aristolochia*
- Region: CHINA (Yunnan)

J. M. Liu

Liu, Ji Ming; 刘济明 ; Liú Jìmíng
1963- First publication: 2011
- Employment: College of Forestry, Guizhou University（贵州大学林学院）
- Research interest: Juglandaceae; Woody Plants [S]
- Published taxa: *Juglans*
- Affiliation: GZAC
- Location of specimens: GZAC
- Region: CHINA (Guizhou)

J. P. Liu

Liu, Jia Pei; 刘家培 ; Liú Jiāpéi
First publication: 1993

- Employment: Horticultural Research Institute, Yunnan Academy of Agricultural Sciences（云南省农业科学院园艺作物研究所）
- Research interest: Rosaceae [S]
- Published taxa: *Malus*
- Region: CHINA (Yunnan)

J. K. Liu

Liu, Jia Kai; 刘甲楷；Liú Jiǎkǎi

First publication: 1981

- Employment: Liuzhou Research Institute of Forestry Science, Guangxi（广西柳州地区林科所）
- Research interest: Poaceae [S]
- Published taxa: *Phyllostachys*
- Region: CHINA (Guangxi)

J. G. Liu

Liu, Jian Guo; Liou, Jian Guo; 刘建国；Liú Jiànguó

1961- First publication: 1992

- Employment: Xinjiang Institute of Biology, Pedology and Desert Research, Chinese Academy of Sciences（中国科学院新疆生物土壤沙漠研究所）
- Research interest: Ranunculaceae [S]
- Published taxa: *Clematis, Pulsatilla, Ranunculus*
- Affiliation: XJBI
- Region: CHINA (Xinjiang)

J. H. Liu

Liu, Jian Hua; 刘建华；Liú Jiànhuá

First publication: 1984

- Employment: Yunnan Institute of Tropical Botany, Chinese Academy of Sciences（中国科学院云南热带植物研究所）
- Research interest: Fabaceae [S]
- Published taxa: *Dalbergia*
- Region: CHINA (Yunnan)

J. L. Liu

Liu, Jian Lin; 刘建林；Liú Jiànlín

1954- First publication: 1989

- Employment: Department of Agriculture, Xichang College（西昌学院农学系）
- Research interest: Acanthaceae, Amaranthaceae, Ericaceae, Lamiaceae, Malvaceae, Melanthiaceae, Musaceae, Oleaceae, Polygonaceae, Rosaceae, Theaceae [S]
- Published taxa: *Achyranthes, Camellia, Docynia, Fagopyrum, Gaultheria, Jasminum, Ligustrum, Mentha, Musa, Osmanthus, Paris, Rostellularia, Sida, Vitex*
- Affiliation: XIAS
- Location of specimens: XIAS
- Region: CHINA

J. Quan Liu

Liu, Jian Quan; 刘建全；Liú Jiànquán; 刘健全

1969- First publication: 1996

- Employment: Northwest Plateau Institute of Biology, Chinese Academy of Sciences; School of Life Sciences, Lanzhou University; College of Life Sciences, Sichuan University（中国科学院西北高原生物研究所；兰州大学生命科学学院；四川大学生命科学学院）
- Research interest: Apiaceae, Asteraceae, Betulaceae, Brassicaceae, Gentianaceae, Poaceae; Plant Systematics [S]
- Published taxa: *Aphragmus, Carpinus, Comastoma, Eutrema, Gentiana, Heracleum, Orinus, Orychophragmus, Ostryopsis, Saussurea, Shangwua, Sinosenecio, Sinoswertia*
- Affiliation: SZ
- Region: CHINA

J. S. Liu

Liu, Jian Sheng; 刘建生；Liú Jiànshēng

1955- First publication: 1988

- Employment: School of Pharmacy, Beijing Medical University; Faculty of Plant Taxonomy, Sichuan Academy of Forestry（北京医科大学药学院；四川省林业科学研究院分类室）
- Research interest: Dipentodontaceae, Lauraceae [S]
- Published taxa: *Dipentodon, Litsea*
- Location of specimens: PEM
- Region: CHINA (Guangxi, Sichuan)

J. W. Liu

Liu, Jian Wei; 刘建伟；Liú Jiànwěi

1962- First publication: 1991

- Employment: Northeast Forestry University（东北林业大学）
- Research interest: Salicaceae [S]
- Published taxa: *Populus*
- Region: CHINA (Henan)

J. F. Liu

Liu, Jiang Feng; 刘江枫；Liú Jiāngfēng

1977- First publication: 2016

- Employment: College of Landscape Architecture, Fujian Agriculture and Forestry University; Management Office of Yushan Scenic Area, Fuzhou（福建农林大学园林学院；福州市于山风景区管理处）
- Research interest: Orchidaceae, Orobanchaceae [S]
- Published taxa: *Bulbophyllum, Christisonia*
- Region: CHINA (Fujian, Guangdong)

Jing Liu

Liu, Jing; 刘静；Liú Jìng

1987- First publication: 2017

- Employment: Guangxi Institute of Botany, Chinese Academy of Sciences（广西壮族自治区中国科学院广西植物研究所）
- Research interest: Rubiaceae; Pteridophytes [S]
- Published taxa: *Spiradiclis*
- Affiliation: IBK
- Region: CHINA (Guangxi)
- IPNI as: J. Liu

J. Liu

Liu, Jun; 刘军；Liú Jūn

1965- **First publication: 1993**

- Employment: Sichuan Agricultural University（四川农业大学）
- Research interest: Loranthaceae, Salicaceae [S]
- Published taxa: *Pleiarina, Populus, Salix*
- Affiliation: SAUF
- Location of specimens: SAUF
- Region: CHINA

G. X. Liou

Liou, G. X.; Liu, Jun Hui; 刘君慧；Liú Jūnhuì

First publication: 1978

- Employment: Henan Agricultural College（河南农学院）
- Research interest: Salicaceae [S]
- Published taxa: *Populus*
- Region: CHINA (Henan)

J. Z. Liu

Liu, Jun Zhe; 刘君哲；Liú Jūnzhé; 劉君哲

1938-1998 **First publication: 1988**

- Employment: Department of Biology, Nankai University（南开大学生物系）
- Research interest: Oleaceae, Plantaginaceae [S]
- Published taxa: *Fraxinus, Plantago*
- Affiliation: NKU
- Location of specimens: NKU
- Region: CHINA

K. Wei Liu

Liu, Ke Wei; 刘可为；Liú Kěwéi

1986- **First publication: 2008**

- Employment: School of Life Sciences, University of Science and Technology of China（中国科学技术大学生命科学学院）
- Research interest: Hypoxidaceae, Orchidaceae [S]
- Published taxa: *Chenorchis, Neuwiedia, Pendulorchis, Sinocurculigo*
- Region: CHINA (Guangdong, Yunnan)

K. M. Liu

Liu, Ke Ming; 刘克明；Liú Kèmíng

1952- **First publication: 1987**

- Employment: Department of Biology, Hunan Normal University; College of Life Sciences, Hunan Normal University（湖南师范大学生物系；湖南师范大学生命科学学院）
- Research interest: Acoraceae, Araceae, Asteraceae, Balsaminaceae, Brassicaceae, Burmanniaceae, Gesneriaceae, Melastomataceae [S]
- Published taxa: *Acorus, Burmannia, Cardamine, Colocasia, Conyza, Impatiens, Phyllagathis, Primulina*
- Affiliation: HNNU
- Location of specimens: HNNU
- Region: CHINA (Hunan)

K. W. Liu

Liu, Ke Wang; 刘克旺；Liú Kèwàng; 劉克旺

1938- **First publication: 1986**

- Employment: Central South College of Forestry（中南林学院）
- Research interest: Betulaceae, Lauraceae, Rosaceae; Woody Plants [S]
- Published taxa: *Actinodaphne, Carpinus, Sorbus*
- Affiliation: CSFI
- Location of specimens: CSFI
- Region: CHINA (Hunan)

Kun Liu

Liu, Kun; 刘坤；Liú Kūn

1989- **First publication: 2014**

- Employment: College of Life Sciences, Anhui Normal University（安徽师范大学生命科学学院）
- Research interest: Amaryllidaceae, Primulaceae; Plants of Anhui [S]
- Published taxa: *Lycoris, Lysimachia*
- Affiliation: ANUB
- Location of specimens: ANUB
- Region: CHINA (Hubei)
- Also as: K. Liu

Kun Liu bis

Liu, Kun; 刘坤；Liú Kūn

1990- **First publication: 2020**

- Employment: Jindong Forest Farm, Yongzhou, Hunan（湖南省永州市金洞林场）
- Research interest: Gesneriaceae [S]
- Published taxa: *Primulina*
- Region: CHINA (Hunan)

L. F. Lau

Lau, Lan Fong; Lau, Lan Fang; 刘兰芳；Liú Lánfāng; 劉蘭芳

1936- **First publication: 1963**

- Employment: Guangxi Institute of Botany, Chinese Academy of Sciences（广西壮族自治区中国科学院广西植物研究所）

- Research interest: Lauraceae, Lythraceae [S]
- Published taxa: *Beilschmiedia, Lagerstroemia*
- Affiliation: SYS
- Location of specimens: SYS
- Region: CHINA (Guangxi)

Lei Liu

Liu, Lei; 刘磊 ; Liú Lěi

First publication: 2020

- Employment: Institute of Grassland Research, Chinese Academy of Agricultural Sciences（中国农业科学院草原研究所）
- Research interest: Fabaceae [S]
- Published taxa: *Astragalus*
- Region: CHINA (Nei Mongol)

L. P. Liu

Liu, Li Pin; 刘立品 ; Liú Lìpǐn; 劉立品

1938- **First publication: 1996**

- Employment: Department of Biology, Qingyang Teachers' College, Gansu（甘肃庆阳高等师范专科学校生物系）
- Research interest: Thymelaeaceae; Plants of Gansu [S]
- Published taxa: *Wikstroemia*
- Affiliation: QYTC
- Location of specimens: QYTC
- Region: CHINA (Gansu)

L. H. Liu

Liu, Li Hua; 刘丽华 ; Liú Lìhuá

1965- **First publication: 1991**

- Employment: Harbin Normal University（哈尔滨师范大学）
- Research interest: Typhaceae [S]
- Published taxa: *Sparganium*
- Region: CHINA (Heilongjiang)

L. F. Liu

Liu, Lian Fen; 刘莲芬 ; Liú Liánfēn

1965- **First publication: 2001**

- Employment: Department of Biology, Liaocheng Normal College（聊城师范学院生物系）
- Research interest: Fabaceae [S]
- Published taxa: *Oxytropis*
- Region: CHINA (Hebei)

L. Liu

Liu, Liang; Liou, Liang; 刘亮 ; Liú Liàng; 劉亮

1933-2001 **First publication: 1960**

- Employment: Sichuan Agricultural College; Institute of Botany, Chinese Academy of Sciences（四川农学院；中国科学院植物研究所）
- Research interest: Poaceae, Ranunculaceae [S]
- Published taxa: *Agrostis, Andropogon, Aristida, Aulacolepis, Batrachium, Bothriochloa, Bromus, Catabrosa, Coelorachis, Coix, Cymbopogon, Danthonia, Deyeuxia, Diandranthus, Digitaria, Elymus, Eragrostiella, Festuca, Halerpestes, Hymenachne, Imperata, Leptoloma, Leucopoa, Miscanthus, Narenga, Neyraudia, Oryzopsis, Phragmites, Poa, Puccinellia, Ranunculus, Sclerodactylon, Spodiopogon, Themeda, Triarrhena, Trisetum, Vulpia*
- Affiliation: PE
- Region: CHINA

Lin H. Liu

Liu, Lin Han; 刘林翰 ; Liú Línhàn; 劉林翰

1936- **First publication: 1999**

- Employment: Hunan Normal University（湖南师范大学）
- Research interest: Berberidaceae, Brassicaceae, Fabaceae, Gesneriaceae, Orchidaceae, Papaveraceae [S]
- Published taxa: *Cardamine, Epimedium, Primulina, Sinolegumenea*
- Affiliation: HNNU
- Location of specimens: HNNU, PE
- Region: CHINA
- IPNI as: L. H. Liu

M. C. Liu

Liu, Mao Chun; 刘茂春 ; Liú Màochūn; 劉茂春

1936- **First publication: 1984**

- Employment: Zhejiang Forestry College（浙江林学院）
- Research interest: Calycanthaceae, Fagaceae, Juglandaceae [S]
- Published taxa: *Carya, Chimonanthus, Fagus, Quercus*
- Region: CHINA (Anhui, Zhejiang)

M. J. Liu

Liu, Meng Jun; 刘孟军 ; Liú Mèngjūn

1965- **First publication: 1994**

- Employment: Research Center of Chinese Jujube, Hebei Agricultural University（河北农业大学中国枣研究中心）
- Research interest: Rhamnaceae [S]
- Published taxa: *Ziziphus*
- Affiliation: JUJ
- Location of specimens: JUJ
- Region: CHINA

M. L. Liu

Liu, Min Lu; 刘珉璐 ; Liú Mínlù

1987- **First publication: 2015**

- Employment: Kunming Institute of Botany, Chinese Academy of Sciences（中国科学院昆明植物研究所）

- Research interest: Scrophulariaceae [S]
- Published taxa: *Pedicularis*
- Region: CHINA (Yunnan)

M. T. Liu

Liu, Ming Ting; 刘名廷 ;Liú Míngtíng; 刘名庭

1933- **First publication: 1979**

- Employment: Xinjiang Institute of Biology, Pedology and Desert Research, Chinese Academy of Sciences（中国科学院新疆生物土壤沙漠研究所）
- Research interest: Tamaricaceae [S]
- Published taxa: *Tamarix*
- Affiliation: TURP
- Location of specimens: TURP, XJBI
- Region: CHINA (Gansu, Xinjiang)

M. G. Liu

Liu, Ming Gang; 刘鸣岗 ; Liú Mínggǎng

1923- **First publication: 1987**

- Employment: Xichang Agricultural College（西昌农业专科学校）
- Research interest: Araceae, Basellaceae, Lemnaceae, Musaceae [S]
- Published taxa: *Lemna, Musa, Spirodela*
- Affiliation: XIAS
- Location of specimens: XIAS
- Region: CHINA (Sichuan)

M. Y. Liou

Liou, Ming Yuan; Liou, Min Yuan; Liu, Ming Yuan; 刘鸣远 ; Liú Míngyuǎn; 劉鳴遠

1925- **First publication: 1981**

- Employment: Department of Biology, Harbin Normal University（哈尔滨师范大学生物系）
- Research interest: Asteraceae, Campanulaceae, Fabaceae, Gentianaceae [S]
- Published taxa: *Adenophora, Artemisia, Gentiana, Trifolium*
- Affiliation: HANU
- Location of specimens: HANU
- Region: CHINA (Heilongjiang)

N. Liu

Liu, Nian; 刘念 ; Liú Niàn

1957- **First publication: 1987**

- Employment: South China Institute of Botany, Chinese Academy of Sciences; Zhongkai University of Agriculture and Engineering（中国科学院华南植物研究所；仲恺农业工程学院）
- Research interest: Cycadaceae, Fabaceae, Zingiberaceae; Plants of S. China [S]
- Published taxa: *Curcuma, Cycas, Hedychium*
- Affiliation: IBSC
- Location of specimens: IBSC
- Region: CHINA

P. L. Liu

Liu, Pei Liang; 刘培亮 ; Liú Péiliàng

1987- **First publication: 2009**

- Employment: College of Life Sciences, Northwest A&F University; College of Life Sciences, Northwest University（西北农林科技大学生命科学学院；西北大学生命科学学院）
- Research interest: Fabaceae, Ranunculaceae [S]
- Published taxa: *Hedysarum, Trollius*
- Region: CHINA

P. S. Liu

Liu, Pei Song; 刘培嵩 ; Liú Péisōng; 劉培嵩

1940- **First publication: 1982**

- Employment: Sichuan Nature Resource Institute（四川省自然资源研究所）
- Research interest: Actinidiaceae, Ericaceae [S]
- Published taxa: *Actinidia, Rhododendron*
- Location of specimens: SR
- Region: CHINA (Sichuan)

P. Y. Liu

Liu, Pei Ying; 刘佩瑛 ; Liú Pèiyīng

First publication: 1984

- Employment: Department of Horticulture, Southwest Agricultural College（西南农学院园艺系）
- Research interest: Araceae [S]
- Published taxa: *Amorphophallus*
- Region: CHINA (Sichuan)

Q. H. Liu

Liu, Qi Hong; 刘启宏 ; Liú Qǐhóng; 劉啟宏

1932-2012 **First publication: 1983**

- Employment: Wuhan Institute of Botany, Chinese Academy of Sciences（中国科学院武汉植物研究所）
- Research interest: Asteraceae, Rubiaceae [S]
- Published taxa: *Dendranthema, Galium*
- Region: CHINA (Hubei)

K. M. Lau

Lau, Kai Man; Lau, Kai Man, Peter; 劉啟文 ; Liú Qǐ wén; 刘启文

1940- **First publication: 2003**

- Employment: Chinese Medical Research Institute（香港中国医学研究所）
- Research interest: Balanophoraceae [S]
- Published taxa: *Balanophora*
- Region: CHINA (Hong Kong)

Q. X. Liu

Liu, Qi Xing; 刘启新 ; Liú Qǐxīn

1958- **First publication: 1987**

- Employment: Institute of Botany, Jiangsu Province; Institute of Botany, Jiangsu Province and Chinese Academy of Sciences（江苏省植物研究所；江苏省中国科学院植物研究所）
- Research interest: Apiaceae, Poaceae; Plants of E. China [S]
- Published taxa: *Deyeuxia, Ferula, Libanotis, Prangos*
- Affiliation: NAS
- Location of specimens: NAS
- Region: CHINA

H. T. Lau

Lau, Hay Tong; 刘起棠；Liú Qǐtáng

First publication: 2015

- Employment: Aletai Gebao Hongma Co., Ltd., Xinjiang（新疆阿勒泰戈宝麻有限公司）
- Research interest: Apocynaceae [S]
- Published taxa: *Poacynum*
- Region: CHINA (Xinjiang)

Qi X. Liu

Liu, Qi Xian; 刘起衔；Liú Qǐxián

1927- **First publication: 1988**

- Employment: Hunan Institute of Forestry Science（湖南省林业科学研究所）
- Research interest: Betulaceae, Ericaceae, Pinaceae, Symplocaceae [S]
- Published taxa: *Abies, Corylus, Rhododendron, Symplocos*
- Region: CHINA (Hunan)
- IPNI as: Q. X. Liu

Q. Liu

Liu, Qiang; 刘强；Liú Qiáng

1980- **First publication: 2014**

- Employment: Yunnan Forestry Technological College; Xishuangbanna Tropical Botanical Garden, Chinese Academy of Sciences（云南林业职业技术学院；中国科学院西双版纳热带植物园）
- Research interest: Magnoliaceae, Orchidaceae [S]
- Published taxa: *Bulbophyllum, Cheirostylis, Coelogyne, Dendrobium, Gastrochilus, Habenaria, Magnolia, Nervilia*
- Region: CHINA (Yunnan)

Q. Q. Liu

Liu, Qing Quan; 刘清泉；Liú Qīngquán; 劉清泉

1919-2015 **First publication: 1993**

- Employment: Forestry Administration of Shanxi（山西省林业厅）
- Research interest: Bignoniaceae, Cupressaceae, Fabaceae, Pinaceae [S]
- Published taxa: *Catalpa, Pinus, Platycladus, Sophora*
- Region: CHINA (Shanxi)

Q. R. Liu

Liu, Quan Ru; 刘全儒；Liú Quánrú

1963- **First publication: 1997**

- Employment: College of Life Sciences, Beijing Normal University（北京师范大学生命科学学院）
- Research interest: Boraginaceae, Celastraceae, Fabaceae, Melanthiaceae, Papaveraceae, Polypodiaceae, Rubiaceae; Plants of N. China [PS]
- Published taxa: *Astragalus, Chionographis, Corydalis, Glyptopetalum, Gymnosporia, Onosma, Ophiorrhiza, Platygyria, Spiradiclis, Trigonotis*
- Affiliation: BNU
- Location of specimens: BNU
- Region: CHINA

R. L. Liu

Liu, Ren Ling; Liu, Ren Lin; **刘仁林；Liú Rénlín**

1958- **First publication: 1993**

- Employment: Jinggangshan Nature Reserve Management Office, Jiangxi; School of Chemistry and Life Science, Gannan Normal University（江西井冈山自然保护区管理处；赣南师范学院化学与生命科学学院）
- Research interest: Ericaceae, Magnoliaceae; Plants of Jinggangshan [S]
- Published taxa: *Manglietia, Rhododendron*
- Affiliation: JN
- Location of specimens: JN
- Region: CHINA (Jiangxi)

Ri L. Liu

Liu, Ri Lin; 刘日林；Liú Rìlín

1968- **First publication: 2019**

- Employment: Administration of Jingning Wangdongyang Alpine Wetland Natural Reserve of Zhejiang Province（浙江省景宁畲族自治县望东垟高山湿地省级自然保护区管理局）
- Research interest: Fagaceae [S]
- Published taxa: *Cyclobalanopsis*
- Region: CHINA (Zhejiang)
- IPNI as: R. L. Liu

J. C. Liu

Liu, Ju Chiang; Liu, Ju Ch'iang; Liu, Ru Qiang; **刘汝强；Liú Rǔ qiáng; 劉汝强**

1895-1987 **First publication: 1927**

- Employment: Department of Pharmacy, Peking Union Medical College; Peking Normal University; Department of Biology, National Northwest University（北平协和医学院药学系；北平师范大学；国立西北大学生物系）
- Research interest: Ephedraceae; Plants of N. China [S]
- Published taxa: *Ephedra*

• Location of specimens: BNU
• Region: CHINA
• IPNI as: Liu

S. W. Liu

Liu, Shang Wu; 刘尚武；Liú Shàngwǔ；劉尚武
1934-2021 **First publication: 1978**
• Employment: Northwest Plateau Institute of Biology, Chinese Academy of Sciences（中国科学院西北高原生物研究所）
• Research interest: Asteraceae, Campanulaceae, Caprifoliaceae, Elaeagnaceae, Gentianaceae [S]
• Published taxa: *Adenophora, Chaetoseris, Cremanthodium, Gentiana, Gentianella, Hippophae, Ligularia, Lomatogoniopsis, Lomatogonium, Lonicera, Metagentiana, Mulgedium, Saussurea, Sinoswertia, Swertia, Syncalathium, Youngia*
• Affiliation: HNWP
• Location of specimens: HNWP
• Region: CHINA

Liou

Liou, Tchen Ngo; Liu, Shên O; Liu, Shên Ê; Liu, Shen E; 刘慎谔；Liú Shèn'è; 劉慎諤
1897-1975 **First publication: 1929**
• Employment: Institute of Botany, National Academy of Peiping; Institute of Forestry and Soil Sciences, Chinese Academy of Sciences（国立北平研究院植物学研究所；中国科学院林业土壤研究所）
• Research interest: Apiaceae, Euphorbiaceae, Fagaceae, Grossulariaceae, Pinaceae, Rhamnaceae, Rosaceae, Rutaceae, Solanaceae; Woody Plants; Fungi. [MPS]
• Published taxa: *Agrimonia, Cerasus, Dictamnus, Euphorbia, Glehnia, Larix, Pinus, Potentilla, Quercus, Rhamnus, Ribes, Solanum, Spiraea*
• Affiliation: IFP
• Location of specimens: IFP, NEAU, PE, SHM
• Region: CHINA

S. X. Liu

Liu, Sheng Xiang; 刘胜祥；Liú Shèngxiáng
1954- **First publication: 1992**
• Employment: Central China Normal University（华中师范大学）
• Research interest: Asteraceae [BS]
• Published taxa: *Aster, Bidens*
• Affiliation: CCNU
• Location of specimens: CCNU
• Region: CHINA (Chongqing, Hunan)

S. L. Liou

Liou, Shou Lu; Liou, Sheo Lu; Liu, Shou Lu; 刘守炉；Liú Shǒulú; 劉守爐
1937- **First publication: 1964**
• Employment: Nanjing Institute of Botany, Chinese Academy of Sciences; Institute of Botany, Jiangsu Province（中国科学院南京植物研究所；江苏省植物研究所）
• Research interest: Apiaceae, Araliaceae, Lamiaceae, Poaceae [S]
• Published taxa: *Acronema, Chamaesium, Cryptotaenia, Festuca, Hydrocotyle, Meeboldia, Physospermopsis, Pimpinella, Sanicula, Sinocarum, Sinolimprichtia, Vitex*
• Affiliation: NAS
• Location of specimens: NAS
• Region: CHINA

S. Y. Liu

Liu, Shou Yang; 刘寿养；Liú Shòuyǎng; 劉壽養
1942-2017 **First publication: 1983**
• Employment: Guangxi College of Traditional Chinese Medicine（广西中医学院）
• Research interest: Araceae, Capparaceae, Convolvulaceae, Fabaceae, Iteaceae, Lamiaceae, Malvaceae, Melastomataceae, Polygonaceae, Rhamnaceae, Rubiaceae, Sabiaceae, Thymelaeaceae, Urticaceae; Medicinal Plants [S]
• Published taxa: *Amorphophallus, Arisaema, Capparis, Dalbergia, Fallopia, Fordiophyton, Grewia, Helicteres, Itea, Merremia, Ophiorrhiza, Pellionia, Polygonum, Sabia, Sageretia, Spiradiclis, Vitex, Wikstroemia*
• Affiliation: GXCM
• Location of specimens: GXCM
• Region: CHINA (Guangxi)

S. R. Liou

Liou, Shu Run; 刘书润；Liú Shūrùn; 劉書潤
1941- **First publication: 1983**
• Employment: Department of Biology, Inner Mongolia University; Department of Biology, Inner Mongolia Education College; Inner Mongolia Normal University（内蒙古大学生物系；内蒙古教育学院生物系；内蒙古师范大学）
• Research interest: Poaceae [S]
• Published taxa: *Festuca*
• Affiliation: HIMC
• Location of specimens: FGC, HIMC, NMTC
• Region: CHINA (Nei Mongol)
• IPNI as: S. R. Liu

S. C. Liu

Liu, Shu Chuan; 劉淑娟；Liú Shūjuān; 刘淑娟
First publication: 2000
• Employment: Department of Life Science, Taiwan Normal University（台湾师范大学生命科学系）

- Research interest: Rosaceae, Zingiberaceae [S]
- Published taxa: *Alpinia, Rubus*
- Region: CHINA (Taiwan)

S. Z. Liou

Liou, Shu Zhen; 刘淑珍 ; Liú Shūzhēn; 劉淑珍
1939- **First publication: 1988**

- Employment: Institute of Forestry and Soil Sciences, Chinese Academy of Sciences; Herbarium, Institute of Applied Ecology, Chinese Academy of Sciences（中国科学院林业土壤研究所；中国科学院沈阳应用生态研究所植物标本馆）
- Research interest: Cannabaceae, Caprifoliaceae, Euphorbiaceae, Orchidaceae, Polemoniaceae, Rutaceae, Simaroubaceae, Solanaceae [S]
- Published taxa: *Cannabis, Euphorbia, Lycium, Neottianthe, Phellodendron, Picrasma, Polemonium, Scabiosa, Solanum*
- Affiliation: IFP
- Location of specimens: IFP
- Region: CHINA (Liaoning)
- Also as: S. Z. Liu

Su Liu

Liu, Su; 刘夙 ; Liú Sù
1982- **First publication: 2019**

- Employment: Shanghai Chenshan Botanical Garden（上海辰山植物园）
- Research interest: Wightiaceae [S]
- Published taxa: Wightiaceae
- Region: [ASIA]

T. S. Liu

Liu, Tang Shui; Liu, Tung Shui; Liu, Tang Rui; Liu, T'ang Jui; Liu, T'ang Shui; 劉棠瑞 ; Liú Tángruì; 刘棠瑞
1911-1997 **First publication: 1951**

- Employment: Botany Department, Taiwan Provincial Museum; Department of Forestry, Taiwan University; Department of Botany, Taiwan University（台湾省立博物馆植物学组；台湾大学森林学系；台湾大学植物学系）
- Research interest: Amaryllidaceae, Apiaceae, Aristolochiaceae, Asphodelaceae, Begoniaceae, Brassicaceae, Caryophyllaceae, Crassulaceae, Gentianaceae, Lamiaceae, Lauraceae, Liliaceae, Malvaceae, Moraceae, Oleaceae, Orchidaceae, Pinaceae, Polygonaceae, Ranunculaceae, Rosaceae, Rubiaceae, Rutaceae, Urticaceae; Plants of Taiwan [S]
- Published taxa: *Abies, Aconitum, Actinodaphne, Allium, Androcorys, Arabis, Aristolochia, Begonia, Bupleurum, Callicarpa, Cardamine, Cephalantheropsis, Cerastium, Cirrhopetalum, Corchorus, Cymbidium, Dendrobium, Dianella, Dianthus, Ficus, Gentiana, Goodyera, Hylophila, Laportea, Ligustrum, Lilium, Liparis, Melicope, Osmanthus, Photinia, Picea, Polygonum, Rubus, Sedum, Stellaria, Theligonum, Trichoglottis, Tricyrtis, Tripterospermum, Tulotis*
- Affiliation: NTUF
- Location of specimens: NTUF
- Region: CHINA (Taiwan)
- Also as: Liu

W. Liu

Liu, Wei; 刘威 ; Liú Wēi
1971- **First publication: 2003**

- Employment: School of Life Sciences, Sun Yat-sen University（中山大学生命科学学院）
- Research interest: Violaceae [S]
- Published taxa: *Viola*
- Region: CHINA (Hunan)

Wei Liu

Liu, Wei; 刘巍 ; Liú Wēi
1982- **First publication: 2007**

- Employment: Institute of Botany, Chinese Academy of Sciences（中国科学院植物研究所）
- Research interest: Fabaceae [S]
- Published taxa: *Glycine*
- Region: CHINA
- IPNI as: W. Liu

W. Q. Liu

Liu, Wei Qiu; 刘蔚秋 ; Liú Wèiqiū
1970- **First publication: 2007**

- Employment: School of Life Sciences, Sun Yat-sen University（中山大学生命科学学院）
- Research interest: Asparagaceae, Ericaceae; Bryophyte [BS]
- Published taxa: *Lyonia, Ophiopogon*
- Affiliation: SYS
- Location of specimens: SYS
- Region: CHINA (Guangdong)

W. Y. Liu

Liu, Wei Yi; 刘蔚漪 ; Liú Wèiyī
1982- **First publication: 2019**

- Employment: Southwest Forestry University（西南林业大学）
- Research interest: Poaceae [S]
- Published taxa: *Dendrocalamus*
- Affiliation: SWFC
- Location of specimens: SWFC
- Region: CHINA (Yunnan)

W. D. Liu

Liu, Wen De; 刘文德 ; Liú Wéndé; 劉文德
1930-2019 **First publication: 1984**

- Employment: Shanxi Institute of Forestry Science（山西省林业科学研究所）
- Research interest: Salicaceae [S]
- Published taxa: *Salix*
- Region: CHINA (Shanxi)

Xi Liu

Liu, Xi; 刘西 ; Liú Xī

1985- **First publication: 2020**

- Employment: Administration of Zhejiang Wuyanling National Natural Reserve（浙江乌岩岭国家级自然保护区管理局）
- Research interest: Oleaceae [S]
- Published taxa: *Osmanthus*
- Region: CHINA (Zhejiang)

X. Z. Liu

Liu, Xian Zhang; 刘宪章 ; Liú Xiànzhāng; 劉憲章

1938- **First publication: 1991**

- Employment: Kunming Institute of Botany, Chinese Academy of Sciences（中国科学院昆明植物研究所）
- Research interest: Asparagaceae, Zingiberaceae [S]
- Published taxa: *Tupistra, Zingiber*
- Region: CHINA (Yunnan)

X. Jun Liu

Liu, Xiang Jun; 刘湘君 ; Liú Xiāngjūn

1964- **First publication: 1989**

- Employment: Department of Biology, Sun Yat-sen University（中山大学生物系）
- Research interest: Caprifoliaceae [S]
- Published taxa: *Lonicera*
- Region: CHINA (Guangdong)

Xiang Jun Liu

Liu, Xiang Jun; 刘祥君 ; Liú Xiángjūn

1959- **First publication: 1992**

- Employment: Department of Biology, Harbin Normal University（哈尔滨师范大学生物系）
- Research interest: Asteraceae, Ranunculaceae [S]
- Published taxa: *Artemisia, Batrachium*
- Region: CHINA (Heilongjiang)
- IPNI as: X. J. Liu

Xiao Lan Liu

Liu, Xiao Lan; 刘小兰 ; Liú Xiǎolán

First publication: 2020

- Employment: School of Life Sciences, Yunnan University（云南大学生命科学学院）
- Research interest: Rubiaceae [S]
- Published taxa: *Hedyotis*
- Region: CHINA (Yunnan)

Xiao L. Liu

Liu, Xiao Lin; 刘小林 ; Liú Xiǎolín

1981- **First publication: 2011**

- Employment: College of Life Sciences, Northwest A&F University（西北农林科技大学生命科学学院）
- Research interest: Fabaceae [S]
- Published taxa: *Astragalus*
- Region: CHINA (Xinjiang)

X. Liu

Liu, Xiao; 刘晓 ; Liú Xiǎo

1975- **First publication: 2002**

- Employment: College of Life Sciences, Northwest University（西北大学生命科学学院）
- Research interest: Pittosporaceae [S]
- Published taxa: *Pittosporum*
- Region: CHINA (Shaanxi)

X. D. Liu

Liu, Xiao Dong; 刘晓东 ; Liú Xiǎodōng; 劉曉東

1940- **First publication: 1976**

- Employment: Citrus Research Institute, Chinese Academy of Agricultural Sciences（中国农业科学院柑橘研究所）
- Research interest: Rutaceae [S]
- Published taxa: *Citrus*
- Affiliation: CIT
- Location of specimens: CIT
- Region: CHINA (Yunnan)
- IPNI as: X. Liu

X. L. Liu

Liu, Xiao Long; 刘晓龙 ; Liú Xiǎolóng

1950- **First publication: 1987**

- Employment: Wuhu School of Traditional Chinese Medicine（安徽省芜湖中医学校）
- Research interest: Araceae, Caryophyllaceae, Convolvulaceae, Crassulaceae, Gesneriaceae, Lamiaceae, Linderniaceae, Mazaceae [S]
- Published taxa: *Chiritopsis, Lindernia, Mazus, Mentha, Merremia, Orostachys, Pinellia, Scutellaria, Silene*
- Affiliation: WUH
- Location of specimens: WUH
- Region: CHINA (Anhui)

X. T. Liu

Liu, Xin tian; 刘心恬 ; Liú Xīntián

1956- **First publication: 1991**

- Employment: Institute of Botany, Jiangsu Province（江苏省植物研究所）
- Research interest: Apiaceae [S]
- Published taxa: *Sanicula, Sinocarum*
- Region: CHINA (Chongqing, Sichuan)

X. C. Liu

Liu, Xin Ce; 刘新策 ; Liú Xīncè

First publication: 1986

- Employment: Forestry Bureau of Rongshui Miao Autonomous County, Guangxi（广西融水苗族自治县林业局）
- Research interest: Poaceae [S]
- Published taxa: *Bambusa*
- Region: CHINA (Guangxi)

Xing Liu

Liu, Xing; 刘星 ; Liú Xīng

1968- First publication: 2019

- Employment: College of Life Sciences, Wuhan University（武汉大学生命科学学院）
- Research interest: Isoetaceae [P]
- Published taxa: *Isoetes*
- Affiliation: WH
- Location of specimens: WH
- Region: CHINA (Yunnan)

X. M. Liu

Liu, Xiu Mei; 刘秀梅 ; Liú Xiùméi; 劉秀梅

1935- First publication: 1987

- Employment: Department of Forestry, Anhui Agricultural College; School of Forestry & Landscape Architecture, Anhui Agricultural University（安徽农学院林学系；安徽农业大学林学与园林学院）
- Research interest: Araliaceae, Betulaceae, Fabaceae, Fagaceae, Moraceae, Rhamnaceae, Rosaceae, Rutaceae, Theaceae [S]
- Published taxa: *Acanthopanax, Betula, Euodia, Morus, Quercus, Rhamnus, Sorbus, Stewartia*
- Affiliation: AAUF
- Location of specimens: AAUF
- Region: CHINA (Anhui)

H. H. Liu

Liu, Hsiou Hsi; Liu, Xiu Xi; Liu, Siu Si; 刘秀熙 ; Liú Xiùxī

1950- First publication: 1981

- Employment: Department of Biology, Xiamen University（厦门大学生物系）
- Research interest: Aquifoliaceae [S]
- Published taxa: *Ilex*
- Affiliation: AU
- Location of specimens: AU
- Region: CHINA (Fujian)

X. P. Liou

Liou, Xue Ping; 刘学平 ; Liú Xuépíng; 劉學平

1932- First publication: 2002

- Employment: School of Traditional Chinese Pharmacy, China Pharmaceutical University（中国药科大学中药学院）
- Research interest: Poaceae [S]
- Published taxa: *Arundinella*
- Region: CHINA (Hubei)

Yan Liu

Liu, Yan; 刘演 ; Liú Yǎn

1968- First publication: 2003

- Employment: Guangxi Institute of Botany, Chinese Academy of Sciences（广西壮族自治区中国科学院广西植物研究所）
- Research interest: Aristolochiaceae, Asparagaceae, Begoniaceae, Dryopteridaceae, Ebenaceae, Ericaceae, Gesneriaceae, Lamiaceae, Orchidaceae, Ranunculaceae, Rubiaceae [PS]
- Published taxa: *Aristolochia, Aspidistra, Begonia, Calanthe, Cheilotheca, Chirita, Chiritopsis, Diospyros, Gastrodia, Hemiboea, Lagarosolen, Lysionotus, Oreocharis, Paraboea, Petrocodon, Petrocosmea, Polystichum, Primulina, Pseudochirita, Salvia, Semiaquilegia, Spiradiclis, Wentsaiboea*
- Affiliation: IBK
- Location of specimens: IBK
- Region: CHINA (Guangxi)

Yan C. Liu

Liu, Yan Chun; 刘艳春 ; Liú Yànchūn

1983- First publication: 2009

- Employment: Kunming Institute of Botany, Chinese Academy of Sciences（中国科学院昆明植物研究所）
- Research interest: Nyssaceae, Poaceae [S]
- Published taxa: *Eulalia, Mastixia, Microstegium, Miscanthus*
- Region: CHINA (Yunnan)
- IPNI as: Y. C. Liu

Y. C. Liu

Liu, Yeh Ching; Liu, Ye Jing; 劉業經 ; Liú Yèjīng; 刘业经

1917-1991 First publication: 1955

- Employment: College of Agriculture, Chung Hsing University（中兴大学农学院）
- Research interest: Adoxaceae, Araliaceae, Asteraceae, Begoniaceae, Caryophyllaceae, Fabaceae, Hydrangeaceae, Lardizabalaceae, Lauraceae, Loranthaceae, Lythraceae, Melastomataceae, Passifloraceae, Pentaphylacaceae, Polygonaceae, Proteaceae, Ranunculaceae, Rhamnaceae, Rosaceae, Rutaceae, Solanaceae, Symplocaceae, Urticaceae; Woody Plants [S]
- Published taxa: *Aralia, Aster, Begonia, Berchemia, Boehmeria, Bredia, Cassia, Clematis, Crotalaria, Desmodium, Dumasia, Eurya, Helicia, Hydrangea, Machilus, Passiflora, Physalis, Polygonum, Ranunculus,*

Rhamnus, Rotala, Rubus, Sageretia, Scurrula, Solanum, Stauntonia, Stellaria, Symplocos, Viburnum, Zanthoxylum
- Affiliation: TCF
- Location of specimens: TCF
- Region: CHINA (Taiwan)

Y. T. Liu

Liu, Yi Tao; 刘怡涛; Liú Yítāo
1955- **First publication: 2002**
- Employment: Kunming Institute of Botany, Chinese Academy of Sciences (中国科学院昆明植物研究所)
- Research interest: Orchidaceae [S]
- Published taxa: *Pholidota*
- Region: CHINA (Yunnan)

Yea C. Liu

Liu, Yea Chen; 劉以誠; Liú Yĭchéng; 刘以诚
1973- **First publication: 2009**
- Employment: Department of Biological Resources, Chiayi University; Department of Forest Biology, Taiwan Forestry Research Institute, Council of Agriculture, "Executive Yuan" (嘉义大学生物资源学系暨研究所;"行政院"农业委员会林业试验所森林生物系)
- Research interest: Athyriaceae, Pteridaceae [P]
- Published taxa: *Adiantum, Anisocampium, Anisocampium, Athyrium, Haplopteris*
- Region: CHINA (Taiwan)

Y. Liu

Liu, Ying; Liou, Ying; 刘瑛; Liú Yīng
1915- ? **First publication: 1941**
- Employment: Fan Memorial Institute of Biology; Institute of Botany, Chinese Academy of Sciences (静生生物调查所;中国科学院植物研究所)
- Research interest: Fabaceae, Ranunculaceae [S]
- Published taxa: *Aconitum, Hedysarum*
- Location of specimens: PE
- Region: CHINA

Y. X. Liou

Liou, Ying Xing; Liou, Ying Hsin; Liou, Ying Sin; Liu, Ying Xin; Liou, f.; 刘媖心; Liú Yīngxīn; 劉媖心
1919-2012 **First publication: 1985**
- Employment: Institute of Desert Research, Chinese Academy of Sciences (中国科学院兰州沙漠研究所)
- Research interest: Apocynaceae, Fabaceae, Polygonaceae, Zygophyllaceae [S]
- Published taxa: *Astragalus, Calligonum, Caragana, Chesneya, Chesniella, Cynanchum, Lespedeza, Sarcozygium, Zygophyllum*
- Affiliation: LZD
- Location of specimens: LZD
- Region: CHINA
- Also as: Liou f.

Ying Liu

Liu, Ying; 刘莹; Liú Yíng
1982- **First publication: 2008**
- Employment: Institute of Botany, Chinese Academy of Sciences; School of Life Sciences, Sun Yat-sen University (中国科学院植物研究所;中山大学生命科学学院)
- Research interest: Asteraceae, Melastomataceae; Plants of S. China [S]
- Published taxa: *Bredia, Faberia, Hainanecio, Parasenecio, Sinosenecio, Tashiroea*
- Affiliation: SYS
- Location of specimens: SYS
- Region: CHINA

Y. Q. Liu

Liu, Yong Qiang; 刘永强; Liú Yǒngqiáng
1965- **First publication: 1999**
- Employment: Shanghai Botanical Garden (上海植物园)
- Research interest: Cyperaceae; Plants of E. China [S]
- Published taxa: *Carex*
- Affiliation: SG
- Region: CHINA (Shanghai)

Y. M. Liu

Liu, Yong Min; 刘勇民; Liú Yǒngmín; 劉勇民
1934- **First publication: 1984**
- Employment: Institute of Materia Medica, Xinjiang Institute for Drug Control (新疆药品检验药物研究所)
- Research interest: Liliaceae; Plants of Xinjiang [S]
- Published taxa: *Fritillaria*
- Affiliation: XJDC
- Location of specimens: XJDC
- Region: CHINA (Xinjiang)

Y. G. Liu

Liu, Yu Guang; 刘玉光; Liú Yùguāng
First publication: 1982
- Employment: Department of Biology, Northwest University (辽宁大学生物系)
- Research interest: Lamiaceae [S]
- Published taxa: *Scutellaria*
- Region: CHINA (Nei Mongol)

Y. W. Law

Law, Yuh Wu; Liu, Yü Hu; Liu, Yu Hu; 刘玉壶; Liú Yùhú; 劉玉壺
1917-2004 **First publication: 1948**
- Employment: Botanical Institute, College of

Agriculture, National Sun Yat-sen University; South China Institute of Botany, Chinese Academy of Sciences（国立中山大学农林植物研究所；中国科学院华南植物研究所）
- Research interest: Actinidiaceae, Magnoliaceae, Pinaceae, Sabiaceae, Schisandraceae [S]
- Published taxa: *Actinidia, Illicium, Larix, Magnolia, Manglietia, Manglietiastrum, Meliosma, Michelia, Parakmeria, Pinus, Sabia, Schisandra, Woonyoungia*
- Affiliation: IBSC
- Location of specimens: IBSC
- Region: CHINA

Y. J. Liu

Liu, Yu Jing; 刘玉晶 ; Liú Yùjīng
1969- **First publication: 1994**
- Employment: Department of Biology, Harbin Normal University（哈尔滨师范大学生物系）
- Research interest: Asteraceae [S]
- Published taxa: *Dendranthema*
- Region: CHINA (Heilongjiang)

Y. L. Liu

Liu, Yu Lan; 刘玉兰 ; Liú Yùlán; 劉玉蘭
1931-2007 **First publication: 1977**
- Employment: Institute of Botany, Northwest Normal College（西北师范学院植物研究所）
- Research interest: Boraginaceae, Polygonaceae, Rosaceae [S]
- Published taxa: *Atraphaxis, Cynoglossum, Ehretia, Heliotropium, Onosma, Polygonum*
- Affiliation: NWTC
- Location of specimens: NWTC
- Region: CHINA

Yu Yu Liu

Liu, Yu Yu; 刘玉雨 ; Liú Yùyǔ
1994- **First publication: 2017**
- Employment: College of Pharmacy, Dali University（大理大学药学院）
- Research interest: Melanthiaceae [S]
- Published taxa: *Paris*
- Region: CHINA (Yunnan)
- IPNI as: Y. Y. Liu

Z. G. Liu

Liu, Zhao Guang; 刘照光 ; Liú Zhàoguāng; 劉照光
1934-2001 **First publication: 1984**
- Employment: Chengdu Institute of Biology, Chinese Academy of Sciences（中国科学院成都生物研究所）
- Research interest: Asparagaceae [S]
- Published taxa: *Polygonatum*
- Location of specimens: CDBI
- Region: CHINA (Sichuan)

Zhen Q. Liu

Liu, Zhen Qian; 刘振乾 ; Liú Zhènqián
First publication: 1983
- Employment: Hunan Institute of Animal Science & Veterinary Medicine（湖南省畜牧兽医研究所）
- Research interest: Araceae [S]
- Published taxa: *Typhonium*
- Region: CHINA (Hunan)
- IPNI as: Z. Q. Liu

Z. H. Liu

Liu, Zhen Hua; 刘振华 ; Liú Zhènhuá; 劉振華
1928- **First publication: 1988**
- Employment: Nanyue Arboretum, Hunan（湖南省南岳树木园）
- Research interest: Ericaceae; Plants of S. Hunan [S]
- Published taxa: *Rhododendron*
- Affiliation: NYA
- Location of specimens: NYA
- Region: CHINA (Hunan)

Zhen W. Liu

Liu, Zhen Wen; 刘振稳 ; Liú Zhènwěn
1980- **First publication: 2009**
- Employment: Kunming Institute of Botany, Chinese Academy of Sciences（中国科学院昆明植物研究所）
- Research interest: Aristolochiaceae, Ericaceae [S]
- Published taxa: *Aristolochia, Pyrola*
- Affiliation: KUN
- Location of specimens: KUN
- Region: CHINA

Z. D. Liu

Liu, Zhen Dong; 刘震东 ; Liú Zhèndōng
1974- **First publication: 2009**
- Employment: West China School of Pharmacy, Sichuan Unieriversity（四川大学华西药学院）
- Research interest: Liliaceae [S]
- Published taxa: *Fritillaria*
- Region: CHINA (Sichuan)

Z. Y. Liu

Liu, Zheng Yu; 刘正宇 ; Liú Zhèngyǔ
1952- **First publication: 1983**
- Employment: Chongqing Institute of Medical Plant Cultivation（重庆市药物种植研究所）
- Research interest: Apiaceae, Asparagaceae, Aspleniaceae, Asteraceae, Athyriaceae, Cyperaceae, Dennstaedtiaceae, Dryopteridaceae, Gesneriaceae, Hymenophyllaceae, Marattiaceae, Moraceae, Polypodiaceae, Primulaceae, Ranunculaceae, Thelypteridaceae; Medicinal Plants; Pteridophytes [PS]
- Published taxa: *Allantodia, Anemone, Angiopteris, Arachniodes, Artocarpus, Asplenium, Athyriopsis,*

Athyrium, Carex, Ctenitis, Cyclosorus, Disporopsis, Dryoathyrium, Dryopteris, Hymenophyllum, Isometrum, Lepidomicrosorium, Lepisorus, Leptogramma, Loxogramme, Lunathyrium, Mecodium, Microlepia, Microsorum, Parathelypteris, Petrocosmea, Polystichum, Primula, Sanicula, Sinosenecio, Stegnogramma
- Affiliation: IMC
- Location of specimens: IMC, PE
- Region: CHINA (Chongqing)

Zhi L. Liu

Liu, Zhi Long; 刘芝龙 ; Liú Zhīlóng
1990- **First publication: 2016**
- Employment: Xishuangbanna Tropical Botanical Garden, Chinese Academy of Sciences（中国科学院西双版纳热带植物园）
- Research interest: Orchidaceae [S]
- Published taxa: *Cheirostylis*
- Region: CHINA (Yunnan)

Z. C. Liu

Liu, Zhong Cheng; 刘忠成 ; Liú Zhōngchéng
First publication: 2018
- Employment: College of Resource Environment and Tourism, Capital Normal University; School of Life Sciences, Sun Yat-sen University（首都师范大学资源环境与旅游学院；中山大学生命科学学院）
- Research interest: Melanthiaceae [S]
- Published taxa: *Chamaelirium*
- Region: CHINA (Jiangxi)

Z. J. Liu

Liu, Zhong Jian; 刘仲健 ; Liú Zhòngjiàn
1958- **First publication: 1998**
- Employment: Shenzhen City Wutongshan Nurseries, Guangdong; China National Orchid Conservation Center; The Orchid Conservation & Research Center of Shenzhen, Guangdong（广东省深圳市梧桐山苗圃总场；全国兰科植物种质资源保护中心；广东省深圳市兰科植物保护研究中心）
- Research interest: Hypoxidaceae, Orchidaceae [S]
- Published taxa: *Apostasia, Arachnis, Bulbophyllum, Calanthe, Cestichis, Changnienia, Chenorchis, Chroniochilus, Cymbidium, Cypripedium, Danxiaorchis, Dendrobium, Eria, Frigidorchis, Gastrochilus, Gunnaria, Holcoglossum, Hygrochilus, Liparis, Liuguishania, Neofinetia, Neuwiedia, Paphiopedilum, Paraholcoglossum, Paraphaius, Pendulorchis, Phalaenopsis, Platystyliparis, Pleione, Renanthera, Singchia, Sinocurculigo, Tsiorchis, Vanda, Vanilla, Wutongshania, Ypsilorchis, Yunorchis*
- Affiliation: NOCC
- Location of specimens: NOCC
- Region: CHINA

Zi Yue Liu

Liu, Zi Yue; 刘子玥 ; Liú Zǐyuè
1992- **First publication: 2018**
- Employment: Shanghai Chenshan Botanical Garden（上海辰山植物园）
- Research interest: Athyriaceae [P]
- Published taxa: *Diplazium*
- Region: CHINA (Guangxi)

Y. Q. Liufu

LiuFu, Yong Qing; 刘付永清 ; Liú-Fù Yǒngqīng
1989- **First publication: 2019**
- Employment: Natural History Museum of Guangxi（广西自然博物馆）
- Research interest: Theaceae [S]
- Published taxa: *Camellia*
- Region: CHINA (Guangxi)

C. S. Leou

Leou, Chong Sheng; Liu, Chong Sheng; **柳重勝 ; Liǔ Chóngshèng; 柳重胜**
First publication: 1990
- Employment: The Experimental Forest, College of Bio-Resources and Agriculture, Taiwan University（台湾大学生物资源暨农学院实验林管理处）
- Research interest: Orchidaceae, Urticaceae [S]
- Published taxa: *Aphyllorchis, Cheirostylis, Erythrodes, Gastrodia, Nervilia, Odontochilus, Parietaria, Tropidia, Zeuxine*
- Region: CHINA (Taiwan)

X. H. Liu

Liu, Xin Hong; 柳新红 ; Liǔ Xīnhóng
1967- **First publication: 2020**
- Employment: Zhejiang Academy of Forestry（浙江省林业科学研究院）
- Research interest: Cucurbitaceae [S]
- Published taxa: *Trichosanthes*
- Region: CHINA (Zhejiang)

C. L. Long

Long, Chun Lin; 龙春林 ; Lóng Chūnlín
1964- **First publication: 1989**
- Employment: Kunming Institute of Botany, Chinese Academy of Sciences; College of Life and Environmental Sciences, Minzu University of China（中国科学院昆明植物研究所；中央民族大学生命与环境科学学院）
- Research interest: Araceae, Asparagaceae, Burmanniaceae, Dioscoreaceae, Orchidaceae, Piperaceae [S]
- Published taxa: *Alocasia, Amorphophallus,*

Aspidistra, Burmannia, Coelogyne, Colocasia, Cymbidium, Dendrobium, Dioscorea, Pholidota, Pinellia, Piper
• Region: CHINA

Chun L. Long

Long, Chun Ling; 龙春玲 ; Lóng Chūnlíng
1988- **First publication: 2015**
• Employment: Jiangxi Provincial Key Laboratory for Bamboo Germplasm Resource and Utilization; Jiangxi Agricultural University（江西省竹子种质资源与利用重点实验室；江西农业大学）
• Research interest: Poaceae [S]
• Published taxa: *Gelidocalamus*
• Region: CHINA (Jiangxi)
• IPNI as: C. L. Long

G. R. Long

Long, Guang Ri; 龙光日 ; Lóng Guāngrì
1952-2011 **First publication: 1990**
• Employment: Liuzhou Timber Company, Guangxi（广西柳州地区木材公司）
• Research interest: Berberidaceae, Juglandaceae [S]
• Published taxa: *Mahonia, Platycarya*
• Location of specimens: IBSC
• Region: CHINA (Guangxi)

H. Long

Long, Hong; 龙红 ; Lóng Hóng
1964- **First publication: 1995**
• Employment: Ji'an Forestry Bureau, Jiangxi（江西吉安地区林业局）
• Research interest: Poaceae [S]
• Published taxa: *Pleioblastus*
• Region: CHINA (Jiangxi)

Y. H. Long

Long, Yao Hwa; 龙耀华 ; Lóng Yàohuá; 龍耀華
1924-2018 **First publication: 1984**
• Employment: Shaanxi Agriculture and Forestry School（陕西省农林学校）
• Research interest: Cupressaceae [S]
• Published taxa: *Metasequoia*
• Region: CHINA (Hubei)

T. L. Long

Long, Ting Lun; 隆廷伦 ; Lóng Tínglún
1966- **First publication: 1989**
• Employment: Wild Animal Resource Survey Team, Sichuan; Sichuan Station of Wildlife Survey and Management（四川省野生动物资源调查队；四川省野生动物资源调查保护管理站）
• Research interest: Poaceae, Taxaceae [S]
• Published taxa: *Torreya, Yushania*
• Region: CHINA (Sichuan)

L. H. Lou

Lou, Lu Huan; 楼炉焕 ; Lóu Lúhuàn; 樓爐煥
1948- **First publication: 2012**
• Employment: School of Forestry and Biotechnology, Zhejiang A&F University（浙江农林大学林业与生物技术学院）
• Research interest: Fabaceae, Rosaceae; Woody Plants [S]
• Published taxa: *Photinia*
• Affiliation: ZJFC
• Location of specimens: HZU, ZJFC
• Region: CHINA (Zhejiang)

Z. C. Lou

Lou, Zhi Cen; Lou, Chih Chen; Lou, Chih Ch'ên; 楼之岑 ; Lóu Zhīcén; 樓之岑
1920-1995 **First publication: 1988**
• Employment: Department of Pharmacognosy, Beijing Medical University（北京医科大学生药学教研室）
• Research interest: Gentianaceae, Orobanchaceae [S]
• Published taxa: *Cistanche, Gentiana*
• Region: CHINA (Gansu, Ningxia)

B. Rong Lu

Lu, Bao Rong; 卢宝荣 ; Lú Bǎoróng
1957- **First publication: 1988**
• Employment: Triticeae Research Institute, Sichuan Agricultural University（四川农业大学小麦研究所）
• Research interest: Poaceae [S]
• Published taxa: *Elymus, Pseudoroegneria, Roegneria*
• Affiliation: SAUT
• Location of specimens: SAUT
• Region: CHINA

Gang Lu

Lu, Gang; 卢刚 ; Lú Gāng
1975- **First publication: 2016**
• Employment: Kadoorie Farm and Botanic Garden（嘉道理农场暨植物园）
• Research interest: Podostemaceae [S]
• Published taxa: *Cladopus, Terniopsis*
• Region: CHINA (Hainan)
• Also as: G. Lu

J. Lu

Lu, Jing; 卢靖 ; Lú Jìng
1974- **First publication: 2007**
• Employment: Dehong Prefecture Forestry Research Institute, Yunnan（云南省德宏州林业科学研究所）
• Research interest: Arecaceae [S]
• Published taxa: *Calamus*

• Region: CHINA (Yunnan)

J. L. Lu

Lu, Jiong Lin; Lu, Giong Lin; 卢炯林 ; Lú Jiǒnglín; 盧炯林
1933- **First publication: 1981**
• Employment: Henan Agricultural College; Henan Agricultural University (河南农学院 ; 河南农业大学)
• Research interest: Orchidaceae, Poaceae; Plants of Henan [S]
• Published taxa: *Bulbophyllum, Dendrobium, Fargesia, Phyllostachys, Pleioblastus, Pseudosasa*
• Affiliation: HEAC
• Location of specimens: HEAC
• Region: CHINA
• Also as: G. L. Lu

Q. M. Lu

Lu, Qi Ming; 卢其明 ; Lú Qímíng
First publication: 1984
• Employment: QingLong County Agriculture Bureau, Guizhou (贵州省晴隆县农业局)
• Research interest: Theaceae [S]
• Published taxa: *Camellia*
• Region: CHINA (Guizhou)

S. L. Lu

Lu, Sheng Lian; Lu, Shen Lian; 卢生莲 ; Lú Shēnglián; 盧生蓮
1940- **First publication: 1984**
• Employment: Northwest Plateau Institute of Biology, Chinese Academy of Sciences (中国科学院西北高原生物研究所)
• Research interest: Poaceae [S]
• Published taxa: *Achnatherum, Agrostis, Calamagrostis, Deyeuxia, Elymus, Festuca, Kengyilia, Leymus, Poa, Roegneria, Stephanachne, Trikeraia*
• Affiliation: HNWP
• Location of specimens: HNWP
• Region: CHINA (Qinghai, Xizang)

X. F. Lu

Lu, Xue Feng; 卢学峰 ; Lú Xuéfēng
1965-2019 **First publication: 1992**
• Employment: Northwest Plateau Institute of Biology, Chinese Academy of Sciences (中国科学院西北高原生物研究所)
• Research interest: Boraginaceae, Orobanchaceae, Plantaginaceae, Poaceae; Plants of Qinghai [S]
• Published taxa: *Eritrichium, Lagotis, Pedicularis, Poa, Trikeraia*
• Affiliation: HNWP
• Location of specimens: HNWP
• Region: CHINA (Gansu, Qinghai)

Yi Jun Lu

Lu, Yi Jun; 卢毅军 ; Lú Yìjūn
1977- **First publication: 2020**
• Employment: Zhejiang University City College (浙江大学城市学院)
• Research interest: Amaryllidaceae [S]
• Published taxa: *Lycoris*
• Region: CHINA (Shaanxi)
• IPNI as: Y. J. Lu

Y. B. Lu

Lu, Yong Bin; 卢永彬 ; Lú Yǒngbīn
1987- **First publication: 2017**
• Employment: Guangxi Institute of Botany, Chinese Academy of Sciences (广西壮族自治区中国科学院广西植物研究所)
• Research interest: Gesneriaceae [S]
• Published taxa: *Petrocodon*
• Region: CHINA (Guangxi)

Y. G. Lu

Lu, Yong Gen; 卢永根 ; Lú Yǒnggēn; 盧永根
1930-2019 **First publication: 1990**
• Employment: South China Agricultural University (华南农业大学)
• Research interest: Poaceae [S]
• Published taxa: *Oryza*
• Region: CHINA

Z. Lu

Lu, Zhu; 卢竹 ; Lú Zhú
1963- **First publication: 1988**
• Employment: Northeast Forestry University (东北林业大学)
• Research interest: Ericaceae, Fabaceae [S]
• Published taxa: *Lespedeza, Rhododendron*
• Region: CHINA (Liaoning)

D. Q. Lu

Lu, De Quan; 鲁德全 ; Lǔ Déquán; 魯德全
1936-2001 **First publication: 1988**
• Employment: Northwest China Institute of Botany, Chinese Academy of Sciences and Shaanxi Province (陕西省中国科学院西北植物研究所)
• Research interest: Caryophyllaceae, Nyctaginaceae [S]
• Published taxa: *Ceodes, Commicarpus, Dianthus, Gypsophila, Oxybaphus*
• Affiliation: WUK
• Location of specimens: WUK
• Region: CHINA

F. J. Lu

Lu, Fa Jun; 鲁法军 ; Lǔ Fǎjūn

1978- **First publication: 2006**
- Employment: College of Life Science, Shandong Normal University（山东师范大学生命科学学院）
- Research interest: Polygonaceae [S]
- Published taxa: *Polygonum*
- Region: CHINA

L. M. Lu

Lu, Li Min; 鲁丽敏；Lǔ Lìmǐn
1986- **First publication: 2016**
- Employment: Institute of Botany, Chinese Academy of Sciences（中国科学院植物研究所）
- Research interest: Vitaceae [S]
- Published taxa: *Cayratia, Cyphostemma, Pseudocayratia*
- Region: CHINA

Run L. Lu

Lu, Run Long; 鲁润龙；Lǔ Rùnlóng; 魯潤龍
1937- **First publication: 1998**
- Employment: Department of Biology, University of Science and Technology of China（中国科学技术大学生物系）
- Research interest: Asteraceae [S]
- Published taxa: *Lactuca*
- Region: CHINA (Anhui)

Y. F. Lu

Lu, Yi Fei; 鲁益飞；Lǔ Yìfēi
1993- **First publication: 2017**
- Employment: College of Life and Environmental Sciences, Hangzhou Normal University（杭州师范大学生命与环境科学学院）
- Research interest: Cyperaceae, Fagaceae, Urticaceae [S]
- Published taxa: *Carex, Cyclobalanopsis, Fimbristylis, Nanocnide*
- Region: CHINA (Zhejiang)

Y. Q. Lu

Lu, Ying Qing; 鲁迎青；Lǔ Yíngqīng
1963- **First publication: 1990**
- Employment: Institute of Botany, Chinese Academy of Sciences（中国科学院植物研究所）
- Research interest: Balsaminaceae [S]
- Published taxa: *Impatiens*
- Location of specimens: PE
- Region: CHINA (Sichuan)

Z. Qiang Lu

Lu, Zhi Qiang; 鲁志强；Lǔ Zhìqiáng
1987- **First publication: 2017**
- Employment: Xishuangbanna Tropical Botanical Garden, Chinese Academy of Sciences（中国科学院西双版纳热带植物园）
- Research interest: Betulaceae, Rhamnaceae [S]
- Published taxa: *Carpinus, Rhamnella*
- Region: CHINA

G. Y. Lu

Lu, Geng Yu; 陆耕宇；Lù Gēngyǔ
1990- **First publication: 2019**
- Employment: School of Traditional Chinese Pharmacy, China Pharmaceutical University（中国药科大学中药学院）
- Research interest: Liliaceae [S]
- Published taxa: *Amana*
- Region: CHINA (Jiangsu)

Jing Lu

Lu, Jing; 陆婧；Lù Jìng
1990- **First publication: 2016**
- Employment: School of Life Sciences, East China Normal University（华东师范大学生命科学学院）
- Research interest: Moraceae [S]
- Published taxa: *Ficus*
- Region: [ASIA]
- IPNI as: J. Lu

J. M. Lu

Lu, Jing Mei; 陆静梅；Lù Jìngméi
1951- **First publication: 1990**
- Employment: Department of Biology, Northeast Normal University（东北师范大学生物系）
- Research interest: Pinaceae [S]
- Published taxa: *Pinus*
- Region: CHINA (Jilin)

L. L. Lou

Lou, Lien Lee; Lou, Lian Li; Lu, Lian Li; 陆莲立；Lù Liánlì; 陸蓮立
1924-2013 **First publication: 1980**
- Employment: Institute of Botany, Jiangsu Province（江苏省植物研究所）
- Research interest: Brassicaceae [S]
- Published taxa: *Cardamine, Chorispora, Cochlearia, Cochleariella, Cochleariopsis, Draba, Pegaeophyton, Platycraspedum, Yinshania*
- Affiliation: NAS
- Region: CHINA
- Also as: L. L. Lu

L. T. Lu

Lu, Ling Ti; Lu, Ling Di; 陆玲娣；Lù Língdì; 陸玲娣
1930-2021 **First publication: 1975**
- Employment: Institute of Botany, Chinese Academy of Sciences（中国科学院植物研究所）
- Research interest: Grossulariaceae, Orobanchaceae,

Rosaceae, Saxifragaceae [S]
- Published taxa: *Amygdalus, Armeniaca, Brandisia, Cotoneaster, Duchesnea, Lauro-cerasus, Malus, Neillia, Photinia, Pygeum, Ribes, Rubus, Sorbus, Spiraea*
- Affiliation: PE
- Region: CHINA

Lu Lu

Lu, Lu; 陆露 ; Lù Lù

1981- **First publication: 2008**
- Employment: Kunming Institute of Botany, Chinese Academy of Sciences（中国科学院昆明植物研究所）
- Research interest: Ericaceae [S]
- Published taxa: *Gaultheria*
- Region: CHINA

M. Z. Lu

Lu, Mao Zhen; 陆毛珍 ; Lù Máozhēn

1979- **First publication: 2006**
- Employment: College of Life Sciences, Northwest Normal University（西北师范大学生命科学学院）
- Research interest: Papaveraceae [S]
- Published taxa: *Meconopsis*
- Region: CHINA (Gansu)

R. L. Lu

Lu, Rui Lin; 陆瑞琳 ; Lù Ruìlín; 陸瑞琳

1935- **First publication: 1989**
- Employment: Shanghai Natural History Museum (Branch of Shanghai Science & Technology Museum)（上海自然博物馆(上海科技馆分馆)）
- Research interest: Oleaceae [S]
- Published taxa: *Osmanthus*
- Affiliation: SHM
- Location of specimens: SHM
- Region: CHINA

S. N. Lu

Lu, Shi Nian; 陆仕念 ; Lù Shìniàn

1965- **First publication: 2009**
- Employment: Forestry Seedlings Experiment Stations, Forestry Bureau of Jingxi County, Guangxi（广西靖西县林业局林业种苗试验站）
- Research interest: Berberidaceae, Gesneriaceae [S]
- Published taxa: *Mahonia, Primulina*
- Region: CHINA (Guangxi)

S. G. Lu

Lu, Shu Gang; 陆树刚 ; Lù Shùgāng

1957- **First publication: 1992**
- Employment: School of Life Sciences, Yunnan University（云南大学生命科学学院）
- Research interest: Cyatheaceae, Dryopteridaceae, Magnoliaceae, Osmundaceae, Polypodiaceae, Taxaceae, Thelypteridaceae; Pteridophytes [P]
- Published taxa: *Alsophila, Aromadendron, Arthromeris, Cephalotaxus, Crypsinus, Dryopteris, Dugandiodendron, Gymnosphaera, Himalayopteris, Houpoea, Lirianthe, Manglietia, Metamagnolia, Metapolypodium, Metathelypteris, Michelia, Microsorum, Osmundastrum, Pachylarnax, Paramagnolia, Parathelypteris, Phymatosorus, Polypodiodes, Selliguea, Thelypteris, Yulania*
- Affiliation: PYU, YUYU
- Location of specimens: PYU, YUYU
- Region: CHINA (Yunnan)

Xiao H. Lu

Lu, Xiao Hong; 陆小鸿 ; Lù Xiǎohóng

First publication: 1984
- Employment: Guangxi Traditional Chinese Medicine Company（广西药材公司）
- Research interest: Asparagaceae, Gesneriaceae, Loganiaceae [S]
- Published taxa: *Aspidistra, Didymostigma, Mitreola, Tupistra*
- Location of specimens: GXMG
- Region: CHINA (Guangxi)

Y. X. Lu

Lu, Yi Xin; 陆益新 ; Lù Yìxīn; 陸益新

1945- **First publication: 1989**
- Employment: Guangxi Institute of Botany（广西植物研究所）
- Research interest: Actinidiaceae, Elaeagnaceae, Rutaceae, Thymelaeaceae [S]
- Published taxa: *Actinidia, Clausena*
- Affiliation: IBK
- Region: CHINA (Guangxi)

Y. L. Lu

Lu, Yong Lun; 陆永伦 ; Lù Yǒnglún

First publication: 1966
- Employment: Department of Biology, Fudan University（复旦大学生物系）
- Research interest: Fabaceae, Poaceae [S]
- Published taxa: *Lespedeza, Melocalamus*
- Region: CHINA (Jiangsu, Zhejiang)

Z. C. Lu

Lu, Zhao Ce; 陆昭岑 ; Lù Zhāocén

1990- **First publication: 2020**
- Employment: Guangxi Institute of Botany, Chinese Academy of Sciences（广西壮族自治区中国科学院广西植物研究所）
- Research interest: Balsaminaceae, Cyperaceae [S]
- Published taxa: *Carex, Impatiens*

- Region: CHINA (Guangxi)

Z. H. Lu

Lu, Zhao Hua; 陆兆华 ; Lù Zhàohuá
1963- **First publication: 1994**
- Employment: Institute of Natural Resources, Heilongjiang Academy of Sciences（黑龙江省科学院自然资源研究所）
- Research interest: Apiaceae, Geraniaceae [S]
- Published taxa: *Geranium*
- Affiliation: HNR
- Location of specimens: HNR
- Region: CHINA (Heilongjiang)

Z. F. Lu

Lu, Zhao Fu; 陆照甫 ; Lù Zhàofǔ
First publication: 1998
- Employment: Baise City Forestry Bureau, Guangxi（广西百色市林业局）
- Research interest: Cycadaceae [S]
- Published taxa: *Cycas*
- Region: CHINA (Guangxi)

Z. M. Lu

Lu, Zhu Min; 陆志敏 ; Lù Zhìmǐn
1962- **First publication: 1997**
- Employment: Ningbo Forestry Bureau, Zhejiang（浙江省宁波市林业局）
- Research interest: Poaceae [S]
- Published taxa: *Phyllostachys*
- Region: CHINA (Zhejiang)

A. M. Lu

Lu, An Min; Lu, An Ming; **路安民 ; Lù Ānmín**
1939- **First publication: 1965**
- Employment: Institute of Botany, Chinese Academy of Sciences（中国科学院植物研究所）
- Research interest: Cucurbitaceae, Hamamelidaceae, Juglandaceae, Juncaceae, Solanaceae [S]
- Published taxa: *Actinostemma, Archihyoscyamus, Baijiania, Carya, Cucumis, Hemsleya, Hodgsonia, Juglans, Juncus, Lycianthes, Lycium, Mandragora, Microlagenaria, Physaliastrum, Physochlaina, Schizopepon, Siraitia, Thladiantha, Withania*
- Affiliation: PE
- Region: CHINA

D. Z. Lu

Lu, Duan Zheng; 路端正 ; Lù Duānzhèng
1943- **First publication: 1992**
- Employment: College of Forestry Resources, Beijing Forestry University（北京林业大学林业资源学院）
- Research interest: Gentianaceae, Grossulariaceae, Primulaceae, Ranunculaceae, Vitaceae; Woody Plants [S]
- Published taxa: *Clematis, Gentiana, Primula, Ribes, Vitis*
- Affiliation: BJFC
- Location of specimens: BJFC
- Region: CHINA (Beijing, Hebei)

S. C. Lu

Lu, Sue Cheng; 路学成 ; Lù Xuéchéng; 路學成
1936- **First publication: 1982**
- Employment: Zhaowuda League Institute of Forestry Science, Inner Mongolia（内蒙古昭乌达盟林业科学研究所）
- Research interest: Salicaceae [S]
- Published taxa: *Populus*
- Region: CHINA (Nei Mongol)

D. Luo

Luo, Dun; 罗敦 ; Luó Dūn
1968- **First publication: 2007**
- Employment: Yachang Wild Orchids National Nature Reserve Administration, Guangxi（广西雅长兰科植物国家级自然保护区管理局）
- Research interest: Orchidaceae [S]
- Published taxa: *Bulbophyllum*
- Region: CHINA (Guangxi)

F. X. Luo

Luo, Feng Xia; 罗凤霞 ; Luó Fèngxiá
1958- **First publication: 2013**
- Employment: Department of Horticulture, Jinling Institute of Technology（金陵科技学院园艺系）
- Research interest: Ericaceae [S]
- Published taxa: *Rhododendron*
- Region: CHINA (Zhejiang)

G. Y. Luo

Luo, Guang Yu; 罗光裕 ; Luó Guāngyù; 羅光裕
1938- **First publication: 1987**
- Employment: Northeast Forestry University（东北林业大学）
- Research interest: Adoxaceae [MS]
- Published taxa: *Sambucus*
- Location of specimens: NEFI
- Region: CHINA (Heilongjiang)

H. C. Luo

Luo, Hai Chao; 罗海潮 ; Luó Hǎicháo; 羅海潮
1940- **First publication: 1992**
- Employment: Shenyang Pharmaceutical University（沈阳药科大学）
- Research interest: Liliaceae [S]
- Published taxa: *Fritillaria*
- Region: CHINA (Liaoning)

H. C. Lo

Lo, Hang Chiang; Luo, Han Qiang; 羅漢強; Luó Hànqiáng; 罗汉强

First publication: 1977

- Employment: Department of Forestry, Taiwan University（台湾大学森林学系）
- Research interest: Malvaceae; Woody Plants [S]
- Published taxa: *Corchorus*
- Affiliation: NTUF
- Region: CHINA (Taiwan)

J. P. Luo

Luo, Ji Peng; 罗集鹏; Luó Jípéng; 羅集鵬

1935- First publication: 1987

- Employment: School of Pharmacy, Beijing Medical University; Guangdong Medical and Pharmaceutical College（北京医科大学药学院；广东医药学院）
- Research interest: Gentianaceae; Medicinal Plants [S]
- Published taxa: *Gentiana*
- Affiliation: GDMP
- Location of specimens: GDMP
- Region: CHINA (Zhejiang)

Jian Luo

Luo, Jian; 罗建; Luó Jiàn

1973- First publication: 2011

- Employment: Xizang Agriculture and Animal Husbandry College（西藏农牧学院）
- Research interest: Campanulaceae, Lamiaceae; Plants of Xizang [S]
- Published taxa: *Cyananthus, Lamiophlomis*
- Affiliation: XZE
- Location of specimens: XZE
- Region: CHINA (Xizang)

Jiang P. Luo

Luo, Jiang Ping; 罗江平; Luó Jiāngpíng

1987- First publication: 2016

- Employment: South China Botanical Garden, Chinese Academy of Sciences（中国科学院华南植物园）
- Research interest: Ranunculaceae [S]
- Published taxa: *Actaea*
- Region: CHINA

J. L. Luo

Luo, Jin Long; 罗金龙; Luó Jīnlóng

1993- First publication: 2017

- Employment: College of Forestry, Central South University of Forestry and Technology（中南林业科技大学林学院）
- Research interest: Orchidaceae [S]
- Published taxa: *Platanthera*
- Region: CHINA (Hunan)

J. Y. Luo

Luo, Jin Yu; 罗金裕; Luó Jīnyù; 羅金裕

1940- First publication: 1983

- Employment: Guangxi Institute of Traditional Medical and Pharmaceutical Sciences（广西中医药研究所）
- Research interest: Celastraceae, Menispermaceae, Salicaceae, Theaceae; Medicinal Plants; Pteridophytes [S]
- Published taxa: *Bennettiodendron, Camellia, Cyclea, Maytenus*
- Affiliation: GXMI
- Location of specimens: GXMI
- Region: CHINA (Guangxi)

K. W. Luo

Luo, Kai Wen; 罗开文; Luó Kāiwén

1980- First publication: 2017

- Employment: Guangxi Forest Inventory & Planning Institute（广西壮族自治区林业勘测设计院）
- Research interest: Arecaceae; Woody Plants [S]
- Published taxa: *Guihaia*
- Affiliation: GXF
- Location of specimens: GXF
- Region: CHINA (Guangxi)

L. Q. Luo

Luo, Li Qun; 罗利群; Luó Lìqún

1950- First publication: 1992

- Employment: Leshan Teachers' College, Sichuan; Department of Biology, Sun Yat-sen University; Department of Environmental and Life Science, Leshan Normal College（四川省乐山教育学院；中山大学生物系；乐山师范学院环境与生命科学系）
- Research interest: Styracaceae [S]
- Published taxa: *Sinojackia*
- Region: CHINA (Sichuan)

M. R. Luo

Luo, Min Rong; 罗敏蓉; Luó Mǐnróng

1980- First publication: 2013

- Employment: College of Horticulture, Northwest A&F University（西北农林科技大学园艺学院）
- Research interest: Ranunculaceae [S]
- Published taxa: *Ranunculus*
- Region: CHINA (Shaanxi)

M. H. Luo

Luo, Ming Hua; 罗明华; Luó Mínghuá

1964- First publication: 2007

- Employment: College of Life Sciences, Sichuan University; Sichuan School of Chinese Materia Medica（四川大学生命科学学院；四川省中药学校）
- Research interest: Zingiberaceae [S]

• Published taxa: *Roscoea*
• Region: CHINA (Yunnan)

P. Luo

Luo, Ping; 罗平 ; Luó Píng

First publication: 1987

• Employment: Forestry Department of Hainan Province（海南省林业局）
• Research interest: Salicaceae [S]
• Published taxa: *Populus*
• Region: CHINA (Hainan)

Q. Luo

Luo, Qiang; 罗强 ; Luó Qiáng

First publication: 2006

• Employment: Department of Agriculture, Xichang College（西昌学院农学系）
• Research interest: Balsaminaceae, Ericaceae, Rosaceae, Theaceae, Woodsiaceae [S]
• Published taxa: *Camellia, Docynia, Eriosoriopsis, Gaultheria, Impatiens*
• Region: CHINA (Sichuan)

Qiong Luo

Luo, Qiong; 罗琼 ; Luó Qióng

1983- **First publication: 2014**

• Employment: The First High School of Zhuxi, Hubei（湖北省竹溪县第一高级中学）
• Research interest: Asteraceae [S]
• Published taxa: *Ligularia*
• Region: CHINA (Hubei)
• IPNI as: Q. Luo

R. L. Luo

Luo, Run Liang; 罗闰良 ; Luó Rùnliáng

1957- **First publication: 1987**

• Employment: Department of Biology, Wuhan University（武汉大学生物系）
• Research interest: Hydrocharitaceae [S]
• Published taxa: *Ottelia*
• Region: CHINA (Guangxi)

R. Q. Luo

Luo, Run Quan; 罗润全 ; Luó Rùnquán

First publication: 2014

• Employment: Amateur（业余爱好者）
• Research interest: Gesneriaceae [S]
• Published taxa: *Primulina*
• Region: CHINA (Guangdong)

S. X. Luo

Luo, Shi Xiao; 罗世孝 ; Luó Shìxiào

First publication: 2018

• Employment: South China Botanical Garden, Chinese Academy of Sciences（中国科学院华南植物园）
• Research interest: Euphorbiaceae [S]
• Published taxa: *Glochidion*
• Region: [ASIA]

X. G. Luo

Luo, Xi Gao; 罗锡高 ; Luó Xīgāo; 羅錫高

1941- **First publication: 1984**

• Employment: Sichuan School of Chinese Materia Medica（四川省中药学校）
• Research interest: Asparagaceae [S]
• Published taxa: *Tupistra*
• Region: CHINA (Sichuan)

H. S. Lo

Lo, Hsien Shui; Luo, Hsien Shui; Luo, Xian Rui; 罗献瑞 ; Luó Xiànruì; 羅獻瑞

1927-2000 **First publication: 1974**

• Employment: South China Institute of Botany, Chinese Academy of Sciences（中国科学院华南植物研究所）
• Research interest: Acanthaceae, Araceae, Meliaceae, Menispermaceae, Rubiaceae, Sapindaceae, Sapotaceae [S]
• Published taxa: *Aglaia, Amesiodendron, Andrographis, Aphania, Arcangelisia, Argostemma, Calophanoides, Ceriscoides, Championella, Cosmianthemum, Cyclea, Damnacanthus, Dimocarpus, Dyschoriste, Echinacanthus, Eranthemum, Graptophyllum, Guihaiothamnus, Gutzlaffia, Gymnostachyum, Hygrophila, Justicia, Keenania, Lasianthus, Lepidagathis, Lepisanthes, Leptodermis, Leptomischus, Leptostachya, Lerchea, Limaciopsis, Mananthes, Mischocarpus, Mouretia, Munronia, Mycetia, Nephelium, Ophiorrhiza, Otophora, Pachygone, Paranephelium, Pararuellia, Pavieasia, Peristrophe, Pseuderanthemum, Pteroptychia, Rostellularia, Rubia, Rungia, Saprosma, Spiradiclis, Staurogyne, Stephania, Strobilanthes, Thunbergia, Tinospora, Typhonium, Urophyllum, Xanthophytum, Xantolis*
• Affiliation: IBSC
• Location of specimens: IBSC
• Region: CHINA

X. Y. Luo

Luo, Xin Yan; 罗新燕 ; Luō Xīnyàn

First publication: 2018

• Employment: Department of Chinese Materia Medica, Guiyang College of Traditional Chinese Medicine（贵阳中医学院药学系）
• Research interest: Convallariaceae [S]
• Published taxa: *Aspidistra*

• Region: CHINA (Chongqing)

Y. Luo

Luo, Yan; 罗艳 ; Luó Yàn

1975- **First publication: 2001**

• Employment: Institute of Botany, Chinese Academy of Sciences; Xishuangbanna Tropical Botanical Garden, Chinese Academy of Sciences（中国科学院植物研究所；中国科学院西双版纳热带植物园）
• Research interest: Actinidiaceae, Ranunculaceae [S]
• Published taxa: *Aconitum, Aquilegia, Delphinium, Saurauia*
• Affiliation: HITBC
• Location of specimens: PE
• Region: CHINA

Y. Y. Luo

Luo, Yan Yan; 罗燕燕 ; Luó Yànyàn

1983- **First publication: 2007**

• Employment: South China Botanical Garden, Chinese Academy of Sciences（中国科学院华南植物园）
• Research interest: Fagaceae [S]
• Published taxa: *Cyclobalanopsis*
• Region: CHINA (Hainan)

Yang Luo

Luo, Yang; 罗扬 ; Luó Yáng

1968- **First publication: 2019**

• Employment: Guizhou Academy of Forestry（贵州省林业科学研究院）
• Research interest: Gesneriaceae [S]
• Published taxa: *Petrocodon*
• Region: CHINA (Guizhou)

Y. B. Luo

Luo, Yi Bo; 罗毅波 ; Luó Yìbō

1964- **First publication: 1994**

• Employment: Institute of Botany, Chinese Academy of Sciences（中国科学院植物研究所）
• Research interest: Orchidaceae, Zingiberaceae [S]
• Published taxa: *Coeloglossum, Cypripedium, Dendrobium, Galearis, Gastrodia, Hedychium, Hemipiliopsis, Leptogastrodia, Listera, Neottia, Pachystoma, Pennilabium, Ponerorchis, Thrixspermum*
• Affiliation: PE
• Location of specimens: PE
• Region: CHINA

Y. X. Luo

Luo, Yun Xiang; 罗运祥 ; Luó Yùnxiáng

First publication: 1992

• Employment: Nanyue Arboretum, Hunan（湖南省南岳树木园）
• Research interest: Aquifoliaceae [S]
• Published taxa: *Ilex*
• Location of specimens: NYA
• Region: CHINA (Hunan)

Qiang Luo

Luo, Qiang; 骆强 ; Luò Qiáng

1965- **First publication: 2009**

• Employment: Department of Environmental and Life Science, Bijie University（毕节学院环境与生命科学系）
• Research interest: Dryopteridaceae, Woodsiaceae; Woody Plants [P]
• Published taxa: *Dryopteris, Polystichum, Woodsia*
• Affiliation: BJ
• Location of specimens: BJ
• Region: CHINA (Guizhou)
• IPNI as: Q. Luo

W. H. Luo

Luo, Wen Hua; 骆文华 ; Luò Wénhuá

1965- **First publication: 2010**

• Employment: Guangxi Institute of Botany, Chinese Academy of Sciences（广西壮族自治区中国科学院广西植物研究所）
• Research interest: Gesneriaceae [S]
• Published taxa: *Chirita, Primulina*
• Region: CHINA (Guangxi)

P. F. Lu

Lu, Pi Fong; 呂碧鳳 ; Lǚ Bìfèng; 吕碧凤

First publication: 2011

• Employment: Taiwan Society of Plant Systematics（台湾植物系统学会）
• Research interest: Selaginellaceae [P]
• Published taxa: *Selaginella*
• Region: CHINA (Taiwan)

C. T. Lu

Lu, Chang Tse; Lu, Chang Tze; Lü, Chang Ze; **呂長澤 ; Lǚ Chángzé; 吕长泽**

First publication: 2009

• Employment: Department of Life Science, Taiwan Normal University（台湾师范大学生命科学系）
• Research interest: Aristolochiaceae [S]
• Published taxa: *Aristolochia, Asarum*
• Region: CHINA (Taiwan)

D. H. Lv

Lv, Ding Hao; 吕定豪 ; Lǚ Dìngháo

1990- **First publication: 2017**

• Employment: School of Pharmacy, Guiyang College of Traditional Chinese Medicine（贵阳中医学院药学院）
• Research interest: Asparagaceae [S]

- Published taxa: *Aspidistra*
- Region: CHINA (Yunnan)

F. Y. Lu

Lu, Fu Yuan; Lu, Fu Yuen; Lü, Fu Yuan; 吕福原；Lǚ Fúyuán; 吕福原

1943- First publication: 1976

- Employment: Department of Forestry and Natural Resources, Chiayi University（台湾嘉义大学森林暨自然资源学系暨研究所）
- Research interest: Anacardiaceae, Araliaceae, Buxaceae, Cannabaceae, Caryophyllaceae, Ebenaceae, Elaeagnaceae, Fabaceae, Hydrangeaceae, Isoetaceae, Lardizabalaceae, Lauraceae, Loranthaceae, Lythraceae, Pentaphylacaceae, Ranunculaceae, Rhamnaceae, Rosaceae, Salicaceae, Styracaceae, Symplocaceae, Urticaceae, Vitaceae, Zingiberaceae; Plants of Taiwan [S]
- Published taxa: *Alpinia, Ampelopsis, Aralia, Berchemia, Boehmeria, Buxus, Cassia, Celtis, Cissus, Cotoneaster, Crotalaria, Desmodium, Dumasia, Elaeagnus, Eurya, Hydrangea, Isoetes, Maba, Machilus, Ranunculus, Rhamnus, Rotala, Rubus, Salix, Sarcococca, Stauntonia, Stellaria, Styrax, Symplocos, Taxillus, Toxicodendron, Vitis*
- Affiliation: CHIA
- Location of specimens: CHIA
- Region: CHINA (Taiwan)

H. Z. Lü

Lü, Hui Zhen; 吕惠珍；Lǚ Huìzhēn

1963- First publication: 2014

- Employment: Guangxi Botanical Garden of Medicinal Plants（广西药用植物园）
- Research interest: Asparagaceae, Gesneriaceae; Medicinal Plants [S]
- Published taxa: *Aspidistra, Primulina*
- Affiliation: GXMG
- Location of specimens: GXMG
- Region: CHINA (Guangxi)

K. C. Lu

Lu, King Cherng; 吕金城；Lǚ Jīnchéng; 吕金城

First publication: 2000

- Employment: Department of Forestry, Chung Hsing University（中兴大学森林学系）
- Research interest: Buxaceae, Cannabaceae, Ebenaceae, Rosaceae, Salicaceae, Styracaceae; Plants of Taiwan [S]
- Published taxa: *Buxus, Celtis, Maba, Rubus, Salix, Sarcococca, Styrax*
- Affiliation: TCF
- Location of specimens: TCF
- Region: CHINA (Taiwan)

M. N. Lu

Lu, Mu Nan; 吕亩南；Lǚ Mǔnán; 吕畝南

1935- First publication: 1999

- Employment: Zhenghe County Agriculture Bureau（福建省政和县农业局）
- Research interest: Rosaceae [S]
- Published taxa: *Armeniaca*
- Region: CHINA (Fujian)

S. Y. Lu

Lu, Sheng You; Leu, Sheng You; Lü, Sheng You; Lu, Sheng Yu; 吕勝由；Lǚ Shèngyóu; 吕胜由

1946- First publication: 1975

- Employment: Department of Forest Biology, Taiwan Forestry Research Institute, Taiwan Provincial Administrative Office; Taiwan Forestry Research Institute, Council of Agriculture, "Executive Yuan"（台湾省政府农林厅林业试验所森林生物系；"行政院"农业委员会林业试验所）
- Research interest: Apocynaceae, Berberidaceae, Buxaceae, Ebenaceae, Elaeagnaceae, Ericaceae, Loranthaceae, Magnoliaceae, Oleaceae, Orchidaceae, Pentaphylacaceae, Piperaceae, Pittosporaceae, Rhamnaceae, Rosaceae, Theaceae; Plants of Taiwan [S]
- Published taxa: *Alyxia, Berberis, Berchemia, Buxus, Calcearia, Camellia, Chionanthus, Corybas, Diospyros, Elaeagnus, Eurya, Michelia, Osmanthus, Peperomia, Piper, Pittosporum, Rhododendron, Rubus, Scurrula*
- Affiliation: TAIF
- Location of specimens: TAIF
- Region: CHINA (Taiwan)
- Also as: S. Y. Leu

T. F. Lü

Lü, Tian Feng; 吕天锋；Lǚ Tiānfēng

First publication: 2019

- Employment: Institute of Botany, Chinese Academy of Sciences（中国科学院植物研究所）
- Research interest: Gesneriaceae [S]
- Published taxa: *Petrocosmea*
- Region: CHINA

W. P. Leu

Leu, Wen Pen; Lü, Wen Bin; 吕文賓；Lǚ Wénbīn; 吕文宾

First publication: 1999

- Employment: Institute of Forestry, Taiwan University（台湾大学森林学研究所）
- Research interest: Asteraceae [S]
- Published taxa: *Blumea*
- Affiliation: HAST

- Location of specimens: HAST
- Region: CHINA (Taiwan)

Y. M. Lv

Lv, Ya Mei; 吕亚媚 ; Lǚ Yàmèi
1990- First publication: 2018
- Employment: College of Forestry, Southwest Forestry University（西南林业大学林学院）
- Research interest: Euphorbiaceae [S]
- Published taxa: *Excoecaria*
- Region: CHINA (Yunnan)

Y. T. Lu

Lu, Yi Tao; 吕益涛 ; Lǚ Yìtāo
1964- First publication: 2000
- Employment: Baiyin Institute for Drug Control, Gansu（甘肃省白银市药品检验所）
- Research interest: Asteraceae [S]
- Published taxa: *Xanthium*
- Region: CHINA (Gansu)

Yong J. Lu

Lu, Yong Jun; Lü, Yong Jun; **吕庸浚 ; Lǚ Yōngjùn**
First publication: 1980
- Employment: Liuzhou Forestry Bureau, Guangxi（广西壮族自治区柳州行政公署林业局）
- Research interest: Pinaceae [S]
- Published taxa: *Abies*
- Location of specimens: IBK
- Region: CHINA (Guangxi)

Z. Y. Lv

Lv, Zhen Yu; 吕振宇 ; Lǚ Zhènyǔ
1995- First publication: 2019
- Employment: School of Life Science, Yunnan Normal University（云南师范大学生命科学学院）
- Research interest: Cornaceae [S]
- Published taxa: *Cornus*
- Region: CHINA (Xizang)

C. G. Ma

Ma, Cheng Gong; Ma, Cheng Gung; 马成功 ; Mǎ Chénggōng; 馬成功
1936-1992 First publication: 1978
- Employment: Institute of Botany, Chinese Academy of Sciences（中国科学院植物研究所）
- Research interest: Amaranthaceae, Chenopodiaceae; Plant Geography [S]
- Published taxa: *Ceratoides, Corispermum*
- Affiliation: PE
- Region: CHINA

C. B. Ma

Ma, Chong Bo; 马崇波 ; Mǎ Chóngbō
1997- First publication: 2020
- Employment: Department of Biology, Zunyi Normal College（遵义师范学院生物系）
- Research interest: Lamiaceae [S]
- Published taxa: *Paraphlomis*
- Region: CHINA (Guizhou)

D. D. Ma

Ma, Dan Dan; 马丹丹 ; Mǎ Dāndān
1982- First publication: 2009
- Employment: School of Forestry and Biotechnology, Zhejiang A&F University; Jiyang College of Zhejiang A&F University（浙江农林大学林业与生物技术学院；浙江农林大学暨阳学院）
- Research interest: Araceae, Betulaceae, Brassicaceae, Liliaceae, Lythraceae, Orobanchaceae, Verbenaceae; Plants of Shanghai [S]
- Published taxa: *Alnus, Arisaema, Hilliella, Lagerstroemia, Rehmannia, Tricyrtis, Verbena*
- Affiliation: ZJFC
- Location of specimens: ZJFC
- Region: CHINA (Yunnan, Zhejiang)

D. Z. Ma

Ma, De Zi; 马德滋 ; Mǎ Dézī; 馬德滋
1933-2013 First publication: 1990
- Employment: Ningxia Agricultural College（宁夏农学院）
- Research interest: Adoxaceae, Asteraceae, Cyperaceae, Lamiaceae, Melanthiaceae, Orobanchaceae, Poaceae; Plants of Ningxia [S]
- Published taxa: *Agrostis, Calamagrostis, Cistanche, Juncellus, Paris, Poa, Taraxacum, Thymus, Viburnum, Xanthium*
- Affiliation: NXAC
- Region: CHINA (Ningxia)

T. S. Ma

Ma, To Shih; 马多士 ; Mǎ Duōshì; 馬多士
1933-2017 First publication: 1990
- Employment: Northwest Forestry College（西北林学院）
- Research interest: Phyllanthaceae [S]
- Published taxa: *Leptopus*

- Location of specimens: NWFC
- Region: CHINA (Shaanxi)

E. W. Ma

Ma, En Wei; 马恩伟 ; Mǎ Ēnwěi; 馬恩偉

1934-2005 **First publication: 1979**

- Employment: Department of Forestry, Inner Mongolia Forestry College（内蒙古林学院林学系）
- Research interest: Betulaceae, Cannabaceae, Fagaceae, Gentianaceae, Rhamnaceae, Rubiaceae, Salicaceae, Ulmaceae [S]
- Published taxa: *Betula, Celtis, Gentiana, Leptodermis, Populus, Rhamnus*
- Affiliation: NMAC, NMFC
- Location of specimens: NMAC, NMFC
- Region: CHINA (Nei Mongol)

G. X. Ma

Ma, Guo Xiang; 马国祥 ; Mǎ Guóxiáng

First publication: 1992

- Employment: Department of Pharmacognosy, China Pharmaceutical University（中国药科大学生药教研室）
- Research interest: Orchidaceae [S]
- Published taxa: *Dendrobium*
- Region: CHINA (Yunnan)

H. X. Ma

Ma, Han Xi; 马汉喜 ; Mǎ Hànxǐ

1964- **First publication: 1993**

- Employment: Mudanjiang Forestry School（牡丹江林业学校）
- Research interest: Asteraceae [S]
- Published taxa: *Artemisia*
- Region: CHINA (Heilongjiang)

H. Ma

Ma, Hong; 马宏 ; Mǎ Hóng

1979- **First publication: 2006**

- Employment: Kunming Institute of Botany, Chinese Academy of Sciences; Research Institute of Resource Insects, Chinese Academy of Forestry（中国科学院昆明植物研究所；中国林业科学研究院资源昆虫研究所）
- Research interest: Begoniaceae, Lamiaceae, Musaceae [S]
- Published taxa: *Begonia, Callicarpa, Musella*
- Region: CHINA (Yunnan)

H. S. Ma

Ma, Hu Sheng; 马虎生 ; Mǎ Hǔ shēng

1986- **First publication: 2017**

- Employment: Guangxi Institute of Botany, Chinese Academy of Sciences（广西壮族自治区中国科学院广西植物研究所）
- Research interest: Gesneriaceae [S]
- Published taxa: *Primulina*
- Region: CHINA (Guangxi)

J. L. Ma

Ma, Ji Long; 马吉龙 ; Mǎ Jílóng

1952- **First publication: 2000**

- Employment: Fengcheng Garden Management Office, Liaoning（辽宁省凤城市园林管理处）
- Research interest: Liliaceae [S]
- Published taxa: *Lilium*
- Region: CHINA (Liaoning)

J. S. Ma

Ma, Jin Shuang; 马金双 ; Mǎ Jīnshuāng

1955- **First publication: 1987**

- Employment: Beijing Medical University; Beijing Normal University; Shanghai Chenshan Botanical Garden（北京医科大学；北京师范大学；上海辰山植物园）
- Research interest: Aristolochiaceae, Celastraceae, Euphorbiaceae, Fabaceae [S]
- Published taxa: *Aristolochia, Euonymus, Euphorbia, Isotrema, Lespedeza, Maytenus*
- Affiliation: BNU, CSH
- Location of specimens: BNU, CSH, PEM
- Region: CHINA

J. Y. Ma

Ma, Jun Ying; 马俊莹 ; Mǎ Jùnyíng

1963- **First publication: 2002**

- Employment: Great Khingan Institute of Forestry Invstigation and Design（大兴安岭地区森林调查规化设计院）
- Research interest: Ericaceae, Onagraceae, Orobanchaceae [S]
- Published taxa: *Boschniakia, Chamaenerion, Empetrum, Vaccinium*
- Region: CHINA (Nei Mongol)

K. P. Ma

Ma, Ke Ping; 马克平 ; Mǎ Kèpíng

1958- **First publication: 1992**

- Employment: Institute of Botany, Chinese Academy of Sciences（中国科学院植物研究所）
- Research interest: Amaranthaceae [S]
- Published taxa: *Kochia, Suaeda*
- Location of specimens: QTC
- Region: CHINA (Heilongjiang)

L. M. Ma

Ma, Li Ming; 马黎明 ; Mǎ Límíng

1963- **First publication: 1991**

- Employment: Institute of Botany, Chinese Academy of Sciences（中国科学院植物研究所）
- Research interest: Campanulaceae, Caprifoliaceae [S]
- Published taxa: *Codonopsis, Cyananthus, Homocodon, Morina*
- Location of specimens: PE
- Region: CHINA

L. S. Ma

Ma, Li Sha; 马丽莎；Mǎ Lìshā

1959- **First publication: 2010**

- Employment: Sichuan Agricultural University（四川农业大学）
- Research interest: Poaceae; Woody Plants [S]
- Published taxa: *Chimonocalamus*
- Affiliation: SIFS
- Location of specimens: SIFS
- Region: CHINA (Sichuan)

Liang Ma

Ma, Liang; 马良；Mǎ Liáng

1989- **First publication: 2016**

- Employment: College of Landscape Architecture, Fujian Agriculture and Forestry University（福建农林大学园林学院）
- Research interest: Orchidaceae [S]
- Published taxa: *Bulbophyllum, Cymbidium, Dendrobium, Gastrodia*
- Region: CHINA (Fujian)

L. Ma

Ma, Ling; 马玲；Mǎ Líng

1979- **First publication: 2003**

- Employment: School of Life Sciences, Inner Mongolia University（内蒙古大学生命科学学院）
- Research interest: Asteraceae [S]
- Published taxa: *Youngia*
- Region: CHINA (Nei Mongol)

L. Y. Ma

Ma, Lü Yi; 马履一；Mǎ Lǚyī

1957- **First publication: 2006**

- Employment: College of Resources and Environment, Beijing Forestry University（北京林业大学资源与环境学院）
- Research interest: Magnoliaceae [S]
- Published taxa: *Magnolia*
- Region: CHINA (Hubei)

N. X. Ma

Ma, Nai Xun; 马乃训；Mǎ Nǎixùn; 馬乃訓

1943- **First publication: 1985**

- Employment: Research Institute of Subtropical Forestry, Chinese Academy of Forestry（中国林业科学研究院亚热带林业研究所）
- Research interest: Poaceae [S]
- Published taxa: *Indocalamus, Phyllostachys*
- Region: CHINA (Zhejiang)

P. Ma

Ma, Ping; 马平；Mǎ Píng

1953- **First publication: 1989**

- Employment: Department of Biology, Inner Mongolia University（内蒙古大学生物系）
- Research interest: Caryophyllaceae [S]
- Published taxa: *Melandrium*
- Region: CHINA (Nei Mongol)

Q. X. Ma

Ma, Qi Xia; 马其侠；Mǎ Qíxiá

1979- **First publication: 2010**

- Employment: South China Botanical Garden, Chinese Academy of Sciences（中国科学院华南植物园）
- Research interest: Loganiaceae [S]
- Published taxa: *Mitreola*
- Region: CHINA (Guangdong)

C. Y. Ma

Ma, Chi Yun; Ma, Qi Yun; 马其云；Mǎ Qíyún; 馬其云

1942- **First publication: 1982**

- Employment: Institute of Pharmacology and Toxicology, Academy of Military Medical Sciences, The Chinese People' s Liberation Army（中国人民解放军军事医学科学院毒物药物研究所）
- Research interest: Convolvulaceae, Fabaceae, Lycopodiaceae [S]
- Published taxa: *Cladrastis, Erycibe, Phlegmariurus, Sophora*
- Affiliation: AMMS
- Location of specimens: AMMS
- Region: CHINA

Q. S. Ma

Ma, Qi Sheng; 马启盛；Mǎ Qǐshèng; 馬啟盛

1943- **First publication: 1999**

- Employment: School of Pharmacy, Beijing Medical University（北京医科大学药学院）
- Research interest: Celastraceae [S]
- Published taxa: *Glyptopetalum*
- Affiliation: PEM
- Region: CHINA

Q. Ma

Ma, Qin; 马琴；Mǎ Qín

1986- **First publication: 2011**

- Employment: School of Life Sciences, Inner Mongolia University（内蒙古大学生命科学学院）
- Research interest: Orobanchaceae [S]

- Published taxa: *Cistanche*
- Region: CHINA (Nei Mongol)

S. Y. Ma

Ma, Shang Ying; 马尚英 ; Mǎ Shàngyīng; 馬尚英

1949- **First publication: 2005**

- Employment: Gansu Forestry Department（甘肃省林业厅）
- Research interest: Salicaceae [S]
- Published taxa: *Populus*
- Region: CHINA (Gansu)
- IPNI as: Sh. Y. Ma

S. T. Ma

Ma, Shu Tai; 马书太 ; Mǎ Shūtài

1955- **First publication: 1983**

- Employment: Shandong College of Traditional Chinese Medicine（山东中医学院）
- Research interest: Dryopteridaceae [PS]
- Published taxa: *Dryopteris*
- Region: CHINA (Shandong)

T. G. Ma

Ma, Tian Gui; 马天贵 ; Mǎ Tiānguì

First publication: 1988

- Employment: Grassland and Animal Husbandry Research Institute of Zhangjiakou, Hebei（河北张家口地区草原畜牧研究所）
- Research interest: Violaceae [S]
- Published taxa: *Viola*
- Region: CHINA (Hebei)

W. L. Ma

Ma, Wei Liang; 马炜梁 ; Mǎ Wěiliáng; 馬煒梁

1936- **First publication: 1991**

- Employment: Department of Biology, East China Normal University（华东师范大学生物系）
- Research interest: Eriocaulaceae; Plant Anatomy [S]
- Published taxa: *Eriocaulon*
- Affiliation: HSNU
- Location of specimens: HSNU
- Region: CHINA

S. S. Mar

Mar, Shek Shing; 馬錫成 ; Mǎ Xīchéng; 马锡成

First publication: 2015

- Employment: Ying Wa College, Hong Kong（香港英华书院）
- Research interest: Burmanniaceae [S]
- Published taxa: *Thismia*
- Region: CHINA (Hong Kong)
- Also as: Mar

X. G. Ma

Ma, Xiang Guang; 马祥光 ; Mǎ Xiángguāng

1986- **First publication: 2013**

- Employment: College of Life Sciences, Sichuan University; Kunming Institute of Botany, Chinese Academy of Sciences（四川大学生命科学学院；中国科学院昆明植物研究所）
- Research interest: Apiaceae [S]
- Published taxa: *Angelica, Bupleurum, Ferula*
- Region: [ASIA]

X. J. Ma

Ma, Xiao Jie; 马晓洁 ; Mǎ Xiǎojié

1981- **First publication: 2007**

- Employment: College of Forestry, South China Agricultural University（华南农业大学林学院）
- Research interest: Primulaceae [S]
- Published taxa: *Ardisia*
- Region: CHINA (Guangdong)

X. T. Ma

Ma, Xin Tang; 马欣堂 ; Mǎ Xīntáng

1964- **First publication: 1994**

- Employment: Institute of Botany, Chinese Academy of Sciences（中国科学院植物研究所）
- Research interest: Campanulaceae, Poaceae [S]
- Published taxa: *Eragrostis, Pankycodon*
- Affiliation: PE
- Region: CHINA

X. D. Ma

Ma, Xing Da; 马兴达 ; Mǎ Xīngdá

1991- **First publication: 2019**

- Employment: Xishuangbanna Tropical Botanical Garden, Chinese Academy of Sciences（中国科学院西双版纳热带植物园）
- Research interest: Begoniaceae, Passifloraceae, Resedaceae [S]
- Published taxa: *Begonia, Passiflora, Stixis*
- Region: CHINA (Yunnan)

Y. Z. Ma

Ma, Yi Zhong; 马宜中 ; Mǎ Yízhōng; 馬宜中

1940- **First publication: 1985**

- Employment: Yunnan Institute of Tropical Botany, Chinese Academy of Sciences（中国科学院云南热带植物研究所）
- Research interest: Orchidaceae [S]
- Published taxa: *Bulbophyllum, Gastrochilus*
- Region: CHINA (Yunnan)

Y. G. Ma

Ma, Yong Kui; Ma, Yong Gui; **马永贵 ; Mǎ Yǒngguì; 馬永貴**

First publication: 1980

- Employment: Kaiyuan County Agriculture Bureau（云南省开远县农业局）
- Research interest: Poaceae [S]
- Published taxa: *Setaria*
- Location of specimens: N
- Region: CHINA (Yunnan)

Y. P. Ma

Ma, Yong Peng; 马永鹏 ; Mǎ Yǒngpéng

1982- First publication: 2012

- Employment: Kunming Institute of Botany, Chinese Academy of Sciences（中国科学院昆明植物研究所）
- Research interest: Ericaceae [S]
- Published taxa: *Rhododendron*
- Region: CHINA (Yunnan)

Y. X. Ma

Ma, Yu Xin; 马玉心 ; Mǎ Yùxīn

1965- First publication: 1997

- Employment: Department of Biology, Mudanjiang Normal University; College of Marine Science, Zhejiang Ocean University（牡丹江师范学院生物系；浙江海洋学院海洋科学学院）
- Research interest: Caryophyllaceae, Iridaceae, Poaceae, Polygonaceae [S]
- Published taxa: *Helictotrichon, Iris, Poa, Polygonum, Spergularia*
- Region: CHINA (Heilongjiang, Zhejiang)

Ma

Ma, Yu Chuan; Ma, Yü Ch'üan; Ma, Yu Quan; 马毓泉 ; Mǎ Yùquán; 馬毓泉

1916-2008 First publication: 1951

- Employment: Department of Botany, Peking University; Department of Biology, Inner Mongolia University（北京大学植物学系；内蒙古大学生物系）
- Research interest: Apiaceae, Asteraceae, Betulaceae, Brassicaceae, Caryophyllaceae, Fabaceae, Gentianaceae, Hydrocharitaceae, Juncaceae, Oleaceae, Orobanchaceae, Poaceae, Polemoniaceae, Potamogetonaceae [S]
- Published taxa: *Betula, Caragana, Cistanche, Cnidium, Dianthus, Festuca, Gentianella, Gentianopsis, Goldbachia, Juncus, Microsisymbrium, Najas, Neotorularia, Orobanche, Ostericum, Oxytropis, Peucedanum, Polemonium, Potamogeton, Seseli, Syringa, Tugarinovia, Yinshania*
- Affiliation: HIMC
- Location of specimens: HIMC, IMDC, PEY
- Region: CHINA

Y. T. Ma

Ma, Yuan Tsun; Ma, Yuan Jun; 马元俊 ; Mǎ Yuánjùn

First publication: 1985

- Employment: Institute for the Control of Pharmaceutical Products, Hubei（湖北省药品检验所）
- Research interest: Convallariaceae [S]
- Published taxa: *Liriope, Tupistra*
- Location of specimens: HIB, IBSC, KUN, PE
- Region: CHINA (Hubei)

Z. X. Ma

Ma, Zheng Xu; 马政旭 ; Mǎ Zhèngxù

2001- First publication: 2017

- Employment: The High School Affiliated to Renmin University of China; Laboratory of Genetics, University of Wisconsin-Madison, Madison, U. S. A.（中国人民大学附属中学；美国威斯康星大学麦迪逊分校）
- Research interest: Araceae, Aristolochiaceae [S]
- Published taxa: *Alocasia, Arisaema, Aristolochia*
- Region: CHINA

Z. G. Ma

Ma, Zhi Gang; 马志刚 ; Mǎ Zhìgāng

1955- First publication: 1993

- Employment: Lanzhou Medical College（兰州医学院）
- Research interest: Orobanchaceae [S]
- Published taxa: *Pedicularis*
- Region: CHINA (Gansu)

Z. Z. Ma

Ma, Zhi Zhong; 马志忠 ; Mǎ Zhìzhōng

1956- First publication: 1993

- Employment: Livestock Department of Dingxi Prefecture（甘肃省定西地区畜牧处）
- Research interest: Orobanchaceae [S]
- Published taxa: *Pedicularis*
- Region: CHINA (Gansu)

Z. H. Ma

Ma, Zhong Hui; 马仲辉 ; Mǎ Zhònghuī

1984- First publication: 2012

- Employment: South China Botanical Garden, Chinese Academy of Sciences; College of Agriculture, Guangxi University（中国科学院华南植物园；广西大学农学院）
- Research interest: Caryophyllaceae, Lamiaceae [S]
- Published taxa: *Callicarpa, Stellaria*
- Affiliation: GAUA
- Location of specimens: GAUA
- Region: CHINA (Hainan, Sichuan)

K. J. Mao

Mao, Ke Jun; 毛克钧 ; Máo Kèjūn

1969- First publication: 1993

- Employment: Department of Forestry, Anhui Agricultural College（安徽农学院林学系）

- Research interest: Poaceae [S]
- Published taxa: *Bambusa, Phyllostachys*
- Region: CHINA (Anhui)

L. Mao

Mao, Ling; 毛玲 ; Máo Líng

1941- **First publication: 1990**

- Employment: Xi'an Botanical Garden, Shaanxi (陕西省西安植物园)
- Research interest: Rosaceae [S]
- Published taxa: *Crataegus*
- Region: CHINA (Shaanxi)

M. H. Mao

Mao, Mei Hong; 毛美红 ; Máo Měihóng

1968- **First publication: 2012**

- Employment: Wuxing A&F Extension Center of Huzhou, Zhejiang (浙江省湖州市吴兴区农林技术推广服务中心)
- Research interest: Rosaceae [S]
- Published taxa: *Rubus*
- Region: CHINA (Zhejiang)

P. I Mao

Mao, Pin I; Mao, Ping I; Mao, Ping Yi; 毛品一 ; Máo Pǐnyī

1926-2014 **First publication: 1964**

- Employment: Southwest Forestry College (西南林学院)
- Research interest: Anacardiaceae, Fagaceae, Malvaceae, Pentaphylacaceae, Rutaceae, Salicaceae; Plants of Yunnan [S]
- Published taxa: *Cyclobalanopsis, Eurya, Fortunella, Populus, Salix, Spondias, Sterculia*
- Affiliation: KUN
- Location of specimens: KUN, SWFC, PE
- Region: CHINA (Yunnan)

R. B. Mao

Mao, Ru Bing; 毛汝兵 ; Máo Rǔbīng

1985- **First publication: 2011**

- Employment: Institute of Botany, Chinese Academy of Sciences (中国科学院植物研究所)
- Research interest: Gesneriaceae [S]
- Published taxa: *Primulina*
- Region: CHINA (Guizhou)

S. Z. Mao

Mao, Shi Zhong; 毛世忠 ; Máo Shìzhōng

1968- **First publication: 2013**

- Employment: Guangxi Institute of Botany, Chinese Academy of Sciences (广西壮族自治区中国科学院广西植物研究所)
- Research interest: Primulaceae [S]
- Published taxa: *Ardisia*
- Region: CHINA (Guangxi, Yunnan)

X. Y. Mao

Mao, Xue Ying; 毛雪莹 ; Máo Xuěyíng; 毛雪瑩

1931- **First publication: 1985**

- Employment: Department of Biology, Hangzhou Normal College (杭州师范学院生物系)
- Research interest: Cyperaceae, Saxifragaceae [S]
- Published taxa: *Carex, Kobresia*
- Affiliation: HTC
- Location of specimens: HTC
- Region: CHINA (Nei Mongol)

Z. M. Mao

Mao, Zu Mei; 毛祖美 ; Máo Zǔměi

1933- **First publication: 1980**

- Employment: Xinjiang Institute of Biology, Pedology and Desert Research, Chinese Academy of Sciences (中国科学院新疆生物土壤沙漠研究所)
- Research interest: Chenopodiaceae, Fabaceae, Liliaceae, Polygonaceae, Zygophyllaceae [S]
- Published taxa: *Calligonum, Tulipa*
- Affiliation: XJBI
- Location of specimens: XJBI
- Region: CHINA (Xinjiang)

X. D. Mei

Mei, Xu Dong; 梅旭东 ; Méi Xùdōng

1972- **First publication: 2018**

- Employment: Jingning County Bureau of Science and Technology, Zhejiang (浙江省景宁县科技局)
- Research interest: Primulaceae [S]
- Published taxa: *Primula*
- Region: CHINA (Zhejiang)

R. X. Meng

Meng, Ren Xian; Meng, Jen Hsien; 蒙仁宪 ; Méng Rénxiàn; 蒙仁憲

1935- **First publication: 1986**

- Employment: Department of Biology, Anhui University (安徽大学生物系)
- Research interest: Crassulaceae, Fabaceae, Polygonaceae [S]
- Published taxa: *Hylotelephium, Lathyrus*
- Affiliation: ANU
- Location of specimens: ANU
- Region: CHINA (Anhui)

T. Meng

Meng, Tao; 蒙涛 ; Méng Tāo

1985- **First publication: 2020**

- Employment: Guangxi Institute of Botany, Chinese Academy of Sciences (广西壮族自治区中国科学院广西植物研究所)

- Research interest: Daphniphyllaceae [S]
- Published taxa: *Daphniphyllum*
- Region: CHINA (Guangxi)

Yuan Meng

Meng, Yuan; 蒙媛 ; Méng Yuàn

1993- **First publication: 2014**

- Employment: College of Forestry and Landscape Architecture, South China Agricultural University; The Orchid Conservation & Research Center of Shenzhen, Guangdong (华南农业大学林学与风景园林学院；广东省深圳市兰科植物保护研究中心)
- Research interest: Orchidaceae [S]
- Published taxa: *Liparis*
- Region: CHINA (Yunnan)
- IPNI as: Y. Meng

D. C. Meng

Meng, De Chang; 孟德昌 ; Mèng Déchāng

First publication: 2020

- Employment: Guangxi Institute of Botany, Chinese Academy of Sciences (广西壮族自治区中国科学院广西植物研究所)
- Research interest: Gesneriaceae [S]
- Published taxa: *Primulina*
- Region: CHINA (Guangxi)

L. Meng

Meng, Lei; 孟雷 ; Mèng Léi

1977- **First publication: 2007**

- Employment: Institute of Botany, Chinese Academy of Sciences (中国科学院植物研究所)
- Research interest: Fabaceae [S]
- Published taxa: *Astragalus*
- Affiliation: BAU
- Region: CHINA (Sichuan)

Q. W. Meng

Meng, Qian Wan; 孟千万 ; Mèng Qiānwàn

1978- **First publication: 2008**

- Employment: Institute of Botany, Chinese Academy of Sciences (中国科学院植物研究所)
- Research interest: Orchidaceae [S]
- Published taxa: *Galearis, Gastrodia, Thrixspermum*
- Region: CHINA (Sichuan)

S. Y. Meng

Meng, Shi Yong; 孟世勇 ; Mèng Shìyǒng

1984- **First publication: 2011**

- Employment: College of Life Sciences, Beijing Normal University; School of Life Sciences, Peking University (北京师范大学生命科学学院；北京大学生命科学学院)
- Research interest: Asteraceae, Celastraceae, Crassulaceae [S]
- Published taxa: *Glyptopetalum, Rhodiola*
- Affiliation: PEY
- Location of specimens: BNU
- Region: CHINA

Y. Meng

Meng, Yan; 孟燕 ; Mèng Yàn

1955- **First publication: 1997**

- Employment: Zhangjiakou Institute for Drug Control (河北省张家口市药检所)
- Research interest: Crassulaceae [S]
- Published taxa: *Rhodiola*
- Region: CHINA (Hebei)

Ying Meng

Meng, Ying; 孟盈 ; Mèng Yíng

1973- **First publication: 2017**

- Employment: College of Bio-resources and Environmental Science, Jishou University (吉首大学生物资源与环境科学学院)
- Research interest: Asparagaceae, Saxifragaceae [S]
- Published taxa: *Heteropolygonatum, Saxifraga*
- Region: CHINA (Hunan)

Y. F. Meng

Meng, Yu Fang; 孟玉芳 ; Mèng Yùfāng

1985- **First publication: 2014**

- Employment: South China Botanical Garden, Chinese Academy of Sciences (中国科学院华南植物园)
- Research interest: Orchidaceae [S]
- Published taxa: *Malaxis*
- Region: CHINA (Yunnan)

X. Y. Miao

Miao, Xin Yuan; 苗馨元 ; Miáo Xīnyuán

First publication: 2017

- Employment: Nanjing Institute of Geology and Palaeontology, Chinese Academy of Sciences (中国科学院南京地质古生物研究所)
- Research interest: Dryopteridaceae [P]
- Published taxa: *Polystichum*
- Region: CHINA (Guizhou)
- IPNI as: Xin Y. Miao

B. M. Miao

Miao, Bo Mao; 缪柏茂 ; Miào Bǎimào

1955- **First publication: 1985**

- Employment: Department of Biology, Fudan University; Shanghai Natural History Museum (Branch of Shanghai Science & Technology Museum) (复旦大学生物系；上海自然博物馆(上海科技馆分馆))
- Research interest: Oleaceae [S]

- Published taxa: *Chionanthus, Jasminum, Ligustrum, Linociera, Olea*
- Location of specimens: SHM
- Region: CHINA

R. H. Miao

Miao, Ru Huai; Miau, Ru Huai; **缪汝槐**; Miào Rǔhuái; **繆汝槐**

1942- **First publication: 1975**

- Employment: Department of Biology, Sun Yat-sen University（中山大学生物系）
- Research interest: Adoxaceae, Apocynaceae, Araliaceae, Arecaceae, Asparagaceae, Caprifoliaceae, Celastraceae, Commelinaceae, Cornaceae, Cyperaceae, Ebenaceae, Ericaceae, Fagaceae, Gentianaceae, Lamiaceae, Lauraceae, Liliaceae, Malvaceae, Melanthiaceae, Melastomataceae, Myrtaceae, Oleaceae, Orobanchaceae, Primulaceae, Pteridaceae, Ranunculaceae, Rosaceae, Rutaceae, Sabiaceae, Sapindaceae, Smilacaceae, Tiliaceae, Zingiberaceae [PS]
- Published taxa: *Acer, Alangium, Anemone, Ardisia, Burretiodendron, Calamus, Callicarpa, Changiodendron, Clematis, Decaspermum, Diospyros, Excentrodendron, Floscopa, Glycosmis, Glyptopetalum, Jasminum, Lilium, Lindenbergia, Lipocarpha, Liriope, Lonicera, Lyonia, Neolitsea, Ophiopogon, Paris, Phoebe, Phyllagathis, Pteris, Pyrenocarpa, Rauvolfia, Rhaphiolepis, Roscoea, Rubus, Schefflera, Smilax, Swertia, Syzygium, Viburnum*
- Affiliation: SYS
- Location of specimens: SYS
- Region: CHINA

B. Q. Min

Min, Bai Qing; **闵伯清**; **Mǐn Bóqīng**

1953- **First publication: 1990**

- Employment: Sichuan School of Chinese Materia Medica（四川省中药学校）
- Research interest: Araceae, Asteraceae, Lamiaceae [S]
- Published taxa: *Arisaema, Aster, Salvia*
- Region: CHINA (Sichuan)

C. L. Min

Min, Cheng Lin; **闵成林**; **Mǐn Chénglín**

1950- **First publication: 1986**

- Employment: Ningxi Forest Bureau, Shaanxi（陕西省宁西林业局）
- Research interest: Lardizabalaceae, Magnoliaceae, Moraceae [S]
- Published taxa: *Magnolia, Morus, Sargentodoxa*
- Region: CHINA (Shaanxi)

T. L. Ming

Ming, Tien Lu; Min, Tian Lu; **闵天禄**; **Mǐn Tiānlù**; **閔天祿**

1937-2021 **First publication: 1979**

- Employment: Kunming Institute of Botany, Chinese Academy of Sciences（中国科学院昆明植物研究所）
- Research interest: Anacardiaceae, Asteraceae, Buxaceae, Ericaceae, Pentaphylacaceae, Ranunculaceae, Sapindaceae, Theaceae [S]
- Published taxa: *Aconitum, Adinandra, Buxus, Camellia, Cleyera, Cremanthodium, Dimocarpus, Drimycarpus, Eurya, Ligularia, Lyonia, Mangifera, Polyspora, Pyrenaria, Ranunculus, Rhododendron, Sapindus, Schima, Spondias, Stewartia, Terminthia, Toxicodendron*
- Affiliation: KUN
- Location of specimens: KUN
- Region: CHINA (Yunnan)

Y. J. Min

Min, Yun Jiang; **闵运江**; **Mǐn Yùnjiāng**

1963- **First publication: 2015**

- Employment: School of Resources and Environmental Engineering, Anhui University（安徽大学资源与环境工程学院）
- Research interest: Polygonaceae [S]
- Published taxa: *Koenigia*
- Region: CHINA (Sichuan, Xizang)

L. Mo

Mo, Ling; **莫凌**; **Mò Líng**

1974- **First publication: 2002**

- Employment: Guangxi Institute of Botany, Chinese Academy of Sciences（广西壮族自治区中国科学院广西植物研究所）
- Research interest: Actinidiaceae [S]
- Published taxa: *Actinidia*
- Region: CHINA (Guangxi)

S. L. Mo

Mo, Sin Li; Mo, Xin Li; **莫新礼**; **Mò Xīnlǐ**; **莫新禮**

1934-1988 **First publication: 1980**

- Employment: Guangxi Forest Inventory & Planning Institute（广西壮族自治区林业勘测设计院）
- Research interest: Capparaceae, Dipterocarpaceae, Euphorbiaceae, Fabaceae, Fagaceae, Hernandiaceae, Lamiaceae, Lardizabalaceae, Malvaceae, Oleandraceae, Phyllanthaceae, Pinaceae, Sapindaceae, Simaroubaceae, Theaceae [PS]
- Published taxa: *Abies, Acrocarpus, Ailanthus, Bostrychanthera, Camellia, Capparis, Castanopsis, Firmiana, Illigera, Lepisanthes, Oleandra, Sauropus, Stauntonia, Trigonostemon, Vatica*
- Affiliation: GXF

- Location of specimens: GXF
- Region: CHINA (Guangxi)
- IPNI as: X. L. Mo

Z. Q. Mo

Mo, Ze Qian; 莫泽乾 ; Mò Zéqián

1963- **First publication: 1989**

- Employment: Department of Biology, Sun Yat-sen University; Guangxi Institute for Drug Control（中山大学生物系；广西药品检验所）
- Research interest: Theaceae [S]
- Published taxa: *Camellia*
- Region: CHINA (Jiangxi)

Merrgen

Merrgen; 莫日根 ; Mòrìgēn

1961- **First publication: 1989**

- Employment: Department of Biology, Inner Mongolia University（内蒙古大学生物系）
- Research interest: Fabaceae; Palynology [S]
- Published taxa: *Caragana*
- Affiliation: HIMC
- Location of specimens: HIMC
- Region: CHINA (Nei Mongol)

C. Mou

Mou, Cun; 牟村 ; Móu Cūn

1983- **First publication: 2020**

- Employment: Hunan Forest Botanical Garden（湖南省森林植物园）
- Research interest: Primulaceae [S]
- Published taxa: *Lysimachia*
- Region: CHINA (Hunan)

F. J. Mou

Mou, Feng Juan; 牟凤娟 ; Móu Fèngjuān

1977- **First publication: 2009**

- Employment: South China Botanical Garden, Chinese Academy of Sciences; Southwest Forestry University（中国科学院华南植物园；西南林业大学）
- Research interest: Rubiaceae, Rutaceae, Zingiberaceae [S]
- Published taxa: *Glycosmis, Roscoea, Rubovietnamia*
- Affiliation: SWFC
- Location of specimens: SWFC
- Region: CHINA (Guangxi, Yunnan)

S. J. Moore

Moore, Shann Jye; 牟善傑 ; Móu Shànjié; 牟善杰

1966-2010 **First publication: 2011**

- Employment: Taiwan Society of Plant Systematics（台湾植物系统学会）
- Research interest: Dennstaedtiaceae, Grammitidaceae [P]
- Published taxa: *Microlepia, Xiphopterella*
- Affiliation: HAST
- Location of specimens: HAST
- Region: [ASIA]

X. Y. Mu

Mu, Xian Yun; 沐先运 ; Mù Xiānyùn

1985- **First publication: 2012**

- Employment: School of Nature Conservation, Beijing Forestry University（北京林业大学自然保护区学院）
- Research interest: Celastraceae, Orchidaceae [S]
- Published taxa: *Celastrus, Holopogon*
- Affiliation: BJFC
- Location of specimens: BJFC
- Region: CHINA

C. T. Moo

Moo, Chuen Tau; Mu, Chun Tao; 穆椿濤 ; Mù Chūntāo; 穆椿涛

First publication: 1978

- Employment: Institute of Botany, Taiwan University（台湾大学植物学研究所）
- Research interest: Zingiberaceae [S]
- Published taxa: *Zingiber*
- Region: CHINA (Taiwan)

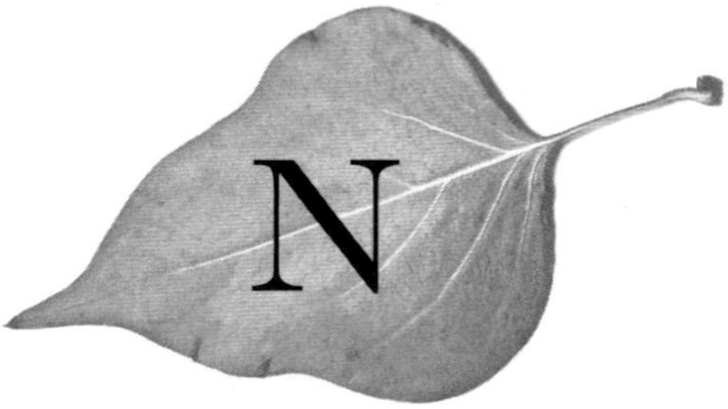

C. H. Nan

Nan, Cheng Hui; 南程慧 ; Nán Chénghuì

1982- **First publication: 2013**

- Employment: Nanjing Forest Police College（南京森林警察学院）
- Research interest: Rosaceae [S]
- Published taxa: *Cerasus*
- Affiliation: NFP
- Region: CHINA (Hubei, Jiangxi)

C. K. Ni

Ni, Chen Kai; 倪陈凯 ; Ní Chénkǎi; 倪陳凱

1940- **First publication: 1982**

- Employment: Department of Biology, Shandong Normal University（山东师范大学生物系）
- Research interest: Amaranthaceae, Poaceae, Woodsiaceae; Plants of Shandong [PS]

- Published taxa: *Amaranthus, Cleistogenes, Woodsia*
- Affiliation: SDNU
- Location of specimens: SDNU
- Region: CHINA (Shandong)

J. B. Ni

Ni, Jing Bo; 倪静波；Ní Jìngbō

First publication: 2019

- Employment: South China Botanical Garden, Chinese Academy of Sciences（中国科学院华南植物园）
- Research interest: Poaceae [S]
- Published taxa: *Melocalamus, Sinosasa*
- Region: [ASIA]

J. M. Ni

Ni, Jing Man; 倪京满；Ní Jīngmǎn

1965- **First publication: 1993**

- Employment: Institute of Medicinal Plants, Lanzhou Medical College（兰州医学院药用植物研究所）
- Research interest: Asparagaceae [S]
- Published taxa: *Asparagus*
- Region: CHINA (Gansu)

W. Y. Ni

Ni, Wei Yong; 倪味咏；Ní Wèiyǒng

1968- **First publication: 2019**

- Employment: Anhui Guniujiang National Nature Reserve Administration（安徽牯牛降国家级自然保护区）
- Research interest: Ranunculaceae [S]
- Published taxa: *Clematis*
- Region: CHINA (Anhui)

C. C. Ni

Ni, Chi Cheng; Ni, Zhi Cheng; 倪志诚；Ní Zhìchéng; 倪志誠

1936- **First publication: 1979**

- Employment: Institute of Botany, Chinese Academy of Sciences（中国科学院植物研究所）
- Research interest: Fabaceae [S]
- Published taxa: *Astragalus, Caragana, Hedysarum*
- Affiliation: XZ
- Location of specimens: PE, XZ
- Region: CHINA (Qinghai, Xizang)

M. X. Nie

Nie, Min Xiang; 聂敏祥；Niè Mǐnxiáng; 聶敏祥

1932- **First publication: 1989**

- Employment: Lushan Botanical Garden, Chinese Academy of Sciences（中国科学院庐山植物园）
- Research interest: Celastraceae, Hydrangeaceae, Rosaceae; Plants Jiangxi [S]
- Published taxa: *Dichroa, Euonymus, Hydrangea, Rubus*
- Affiliation: LBG
- Location of specimens: LBG, PE, SHM
- Region: CHINA (Jiangxi)

S. Q. Nie

Nie, Shao Quan; Nie, Shou Chuan; 聂绍荃；Niè Shàoquán; 聶紹荃

1933-2005 **First publication: 1982**

- Employment: Northeast Forestry Institute; Northeast Forestry University（东北林学院；东北林业大学）
- Research interest: Pinaceae, Rosaceae, Ulmaceae [S]
- Published taxa: *Amygdalus, Cerasus, Crataegus, Picea, Ulmus*
- Affiliation: NEFI
- Location of specimens: NEFI
- Region: CHINA (Heilongjiang)
- Also as: S. C. Nie

Z. L. Nie

Nie, Ze Long; 聂泽龙；Niè Zélóng

1974- **First publication: 2013**

- Employment: Kunming Institute of Botany, Chinese Academy of Sciences; College of Bio-resources and Environmental Science, Jishou University（中国科学院昆明植物研究所；吉首大学生物资源与环境科学学院）
- Research interest: Oxalidaceae, Rubiaceae, Vitaceae; Plants of Hunan [S]
- Published taxa: *Nekemias, Oxalis, Pseudogalium, Rubia*
- Affiliation: JIU
- Location of specimens: JIU
- Region: CHINA

X. Q. Ning

Ning, Xiao Qing; 宁小清；Níng Xiǎoqīng

1966- **First publication: 2010**

- Employment: Guangxi College of Traditional Chinese Medicine（广西中医学院）
- Research interest: Capparaceae, Melastomataceae; Medicinal Plants [S]
- Published taxa: *Capparis, Fordiophyton*
- Affiliation: GXCM
- Location of specimens: GXCM
- Region: CHINA (Guangxi)

Z. H. Ning

Ning, Zhu Hua; 宁祝华；Níng Zhùhuá

1961- **First publication: 1987**

- Employment: Botanical Laboratory, Northeast Forestry Institute（东北林业大学植物研究室）

• Research interest: Adoxaceae, Rhamnaceae [S]
• Published taxa: *Adoxa, Rhamnus*
• Region: CHINA

Z. L. Ning

Ning, Zu Lin; 宁祖林 ; Níng Zǔlín
1977- **First publication: 2006**
• Employment: Wuhan Botanical Garden, Chinese Academy of Sciences; South China Botanical Garden, Chinese Academy of Sciences (中国科学院武汉植物园；中国科学院华南植物园)
• Research interest: Brassicaceae, Gesneriaceae, Violaceae [S]
• Published taxa: *Neomartinella, Primulina, Viola*
• Region: CHINA

C. S. Niu

Niu, Chun San; 牛春山 ; Niú Chūnshān
1904-1999 **First publication: 1990**
• Employment: Northwest Forestry College (西北林学院)
• Research interest: Ebenaceae, Oleaceae, Salicaceae; Woody Plants [S]
• Published taxa: *Diospyros, Forsythia, Salix*
• Affiliation: NWFC
• Location of specimens: NWFC
• Region: CHINA (Shaanxi)

L. X. Niu

Niu, Li Xin; 牛立新 ; Niú Lìxīn
1963- **First publication: 1995**
• Employment: Department of Horticulture, Northwest Agricultural University (西北农业大学园艺系)
• Research interest: Vitaceae [S]
• Published taxa: *Vitis*
• Region: CHINA (Shaanxi)

D. X. Nong

Nong, Dong Xin; 农东新 ; Nóng Dōngxīn
1985- **First publication: 2010**
• Employment: Guangxi Institute of Botany, Chinese Academy of Sciences; Guangxi Botanical Garden of Medicinal Plants (广西壮族自治区中国科学院广西植物研究所；广西药用植物园)
• Research interest: Asparagaceae, Cucurbitaceae, Ebenaceae, Gesneriaceae; Plants of Shiwandashan [S]
• Published taxa: *Aspidistra, Diospyros, Lysionotus, Peliosanthes, Trichosanthes*
• Affiliation: GXMG
• Location of specimens: GXMG
• Region: CHINA (Guangxi)

Z. L. Nong

Nong, Zhi Lin; 农植林 ; Nóng Zhílín; 農植林
1933- **First publication: 1993**
• Employment: Jiangxi Agricultural University (江西农业大学)
• Research interest: Aquifoliaceae, Fagaceae, Magnoliaceae [S]
• Published taxa: *Michelia*
• Affiliation: JXAU
• Location of specimens: JXAU
• Region: CHINA (Jiangxi)

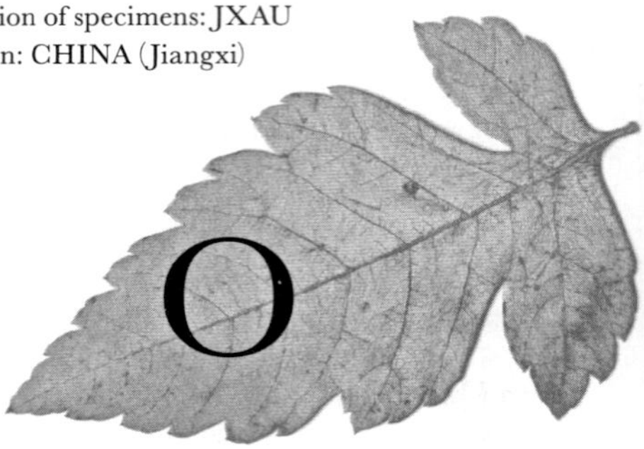

C. H. Ou

Ou, Chern Hsiung; Au, Chen Hsiung; Ou, Chen Xiong; 歐辰雄 ; Ōu Chénxióng; 欧辰雄
First publication: 1976
• Employment: Department of Forestry, Chung Hsing University (中兴大学森林学系)
• Research interest: Adoxaceae, Anacardiaceae, Asteraceae, Begoniaceae, Buxaceae, Cannabaceae, Ebenaceae, Elaeagnaceae, Loranthaceae, Melastomataceae, Passifloraceae, Polygonaceae, Ranunculaceae, Rhamnaceae, Rosaceae, Salicaceae, Solanaceae, Styracaceae; Woody Plants [S]
• Published taxa: *Aster, Begonia, Bredia, Buxus, Celtis, Clematis, Elaeagnus, Eupatorium, Maba, Passiflora, Physalis, Polygonum, Rhamnus, Rubus, Salix, Sarcococca, Solanum, Styrax, Taxillus, Toxicodendron, Viburnum*
• Affiliation: TCF
• Location of specimens: CHIA
• Region: CHINA (Taiwan)

D. Y. Ou

Ou, Dan Yan; 欧丹燕 ; Ōu Dānyàn
1975- **First publication: 2010**
• Employment: Landscape Administration Department of Putuo, Zhejiang; Putuo Forest Ecosystem Research and Observation Station, Zhejiang (浙江普陀山园林管理处；浙江普陀山森林生态系统定位观测研究站)
• Research interest: Asteraceae, Lamiaceae [S]
• Published taxa: *Caryopteris, Cirsium*
• Region: CHINA (Zhejiang)

L. J. Ou

Ou, Li Jun; 欧立军 ; Ōu Lìjūn
1976- **First publication: 2013**
- Employment: College of Biological and Food Engineering, Huaihua University（怀化学院生物与食品工程学院）
- Research interest: Amaryllidaceae [S]
- Published taxa: *Lycoris*
- Region: CHINA (Hunan)

J. C. Ou

Ou, Jun Chin; 歐潤芝 ; Ōu Rùnzhī; 欧润芝
First publication: 1976
- Employment: Research Institute of Chinese Medicine（中国医药研究所）
- Research interest: Melastomataceae [S]
- Published taxa: *Melastoma*
- Region: CHINA (Taiwan)

Shan Hua Ou

Ou, Shan Hua; 欧善华 ; Ōu Shànhuá; 歐善華
1937- **First publication: 1985**
- Employment: Shanghai Normal University（上海师范大学）
- Research interest: Schisandraceae; Seed Plants [S]
- Published taxa: *Illicium*
- Affiliation: SHTU
- Location of specimens: SHTU
- Region: CHINA (Zhejiang)

X. Ouyang

Ouyang, Xiong; 欧阳雄 ; Ōuyáng Xióng
1970- **First publication: 2005**
- Employment: Lianhua Hill Garden of Shenzhen City（深圳市莲花山花木园）
- Research interest: Orchidaceae [S]
- Published taxa: *Paphiopedilum*
- Region: CHINA (Yunnan)

P

B. R. Pan

Pan, Bo Rong; 潘伯荣 ; Pān Bóróng; 潘伯榮
1946- **First publication: 2010**
- Employment: Xinjiang Institute of Ecology and Geography, Chinese Academy of Sciences（中国科学院新疆生态与地理研究所）
- Research interest: Elaeagnaceae, Polygonaceae [S]
- Published taxa: *Calligonum*
- Affiliation: TURP
- Location of specimens: TURP
- Region: CHINA (Xinjiang)

B. Pan bis

Pan, Bo; 潘勃 ; Pān Bó
1982- **First publication: 2010**
- Employment: Institute of Botany, Chinese Academy of Sciences; Xishuangbanna Tropical Botanical Garden, Chinese Academy of Sciences（中国科学院植物研究所；中国科学院西双版纳热带植物园）
- Research interest: Fabaceae [S]
- Published taxa: *Apios, Dumasia, Haymondia, Neustanthus, Pseudarthria, Pueraria, Teyleria, Toxicopueraria*
- Region: CHINA (Yunnan)
- Also as: Bo Pan bis

C. C. Pan

Pan, Cheng Chun; 潘成椿 ; Pān Chéngchūn
1967- **First publication: 2017**
- Employment: Administration of Zhejiang Jiulongshan National Natural Reserve（浙江九龙山国家级自然保护区）
- Research interest: Asteraceae [S]
- Published taxa: *Aster*
- Region: CHINA (Zhejiang)

J. T. Pan

Pan, Jin Tang; 潘锦堂 ; Pān Jǐntáng; 潘錦堂
1933-2004 **First publication: 1978**
- Employment: Northwest Plateau Institute of Biology, Chinese Academy of Sciences（中国科学院西北高原生物研究所）
- Research interest: Apiaceae, Asteraceae, Celastraceae, Grossulariaceae, Hydrangeaceae, Ranunculaceae, Saxifragaceae [S]
- Published taxa: *Astilbe, Bergenia, Chrysosplenium, Delphinium, Deutzia, Heracleum, Ligusticum, Parnassia, Pleurospermum, Ribes, Rodgersia, Saussurea, Saxifraga*
- Affiliation: HNWP
- Region: CHINA

K. Y. Pan

Pan, Kai Yu; 潘开玉 ; Pān Kāiyù; 潘開玉
1937- **First publication: 1979**
- Employment: Institute of Botany, Chinese Academy of Sciences（中国科学院植物研究所）
- Research interest: Apiaceae, Asteraceae, Gesneriaceae, Hamamelidaceae, Paeoniaceae [S]

- Published taxa: *Aeschynanthus, Ancylostemon, Anna, Aster, Beccarinda, Boeica, Bournea, Briggsia, Briggsiopsis, Corallodiscus, Disanthus, Hemiboea, Heteropappus, Isometrum, Ligusticum, Loxostigma, Oreocharis, Paeonia, Paraboea, Saussurea, Senecio, Tremacron*
- Affiliation: PE
- Region: CHINA

Kun Pan

Pan, Kun; 潘坤 ; Pān Kūn

1983- **First publication: 2012**

- Employment: Hainan Institute of Tropical Bioscience and Biotechnology（海南热带生物技术研究所）
- Research interest: Magnoliaceae [S]
- Published taxa: *Michelia*
- Region: CHINA (Hainan)
- IPNI as: K. Fan

S. L. Pan

Pan, Sheng Li; 潘胜利 ; Pān Shènglì; 潘勝利

1945- **First publication: 1983**

- Employment: Shanghai First Medical College; School of Pharmacy, Shanghai Medical University（上海第一医学院；上海医科大学药学院）
- Research interest: Apiaceae, Araliaceae [S]
- Published taxa: *Bupleurum, Eleutherococcus*
- Affiliation: SHMU
- Location of specimens: SHMU
- Region: CHINA

S. H. Pan

Pan, Shi Hua; 潘士华 ; Pān Shìhuá

1964- **First publication: 2003**

- Employment: Shanghai Forestry Station（上海市林业总站）
- Research interest: Taxodiaceae [S]
- Published taxa: × *Taxodiomeria*
- Region: [cult.]

W. W. Pan

Pan, Wen Wen; 潘温文 ; Pān Wēnwén

1987- **First publication: 2020**

- Employment: Lishui Vocational and Technical College（丽水职业技术学院）
- Research interest: Boraginaceae [S]
- Published taxa: *Omphalotrigonotis*
- Region: CHINA (Zhejiang)

Xiao L. Pan

Pan, Xiao Ling; 潘晓玲 ; Pān Xiǎolíng

1963-2006 **First publication: 1991**

- Employment: Department of Biology, Xinjiang University（新疆大学生物系）
- Research interest: Amaryllidaceae, Asphodelaceae, Caryophyllaceae, Ephedraceae, Primulaceae, Ranunculaceae, Solanaceae, Violaceae [S]
- Published taxa: *Allium, Androsace, Clematis, Ephedra, Eremurus, Silene, Solanum, Viola*
- Region: CHINA (Xinjiang)

Y. Z. Pan

Pan, Yue Zhi; 潘跃芝 ; Pān Yuèzhī

1973- **First publication: 2008**

- Employment: Kunming Institute of Botany, Chinese Academy of Sciences（中国科学院昆明植物研究所）
- Research interest: Asteraceae [S]
- Published taxa: *Ligularia*
- Region: CHINA (Yunnan)

Y. Y. Pan

Pan, Yun Yun; 潘云云 ; Pān Yúnyún

1987- **First publication: 2020**

- Employment: The Orchid Conservation & Research Center of Shenzhen, Guangdong（广东省深圳市兰科植物保护研究中心）
- Research interest: Orchidaceae [S]
- Published taxa: *Arundina, Paphiopedilum*
- Region: CHINA (Yunnan)

Z. H. Pan

Pan, Ze Hui; 潘泽惠 ; Pān Zéhuì; 潘澤惠

1938- **First publication: 1981**

- Employment: Institute of Botany, Jiangsu Province（江苏省植物研究所）
- Research interest: Apiaceae, Ericaceae [S]
- Published taxa: *Acronema, Angelica, Heracleum, Ligusticum, Ostericum, Pimpinella, Pleurospermum, Pternopetalum, Vaccinium*
- Affiliation: NAS
- Location of specimens: NAS
- Region: CHINA

Z. F. Pan

Pan, Zhu Fong; Pan, Zhu Feng; 潘翥峰 ; Pān Zhùfēng

First publication: 1992

- Employment: Institute of Mountain Hazards and Environment, Chinese Academy of Sciences（中国科学院水利部成都山地灾害与环境研究所）
- Research interest: Berberidaceae [S]
- Published taxa: *Mahonia*
- Region: CHINA (Sichuan)

B. Pan

Pan, Bo; 盘波 ; Pán Bō

1982- **First publication: 2008**

- Employment: Guangxi Institute of Botany, Chinese

Academy of Sciences（广西壮族自治区中国科学院广西植物研究所）
- Research interest: Asparagaceae, Gesneriaceae, Rubiaceae [S]
- Published taxa: *Aspidistra, Briggsia, Chirita, Chiritopsis, Hemiboea, Oreocharis, Paraboea, Petrocodon, Petrocosmea, Primulina, Spiradiclis, Wentsaiboea*
- Affiliation: IBK
- Location of specimens: IBK
- Region: CHINA (Guangxi, Yunnan)
- Also as: Bo Pan

Pang

Pang, Jin Hu; 庞金虎；Páng Jīnhǔ; 龐金虎

1939- **First publication: 1983**

- Employment: Laboratory of Ecology, Kunming Branch, Chinese Academy of Sciences（中国科学院昆明分院生态室）
- Research interest: Oleaceae [S]
- Published taxa: *Osmanthus*
- Region: CHINA (Yunnan)

C. Pei

Pei, Chien; P'ei, Chien; Pei, Jian; 裴鉴；Péi Jiàn; 裴鑒

1902-1969 **First publication: 1932**

- Employment: Department of Botany, Biological Laboratory of Science Society of China; National Institute of Botany, Academia Sinica; Institute of Botany, Jiangsu Province（中国科学社生物研究所植物部；国立中央研究院植物研究所；江苏省植物研究所）
- Research interest: Actinidiaceae, Araceae, Asparagaceae, Betulaceae, Brassicaceae, Chloranthaceae, Dioscoreaceae, Lamiaceae, Magnoliaceae, Ranunculaceae, Saururaceae, Verbenaceae [S]
- Published taxa: *Actinidia, Anemone, Aspidistra, Betula, Callicarpa, Caryopteris, Chloranthus, Clematis, Clerodendrum, Gymnotheca, Magnolia, Marrubium, Pinellia, Plectranthus, Premna, Radicula, Vitex*
- Affiliation: NAS
- Location of specimens: NAS
- Region: CHINA

S. J. Pei

Pei, Sheng Ji; Pei, Seng Ji; 裴盛基；Péi Shèngjī

1938- **First publication: 1981**

- Employment: Yunnan Institute of Tropical Botany, Chinese Academy of Sciences; Kunming Institute of Botany, Chinese Academy of Sciences（中国科学院云南热带植物研究所；中国科学院昆明植物研究所）
- Research interest: Arecaceae, Celastraceae [S]
- Published taxa: *Calamus, Maytenus*
- Affiliation: HITBC, KUN
- Region: CHINA (Yunnan)

Y. L. Pei

Pei, Yan Long; 裴颜龙；Péi Yánlóng

1964- **First publication: 1995**

- Employment: Institute of Botany, Chinese Academy of Sciences（中国科学院植物研究所）
- Research interest: Paeoniaceae [S]
- Published taxa: *Paeonia*
- Region: CHINA (Hubei)

C. L. Peng

Peng, Chun Liang; 彭春良；Péng Chūnliáng

1963- **First publication: 1989**

- Employment: Hunan Forest Botanical Garden（湖南省森林植物园）
- Research interest: Ericaceae, Euphorbiaceae, Magnoliaceae, Rosaceae [S]
- Published taxa: *Magnolia, Mallotus, Michelia, Parakmeria, Rhododendron, Stranvaesia*
- Region: CHINA (Hunan)

D. T. Peng

Peng, De Tai; 彭德太；Péng Détài

1936- **First publication: 1991**

- Employment: Lichuan Traditional Chinese Medicine Company, Hubei（湖北省利川市中药材公司）
- Research interest: Asparagaceae [S]
- Published taxa: *Tupistra*
- Region: CHINA (Hubei)

D. H. Peng

Peng, Dong Hui; 彭东辉；Péng Dōnghuī

1971- **First publication: 2013**

- Employment: College of Landscape Architecture, Fujian Agriculture and Forestry University（福建农林大学园林学院）
- Research interest: Melastomataceae, Orchidaceae [S]
- Published taxa: *Bredia, Changnienia*
- Region: CHINA

G. F. Peng

Peng, Guang Fang; 彭广芳；Péng Guǎngfāng; 彭廣芳

1929- **First publication: 1999**

- Employment: Shandong Institute of Traditional Chinese Medicine（山东省中医药研究所）
- Research interest: Asteraceae; Medicinal Plants [S]
- Published taxa: *Dendranthema*
- Affiliation: SDMP
- Region: CHINA (Shandong)

H. Peng

Peng, Hua; 彭华 ; Péng Huá

1959- **First publication: 1991**

- Employment: Kunming Institute of Botany, Chinese Academy of Sciences（中国科学院昆明植物研究所）
- Research interest: Acanthaceae, Apocynaceae, Aquifoliaceae, Araliaceae, Asteraceae, Ericaceae, Lamiaceae, Nyssaceae, Orchidaceae, Pittosporaceae, Poaceae, Primulaceae, Rosaceae, Salicaceae, Scrophulariaceae; Plant Systematics [S]
- Published taxa: *Arthraxon, Buddleja, Chelonopsis, Dendropanax, Digitaria, Eulalia, Flacourtia, Gerbera, Hemipilia, Ilex, Isodon, Mastixia, Matsumurella, Melanoseris, Microstegium, Miscanthus, Paraphlomis, Parasenecio, Phlomoides, Pittosporum, Pyrola, Sadiria, Salvia, Schnabelia, Sorbus, Vincetoxicum, Wuacanthus*
- Affiliation: KUN
- Location of specimens: KUN
- Region: CHINA (Yunnan)

H. S. Peng

Peng, Hua Sheng; 彭华胜 ; Péng Huáshèng

1975- **First publication: 2017**

- Employment: College of Pharmacy, Anhui University of Chinese Medicine（安徽中医药大学药学院）
- Research interest: Apiaceae, Papaveraceae; Medicinal Plants [S]
- Published taxa: *Corydalis, Peucedanum*
- Affiliation: ACM
- Location of specimens: ACM
- Region: CHINA (Anhui)

H. Z. Peng

Peng, Hua Zheng; 彭华正 ; Péng Huázhèng

First publication: 2020

- Employment: Zhejiang Academy of Forestry（浙江省林业科学研究院）
- Research interest: Cucurbitaceae [S]
- Published taxa: *Trichosanthes*
- Region: CHINA (Zhejiang)

C. I Peng

Peng, Ching I; Peng, Jing Yi; **彭鏡毅 ; Péng Jìngyì; 彭镜毅**

1950-2018 **First publication: 1984**

- Employment: Herbarium, Institute of Botany, "Academia Sinica"; Institute of Plant and Microbial Biology, "Academia Sinica"; Herbarium, Biodiversity Research Center, "Academia Sinica"（中研院植物研究所；中研院植物暨微生物学研究所；中研院生物多样性研究中心）
- Research interest: Asparagaceae, Asteraceae, Begoniaceae, Commelinaceae, Gentianaceae, Liliaceae, Onagraceae, Primulaceae, Urticaceae; Plants of Taiwan [S]
- Published taxa: *Aspidistra, Begonia, Belosynapsis, Blumea, Eupatorium, Gentiana, Ixeridium, Ludwigia, Lysimachia, Parasenecio, Pouzolzia, Pterocypsela, Senecio, Tricyrtis, Youngia*
- Affiliation: HAST
- Location of specimens: HAST
- Region: CHINA (Taiwan)

J. S. Peng

Peng, Jiu Sheng; 彭九生 ; Péng Jiǔshēng

First publication: 2018

- Employment: Jiangxi Academy of Forestry（江西省林业科学院）
- Research interest: Poaceae [S]
- Published taxa: *Phyllostachys*
- Region: CHINA (Jiangxi)

L. J. Peng

Peng, Long Jin; 彭隆金 ; Péng Lóngjīn

1941-2017 **First publication: 1989**

- Employment: Kunming Institute of Botany, Chinese Academy of Sciences（中国科学院昆明植物研究所）
- Research interest: Asparagaceae, Liliaceae [S]
- Published taxa: *Aspidistra, Lilium*
- Region: CHINA

K. S. Pang

Pang, Kuen Shum; 彭權森 ; Péng Quánsēn; 彭权森

1961- **First publication: 2014**

- Employment: Hong Kong Herbarium, Agriculture, Fisheries and Conservation Department（香港渔农自然护理署香港植物标本室）
- Research interest: Betulaceae; Plants of Hong Kong [S]
- Published taxa: *Carpinus*
- Affiliation: HK
- Region: CHINA (Hong Kong)

T. Peng

Peng, Tao; 彭涛 ; Péng Tāo

1977- **First publication: 2014**

- Employment: School of Life Sciences, Guizhou Normal University（贵州师范大学生命科学学院）
- Research interest: Gesneriaceae [BS]
- Published taxa: *Primulina*
- Affiliation: GNUB
- Location of specimens: GNUB
- Region: CHINA (Guizhou)

W. D. Peng

Peng, Wei Dong; 彭卫东 ; Péng Wèidōng

1963- **First publication: 1986**

- Employment: Shandong Agricultural University（山东农业大学）

- Research interest: Asteraceae, Cucurbitaceae, Rosaceae [S]
- Published taxa: *Crataegus, Ligularia, Pyrus*
- Affiliation: SDAU
- Location of specimens: SDAU
- Region: CHINA (Gansu, Shandong)

X. M. Peng

Peng, Xiao Ming; 彭小明 ; Péng Xiǎomíng

1981- **First publication: 2011**

- Employment: Jiangxi Province Forestry Survey Planning Institute（江西省林业调查规划研究院）
- Research interest: Lamiaceae [S]
- Published taxa: *Callicarpa*
- Region: CHINA (Yunnan)

Y. Q. Peng

Peng, Yan Qiong; 彭艳琼 ; Péng Yànqióng

1974- **First publication: 2014**

- Employment: Xishuangbanna Tropical Botanical Garden, Chinese Academy of Sciences（中国科学院西双版纳热带植物园）
- Research interest: Moraceae [S]
- Published taxa: *Ficus*
- Region: CHINA (Yunnan)

Y. C. Peng

Peng, Yang Cheng; 彭阳城 ; Péng Yángchéng

First publication: 2020

- Employment: College of Life Sciences, Hunan Normal University（湖南师范大学生命科学学院）
- Research interest: Balsaminaceae [S]
- Published taxa: *Impatiens*
- Region: CHINA (Xizang)

Ying L. Peng

Peng, Ying Li; 彭盈丽 ; Péng Yínglì

1993- **First publication: 2019**

- Employment: Forestry College, Fujian Agriculture and Forestry University（福建农林大学林学院）
- Research interest: Orchidaceae [S]
- Published taxa: *Cymbidium*
- Region: CHINA (Yunnan)

Y. D. Peng

Peng, Yu De; 彭玉德 ; Péng Yùdé

1980- **First publication: 2015**

- Employment: Guangxi Botanical Garden of Medicinal Plants（广西药用植物园）
- Research interest: Aristolochiaceae, Ebenaceae; Medicinal Plants [S]
- Published taxa: *Aristolochia, Diospyros*
- Affiliation: GXMG
- Location of specimens: GXMG
- Region: CHINA (Guangxi)

Y. L. Peng

Peng, Yu Lan; 彭玉兰 ; Péng Yùlán

1975- **First publication: 2004**

- Employment: Chengdu Institute of Biology, Chinese Academy of Sciences（中国科学院成都生物研究所）
- Research interest: Asteraceae, Ericaceae, Papaveraceae [S]
- Published taxa: *Corydalis, Humbertacalia, Rhododendron, Youngia*
- Affiliation: CDBI
- Location of specimens: CDBI
- Region: CHINA (Sichuan)

Z. Q. Peng

Peng, Ze Qiu; 彭泽球 ; Péng Zéqiú

First publication: 2015

- Employment: South China Botanical Garden, Chinese Academy of Sciences（中国科学院华南植物园）
- Research interest: Apocynaceae [S]
- Published taxa: *Hoya*
- Region: CHINA (Yunnan)

Z. X. Peng

Peng, Ze Xiang; Peng, Tse Xiang; Peng, Tse Hsiang; Pong, Tse Siang; 彭泽祥 ; Péng Zéxiáng; 彭澤祥

1924- **First publication: 1982**

- Employment: Department of Biology, Lanzhou University（兰州大学生物系）
- Research interest: Apiaceae, Asteraceae, Fabaceae, Fagaceae, Lardizabalaceae, Melanthiaceae, Plumbaginaceae, Polygalaceae, Ranunculaceae, Urticaceae [S]
- Published taxa: *Acantholimon, Ceratostigma, Goniolimon, Holboellia, Ligularia, Ligusticum, Limonium, Lithocarpus, Paris, Pilea, Plumbago, Polygala, Ranunculus, Thermopsis, Ypsilandra*
- Affiliation: LZU
- Location of specimens: LZU
- Region: CHINA
- Also as: T. X. Peng; T. H. Peng

X. M. Pi

Pi, Xi Ming; 皮锡铭 ; Pí Xīmíng; 皮錫銘

1932-1992 **First publication: 1991**

- Employment: Department of Biology, Xinjiang University（新疆大学生物系）
- Research interest: Boraginaceae, Caryophyllaceae [S]
- Published taxa: *Cerastium, Silene*
- Affiliation: XJU
- Location of specimens: XJU
- Region: CHINA (Xinjiang)

X. F. Pu

Pu, Xu Feng; 蒲旭峰 ; Pú Xùfēng

1963- First publication: 1992

- Employment: Chengdu College of Traditional Chinese Medicine（成都中医学院）
- Research interest: Ranunculaceae [S]
- Published taxa: *Cimicifuga*
- Region: CHINA (Sichuan)

C. X. Pu

Pu, Chun Xia; 普春霞 ; Pǔ Chūnxiá

1977- First publication: 2012

- Employment: Kunming Institute of Botany, Chinese Academy of Sciences（中国科学院昆明植物研究所）
- Research interest: Lamiaceae [S]
- Published taxa: *Elsholtzia*
- Affiliation: YNTCM
- Location of specimens: YNTCM
- Region: CHINA (Sichuan)

F. T. Pu

Pu, Fa Ting; Pu, Fa Ding; 溥发鼎 ; Pǔ Fādǐng; 溥發鼎

1936- First publication: 1978

- Employment: Chengdu Institute of Biology, Chinese Academy of Sciences（中国科学院成都生物研究所）
- Research interest: Apiaceae, Araliaceae, Fagaceae [S]
- Published taxa: *Angelica, Anthriscus, Carum, Chamaesciadium, Heracleum, Hydrocotyle, Ligusticum, Meeboldia, Notopterygium, Oenanthe, Ostericum, Pachypleurum, Peucedanum, Physospermopsis, Pimpinella, Pleurospermum, Pternopetalum, Sanicula, Sinocarum, Trachydium, Vicatia*
- Affiliation: CDBI
- Location of specimens: CDBI
- Region: CHINA

C. Z. Qi

Qi, Chun Zhang; Qi, J.; 戚春章 ; Qī Chūnzhāng

First publication: 2017

- Employment: The Institute of Vegetables, Chinese Academy of Agricultural Sciences（中国农业科学院蔬菜研究所）
- Research interest: Cucurbitaceae [S]
- Published taxa: *Cucumis*
- Affiliation: IVH
- Location of specimens: IVH
- Region: CHINA (Yunnan)
- IPNI as: J. Qi

C. W. Chi

Chi, Chin Wen; Qi, Jing Wen; 戚经文 ; Qī Jīngwén; 戚經文

1916-1990 First publication: 1948

- Employment: College of Agriculture, National Sun Yat-sen University（国立中山大学农学院）
- Research interest: Theaceae [S]
- Published taxa: *Camellia*
- Location of specimens: SYS
- Region: CHINA

H. R. Qi

Qi, Hui Rong; 齐辉荣 ; Qí Huīróng; 齊輝榮

1938- First publication: 1985

- Employment: Forestry Bureau of Liangping County, Sichuan（四川省梁平县林业局）
- Research interest: Cyperaceae, Poaceae [S]
- Published taxa: *Dendrocalamus, Neosinocalamus, Phyllostachys*
- Region: CHINA (Sichuan)

Y. D. Qi

Qi, Yao Dong; 齐耀东 ; Qí Yàodōng

1971- First publication: 2004

- Employment: Institute of Botany, Chinese Academy of Sciences（中国科学院植物研究所）
- Research interest: Liliaceae, Thymelaeaceae [S]
- Published taxa: *Wikstroemia*
- Affiliation: IMD
- Region: CHINA (Yunnan)

C. J. Qi

Qi, Cheng Jing; 祁承经 ; Qí Chéngjīng; 祁承經

1931- First publication: 1981

- Employment: Central South College of Forestry（中南林学院）
- Research interest: Aquifoliaceae, Araliaceae, Betulaceae, Elaeagnaceae, Fagaceae, Garryaceae, Grossulariaceae, Lauraceae, Malvaceae, Oleaceae, Pinaceae, Rosaceae, Styracaceae; Woody Plants [S]
- Published taxa: *Actinodaphne, Aucuba, Carpinus, Cyclobalanopsis, Elaeagnus, Hunaniopanax, Ilex, Linociera, Machilus, Pinus, Reevesia, Ribes, Sinojackia, Sorbus, Stranvaesia*
- Affiliation: CSFI
- Location of specimens: CSFI
- Region: CHINA (Hunan)

Z. C. Qi

Qi, Zhe Chen; 祁哲晨 ; Qí Zhéchén

1986- **First publication: 2016**

- Employment: College of Life Sciences, Zhejiang Sci-Tech University（浙江理工大学生命科学学院）
- Research interest: Smilacaceae [S]
- Published taxa: *Smilax*
- Region: [ASIA]

S. S. Chien

Chien, Sung Shu; Ch'ien, Ch'ung Shu; Ch'ien, Sung Shu; Qian, Chong Shu; 钱崇澍 ; Qián Chóngshù; 錢崇澍

1883-1965 **First publication: 1916**

- Employment: Biological Laboratory of Science Society of China; Institute of Systematic Botany, Academia Sinica; Institute of Botany, Chinese Academy of Sciences（中国科学社生物研究所；中国科学院植物分类研究所；中国科学院植物研究所）
- Research interest: Berberidaceae, Caprifoliaceae, Cornaceae, Daphniphyllaceae, Fabaceae, Iridaceae, Lauraceae, Orchidaceae, Primulaceae, Theaceae, Urticaceae [PS]
- Published taxa: *Camellia, Campylotropis, Changnienia, Cornus, Cypripedium, Daphniphyllum, Hemipilia, Indigofera, Iris, Liparis, Litsea, Lonicera, Lysimachia, Maackia, Oreorchis, Pellionia, Podophyllum, Stewartia*
- Region: CHINA

G. Z. Qian

Qian, Guan Ze; 钱关泽 ; Qián Guānzé

1965- **First publication: 1999**

- Employment: College of Life Science, Liaocheng University; Research Institute of Subtropical Forestry, Chinese Academy of Forestry; Institute of Botany, Chinese Academy of Sciences（聊城大学生命科学学院；中国林业科学研究院亚热带林业研究所；中国科学院植物研究所）
- Research interest: Fabaceae, Rosaceae [S]
- Published taxa: *Malus, Oxytropis*
- Region: CHINA

H. Qian

Qian, Hong; 钱宏 ; Qián Hóng

1957- **First publication: 1988**

- Employment: Institute of Applied Ecology, Chinese Academy of Sciences（中国科学院沈阳应用生态研究所）
- Research interest: Rhamnaceae [S]
- Published taxa: *Berchemiella*
- Location of specimens: AAUF
- Region: CHINA

H. J. Qian

Qian, Hong Jiang; Qian, Hong Qiang; 钱洪强 ; Qián Hóngqiáng

First publication: 1983

- Employment: Southwest Forestry College（西南林学院）
- Research interest: Fagaceae [S]
- Published taxa: *Lithocarpus*
- Region: CHINA (Yunnan)

J. J. Chien

Chien, Jia Ju; Chien, Chia Chü; Ch'ien, Chia Chü; Qian, Jia Ju; 钱家驹 ; Qián Jiājū; 錢家駒

1922-1984 **First publication: 1957**

- Employment: Department of Biology, Northeast Normal University; Department of Geography, Northeast Normal University（东北师范大学生物系；东北师范大学地理系）
- Research interest: Athyriaceae, Pinaceae; Plants of N. E. China [PS]
- Published taxa: *Abies, Athyrium, Lunathyrium*
- Affiliation: NENU
- Location of specimens: JLMP, NENU
- Region: CHINA (Heilongjiang)

J. Qian

Qian, Jie; 钱洁 ; Qián Jié

1975- **First publication: 2003**

- Employment: Department of Biology, Yunnan University; Kunming Institute of Botany, Chinese Academy of Sciences（云南大学生物系；中国科学院昆明植物研究所）
- Research interest: Poaceae [S]
- Published taxa: *Achnatherum*
- Region: CHINA (Yunnan)

L. Qian

Qian, Li; 钱力 ; Qián Lì

1988- **First publication: 2008**

- Employment: College of Life and Environmental Sciences, Hangzhou Normal University（杭州师范大学生命与环境科学学院）
- Research interest: Balsaminaceae, Rosaceae [S]
- Published taxa: *Impatiens, Rosa, Rubus*
- Region: CHINA (Zhejiang)

M. Qian

Qian, Ming; 钱明 ; Qián Míng; 錢明

1925-1992 **First publication: 1987**

- Employment: Department of Biology, Shanghai Normal University（上海师范大学生物系）
- Research interest: Mazaceae; Seed Plants [S]
- Published taxa: *Mazus*
- Affiliation: SHTU
- Location of specimens: SHTU

- Region: CHINA (Fujian)

Q. X. Qian

Qian, Qi Xia; 钱奇霞 ; Qián Qíxiá

1976- **First publication: 2019**

- Employment: School of Landscape Architecture, Zhejiang A&F University (浙江农林大学风景园林与建筑学院)
- Research interest: Poaceae [S]
- Published taxa: *Pleioblastus*
- Region: CHINA (Zhejiang)

S. X. Qian

Qian, Shi Xin; 钱士心 ; Qián Shìxīn; 錢士心

1932- **First publication: 1985**

- Employment: Shanghai Railway Medical College; School of Medicine, Shanghai Railway University (上海铁道医学院；上海铁道大学医学院)
- Research interest: Berberidaceae, Brassicaceae, Cyperaceae, Rosaceae; Plants of E. China [S]
- Published taxa: *Carex, Crataegus, Epimedium, Hilliella*
- Affiliation: SG
- Location of specimens: SG
- Region: CHINA

X. H. Qian

Qian, Xiao Hu; Chien, Hsiao Hu; Ch'ien, Hsiao Hu; **钱啸虎 ; Qián Xiàohǔ; 錢嘯虎**

1928-2000 **First publication: 1980**

- Employment: Department of Biology, Anhui Normal University (安徽师范大学生物系)
- Research interest: Amaryllidaceae, Ixioliriaceae [S]
- Published taxa: *Ixiolirion*
- Affiliation: ANUB
- Location of specimens: ANUB
- Region: CHINA (Xinjiang)

Y. Y. Qian

Qian, Yi Yong; 钱义咏 ; Qián Yìyǒng; 錢義詠

1930- **First publication: 1985**

- Employment: Simao Forestry Bureau, Yunnan (云南省思茅行署林业局)
- Research interest: Amaranthaceae, Apiaceae, Asparagaceae, Asteraceae, Balanophoraceae, Begoniaceae, Campanulaceae, Caprifoliaceae, Celastraceae, Colchicaceae, Convolvulaceae, Cyperaceae, Fabaceae, Gesneriaceae, Hamamelidaceae, Juncaceae, Lamiaceae, Liliaceae, Malvaceae, Myrtaceae, Orchidaceae, Orobanchaceae, Poaceae, Primulaceae, Pteridaceae, Ranunculaceae, Rosaceae, Saxifragaceae, Symplocaceae, Thymelaeaceae, Urticaceae, Zingiberaceae; Plants of S. Yunnan [S]
- Published taxa: *Adenophora, Adiantum, Ainsliaea, Albizia, Anisachne, Argyreia, Balanophora, Begonia, Brachycorythis, Callicarpa, Cassia, Chirita, Cyperus, Dalbergia, Dipsacus, Disporum, Erianthus, Eriosolena, Fimbristylis, Galactia, Globba, Grewia, Hedychium, Juncus, Kaempferia, Lilium, Lysimachia, Millettia, Oenanthe, Ophiopogon, Parnassia, Pellionia, Podocarpium, Premna, Pseudoraphis, Psilotrichum, Rubus, Sacciolepis, Saxifraga, Scleria, Shuteria, Sopubia, Sterculia, Symplocos, Syzygium, Tetrathyrium, Thalictrum, Zingiber*
- Affiliation: SMAO
- Location of specimens: SMAO
- Region: CHINA (Yunnan)

Zi G. Qian

Qian, Zi Gang; 钱子刚 ; Qián Zǐgāng

1962- **First publication: 1992**

- Employment: Department of Chinese Materia Medica, Yunnan University of Traditional Chinese Medicine (云南中医学院中药系)
- Research interest: Fabaceae [S]
- Published taxa: *Astragalus, Chesneya*
- Affiliation: YNTCM
- Region: CHINA (Yunnan)
- IPNI as: Z. G. Qian

C. Z. Qiao

Qiao, Chuan Zhuo; 乔传卓 ; Qiáo Chuánzhuó; 喬傳卓

1938-2019 **First publication: 1987**

- Employment: College of Pharmacy, Second Military Medical University (第二军医大学药学院)
- Research interest: Chloranthaceae, Rosaceae, Solanaceae [S]
- Published taxa: *Armeniaca, Datura, Sarcandra*
- Location of specimens: SMMU-BH
- Region: CHINA

Q. Qiao

Qiao, Qin; 乔琴 ; Qiáo Qín

1981- **First publication: 2008**

- Employment: Kunming Institute of Botany, Chinese Academy of Sciences (中国科学院昆明植物研究所)
- Research interest: Asparagaceae [S]
- Published taxa: *Rohdea*
- Region: CHINA (Yunnan)

Y. C. Qiao

Qiao, Ying Chang; 乔应常 ; Qiáo Yīngcháng

1952- **First publication: 1983**

- Employment: Xuchang City Forestry Bureau, Henan (河南省许昌市林业局)
- Research interest: Magnoliaceae [S]
- Published taxa: *Magnolia*

• Region: CHINA (Henan)

K. F. Ching

Ching, Kuo Feng; Qin, Guo Feng; 秦国峰 ; Qín Guófēng

First publication: 1978

• Employment: Ningxia Institute of Agricultural Sciences（宁夏农业科学研究所）
• Research interest: Solanaceae [S]
• Published taxa: *Lycium*
• Region: CHINA (Ningxia)

Ching

Ching, Ren Chang; Qin, Ren Chang; Ch'in, Jên Ch'ang; 秦仁昌 ; Qín Rénchāng

1898-1986 **First publication: 1929**

• Employment: Natural History Museum, Academia Sinica; National Institute of Botany, Academia Sinica; Institute of Systematic Botany, Academia Sinica; Institute of Botany, Chinese Academy of Sciences（国立中央研究院自然博物馆；国立中央研究院植物研究所；中国科学院植物分类研究所；中国科学院植物研究所）
• Research interest: Arecaceae, Aspleniaceae, Asteraceae, Athyriaceae, Betulaceae, Blechnaceae, Bolbitidaceae, Clethraceae, Cyatheaceae, Cystopteridaceae, Davalliaceae, Dennstaedtiaceae, Dicranopteridaceae, Didymochlaenaceae, Diplaziopsidaceae, Dipteridaceae, Drynariaceae, Dryopteridaceae, Equisetaceae, Gleicheniaceae, Hymenophyllaceae, Hypodematiaceae, Lindsaeaceae, Lomariopsidaceae, Loxogrammaceae, Lycopodiaceae, Lygodiaceae, Marattiaceae, Oleaceae, Oleandraceae, Onocleaceae, Ophioglossaceae, Orchidaceae, Osmundaceae, Plagiogyriaceae, Pleurosoriopsidaceae, Polypodiaceae, Pteridaceae, Pteridryaceae, Rhachidosoraceae, Selaginellaceae, Stenochlaenaceae, Tectariaceae, Thelypteridaceae, Vittariaceae, Woodsiaceae; Pteridophytes [PS]
• Published taxa: *Abacopteris, Acrophorus, Acrorumohra, Adiantum, Aleuritopteris, Allantodia, Allosorus, Alsophila, Angiopteris, Arachniodes, Araiostegia, Archangiopteris, Arcypteris, Arthromeris, Aspidium, Asplenium, Athyriopsis, Athyrium, Belvisia, Betula,* Bolbitidaceae, *Bolbitis, Botrychium, Botrypus, Callipteris, Calymella, Campium, Campyloneurum, Ceterachopsis, Ceterach, Cheilanthes, Cheilanthopsis, Cheilosoria, Chieniopteris, Chieniopteris, Christensenia, Clethra, Colysis, Coniogramme, Cornopteris, Craspedosorus, Crepidomanes, Cryptogramma, Ctenitis, Ctenitopsis, Cyathea, Cyclogramma, Cyclosorus, Cyrtogonellum, Cyrtomidictyum, Cyrtomium, Cystoathyrium, Cystopteris, Davallia, Davallodes, Dennstaedtia, Diacalpe, Diblemma,* Dicranopteridaceae, *Dicranopteris, Dictymia, Dictyocline, Dictyodroma,* Didymochlaenaceae, *Diphasiastrum, Diplaziopsis, Diplazium, Diplopterygium,* Drynariaceae, *Drynaria, Drynariopsis, Dryoathyrium,* Dryopteridaceae, *Dryopteris, Egenolfia, Elaphoglossum, Emodiopteris, Eriosoriopsis, Forsythia, Glaphyropteridopsis, Gleichenella, Goniopteris, Gonocormus, Grammitis, Gymnocarpium, Gymnopteris, Gymnosphaera, Haplodictyum, Hemigramma, Hemistachyum, Hicriopteris, Hippochaete, Holcosorus, Holostachyum, Humata, Huperzia, Hymenolepis, Hymenophyllum,* Hypodematiaceae, *Hypodematium, Hypolepis, Lastrea, Lastreopsis, Lemmaphyllum, Lepidogrammitis, Lepidomicrosorium, Lepisorus, Leptochilus, Leptogramma, Leptolepidium, Leucostegia, Lindsaea, Lithostegia, Lomagramma, Lomaria, Lomariopsis,* Loxogrammaceae, *Loxogramme, Lunathyrium, Lycopodium, Lygodium, Macrothelypteris, Matteuccia, Mecodium, Mesoneuron, Mesopteris, Metapolypodium, Metathelypteris, Microchlaena, Microlepia, Microsorum, Monachosorum, Monomelangium, Myrmecophila, Neoathyrium, Neocheiropteris, Neolepisorus, Neottopteris, Nothoperanema, Odontosoria,* Oleandraceae, *Oleandra, Onychium, Ophioglossum, Osmunda, Palhinhaea, Paradavallodes, Paragramma, Parapolystichum, Parathelypteris, Pellaea, Peranema, Phanerophlebiopsis, Phegopteris, Phlegmariurus, Phyllitis, Phymatodes, Phymatopsis, Phymatopteris, Plagiogyria, Pleocnemia, Pleurosoriopsidaceae, Polypodiastrum, Polypodiodes, Polypodium, Prosaptia, Protowoodsia, Pseudocyclosorus, Pseudocystopteris, Pseudodrynaria, Pseudophegopteris, Pteretis,* Pteridaceae, *Pteridium, Pteridrys, Pteris, Pyrrosia, Rhachidosorus, Rumohra, Saxiglossum, Schizoloma, Selaginella, Selenodesmium, Selliguea, Stegnogramma,* Stenochlaenaceae, *Stenochlaena, Stenoloma, Sticherus, Struthiopteris, Tectaria, Thelypteris, Trachycarpus, Triblemma, Tricholepidium, Trichomanes, Trichoneuron, Trogostolon, Vandenboschia, Vittariaceae, Vittaria, Woodsia, Woodwardia*
• Affiliation: PE
• Location of specimens: CQNM, KUN, N, NAS, PE, SWFC
• Region: CHINA

W. H. Qin

Qin, Wei Hua; 秦卫华 ; Qín Wèihuá

First publication: 2020

• Employment: Nanjing Institute of Environmental Sciences, Ministry of Ecology and Enlightenment（生

态环境部南京环境科学研究所）
- Research interest: Gesneriaceae [S]
- Published taxa: Petrocodon
- Region: CHINA (Guangxi)

X. K. Qin

Qin, Xiang Kun; 秦祥堃 ; Qín Xiángkūn
1950- **First publication: 1996**
- Employment: Shanghai Natural History Museum (Branch of Shanghai Science & Technology Museum) （上海自然博物馆(上海科技馆分馆)）
- Research interest: Oleaceae; Plants of Shanghai [S]
- Published taxa: *Forsythia, Fraxinus, Ligustrum, Syringa*
- Affiliation: SHM
- Location of specimens: SHM
- Region: CHINA

X. S. Qin

Qin, Xin Sheng; 秦新生 ; Qín Xīnshēng
1979- **First publication: 2006**
- Employment: College of Forestry, South China Agricultural University（华南农业大学林学院）
- Research interest: Asclepiadaceae, Celastraceae, Euphorbiaceae, Magnoliaceae, Putranjivaceae [S]
- Published taxa: *Acalypha, Drypetes, Manglietia, Maytenus*
- Affiliation: CANT
- Location of specimens: CANT
- Region: CHINA (Guangdong, Hainan)

Zhong S. Qin

Qin, Zhong Shi; 秦忠时 ; Qín Zhōngshí; 秦忠時
1943- **First publication: 1992**
- Employment: Institute of Forestry and Soil Sciences, Chinese Academy of Sciences（中国科学院林业土壤研究所）
- Research interest: Amaranthaceae, Poaceae [S]
- Published taxa: *Chenopodium, Hordeum*
- Affiliation: IFP
- Location of specimens: IFP
- Region: CHINA (Liaoning)

D. H. Qin

Qin, De Hai; 覃德海 ; Qín Déhǎi
1953-2011 **First publication: 1988**
- Employment: Guangxi Institute of Traditional Medical and Pharmaceutical Sciences（广西中医药研究所）
- Research interest: Acanthaceae, Begoniaceae, Cucurbitaceae, Gesneriaceae, Hypoxidaceae, Loganiaceae, Moraceae, Pentaphylacaceae, Rubiaceae, Zingiberaceae; Medicinal Plants [S]
- Published taxa: *Adinandra, Amomum, Begonia, Chirita, Chiritopsis, Curculigo, Ficus, Gynostemma, Mitreola, Oreocharis, Paraboea, Spiradiclis, Strobilanthes, Wentsaiboea, Zingiber*
- Affiliation: GXMI
- Location of specimens: GXMI
- Region: CHINA (Guangxi)

H. N. Qin

Qin, Hai Ning; 覃海宁 ; Qín Hǎiníng
1960- **First publication: 1989**
- Employment: Institute of Botany, Chinese Academy of Sciences（中国科学院植物研究所）
- Research interest: Balsaminaceae, Berberidaceae, Fabaceae, Lardizabalaceae, Nyssaceae, Symplocaceae [S]
- Published taxa: *Afgekia, Akebia, Archakebia, Holboellia, Impatiens, Mahonia, Nyssa, Parvatia, Stauntonia, Symplocos*
- Affiliation: PE
- Region: CHINA

Q. M. Qin

Qin, Qiao Mei; 覃俏梅 ; Qín Qiàoméi
First publication: 2019
- Employment: South China Botanical Garden, Chinese Academy of Sciences（中国科学院华南植物园）
- Research interest: Poaceae [S]
- Published taxa: *Melocalamus, Sinosasa*
- Region: [ASIA]

Ying Qin

Qin, Ying; 覃营 ; Qín Yíng
1988- **First publication: 2018**
- Employment: College of Life Sciences, Guangxi Normal University; Guangxi Institute of Botany, Chinese Academy of Sciences（广西师范大学生命科学学院；广西壮族自治区中国科学院广西植物研究所）
- Research interest: Gesneriaceae, Orchidaceae [S]
- Published taxa: *Platanthera, Primulina*
- Region: CHINA (Guangxi)

Y. H. Qin

Qin, Yong Hua; 覃永华 ; Qín Yǒnghuá
1981- **First publication: 2017**
- Employment: Guangxi Forest Inventory & Planning Institute（广西壮族自治区林业勘测设计院）
- Research interest: Begoniaceae; Woody Plants [S]
- Published taxa: *Begonia*
- Affiliation: GXF
- Location of specimens: GXF
- Region: CHINA (Guangxi)

H. S. Kiu

Kiu, Hua Shing; Kiu, Hua Sing; Chiu, Hua Hsing; Ch'iu, Hua Hsing; Qiu, Hua Xing; 丘华兴; Qiū Huáxīng; 丘華興

1929- **First publication: 1974**

- Employment: South China Institute of Botany, Chinese Academy of Sciences（中国科学院华南植物研究所）
- Research interest: Amaranthaceae, Convolvulaceae, Euphorbiaceae, Goodeniaceae, Loranthaceae, Malvaceae, Opiliaceae, Phyllanthaceae, Proteaceae, Santalaceae [S]
- Published taxa: *Acalypha, Aerva, Alchornea, Antidesma, Aporosa, Arceuthobium, Calogyne, Champereia, Cleistanthus, Croton, Decaschistia, Firmiana, Helicia, Helixanthera, Korthalsella, Lasiococca, Loranthus, Mallotus, Merremia, Psilotrichopsis, Psilotrichum, Scurrula, Strophioblachia, Taxillus, Trigonostemon, Viscum*
- Affiliation: IBSC
- Region: CHINA

H. L. Chiu

Chiu, Hui Lung; 邱輝龍; Qiū Huīlóng; 邱辉龙

First publication: 2011

- Employment: Taiwan Agricultural Research Institute, Council of Agriculture, "Executive Yuan"（"行政院"农业委员会农业试验所）
- Research interest: Musaceae [S]
- Published taxa: *Musa*
- Region: CHINA (Taiwan)

J. X. Qiu

Qiu, Jin Xing; 邱金兴; Qiū Jīnxīng

First publication: 1989

- Employment: Jiangxi Institute of Forestry Science（江西省林业科学研究所）
- Research interest: Ericaceae [S]
- Published taxa: *Vaccinium*
- Region: CHINA (Jiangxi)

Jing Qiu

Qiu, Jing; 邱靖; Qiū Jìng

1982- **First publication: 2019**

- Employment: College of Biology and the Environment, Nanjing Forestry University; Sanjiang University（南京林业大学生物与环境学院；三江学院）
- Research interest: Rosaceae [S]
- Published taxa: *Sorbus*
- Region: CHINA (Jiangxi)

J. Qiu

Qiu, Juan; 邱娟; Qiū Juān

First publication: 2019

- Employment: College of Grassland and Environment Sciences, Xinjiang Agricultural University（新疆农业大学草业与环境科学学院）
- Research interest: Asteraceae [S]
- Published taxa: *Crepis*
- Region: CHINA (Xinjiang)

J. Z. Qiu

Qiu, Jun Zhuan; 邱均专; Qiū Jūnzhuān

1962- **First publication: 1990**

- Employment: Institute of Botany, Chinese Academy of Sciences（中国科学院植物研究所）
- Research interest: Campanulaceae [S]
- Published taxa: *Adenophora*
- Region: CHINA

L. C. Chiu

Chiu, Lee Ching; Chiu, Lien Ching; Ch'iu, Lien Ch'ing; 邱莲卿; Qiū Liánqīng; 邱蓮卿

1931- **First publication: 1979**

- Employment: Shanghai Natural History Museum (Branch of Shanghai Science & Technology Museum)（上海自然博物馆(上海科技馆分馆)）
- Research interest: Caprifoliaceae; Plant Ecology [S]
- Published taxa: *Valeriana*
- Affiliation: SHM
- Location of specimens: SHM
- Region: CHINA

S. T. Chiu

Chiu, Shau Ting; Qiu, Shao Ting; 邱少婷; Qiū Shàotíng

1961- **First publication: 1996**

- Employment: Museum of Natural Science（自然科学博物馆）
- Research interest: Caprifoliaceae, Loranthaceae [S]
- Published taxa: *Taxillus*
- Affiliation: TNM
- Location of specimens: TNM
- Region: CHINA (Taiwan)

S. H. Qiu

Qiu, Shu Hua; 邱淑华; Qiū Shūhuá

1939- **First publication: 1979**

- Employment: Chengdu Institute for Drug Control, Sichuan（四川省成都市药品检验所）
- Research interest: Apiaceae [S]
- Published taxa: *Ligusticum*
- Location of specimens: CDC
- Region: CHINA (Sichuan)

W. L. Chiou

Chiou, Wen Liang; 邱文良; Qiū Wénliáng

1953- **First publication: 2009**

- Employment: Taiwan Forestry Research Institute, Council of Agriculture, "Executive Yuan" (“行政院”农业委员会林业试验所)
- Research interest: Athyriaceae, Polypodiaceae, Pteridaceae, Selaginellaceae; Pteridophytes [P]
- Published taxa: *Adiantum, Anisocampium, Athyrium, Deparia, Pteris, Selaginella, Xiphopterella*
- Affiliation: TAIF
- Location of specimens: TAIF
- Region: CHINA (Taiwan)

Y. L. Qiu

Qiu, Yan Lian; 邱燕连 ; Qiū Yànlián

1987- **First publication: 2013**

- Employment: College of Agriculture, Hainan University (海南大学农学院)
- Research interest: Gesneriaceae [S]
- Published taxa: *Didymocarpus*
- Region: CHINA (Fujian)

Z. J. Qiu

Qiu, Zhi Jing; 邱志敬 ; Qiū Zhìjìng

1981- **First publication: 2015**

- Employment: Fairy Lake Botanical Garden, Shenzhen & Chinese Academy of Sciences (深圳市中国科学院仙湖植物园)
- Research interest: Gesneriaceae [S]
- Published taxa: *Petrocosmea, Primulina*
- Affiliation: SZG
- Location of specimens: SZG
- Region: CHINA

P. L. Chiu

Chiu, Pao Ling; Chiu, Pao Lin; Qiu, Bao Lin; 裘宝林 ; Qiú Bǎolín; 裘寶林

1936- **First publication: 1974**

- Employment: Hangzhou Botanical Garden (杭州植物园)
- Research interest: Aceraceae, Adoxaceae, Berberidaceae, Caprifoliaceae, Iridaceae, Magnoliaceae, Malvaceae, Pittosporaceae, Plagiogyriaceae, Rosaceae, Sapindaceae, Staphyleaceae, Theaceae, Tiliaceae, Vitaceae [PS]
- Published taxa: *Acer, Camellia, Corchoropsis, Euscaphis, Gymnospermium, Iris, Leontice, Magnolia, Photinia, Pittosporum, Plagiogyria, Rubus, Stewartia, Tilia, Viburnum, Vitis*
- Affiliation: HHBG
- Location of specimens: HHBG, ZNU
- Region: CHINA (Zhejiang)

Li H. Qiu

Qiu, Li Hong; 裘利洪 ; Qiú Lìhóng

1971- **First publication: 2018**

- Employment: Jiangxi Agricultural University (江西农业大学)
- Research interest: Aceraceae, Taxaceae [S]
- Published taxa: *Taxus*
- Affiliation: JXAU
- Location of specimens: JXAU
- Region: CHINA (Jiangxi)

P. S. Chiu

Chiu, Pei Shi; Chiu, Pei Hsi; Chiu, Pei Xi; Qiu, Pei Xi; 裘佩熹 ; Qiú Pèixī

1919-1987 **First publication: 1959**

- Employment: Department of Biology, East China Normal University; Department of Biology, Shanghai Normal University (华东师范大学生物系 ; 上海师范大学生物系)
- Research interest: Athyriaceae, Blechnaceae, Dryopteridaceae, Gleicheniaceae, Hymenophyllaceae, Lycopodiaceae; Pteridophytes [PS]
- Published taxa: *Allantodia, Athyrium, Ctenitis, Dryopsis, Egenolfia, Hicriopteris, Huperzia, Stenochlaena, Vandenboschia, Woodwardia*
- Affiliation: HSNU
- Location of specimens: HSNU, PE
- Region: CHINA
- Also as: P. C. Chiu

L. D. Chow

Chow, Liang Dong; 仇良栋 ; Qiú Liángdòng; 仇良棟

1929-1997 **First publication: 1975**

- Employment: Guangzhou Institute for Drug Control (广州市药品检验所)
- Research interest: Aristolochiaceae, Salicaceae [S]
- Published taxa: *Aristolochia, Salix*
- Region: CHINA (Guangdong)

X. C. Qu

Qu, Xin Cheng; 屈信成 ; Qū Xìnchéng

1966- **First publication: 2015**

- Employment: Guangxi Institute of Chinese Medicine & Pharmaceutical Science (广西中医药研究院)
- Research interest: Orchidaceae [S]
- Published taxa: *Anoectochilus*
- Region: CHINA (Guangxi)

Y. F. Qu

Qu, Yan Fei; 屈燕飞 ; Qū Yànfēi

1981- **First publication: 2009**

- Employment: College of Life Sciences, Northwest Normal University (西北师范大学生命科学学院)
- Research interest: Rosaceae [S]
- Published taxa: *Amygdalus*

- Region: CHINA (Gansu)

C. Y. Qu

Qu, Chang You; 曲畅游；Qū Chàngyóu

1966- **First publication: 2006**

- Employment: Key Laboratory of Plant Stress, Shandong Normal University; College of Life Science, Qufu Normal University（山东师范大学逆境植物重点实验室；曲阜师范大学生命科学学院）
- Research interest: Polygonaceae [S]
- Published taxa: *Polygonum*
- Region: CHINA

K. L. Chu

Chu, Kuei Ling; Ch'ü, Kuei Ling; Chu, Chung Hsiang; Ch'ü, Chung Hsiang; 曲桂龄；Qū Guìlíng 曲桂龄；曲仲湘

1905-1990 **First publication: 1938**

- Employment: Biological Laboratory of Science Society of China; Department of Botany, Institute of Biology, The Science Institute of West China（中国科学社生物研究所；中国西部科学院生物研究所植物部）
- Research interest: Cyperaceae [S]
- Published taxa: *Carex*
- Location of specimens: CQNM, PE, SCFI
- Region: CHINA
- Also as: C. H. Chu

H. Qu

Qu, Hong; 曲红；Qū Hóng

1972- **First publication: 2006**

- Employment: School of Nature Conservation, Beijing Forestry University（北京林业大学自然保护区学院）
- Research interest: Liliaceae [S]
- Published taxa: *Lilium*
- Region: CHINA (Beijing)

S. Qu

Qu, Shang; 曲上；Qū Shàng

1987- **First publication: 2018**

- Employment: Institute of Botany, Chinese Academy of Sciences（中国科学院植物研究所）
- Research interest: Cyperaceae [S]
- Published taxa: *Carex*
- Region: CHINA (Chongqing)

S. Z. Qu

Qu, Shi Zeng; Chu, Shin Tseng; Qu, Shi Ceng; 曲式曾；Qū Shìzēng

1926- **First publication: 1979**

- Employment: Northwest Forestry College（西北林学院）
- Research interest: Celastraceae, Fagaceae, Lardizabalaceae, Oleaceae, Paulowniaceae, Pinaceae, Styracaceae; Woody Plants [S]
- Published taxa: *Euonymus, Fraxinus, Paulownia, Pseudotsuga, Quercus, Sargentodoxa, Styrax, Syringa*
- Affiliation: NWFC
- Location of specimens: NWFC
- Region: CHINA (Anhui, Hubei, Shaanxi, Sichuan)
- Also as: S. C. Qu

M. H. Quan

Quan, Miao Hua; 全妙华；Quán Miàohuá

1971- **First publication: 2012**

- Employment: College of Biological and Food Engineering, Huaihua University（怀化学院生物与食品工程学院）
- Research interest: Amaryllidaceae [S]
- Published taxa: *Lycoris*
- Region: CHINA (Hunan)

C. W. Chiuan

Chiuan, Chin Wu; Quan, Zhen Wu; 全振武；Quán Zhènwǔ

1935-2019 **First publication: 1980**

- Employment: Nanyang Institute of Forestry Science, Henan（河南省南阳地区林科所）
- Research interest: Salicaceae [S]
- Published taxa: *Populus*
- Region: CHINA (Henan)

T. F. Que

Que, Tian Fu; 阙天福；Què Tiānfú

1962- **First publication: 2005**

- Employment: Shanghang County Forestry Bureau, Fujian（福建上杭县林业局）
- Research interest: Lauraceae [S]
- Published taxa: *Machilus*
- Region: CHINA (Fujian)

Z. Y. Que

Que, Zai Ying; 阙再昊；Què Zàiyīng

First publication: 1981

- Employment: Department of Forestry, Sichuan Agricultural College（四川农学院林学系）
- Research interest: Cupressaceae [S]
- Published taxa: *Cunninghamia*
- Region: CHINA (Sichuan)

G. Y. Rao

Rao, Guang Yuan; 饶广远 ; Ráo Guǎngyuǎn

1962- **First publication: 1988**

- Employment: Northwest China Institute of Botany, Chinese Academy of Sciences and Shaanxi Province; School of Life Sciences, Peking University（陕西省中国科学院西北植物研究所；北京大学生命科学学院）
- Research interest: Crassulaceae, Rosaceae [S]
- Published taxa: *Hylotelephium, Rhodiola, Sedum*
- Affiliation: PEY
- Location of specimens: PEY
- Region: CHINA

W. Y. Rao

Rao, Wei Yuan; 饶伟源 ; Ráo Wěiyuán

1963- **First publication: 1995**

- Employment: Guangxi Institute of Traditional Medical and Pharmaceutical Sciences（广西中医药研究所）
- Research interest: Gesneriaceae [S]
- Published taxa: *Paraboea*
- Location of specimens: GXMI
- Region: CHINA (Guizhou)

W. H. Rao

Rao, Wen Hui; 饶文辉 ; Ráo Wénhuī

1978- **First publication: 2010**

- Employment: The Orchid Conservation & Research Center of Shenzhen, Guangdong（广东省深圳市兰科植物保护研究中心）
- Research interest: Orchidaceae [S]
- Published taxa: *Bulbophyllum, Cheirostylis, Dendrobium, Gastrochilus, Pendulorchis*
- Affiliation: NOCC
- Location of specimens: NOCC
- Region: CHINA (Yunnan)

B. Q. Ren

Ren, Bao Qing; 任保青 ; Rén Bǎoqīng

1979- **First publication: 2014**

- Employment: Taiyuan Botanical Garden（太原植物园）
- Research interest: Betulaceae [S]
- Published taxa: *Betula*
- Region: CHINA (Hainan)

B. J. Jen

Jen, Bu Jun; Jen, P. C.; Ren, Bu Jun; **任步钧 ; Rèn Bùjūn; 任步鈞**

1938- **First publication: 1980**

- Employment: Forest Botanical Garden of Heilongjiang Province（黑龙江省森林植物园）
- Research interest: Rosaceae [S]
- Published taxa: *Crataegus, Spiraea*
- Affiliation: HFBG
- Location of specimens: HFBG
- Region: CHINA (Heilongjiang)
- Also as: P. C. Jen

C. Ren

Ren, Chen; 任琛 ; Rén Chēn

1983- **First publication: 2014**

- Employment: South China Botanical Garden, Chinese Academy of Sciences（中国科学院华南植物园）
- Research interest: Asteraceae [S]
- Published taxa: *Cissampelopsis, Cremanthodium, Japonicalia, Parasenecio, Senecio, Synotis, Taimingasa*
- Affiliation: IBSC
- Region: [ASIA]

J. W. Ren

Ren, Ji Wen; 任继文 ; Rén Jìwén

1964- **First publication: 1996**

- Employment: Gansu Forestry Technological College（甘肃林业职业技术学院）
- Research interest: Apocynaceae, Celastraceae; Plants of Gansu [S]
- Published taxa: *Euonymus, Periploca*
- Affiliation: GSFS
- Location of specimens: GSFS
- Region: CHINA (Gansu)

J. Z. Ren

Ren, Jin Zhou; 任进舟 ; Rén Jìnzhōu

First publication: 1987

- Employment: Herbarium, Nanjing Pharmaceutical College（南京药学院标本室）
- Research interest: Liliaceae; Medicinal Plants [S]
- Published taxa: *Fritillaria*
- Affiliation: CPU
- Region: CHINA (Gansu)

M. X. Ren

Ren, Ming Xun; 任明讯 ; Rén Míngxùn

1976- **First publication: 2019**

- Employment: College of Horticulture and Landscape Architecture, Hainan University（海南大学园艺园林学院）
- Research interest: Celastraceae, Gesneriaceae, Malpighiaceae; Plant Evolution [S]
- Published taxa: *Hiptage, Oreocharis, Parnassia*
- Affiliation: HUTB
- Location of specimens: HUTB
- Region: CHINA (Chongqing, Yunnan)

S. X. Ren

Ren, Shan Xiang; 任善相 ; Rén Shànxiāng

1920- **First publication: 1991**

- Employment: Department of Biology, Sun Yat-sen University（中山大学生物系）
- Research interest: Cannabaceae, Theaceae; Plants of S. China [S]
- Published taxa: *Camellia, Trema, Tutcheria*
- Affiliation: SYS
- Region: CHINA

H. W. Jen

Jen, Hsien Wei; Ren, Xian Wei; **任宪威 ; Rén Xiànwēi; 任憲威**

1928-1997 **First publication: 1975**

- Employment: College of Resources and Environment, Beijing Forestry University（北京林业大学森林资源与环境学院）
- Research interest: Fabaceae, Fagaceae, Lamiaceae, Pinaceae [S]
- Published taxa: *Astragalus, Castanopsis, Cyclobalanopsis, Elsholtzia, Lithocarpus, Picea, Quercus, Scutellaria, Vitex*
- Affiliation: BJFC
- Location of specimens: BJFC
- Region: CHINA

Y. Ren

Ren, Yi; 任毅 ; Rén Yì

1959-2019 **First publication: 1992**

- Employment: College of Life Sciences, Northwest University; College of Life Sciences, Shaanxi Normal University（西北大学生命科学学院；陕西师范大学生命科学学院）
- Research interest: Adoxaceae, Araliaceae, Hypericaceae, Pittosporaceae, Poaceae, Ranunculaceae [S]
- Published taxa: *Bashania, Hydrocotyle, Hypericum, Pittosporum, Viburnum*
- Affiliation: SANU, WNU
- Location of specimens: SANU, WNU
- Region: CHINA (Shaanxi)

Y. H. Ren

Ren, Yun He; 任云和 ; Rén Yúnhé; 任雲和

1937- **First publication: 1983**

- Employment: Nanzhao County Forestry Bureau, Henan（河南省南召县林业局）
- Research interest: Magnoliaceae [S]
- Published taxa: *Magnolia*
- Region: CHINA (Henan)

Z. X. Ren

Ren, Zong Xin; 任宗昕 ; Rén Zōngxīn

1982- **First publication: 2011**

- Employment: Kunming Institute of Botany, Chinese Academy of Sciences（中国科学院昆明植物研究所）
- Research interest: Orchidaceae [S]
- Published taxa: *Calanthe*
- Region: CHINA (Yunnan)

Z. Z. Ru

Ru, Zheng Zhong; 茹正忠 ; Rú Zhèngzhōng

1957- **First publication: 2006**

- Employment: Shenzhen City Wutongshan Nurseries, Guangdong（广东省深圳市梧桐山苗圃总场）
- Research interest: Orchidaceae [S]
- Published taxa: *Phalaenopsis*
- Region: CHINA (Sichuan)

Y. Z. Ruan

Ruan, Yun Zhen; 阮云珍 ; Ruǎn Yúnzhēn; 阮雲珍

1936- **First publication: 1981**

- Employment: South China Institute of Botany, Chinese Academy of Sciences（中国科学院华南植物研究所）
- Research interest: Droseraceae, Nepenthaceae, Rubiaceae [S]
- Published taxa: *Damnacanthus, Drosera, Morinda, Prismatomeris*
- Affiliation: IBSC
- Region: CHINA

R. Sa

Sa, Ren; Sha, Ren; **萨仁 ; Sà Rén**

1972- **First publication: 1996**

- Employment: Department of Ecology and Environmental Science, Inner Mongolia University; Institute of Botany, Chinese Academy of Sciences（内蒙古大学生态与环境科学系；中国科学院植物研究所）
- Research interest: Fabaceae [S]
- Published taxa: *Dumasia, Erythrina, Hedysarum, Mucuna*
- Affiliation: PE
- Region: CHINA
- IPNI as: R. Sha

Sayit

Sayit, Abdukerim; 萨依提·阿布都克里木；Sàyītí Ābùdūkèlǐmù

First publication: 1991

- Employment: Xinjiang Institute of Biology, Pedology and Desert Research, Chinese Academy of Sciences（中国科学院新疆生物土壤沙漠研究所）
- Research interest: Caprifoliaceae [S]
- Published taxa: *Cephalaria*
- Region: CHINA (Xinjiang)

W. L. Sha

Sha, Wen Lan; 沙文兰；Shā Wénlán

1935- First publication: 1981

- Employment: Guangxi Research Centre of Natural Materia Medica（广西天然药物研究中心）
- Research interest: Celastraceae, Colchicaceae, Fabaceae, Linaceae, Primulaceae, Rubiaceae [S]
- Published taxa: *Disporum, Gueldenstaedtia, Lysimachia, Maytenus, Ophiorrhiza, Spiradiclis, Tirpitzia, Uraria*
- Region: CHINA (Guangxi)

J. L. Shan

Shan, Jia Lin; 单家林；Shàn Jiālín

1964- First publication: 1999

- Employment: South China University of Tropical Agriculture（华南热带农业大学）
- Research interest: Cleomaceae [S]
- Published taxa: *Cleome*
- Region: CHINA (Hainan)

R. H. Shan

Shan, Ren Hwa; Shan, Jên Hua; Shan, Ren Hua; 单人骅；Shàn Rénhuá; 單人驊

1909-1986 First publication: 1936

- Employment: National Institute of Zoology and Botany, Academia Sinica; National Institute of Botany, Academia Sinica; Nanjing Botanical Garden Mem. Sun Yat-Sen, Institute of Botany, Chinese Academy of Sciences; Nanjing Botanical Garden Mem. Sun Yat-Sen, Chinese Academy of Sciences; Nanjing Institute of Botany, Chinese Academy of Sciences; Institute of Botany, Jiangsu Province（国立中央研究院动植物研究所；国立中央研究院植物研究所；中国科学院植物研究所南京中山植物园；中国科学院南京中山植物园；中国科学院南京植物研究所；江苏省植物研究所）
- Research interest: Apiaceae, Araliaceae [S]
- Published taxa: *Acronema, Angelica, Arcuatopterus, Bupleurum, Carum, Chamaesciadium, Chamaesium, Chuanminshen, Cortiella, Cyclorhiza, Eriocycla, Ferula, Harrysmithia, Heracleum, Hydrocotyle, Libanotis, Ligusticum, Nothosmyrnium, Notopterygium, Osmorhiza, Ostericum, Pachypleurum, Peucedanum, Physospermopsis, Pimpinella, Pleurospermum, Pternopetalum, Sanicula, Seseli, Sinocarum, Sinolimprichtia, Trachydium, Vicatia*
- Affiliation: NAS
- Location of specimens: NAS
- Region: CHINA
- IPNI as: R. H. Shen

H. Shang

Shang, Hui; 商辉；Shāng Huī

1986- First publication: 2015

- Employment: Shanghai Chenshan Botanical Garden（上海辰山植物园）
- Research interest: Dennstaedtiaceae, Dryopteridaceae; Pteridophytes [P]
- Published taxa: *Dryopteris, Hiya*
- Affiliation: CSH
- Location of specimens: CSH
- Region: [AISA]

C. Shang

Shang, Ce; 尚策；Shàng Cè

1988- First publication: 2016

- Employment: School of Nature Conservation, Beijing Forestry University（北京林业大学自然保护区学院）
- Research interest: Salicaceae, Thymelaeaceae [S]
- Published taxa: *Dianyuea, Populus, Wikstroemia*
- Location of specimens: BJFC
- Region: CHINA

F. J. Shang

Shang, Fang Jian; 尚方剑；Shàng Fāngjiàn

1988- First publication: 2016

- Employment: School of Landscape Architecture, Northeast Forestry University（东北林业大学园林学院）
- Research interest: Iridaceae [S]
- Published taxa: *Iris*
- Region: CHINA (Heilongjiang)

Z. Y. Shang

Shang, Zong Yan; 尚宗燕 ; Shàng Zōngyàn

1976- **First publication: 1985**

- Employment: Xi' an Botanical Garden, Shaanxi（陕西省西安植物园）
- Research interest: Anacardiaceae [S]
- Published taxa: *Toxicodendron*
- Region: CHINA (Shaanxi)

H. Shao

Shao, Hong; 邵宏 ; Shào Hóng

1964- **First publication: 1994**

- Employment: Department of Biology and Genetics, Beijing Medical University（北京医科大学生物遗传教研室）
- Research interest: Celastraceae, Gnetaceae [S]
- Published taxa: *Gnetum, Maytenus*
- Region: CHINA

J. X. Shao

Shao, Ji Xing; 邵际兴 ; Shào Jìxīng; 邵際興

1941-? **First publication: 1987**

- Employment: Baishuijiang Natural Reserve Administrative Bureau, Gansu（甘肃白水江自然保护区管理局）
- Research interest: Poaceae [S]
- Published taxa: *Fargesia*
- Region: CHINA (Gansu)

J. R. Shao

Shao, Ji Rong; 邵继荣 ; Shào Jìróng

1958- **First publication: 2011**

- Employment: College of Life Sciences, Sichuan Agricultural University（四川农业大学生命科学学院）
- Research interest: Polygonaceae [S]
- Published taxa: *Fagopyrum*
- Region: CHINA (Sichuan)

J. C. Shao

Shao, Jian Chu; 邵建初 ; Shào Jiànchū

1953- **First publication: 2009**

- Employment: Xinjiang Uygur Autonomous Region Institute for Food and Drug Control（新疆维吾尔自治区食品药品检验所）
- Research interest: Papaveraceae [S]
- Published taxa: *Papaver*
- Region: CHINA (Xinjiang)

J. Z. Shao

Shao, Jian Zhang; Shao, Chian Zhang; 邵建章 ; Shào Jiànzhāng

1937- **First publication: 1986**

- Employment: Anhui Normal University（安徽师范大学）
- Research interest: Asparagaceae, Brassicaceae, Caryophyllaceae, Liliaceae, Primulaceae, Rosaceae, Thymelaeaceae, Violaceae [S]
- Published taxa: *Cardamine, Cochlearia, Daphne, Fritillaria, Lilium, Polygonatum, Rosa, Stimpsonia, Wikstroemia*
- Affiliation: ANUB
- Location of specimens: ANUB
- Region: CHINA (Anhui)
- Also as: C. Z. Shao

J. W. Shao

Shao, Jian Wen; 邵剑文 ; Shào Jiànwén

1975- **First publication: 2004**

- Employment: College of Life Sciences, Anhui Normal University（安徽师范大学生命科学学院）
- Research interest: Primulaceae; Plants of Anhui [S]
- Published taxa: *Lysimachia, Primula*
- Affiliation: ANUB
- Location of specimens: ANUB
- Region: CHINA (Anhui)

Q. Q. Shao

Shao, Qi Quan; 邵启全 ; Shào Qǐquán

1932- **First publication: 1981**

- Employment: Institute of Genetics, Academia Sinica（中国科学院遗传研究所）
- Research interest: Poaceae [S]
- Published taxa: *Hordeum*
- Region: CHINA (Xizang)

W. Shao

Shao, Wen; 邵文 ; Shào Wén

1979- **First publication: 2011**

- Employment: School of Life Sciences, Yunnan University; Shanghai Chenshan Botanical Garden（云南大学生命科学学院；上海辰山植物园）
- Research interest: Polypodiaceae [P]
- Published taxa: *Himalayopteris*
- Region: CHINA (Yunnan)

W. H. Shao

Shao, Wen Hao; 邵文豪 ; Shào Wénháo

1981- **First publication: 2007**

- Employment: Research Institute of Subtropical Forestry, Chinese Academy of Forestry（中国林业科学研究院亚热带林业研究所）
- Research interest: Rosaceae [S]
- Published taxa: *Malus*
- Region: CHINA (Shandong)

C. W. She

She, Chao Wen; 佘朝文 ; Shé Cháowén

1964- **First publication: 2013**
- Employment: College of Biological and Food Engineering, Huaihua University（怀化学院生物与食品工程学院）
- Research interest: Amaryllidaceae [S]
- Published taxa: *Lycoris*
- Region: CHINA (Hunan)

M. L. Sheh

Sheh, Men Lan; She, Meng Lan; 佘孟兰；Shé Mènglán; 佘孟蘭

1925- **First publication: 1979**
- Employment: Institute of Botany, Jiangsu Province（江苏省植物研究所）
- Research interest: Apiaceae, Araliaceae [S]
- Published taxa: *Arcuatopterus, Bupleurum, Chuanminshen, Cortiella, Cyclorhiza, Harrysmithia, Heracleum, Hydrocotyle, Libanotis, Ligusticum, Notopterygium, Peucedanum, Sanicula, Selinum, Seseli*
- Affiliation: NAS
- Location of specimens: NAS
- Region: CHINA
- Also as: Sheh; • IPNI as: M. G. Sheh

J. Y. Shen

Shen, Jian Yong; 申健勇；Shēn Jiànyǒng

1986- **First publication: 2018**
- Employment: Xishuangbanna Tropical Botanical Garden, Chinese Academy of Sciences（中国科学院西双版纳热带植物园）
- Research interest: Apocynaceae, Aristolochiaceae, Begoniaceae, Celastraceae, Passifloraceae [S]
- Published taxa: *Aristolochia, Begonia, Cynanchum, Passiflora, Salacia*
- Region: CHINA (Yunnan)

B. A. Shen

Shen, Bao An; 沈保安；Shěn Bǎo'ān

1957- **First publication: 1987**
- Employment: Wuhu Institute for Drug Control, Anhui（安徽省芜湖市药品检验所）
- Research interest: Campanulaceae, Convolvulaceae, Paeoniaceae [S]
- Published taxa: *Asyneuma, Merremia, Paeonia*
- Region: CHINA (Anhui)

C. D. Shen

Shen, Chao Dong; 沈朝栋；Shěn Cháodòng

1963- **First publication: 1997**
- Employment: Faculty of Botany, Zhejiang Agricultural University（浙江农业大学植物教研室）
- Research interest: Smilacaceae; Woody Plants [S]
- Published taxa: *Smilax*
- Affiliation: HZU, ZAU
- Location of specimens: HZU, ZAU
- Region: CHINA (Guizhou)

C. Q. Shen

Shen, Cheng Quan; 沈承权；Shěn Chéngquán

First publication: 1991
- Employment: Nanchong Institute of Forest Science, Sichuan（四川南充地区林科所）
- Research interest: Poaceae [S]
- Published taxa: *Phyllostachys*
- Region: CHINA (Sichuan)

C. Z. Shen

Shen, Chu Ze; 沈初泽；Shěn Chūzé

1990- **First publication: 2020**
- Employment: College of Life Sciences, Beijing Normal University（北京师范大学生命科学学院）
- Research interest: Asteraceae [S]
- Published taxa: *Chrysanthemum*
- Region: CHINA (Hubei, Hunan)

K. M. Shen

Shen, Kuan Mien; Shen, Guan Mian; 沈观冕；Shěn Guānmiǎn; 沈觀冕

1935-2017 **First publication: 1975**
- Employment: Xinjiang Institute of Biology, Pedology and Desert Research; Xinjiang Institute of Ecology and Geography, Chinese Academy of Sciences（新疆生物土壤沙漠研究所；中国科学院新疆生态与地理研究所）
- Research interest: Apiaceae, Asteraceae, Polygonaceae [S]
- Published taxa: *Calligonum, Ferula, Saussurea*
- Affiliation: XJBI
- Location of specimens: XJBI
- Region: CHINA (Xinjiang)
- Also as: G. M. Shen

H. M. Shen

Shen, Hong Mei; 沈红梅；Shěn Hóngméi

1966- **First publication: 1994**
- Employment: College of Pharmacy, Second Military Medical University（第二军医大学药学院）
- Research interest: Rosaceae [S]
- Published taxa: *Armeniaca*
- Region: CHINA (Yunnan)

L. D. Shen

Shen, Lian De; Shen, Lian Te; 沈联德；Shěn Liándé; 沈聯德

1930-2010 **First publication: 1970**
- Employment: Department of Pharmacy, Sichuan Medical College（四川医学院药学系）

- Research interest: Campanulaceae, Cucurbitaceae; Medicinal Plants [S]
- Published taxa: *Codonopsis, Hemsleya*
- Affiliation: WCU
- Location of specimens: WCU
- Region: CHINA (Sichuan)

R. J. Shen

Shen, Ru Jiang; 沈如江 ; Shěn Rújiāng
1980- **First publication: 2010**
- Employment: School of Life Sciences, Sun Yat-sen University（中山大学生命科学学院）
- Research interest: Gesneriaceae [S]
- Published taxa: *Chiritopsis*
- Region: CHINA (Guangdong)

S. D. Shen

Shen, Shu Duan; 沈淑端 ; Shěn Shūduān
First publication: 2001
- Employment: Department of Life Science, Taiwan Normal University（台湾师范大学生命科学系）
- Research interest: Boraginaceae [S]
- Published taxa: *Trigonotis*
- Region: CHINA (Taiwan)

X. S. Shen

Shen, Xian Sheng; 沈显生 ; Shěn Xiǎnshēng
1956- **First publication: 1989**
- Employment: Anhui College of Education; School of Life Sciences, University of Science and Technology of China（安徽教育学院；中国科学技术大学生命科学学院）
- Research interest: Asteraceae, Hydrocharitaceae, Liliaceae, Oxalidaceae, Poaceae, Vitaceae [S]
- Published taxa: *Lactuca, Oxalis, Sporobolus, Tulipa, Vallisneria, Vitis*
- Affiliation: ACE
- Location of specimens: ACE
- Region: CHINA (Anhui)

X. L. Shen

Shen, Xiang Lin; 沈湘林 ; Shěn Xiānglín
1956- **First publication: 1992**
- Employment: Huzhou Forestry Science and Technology Institute, Zhejiang（浙江省湖州市林业科学研究所）
- Research interest: Fagaceae [S]
- Published taxa: *Quercus*
- Region: CHINA (Zhejiang)

Xiao L. Shen

Shen Xiao Lin; 沈晓琳 ; Shěn Xiǎolín
1975- **First publication: 2015**
- Employment: Guangxi Institute of Botany, Chinese Academy of Sciences（广西壮族自治区中国科学院广西植物研究所）
- Research interest: Dryopteridaceae [P]
- Published taxa: *Polystichum*
- Region: CHINA (Guangxi)

Y. G. Shen

Shen, Yun Guang; 沈云光 ; Shěn Yúnguāng
1973- **First publication: 2004**
- Employment: Kunming Institute of Botany, Chinese Academy of Sciences（中国科学院昆明植物研究所）
- Research interest: Iridaceae [S]
- Published taxa: *Iris*
- Region: CHINA (Yunnan)

Z. H. Shen

Shen, Ze Hao; 沈泽昊 ; Shěn Zéhào
1968- **First publication: 2005**
- Employment: College of Environmental Sciences, Peking University（北京大学环境学院）
- Research interest: Caryophyllaceae [S]
- Published taxa: *Arenaria*
- Region: CHINA (Hubei)

C. F. Shen

Shen, Chung Fu; Shen, Zhong Fu; **沈中桴 ; Shěn Zhōngfú**
1957- **First publication: 1994**
- Employment: Department of Forestry, Taiwan University（台湾大学森林学系）
- Research interest: Cycadaceae, Fagaceae [S]
- Published taxa: *Castanopsis, Cycas, Lithocarpus, Quercus*
- Region: CHINA (Taiwan)

Z. A. Shen

Shen, Zu An; 沈祖安 ; Shěn Zǔ'ān
1927- **First publication: 1984**
- Employment: Department of Biology, Anhui University（安徽大学生物系）
- Research interest: Lamiaceae, Lauraceae, Poaceae [S]
- Published taxa: *Salvia*
- Affiliation: ANU
- Location of specimens: ANU
- Region: CHINA (Anhui)

G. Y. Sheng

Sheng, Guo Ying; 盛国英 ; Shèng Guóyīng; 盛國英
1936- **First publication: 1981**
- Employment: Institute of Botany, Jiangsu Province; Institute of Botany, Jiangsu Province and Chinese Academy of Sciences（江苏省植物研究所；江苏省中国科学院植物研究所）
- Research interest: Lamiaceae, Poaceae [S]

- Published taxa: *Ampelocalamus, Clerodendrum, Dimeria, Pleioblastus, Pogonatherum, Pseudosasa, Setaria*
- Affiliation: NAS
- Region: CHINA

M. Y. Sheng

Sheng, Mao Yin; 盛茂银 ; Shèng Màoyín

1980- **First publication: 2011**

- Employment: School of Life Sciences, Nanjing University (南京大学生命科学学院)
- Research interest: Berberidaceae [S]
- Published taxa: *Epimedium*
- Region: CHINA (Guizhou)

B. L. Shih

Shih, Bing Ling; Shi, Bing Lin; **施炳霖 ; Shī Bǐnglín**

First publication: 1995

- Employment: Department of Biological Sciences, Sun Yat-sen University, Taiwan (台湾中山大学生物科学系)
- Research interest: Urticaceae [S]
- Published taxa: *Boehmeria, Boehmeria, Dendrocnide, Elatostema, Pilea*
- Region: CHINA (Taiwan)

S. Shi

Shi, Shi; 施诗 ; Shī Shī

1988- **First publication: 2015**

- Employment: School of Life Sciences, Sun Yat-sen University (中山大学生命科学学院)
- Research interest: Aquifoliaceae [S]
- Published taxa: *Ilex*
- Region: CHINA (Jiangxi)

S. H. Shi

Shi, Su Hua; 施苏华 ; Shī Sūhuá

1956- **First publication: 1990**

- Employment: School of Life Sciences, Sun Yat-sen University (中山大学生命科学学院)
- Research interest: Asteraceae, Lindsaeaceae, Pentaphylacaceae, Thelypteridaceae [S]
- Published taxa: *Cleyera, Lindsaea, Packera, Pronephrium, Ternstroemia*
- Region: CHINA

W. L. Shih

Shih, Wen Liang; Shi, Wen Liang; **施文良 ; Shī Wénliáng**

First publication: 1976

- Employment: Pharmaceutical Standards Office, Yunnan (云南省药品标准办公室)
- Research interest: Gentianaceae [S]
- Published taxa: *Anagallidium, Swertia*
- Location of specimens: YIM
- Region: CHINA (Yunnan)

X. C. Shi

Shi, Xiao Chun; 施晓春 ; Shī Xiǎochūn

1970- **First publication: 2002**

- Employment: Baoshan Administrative Bureau of Gaoligong Mountain National Nature Reserve, Yunnan (云南省高黎贡山国家级自然保护区保山管理局)
- Research interest: Araliaceae, Orchidaceae [S]
- Published taxa: *Aralia, Cymbidium, Pendulorchis*
- Region: CHINA (Yunnan)

Y. L. Shi

Shi, You Li; 施有立 ; Shī Yǒulì

First publication: 1990

- Employment: Anhui College of Traditional Chinese Medicine (安徽中医学院)
- Research interest: Crassulaceae [S]
- Published taxa: *Sedum*
- Region: CHINA (Anhui)

F. C. Shi

Shi, Fu Chen; 石福臣 ; Shí Fúchén

1966- **First publication: 2006**

- Employment: Northeast Forestry University; College of Life Sciences, Nankai University (东北林业大学 ; 南开大学生命科学学院)
- Research interest: Fabaceae; Plant Ecology [S]
- Published taxa: *Caragana*
- Affiliation: NKU
- Region: CHINA

J. L. Shi

Shi, Jin Li; 石晋丽 ; Shí Jìnlì

1967- **First publication: 1995**

- Employment: Department of Chinese Materia Medica, Beijing University of Chinese Medicine (北京中医药大学中药系)
- Research interest: Lamiaceae [S]
- Published taxa: *Mosla*
- Region: CHINA (Jiangxi)

L. Shi

Shi, Lei; 石雷 ; Shí Léi

1967- **First publication: 1994**

- Employment: Institute of Botany, Chinese Academy of Sciences (中国科学院植物研究所)
- Research interest: Polypodiaceae, Pteridaceae [P]
- Published taxa: *Aleuritopteris, Colysis, Lepidomicrosorium, Microsorum, Neolepisorus*
- Region: CHINA

X. G. Shi

Shi, Xiang Gang; 石祥刚 ; Shí Xiánggāng

1978- **First publication: 2005**

- Employment: School of Life Sciences, Sun Yat-sen University（中山大学生命科学学院）
- Research interest: Gesneriaceae, Pentaphylacaceae, Theaceae; Plants of S. China [S]
- Published taxa: *Camellia, Didymostigma, Eurya*
- Affiliation: SYS
- Location of specimens: SYS
- Region: CHINA

C. N. Shih

Shih, Chi Nong; Schih, Chi Nong; 石植农；Shí Zhínóng; 石植農

First publication: 1957

- Research interest: Orobanchaceae [S]
- Published taxa: *Rehmannia*
- Region: CHINA

C. Shih

Shih, Chu; Shi, Zhu; 石铸；Shí Zhù; 石鑄

1934-2005 **First publication: 1963**

- Employment: Institute of Botany, Chinese Academy of Sciences（中国科学院植物研究所）
- Research interest: Actinidiaceae, Asteraceae, Euphorbiaceae [S]
- Published taxa: *Ajania, Ajaniopsis, Alfredia, Anaphalis, Brachanthemum, Cancrinia, Centaurea, Cephalorrhynchus, Chaetoseris, Cicerbita, Cirsium, Clematoclethra, Cousinia, Crepis, Dendranthema, Diplazoptilon, Dolomiaea, Dubyaea, Echinops, Eupatorium, Faberia, Faberiopsis, Hippolytia, Ixeridium, Ixeris, Jurinea, Mulgedium, Myriactis, Nabalus, Notoseris, Opisthopappus, Paraixeris, Paraprenanthes, Prenanthes, Pterocypsela, Pyrethrum, Saussurea, Scorzonera, Sonchus, Soroseris, Stenoseris, Stilpnolepis, Symphyllia, Syncalathium, Vladimiria, Youngia*
- Affiliation: PE
- Region: CHINA

S. D. Shi

Shi, Sheng De; 时圣德；Shí Shèngdé; 時聖德

1938- **First publication: 1994**

- Employment: Guizhou Botanical Garden（贵州省植物园）
- Research interest: Actinidiaceae [S]
- Published taxa: *Actinidia*
- Region: CHINA (Guizhou)

C. D. Shi

Shi, Chuan Duo; 史传铎；ShǐChuánduó; 史傳鐸

1937- **First publication: 1999**

- Employment: Shandong Institute of Pomology（山东省果树研究所）
- Research interest: Rosaceae [S]
- Published taxa: *Cerasus*
- Region: CHINA (Shandong)

J. H. Shi

Shi, Jing Hua; 史京华；Shǐ Jīnghuá

1979- **First publication: 2005**

- Employment: Institute of Botany, Chinese Academy of Sciences（中国科学院植物研究所）
- Research interest: Ranunculaceae [S]
- Published taxa: *Clematis*
- Region: CHINA (Xizang)

J. Y. Shi

Shi, Jun Yi; 史军义；Shǐ Jūnyì

1958- **First publication: 2005**

- Employment: Flower Research and Development Center of Southwest China, Chinese Academy of Forestry（中国林业科学研究院西南花卉研究开发中心）
- Research interest: Poaceae [S]
- Published taxa: *Bashania, Chimonocalamus, Fargesia, Indocalamus, Lingnania, Thamnocalamus, Yushania*
- Region: CHINA

W. T. Shi

Shi, Wen Tsun; 史文俊；Shǐ Wénjùn

1935- **First publication: 1984**

- Employment: Ji'an Institute of Forestry Science, Jiangxi（江西省吉安市林业科学研究所）
- Research interest: Theaceae [S]
- Published taxa: *Camellia*
- Region: CHINA (Jiangxi)

Z. J. Shi

Shi, Zheng Jun; 史正军；Shǐ Zhèngjūn

1979- **First publication: 2019**

- Employment: Southwest Forestry University（西南林业大学）
- Research interest: Poaceae [S]
- Published taxa: *Dendrocalamus*
- Region: CHINA (Yunnan)

W. S. Shu

Shu, Wen Sheng; 束文圣；Shù Wénshèng

1968- **First publication: 2003**

- Employment: School of Life Sciences, Sun Yat-sen University（中山大学生命科学学院）
- Research interest: Violaceae [S]
- Published taxa: *Viola*
- Region: CHINA (Hunan)

Y. M. Shui

Shui, Yu Min; 税玉民；Shuì Yùmín

1966- **First publication: 1994**

- Employment: Yunnan Forestry School; Department of Biology, Yunnan University; Kunming Institute of Botany, Chinese Academy of Sciences（云南省林业学校；云南大学生物系；中国科学院昆明植物研究所）
- Research interest: Acanthaceae, Annonaceae, Araliaceae, Asparagaceae, Balsaminaceae, Begoniaceae, Celastraceae, Connaraceae, Cornaceae, Cycadaceae, Gesneriaceae, Lauraceae, Magnoliaceae, Melanthiaceae, Melastomataceae, Orchidaceae, Orobanchaceae, Polygalaceae, Primulaceae, Rubiaceae, Schisandraceae, Sladeniaceae, Thymelaeaceae, Urticaceae [S]
- Published taxa: *Alseodaphne, Amitostigma, Ancylostemon, Anoectochilus, Begonia, Connarus, Cornus, Cycas, Daphne, Didymocarpus, Elatostema, Goniothalamus, Helonias, Hemiboea, Impatiens, Lindenbergia, Litostigma, Loxostigma, Lysimachia, Magnolia, Manglietia, Michelia, Microtropis, Oreocharis, Oxyspora, Paraboea, Pararuellia, Peliosanthes, Pentapanax, Petrocodon, Petrocosmea, Polygala, Ponerorchis, Raphiocarpus, Ridsdalea, Rothmannia, Rourea, Santaloides, Schisandra, Sladenia, Spiradiclis, Thrixspermum, Tremacron, Ypsilandra*
- Affiliation: KUN, YFS
- Location of specimens: KUN, YCP, YFS
- Region: CHINA (Yunnan)

Sima

Sima, Yong Keng; Sima, Yong Kang; 司马永康；Sīmǎ Yǒngkāng

1967- **First publication: 2001**

- Employment: Yunnan Academy of Forestry（云南省林业科学院）
- Research interest: Cephalotaxaceae, Magnoliaceae, Orchidaceae [S]
- Published taxa: *Aromadendron, Cremastra, Dugandiodendron, Houpoea, Lirianthe, Magnolia, Manglietia, Metamagnolia, Michelia, Pachylarnax, Paramagnolia, Yulania*
- Affiliation: YCP
- Location of specimens: YAF, YCP
- Region: CHINA (Yunnan)

C. Song

Song, Chao; 宋超；Sòng Chāo

1978- **First publication: 2008**

- Employment: Zhejiang Sci-Tech University（浙江理工大学）
- Research interest: Cyperaceae [S]
- Published taxa: *Carex*
- Region: CHINA (Zhejiang)

G. Q. Song

Song, Gui Qing; 宋桂卿；Sòng Guìqīng

1941- **First publication: 1994**

- Employment: Department of Biology, Nanjing University（南京大学生物系）
- Research interest: Poaceae [S]
- Published taxa: *Poa*
- Affiliation: N
- Region: CHINA

W. C. Sung

Sung, Wan Chih; Song, Wan Zhi; 宋万志；Sòng Wànzhì; 宋萬志

1933- **First publication: 1974**

- Employment: Institute of Materia Medica, Chinese Academy of Medical Sciences（中国医学科学院药物研究所）
- Research interest: Berberidaceae, Schisandraceae [S]
- Published taxa: *Berberis*
- Affiliation: IMM
- Region: CHINA

X. Q. Song

Song, Xi Qiang; 宋希强；Sòng Xīqiáng

1972- **First publication: 2008**

- Employment: Institute of Botany, Chinese Academy of Sciences（中国科学院植物研究所）
- Research interest: Orchidaceae [S]
- Published taxa: *Gastrodia, Thrixspermum*
- Region: CHINA (Sichuan)

X. H. Song

Song, Xiang Hou; 宋祥后；Sòng Xiánghòu

1955- **First publication: 1984**

- Employment: Department of Forestry, Nanjing Forestry College（南京林学院林学系）
- Research interest: Altingiaceae, Lauraceae, Magnoliaceae, Oleaceae, Putranjivaceae, Rhamnaceae [S]
- Published taxa: *Altingia, Cryptocarya, Drypetes, Machilus, Manglietia, Osmanthus, Rhamnus*
- Location of specimens: NF
- Region: CHINA

Y. Song

Song, Yi; 宋颐；Sòng Yí

First publication: 2011

- Employment: Institute of Botany, University of Neuchâtel, Switzerland（瑞士纳沙泰尔大学生物研究所）
- Research interest: Balsaminaceae [S]
- Published taxa: *Impatiens*
- Region: CHINA (Sichuan)

Yu Song bis

Song, Yu; 宋钰; Sòng Yù

First publication: 2020

- Employment: Xishuangbanna Tropical Botanical Garden, Chinese Academy of Sciences (中国科学院西双版纳热带植物园)
- Research interest: Lauraceae [S]
- Published taxa: *Neocinnamomeae*
- Region: CHINA (Yunnan)

Z. Q. Song

Song, Zhu Qiu; 宋柱秋; Sòng Zhùqiū

1985- **First publication: 2014**

- Employment: Administrative Bureau of Dinghushan National Nature Reserve, South China Botanical Garden, Chinese Academy of Sciences; South China Botanical Garden, Chinese Academy of Sciences (中国科学院华南植物园鼎湖山国家级自然保护区管理局; 中国科学院华南植物园)
- Research interest: Fabaceae, Rubiaceae [S]
- Published taxa: *Cladrastis, Foonchewia, Millettia, Mycetia*
- Affiliation: GXNM
- Location of specimens: GXNM
- Region: CHINA

Soong

Soong, Tse Pu; Soong, Tze Pu; Song, Zi Pu; 宋滋圃; Sòng Zīpǔ

1925-2008 **First publication: 1975**

- Employment: Department of Biology, Sichuan University (四川大学生物系)
- Research interest: Alangiaceae, Amaranthaceae, Berberidaceae, Garryaceae, Gesneriaceae, Helwingiaceae, Nyssaceae, Sapindaceae [S]
- Published taxa: *Acer, Acroglochin, Aucuba, Axyris, Camptotheca, Didymocarpus, Helwingia, Mahonia, Mastixia, Nyssa*
- Affiliation: SZ
- Location of specimens: SZ
- Region: CHINA (Sichuan)
- Also as: Z. P. Soong; Z. P. Song

Su

Institute of Botany, Jiangsu Province and Chinese Academy of Sciences; Jiang Su Zhi Wu Suo; Su 苏 Sū

First publication: 1982

- Employment: Institute of Botany, Jiangsu Province and Chinese Academy of Sciences (江苏省中国科学院植物研究所)
- Research interest: Apiaceae [S]
- Published taxa: *Ferula*
- Region: CHINA (Jiangsu)
- Organization

H. J. Su

Su, Horng Jye; Su, Hong Ji; Su, Hung Chieh; 蘇鴻傑; Sū Hóngjié; 苏鸿杰

1943-2020 **First publication: 1971**

- Employment: Herbarium, Department of Forestry, Taiwan University (台湾大学森林学系腊叶标本馆)
- Research interest: Orchidaceae, Rosaceae. [MS]
- Published taxa: *Androcorys, Cephalantheropsis, Cirrhopetalum, Cymbidium, Epipactis, Goodyera, Hippeophyllum, Hylophila, Liparis, Listera, Phaius, Photinia, Ponerorchis, Trichoglottis, Tulotis*
- Affiliation: NTUF
- Location of specimens: NTUF
- Region: CHINA (Taiwan)

Hong Y. Su

Su, Hong Yan; 苏鸿雁; Sū Hóngyàn

1967- **First publication: 2000**

- Employment: Department of Biology, Dali Teachers' College (云南大理师范高等专科学校生物系)
- Research interest: Lamiaceae [S]
- Published taxa: *Clinopodium*
- Region: CHINA (Yunnan)

J. X. Su

Su, Jun Xia; 苏俊霞; Sū Jùnxiá

1974- **First publication: 2012**

- Employment: School of Life Science, Shanxi Normal University; Institute of Botany, Chinese Academy of Sciences (山西师范大学生命科学学院; 中国科学院植物研究所)
- Research interest: Brassicaceae, Resedaceae [S]
- Published taxa: *Borthwickia*
- Affiliation: LINF
- Location of specimens: LINF
- Region: CHINA (Yunnan)

L. Y. Su

Su, Lan Ying; 苏兰英; Sū Lányīng

1990- **First publication: 2019**

- Employment: Guangxi Normal University; Guangxi Institute of Botany, Chinese Academy of Sciences (广西师范大学; 广西壮族自治区中国科学院广西植物研究所)
- Research interest: Gesneriaceae [S]
- Published taxa: *Petrocodon*
- Region: CHINA (Taiwan)

L. Su

Su, Lei; 苏蕾; Sū Lěi

1992- **First publication: 2016**

- Employment: School of Landscape Architecture, Northeast Forestry University (东北林业大学园林学

院）
• Research interest: Iridaceae [S]
• Published taxa: *Iris*
• Region: CHINA (Heilongjiang)

M. H. Su

Su, Mong Huai; 蘇夢淮；Sū Mènghuái; 苏梦淮
1968- First publication: 2004
• Employment: Department of Forestry and Nature Conservation, Chinese Culture University（中国文化大学森林暨自然保育学系）
• Research interest: Theaceae [S]
• Published taxa: *Camellia, Pyrenaria*
• Region: CHINA (Taiwan)

P. L. Su

Su, Pi Lin; 苏丕林；Sū Pīlín; 蘇丕林
1934-2017 First publication: 1979
• Employment: Jingzhou Institute of Forestry Science, Hubei（湖北省荆州地区林科所）
• Research interest: Oleaceae [S]
• Published taxa: *Fraxinus*
• Region: CHINA (Hubei)

S. W. Su

Su, Song Wang; 苏宋旺；Sū Sòngwàng; 蘇宋旺
1930- First publication: 1982
• Employment: Department of Biology, Anhui University; School of Life Sciences, Anhui University（安徽大学生物系；安徽大学生命科学学院）
• Research interest: Apiaceae, Cyperaceae, Lamiaceae, Verbenaceae [S]
• Published taxa: *Carex, Ferula, Salvia, Teucrium*
• Affiliation: ANU
• Location of specimens: ANU
• Region: CHINA (Anhui)

X. X. Su

Su, Xiang Xiu; 苏享修；Sū Xiǎngxiū
1962- First publication: 2019
• Employment: College of Landscape Architecture, Fujian Agriculture and Forestry University（福建农林大学园林学院）
• Research interest: Melastomataceae [S]
• Published taxa: *Tashiroea*
• Region: CHINA (Fujian)

X. Su

Su, Xu; 苏旭；Sū Xù
1980- First publication: 2007
• Employment: Northwest Plateau Institute of Biology, Chinese Academy of Sciences; School of Life Sciences, Lanzhou University; College of Life and Geographical Sciences, Qinghai Normal University（中国科学院西北高原生物研究所；兰州大学生命科学学院；青海师范大学生命与地理科学学院）
• Research interest: Poaceae [S]
• Published taxa: *Leymus, Orinus*
• Region: CHINA (Qinghai, Sichuan, Xizang)

Y. J. Su

Su, Ying Juan; 苏应娟；Sū Yīngjuān
1965- First publication: 1997
• Employment: School of Life Sciences, Sun Yat-sen University（中山大学生命科学学院）
• Research interest: Berberidaceae [S]
• Published taxa: *Dysosma*
• Region: CHINA (Hubei)

Yong Y. Su

Su, Yong Yu; 苏咏娱；Sū Yǒngyú
1992- First publication: 2014
• Employment: College of Forestry and Landscape Architecture, South China Agricultural University; The Orchid Conservation & Research Center of Shenzhen, Guangdong（华南农业大学林学与风景园林学院；广东省深圳市兰科植物保护研究中心）
• Research interest: Orchidaceae [S]
• Published taxa: *Liparis*
• Region: CHINA (Yunnan)
• IPNI as: Y. Y. Su

Z. Y. Su

Su, Zhi Yun; Shu, Tsi Yun; 苏志云；Sū Zhìyún; 蘇志雲
1936- First publication: 1980
• Employment: Kunming Institute of Botany, Chinese Academy of Sciences（中国科学院昆明植物研究所）
• Research interest: Papaveraceae, Theaceae [S]
• Published taxa: *Corydalis, Schima*
• Affiliation: KUN
• Region: CHINA
• Also as: T. Y. Su; T. Y. Shu

Z. W. Su

Su, Zhong Wu; 苏中武；Sū Zhōngwǔ；蘇中武
1917-2011 First publication: 2001
• Employment: College of Pharmacy, Second Military Medical University（第二军医大学药学院）
• Research interest: Araliaceae [S]
• Published taxa: *Aralia*
• Location of specimens: SMMU-BH
• Region: CHINA (Yunnan)

Z. M. Su

Su, Zong Ming; 苏宗明；Sū Zōngmíng; 蘇宗明
1935- First publication: 1985
• Employment: Guangxi Institute of Botany（广西植物

研究所）
• Research interest: Theaceae [S]
• Published taxa: *Camellia*
• Region: CHINA (Guangxi)

H. Y. Su

Su, Ho Yi; Su, He Yi; 粟和毅；Sù Héyì
1937- **First publication: 1979**
• Employment: Department of Biology, Sichuan University（四川大学生物系）
• Research interest: Cornaceae, Davidiaceae, Pittosporaceae, Sapindaceae [S]
• Published taxa: *Acer, Alangium, Pittosporum*
• Affiliation: SZ
• Location of specimens: SZ
• Region: CHINA (Sichuan)

B. S. Sun

Sun, Bi Sin; Sun, Bi Shin; Sun, Bi Xing; 孙必兴；Sūn Bìxīng; 孫必興
1921-2002 **First publication: 1964**
• Employment: Department of Biology, Yunnan University; School of Life Sciences, Yunnan University（云南大学生物系；云南大学生命科学学院）
• Research interest: Capparaceae, Cleomaceae, Fagaceae, Poaceae, Scrophulariaceae [S]
• Published taxa: *Achnatherum, Agrostis, Anthoxanthum, Arthraxon, Arundinella, Bosciopsis, Bromus, Buddleja, Capparis, Chloris, Cleome, Crateva, Cymbopogon, Deschampsia, Deyeuxia, Dichanthium, Dimeria, Elymus, Eragrostis, Eulalia, Festuca, Garnotia, Harpachne, Helictotrichon, Heteropogon, Hyparrhenia, Lithocarpus, Microchloa, Microstegium, Paspalum, Pennisetum, Phacelurus, Phragmites, Rhytachne, Roegneria, Rubimons, Themeda, Urochloa*
• Affiliation: YUKU
• Location of specimens: YUKU
• Region: CHINA (Yunnan)

C. R. Sun

Sun, Cheng Ren; 孙成仁；Sūn Chéngrén; 孫成仁
1944-2010 **First publication: 1988**
• Employment: Nanchong Normal School, Sichuan（四川省南充师范学院）
• Research interest: Schisandraceae [S]
• Published taxa: *Schisandra*
• Affiliation: SITC
• Location of specimens: SITC
• Region: CHINA (Gansu)

T. Y. Sun

Sun, Tai Yang; Sun, Dai Yang; 孙岱阳；Sūn Dàiyáng; 孫岱陽
1914-1990 **First publication: 1985**
• Employment: Inner Mongolia Forestry College（内蒙古林学院）
• Research interest: Salicaceae; Woody Plants [S]
• Published taxa: *Populus*
• Affiliation: BJFC
• Location of specimens: BJFC, HIMC, NMAC, NMFC
• Region: CHINA (Nei Mongol)

H. Sun

Sun, Hang; 孙航；Sūn Háng
1963- **First publication: 1996**
• Employment: Kunming Institute of Botany, Chinese Academy of Sciences（中国科学院昆明植物研究所）
• Research interest: Apiaceae, Asteraceae, Berberidaceae, Brassicaceae, Campanulaceae, Euphorbiaceae, Fabaceae, Fagaceae, Gesneriaceae, Orchidaceae, Papaveraceae, Poaceae, Polygonaceae, Primulaceae, Rhamnaceae, Rosaceae, Rubiaceae, Thymelaeaceae, Urticaceae; Plants of Xizang [S]
• Published taxa: *Abarema, Aconogonon, Afgekia, Bupleurum, Callerya, Capillipedium, Carpesium, Cyclobalanopsis, Cypripedium, Entada, Epimedium, Indigofera, Lithocarpus, Meconopsis, Pankycodon, Parasyncalathium, Primula, Primulina, Pseudocodon, Pseudogalium, Rubus, Sageretia, Salweenia, Saussurea, Senegalia, Shangrilaia, Solms-laubachia, Soroseris, Tsaiodendron, Wikstroemia, Youngia, Zhengyia*
• Affiliation: KUN
• Location of specimens: KUN
• Region: CHINA (Yunnan)

Hao Sun

Sun, Hao; 孙灏；Sūn Hào
1969- **First publication: 2003**
• Employment: School of Life Sciences, University of Science and Technology of China（中国科学技术大学生命科学学院）
• Research interest: Oxalidaceae [S]
• Published taxa: *Oxalis*
• Region: CHINA (Anhui)

H. J. Sun

Sun, Hua Jun; 孙华君；Sūn Huájūn
First publication: 1994
• Employment: College of Pharmacy, Second Military Medical University（第二军医大学药学院）
• Research interest: Solanaceae [S]
• Published taxa: *Datura*
• Region: CHINA (Zhejiang)

H. M. Sun

Sun, Hua Mei; 孙华美；Sūn Huáměi; 孫華美

1942- First publication: 1994
- Employment: Huazhong Agricultural University（华中农业大学）
- Research interest: Actinidiaceae [S]
- Published taxa: *Actinidia*
- Region: CHINA (Hubei)

J. L. Sun

Sun, Ji Liang; 孙吉良 ; Sūn Jíliáng
1952- First publication: 1982
- Employment: Yunnan Institute of Tropical Botany, Chinese Academy of Sciences（中国科学院云南热带植物研究所）
- Research interest: Poaceae; Plants of Shanghai [S]
- Published taxa: *Dendrocalamus*
- Affiliation: SHM
- Location of specimens: SHM
- Region: CHINA (Yunnan)

J. Z. Sun

Sun, Ji Zhou; 孙继周 ; Sūn Jìzhōu; 孙纪周
1944- First publication: 1990
- Employment: Department of Biology, Lanzhou University（兰州大学生物系）
- Research interest: Brassicaceae, Fabaceae, Juncaceae, Lardizabalaceae, Orobanchaceae, Poaceae, Rosaceae, Rutaceae [S]
- Published taxa: *Cardamine, Holboellia, Pedicularis*
- Affiliation: LZU
- Location of specimens: LZU
- Region: CHINA (Gansu)

Jiao Sun

Sun, Jiao; 孙骄 ; Sūn Jiāo
First publication: 2020
- Employment: Wuhan Botanical Garden, Chinese Academy of Sciences（中国科学院武汉植物园）
- Research interest: Primulaceae [S]
- Published taxa: *Primula*
- Region: CHINA (Hubei)

J. W. Sun

Sun, Ju Wen; 孙居文 ; Sūn Jūwén
1961- First publication: 1993
- Employment: Shandong Forestry School; Forestry College, Shandong Agricultural University（山东省林业学校；山东农业大学林学院）
- Research interest: Lamiaceae, Rosaceae; Plants of Shandong [S]
- Published taxa: *Malus, Vitex*
- Affiliation: SDFS
- Location of specimens: SDFS
- Region: CHINA (Shandong)

K. Sun

Sun, Kun; 孙坤 ; Sūn Kūn
1963- First publication: 1992
- Employment: Department of Biology, Northwest Normal University（西北师范大学生物系）
- Research interest: Elaeagnaceae, Paeoniaceae, Ranunculaceae, Typhaceae, Violaceae; Plant Systematics [S]
- Published taxa: *Clematis, Hippophae, Paeonia, Sparganium, Viola*
- Affiliation: NWTC
- Location of specimens: NWTC
- Region: CHINA (Gansu)

L. Yong Sun

Sun, Li Yong; 孙李勇 ; Sūn Lǐyǒng
1991- First publication: 2019
- Employment: College of Biology and the Environment, Nanjing Forestry University（南京林业大学生物与环境学院）
- Research interest: Lythraceae [S]
- Published taxa: *Trapa*
- Region: CHINA (Jiangsu)

L. Y. Sun

Sun, Li Yuan; 孙立元 ; Sūn Lìyuán; 孫立元
1934- First publication: 1991
- Employment: Hebei Agricultural University（河北农业大学）
- Research interest: Rosaceae [S]
- Published taxa: *Crataegus*
- Region: CHINA (Hebei)

M. S. Sun

Sun, Mao Sheng; 孙茂盛 ; Sūn Màoshèng
1963- First publication: 2011
- Employment: Faculty of Natural Resources, Southwest Forestry University（西南林学院资源学院）
- Research interest: Poaceae [S]
- Published taxa: *Fargesia*
- Region: CHINA (Yunnan)

Mei Sun

Sun, Mei; 孫梅 ; Sūn Méi; 孙梅
First publication: 2017
- Employment: School of Biological Sciences, The University of Hong Kong（香港大学生物科学学院）
- Research interest: Orchidaceae [S]
- Published taxa: *Spiranthes*
- Region: CHINA (Hainan, Yunnan)

M. Sun

Sun, Miao; 孙苗 ; Sūn Miáo

1983- **First publication: 2010**
- Employment: Institute of Botany, Chinese Academy of Sciences（中国科学院植物研究所）
- Research interest: Elaeagnaceae [S]
- Published taxa: *Elaeagnus*
- Region: CHINA (Chongqing)

Ming Sun
Sun, Ming; 孙明 ; Sūn Míng
1980- **First publication: 2018**
- Employment: School of Landscape Architecture, Beijing Forestry University（北京林业大学园林学院）
- Research interest: Asteraceae [S]
- Published taxa: *Chrysanthemum*
- Region: CHINA (Shandong)
- IPNI as: M. Sun

Q. S. Sun
Sun, Qi Shi; Sun, Chi Shi; **孙启时 ; Sūn Qǐshí; 孫啟時**
1945- **First publication: 1992**
- Employment: Shenyang Pharmaceutical University（沈阳药科大学）
- Research interest: Amaryllidaceae, Asparagaceae, Liliaceae, Tofieldiaceae [S]
- Published taxa: *Allium, Erythronium, Fritillaria, Gagea, Hosta, Lilium, Tofieldia*
- Affiliation: SYPC
- Location of specimens: SYPC
- Region: CHINA (Heilongjiang, Jilin, Liaoning, Nei Mongol)

Q. Sun
Sun, Qian; 孙茜 ; Sūn Qiàn
1984- **First publication: 2010**
- Employment: Institute of Botany, Chinese Academy of Sciences（中国科学院植物研究所）
- Research interest: Poaceae [S]
- Published taxa: *Miscanthus*
- Region: CHINA (Yunnan)

Q. W. Sun
Sun, Qing Wen; 孙庆文 ; Sūn Qìngwén
1978- **First publication: 2010**
- Employment: Guiyang College of Traditional Chinese Medicine（贵阳中医学院）
- Research interest: Asparagaceae, Gesneriaceae, Selaginellaceae; Medicinal Plants [S]
- Published taxa: *Aspidistra, Oreocharis, Selaginella, Tremacron*
- Affiliation: GZTM
- Location of specimens: GZTM
- Region: CHINA (Guizhou)

Q. Y. Sun
Sun, Qing Ye; 孙庆业 ; Sūn Qìngyè
1964- **First publication: 1999**
- Employment: School of Life Sciences, Anhui University（安徽大学生命科学学院）
- Research interest: Adoxaceae, Poaceae, Polygonaceae [S]
- Published taxa: *Polygonum, Viburnum*
- Affiliation: ANU
- Location of specimens: ANU
- Region: CHINA (Anhui, Shaanxi)

S. S. Sun
Sun, San Sheng; 孙三省 ; Sūn Sānshěng
1941- **First publication: 1989**
- Employment: Air Force Medical College（空军医学高等专科学校）
- Research interest: Oleaceae [S]
- Published taxa: *Fraxinus*
- Region: CHINA

Shao C. Sun
Sun, Shao Chi; 孙绍棋 ; Sūn Shàoqí 孫紹棋，孙绍祺
1941- **First publication: 1986**
- Employment: Sichuan Institute of Chinese Materia Medica（四川省中药研究所）
- Research interest: Orchidaceae [S]
- Published taxa: *Dendrobium*
- Location of specimens: SM
- Region: CHINA (Sichuan)
- IPNI as: S. C. Sun

W. B. Sun
Sun, Wei Bang; 孙卫邦 ; Sūn Wèibāng
1964- **First publication: 1999**
- Employment: Institute of Botany, Chinese Academy of Sciences（中国科学院昆明植物研究所）
- Research interest: Magnoliaceae [S]
- Published taxa: *Magnolia, Yulania*
- Region: CHINA

S. C. Sun
Sun, Siang Chung; Sun, Xiang Zhong; Sun, Hsiang Chung; 孙祥钟 ; Sūn Xiángzhōng; 孫祥鐘
1908-1994 **First publication: 1946**
- Employment: Department of Biology, Wuhan University（武汉大学生物系）
- Research interest: Alismataceae, Aquifoliaceae, Araliaceae, Caprifoliaceae, Hydrocharitaceae, Poaceae, Potamogetonaceae; Aquatic Plants [S]
- Published taxa: *Alisma, Eragrostis, Ilex, Ottelia, Panax, Potamogeton, Sagittaria, Viburnum*
- Affiliation: WH
- Location of specimens: WH

• Region: CHINA
• Also as: X. Z. Sun; • IPNI as: S. C. Wang

Y. Z. Sun

Sun, Yon Zai; Sun, Hsiung Tsai; Sun, Hsiung T'sai; Sun Xiong Chai; **孙雄才**; **Sūn Xióngcái**; **孫雄才**
1898-1964 First publication: 1932
• Employment: Department of Botany, Biological Laboratory of Science Society of China; Nanjing Pharmaceutical College; Nanjing Institute of Materia Medica（中国科学社生物研究所植物部；南京药学院；南京药物研究所）
• Research interest: Lamiaceae [S]
• Published taxa: *Chienodoxa, Dracocephalum, Dysophylla, Elsholtzia, Hanceola, Meehania, Orthosiphon, Paraphlomis, Phlomis, Plectranthus, Pogostemon, Salvia, Scutellaria, Teucrium*
• Affiliation: CPU
• Location of specimens: CPU
• Region: CHINA
• Also as: Sun

X. D. Sun

Sun, Xiu Dian; **孙秀殿**; **Sūn Xiùdiàn**
1963- First publication: 2001
• Employment: Zhalantun Forestry School, Inner Mongolia（内蒙古扎兰屯林业学校）
• Research interest: Asteraceae [S]
• Published taxa: *Neo-taraxacum, Taraxacum*
• Region: CHINA (Nei Mongol)

X. G. Sun

Sun, Xue Gang; **孙学刚**; **Sūn Xuégāng**
1960- First publication: 1990
• Employment: College of Forestry, Gansu Agricultural University（甘肃农业大学林学院）
• Research interest: Apocynaceae, Caprifoliaceae, Celastraceae, Cornaceae, Ericaceae, Fabaceae, Hydrangeaceae, Rosaceae, Salicaceae; Plants of Gansu [S]
• Published taxa: *Cornus, Deutzia, Euonymus, Indigofera, Kerria, Lonicera, Rhododendron, Rubus, Salix, Tylophora*
• Affiliation: GAUF
• Location of specimens: GAUF
• Region: CHINA (Gansu)

Y. Sun

Sun, Yi; **孙逸**; **Sūn Yì**
1984- First publication: 2012
• Employment: College of Life Sciences, Zhejiang University（浙江大学生命科学学院）
• Research interest: Rosaceae [S]
• Published taxa: *Rubus*
• Region: CHINA (Xizang, Yunnan)

Y. H. Sun

Sun, Yong Hua; **孙永华**; **Sūn Yǒnghuá**; **孫永華**
1934- First publication: 1987
• Employment: Xi' an Botanical Garden, Shaanxi（陕西省西安植物园）
• Research interest: Poaceae [S]
• Published taxa: *Stipa*
• Affiliation: XBGH
• Location of specimens: XBGH
• Region: CHINA

Y. Shuai Sun

Sun, Yong Shuai; **孙永帅**; **Sūn Yǒngshuài**
1985- First publication: 2019
• Employment: Xishuangbanna Tropical Botanical Garden, Chinese Academy of Sciences（中国科学院西双版纳热带植物园）
• Research interest: Rhamnaceae [S]
• Published taxa: *Rhamnella*
• Region: CHINA (Hainan)

Y. Y. Sun

Sun, Yue Yin; **孙岳胤**; **Sūn Yuèyìn**
1964- First publication: 2005
• Employment: Mudanjiang Forestry Research Institute, Heilongjiang（黑龙江省牡丹江林业科学研究所）
• Research interest: Pinaceae [S]
• Published taxa: *Abies*
• Region: CHINA (Heilongjiang)

Y. J. Sun

Sun, Yong Jiu; **孙永久**; **Sūn Yǒngjiǔ**; **孫永久**
1933- First publication: 1991
• Employment: Liaoning College of Traditional Chinese Medicine（辽宁中医学院）
• Research interest: Rhamnaceae [S]
• Published taxa: *Ziziphus*
• Location of specimens: LNCM
• Region: CHINA (Liaoning)

Z. Y. Sun

Sun, Zhi Ying; **孙稚颖**; **Sūn Zhìyǐng**
1971- First publication: 2005
• Employment: College of Life Science, Shandong Normal University（山东师范大学生命科学学院）
• Research interest: Brassicaceae, Lamiaceae [S]
• Published taxa: *Lepidium, Sisymbrium, Stachys*
• Location of specimens: SDCM
• Region: CHINA (Shandong)

Z. S. Sun

Sun, Zhong Shuai; 孙中帅 ; Sūn Zhōngshuài
1984- **First publication: 2015**
- Employment: College of Life Sciences, Zhejiang University（浙江大学生命科学学院）
- Research interest: Smilacaceae [S]
- Published taxa: *Smilax*
- Region: [WORLD]

T

Y. F. Tan

Tan, Yuan Feng; 谈远锋 ; Tán Yuǎnfēng
1978- **First publication: 2012**
- Employment: Guangxi College of Traditional Chinese Medicine（广西中医学院）
- Research interest: Capparaceae; Medicinal Plants [S]
- Published taxa: *Capparis*
- Affiliation: GXCM
- Location of specimens: GXCM
- Region: CHINA (Guangxi)

D. Y. Tan

Tan, Dun Yan; 谭敦炎 ; Tán Dūnyán
1963- **First publication: 2000**
- Employment: College of Forestry, Xinjiang Agricultural University; Institute of Botany, Chinese Academy of Sciences（新疆农业大学林学院；中国科学院植物研究所）
- Research interest: Liliaceae; Plants of Xinjiang [S]
- Published taxa: *Amana, Tulipa*
- Affiliation: XJA
- Location of specimens: XJA
- Region: CHINA (Xinjiang, Zhejiang)

J. B. Tan

Tan, Jin Bo; 谭进波 ; Tán Jìnbō
1987- **First publication: 2014**
- Employment: College of Life Sciences, Sichuan University（四川大学生命科学学院）
- Research interest: Apiaceae [S]
- Published taxa: *Pternopetalum*
- Region: CHINA (Sichuan)

K. Tan

Tan, Ke; 谭珂 ; Tán Kē
1989- **First publication: 2019**
- Employment: College of Ecology and Environment, Hainan University（海南大学生态与环境学院）
- Research interest: Malpighiaceae [S]
- Published taxa: *Hiptage*
- Region: CHINA (Yunnan)

P. C. Tam

Tam, Pui Cheung; Tuam Pui Cheung; Tan, Pei Xiang; 谭沛祥 ; Tán Pèixiáng; 譚沛祥
1919-1991 **First publication: 1978**
- Employment: South China Institute of Botany, Chinese Academy of Sciences（中国科学院华南植物研究所）
- Research interest: Balanophoraceae, Crypteroniaceae, Ericaceae, Fagaceae, Santalaceae [S]
- Published taxa: *Balanophora, Cyclobalanopsis, Dendrotrophe, Enkianthus, Henslowia, Osyris, Pyrularia, Rhododendron, Thesium, Vaccinium*
- Affiliation: IBK, IBSC
- Location of specimens: IBK, IBSC
- Region: CHINA

S. X. Tan

Tan, Shi Xian; 谭仕贤 ; Tán Shìxián; 譚士賢
1931-2006 **First publication: 1987**
- Employment: Sichuan Institute of Chinese Materia Medica Cultivation（四川中药栽培研究所）
- Research interest: Aristolochiaceae; Medicinal Plants [S]
- Published taxa: *Aristolochia*
- Affiliation: IMC
- Location of specimens: IMC
- Region: CHINA (Chongqing)

Y. J. Tan

Tan, Yong Ji ; 谭永济 ; Tán Yǒngjì
First publication: 1983
- Employment: Tea Research Institute, Chinese Academy of Agricultural Sciences（中国农业科学院茶叶研究所）
- Research interest: Theaceae [S]
- Published taxa: *Camellia*
- Affiliation: TEA
- Location of specimens: SYS, TEA
- Region: CHINA (Yunnan)

Y. H. Tan

Tan, Yun Hong; 谭运洪 ; Tán Yùnhóng
1979- **First publication: 2012**
- Employment: Xishuangbanna Tropical Botanical Garden, Chinese Academy of Sciences（中国科学院西双版纳热带植物园）
- Research interest: Annonaceae, Apocynaceae,

Aristolochiaceae, Asparagaceae, Balsaminaceae, Begoniaceae, Ericaceae, Euphorbiaceae, Gesneriaceae, Lamiaceae, Lauraceae, Linaceae, Malpighiaceae, Metteniusaceae, Orchidaceae, Piperaceae, Primulaceae, Rubiaceae, Zingiberaceae; Plants of S. E. Asia [S]
- Published taxa: *Acranthera, Agapetes, Alphonsea, Amblyanthopsis, Amomum, Aristolochia, Begonia, Biermannia, Canthium, Coelogyne, Curcuma, Demorchis, Didymocarpus, Gastrochilus, Gastrodia, Hedychium, Hemiboea, Henckelia, Hiptage, Impatiens, Jasminanthes, Marsdenia, Neocinnamomeae, Ophiorrhiza, Oreocharis, Petrocosmea, Piper, Platea, Polyalthia, Premna, Primula, Reinwardtia, Trivalvaria, Tsaiodendron, Tupistra, Wuodendron*
- Affiliation: HITBC
- Location of specimens: HITBC
- Region: CHINA (Yunnan); MYANMAR

Z. M. Tan

Tan, Zhong Ming; Tan, Chung Ming; **谭仲明**; Tán Zhòngmíng; **譚仲明**

1939-2001 **First publication: 1989**

- Employment: Department of Biology, Sichuan University（四川大学生物系）
- Research interest: Aquifoliaceae, Brassicaceae, Geraniaceae, Rutaceae, Sapindaceae [S]
- Published taxa: *Acer, Boenninghausenia, Cardamine, Draba, Geranium, Ilex, Orixa, Orychophragmus, Toddalia, Zanthoxylum*
- Affiliation: SZ
- Location of specimens: SZ
- Region: CHINA (Sichuan)
- Also as: C. M. Tan

G. G. Tang

Tang, Geng Guo; **汤庚国**; Tāng Gēngguó

1950- **First publication: 1984**

- Employment: Department of Forestry, Nanjing Forestry University（南京林业大学林学系）
- Research interest: Fabaceae, Poaceae, Sapindaceae; Plants of Hubei [S]
- Published taxa: *Acer, Cladrastis, Phyllostachys, Sasa*
- Affiliation: NF
- Location of specimens: NF
- Region: CHINA (Hubei)

Huan Tang

Tang, Huan; **汤欢**; Tāng Huān

1986- **First publication: 2016**

- Employment: College of Forestry, Sichuan Agricultural University（四川农业大学林学院）
- Research interest: Orchidaceae [S]
- Published taxa: *Odontochilus*
- Region: CHINA (Guangxi)

J. S. Tang

Tang, Jing Shan; **汤儆杉**; Tāng Jǐngshān

1958- **First publication: 1985**

- Employment: Institute of Botany, Jiangsu Province; Nanjing Botanical Garden Mem. Sun Yat-Sen, Chinese Academy of Sciences（江苏省植物研究所；中国科学院南京中山植物园）
- Research interest: Asparagaceae, Poaceae [S]
- Published taxa: *Fusifilum, Physodia, Ptilagrostis*
- Region: [WORLD]

T. H. Tang

Tang, Teng Han; Tang, T'êng Han; **汤腾汉**; Tāng Ténghàn; **湯騰漢**

1900-1988 **First publication: 1926**

- Employment: National University of Tsingtao; Department of Chemistry, Shandong University（国立青岛大学；山东大学化学系）
- Research interest: Ephedraceae [S]
- Published taxa: *Ephedra*
- Region: CHINA

Y. C. Tang

Tang, Yan Cheng; Tang, Yen Cheng; T'ang, Yen Ch'êng; **汤彦承**; Tāng Yànchéng; **湯彥承**

1926-2016 **First publication: 1963**

- Employment: Institute of Botany, Chinese Academy of Sciences（中国科学院植物研究所）
- Research interest: Actinidiaceae, Adoxaceae, Amaryllidaceae, Apiaceae, Asparagaceae, Cannabaceae, Caprifoliaceae, Cyperaceae, Liliaceae, Menispermaceae, Poaceae, Stachyuraceae, Styracaceae [S]
- Published taxa: *Agrostis, Allium, Carex, Celtis, Clematoclethra, Cyclea, Fimbristylis, Huodendron, Kobresia, Ligusticum, Lonicera, Machaerina, Morina, Polygonatum, Rehderodendron, Sambucus, Scilla, Stachyurus, Streptopus*
- Affiliation: PE
- Region: CHINA
- IPNI as: Y. C. Tong

Z. C. Tang

Tang, Zhao Cheng; **汤兆成**; Tāng Zhàochéng; **湯兆成**

1937- **First publication: 1995**

- Employment: Suichang Institute of Forestry, Zhejiang（浙江省遂昌县林业科学研究所）
- Research interest: Taxaceae [S]
- Published taxa: *Torreya*
- Region: CHINA (Zhejiang)

Z. X. Tang

Tang, Zong Xiao; 汤宗孝 ; Tāng Zōngxiào; 湯宗孝

1938- **First publication: 1984**

- Employment: Sichuan Institute of Grassland（四川省草原研究所）
- Research interest: Poaceae [S]
- Published taxa: *Aristida, Dactylis*
- Location of specimens: HON
- Region: CHINA (Sichuan)

C. L. Tang

Tang, Chang Lin; 唐昌林 ; Táng Chānglín

1934- **First publication: 1986**

- Employment: Mianyang Institute for Drug Control, Sichuan（四川省绵阳地区药检所）
- Research interest: Caryophyllaceae, Polygonaceae, Rosaceae [S]
- Published taxa: *Silene, Sorbus*
- Affiliation: MYDC, WUK
- Location of specimens: MYDC, WUK
- Region: CHINA

G. D. Tang

Tang, Guang Da; 唐光大 ; Táng Guāngdà

1982- **First publication: 2015**

- Employment: College of Forestry and Landscape Architecture, South China Agricultural University; The Orchid Conservation & Research Center of Shenzhen, Guangdong（华南农业大学林学与风景园林学院；广东省深圳市兰科植物保护研究中心）
- Research interest: Dryopteridaceae, Melastomataceae, Orchidaceae, Orobanchaceae, Tectariaceae [PS]
- Published taxa: *Cestichis, Christisonia, Fordiophyton, Platystyliparis, Polystichum, Tectaria*
- Affiliation: CANT
- Location of specimens: CANT
- Region: CHINA

H. Tang

Tang, Hui; 唐辉 ; Táng Huī

1972- **First publication: 2011**

- Employment: Guangxi Institute of Botany, Chinese Academy of Sciences（广西壮族自治区中国科学院广西植物研究所）
- Research interest: Gesneriaceae [S]
- Published taxa: *Chirita*
- Region: CHINA (Guangxi)

Tang

Tang, Tsin; Tang, Jin; Tang, Chin; T'ang, Chin; 唐进 ; Táng Jìn; 唐進

1897-1984 **First publication: 1937**

- Employment: Fan Memorial Institute of Biology; Institute of Botany, Chinese Academy of Sciences（静生生物调查所；中国科学院植物研究所）
- Research interest: Amaryllidaceae, Asparagaceae, Celastraceae, Colchicaceae, Cyperaceae, Liliaceae, Melanthiaceae, Moraceae, Nartheciaceae, Orchidaceae, Smilacaceae, Stachyuraceae; Monocotyledons [S]
- Published taxa: *Aletris, Allium, Amitostigma, Ania, Aphyllorchis, Arachnis, Asparagus, Biermannia, Bletilla, Blysmus, Broussonetia, Bulbophyllum, Calanthe, Campylandra, Carex, Ceratostylis, Cheirostylis, Chrysoglossum, Cirrhopetalum, Collabium, Corybas, Cudrania, Cyperus, Dendrobium, Desmotrichum, Diglyphosa, Diphylax, Disporum, Eleocharis, Epipactis, Eria, Erythrodes, Eulophia, Fimbristylis, Fuirena, Goodyera, Habenaria, Hemipilia, Herminium, Hetaeria, Heterosmilax, Hexonix, Hypolytrum, Kobresia, Lilium, Liparis, Lipocarpha, Liriope, Listera, Malaxis, Mapania, Mariscus, Micropera, Mischobulbum, Monocelastrus, Myrmechis, Neottia, Nephelaphyllum, Nervilia, Odontochilus, Ophiopogon, Orchis, Panisea, Paphiopedilum, Paris, Pecteilis, Pelatantheria, Peliosanthes, Peristylus, Phalaenopsis, Platanthera, Pleione, Polygonatum, Pomatocalpa, Pycreus, Saccolabium, Sarcanthus, Sarcochilus, Sarcopodium, Scirpus, Scleria, Siraitos, Smilacina, Smilax, Stachyurus, Stauropsis, Streptopus, Sunipia, Thrixspermum, Trichoglottis, Tupistra, Vanda, Veratrum*
- Affiliation: PE
- Region: CHINA

K. S. Tang

Tang, Kai Shan; 唐开山 ; Táng Kāishān; 唐開山

1939- **First publication: 2010**

- Employment: Loudi City Forestry Bureau, Hunan（湖南省娄底市林业局）
- Research interest: Aquifoliaceae [S]
- Published taxa: *Ilex*
- Region: CHINA (Hunan)

M. Tang

Tang, Ming; 唐明 ; Táng Míng

1984- **First publication: 2014**

- Employment: South China Botanical Garden, Chinese Academy of Sciences（中国科学院华南植物园）
- Research interest: Asteraceae [S]
- Published taxa: *Senecio, Synotis*
- Region: [ASIA]

M. D. Tang

Tang, Ming De; 唐明德 ; Táng Míngdé

First publication: 1990
• Employment: Hunan Agricultural College（湖南农学院）
• Research interest: Theaceae [S]
• Published taxa: *Camellia*
• Region: CHINA (Yunnan)

M. S. Tang

Tang, Mo Shih; 唐默詩；Táng Mòshī; 唐默诗
1969- **First publication: 2013**
• Employment: Department of Pharmaceutical Science and Technology, Chung Hwa University of Medical Technology（中华医事科技大学制药工程系）
• Research interest: Orchidaceae [S]
• Published taxa: *Tropidia*
• Region: CHINA (Taiwan)

S. C. Tang

Tang, Sai Chun; 唐赛春；Táng Sàichūn
1973- **First publication: 1999**
• Employment: Guangxi Institute of Botany, Chinese Academy of Sciences（广西壮族自治区中国科学院广西植物研究所）
• Research interest: Asparagaceae, Celastraceae, Ericaceae, Lauraceae, Primulaceae [S]
• Published taxa: *Aspidistra, Lysimachia, Machilus, Parnassia*
• Affiliation: IBK
• Location of specimens: IBK
• Region: CHINA (Guangxi)

W. Tang

Tang, William; 唐威廉；Táng Wēilián
First publication: 1999
• Employment: Fairchild Tropical Botanic Garden, U.S.A.（美国费尔柴尔德热带植物园）
• Research interest: Cycadaceae [S]
• Published taxa: *Cycas*
• Region: [ASIA]

W. X. Tang

Tang, Wen Xiu; 唐文秀；Táng Wénxiù
1973- **First publication: 2008**
• Employment: Guangxi Institute of Botany, Chinese Academy of Sciences（广西壮族自治区中国科学院广西植物研究所）
• Research interest: Gesneriaceae [S]
• Published taxa: *Chirita*
• Region: CHINA (Guangxi)

S. H. Tang

Tang, Si Hua; 唐锡华；Táng Xīhuá; 唐錫華
1922-1999 **First publication: 1982**
• Employment: Institute of Plant Physiology, Chinese Academy of Sciences（中国科学院上海植物生理研究所）
• Research interest: Poaceae [S]
• Published taxa: × *Oryticum*
• Region: [cult.]

S. Y. Tang

Tang, Sin Yao; Tang, Xin Yao; **唐心曜；Táng Xīnyào**
1934- **First publication: 1983**
• Employment: Department of Pharmacognosy, Sichuan Medical College（四川医学院生药学教研室）
• Research interest: Liliaceae [S]
• Published taxa: *Fritillaria*
• Affiliation: WCU
• Location of specimens: WCU
• Region: CHINA (Sichuan)

Y. Tang

Tang, Ya; 唐亚；Táng Yà
1963- **First publication: 1988**
• Employment: Southwest Forestry College; Chengdu Institute of Biology, Chinese Academy of Sciences; College of Architecture & Environment, Sichuan University（西南林学院；中国科学院成都生物研究所；四川大学建筑与环境学院）
• Research interest: Elaeocarpaceae, Malvaceae, Orobanchaceae; Gymnospermae [S]
• Published taxa: *Abutilon, Corchoropsis, Diplodiscus, Elaeocarpus, Hibiscus, Malva, Pedicularis, Sloanea, Sterculia, Tilia*
• Affiliation: CDBI
• Location of specimens: CDBI, SWFC
• Region: CHINA

Ying Tang

Tang, Ying; 唐颖；Táng Yǐng
1987- **First publication: 2015**
• Employment: Kunming Institute of Botany, Chinese Academy of Sciences（中国科学院昆明植物研究所）
• Research interest: Orchidaceae [S]
• Published taxa: *Hemipilia*
• Affiliation: SCFI
• Region: CHINA (Fujian)

Yu Tang

Yu, Tang; 唐宇；Táng Yǔ
1954- **First publication: 2010**
• Employment: College of Food Science and Technology, Sichuan Tourism University; College of Life Sciences, Sichuan Agricultural University（四川旅游学院食品学院；四川农业大学生命科学学院）
• Research interest: Polygonaceae [S]
• Published taxa: *Fagopyrum*

• Region: CHINA (Sichuan)
• IPNI as: T. Yu

C. Z. Tang

Tang, Chen Zi; Tang, Zhen Zi; **唐振缁**; Táng Zhènzī
1934- **First publication: 1977**
• Employment: South China Institute of Botany, Chinese Academy of Sciences (中国科学院华南植物研究所)
• Research interest: Araceae, Arecaceae, Orchidaceae [S]
• Published taxa: *Calanthe, Chuniophoenix, Dendrobium, Oxystophyllum, Paphiopedilum, Paraphaius, Phaius, Phalaenopsis, Pleione, Typhonium, Vanda*
• Region: CHINA
• Also as: Z. Z. Tang

G. F. Tao

Tao, Guang Fu; 陶光复; Táo Guāngfù; **陶光復**
1946-2006 **First publication: 1985**
• Employment: Wuhan Institute of Botany, Chinese Academy of Sciences (中国科学院武汉植物研究所)
• Research interest: Lauraceae, Ranunculaceae [S]
• Published taxa: *Cinnamomum, Clematis, Delphinium, Thalictrum*
• Region: CHINA (Huibei)

G. D. Tao

Tao, Guo Da; 陶国达; Táo Guódá; **陶國達**
1939- **First publication: 1983**
• Employment: Yunnan Institute of Tropical Botany, Chinese Academy of Sciences; Xishuangbanna Tropical Botanical Garden, Chinese Academy of Sciences (中国科学院云南热带植物研究所；中国科学院西双版纳热带植物园)
• Research interest: Cycadaceae, Dipterocarpaceae, Theaceae, Urticaceae [S]
• Published taxa: *Cycas, Elatostema, Pyrenaria, Vatica*
• Affiliation: HITBC
• Location of specimens: HITBC
• Region: CHINA (Yunnan)

R. Tao

Tao, Ran; 陶然; Táo Rán
First publication: 1991
• Employment: Guiyang College of Traditional Chinese Medicine (贵阳中医学院)
• Research interest: Trilliaceae [S]
• Published taxa: *Paris*
• Region: CHINA (Guizhou)

X. L. Tao

Tao, Xiu Liu; 陶秀林; Táo Xiùlín
First publication: 1982
• Employment: Guangxi Forestry Research Institute (广西林业科学研究所)
• Research interest: Poaceae [S]
• Published taxa: *Chimonobambusa, Dendrocalamopsis*
• Region: CHINA (Guangxi)

N. C. Tao

Tao, Nin Chou; 陶银周; Tao Yínzhōu
1936-1996 **First publication: 1985**
• Employment: Lin' an Forestry Institute, Zhejiang (浙江省临安县林业科学研究所)
• Research interest: Juglandaceae [S]
• Published taxa: *Carya*
• Region: CHINA (Anhui)

B. Tian

Tian, Bin; 田斌; Tián Bīn
1983- **First publication: 2010**
• Employment: School of Life Sciences, Lanzhou University (兰州大学生命科学学院)
• Research interest: Betulaceae [S]
• Published taxa: *Ostryopsis*
• Region: CHINA (Yunnan)

D. K. Tian

Tian, Dai Ke; 田代科; Tián Dàikē
1968- **First publication: 2000**
• Employment: Kunming Institute of Botany, Chinese Academy of Sciences; Shanghai Chenshan Botanical Garden (中国科学院昆明植物研究所；上海辰山植物园)
• Research interest: Begoniaceae, Brassicaceae, Nelumbonaceae [S]
• Published taxa: *Begonia, Eutrema*
• Affiliation: CSH
• Location of specimens: CSH
• Region: CHINA

G. H. Tian

Tian, Guo Hang; 田国行; Tián Guóháng
1966- **First publication: 2004**
• Employment: College of Forestry and Horticulture, Henan Agricultural University (河南农业大学林学园艺学院)
• Research interest: Magnoliaceae [S]
• Published taxa: *Yulania*
• Region: CHINA (Henan)

H. Z. Tian

Tian, Huai Zhen; 田怀珍; Tián Huáizhēn
1981- **First publication: 2008**
• Employment: South China Botanical Garden,

Chinese Academy of Sciences; School of Life Sciences, East China Normal University（中国科学院华南植物园；华东师范大学生命科学学院）
- Research interest: Orchidaceae [S]
- Published taxa: *Anoectochilus, Chamaegastrodia, Liparis, Platanthera*
- Affiliation: HSNU
- Region: CHINA

J. J. Tian

Tian, Jian Jun; 田建军；Tián Jiànjūn

1956- **First publication: 1997**

- Employment: Institute of Chinese Materia Medica, China Academy of Chinese Medical Sciences（中国中医研究院中药研究所）
- Research interest: Crassulaceae [S]
- Published taxa: *Rhodiola*
- Region: CHINA (Hebei)

J. Tian

Tian, Jing; 田径；Tián Jìng

1985- **First publication: 2016**

- Employment: College of Life Sciences, Hunan Normal University（湖南师范大学生命科学学院）
- Research interest: Melastomataceae [S]
- Published taxa: *Phyllagathis*
- Region: CHINA (Guangxi)

Q. Tian

Tian, Qi; 田旗；Tián Qí

1971- **First publication: 2008**

- Employment: Shanghai Botanical Garden; Shanghai Institute of Landscape Gardening Science（上海植物园；上海园林科学研究所）
- Research interest: Apiaceae [S]
- Published taxa: *Peucedanum*
- Location of specimens: CSH
- Region: CHINA (Zhejiang)

X. L. Tian

Tian, Xiao Ling; 田晓玲；Tián Xiǎolíng

First publication: 2019

- Employment: College of Forest Resources and Environment, Nanjing Forestry University（南京林业大学森林资源与环境学院）
- Research interest: Ericaceae [S]
- Published taxa: *Rhododendron*
- Region: CHINA (Yunnan)

X. J. Tian

Tian, Xing Jun; 田兴军；Tián Xīngjūn

1961- **First publication: 1988**

- Employment: Northeast Forestry University; School of Life Sciences, Nanjing University（东北林业大学；南京大学生命科学学院）
- Research interest: Berberidaceae, Ranunculaceae, Rosaceae; Plant Ecology [S]
- Published taxa: *Crataegus, Epimedium, Thalictrum*
- Affiliation: N
- Region: CHINA

Y. Tian

Tian, Ye; 田野；Tián Yě

First publication: 2020

- Employment: School of Life Sciences, Yunnan University（云南大学生命科学学院）
- Research interest: Oxalidaceae [S]
- Published taxa: *Oxalis*
- Region: CHINA (Yunnan)

Y. Q. Tian

Tian, Ying Qiu; 田迎秋；Tián Yíngqiū

1981- **First publication: 2017**

- Employment: Maize Research Institute, Sichuan Agricultural University（四川农业大学玉米研究所）
- Research interest: Orchidaceae [S]
- Published taxa: *Dendrobium*
- Region: CHINA (Yunnan)

W. X. Tong

Tong, Wen Xuan; 同文轩；Tóng Wénxuān; 同文軒

1935- **First publication: 1992**

- Employment: Lanzhou Institute of Animal Science, Chinese Academy of Agricultural Sciences（中国农业科学院兰州畜牧研究所）
- Research interest: Poaceae; Herbaceous Plants [S]
- Published taxa: *Pennisetum*
- Affiliation: LZAH
- Location of specimens: LZAH
- Region: CHINA (Shaanxi)

S. Q. Tong

Tong, Shao Quan; 童绍全；Tóng Shàoquán; 童紹全

1935- **First publication: 1985**

- Employment: Kunming Institute of Botany, Chinese Academy of Sciences（中国科学院昆明植物研究所）
- Research interest: Arecaceae, Costaceae, Zingiberaceae; Plants of Yunnan [S]
- Published taxa: *Alpinia, Amomum, Boesenbergia, Costus, Curcuma, Hedychium, Kaempferia, Lanxangia, Meistera, Paramomum, Plagiostachys, Roscoea, Stahlianthus, Wurfbainia, Zingiber*
- Affiliation: HITBC, KUNE
- Region: CHINA

T. J. Tong

Tong, Tian Jing; 童恬静；Tóng Tiánjìng

1991- **First publication: 2017**

- Employment: South China Botanical Garden, Chinese Academy of Sciences（中国科学院华南植物园）
- Research interest: Asteraceae [S]
- Published taxa: *Senecio, Synotis*
- Region: [ASIA]

Y. Tong

Tong, Yi; 童毅；Tóng Yì

1988- **First publication: 2016**

- Employment: South China Botanical Garden, Chinese Academy of Sciences; Shanghai Chenshan Botanical Garden; College of Pharmacy, Guangzhou University of Chinese Medicine（中国科学院华南植物园；上海辰山植物园；广州中医药大学中药学院）
- Research interest: Acanthaceae, Begoniaceae, Melanthiaceae [S]
- Published taxa: *Begonia, Chionographis, Justicia*
- Region: CHINA

Y. H. Tong

Tong, Yi Hua; 童毅华；Tóng Yìhuá

1986- **First publication: 2013**

- Employment: South China Botanical Garden, Chinese Academy of Sciences（中国科学院华南植物园）
- Research interest: Betulaceae, Ebenaceae, Ericaceae, Fagaceae, Lamiaceae, Poaceae, Rosaceae, Rubiaceae, Urticaceae [S]
- Published taxa: *Agapetes, Argentina, Carpinus, Diospyros, Khoonmengia, Pilea, Prunus, Quercus, Rubovietnamia, Schizostachyum, Teucrium, Vaccinium*
- Affiliation: IBSC
- Location of specimens: IBSC
- Region: CHINA

R. H. Tu

Tu, Rong Hui; 涂蓉慧；Tú Rónghuì

1994- **First publication: 2018**

- Employment: College of Forestry, Central South University of Forestry and Technology（中南林业科技大学林学院）
- Research interest: Rubiaceae [S]
- Published taxa: *Ophiorrhiza*
- Region: CHINA (Yunnan)

T. Y. Tu

Tu, Tie Yao; 涂铁要；Tú Tiěyào

1979- **First publication: 2013**

- Employment: South China Botanical Garden, Chinese Academy of Sciences（中国科学院华南植物园）
- Research interest: Fabaceae, Fagaceae, Solanaceae; Plants of S. China [S]
- Published taxa: *Bauhinia, Quercus*
- Affiliation: IBSC
- Region: CHINA (Guangdong, Yunnan)

W. H. Tu

Tu, Wen Hui; 涂文辉；Tú Wénhuī

1996- **First publication: 2020**

- Employment: College of Forestry and Landscape Architecture, South China Agricultural University（华南农业大学林学与风景园林学院）
- Research interest: Begoniaceae [S]
- Published taxa: *Begonia*
- Region: CHINA (Guangdong)

X. D. Tu

Tu, Xiong De; 涂雄德；Tú Xióngdé

1994- **First publication: 2020**

- Employment: College of Landscape Architecture, Fujian Agriculture and Forestry University（福建农林大学园林学院）
- Research interest: Orchidaceae [S]
- Published taxa: *Liparis*
- Region: CHINA (Guangxi)

P. F. Tu

Tu, Peng Fei; 屠鹏飞；Tú Péngfēi

1963- **First publication: 1990**

- Employment: School of Pharmacy, Beijing Medical University（北京医科大学药学院）
- Research interest: Campanulaceae, Orobanchaceae [S]
- Published taxa: *Adenophora, Cistanche*
- Region: CHINA

Y. L. Tu

Tu, Yu Lin; 屠玉麟；Tú Yùlín

1941- **First publication: 1984**

- Employment: Department of Geography, Guiyang Normal College（贵阳师范学院地理系）
- Research interest: Juglandaceae, Liliaceae, Pinaceae, Rubiaceae [S]
- Published taxa: *Abies*
- Affiliation: GNUG
- Location of specimens: GNUG
- Region: CHINA (Guizhou)

Tolgor

Tolgor; 图力古尔；Túlìgǔěr

First publication: 1991

- Employment: Jilin Agricultural University（吉林农业大学）
- Research interest: Amaryllidaceae, Ranunculaceae [S]
- Published taxa: *Allium, Aconitum*
- Region: CHINA (Nei Mongol)

D. D. Tao

Tao, De Ding; 陶德定 ; Táo Dédìng
1937-2013 First publication: 1983

- Employment: Kunming Institute of Botany, Chinese Academy of Sciences (中国科学院昆明植物研究所)
- Research interest: Amaranthaceae, Araliaceae, Aristolochiaceae, Asparagaceae, Bignoniaceae, Loranthaceae, Menispermaceae, Opiliaceae, Orobanchaceae, Phrymaceae, Ranunculaceae, Rutaceae, Santalaceae, Sapotaceae [S]
- Published taxa: *Aralia, Aristolochia, Aspidistra, Champereia, Clausena, Cyrtandromoea, Dendrotrophe, Dichocarpum, Diploknema, Euodia, Fernandoa, Glycosmis, Lindenbergia, Phacellaria, Phtheirospermum, Psilotrichum, Stephania, Stereospermum, Taxillus, Thesium, Xizangia, Zanthoxylum*
- Affiliation: KUN
- Location of specimens: KUN, PE
- Region: CHINA (Yunnan)

S. B. Wan

Wan, Shao Bin; 万绍滨 ; Wàn Shàobīn; 万绍宾
1926-1998 First publication: 1983

- Employment: Department of Biology, Hunan Normal College (湖南师范学院生物系)
- Research interest: Betulaceae, Fagaceae [S]
- Published taxa: *Alnus*
- Affiliation: HNNU
- Location of specimens: HNNU
- Region: CHINA (Hunan)

W. H. Wan

Wan, Wen Hao; 万文豪 ; Wàn Wénháo; 萬文豪
1934- First publication: 1991

- Employment: Department of Biology, Jiangxi University (江西大学生物系)
- Research interest: Lythraceae, Trapoideae [S]
- Published taxa: *Trapa*
- Affiliation: JXU
- Location of specimens: JXU
- Region: CHINA (Jiangxi)

X. S. Wan

Wan, Xu Shan; 万绪山 ; Wàn Xùshān
1956- First publication: 1992

- Employment: Department of Traditional Chinese Pharmacy, Liaoning College of Traditional Chinese Medicine (辽宁中医学院中药系)
- Research interest: Plantaginaceae [S]
- Published taxa: *Plantago*
- Region: CHINA (Liaoning)

Y. Wan

Wan, Yu; 万煜 ; Wàn Yù; 萬煜
1937-1988 First publication: 1984

- Employment: Guangxi School of Pharmacy (广西药科学校)
- Research interest: Annonaceae, Apocynaceae, Asparagaceae, Begoniaceae, Commelinaceae, Lilicaceae, Menispermaceae, Rosaceae, Theaceae; Medicinal Plants [S]
- Published taxa: *Aganosma, Asparagus, Aspidistra, Begonia, Camellia, Fissistigma, Ophiopogon, Peliosanthes, Polygonatum, Porandra, Raphistemma, Rosa, Tinospora, Tupistra*
- Affiliation: GXSP
- Location of specimens: GXMI, GXSP
- Region: CHINA (Guangxi)

F. T. Wang

Wang, Fa Tsuan; Wang, Fa Zuan; 汪发缵 ; Wāng Fāzuǎn; 汪發纘
1899-1985 First publication: 1934

- Employment: Fan Memorial Institute of Biology; Institute of Botany, National Academy of Peiping; Institute of Systematic Botany, Academia Sinica; Institute of Botany, Chinese Academy of Sciences (静生生物调查所；国立北平研究院植物学研究所；中国科学院植物分类研究所；中国科学院植物研究所)
- Research interest: Amaryllidaceae, Araceae, Asparagaceae, Celastraceae, Colchicaceae, Cyperaceae, Eriocaulaceae, Fabaceae, Garryaceae, Liliaceae, Melanthiaceae, Moraceae, Myristicaceae, Nartheciaceae, Orchidaceae, Pittosporaceae, Smilacaceae, Stachyuraceae; Monocotyledons [S]
- Published taxa: *Aletris, Allium, Amitostigma, Androcorys, Ania, Aphyllorchis, Arachnis, Asparagus, Aspidistra, Astragalus, Aucuba, Bauhinia, Biermannia, Bletilla, Blysmus, Broussonetia, Bulbophyllum, Caesalpinia, Calanthe, Campylandra, Carex, Ceratostylis, Cheirostylis, Chionographis, Chrysoglossum, Cirrhopetalum, Collabium, Corybas, Cudrania, Cyperus, Cypripedium, Dendrobium, Desmotrichum, Diglyphosa, Diphylax, Disporum, Diuranthera, Dumasia, Eleocharis, Epipactis, Eria, Eriocaulon, Erythrodes, Fimbristylis, Flemingia,*

Fuirena, Goodyera, Habenaria, Hemipilia, Herminium, Hetaeria, Heterosmilax, Hexonix, Hypolytrum, Knema, Kobresia, Lilium, Liparis, Lipocarpha, Liriope, Listera, Malaxis, Mapania, Mariscus, Micropera, Mischobulbum, Monocelastrus, Morus, Myrmechis, Neottia, Nephelaphyllum, Nervilia, Odontochilus, Oligobotrya, Ophiopogon, Orchis, Panisea, Paphiopedilum, Paris, Pecteilis, Pelatantheria, Peliosanthes, Peristylus, Phalaenopsis, Phyllomphax, Pittosporum, Platanthera, Pleione, Pogonia, Polygonatum, Pomatocalpa, Porolabium, Pycreus, Robiquetia, Rohdea, Saccolabium, Sarcanthus, Sarcochilus, Sarcopodium, Scilla, Scirpus, Scleria, Siraitos, Smilacina, Smilax, Smithorchis, Stachyurus, Stauropsis, Streptopus, Sunipia, Thrixspermum, Trichoglottis, Tsaiorchis, Tupistra, Typhonium, Vanda, Veratrum, Ypsilandra

- Affiliation: PE
- Location of specimens: PE
- Region: CHINA

G. X. Wang

Wang, Guang Xi; 汪光熙 ; Wāng Guāngxī
1958- **First publication: 1994**

- Employment: Wuhan Institute of Botany, Chinese Academy of Sciences; Graduate School of Agriculture, Kyoto University, Japan（中国科学院武汉植物研究所；日本京都大学农学研究科）
- Research interest: Pontederiaceae [S]
- Published taxa: *Monochoria, Pontederia*
- Region: [ASIA]

H. B. Wang

Wang, Hai Bo; 汪海波 ; Wāng Hǎibō
First publication: 2008

- Employment: Leshan Greenfield Technology Service Co., Ltd., Sichuan（四川乐山市绿野科技服务有限公司）
- Research interest: Orchidaceae [S]
- Published taxa: *Dendrobium*
- Region: CHINA (Sichuan)

Jian Wang

Wang, Jian; 汪健 ; Wāng Jiàn
1986- **First publication: 2012**

- Employment: College of Forestry, Southwest Forestry University（西南林业大学林学院）
- Research interest: Apocynaceae, Crassulaceae [S]
- Published taxa: *Cynanchum, Sinocrassula*
- Region: CHINA (Yunnan)

J. W. Wang

Wang, Jin Wu; 汪劲武 ; Wāng Jìnwǔ ; 汪勁武
1927- **First publication: 1988**

- Employment: Department of Biology, Peking University（北京大学生物系）
- Research interest: Violaceae; Plants of Hebei [S]
- Published taxa: *Viola*
- Affiliation: PEY
- Location of specimens: PEY
- Region: CHINA (Beijing, Hebei)

M. Wang

Wang, Mao; 汪矛 ; Wāng Máo
1948- **First publication: 1988**

- Employment: Jilin Agricultural University（吉林农业大学）
- Research interest: Caprifoliaceae; Plant Anatomy [S]
- Published taxa: *Metalonicera*
- Affiliation: BAU
- Region: CHINA (Jilin)

P. Wang

Wang, Ping; 汪萍 ; Wāng Píng
First publication: 2002

- Employment: Guiyang No.8 High School, Guizhou（贵州省贵阳市第八中学）
- Research interest: Salicaceae [S]
- Published taxa: *Homalium*
- Region: CHINA (Guangdong)

Q. S. Wang

Wang, Qian Sheng; 汪前生 ; Wāng Qiánshēng
1937-2006 **First publication: 1987**

- Employment: Wuhan Institute of Botany, Chinese Academy of Sciences（中国科学院武汉植物研究所）
- Research interest: Araliaceae, Cyperaceae; Plants of Hubei [S]
- Published taxa: *Carex, Eleutherococcus*
- Affiliation: HIB
- Location of specimens: HIB
- Region: CHINA (Hubei)

R. B. Wang

Wang, Rong Bin; 汪荣斌 ; Wāng Róngbīn
1978- **First publication: 2019**

- Employment: College of Life Sciences, Anhui Normal University; Anhui College of Traditional Chinese Medicine（安徽师范大学生命科学学院；安徽中医药高等专科学校）
- Research interest: Ranunculaceae [S]
- Published taxa: *Clematis*
- Region: CHINA (Anhui)

Shu L. Wang

Wang, Shu Li; 汪书丽 ; Wāng Shūlì
1983- **First publication: 2011**

- Employment: Xizang Agriculture and Animal

Husbandry College（西藏农牧学院）
- Research interest: Campanulaceae, Lamiaceae; Plants of Xizang [S]
- Published taxa: *Cyananthus, Lamiophlomis*
- Affiliation: XZE
- Location of specimens: XZE
- Region: CHINA (Xizang)

X. F. Wang
Wang, Xiao Fan; 汪小凡；Wāng Xiǎofán
1965- **First publication: 2018**
- Employment: College of Life Sciences, Wuhan University（武汉大学生命科学学院）
- Research interest: Alismataceae, Poaceae, Rosaceae, Rubiaceae [S]
- Published taxa: *Rubia*
- Affiliation: WH, XYTC
- Location of specimens: WH
- Region: CHINA (Hubei)

X. L. Wang
Wang, Xiao Lan; 汪小兰；Wāng Xiǎolán
First publication: 1987
- Employment: Beijing Forestry University（北京林业大学）
- Research interest: Theaceae [S]
- Published taxa: *Camellia*
- Region: CHINA (Guangxi)

Xiao Q. Wang
Wang, Xiao Quan; 汪小全；Wāng Xiǎoquán
1968- **First publication: 2003**
- Employment: Institute of Botany, Chinese Academy of Sciences（中国科学院植物研究所）
- Research interest: Orobanchaceae, Paeoniaceae, Ranunculaceae [S]
- Published taxa: *Paeonia, Pedicularis*
- Affiliation: PE
- Location of specimens: PE
- Region: CHINA

A. H. Wang
Wang, Ai Hua; 王爱华；Wáng Àihuá
1985- **First publication: 2017**
- Employment: South China Botanical Garden, Chinese Academy of Sciences（中国科学院华南植物园）
- Research interest: Pteridaceae [P]
- Published taxa: *Adiantum*
- Region: CHINA (Guangxi)

An H. Wang
Wang, An Hu; 王安虎；Wáng Ānhǔ
First publication: 2007
- Employment: Xichang University（西昌学院）
- Research interest: Polygonaceae [S]
- Published taxa: *Fagopyrum*
- Region: CHINA (Sichuan)

B. Y. Wang
Wang, Bau Yung; Wang, Bau Yun; 王宝云；Wáng Bǎoyún; 王寶雲
First publication: 1960
- Employment: Northeast Forestry Institute（东北林学院）
- Research interest: Ranunculaceae [S]
- Published taxa: *Aconitum*
- Region: CHINA (Heilongjiang)

B. Z. Wang
Wang, Ben Zhong; 王本忠；Wáng Běnzhōng
1971- **First publication: 2020**
- Employment: Administration Bureau of Gaowangjie National Natural Reserve, Hunan（湖南高望界国家级自然保护区管理局）
- Research interest: Fagaceae [S]
- Published taxa: *Quercus*
- Region: CHINA (Hunan)

B. N. Wang
Wang, Bi Nong; 王必农；Wáng Bìnóng; 王必農
1941-2016 **First publication: 1986**
- Employment: Sichuan Jinfo Mountain Nature Reserve（四川金佛山自然保护区）
- Research interest: Liliaceae [S]
- Published taxa: *Lilium*
- Region: CHINA (Chongqing)

B. Wang
Wang, Bing; Wang, Bin 王兵 Wáng Bīng
1957- **First publication: 1989**
- Employment: Xinjiang Bayi Agricultural College（新疆八一农学院）
- Research interest: Lamiaceae, Ranunculaceae [S]
- Published taxa: *Delphinium, Nepeta, Perovskia*
- Affiliation: XJA
- Location of specimens: XJA
- Region: CHINA (Xinjiang)

Bing Wang
Wang, Bing; 王冰；Wáng Bīng
First publication: 1991
- Employment: Liaoning College of Traditional Chinese Medicine（辽宁中医学院）
- Research interest: Rhamnaceae [S]
- Published taxa: *Ziziphus*
- Region: CHINA (Liaoning)

B. M. Wang

Wang, Bing Mou; 王炳谋 ; Wáng Bǐngmóu

1984- **First publication: 2016**

- Employment: Guangzhou Panyu Central Hospital（广东省番禺中心医院）
- Research interest: Asparagaceae, Begoniaceae, Ericaceae, Gesneriaceae, Orchidaceae, Rubiaceae [S]
- Published taxa: *Agapetes, Aspidistra, Begonia, Bulbophyllum, Primulina, Spiradiclis*
- Region: CHINA

B. S. Wang

Wang, Ba San; Wong, Bo Sun; Wang, Pai Sun; Wang, Bai Sun; 王伯荪 ; Wáng Bósūn

1931- **First publication: 1961**

- Employment: Department of Biology, Sun Yat-sen University（中山大学生物系）
- Research interest: Blechnaceae, Dennstaedtiaceae, Lindsaeaceae, Pteridaceae, Thelypteridaceae; Plants of Guangdong [P]
- Published taxa: *Hypolepis, Lindsaea, Microlepia, Pronephrium, Vittaria, Woodwardia*
- Affiliation: SYS
- Location of specimens: SYS
- Region: CHINA (Guangdong)

C. L. Wang

Wang, Ceng Lin; 王层林 ; Wáng Cénglín

1974- **First publication: 2009**

- Employment: School of Forestry & Landscape Architecture, Anhui Agricultural University（安徽农业大学林学与园林学院）
- Research interest: Rosaceae [S]
- Published taxa: *Sorbus*
- Region: CHINA (Anhui)

C. B. Wang

Wang, Chang Bao; 王长宝 ; Wáng Chángbǎo

1972- **First publication: 2011**

- Employment: College of Life Sciences, Sichuan University; College of Life Sciences, Jiamusi University（四川大学生命科学学院；佳木斯大学生命科学学院）
- Research interest: Apiaceae [S]
- Published taxa: *Bupleurum*
- Region: CHINA (Guizhou)

C. Y. Wang

Wang, Chang Yong; Wang, Chung Yong; 王长墉 ; Wáng Chángyōng; 王長墉

1933-? **First publication: 1984**

- Employment: Shandong College of Traditional Chinese Medicine（山东中医学院）
- Research interest: Polypodiaceae [PS]
- Published taxa: *Phymatopsis*
- Region: CHINA (Shandong)

C. P. Wang

Wang, Chao Pin; 王朝品 ; Wáng Cháopǐn

1920-1998 **First publication: 1986**

- Employment: Department of Grassland, Inner Mongolia College of Agriculture and Animal Husbandry（内蒙古农牧学院草原系）
- Research interest: Poaceae [S]
- Published taxa: *Cleistogenes, Elymus, × Oryticum, Phyllostachys, Roegneria, Stipa*
- Location of specimens: NMAC
- Region: CHINA

Chen Wang

Wang, Chen; 王臣 ; Wáng Chén

1964- **First publication: 1992**

- Employment: Department of Biology, Harbin Normal University（哈尔滨师范大学生物系）
- Research interest: Ranunculaceae, Violaceae [S]
- Published taxa: *Batrachium*
- Affiliation: HANU
- Location of specimens: HANU
- Region: CHINA (Heilongjiang)

C. H. Wang

Wang, Chun Hui; 王春晖 ; Wáng Chūnhuī

1992- **First publication: 2018**

- Employment: College of Life Sciences, Wuhan University（武汉大学生命科学学院）
- Research interest: Rubiaceae [S]
- Published taxa: *Rubia*
- Region: CHINA (Hubei)

C. J. Wang

Wang, Cong Jiao; 王从皎 ; Wáng Cóngjiǎo; 王從皎

1927-? **First publication: 1988**

- Employment: Southwest Forestry College（西南林学院）
- Research interest: Betulaceae, Theaceae [S]
- Published taxa: *Betula, Camellia, Carpinus, Corylus*
- Location of specimens: SWFC
- Region: CHINA (Yunnan)

D. M. Wang

Wang, Da Ming; 王达明 ; Wáng Dámíng; 王達明

1940- **First publication: 1981**

- Employment: Yunnan Forestry College（云南林学院）
- Research interest: Dipterocarpaceae, Fagaceae [S]
- Published taxa: *Cyclobalanopsis, Hopea*
- Location of specimens: YAF, YCP

• Region: CHINA (Yunnan)

D. Q. Wang

Wang, De Qun; 王德群 ; Wáng Déqún
1951- **First publication: 1987**

- Employment: Anhui College of Traditional Chinese Medicine (安徽中医学院)
- Research interest: Aristolochiaceae, Asparagaceae, Campanulaceae, Commelinaceae, Crassulaceae, Liliaceae, Ranunculaceae, Violaceae; Medicinal Plants [S]
- Published taxa: *Adenophora, Asarum, Codonopsis, Commelina, Fritillaria, Hosta, Sedum, Semiaquilegia, Viola*
- Affiliation: ACM
- Location of specimens: ACM
- Region: CHINA (Anhui)

D. Y. Wang

Wang, De Yin; 王德银 ; Wáng Déyín; 王德銀
1944- **First publication: 1982**

- Employment: Sichuan Institute of Forest Science (四川省林业科学研究所)
- Research interest: Cupressaceae, Cycadaceae [S]
- Published taxa: *Cunninghamia, Cycas*
- Region: CHINA (Sichuan)

D. Yue Wang

Wang, Ding Yue; Wang, Ding Yao; 王定跃 ; Wáng Dìngyuè
1962- **First publication: 1996**

- Employment: Fairy Lake Botanical Garden, Shenzhen & Chinese Academy of Sciences (深圳市中国科学院仙湖植物园)
- Research interest: Cycadaceae, Theaceae; Plants of E. China [S]
- Published taxa: *Cycas*
- Affiliation: SZG
- Location of specimens: SZG
- Region: CHINA

D. Wang

Wang, Dong; 王东 ; Wáng Dōng
1964- **First publication: 2002**

- Employment: College of Life Sciences, Wuhan University; School of Life Sciences, Central China Normal University (武汉大学生命科学学院 ; 华中师范大学生命科学学院)
- Research interest: Haloragaceae, Papaveraceae; Medicinal Plants [S]
- Published taxa: *Corydalis, Myriophyllum*
- Affiliation: CCNU, HZTC, SXMP
- Location of specimens: CCNU, HZTC, SXMP
- Region: CHINA

F. G. Wang

Wang, Fa Guo; 王发国 ; Wáng Fāguó
1978- **First publication: 2002**

- Employment: South China Institute of Botany, Chinese Academy of Sciences; South China Botanical Garden, Chinese Academy of Sciences (中国科学院华南植物研究所 ; 中国科学院华南植物园)
- Research interest: Begoniaceae, Davalliaceae, Dryopteridaceae, Fagaceae, Hypodematiaceae, Lauraceae, Magnoliaceae, Pteridaceae, Saxifragaceae, Symplocaceae, Tectariaceae [PS]
- Published taxa: *Adiantum, Begonia, Bolbitis, Cinnamomum, Davallia, Elaphoglossum, Hypodematium, Hypoderris, Lithocarpus, Manglietia, Saxifraga, Symplocos*
- Region: CHINA

F. S. Wang

Wang, Fa Song; 王发松 ; Wáng Fāsōng
1969- **First publication: 2000**

- Employment: School of Life Sciences, Sun Yat-sen University; Hubei Minzu University (中山大学生命科学学院 ; 湖北民族大学)
- Research interest: Gesneriaceae, Hypericaceae, Vitaceae [S]
- Published taxa: *Didymocarpus, Hypericum, Vitis*
- Region: CHINA

G. T. Wang

Wang, Gang Tao; 王刚涛 ; Wáng Gāngtāo
1990- **First publication: 2018**

- Employment: South China Botanical Garden, Chinese Academy of Sciences (中国科学院华南植物园)
- Research interest: Rubiaceae [S]
- Published taxa: *Hedyotis*
- Region: CHINA (Guangdong)

G. C. Wang

Wang, Gui Chen; 王贵臣 ; Wáng Guìchén
First publication: 1984

- Employment: The Institute of Vegetables, Chinese Academy of Agricultural Sciences (中国农业科学院蔬菜研究所)
- Research interest: Cucurbitaceae [S]
- Published taxa: *Cucumis*
- Region: CHINA (Shandong)

Guo C. Wang

Wang, Guo Chang; 王国昌 ; Wáng Guóchāng; 王國昌
1934-2016 **First publication: 1990**

- Employment: South China Agricultural University (华南农业大学)
- Research interest: Poaceae [S]

- Published taxa: *Oryza*
- Region: CHINA

G. H. Wang

Wang, Guo Hong; 王国宏 ; Wáng Guóhóng
1963- **First publication: 1995**
- Employment: College of Forestry, Gansu Agricultural University (甘肃农业大学林学院)
- Research interest: Cannabaceae, Ericaceae, Pittosporaceae, Salicaceae, Saxifragaceae [S]
- Published taxa: *Celtis, Pittosporum, Rhododendron, Salix, Saxifraga*
- Location of specimens: GAUF
- Region: CHINA (Gansu)

K. H. Wang

Wang, Kuo Hsiung; 王國雄 ; Wáng Guóxióng; 王国雄
First publication: 2019
- Employment: Institute of Ecology and Evolutionary Biology, Taiwan University (台湾大学生态学与演化生物学研究所)
- Research interest: Orchidaceae [S]
- Published taxa: *Cyrtosia*
- Region: CHINA (Taiwan)

H. X. Wang

Wang, Hai Xia; 王海霞 ; Wáng Hǎixiá
First publication: 2018
- Employment: Jiangxi Academy of Forestry (江西省林业科学院)
- Research interest: Poaceae [S]
- Published taxa: *Phyllostachys*
- Region: CHINA (Jiangxi)

H. J. Wang

Wang, Han Jin; 王汉津 ; Wáng Hànjīn; 王漢津
1929-2002 **First publication: 1978**
- Employment: Department of Biology, Fudan University (复旦大学生物系)
- Research interest: Caprifoliaceae, Crassulaceae, Valerianaceae; Plant of Shanghai [S]
- Published taxa: *Leycesteria, Lonicera, Patrinia, Sedum*
- Affiliation: FUS
- Location of specimens: FUS
- Region: CHINA
- IPNI as: G. J. Wang

Hao Wang

Wang, Hao; 王豪 ; Wáng Háo
1994- **First publication: 2020**
- Employment: College of Life Sciences, Southwest University (西南大学生命科学学院)
- Research interest: Crassulaceae [S]
- Published taxa: *Rhodiola*
- Region: CHINA (Xizang)

H. S. Wang

Wang, He Sheng; 王荷生 ; Wáng Héshēng
1929- **First publication: 1983**
- Employment: Institute of Geography, Chinese Academy of Sciences (中国科学院地理研究所)
- Research interest: Theaceae [S]
- Published taxa: *Camellia*
- Region: CHINA

Heng C. Wang

Wang, Heng Chang; 王恒昌 ; Wáng Héngchāng
1968- **First publication: 2013**
- Employment: Wuhan Botanical Garden, Chinese Academy of Sciences (中国科学院武汉植物园)
- Research interest: Menispermaceae, Rosaceae [S]
- Published taxa: *Argentina, Stephania*
- Affiliation: HIB
- Location of specimens: HIB
- Region: CHINA (Guangxi, Xizang)

Hong Wang bis

Wang, Hong; 王红 ; Wáng Hóng
1964- **First publication: 2005**
- Employment: Kunming Institute of Botany, Chinese Academy of Sciences (中国科学院昆明植物研究所)
- Research interest: Cucurbitaceae, Orchidaceae, Orobanchaceae, Pentaphylacaceae, Scrophulariaceae [S]
- Published taxa: *Calanthe, Eurya, Pedicularis, Pterygiella, Thladiantha*
- Affiliation: KUN
- Location of specimens: KUN
- Region: CHINA (Yunnan)
- IPNI as: H. Wang

Hong Wang

Wang, Hong; 王泓 ; Wáng Hóng
1971- **First publication: 2005**
- Employment: College of Life Sciences, Zhejiang University; College of Life and Environmental Sciences, Hangzhou Normal University (浙江大学生命科学学院 ; 杭州师范大学生命与环境科学学院)
- Research interest: Cyperaceae [S]
- Published taxa: *Carex*
- Region: CHINA (Guangxi, Zhejiang)
- IPNI as: H. Wang

H. Wang

Wang, Hong; 王洪 ; Wáng Hóng
1955- **First publication: 1994**
- Employment: Xishuangbanna Tropical Botanical Garden, Chinese Academy of Sciences (中国科学院

西双版纳热带植物园）
• Research interest: Meliaceae, Musaceae; Plants of Yunnan [S]
• Published taxa: *Amoora, Musa*
• Affiliation: HITBC
• Location of specimens: HITBC
• Region: CHINA (Yunnan)

Huan C. Wang
Wang, Huan Chong; 王焕冲；Wáng Huànchōng
1980- **First publication: 2013**
• Employment: School of Life Sciences, Yunnan University（云南大学生命科学学院）
• Research interest: Apiaceae, Gesneriaceae, Orobanchaceae, Rosaceae, Urticaceae; Plants of Yunnan [S]
• Published taxa: *Acronema, Bupleurum, Petrocosmea, Pilea, Potentilla, Prunus, Pterygiella, Rubus*
• Affiliation: YUKU
• Location of specimens: YUKU
• Region: CHINA

Hui Wang bis
Wang, Hui; 王晖；Wáng Huī
1982- **First publication: 2020**
• Employment: Fairy Lake Botanical Garden, Shenzhen & Chinese Academy of Sciences（深圳市中国科学院仙湖植物园）
• Research interest: Asclepiadaceae, Hymenophyllaceae; Pteridophytes [PS]
• Published taxa: *Crepidomanes, Hoya*
• Affiliation: SZG
• Location of specimens: SZG
• Region: CHINA
• IPNI as: Wang Hui

H. Q. Wang
Wang, Hui Qin; 王徽勤；Wáng Huīqín
1934- **First publication: 1981**
• Employment: Department of Biology, Wuhan University（武汉大学生物系）
• Research interest: Alismataceae, Hydrocharitaceae, Poaceae, Potamogetonaceae [S]
• Published taxa: *Alisma, Eragrostis, Najas, Ottelia, Potamogeton, Sagittaria*
• Affiliation: WH
• Location of specimens: WH
• Region: CHINA

J. M. Wang
Wang, Ji Mei; 王继梅；Wáng Jìméi
1972- **First publication: 2010**
• Employment: College of Life Science, Qufu Normal University; jinxiang No.2 Middle School, Shandong（曲阜师范大学生命科学学院；山东省金乡县第二中学）
• Research interest: Asteraceae [S]
• Published taxa: *Chrysanthemum*
• Region: CHINA

Jia G. Wang
Wang, Jia Guo; 王加国；Wáng Jiāguó
1989- **First publication: 2016**
• Employment: Guizhou Normal University; College of Forestry, Guizhou University（贵州师范大学；贵州大学林学院）
• Research interest: Asparagaceae [S]
• Published taxa: *Polygonatum*
• Location of specimens: GZAC
• Region: CHINA (Guizhou)
• IPNI as: J. G. Wang

J. Z. Wang
Wang, Jian Zhong; 王建中；Wáng Jiànzhōng
1952- **First publication: 1989**
• Employment: Beijing Forestry University（北京林业大学）
• Research interest: Athyriaceae, Dryopteridaceae, Equisetaceae, Grossulariaceae, Lamiaceae, Polypodiaceae [PS]
• Published taxa: *Athyrium, Dryopteris, Hippochaete, Neoathyrium, Phymatopsis, Ribes, Schizonepeta*
• Location of specimens: BJFC
• Region: CHINA

J. Wang
Wang, Jian; 王健；Wáng Jiàn
First publication: 2006
• Employment: Aletai Research Institute of Forestry, Xinjiang（新疆阿勒泰地区林业科学研究所）
• Research interest: Betulaceae [S]
• Published taxa: *Betula*
• Region: CHINA (Xinjiang)

Jian Wang tris
Wang, Jian; 王健；Wáng Jiàn
1959- **First publication: 2016**
• Employment: Brisbane Botanic Gardens, Australia（澳大利亚布里斯班植物园）
• Research interest: Asparagaceae, Asteraceae [S]
• Published taxa: *Lagenophora, Lomandra, Solenogyne*
• Region: AUSTRALIA

Jian S. Wang
Wang, Jian Sheng; 王健生；Wáng Jiànshēng
First publication: 2020
• Employment: Jinhua Polytechnic, Zhejiang（金华职

业技术学院）
- Research interest: Balsaminaceae [S]
- Published taxa: *Impatiens*
- Region: CHINA (Fujian)

J. Y. Wang

Wang, Jie Yu; 王洁雨；Wáng Jiéyǔ
1992- **First publication: 2017**
- Employment: College of Forestry and Landscape Architecture, South China Agricultural University; The Orchid Conservation & Research Center of Shenzhen, Guangdong（华南农业大学林学与风景园林学院；广东省深圳市兰科植物保护研究中心）
- Research interest: Orchidaceae [S]
- Published taxa: *Bulbophyllum*
- Region: CHINA (Yunnan)

Jing Q. Wang

Wang, Jing Quan; 王景权；Wáng Jǐngquán; 王景權
1943- **First publication: 2002**
- Employment: Forestry Bureau, Heilongjiang Farms & Land Reclamation Administration（黑龙江省农垦总局林业局）
- Research interest: Salicaceae [S]
- Published taxa: *Salix*
- Region: CHINA (Heilongjiang)
- IPNI as: J. Q. Wang

J. X. Wang

Wang, Jing Xiang; 王景祥；Wáng Jǐngxiáng
1924- **First publication: 1981**
- Employment: Zhejiang Forestry College（浙江林学院）
- Research interest: Daphniphyllaceae [S]
- Published taxa: *Daphniphyllum*
- Location of specimens: IBSC
- Region: CHINA

Jing Wang

Wang, Jing; 王静；Wáng Jìng
1980- **First publication: 2009**
- Employment: South China Botanical Garden, Chinese Academy of Sciences（中国科学院华南植物园）
- Research interest: Annonaceae, Gesneriaceae [S]
- Published taxa: *Dasymaschalon, Primulina*
- Region: [ASIA]

Jing H. Wang

Wang, Jing Hua; 王静华；Wáng Jìnghuá
1962- **First publication: 2005**
- Employment: Kunming Institute of Botany, Chinese Academy of Sciences（中国科学院昆明植物研究所）
- Research interest: Pentaphylacaceae [S]
- Published taxa: *Eurya*
- Affiliation: KUN
- Region: CHINA (Yunnan)
- IPNI as: J. H. Wang

J. Q. Wang

Wang, Jing Quan; 王镜泉；Wáng Jìngquán; 王鏡泉
1938- **First publication: 1980**
- Employment: Faculty of Plant Taxonomy, Gansu Normal University（甘肃师范大学植物分类研究室）
- Research interest: Boraginaceae, Salicaceae, Zygophyllaceae [S]
- Published taxa: *Eritrichium, Salix*
- Affiliation: NWTC
- Location of specimens: NWTC
- Region: CHINA (Gansu)

Jiu L. Wang

Wang, Jiu Li; 王久利；Wáng Jiǔlì
1991- **First publication: 2018**
- Employment: Northwest Plateau Institute of Biology, Chinese Academy of Sciences（中国科学院西北高原生物研究所）
- Research interest: Gentianaceae [S]
- Published taxa: *Halenia*
- Region: CHINA (Sichuan)

Juan Wang

Wang, Juan; 王娟；Wáng Juān
1966- **First publication: 2008**
- Employment: Faculty of Natural Resources, Southwest Forestry University（西南林学院资源学院）
- Research interest: Gentianaceae, Primulaceae [S]
- Published taxa: *Gentiana, Paralysimachia*
- Region: CHINA (Yunnan)
- IPNI as: J. Wang

J. F. Wang

Wang, Jun Feng; 王军峰；Wáng Jūnfēng
1980- **First publication: 2017**
- Employment: Lishui Forestry Institute, Zhejiang（浙江省丽水市林业科学研究院）
- Research interest: Lamiaceae [S]
- Published taxa: *Salvia*
- Region: CHINA (Zhejiang)

Jun Wang tris

Wang, Jun; 王君；Wáng Jūn
1991- **First publication: 2020**
- Employment: Xinyang Normal University（信阳师范学院）
- Research interest: Aristolochiaceae [S]
- Published taxa: *Isotrema*

- Region: CHINA (Guangxi, Yunnan)
- IPNI as: Jun Wang

Jun Wang

Wang, Jun; 王俊 ; Wáng Jùn

1957- **First publication: 2009**

- Employment: College of Life Sciences, Ningxia University（宁夏大学生命科学学院）
- Research interest: Geraniaceae [S]
- Published taxa: *Geranium*
- Region: CHINA (Ningxia)
- IPNI as: J. Wang

Jun Wang bis

Wang, Jun; 王俊 ; Wáng Jùn

1982- **First publication: 2010**

- Employment: South China Botanical Garden, Chinese Academy of Sciences（中国科学院华南植物园）
- Research interest: Asteraceae [S]
- Published taxa: *Ainsliaea*
- Region: CHINA (Guangdong)
- IPNI as: J. Wang

K. Y. Wang

Wang, Kai Yun; 王开运 ; Wáng Kāiyùn

1960- **First publication: 1988**

- Employment: Northwest Forestry College（西北林学院）
- Research interest: Betulaceae, Cornaceae, Pinaceae, Styracaceae; Woody Plants [S]
- Published taxa: *Carpinus, Cornus, Pseudotsuga, Styrax*
- Affiliation: NWFC
- Region: CHINA (Shaanxi)

K. L. Wang

Wang, Kang Lin; 王慷林 ; Wáng Kānglín

1964- **First publication: 2002**

- Employment: Kunming Institute of Botany, Chinese Academy of Sciences; Southwest Forestry University（中国科学院昆明植物研究所；西南林业大学）
- Research interest: Arecaceae, Poaceae [S]
- Published taxa: *Calamus, Dendrocalamus*
- Location of specimens: KUN
- Region: CHINA (Yunnan)

K. Q. Wang

Wang, Ke Qing; 王可青 ; Wáng Kěqīng

1968- **First publication: 2003**

- Employment: Institute of Botany, Chinese Academy of Sciences（中国科学院植物研究所）
- Research interest: Aspleniaceae [P]
- Published taxa: *Asplenium*
- Region: CHINA

L. C. Wang

Wang, Lan Chow; Wang, Lan Zhou; 王兰州 ; Wáng Lánzhōu

1952- **First publication: 1986**

- Employment: Department of Forestry, South China Agricultural University; Department of Biology, Northwest Normal University（华南农业大学林学系；西北师范大学生物系）
- Research interest: Apocynaceae, Campanulaceae, Celastraceae, Cornaceae, Dipterocarpaceae, Fabaceae, Hydrangeaceae, Lauraceae, Polygonaceae, Ranunculaceae, Rosaceae; Plants of Gansu [S]
- Published taxa: *Aconitum, Campanula, Cornus, Deutzia, Euonymus, Indigofera, Kerria, Lindera, Litsea, Polygonum, Tylophora, Vatica*
- Affiliation: NWUB
- Location of specimens: GAUF, NWUB
- Region: CHINA
- Also as: L. Z. Wang

Lei Wang

Wang, Lei; 王磊 ; Wáng Lěi

1943- **First publication: 1990**

- Employment: Department of Horticulture, Xinjiang Bayi Agricultural College（新疆八一农学院园艺系）
- Research interest: Rosaceae [S]
- Published taxa: *Prunus*
- Region: CHINA (Xinjiang)
- IPNI as: L. Wang

Lei Wang bis

Wang, Lei; 王蕾 ; Wáng Lěi

1977- **First publication: 2018**

- Employment: College of Resource Environment and Tourism, Capital Normal University（首都师范大学资源环境与旅游学院）
- Research interest: Saxifragaceae [S]
- Published taxa: *Saxifraga*
- Region: CHINA (Hunan, Jiangxi)
- IPNI as: L. Wang; Lei Wang

Li Wang

Wang, Li; 王丽 ; Wáng Lì

1983- **First publication: 2010**

- Employment: Institute of Botany, Chinese Academy of Sciences（中国科学院植物研究所）
- Research interest: Polypodiaceae [P]
- Published taxa: *Lemmaphyllum, Lepidomicrosorium, Lepisorus, Neolepisorus*
- Region: CHINA

• IPNI as: L. Wang

Li Song Wang

Wang, Li Song; 王利松 ; Wáng Lìsōng
1976- **First publication: 2016**

• Employment: Kunming Institute of Botany, Chinese Academy of Sciences; Institute of Botany, Chinese Academy of Sciences（中国科学院昆明植物研究所；中国科学院植物研究所）
• Research interest: Apiaceae, Poaceae [S]
• Published taxa: *Digitaria, Pternopetalum, Sium*
• Affiliation: PE
• Location of specimens: PE
• Region: CHINA (Yunnan)
• IPNI as: Li S. Wang

L. Z. Wang

Wang, Lian Zheng; 王连铮 ; Wáng Liánzhēng; 王連錚
1930-2018 **First publication: 1983**

• Employment: Heilongjiang Academy of Agricultural Sciences（黑龙江省农业科学院）
• Research interest: Fabaceae [S]
• Published taxa: *Glycine*
• Region: CHINA (Heilongjiang)

L. M. Wang

Wang, Liang Min; 王良民 ; Wáng Liángmín
1955- **First publication: 1984**

• Employment: College of Forestry, Shanxi Agricultural University; Beijing Forestry College（山西农业大学林学院；北京林学院）
• Research interest: Celastraceae, Fagaceae [S]
• Published taxa: *Euonymus, Quercus*
• Affiliation: SXAU
• Location of specimens: SXAU
• Region: CHINA

Ling Wang

Wang, Ling; 王玲 ; Wáng Líng
1972- **First publication: 2012**

• Employment: School of Landscape Architecture, Northeast Forestry University（东北林业大学园林学院）
• Research interest: Brassicaceae, Iridaceae [S]
• Published taxa: *Iris, Orychophragmus*
• Region: CHINA (Heilongjiang, Jilin, Liaoning)
• IPNI as: L. Wang

L. S. Wang

Wang, Ling Shi; 王凌诗 ; Wáng Língshī
1963- **First publication: 1993**

• Employment: Department of Biology, Harbin Normal University（哈尔滨师范大学生物系）
• Research interest: Asteraceae [S]
• Published taxa: *Artemisia*
• Region: CHINA (Heilongjiang)

Long Wang bis

Wang, Long; 王龙 ; Wáng Lóng
1988- **First publication: 2016**

• Employment: College of Science, Sichuan Agricultural University（四川农业大学理学院）
• Research interest: Lamiaceae [S]
• Published taxa: *Salvia*
• Region: CHINA (Yunnan)
• IPNI as: L. Wang

Long Wang

Wang, Long; 王龙 ; Wáng Lóng
1991- **First publication: 2015**

• Employment: South China Botanical Garden, Chinese Academy of Sciences（中国科学院华南植物园）
• Research interest: Asteraceae [S]
• Published taxa: *Cremanthodium, Ligularia*
• Region: [ASIA]
• IPNI as: L. Wang

Long Wang tris

Wang, Long; 王龙 ; Wáng Lóng
First publication: 2019

• Employment: Department of Traditional Chinese Medicine Resources, China Pharmaceutical University（中国药科大学中药资源学教研室）
• Research interest: Liliaceae [S]
• Published taxa: *Amana*
• Region: CHINA (Jiangsu)
• IPNI as: L. Wang

Long Y. Wang

Wang, Long Yuan; 王龙远 ; Wáng Lóngyuǎn
1985- **First publication: 2018**

• Employment: School of Life Sciences, Sun Yat-sen University; Zhongkai University of Agriculture and Engineering（中山大学生命科学学院；仲恺农业工程学院）
• Research interest: Rosaceae [S]
• Published taxa: *Pourthiaea, Stranvaesia*
• Region: CHINA

L. R. Wang

Wang, Luo Rong; 王罗荣 ; Wáng Luōróng; 王羅榮
1939- **First publication: 2006**

• Employment: General Station for Forest Pest and Disease Control and Quarantine in Hubei Province（湖北省林木种苗管理总站）
• Research interest: Magnoliaceae [S]
• Published taxa: *Magnolia*

• Region: CHINA (Hubei)

M. L. Wang

Wang, Ma Li; 王玛丽 ; Wáng Mǎlì

1963- **First publication: 2004**

- Employment: College of Life Sciences, Northwest University（西北大学生命科学学院）
- Research interest: Woodsiaceae; Bryophyte; Pteridophytes. [BP]
- Published taxa: *Deparioideae, Rhachidosoroideae*
- Affiliation: WNU
- Location of specimens: WNU
- Region: CHINA (Shaanxi)

M. C. Wang

Wang, Ming Chin; Wang, Ming Jin; Wang, Ming Kin; 王名金 ; Wáng Míngjīn

1926-2018 **First publication: 1954**

- Employment: Institute of Botany, Chinese Academy of Sciences（中国科学院植物研究所）
- Research interest: Celastraceae [S]
- Published taxa: *Euonymus*
- Location of specimens: HZU, NAS
- Region: CHINA (Jiangxi)
- Also as: M. K. Wang

M. Chang Wang

Wang, Ming Chang; 王明昌 ; Wáng Míngchāng

1934- **First publication: 1988**

- Employment: Northwest Forestry College（西北林学院）
- Research interest: Magnoliaceae, Papaveraceae, Sapindaceae; Woody Plants [S]
- Published taxa: *Acer, Magnolia, Meconopsis*
- Affiliation: NWFC
- Location of specimens: NWFC
- Region: CHINA (Shaanxi)

N. Wang

Wang, Ning; 王宁 ; Wáng Níng

1962- **First publication: 1989**

- Employment: Wuhu School of Traditional Chinese Medicine（安徽省芜湖中医学校）
- Research interest: Ranunculaceae [S]
- Published taxa: *Anemone*
- Affiliation: BJM
- Location of specimens: WUH
- Region: CHINA (Anhui)

N. Z. Wang

Wang, Ning Zhu; 王宁珠 ; Wáng Níngzhū; 王寧珠

1940- **First publication: 1985**

- Employment: Wuhan Institute of Botany, Chinese Academy of Sciences（中国科学院武汉植物研究所）
- Research interest: Hydrocharitaceae [S]
- Published taxa: *Najas*
- Region: CHINA

Pan Wang

Wang, Pan; 王盼 ; Wáng Pàn

1989- **First publication: 2018**

- Employment: Administration of Dapanshan National Natural Reserve, Zhejiang（浙江省大盘山国家级自然保护区管理局）
- Research interest: Thymelaeaceae [S]
- Published taxa: *Daphne*
- Region: CHINA (Zhejiang)
- IPNI as: P. Wang

P. S. Wang

Wang, Pei Shan; 王培善 ; Wáng Péishàn

1936- **First publication: 1983**

- Employment: Institute of Biology, Guizhou Academy of Sciences（贵州省科学院生物研究所）
- Research interest: Athyriaceae, Cystopteridaceae, Dennstaedtiaceae, Dryopteridaceae, Hymenophyllaceae, Lycopodiaceae, Polypodiaceae, Pteridaceae, Rosaceae, Sabiaceae, Selaginellaceae, Thelypteridaceae, Woodsiaceae; Pteridophytes [PS]
- Published taxa: *Allantodia, Athyriopsis, Cheilosoria, Coniogramme, Crepidomanes, Ctenitis, Cyclosorus, Cyrtogonellum, Cyrtomium, Cystopteris, Dryoathyrium, Dryopteris, Huperzia, Lepidomicrosorium, Microlepia, Neolepisorus, Phymatopteris, Polypodiodes, Polystichum, Pteris, Rubus, Sabia, Selaginella, Woodsia*
- Affiliation: HGAS
- Location of specimens: HGAS
- Region: CHINA (Guizhou)

Ping S. Wang

Wang, Ping Sheng; 王平盛 ; Wáng Píngshèng

First publication: 1983

- Employment: Tea Research Institute, Yunnan Academy of Agricultural Sciences（云南省农业科学院茶叶研究所）
- Research interest: Theaceae [S]
- Published taxa: *Camellia*
- Region: CHINA (Yunnan)
- IPNI as: P. S. Wang

P. Y. Wang

Wang, Ping Yuan; 王平元 ; Wáng Píngyuán

1985- **First publication: 2016**

- Employment: Xishuangbanna Tropical Botanical Garden, Chinese Academy of Sciences（中国科学院西双版纳热带植物园）
- Research interest: Poaceae [S]

• Published taxa: *Dendrocalamus*
• Region: CHINA (Yunnan)

P. L. Wang

Wang, Ping Li; 王萍莉 ; Wáng Pínglì
1936- **First publication: 2004**
• Employment: Chengdu Institute of Biology, Chinese Academy of Sciences（中国科学院成都生物研究所）
• Research interest: Nothofagaceae; Palynology [S]
• Published taxa: *Nothofagus*
• Affiliation: CDBI
• Region: CHINA

Qi Wang

Wang, Qi; 王祺 ; Wáng Qí
1973- **First publication: 2001**
• Employment: Department of Geology, Peking University（北京大学地质学系）
• Research interest: Fabaceae [S]
• Published taxa: *Oxytropis*
• Region: CHINA (Xinjiang)
• IPNI as: Q. Wang

C. W. Wang

Wang, Chi Wu; Wang, Ch'i Wu; Wang, Qi Wu; 王启无 ; Wáng Qǐwú; 王啟無
1913-1987 **First publication: 1941**
• Employment: Fan Memorial Institute of Biology（静生生物调查所）
• Research interest: Celastraceae; Bryophyte; Woody Plants [BS]
• Published taxa: *Euonymus*
• Location of specimens: LBG, KUN, NAS, NF, PE
• Region: CHINA (Yunnan)

Qian Wang

Wang, Qian; 王茜 ; Wáng Qiàn
1987- **First publication: 2016**
• Employment: College of Life Sciences, Southwest University（西南大学生命科学学院）
• Research interest: Balsaminaceae, Begoniaceae, Pentaphylacaceae [S]
• Published taxa: *Eurya, Impatiens*
• Affiliation: SWCTU
• Location of specimens: SWCTU
• Region: CHINA (Hubei)
• IPNI as: Qiang Wang; Q. Wang

Qiang Wang

Wang, Qiang; 王强 ; Wáng Qiáng
1982- **First publication: 2015**
• Employment: Institute of Botany, Chinese Academy of Sciences（中国科学院植物研究所）
• Research interest: Campanulaceae, Lamiaceae [S]
• Published taxa: *Codonopsis, Himalacodon, Microtoena, Pseudocodon*
• Affiliation: PE
• Location of specimens: PE
• Region: CHINA
• IPNI as: Q. Wang

Q. F. Wang

Wang, Qing Feng; 王青锋 ; Wáng Qīngfēng
1968- **First publication: 2002**
• Employment: Wuhan Botanical Garden, Chinese Academy of Sciences（中国科学院武汉植物园）
• Research interest: Alismataceae, Aristolochiaceae, Asparagaceae, Balsaminaceae, Campanulaceae, Crassulaceae, Cucurbitaceae, Hydrocharitaceae, Isoetaceae, Melanthiaceae, Menispermaceae, Orchidaceae, Passifloraceae; Aquatic Plants; Plants of E. Africa [PS]
• Published taxa: *Adenia, Asarum, Aspidistra, Cissampelos, Gastrodia, Impatiens, Isoetes, Lobelia, Ottelia, Paris, Polystachya, Sagittaria, Sedum, Zehneria*
• Affiliation: HIB, WH
• Location of specimens: HIB, WH
• Region: CHINA; [AFRICA]

Q. J. Wang

Wang, Qing Jiang; 王清江 ; Wáng Qīngjiāng
1918-2003 **First publication: 1982**
• Employment: Department of Biology, Xiamen University（厦门大学生物系）
• Research interest: Staphyleaceae [S]
• Published taxa: *Euscaphis*
• Affiliation: AU
• Location of specimens: AU
• Region: CHINA (Fujian)

Qing L. Wang

Wang, Qing Long; 王清隆 ; Wáng Qīnglóng
1983- **First publication: 2012**
• Employment: College of Horticulture and Landscape Architecture, Hainan University; Tropical Crops Genetic Resources Institute, Chinese Academy of Tropical Agricultural Sciences（海南大学园艺园林学院；中国热带农业科学院热带作物品种资源研究所）
• Research interest: Cyperaceae; Plants of Hainan [S]
• Published taxa: *Carex*
• Affiliation: ATCH
• Location of specimens: ATCH
• Region: CHINA (Hainan)
• IPNI as: Q. L. Wang

Q. B. Wang

Wang, Qing Bin; 王庆斌；Wáng Qìngbīn; 王慶斌

1947- **First publication: 1994**

- Employment: Guizhou Botanical Garden（贵州省植物园）
- Research interest: Actinidiaceae [S]
- Published taxa: *Actinidia*
- Region: CHINA (Guizhou)

Q. L. Wang

Wang, Qing Li; 王庆礼；Wáng Qìnglǐ

1954- **First publication: 1984**

- Employment: Institute of Forestry and Soil Sciences, Chinese Academy of Sciences（中国科学院林业土壤研究所）
- Research interest: Buxaceae, Pinaceae, Rosaceae, Taxaceae [S]
- Published taxa: *Buxus, Pinus, Prunus, Rosa, Taxus*
- Affiliation: IFP
- Region: CHINA (Liaoning)

Ching J. Wang

Wang, Ching Jui; Wang, Ch'ing Jui; Wang, Qing Rui; 王庆瑞；Wáng Qìngruì; 王慶瑞

1928- **First publication: 1980**

- Employment: Northwest Normal College（西北师范学院）
- Research interest: Asphodelaceae, Boraginaceae, Papaveraceae, Violaceae. [MS]
- Published taxa: *Corydalis, Hemerocallis, Lappula, Trigonotis, Viola*
- Affiliation: NWTC
- Location of specimens: NWTC
- Region: CHINA
- Also as: Q. R. Wang

Qiu L. Wang

Wang, Qiu Ling; 王秋玲；Wáng Qiūlíng

1981- **First publication: 2011**

- Employment: Department of Chinese Medicine Resources, Beijing University of Chinese Medicine（北京中医药大学中药资源系）
- Research interest: Lamiaceae [S]
- Published taxa: *Salvia*
- Region: CHINA (Sichuan)
- IPNI as: Q. L. Wang

C. M. Wang

Wang, Chiou Mei; Wang, Qiu Mei; 王秋美；Wáng Qiūměi

1963- **First publication: 1990**

- Employment: Department of Forestry, Chung Hsing University（中兴大学森林学系）
- Research interest: Rhamnaceae, Rosaceae [S]
- Published taxa: *Berchemia, Rhamnus, Sageretia*
- Affiliation: TNM
- Location of specimens: TNM
- Region: CHINA (Taiwan)

Q. P. Wang

Wang, Qiu Ping; 王秋萍；Wáng Qiūpíng

1994- **First publication: 2019**

- Employment: School of Life Sciences, Yunnan University（云南大学生命科学学院）
- Research interest: Rosaceae [S]
- Published taxa: *Rubus*
- Region: CHINA (Yunnan)

J. L. Wang

Wang, Jen Li; 王仁禮；Wáng Rénlǐ; 王仁礼

1908-1988 **First publication: 1967**

- Employment: Taiwan Forestry Research Institute, Taiwan Provincial Administrative Office（台湾省政府农林厅林业试验所）
- Research interest: Lamiaceae [S]
- Published taxa: *Callicarpa*
- Region: CHINA (Taiwan)

R. S. Wang

Wang, Ren Shi; 王仁师；Wáng Rénshī; 王仁師

1937- **First publication: 1985**

- Employment: Department of Forestry, Southwest Forestry College（西南林学院林业系）
- Research interest: Poaceae [S]
- Published taxa: *Ampelocalamus*
- Location of specimens: SWFC
- Region: CHINA (Yunnan)

R. Z. Wang

Wang, Ren Zi; 王仁梓；Wáng Rénzǐ

1939- **First publication: 1982**

- Employment: Shaanxi Institute of Pomology（陕西省果树研究所）
- Research interest: Actinidiaceae [S]
- Published taxa: *Actinidia*
- Region: CHINA (Shaanxi)

R. W. Wang

Wang, Rong Wei; 王荣伟；Wáng Róngwěi

1971- **First publication: 2013**

- Employment: Tonglingshan National Forest Park, Zhejiang（浙江铜铃山国家森林公园）
- Research interest: Rubiaceae [S]
- Published taxa: *Rubia*
- Region: CHINA (Zhejiang)

Rong Z. Wang

Wang, Rong Zhang; 王荣璋；Wáng Róngzhāng

First publication: 1983

- Employment: Sichuan Institute of Forest Science（四川省林业科学研究所）
- Research interest: Mimosaceae [S]
- Published taxa: *Albizia*
- Region: CHINA (Sichuan)

R.J. Wang

Wang, Rui Jiang; 王瑞江; Wáng Ruìjiāng
1968- **First publication: 1999**

- Employment: South China Institute of Botany, Chinese Academy of Sciences; South China Botanical Garden, Chinese Academy of Sciences（中国科学院华南植物研究所；中国科学院华南植物园）
- Research interest: Annonaceae, Aristolochiaceae, Fagaceae, Oleaceae, Ranunculaceae, Rubiaceae, Solanaceae [S]
- Published taxa: *Alkekengi, Clematis, Cyathocalyx, Cyclobalanopsis, Dimetia, Foonchewia, Hedyotis, Isotrema, Leptodermis, Ligustrum, Lycium, Oldenlandia, Scleromitrion, Spiradiclis, Uvaria*
- Affiliation: IBSC
- Location of specimens: IBSC
- Region: CHINA

R. H. Wang

Wang, Run Hui; 王润辉; Wáng Rùnhuī
1974- **First publication: 2009**

- Employment: Guangdong Academy of Forestry（广东省林业科学研究院）
- Research interest: Poaceae [S]
- Published taxa: *Bambusa*
- Region: CHINA (Guangdong)

S. N. Wang

Wang, Shao Neng; 王绍能; Wáng Shàonéng
1974- **First publication: 2005**

- Employment: Administration Bureau of Guangxi Mao' er Mountain National Nature Reserve（广西猫儿山国家级自然保护区管理局）
- Research interest: Cyperaceae [S]
- Published taxa: *Carex*
- Region: CHINA (Guangxi)

S. X. Wang

Wang, Sheng Xin; 王生新; Wáng Shēngxīn
1932-2019 **First publication: 1982**

- Employment: Northwest Plateau Institute of Biology, Chinese Academy of Sciences（中国科学院西北高原生物研究所）
- Research interest: Ericaceae [S]
- Published taxa: *Rhododendron*
- Region: CHINA (Qinghai)

S. M. Wang

Wang, Sheng Mei; 王圣梅; Wáng Shèngméi; 王聖梅
1940-2013 **First publication: 1995**

- Employment: Wuhan Institute of Botany, Chinese Academy of Sciences（中国科学院武汉植物研究所）
- Research interest: Actinidiaceae [S]
- Published taxa: *Actinidia*
- Region: CHINA (Hubei)

Shi Y. Wang

Wang, Shi Yun; 王诗云; Wáng Shīyún
First publication: 1984

- Employment: Wuhan Institute of Botany, Chinese Academy of Sciences（中国科学院武汉植物研究所）
- Research interest: Poaceae [S]
- Published taxa: *Phyllostachys*
- Location of specimens: HIB
- Region: CHINA (Hunan)
- IPNI as: S. Y. Wang

S. F. Wang

Wang, Shu Fen; 王淑芬; Wáng Shūfēn
1936- **First publication: 1985**

- Employment: Department of Biology, Sichuan University（四川大学生物系）
- Research interest: Melanthiaceae [S]
- Published taxa: *Paris*
- Region: CHINA (Sichuan)

Shu Y. Wang

Wang, Shu Yun; 王淑云; Wáng Shūyún; 王淑雲
1937- **First publication: 1995**

- Employment: Dalian Medical University（大连医科大学）
- Research interest: Asteraceae [S]
- Published taxa: *Saussurea*
- Region: CHINA (Liaoning)

S. H. Wang

Wang, Shu Hsiou; 王蜀秀; Wáng Shǔxiù
1936- **First publication: 1979**

- Employment: Institute of Botany, Chinese Academy of Sciences（中国科学院植物研究所）
- Research interest: Nymphaeaceae, Paeoniaceae, Ranunculaceae [S]
- Published taxa: *Paeonia, Thalictrum*
- Affiliation: PE
- Region: CHINA

Shu Wang

Wang, Shu; 王曙; Wáng Shǔ
1957- **First publication: 2009**

- Employment: West China School of Pharmacy, Sichuan Univerisity（四川大学华西药学院）

- Research interest: Liliaceae [S]
- Published taxa: *Fritillaria*
- Affiliation: WCU
- Location of specimens: WCU
- Region: CHINA (Sichuan)

S. Wang

Wang, Song; 王松 ; Wáng Sōng

1955- **First publication: 1989**

- Employment: Department of Biology, Yunnan University（云南大学生物系）
- Research interest: Poaceae [S]
- Published taxa: *Dichanthium, Elymus, Eragrostis, Eulalia, Harpachne, Helictotrichon, Heteropogon, Themeda*
- Affiliation: YUKU
- Location of specimens: YUKU
- Region: CHINA (Yunnan)

S. W. Wang

Wang, Su Wen; 王苏文 ; Wáng Sūwén

First publication: 1994

- Employment: Lianyungang Waterfront Park（连云港海滨公园）
- Research interest: Lamiaceae [S]
- Published taxa: *Vitex*
- Region: CHINA (Jiangsu)

S. Y. Wang

Wang, Sui Yi; 王遂义 ; Wáng Suìyì; 王遂義

1933-2003 **First publication: 1980**

- Employment: College of Agronomy, Henan Agricultural University（河南农业大学农学院）
- Research interest: Balsaminaceae, Betulaceae, Cannabaceae, Euphorbiaceae, Fabaceae, Fagaceae, Hydrangeaceae, Magnoliaceae, Papaveraceae, Phyllanthaceae, Pinaceae, Ranunculaceae, Rosaceae, Salicaceae, Saxifragaceae, Ulmaceae, Vitaceae; Plants of Henan [S]
- Published taxa: *Betula, Campylotropis, Carpinus, Celtis, Cercis, Chrysosplenium, Clematis, Corydalis, Crataegus, Delphinium, Dicranostigma, Impatiens, Lathyrus, Magnolia, Malus, Pinus, Populus, Potentilla, Pyrus, Quercus, Sapium, Schizophragma, Securinega, Ulmus, Vitis*
- Affiliation: HEAC
- Location of specimens: HEAC
- Region: CHINA (Henan)

T. Wang

Wang, Tao; 王涛 ; Wáng Tāo

1986- **First publication: 2016**

- Employment: College of Science, Sichuan Agricultural University; Institute of Chinese Medicinal Materials, Mianyang Academy of Agricultural Sciences, Sichuan（四川农业大学理学院；四川省绵阳市农业科学研究院中药材研究所）
- Research interest: Lamiaceae [S]
- Published taxa: *Salvia*
- Region: CHINA (Yunnan)

T. Z. Wang

Wang, Tian Zhi; 王天志 ; Wàng Tiānzhì

First publication: 1989

- Employment: College of Pharmacy, West China University of Medical Sciences（华西医科大学药学院）
- Research interest: Ranunculaceae [S]
- Published taxa: *Coptis*
- Affiliation: WCU
- Location of specimens: WCU
- Region: CHINA (Sichuan)

T. J. Wang

Wang, Tie Juan; 王铁娟 ; Wáng Tiějuān

1969- **First publication: 2000**

- Employment: Correspondence Department, Inner Mongolia Education College（内蒙古教育学院函授部）
- Research interest: Asteraceae, Rosaceae [S]
- Published taxa: *Spiraea*
- Affiliation: NMTC
- Location of specimens: NMTC
- Region: CHINA (Nei Mongol)

T. S. Wang

Wang, Tieh Seng; 王铁僧 ; Wáng Tiěsēng; 王鐵僧

1933-2009 **First publication: 1986**

- Employment: Institute of Botany, Jiangsu Province and Chinese Academy of Sciences（江苏省中国科学院植物研究所）
- Research interest: Apiaceae [S]
- Published taxa: *Heracleum, Nothosmyrnium*
- Location of specimens: NAS
- Region: CHINA

T. F. Wang

Wang, Ting Fen; 王庭芬 ; Wáng Tíngfēn

1927-2011 **First publication: 1965**

- Employment: Northeast Forestry Institute（东北林学院）
- Research interest: Poaceae [S]
- Published taxa: *Calamagrostis*
- Region: CHINA (Heilongjiang)

Ting Wang

Wang, Ting; 王婷 ; Wáng Tíng

1971- **First publication: 2017**

- Employment: College of Forestry, Henan Agricultural University（河南农业大学林学院）
- Research interest: Boraginaceae [S]
- Published taxa: *Oreocharis*
- Region: CHINA (Shaanxi)
- IPNI as: T. Wang

Ting Wang tris

Wang, Ting; 王婷；**Wáng Tíng**

1993- **First publication: 2020**

- Employment: College of Biodiversity Conservation, Southwest Forestry University（西南林业大学生物多样性保护学院）
- Research interest: Marattiaceae [P]
- Published taxa: *Angiopteris*
- Region: CHINA (Hainan)

Ting Wang bis

Wang, Ting; 王挺；**Wáng Tǐng**

1984- **First publication: 2020**

- Employment: Hangzhou Botanical Garden（杭州植物园）
- Research interest: Amaryllidaceae; Plants of Hangzhou [S]
- Published taxa: *Lycoris*
- Affiliation: HHBG
- Location of specimens: HHBG
- Region: CHINA (Shaanxi)
- IPNI as: T. Wang

W. X. Wang

Wang, Wan Xian; 王万贤；**Wáng Wànxián**; 王萬賢

1949- **First publication: 1984**

- Employment: Department of Biology, Hubei University; Department of Life Sciences, Hubei University（湖北大学生物系；湖北大学生命科学系）
- Research interest: Araliaceae, Malvaceae, Onagraceae, Potamogetonaceae; Aquatic Plants [S]
- Published taxa: *Aralia, Epilobium, Potamogeton, Tilia*
- Affiliation: EU
- Location of specimens: EU
- Region: CHINA (Hubei)

W. Wang

Wang, Wei; 王薇；**Wáng Wēi**

1912-1991 **First publication: 1958**

- Employment: Institute of Forestry and Soil Sciences, Chinese Academy of Sciences; Institute of Applied Ecology, Chinese Academy of Sciences（中国科学院林业土壤研究所；中国科学院沈阳应用生态研究所）
- Research interest: Adoxaceae, Amaranthaceae, Asteraceae, Oleaceae [PS]
- Published taxa: *Anaphalis, Artemisia, Cacalia, Chenopodium, Cirsium, Corispermum, Heteropappus, Sambucus, Syringa*
- Affiliation: IFP
- Location of specimens: IFP
- Region: CHINA

W. Q. Wang

Wang, Wei Qin; 王为勤；**Wáng Wéiqín**

First publication: 1992

- Employment: Institute of Forestry and Soil Sciences, Chinese Academy of Sciences（中国科学院林业土壤研究所）
- Research interest: Solanaceae [S]
- Published taxa: *Solanum*
- Location of specimens: IFP
- Region: CHINA (Liaoning)

W. Y. Wang

Wang, Wei Yi; 王为义；**Wáng Wéiyì**; 王為義

1937-1990 **First publication: 1982**

- Employment: Northwest Plateau Institute of Biology, Chinese Academy of Sciences（中国科学院西北高原生物研究所）
- Research interest: Asteraceae, Ericaceae [S]
- Published taxa: *Rhododendron, Saussurea*
- Location of specimens: HNWP
- Region: CHINA (Qinghai)

W. E. Wang

Wang, Wei En; 王维恩；**Wáng Wéi'ēn**

1972- **First publication: 2008**

- Employment: Northwest Plateau Institute of Biology, Chinese Academy of Sciences（中国科学院西北高原生物研究所）
- Research interest: Papaveraceae [S]
- Published taxa: *Meconopsis*
- Region: CHINA (Qinghai)

Wei Wang

Wang, Wei; 王伟；**Wáng Wěi**

1978- **First publication: 2009**

- Employment: Institute of Botany, Chinese Academy of Sciences（中国科学院植物研究所）
- Research interest: Balsaminaceae, Menispermaceae, Ranunculaceae, Resedaceae; Plant Systematics [S]
- Published taxa: *Aquilegia, Borthwickia, Delphinium, Elissarrhena, Gymnaconitum, Impatiens, Menispermum, Rupertiella*
- Affiliation: PE
- Region: CHINA

W. T. Wang

Wang, Wen Tsai; Wang, Wên Ts'ai; Wang, Wen Cai;

王文采; Wáng Wéncǎi

1926- **First publication: 1957**

- Employment: Institute of Botany, Chinese Academy of Sciences（中国科学院植物研究所）
- Research interest: Actinidiaceae, Annonaceae, Apocynaceae, Boraginaceae, Brassicaceae, Circaeasteraceae, Cupressaceae, Cyperaceae, Euphorbiaceae, Fabaceae, Gesneriaceae, Hydrangeaceae, Hypericaceae, Lamiaceae, Lauraceae, Metteniusaceae, Moraceae, Myristicaceae, Paeoniaceae, Papaveraceae, Pittosporaceae, Proteaceae, Ranunculaceae, Sapindaceae, Saxifragaceae, Urticaceae, Vitaceae [S]
- Published taxa: *Acalypha, Aconitum, Adonis, Aeschynanthus, Allocheilos, Allostigma, Ampelopsis, Ancylostemon, Anemoclema, Anemonastrum, Anemone, Anna, Arabidopsis, Arabis, Artocarpus, Batrachium, Beccarinda, Boehmeria, Bournea, Braya, Briggsia, Buxiphyllum, Calathodes, Callianthemum, Caltha, Cardamine, Caryodaphnopsis, Cayratia, Ceratocephala, Chamabainia, Chienia, Chirita, Chiritopsis, Clematis, Clematoclethra, Coptis, Corallodiscus, Corydalis, Croton, Cynanchum, Dayaoshania, Debregeasia, Deinocheilos, Deinostigma, Delphinium, Deltocheilos, Desmos, Deutzia, Dichocarpum, Dichroa, Didissandra, Didymocarpus, Didymostigma, Dilophia, Dimocarpus, Dolicholoma, Draba, Dracocephalum, Elatostema, Enicosanthellum, Eranthis, Eritrichium, Euphorbia, Eutrema, Ficus, Fissistigma, Glochidocaryum, Goniothalamus, Gyrocheilos, Gyrogyne, Halerpestes, Helicia, Heliciopsis, Hemiboea, Hemiboeopsis, Hemilophia, Henckelia, Horsfieldia, Hydrangea, Hypericum, Isometrum, Isopyrum, Kingdonia, Kobresia, Lagarosolen, Laportea, Lappula, Lecanthus, Lepechiniella, Loxostigma, Lysionotus, Maackia, Mallotus, Marsdenia, Meconopsis, Melodinus, Mercurialis, Messerschmidia, Metabriggsia, Metaeritrichium, Metanemone, Metapetrocosmea, Metapilea, Microula, Miliusa, Mitrephora, Nekemias, Neolitsea, Neomartinella, Omphalotrigonotis, Onosma, Opithandra, Oreocharis, Oresitrophe, Paeonia, Paraboea, Paraisometrum, Parthenocissus, Pellionia, Petrocodon, Petrocosmea, Phaeanthus, Pilea, Pittosporopsis, Pittosporum, Pouzolzia, Pseudochirita, Ranunculus, Rhynchoglossum, Rhynchotechum, Sabina, Schistolobos, Scutellaria, Sinojohnstonia, Sinosophiopsis, Smelowskia, Tanakea, Tengia, Tetrastigma, Thalictrum, Thamnocharis, Trigonotis, Trollius, Urtica, Uvaria, Vincetoxicum, Vitis, Wangia, Xerospermum*
- Affiliation: PE
- Location of specimens: PE
- Region: CHINA

W. G. Wang

Wang, Wen Guang; 王文广; Wáng Wénguǎng

1989- **First publication: 2019**

- Employment: Xishuangbanna Tropical Botanical Garden, Chinese Academy of Sciences; Fairy Lake Botanical Garden, Shenzhen & Chinese Academy of Sciences（中国科学院西双版纳热带植物园；深圳市中国科学院仙湖植物园）
- Research interest: Begoniaceae [S]
- Published taxa: *Begonia*
- Region: CHINA (Xizang, Yunnan)

Wen Q. Wang

Wang, Wen Quan; 王文泉; Wáng Wénquán

1963- **First publication: 2012**

- Employment: Chinese Academy of Tropical Agricultural Sciences（中国热带农业科学院）
- Research interest: Fabaceae [S]
- Published taxa: *Dalbergia*
- Region: CHINA (Hainan)

X. Q. Wang

Wang, Xi Qu; 王希蕖; Wáng Xīqú

1942- **First publication: 1992**

- Employment: Institute of Botany, Jiangsu Province（江苏省植物研究所）
- Research interest: Hamamelidaceae; Plants of E. China [S]
- Published taxa: *Shaniodendron*
- Affiliation: NAS
- Location of specimens: NAS
- Region: CHINA (Jiangsu)

Xi L. Wang

Wang, Xi Long; 王喜龙; Wáng Xǐlóng

1982- **First publication: 2019**

- Employment: Tibet Plateau Institute of Biology（西藏自治区高原生物研究所）
- Research interest: Orchidaceae [S]
- Published taxa: *Bulbophyllum*
- Affiliation: XZ
- Location of specimens: XZ
- Region: CHINA (Xizang)

X. R. Wang

Wang, Xian Rong; 王贤荣; Wáng Xiánróng

1966- **First publication: 1998**

- Employment: College of Forest Resources and Environment, Nanjing Forestry University（南京林业大学森林资源与环境学院）
- Research interest: Oleaceae, Phyllanthaceae, Rosaceae, Ulmaceae; Plants of N. China [S]
- Published taxa: *Bischofia, Cerasus, Chengiodendron, Ulmus*

- Affiliation: NF
- Location of specimens: NF
- Region: CHINA

Xian J. Wang

Wang, Xian Jia; Wang, X. G.; 王显家；Wáng Xiǎnjiā; 王顯家

1942- **First publication: 1997**

- Employment: Fenghua Forestry Bureau, Zhejiang（浙江省奉化市林业局）
- Research interest: Poaceae [S]
- Published taxa: *Phyllostachys*
- Region: CHINA (Zhejiang)

H. D. Wong

Wong, Hin Dzi; Wang, Hsien Chih; Wang, Xian Zhi; 王显智；Wáng Xiǎnzhì; 王顯智

First publication: 1935

- Employment: Botanical Institute, College of Agriculture, National Sun Yat-sen University（国立中山大学农林植物研究所）
- Research interest: Malvaceae [S]
- Published taxa: *Tilia*
- Region: CHINA (Guangdong)

X. X. Wang

Wang, Xiao Xia; 王小夏；Wáng Xiǎoxià

1967- **First publication: 2009**

- Employment: ChangTing No.2 Middle School of Fujian（福建省长汀第二中学）
- Research interest: Pteridaceae [P]
- Published taxa: *Coniogramme*
- Region: CHINA (Fujian)

X. D. Wang

Wang, Xiao Dong; 王晓东；Wáng Xiǎodōng

1966- **First publication: 1992**

- Employment: Institute of Botany, Northwest Normal University（西北师范大学植物研究所）
- Research interest: Boraginaceae, Violaceae, Vitaceae [S]
- Published taxa: *Lappula, Viola, Vitis*
- Affiliation: NWTC
- Region: CHINA

Xiao M. Wang

Wang, Xiao Ming; 王晓明；Wáng Xiǎomíng

1963- **First publication: 2006**

- Employment: Shenzhen Municipal Administration（深圳市城市管理局）
- Research interest: Sapindaceae [S]
- Published taxa: *Acer*
- Region: CHINA (Guangdong)
- IPNI as: X. M. Wang

X. Yu Wang

Wang, Xiao Yu; 王晓宇；Wáng Xiǎoyǔ

1970- **First publication: 2010**

- Employment: College of Life Sciences, Guizhou University（贵州大学生命科学学院）
- Research interest: Crassulaceae, Gesneriaceae; Bryophyte [S]
- Published taxa: *Petrocosmea, Sedum*
- Affiliation: GACP
- Region: CHINA (Guizhou)

X. Yun Wang

Wang, Xiao Yun; 王晓云；Wáng Xiǎoyún

First publication: 2019

- Employment: Amateur（业余爱好者）
- Research interest: Araceae, Hymenoophyllaceae [PS]
- Published taxa: *Arisaema, Crepidomanes*
- Region: CHINA (Guangdong)

X. Y. Wang

Wang, Xiao Ying; 王筱英；Wáng Xiǎoyīng

1938- **First publication: 1997**

- Employment: Guizhou Academy of Sciences（贵州省科学院）
- Research interest: Athyriaceae, Cystopteridaceae, Dryopteridaceae, Lycopodiaceae, Polypodiaceae, Pteridaceae, Selaginellaceae [P]
- Published taxa: *Allantodia, Coniogramme, Cyrtogonellum, Cystopteris, Dryoathyrium, Dryopteris, Huperzia, Phymatopteris, Polypodiodes, Polystichum, Pteris, Selaginella*
- Region: CHINA (Guizhou)

X. G. Wang

Wang, Xin Gui; 王新桂；Wáng Xīnguì

1967- **First publication: 2002**

- Employment: Guangxi Institute of Botany, Chinese Academy of Sciences（广西壮族自治区中国科学院广西植物研究所）
- Research interest: Actinidiaceae [S]
- Published taxa: *Actinidia*
- Region: CHINA (Guangxi)

X. J. Wang

Wang, Xiu Juan; 王秀娟；Wáng Xiùjuān

1978- **First publication: 2004**

- Employment: School of Life Sciences, Sun Yat-sen University（中山大学生命科学学院）
- Research interest: Theaceae [S]
- Published taxa: *Camellia*
- Region: CHINA (Guangdong)

X. W. Wang

Wang, Xue Wen; 王学文；Wáng Xuéwén; 王學文

1947- **First publication: 1984**

- Employment: Anhui Institute of Biology（安徽省生物研究所）
- Research interest: Crassulaceae, Lamiaceae, Ranunculaceae [S]
- Published taxa: *Clematis, Scutellaria, Sedum*
- Affiliation: ACE
- Location of specimens: ACE, AIB, IBSC
- Region: CHINA (Anhui)

X. M. Wang

Wang, Xue Ming; Wang, Xie Ming; 王雪明 ; Wáng Xuěmíng

1946- **First publication: 1985**

- Employment: Guizhou Institute of Biology（贵州省生物研究所）
- Research interest: Altingiaceae, Apocynaceae, Fagaceae, Hamamelidaceae, Lauraceae, Magnoliaceae, Rosaceae; Plants of S. W. China [S]
- Published taxa: *Cyclobalanopsis, Distylium, Gongronema, Michelia, Phoebe, Photinia, Semiliquidambar*
- Affiliation: TIE
- Region: CHINA (Guizhou)

Ya L. Wang

Wang, Ya Ling; 王亚玲 ; Wáng Yàlíng

1971- **First publication: 2013**

- Employment: Xi' an Botanical Garden, Shaanxi; Qinling National Botanical Garden; Fairy Lake Botanical Garden, Shenzhen & Chinese Academy of Sciences; Palm Landscape Architecture Co., Ltd.（陕西省西安植物园；秦岭国家植物园；深圳市中国科学院仙湖植物园；棕榈园林股份有限公司）
- Research interest: Magnoliaceae [S]
- Published taxa: *Magnolia*
- Region: CHINA
- IPNI as: Y. L. Wang

Yan Wang

Wang, Yan; 王雁 ; Wáng Yàn

1969- **First publication: 2015**

- Employment: Research Institute of Forestry, Chinese Academy of Forestry（中国林业科学研究院林业研究所）
- Research interest: Orchidaceae [S]
- Published taxa: *Dendrobium, Phalaenopsis*
- Region: CHINA (Guangxi, Yunnan)

Yang C. Wang

Wang, Yang Cai; 王阳才 ; Wáng Yángcái

1959- **First publication: 1992**

- Employment: Department of Biology, Yunnan College of Education（云南教育学院生物系）
- Research interest: Asparagaceae, Poaceae [S]
- Published taxa: *Agrostis*
- Affiliation: YCE
- Location of specimens: YCE
- Region: CHINA (Yunnan)

Yi F. Wang

Wang, Yi Feng; 王一峰 ; Wáng Yīfēng

1964- **First publication: 1994**

- Employment: College of Life Sciences, Northwest Normal University（西北师范大学生命科学学院）
- Research interest: Asteraceae, Caprifoliaceae, Orobanchaceae, Saxifragaceae; Plants of Gansu [S]
- Published taxa: *Dipelta, Euphrasia, Saussurea, Saxifraga*
- Affiliation: NWTC, NWUB
- Location of specimens: NWTC, NWUB
- Region: CHINA (Gansu)

Yi Fu Wang

Wang, Yi Fu; 王義富 ; Wáng Yìfù; 王义富

First publication: 2014

- Employment: Dr. Cecilia Koo Botanic Conservation Center（辜严倬云植物保种中心）
- Research interest: Orchidaceae [S]
- Published taxa: *Bulbophyllum, Listera*
- Region: CHINA (Taiwan)

Yin Z. Wang

Wang, Yin Zheng; 王印政 ; Wáng Yìnzhèng

1960- **First publication: 1995**

- Employment: Institute of Botany, Chinese Academy of Sciences（中国科学院植物研究所）
- Research interest: Apiaceae, Gesneriaceae, Lamiaceae, Thymelaeaceae [S]
- Published taxa: *Chirita, Daphne, Lagochilus, Ligusticopsis, Ligusticum, Microchirita, Petrocodon, Petrocosmea, Primulina, Whytockia, Wikstroemia*
- Affiliation: PE
- Location of specimens: PE
- Region: CHINA
- Also as: Y. Z. Wang

Ying Wang

Wang, Ying; 王英 ; Wáng Yīng

First publication: 1988

- Employment: School of Pharmacy, Beijing Medical University（北京医科大学药学院）
- Research interest: Gentianaceae [S]
- Published taxa: *Gentiana*
- Region: CHINA (Gansu)

Y. M. Wang

Wang, Ying Ming; 王映明 ; Wáng Yìngmíng

1938- First publication: 1991
- Employment: Wuhan Institute of Botany, Chinese Academy of Sciences（中国科学院武汉植物研究所）
- Research interest: Asclepiadaceae; Plant Ecology [S]
- Published taxa: *Marsdenia*
- Affiliation: HIB
- Location of specimens: HIB
- Region: CHINA (Hubei)

Y. Q. Wang

Wang, Ying Qiang; 王英强；Wáng Yīngqiáng
1967- First publication: 1995
- Employment: Zhongkai University of Agriculture and Engineering; School of Life Sciences, South China Normal University（仲恺农业工程学院；华南师范大学生命科学学院）
- Research interest: Aquifoliaceae, Fabaceae, Gesneriaceae, Rosaceae [S]
- Published taxa: *Ilex, Oreocharis, Ormosia, Petrocodon, Rosa*
- Region: CHINA (Guangdong, Guizhou)

Y. W. Wang

Wang, Ying Wei; 王英伟；Wáng Yīngwěi
1978- First publication: 2003
- Employment: Institute of Botany, Chinese Academy of Sciences（中国科学院植物研究所）
- Research interest: Papaveraceae [S]
- Published taxa: *Corydalis*
- Region: CHINA

Ying Wang tris

Wang, Ying; 王莹；Wáng Yíng
1989- First publication: 2015
- Employment: Shanghai Chenshan Botanical Garden（上海辰山植物园）
- Research interest: Pteridaceae [S]
- Published taxa: *Adiantum*
- Region: CHINA (Yunnan)
- IPNI as: Y. Wang

Ying Wang tetrakis

Wang, Ying; 王影；Wáng Yǐng
1981- First publication: 2018
- Employment: College of Life Sciences, Anhui Normal University（安徽师范大学生命科学学院）
- Research interest: Primulaceae [S]
- Published taxa: *Lysimachia*
- Region: CHINA (Anhui)
- IPNI as: Y. Wang

Yong Wang tris

Wang, Yong; 王永；Wáng Yǒng
1988- First publication: 2004
- Employment: Department of Chinese Materia Medica, Guiyang College of Traditional Chinese Medicine; Guizhou Botanical Garden（贵阳中医学院药学系；贵州省植物园）
- Research interest: Asparagaceae [S]
- Published taxa: *Aspidistra*
- Region: CHINA (Guizhou)
- IPNI as: Y. Wang

Y. X. Wang

Wang, Yong Xiao; 王永孝；Wáng Yǒngxiào
1916-2006 First publication: 1982
- Employment: Shandong Institute of Forestry（山东省林业研究所）
- Research interest: Salicaceae [S]
- Published taxa: *Populus*
- Location of specimens: SDFI
- Region: CHINA (Shandong)

Yong Wang

Wang, Yong; 王勇；Wáng Yǒng
1968- First publication: 2002
- Employment: Wuhan Botanical Garden, Chinese Academy of Sciences（中国科学院武汉植物园）
- Research interest: Aristolochiaceae, Plantaginaceae [S]
- Published taxa: *Asarum, Plantago*
- Region: CHINA (Chongqing)
- IPNI as: Y. Wang

Y. P. Wang

Wang, You Ping; 王幼平；Wáng Yòupíng
1965- First publication: 1994
- Employment: Department of Biology, Sichuan University（四川大学生物系）
- Research interest: Apiaceae [S]
- Published taxa: *Notopterygium*
- Region: CHINA (Sichuan)

Yu B. Wang

Wang, Yu Bing; 王玉兵；Wáng Yùbīng
1977- First publication: 2019
- Employment: Biotechnology Research Center, China Three Gorges University（三峡大学生物技术研究中心）
- Research interest: Crassulaceae [S]
- Published taxa: *Sedum*
- Location of specimens: GXF
- Region: CHINA (Hubei)
- IPNI as: Y. B. Wang

Yu J. Wang

Wang, Yu Jin; 王玉金；Wáng Yùjīn
1975- First publication: 2003

- Employment: Northwest Plateau Institute of Biology, Chinese Academy of Sciences; School of Life Sciences, Lanzhou University（中国科学院西北高原生物研究所；兰州大学生命科学学院）
- Research interest: Asteraceae, Poaceae [S]
- Published taxa: *Achnatherum, Saussurea, Shangwua, Soroseris*
- Region: CHINA
- IPNI as: Y. J. Wang

Y. S. Wang

Wang, Yu Sheng; 王育生；Wáng Yùshēng

1938- **First publication: 1984**

- Employment: Guilin Medical College（桂林医学专科学校）
- Research interest: Actinidiaceae, Berberidaceae, Betulaceae [S]
- Published taxa: *Carpinus, Dysosma, Mahonia, Ostrya, Saurauia*
- Affiliation: GLMC
- Location of specimens: GLMC
- Region: CHINA (Guangxi)

Y. Y. Wang

Wang, Yue Ying; 王月英；Wáng Yuèyīng

1964- **First publication: 2006**

- Employment: Institute of Subtropical Crops, Zhejiang Academy of Agricultural Sciences（浙江省农业科学院亚热带作物研究所）
- Research interest: Poaceae [S]
- Published taxa: *Dendrocalamopsis*
- Region: CHINA (Zhejiang)

Yue Y. Wang

Wang, Yue Yun; 王悦云；Wáng Yuèyún

1978- **First publication: 2010**

- Employment: Guiyang College of Traditional Chinese Medicine（贵阳中医学院）
- Research interest: Berberidaceae [S]
- Published taxa: *Epimedium*
- Location of specimens: GZTM
- Region: CHINA (Guizhou)
- IPNI as: Y. Y. Wang

Y. Hu Wang

Wang, Yue Hu; 王跃虎；Wáng Yuèhǔ

1968- **First publication: 2017**

- Employment: Kunming Institute of Botany, Chinese Academy of Sciences（中国科学院昆明植物研究所）
- Research interest: Melanthiaceae [S]
- Published taxa: *Paris*
- Region: CHINA (Yunnan)
- IPNI as: Y. H. Wang

Y. H. Wang

Wang, Yue Hua; 王跃华；Wáng Yuèhuá

1957- **First publication: 2003**

- Employment: School of Life Sciences, Yunnan University（云南大学生命科学学院）
- Research interest: Apiaceae, Apocynaceae, Araceae, Magnoliaceae, Poaceae [S]
- Published taxa: *Acronema, Alocasia, Deyeuxia, Englerarum, Magnolia, Michelia, Vincetoxicum*
- Affiliation: YUKU
- Location of specimens: YUKU
- Region: CHINA (Yunnan)

Yue Wang

Wang, Yue; 王越；Wáng Yuè

1978- **First publication: 2008**

- Employment: Zhejiang Senhe Seed Co., Ltd.（浙江森禾种业股份有限公司）
- Research interest: Gesneriaceae [S]
- Published taxa: *Chirita, Chiritopsis, Primulina*
- Region: CHINA

Y. C. Wang

Wang, Yun Chang; Wang, Yun Zhang; 王云章；Wáng Yúnzhāng; 王雲章

1906-2012 **First publication: 1934**

- Employment: Institute of Botany, National Academy of Peiping（国立北平研究院植物学研究所）
- Research interest: Solanaceae [MS]
- Published taxa: *Lycium*
- Region: CHINA
- Also as: Y. Z. Wang

Ze H. Wang

Wang, Ze Huan; 王泽欢；Wáng Zéhuān

1986- **First publication: 2011**

- Employment: Kunming Institute of Botany, Chinese Academy of Sciences（中国科学院昆明植物研究所）
- Research interest: Asteraceae, Primulaceae [S]
- Published taxa: *Faberia, Lysimachia, Melanoseris, Paraprenanthes, Sadiria, Sinoseris*
- Region: CHINA
- Also as: Z. H. Wang

Z. Wang

Wang, Zhan; Wang, Chan; Wang, Tsang; Wang, Than; Wang, Chang; 王战；Wáng Zhàn; 王义仕

1910-2000 **First publication: 1955**

- Employment: Institute of Forestry and Soil Sciences, Chinese Academy of Sciences（中国科学院林业土壤研究所）
- Research interest: Betulaceae, Hydrangeaceae, Malvaceae, Pinaceae, Salicaceae, Ulmaceae [S]
- Published taxa: *Betula, Larix, Philadelphus, Pinus,*

Populus, Salix, Tilia, Ulmus
- Affiliation: IFP
- Location of specimens: IFP
- Region: CHINA
- Also as: C. Wang

Zhang R. Wang

Wang, Zhang Rong; 王章荣; Wáng Zhāngróng; 王章榮
1932- **First publication: 2012**
- Employment: College of Forest Resources and Environment, Nanjing Forestry University（南京林业大学森林资源与环境学院）
- Research interest: Magnoliaceae [S]
- Published taxa: *Liriodendron*
- Region: [cult.]

Chen H. Wang

Wang, Chen Hwa; Wang, Chên Hua; Wang, Zhen Hua; 王振华; Wáng Zhènhuá; 王振華
1908-1976 **First publication: 1936**
- Employment: Botanical Survey of North-Western China, National Academy of Peiping（国立北平研究院西北植物调查所）
- Research interest: Celastraceae [S]
- Published taxa: *Celastrus, Euonymus*
- Region: CHINA

Jen Y. Wang

Wang, Jen Yu; 王振宇; Wáng Zhènyǔ
First publication: 2018
- Employment: Taiwan University College of Medicine（台湾大学医学院医学系）
- Research interest: Asteraceae [S]
- Published taxa: *Emilia*
- Region: CHINA (Taiwan)
- IPNI as: J. Y. Wang

Zhen Z. Wang

Wang, Zhen Zhong; 王振忠; Wáng Zhènzhōng
1953-2007 **First publication: 2007**
- Employment: Xiamen Botanical Garden（厦门市园林植物园）
- Research interest: Poaceae [S]
- Published taxa: *Drepanostachyum*
- Region: CHINA (Fujian)

J. C. Wang

Wang, Jenn Che; Wang, Zhen Zhe; 王震哲; Wáng Zhènzhé
1953- **First publication: 1990**
- Employment: Department of Life Science, Taiwan Normal University（台湾师范大学生命科学系）
- Research interest: Acanthaceae, Apiaceae, Araceae, Aristolochiaceae, Asteraceae, Boraginaceae, Crassulaceae, Gentianaceae, Gesneriaceae, Linderniaceae, Phyllanthaceae, Violaceae, Zingiberaceae [S]
- Published taxa: *Alpinia, Arisaema, Aristolochia, Asarum, Bonnaya, Breynia, Craterostigma, Emilia, Gentiana, Glochidion, Lepidagathis, Lomatogonium, Oreomyrrhis, Rhynchotechum, Sedum, Torenia, Trigonotis, Tripterospermum, Vandellia, Viola*
- Affiliation: TNU
- Location of specimens: TNU
- Region: CHINA (Taiwan)

Z. T. Wang

Wang, Zheng Tao; 王峥涛; Wáng Zhēngtāo
1956- **First publication: 1993**
- Employment: China Pharmaceutical University; Institute of Chinese Materia Medica, Shanghai University of Traditional Chinese Medicine（中国药科大学；上海中医药大学中药研究所）
- Research interest: Campanulaceae, Gentianaceae [S]
- Published taxa: *Codonopsis, Gentiana*
- Region: CHINA

Zh. Wang

Wang, Zheng; 王筝; Wáng Zhēng
1956- **First publication: 1999**
- Employment: Institute of Botany, Chinese Academy of Sciences（中国科学院植物研究所）
- Research interest: Ranunculaceae [S]
- Published taxa: *Cimicifuga*
- Region: CHINA

Z. P. Wang

Wang, Zheng Ping; Wang, Cheng Ping; 王正平; Wáng Zhèngpíng
1929- **First publication: 1962**
- Employment: Nanjing University（南京大学）
- Research interest: Cucurbitaceae, Cyperaceae, Poaceae [S]
- Published taxa: *Acidosasa, Carex, Chimonocalamus, Fargesia, Gynostemma, Indocalamus, Indosasa, Oligostachyum, Phyllostachys, Pleioblastus, Pseudosasa, Trirostellum, Yushania*
- Affiliation: N
- Location of specimens: N
- Region: CHINA

Z. Ming Wang

Wang, Zhi Ming; 王志明; Wáng Zhìmíng
First publication: 1999
- Employment: Henan Education College of Profession Cadre（河南省职业干部教育学院）
- Research interest: Rosaceae [S]

- Published taxa: *Armeniaca*
- Region: CHINA (Liaoning)

C. C. Wang

Wang, Chih Chiang; 王志強；Wáng Zhìqiáng; 王志强

First publication: 1999

- Employment: Experimental Forest Management Office, College of Agriculture, Chung Hsing University; Department of Forestry, Chung Hsing University; College of Tourism and Leisure, Penghu University of Science and Technology（中兴大学农学院实验林管理处；中兴大学森林学系；澎湖科技大学观光休闲学院）
- Research interest: Melastomataceae, Rosaceae, Symplocaceae, Zingiberaceae; Plants of Taiwan [S]
- Published taxa: *Alpinia, Cotoneaster, Memecylon, Symplocos*
- Affiliation: PPI
- Location of specimens: PPI
- Region: CHINA (Taiwan)
- Also as: Chih C. Wang

Zhi W. Wang

Wang, Zhi Wei; 王志威；Wáng Zhìwēi

1986- **First publication: 2019**

- Employment: School of Pharmacy, Guizhou University of Traditional Chinese Medicine（贵州中医药大学药学院）
- Research interest: Aristolochiaceae, Berberidaceae [S]
- Published taxa: *Dysosma, Isotrema*
- Region: CHINA (Guizhou, Hainan)
- IPNI as: Z. W. Wang

Z. X. Wang

Wang, Zhi Xin; 王志新；Wáng Zhìxīn

1981- **First publication: 2013**

- Employment: College of Life Sciences, Sichuan University（四川大学生命科学学院）
- Research interest: Apiaceae [S]
- Published taxa: *Spuriopimpinella*
- Region: CHINA

Z. Y. Wang

Wang, Zhi Yong; 王志勇；Wáng Zhìyǒng

First publication: 1994

- Employment: Herbarium, Central South College of Forestry（中南林学院森林植物标本室）
- Research interest: Salicaceae [S]
- Published taxa: *Salix*
- Region: CHINA (Hunan)

Z. R. Wang

Wang, Zhong Ren; 王中仁；Wáng Zhōngrén

1939- **First publication: 1982**

- Employment: Institute of Botany, Chinese Academy of Sciences（中国科学院植物研究所）
- Research interest: Aspleniaceae, Athyriaceae, Cystopteridaceae, Dryopteridaceae [P]
- Published taxa: *Allantodia, Asplenium, Athyriopsis, Athyrium, Cornopteris, Cystopteris, Deparia, Diplazium, Dryopteris, Gymnocarpium, Lunathyrium, Neoathyrium, Pseudocystopteris*
- Affiliation: PE
- Region: CHINA
- IPNI as: Z. B. Wang

Chung H. Wang

Wang, Chung Hsin; Wang, Zhong Xin; 王忠信；Wáng Zhōngxìn

1940- **First publication: 1975**

- Employment: Shaanxi Institute of Forestry（陕西省林业科学研究所）
- Research interest: Salicaceae [PS]
- Published taxa: *Populus*
- Region: CHINA (Shaanxi)

Z. Z. Wang

Wang, Zhong Zhuang; 王忠壮；Wáng Zhōngzhuàng

1964- **First publication: 1994**

- Employment: College of Pharmacy, Second Military Medical University（第二军医大学药学院）
- Research interest: Araliaceae [S]
- Published taxa: *Aralia*
- Region: CHINA

Z. L. Wang

Wang, Zhong Lang; 王仲朗；Wáng Zhònglǎng

1967- **First publication: 1999**

- Employment: Kunming Institute of Botany, Chinese Academy of Sciences（中国科学院昆明植物研究所）
- Research interest: Araceae [S]
- Published taxa: *Sauromatum, Typhonium*
- Region: CHINA (Yunnan)

Z. N. Wang

Wang, Zhu Nian; 王祝年；Wáng Zhùnián

1962- **First publication: 2019**

- Employment: Tropical Crops Genetic Resources Institute, Chinese Academy of Tropical Agricultural Sciences（中国热带农业科学院热带作物品种资源研究所）
- Research interest: Rubiaceae; Medicinal Plants [S]
- Published taxa: *Hedyotis*
- Affiliation: ATCH
- Location of specimens: ATCH
- Region: CHINA (Hainan)

Chu H. Wang

Wang, Chu Hao; Wang, Zhu Hao; 王铸豪; **Wáng Zhùháo**; 王鑄豪

1923-2008 **First publication: 1959**

- Employment: South China Institute of Botany, Chinese Academy of Sciences; South China Botanical Garden, Chinese Academy of Sciences (中国科学院华南植物研究所; 中国科学院华南植物园)
- Research interest: Dennstaedtiaceae, Dipteridaceae, Dryopteridaceae, Hymenophyllaceae, Lindsaeaceae, Marattiaceae, Polypodiaceae, Pteridaceae, Pteridryaceae, Selaginellaceae, Tectariaceae; Pteridophytes [PS]
- Published taxa: *Angiopteris, Arachniodes, Bolbitis, Colysis, Crepidomanes, Ctenitis, Ctenitopsis, Dryopteris, Hypolepis, Lepidogrammitis, Lepisorus, Lindsaea, Microlepia, Phymatodes, Pleocnemia, Pteridrys, Pteris, Selaginella, Selenodesmium, Tectaria*
- Affiliation: IBSC
- Region: CHINA
- Also as: Z. H. Wang; • IPNI as: C. H. Wang

T. H. Wang

Wang, Tsung Hsuin; Wang, Tsung Hsün; Wang, Zong Xun; 王宗训; **Wáng Zōngxùn**; 王宗訓

1919-2000 **First publication: 1979**

- Employment: Institute of Botany, Chinese Academy of Sciences (中国科学院植物研究所)
- Research interest: Berberidaceae [S]
- Published taxa: *Dysosma*
- Region: CHINA (Guizhou)

T. P. Wang

Wang, Tso Pin; Wang, Tso Ping; Wang, Zuo Bin; 王作宾; **Wáng Zuòbīn**; 王作賓

1902-1989 **First publication: 1934**

- Employment: Botanical Survey of North-Western China, National Academy of Peiping; Northwest China Institute of Botany, Chinese Academy of Sciences and Shaanxi Province (国立北平研究院西北植物调查所; 陕西省中国科学院西北植物研究所)
- Research interest: Fabaceae, Papaveraceae, Saxifragaceae; Plants of Shaanxi [S]
- Published taxa: *Bergenia, Corydalis, Oxytropis*
- Affiliation: WUK
- Location of specimens: PE, WUK
- Region: CHINA (Hebei, Shaanxi)

Wang Hsie

Cooperation Group of Parashorea chinensis; Wang Tian Shu Hsie Zuo Zu; Wang Hsie; 望协; **Wàng Xié**

First publication: 1977

- Employment: Cooperation Group of *Parashorea chinensis* (望天树协作组)
- Research interest: Dipterocarpaceae [S]
- Published taxa: *Parashorea*
- Region: CHINA (Yunnan)
- Organization

F. N. Wei

Wei, Fa Nan; 韦发南; **Wéi Fānán**; 韋發南

1941- **First publication: 1979**

- Employment: Guangxi Institute of Botany, Chinese Academy of Sciences (广西壮族自治区中国科学院广西植物研究所)
- Research interest: Acoraceae, Araliaceae, Arecaceae, Berberidaceae, Boraginaceae, Clusiaceae, Cycadaceae, Euphorbiaceae, Lamiaceae, Lardizabalaceae, Lauraceae, Magnoliaceae, Malpighiaceae, Oleaceae, Primulaceae [S]
- Published taxa: *Acorus, Beilschmiedia, Berberis, Bostrychanthera, Cinnamomum, Cryptocarya, Cycas, Ehretia, Euphorbia, Evodiopanax, Excoecaria, Fraxinus, Garcinia, Guihaia, Hiptage, Lysimachia, Machilus, Manglietia, Neocinnamomum, Phoebe, Stauntonia, Trachycarpus*
- Affiliation: IBK
- Location of specimens: IBK
- Region: CHINA

F. M. Wei

Wei, Fu Min; 韦福民; **Wéi Fúmín**

1965- **First publication: 2006**

- Employment: Administration of Dapanshan National Natural Reserve, Zhejiang (浙江省大盘山国家级自然保护区管理局)
- Research interest: Rosaceae [S]
- Published taxa: *Rosa*
- Region: CHINA (Zhejiang)

H. J. Wei

Wei, Hong Jin; 韦宏金; **Wéi Hóngjīn**

1969- **First publication: 2018**

- Employment: Shanghai Chenshan Botanical Garden (上海辰山植物园)
- Research interest: Athyriaceae, Dryopteridaceae; Pteridophytes [P]
- Published taxa: *Diplazium, Polystichum*
- Affiliation: CSH
- Location of specimens: CSH
- Region: CHINA (Guangxi)

J. J. Wei

Wei, Jia Jia; 韦佳佳; **Wéi Jiājiā**

1991- **First publication: 2016**

- Employment: Guangxi Institute of Botany, Chinese

Academy of Sciences; School of Life Sciences, Yunnan University (广西壮族自治区中国科学院广西植物研究所 ; 云南大学生命科学学院)
- Research interest: Gesneriaceae [S]
- Published taxa: *Oreocharis*
- Region: CHINA (Guangxi)

J. Wei

Wei, Jin; 韦瑾 ; Wéi Jǐn

First publication: 2020

- Employment: School of Pharmaceutical Science, Kunming Medical University (昆明医科大学药学院)
- Research interest: Apiaceae [S]
- Published taxa: *Pleurospermopsis*
- Region: [ASIA]

R. X. Wei

Wei, Ruo Xun; 韦若勋 ; Wéi Ruòxūn

1975- **First publication: 2019**

- Employment: Department of Biology, Zunyi Normal College (遵义师范学院生物系)
- Research interest: Crassulaceae, Poaceae [S]
- Published taxa: *Sedum*
- Affiliation: ZY
- Location of specimens: ZY
- Region: CHINA (Guizhou)

S. Q. Wei

Wei, Si Qi; 韦思奇 ; Wéi Sīqí; 韋思奇

1925-1992 **First publication: 1984**

- Employment: Zhejiang Provincial Museum (浙江省博物馆)
- Research interest: Fabaceae [S]
- Published taxa: *Piptanthus, Thermopsis*
- Affiliation: ZM
- Location of specimens: ZM
- Region: CHINA

S. J. Wei

Wei, Song Ji; 韦松基 ; Wéi Sōngjī

1952- **First publication: 1986**

- Employment: Guangxi College of Traditional Chinese Medicine (广西中医学院)
- Research interest: Araceae, Rubiaceae [S]
- Published taxa: *Amorphophallus, Ophiorrhiza, Spiradiclis*
- Location of specimens: GXCM
- Region: CHINA (Guangxi)

X. W. Wei

Wei, Xing Wei; 韦星伟 ; Wéi Xīngwěi; 韋星偉

1946-1982 **First publication: 1982**

- Employment: Department of Forestry, South China Agricultural College (华南农学院林学系)
- Research interest: Arecaceae, Moraceae, Primulaceae [S]
- Published taxa: *Ardisia, Broussonetia, Livistona*
- Region: CHINA (Guangdong)

Y. G. Wei

Wei, Yi Gang; 韦毅刚 ; Wéi Yìgāng

1967- **First publication: 1995**

- Employment: Guangxi Institute of Botany, Chinese Academy of Sciences (广西壮族自治区中国科学院广西植物研究所)
- Research interest: Acanthaceae, Asparagaceae, Begoniaceae, Gesneriaceae, Ranunculaceae, Urticaceae [S]
- Published taxa: *Anna, Aspidistra, Begonia, Boeica, Briggsia, Chirita, Chiritopsis, Clematis, Didymocarpus, Elatostema, Elatostematoides, Glabrella, Hemiboea, Lagarosolen, Litostigma, Oreocharis, Paraboea, Paralagarosolen, Pellionia, Petrocodon, Petrocosmea, Pilea, Primulina, Pseudochirita, Raphiocarpus, Strobilanthes*
- Affiliation: IBK
- Location of specimens: IBK
- Region: CHINA

Y. Wei

Wei, Yu; Wei, Zhan Ye; 韦宇 ; Wéi Yǔ ; 韦占业

1931-1991 **First publication: 1980**

- Employment: Guangxi Forest Inventory & Planning Institute (广西壮族自治区林业勘测设计院)
- Research interest: Fabaceae [S]
- Published taxa: *Acrocarpus*
- Location of specimens: GXF
- Region: CHINA (Guangxi)

Y. T. Wei

Wei, Yue Tsung; Wei, Yu Tsung; Wei, Yu Zong; 韦裕宗 ; Wéi Yùzōng; 韋裕宗

1936- **First publication: 1979**

- Employment: Guangxi Institute of Botany (广西植物研究所)
- Research interest: Fabaceae, Lauraceae [S]
- Published taxa: *Amphicarpaea, Atylosia, Beilschmiedia, Cajanus, Dumasia, Endiandra, Flemingia, Rhynchosia*
- Affiliation: IBK
- Region: CHINA (Guangxi)

Z. Wei

Wei, Zhi; 韦直 ; Wéi Zhí; 韋直

1929- **First publication: 1981**

- Employment: Zhejiang Museum of Natural History (浙江自然博物馆)
- Research interest: Fabaceae, Polygonaceae [S]

- Published taxa: *Antheroporum, Callerya, Craspedolobium, Crotalaria, Derris, Fordia, Millettia, Ormosia, Polygonum, Tephrosia, Trifolium, Whitfordiodendron*
- Affiliation: ZM
- Location of specimens: ZM
- Region: CHINA

R. Wei

Wei, Ran; 卫然 ; Wèi Rán

1985- **First publication: 2012**

- Employment: Institute of Botany, Chinese Academy of Sciences (中国科学院植物研究所)
- Research interest: Athyriaceae; Pteridophytes [P]
- Published taxa: *Anisocampium, Athyrium, Diplazium, Lepisorus*
- Affiliation: PE
- Region: CHINA

Yun Wei

Wei, Yun; 卫云 ; Wèi Yún; 衛雲

1936- **First publication: 1984**

- Employment: Shandong College of Traditional Chinese Medicine (山东中医学院)
- Research interest: Dryopteridaceae [P]
- Published taxa: *Polystichum*
- Region: CHINA (Shandong)
- IPNI as: Y. Wei

C. F. Wei

Wei, Chao Fen; Wei, Zhao Fen; 卫兆芬 ; Wèi Zhàofēn; 衛兆芬

1934- **First publication: 1963**

- Employment: South China Institute of Botany, Chinese Academy of Sciences (中国科学院华南植物研究所)
- Research interest: Arecaceae, Fabaceae, Hydrangeaceae, Ochnaceae, Theaceae, Thymelaeaceae [S]
- Published taxa: *Arenga, Calamus, Camellia, Cardiandra, Cercis, Cochlianthus, Daphne, Gomphia, Hydrangea, Lysidice, Nogra, Schizophragma, Spatholobus*
- Affiliation: IBSC
- Region: CHINA

H. T. Wei

Wei, Hong Tu; 魏宏图 ; Wèi Hóngtú; 魏宏圖

1938- **First publication: 1982**

- Employment: Institute of Botany, Jiangsu Province; Institute of Botany, Jiangsu Province and Chinese Academy of Sciences (江苏省植物研究所 ; 江苏省中国科学院植物研究所)
- Research interest: Hamamelidaceae [S]
- Published taxa: *Parrotia, Shaniodendron*
- Region: CHINA (Anhui, Jiangsu)

K. Y. Wei

Wei, Kai Yun; 魏开云 ; Wèi Kāiyún

1962- **First publication: 2003**

- Employment: College of Landscape Architecture, Southwest Forestry University (西南林学院园林学院)
- Research interest: Sapindaceae [S]
- Published taxa: *Acer*
- Region: CHINA (Yunnan)

L. Wei

Wei, Lai; 魏来 ; Wèi Lái

1984- **First publication: 2007**

- Employment: Institute of Botany, Chinese Academy of Sciences; College of Life Sciences, Beijing Normal University (中国科学院植物研究所 ; 北京师范大学生命科学学院)
- Research interest: Boraginaceae, Lamiaceae [S]
- Published taxa: *Heterolamium, Myosotis*
- Affiliation: BNU
- Region: CHINA (Sichuan, Yunnan)

N. Wei

Wei, Neng; 魏能 ; Wèi Néng

1993- **First publication: 2020**

- Employment: Wuhan Botanical Garden, Chinese Academy of Sciences (中国科学院武汉植物园)
- Research interest: Cucurbitaceae [S]
- Published taxa: *Peponium, zehneria*
- Location of specimens: HIB
- Region: [AFRICA]
- Also as: Neng Wei

X. Wei

Wei, Xing; 魏星 ; Wèi Xīng

1971- **First publication: 2000**

- Employment: College of Life Sciences, Beijing Normal University (北京师范大学生命科学学院)
- Research interest: Liliaceae [S]
- Published taxa: *Tulipa*
- Region: CHINA (Xinjiang)

X. H. Wei

Wei, Xiu Hua; 魏秀华 ; Wèi Xiùhuá

1977- **First publication: 2008**

- Employment: Triticeae Research Institute, Sichuan Agricultural University (四川农业大学小麦研究所)
- Research interest: Poaceae [S]
- Published taxa: *Roegneria*
- Region: [cult.]

X. P. Wei

Wei, Xue Ping; 魏雪苹 ; Wèi Xuěpíng

1986- **First publication: 2013**

- Employment: Institute of Botany, Chinese Academy of Sciences（中国科学院植物研究所）
- Research interest: Polypodiaceae [P]
- Published taxa: *Lemmaphyllum*
- Region: CHINA

Yan Wei

Wei, Yan; 魏岩 ; Wèi Yán

1966- **First publication: 1999**

- Employment: Xinjiang Agricultural University（新疆农业大学）
- Research interest: Asteraceae [S]
- Published taxa: *Aster, Brachyactis, Erigeron, Galatella*
- Region: CHINA (Xinjiang)
- IPNI as: Y. Wei

Y. K. Wei

Wei, Yu Kun; 魏宇昆 ; Wèi Yǔkūn

1976- **First publication: 2019**

- Employment: Shanghai Chenshan Botanical Garden（上海辰山植物园）
- Research interest: Lamiaceae [S]
- Published taxa: *Salvia*
- Affiliation: CSH
- Location of specimens: CSH
- Region: CHINA (Hunan)

Z. X. Wei

Wei, Zhao Xiang; 魏兆祥 ; Wèi Zhàoxiáng

1933-2017 **First publication: 1993**

- Employment: Kunming Institute of Botany, Chinese Academy of Sciences（中国科学院昆明植物研究所）
- Research interest: Araceae [S]
- Published taxa: *Colocasia*
- Region: CHINA (Yunnan)

Z. D. Wei

Wei, Zhi Dan; 魏志丹 ; Wèi Zhìdān

1979- **First publication: 2007**

- Employment: Kunming Institute of Botany, Chinese Academy of Sciences（中国科学院昆明植物研究所）
- Research interest: Begoniaceae [S]
- Published taxa: *Begonia*
- Region: CHINA (Yunnan)

D. S. Wen

Wen, Du Su; 温都苏 ; Wēn Dūsū; 溫都蘇

1936- **First publication: 1982**

- Employment: Grassland Research Institute, Inner Mongolia Academy of Agricultural & Animal Husbandry Sciences（内蒙古农牧业科学院草原研究所）
- Research interest: Asteraceae [S]
- Published taxa: *Saussurea*
- Region: CHINA (Nei Mongol)

F. Wen

Wen, Fang; 温放 ; Wēn Fàng

1976- **First publication: 2008**

- Employment: Guangxi Institute of Botany, Chinese Academy of Sciences（广西壮族自治区中国科学院广西植物研究所）
- Research interest: Gesneriaceae, Urticaceae [S]
- Published taxa: *Anna, Boeica, Briggsia, Chirita, Chiritopsis, Didymocarpus, Elatostema, Glabrella, Hemiboea, Lagarosolen, Litostigma, Oreocharis, Paraboea, Pellionia, Petrocodon, Petrocosmea, Primulina*
- Affiliation: IBK
- Location of specimens: IBK
- Region: CHINA

H. Z. Wen

Wen, Hai Zhen; 温海珍 ; Wēn Hǎizhēn

1987- **First publication: 2012**

- Employment: South China Botanical Garden, Chinese Academy of Sciences（中国科学院华南植物园）
- Research interest: Oleaceae, Rubiaceae [S]
- Published taxa: *Foonchewia, Ligustrum*
- Region: CHINA (Guangdong)

T. H. Wen

Wen, Tai Hui; 温太辉 ; Wēn Tàihuī; 溫太輝

1923-1993 **First publication: 1978**

- Employment: Zhejiang Institute of Forestry（浙江省林业科学研究所）
- Research interest: Poaceae [S]
- Published taxa: *Acidosasa, Ampelocalamus, Arundinaria, Bambusa, Bashania, Chimonobambusa, Clavinodum, Dendrocalamus, Fargesia, Ferrocalamus, Gelidocalamus, Indocalamus, Indosasa, Lingnania, Neohouzeaua, Neosinocalamus, Oreocalamus, Phyllostachys, Pleioblastus, Pseudosasa, Qiongzhuea, Racemobambos, Sasa, Schizostachyum, Semiarundinaria, Shibataea, Sinobambusa, Sinocalamus, Yushania*
- Affiliation: ZJFI
- Location of specimens: ZJFI
- Region: CHINA

Z. J. Wen

Wen, Zhao Jie; 温兆捷 ; Wēn Zhàojié

1993- **First publication: 2019**

- Employment: College of Life Science and Technology, Central South University of Forestry and Technology（中南林业科技大学生命科学与技术学院）
- Research interest: Rubiaceae [S]
- Published taxa: *Spiradiclis*
- Region: CHINA (Guangxi)

Z. Y. Wen

Wen, Zhen Ying; 温振英；Wēn Zhènyīng

1993- **First publication: 2019**

- Employment: College of Landscape Architecture, Fujian Agriculture and Forestry University（福建农林大学园林学院）
- Research interest: Melastomataceae [S]
- Published taxa: *Bredia*
- Region: CHINA (Yunnan)

B. Wen

Wen, Bin; 文斌；Wén Bīn

1961- **First publication: 2001**

- Employment: Xishuangbanna Tropical Botanical Garden, Chinese Academy of Sciences（中国科学院西双版纳热带植物园）
- Research interest: Poaceae [S]
- Published taxa: *Gigantochloa*
- Region: CHINA (Yunnan)

H. Q. Wen

Wen, He Qun; 文和群；Wén Héqún

1957-2013 **First publication: 1984**

- Employment: Guangxi Institute of Botany, Chinese Academy of Sciences（广西壮族自治区中国科学院广西植物研究所）
- Research interest: Aristolochiaceae, Boraginaceae, Fabaceae, Gesneriaceae [S]
- Published taxa: *Allocheilos, Aristolochia, Chirita, Ehretia, Euchresta, Hemiboea, Pithecellobium*
- Affiliation: IBK
- Region: CHINA (Guangxi)

J. Wen

Wen, Jun; 文军；Wén Jūn

1963- **First publication: 1993**

- Employment: Smithsonian Institution, U.S.A.; Field Museum of Natural History, Chicago, U.S.A.（美国史密森学会；美国芝加哥自然博物馆）
- Research interest: Altingiaceae, Anacardiaceae, Araliaceae, Asteraceae, Fabaceae, Nyssaceae, Rosaceae, Rutaceae, Staphyleaceae, Vitaceae [S]
- Published taxa: *Ampelocissus, Aralia, Brassaiopsis, Caragana, Causonis, Cayratia, Chesneya, Chesniella, Hedera, Hedysarum, Liquidambar, Melicope, Metapanax, Nekemias, Nyssa, Oreoseris, Panax, Prunus, Pseudocayratia, Searsia, Staphylea, Tetrastigma, Trevesia, Zanthoxylum*
- Region: [WORLD]

X. Y. Wen

Wen, Xiang Ying; 文香英；Wén Xiāngyīng

1972- **First publication: 2007**

- Employment: South China Botanical Garden, Chinese Academy of Sciences（中国科学院华南植物园）
- Research interest: Rubiaceae [S]
- Published taxa: *Leptodermis*
- Region: CHINA

X. K. Wen

Wen, Xuan Kai; 文选开；Wén Xuǎnkāi

First publication: 1982

- Employment: Xiangxi Institute of Forestry, Hunan（湖南湘西自治州林科所）
- Research interest: Theaceae [S]
- Published taxa: *Camellia*
- Region: CHINA (Hunan)

D. M. Weng

Weng, Dong Ming; 翁东明；Wēng Dōngmíng

1966- **First publication: 2009**

- Employment: Administration of Zhejiang Qingliangfeng National Natural Reserve（浙江清凉峰国家级自然保护区管理局）
- Research interest: Cyperaceae [S]
- Published taxa: *Carex*
- Region: CHINA (Zhejiang)

C. T. Wong

Wong, Ching Tien; 翁景田；Wēng Jǐngtián

First publication: 2010

- Employment: Tzeng-Wen Orchids, Taiwan（台湾曾文兰园）
- Research interest: Orchidaceae [S]
- Published taxa: × *Aeridsonia*
- Region: CHINA (Taiwan)

H. Q. Wu

Wu, Hong Qi; 乌弘奇；Wū Hóngqí

1958- **First publication: 1986**

- Employment: Northeast Forestry University（东北林业大学）
- Research interest: Pinaceae [S]
- Published taxa: *Picea*
- Region: CHINA (Nei Mongol)

Gaowua

Gaowua; Wuyungaowua; Gao, Wua; 乌云高娃；Wūyúngāowá; 烏雲高娃，高瓦

1941- First publication: 1979
- Employment: Institute of Grassland Research, Chinese Academy of Agricultural Sciences（中国农业科学院草原研究所）
- Research interest: Poaceae [S]
- Published taxa: *Roegneria*
- Region: CHINA (Nei Mongol)
- IPNI as: W. Gao

H. S. Wu

Wu, Hua Song; 邬华松；Wū Huásōng

1965- First publication: 2015
- Employment: Spice and Beverage Research Institute, Chinese Academy of Tropical Agricultural Sciences（中国热带农业科学院香料饮料研究所）
- Research interest: Piperaceae [S]
- Published taxa: *Piper*
- Region: CHINA (Hainan)

J. L. Wu

Wu, Jia Lin; 邬家林；Wū Jiālín; 鄔家林

1938- First publication: 1989
- Employment: Sichuan School of Chinese Materia Medica（四川省中药学校）
- Research interest: Aristolochiaceae, Berberidaceae, Oleaceae, Orchidaceae; Medicinal Plants [S]
- Published taxa: *Aristolochia, Asarum, Cypripedium, Dysosma, Fraxinus, Podophyllum*
- Affiliation: EMA
- Location of specimens: EMA
- Region: CHINA (Chongqing, Sichuan)

Q. X. Wu

Wu, Qi Xin; 巫启新；Wū Qǐxīn; 巫啟新

1940- First publication: 1985
- Employment: Guizhou Research Institute of Forestry（贵州省林业科学研究所）
- Research interest: Poaceae [S]
- Published taxa: *Chimonobambusa*
- Region: CHINA (Guizhou)

Cun J. Wu

Wu, Cun Jian; 毋存俭；Wú Cúnjiǎn; 毋存儉

1945- First publication: 2006
- Employment: Bamboo Research Institute of Boai County, Henan（河南省博爱县竹子科学研究所）
- Research interest: Poaceae [S]
- Published taxa: *Phyllostachys*
- Region: CHINA (Henan)
- IPNI as: C. J. Wu

X. Y. Wu

Wu, Xu Yan; 毋绪燕；Wú Xùyàn; 毋緒燕

1939- First publication: 1985
- Employment: Northwest China Institute of Botany, Chinese Academy of Sciences and Shaanxi Province（陕西省中国科学院西北植物研究所）
- Research interest: Asteraceae, Cucurbitaceae [S]
- Published taxa: *Saussurea*
- Affiliation: WUK
- Location of specimens: WUK
- Region: CHINA (Shaanxi)

C. C. Wu

Wu, Chang Chun; 吴长春；Wú Chángchūn; 吳長春

1905-1974 First publication: 1964
- Employment: Department of Biology, Hangzhou University（杭州大学生物系）
- Research interest: Primulaceae [S]
- Published taxa: *Lysimachia*
- Location of specimens: HZU
- Region: CHINA (Zhejiang)

Cheng J. Wu

Wu, Cheng Jie; 吴澄杰；Wú Chéngjié

First publication: 1985
- Employment: Jiangyin Health Bureau, Jiangsu（江苏省江阴市卫生局）
- Research interest: Liliaceae [S]
- Published taxa: *Fritillaria*
- Region: CHINA (Jiangsu)
- IPNI as: C. J. Wu

D. C. Wu

Wu, De Cheng; 吴德成；Wú Déchéng; 吳德成

1937-2012 First publication: 1979
- Employment: Plant Resources Laboratory, Heilongjiang Institute of Natural Resources（黑龙江省自然资源研究所植物资源研究室）
- Research interest: Araceae, Ranunculaceae; Plant Ecology [S]
- Published taxa: *Arisaema, Ranunculus*
- Affiliation: HNR
- Location of specimens: HNR
- Region: CHINA (Liaoning)

T. L. Wu

Wu, Te Lin; Wu, Te Ling; Wu, De Lin; 吴德邻；Wú Délín; 吳德鄰

1934- First publication: 1963
- Employment: South China Institute of Botany, Chinese Academy of Sciences（中国科学院华南植物研究所）
- Research interest: Arecaceae, Cornaceae, Costaceae, Euphorbiaceae, Fabaceae, Hydrocharitaceae, Lowiaceae, Marantaceae, Melastomataceae, Pandanaceae, Zingiberaceae [BS]

- Published taxa: *Achasma, Albizia, Alpinia, Amomum, Archidendron, Chuniophoenix, Costus, Cylindrokelupha, Fordiophyton, Hedychium, Hornstedtia, Monolophus, Orchidantha, Ottelia, Pandanus, Phrynium, Plagiostachys, Pyrgophyllum, Roscoea, Sonerila, Swida, Trigonostemon, Vigna, Zingiber, Zygia*
- Affiliation: IBSC
- Location of specimens: IBSC
- Region: CHINA

D. F. Wu

Wu, Di Fei; 吴棣飞 ; Wú Dìfēi

1980- **First publication: 2012**

- Employment: Wenzhou Park Management Office, Zhejiang（浙江省温州市公园管理处）
- Research interest: Cyperaceae [S]
- Published taxa: *Carex*
- Region: CHINA (Zhejiang)

D. H. Wu

Wu, Dong Hao; 吴东浩 ; Wú Dōnghào

1967- **First publication: 2018**

- Employment: Lishui Municipal Administration of Market Supervision, Zhejiang（浙江省丽水市市场监督管理局）
- Research interest: Primulaceae [S]
- Published taxa: *Primula*
- Region: CHINA (Zhejiang)

T. C. Wu

Wu, Tung Cheng; 吴栋成 ; Wú Dòngchéng; 吳棟成

1939- **First publication: 1978**

- Employment: Guangdong Institute of Medicine and Health（广东省医药卫生研究所）
- Research interest: Ericaceae [S]
- Published taxa: *Rhododendron*
- Region: CHINA (Guangdong)

K. F. Wu

Wu, Kuo Fang; Wu, Guo Fang; **吴国芳 ; Wú Guófāng; 吳國芳**

1930-1997 **First publication: 1978**

- Employment: Department of Biology, East China Normal University（华东师范大学生物系）
- Research interest: Berberidaceae, Buxaceae, Chloranthaceae, Ericaceae, Juncaceae [S]
- Published taxa: *Chloranthus, Epimedium, Juncus, Luzula, Monotropastrum, Sarcococca*
- Affiliation: HSNU
- Location of specimens: HSNU
- Region: CHINA

H. Wu

Wu, Han; 吴翰 ; Wú Hàn; 吳翰

1926-1993 **First publication: 1986**

- Employment: Department of Agricultural Biology, South China Agricultural University（华南农业大学农业生物系）
- Research interest: Rubiaceae [S]
- Published taxa: *Mussaenda*
- Location of specimens: SCAUB
- Region: CHINA (Guangdong)

J. K. Wu

Wu, Jia Kun; 吴家坤 ; Wú Jiākūn; 吳家坤

1935- **First publication: 1985**

- Employment: Nanjing Pharmaceutical College; China Pharmaceutical University（南京药学院；中国药科大学）
- Research interest: Asparagaceae, Campanulaceae, Caprifoliaceae, Cyatheaceae, Dipterocarpaceae, Fabaceae, Liliaceae, Polygonaceae [PS]
- Published taxa: *Alsophila, Campanula, Cephalaria, Dipsacus, Fritillaria, Rheum, Scabiosa, Shorea, Sinolegumenea, Tupistra*
- Region: CHINA

J. R. Wu

Wu, Jia Rong; 吴家荣 ; Wú Jiāróng; 吳家榮

1930- **First publication: 1986**

- Employment: Faculty of Chinese Pharmacy, Guiyang College of Traditional Chinese Medicine（贵阳中医学院中药鉴定学教研组）
- Research interest: Convolvulaceae, Loranthaceae, Violaceae [S]
- Published taxa: *Ipomoea, Pharbitis, Taxillus*
- Affiliation: GZTM
- Location of specimens: GZTM
- Region: CHINA (Guizhou)

J. Q. Wu

Wu, Jin Qing; 吴金清 ; Wú Jīnqīng

1965- **First publication: 2000**

- Employment: Wuhan Botanical Garden, Chinese Academy of Sciences（中国科学院武汉植物园）
- Research interest: Brassicaceae, Caryophyllaceae, Primulaceae; Plants of Hubei [S]
- Published taxa: *Lysimachia, Orychophragmus, Pseudostellaria*
- Affiliation: HIB
- Location of specimens: HIB
- Region: CHINA (Hubei)

J. H. Wu

Wu, Jin Hua; 吳進華 ; Wú Jìnhuá; 吴进华

First publication: 2018

- Employment: Nantou Forest District Office, Forestry Bureau, Council of Agriculture, "Executive Yuan" （"行政院"农业委员会林务局南投林区管理处）
- Research interest: Orchidaceae [S]
- Published taxa: *Gastrochilus*
- Region: CHINA (Taiwan)

J. T. Wu

Wu, Jiunn Tzong; Wu, Jiunn Tsong; Wu, Jun Zong; 吳俊宗；Wú Jùnzōng; 吴俊宗

1949- **First publication: 1975**

- Employment: Herbarium, Institute of Botany, "Academia Sinica"（中研院植物研究所标本馆）
- Research interest: Lamiaceae; Algae. [AS]
- Published taxa: *Salvia*
- Affiliation: HAST
- Region: CHINA (Taiwan)

L. F. Wu

Wu, Lan Fen; 吴兰芬；Wú Lánfēn

1985- **First publication: 2012**

- Employment: South China Botanical Garden, Chinese Academy of Sciences（中国科学院华南植物园）
- Research interest: Celastraceae [S]
- Published taxa: *Euonymus*
- Region: CHINA (Guangdong)

L. Wu

Wu, Lei; 吴磊；Wú Lěi

1986- **First publication: 2011**

- Employment: Guangxi Institute of Botany, Chinese Academy of Sciences; College of Life Sciences, Beijing Normal University; College of Forestry, Central South University of Forestry and Technology（广西壮族自治区中国科学院广西植物研究所；北京师范大学生命科学学院；中南林业科技大学林学院）
- Research interest: Aristolochiaceae, Asparagaceae, Ericaceae, Gesneriaceae, Lauraceae, Melanthiaceae, Orchidaceae, Ranunculaceae, Rubiaceae [S]
- Published taxa: *Aristolochia, Aspidistra, Boeica, Briggsia, Cheilotheca, Chionographis, Hedyotis, Leptomischus, Liparis, Litsea, Ophiorrhiza, Platanthera, Primulina, Semiaquilegia, Spiradiclis*
- Region: CHINA

L. H. Wu

Wu, Li Hong; 吴立宏；Wú Lìhóng

1966- **First publication: 1997**

- Employment: Luoyang Agricultural College, Henan; School of Life Sciences, Sun Yat-sen University; Shanghai University of Traditional Chinese Medicine; Shanghai R&D Center for Standardization of Chinese Medicines（河南省洛阳农业高等专科学校；中山大学生命科学学院；上海中医药大学；上海市中药标准化研究中心）
- Research interest: Ericaceae, Gentianaceae, Hypericaceae, Papaveraceae [S]
- Published taxa: *Dicranostigma, Gentiana, Hypericum, Rhododendron*
- Region: CHINA

Lin F. Wu

Wu, Lin Fang; 吴林芳；Wú Línfāng

First publication: 2018

- Employment: Guangzhou Linfang Eco-Technology Co., Ltd.（广州林芳生态科技有限公司）
- Research interest: Orchidaceae [S]
- Published taxa: *Platanthera*
- Region: CHINA (Guangdong)
- IPNI as: L. F. Wu

Long H. Wu

Wu, Long Hua; 吴龙华；Wú Lónghuá

1969- **First publication: 2012**

- Employment: Institute of Soil Science, Chinese Academy of Sciences（中国科学院南京土壤研究所）
- Research interest: Crassulaceae [S]
- Published taxa: *Sedum*
- Region: CHINA (Zhejiang)
- IPNI as: L. H. Wu

M. Jiang Wu

Wu, Ming Jiang; 吴明江；Wú Míngjiāng

1963- **First publication: 2000**

- Employment: Department of Biology, Keshan Teachers' College, Jilin（吉林省克山师范专科学校生物系）
- Research interest: Typhaceae [S]
- Published taxa: *Typha*
- Region: CHINA (Jilin)

M. J. Wu

Wu, Ming Jou; 吳明洲；Wú Míngzhōu; 吴明洲

First publication: 1992

- Employment: Graduate Institute of Biological Resource and Technology, Hualien University of Education（花莲教育大学生物资源与科技研究所）
- Research interest: Asteraceae, Fabaceae, Lamiaceae, Nyctaginaceae, Phyllanthaceae [BS]
- Published taxa: *Boerhavia, Centratherum, Indigofera, Phyllanthus, Scutellaria*
- Region: CHINA (Taiwan)

M. H. Wu

Wu, Ming Hsiang; Wu, Ming Xiang; 吳鳴翔；Wú Míngxiáng; 吴鸣翔

1936- **First publication: 1976**

- Employment: Qingyuan Wanli Forest Farm, Zhejiang; Qingyuan Forestry Bureau, Zhejiang（浙江省庆元县万里林场；浙江省庆元县林业局）
- Research interest: Fagaceae, Magnoliaceae, Pinaceae [S]
- Published taxa: *Abies, Fagus, Michelia*
- Region: CHINA (Zhejiang)
- IPNI as: M. X. Wu

Q. G. Wu

Wu, Qi Gen; 吴七根；Wú Qīgēn; 吳七根

1936- **First publication: 1996**

- Employment: South China Institute of Botany, Chinese Academy of Sciences（中国科学院华南植物研究所）
- Research interest: Zingiberaceae [S]
- Published taxa: *Zingiber*
- Region: CHINA (Yunnan)

Chi C. Wu

Wu, Chi Chih; 吳啟智；Wú Qǐzhì; 吴启智

First publication: 2003

- Employment: Institute of Botany, "Academia Sinica"（中研院植物研究所）
- Research interest: Pentaphylacaceae [S]
- Published taxa: *Eurya*
- Region: CHINA (Taiwan)

C. J. Wu

Wu, Ching Ju; Wu, Qing Ru; 吴庆如；Wú Qìngrú; 吳慶如

1934- **First publication: 1984**

- Employment: Department of Biology, Inner Mongolia University（内蒙古大学生物系）
- Research interest: Gentianaceae; Plants of Nei Mongol [S]
- Published taxa: *Crawfurdia, Gentiana, Tripterospermum*
- Affiliation: HIMC
- Location of specimens: HIMC, IMDC
- Region: CHINA (Nei Mongol)

Y. F. Wu

Wu, Yeng Fen; Wu, Yong Fen; Wu, Young Fen; Wu, Rong Fen; 吴容芬；Wú Róngfēn; 吳容芬

1922-2001 **First publication: 1963**

- Employment: South China Institute of Botany, Chinese Academy of Sciences（中国科学院华南植物研究所）
- Research interest: Magnoliaceae, Sabiaceae, Symplocaceae [S]
- Published taxa: *Manglietia, Michelia, Sabia, Symplocos*

- Affiliation: IBSC
- Region: CHINA

Shi H. Wu

Wu, Shi Hua; 吴诗华；Wú Shīhuá

First publication: 1981

- Employment: Anhui Agricultural College（安徽农学院）
- Research interest: Poaceae [S]
- Published taxa: *Phyllostachys*
- Region: CHINA (Anhui)
- IPNI as: S. H. Wu

S. F. Wu

Wu, Shi Fu; 吴世福；Wú Shìfú; 吳世福

1946- **First publication: 1990**

- Employment: Department of Biology, Shanghai Teachers' College of Technology（上海技术师范学院生物系）
- Research interest: Athyriaceae, Dryopteridaceae, Plagiogyriaceae, Polypodiaceae; Pteridophytes [P]
- Published taxa: *Arachniodes, Athyriopsis, Athyrium, Cornopteris, Cyrtomium, Dryopteris, Neolepisorus, Phanerophlebiopsis, Plagiogyria, Polystichum*
- Affiliation: SHCT, SHTU
- Location of specimens: SHCT, SHTU
- Region: CHINA (Hunan)

S. Wu

Wu, Shuang; 吴双；Wú Shuāng

1962- **First publication: 2018**

- Employment: Guangxi Association for Science and Technology（广西科学技术协会）
- Research interest: Hydrocharitaceae [S]
- Published taxa: *Ottelia*
- Region: CHINA (Guangxi)

Wan C. Wu

Wu, Wan Chun; 吴万春；Wú Wànchūn; 吳萬春

1928- **First publication: 1985**

- Employment: South China Agricultural University（华南农业大学）
- Research interest: Poaceae [S]
- Published taxa: *Eremochloa, Microstegium, Oryza*
- Location of specimens: SCAUB
- Region: CHINA (Guangdong, Hainan, Yunnan)

W. H. Wu

Wu, Wang Hui; 吴望辉；Wú Wànghuī

1985- **First publication: 2011**

- Employment: Guangxi Institute of Botany, Chinese Academy of Sciences（广西壮族自治区中国科学院广西植物研究所）
- Research interest: Gesneriaceae [S]

- Published taxa: *Chirita, Chiritopsis, Hemiboea, Petrocodon, Primulina*
- Region: CHINA (Guangxi)

W. S. Wu

Wu, Wei Sheng; 吴伟生 ; Wú Wěishēng

1964- **First publication: 1992**

- Employment: Nanyue Arboretum, Hunan（湖南省南岳树木园）
- Research interest: Aquifoliaceae; Plants of Nanyue [S]
- Published taxa: *Ilex*
- Affiliation: NYA
- Location of specimens: NYA
- Region: CHINA (Hunan)

W. Wu

Wu, Wen; 吴文 ; Wú Wén

First publication: 1992

- Employment: Wuhu School of Traditional Chinese Medicine（安徽省芜湖中医学校）
- Research interest: Araceae, Lamiaceae [S]
- Published taxa: *Scutellaria*
- Affiliation: WUH
- Location of specimens: WUH
- Region: CHINA (Anhui)

W. C. Wu

Wu, Wen Chen; Wu, Wen Chên; Wu, Yün Chên; Wu, Wen Cheng; Wu, Yun Zhen; 吴韫珍 ; Wú Wēnzhēn; 吳韞珍

1899-1941 **First publication: 1936**

- Employment: Department of Biology, National Tsing Hua University（国立清华大学生物系）
- Research interest: Asteraceae, Caryophyllaceae [S]
- Published taxa: *Chrysanthemum, Psammosilene*
- Location of specimens: PEY
- Region: CHINA (Yunnan)

X. H. Wu

Wu, Xia Hua; 吴夏华 ; Wú Xiàhuá

1973- **First publication: 2015**

- Employment: Qingyuan Forestry Bureau, Zhejiang（浙江省庆元县林业局）
- Research interest: Magnoliaceae [S]
- Published taxa: *Michelia*
- Region: CHINA (Zhejiang)

X. Z. Wu

Wu, Xiang Zhu; 吴相祝 ; Wú Xiāngzhù

1959- **First publication: 2009**

- Employment: Xianju Forestry Bureau, Zhejiang（浙江省仙居县林业局）
- Research interest: Rosaceae [S]
- Published taxa: *Armeniaca*
- Region: CHINA (Zhejiang)

X. F. Wu

Wu, Xun Feng; 吴训锋 ; Wú Xùnfēng

1965- **First publication: 2020**

- Employment: Yunnan Forestry Technological College（云南林业职业技术学院）
- Research interest: Orchidaceae [S]
- Published taxa: *Cheirostylis*
- Region: CHINA (Yunnan)

Y. P. Wu

Wu, Yi Ping; 吴依平 ; Wú Yīpíng

1954- **First publication: 1984**

- Employment: Department of Biology, East China Normal University（华东师范大学生物系）
- Research interest: Dryopteridaceae [P]
- Published taxa: *Arachniodes*
- Region: CHINA (Zhejiang)

Y. C. Wu

Wu, Yin Chan; Wu, Yin Ch'an; 吴印禅 ; Wú Yìnchán; 吳印禪

1902-1959 **First publication: 1932**

- Employment: Botanical Institute, College of Agriculture, National Sun Yat-sen University; South China Institute of Botany, Chinese Academy of Sciences（国立中山大学农林植物研究所；中国科学院华南植物研究所）
- Research interest: Aristolochiaceae, Athyriaceae, Hydrangeaceae, Lardizabalaceae, Polypodiaceae; Pteridophytes [PS]
- Published taxa: *Aristolochia, Dichroa, Diplazium, Holboellia, Polypodium*
- Affiliation: IBSC
- Region: CHINA

Y. S. Wu

Wu, Ying Siang; Wu, Ying Hsiang; Wu, Ying Xiang; 吴应祥 ; Wú Yīngxiáng; 吳應祥

1915-2005 **First publication: 1980**

- Employment: Institute of Botany, Chinese Academy of Sciences（中国科学院植物研究所）
- Research interest: Orchidaceae [S]
- Published taxa: *Cymbidium*
- Region: CHINA (Sichuan)

Yu Wu

Wu, Yu; 吴玉 ; Wú Yù

1994- **First publication: 2019**

- Employment: College of Life Sciences, Hunan Normal University（湖南师范大学生命科学学院）
- Research interest: Primulaceae, Rosaceae [S]
- Published taxa: *Lysimachia, Prunus*

- Region: CHINA
- IPNI as: Y. Wu

Y. H. Wu

Wu, Yu Hu; 吴玉虎 ; **Wú Yùhǔ**

1951- **First publication: 1992**

- Employment: Northwest Plateau Institute of Biology, Chinese Academy of Sciences (中国科学院西北高原生物研究所)
- Research interest: Brassicaceae, Elaeagnaceae, Fabaceae, Lamiaceae, Mazaceae, Plumbaginaceae, Poaceae, Tamaricaceae [S]
- Published taxa: *Astragalus, Caragana, Christolea, Corethrodendron, Deyeuxia, Elymus, Hedysarum, Hippophae, Kengyilia, Lancea, Leymus, Limonium, Melilotoides, Oxytropis, Pennisetum, Roegneria, Salvia, Tamarix, Vicia*
- Affiliation: HNWP
- Location of specimens: HNWP
- Region: CHINA (Qinghai)

Yue Wu

Wu, Yue; 吴越 ; **Wú Yuè**

First publication: 1984

- Employment: Shaanxi Agriculture and Forestry School (陕西省农林学校)
- Research interest: Cupressaceae [S]
- Published taxa: *Metasequoia*
- Region: CHINA (Hubei)
- IPNI as: Y. Wu

Ze M. Wu

Wu, Ze Min; 吴泽民 ; **Wú Zémín**; 吳澤民

1944- **First publication: 1988**

- Employment: Department of Forestry, Anhui Agricultural College (安徽农学院林学系)
- Research interest: Elaeagnaceae, Lardizabalaceae, Rosaceae [S]
- Published taxa: *Elaeagnus, Rosa, Rubus, Sargentodoxa*
- Affiliation: AAUF
- Region: CHINA (Anhui)
- Also as: T. M. Wu

Z. Y. Wu

Wu, Zeng Yuan; 吴增源 ; **Wú Zēngyuán**

1987- **First publication: 2011**

- Employment: Kunming Institute of Botany, Chinese Academy of Sciences (中国科学院昆明植物研究所)
- Research interest: Urticaceae [S]
- Published taxa: *Elatostema*
- Region: CHINA (Yunnan)
- Also as: Zeng Y. Wu

S. H. Wu

Wu, Shiew Hung; Wu, Zhao Hong; 吴兆洪 ; **Wú Zhàohóng**; 吳兆洪

1934- **First publication: 1964**

- Employment: South China Institute of Botany, Chinese Academy of Sciences (中国科学院华南植物研究所)
- Research interest: Aspleniaceae, Athyriaceae, Cyatheaceae, Dennstaedtiaceae, Dryopteridaceae, Marattiaceae, Ophioglossaceae, Pteridaceae, Urticaceae, Woodsiaceae; Pteridophytes [PS]
- Published taxa: *Acrophorus, Angiopteris, Asplenium, Bolbitis, Ceterachopsis, Cyathea, Diacalpe, Diplazium, Elaphoglossum, Eriosoriopsis, Monomelangium, Neottopteris, Pellionia, Peranema, Pteridium, Pteris, Sceptridium, Woodsia*
- Affiliation: IBSC
- Region: CHINA

Z. L. Wu

Wu, Zhen Lan; 吴珍兰 ; **Wú Zhēnlán**; 吳珍蘭

1939- **First publication: 1981**

- Employment: Northwest Plateau Institute of Biology, Chinese Academy of Sciences (中国科学院西北高原生物研究所)
- Research interest: Adoxaceae, Asparagaceae, Orobanchaceae, Poaceae [S]
- Published taxa: *Achnatherum, Anthoxanthum, Calamagrostis, Deschampsia, Glyceria, Helictotrichon, Koeleria, Melica, Oryzopsis, Pedicularis, Piptatherum, Polygonatum, Ptilagrostis, Sinadoxa, Trisetum*
- Affiliation: HNWP
- Region: CHINA (Qinghai)

Z. H. Wu

Wu, Zhen Hai; 吴振海 ; **Wú Zhènhǎi**

1964- **First publication: 1988**

- Employment: Northwest China Institute of Botany, Chinese Academy of Sciences and Shaanxi Province; College of Life Sciences, Northwest A&F University (陕西省中国科学院西北植物研究所 ; 西北农林科技大学生命科学学院)
- Research interest: Fabaceae, Orchidaceae; Plants of Shaanxi [S]
- Published taxa: *Astragalus, Chusua, Oxytropis*
- Affiliation: WUK
- Location of specimens: WUK
- Region: CHINA

C. Y. Wu

Wu, Cheng Yih; Wu, Cheng I; Wu Chêng I; Wu, Zheng Yi; 吴征镒 ; **Wú Zhēngyì**; 吳征鎰

1916-2013 **First publication: 1936**

- Employment: Department of Biology, National

Tsing Hua University; Institute of Sciences, National Southwestern Associated University; Institute of Botany, Chinese Academy of Sciences; Kunming Institute of Botany, Chinese Academy of Sciences（国立清华大学生物系；国立西南联合大学理科研究所；中国科学院植物研究所；中国科学院昆明植物研究所）

- Research interest: Acanthaceae, Achariaceae, Actinidiaceae, Adoxaceae, Anacardiaceae, Annonaceae, Apiaceae, Apocynaceae, Aquifoliaceae, Araceae, Araliaceae, Aristolochiaceae, Aspleniaceae, Asteraceae, Athyriaceae, Begoniaceae, Berberidaceae, Bignoniaceae, Brassicaceae, Buxaceae, Campanulaceae, Caprifoliaceae, Caryophyllaceae, Celastraceae, Clethraceae, Clusiaceae, Combretaceae, Commelinaceae, Connaraceae, Convolvulaceae, Cornaceae, Cucurbitaceae, Diapensiaceae, Dipterocarpaceae, Ebenaceae, Elaeocarpaceae, Ericaceae, Euphorbiaceae, Fabaceae, Garryaceae, Gentianaceae, Gesneriaceae, Hamamelidaceae, Hernandiaceae, Icacinaceae, Iteaceae, Lamiaceae, Lardizabalaceae, Lauraceae, Loganiaceae, Magnoliaceae, Malvaceae, Mazaceae, Melastomataceae, Meliaceae, Menispermaceae, Metteniusaceae, Moraceae, Myristicaceae, Nyssaceae, Oleaceae, Opiliaceae, Orobanchaceae, Papaveraceae, Piperaceae, Pittosporaceae, Polygalaceae, Primulaceae, Proteaceae, Ranunculaceae, Rhamnaceae, Rosaceae, Rubiaceae, Sabiaceae, Salicaceae, Santalaceae, Sapindaceae, Sapotaceae, Saxifragaceae, Smilacaceae, Solanaceae, Stachyuraceae, Staphyleaceae, Styracaceae, Symplocaceae, Theaceae, Thymelaeaceae, Urticaceae, Violaceae, Vitaceae [S]
- Published taxa: *Acanthus, Acer, Acranthera, Actinidia, Adenophora, Aglaia, Ajuga, Alangium, Allantodia, Allomorphia, Alyxia, Amoora, Ancylostemon, Androsace, Anemone, Anisodus, Anthriscus, Aralia, Archakebia, Arctous, Ardisia, Arenaria, Argyreia, Arisaema, Aristolochia, Artabotrys, Artocarpus, Asplenium, Astilbe, Aucuba, Beccarinda, Beesia, Begonia, Bennettiodendron, Berberis, Berchemia, Bergenia, Blastus, Blumea, Brachytome, Buchanania, Bupleurum, Calcareoboea, Callicarpa, Calophanoides, Campanula, Cardamine, Cardiochlamys, Cardioteucris, Caryopteris, Casearia, Cayratia, Celastrus, Cerastium, Championella, Chaydaia, Chelonopsis, Chirita, Circaeocarpus, Clerodendranthus, Clerodendrum, Clethra, Clinopodium, Codonopsis, Coleus, Colquhounia, Comanthosphace, Combretum, Corchoropsis, Corydalis, Corylopsis, Cotinus, Cotoneaster, Crawfurdia, Cyananthus, Cyathella, Dendrobenthamia, Dendrotrophe, Desmos, Deutzianthus, Dichotomanthes, Dicranostigma, Didissandra, Didymocarpus, Diflugossa, Dimocarpus, Diospyros, Distyliopsis, Distylium, Dolichandrone, Dracocephalum, Drimycarpus, Dysophylla, Dysoxylum, Elaeocarpus, Elsholtzia, Embelia, Epimedium, Erycibe, Euchresta, Euonymus, Euphorbia, Eustigma, Ficus, Fissistigma, Flemingia, Fordiophyton, Fraxinus, Galeobdolon, Galium, Gamblea, Garcinia, Gardneria, Gaultheria, Gerbera, Glechoma, Glyptopetalum, Goldfussia, Gomphostemma, Graptophyllum, Grewia, Gynostemma, Hanceola, Hapaline, Helicia, Heliciopsis, Hemiboea, Hemsleya, Heracleum, Heterolamium, Hibiscus, Holboellia, Hopea, Horsfieldia, Houpoea, Hovenia, Huodendron, Hydrocotyle, Hymenochlaena, Hyssopus, Ilex, Illigera, Incarvillea, Inula, Ipomoea, Itea, Itoa, Ixora, Jasminum, Keiskea, Kinostemon, Lagochilus, Lamiophlomis, Laportea, Lasianthus, Leonurus, Lepidium, Leucothoë, Lirianthe, Lobelia, Loeseneriella, Lonicera, Lophanthus, Lycianthes, Lycopus, Lyonia, Lysimachia, Lysionotus, Mackaya, Maesa, Mahonia, Mallotus, Mananthes, Mangifera, Manglietia, Mastixia, Maytenus, Mazus, Meconopsis, Medinilla, Meehania, Meliosma, Melissa, Memecylon, Mentha, Merremia, Merrilliopanax, Metastachydium, Michelia, Micromeria, Microtoena, Morus, Mosla, Mussaenda, Myrsine, Nandina, Nepeta, Nephelium, Neuropeltis, Nosema, Nothapodytes, Notochaete, Oenanthe, Oreocharis, Ornithoboea, Orthodon, Osbeckia, Ostericum, Oyama, Pachylarnax, Pachysandra, Panax, Panzeria, Paraboea, Paraphlomis, Pararuellia, Parastyrax, Parnassia, Pedicularis, Perilepta, Perilla, Peristrophe, Petrocosmea, Peucedanum, Phlomis, Phoebe, Phtheirospermum, Phyllagathis, Phyllophyton, Physospermopsis, Pimpinella, Pittosporopsis, Pittosporum, Plagiopetalum, Planchonella, Pleiosorbus, Pogostemon, Polyalthia, Polygala, Porana, Pothos, Premna, Psammosilene, Pseuderanthemum, Pseudocerastium, Pteracanthus, Pternopetalum, Pterospermum, Pygeum, Pyrenaria, Pyrrothrix, Rabdosia, Radermachera, Rapanea, Rehderodendron, Rhamnoneuron, Rhamnus, Rhodostegiella, Rinorea, Rodgersia, Rostellularia, Rostrinucula, Roureopsis, Sabia, Sageretia, Salacia, Salomonia, Salvia, Saniculiphyllum, Sapindus, Sarcococca, Sarcopyramis, Saxifraga, Schnabelia, Scopolia, Scutellaria, Seseli, Shortia, Shuteria, Silene, Sinadoxa, Siphocranion, Skapanthus, Smilax, Solanum, Solena, Sonerila, Sopubia, Sorbaria, Spatholirion, Spondias, Sporoxeia, Stachys, Stachyurus, Stauntonia, Staurogyne, Stellaria, Stephania, Stereospermum, Stewartia, Streptolirion,*

Styrax, Symplocos, Taraktogenos, Terminthia, Tetradoxa, Tetraglochidium, Tetrastigma, Teucrium, Thesium, Thladiantha, Thoreliella, Thunbergia, Thymus, Toona, Toxicodendron, Toxocarpus, Trichosanthes, Tripterospermum, Turpinia, Typhonium, Vaccinium, Viburnum, Vincetoxicum, Vitex, Walsura, Wenchengia, Xanthophyllum, Xantolis, Xizangia, Yunnanopilia
- Affiliation: KUN
- Location of specimens: IBK, IBSC, KUN, PE, PEY, WUK
- Region: CHINA

Z. K. Wu

Wu, Zhi Kun; 吴之坤 ; Wú Zhīkūn

1980- **First publication: 2011**
- Employment: Kunming Institute of Botany, Chinese Academy of Sciences（中国科学院昆明植物研究所）
- Research interest: Apocynaceae, Gesneriaceae, Papaveraceae, Primulaceae [S]
- Published taxa: *Ceropegia, Meconopsis, Oreocharis, Primula*
- Region: CHINA (Yunnan)

Z. M. Wu

Wu, Zhi Min; 吴志敏 ; Wú Zhìmǐn

1963- **First publication: 1988**
- Employment: College of Forestry, South China Agricultural University（华南农业大学林学院）
- Research interest: Cannabaceae, Clusiaceae, Poaceae; Plants of Guangdong [S]
- Published taxa: *Acidosasa, Arundinaria, Bambusa, Garcinia, Indocalamus, Indosasa, Phyllostachys, Pleioblastus, Sinocalamus, Trema*
- Affiliation: CANT
- Region: CHINA (Guangdong, Guangxi)

C. N. Wu

Wu, Chi Nan; 吴志南 ; Wú Zhìnán; 吳志南

1940- **First publication: 1983**
- Employment: Guangdong Institute for Drug Control（广东省药品检验所）
- Research interest: Ericaceae [S]
- Published taxa: *Rhododendron*
- Region: CHINA (Guangdong)

X. J. Wu

Wu, Xian Jin; 伍贤进 ; Wǔ Xiánjìn

1964- **First publication: 2013**
- Employment: College of Biological and Food Engineering, Huaihua University（怀化学院生物与食品工程学院）
- Research interest: Araceae [S]
- Published taxa: *Pinellia*
- Region: CHINA (Hunan)

Y. T. Wu

Wu, Yu Ting; 伍煜庭 ; Wǔ Yùtíng

1939- **First publication: 1979**
- Employment: Department of Biology, Sichuan University（四川大学生物系）
- Research interest: Anacardiaceae, Asteraceae, Sapindaceae [S]
- Published taxa: *Acer, Chrysanthemum, Cotinus, Rhus*
- Affiliation: SZ
- Location of specimens: SZ
- Region: CHINA (Sichuan)

Zhao W. Wu

Wu, Zhao Wen; 伍兆文 ; Wǔ Zhàowén

First publication: 2019
- Employment: School of Life Sciences, Nanchang University; Institute of Botany, Chinese Academy of Sciences（南昌大学生命科学学院；中国科学院植物研究所）
- Research interest: Gesneriaceae [S]
- Published taxa: *Hemiboea*
- Region: CHINA (Guizhou)
- IPNI as: Z. W. Xu

J. Y. Wu

Wu, Jian Yong; 武建勇 ; Wǔ Jiànyǒng

1977- **First publication: 2009**
- Employment: Nanjing Institute of Environmental Sciences, Ministry of Environmental Protection（环境保护部南京环境科学研究所）
- Research interest: Asparagaceae, Berberidaceae [S]
- Published taxa: *Aspidistra, Mahonia*
- Region: CHINA (Guangxi, Guizhou)

K. Y. Wu

Wu, Kong Yun; 武孔云 ; Wǔ Kǒngyún

First publication: 1991
- Employment: Guiyang College of Traditional Chinese Medicine（贵阳中医学院）
- Research interest: Trilliaceae [S]
- Published taxa: *Paris*
- Region: CHINA (Guizhou)

S. K. Wu

Wu, Su Kung; Wu, Shu Gong; Wu, Su Gong; **武素功 ; Wǔ Sùgōng**

1935-2013 **First publication: 1976**
- Employment: Kunming Institute of Botany, Chinese Academy of Sciences（中国科学院昆明植物研究所）
- Research interest: Annonaceae, Araceae, Araliaceae, Aristolochiaceae, Asparagaceae, Aspleniaceae, Athyriaceae, Balsaminaceae, Blechnaceae,

Caprifoliaceae, Caryophyllaceae, Crassulaceae, Cyatheaceae, Dennstaedtiaceae, Dryopteridaceae, Fabaceae, Gentianaceae, Hymenophyllaceae, Lamiaceae, Lycopodiaceae, Moraceae, Orchidaceae, Pittosporaceae, Polypodiaceae, Primulaceae, Pteridaceae, Ranunculaceae, Rubiaceae, Saxifragaceae, Selaginellaceae, Tectariaceae, Thelypteridaceae, Woodsiaceae; Pteridophytes [PS]
- Published taxa: *Aleuritopteris, Allantodia, Androsace, Arachniodes, Arenaria, Arisaema, Aristolochia, Arthromeris, Artocarpus, Asplenium, Astragalus, Athyrium, Bolbitis, Clerodendrum, Coniogramme, Crepidomanes, Crypsinus, Ctenitis, Cyclogramma, Cyclosorus, Cyrtogonellum, Cyrtomium, Delphinium, Diacalpe, Drynaria, Dryopteris, Egenolfia, Emodiopteris, Gentiana, Gymnosphaera, Huperzia, Impatiens, Kontumia, Lepisorus, Leptolepidium, Loxogramme, Lunathyrium, Merrilliopanax, Metathelypteris, Microsorum, Nervilia, Onychium, Oxytropis, Peliosanthes, Phaius, Phymatopsis, Pittosporum, Platygyria, Polyalthia, Polypodiastrum, Polypodiodes, Polypodium, Polystichum, Pseudocyclosorus, Pseudocystopteris, Pseudophegopteris, Pteris, Pyrrosia, Rhodiola, Saxifraga, Selaginella, Sinocrassula, Tectaria, Tricholepidium, Trichomanes, Valeriana, Vittaria, Wendlandia, Woodsia, Woodwardia*
- Affiliation: KUN
- Location of specimens: KUN, SCFI, PE
- Region: CHINA
- Also as: S. G. Wu

Y. B. Wu

Wu, Yu Bi; 武玉璧 ; Wǔ Yùbì

1940- **First publication: 1994**

- Employment: Institute of Sericulture, Hebei Academy of Agriculture and Forestry Sciences (河北省农林科学院蚕桑研究所)
- Research interest: Moraceae [S]
- Published taxa: *Morus*
- Region: CHINA (Hebei)

Wuzhi

Wuhan Botanical Garden, Chinese Academy of Sciences; Wu Han Zhi Wu Yuan; Wuzhi; 武植 ; Wǔ Zhí

First publication: 1979

- Employment: Wuhan Institute of Botany, Chinese Academy of Sciences (中国科学院武汉植物研究所)
- Research interest: Celastraceae, Fagaceae, Rosaceae [S]
- Published taxa: *Celastrus, Exochorda, Quercus, Rubus*
- Region: CHINA (Hubei)
- Organization

Z. F. Wu

Wu, Zu Fa; 武祖发 ; Wǔ Zǔfā; 武祖發

1936- **First publication: 1990**

- Employment: Department of Chinese Materia Medica, Anhui College of Traditional Chinese Medicine (安徽中医学院中药系)
- Research interest: Crassulaceae [S]
- Published taxa: *Sedum*
- Region: CHINA (Anhui)

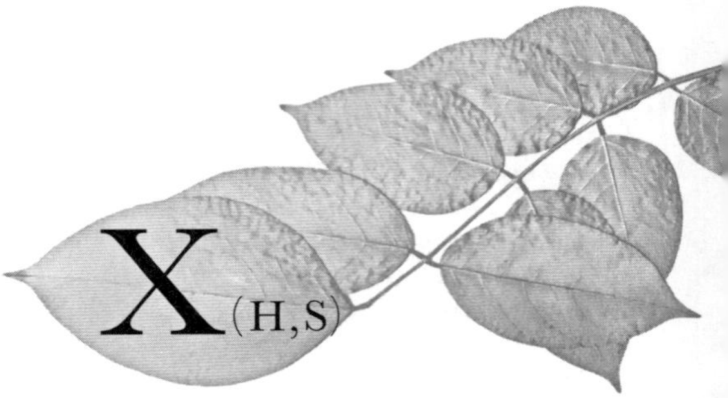

H. C. Xi

Xi, Hou Cheng; 郗厚诚 ; Xī Hòuchéng

1986- **First publication: 2019**

- Employment: Xishuangbanna Tropical Botanical Garden, Chinese Academy of Sciences; Guiyang Medicinal Botanical Garden (中国科学院西双版纳热带植物园 ; 贵阳药用植物园)
- Research interest: Begoniaceae, Berberidaceae [S]
- Published taxa: *Begonia, Dysosma*
- Location of specimens: GYBG
- Region: CHINA (Guizhou, Yunnan)

J. Q. Xi

Xi, Jing Qing; 奚镜清 ; Xī Jìngqīng; 奚鏡清

1925- **First publication: 1987**

- Employment: Department of Pharmacy, Zhejiang Medical University (浙江医科大学药学系)
- Research interest: Dioscoreaceae, Dipsacaceae, Smilacaceae, Solanaceae, Stemonaceae [S]
- Published taxa: *Dioscorea*
- Affiliation: ZMU
- Location of specimens: ZMU
- Region: CHINA (Zhejiang)

H. H. Xi

Xi, Hui Hui; 席辉辉 ; Xí Huīhuī

First publication: 2020

- Employment: Kunming Institute of Botany, Chinese Academy of Sciences (中国科学院昆明植物研究所)
- Research interest: Begoniaceae [S]
- Published taxa: *Begonia*
- Region: CHINA (Yunnan)

B. S. Xia

Xia, Bo Shun; 夏伯顺；Xià Bóshùn

1983- **First publication: 2017**

- Employment: Wuhan Botanical Garden, Chinese Academy of Sciences（中国科学院武汉植物园）
- Research interest: Lauraceae [S]
- Published taxa: *Neocinnamomum*
- Region: CHINA (Guangxi)

Chang Y. Xia

Xia, Chang Ying; 夏常英；Xià Chángyīng

1994- **First publication: 2019**

- Employment: College of Life Sciences, Southwest University; Institute of Botany, Chinese Academy of Sciences（西南大学生命科学学院；中国科学院植物研究所）
- Research interest: Balsaminaceae [S]
- Published taxa: *Impatiens*
- Region: CHINA (Guangxi, Yunnan)

C. Xia

Xia, Chun; 夏纯；Xià Chún

1987- **First publication: 2013**

- Employment: South China Botanical Garden, Chinese Academy of Sciences（中国科学院华南植物园）
- Research interest: Acanthaceae [S]
- Published taxa: *Phlogacanthus*
- Region: CHINA (Yunnan)

D. Y. Xia

Xia, De Yun; 夏德云；Xià Déyún

1939-2008 **First publication: 1986**

- Employment: Kunming Institute of Botany, Chinese Academy of Sciences（中国科学院昆明植物研究所）
- Research interest: Begoniaceae [S]
- Published taxa: *Begonia*
- Region: CHINA (Yunnan)

K. C. Hsia

Hsia, Kuang Cheng; Xia, Guang Cheng; **夏光成；Xià Guāngchéng**

1929- **First publication: 1964**

- Employment: Tianjin Institute of Pharmacology and Drug Inspection（天津市药品检验药物研究所）
- Research interest: Gentianaceae, Liliaceae, Rubiaceae; Medicinal Plants [S]
- Published taxa: *Fritillaria, Gentiana, Uncaria*
- Affiliation: TJMP
- Location of specimens: IMD, TJMP
- Region: CHINA

G. H. Xia

Xia, Guo Hua; 夏国华；Xià Guóhuá

1980- **First publication: 2009**

- Employment: School of Forestry and Biotechnology, Zhejiang A&F University（浙江农林大学林业与生物技术学院）
- Research interest: Apiaceae, Asparagaceae, Berberidaceae, Caryophyllaceae, Orobanchaceae, Rosaceae, Zingiberaceae; Plants of Zhejiang [S]
- Published taxa: *Epimedium, Globba, Liriope, Ostericum, Photinia, Pseudostellaria, Rehmannia*
- Affiliation: ZJFC
- Location of specimens: ZJFC
- Region: CHINA (Zhejiang)

N. H. Xia

Xia, Nian He; 夏念和；Xià Niànhé

1963- **First publication: 1993**

- Employment: South China Institute of Botany, Chinese Academy of Sciences; South China Botanical Garden, Chinese Academy of Sciences（中国科学院华南植物研究所；中国科学院华南植物园）
- Research interest: Acanthaceae, Apocynaceae, Asteraceae, Betulaceae, Ebenaceae, Ericaceae, Euphorbiaceae, Fagaceae, Gesneriaceae, Lamiaceae, Lauraceae, Magnoliaceae, Melastomataceae, Menispermaceae, Myrtaceae, Piperaceae, Poaceae, Rhamnaceae, Rosaceae, Rubiaceae, Santalaceae, Sapindaceae, Urticaceae, Zingiberaceae [S]
- Published taxa: *Acanthus, Aesculus, Agapetes, Amomum, Ampelocalamus, Annamocalamus, Argentina, Arundinaria, Bambusa, Beilschmiedia, Blastus, Bonia, Carpinus, Castanopsis, Chimonobambusa, Chimonocalamus, Croton, Curcuma, Dendrocalamus, Dendrotrophe, Diospyros, Frangula, Gaoligongshania, Gardenia, Gigantochloa, Houpoea, Hoya, Justicia, Khoonmengia, Lepisanthes, Lirianthe, Magnolia, Manglietia, Melocalamus, Michelia, Oreocharis, Oyama, Pachylarnax, Parakmeria, Peristrophe, Phyllostachys, Pilea, Piper, Prunus, Pseudosasa, Quercus, Rubovietnamia, Saussurea, Schizostachyum, Sinopora, Stephania, Strobilanthes, Syndiclis, Syzygium, Teucrium, Vaccinium, Woonyoungia, Wuacanthus, Yulania, Zingiber*
- Affiliation: IBSC
- Region: CHINA

Quan Xia

Xia, Quan; 夏泉；Xià Quán

1957- **First publication: 1990**

- Employment: Department of Biology, Lanzhou University（兰州大学生物系）
- Research interest: Lardizabalaceae, Sargentodoxaceae [S]
- Published taxa: *Holboellia*

- Affiliation: LZU, NWTC
- Region: CHINA (Gansu)

Q. Xia

Xia, Qun; 夏群 ; Xià Qún

1949- **First publication: 1989**

- Employment: Institute of Botany, Chinese Academy of Sciences（中国科学院植物研究所）
- Research interest: Cyatheaceae [P]
- Published taxa: *Alsophila*
- Region: CHINA

W. Y. Hsia

Hsia, Wei Ying; Xia, Wei Ying; **夏纬瑛 ; Xià Wěiyīng; 夏緯瑛**

1896-1987 **First publication: 1936**

- Employment: Institute of Botany, National Academy of Peiping（国立北平研究院植物学研究所）
- Research interest: Pinaceae; Plants of N. China [S]
- Published taxa: *Pinus*
- Affiliation: PE
- Location of specimens: BJFC, PE
- Region: CHINA (Anhui)

Y. M. Xia

Xia, Yong Mei; 夏咏梅 ; Xià Yǒngméi; 夏永梅

1963- **First publication: 1987**

- Employment: Xishuangbanna Tropical Botanical Garden, Chinese Academy of Sciences（中国科学院西双版纳热带植物园）
- Research interest: Zingiberaceae [S]
- Published taxa: *Alpinia, Amomum, Plagiostachys, Zingiber*
- Region: CHINA (Yunnan)

Z. D. Xia

Xia, Zhen Dai; 夏振岱 ; Xià Zhèndài

1935- **First publication: 1996**

- Employment: Institute of Botany, Chinese Academy of Sciences（中国科学院植物研究所）
- Research interest: Fabaceae [S]
- Published taxa: *Vicia*
- Affiliation: PE
- Region: CHINA

C. Y. Sia

Sia, Cheng Yin; Xia, Cheng Yin; Xia, Zheng Yin; **夏政寅 ; Xià Zhèngyín**

1924-2019 **First publication: 1988**

- Employment: Chengdu Wangjiang Tower Park, Sichuan（四川省成都望江楼公园）
- Research interest: Poaceae [S]
- Published taxa: *Bambusa, Dendrocalamus*
- Region: CHINA (Sichuan)
- Also as: C. Y. Xia

Z. Xia

Xia, Zhi; 夏至 ; Xià Zhì

1974- **First publication: 2012**

- Employment: College of Agronomy, Henan Agricultural University（河南农业大学农学院）
- Research interest: Gesneriaceae [S]
- Published taxa: *Microchirita*
- Region: CHINA (Yunnan)

Y. L. Xiang

Xiang, Yin Long; 相银龙 ; Xiāng Yínlóng

1985- **First publication: 2010**

- Employment: College of Life Sciences, Hunan Normal University（湖南师范大学生命科学学院）
- Research interest: Balsaminaceae [S]
- Published taxa: *Impatiens*
- Region: CHINA (Hunan)

C. L. Xiang

Xiang, Chun Lei; 向春雷 ; Xiàng Chūnléi

1984- **First publication: 2008**

- Employment: Kunming Institute of Botany, Chinese Academy of Sciences（中国科学院昆明植物研究所）
- Research interest: Lamiaceae [S]
- Published taxa: *Caryopteris, Chelonopsis, Elsholtzia, Isodon, Matsumurella, Nepeta, Paraphlomis, Phlomoides, Salvia, Schnabelia, Scutellaria, Siphocranion, Teucrium*
- Affiliation: KUN
- Location of specimens: KUN
- Region: CHINA (Yunnan)

G. X. Xiang

Xiang, Guo Xi; 向国喜 ; Xiàng Guóxǐ

1958- **First publication: 1991**

- Employment: Forestry Bureau of Dukou Municipal, Sichuan（四川省渡口市林业局）
- Research interest: Theaceae [S]
- Published taxa: *Camellia*
- Region: CHINA (Sichuan)

J. Y. Xiang

Xiang, Jian Ying; 向建英 ; Xiàng Jiànyīng

1976- **First publication: 2012**

- Employment: College of Biodiversity Conservation, Southwest Forestry University（西南林业大学生物多样性保护学院）
- Research interest: Dryopteridaceae, Malvaceae, Marattiaceae [PS]
- Published taxa: *Angiopteris, Bolbitis, Firmiana*
- Region: [ASIA]

L. L. Xiang

Xiang, Li Lin; 向莉琳 ; Xiàng Lìlín

1967- **First publication: 1994**

- Employment: Beijing Museum of Natural History（北京自然博物馆）
- Research interest: Dryopteridaceae [P]
- Published taxa: *Polystichum*
- Region: CHINA (Yunnan)

C. B. Shang

Shang, Chih Bei; Xiang, Qi Bai; 向其柏 ; Xiàng Qíbǎi

1935- **First publication: 1974**

- Employment: Department of Forestry, Nanjing Forestry College; Department of Forestry, Nanjing Forestry University; College of Forest Resources and Environment, Nanjing Forestry University（南京林学院林学系；南京林业大学林学系；南京林业大学森林资源与环境学院）
- Research interest: Aquifoliaceae, Araliaceae, Lauraceae, Magnoliaceae, Oleaceae, Rosaceae [S]
- Published taxa: *Acanthopanax, Aralia, Brassaiopsis, Cerasus, Chengiodendron, Chengiopanax, Coudenbergia, Dendropanax, Eleutherococcus, Evodiopanax, Fraxinus, Gamblea, Heteropanax, Ilex, Liriodendron, Macropanax, Merrilliopanax, Nothopanax, Pentapanax, Phoebe, Polyscias, Schefflera*
- Affiliation: NF
- Location of specimens: NF
- Region: CHINA

Q. P. Xiang

Xiang, Qiao Ping; 向巧萍 ; Xiàng Qiǎopíng

1965- **First publication: 1997**

- Employment: Institute of Botany, Chinese Academy of Sciences（中国科学院植物研究所）
- Research interest: Cupressaceae, Pinaceae; Gymnospermae [S]
- Published taxa: *Abies, Cupressus*
- Affiliation: PE
- Location of specimens: PE
- Region: [ASIA]

Q. Y. Xiang

Xiang, Qiu Yun; 向秋云 ; Xiàng Qiūyún

1962- **First publication: 1987**

- Employment: Institute of Botany, Chinese Academy of Sciences（中国科学院植物研究所）
- Research interest: Actinidiaceae, Apocynaceae, Buxaceae, Cornaceae [S]
- Published taxa: *Clematoclethra, Cornus, Gonolobus, Pachysandra*
- Region: CHINA

X. G. Xiang

Xiang, Xiao Guo; 向小果 ; Xiàng Xiǎoguǒ

1982- **First publication: 2012**

- Employment: Institute of Botany, Chinese Academy of Sciences（中国科学院植物研究所）
- Research interest: Gesneriaceae, Orchidaceae [S]
- Published taxa: *Cephalanthera, Hemiboea, Oreocharis, Shizhenia*
- Affiliation: PE
- Location of specimens: PE
- Region: CHINA

Y. H. Xiang

Xiang, Ying Hai; 向应海 ; Xiàng Yīnghǎi; 向應海

1936- **First publication: 1990**

- Employment: Guizhou Institute of Biology（贵州省生物研究所）
- Research interest: Sabiaceae; Plants of Guizhou [S]
- Published taxa: *Sabia*
- Affiliation: HGAS
- Location of specimens: HGAS
- Region: CHINA (Guizhou)

Zu H. Xiang

Xiang, Zu Heng; 向祖恒 ; Xiàng Zǔhéng

1963- **First publication: 2018**

- Employment: Longshan County Forestry Bureau, Hunan（湖南省龙山县林业局）
- Research interest: Rosaceae [S]
- Published taxa: *Prunus*
- Region: CHINA (Hunan)
- IPNI as: Z. H. Xiang

C. F. Xiao

Xiao, Chun Fen; 肖春芬 ; Xiāo Chūnfēn

1963- **First publication: 2017**

- Employment: Xishuangbanna Tropical Botanical Garden, Chinese Academy of Sciences（中国科学院西双版纳热带植物园）
- Research interest: Lowiaceae [S]
- Published taxa: *Orchidantha*
- Affiliation: HITBC
- Location of specimens: HITBC
- Region: CHINA (Yunnan)

H. X. Xiao

Xiao, Hong Xing; 肖洪兴 ; Xiāo Hóngxìng

1963- **First publication: 2012**

- Employment: School of Life Sciences, Northeast Normal University（东北师范大学生命科学学院）
- Research interest: Poaceae; Plants of N. E. China [S]
- Published taxa: *Leymus*
- Affiliation: NENU
- Region: CHINA (Jilin, Nei Mongol)

J. W. Xiao

Xiao, Jia Wei; 肖佳伟; Xiāo Jiāwěi

1992- **First publication: 2017**

- Employment: Jishou University（吉首大学）
- Research interest: Asparagaceae, Asteraceae [S]
- Published taxa: *Aster, Heteropolygonatum*
- Region: CHINA

J. B. Xiao

Xiao, Jia Bin; 肖家斌; Xiāo Jiābīn

1969- **First publication: 2006**

- Employment: Wuyishan City Forestry Bureau, Fujian（福建省武夷山市林业局）
- Research interest: Betulaceae [S]
- Published taxa: *Betula*
- Region: CHINA (Fujian)

K. S. Xiao

Xiao, Kai Sheng; 肖开生; Xiāo Kāishēng

First publication: 1985

- Employment: Jiangsu Institute of Forestry（江苏省林业科学研究所）
- Research interest: Poaceae [S]
- Published taxa: *Sinobambusa*
- Region: CHINA (Jiangsu)

M. Y. Xiao

Xiao, Mian Yun; 肖绵韵; Xiāo Miányùn; 蕭綿韻

1932-2005 **First publication: 1982**

- Employment: Department of Forestry, South China Agricultural College（华南农学院林学系）
- Research interest: Arecaceae, Primulaceae; Plants of S. China [S]
- Published taxa: *Ardisia, Livistona*
- Affiliation: CANT
- Location of specimens: CANT
- Region: CHINA (Guangdong)

P. K. Hsiao

Hsiao, Pei Ken; Xiao, Pei Gen; 肖培根; Xiāo Péigēn; 蕭培根

1931- **First publication: 1964**

- Employment: Institute of Medicinal Plant Development, Chinese Academy of Medical Sciences; Institute of Medicinal Plant Development, Chinese Academy of Medical Sciences（中国医学科学院药用植物研究所；中国医学科学院药用植物资源开发研究所）
- Research interest: Berberidaceae, Fabaceae, Gentianaceae, Liliaceae, Polygonaceae, Ranunculaceae, Rubiaceae [S]
- Published taxa: *Aconitum, Aquilegia, Astragalus, Berberis, Cimicifuga, Epimedium, Fritillaria, Gentiana, Mahonia, Rheum, Rubia*
- Affiliation: IMD
- Location of specimens: IMD
- Region: CHINA

Q. Y. Xiao

Xiao, Qun Ying; 肖群英; Xiāo Qúnyīng

1987- **First publication: 2017**

- Employment: College of Life Sciences, Sichuan University（四川大学生命科学学院）
- Research interest: Apiaceae [S]
- Published taxa: *Semenovia, Tetrataenium*
- Region: CHINA (Xizang, Yunnan)

Y. Shiao

Shiao, Yung; Xiao, Rong; 肖溶; Xiāo Róng; 蕭溶

1940- **First publication: 1977**

- Employment: Institute of Botany, Yunnan Province（云南省植物研究所）
- Research interest: Araceae; Scientific Illustrator [S]
- Published taxa: *Arisaema, Epipremnopsis, Typhonium*
- Affiliation: KUN
- Region: CHINA

X. J. Xiao

Xiao, Xin Ju; Xiao, Xin Jun; 肖新菊; Xiāo Xīnjú

1978- **First publication: 2012**

- Employment: The Orchid Conservation & Research Center of Shenzhen, Guangdong（广东省深圳市兰科植物保护研究中心）
- Research interest: Orchidaceae [S]
- Published taxa: *Coelogyne, Holcoglossum, Pendulorchis*
- Region: CHINA

Y. Xiao

Xiao, Yan; 肖艳; Xiāo Yàn

1988- **First publication: 2015**

- Employment: Shanghai Chenshan Botanical Garden; Jishou University（上海辰山植物园；吉首大学）
- Research interest: Brassicaceae [S]
- Published taxa: *Eutrema*
- Location of specimens: CSH
- Region: CHINA (Hunan)

Y. E Xiao

Xiao, Yue E; 肖月娥; Xiāo Yuè'é

1979- **First publication: 2020**

- Employment: Shanghai Botanical Garden（上海植物园）
- Research interest: Iridaceae [S]
- Published taxa: *Iris*
- Region: CHINA

A. Hsiao

Hsiao, Arthur; Hsiao, Jin Long; Xiao, Jin Long; **蕭錦隆**; Xiāo Jǐnlóng; **萧锦隆**

First publication: 1998

- Employment: Department of Botany, Taiwan University（台湾大学植物学系）
- Research interest: Araceae, Lamiaceae [S]
- Published taxa: *Schismatoglottis, Scutellaria*
- Region: CHINA (Taiwan)
- Also as: J. L. Hsiao

L. P. Siu

Siu, Lai Ping; **蕭麗萍**; Xiāo Lìpíng; **萧丽萍**

First publication: 2002

- Employment: Kadoorie Farm and Botanic Garden（嘉道理农场暨植物园）
- Research interest: Orchidaceae [S]
- Published taxa: *Anoectochilus, Trichotosia*
- Region: CHINA (Guangdong, Hainan)

C. F. Hsieh

Hsieh, Chang Fu; Xie, Chang Fu; **謝長富**; Xiè Chángfù; **谢长富**

1947- **First publication: 1974**

- Employment: Institute of Botany, Taiwan University（台湾大学植物学研究所）
- Research interest: Acanthaceae, Cupressaceae, Ericaceae, Pentaphylacaceae, Ranunculaceae, Rosaceae, Theaceae, Violaceae [S]
- Published taxa: *Aconitum, Camellia, Cheilotheca, Chimaphila, Cleyera, Eurya, Goldfussia, Juniperus, Justicia, Parachampionella, Pyrenaria, Rubus, Semnostachya, Strobilanthes, Triaenacanthus, Viola*
- Affiliation: TAI
- Location of specimens: TAI
- Region: CHINA (Taiwan)

C. K. Hsieh

Hsieh, Chen Ko; Xie, Cheng Ke; **謝成科**; Xiè Chéngkē; **謝成科**

1913-2006 **First publication: 1984**

- Employment: Department of Pharmacognosy, Sichuan Medical College; College of Pharmacy, West China University of Medical Sciences（四川医学院生药学教研室；华西医科大学药学院）
- Research interest: Araliaceae, Aristolochiaceae, Ranunculaceae, Zingiberaceae [S]
- Published taxa: *Aristolochia, Acanthopanax, Coptis, Curcuma*
- Location of specimens: WCU
- Region: CHINA (Chongqing, Sichuan)

C. P. Xie

Xie, Chun Ping; **谢春平**; Xiè Chūnpíng

1980- **First publication: 2007**

- Employment: College of Forest Resources and Environment, Nanjing Forestry University（南京林业大学森林资源与环境学院）
- Research interest: Rosaceae [S]
- Published taxa: *Cerasus*
- Affiliation: NFP
- Region: CHINA (Fujian)

D. Xie

Xie, Dan; **谢丹**; Xiè Dān

1995- **First publication: 2017**

- Employment: Institute of Botany, Chinese Academy of Sciences（中国科学院植物研究所）
- Research interest: Campanulaceae, Phytolaccaceae [S]
- Published taxa: *Adenophora, Phytolacca*
- Region: CHINA

D. F. Xie

Xie, Deng Feng; **谢登峰**; Xiè Dēngfēng

First publication: 2020

- Employment: College of Life Sciences, Sichuan University（四川大学生命科学学院）
- Research interest: Amaryllidaceae [S]
- Published taxa: *Allium*
- Region: CHINA (Sichuan)

T. Y. Hsieh

Hsieh, Tung Yu; **謝東佑**; Xiè Dōngyòu; **谢东佑**

1974- **First publication: 2007**

- Employment: Department of Horticulture, Chung Hsing University（中兴大学园艺学系）
- Research interest: Gentianaceae, Lycopodiaceae [S]
- Published taxa: *Gentiana, Phlegmariurus*
- Region: CHINA (Taiwan)

D. M. Xie

Xie, Dong Mei; **谢冬梅**; Xiè Dōngméi

1975- **First publication: 2014**

- Employment: Anhui University of Chinese Medicine（安徽中医药大学）
- Research interest: Crassulaceae [S]
- Published taxa: *Sedum*
- Region: CHINA (Anhui)

G. C. Xie

Xie, Gao Chang; **谢高昌**; Xiè Gāochāng

1956- **First publication: 2014**

- Employment: The Orchid Conservation & Research Center of Shenzhen, Guangdong（广东省深圳市兰科植物保护研究中心）
- Research interest: Orchidaceae [S]
- Published taxa: *Calanthe*

• Region: CHINA (Yunnan)

H. Xie

Xie, Hang; 谢航 ; Xiè Háng

1962- **First publication: 1994**

• Employment: Department of Biology, Northeast Normal University (东北师范大学生物系)

• Research interest: Boraginaceae, Fabaceae, Hydrangeaceae, Rosaceae, Typhaceae; Woody Plants [S]

• Published taxa: *Caragana, Cynoglossum, Philadelphus, Rosa, Typha*

• Affiliation: NENU

• Location of specimens: NENU

• Region: CHINA

Jin Xie

Xie, Jin; 谢晋 ; Xiè Jìn

First publication: 2019

• Employment: School of Pharmacy, Anhui Medical University (安徽医科大学药学院)

• Research interest: Campanulaceae, Ranunculaceae [S]

• Published taxa: *Codonopsis, Ranunculus*

• Region: CHINA (Anhui)

• IPNI as: J. Xie

K. M. Xie

Xie, Kai Ming; 谢开明 ; Xiè Kāimíng; 謝開明

1912-2003 **First publication: 1983**

• Employment: Liangshan Institute of Forest Science, Sichuan (四川省凉山州林科所)

• Research interest: Araceae [S]

• Published taxa: *Spirodela*

• Region: CHINA (Sichuan)

L. Xie

Xie, Lei; 谢磊 ; Xiè Lěi

1977- **First publication: 2005**

• Employment: Institute of Botany, Chinese Academy of Sciences; Beijing Forestry University (中国科学院植物研究所 ; 北京林业大学)

• Research interest: Hamamelidaceae, Ranunculaceae [S]

• Published taxa: *Clematis, Thalictrum*

• Affiliation: BJFC

• Location of specimens: BJFC

• Region: CHINA

L. S. Xie

Xie, Li Shan; 谢立山 ; Xiè Lìshān

1951- **First publication: 1980**

• Employment: Kunming Institute of Botany, Chinese Academy of Sciences (中国科学院昆明植物研究所)

• Research interest: Araceae, Theaceae [S]

• Published taxa: *Arisaema, Camellia*

• Location of specimens: KUN

• Region: CHINA (Guizhou, Yunnan)

Q. Z. Xie

Xie, Quan Zhong; 谢权中 ; Xiè Quánzhōng; 謝權中

1933-2008 **First publication: 1981**

• Employment: Department of Biology, Nanjing University (南京大学生物系)

• Research interest: Cucurbitaceae, Poaceae [S]

• Published taxa: *Acidosasa, Trirostellum*

• Region: CHINA

S. M. Xie

Xie, Si Min; 谢思敏 ; Xiè Sīmǐn; 謝思敏

1937- **First publication: 1997**

• Employment: Shanxi Agricultural University (山西农业大学)

• Research interest: Rosaceae [S]

• Published taxa: *Cerasus*

• Region: CHINA (Shanxi)

S. I Hsieh

Hsieh, Szu I; Hsieh, Si-I; **謝思怡 ; Xiè Sīyí; 谢思怡**

First publication: 2018

• Employment: Department of Forestry, The Affiliated Taichung Senior Agricultural Vocational High School of Chung Hsing University (中兴大学附属台中高级农业职业学校森林科)

• Research interest: Orchidaceae [S]

• Published taxa: *Gastrochilus*

• Region: CHINA (Taiwan)

W. C. Shieh

Shieh, Wang Chueng; Xie, Wan Quan; **謝萬權 ; Xiè Wànquán; 谢万权**

1929- **First publication: 1966**

• Employment: Department of Botany, Chung Hsing University (中兴大学植物学系)

• Research interest: Cystopteridaceae, Dennstaedtiaceae, Dryopteridaceae, Lindsaeaceae, Marattiaceae, Pteridaceae, Thelypteridaceae; Pteridophytes [PS]

• Published taxa: *Acrorumohra, Acystopteris, Adiantum, Archangiopteris, Cheilanthes, Christella, Cyclosorus, Dennstaedtia, Dryopteris, Gymnocarpium, Lindsaea, Microlepia, Monachosorum, Paesia, Pronephrium, Pteridium, Tapeinidium, Thelypteris*

• Affiliation: TCB

• Location of specimens: TCB

• Region: CHINA (Taiwan)

• Also as: Shieh; • IPNI as: W. H. Shieh

W. Y. Xie

Xie, Wen Yuan; 谢文远 ; Xiè Wényuǎn
1985- **First publication: 2013**
- Employment: School of Forestry and Biotechnology, Zhejiang A&F University; Forest Resources Monitoring Center of Zhejiang Province（浙江农林大学林业与生物技术学院；浙江省森林资源监测中心）
- Research interest: Apiaceae, Brassicaceae, Cucurbitaceae, Lamiaceae, Potamogetonaceae, Rosaceae [S]
- Published taxa: *Cerasus, Hilliella, Ostericum, Potamogeton, Salvia, Sanicula, Trichosanthes*
- Region: CHINA (Zhejiang)

Y. F. Xie

Xie, Yi Fei; 谢宜飞 ; Xiè Yífēi
First publication: 2018
- Employment: School of Nature Conservation, Beijing Forestry University（北京林业大学自然保护区学院）
- Research interest: Elaeocarpaceae [S]
- Published taxa: *Sloanea*
- Region: CHINA (Yunnan)

Y. T. Hsieh

Hsieh, Yin Tang; Xie, Yin Tang; **谢寅堂 ; Xiè Yíntáng; 謝寅堂**
1925-2012 **First publication: 1983**
- Employment: College of Life Sciences, Northwest University（西北大学生命科学学院）
- Research interest: Athyriaceae, Dryopteridaceae, Polypodiaceae, Pteridaceae, Woodsiaceae; Pteridophytes [P]
- Published taxa: *Acrorumohra, Arachniodes, Athyrium, Coniogramme, Cyrtogonellum, Dryoathyrium, Dryopteris, Phanerophlebiopsis, Polypodiodes, Sorolepidium, Woodsia*
- Affiliation: WNU
- Location of specimens: WNU
- Region: CHINA (Shaanxi)
- Also as: Y. T. Xie

Z. G. Xie

Xie, Zheng Guo; 谢镇国 ; Xiè Zhènguó
1965- **First publication: 2015**
- Employment: Leigongshan National Nature Reserve Administration Bureau, Guizhou（贵州雷公山国家级自然保护区管理局）
- Research interest: Ericaceae [S]
- Published taxa: *Rhododendron*
- Region: CHINA (Guizhou)

Z. M. Xie

Xie, Zhi Ming; 谢志明 ; Xiè Zhìmíng
1958- **First publication: 2002**
- Employment: Natural History Museum of Guangxi（广西自然博物馆）
- Research interest: Rubiaceae; Plants of Guangxi [S]
- Published taxa: *Ophiorrhiza, Spiradiclis*
- Affiliation: GXNM
- Location of specimens: GXNM
- Region: CHINA (Guangxi)

Zhong W. Xie

Xie, Zhong Wen; 谢中稳 ; Xiè Zhōngwěn
1962- **First publication: 1998**
- Employment: Institute of Botany, Chinese Academy of Sciences（中国科学院植物研究所）
- Research interest: Paeoniaceae [S]
- Published taxa: *Paeonia*
- Region: CHINA (Henan)

Z. W. Xie

Xie, Zong Wan; Hsieh, Tsung Wan; **谢宗万 ; Xiè Zōngwàn; 謝宗萬**
1924-2004 **First publication: 1987**
- Employment: Institute of Chinese Materia Medica, China Academy of Chinese Medical Sciences（中国中医研究院中药研究所）
- Research interest: Aizoaceae, Amaranthaceae, Apocynaceae, Magnoliaceae, Oleaceae, Rubiaceae [S]
- Published taxa: *Fraxinus, Gardenia, Magnolia*
- Affiliation: CMMI
- Location of specimens: CMMI
- Region: CHINA

T. H. Hsieh

Hsieh, Tsung Hsin; Xie, Zong Xin; **謝宗欣 ; Xiè Zōngxīn; 谢宗欣**
1963- **First publication: 1994**
- Employment: Department of Natural Science Education, Tainan Teachers' College（台南师范学院自然科学教育系）
- Research interest: Aristolochiaceae, Burmanniaceae, Lamiaceae, Mazaceae, Menyanthaceae, Zygophyllaceae [S]
- Published taxa: *Asarum, Clinopodium, Mazus, Nymphoides, Paraphlomis, Scutellaria, Teucrium, Thismia, Tribulus*
- Region: CHINA (Taiwan)

H. J. Xin

Xin, Hai Jing; 辛海静 ; Xīn Hǎijìng
1985- **First publication: 2010**
- Employment: South China Botanical Garden, Chinese Academy of Sciences（中国科学院华南植物园）
- Research interest: Acanthaceae [S]

• Published taxa: *Ophiorrhiziphyllon*
• Region: VETNAM

Z. M. Xin

Xin, Zhi Ming; 辛智鸣 ; Xīn Zhìmíng
1984- **First publication: 2016**
• Employment: Experimental Center of Desert Forestry, Chinese Academy of Forestry（中国林业科学研究院沙漠林业实验中心）
• Research interest: Caryophyllaceae [S]
• Published taxa: *Silene*
• Region: CHINA (Nei Mongol)

Z. B. Xin

Xin, Zi Bing; 辛子兵 ; Xīn Zǐbīng
1990- **First publication: 2018**
• Employment: Guangxi Institute of Botany, Chinese Academy of Sciences（广西壮族自治区中国科学院广西植物研究所）
• Research interest: Gesneriaceae [S]
• Published taxa: *Primulina*
• Region: CHINA (Guangxi)

F. W. Xing

Xing, Fu Wu; 邢福武 ; Xíng Fúwǔ
1956- **First publication: 1991**
• Employment: South China Institute of Botany, Chinese Academy of Sciences; South China Botanical Garden, Chinese Academy of Sciences（中国科学院华南植物研究所；中国科学院华南植物园）
• Research interest: Arecaceae, Balanophoraceae, Balsaminaceae, Begoniaceae, Berberidaceae, Boraginaceae, Celastraceae, Davalliaceae, Dioscoreaceae, Dryopteridaceae, Euphorbiaceae, Fagaceae, Gesneriaceae, Hypodematiaceae, Loganiaceae, Magnoliaceae, Meliaceae, Orchidaceae, Polygalaceae, Primulaceae, Pteridaceae, Putranjivaceae, Rubiaceae, Rutaceae, Saxifragaceae, Symplocaceae, Violaceae, Zingiberaceae; Plants of S. China [PS]
• Published taxa: *Acalypha, Adiantum, Anoectochilus, Ardisia, Balanophora, Begonia, Blachia, Bolbitis, Calanthe, Cephalanthera, Chamaegastrodia, Clausena, Danxiaorchis, Davallia, Dioscorea, Drypetes, Ehretia, Elaphoglossum, Guihaia, Hedyotis, Hetaeria, Hypodematium, Impatiens, Liparis, Mahonia, Malaxis, Manglietia, Maytenus, Michelia, Microtropis, Mitreola, Munronia, Paraboea, Paraphaius, Polygala, Pteris, Quercus, Saxifraga, Symplocos, Viola, Zingiber*
• Affiliation: IBSC
• Location of specimens: ATCH, IBSC
• Region: CHINA

K. H. Shing

Shing, Kung Hsia; Hsing, Kung Hsia; Xing, Gong Xia; Shing, Gung Hsia; 邢公侠 ; Xíng Gōngxiá; 邢公俠
1929- **First publication: 1979**
• Employment: Institute of Botany, Chinese Academy of Sciences（中国科学院植物研究所）
• Research interest: Athyriaceae, Dryopteridaceae, Hypodematiaceae, Onocleaceae, Polypodiaceae, Pteridaceae, Selaginellaceae, Thelypteridaceae; Pteridophytes [P]
• Published taxa: *Adiantum, Athyrium, Cheilosoria, Coniogramme, Ctenitis, Cyclogramma, Cyclosorus, Cyrtomium, Dryopteris, Hypodematium, Lepidomicrosorium, Lepisorus, Leptolepidium, Lunathyrium, Macrothelypteris, Matteuccia, Metathelypteris, Neolepisorus, Onychium, Paragymnopteris, Parathelypteris, Polypodium, Polystichum, Pseudocyclosorus, Pyrrosia, Selaginella, Stegnogramma*
• Affiliation: PE
• Location of specimens: PE
• Region: CHINA
• Also as: K. H. Hsing

J. Q. Xing

Xing, Ji Qing; 邢吉庆 ; Xíng Jíqìng; 邢吉慶
1936- **First publication: 1987**
• Employment: Xi' an Botanical Garden, Shaanxi（陕西省西安植物园）
• Research interest: Asparagaceae; Plants of Shaanxi [S]
• Published taxa: *Diuranthera*
• Affiliation: XBGH
• Location of specimens: XBGH, WUK
• Region: CHINA (Shaanxi)

J. W. Xing

Xing, Jun Wu; 邢军武 ; Xíng Jūnwǔ
1956- **First publication: 2018**
• Employment: Institute of Oceanology, Chinese Academy of Sciences（中国科学院海洋研究所）
• Research interest: Amaranthaceae [S]
• Published taxa: *Suaeda*
• Region: CHINA (Shandong)

Q. Xing

Xing, Quan; 邢全 ; Xíng Quán
1971- **First publication: 2006**
• Employment: Institute of Botany, Chinese Academy of Sciences（中国科学院植物研究所）
• Research interest: Gesneriaceae [S]
• Published taxa: *Chirita*
• Region: CHINA (Guangxi)

B. H. Xiong

Xiong, Bing Hong; 熊秉红 ; Xióng Bǐnghóng

First publication: 2019

- Employment: South China Botanical Garden, Chinese Academy of Sciences（中国科学院华南植物园）
- Research interest: Magnoliaceae [S]
- Published taxa: *Yulania*
- Region: CHINA (Guizhou)

C. H. Hsing

Hsing, Chi Hua; 熊济华 ; Xióng Jìhuá; 熊濟華

1923- **First publication: 1986**

- Employment: Southwest Agricultural University（西南农业大学）
- Research interest: Amaranthaceae, Caprifoliaceae, Rosaceae, Theaceae [S]
- Published taxa: *Camellia, Morina*
- Affiliation: HWA
- Location of specimens: HWA, SCFI, SZ
- Region: CHINA (Chongqing, Sichuan)

W. Y. Hsung

Hsung, Wen Yu; Hsiung, Wen Yue; Xiong, Wen Yu; 熊文愈 ; Xióng Wényù

1915-2014 **First publication: 1977**

- Employment: Nanjing Technological College of Forest Products（南京林产工业学院）
- Research interest: Poaceae [S]
- Published taxa: *Arundinaria, Indosasa, Phyllostachys, Pleioblastus*
- Region: CHINA
- IPNI as: W. Y. Hsiung

X. Y. Xiong

Xiong, Xing Yao; 熊兴耀 ; Xióng Xīngyào

First publication: 1991

- Employment: Hunan Agricultural College（湖南农学院）
- Research interest: Actinidiaceae [S]
- Published taxa: *Actinidia*
- Location of specimens: IBK
- Region: CHINA (Hunan)

X. H. Xiong

Xiong, Xian-Hua; 熊先华 ; Xióng Xiānhuá

1989- **First publication: 2019**

- Employment: Chengdu Institute of Biology, Chinese Academy of Sciences（中国科学院成都生物研究所）
- Research interest: Rosaceae [S]
- Published taxa: *Rubus*
- Region: CHINA (Sichuan)

Y. X. Xiong

Xiong, Yuan Xin; 熊源新 ; Xióng Yuánxīn

1954- **First publication: 1996**

- Employment: Guizhou Agricultural College; College of Life Sciences, Guizhou University（贵州农学院；贵州大学生命科学学院）
- Research interest: Balsaminaceae, Orchidaceae; Bryophyte [BS]
- Published taxa: *Corybas, Impatiens*
- Affiliation: GACP
- Location of specimens: GACP
- Region: CHINA (Guizhou)

Z. T. Xiong

Xiong, Zhi Ting; 熊治廷 ; Xióng Zhìtíng

1955- **First publication: 1985**

- Employment: Department of Biology, Wuhan University; Institute of Botany, Chinese Academy of Sciences（武汉大学生物系；中国科学院植物研究所）
- Research interest: Asphodelaceae, Lythraceae [S]
- Published taxa: *Hemerocallis, Trapa*
- Region: CHINA

P. S. Hsu

Hsu, Ping Sheng; Xu, Bing Sheng; 徐炳声 ; Xú Bǐngshēng; 徐炳聲

1924-2016 **First publication: 1964**

- Employment: Department of Biology, Fudan University（复旦大学生物系）
- Research interest: Actinidiaceae, Adoxaceae, Amaryllidaceae, Apiaceae, Araliaceae, Asparagaceae, Asteraceae, Caprifoliaceae, Celastraceae, Crassulaceae, Ericaceae, Fabaceae, Hydrangeaceae, Juglandaceae, Lamiaceae, Oleaceae, Pentaphylacaceae, Rosaceae, Staphyleaceae; Plants of Shanghai [S]
- Published taxa: *Actinidia, Bupleurum, Celastrus, Clerodendrum, Cyclocarya, Dendranthema, Eleutherococcus, Eurya, Euscaphis, Hydrangea, Indigofera, Lespedeza, Ligustrum, Liriope, Lonicera, Lycoris, Patrinia, Photinia, Rosa, Sedum, Vaccinium, Viburnum*
- Affiliation: FUS
- Location of specimens: FUS
- Region: CHINA

Bo Xu

Xu, Bo; 徐波 ; Xú Bō

1983- **First publication: 2009**

- Employment: Yunnan Normal University; Kunming Institute of Botany, Chinese Academy of Sciences; Southwest Forestry University（云南师范大学；中国科学院昆明植物研究所；西南林业大学）
- Research interest: Lamiaceae, Papaveraceae [S]

- Published taxa: *Eriophyton, Meconopsis*
- Region: CHINA (Xizang)

Bo Xu bis

Xu, Bo; 徐波 ; Xú Bō

1983- **First publication: 2013**

- Employment: Chengdu Institute of Biology, Chinese Academy of Sciences (中国科学院成都生物研究所)
- Research interest: Fabaceae [S]
- Published taxa: *Campylotropis, Flemingia, Lespedeza*
- Affiliation: CDBI
- Location of specimens: CDBI
- Region: CHINA

C. L. Xu

Xu, Chang Lin; 徐长林 ; Xú Chánglín

1957- **First publication: 2016**

- Employment: Pratacultural College, Gansu Agricultural University (甘肃农业大学草业学院)
- Research interest: Fabaceae [S]
- Published taxa: *Melilotoides*
- Region: CHINA (Gansu)

C. D. Xu

Xu, Cheng Dong; 徐成东 ; Xú Chéngdōng

1964- **First publication: 2007**

- Employment: School of Life Sciences, Yunnan University (云南大学生命科学学院)
- Research interest: Polypodiaceae [P]
- Published taxa: *Arthromeris*
- Region: CHINA (Yunnan)

F. S. Hsu

Hsu, Fei Shuang; 徐飛霜 ; Xú Fēishuāng; 徐飞霜

First publication: 2009

- Employment: Chung Hsing University (中兴大学)
- Research interest: Pteridaceae [P]
- Published taxa: *Adiantum*
- Region: CHINA (Taiwan)

G. J. Xu

Xu, Guo Jun; 徐国钧 ; Xú Guójūn; 徐國鈞

1922-2005 **First publication: 1990**

- Employment: School of Traditional Chinese Pharmacy, China Pharmaceutical University (中国药科大学中药学院)
- Research interest: Campanulaceae, Orchidaceae, Zingiberaceae [S]
- Published taxa: *Adenophora, Alpinia, Codonopsis, Dendrobium, Hedychium*
- Location of specimens: CPU
- Region: CHINA

G. R. Xu

Xu, Guo Rui; 徐国瑞 ; Xú Guóruì

1986- **First publication: 2011**

- Employment: College of Forestry, Guizhou University (贵州大学林学院)
- Research interest: Juglandaceae [S]
- Published taxa: *Juglans*
- Region: CHINA (Guizhou)

K. S. Hsu

Hsu, Kuo Shih; Xu, Guo Shi; **徐國士 ; Xú Guóshì; 徐国士**

1942- **First publication: 1978**

- Employment: Dong Hwa University, Taiwan; Taiwan Science Education Center (台湾东华大学 ; 台湾科学教育馆)
- Research interest: Commelinaceae [S]
- Published taxa: *Amischotolype*
- Region: CHINA (Taiwan)

Han F. Xu

Xu, Han Feng; 徐含锋 ; Xú Hánfēng

1992- **First publication: 2018**

- Employment: College of Agriculture, Guangxi University (广西大学农学院)
- Research interest: Caryophyllaceae [S]
- Published taxa: *Stellaria*
- Region: CHINA (Sichuan)
- IPNI as: H. F. Xu

H. Xu

Xu, Han; 徐晗 ; Xú Hán

1981- **First publication: 2008**

- Employment: Institute of Botany, Chinese Academy of Sciences; Chinese Academy of Inspection and Quarantine (中国科学院植物研究所 ; 中国检验检疫科学研究院)
- Research interest: Gesneriaceae [S]
- Published taxa: *Chirita*
- Region: CHINA (Yunnan)

H. F. Xu

Xu, Hong Feng; 徐洪峰 ; Xú Hóngfēng

1975- **First publication: 2017**

- Employment: Jingning Center of Ecology and Forestry Development, Jingning, Zhejiang (浙江省景宁畲族自治县生态林业发展中心)
- Research interest: Rosaceae [S]
- Published taxa: *Cerasus*
- Region: CHINA (Zhejiang)

H. M. Xu

Xu, Hong Mei; 徐红梅 ; Xú Hóngméi

1968- **First publication: 2006**

- Employment: Beijing University of Agriculture (北京

农学院）
- Research interest: Asparagaceae, Poaceae [S]
- Published taxa: *Polygonatum, Setaria*
- Region: CHINA (Beijing)

L. R. Xu

Xu, Lang Rang; Xu, Lang Ran; Shu, Lon Rhan; Hsu, Lang Rang; Shue, Long Zhan; 徐朗然 ; Xú Lǎngrán
1936-2020 **First publication: 1980**
- Employment: Northwest China Institute of Botany, Chinese Academy of Sciences and Shaanxi Province; College of Life Sciences, Northwest A&F University（陕西省中国科学院西北植物研究所；西北农林科技大学生命科学学院）
- Research interest: Apiaceae, Fabaceae, Geraniaceae, Liliaceae, Oxalidaceae [S]
- Published taxa: *Astragalus, Caragana, Corethrodendron, Fritillaria, Gagea, Geranium, Hedysarum, Oxalis, Oxytropis, Thermopsis*
- Affiliation: WUK
- Location of specimens: WUK
- Region: CHINA
- Also as: L. R. Hsu; L. R. Shu; L. Z. Shue

L. G. Xu

Xu, Li Guo; 徐利国 ; Xú Lìguó; 徐利國
1936- **First publication: 1986**
- Employment: Sichuan Institute of Chinese Materia Medica（四川省中药研究所）
- Research interest: Orchidaceae [S]
- Published taxa: *Dendrobium*
- Affiliation: SM
- Region: CHINA (Chongqing)

Lian G. Xu

Xu, Lian Gen; 徐连根 ; Xú Liángēn
First publication: 1988
- Employment: Shanghai Botanical Garden（上海植物园）
- Research interest: Juglandaceae [S]
- Published taxa: *Cyclocarya*
- Region: CHINA (Anhui, Zhejiang)
- IPNI as: L. G. Xu

Lian S. Xu

Xu, Lian Sheng; 徐连升 ; Xú Liánshēng
1991- **First publication: 2016**
- Employment: Institute of Botany, Chinese Academy of Sciences（中国科学院植物研究所）
- Research interest: Asteraceae [S]
- Published taxa: *Nabalus, Parasenecio*
- Region: CHINA

L. Xu

Xu, Liang; 徐良 ; Xú Liáng
1954- **First publication: 2004**
- Employment: The Research Section of Herbal Resources, Guangzhou University of Chinese Medicine（广州中医药大学中药资源研究室）
- Research interest: Gesneriaceae [S]
- Published taxa: *Paraboea*
- Region: CHINA (Guangxi)

L. C. Xu

Xu, Ling Chuan; 徐凌川 ; Xú Língchuān
1962- **First publication: 1989**
- Employment: Department of Chinese Materia Medica, Shandong College of Traditional Chinese Medicine（山东中医学院中药系）
- Research interest: Apiaceae [S]
- Published taxa: *Libanotis*
- Location of specimens: SDCM
- Region: CHINA (Shandong)

L. S. Xu

Xu, Luo Shan; 徐珞珊 ; Xú Luòshān
1938- **First publication: 1997**
- Employment: School of Traditional Chinese Pharmacy, China Pharmaceutical University（中国药科大学中药学院）
- Research interest: Asteraceae, Zingiberaceae [S]
- Published taxa: *Alpinia, Ligularia*
- Region: CHINA

M. Z. Xu

Xu, Mei Zhen; 徐梅珍 ; Xú Méizhēn
1991- **First publication: 2020**
- Employment: South China Botanical Garden, Chinese Academy of Sciences（中国科学院华南植物园）
- Research interest: Gesneriaceae [S]
- Published taxa: *Primulina*
- Region: CHINA (Jiangxi)

M. D. Xu

Xu, Ming De; 徐铭德 ; Xú Míngdé
First publication: 1989
- Employment: Amateur（业余爱好者）
- Research interest: Apiaceae [S]
- Published taxa: *Libanotis*
- Region: CHINA (Shandong)

Q. S. Hsue

Hsue, Qing Song; 徐清松 ; Xú Qīngsōng
First publication: 1978
- Employment: Ya County Forestry Bureau, Hainan（海南省崖县林业局）
- Research interest: Dipterocarpaceae [S]

- Published taxa: *Hopea*
- Region: CHINA (Hainan)

Q. Xu

Xu, Qing; 徐晴; Xú Qíng

1987- **First publication: 2014**

- Employment: Institute of Botany, Chinese Academy of Sciences; College of Landscape Architecture, Fujian Agriculture and Forestry University（中国科学院植物研究所；福建农林大学园林学院）
- Research interest: Orchidaceae [S]
- Published taxa: *Dendrobium*
- Region: CHINA (Yunnan)

Y. Z. Hsu

Hsu, Yung Zhang; Xu, Rong Zhang; **徐荣章**; Xú Róngzhāng

1935-2006 **First publication: 1985**

- Employment: Lin'an Forestry Institute, Zhejiang（浙江省临安县林业科学研究所）
- Research interest: Juglandaceae [S]
- Published taxa: *Carya*
- Region: CHINA (Anhui)

Shi C. Hsu

Hsu, Shi Chu; Xu, Shi Ju; 徐士菊; Xú Shìjú

First publication: 1966

- Employment: Department of Biology, Fudan University（复旦大学生物系）
- Research interest: Adoxaceae; [S]
- Published taxa: *Viburnum*
- Region: CHINA
- IPNI as: S. C. Hsu

S. M. Xu

Xu, Shun Mei; 徐顺梅; Xú Shùnméi; **徐順梅**

1937- **First publication: 1989**

- Employment: Department of Biology, Anhui University（安徽大学生物系）
- Research interest: Cyperaceae [S]
- Published taxa: *Carex*
- Region: CHINA (Anhui)

S. J. Xu

Xu, Song Jun; 徐颂军; Xú Sòngjūn

1962- **First publication: 1987**

- Employment: South China Normal University（华南师范大学）
- Research interest: Malvaceae, Saxifragaceae [S]
- Published taxa: *Chrysosplenium, Reevesia, Sterculia*
- Region: CHINA

T. L. Xu

Xu, Tian Lu; 徐天禄; Xú Tiānlù

First publication: 1993

- Employment: Institute of Biology, Guizhou Academy of Sciences（贵州省科学院生物研究所）
- Research interest: Brassicaceae, Celastraceae, Nartheciaceae, Primulaceae, Rosaceae [S]
- Published taxa: *Aletris, Cardamine, Euonymus, Rapanea, Rosa, Rubus*
- Region: CHINA (Guizhou)

T. Z. Hsu

Hsu, Ting Zhi; Xu, Ting Zhi; Shu, Ting Chi; **徐廷志**; Xú Tíngzhì

1941-2001 **First publication: 1977**

- Employment: Kunming Institute of Botany, Chinese Academy of Sciences（中国科学院昆明植物研究所）
- Research interest: Aceraceae, Combretaceae, Ericaceae, Proteaceae, Sapindaceae, Staphyleaceae, Tapisciaceae, Thymelaeaceae [S]
- Published taxa: *Acer, Cassiope, Chiogenes, Combretum, Daphne, Enkianthus, Gaultheria, Heliciopsis, Leucothoë, Lyonia, Staphylea, Tapiscia, Turpinia*
- Affiliation: KUN
- Region: CHINA
- Also as: T. C. Shu

W. Y. Hsu

Hsu, Wei Ying; Hsü, Wei Ying; Xu, Wei Ying; **徐纬英**; Xú Wěiyīng; **徐緯英**

1916-2009 **First publication: 1982**

- Employment: Research Institute of Forestry, Chinese Academy of Forestry（中国林业科学研究院林业研究所）
- Research interest: Salicaceae [S]
- Published taxa: *Populus*
- Region: CHINA (Beijing, Jilin, Nei Mongol)

W. Xu

Xu, Wei; 徐炜; Xú Wěi

First publication: 1989

- Employment: Fuzhou Institute of Landscape Gardening Science（福州市园林研究所）
- Research interest: Apocynaceae [S]
- Published taxa: *Hoya*
- Region: CHINA (Fujian)

Wen B. Xu

Xu, Wen Bin; 徐文斌; Xú Wénbīn

1983- **First publication: 2015**

- Employment: Wuhan Botanical Garden, Chinese Academy of Sciences（中国科学院武汉植物园）
- Research interest: Caprifoliaceae, Lauraceae [S]
- Published taxa: *Lonicera, Neocinnamomum*
- Region: CHINA (Guangxi, Guizhou)

W. D. Xu

Xu, Wen Duo; 徐文铎 ; Xú Wénduó; 徐文鐸

1935- **First publication: 1994**

- Employment: Institute of Applied Ecology, Chinese Academy of Sciences（中国科学院沈阳应用生态研究所）
- Research interest: Pinaceae [S]
- Published taxa: *Picea*
- Region: CHINA (Nei Mongol)

W. F. Xu

Xu, Wen Fen; 徐文芬 ; Xú Wénfēn

1964- **First publication: 2003**

- Employment: Department of Chinese Materia Medica, Guiyang College of Traditional Chinese Medicine; Chinese Medicine Institute of Guizhou Institute of Traditional Chinese Medicine（贵阳中医学院药学系；贵州省中医药研究院中药研究所）
- Research interest: Asparagaceae, Berberidaceae [S]
- Published taxa: *Aspidistra, Epimedium*
- Location of specimens: GZTM
- Region: CHINA (Guizhou)

H. H. Hsue

Hsue, Hsiang Hao; Hsue, Hsiang How; Hsu, Hsiang Hao; Hsü, Hsiang Hao; Xu, Xiang Hao; 徐祥浩 ; Xú Xiánghào

1920-2017 **First publication: 1963**

- Employment: Department of Agricultural Biology, South China Agricultural University（华南农业大学农业生物系）
- Research interest: Malvaceae, Rubiaceae, Sapindaceae, Sterculiaceae [S]
- Published taxa: *Erythropsis, Firmiana, Litchi, Mussaenda, Pterospermum, Reevesia, Sterculia, Tsiangia*
- Affiliation: CANT
- Location of specimens: CANT, SCAUB, SN
- Region: CHINA

X. M. Xu

Xu, Xiang Ming; 徐向明 ; Xú Xiàngmíng

1973- **First publication: 2005**

- Employment: Lianhua Hill Garden of Shenzhen City（深圳市莲花山花木园）
- Research interest: Orchidaceae [S]
- Published taxa: *Cymbidium, Paphiopedilum*
- Region: CHINA (Yunnan)

X. D. Xu

Xu, Xiao Dan; 徐晓丹 ; Xú Xiǎodān

First publication: 2018

- Employment: Faculty of Art and Communication, Kunming University of Science and Technology（昆明理工大学艺术与传媒学院）
- Research interest: Asteraceae [S]
- Published taxa: *Oreoseris*
- Region: [WORLD]

Y. P. Hsu

Hsu, Ying Peng; Hsu, Yang Pong; Hsu, Yang Peng; Hsu, Ying Ben; Xu, Yang Peng; 徐养鹏 ; Xú Yǎngpéng; 徐養鵬

1933- **First publication: 1974**

- Employment: Northwest China Institute of Botany, Chinese Academy of Sciences and Shaanxi Province（陕西省中国科学院西北植物研究所）
- Research interest: Athyriaceae, Dryopteridaceae, Hymenophyllaceae, Pteridaceae, Selaginellaceae; Pteridophytes [PS]
- Published taxa: *Aleuritopteris, Allantodia, Athyrium, Coniogramme, Dryoathyrium, Dryopteris, Lunathyrium, Mecodium, Polystichum, Selaginella*
- Affiliation: WUK
- Location of specimens: WUK
- Region: CHINA

Y. Hsu

Hsu, Yin; Xu, Yin; 徐垠 ; Xú Yín

1931- **First publication: 1974**

- Employment: Shanghai Institute of Materia Medica, Chinese Academy of Sciences（中国科学院上海药物研究所）
- Research interest: Amaryllidaceae [S]
- Published taxa: *Lycoris*
- Region: CHINA

Y. C. Hsu

Hsu, Yung Chun; Hsü, Yun Chun; Hsü, Yung Ch'un; Hsu, Ying Chun; Xu, Yong Chun; 徐永椿 ; Xú Yǒngchūn

1910-1993 **First publication: 1975**

- Employment: Yunnan Forestry College（云南林学院）
- Research interest: Arecaceae, Betulaceae, Elaeocarpaceae, Fagaceae, Malvaceae, Salicaceae [S]
- Published taxa: *Bennettiodendron, Betula, Burretiodendron, Castanopsis, Cyclobalanopsis, Elaeocarpus, Grewia, Lithocarpus, Quercus, Sloanea, Trachycarpus*
- Affiliation: SWFC
- Location of specimens: SWFC
- Region: CHINA (Yunnan)
- Also as: Y. T. Hsu

Y. Xu

Xu, Yuan; 徐源 ; Xú Yuán

1988- **First publication: 2015**

- Employment: College of Life Sciences, South China Agricultural University（华南农业大学生命科学学院）
- Research interest: Primulaceae [S]

- Published taxa: *Primula*
- Region: CHINA

Y. J. Xu

Xu, Yuan Jie; 徐远杰 ; Xú Yuǎnjié

1980- **First publication: 2007**

- Employment: College of Landscape Architecture, Southwest Forestry University（西南林学院园林学院）
- Research interest: Celastraceae [S]
- Published taxa: *Glyptopetalum*
- Region: CHINA (Yunnan)

Y. L. Xu

Xu, Yao Liang; 徐跃良 ; Xú Yuèliáng; 徐耀良

1964- **First publication: 1992**

- Employment: Zhejiang Museum of Natural History（浙江自然博物馆）
- Research interest: Asteraceae, Balsaminaceae, Lamiaceae, Poaceae, Primulaceae, Ranunculaceae, Rosaceae; Plants of Zhejiang [S]
- Published taxa: *Anemone, Impatiens, Paraphlomis, Phyllostachys, Rosa, Stimpsonia, Youngia*
- Affiliation: ZM
- Location of specimens: ZM
- Region: CHINA

Z. L. Xu

Xu, Zeng Lai; 徐增莱 ; Xú Zēnglái

1968- **First publication: 2004**

- Employment: Institute of Botany, Jiangsu Province and Chinese Academy of Sciences（江苏省中国科学院植物研究所）
- Research interest: Cyperaceae, Dioscoreaceae, Euphorbiaceae; Medicinal Plants [S]
- Published taxa: *Bolboschoenus, Croton, Dioscorea*
- Affiliation: NAS
- Region: CHINA

Z. G. Xu

Xu, Zheng Gang; 徐正刚 ; Xú Zhènggāng

First publication: 2020

- Employment: College of Life Science and Technology, Central South University of Forestry and Technology（中南林业科技大学生命科学与技术学院）
- Research interest: Theaceae [S]
- Published taxa: *Camellia*
- Region: CHINA (Hainan)

Z. F. Hsu

Hsu, Ze Fu; 徐子富 ; Xú Zǐfù

First publication: 2003

- Employment: Institute of Botany, "Academia Sinica"（中研院植物研究所）
- Research interest: Pentaphylacaceae [S]
- Published taxa: *Eurya*
- Region: CHINA (Taiwan)

B. Q. Xu

Xu, Bing Qiang; 许炳强 ; Xǔ Bǐngqiáng

1972- **First publication: 2005**

- Employment: South China Botanical Garden, Chinese Academy of Sciences（中国科学院华南植物园）
- Research interest: Asteraceae, Oleaceae [S]
- Published taxa: *Ligustrum, Osmanthus, Saussurea*
- Region: CHINA

C. J. Hsu

Hsu, Chung Jou; 許重洲 ; Xǔ Chóngzhōu; 许重洲

First publication: 2002

- Employment: Pingtung University of Science and Technology（屏东科技大学）
- Research interest: Burmanniaceae [S]
- Published taxa: *Thismia*
- Region: CHINA (Taiwan)

Y. C. F. Su

Su, Chuan Fang, Yvonne; Su, Chuan Fang; 許傳芳 ; Xǔ Chuánfāng; 许传芳

1976- **First publication: 2001**

- Employment: School of Biological Sciences, The University of Hong Kong（香港大学生物科学学院）
- Research interest: Annonaceae [S]
- Published taxa: *Craibella, Pseuduvaria, Uvaria*
- Region: [ASIA]

C. Q. Xu

Xu, Chun Quan; Hsu, Chun Chuan; 许春泉 ; Xǔ Chūnquán; 许春全

1926- **First publication: 1977**

- Employment: Shenyang Pharmaceutical College（沈阳药学院）
- Research interest: Papaveraceae [S]
- Published taxa: *Corydalis*
- Affiliation: SYPC
- Location of specimens: SYPC
- Region: CHINA (Liaoning)
- Also as: C. C. Hsu

D. X. Xu

Xu, Dong Xian; 许东先 ; Xǔ Dōngxiān

1986- **First publication: 2014**

- Employment: College of Life Sciences, Beijing Normal University（北京师范大学生命科学学院）
- Research interest: Fabaceae [S]
- Published taxa: *Cladrastis*
- Region: CHINA (Guangxi)

Han Xu

Xu, Han; 许涵 ; Xǔ Hán

1981- **First publication: 2011**

- Employment: Research Institute of Tropical Forestry, Chinese Academy of Forestry（中国林业科学研究院热带林业研究所）
- Research interest: Aristolochiaceae, Cyperaceae, Orchidaceae, Triuridaceae [S]
- Published taxa: *Aristolochia, Carex, Sciaphila, Zeuxine*
- Region: CHINA (Hainan)

C. C. Hsu

Hsu, Chien Chang; Hsu, Chien Ch'ang; Hsu, Chien Chieng; Shü, Chien Tsang; Kyoda, Kurasono; Xu, Jian Chang; 許建昌 ; Xǔ Jiànchāng; 许建昌

1932- **First publication: 1962**

- Employment: School of Science, The University of Tokyo, Japan; Department of Botany, Taiwan University（日本东京大学理学部；台湾大学植物学系）
- Research interest: Orchidaceae, Poaceae [S]
- Published taxa: *Brachypodium, Capillipedium, Deyeuxia, Digitaria, Hymenachne, Leptaspis, Neohusnotia, Odontochilus, Panicum, Spodiopogon, Thaumastochloa, Thrixspermum*
- Location of specimens: TAI
- Region: CHINA (Taiwan)

J. C. Xu

Xu, Jian Chu; 许建初 ; Xǔ Jiànchū

1964- **First publication: 1998**

- Employment: Kunming Institute of Botany, Chinese Academy of Sciences（中国科学院昆明植物研究所）
- Research interest: Euphorbiaceae [S]
- Published taxa: *Excoecaria*
- Region: CHINA (Yunnan)

J. M. Xu

Xu, Jie Mei; 许介眉 ; Xǔ Jièméi; 許介眉

1938- **First publication: 1979**

- Employment: Department of Biology, Sichuan University（四川大学生物系）
- Research interest: Amaryllidaceae, Apiaceae, Asparagaceae, Brassicaceae, Grossulariaceae, Liliaceae, Smilacaceae [S]
- Published taxa: *Allium, Heteropolygonatum, Ligusticum, Lilium, Ophiopogon, Orychophragmus, Ribes, Smilax*
- Affiliation: SZ
- Region: CHINA (Sichuan)

K. W. Xu

Xu, Ke Wang; 许可旺 ; Xǔ Kěwàng

1991- **First publication: 2017**

- Employment: School of Life Sciences, Sun Yat-sen University（中山大学生命科学学院）
- Research interest: Aquifoliaceae, Aspleniaceae [PS]
- Published taxa: *Asplenium, Hymenasplenium, Ilex*
- Region: [ASIA]

M. Xu

Xu, Min; 许敏 ; Xǔ Mǐn

First publication: 2019

- Employment: Forest Inventory and Planning Institute of Tibet Autonomous Region（西藏自治区林业调查规划研究院）
- Research interest: Magnoliaceae [S]
- Published taxa: *Yulania*
- Region: CHINA (Yunnan)

Sheue

Sheue, Chiou Rong; 許秋容 ; Xǔ Qiūróng; 许秋容

First publication: 2003

- Employment: Department of Biological Resources, Chiayi University; Department of Life Sciences, Chung Hsing University（嘉义大学生物资源学系暨研究所；中兴大学生命科学系）
- Research interest: Rhizophoraceae [S]
- Published taxa: *Ceriops, Kandelia*
- Region: [WORLD]

Shih C. Hsu

Hsu, Shih Chung; 許世忠 ; Xǔ Shìzhōng; 许世忠

First publication: 2005

- Employment: Biodiversity Research Center, "Academia Sinica"（中研院生物多样性研究中心）
- Research interest: Orchidaceae [S]
- Published taxa: *Geesinkorchis*
- Region: [ASIA]

S. F. Xu

Xu, Shui Feng; 许水锋 ; Xǔ Shuǐfēng

1987- **First publication: 2009**

- Employment: College of Life and Environmental Sciences, Hangzhou Normal University（杭州师范大学生命与环境科学学院）
- Research interest: Cyperaceae [S]
- Published taxa: *Carex*
- Region: CHINA (Zhejiang)

T. C. Hsu

Hsu, Tian Chuan; Hsu, Tien Chuan; Hsu, Tien Chung; 許天銓 ; Xǔ Tiānquán; 许天铨

First publication: 2006

- Employment: Institute of Ecology and Evolutionary Biology, Taiwan University（台湾大学生态学与演化生物学研究所）

- Research interest: Asteraceae, Athyriaceae, Gentianaceae, Hymenophyllaceae, Melastomataceae, Orchidaceae, Polygonaceae, Polypodiaceae, Rubiaceae [PS]
- Published taxa: *Bredia, Bulbophyllum, Calymmodon, Corybas, Dendrobium, Deparia, Didymoplexis, Diplazium, Gastrochilus, Gastrodia, Gentiana, Hayata, Hymenophyllum, Ixeridium, Koenigia, Kuhlhasseltia, Lecanorchis, Liparis, Luisia, Neottia, Nervilia, Oberonia, Oreogrammitis, Peristylus, Persicaria, Pinalia, Prosaptia, Radiogrammitis, Scleromitrion, Tripterospermum*
- Region: CHINA (Taiwan)

W. B. Xu

Xu, Wei Bin; 许为斌 ; Xǔ Wéibīn

1980- **First publication: 2008**

- Employment: Guangxi Institute of Botany, Chinese Academy of Sciences（广西壮族自治区中国科学院广西植物研究所）
- Research interest: Asparagaceae, Gesneriaceae, Lauraceae, Primulaceae, Rubiaceae [S]
- Published taxa: *Aspidistra, Chirita, Chiritopsis, Hemiboea, Lagarosolen, Lysimachia, Machilus, Ophiopogon, Oreocharis, Paraboea, Petrocodon, Petrocosmea, Primulina, Rubovietnamia, Spiradiclis, Wentsaiboea*
- Affiliation: IBK
- Location of specimens: IBK
- Region: CHINA (Guangxi)

X. G. Xu

Xu, Xiao Gang; 许晓岗 ; Xǔ Xiǎogǎng

1968- **First publication: 2016**

- Employment: College of Biology and the Environment, Nanjing Forestry University（南京林业大学生物与环境学院）
- Research interest: Dryopteridaceae, Lycopodiaceae, Rosaceae; Plants of E. China [P]
- Published taxa: *Huperzia, Pleocnemia*
- Affiliation: NF
- Location of specimens: NF
- Region: [ASIA]

Xue M. Xu

Xu, Xue Min; 许雪敏 ; Xǔ Xuěmǐn

First publication: 2020

- Employment: College of Life Sciences, Beijing Normal University（北京师范大学生命科学学院）
- Research interest: Boraginaceae [S]
- Published taxa: *Trigonotis*
- Region: CHINA (Xizang)

Y. H. Xu

Xu, Yi Hua; 许奕华 ; Xǔ Yìhuá

1972- **First publication: 1997**

- Employment: Department of Biology, Beijing Normal University（北京师范大学生物系）
- Research interest: Fabaceae [S]
- Published taxa: *Astragalus*
- Region: CHINA (Yunnan)

Y. S. Hsu

Xu, Ying Su; 許熒素 ; Xǔ Yǐngsù; 许荧素

First publication: 2003

- Employment: Department of Forestry and Natural Resources, Chiayi University（嘉义大学森林暨自然资源学系暨研究所）
- Research interest: Phyllanthaceae [S]
- Published taxa: *Glochidion*
- Region: CHINA (Taiwan)

Y. K. Xu

Xu, Yuan Ke; 许元科 ; Xǔ Yuánkē

1968- **First publication: 2012**

- Employment: Forestry Bureau of Jingning She Autonomous County, Zhejiang（浙江省景宁畲族自治县林业局）
- Research interest: Rosaceae [S]
- Published taxa: *Cerasus*
- Region: CHINA (Zhejiang)

Z. F. Xu

Xu, Zai Fu; 许再富 ; Xǔ Zàifù; 許再富

1939- **First publication: 2004**

- Employment: Xishuangbanna Tropical Botanical Garden, Chinese Academy of Sciences（中国科学院西双版纳热带植物园）
- Research interest: Araceae [S]
- Published taxa: *Alocasia, Arisaema, Colocasia*
- Region: CHINA (Yunnan)

T. W. Hsu

Hsu, Tsai Wen; Xu, Zai Wen; 許再文 ; Xǔ Zàiwén; 许再文

First publication: 1999

- Employment: Endemic Species Research Institute, Council of Agriculture, "Executive Yuan"（"行政院"农业委员会特有生物研究保育中心）
- Research interest: Vitaceae [S]
- Published taxa: *Pseudocayratia*
- Region: CHINA (Taiwan)

Z. R. Xu

Xu, Zhao Ran; 许兆然 ; Xǔ Zhàorán

1957- **First publication: 1985**

- Employment: Department of Biology, Sun Yat-sen University（中山大学生物系）

- Research interest: Apocynaceae, Celastraceae, Elaeagnaceae, Gesneriaceae, Lamiaceae, Lauraceae, Primulaceae, Ranunculaceae, Rhamnaceae, Sapindaceae, Stachyuraceae, Theaceae [S]
- Published taxa: *Acer, Callicarpa, Camellia, Clematis, Elaeagnus, Euonymus, Hoya, Lysimachia, Melodinus, Neolitsea, Paraboea, Primula, Rhamnus, Rhytidophyllum, Stachyurus*
- Location of specimens: SCAUB
- Region: CHINA; THAILAND

C. T. Shii

Shii, Chou Tou; 許圳塗 ; Xǔ Zhèntú; 许圳涂

First publication: 2011

- Employment: Department of Horticulture and Landscape Architecture, Taiwan University（台湾大学园艺与景观学系）
- Research interest: Musaceae [S]
- Published taxa: *Musa*
- Region: CHINA (Taiwan)

Xuri

Xuri, Xu Ri; Ri, Xu; 旭日 ; Xùrì

1989- **First publication: 2018**

- Employment: School of Ecology and Environment, Inner Mongolia University（内蒙古大学生态与环境学院）
- Research interest: Fabaceae [S]
- Published taxa: *Astragalus*
- Region: CHINA (Nei Mongol)
- IPNI as: Xu Ri

S. J. Hsuan

Hsuan, Shwe Jye; Hsuan, Shwu Jue; Xuan, Shu Jie; 宣淑洁 ; Xuān Shūjié; 宣淑潔

1932-1972 **First publication: 1965**

- Employment: Kunming Branch Institute, Institute of Botany, Chinese Academy of Sciences; Kunming Institute of Botany, Chinese Academy of Sciences（中国科学院植物研究所昆明分所；中国科学院昆明植物研究所）
- Research interest: Lamiaceae [S]
- Published taxa: *Clinopodium, Dysophylla, Lagochilus, Microtoena, Nepeta, Orthodon, Perilla*
- Affiliation: KUN
- Region: CHINA (Yunnan)

B. Xue

Xue, Bine; Xue, Bin E; 薛彬娥 ; Xuē Bīn'é

1986- **First publication: 2011**

- Employment: South China Botanical Garden, Chinese Academy of Sciences（中国科学院华南植物园）
- Research interest: Annonaceae, Boraginaceae [S]
- Published taxa: *Alphonsea, Goniothalamus, Marsypopetalum, Meiogyne, Monoon, Polyalthia, Trigonotis, Wangia, Wuodendron*
- Affiliation: IBSC
- Region: CHINA

D. W. Xue

Xue, Da Wei; 薛大伟 ; Xuē Dàwěi

1978- **First publication: 2004**

- Employment: Kunming Institute of Botany, Chinese Academy of Sciences（中国科学院昆明植物研究所）
- Research interest: Primulaceae [S]
- Published taxa: *Primula*
- Region: CHINA (Yunnan)

D. Xue

Xue, Dan; 薛丹 ; Xuē Dān

1984- **First publication: 2007**

- Employment: West China School of Pharmacy, Sichuan Univerisity（四川大学华西药学院）
- Research interest: Melanthiaceae [S]
- Published taxa: *Paris*
- Region: CHINA (Sichuan)

Hsueh

Hsueh, Chi Ju; Xue, Ji Ru; Hsueh, Ji Ru; Shien, Ji Ru; 薛纪如 ; Xuē Jìrú; 薛紀如

1921-1999 **First publication: 1979**

- Employment: Yunnan Forestry College; Southwest Forestry College（云南林学院；西南林学院）
- Research interest: Pinaceae, Poaceae [S]
- Published taxa: *Ampelocalamus, Bambusa, Chimonobambusa, Chimonocalamus, Dendrocalamus, Fargesia, Gaoligongshania, Indocalamus, Indosasa, Keteleeria, Melocalamus, Pinus, Qiongzhuea, Schizostachyum, Sinocalamus, Yushania*
- Affiliation: SWFC
- Location of specimens: SWFC
- Region: CHINA

Hsueh f.

Hsueh, Jia Rong; Hsueh, f.; Xue, Jia Rong; 薛嘉榕 ; Xuē Jiāróng

1951-2001 **First publication: 1991**

- Employment: Southwest Forestry University（西南林业大学）
- Research interest: Poaceae [S]
- Published taxa: *Dinochloa, Neosinocalamus*
- Region: CHINA (Yunnan)
- IPNI as: Jia R. Xue

X. J. Xue

Xue, Xiang Ji; 薛祥骥 ; Xuē Xiángjì; 薛祥驥

1934- **First publication: 1983**

- Employment: Department of Pharmacy, Zhejiang Medical University（浙江医科大学药学系）
- Research interest: Araceae, Araliaceae, Asparagaceae, Cucurbitaceae, Iridaceae, Valerianaceae [S]
- Published taxa: *Acanthopanax, Asparagus, Gynostemma, Hemsleya, Iris, Polygonatum*
- Affiliation: ZMU
- Location of specimens: ZMU
- Region: CHINA (Zhejiang)

Y. L. Hsueh

Hsueh, Yein Ling; 薛燕璘 ; Xuē Yànlín

First publication: 2011

- Employment: Department of Forestry and Natural Resources, Chiayi University（嘉义大学森林暨自然资源学系暨研究所）
- Research interest: Isoetaceae [P]
- Published taxa: *Isoetes*
- Region: CHINA (Taiwan)

Z. W. Xue

Xue, Zhao Wen; 薛兆文 ; Xuē Zhàowén

1943- **First publication: 1986**

- Employment: Anhui Institute of Biology（安徽省生物研究所）
- Research interest: Lamiaceae, Ranunculaceae [S]
- Published taxa: *Clematis, Scutellaria*
- Region: CHINA (Anhui)

J. D. Ya

Ya, Ji Dong; 亚吉东 ; Yà Jídōng

1987- **First publication: 2019**

- Employment: Kunming Institute of Botany, Chinese Academy of Sciences（中国科学院昆明植物研究所）
- Research interest: Apocynaceae, Gentianaceae, Orchidaceae [S]
- Published taxa: *Bulbophyllum, Cylindrolobus, Gentianella, Marsdenia*
- Region: CHINA

J. Z. Yan

Yan, Ji Zhe; 闫吉喆 ; Yán Jízhé; 閆吉喆

1940- **First publication: 1981**

- Employment: Anshan Institute of Forestry Science, Liaoning（辽宁省鞍山市林业科学研究所）
- Research interest: Salicaceae [S]
- Published taxa: *Salix*
- Region: CHINA (Liaoning)

L. C. Yan

Yan, Li Chun; 闫丽春 ; Yán Lìchūn

1973- **First publication: 2018**

- Employment: Xishuangbanna Tropical Botanical Garden, Chinese Academy of Sciences（中国科学院西双版纳热带植物园）
- Research interest: Celastraceae, Passifloraceae; Plants of Yunnan [S]
- Published taxa: *Passiflora, Salacia*
- Affiliation: HITBC
- Location of specimens: HITBC
- Region: CHINA (Yunnan)

S. X. Yan

Yan, Shuang Xi; 闫双喜 ; Yán Shuāngxǐ

1963- **First publication: 2005**

- Employment: Henan Agricultural University（河南农业大学）
- Research interest: Ranunculaceae [S]
- Published taxa: *Clematis*
- Region: CHINA (Henan)

T. K. Yen

Yen, Tsu Kiang; Yang, Chu Jiang; 严楚江 ; **Yán Chǔjiāng; 嚴楚江**

1900-1978 **First publication: 1964**

- Employment: Department of Biology, Xiamen University（厦门大学生物系）
- Research interest: Orchidaceae [S]
- Published taxa: *Cymbidium*
- Region: CHINA
- IPNI as: T. C. Yen

H. J. Yan

Yan, Han Jing; 严寒静 ; Yán Hánjìng

1972- **First publication: 2011**

- Employment: School of Life Sciences, Sun Yat-sen University（中山大学生命科学学院）
- Research interest: Polygonaceae [S]
- Published taxa: *Fallopia*
- Region: CHINA (Guangxi)

K. C. Yen

Yen, Ke Chien; Yan, Ke Jian; 严克俭 ; **Yán Kèjiǎn**

1964- **First publication: 1993**

- Employment: Guangxi Institute of Traditional Medical and Pharmaceutical Sciences; Guangxi

Institute of Chinese Medicine & Pharmaceutical Science（广西中医药研究所；广西中医药研究院）
- Research interest: Asparagaceae, Berberidaceae, Lamiaceae, Rubiaceae [S]
- Published taxa: *Aspidistra, Epimedium, Mycetia, Paraphlomis*
- Affiliation: GXMI
- Location of specimens: GXMI
- Region: CHINA (Guangxi)
- Also as: K. J. Yan

L. J. Yan

Yan, Li Jiao; 严力蛟; Yán Lìjiāo

1959- **First publication: 2014**

- Employment: College of Life Sciences, Zhejiang University（浙江大学生命科学学院）
- Research interest: Gesneriaceae [S]
- Published taxa: *Primulina*
- Region: CHINA (Fujian, Guangxi)

Y. H. Yan

Yan, Yue Hong; 严岳鸿; Yán Yuèhóng

1974- **First publication: 2004**

- Employment: South China Botanical Garden, Chinese Academy of Sciences; Shanghai Chenshan Botanical Garden（中国科学院华南植物园；上海辰山植物园）
- Research interest: Athyriaceae, Begoniaceae, Dennstaedtiaceae, Dryopteridaceae, Lycopodiaceae, Magnoliaceae, Pteridaceae; Pteridophytes [PS]
- Published taxa: *Adiantum, Begonia, Diplazium, Dryopteris, Huperzia, Magnolia, Michelia, Microlepia, Pteris*
- Affiliation: CSH
- Location of specimens: CSH, HUST
- Region: CHINA

P. Yan

Yan, Ping; 阎平; Yán Píng

1962- **First publication: 1996**

- Employment: College of Life Sciences, Shihezi University（石河子大学生命科学学院）
- Research interest: Fabaceae, Ixioliriaceae; Plants of Xinjiang [S]
- Published taxa: *Astragalus, Ixiolirion, Oxytropis*
- Affiliation: SHI
- Location of specimens: SHI
- Region: CHINA (Xinjiang)

W. M. Yan

Yan, Wen Mei; 阎文玫; Yán Wénméi

1959- **First publication: 1990**

- Employment: Faculty of Chinese Pharmacy, Beijing College of Traditional Chinese Medicine（北京中医学院中药鉴定室）
- Research interest: Berberidaceae [S]
- Published taxa: *Epimedium*
- Region: CHINA (Guizhou)

H. F. Yan

Yan, Hai Fei; 颜海飞; Yán Hǎifēi

1979- **First publication: 2012**

- Employment: South China Botanical Garden, Chinese Academy of Sciences（中国科学院华南植物园）
- Research interest: Orchidaceae, Primulaceae [S]
- Published taxa: *Liparis, Lysimachia*
- Region: CHINA (Guangxi, Sichuan)

C. Yen

Yen, Chi; Yan, Ji; 颜济; Yán Jì; 顏濟

1924- **First publication: 1983**

- Employment: Triticeae Research Institute, Sichuan Agricultural University（四川农业大学小麦研究所）
- Research interest: Poaceae [S]
- Published taxa: *Anthosachne, Australopyrum, Douglasdeweya, Kengyilia, Leymus, Roegneria, Triticum*
- Location of specimens: SAUT
- Region: CHINA

K. Y. Yen

Yen, Kun Ying; 顏焜熒; Yán Kūnyíng; 颜焜荧

1924-2018 **First publication: 1963**

- Employment: Taipei Medical University（台北医学大学）
- Research interest: Apiaceae [S]
- Published taxa: *Angelica*
- Region: CHINA (Taiwan)

L. H. Yan

Yan, Li Hong; 颜立红; Yán Lìhóng

1965- **First publication: 1995**

- Employment: Hunan Forest Botanical Garden（湖南省森林植物园）
- Research interest: Ericaceae, Euphorbiaceae, Magnoliaceae [S]
- Published taxa: *Magnolia, Mallotus, Michelia, Parakmeria, Rhododendron*
- Region: CHINA (Hunan)

S. H. Yen

Yen, Shen Horn; 顏聖紘; Yán Shènghóng; 颜圣纮

First publication: 1997

- Employment: Institute of Life Sciences, Sun Yat-sen University（中山大学生命科学研究所）
- Research interest: Plantaginaceae [S]
- Published taxa: *Limnophila*
- Region: CHINA (Taiwan)

S. Z. Yan

Yan, Su Zhu; 颜素珠 ; Yán Sùzhū; 顏素珠

1934- **First publication: 1981**

- Employment: Department of Biology, Jinan University（暨南大学生物系）
- Research interest: Hamamelidaceae, Hydrocharitaceae, Pittosporaceae, Theaceae [S]
- Published taxa: *Hartia, Ottelia, Pittosporum, Stewartia, Vallisneria*
- Affiliation: SYS
- Location of specimens: SYS
- Region: CHINA

M. S. Yan

Yan, Min Shen; Yan, Min Sheng; **晏民生 ; Yàn Mínshēng**

1950- **First publication: 1989**

- Employment: Northwest Normal College（西北师范学院）
- Research interest: Paeoniaceae, Papaveraceae, Ranunculaceae [S]
- Published taxa: *Clematis, Corydalis, Paeonia*
- Region: CHINA (Gansu)

Yu H. Yan

Yan, Yu Hong; 晏雨鸿 ; Yàn Yǔhóng

1975- **First publication: 2006**

- Employment: Xishuangbanna Tropical Botanical Garden, Chinese Academy of Sciences（中国科学院西双版纳热带植物园）
- Research interest: Asparagaceae [S]
- Published taxa: *Dracaena*
- Region: CHINA (Yunnan)

H. J. Yang

Yang, Hai Jun; 羊海军 ; Yáng Hǎijūn

1980- **First publication: 2011**

- Employment: Center of Experimental Teaching for Common Basic Courses, South China Agricultural University（华南农业大学公共基础课实验教学中心）
- Research interest: Aristolochiaceae, Asparagaceae, Cyperaceae, Orchidaceae [S]
- Published taxa: *Aristolochia, Carex, Polygonatum, Zeuxine*
- Location of specimens: CANT
- Region: CHINA (Hainan, Zhejiang)

W. J. Yang

Yang, Wen Jing; 阳文静 ; Yáng Wénjìng

1983- **First publication: 2009**

- Employment: Institute of Botany, Chinese Academy of Sciences（中国科学院植物研究所）
- Research interest: Ranunculaceae [S]
- Published taxa: *Clematis*
- Region: CHINA

Yi Yang

Yang, Yi; 阳亿 ; Yáng Yì

1992- **First publication: 2017**

- Employment: Kunming Institute of Botany, Chinese Academy of Sciences（中国科学院昆明植物研究所）
- Research interest: Aquifoliaceae, Rhamnaceae [S]
- Published taxa: *Ilex, Sageretia*
- Region: CHINA
- IPNI as: Y. Yang

Bo Y. Yang

Yang, Bo Yun; 杨柏云 ; Yáng Bǎiyún

1963- **First publication: 2011**

- Employment: School of Life Science and Food Engineering, Nanchang University（南昌大学生命科学与食品工程学院）
- Research interest: Orchidaceae [S]
- Published taxa: *Calanthe*
- Affiliation: JXU
- Region: CHINA (Jiangxi)
- Also as: Bo Yun Yang; • IPNI as: B. Y. Yang

B. M. Yang

Yang, Bao Min; 杨保民 ; Yáng Bǎomín; 楊保民

1928-1996 **First publication: 1978**

- Employment: Hunan Normal College（湖南师范学院）
- Research interest: Amaranthaceae, Berberidaceae, Poaceae, Ranunculaceae [S]
- Published taxa: *Acidosasa, Bambusa, Berberis, Clematis, Epimedium, Gelidocalamus, Indocalamus, Indosasa, Pleioblastus, Pseudosasa, Yushania*
- Affiliation: HNNU
- Location of specimens: HNNU
- Region: CHINA (Hunan)

Bin Yang

Yang, Bin; 杨斌 ; Yáng Bīn

1990- **First publication: 2015**

- Employment: Southeast Asia Biodiversity Research Institute, Chinese Academy of Sciences; Xishuangbanna Tropical Botanical Garden, Chinese Academg of Sciences（中国科学院东南亚生物多样性研究中心；中国科学院西双版纳热带植物园）
- Research interest: Annonaceae, Aristolochiaceae, Balsaminaceae, Ericaceae, Gesneriaceae, Linaceae, Malpighiaceae, Orchidaceae, Primulaceae, Rubiaceae [S]
- Published taxa: *Acranthera, Agapetes, Aristolochia, Biermannia, Coelogyne, Didymocarpus, Goniothalamus, Henckelia, Hiptage, Impatiens, Primula, Reinwardtia, Trivalvaria*

- Region: [ASIA]
- IPNI as: B. Yang

T. Y. Yang

Yang, Tsai Yeong; Yang, Cai Yong; 楊彩勇 ; Yáng Cǎiyǒng; 杨彩勇

First publication: 1967

- Employment: Institute of Forestry, Taiwan University（台湾大学森林学研究所）
- Research interest: Rosaceae [S]
- Published taxa: *Rubus*
- Region: CHINA (Taiwan)

C. P. Yang

Yang, Chang Ping; 杨昌平 ; Yáng Chāngpíng; 杨昌萍

1957- **First publication: 1985**

- Employment: Hubei Traditional Chinese Medicine Company（湖北省中药材公司）
- Research interest: Liliaceae [S]
- Published taxa: *Fritillaria*
- Region: CHINA (Hubei)

Chang Y. Yang

Yang, Chang You; 杨昌友 ; Yáng Chāngyǒu; 楊昌友

1928-2016 **First publication: 1978**

- Employment: College of Forestry, Xinjiang Agricultural University（新疆农业大学林学院）
- Research interest: Amaryllidaceae, Aspleniaceae, Asteraceae, Boraginaceae, Caryophyllaceae, Crassulaceae, Cupressaceae, Cystopteridaceae, Dryopteridaceae, Ericaceae, Fabaceae, Geraniaceae, Grossulariaceae, Lamiaceae, Liliaceae, Polygonaceae, Ranunculaceae, Rosaceae, Salicaceae, Urticaceae; Pteridophytes [PS]
- Published taxa: *Allium, Asplenium, Atraphaxis, Delphinium, Dianthus, Fritillaria, Geranium, Gymnocarpium, Hedysarum, Juniperus, Lappula, Ligularia, Nepeta, Oxytropis, Padus, Perovskia, Polystichum, Populus, Pyrola, Rhodiola, Ribes, Rumex, Sabina, Salix, Sorbus, Thermopsis, Urtica*
- Affiliation: XJA
- Location of specimens: XJA
- Region: CHINA (Xinjiang)

C. X. Yang

Yang, Chen Xuan; 杨晨璇 ; Yáng Chénxuán

1989- **First publication: 2020**

- Employment: Xishuangbanna Tropical Botanical Garden, Chinese Academy of Sciences（中国科学院西双版纳热带植物园）
- Research interest: Asteraceae [S]
- Published taxa: *Ainsliaea*
- Region: CHINA (Yunnan)

C. H. Yang

Yang, Cheng Hua; 杨成华 ; Yáng Chénghuá

1959- **First publication: 1997**

- Employment: Guizhou Academy of Forestry（贵州省林业科学研究院）
- Research interest: Amaryllidaceae, Ericaceae, Theaceae; Plants of Guizhou [S]
- Published taxa: *Camellia, Lycoris, Rhododendron*
- Affiliation: GF
- Location of specimens: GF
- Region: CHINA (Guizhou)

C. J. Yang

Yang, Cheng Jin; 杨成金 ; Yáng Chéngjīn

First publication: 2017

- Employment: Yunnan Baiyao Group Co., Ltd.（云南白药集团股份有限公司）
- Research interest: Begoniaceae, Melanthiaceae [S]
- Published taxa: *Begonia, Paris*
- Region: CHINA (Yunnan)

Cheng Y. Yang

Yang, Cheng Yuan; 杨成源 ; Yáng Chéngyuán

1958- **First publication: 2007**

- Employment: Xishuangbanna Tropical Botanical Garden, Chinese Academy of Sciences（中国科学院西双版纳热带植物园）
- Research interest: Arecaceae [S]
- Published taxa: *Calamus*
- Region: CHINA (Yunnan)

C. Z. Yang

Yang, Cheng Zi; 杨成梓 ; Yáng Chéngzǐ

1972- **First publication: 2015**

- Employment: College of Pharmacy, Fujian University of Traditional Chinese Medicine（福建中医药大学药学院）
- Research interest: Gesneriaceae [S]
- Published taxa: *Oreocharis*
- Region: CHINA (Fujian)

C. D. Yang

Yang, Chuan Dong; 杨传东 ; Yáng Chuándōng

1957- **First publication: 2008**

- Employment: Fanjingshan National Nature Reserve Administration Bureau, Guizhou（贵州梵净山国家级自然保护区管理局）
- Research interest: Amaryllidaceae, Crassulaceae, Rubiaceae; Plants of Fanjingshan [S]
- Published taxa: *Allium, Ophiorrhiza, Sedum*
- Affiliation: FAN
- Location of specimens: FAN
- Region: CHINA (Guizhou)

C. S. Yang

Yang, Chun Shu; 杨春澍 ; Yáng Chūnshù; 楊春澍

1933- **First publication: 1975**

- Employment: School of Chinese Materia Medica, Beijing University of Chinese Medicine（北京中医药大学中药学院）
- Research interest: Aristolochiaceae, Illiciaceae [S]
- Published taxa: *Asarum*
- Affiliation: BCMM
- Location of specimens: BCMM
- Region: CHINA

C. Y. Yang

Yang, Chun Yu; 杨纯瑜 ; Yáng Chúnyú; 楊純瑜

1948- **First publication: 1982**

- Employment: Academy of Military Medical Sciences, The Chinese People's Liberation Army（中国人民解放军军事医学科学院）
- Research interest: Fabaceae, Lycopodiaceae [PS]
- Published taxa: *Crotalaria, Huperzia, Palhinhaea, Phlegmariurus*
- Affiliation: AMMS
- Location of specimens: AMMS
- Region: CHINA

D. P. Yang

Yang, De Po; 杨得坡 ; Yáng Dépō

1962- **First publication: 2002**

- Employment: School of Life Sciences, Sun Yat-sen University（中山大学生命科学学院）
- Research interest: Hypericaceae [S]
- Published taxa: *Hypericum*
- Region: CHINA

Feng Yang

Yang, Feng; 杨凤 ; Yáng Fèng

1994- **First publication: 2020**

- Employment: School of Life Sciences, Yunnan University（云南大学生命科学学院）
- Research interest: Caryophyllaceae [S]
- Published taxa: *Stellaria*
- Region: CHINA (Sichuan, Yunnan)

F. S. Yang

Yang, Fu Sheng; 杨福生 ; Yáng Fúshēng

1974- **First publication: 2003**

- Employment: Institute of Botany, Chinese Academy of Sciences（中国科学院植物研究所）
- Research interest: Orobanchaceae, Papaveraceae, Scrophulariaceae [S]
- Published taxa: *Pedicularis*
- Affiliation: PE
- Location of specimens: PE
- Region: CHINA (Sichuan, Xizang)

Gang Yang

Yang, Gang; 杨刚 ; Yáng Gāng

1959- **First publication: 2008**

- Employment: Institute of Grassland, Xinjiang Academy of Animal Sciences（新疆畜牧科学院草原研究所）
- Research interest: Amaranthaceae [S]
- Published taxa: *Krascheninnikovia*
- Region: CHINA (Xinjiang)

G. Yang

Yang, Guang; 杨光 ; Yáng Guāng

1964- **First publication: 1998**

- Employment: Institute of Botany, Jiangsu Province and Chinese Academy of Sciences（江苏省中国科学院植物研究所）
- Research interest: Brassicaceae [S]
- Published taxa: *Barbarea, Cardamine, Chorispora, Eurycarpus, Eutrema, Neotorularia, Orychophragmus, Pegaeophyton, Platycraspedum, Sisymbriopsis, Solms-laubachia, Synstemon, Taphrospermum, Yinshania*
- Region: CHINA

G. H. Yang

Yang, Guang Hui; Yang, Kuang Hui; **杨光辉 ; Yáng Guānghuī; 楊光輝**

1930-2013 **First publication: 1987**

- Employment: Sichuan Agricultural College（四川农学院）
- Research interest: Nartheciaceae, Poaceae [S]
- Published taxa: *Aletris*
- Affiliation: SAU
- Location of specimens: CDBI, PE, SAU, SCFI, SHM, SZ
- Region: CHINA (Sichuan)

G. S. Yang

Yang, Guang Sui; 杨光穗 ; Yáng Guāngsuì

1972- **First publication: 2012**

- Employment: Tropical Crops Genetic Resources Institute, Chinese Academy of Tropical Agricultural Sciences（中国热带农业科学院热带作物品种资源研究所）
- Research interest: Orchidaceae [S]
- Published taxa: *Cleisostoma, Cymbidium, Panisea*
- Region: CHINA (Hainan)

G. Y. Yang

Yang, Guang Yao; 杨光耀 ; Yáng Guāngyào

1962- **First publication: 1993**

- Employment: College of Forestry, Jiangxi Agricultural University（江西农业大学林学院）
- Research interest: Poaceae [S]
- Published taxa: *Acidosasa, Arundinaria,*

Gelidocalamus, Sinarundinaria
- Affiliation: JXAU
- Location of specimens: JXAU
- Region: CHINA

G. T. Yang

Yang, Guo Ting; 杨国亭 ; Yáng Guótíng

First publication: 1991

- Employment: Northeast Forestry University（东北林业大学）
- Research interest: Typhaceae [S]
- Published taxa: *Sparganium*
- Region: CHINA (Heilongjiang)

K. C. Yang

Yang, Kuoh Cheng; Yang, Guo Zhen; 楊國禎 ; Yáng Guózhēn; 杨国祯

First publication: 1996

- Employment: Department of Forest Biology, Taiwan Forestry Research Institute, Taiwan Provincial Administrative Office（台湾省政府农林厅林业试验所森林生物系）
- Research interest: Fabaceae, Melanthiaceae, Salicaceae [S]
- Published taxa: *Daiswa, Ormosia, Paris, Salix*
- Location of specimens: HAST
- Region: CHINA (Taiwan)

H. P. Yang

Yang, Han Pi; Yang, Han Bi; 杨汉碧 ; Yáng Hànbì; 楊漢碧

1930- **First publication: 1979**

- Employment: Institute of Botany, Chinese Academy of Sciences（中国科学院植物研究所）
- Research interest: Ericaceae, Mazaceae, Orobanchaceae, Phrymaceae, Plantaginaceae, Scrophulariaceae [S]
- Published taxa: *Lagotis, Mazus, Mimulus, Pedicularis, Phyllodoce, Rhododendron*
- Affiliation: PE
- Region: CHINA

H. Q. Yang

Yang, Han Qi; 杨汉奇 ; Yáng Hànqí

1974- **First publication: 2006**

- Employment: Kunming Institute of Botany, Chinese Academy of Sciences; Research Institute of Resource Insects, Chinese Academy of Forestry（中国科学院昆明植物研究所；中国林业科学研究院资源昆虫研究所）
- Research interest: Poaceae [S]
- Published taxa: *Cephalostachyum, Chimonobambusa, Dendrocalamus, Fargesia*
- Region: CHINA (Yunnan)

H. W. Yang

Yang, Hao Wei; 杨好伟 ; Yáng Hǎowěi

1954- **First publication: 1994**

- Employment: Henan Agricultural University（河南农业大学）
- Research interest: Balsaminaceae, Scrophulariaceae [S]
- Published taxa: *Impatiens, Scrophularia*
- Region: CHINA (Henan)

H. Z. Yang

Yang, Hu Zhao; 杨胡朝 ; Yáng Húzhāo

First publication: 1987

- Employment: Zhouqu County Pharmaceutical Company（舟曲县医药公司）
- Research interest: Liliaceae [S]
- Published taxa: *Fritillaria*
- Region: CHINA (Gansu)

H. B. Yang

Yang, Hu Biao; 杨虎彪 ; Yáng Hǔbiāo

1983- **First publication: 2012**

- Employment: Tropical Crops Genetic Resources Institute, Chinese Academy of Tropical Agricultural Sciences（中国热带农业科学院热带作物品种资源研究所）
- Research interest: Cyperaceae, Fabaceae, Poaceae [S]
- Published taxa: *Carex*
- Affiliation: ATCH
- Location of specimens: ATCH
- Region: CHINA (Hainan)

J. Yang

Yang, Ji; 杨继 ; Yáng Jì

1961- **First publication: 1989**

- Employment: Department of Biology, Peking University（北京大学生物系）
- Research interest: Asteraceae, Liliaceae, Violaceae [S]
- Published taxa: *Viola*
- Affiliation: PEY
- Region: CHINA (Hebei)

Jie Yang

Yang, Jie; 杨劼 ; Yáng Jié

1965- **First publication: 2006**

- Employment: School of Life Sciences, Inner Mongolia University（内蒙古大学生命科学学院）
- Research interest: Asteraceae, Cyperaceae, Liliaceae, Poaceae [S]
- Published taxa: *Agropyron, Carex, Chrysanthemum, Gagea*
- Region: CHINA (Nei Mongol)

Jin C. Yang

Yang, Jin Cai; 杨金财 ; Yáng Jīncái

1988- **First publication: 2014**

- Employment: College of Agriculture, Guangxi University; Guangxi Institute of Botany, Chinese Academy of Sciences（广西大学农学院；广西壮族自治区中国科学院广西植物研究所）
- Research interest: Asparagaceae [S]
- Published taxa: *Aspidistra*
- Region: CHINA (Guangxi)
- IPNI as: J. C. Yang

J. X. Yang

Yang, Jin Xiang; 杨金祥 ; Yáng Jīnxiáng; 楊金祥

1936- **First publication: 1983**

- Employment: Northwest China Institute of Botany, Chinese Academy of Sciences and Shaanxi Province（陕西省中国科学院西北植物研究所）
- Research interest: Gentianaceae, Liliaceae, Primulaceae, Rosaceae; Plants of Shaanxi [S]
- Published taxa: *Androsace, Cerasus, Fritillaria, Lomatogonium, Primula, Swertia*
- Affiliation: WUK
- Location of specimens: WUK
- Region: CHINA (Shaanxi)

J. Y. Yang

Yang, Jiu Yan; 杨九艳 ; Yáng Jiǔyàn

First publication: 1991

- Employment: Inner Mongolia University（内蒙古大学）
- Research interest: Chenopodiaceae [S]
- Published taxa: *Ceratoides*
- Region: CHINA (Nei Mongol)

Zun Yang

Yang, Zun; Yang, Jun; **杨俊 ; Yáng Jùn**

1961- **First publication: 2019**

- Employment: Anhui University of Chinese Medicine（安徽中医药大学）
- Research interest: Ranunculaceae [S]
- Published taxa: *Ranunculus*
- Region: CHINA (Anhui)

J. L. Yang

Yang, Jun Liang; 杨俊良 ; Yáng Jùnliáng; 楊俊良

1930- **First publication: 1983**

- Employment: Triticeae Research Institute, Sichuan Agricultural University（四川农业大学小麦研究所）
- Research interest: Poaceae [S]
- Published taxa: *Achnatherum, Agrostis, Anthosachne, Australopyrum, Calamagrostis, Douglasdeweya, Kengyilia, Leymus, Roegneria, Trikeraia, Tripogon*
- Affiliation: SAU, SAUT
- Location of specimens: SAU, SAUT
- Region: CHINA

Jun Yang bis

Yang, Jun; 杨珺 ; Yáng Jùn

1987- **First publication: 2017**

- Employment: Kunming Institute of Botany, Chinese Academy of Sciences（中国科学院昆明植物研究所）
- Research interest: Melanthiaceae, Piperaceae [S]
- Published taxa: *Paris, Piper*
- Region: CHINA (Hubei, Yunnan)

L. E Yang

Yang, Li E; 杨丽娥 ; Yáng Lì'é

1990- **First publication: 2017**

- Employment: Kunming Institute of Botany, Chinese Academy of Sciences（中国科学院昆明植物研究所）
- Research interest: Gesneriaceae, Rubiaceae [S]
- Published taxa: *Oreocharis, Pseudogalium, Rubia*
- Region: CHINA (Yunnan)

Li H. Yang

Yang, Li Hua; 杨丽华 ; Yáng Lìhuá

1985- **First publication: 2015**

- Employment: South China Botanical Garden, Chinese Academy of Sciences; Huizhou City Forestry Scientific Institute of Guangdong Province（中国科学院华南植物园；广东省惠州市林业科学研究所）
- Research interest: Begoniaceae, Gesneriaceae, Rubiaceae [S]
- Published taxa: *Begonia, Hedyotis, Oreocharis, Primulina*
- Region: CHINA
- Also as: Li Hua Yang

L. J. Yang

Yang, Lian Ju; 杨连菊 ; Yáng Liánjú

1954- **First publication: 1995**

- Employment: Institute of Chinese Materia Medica, China Academy of Chinese Medical Sciences（中国中医研究院中药研究所）
- Research interest: Caprifoliaceae [S]
- Published taxa: *Dipsacus*
- Region: CHINA (Yunnan)

Lin Yang

Yang, Lin; 杨林 ; Yáng Lín

1965- **First publication: 1998**

- Employment: Sichuan Agricultural University（四川农业大学）
- Research interest: Poaceae, Taxaceae; Woody Plants [S]
- Published taxa: *Bambusa, Bashania, Fargesia, Torreya, Yushania*

• Affiliation: SIFS
• Location of specimens: SIFS
• Region: CHINA (Guizhou, Sichuan)

Lin Yang bis

Yang, Lin; 杨琳 ; Yáng Lín
1974- **First publication: 2000**
• Employment: Department of Biology, Dali Teachers' College（大理师范高等专科学校生物系）
• Research interest: Ranunculaceae [S]
• Published taxa: *Anemone*
• Region: CHINA (Yunnan)
• IPNI as: L. Yang

L. H. Yang

Yang, Lu Hong; 杨鲁红 ; Yáng Lǔhóng
1976- **First publication: 2010**
• Employment: School of Life Sciences, Yunnan University; School of Life Science, Shanxi Normal University（云南大学生命科学学院；山西师范大学生命科学学院）
• Research interest: Polypodiaceae [P]
• Published taxa: *Metapolypodium*
• Region: CHINA

M. Z. Yang

Yang, Ming Zhu; 杨明珠 ; Yáng Míngzhū; 楊明珠
1941-2012 **First publication: 1988**
• Employment: Guizhou Institute of Biology（贵州省生物研究所）
• Research interest: Rosaceae, Theaceae [S]
• Published taxa: *Camellia, Photinia*
• Region: CHINA (Guizhou)

P. H. Yang

Yang, Ping Hou; 杨平厚 ; Yáng Pínghòu
1957- **First publication: 1988**
• Employment: Northwest Forestry College; College of Forestry, Northwest A&F University（西北林学院；西北农林科技大学林学院）
• Research interest: Malvaceae, Orchidaceae, Papaveraceae; Woody Plants [S]
• Published taxa: *Liparis, Meconopsis, Neottia, Tilia*
• Affiliation: NWFC
• Location of specimens: NWFC
• Region: CHINA (Shaanxi)

P. Yang

Yang, Ping; 杨坪 ; Yáng Píng
First publication: 2007
• Employment: Xichang University（西昌学院）
• Research interest: Polygonaceae [S]
• Published taxa: *Fagopyrum*
• Region: CHINA (Sichuan)

C. C. Yang

Yang, Chien Chow; Yang, Ching Chow; Yang, Qin Zhou; 杨钦周 ; Yáng Qīnzhōu; 楊欽周
1933- **First publication: 1978**
• Employment: Sichuan Forestry Inventory and Planning Institute; Sichuan Forestry Exploration and Design Institute（四川省林业调查规划院；四川省林业勘察设计研究院）
• Research interest: Betulaceae, Fagaceae, Hydrangeaceae [S]
• Published taxa: *Betula, Carpinus, Corylus, Fagus, Hydrangea, Pileostegia, Schizophragma*
• Region: CHINA (Sichuan)

Q. E. Yang

Yang, Qin Er; 杨亲二 ; Yáng Qīn'èr
1964- **First publication: 1990**
• Employment: Institute of Botany, Chinese Academy of Sciences; South China Botanical Garden, Chinese Academy of Sciences（中国科学院植物研究所；中国科学院华南植物园）
• Research interest: Adoxaceae, Asteraceae, Caprifoliaceae, Ranunculaceae, Salicaceae, Sapindaceae, Violaceae [S]
• Published taxa: *Acer, Aconitum, Actaea, Anemone, Asteropyrum, Cremanthodium, Delphinium, Faberia, Hainanecio, Japonicalia, Ligularia, Lonicera, Parasenecio, Ranunculus, Senecio, Sinosenecio, Synotis, Taimingasa, Thalictrum, Viburnum, Viola, Xylosma*
• Affiliation: IBSC, PE
• Region: CHINA

Q. H. Yang

Yang, Qing Hua; 杨庆华 ; Yáng Qìnghuá
1980- **First publication: 2007**
• Employment: Shanghai Botanical Garden; Shanghai Chenshan Botanical Garden（上海植物园；上海辰山植物园）
• Research interest: Apiaceae, Orchidaceae; Cultivated Plants [S]
• Published taxa: *Chusua, Peucedanum*
• Affiliation: CSH
• Location of specimens: CSH
• Region: CHINA (Shaanxi, Zhejiang)

Q. S. Yang

Yang, Qiu Sheng; 杨秋生 ; Yáng Qiūshēng
1958- **First publication: 1989**
• Employment: Henan Agricultural University（河南农业大学）
• Research interest: Ranunculaceae [S]
• Published taxa: *Delphinium*
• Region: CHINA (Henan)

R. J. Yang

Yang, Ren Jun; 杨人俊 ; Yáng Rénjùn; 楊人俊
1928- **First publication: 1984**
- Employment: Shenyang Agricultural College（沈阳农学院）
- Research interest: Poaceae [S]
- Published taxa: *Microstegium*
- Affiliation: SYAU
- Location of specimens: SYAU
- Region: CHINA (Yunnan)

Shao Y. Yang

Yang, Shao Yong; 杨少永 ; Yáng Shàoyǒng
1964- **First publication: 2008**
- Employment: College of Landscape Architecture, Southwest Forestry University（西南林学院园林学院）
- Research interest: Gentianaceae, Primulaceae [S]
- Published taxa: *Gentiana, Paralysimachia*
- Region: CHINA (Yunnan)
- IPNI as: S. Y. Yang

Shao Z. Yang

Yang, Shao Zong; 杨少宗 ; Yáng Shàozōng
1974- **First publication: 2020**
- Employment: Zhejiang Academy of Forestry（浙江省林业科学研究院）
- Research interest: Boraginaceae [S]
- Published taxa: *Omphalotrigonotis*
- Region: CHINA (Zhejiang)

S. C. Yang

Yang, Shao Cheng; 杨绍诚 ; Yáng Shàochéng; 楊紹誠
1935-2017 **First publication: 1988**
- Employment: Wenshan Forestry Bureau, Yunnan（云南省文山州林业局）
- Research interest: Magnoliaceae [S]
- Published taxa: *Manglietia, Michelia*
- Location of specimens: YCP
- Region: CHINA (Yunnan)

S. Z. Yang

Yang, Shao Zeng; 杨绍增 ; Yáng Shàozēng; 楊紹增
1937-2008 **First publication: 1981**
- Employment: Yunnan Academy of Forestry（云南省林业科学院）
- Research interest: Dipterocarpaceae [S]
- Published taxa: *Hopea*
- Location of specimens: YAF, YCP
- Region: CHINA (Yunnan)

Sheng Z. Yang

Yang, Sheng Zehn; Yang, Sheng Ren; 楊勝任 ; Yáng Shèngrèn; 杨胜任
First publication: 1996
- Employment: Department of Forestry, Pingtung University of Science and Technology（屏东科技大学森林系）
- Research interest: Burmanniaceae, Convolvulaceae, Gentianaceae, Orobanchaceae, Pentaphylacaceae, Theaceae [S]
- Published taxa: *Argyreia, Eurya, Pyrenaria, Striga, Swertia, Thismia*
- Affiliation: PPI
- Location of specimens: PPI
- Region: CHINA (Taiwan)

Shi H. Yang

Yang, Shi Hai; 杨时海 ; Yáng Shíhǎi
1981- **First publication: 2009**
- Employment: Grassland Research Institute, Qinghai Academy of Animal and Veterinary Medicine（青海省畜牧兽医科学院草原研究所）
- Research interest: Ranunculaceae [S]
- Published taxa: *Adonis*
- Region: CHINA (Qinghai)

S. X. Yang

Yang, Shi Xiong; 杨世雄 ; Yáng Shìxióng
1963- **First publication: 1997**
- Employment: Kunming Institute of Botany, Chinese Academy of Sciences（中国科学院昆明植物研究所）
- Research interest: Theaceae [S]
- Published taxa: *Camellia, Polyspora, Pyrenaria*
- Affiliation: KUN
- Region: CHINA (Yunnan)

Shu Z. Yang

Yang, Shu Zhen; 杨淑贞 ; Yáng Shūzhēn
1963- **First publication: 2008**
- Employment: Administration of Zhejiang Tianmushan National Natural Reserve（浙江天目山国家级自然保护区管理局）
- Research interest: Balsaminaceae [S]
- Published taxa: *Impatiens*
- Region: CHINA (Zhejiang)

S. Y. Yang

Yang, Si Yuan; 杨思源 ; Yáng Sīyuán; 楊思源
1944- **First publication: 1981**
- Employment: Landscape Office, Urban Construction Bureau of Dukou Municipal, Sichuan（四川省渡口市城建局园林处）
- Research interest: Cycadaceae [S]
- Published taxa: *Cycas*
- Region: CHINA (Sichuan, Yunnan)

S. L. Yang

Yang, Si Lin; Yang, Si Ling; 杨四林 ; Yáng Sìlín

First publication: 1996

- Employment: Fairchild Tropical Botanic Garden, U.S.A.（美国费尔柴尔德热带植物园）
- Research interest: Cycadaceae [S]
- Published taxa: *Cycas, Epicycas*
- Region: [ASIA]

T. D. Yang

Yang, Ting Dong; 杨廷栋；Yáng Tíngdòng; 楊廷棟

1939-2013 First publication: 1993

- Employment: Xi'an Botanical Garden, Shaanxi（陕西省西安植物园）
- Research interest: Magnoliaceae [S]
- Published taxa: *Magnolia*
- Region: [cult.]

W. L. Yang

Yang, Wang Li; 杨旺利；Yáng Wànglì

1975- First publication: 2018

- Employment: Forestry Science and Technology Promotion Center of Fu'an City, Fujian（福建省福安市林业科学技术推广中心）
- Research interest: Orchidaceae [S]
- Published taxa: *Dendrobium*
- Region: CHINA (Fujian)

W. Yang

Yang, Wen; 杨文；Yáng Wén

1980- First publication: 2015

- Employment: College of Forestry, Central South University of Forestry and Technology; Hunan Prospectiong Designing & Research General Institute for Agriculture Forestry & Industry（中南林业科技大学林学院；湖南省农林工业勘察设计研究总院）
- Research interest: Styracaceae [S]
- Published taxa: *Styrax*
- Region: CHINA (Hunan)

X. L. Yang

Yang, Xi Ling; Yang, Xi Lin; 杨锡麟；Yáng Xīlín; 楊錫麟

1931-2008 First publication: 1980

- Employment: Department of Biology, Inner Mongolia Normal College（内蒙古师范学院生物系）
- Research interest: Poaceae [S]
- Published taxa: *Aeluropus, Agropyron, Elymus, Leymus, Panicum, Roegneria, Stipa, Tripogon*
- Affiliation: NMTC
- Location of specimens: NMTC
- Region: CHINA

H. L. Yang

Yang, Hsi Lin; Yang, Hsi Ling; Yang, Xi Lin; Yang, Xi Ling; 杨喜林；Yáng Xǐlín; 楊喜林

1934- First publication: 1981

- Employment: Institute of Desert Research, Chinese Academy of Sciences（中国科学院兰州沙漠研究所）
- Research interest: Asteraceae, Brassicaceae, Salicaceae [S]
- Published taxa: *Alyssum, Dimorphostemon, Hexinia, Lepidium, Neotorularia, Oreoloma, Populus, Pugionium, Salix, Torularia*
- Location of specimens: LZD
- Region: CHINA

Yen C. Yang

Yang, Yen Chin; Yang, Hsien Chin; Yang, Xian Jin; 杨衔晋；Yáng Xiánjìn; 楊銜晉

1913-1984 First publication: 1939

- Employment: College of Agricultural Sciences, Fudan University; Department of Forestry, Northeast Agricultural College; Northeast Forestry Institute（复旦大学农学院；东北农学院森林系；东北林学院）
- Research interest: Fabaceae, Hamamelidaceae, Lauraceae, Rosaceae [S]
- Published taxa: *Actinodaphne, Alysicarpus, Christia, Corylopsis, Geum, Litsea, Machilus, Neolitsea, Podocarpium, Uraria*
- Affiliation: NEFI
- Region: CHINA
- IPNI as: Y. C. Yang

X. Yang

Yang, Xue; 杨雪；Yáng Xuě

1968- First publication: 1993

- Employment: Kunming Institute of Botany, Chinese Academy of Sciences（中国科学院昆明植物研究所）
- Research interest: Phrymaceae, Poaceae [S]
- Published taxa: *Cyrtandromoea, Microstegium, Pennisetum*
- Affiliation: KUN
- Region: CHINA (Yunnan)

Y. L. Yang

Yang, Ya Ling; 杨雅玲；Yáng Yǎlíng; 楊雅玲

1933- First publication: 1976

- Employment: Department of Biology, Nanjing University（南京大学生物系）
- Research interest: Cyperaceae, Poaceae [S]
- Published taxa: *Carex, Dimeria, Indocalamus, Monocladus, Pseudosasa*
- Location of specimens: N
- Region: CHINA

Y. B. Yang

Yang, Yan Bing; 杨焱冰；Yáng Yànbīng

1993- First publication: 2016

- Employment: College of Forestry, Guizhou University（贵州大学林学院）
- Research interest: Brassicaceae [S]
- Published taxa: *Cardamine*
- Region: CHINA (Guizhou)

Y. Yang

Yang, Yong; 杨永；Yáng Yǒng

1974- **First publication: 2000**

- Employment: Institute of Botany, Chinese Academy of Sciences（中国科学院植物研究所）
- Research interest: Ephedraceae, Lauraceae, Ranunculaceae; Gymnospermae [S]
- Published taxa: *Beilschmiedia, Caltha, Caryodaphnopsis, Ephedra, Phoebe*
- Affiliation: PE
- Location of specimens: PE
- Region: CHINA

Y. C. Yang

Yang, Yung Chang; Yang, Yong Chang; 杨永昌；Yáng Yǒngchāng; 楊永昌

1927- **First publication: 1980**

- Employment: Northwest Plateau Institute of Biology, Chinese Academy of Sciences（中国科学院西北高原生物研究所）
- Research interest: Asparagaceae, Cyperaceae, Plumbaginaceae, Poaceae, Primulaceae [S]
- Published taxa: *Agrostis, Androsace, Baeothryon, Blysmocarex, Bolboschoenus, Carex, Kobresia, Limonium, Polygonatum, Schoenoplectus*
- Affiliation: HNWP
- Location of specimens: HNWP
- Region: CHINA

Y. K. Yang

Yang, Yong Kang; 杨永康；Yáng Yǒngkāng

1931- **First publication: 1987**

- Employment: Nanjing Pharmaceutical College; China Pharmaceutical University（南京药学院；中国药科大学）
- Research interest: Asparagaceae, Berberidaceae, Campanulaceae, Caprifoliaceae, Cyatheaceae, Dipterocarpaceae, Fabaceae, Lamiaceae, Liliaceae, Polygonaceae, Ranunculaceae, Zingiberaceae [PS]
- Published taxa: *Adenanthera, Alsophila, Anemone, Campanula, Caryopteris, Cephalaria, Dalbergia, Dipsacus, Epimedium, Fritillaria, Hopea, Rheum, Scabiosa, Shorea, Sinolegumenea, Tupistra, Vatica, Zingiber*
- Location of specimens: YAF
- Region: CHINA

Y. P. Yang

Yang, Yong Ping; 杨永平；Yáng Yǒngpíng

1965- **First publication: 1990**

- Employment: Kunming Institute of Botany, Chinese Academy of Sciences（中国科学院昆明植物研究所）
- Research interest: Asparagaceae [S]
- Published taxa: *Ophiopogon, Polygonatum*
- Affiliation: KUN
- Location of specimens: KUN
- Region: CHINA (Yunnan)

Yu M. Yang

Yang, Yu Ming; 杨宇明；Yáng Yǔmíng

1955- **First publication: 2007**

- Employment: Southwest Forestry University（西南林业大学）
- Research interest: Poaceae [S]
- Published taxa: *Dinochloa, Fargesia, Schizostachyum*
- Affiliation: SWFC
- Location of specimens: SWFC
- Region: CHINA (Sichuan,Yunnan)
- IPNI as: Y. M. Yang

Yuen P. Yang

Yang, Yuen Po; Yang, Yuan Bo; 楊遠波；Yáng Yuǎnbō; 杨远波

1943- **First publication: 1989**

- Employment: Department of Biological Sciences, Sun Yat-sen University, Taiwan; Institute of Life Sciences, Sun Yat-sen University, Taiwan; Department of Bioresources, Da-Yeh University（台湾中山大学生物科学系；台湾中山大学生命科学研究所；大叶大学生物资源学系）
- Research interest: Berberidaceae, Buxaceae, Celastraceae, Elaeagnaceae, Ericaceae, Eriocaulaceae, Helwingiaceae, Lamiaceae, Loranthaceae, Melastomataceae, Oleaceae, Pentaphylacaceae, Plantaginaceae, Primulaceae, Rhizophoraceae, Rosaceae, Theaceae, Urticaceae [S]
- Published taxa: *Ardisia, Berberis, Boehmeria, Buxus, Callicarpa, Camellia, Ceriops, Chionanthus, Dendrocnide, Elaeagnus, Elatostema, Eriocaulon, Euonymus, Eurya, Helwingia, Limnophila, Maesa, Medinilla, Melastoma, Pilea, Rhaphiolepis, Rhododendron, Rubus, Scurrula*
- Location of specimens: TAIF
- Region: CHINA (Taiwan)

Y. Y. Yang

Yang, Yuan You; 杨远攸；Yáng Yuǎnyōu

First publication: 1978

- Employment: Hainan Institute of Forestry Science（海南林业科学研究所）
- Research interest: Dipterocarpaceae [S]

- Published taxa: *Hopea*
- Region: CHINA (Hainan)

Y. H. Yang

Yang, Yun Hua; 杨蕴华 ; Yáng Yùnhuá
First publication: 1987

- Employment: Pingwu County Institute of Chinese Materia Medica, Sichuan (四川省平武县中药研究所)
- Research interest: Liliaceae [S]
- Published taxa: *Fritillaria*
- Region: CHINA (Sichuan)

Z. H. Yang

Yang, Zen Hong; 杨增宏 ; Yáng Zēnghóng; 楊增宏
1937-2017 **First publication: 1988**

- Employment: Kunming Institute of Botany, Chinese Academy of Sciences (中国科学院昆明植物研究所)
- Research interest: Ericaceae, Sapotaceae [S]
- Published taxa: *Diploknema, Rhododendron*
- Region: CHINA (Yunnan)

Z. L. Yang

Yang, Zheng Lu; 杨祯禄 ; Yáng Zhēnlù; 楊禎祿
1941- **First publication: 1987**

- Employment: Sichuan School of Chinese Materia Medica (四川省中药学校)
- Research interest: Aristolochiaceae, Asparagaceae [S]
- Published taxa: *Aristolochia, Asarum, Tupistra*
- Affiliation: EMA
- Location of specimens: EMA
- Region: CHINA (Sichuan)

Z. Y. Yang

Yang, Zhen Yan; 杨振艳 ; Yáng Zhènyàn
1983- **First publication: 2019**

- Employment: Kunming Institute of Botany, Chinese Academy of Sciences (中国科学院昆明植物研究所)
- Research interest: Melanthiaceae [S]
- Published taxa: *Paris*
- Region: CHINA (Yunnan)

Zheng H. Yang

Yang, Zheng Hua; 杨正华 ; Yáng Zhènghuá
1974- **First publication: 2007**

- Employment: Dehong Prefecture Forestry Research Institute, Yunnan (云南省德宏州林业科学研究所)
- Research interest: Arecaceae [S]
- Published taxa: *Calamus*
- Region: CHINA (Yunnan)

Jeng J. Yang

Yang, Jeng Jung; Yang, Zheng Zhong; 楊正仲 ; Yáng Zhèngzhòng; 杨正仲
First publication: 1998

- Employment: Department of Life Science, Taiwan Normal University (台湾师范大学生命科学系)
- Research interest: Zingiberaceae [S]
- Published taxa: *Alpinia*
- Region: CHINA (Taiwan)

Z. R. Yang

Yang, Zhi Rong; 杨志荣 ; Yáng Zhìróng
1975- **First publication: 2007**

- Employment: Institute of Botany, Chinese Academy of Sciences (中国科学院植物研究所)
- Research interest: Ericaceae, Schisandraceae [S]
- Published taxa: *Rhododendron, Schisandra*
- Affiliation: PE
- Region: CHINA

T. Y. A. Yang

Yang, Tsung Yu, Aleck; Yang, Aleck T. Y.; Yang, Aleck; Yang, Tsung Yu; 楊宗愈 ; Yáng Zōngyù 杨宗愈 , 杨中宇
1961- **First publication: 1991**

- Employment: Botany Department, Museum of Natural Science; Department of Life Sciences, Chung Hsing University (自然科学博物馆植物学组 ; 中兴大学生命科学系)
- Research interest: Melastomataceae, Musaceae, Ranunculaceae, Theaceae [S]
- Published taxa: *Aconitum, Actaea, Camellia, Cimicifuga, Clematis, Musa, Phyllagathis, Sonerila*
- Affiliation: TNM, TUNG
- Region: CHINA (Taiwan)

Z. Z. Yang

Yang, Zong Zong; 杨宗宗 ; Yáng Zōngzōng
1984- **First publication: 2019**

- Employment: Yang' s Herbarium, Xinjiang (杨氏植物标本馆)
- Research interest: Ranunculaceae [S]
- Published taxa: *Aconitum, Clematis*
- Region: CHINA (Xinjiang)

C. Y. Yao

Yao, Chang Yu; 姚昌豫 ; Yáo Chāngyù
1936- **First publication: 1980**

- Employment: Hangzhou Botanical Garden (杭州植物园)
- Research interest: Poaceae [S]
- Published taxa: *Phyllostachys*
- Region: CHINA

T. S. Yao

Yao, Te Shen; Yao, De Shen; 姚德生 ; Yáo Déshēng
1957- **First publication: 1987**

- Employment: Gansu Forestry Technological College (甘肃林业职业技术学院)

- Research interest: Apocynaceae, Celastraceae, Fabaceae, Rosaceae, Salicaceae; Plants of Gansu [S]
- Published taxa: *Albizia, Euonymus, Periploca, Populus, Rubus*
- Affiliation: GSFS
- Location of specimens: GSFS
- Region: CHINA (Gansu)
- Also as: D. S. Yao

K. Yao

Yao, Kan; Yao, Gan; **姚淦**; Yáo Gàn

1937- **First publication: 1979**

- Employment: Institute of Botany, Jiangsu Province（江苏省植物研究所）
- Research interest: Adoxaceae, Apiaceae, Aquifoliaceae, Elaeagnaceae, Gentianaceae, Grossulariaceae, Hamamelidaceae, Lamiaceae, Liliaceae, Primulaceae, Rosaceae, Rubiaceae [S]
- Published taxa: *Adoxa, Ardisia, Crawfurdia, Damnacanthus, Elaeagnus, Fritillaria, Gmelina, Hamamelis, Ilex, Photinia, Pimpinella, Rapanea, Ribes*
- Affiliation: NAS
- Location of specimens: NAS, XZE
- Region: CHINA
- Also as: G. Yao

Gang Yao

Yao, Gang; **姚纲**; Yáo Gāng

1984- **First publication: 2013**

- Employment: Kunming Institute of Botany, Chinese Academy of Sciences（中国科学院昆明植物研究所）
- Research interest: Caryophyllaceae, Lamiaceae, Phyllanthaceae [S]
- Published taxa: *Dichodon, Glochidion, Odontostemma, Pogostemon, Solitaria*
- Region: CHINA

K. W. Yao

Yao, Kwan Wu; Yao, Guan Hu; **姚关琥**; Yáo Guānhǔ; **姚關琥**

1947- **First publication: 1982**

- Employment: Department of Biology, East China Normal University（华东师范大学生物系）
- Research interest: Athyriaceae, Dryopteridaceae, Thelypteridaceae; Pteridophytes [P]
- Published taxa: *Allantodia, Ctenitis, Cyclosorus, Dryopteris*
- Affiliation: HSNU
- Region: CHINA (Zhejiang)
- Also as: K. Yao

H. Yao

Yao, Hong; **姚红**; Yáo Hóng; **姚虹**

1967- **First publication: 1994**

- Employment: Department of Pharmacy, Zhejiang Medical University（浙江医科大学药学系）
- Research interest: Asparagaceae, Cucurbitaceae [S]
- Published taxa: *Asparagus, Hemsleya, Polygonatum*
- Region: CHINA (Zhejiang)

Q. W. Yao

Yao, Qing Wei; **姚庆渭**; Yáo Qìngwèi; **姚慶渭**

1921- **First publication: 1980**

- Employment: Nanjing Forestry Shcool（南京林业学校）
- Research interest: Bignoniaceae, Fabaceae [S]
- Published taxa: *Catalpa, Cladrastis, Gymnocladus, Ormosia*
- Affiliation: NFP
- Location of specimens: NFP
- Region: CHINA

X. H. Yao

Yao, Xiao Hong; **姚小洪**; Yáo Xiǎohóng

1975- **First publication: 2007**

- Employment: Wuhan Botanical Garden, Chinese Academy of Sciences（中国科学院武汉植物园）
- Research interest: Styracaceae [S]
- Published taxa: *Sinojackia*
- Region: CHINA (Hubei)

Y. Y. Yao

Yao, Yu Ying; **姚育英**; Yáo Yùyīng

1932- **First publication: 1987**

- Employment: Institute of Desert Research, Chinese Academy of Sciences（中国科学院兰州沙漠研究所）
- Research interest: Asteraceae, Rosaceae [S]
- Published taxa: *Prunus, Saussurea*
- Affiliation: LZD
- Region: CHINA

B. J. Ye

Ye, Bao Jian; **叶宝鉴**; Yè Bǎojiàn

1989- **First publication: 2019**

- Employment: Forestry College, Fujian Agriculture and Forestry University（福建农林大学林学院）
- Research interest: Gesneriaceae [S]
- Published taxa: *Primulina*
- Region: CHINA (Fujian)

C. R. Yeh

Yeh, Chuan Rong; **葉川榮**; Yè Chuānróng; **叶川荣**

First publication: 2008

- Employment: Department of Education, Kaohsiung Normal University（高雄师范大学教育系）
- Research interest: Melastomataceae, Orchidaceae [S]
- Published taxa: *Bredia, Gastrodia*
- Region: CHINA (Taiwan)

C. X. Ye

Ye, Chuang Xing; 叶创兴 ; Yè Chuàngxīng; 葉創興
1946- **First publication: 1982**
- Employment: School of Life Sciences, Sun Yat-sen University（中山大学生命科学学院）
- Research interest: Gesneriaceae, Pentaphylacaceae, Theaceae [S]
- Published taxa: *Camellia, Didymostigma, Eurya, Hartia, Polyspora, Stewartia, Tutcheria*
- Affiliation: SYS
- Location of specimens: SYS
- Region: CHINA

D. P. Ye

Ye. De Ping; 叶德平 ; Yè Dépíng
1977-2020 **First publication: 2014**
- Employment: Puer Forestry Bureau, Yunnan（云南省普洱市林业局）
- Research interest: Orchidaceae [S]
- Published taxa: *Bulbophyllum, Coelogyne, Dendrobium, Gastrochilus, Luisia, Nervilia, Oberonia, Pholidota, Thrixspermum, Thunia, Thuniopsis*
- Region: CHINA (Yunnan)

G. H. Ye

Ye, Guang Han; 叶光汉 ; Yè Guānghàn; 葉光漢
1938-2005 **First publication: 1980**
- Employment: Department of Biology, Nanjing University（南京大学生物系）
- Research interest: Poaceae [S]
- Published taxa: *Acidosasa, Fargesia, Indosasa, Oligostachyum, Phyllostachys, Pleioblastus, Pseudosasa, Yushania*
- Affiliation: N
- Location of specimens: N
- Region: CHINA

G. Z. Ye

Ye, Guang Zheng; 叶光正 ; Yè Guāngzhèng; 葉光正
1936- **First publication: 1992**
- Employment: Department of Biology, Yunnan College of Education（云南教育学院生物系）
- Research interest: Asparagaceae, Dracaenaceae [S]
- Published taxa: *Dracaena*
- Affiliation: YCE
- Location of specimens: YCE
- Region: CHINA (Yunnan)

K. L. Yip

Yip, Kwok Leung; 葉國梁 ; Yè Guóliáng; 叶国梁
1969- **First publication: 2006**
- Employment: Hong Kong Herbarium, Agriculture, Fisheries and Conservation Department（香港渔农自然护理署香港植物标本室）
- Research interest: Koeberliniaceae, Lauraceae, Myrtaceae [S]
- Published taxa: *Koeberlinia, Syndiclis, Syzygium*
- Region: CHINA (Hong Kong)

H. Ye

Ye, Hang; 叶航 ; Yè Háng
1981- **First publication: 2012**
- Employment: Guangxi Forestry Research Institute（广西壮族自治区林业科学研究院）
- Research interest: Theaceae [S]
- Published taxa: *Camellia*
- Region: CHINA (Guangxi)

H. Y. Yeh

Yeh, Hong Yih; 葉宏毅 ; Yè Hóngyì; 叶宏毅
First publication: 2000
- Employment: Department of Botany, Taiwan University（台湾大学植物学系）
- Research interest: Araceae [S]
- Published taxa: *Schismatoglottis*
- Region: CHINA (Taiwan)

H. G. Ye

Ye, Hua Gu; 叶华谷 ; Yè Huágǔ
1956- **First publication: 1994**
- Employment: South China Institute of Botany, Chinese Academy of Sciences; South China Botanical Garden, Chinese Academy of Sciences（中国科学院华南植物研究所；中国科学院华南植物园）
- Research interest: Aquifoliaceae, Asteraceae, Begoniaceae, Buxaceae, Euphorbiaceae, Fagaceae, Lauraceae, Loganiaceae, Pentaphylacaceae, Rhamnaceae, Rosaceae, Saxifragaceae, Symplocaceae; Plants of S. China [S]
- Published taxa: *Acalypha, Ainsliaea, Begonia, Buxus, Chrysosplenium, Cinnamomum, Cleyera, Croton, Frangula, Ilex, Lithocarpus, Mitreola, Prunus, Symplocos*
- Affiliation: IBSC
- Location of specimens: IBSC
- Region: CHINA (Guangdong, Hainan)

J. F. Ye

Ye, Jian Fei; 叶建飞 ; Yè Jiànfēi
1986- **First publication: 2020**
- Employment: Beijing Botanical Garden, Institute of Botany, Chinese Academy of Sciences（中国科学院植物研究所北京植物园）
- Research interest: Apiaceae [S]
- Published taxa: *Pternopetalum*
- Affiliation: PE
- Location of specimens: PE
- Region: CHINA (Sichuan)

K. Ye

Ye, Kang; 叶康；Yè Kāng

1981- **First publication: 2020**

- Employment: Shanghai Chenshan Botanical Garden（上海辰山植物园）
- Research interest: Rosaceae [S]
- Published taxa: *Rubus*
- Region: CHINA (Anhui)

L. X. Ye

Ye, Li Xin; 叶立新；Yè Lìxīn

1968- **First publication: 2017**

- Employment: Administration of Zhejiang Fengyangshan-Baishanzu National Nature Reserve, Zhejiang（浙江凤阳山 - 百山祖国家级自然保护区管理局）
- Research interest: Lamiaceae, Rosaceae [S]
- Published taxa: *Callicarpa, Cerasus*
- Region: CHINA (Zhejiang)

N. G. Ye

Ye, Neng Gan; 叶能干；Yè Nénggàn; 葉能幹

1934- **First publication: 1988**

- Employment: Guizhou Agricultural College（贵州农学院）
- Research interest: Cucurbitaceae [S]
- Published taxa: *Trichosanthes*
- Region: CHINA (Guizhou)

P. C. Yieh

Yieh, Pei Chong; Ip, Pei Chong; 叶培忠；Yè Péizhōng; 葉培忠

1899-1978 **First publication: 1942**

- Employment: Nanjing Forestry College（南京林学院）
- Research interest: Hamamelidaceae, Magnoliaceae [S]
- Published taxa: *Liriodendron, Loropetalum*
- Region: [cult.]
- Also as: Yieh

Q. L. Ye

Ye, Qin Liang; 叶钦良；Yè Qīnliáng

1971- **First publication: 2018**

- Employment: Zijin Baixi Provincial Nature Reserve Management Office, Guangdong（广东紫金白溪省级自然保护区管理处）
- Research interest: Orchidaceae [S]
- Published taxa: *Platanthera*
- Region: CHINA (Guangdong)

C. L. Yeh

Yeh, Ching Long; 葉慶龍；Yè Qìnglóng; 叶庆龙

First publication: 2006

- Employment: Department of Forestry, Pingtung University of Science and Technology（屏东科技大学森林系）
- Research interest: Melastomataceae, Musaceae, Orchidaceae, Urticaceae, Zingiberaceae [S]
- Published taxa: *Bredia, Erythrodes, Musa, Nervilia, Parietaria, Tropidia, Zingiber*
- Region: CHINA (Taiwan)

W. H. Ye

Ye, Wan Hui; 叶万辉；Yè Wànhuī

1963- **First publication: 1996**

- Employment: Heilongjiang College of Traditional Chinese Medicine（黑龙江中医学院）
- Research interest: Araliaceae, Asteraceae [S]
- Published taxa: *Aralia, Erigeron*
- Region: CHINA (Heilongjiang)

W. C. Ye

Ye, Wen Cai; 叶文才；Yè Wéncái

1962- **First publication: 1989**

- Employment: Wuhu School of Traditional Chinese Medicine（安徽省芜湖中医学校）
- Research interest: Lamiaceae, Ranunculaceae [S]
- Published taxa: *Anemone, Scutellaria*
- Region: CHINA (Anhui)

X. Y. Ye

Ye, Xi Yang; 叶喜阳；Yè Xǐyáng

1980- **First publication: 2017**

- Employment: School of Forestry and Biotechnology, Zhejiang A&F University（浙江农林大学林业与生物技术学院）
- Research interest: Asteraceae [S]
- Published taxa: *Aster*
- Location of specimens: ZJFC
- Region: CHINA (Zhejiang)

Xia Y. Ye

Ye, Xia Ying; 叶夏英；Yè Xiàyīng

1990- **First publication: 2020**

- Employment: Agronomy and Life Science Department, Zhaotong University（昭通学院农学与生命科学学院）
- Research interest: Poaceae [S]
- Published taxa: *Fargesia*
- Region: CHINA (Yunnan)

X. B. Ye

Ye, Xiang Bin; 叶向斌；Yè Xiàngbīn

1963- **First publication: 1988**

- Employment: Department of Forestry, South China Agricultural University; Zhongkai University of Agriculture and Engineering（华南农业大学林学系；

仲恺农业工程学院）
• Research interest: Gesneriaceae, Poaceae, Zingiberaceae [S]
• Published taxa: *Acidosasa, Arundinaria, Curcuma, Indocalamus, Sasa, Titanotrichum*
• Region: CHINA (Guangdong)

X. E. Ye

Ye, Xing Er; 叶幸儿 ; Yè Xìng'ér
1991- **First publication: 2016**
• Employment: South China Botanical Garden, Chinese Academy of Sciences（中国科学院华南植物园）
• Research interest: Rubiaceae, Zingiberaceae [S]
• Published taxa: *Amomum, Gardenia*
• Region: CHINA

Y. M. Ye

Ye, Yin Min; 叶荫民 ; Yè Yīnmín; 葉蔭民
1929- **First publication: 1976**
• Employment: Citrus Research Institute, Chinese Academy of Agricultural Sciences（中国农业科学院柑橘研究所）
• Research interest: Rutaceae [S]
• Published taxa: *Citrus*
• Affiliation: CIT
• Location of specimens: CIT
• Region: CHINA (Guangxi, Yunnan)
• IPNI as: Y. Ye

Y. Q. Ye

Ye, Yu Qing; 叶育青 ; Yè Yùqīng
First publication: 1987
• Employment: Shanghai Traditional Chinese Medicine Company（上海中药材公司）
• Research interest: Liliaceae [S]
• Published taxa: *Fritillaria*
• Region: CHINA (Xizang)

Y. S. Ye

Ye, Yu Shi; 叶育石 ; Yè Yùshí
1978- **First publication: 2004**
• Employment: South China Botanical Garden, Chinese Academy of Sciences（中国科学院华南植物园）
• Research interest: Asteraceae, Begoniaceae, Celastraceae, Euphorbiaceae, Malvaceae, Marantaceae, Meliaceae, Zingiberaceae; Plants of S. China [S]
• Published taxa: *Acalypha, Ainsliaea, Alpinia, Amomum, Begonia, Euonymus, Malva, Munronia, Phrynium, Zingiber*
• Affiliation: IBSC
• Location of specimens: IBSC
• Region: CHINA (Guangdong, Hainan)

Z. J. Ye

Ye, Zheng Ji; 叶增基 ; Yè Zēngjī; 葉增基
1941- **First publication: 2003**
• Employment: Shanghai Forestry Station（上海市林业总站）
• Research interest: Taxodiaceae [S]
• Published taxa: × *Taxodiomeria*
• Region: [cult.]

H. Y. Ye

Ye, Hong Yu; 曳宏玉 ; Yè Hóngyù
1957- **First publication: 1993**
• Employment: Shanxi Academy of Forestry Survey, Planning and Design（山西省林业勘测设计院）
• Research interest: Bignoniaceae, Cupressaceae, Fabaceae, Pinaceae [S]
• Published taxa: *Catalpa, Pinus, Platycladus, Sophora*
• Region: CHINA (Shanxi)

T. S. Yi

Yi, Ting Shuang; 伊廷双 ; Yī Tíngshuāng
1973- **First publication: 2001**
• Employment: Kunming Institute of Botany, Chinese Academy of Sciences（中国科学院昆明植物研究所）
• Research interest: Anacardiaceae, Araceae, Fabaceae [S]
• Published taxa: *Arisaema, Pseudarthria, Searsia*
• Affiliation: KUN
• Region: CHINA (Yunnan)

X. G. Yi

Yi, Xian Gui; 伊贤贵 ; Yī Xiánguì
1982- **First publication: 2007**
• Employment: College of Forest Resources and Environment, Nanjing Forestry University（南京林业大学森林资源与环境学院）
• Research interest: Rosaceae; Plants of E. China [S]
• Published taxa: *Cerasus*
• Affiliation: NF
• Location of specimens: NF
• Region: CHINA (Fujian)

Q. F. Yi

Yi, Qi Fei; 易绮斐 ; Yì Qǐfěi
1971- **First publication: 2009**
• Employment: South China Botanical Garden, Chinese Academy of Sciences（中国科学院华南植物园）
• Research interest: Magnoliaceae [S]
• Published taxa: *Michelia*
• Region: CHINA (Yunnan)

R. Yi

Yi, Ran; 易冉 ; Yì Rǎn
1994- **First publication: 2019**

- Employment: College of Life Sciences, Henan Agricultural University（河南农业大学生命科学学院）
- Research interest: Gesneriaceae [S]
- Published taxa: *Oreocharis*
- Region: CHINA (Fujian)

S. R. Yi

Yi, Si Rong; 易思荣 ; Yì Sīróng

1972- **First publication: 2010**

- Employment: Chongqing Institute of Medical Plant Cultivation（重庆市药物种植研究所）
- Research interest: Asparagaceae, Orchidaceae; Medicinal Plants [S]
- Published taxa: *Aspidistra, Gastrochilus*
- Affiliation: IMC
- Location of specimens: IMC
- Region: CHINA (Chongqing)

T. P. Yi

Yi, Tong Pei; 易同培 ; Yì Tóngpéi

1933- **First publication: 1980**

- Employment: Sichuan Forestry School; Dujiangyan Campus, Sichuan Agricultural University; College of Tourism, Sichuan Agricultural University（四川省林业学校；四川农业大学都江堰分校；四川农业大学旅游学院）
- Research interest: Betulaceae, Fagaceae, Magnoliaceae, Poaceae, Taxaceae, Ulmaceae [S]
- Published taxa: *Acidosasa, Ampelocalamus, Bambusa, Bashania, Carpinus, Castanopsis, Chimonobambusa, Chimonocalamus, Dendrocalamus, Drepanostachyum, Fargesia, Indocalamus, Indosasa, Lingnania, Magnolia, Melocalamus, Menstruocalamus, Michelia, Monocladus, Neomicrocalamus, Neosinocalamus, Patellocalamus, Phyllostachys, Pleioblastus, Pseudosasa, Qiongzhuea, Schizostachyum, Sinobambusa, Sinocalamus, Thamnocalamus, Torreya, Ulmus, Yushania*
- Affiliation: SIFS
- Location of specimens: SIFS
- Region: CHINA

X. Y. Yi

Yi, Xin Yu; 易心钰 ; Yì Xīnyù

1989- **First publication: 2019**

- Employment: Central South University of Forestry and Technology（中南林业科技大学）
- Research interest: Campanulaceae [S]
- Published taxa: *Adenophora*
- Region: CHINA (Hunan)

T. H. Ying

Ying, Te Hsiao; 殷德孝 ; Yīn Déxiào

1943-2001 **First publication: 1990**

- Employment: Altay Biochemical Factory, Xinjiang（新疆阿勒泰生化厂）
- Research interest: Paeoniaceae [S]
- Published taxa: *Paeonia*
- Region: CHINA (Xinjiang)

J. T. Yin

Yin, Jian Tao; 殷建涛 ; Yīn Jiàntāo

1976- **First publication: 2004**

- Employment: Xishuangbanna Tropical Botanical Garden, Chinese Academy of Sciences（中国科学院西双版纳热带植物园）
- Research interest: Araceae [S]
- Published taxa: *Alocasia, Amorphophallus, Arisaema, Colocasia, Englerarum*
- Affiliation: HITBC
- Location of specimens: HITBC
- Region: CHINA (Yunnan)

S. F. Yin

Yin, Shu Fen; 殷淑芬 ; Yīn Shūfēn

1935- **First publication: 1983**

- Employment: Anhui Institute for Drug Control（安徽省药品检验所）
- Research interest: Liliaceae [S]
- Published taxa: *Fritillaria*
- Region: CHINA (Anhui)

H. X. Yin

Yin, Hong Xiang; 尹鸿翔 ; Yǐn Hóngxiáng

1979- **First publication: 2007**

- Employment: School of Ethnic Medicine, Chengdu University of Traditional Chinese Medicine（成都中医药大学民族医药学院）
- Research interest: Melanthiaceae [S]
- Published taxa: *Paris*
- Region: CHINA (Sichuan)

J. M. Yin

Yin, Jun Mei; 尹俊梅 ; Yǐn Jùnméi

1968- **First publication: 2012**

- Employment: Tropical Crops Genetic Resources Institute, Chinese Academy of Tropical Agricultural Sciences（中国热带农业科学院热带作物品种资源研究所）
- Research interest: Orchidaceae [S]
- Published taxa: *Cymbidium, Panisea*
- Region: CHINA (Hainan)

M. Y. Yin

Yin, Ming Yun; 尹明云 ; Yǐn Míngyún

1996- **First publication: 2019**

- Employment: School of Life Sciences, Yunnan University（云南大学生命科学学院）

• Research interest: Orobanchaceae [S]
• Published taxa: *Pterygiella*
• Region: CHINA (Yunnan)

R. Yin

Yin, Rui; 尹睿; Yǐn Ruì
1965- **First publication: 1995**
• Employment: Institute of Applied Ecology, Chinese Academy of Sciences（中国科学院沈阳应用生态研究所）
• Research interest: Asteraceae, Rosaceae [S]
• Published taxa: *Tephroseris*
• Affiliation: SYAU
• Location of specimens: SYAU
• Region: CHINA (Liaoning)

W. Q. Yin

Yin, Wen Qing; 尹文清; Yǐn Wénqīng
1927- **First publication: 1977**
• Employment: Kunming Institute of Botany, Chinese Academy of Sciences（中国科学院昆明植物研究所）
• Research interest: Bignoniaceae, Euphorbiaceae, Nyssaceae, Pittosporaceae [S]
• Published taxa: *Incarvillea, Nyssa, Pittosporum*
• Affiliation: KUN
• Location of specimens: KUN
• Region: CHINA (Yunnan)
• Also as: W. C. Yin

W. Y. Yin

Yin, Wu Yuan; 尹五元; Yǐn Wǔ yuán
1957- **First publication: 1990**
• Employment: Southwest Forestry College（西南林学院）
• Research interest: Sapindaceae; Plants of Yunnan [S]
• Published taxa: *Aesculus*
• Affiliation: SWFC
• Location of specimens: SWFC
• Region: CHINA (Yunnan)

Y. Y. Yin

Yin, Ya Yi; 尹雅宜; Yǐn Yǎyí
1988- **First publication: 2016**
• Employment: The Orchid Conservation & Research Center of Shenzhen, Guangdong（广东省深圳市兰科植物保护研究中心）
• Research interest: Orchidaceae [S]
• Published taxa: *Apostasia*
• Region: CHINA (Guangdong)

Z. F. Yin

Yin, Zeng Fang; 尹增芳; Yǐn Zēngfāng
1966- **First publication: 2019**
• Employment: College of Biology and the Environment, Nanjing Forestry University（南京林业大学生物与环境学院）
• Research interest: Lythraceae [S]
• Published taxa: *Trapa*
• Region: CHINA (Jiangsu)

Z. T. Yin

Yin, Zu Tang; Yin, Tsu Tang; 尹祖棠; Yǐn Zǔtáng
1931-2012 **First publication: 1985**
• Employment: Department of Biology, Beijing Normal University（北京师范大学生物系）
• Research interest: Caprifoliaceae, Fabaceae, Rosaceae; Plants of Hebei, Plants of Beijing [S]
• Published taxa: *Astragalus, Dipsacus, Potentilla*
• Affiliation: BNU
• Location of specimens: BNU
• Region: CHINA

T. S. Ying

Ying, Tsun Shen; Ying, Jun Sheng; 应俊生; Yīng Jùnshēng; 應俊生
1934- **First publication: 1979**
• Employment: Institute of Botany, Chinese Academy of Sciences（中国科学院植物研究所）
• Research interest: Berberidaceae [S]
• Published taxa: *Berberis, Dysosma, Epimedium, Mahonia, Sinopodophyllum*
• Affiliation: PE
• Location of specimens: PE
• Region: CHINA

S. S. Ying

Ying, Shao Shun; 應紹舜; Yīng Shàoshùn; 应绍舜
1941- **First publication: 1970**
• Employment: School of Forestry and Resources Conservation, Taiwan University（台湾大学森林环境暨资源学系）
• Research interest: Acanthaceae, Adoxaceae, Amaryllidaceae, Apiaceae, Apocynaceae, Araceae, Araliaceae, Aristolochiaceae, Asparagaceae, Asphodelaceae, Asteraceae, Balanophoraceae, Begoniaceae, Betulaceae, Boraginaceae, Brassicaceae, Buxaceae, Cactaceae, Campanulaceae, Caryophyllaceae, Celastraceae, Colchicaceae, Commelinaceae, Cornaceae, Costaceae, Crassulaceae, Cucurbitaceae, Daphniphyllaceae, Diapensiaceae, Ebenaceae, Elaeagnaceae, Elaeocarpaceae, Ericaceae, Eriocaulaceae, Euphorbiaceae, Fabaceae, Fagaceae, Gentianaceae, Gesneriaceae, Grossulariaceae, Hamamelidaceae, Hydrangeaceae, Hypericaceae, Iridaceae, Lamiaceae, Lauraceae, Liliaceae, Linderniaceae, Loranthaceae, Malvaceae, Mazaceae, Melanthiaceae, Melastomataceae,

Meliaceae, Menispermaceae, Moraceae, Musaceae, Onagraceae, Orchidaceae, Orobanchaceae, Oxalidaceae, Pentaphylacaceae, Phrymaceae, Pinaceae, Plantaginaceae, Poaceae, Polygonaceae, Primulaceae, Proteaceae, Ranunculaceae, Rhamnaceae, Rosaceae, Rubiaceae, Rutaceae, Salicaceae, Sapindaceae, Saxifragaceae, Schisandraceae, Solanaceae, Symplocaceae, Theaceae, Thymelaeaceae, Triuridaceae, Urticaceae, Verbenaceae, Violaceae, Vitaceae; Plants of Taiwan [S]

- Published taxa: *Abelmoschus, Acalypha, Acampe, Acer, Actinodaphne, Adenophora, Allium, Alysicarpus, Amitostigma, Ampelopsis, Androcorys, Anemone, Angelica, Anoectochilus, Appendicula, Arabis, Aralia, Arenaria, Argostemma, Aristolochia, Arundina, Arundo, Asarum, Ascolabium, Aspidistra, Aster, Balanophora, Barbarea, Barthea, Begonia, Belamcanda, Berchemia, Bidens, Bletilla, Boehmeria, Brachycorythis, Brassica, Bredia, Bulbophyllum, Buxus, Calanthe, Callerya, Callicarpa, Camellia, Canavalia, Cardamine, Cardiandra, Carpinus, Caryopteris, Castanopsis, Cephalanthera, Cephalantheropsis, Cerastium, Cheilotheca, Cheirostylis, Chiloschista, Chimaphila, Cinnamomum, Circaea, Cissus, Citrus, Clematis, Clinopodium, Cocculus, Coeloglossum, Collabiopsis, Commelina, Costus, Crepis, Crotalaria, Cryptostylis, Cymbidium, Cypripedium, Daphne, Daphniphyllum, Dendranthema, Dendrobium, Desmodium, Deutzia, Dianella, Dianthus, Diploprora, Disporopsis, Disporum, Dolichos, Dysophylla, Ehretia, Elaeagnus, Elaeocarpus, Elymus, Emilia, Enkianthus, Ephemerantha, Epilobium, Epithema, Eria, Eriocaulon, Erythrina, Eulophia, Euonymus, Euphorbia, Euphrasia, Eurya, Ficus, Gaillardia, Gastrochilus, Gastrodia, Gaultheria, Gentiana, Glechoma, Glossogyne, Gnaphalium, Gomphostemma, Goodyera, Grossularia, Gynura, Habenaria, Hedyotis, Helicia, Heloniopsis, Hetaeria, Heteropappus, Himalaiella, Hoya, Hydrangea, Hydrosme, Hylophila, Hypericum, Illicium, Indigofera, Inula, Iris, Isodon, Ixeridium, Jacobaea, Lamium, Lasianthus, Lecanorchis, Lecanthus, Lespedeza, Lilium, Lindera, Liparis, Liriope, Listera, Litsea, Lotus, Luisia, Lysimachia, Maba, Maclura, Macodes, Malaxis, Malus, Mazus, Medinilla, Melanthera, Mentha, Microtatorchis, Mimulus, Monotropa, Musa, Myriactis, Myrmechis, Nervilia, Oberonia, Octarrhena, Odontochilus, Orchis, Oreorchis, Oxalis, Pachysandra, Pachystoma, Paederia, Panicum, Parachampionella, Paris, Pasania, Pectiantia, Peliosanthes, Pellionia, Peristylus, Phaius, Phedimus, Photinia, Picris, Pieris, Pilea, Platanthera, Plectranthus, Pleione, Podochilus, Poinsettia, Polygonatum, Polygonum, Polyspora, Ponerorchis, Potentilla, Pouzolzia, Prinsepia, Prunella, Prunus, Pseudognaphalium, Quercus, Reynoutria, Rhaphiolepis, Rhododendron, Rhynchotechum, Richardia, Rohdea, Rosa, Rostellularia, Rubus, Saccolabium, Salix, Salvia, Schoenorchis, Sciaphila, Scutellaria, Sedum, Senecio, Shortia, Sida, Silene, Solanum, Sorbus, Spergularia, Stachytarpheta, Stellaria, Swida, Swietenia, Sycopsis, Symplocos, Synurus, Taeniophyllum, Tainia, Tangshuia, Taxillus, Thelasis, Thrixspermum, Thyrocarpus, Tithymalus, Torenia, Trichoglottis, Tricyrtis, Trillium, Tropidia, Tsuga, Tulotis, Tupistra, Tylophora, Urtica, Vaccinium, Vanda, Vanilla, Veratrum, Veronica, Vexillabium, Viburnum, Viola, Vitex, Vitis, Wahlenbergia, Weberocereus, Wollastonia, Youngia, Zehneria, Zeuxine*
- Affiliation: NTUF
- Location of specimens: NTUF
- Region: CHINA (Taiwan)

C. H. You

You, Cun Hou; 尤存厚 ; Yóu Cúnhòu

1927-1989 **First publication: 1983**

- Employment: Liangshan Institute of Forest Science, Sichuan（四川省凉山州林科所）
- Research interest: Araceae [S]
- Published taxa: *Lemna*
- Region: CHINA (Sichuan)

C. X. You

You, Cheng Xia; 游承侠 ; Yóu Chéngxiá; 遊承俠

1948- **First publication: 1985**

- Employment: Kunming Institute of Botany, Chinese Academy of Sciences（中国科学院昆明植物研究所）
- Research interest: Hydrocharitaceae [S]
- Published taxa: *Ottelia*
- Region: CHINA (Guizhou)

S. S. You

You, Shui Shen; You, Shui Sheng; **游水生 ; Yóu Shuǐ shēng**

1953- **First publication: 1992**

- Employment: Fujian Forestry College（福建林学院）
- Research interest: Poaceae; Woody Plants [S]
- Published taxa: *Acidosasa, Oligostachyum, Phyllostachys*
- Affiliation: FJFC
- Location of specimens: FJFC
- Region: CHINA (Fujian)

C. C. Yu

Yu, Chih Chieh; 游旨价 ; Yóu Zhǐjiè

First publication: 2014

- Employment: School of Forestry and Resources Conservation, Taiwan University (台湾大学森林环境暨资源学系)
- Research interest: Berberidaceae [S]
- Published taxa: *Alloberberis, Berberis, Mahonia, Moranothamnus*
- Location of specimens: HAST
- Region: CHINA (Taiwan)

B. P. Yu

Yu, Bao Ping; Yu, Baoping; 于保平; Yú Bǎopíng

1961- **First publication: 1991**

- Employment: College of Forestry, South China Agricultural University (华南农业大学林学院)
- Research interest: Fagaceae [S]
- Published taxa: *Castanopsis*
- Region: CHINA (Hainan)

P. Yu

Yu, Po; Yu, Bo; 于波; Yú Bō

First publication: 1984

- Employment: Kulun Banner Forestry Bureau, Juu Uda, Inner Mongolia (内蒙古昭盟库伦旗林业局)
- Research interest: Salicaceae [S]
- Published taxa: *Populus*
- Region: CHINA (Nei Mongol)

D. Yu

Yu, Dan; 于丹; Yú Dān

1957- **First publication: 1992**

- Employment: Institute of Botany, Northeast Forestry University; College of Life Sciences, Wuhan University (东北林业大学植物研究所;武汉大学生命科学学院)
- Research interest: Haloragaceae, Plantaginaceae, Typhaceae [S]
- Published taxa: *Hippuris, Myriophyllum, Sparganium*
- Region: CHINA

H. Q. Yu

Yu, Hai Qing; 于海清; Yú Hǎiqīng

1978- **First publication: 2008**

- Employment: Triticeae Research Institute, Sichuan Agricultural University (四川农业大学小麦研究所)
- Research interest: Poaceae [S]
- Published taxa: *Roegneria, Trichopyrum*
- Region: [cult.]

Hui Yu

Yu, Hui; 于慧; Yú Huì

1974- **First publication: 2004**

- Employment: South China Botanical Garden, Chinese Academy of Sciences (中国科学院华南植物园)
- Research interest: Cornaceae, Poaceae, Rhamnaceae, Rosaceae [S]
- Published taxa: *Dendrobenthamia, Frangula, Kengia, Prunus, Pseudopogonatherum*
- Region: CHINA

J. X. Yu

Yu, Ji Xiang; 于吉祥; Yú Jíxiáng

1958- **First publication: 1989**

- Employment: Shanxi Institute of Forestry Science (山西省林业科学研究所)
- Research interest: Sapindaceae [S]
- Published taxa: *Acer*
- Region: CHINA (Shanxi)

J. H. Yu

Yu, Jing Hua; 于景华; Yú Jǐnghuá

1972- **First publication: 2010**

- Employment: Northeast Forestry University (东北林业大学)
- Research interest: Gentianaceae, Ranunculaceae [S]
- Published taxa: *Gentiana, Pulsatilla*
- Region: CHINA (Nei Mongol)

L. M. Yu

Yu, Li Min; 于立敏; Yú Lìmǐn

1974- **First publication: 2018**

- Employment: Xianrendong National Natural Reserve Administrative Bureau, Liaoning (辽宁仙人洞国家级自然保护区管理局)
- Research interest: Balsaminaceae, Fabaceae, Ranunculaceae, Violaceae [S]
- Published taxa: *Impatiens, Ranunculus, Vicia, Viola*
- Region: CHINA (Liaoning)

L. J. Yu

Yu, Li Jie; 于丽杰; Yú Lìjié

1961- **First publication: 1994**

- Employment: Department of Biology, Harbin Normal University (哈尔滨师范大学生物系)
- Research interest: Asteraceae [S]
- Published taxa: *Dendranthema*
- Region: CHINA (Heilongjiang)

L. L. Yu

Yu, Ling Long; 於玲珑; Yú Línglóng; 於玲瓏

1938- **First publication: 1983**

- Employment: Hangzhou Botanical Garden (杭州植物园)
- Research interest: Actinidiaceae, Styracaceae; Woody Plants [S]
- Published taxa: *Actinidia, Styrax*
- Affiliation: HHBG

• Region: CHINA (Zhejiang)

S. X. Yu

Yu, Sheng Xiang; 于胜祥 ; Yú Shèngxiáng

1977- **First publication: 2008**

• Employment: Institute of Botany, Chinese Academy of Sciences（中国科学院植物研究所）
• Research interest: Balsaminaceae [S]
• Published taxa: *Impatiens*
• Affiliation: PE
• Location of specimens: PE
• Region: CHINA

S. L. Yu

Yu, Shun Li; 于顺利 ; Yú Shùnlì

1965- **First publication: 1997**

• Employment: Institute of Botany, Chinese Academy of Sciences（中国科学院植物研究所）
• Research interest: Polypodiaceae [P]
• Published taxa: *Lepisorus*
• Region: CHINA

Shuo Yu

Yu, Shuo; 于硕 ; Yú Shuò

1985- **First publication: 2014**

• Employment: East China Normal University（华东师范大学）
• Research interest: Ruppiaceae [S]
• Published taxa: *Ruppia*
• Region: CHINA

W. T. Yu

Yu, Wen Tao; 于文涛 ; Yú Wéntāo

1984- **First publication: 2011**

• Employment: Kunming Institute of Botany, Chinese Academy of Sciences（中国科学院昆明植物研究所）
• Research interest: Boraginaceae [S]
• Published taxa: *Microula*
• Region: CHINA (Qinghai, Sichuan)

Y. F. Yu

Yu, Yong Fu; 于永福 ; Yú Yǒngfú

1967- **First publication: 1998**

• Employment: Institute of Botany, Chinese Academy of Sciences（中国科学院植物研究所）
• Research interest: Cupressaceae, Ephedraceae, Gnetaceae, Taxodiaceae [S]
• Published taxa: *Ephedra, Gnetum, Juniperus, Sabina*
• Affiliation: PE
• Location of specimens: PE
• Region: CHINA

C. Y. Yu

Yu, Chao Ying; Yu, Zhao Ying; 于兆英 ; Yú Zhàoyīng; 於兆英

1934-1993 **First publication: 1974**

• Employment: Northwest China Institute of Botany, Chinese Academy of Sciences and Shaanxi Province（陕西省中国科学院西北植物研究所）
• Research interest: Salicaceae, Thymelaeaceae [S]
• Published taxa: *Populus, Salix, Wikstroemia*
• Affiliation: WUK
• Location of specimens: WUK
• Region: CHINA (Shaanxi)
• Also as: Z. Y. Yu

K. D. Yu

Yu, Kuo Dian; Yu, Guo Dian; 余国奠 ; Yú Guódiàn; 余國奠

1938- **First publication: 1980**

• Employment: Department of Pharmacognosy, Nanjing Pharmaceutical College（南京药学院生药学教研室）
• Research interest: Liliaceae, Poaceae; Medicinal Plants [S]
• Published taxa: *Fritillaria, Setaria*
• Affiliation: CPU
• Location of specimens: CPU
• Region: CHINA (Hubei)
• Also as: G. D. Yu

H. Yu

Yu, Hong; 余鸿 ; Yú Hóng

First publication: 2003

• Employment: Kunming Plastic Factory, Yunnan; Kunming Center of Biological Resources & Biodiversity Researches, Yunnan（云南省昆明市塑料厂; 云南省昆明生物资源与多样性研究中心）
• Research interest: Magnoliaceae, Orchidaceae [S]
• Published taxa: *Cremastra, Magnolia, Michelia*
• Region: CHINA (Yunnan)
• Also as: Hong Yu

H. L. Yu

Yu, Huo Liang; 余火亮 ; Yú Huǒliàng

1961- **First publication: 1999**

• Employment: Administration Committee of Wuyishan Scenery District, Fujian（福建省武夷山风景名胜区管理委员会）
• Research interest: Poaceae [S]
• Published taxa: *Phyllostachys*
• Region: CHINA (Fujian)

L. Y. Yu

Yu, Li Ying; 余丽莹 ; Yú Lìyíng

1974- **First publication: 2002**

• Employment: Guangxi Botanical Garden of Medicinal Plants（广西药用植物园）

- Research interest: Aristolochiaceae, Asparagaceae, Ebenaceae; Medicinal Plants [S]
- Published taxa: *Aristolochia, Aspidistra, Diospyros, Peliosanthes*
- Affiliation: GXMG
- Location of specimens: GXMG
- Region: CHINA (Guangxi)

Q. Z. Yu

Yu, Qing Zhu; 余清珠 ; Yú Qīngzhū

First publication: 1986

- Employment: Shaanxi Agriculture and Forestry School（陕西省农林学校）
- Research interest: Araliaceae, Ericaceae [S]
- Published taxa: *Kalopanax, Rhododendron*
- Region: CHINA

S. K. Yu

Yu, Sheng Kun; 余勝焜 ; Yú Shèngkūn; 余胜焜

First publication: 2013

- Employment: Amateur（业余爱好者）
- Research interest: Orchidaceae [S]
- Published taxa: *Aphyllorchis, Gastrochilus*
- Region: CHINA (Taiwan)

S. C. Yu

Yu, Shi Chun; 余世春 ; Yú Shìchūn

First publication: 1992

- Employment: Anhui Institute for Drug Control（安徽省药品检验所）
- Research interest: Liliaceae [S]
- Published taxa: *Fritillaria*
- Region: CHINA (Hubei, Sichuan)

Shi X. Yu

Yu, Shi Xiao; 余世孝 ; Yú Shìxiào

1962- **First publication: 2011**

- Employment: School of Life Sciences, Sun Yat-sen University（中山大学生命科学学院）
- Research interest: Polygonaceae [S]
- Published taxa: *Fallopia*
- Region: CHINA (Guangxi)

W. Yu

Yu, Wei; 余伟 ; Yú Wěi

First publication: 1992

- Employment: Beijing Medical University（北京医科大学）
- Research interest: Aristolochiaceae [S]
- Published taxa: *Aristolochia*
- Region: CHINA (Anhui, Jiangxi)

X. Y. Yu

Yu, Xiang Yun; 余湘云 ; Yú Xiāngyún; 余湘雲

1939- **First publication: 1989**

- Employment: Department of Biology, Shanxi University（山西大学生物系）
- Research interest: Ranunculaceae; Plants of Shanxi [S]
- Published taxa: *Anemone*
- Affiliation: SXU
- Location of specimens: SXU
- Region: CHINA (Shanxi)

Yong F. Yu

Yu, Yong Fu; 余永富 ; Yú Yǒngfù

1972- **First publication: 2015**

- Employment: Leigongshan National Nature Reserve Administration Bureau, Guizhou（贵州雷公山国家级自然保护区管理局）
- Research interest: Ericaceae [S]
- Published taxa: *Rhododendron*
- Region: CHINA (Guizhou)

Y. H. Yu

Yu, Yuan Hu; 余元虎 ; Yú Yuánhǔ

First publication: 1987

- Employment: Pingwu County Institute of Chinese Materia Medica, Sichuan（四川省平武县中药研究所）
- Research interest: Liliaceae [S]
- Published taxa: *Fritillaria*
- Region: CHINA (Sichuan)

T. T. Yu

Yu, Tse Tsun; Yu, Te Tsun; Yü, Tê Chün; Yü, Tê Chun; Yu, De Jun; 俞德浚 ; Yú Déjùn

1908-1986 **First publication: 1940**

- Employment: Fan Memorial Institute of Biology; Institute of Systematic Botany, Academia Sinica; Institute of Botany, Chinese Academy of Sciences（静生生物调查所；中国科学院植物分类研究所；中国科学院植物研究所）
- Research interest: Fabaceae, Rosaceae [S]
- Published taxa: *Acomastylis, Amygdalus, Armeniaca, Astragalus, Cerasus, Chaenomeles, Cotoneaster, Duchesnea, Erythrina, Lauro-cerasus, Maddenia, Malus, Neillia, Osteomeles, Padus, Photinia, Potentilla, Pygeum, Pyracantha, Pyrus, Rosa, Rubus, Sanguisorba, Sibbaldia, Sorbus, Spiraea, Stranvaesia, Taihangia, Waldsteinia*
- Affiliation: CQNM, PE
- Location of specimens: CQNM, PE, KUN
- Region: CHINA

Z. H. Yu

Yu, Ze Jun; 俞泽华 ; Yú Zéhuá; 俞澤華

1933- **First publication: 1980**

- Employment: Nanjing University（南京大学）
- Research interest: Poaceae [S]

- Published taxa: *Phyllostachys*
- Affiliation: N
- Location of specimens: N
- Region: CHINA

Z. X. Yu

Yu, Zhi Xiong; Yu, Ze Jun; **俞志雄 ; Yú Zhìxióng**

1938- **First publication: 1988**

- Employment: Jiangxi Agricultural University（江西农业大学）
- Research interest: Anacardiaceae, Lamiaceae, Magnoliaceae, Rosaceae, Sapindaceae [S]
- Published taxa: *Acer, Callicarpa, Manglietia, Neillia, Rhus, Rosa, Rubus, Sinomanglietia, Sorbus, Spiraea*
- Affiliation: JXAU
- Location of specimens: JXAU
- Region: CHINA (Jiangxi)

Z. Z. Yu

Yu, Zhi Zhou; 俞志洲 ; Yú Zhìzhōu

1936- **First publication: 1994**

- Employment: Hangzhou Botanical Garden（杭州植物园）
- Research interest: Amaryllidaceae [S]
- Published taxa: *Lycoris*
- Region: CHINA (Gansu, Hubei)

F. L. Yu

Yu, Fu Lian; 虞富莲 ; Yú Fùlián; 虞富蓮

1939- **First publication: 1983**

- Employment: Tea Research Institute, Chinese Academy of Agricultural Sciences（中国农业科学院茶叶研究所）
- Research interest: Theaceae [S]
- Published taxa: *Camellia*
- Affiliation: TEA
- Location of specimens: TEA
- Region: CHINA (Yunnan)

Hong Yu

Yu, Hong; 虞泓 ; Yú Hóng

1962- **First publication: 2005**

- Employment: School of Life Sciences, Yunnan University（云南大学生命科学学院）
- Research interest: Orchidaceae [S]
- Published taxa: *Epigeneium*
- Region: CHINA (Yunnan)

Y. C. Yu

Yu, Ying Chun; 禹迎春 ; Yǔ Yíngchūn

First publication: 2019

- Employment: Yangzhou Dayu Scenic Bamboo Garden, Jiangsu（扬州大禹风景竹园）
- Research interest: Poaceae [S]
- Published taxa: *Phyllostachys*
- Region: CHINA (Jiangsu)

Z. D. Yu

Yu, Zai Ding; 禹在定 ; Yǔ Zàidìng

First publication: 2019

- Employment: Yangzhou Dayu Scenic Bamboo Garden, Jiangsu（扬州大禹风景竹园）
- Research interest: Poaceae [S]
- Published taxa: *Phyllostachys*
- Region: CHINA (Jiangsu)

W. B. Yu

Yu, Wen Bin; 郁文彬 ; Yù Wénbīn

1982- **First publication: 2008**

- Employment: Kunming Institute of Botany, Chinese Academy of Sciences; Xishuangbanna Tropical Botanical Garden, Chinese Academy of Sciences（中国科学院昆明植物研究所；中国科学院西双版纳热带植物园）
- Research interest: Celastraceae, Lamiaceae, Lauraceae, Orobanchaceae, Ranunculaceae [S]
- Published taxa: *Anemone, Callicarpa, Christisonia, Gymnosporia, Neocinnamomeae, Pedicularis, Pseudobartsia*
- Affiliation: HITBC
- Region: CHINA

C. H. Yu

Yu, Cheng Hung; 喻诚鸿 ; Yù Chénghóng; 喻誠鴻

1922-1993 **First publication: 1974**

- Employment: South China Institute of Botany, Chinese Academy of Sciences（中国科学院华南植物研究所）
- Research interest: Asteraceae [S]
- Published taxa: *Blumea*
- Region: CHINA

F. Q. Yu

Yu, Feng Qiong; 喻奉琼 ; Yù Fèngqióng

1991- **First publication: 2017**

- Employment: College of Life Sciences, Southwest University（西南大学生命科学学院）
- Research interest: Orchidaceae [S]
- Published taxa: *Calanthe*
- Region: CHINA (Chongqing)

F. G. Yu

Yu, Fu Gen; 喻富根 ; Yù Fùgēn; 胡喻陈

1965- **First publication: 1991**

- Employment: Nanjing University（南京大学）
- Research interest: Poaceae [S]
- Published taxa: *Polyanthus*
- Region: CHINA (Hunan)
- IPNI as: Y. C. Hu

X. L. Yu

Yu, Xun Lin; 喻勋林；Yù Xūnlín

1964- **First publication: 2014**

- Employment: College of Forestry, Central South University of Forestry and Technology（中南林业科技大学林学院）
- Research interest: Begoniaceae, Fabaceae, Gesneriaceae, Orchidaceae, Primulaceae, Saxifragaceae, Styracaceae; Plants of Hunan [S]
- Published taxa: *Apios, Astragalus, Begonia, Chrysosplenium, Lysimachia, Petrocodon, Platanthera, Primula, Primulina, Styrax*
- Affiliation: CSFI
- Location of specimens: CSFI
- Region: CHINA (Hunan)

Zhi Y. Yu

Yu, Zhi Yong; 喻智勇；Yù Zhìyǒng

1967- **First publication: 2003**

- Employment: Fenshuiling National Nature Reserve Administration Bureau, Jinping, Yunnan（云南金平分水岭国家级自然保护区管理局）
- Research interest: Cyatheaceae, Melanthiaceae, Melastomataceae [PS]
- Published taxa: *Alsophila, Fordiophyton, Ypsilandra*
- Region: CHINA (Yunnan)
- IPNI as: Y. Z. Yu

Yu Nung

Henan Agronomy College; Yu Nung; **豫农；**Yù Nóng

First publication: 1981

- Employment: Henan Agricultural College（河南农学院）
- Research interest: Salicaceae [S]
- Published taxa: *Populus*
- Region: CHINA (Henan)
- Organization

C. C. Yuan

Yuan, Chang Chi; Yuan, Ch'ang Chi; Yuan, Chang Qi; **袁昌齐；Yuán Chāngqí; 袁昌齊**

1934- **First publication: 1980**

- Employment: Institute of Botany, Jiangsu Province（江苏省植物研究所）
- Research interest: Apiaceae, Brassicaceae [S]
- Published taxa: *Angelica, Arabis, Eriocycla, Ostericum, Selinum*
- Affiliation: NAS
- Region: CHINA
- Also as: C. Q. Yuan

J. L. Yuan

Yuan, Jin Ling; 袁金玲；Yuán Jīnlíng

First publication: 2018

- Employment: Research Institute of Subtropical Forestry, Chinese Academy of Forestry（中国林业科学研究院亚热带林业研究所）
- Research interest: Poaceae [S]
- Published taxa: *Bambusa*
- Region: CHINA (Zhejiang)

L. X. Yuan

Yuan, Lang Xing; 袁浪兴；Yuán Làngxìng

1996- **First publication: 2019**

- Employment: College of Tropical Agriculture and Forestry, Hainan University; Tropical Crops Genetic Resources Institute, Chinese Academy of Tropical Agricultural Sciences（海南大学热带农林学院；中国热带农业科学院热带作物品种资源研究所）
- Research interest: Rubiaceae [S]
- Published taxa: *Hedyotis*
- Region: CHINA (Hainan)

M. D. Yuan

Yuan, Ming Deng; 袁明灯；Yuán Míngdēng

First publication: 2020

- Employment: South China Botanical Garden, Chinese Academy of Sciences（中国科学院华南植物园）
- Research interest: Rubiaceae [S]
- Published taxa: *Involucrella*
- Region: CHINA (Guangxi)

Qian Yuan

Yuan, Qian; 袁慊；Yuán Qiàn

1990- **First publication: 2014**

- Employment: Institute of Botany, Chinese Academy of Sciences（中国科学院植物研究所）
- Research interest: Asteraceae [S]
- Published taxa: *Himalaiella, Saussurea*
- Region: [ASIA]

Q. Yuan

Yuan, Qiong; 袁琼；Yuán Qióng

1977- **First publication: 2006**

- Employment: South China Botanical Garden, Chinese Academy of Sciences（中国科学院华南植物园）
- Research interest: Asteraceae, Ranunculaceae [S]
- Published taxa: *Actaea, Anemone, Asteropyrum, Dolomiaea, Doronicum, Sphagneticola*
- Affiliation: IBSC
- Region: CHINA

S. Yuan

Yuan, Shuai; 袁帅；Yuán Shuài

1989- **First publication: 2017**

- Employment: South China Botanical Garden, Chinese Academy of Sciences（中国科学院华南植物园）

- Research interest: Primulaceae [S]
- Published taxa: *Primula*
- Region: CHINA (Sichuan)

X. Y. Yuan

Yuan, Xiao Ying; 袁晓颖；Yuán Xiǎoyǐng

1950- **First publication: 1985**

- Employment: Northeast Forestry University（东北林业大学）
- Research interest: Cyperaceae, Pinaceae [S]
- Published taxa: *Carex, Picea, Pinus*
- Region: CHINA (Heilongjiang)

Y. W. Yuan

Yuan, Yao Wu; 袁耀武；Yuán Yàowǔ

First publication: 2010

- Employment: Department of Biology, University of Washington, U.S.A.; Department of Plant Biology, University of Georgia, U.S.A.（美国华盛顿大学生物系；美国乔治亚大学植物生物学系）
- Research interest: Lamiaceae [S]
- Published taxa: *Volkameria*
- Region: [WORLD]

Y. Yuan

Yuan, Yi; 袁艺；Yuán Yì

First publication: 2012

- Employment: School of Architecture, Southwest Jiaotong University（西南交通大学建筑学院）
- Research interest: Dennstaedtiaceae [P]
- Published taxa: *Microlepia*
- Region: CHINA (Guangdong)

Y. M. Yuan

Yuan, Yong Ming; 袁永明；Yuán Yǒngmíng

1962- **First publication: 1992**

- Employment: Department of Biology, Lanzhou University; Institute of Botany, University of Neuchâtel, Switzerland; R&D Center, Firmenich Aromatics (China)Co., Ltd.（兰州大学生物系；瑞士纳沙泰尔大学生物研究所；芬美意香料(中国)有限公司研发中心）
- Research interest: Asteraceae, Balsaminaceae, Fabaceae, Gentianaceae [S]
- Published taxa: *Impatiens, Sinogentiana, Tephroseris, Thermopsis*
- Region: CHINA

Z. Z. Yuan

Yuan, Zhen Zhen; Yuan, Z.; 袁珍珍；Yuán Zhēnzhēn

First publication: 2017

- Employment: The Institute of Vegetables, Chinese Academy of Agricultural Sciences（中国农业科学院蔬菜研究所）
- Research interest: Cucurbitaceae [S]
- Published taxa: *Cucumis*
- Region: CHINA (Yunnan)
- IPNI as: Z. Yuan

J. J. Yue

Yue, Jin Jun; 岳晋军；Yuè Jìnjūn

First publication: 2018

- Employment: Research Institute of Subtropical Forestry, Chinese Academy of Forestry（中国林业科学研究院亚热带林业研究所）
- Research interest: Poaceae [S]
- Published taxa: *Bambusa*
- Region: CHINA (Zhejiang)

S. C. Yueh

Yueh, Song Chien; Yueh, Sung Chien; Yue, Song Jian; 岳松健；Yuè Sōngjiàn

1927-2001 **First publication: 1983**

- Employment: Department of Pharmacognosy, Sichuan Medical College（四川医学院生药学教研室）
- Research interest: Fabaceae, Liliaceae [S]
- Published taxa: *Fritillaria*
- Affiliation: WCU
- Location of specimens: WCU
- Region: CHINA (Sichuan)

Z. S. Yue

Yue, Zong Shu; 岳中枢；Yuè Zhōngshū; 岳中樞

1934- **First publication: 1987**

- Employment: Kunming Institute of Botany, Chinese Academy of Sciences（中国科学院昆明植物研究所）
- Research interest: Magnoliaceae [S]
- Published taxa: *Michelia*
- Region: [cult.]

C. H. Yueh

Yueh, Chun Hsi; Yueh, Chung Hsi; Yue, Zong Xi; Yue, Chong Xi; 乐崇熙；Yuè Chóngxī; 樂崇熙

1932- **First publication: 1974**

- Employment: Institute of Chinese Materia Medica, China Academy of Chinese Medical Sciences（中国中医研究院中药研究所）
- Research interest: Cucurbitaceae, Polygonaceae [S]
- Published taxa: *Trichosanthes*
- Affiliation: CMMI
- Location of specimens: CMMI
- Region: [WORLD]

J. P. Yue

Yue, Ji Pei; 乐霁培；Yuè Jìpéi

1974- **First publication: 2004**

- Employment: Kunming Institute of Botany, Chinese Academy of Sciences（中国科学院昆明植物研究所）

- Research interest: Brassicaceae, Fabaceae [S]
- Published taxa: *Draba, Salweenia, Shangrilaia, Solms-laubachia*
- Region: CHINA (Sichuan, Yunnan, Xizang)

T. Y. Yao

Yao, Tien Yu; Lo, Tien Yu; Lo, T'ien Yü; Lao, Tien Yu; Yue, Tian Yu; 乐天宇 ; Yuè Tiānyǔ ; 樂天宇 , 乐天愚

1901-1984 First publication: 1935

- Employment: Provincial Henan University; Chinese Academy of Forestry (河南大学 ; 中国林业科学研究院)
- Research interest: Betulaceae, Pinaceae [S]
- Published taxa: *Ostryopsis, Pinus*
- Location of specimens: PE
- Region: CHINA (Gansu, Ningxia, Shaanxi, Shanxi)
- Also as: T. Y. Lo; 陕甘宁盆地植物志(Basin Flora of Shaanxi-Gansu-Ningxia)

P. Yun

Yun, Po; 云波 ; Yún Bō

First publication: 1995

- Employment: Gejiu City No.2 Middle School, Yunnan (云南省个旧市第二中学)
- Research interest: Cycadaceae [S]
- Published taxa: *Cycas*
- Region: CHINA (Yunnan)

Y. Y. Zan

Zan, Yan Yan; 昝艳燕 ; Zǎn Yànyàn

1971- First publication: 2005

- Employment: Wuhan Botanical Garden, Chinese Academy of Sciences; Shennongjia Nature Reserve Administration Bureau, Hubei (中国科学院武汉植物园 ; 湖北神农架自然保护区管理局)
- Research interest: Orobanchaceae [S]
- Published taxa: *Triaenophora*
- Region: CHINA (Hubei)

D. K. Zang

Zang, De Kui; 臧德奎 ; Zāng Dékuí; 臧得奎

1966- First publication: 1992

- Employment: Forestry College, Shandong Agricultural University (山东农业大学林学院)
- Research interest: Asteraceae, Lamiaceae, Ranunculaceae, Rhamnaceae, Rosaceae, Stemonaceae [S]
- Published taxa: *Cerasus, Dendranthema, Pulsatilla, Pyrus, Rhamnus, Sorbus, Spiraea, Stemona, Vitex*
- Location of specimens: SDFGR
- Region: CHINA (Shandong)

C. J. Tseng

Tseng, Chang Jiang; Tsêng,Ts'ang Chiang; Zeng, Cang Jiang; 曾沧江 ; Zēng Cāngjiāng; 曾滄江

1928-1982 First publication: 1965

- Employment: Department of Biology, Xiamen University (厦门大学生物系)
- Research interest: Aquifoliaceae, Araliaceae, Meliaceae [S]
- Published taxa: *Dendropanax, Euaraliopsis, Ilex, Panax, Schefflera, Toona*
- Affiliation: AU
- Location of specimens: AU
- Region: CHINA
- Also as: C. Tseng; Tseng

F. A. Zeng

Zeng, Fan An; 曾范安 ; Zēng Fàn'ān; 曾範安

1940- First publication: 1985

- Employment: Guizhou Research Institute of Forestry (贵州省林业科学研究所)
- Research interest: Theaceae [S]
- Published taxa: *Camellia*
- Affiliation: GF
- Location of specimens: GF
- Region: CHINA (Guizhou)

J. Zeng

Zeng, Jie; 曾杰 ; Zēng Jié

1969- First publication: 2008

- Employment: Research Institute of Tropical Forestry, Chinese Academy of Forestry (中国林业科学研究院热带林业研究所)
- Research interest: Betulaceae [S]
- Published taxa: *Betula*
- Region: CHINA (Fujian, Hainan)

L. Zeng

Zeng, Ling; 曾玲 ; Zēng Líng

1959- First publication: 1993

- Employment: Natural History Museum of Guangxi (广西自然博物馆)
- Research interest: Asparagaceae, Gesneriaceae; Plants of Guangxi [S]
- Published taxa: *Aspidistra, Chirita, Chiritopsis, Lagarosolen, Paraboea*
- Affiliation: GXNM
- Location of specimens: GXNM

• Region: CHINA (Guangxi)

Tsen

Tsen, Mill; Tseng, Mien Chih; Zeng, Mian Zhi; Zeng, Mian; 曾勉；Zēng Miǎn; 曾勉之

1901-1988 First publication: 1942

- Employment: Department of Horticulture, College of Agriculture, National Central University; Citrus Research Institute, Chinese Academy of Agricultural Sciences（国立中央大学农学院园艺系；中国农业科学院柑橘研究所）
- Research interest: Brassicaceae, Rutaceae [S]
- Published taxa: *Brassica*
- Affiliation: CIT
- Location of specimens: PE
- Region: CHINA

C. C. Tseng

Tseng, Chiao, Charles; Tseng, Chiao; Tsêng, Ch'iao; 曾樵；Zēng Qiáo

1932- First publication: 1957

- Employment: Taiwan University; University of California, Los Angeles, U.S.A.（台湾大学；美国加州大学洛杉矶分校）
- Research interest: Apiaceae, Lamiaceae [S]
- Published taxa: *Aletes, Callicarpa*
- Region: CHINA (Taiwan); UNITED STATES
- Also as: C. Tseng; Tseng

Q. W. Zeng

Zeng, Qing Wen; 曾庆文；Zēng Qìngwén

1963-2012 First publication: 2004

- Employment: South China Botanical Garden, Chinese Academy of Sciences（中国科学院华南植物园）
- Research interest: Magnoliaceae [S]
- Published taxa: *Magnolia, Manglietia, Michelia*
- Affiliation: IBSC
- Region: CHINA

S. Jin Zeng

Zeng, Si Jin; 曾思金；Zēng Sījīn

1989- First publication: 2016

- Employment: College of Forestry and Landscape Architecture, South China Agricultural University（华南农业大学林学与风景园林学院）
- Research interest: Melastomataceae [S]
- Published taxa: *Bredia, Fordiophyton*
- Region: CHINA

S. J. Zeng

Zeng, Song Jun; 曾宋君；Zēng Sòngjūn

1965- First publication: 2010

- Employment: South China Botanical Garden, Chinese Academy of Sciences（中国科学院华南植物园）
- Research interest: Orchidaceae [S]
- Published taxa: *Dendrobium*
- Region: CHINA (Guangdong)

W. Z. Zeng

Zeng, Wan Zhang; 曾万章；Zēng Wànzhāng; 曾萬章

1935- First publication: 1986

- Employment: Department of Chinese Medicine, Chengdu College of Traditional Chinese Medicine（成都中医学院中药系）
- Research interest: Asparagaceae, Cucurbitaceae, Liliaceae, Phrymaceae [S]
- Published taxa: *Polygonatum*
- Affiliation: CDCM
- Location of specimens: CDCM
- Region: CHINA (Sichuan)

W. G. Zeng

Zeng, Wei Guang; 曾维光；Zēng Wéiguāng

First publication: 1992

- Employment: Aba Forestry Bureau, Sichuan（四川省阿坝州林业局）
- Research interest: Rosaceae [S]
- Published taxa: *Malus*
- Region: CHINA (Sichuan)

H. Y. Tzeng

Tzeng, Hsy Yu; 曾喜育；Zēng Xǐyù

First publication: 2006

- Employment: Department of Forestry, Chung Hsing University（中兴大学林学系）
- Research interest: Asparagaceae [S]
- Published taxa: *Heteropolygonatum*
- Region: CHINA (Taiwan)

S. L. Tseng

Tseng, Shiao Lien; 曾孝濂；Zēng Xiàolián

1938- First publication: 1977

- Employment: Institute of Botany, Yunnan Province（云南省植物研究所）
- Research interest: Araceae; Scientific Illustrator [S]
- Published taxa: *Typhonium*
- Affiliation: KUN
- Region: CHINA (Yunnan)

Xin Y. Zeng

Zeng, Xin Yu; 曾新宇；Zēng Xīnyǔ

1956- First publication: 2005

- Employment: Hangzhou Botanical Garden（杭州植物园）
- Research interest: Poaceae [S]
- Published taxa: *Phyllostachys*
- Affiliation: HHBG

- Location of specimens: HHBG
- Region: CHINA (Zhejiang)
- IPNI as: X. Y. Zeng

Y. H. Tseng

Tseng, Yen Hsueh; Zeng, Yan Xue;
曾彥學; Zēng Yànxué; **曾彦学**

First publication: 1998

- Employment: Institute of Forestry, Taiwan University; Department of Forestry, Chung Hsing University（台湾大学森林学研究所；中兴大学森林学系）
- Research interest: Apocynaceae, Asparagaceae, Asteraceae, Buxaceae, Cannabaceae, Colchicaceae, Ebenaceae, Ericaceae, Melastomataceae, Moraceae, Salicaceae, Styracaceae, Zingiberaceae [S]
- Published taxa: *Alpinia, Buxus, Celtis, Cirsium, Disporum, Ficus, Heteropolygonatum, Maba, Maianthemum, Memecylon, Polygonatum, Rhododendron, Salix, Sarcococca, Styrax, Tylophora*
- Region: CHINA (Taiwan)

Y. Q. Zeng

Zeng, Yi Quan; **曾义泉**; Zēng Yìquán
1950- **First publication: 1979**

- Employment: Chengdu Institute for Drug Control, Sichuan（四川省成都市药品检验所）
- Research interest: Apiaceae [S]
- Published taxa: *Ligusticum*
- Affiliation: CDC
- Location of specimens: CDC
- Region: CHINA (Sichuan)

Y. Zeng

Zeng, Yi; **曾翼**; Zēng Yì
1988- **First publication: 2014**

- Employment: South China Botanical Garden, Chinese Academy of Sciences（中国科学院华南植物园）
- Research interest: Poaceae [S]
- Published taxa: *Gigantochloa*
- Region: CHINA

Y. P. Zeng

Zeng, You Pai; **曾佑派**; Zēng Yòupài

First publication: 2021

- Employment: South China Botanical Garden, Chinese Academy of Sciences（中国科学院华南植物园）
- Research interest: Ranunculaceae [S]
- Published taxa: *Thalictrum*
- Region: CHINA (Yunnan)

Yu H. Tseng

Tseng, Yu Hsin; **曾妤馨**; Zēng Yúxīn

First publication: 2014

- Employment: Institute of Ecology and Evolutionary Biology, Taiwan University（台湾大学生态学与演化生物学研究所）
- Research interest: Urticaceae [S]
- Published taxa: *Elatostematoides, Elatostema*
- Region: CHINA (Taiwan)
- Also as: Yu Hsin Tseng

D. T. Zhai

Zhai, Da Tong; **翟大彤**; Zhái Dàtóng
1965- **First publication: 1996**

- Employment: Teachers' College, Shanxi University（山西大学师范学院）
- Research interest: Asteraceae [S]
- Published taxa: *Taraxacum*
- Affiliation: LINF
- Location of specimens: LINF
- Region: CHINA (Xinjiang)

J. W. Zhai

Zhai, Jun Wen; **翟俊文**; Zhái Jùnwén
1985- **First publication: 2013**

- Employment: College of Landscape Architecture, Fujian Agriculture and Forestry University（福建农林大学园林学院）
- Research interest: Orchidaceae [S]
- Published taxa: *Bulbophyllum, Calanthe, Changnienia, Danxiaorchis, Paraphaius*
- Region: CHINA

W. Chai

Chai, Wei; Zhai, Wei; **翟伟**; Zhái Wěi
1981- **First publication: 2010**

- Employment: College of Life Sciences, Shihezi University（石河子大学生命科学学院）
- Research interest: Fabaceae [S]
- Published taxa: *Astragalus*
- Location of specimens: SHI
- Region: CHINA (Xinjiang)

M. Zhan

Zhan, Ming; **詹明**; Zhān Míng
1963- **First publication: 1987**

- Employment: Northwest Plateau Institute of Biology, Chinese Academy of Sciences（中国科学院西北高原生物研究所）
- Research interest: Cyperaceae [S]
- Published taxa: *Baeothryon, Bolboschoenus, Schoenoplectus*
- Region: CHINA

X. H. Zhan

Zhan, Xuan Huai; **詹选怀**; Zhān Xuǎnhuái
1964- **First publication: 2017**

- Employment: Lushan Botanical Garden, Chinese Academy of Sciences (中国科学院庐山植物园)
- Research interest: Melastomataceae; Pteridophytes [S]
- Published taxa: *Bredia*
- Affiliation: LBG
- Location of specimens: LBG
- Region: CHINA (Jiangxi)

A. L. Chang

Chang, Ao Luo; Zhang, Ao Luo; 张敖罗; Zhāng Áoluō; 張敖羅

1935- **First publication: 1982**

- Employment: Kunming Institute of Botany, Chinese Academy of Sciences (中国科学院昆明植物研究所)
- Research interest: Ericaceae [S]
- Published taxa: *Rhododendron*
- Region: CHINA (Yunnan)

B. N. Chang

Chang, Ben Neng; Zhang, Ben Neng; 张本能; Zhāng Běnnéng; 張本能

1938-2010 **First publication: 1982**

- Employment: Guangxi Institute of Botany; Department of Biology, Sichuan Normal University (广西植物研究所; 四川师范大学生物系)
- Research interest: Begoniaceae, Fabaceae, Illiciaceae, Menispermaceae, Schisandraceae [S]
- Published taxa: *Begonia, Illicium, Stephania*
- Affiliation: IBK, SCNU
- Location of specimens: IBK, SCNU
- Region: CHINA (Guangxi)

B. Y. Zhang

Zhang, Bing Yan; 张炳炎; Zhāng Bǐngyán; 張炳炎

1937-? **First publication: 1995**

- Employment: Institute of Plant Protection, Gansu Academy of Agricultural Science (甘肃省农业科学院植物保护研究所)
- Research interest: Apiaceae, Dryopteridaceae [PS]
- Published taxa: *Ligusticum, Polystichum*
- Region: CHINA (Gansu)

Bo Y. Zhang

Zhang, Bo Yu; 张伯誉; Zhāng Bóyù; 張伯譽

1936- **First publication: 2001**

- Employment: Chongqing Normal College (重庆师范学院)
- Research interest: Dryopteridaceae [S]
- Published taxa: *Polystichum*
- Region: CHINA (Chongqing)

Cai F. Zhang

Zhang, Cai Fei; 张彩飞; Zhāng Cǎifēi

1985- **First publication: 2013**

- Employment: Institute of Botany, Chinese Academy of Sciences; Wuhan Botanical Garden, Chinese Academy of Sciences (中国科学院植物研究所; 中国科学院武汉植物园)
- Research interest: Asteraceae [S]
- Published taxa: *Pertya*
- Region: CHINA
- IPNI as: C. F. Zhang

C. M. Zhang

Zhang, Can Ming; 张灿明; Zhāng Cànmíng

1963- **First publication: 1990**

- Employment: Hunan Institute of Forestry Science (湖南省林业科学研究所)
- Research interest: Aspleniaceae, Betulaceae, Dryopteridaceae, Ericaceae, Plagiogyriaceae, Pteridaceae, Thelypteridaceae; Pteridophytes [PS]
- Published taxa: *Adiantum, Asplenium, Corylus, Cyclosorus, Dryopteris, Plagiogyria, Pteris, Rhododendron, Thelypteris*
- Affiliation: HUIF
- Location of specimens: HUIF
- Region: CHINA (Hunan)

C. Q. Zhang

Zhang, Chang Qin; 张长芹; Zhāng Chángqín

1953- **First publication: 2003**

- Employment: Kunming Institute of Botany, Chinese Academy of Sciences (中国科学院昆明植物研究所)
- Research interest: Asparagaceae, Ericaceae, Primulaceae [S]
- Published taxa: *Primula, Rhododendron, Rohdea*
- Region: CHINA (Yunnan)

C. F. Zhang

Zhang, Chao Fang; 张朝芳; Zhāng Cháofāng; 張朝芳

1923-2002 **First publication: 1983**

- Employment: Department of Biology, Hangzhou University (杭州大学生物系)
- Research interest: Aspleniaceae, Dryopteridaceae, Hymenophyllaceae, Lycopodiaceae, Thelypteridaceae; Pteridophytes [P]
- Published taxa: *Arachniodes, Arachniodes, Asplenium, Crepidomanes, Ctenitis, Cyclosorus, Dryopteris, Hymenophyllum, Phlegmariurus, Thelypteris*
- Affiliation: HZU
- Location of specimens: HZU
- Region: CHINA (Zhejiang)
- IPNI as: Z. F. Zhang

C. H. Zhang

Zhang, Chun Hong; 张春红; Zhāng Chūnhóng

1975- **First publication: 2016**

- Employment: Baotou Medical College (包头医学院)
- Research interest: Orobanchaceae [S]
- Published taxa: *Rehmannia*
- Region: CHINA (Nei Mongol)

C. L. Zhang

Zhang, Chun Lin; 张春林; Zhāng Chūnlín
1964- **First publication: 1993**

- Employment: Northwest China Institute of Botany, Chinese Academy of Sciences and Shaanxi Province (陕西省中国科学院西北植物研究所)
- Research interest: Fabaceae [S]
- Published taxa: *Oxytropis*
- Region: CHINA (Gansu)

C. Y. Zhang

Zhang, Cun Yi; 张存义; Zhāng Cúnyì
1951- **First publication: 1995**

- Employment: Puyang Institute of Forestry Science, Henan (河南省濮阳林业科学研究所)
- Research interest: Paulowniaceae [S]
- Published taxa: *Paulownia*
- Region: CHINA (Henan)

D. M. Zhang

Zhang, Da Ming; 张大明; Zhāng Dàmíng
1951- **First publication: 2004**

- Employment: Institute of Botany, Chinese Academy of Sciences (中国科学院植物研究所)
- Research interest: Colchicaceae, Liliaceae, Paeoniaceae [S]
- Published taxa: *Disporum, Paeonia*
- Affiliation: PE
- Location of specimens: PE
- Region: CHINA (Chongqing)

D. G. Zhang

Zhang, Dai Gui; 张代贵; Zhāng Dàiguì
1963- **First publication: 2008**

- Employment: College of Resources and Environmental Science, Jishou University (吉首大学资源与环境科学学院)
- Research interest: Asteraceae, Berberidaceae, Campanulaceae, Caryophyllaceae, Mazaceae, Oxalidaceae, Phytolaccaceae, Rosaceae, Saxifragaceae, Urticaceae; Plants of Hunan [S]
- Published taxa: *Adenophora, Epimedium, Mazus, Oxalis, Phytolacca, Prunus, Saxifraga, Silene, Sinosenecio, Youngia, Zhengyia*
- Affiliation: JIU
- Location of specimens: JIU
- Region: CHINA

D. S. Zhang

Zhang, De Shun; 张德舜; Zhāng Déshùn
First publication: 1988

- Employment: Department of Landscape, Beijing Forestry University (北京林业大学园林系)
- Research interest: Pinaceae [S]
- Published taxa: *Larix*
- Region: CHINA (Hebei)

D. K. Zhang

Zhang, Deng Ke; 张登科; Zhāng Dēngkē
First publication: 1992

- Employment: Taibai County Traditional Chinese Medicine Company (陕西省太白县药材公司)
- Research interest: Liliaceae, Polygonaceae [S]
- Published taxa: *Fritillaria, Rheum*
- Region: CHINA (Shaanxi)

D. M. Chang

Chang, Dian Mine; Chang, Dian Min; Zhang, Dian Min; **张佃民; Zhāng Diànmín; 張佃民**
1934- **First publication: 1978**

- Employment: Xinjiang Institute of Biology, Pedology and Desert Research, Chinese Academy of Sciences (中国科学院新疆生物土壤沙漠研究所)
- Research interest: Poaceae; Plants of Xinjiang [S]
- Published taxa: *Festuca*
- Affiliation: XJBI
- Location of specimens: XJBI
- Region: CHINA (Xinjiang)

D. X. Zhang

Zhang, Dian Xiang; 张奠湘; Zhāng Diànxiāng
1963- **First publication: 1993**

- Employment: South China Institute of Botany, Chinese Academy of Sciences; South China Botanical Garden, Chinese Academy of Sciences (中国科学院华南植物研究所；中国科学院华南植物园)
- Research interest: Burmanniaceae, Corsiaceae, Fabaceae, Lamiaceae, Oleaceae, Orchidaceae, Primulaceae, Rubiaceae, Rutaceae, Santalaceae; Plant Systematics [S]
- Published taxa: *Bauhinia, Burmannia, Caesalpinia, Callicarpa, Corsiopsis, Glycosmis, Jasminum, Mussaenda, Phaius, Primula, Rubovietnamia, Schizomussaenda, Viscum*
- Affiliation: IBSC
- Location of specimens: IBSC
- Region: CHINA

D. C. Zhang

Zhang, Ding Cheng; 张定成; Zhāng Dìngchéng; 張定成
1939-2003 **First publication: 1986**

- Employment: Department of Biology, Anhui Normal

University（安徽师范大学生物系）
• Research interest: Asparagaceae, Brassicaceae, Crassulaceae, Liliaceae, Magnoliaceae, Rosaceae, Thymelaeaceae [S]
• Published taxa: *Cardamine, Cochlearia, Daphne, Fritillaria, Lilium, Michelia, Polygonatum, Rosa, Sedum, Wikstroemia*
• Affiliation: ANUB
• Location of specimens: ANUB
• Region: CHINA (Anhui)

D. L. Zhang
Zhang, Dong Lin; 张冬林；Zhāng Dōnglín
1968- **First publication: 2010**
• Employment: University of Maine, U.S.A.（美国缅因大学）
• Research interest: Magnoliaceae [S]
• Published taxa: *Yulania*
• Location of specimens: CSFI
• Region: CHINA (Sichuan)

F. H. Zhang
Zhang, Fa Hai; 张发海；Zhāng Fāhǎi
1955- **First publication: 1984**
• Employment: Department of Forestry, Guizhou Agricultural College（贵州农学院林学系）
• Research interest: Taxaceae [S]
• Published taxa: *Amentotaxus*
• Region: CHINA (Guizhou)

F. Zhang
Zhang, Fan; 张帆；Zhāng Fān
1993- **First publication: 2018**
• Employment: College of Forestry, Central South University of Forestry and Technology（中南林业科技大学林学院）
• Research interest: Fabaceae [S]
• Published taxa: *Apios*
• Region: CHINA

F. G. Zhang
Zhang, Fang Gang; 张方钢；Zhāng Fānggāng
1958- **First publication: 2003**
• Employment: Zhejiang Museum of Natural History（浙江自然博物馆）
• Research interest: Balsaminaceae, Rosaceae; Plants of Zhejiang [S]
• Published taxa: *Impatiens, Lauro-cerasus, Rosa, Rubus*
• Affiliation: ZM
• Location of specimens: ZM
• Region: CHINA (Zhejiang)

F. S. Zhang
Zhang, Fang Szu; Zhang, Fang Ci; **张芳赐；Zhāng Fāngcì; 張芳賜**
1932- **First publication: 1980**
• Employment: Yunnan Agricultural University（云南农业大学）
• Research interest: Theaceae [S]
• Published taxa: *Camellia*
• Region: CHINA (Yunnan)
• Also as: F. C. Zhang

F. Y. Zhang
Zhang, Fen Yao; 张芬耀；Zhāng Fēnyào
1986- **First publication: 2010**
• Employment: Forest Resources Monitoring Center of Zhejiang Province（浙江省森林资源监测中心）
• Research interest: Primulaceae, Rosaceae [S]
• Published taxa: *Ardisia, Cerasus*
• Region: CHINA (Zhejiang)

F. L. Chang
Chang, Fu Lai; 張福來；Zhāng Fúlái; 张福来
First publication: 2006
• Employment: Hwuluduen Orchids, Taiwan（台湾葫芦墩兰园）
• Research interest: Orchidaceae [S]
• Published taxa: × *Changara*, × *Hsuara*
• Region: CHINA (Taiwan)

G. M. Zhang
Zhang, Gang Min; 张钢民；Zhāng Gāngmín
1967- **First publication: 2002**
• Employment: Institute of Botany, Chinese Academy of Sciences（中国科学院植物研究所）
• Research interest: Pteridaceae; Pteridophytes [P]
• Published taxa: *Aleuritopteris, Argyrochosma, Cryptogramma, Leptolepidium*
• Affiliation: BJFC, HBFC
• Location of specimens: BJFC, HBFC
• Region: CHINA

G. C. Zhang
Zhang, Ge Chen; Zhang, Jason; Zhang, Ge Chen, Jason; **张戈宸；Zhāng Gēchén**
1992- **First publication: 2011**
• Employment: Rockwood Summit High School, Missouri, U.S.A.（美国密苏里州罗克伍德萨米特高中）
• Research interest: Balsaminaceae [S]
• Published taxa: *Impatiens*
• Region: CHINA (Sichuan)

Gui L. Zhang
Zhang, Gui Liang; 张贵良；Zhāng Guìliáng
1977- **First publication: 2017**

- Employment: Hekou Yao Autonomous County Forestry and Grassland Bureau, Yunnan（河口瑶族自治县林业和草原局）
- Research interest: Gesneriaceae, Sterculiaceae [S]
- Published taxa: *Firmiana, Loxostigma, Paraboea*
- Region: CHINA (Yunnan)

G. Y. Zhang

Zhang, Gui Yi; Chang, Gui Yi; 张贵一 ; Zhāng Guìyī; 張貴一

1935-2013 **First publication: 1987**

- Employment: Department of Biology, Harbin Normal University（哈尔滨师范大学生物系）
- Research interest: Asteraceae, Caryophyllaceae, Ranunculaceae [S]
- Published taxa: *Artemisia, Batrachium, Dendranthema, Dianthus*
- Affiliation: HANU
- Location of specimens: HANU
- Region: CHINA (Heilongjiang, Jilin, Liaoning)

Gui C. Zhang

Zhang, Gui Cai; 张桂才 ; Zhāng Guìcái; 張桂才

1936- **First publication: 1994**

- Employment: South China Institute of Botany, Chinese Academy of Sciences（中国科学院华南植物研究所）
- Research interest: Saxifragaceae [S]
- Published taxa: *Chrysosplenium*
- Location of specimens: IBSC
- Region: CHINA (Guangxi)

G. Z. Zhang

Zhang, Gui Zhen; 张桂珍 ; Zhāng Guìzhēn

First publication: 1984

- Employment: Institute of Materia Medica, Xinjiang Institute for Drug Control（新疆药品检验药物研究所）
- Research interest: Liliaceae [S]
- Published taxa: *Fritillaria*
- Location of specimens: XJDC
- Region: CHINA (Xinjiang)

G. J. Zhang

Zhang, Guo Jin; 张国进 ; Zhāng Guójìn

1989- **First publication: 2013**

- Employment: Institute of Botany, Chinese Academy of Sciences（中国科学院植物研究所）
- Research interest: Asteraceae [S]
- Published taxa: *Aster*
- Region: CHINA

G. L. Zhang

Zhang, Guo Liang; Chang, Kuo Liang; 张国梁 ; Zhāng Guóliáng; 張國樑

1934- **First publication: 1985**

- Employment: Department of Biology, Lanzhou University（兰州大学生物系）
- Research interest: Brassicaceae, Fagaceae, Poaceae; Plants of Gansu [S]
- Published taxa: *Aeluropus, Cardamine, Lithocarpus, Roegneria*
- Affiliation: LZU
- Location of specimens: LZD
- Region: CHINA (Gansu)

G. Q. Zhang

Zhang, Guo Qiang; 张国强 ; Zhāng Guóqiáng

1978- **First publication: 2013**

- Employment: The Orchid Conservation & Research Center of Shenzhen, Guangdong（广东省深圳市兰科植物保护研究中心）
- Research interest: Orchidaceae [S]
- Published taxa: *Cymbidium, Holcoglossum, Liparis, Pendulorchis, Yoania, Yunorchis*
- Region: CHINA

H. D. Zhang

Zhang, Hai Dao; Zhang, Hai Tau; 张海道 ; Zhāng Hǎidào; 張海道

1928- **First publication: 1965**

- Employment: Jiangxi Institute of Materia Medica（江西省药物研究所）
- Research interest: Apiaceae, Apocynaceae, Calycanthaceae [S]
- Published taxa: *Cyathella, Chimonanthus, Ligusticum*
- Affiliation: JXM
- Location of specimens: IMD, JXM
- Region: CHINA
- Also as: H. T. Zhang

H. Q. Zhang

Zhang, Hai Qin; 张海琴 ; Zhāng Hǎiqín

1977- **First publication: 2009**

- Employment: Triticeae Research Institute, Sichuan Agricultural University（四川农业大学小麦研究所）
- Research interest: Poaceae [S]
- Published taxa: *Asperella, Connorochloa, Leymus*
- Affiliation: SAUT
- Location of specimens: SAUT
- Region: CHINA

H. Y. Zhang

Zhang, Hai Yang; 张海洋 ; Zhāng Hǎiyáng

1954- **First publication: 1985**

- Employment: Normal College, Jiamusi University（佳木斯大学师范学院）
- Research interest: Solanaceae [S]
- Published taxa: *Solanum*

• Region: CHINA

H. F. Zhang

Zhang, Han Fu; 张汉夫；Zhāng Hànfū

1962- **First publication: 2012**

• Employment: Hanggai town, Anji, Zhejiang（浙江省安吉县杭垓镇）

• Research interest: Poaceae [S]

• Published taxa: *Phyllostachys*

• Region: CHINA (Zhejiang)

H. J. Zhang

Zhang, Han Jie; 张翰杰；Zhāng Hànjié 張翰傑，张瀚杰

1939-2007 **First publication: 1985**

• Employment: Yakeshi Forestry Administration Bureau, Inner Mongolia（内蒙古牙克石林业管理局）

• Research interest: Pinaceae [S]

• Published taxa: *Pinus*

• Region: CHINA (Nei Mongol)

H. Zhang

Zhang, Hao; Chang, Hao; 张浩；Zhāng Hào

1950- **First publication: 1984**

• Employment: Department of Pharmacognosy, Sichuan Medical College; College of Pharmacy, West China University of Medical Sciences; West China School of Pharmacy, Sichuan Univerisity（四川医学院生药学教研室；华西医科大学药学院；四川大学华西药学院）

• Research interest: Aristolochiaceae, Asteraceae, Crassulaceae, Melanthiaceae, Zingiberaceae [S]

• Published taxa: *Aristolochia, Curcuma, Erigeron, Paris, Rhodiola*

• Affiliation: WCU

• Location of specimens: WCU

• Region: CHINA (Sichuan)

• Also as: Hao Zhang

H. R. Zhang

Zhang, Hao Rang; 张浩然；Zhāng Hàorán

1969- **First publication: 1998**

• Employment: Southwest Forestry University（西南林业大学）

• Research interest: Poaceae [S]

• Published taxa: *Fargesia*

• Region: CHINA (Yunnan)

H. M. Chang

Chang, Ho Ming; 張和明；Zhāng Hémíng; 张和明

First publication: 2001

• Employment: Department of Biology, Taiwan Normal University（台湾师范大学生物系）

• Research interest: Lycopodiaceae, Selaginellaceae [P]

• Published taxa: *Huperzia, Selaginella*

• Region: CHINA (Taiwan)

Ho T. Chang

Chang, Ho Tseng; Chang, He Zeng; Zhang, He Zeng; 张盍曾；Zhāng Hézēng; 張盍曾

1939-2016 **First publication: 1975**

• Employment: Northwest Plateau Institute of Biology, Chinese Academy of Sciences（中国科学院西北高原生物研究所）

• Research interest: Apiaceae [S]

• Published taxa: *Ligusticum, Notopterygium, Pachypleurum*

• Region: CHINA (Xizang)

• Also as: H. T. Chang

Hung T. Chang

Chang, Hung Ta; Zhang, Hong Da; 张宏达；Zhāng Hóngdá; 張宏達

1914-2016 **First publication: 1948**

• Employment: Department of Biology, Sun Yat-sen University（中山大学生物系）

• Research interest: Acanthaceae, Altingiaceae, Aquifoliaceae, Caprifoliaceae, Centroplacaceae, Cycadaceae, Dipterocarpaceae, Elaeocarpaceae, Fabaceae, Fagaceae, Hamamelidaceae, Iteaceae, Lamiaceae, Lauraceae, Magnoliaceae, Malvaceae, Myrtaceae, Oleaceae, Pentaphylacaceae, Pittosporaceae, Rhamnaceae, Rosaceae, Stachyuraceae, Theaceae [S]

• Published taxa: *Actinodaphne, Adinandra, Altingia, Andrographis, Anneslea, Apterosperma, Baphicacanthus, Beilschmiedia, Bhesa, Callicarpa, Camellia, Chunia, Cinnamomum, Cleyera, Corylopsis, Cryptocarya, Cycas, Decaspermum, Distylium, Elaeocarpus, Eurya, Euryodendron, Exbucklandia, Excentrodendron, Gordonia, Grewia, Hamamelis, Hartia, Ilex, Itea, Kurrimia, Ligustrum, Linociera, Liquidambar, Lithocarpus, Litsea, Lonicera, Loropetalum, Machilus, Magnolia, Manglietia, Michelia, Myxopyrum, Neolitsea, Osmanthus, Paramanglietia, Parapyrenaria, Pittosporum, Premna, Pyrenaria, Pyrenocarpa, Rhodoleia, Rhynchosia, Rubus, Schima, Semiliquidambar, Sinowilsonia, Sloanea, Stachyurus, Stewartia, Sycopsis, Syzygium, Ternstroemia, Tilia, Tutcheria, Vatica, Ziziphus*

• Affiliation: SYS

• Location of specimens: SYS

• Region: CHINA

• Also as: H. T. Chang

H. W. Zhang

Zhang, Hong Wei; 张宏伟；Zhāng Hóngwěi

1966- **First publication: 2008**

• Employment: Administration of Zhejiang

Qingliangfeng National Natural Reserve (浙江清凉峰国家级自然保护区管理局)
- Research interest: Brassicaceae, Caryophyllaceae, Cyperaceae, Polygonaceae [S]
- Published taxa: *Carex, Cerastium, Persicaria, Sinalliaria*
- Region: CHINA (Zhejiang)

H. H. Zhang

Zhang, Hua Hai; 张华海; Zhāng Huáhǎi
1955- **First publication: 1993**
- Employment: Guizhou Provincial Administration Station for Wildlife (贵州省野生动植物管理站)
- Research interest: Araceae, Theaceae; Woody Plants [S]
- Published taxa: *Arisaema, Camellia*
- Affiliation: GFS
- Location of specimens: GFS, GZAC
- Region: CHINA (Guizhou)

H. J. Chang

Chang, Huey Ju; Zhang, Hui Zhou; 張惠珠; Zhāng Huìzhū; 张惠珠
First publication: 1975
- Employment: Institute of Botany, Taiwan University; Taiwan Forestry Research Institute, Taiwan Provincial Administrative Office (台湾大学植物学研究所; 台湾省政府农林厅林业试验所)
- Research interest: Paulowniaceae [S]
- Published taxa: *Paulownia*
- Region: CHINA (Taiwan)

J. L. Zhang

Zhang, Ji Lin; 张吉林; Zhāng Jílín; 張吉林
1936- **First publication: 1981**
- Employment: Sichuan School of Chinese Materia Medica (四川省中药学校)
- Research interest: Asparagaceae [S]
- Published taxa: *Aspidistra*
- Region: CHINA (Sichuan)

J. Q. Zhang

Zhang, Ji Quan; 张吉全; Zhāng Jíquán; 張吉全
1936- **First publication: 1982**
- Employment: Guizhou Research Institute of Forestry (贵州省林业科学研究所)
- Research interest: Poaceae [S]
- Published taxa: *Arundinaria, Phyllostachys*
- Region: CHINA (Guizhou)

Ji J. Zhang

Zhang, Ji Jun; 张记军; Zhāng Jìjūn
First publication: 2019
- Employment: College of Resource Environment and Tourism, Capital Normal University (首都师范大学资源环境与旅游学院)
- Research interest: Saxifragaceae [S]
- Published taxa: *Saxifraga*
- Region: CHINA (Hunan)

J. M. Zhang

Zhang, Ji Min; 张继敏; Zhāng Jìmǐn
1966- **First publication: 1999**
- Employment: Northwest China Institute of Botany, Chinese Academy of Sciences and Shaanxi Province (陕西省中国科学院西北植物研究所)
- Research interest: Crassulaceae, Primulaceae [S]
- Published taxa: *Hylotelephium, Myrsine*
- Region: CHINA

Ji Zu Zhang

Zhang, Ji Zu; 张继祖; Zhāng Jìzǔ; 張繼祖
1937-2002 **First publication: 1985**
- Employment: Xi' an Botanical Garden, Shaanxi (陕西省西安植物园)
- Research interest: Anacardiaceae [S]
- Published taxa: *Toxicodendron*
- Location of specimens: XBGH
- Region: CHINA (Shaanxi)
- IPNI as: J. Z. Zhang

J. Y. Zhang

Zhang, Jia Yan; 张加延; Zhāng Jiāyán; 張加延
1939- **First publication: 1989**
- Employment: Liaoning Institute of Pomology (辽宁省果树科学研究所)
- Research interest: Rosaceae [S]
- Published taxa: *Armeniaca*
- Region: CHINA (Liaoning)

J. X. Zhang

Zhang, Jia Xun; 张家勋; Zhāng Jiāxūn
First publication: 1992
- Employment: Zhengzhou University of Aeronautics (郑州航空工业管理学院)
- Research interest: Paeoniaceae [S]
- Published taxa: *Paeonia*
- Region: CHINA (Henan, Hunan, Gansu, Shaanxi)

J. H. Zhang

Zhang, Jian Hou; 张建侯; Zhāng Jiànhóu; 張建侯
1937- **First publication: 1983**
- Employment: Yunnan Institute of Tropical Botany, Chinese Academy of Sciences (中国科学院云南热带植物研究所)
- Research interest: Dipterocarpaceae [S]
- Published taxa: *Vatica*
- Region: CHINA (Yunnan)

J. J. Zhang

Zhang, Jian Jun; 张建军 ; Zhāng Jiànjūn

1957- **First publication: 2003**

- Employment: Forest & Fruit Tree Research Institute, Shanghai Academy of Agricultural Sciences（上海农业科学院林木果树研究所）
- Research interest: Taxodiaceae [S]
- Published taxa: × *Taxodiomeria*
- Region: [cult.]

Jian Q. Zhang

Zhang, Jian Qiang; 张建强 ; Zhāng Jiànqiáng

1987- **First publication: 2015**

- Employment: College of Life Sciences, Shaanxi Normal University（陕西师范大学生命科学学院）
- Research interest: Crassulaceae; Plants of Qinghai-Xizang Plateau; Plants of Qinling [S]
- Published taxa: *Rhodiola*
- Affiliation: SANU
- Location of specimens: SANU
- Region: CHINA (Sichuan)
- IPNI as: J. Q. Zhang

J. W. Zhang

Zhang, Jian Wen; 张建文 ; Zhāng Jiànwén

1980- **First publication: 2011**

- Employment: Kunming Institute of Botany, Chinese Academy of Sciences（中国科学院昆明植物研究所）
- Research interest: Asteraceae [S]
- Published taxa: *Crepidiastrum, Faberia, Melanoseris, Parasyncalathium, Youngia*
- Affiliation: KUN
- Location of specimens: KUN
- Region: CHINA

J. Yong Zhang

Zhang, Jian Yong; 张建勇 ; Zhāng Jiànyǒng

1956- **First publication: 2000**

- Employment: Shenzhen City Wutongshan Nurseries, Guangdong; The Orchid Conservation & Research Center of Shenzhen, Guangdong（广东省深圳市梧桐山苗圃总场；广东省深圳市兰科植物保护研究中心）
- Research interest: Orchidaceae [S]
- Published taxa: *Cymbidium, Paphiopedilum*
- Region: CHINA

Jian Z. Zhang

Zhang, Jian Zhong; 张建忠 ; Zhāng Jiànzhōng

First publication: 1985

- Employment: Herbarium, Shigatse Medicine Company, Xizang（西藏日喀则药材公司标本室）
- Research interest: Liliaceae [S]
- Published taxa: *Fritillaria*
- Region: CHINA (Xizang)
- IPNI as: J. Z. Zhang

J. L. Chang

Chang, Jin Lun; Zhang, Jin Lun; Chang, J. I.; 张进伦 ; Zhāng Jìnlún

1963- **First publication: 1984**

- Employment: Chongqing Institute of Medical Plant Cultivation（重庆市药物种植研究所）
- Research interest: Dryopteridaceae [P]
- Published taxa: *Ctenitis*
- Region: CHINA (Chongqing)
- IPNI as: J. I. Chang

J. N. Zhang

Zhang, Jin Ning; 张景宁 ; Zhāng Jǐngníng; 張景寧

1937- **First publication: 1998**

- Employment: College of Forestry, South China Agricultural University（华南农业大学林学院）
- Research interest: Orchidaceae [S]
- Published taxa: *Cymbidium, Liuguishania, Wutongshania*
- Region: CHINA (Guangdong)

J. Feng Zhang

Zhang, Jing Feng; 张静峰 ; Zhāng Jìngfēng

1975- **First publication: 2015**

- Employment: South China Botanical Garden, Chinese Academy of Sciences（中国科学院华南植物园）
- Research interest: Apocynaceae [S]
- Published taxa: *Hoya*
- Region: CHINA (Yunnan)
- IPNI as: J. F. Zhang

Jun Zhang

Zhang, Jun; 张军 ; Zhāng Jūn

1982- **First publication: 2018**

- Employment: Chongqing Institute of Medical Plant Cultivation（重庆市药物种植研究所）
- Research interest: Celastraceae, Cyperaceae; Medicinal Plants [S]
- Published taxa: *Carex, Parnassia*
- Affiliation: IMC
- Location of specimens: IMC
- Region: CHINA (Chongqing)
- IPNI as: J. Zhang

Kai Zhang

Zhang, Kai; 张凯 ; Zhāng Kǎi

1987- **First publication: 2019**

- Employment: South China Botanical Garden, Chinese Academy of Sciences（中国科学院华南植物园）
- Research interest: Oleaceae [S]
- Published taxa: *Jasminum*

- Region: CHINA (Yunnan)
- IPNI as: K. Zhang

K. Zhang

Zhang, Ke; 张珂 ; Zhāng Kē
1967- **First publication: 2014**
- Employment: College of Pharmacy, Anhui University of Chinese Medicine（安徽中医药大学药学院）
- Research interest: Liliaceae, Violaceae [S]
- Published taxa: *Amana, Viola*
- Location of specimens: ACM
- Region: CHINA (Anhui)

Kun C. Chang

Chang, Kun Cheng; 張坤城 ; Zhāng Kūnchéng; 张坤城
First publication: 2011
- Employment: Department of Forestry, Chung Hsing University（中兴大学森林学系）
- Research interest: Melastomataceae, Rosaceae [S]
- Published taxa: *Cotoneaster, Memecylon,*
- Region: CHINA (Taiwan)
- IPNI as: K. C. Chang

L. F. Zhang

Zhang, Lai Fa; 张来发 ; Zhāng Láifā; 張來發
1938- **First publication: 1990**
- Employment: Department of Biology, Shanghai Teachers' College of Technology（上海技术师范学院生物系）
- Research interest: Athyriaceae; Medicinal Plants [P]
- Published taxa: *Athyrium*
- Affiliation: SHCT
- Location of specimens: SHCT
- Region: CHINA (Hunan)

L. B. Zhang

Zhang, Li Bin; 张立彬 ; Zhāng Lìbīn
1962- **First publication: 1989**
- Employment: Hebei Agrotechnical Teachers' College; Department of Horticulture and Landscape Architecture, Hebei Normal University Of Science & Technology（河北农业技术师范学院；河北科技师范学院园艺园林系）
- Research interest: Rosaceae [S]
- Published taxa: *Armeniaca*
- Region: CHINA (Hebei)

L. C. Zhang

Zhang, Li Cun; 张立存 ; Zhāng Lìcún
1988- **First publication: 2017**
- Employment: College of Life Sciences, Nanjing Agricultural University（南京农业大学生命科学学院）
- Research interest: Berberidaceae [S]
- Published taxa: *Berberis*
- Region: CHINA (Sichuan)

Li Bing Zhang

Zhang, Li Bing; 张丽兵 ; Zhāng Lìbīng
1966- **First publication: 1994**
- Employment: Chengdu Institute of Biology, Chinese Academy of Sciences; Missouri Botanical Garden, U.S.A.（中国科学院成都生物研究所；美国密苏里植物园）
- Research interest: Anisophylleaceae, Aspleniaceae, Asteraceae, Athyriaceae, Balsaminaceae, Boraginaceae, Borthwickiaceae, Didymochlaenaceae, Dryopteridaceae, Fabaceae, Gesneriaceae, Hypodematiaceae, Lamiaceae, Lycopodiaceae, Ophioglossaceae, Polypodiaceae, Primulaceae, Pteridaceae, Pteridryaceae, Selaginellaceae, Solanaceae, Tectariaceae, Woodsiaceae; Pteridophytes [PS]
- Published taxa: *Aleuritopteris, Anisophyllea, Arachniodes, Asplenium, Athyrium,* Borthwickiaceae, *Callicarpa, Ctenitis, Dendrolycopodium,* Didymochlaenaceae, *Draconopteris, Dryopteris, Eritrichium, Gastoniella, Hovenkampia, Humbertacalia, Huperzia, Hymenasplenium, Hypodematium, Impatiens, Leptochilus, Lespedeza, Lunathyrium, Lycianthes, Lycopodioides, Lycopodium, Malaifilix, Megalastrum, Ophioderma, Palhinhaea, Petrocosmea, Phlegmariurus, Pleocnemia, Polydictyum, Polystichum, Premna, Primula,* Pteridryaceae, *Pteridrys, Pteris, Pyrrosia, Selaginella, Solanum, Soldanella, Spinulum, Tectaria, Woodsia, Youngia*
- Affiliation: CDBI
- Location of specimens: CDBI, CTC
- Region: [WORLD]

L. R. Zhang

Zhang, Li Rong; 张丽荣 ; Zhāng Lìróng
1975- **First publication: 2013**
- Employment: College of Biological Sciences and Technology, Beijing Forestry University（北京林业大学生物科学与技术学院）
- Research interest: Balsaminaceae [S]
- Published taxa: *Impatiens*
- Region: CHINA (Guangxi)

Li X. Zhang

Zhang, Li Xia; 张丽霞 ; Zhāng Lìxiá
1975- **First publication: 2019**
- Employment: Yunnan Branch, Institute of Medicinal Plant Development, Chinese Academy of Medical Sciences（中国医学科学院药用植物研究所云南分所）
- Research interest: Zingiberaceae [S]
- Published taxa: *Curcuma*

- Location of specimens: IMDY
- Region: CHINA (Yunnan)

Liang Zhang

Zhang, Liang; 张良 ; Zhāng Liáng

1985- **First publication: 2013**

- Employment: Kunming Institute of Botany, Chinese Academy of Sciences; Chengdu Institute of Biology, Chinese Academy of Sciences（中国科学院昆明植物研究所；中国科学院成都生物研究所）
- Research interest: Aspleniaceae, Didymochlaenaceae, Dryopteridaceae, Polypodiaceae, Pteridaceae, Pteridryaceae, Selaginellaceae; Pteridophytes [PS]
- Published taxa: *Arachniodes, Didymochlaena, Draconopteris, Gastoniella, Hymenasplenium, Leptochilus, Polydictyum, Polystichum,* Pteridryaceae, *Pteridrys, Pteris, Selaginella*
- Affiliation: CDBI
- Location of specimens: CDBI
- Region: CHINA

L. J. Zhang

Zhang, Lin Jing; 张林静 ; Zhāng Línjìng

1969- **First publication: 2015**

- Employment: School of Life Science, Shanxi Normal University（山西师范大学生命科学学院）
- Research interest: Balsaminaceae, Zygophyllaceae [S]
- Published taxa: *Impatiens*
- Affiliation: LINF
- Location of specimens: LINF
- Region: CHINA (Guangxi)

L. L. Zhang

Zhang, Lin Lin; 张林林 ; Zhāng Línlín

1982- **First publication: 2008**

- Employment: South China Botanical Garden, Chinese Academy of Sciences（中国科学院华南植物园）
- Research interest: Poaceae [S]
- Published taxa: *Schizostachyum*
- Region: CHINA (Hainan)

Lin Zhang

Zhang, Lin; 张琳 ; Zhāng Lín

1987- **First publication: 2016**

- Employment: Xinyang Normal University（信阳师范学院）
- Research interest: Colchicaceae [S]
- Published taxa: *Disporum*
- Region: CHINA

L. Zhang

Zhang, Ling; 张玲 ; Zhāng Líng

1970- **First publication: 2008**

- Employment: Xishuangbanna Tropical Botanical Garden, Chinese Academy of Sciences（中国科学院西双版纳热带植物园）
- Research interest: Dioscoreaceae [S]
- Published taxa: *Tacca*
- Region: CHINA (Yunnan)

Ling Zhang

Zhang, Ling; 张玲 ; Zhāng Líng

1975- **First publication: 2019**

- Employment: College of Pharmacy, Anhui University of Chinese Medicine（安徽中医药大学药学院）
- Research interest: Campanulaceae [S]
- Published taxa: *Adenophora, Codonopsis*
- Region: CHINA (Anhui)

M. D. Zhang

Zhang, Mei De; Chang, Mei De; **张美德 ; Zhāng Měidé**

1978- **First publication: 2006**

- Employment: Kunming Institute of Botany, Chinese Academy of Sciences（中国科学院昆明植物研究所）
- Research interest: Primulaceae [S]
- Published taxa: *Lysimachia*
- Region: CHINA (Yunnan)

M. J. Zhang

Zhang, Mei Jiao; 张美娇 ; Zhāng Měijiāo

1994- **First publication: 2019**

- Employment: School of Life Sciences, East China Normal University（华东师范大学生命科学学院）
- Research interest: Asteraceae [S]
- Published taxa: *Ainsliaea*
- Region: CHINA (Fujian)

M. C. Chang

Chang, Mei Chen; Zhang, Mei Zhen; **张美珍 ; Zhāng Měizhēn; 張美珍**

1933- **First publication: 1980**

- Employment: Shanghai Natural History Museum (Branch of Shanghai Science & Technology Museum)（上海自然博物馆(上海科技馆分馆)）
- Research interest: Dioscoreaceae, Oleaceae, Ranunculaceae [S]
- Published taxa: *Clematis, Dioscorea, Forsythia, Ligustrum, Syringa*
- Affiliation: SHM
- Location of specimens: SHM
- Region: CHINA

Meng Zhang

Zhang, Meng; 张蒙 ; Zhāng Méng

1995- **First publication: 2019**

- Employment: South China Botanical Garden, Chinese Academy of Sciences（中国科学院华南植物园）
- Research interest: Asteraceae [S]

- Published taxa: *Cremanthodium*
- Region: CHINA (Yunnan)
- IPNI as: M. Zhang

M. H. Zhang

Zhang, Meng Hua; 张梦华 ; Zhāng Mènghuá

1993- **First publication: 2017**

- Employment: College of Bio-resources and Environmental Science, Jishou University（吉首大学生物资源与环境科学学院）
- Research interest: Saxifragaceae [S]
- Published taxa: *Saxifraga*
- Region: CHINA (Hunan)

Mian Zhang

Zhang, Mian; 张勉 ; Zhāng Miǎn

1962- **First publication: 1997**

- Employment: School of Traditional Chinese Pharmacy, China Pharmaceutical University（中国药科大学中药学院）
- Research interest: Asteraceae; Medicinal Plants [S]
- Published taxa: *Ligularia*
- Affiliation: CPU, SXAU
- Location of specimens: CPU, SXAU
- Region: CHINA (Yunnan)
- Also as: M. Zhang

M. L. Zhang

Zhang, Ming Li; 张明理 ; Zhāng Mínglǐ

1959-2017 **First publication: 1997**

- Employment: Institute of Botany, Chinese Academy of Sciences; Xinjiang Institute of Ecology and Geography, Chinese Academy of Sciences（中国科学院植物研究所；中国科学院新疆生态与地理研究所）
- Research interest: Amaranthaceae, Asteraceae, Capparaceae, Caryophyllaceae, Cleomaceae, Fabaceae, Papaveraceae [S]
- Published taxa: *Arivela, Capparis, Caragana, Corispermum, Corydalis, Cremanthodium, Hartmaniella, Neobotrydium, Phyllolobium*
- Affiliation: PE, WUK
- Location of specimens: PE, WUK
- Region: CHINA
- IPNI as: M. Zhang

P. K. Chang

Chang, Pei Kao; 张培杲 ; Zhāng Péigǎo; 張培杲

First publication: 1960

- Employment: Northeast Forestry Institute（东北林学院）
- Research interest: Ranunculaceae [S]
- Published taxa: *Aconitum*
- Region: CHINA (Heilongjiang)

P. X. Zhang

Zhang, Pei Xin; 张培新 ; Zhāng Péixīn

1953- **First publication: 1985**

- Employment: Anji Forestry Bureau, Zhejiang（浙江省安吉县林业局）
- Research interest: Poaceae [S]
- Published taxa: *Indocalamus, Phyllostachys*
- Region: CHINA (Zhejiang)

P. C. Zhang

Zhang, Peng Chong; 张鹏翀 ; Zhāng Péngchōng

1982- **First publication: 2020**

- Employment: Hangzhou Botanical Garden（杭州植物园）
- Research interest: Amaryllidaceae [S]
- Published taxa: *Lycoris*
- Region: CHINA (Shaanxi)

P. Y. Zhang

Zhang, Pan Yung; Zhang, Peng Yun; Zhang, Peng Yong; 张鹏云 ; Zhāng Péngyún; 張鵬雲

1921-1994 **First publication: 1984**

- Employment: Department of Biology, Lanzhou University（兰州大学生物系）
- Research interest: Fabaceae, Tamaricaceae [S]
- Published taxa: *Myricaria, Tamarix*
- Affiliation: LZU
- Location of specimens: LZU
- Region: CHINA

Q. H. Zhang

Zhang, Qi Hong; 张其鸿 ; Zhāng Qíhóng

First publication: 1987

- Employment: Department of Pharmacy, Second Military Medical University（第二军医大学药学系）
- Research interest: Chloranthaceae [S]
- Published taxa: *Sarcandra*
- Region: CHINA

Q. T. Zhang

Zhang, Qi Tai; 张启泰 ; Zhāng Qǐtài; 張啟泰

1943-2014 **First publication: 1988**

- Employment: Kunming Institute of Botany, Chinese Academy of Sciences（中国科学院昆明植物研究所）
- Research interest: Araceae, Sapotaceae [S]
- Published taxa: *Arisaema, Diploknema*
- Region: CHINA (Yunnan)

Q. X. Zhang

Zhang, Qi Xiang; 张启翔 ; Zhāng Qǐxiáng

1956- **First publication: 2008**

- Employment: School of Landscape Architecture, Beijing Forestry University（北京林业大学园林学院）
- Research interest: Gesneriaceae [S]

- Published taxa: *Chirita, Chiritopsis*
- Region: CHINA (Guangxi)

Qian Zhang

Zhang, Qian; 张倩；Zhāng Qiàn

1987- **First publication: 2015**

- Employment: College of Life Sciences, Sichuan Agricultural University（四川农业大学生命科学学院）
- Research interest: Polygonaceae [S]
- Published taxa: *Fagopyrum*
- Region: CHINA (Sichuan)

Qiang Zhang

Zhang, Qiang; 张强；Zhāng Qiáng

1979- **First publication: 2012**

- Employment: Guangxi Institute of Botany, Chinese Academy of Sciences（广西壮族自治区中国科学院广西植物研究所）
- Research interest: Chloranthaceae, Gesneriaceae, Ranunculaceae [S]
- Published taxa: *Hemiboea, Petrocodon, Petrocosmea, Primulina, Semiaquilegia*
- Affiliation: IBK
- Location of specimens: IBK
- Region: CHINA (Guangxi)

Q. R. Zhang

Zhang, Qiao Rong; 张桥蓉；Zhāng Qiáoróng

1984- **First publication: 2019**

- Employment: Kunming Institute of Botany, Chinese Academy of Sciences（中国科学院昆明植物研究所）
- Research interest: Gentianaceae [S]
- Published taxa: *Gentianella*
- Region: CHINA (Xinjiang)

Q. Zhang

Zhang, Qing; 张青；Zhāng Qīng; 张清

First publication: 1989

- Employment: Department of Biology, Anhui University（安徽大学生物系）
- Research interest: Cyperaceae [S]
- Published taxa: *Carex*
- Region: CHINA (Anhui)

Q. B. Zhang

Zhang, Qing Bin; 张清斌；Zhāng Qīngbīn

1953- **First publication: 1991**

- Employment: Institute of Grassland, Xinjiang Academy of Animal Sciences（新疆畜牧科学院草原研究所）
- Research interest: Poaceae [S]
- Published taxa: *Elymus*
- Region: CHINA (Xinjiang)

Q. Q. Chang

Chang, Qing Qi; Zhang, Qing Qi; 张清其；Zhāng Qīngqí; 張清其

1935- **First publication: 1982**

- Employment: Department of Biology, Fujian Normal University; College of Life Sciences, Fujian Normal University（福建师范大学生物系；福建师范大学生命科学学院）
- Research interest: Actinidiaceae, Rubiaceae; Plants of Fujian [S]
- Published taxa: *Actinidia, Lasianthus*
- Affiliation: FNU
- Location of specimens: FNU
- Region: CHINA (Fujian)
- Also as: Q. Q. Zhang

C. E. Chang

Chang, Ching En; Chang, Chin Ann; Chang, Ch'ing Nen; Zhang, Qing En; Chang, Ching Un; 張慶恩；Zhāng Qìng'ēn; 张庆恩

First publication: 1963

- Employment: Department of Forest Resources Management, Pingtung Polytechnic Institute（屏东技术学院森林资源系）
- Research interest: Apocynaceae, Arecaceae, Celastraceae, Clusiaceae, Elaeocarpaceae, Eriocaulaceae, Lauraceae, Myrtaceae, Phyllanthaceae, Rosaceae, Rutaceae, Thymelaeaceae; Plants of Taiwan [S]
- Published taxa: *Antidesma, Calamus, Cinnamomum, Daphne, Elaeocarpus, Endiandra, Eriocaulon, Garcinia, Litsea, Maytenus, Phellodendron, Rubus, Skimmia, Syzygium, Trachelospermum, Wikstroemia*
- Affiliation: PPI
- Location of specimens: HAST, PPI
- Region: CHINA (Taiwan)

C. L. Chang

Chang, Ching Lian; 张庆连；Zhāng Qìnglián; 張慶連

1946- **First publication: 1980**

- Employment: Huojia County Forestry Bureau, Henan（河南省获嘉县林业局）
- Research interest: Betulaceae, Cannabaceae, Fagaceae, Pinaceae, Ranunculaceae, Rosaceae [S]
- Published taxa: *Betula, Carpinus, Celtis, Clematis, Pinus, Pyrus, Quercus*
- Region: CHINA (Henan)

Q. G. Zhang

Zhang, Qiu Gen; 张秋根；Zhāng Qiūgēn; 張秋根

1949- **First publication: 1983**

- Employment: Jiangxi Agricultural University（江西农业大学）
- Research interest: Anacardiaceae [S]

- Published taxa: *Rhus*
- Location of specimens: JXAU
- Region: CHINA (Jiangxi)

Qun Zhang

Zhang, Qun; 张群 ; Zhāng Qún

First publication: 2019

- Employment: Jinguangsi Provincial Nature Reserve, Yongping, Dali, Yunnan（云南省大理永平金光寺省级自然保护区）
- Research interest: Magnoliaceae [S]
- Published taxa: *Yulania*
- Region: CHINA (Yunnan)

R. T. Zhang

Zhang, Rao Ting; 张娆挺 ; Zhāng Ráotǐng; 張嬈挺

1935- **First publication: 1985**

- Employment: Department of Biology, Xiamen University（厦门大学生物系）
- Research interest: Acanthaceae; Plants of Fujian [S]
- Published taxa: *Acanthus*
- Affiliation: AU
- Location of specimens: AU
- Region: CHINA (Fujian)

R. B. Zhang

Zhang, Ren Bo; 张仁波 ; Zhāng Rénbō

1977- **First publication: 2015**

- Employment: Department of Biology, Zunyi Normal College（遵义师范学院生物系）
- Research interest: Crassulaceae, Gesneriaceae, Lamiaceae; Plants of Guizhou [S]
- Published taxa: *Didissandra, Paraphlomis, Petrocodon, Primulina, Sedum*
- Affiliation: ZY
- Location of specimens: ZY
- Region: CHINA (Guizhou)

R. Zhang

Zhang, Rong; 张荣 ; Zhāng Róng

1960- **First publication: 1993**

- Employment: College of Pharmacy, Second Military Medical University（第二军医大学药学院）
- Research interest: Poaceae [S]
- Published taxa: *Cymbopogon*
- Region: CHINA (Sichuan, Yunnan)

Rong Zhang

Zhang, Rong; 张荣 ; Zhāng Róng

1988- **First publication: 2018**

- Employment: Kunming Institute of Botany, Chinese Academy of Sciences（中国科学院昆明植物研究所）
- Research interest: Fabaceae [S]
- Published taxa: *Pseudarthria*
- Region: CHINA (Yunnan)
- IPNI as: R. Zhang

R. J. Zhang

Zhang, Rong Jing; 张荣京 ; Zhāng Róngjīng

1979- **First publication: 2006**

- Employment: South China Botanical Garden, Chinese Academy of Sciences（中国科学院华南植物园）
- Research interest: Magnoliaceae, Meliaceae; Plants of Hainan [S]
- Published taxa: *Magnolia, Munronia*
- Affiliation: SCAUB
- Location of specimens: CANT, SCAUB
- Region: CHINA (Fujian, Hainan)

R. S. Zhang

Zhang, Ru Song; 张如松 ; Zhāng Rúsōng

1950- **First publication: 1983**

- Employment: Department of Pharmacy, Zhejiang Medical University（浙江医科大学药学系）
- Research interest: Araliaceae [S]
- Published taxa: *Acanthopanax*
- Region: CHINA (Zhejiang)

Rui Zhang bis

Zhang, Rui; 张锐 ; Zhāng Ruì

1984- **First publication: 2020**

- Employment: Shanghai Chenshan Botanical Garden（上海辰山植物园）
- Research interest: Pteridaceae [P]
- Published taxa: *Ceratopteris*
- Affiliation: CSH
- Location of specimens: CSH
- Region: CHINA (Hainan)

R. L. Zhang

Zhang, Rui Li; 张睿鹂 ; Zhāng Ruìlí

1979- **First publication: 2016**

- Employment: School of Landscape Architecture, Beijing University of Agriculture（北京农学院园林学院）
- Research interest: Gesneriaceae [S]
- Published taxa: *Petrocodon, Primulina*
- Region: CHINA (Guangdong, Guangxi)

R. H. Chang

Chang, Roh Hwei; Zhang, Ruo Hui; 张若蕙 ; Zhāng Ruòhuì; 張若蕙

1931-2001 **First publication: 1979**

- Employment: Zhejiang Forestry College（浙江林学院）
- Research interest: Calycanthaceae, Fabaceae, Juglandaceae, Lardizabalaceae [S]
- Published taxa: *Carya, Chimonanthus, Juglans, Ormosia, Stauntonia*

- Affiliation: ZJFC
- Location of specimens: ZJFC
- Region: CHINA

S. Yun Chang

Chang, Shao Yun; Zhang, Shao Yun; 张绍云 ; Zhāng Shàoyún; 张绍芸

1955- **First publication: 1983**

- Employment: Simao Institute of Chinese Herbal Medicine, Yunnan（云南省思茅中草药研究所）
- Research interest: Balanophoraceae; Medicinal Plants [S]
- Published taxa: *Balanophora*
- Affiliation: SMN
- Location of specimens: SMN
- Region: CHINA (Yunnan)

Sheng L. Zhang

Zhang, Sheng Lin; 张盛林 ; Zhāng Shènglín

First publication: 1994

- Employment: Department of Horticulture, Southwest Agricultural College（西南农学院园艺系）
- Research interest: Araceae [S]
- Published taxa: *Amorphophallus*
- Region: CHINA (Sichuan)

S. B. Zhang

Zhang, Shi Bao; 张石宝 ; Zhāng Shíbǎo

1970- **First publication: 2018**

- Employment: Kunming Institute of Botany, Chinese Academy of Sciences（中国科学院昆明植物研究所）
- Research interest: Orchidaceae [S]
- Published taxa: *Pleione*
- Region: CHINA (Guangxi, Yunnan)

S. G. Zhang

Zhang, Shi Gang; 张时刚 ; Zhāng Shígāng

First publication: 2005

- Employment: Inmol Laboratory of Biotechnology of Yunnan（云南英茂生物技术实验室）
- Research interest: Orchidaceae [S]
- Published taxa: *Epigeneium*
- Region: CHINA (Yunnan)

S. C. Zhang

Zhang, Shi Cai; 张士才 ; Zhāng Shìcái

1960- **First publication: 1989**

- Employment: Gansu Desert Control Research Institute（甘肃省治沙研究所）
- Research interest: Fabaceae [S]
- Published taxa: *Caragana*
- Region: CHINA (Gansu)

S. L. Zhang

Zhang, Shi Liang; 张士良 ; Zhāng Shìliáng

1931- **First publication: 1987**

- Employment: Sichuan School of Chinese Materia Medica（四川省中药学校）
- Research interest: Saururaceae, Zingiberaceae; Medicinal Plants [S]
- Published taxa: *Houttuynia, Zingiber*
- Affiliation: EMA
- Location of specimens: EMA
- Region: CHINA (Sichuan)

S. Z. Zhang

Zhang, Shou Zhou; 张寿洲 ; Zhāng Shòuzhōu

1964- **First publication: 1990**

- Employment: Department of Biology, Inner Mongolia University; Fairy Lake Botanical Garden, Shenzhen & Chinese Academy of Sciences（内蒙古大学生物系；深圳市中国科学院仙湖植物园）
- Research interest: Araceae, Begoniaceae, Gesneriaceae, Magnoliaceae, Zygophyllaceae; Pteridophytes [S]
- Published taxa: *Begonia, Magnolia, Petrocosmea, Tetraena*
- Affiliation: SZG
- Location of specimens: SZG
- Region: CHINA

Shu D. Zhang

Zhang, Shu Dong; 张书东 ; Zhāng Shūdōng

1979- **First publication: 2008**

- Employment: Kunming Institute of Botany, Chinese Academy of Sciences（中国科学院昆明植物研究所）
- Research interest: Ericaceae, Melanthiaceae, Nartheciaceae, Rhamnaceae, Rosaceae [S]
- Published taxa: *Aletris, Paris, Rhododendron*
- Affiliation: KUN
- Location of specimens: KUN
- Region: CHINA (Yunnan)

S. L. Chang

Chang, Shu Lin; 张书林 ; Zhāng Shūlín; 張書林

1935- **First publication: 1979**

- Employment: Xiongyue Institute of Agricultural Science, Liaoning（辽宁省熊岳农科所）
- Research interest: Ulmaceae [S]
- Published taxa: *Ulmus*
- Region: CHINA (Liaoning)

S. M. Zhang

Zhang, Shu Mei; 张淑梅 ; Zhāng Shūméi

1963- **First publication: 2017**

- Employment: Dalian Natural History Museum（大连自然博物馆）

• Research interest: Balsaminaceae, Campanulaceae, Fabaceae, Lamiaceae, Ranunculaceae, Violaceae; Plants of N. E. China; Fungi [S]
• Published taxa: *Adenophora, Ajuga, Impatiens, Meehania, Mosla, Phlomoides, Ranunculus, Vicia, Viola*
• Affiliation: DNHM
• Location of specimens: DNHM
• Region: CHINA (Liaoning)

S. X. Zhang

Zhang, Shu Xian; 张淑贤 ; Zhāng Shūxián; 張淑賢
1930- **First publication: 1987**
• Employment: Northwest University (西北大学)
• Research interest: Liliaceae, Poaceae [S]
• Published taxa: *Fritillaria*
• Affiliation: WNU
• Location of specimens: WNU
• Region: CHINA (Shaanxi)

S. F. Zhang

Zhang, Shu Fan; 张树藩 ; Zhāng Shùfān; 張樹藩
1937- **First publication: 1983**
• Employment: Wuhan Institute of Botany, Chinese Academy of Sciences (中国科学院武汉植物研究所)
• Research interest: Asteraceae [S]
• Published taxa: *Dendranthema*
• Region: CHINA (Hubei)

S. J. Zhang

Zhang, Shu Jie; 张树杰 ; Zhāng Shùjié
1963- **First publication: 1995**
• Employment: Liaoning Institute of Sand Fixation and Forestation (辽宁省固沙造林研究所)
• Research interest: Pinaceae [S]
• Published taxa: *Pinus*
• Region: CHINA (Liaoning)

S. R. Zhang

Zhang, Shu Ren; 张树仁 ; Zhāng Shùrén
1962- **First publication: 1995**
• Employment: Institute of Botany, Chinese Academy of Sciences (中国科学院植物研究所)
• Research interest: Cyperaceae [S]
• Published taxa: *Carex, Cyperus, Fimbristylis, Kobresia, Schoenoplectus*
• Affiliation: PE
• Location of specimens: PE
• Region: CHINA

Shui L. Zhang

Zhang, Shui Li; 张水利 ; Zhāng Shuǐlì
1969- **First publication: 2020**
• Employment: College of Pharmaceutical Science, Zhejiang Chinese Medical University (浙江中医药大学药学院)
• Research interest: Araliaceae [S]
• Published taxa: *Eleutherococcus*
• Region: CHINA (Zhejiang)

S. Q. Zhang

Zhang, Su Qin; 张素芹 ; Zhāng Sùqín
First publication: 1999
• Employment: Shandong Institute of Traditional Chinese Medicine (山东省中医药研究所)
• Research interest: Asteraceae; Medicinal Plants [S]
• Published taxa: *Dendranthema*
• Affiliation: SDMP
• Region: CHINA (Shandong)

Tao Zhang

Zhang, Tao; 张涛 ; Zhāng Tāo
1982- **First publication: 2016**
• Employment: Administration of Xiaozhaizigou National Nature Reserve, Sichuan (四川省小寨子沟国家级自然保护区管理局)
• Research interest: Ranunculaceae [S]
• Published taxa: *Caltha*
• Region: CHINA (Sichuan)

T. L. Zhang

Zhang, Tian Lun; 张天伦 ; Zhāng Tiānlún
1955- **First publication: 1994**
• Employment: Guizhou Institute of Traditional Chinese Medicine (贵州省中药研究所)
• Research interest: Berberidaceae [S]
• Published taxa: *Epimedium*
• Location of specimens: GZTM
• Region: CHINA (Guizhou)

T. X. Zhang

Zhang, Tian Xi; 张天锡 ; Zhāng Tiānxī; 張天錫
1942- **First publication: 1983**
• Employment: Nanzhao County Forestry Bureau, Henan (河南省南召县林业局)
• Research interest: Magnoliaceae [S]
• Published taxa: *Magnolia*
• Region: CHINA (Henan)

T. J. Zhang

Zhang, Tie Jun; 张铁军 ; Zhāng Tiějūn
1962- **First publication: 1992**
• Employment: Tianjin Institute of Pharmaceutical Research (天津药物研究院)
• Research interest: Campanulaceae, Liliaceae [S]
• Published taxa: *Lobelia*
• Affiliation: TIPR
• Location of specimens: TIPR

• Region: CHINA

T. C. Chang

Chang, Ting Chien; Zhang, Ting Zhen; 张廷桢；Zhāng Tíngzhēn; 張廷楨

1938- First publication: 1981

- Employment: Shaanxi Institute of Forestry; Northwest Forestry College（陕西省林业科学研究所；西北林学院）
- Research interest: Cupressaceae, Salicaceae [S]
- Published taxa: *Populus, Sabina*
- Location of specimens: YL
- Region: CHINA (Shaanxi)
- Also as: T. Z. Zhang

Tong L. Zhang

Zhang, Tong Lin; 张同林；Zhāng Tónglín

1978- First publication: 2008

- Employment: Northwest Plateau Institute of Biology, Chinese Academy of Sciences（中国科学院西北高原生物研究所）
- Research interest: Poaceae [S]
- Published taxa: *Leymus, Orinus*
- Region: CHINA (Gansu, Qinghai)

W. Q. Zhang

Zhang, Wei Qian; 张维谦；Zhāng Wéiqiān

1962- First publication: 2002

- Employment: Weixin County Forestry Bureau, Yunnan（云南省威信县林业局）
- Research interest: Pinaceae [S]
- Published taxa: *Keteleeria*
- Region: CHINA (Yunnan)

Wei Zhang

Zhang, Wei; 张伟；Zhāng Wěi

1987- First publication: 2019

- Employment: Kunming Institute of Botany, Chinese Academy of Sciences（中国科学院昆明植物研究所）
- Research interest: Orchidaceae [S]
- Published taxa: *Pleione*
- Region: CHINA (Guangxi, Yunnan)
- IPNI as: W. Zhang

W. G. Zhang

Zhang, Wen Gen; 张文根；Zhāng Wéngēn

1983- First publication: 2015

- Employment: Jiangxi Agricultural University（江西农业大学）
- Research interest: Poaceae, Taxaceae [S]
- Published taxa: *Gelidocalamus, Taxus*
- Region: CHINA (Jiangxi)

Wen H. Zhang

Zhang, Wen Heng; 张文衡；Zhāng Wénhéng

1976- First publication: 2008

- Employment: Harvard University Herbaria, U.S.A.（美国哈佛大学植物标本馆）
- Research interest: Orchidaceae [S]
- Published taxa: *Spiranthes*
- Region: CHINA (Gansu)

W. H. Zhang

Zhang, Wen Hui; 张文辉；Zhāng Wénhuī

1955- First publication: 1984

- Employment: Northwest Forestry College; College of Forestry, Northwest A&F University（西北林学院；西北农林科技大学林学院）
- Research interest: Fagaceae [S]
- Published taxa: *Cyclobalanopsis, Quercus*
- Affiliation: NWFC
- Location of specimens: NWFC
- Region: CHINA (Shaanxi)

W. J. Chang

Chang, Wen Jin; Zhang, Wen Jin; 张文锦；Zhāng Wénjǐn; 張文錦

1933-2011 First publication: 1979

- Employment: Peng County Institute of Chinese Herbal Medicine, Sichuan; Pengzhou Institute for Drug Control, Sichuan（四川省彭县中草药研究所；四川省彭州市药品检验所）
- Research interest: Asteraceae, Cucurbitaceae, Ranunculaceae [S]
- Published taxa: *Aconitum, Delphinium, Hemsleya, Ligularia, Trichosanthes*
- Region: CHINA (Sichuan)
- Also as: W. J. Zhang

Wen J. Zhang

Zhang, Wen Ju; 张文驹；Zhāng Wénjū

1965- First publication: 1993

- Employment: Kunming Institute of Botany, Chinese Academy of Sciences（中国科学院昆明植物研究所）
- Research interest: Theaceae [S]
- Published taxa: *Camellia*
- Region: CHINA (Yunnan)

W. L. Zhang

Zhang, Wen Liu; 张文柳；Zhāng Wénliǔ

1988- First publication: 2017

- Employment: Xishuangbanna Tropical Botanical Garden, Chinese Academy of Sciences（中国科学院西双版纳热带植物园）
- Research interest: Orchidaceae [S]
- Published taxa: *Habenaria*
- Region: CHINA (Yunnan)

W. Y. Zhang

Zhang, Wen Yan; 张文燕；Zhāng Wényàn; 張文燕
1943- **First publication: 1993**
- Employment: Research Institute of Subtropical Forestry, Chinese Academy of Forestry（中国林业科学研究院亚热带林业研究所）
- Research interest: Poaceae [S]
- Published taxa: *Phyllostachys, Pleioblastus*
- Region: CHINA (Zhejiang)

X. N. Zhang

Zhang, Xian Nu; 张显努；Zhāng Xiǎnnǔ；張顯努
1937-2018 **First publication: 1984**
- Employment: Horticultural Research Institute, Yunnan Academy of Agricultural Sciences（云南省农业科学院园艺作物研究所）
- Research interest: Rutaceae [S]
- Published taxa: *Poncirus*
- Region: CHINA (Yunnan)

X. C. Zhang

Zhang, Xian Chun; 张宪春；Zhāng Xiànchūn
1964- **First publication: 1991**
- Employment: Institute of Botany, Chinese Academy of Sciences（中国科学院植物研究所）
- Research interest: Aspleniaceae, Athyriaceae, Davalliaceae, Dennstaedtiaceae, Diplaziopsidaceae, Dryopteridaceae, Gleicheniaceae, Hymenophyllaceae, Lycopodiaceae, Osmundaceae, Plagiogyriaceae, Polypodiaceae, Pteridaceae, Rhachidosoraceae, Selaginellaceae, Thelypteridaceae; Pteridophytes [P]
- Published taxa: *Adiantum, Aleuritopteris, Anisocampium, Antrophyum, Asplenium, Athyrium, Caobangia, Colysis, Coryphopteris, Cyclosorus, Davallia, Deparia,* Diplaziopsidaceae, *Diplazium, Diplopterygium, Goniophlebium, Haplopteris, Hemionitis, Huperzia, Hymenophyllum, Kaulinia, Lemmaphyllum, Lepidomicrosorium, Leptochilus, Leptolepidium, Lycopodium, Micropolypodium, Neolepisorus, Osmundastrum, Paragymnopteris, Parathelypteris, Phlegmariurus, Plagiogyria, Platygyria, Pteridium,* Rhachidosoraceae, *Selaginella, Selliguea, Stegnogramma, Teratophyllum, Vittaria*
- Affiliation: PE
- Location of specimens: PE
- Region: CHINA

X. Liang Zhang

Zhang, Xiao Liang; 张小亮；Zhāng Xiǎoliàng
1971- **First publication: 1998**
- Employment: Department of Biology, Sichuan Union University（四川联合大学生物系）
- Research interest: Brassicaceae [S]
- Published taxa: *Orychophragmus*
- Region: CHINA (Hubei)

H. P. Zhang

Zhang, Hsiao Ping; Zhang, Xiao Ping; 张小平；Zhāng Xiǎopíng
1957- **First publication: 1985**
- Employment: Department of Biology, Anhui Normal University; College of Life Sciences, Anhui Normal University（安徽师范大学生物系；安徽师范大学生命科学学院）
- Research interest: Asteraceae, Caryophyllaceae, Crassulaceae, Hydrangeaceae, Lamiaceae, Primulaceae, Saxifragaceae, Thymelaeaceae [S]
- Published taxa: *Chrysosplenium, Hydrangea, Lysimachia, Pseudocerastium, Rabdosia, Sedum, Wikstroemia*
- Affiliation: ANUB
- Location of specimens: ANUB
- Region: CHINA (Anhui)
- Also as: X. P. Zhang

Xiao F. Zhang

Zhang, Xiao Feng; 张晓峰；Zhāng Xiǎofēng
1954- **First publication: 2008**
- Employment: Northwest Plateau Institute of Biology, Chinese Academy of Sciences（中国科学院西北高原生物研究所）
- Research interest: Papaveraceae [S]
- Published taxa: *Meconopsis*
- Region: CHINA (Qinghai)
- IPNI as: X. F. Zhang

X. H. Zhang

Zhang, Xin Hua; 张新华；Zhāng Xīnhuá
1978- **First publication: 2005**
- Employment: South China Botanical Garden, Chinese Academy of Sciences（中国科学院华南植物园）
- Research interest: Magnoliaceae [S]
- Published taxa: *Michelia*
- Region: [ASIA]

X. Zhang

Zhang, Xin; 张鑫；Zhāng Xīn
1984- **First publication: 2007**
- Employment: College of Biological Sciences and Technology, Beijing Forestry University; College of Forestry, Northwest A&F University（北京林业大学生物科学与技术学院；西北农林科技大学林学院）
- Research interest: Gentianaceae, Tectariaceae [S]
- Published taxa: *Comastoma, Tectaria*
- Location of specimens: BJFC
- Region: [WORLD]
- IPNI as: Xin Zhang

X. J. Zhang

Zhang, Xin Jian; 张信坚 ; Zhāng Xìnjiān
1993- **First publication: 2018**
- Employment: School of Life Sciences, Sun Yat-sen University (中山大学生命科学学院)
- Research interest: Saxifragaceae [S]
- Published taxa: *Saxifraga*
- Region: CHINA (Hunan, Jiangxi)

X. X. Zhang

Zhang, Xing Xiang; 张兴祥 ; Zhāng Xīngxiáng; 張興祥
1938- **First publication: 1986**
- Employment: Heilongjiang Forestry Department (黑龙江省林业厅)
- Research interest: Pinaceae [S]
- Published taxa: *Pinus*
- Region: CHINA (Heilongjiang, Nei Mongol)

X. F. Zhang

Zhang, Xiu Fu; 张秀伏 ; Zhāng Xiùfú
1964- **First publication: 1995**
- Employment: Institute of Desert Research, Chinese Academy of Sciences (中国科学院兰州沙漠研究所)
- Research interest: Apiaceae, Brassicaceae, Ranunculaceae [S]
- Published taxa: *Bupleurum*
- Affiliation: LZD
- Location of specimens: LZD
- Region: CHINA (Shaanxi)

S. S. Chang

Chang, Siu Shih; Zhang, Xiu Shi; 张秀实 ; Zhāng Xiùshí; 張秀實
1918-2003 **First publication: 1984**
- Employment: Guizhou Academy of Sciences (贵州省科学院)
- Research interest: Cornaceae, Ericaceae, Moraceae, Sapindaceae; Plants of S. W. China [S]
- Published taxa: *Acer, Artocarpus, Cudrania, Dendrobenthamia, Ficus, Morus, Rhododendron*
- Affiliation: HGAS
- Location of specimens: HGAS, HWA, PE, SCFI
- Region: CHINA
- Also as: X. S. Zhang

Xiu Y. Zhang

Zhang, Xiu Yue; 张秀岳 ; Zhāng Xiùyuè
1968- **First publication: 2017**
- Employment: College of Life and Environmental Sciences, Hangzhou Normal University; Zhejiang Wuyi Forestry Farm (杭州师范大学生命与环境科学学院 ; 浙江省武义县林场)
- Research interest: Sapindaceae [S]
- Published taxa: *Acer*
- Region: CHINA (Zhejiang)
- IPNI as: X. Y. Zhang

H. Z. Zhang

Zhang, Hsue Zhong; Zhang, Hs. Z.; Chang, Hsuch Chung; Zhang, Xue Zhong; 张学忠 ; Zhāng Xuézhōng
First publication: 1988
- Employment: Department of Biology, Lanzhou University (兰州大学生物系)
- Research interest: Tamaricaceae [S]
- Published taxa: *Tamarix*
- Region: CHINA (Gansu)
- Also as: Hsue Z. Zhang; Hs. Z. Zhang

X. S. Zhang

Zhang, Xue Song; 张雪松 ; Zhāng Xuěsōng
1966- **First publication: 2003**
- Employment: Technology Promotion Station of Forest Management Bureau of Great Khingan (大兴安岭林业管理局森林经营局技术推广站)
- Research interest: Salicaceae [S]
- Published taxa: *Populus*
- Region: CHINA (Heilongjiang)

Ya Z. Zhang

Zhang, Ya Zhou; 张亚洲 ; Zhāng Yàzhōu
1995- **First publication: 2019**
- Employment: Kunming Institute of Botany, Chinese Academy of Sciences (中国科学院昆明植物研究所)
- Research interest: Asteraceae [S]
- Published taxa: *Saussurea*
- Region: CHINA (Sichuan)
- IPNI as: Y. Z. Zhang

Y. F. Chang

Chang, Yan Fu; Zhang, Yan Fu; 张彦福 ; Zhāng Yànfú; 張彥福
1939-2009 **First publication: 1983**
- Employment: Xinjiang College of Traditional Chinese Medicine (新疆中医学校)
- Research interest: Lamiaceae [S]
- Published taxa: *Nepeta*
- Region: CHINA (Xinjiang)

Y. M. Zhang

Zhang, Yan Min; 张艳敏 ; Zhāng Yànmǐn
1958- **First publication: 1990**
- Employment: Shandong Forestry School (山东省林业学校)
- Research interest: Crassulaceae, Cyperaceae, Polygonaceae; Bryophyte [S]
- Published taxa: *Carex, Polygonum, Sedum*
- Affiliation: SDFS
- Location of specimens: SDFS

- Region: CHINA (Shandong)

Yan J. Zhang

Zhang, Yan Jun; 张燕君；Zhāng Yànjūn
1982- **First publication: 2009**
- Employment: Wuhan Botanical Garden, Chinese Academy of Sciences（中国科学院武汉植物园）
- Research interest: Berberidaceae [S]
- Published taxa: *Epimedium*
- Affiliation: HIB
- Location of specimens: HIB
- Region: CHINA (Hubei)

Y. N. Chang

Chang, Yan Ni; 張燕郳；Zhāng Yànní; 张燕郳
First publication: 2013
- Employment: Nantou Forest District Office, Forestry Bureau, Council of Agriculture, "Executive Yuan"（"行政院"农业委员会林务局南投林区管理处）
- Research interest: Orchidaceae [S]
- Published taxa: *Bulbophyllum, Goodyera, Nervilia, Oberonia*
- Region: CHINA (Taiwan)

Y. G. Zhang

Zhang, Yao Guang; 张耀广; Zhāng Yàoguǎng
1990- **First publication: 2017**
- Employment: College of Life Sciences, Henan Agricultural University（河南农业大学生命科学学院）
- Research interest: Boraginaceae [S]
- Published taxa: *Oreocharis*
- Region: CHINA (Shaanxi)

Y. J. Zhang

Zhang, Yao Jia; 张耀甲；Zhāng Yàojiǎ; 張耀甲
1934-2021 **First publication: 1984**
- Employment: Department of Biology, Lanzhou University（兰州大学生物系）
- Research interest: Betulaceae, Fagaceae, Ranunculaceae, Tamaricaceae [S]
- Published taxa: *Betula, Lithocarpus, Myricaria, Ranunculus*
- Affiliation: LZU
- Location of specimens: LZU
- Region: CHINA (Gansu)

Yi H. Chang

Chang, Yi Han; 張藝翰；Zhāng Yìhàn; 张艺翰
1970- **First publication: 2014**
- Employment: Taiwan Forestry Research Institute, Council of Agriculture, "Executive Yuan"（"行政院"农业委员会林业试验所）
- Research interest: Dryopteridaceae, Pteridaceae, Thelypteridaceae; Pteridophytes [P]
- Published taxa: *Amauropelta, Christella, Cyrtomium, Dryopteris, Haplopteris*
- Affiliation: TAIF
- Region: CHINA (Taiwan)
- IPNI as: Y. H. Chang

Yi Zhang

Zhang, Yi; 张毅；Zhāng Yì
1957- **First publication: 1999**
- Employment: Shandong Institute of Pomology（山东省果树研究所）
- Research interest: Rosaceae [S]
- Published taxa: *Cerasus*
- Region: CHINA (Shandong)

Yi Zhang bis

Zhang, Yi; 张熠；Zhāng Yì
First publication: 2010
- Employment: Yunnan Yelantang Biotechnology Co., Ltd.（云南野兰堂生物科技有限公司）
- Research interest: Orchidaceae [S]
- Published taxa: *Stereochilus*
- Region: CHINA (Yunnan)
- IPNI as: Y. Zhang

Yin H. Zhang

Zhang, Yin Hong; 张荫鸿；Zhāng Yīnhóng
First publication: 1987
- Employment: Tongling Institute for Drug Control, Anhui（安徽省铜陵市药检所）
- Research interest: Liliaceae [S]
- Published taxa: *Fritillaria*
- Region: CHINA (Anhui)

Yong H. Zhang

Zhang, Yong Hong; 张永洪；Zhāng Yǒnghóng
1975- **First publication: 2006**
- Employment: Kunming Institute of Botany, Chinese Academy of Sciences; School of Life Science, Yunnan Normal University（中国科学院昆明植物研究所；云南师范大学生命科学学院）
- Research interest: Orchidaceae, Thymelaeaceae [S]
- Published taxa: *Cypripedium, Wikstroemia*
- Affiliation: YNUB
- Region: CHINA (Sichuan, Yunnan)

Y. T. Chang

Chang, Yong Tian; Zhang, Yong Tian; 张永田；Zhāng Yǒngtián; 張永田
1936- **First publication: 1963**
- Employment: Institute of Botany, Chinese Academy of Sciences; Fujian Institute of Subtropical Botany（中国科学院植物研究所；福建省亚热带植物研究所）
- Research interest: Amaranthaceae, Asteraceae,

Euphorbiaceae, Fagaceae, Lamiaceae, Malvaceae, Molluginaceae, Rosaceae, Santalaceae [S]
- Published taxa: *Alternanthera, Baliospermum, Blachia, Castanopsis, Corchoropsis, Crataegus, Croton, Cyclobalanopsis, Dendrotrophe, Eclipta, Fagus, Hibiscus, Lithocarpus, Maddenia, Mollugo, Ostodes, Paraphlomis, Quercus, Rubus, Trigonostemon*
- Affiliation: FJSI
- Location of specimens: FJSI, PE, SHM
- Region: CHINA

Yo. Zhang

Zhang, Yong; 张勇 ; Zhāng Yǒng

1963- **First publication: 1994**
- Employment: Department of Biology, Beijing Normal University（北京师范大学生物系）
- Research interest: Rosaceae; Plants of Gansu [S]
- Published taxa: *Potentilla*
- Affiliation: ZYTC
- Location of specimens: BJFC, ZYTC
- Region: CHINA (Hebei)

Yong Zhang

Zhang, Yong; 张勇 ; Zhāng Yǒng

1979- **First publication: 2002**
- Employment: Institute of Botany, Jiangsu Province and Chinese Academy of Sciences（江苏省中国科学院植物研究所）
- Research interest: Helwingiaceae [S]
- Published taxa: *Helwingia*
- Region: CHINA (Zhejiang)
- IPNI as: Yo. Zhang

Y. H. Zhang

Zhang, Yu Hua; Chang, Yu Hua; 张渝华 ; Zhāng Yúhuá; 張渝華

1939- **First publication: 1977**
- Employment: Institute of Pharmacy, Zhejiang Insitutute of Medical Sciences; Institute of Forestry and Soil Sciences, Chinese Academy of Sciences（浙江医学研究院药物研究所；中国科学院林业土壤研究所）
- Research interest: Apiaceae, Brassicaceae, Convolvulaceae, Papaveraceae, Rutaceae; Medicinal Plants [S]
- Published taxa: *Aniseia, Arabis, Cochleariella, Cochleariopsis, Corydalis, Dictamnus, Glehnia, Hilliella, Pternopetalum, Yinshania*
- Affiliation: ZJMA
- Region: CHINA
- Also as: Y. H. Chang

Y. J. Chang

Chang, Yu Jun; Zhang, Yu Jun; 张玉钧 ; Zhāng Yùjūn; 張玉均

1965- **First publication: 1991**
- Employment: College of Forestry Resources, Beijing Forestry University（北京林业大学林业资源学院）
- Research interest: Fabaceae, Lamiaceae; Woody Plants [S]
- Published taxa: *Astragalus, Elsholtzia, Scutellaria, Vitex*
- Affiliation: BJFC
- Region: CHINA (Beijing)

Y. L. Chang

Chang, Yui Liang; Chang, Yu Liang; Chang, Yü Liang; Zhang, Yu Liang; 张玉良 ; Zhāng Yùliáng; 張玉良

1923-1977 **First publication: 1955**
- Employment: Institute of Forestry and Soil Sciences, Chinese Academy of Sciences; Institute of Applied Ecology, Chinese Academy of Sciences（中国科学院林业土壤研究所；中国科学院沈阳应用生态研究所）
- Research interest: Boraginaceae, Brassicaceae, Cyperaceae, Ericaceae, Geraniaceae, Lythraceae, Plantaginaceae, Polygonaceae, Salicaceae [S]
- Published taxa: *Callitriche, Carex, Cyperus, Eleocharis, Erysimum, Geranium, Isatis, Monotropastrum, Myosotis, Polygonum, Pyrola, Rorippa, Salix, Scirpus, Trapa*
- Affiliation: IFP
- Location of specimens: IFP, NEAU
- Region: CHINA

Y. W. Zhang

Zhang, Yu Wu; 张玉武 ; Zhāng Yùwǔ

1963- **First publication: 2001**
- Employment: Fanjing Mountain Ecological Station, Guizhou Academy of Sciences（贵州省科学院梵净山生态站）
- Research interest: Orchidaceae; Plants of Guizhou [S]
- Published taxa: *Dendrobium*
- Affiliation: HGAS
- Location of specimens: HGAS
- Region: CHINA (Guizhou)

Y. X. Zhang

Zhang, Yu Xiao; 张玉霄 ; Zhāng Yùxiāo

1981- **First publication: 2010**
- Employment: Yunnan Academy of Biodiversity, Southwest Forestry University; Kunming Institute of Botany, Chinese Academy of Sciences（西南林业大学云南生物多样性研究院；中国科学院昆明植物研究所）
- Research interest: Poaceae [S]
- Published taxa: *Acidosasa, Dendrocalamus, Hsuehochloa, Oldeania, Pseudosasa, Yushania*

- Region: CHINA (Yunnan)

Y. Zhang

Zhang, Yuan; 张源 ; Zhāng Yuán

1955- **First publication: 1989**

- Employment: Department of Biology, Jiangxi University (江西大学生物系)
- Research interest: Ericaceae [S]
- Published taxa: *Vaccinium*
- Region: CHINA (Jiangxi)

Yue Zhang

Zhang, Yue; 张悦 ; Zhāng Yuè

1962- **First publication: 2002**

- Employment: Institute of Natural Resources, Heilongjiang Academy of Sciences (黑龙江省科学院自然资源研究所)
- Research interest: Ericaceae, Onagraceae, Orobanchaceae [S]
- Published taxa: *Boschniakia, Chamaenerion, Empetrum, Vaccinium*
- Region: CHINA (Nei Mongol)

Yue J. Zhang

Zhang, Yue Jin; 张跃进 ; Zhāng Yuèjìn

1960- **First publication: 1991**

- Employment: Northwest China Institute of Botany, Chinese Academy of Sciences and Shaanxi Province (陕西省中国科学院西北植物研究所)
- Research interest: Berberidaceae; Gymnospermae [S]
- Published taxa: *Berberis*
- Affiliation: WUK
- Location of specimens: WUK
- Region: CHINA (Shaanxi)
- IPNI as: Y. J. Zhang

Y. Z. Zhang

Zhang, Yun Zhong; 张云忠 ; Zhāng Yúnzhōng

1956- **First publication: 1991**

- Employment: Forestry Bureau of Dukou Municipal, Sichuan (四川省渡口市林业局)
- Research interest: Theaceae [S]
- Published taxa: *Camellia*
- Region: CHINA (Sichuan)

Y. B. Chang

Chang, Yin Bin; Zhang, Yun Bing; Chang, Yi Bi; Chang, Yun Bing; 张韵冰 ; Zhāng Yùnbīng; 張韻冰

1921-2019 **First publication: 1981**

- Employment: Northeast Forestry Institute (东北林学院)
- Research interest: Asteraceae, Burmanniaceae, Celastraceae, Melastomataceae, Orchidaceae, Polygonaceae, Rosaceae, Rutaceae, Saxifragaceae [S]
- Published taxa: *Agrimonia, Anoectochilus, Burmannia, Citrus, Euonymus, Fordiophyton, Klasea, Olgaea, Pertya, Polygonum, Prunus, Rosa, Rubus, Saxifraga, Spiraea*
- Location of specimens: NEFI
- Region: CHINA (Zhejiang)

Zhan Y. Zhang

Zhang, Zhan Ying; Zhang, Zan Ying; 张赞英 ; Zhāng Zànyīng; 張讚英

1945- **First publication: 1987**

- Employment: Kunming Institute of Botany, Chinese Academy of Sciences (中国科学院昆明植物研究所)
- Research interest: Theaceae [S]
- Published taxa: *Camellia*
- Region: CHINA (Guizhou)

C. Y. Chang

Chang, Che Yung; Chang, Tseh Yung; Chang, Chieh Yun; Zhang, Ze Rong; 张泽荣 ; Zhāng Zéróng; 張澤榮

1932-1997 **First publication: 1966**

- Employment: Department of Biology, Sichuan University (四川大学生物系)
- Research interest: Actinidiaceae, Celastraceae, Dipentodontaceae, Elaeagnaceae, Sabiaceae, Sapindaceae, Thymelaeaceae [S]
- Published taxa: *Acer, Actinidia, Clematoclethra, Daphne, Elaeagnus, Euonymus, Gymnosporia, Maytenus, Meliosma, Perrottetia, Sabia, Wikstroemia*
- Affiliation: SZ
- Location of specimens: SCFI, SZ
- Region: CHINA (Sichuan, Xizang, Yunnan)

C. C. Chang

Chang, Chao Chien; Chang, Chao Ch'ien; Zhang, Zhao Qian; 张肇骞 ; Zhāng Zhàoqiān; 張肇騫

1900-1972 **First publication: 1933**

- Employment: Department of Biology, National Central University; Fan Memorial Institute of Biology; China Foundation for the Promotion of Education and Culture; Institute of Systematic Botany, Academia Sinica; Institute of Botany, Chinese Academy of Sciences; South China Institute of Botany, Chinese Academy of Sciences (国立中央大学生物系；静生生物调查所；中华教育文化基金董事会；中国科学院植物分类研究所；中国科学院植物研究所；中国科学院华南植物研究所)
- Research interest: Asteraceae, Poaceae, Ranunculaceae [S]
- Published taxa: *Anaphalis, Anemone, Aster, Blumea, Calotis, Chrysanthemum, Cicerbita, Gelidocalamus, Heteroplexis, Lactuca, Ligularia, Paraprenanthes, Prenanthes, Saussurea, Scorzonera, Senecio, Stenoseris, Vernonia*

- Affiliation: IBSC
- Location of specimens: IBSC
- Region: CHINA

C. T. Chang

Chang, Che Tseng; 张哲增 ; Zhāng Zhézēng

1931- **First publication: 1974**

- Employment: South China Institute of Botany, Chinese Academy of Sciences（中国科学院华南植物研究所）
- Research interest: Asteraceae [S]
- Published taxa: *Blumea*
- Region: CHINA (Yunnan)

C. W. Chang

Chang, Chen Wan; Zhang, Zhen Wan; 张振万 ; Zhāng Zhènwàn; 張振萬

1924-1997 **First publication: 1979**

- Employment: Northwest China Institute of Botany, Chinese Academy of Sciences and Shaanxi Province（陕西省中国科学院西北植物研究所）
- Research interest: Actinidiaceae, Fabaceae [S]
- Published taxa: *Actinidia, Astragalus, Caesalpinia, Caragana, Lathyrus, Maackia, Medicago, Melissitus, Oxytropis*
- Affiliation: WUK
- Location of specimens: WUK
- Region: CHINA

Chih Y. Chang

Chang, Chih Yi; 張之毅 ; Zhāng Zhīyì; 张之毅

First publication: 2019

- Employment: Department of Forestry, Chung Hsing University（中兴大学森林学系）
- Research interest: Asteraceae [S]
- Published taxa: *Cirsium*
- Region: CHINA (Taiwan)

C. Yu Chang

Chang, Chi Yu; Chang, Chih Yu; Zhang, Zhi Yu; 张芝玉 ; Zhāng Zhīyù; 張芝玉

1937- **First publication: 1982**

- Employment: Institute of Botany, Chinese Academy of Sciences（中国科学院植物研究所）
- Research interest: Melanthiaceae; Plant Systematics [S]
- Published taxa: *Paris*
- Affiliation: SMMU-BH
- Region: CHINA

Zhi F. Zhang

Zhang, Zhi Feng; 张志峰 ; Zhāng Zhìfēng

First publication: 2010

- Employment: Ethnic Pharmaceutical Institute, Southwest University for Nationalities（西南民族大学民族药物研究所）
- Research interest: Asteraceae [S]
- Published taxa: *Erigeron*
- Region: CHINA (Sichuan)
- IPNI as: Z. F. Zhang

Z. G. Zhang

Zhang, Zhi Guang; 张志光 ; Zhāng Zhìguāng; 張志光

1934- **First publication: 2004**

- Employment: Hunan Normal University（湖南师范大学）
- Research interest: Asteraceae. [MS]
- Published taxa: *Aster*
- Region: CHINA (Hubei)

Z. X. Zhang

Zhang, Zhi Xiang; 张志翔 ; Zhāng Zhìxiáng

1960- **First publication: 1999**

- Employment: College of Biological Sciences and Technology, Beijing Forestry University; School of Nature Conservation, Beijing Forestry University（北京林业大学生物科学与技术学院；北京林业大学自然保护区学院）
- Research interest: Celastraceae, Elaeocarpaceae, Eriocaulaceae, Magnoliaceae, Salicaceae, Saxifragaceae [S]
- Published taxa: *Celastrus, Dianyuea, Eriocaulon, Glyptopetalum, Manglietia, Microtropis, Parnassia, Salix, Saxifraga, Sloanea*
- Affiliation: BJFC
- Location of specimens: BJFC
- Region: CHINA

Z. Ying Zhang

Zhang, Zhi Ying; Chang, Chih Ying; 张志英 ; Zhāng Zhìyīng; 張志英

1937-2011 **First publication: 1980**

- Employment: Northwest China Institute of Botany, Chinese Academy of Sciences and Shaanxi Province; Xianyang College of Traditional Chinese Medicine（陕西省中国科学院西北植物研究所；咸阳中医学院）
- Research interest: Aquifoliaceae, Asteraceae, Boraginaceae, Ebenaceae, Oleaceae, Rubiaceae, Salicaceae, Scrophulariaceae, Styracaceae; Plants of Shaanxi [S]
- Published taxa: *Buddleja, Cacalia, Diospyros, Ilex, Leptodermis, Ligustrum, Rubia, Senecio, Sinojohnstonia, Styrax, Xylosma*
- Affiliation: WUK
- Location of specimens: WUK
- Region: CHINA (Gansu, Shaanxi)

Zhi Y. Zhang

Zhang, Zhi Yun; 张志耘 ; Zhāng Zhìyún

1950- **First publication: 1979**

- Employment: Institute of Botany, Chinese Academy of Sciences（中国科学院植物研究所）
- Research interest: Cucurbitaceae, Juncaceae, Orobanchaceae, Pittosporaceae, Solanaceae, Stachyuraceae [S]
- Published taxa: *Actinostemma, Anisodus, Cistanche, Hodgsonia, Juncus, Lycianthes, Orobanche, Physaliastrum, Pittosporum, Schizopepon, Siraitia, Stachyurus, Thladiantha*
- Affiliation: PE
- Region: CHINA

Z. Zhang

Zhang, Zhi; 张智 ; Zhāng Zhì

1942- **First publication: 1989**

- Employment: Anhui Agricultural College（安徽农学院）
- Research interest: Cucurbitaceae [S]
- Published taxa: *Gynostemma, Thladiantha*
- Affiliation: AAUB
- Location of specimens: AAUB
- Region: CHINA (Anhui)

Z. X. Chang

Chang, Zhi Xiang; 張智翔 ; Zhāng Zhìxiáng; 张智翔

First publication: 2020

- Employment: Tsing Hua University, Taiwan（台湾清华大学）
- Research interest: Aspleniaceae [P]
- Published taxa: *Asplenium*
- Region: CHINA (Taiwan)

Zhong S. Zhang

Zhang, Zhong Shuai; 张中帅 ; Zhāng Zhōngshuài

1990- **First publication: 2016**

- Employment: Institute of Botany, Chinese Academy of Sciences（中国科学院植物研究所）
- Research interest: Poaceae [S]
- Published taxa: *Achnatherum, Ptilagrostis*
- Region: CHINA
- IPNI as: Z. S. Zhang

Z. B. Zhang

Zhang, Zi Bin; 张自斌 ; Zhāng Zìbīn

1978- **First publication: 2015**

- Employment: Flowers Research Institute, Guangxi Academy of Agricultural Sciences（广西农业科学院花卉研究所）
- Research interest: Orchidaceae [S]
- Published taxa: *Habenaria, Oreorchis*
- Region: CHINA (Guangxi)

Z. S. Zhang

Zhang, Zong Shi; 张宗师 ; Zhāng Zōngshī

1966?- **First publication: 1994**

- Employment: Guizhou Botanical Garden（贵州省植物园）
- Research interest: Actinidiaceae [S]
- Published taxa: *Actinidia*
- Region: CHINA (Guizhou)

C. I. Chang

Chang, Chun Iao; Chang, Zung Yao; 张宗尧 ; Zhāng Zōngyáo; 張宗堯

1930-1997 **First publication: 1981**

- Employment: Henan Agricultural University（河南农业大学）
- Research interest: Fagaceae [S]
- Published taxa: *Quercus*
- Location of specimens: HEAC
- Region: CHINA (Henan)
- Also as: Z. Y. Chang

D. Y. Zhang

Zhang, Di Yang; 章迪杨 ; Zhāng Díyáng

1992- **First publication: 2020**

- Employment: College of Landscape Architecture, Fujian Agriculture and Forestry University（福建农林大学园林学院）
- Research interest: Orchidaceae [S]
- Published taxa: *Cymbidium*
- Region: CHINA (Yunnan)

Hui Z. Zhang

Zhang, Hui Zhi; 章恢志 ; Zhāng Huīzhì

1911-1991 **First publication: 2015**

- Employment: Department of Horticulture, Huazhong Agricultural University（华中农业大学园艺系）
- Research interest: Rosaceae [S]
- Published taxa: *Eriobotrya*
- Region: CHINA (Sichuan)
- IPNI as: H. Z. Zhang

S. Y. Chang

Chang, Shao Yao; Zhang, Shao Yao; 章绍尧 ; Zhāng Shàoyáo; 章紹堯

1914-2001 **First publication: 1963**

- Employment: Hangzhou Botanical Garden（杭州植物园）
- Research interest: Calycanthaceae; Woody Plants [S]
- Published taxa: *Calycanthus, Sinocalycanthus*
- Affiliation: HHBG
- Location of specimens: HHBG, PE
- Region: CHINA

W. P. Zhang

Zhang, Wei Ping; Zhang, Wi Pien; 章伟平 ; Zhāng Wěipíng

1963- **First publication: 1988**

- Employment: Southwest Forestry College（西南林学院）
- Research interest: Poaceae [S]
- Published taxa: *Chimonobambusa, Schizostachyum*
- Affiliation: SWFC
- Location of specimens: SWFC
- Region: CHINA (Yunnan)

A. C. Chao

Chao, Ai Cheng; Chao, Ai Chêng; Chao, Ai Chên; Zhao, Ai Zhen; 赵爱真 ; Zhào Àizhēn; 趙愛真

1911-? **First publication: 1958**

- Employment: Department of Biology, Sun Yat-sen University（中山大学生物系）
- Research interest: Combretaceae [S]
- Published taxa: *Terminalia, Combretum*
- Location of specimens: SYS
- Region: CHINA

B. Zhao

Zhao, Bing; 赵冰 ; Zhào Bīng

1980- **First publication: 2007**

- Employment: School of Landscape Architecture, Beijing Forestry University（北京林业大学园林学院）
- Research interest: Calycanthaceae [S]
- Published taxa: *Chimonanthus*
- Region: CHINA (Hubei)

B. X. Zhao

Zhao, Bing Xiang; 赵炳祥 ; Zhào Bǐngxiáng

First publication: 1998

- Employment: Department of Biology, Sichuan Union University（四川联合大学生物系）
- Research interest: Brassicaceae [S]
- Published taxa: *Orychophragmus*
- Region: CHINA (Shaanxi)

Bo Zhao

Zhao, Bo; 赵博 ; Zhào Bó

1981- **First publication: 2012**

- Employment: Guangxi Institute of Botany, Chinese Academy of Sciences（广西壮族自治区中国科学院广西植物研究所）
- Research interest: Gesneriaceae [S]
- Published taxa: *Primulina*
- Region: CHINA (Guangxi)

C. H. Zhao

Zhao, Chang Heng; 赵昌恒 ; Zhào Chānghéng

1968- **First publication: 1993**

- Employment: Department of Forestry, Anhui Agricultural College（安徽农学院林学系）
- Research interest: Poaceae [S]
- Published taxa: *Bambusa, Phyllostachys*
- Region: CHINA (Anhui)

C. Y. Chao

Chao, Chuan Ying; 趙傳纓 ; Zhào Chuányīng; 赵传缨

1920- **First publication: 1961**

- Employment: Institute of Botany, Taiwan University（台湾大学植物学研究所）
- Research interest: Apiaceae, Araliaceae [S]
- Published taxa: *Angelica, Bupleurum, Hydrocotyle, Oenanthe*
- Region: CHINA (Taiwan)

T. C. Chao

Chao, Ta Chang; Chao, Ta Ch'ang; Zhao, Da Chang; 赵大昌 ; Zhào Dàchāng; 趙大昌

1926- **First publication: 1955**

- Employment: Herbarium, Institute of Applied Ecology, Chinese Academy of Sciences（中国科学院沈阳应用生态研究所植物标本馆）
- Research interest: Oleaceae [S]
- Published taxa: *Syringa*
- Affiliation: IFP
- Location of specimens: IFP
- Region: CHINA (Liaoning)

D. W. Zhao

Zhao, Dong Wu; 赵东武 ; Zhào Dōngwǔ

1972- **First publication: 2007**

- Employment: Xinzheng City Forestry Bureau, Henan（河南省新郑市林业局）
- Research interest: Magnoliaceae [S]
- Published taxa: *Yulania*
- Region: CHINA (Henan)

F. Z. Zhao

Zhao, Fa Zhu; 赵法珠 ; Zhào Fǎzhū; 趙法珠

1935- **First publication: 1991**

- Employment: Pingyi County Forestry Bureau, Shandong（山东省平邑县林业局）
- Research interest: Betulaceae [S]
- Published taxa: *Carpinus*
- Region: CHINA (Shandong)

F. Zhao

Zhao, Fei; 赵飞 ; Zhào Fēi

1989- **First publication: 2017**

- Employment: Kunming Institute of Botany, Chinese Academy of Sciences（中国科学院昆明植物研究所）
- Research interest: Lamiaceae [S]
- Published taxa: *Scutellaria*

• Region: CHINA (Yunnan)

H. T. Zhao

Zhao, Hou Tao; 赵厚涛 ; Zhào Hòutāo

1985- **First publication: 2010**

• Employment: Kunming Institute of Botany, Chinese Academy of Sciences（中国科学院昆明植物研究所）
• Research interest: Gesneriaceae; Pteridophytes [S]
• Published taxa: *Petrocosmea*
• Affiliation: GYBG
• Location of specimens: GYBG
• Region: CHINA (Yunnan)

H. R. Zhao

Zhao, Hui Ru; 赵惠如 ; Zhào Huìrú; 趙惠如

1913-2000 **First publication: 1985**

• Employment: Department of Biology, Nanjing Normal College（南京师范学院生物系）
• Research interest: Poaceae [S]
• Published taxa: *Ischaemum, Phyllostachys, Pseudosasa*
• Affiliation: NJNU
• Location of specimens: N, NJNU
• Region: CHINA

J. R. Zhao

Zhao, Jia Rong; 赵家荣 ; Zhào Jiāróng

1952- **First publication: 2007**

• Employment: Wuhan Botanical Garden, Chinese Academy of Sciences（中国科学院武汉植物园）
• Research interest: Polygonaceae [S]
• Published taxa: *Polygonum*
• Region: CHINA (Hainan)

C. T. Chao

Chao, Chien Ti; 趙建棣 ; Zhào Jiàndì; 赵建棣

First publication: 2011

• Employment: School of Life Science, Taiwan Normal University; Department of Forestry, Chung Hsing University（台湾师范大学生命科学学院；中兴大学林学系）
• Research interest: Apocynaceae, Asparagaceae, Colchicaceae [S]
• Published taxa: *Disporum, Heteropolygonatum, Maianthemum, Polygonatum, Tylophora*
• Region: CHINA (Taiwan)

J. Zhao

Zhao, Jie; 赵杰 ; Zhào Jié

1965- **First publication: 2007**

• Employment: Xinzheng City Forestry Bureau, Henan（河南省新郑市林业局）
• Research interest: Magnoliaceae [S]
• Published taxa: *Yulania*
• Region: CHINA (Henan)

Jun H. Zhao

Zhao, Jun Hua; 赵俊华 ; Zhào Jùnhuá

1955- **First publication: 2011**

• Employment: Guiyang College of Traditional Chinese Medicine（贵阳中医学院）
• Research interest: Pteridaceae, Selaginellaceae [P]
• Published taxa: *Pteris, Selaginella*
• Location of specimens: GZTM
• Region: CHINA (Guizhou)
• IPNI as: J. H. Zhao

L. H. Zhao

Zhao, Li Hua; 赵丽华 ; Zhào Lìhuá

1985- **First publication: 2014**

• Employment: College of Life Sciences, Sichuan University（四川大学生命科学学院）
• Research interest: Asparagaceae [S]
• Published taxa: *Polygonatum*
• Region: CHINA (Yunnan)

L. N. Zhao

Zhao, Li Na; 赵莉娜 ; Zhào Lìnà

1985- **First publication: 2020**

• Employment: Institute of Botany, Chinese Academy of Sciences（中国科学院植物研究所）
• Research interest: Lauraceae [S]
• Published taxa: *Phoebe*
• Region: CHINA (Yunnan)

L. Q. Zhao

Zhao, Li Qing; 赵利清 ; Zhào Lìqīng

1979- **First publication: 2003**

• Employment: School of Life Sciences, Inner Mongolia University（内蒙古大学生命科学学院）
• Research interest: Asteraceae, Caryophyllaceae, Cyperaceae, Fabaceae, Gentianaceae, Lamiaceae, Liliaceae, Poaceae, Ranunculaceae, Rhamnaceae, Rosaceae [S]
• Published taxa: *Agropyron, Anagallidium, Astragalus, Caragana, Carex, Chrysanthemum, Dracocephalum, Gagea, Pulsatilla, Rhamnus, Rosa, Silene, Stipa*
• Affiliation: HIMC
• Location of specimens: HIMC
• Region: CHINA (Nei Mongol)

Liang Zhao

Zhao, Liang; 赵亮 ; Zhào Liàng

1982- **First publication: 2013**

• Employment: College of Life Sciences, Northwest A&F University（西北农林科技大学生命科学学院）
• Research interest: Ranunculaceae [S]
• Published taxa: *Ranunculus*
• Affiliation: WUK
• Region: CHINA (Shaanxi)

• IPNI as: L. Zhao

L. Zhao

Zhao, Ling; 赵泠; Zhào Líng; 趙泠

1923-2009 **First publication: 1988**

• Employment: Shenyang Agricultural University (沈阳农业大学)
• Research interest: Acanthaceae, Betulaceae [S]
• Published taxa: *Alnus, Corylus*
• Affiliation: SYAUF
• Location of specimens: SYAUF
• Region: CHINA (Liaoning)

M. H. Zhao

Zhao, Mei Hua; 赵美华; Zhào Měihuá; 趙美華

1934- **First publication: 1979**

• Employment: Inner Mongolia Forestry College (内蒙古林学院)
• Research interest: Polygonaceae, Zygophyllaceae [S]
• Published taxa: *Atraphaxis*
• Affiliation: NMAC, NMFC
• Region: CHINA (Nei Mongol)

M. X. Zhao

Zhao, Ming Xu; 赵明旭; Zhào Míngxù

1984- **First publication: 2017**

• Employment: Kunming Institute of Survey and Design, State Forestry Bureau (国家林业局昆明勘察设计院)
• Research interest: Polypodiaceae [P]
• Published taxa: *Leptochilus*
• Region: CHINA (Yunnan)

N. X. Zhao

Zhao, Nan Xian; 赵南先; Zhào Nánxiān

1959- **First publication: 1992**

• Employment: Anhui Institute of Biology; South China Institute of Botany, Chinese Academy of Sciences (安徽省生物研究所; 中国科学院华南植物研究所)
• Research interest: Poaceae [P]
• Published taxa: *Arundinella, Bromus, Deyeuxia, Kengia, Orinus, Pseudopogonatherum, Stipa*
• Affiliation: AIB
• Location of specimens: AIB
• Region: CHINA

N. Chao

Chao, Neng; Chao, Liang Neng; Zhao, Neng; Zhao, Liang Neng; 赵能; Zhào Néng; 赵良能

1928- **First publication: 1974**

• Employment: Sichuan Academy of Forestry (四川省林业科学研究院)
• Research interest: Betulaceae, Cupressaceae, Fabaceae, Hydrangeaceae, Lauraceae, Rutaceae, Salicaceae [S]
• Published taxa: *Balsamiflua, Beilschmiedia, Betula, Chosenia, Cinnamomum, Cryptocarya, Cupressus, Litsea, Machilus, Ormosia, Phoebe, Pleiarina, Populus, Salix, Schizophragma, Zanthoxylum*
• Affiliation: SCFI
• Location of specimens: SAUF, SCFI
• Region: CHINA
• Also as: N. Zhao

C. S. Chao

Chao, Chi Son; Zhao, Qi Seng; 赵奇僧; Zhào Qísēng; 趙奇僧

1936- **First publication: 1963**

• Employment: Nanjing Forestry College; Nanjing Forestry University (南京林学院; 南京林业大学)
• Research interest: Fagaceae, Lauraceae, Poaceae; Gymnospermae [S]
• Published taxa: *Acidosasa, Ampelocalamus, Arundinaria, Castanopsis, Chimonobambusa, Gelidocalamus, Indocalamus, Indosasa, Machilus, Phyllostachys, Pleioblastus, Pseudosasa, Racemobambos, Sasa, Sinarundinaria, Sinobambusa, Thamnocalamus*
• Affiliation: NF
• Location of specimens: NF
• Region: CHINA

Q. S. Zhao

Zhao, Qing Sheng; Cao, Ching Sen; 赵清盛; Zhào Qīngshèng; 趙清盛

1941- **First publication: 1983**

• Employment: Department of Biology, Sichuan University (四川大学生物系)
• Research interest: Bignoniaceae [S]
• Published taxa: *Incarvillea*
• Affiliation: SZ
• Location of specimens: CDBI, SZ
• Region: CHINA (Sichuan)

R. N. Zhao

Zhao, Ru Neng; 赵汝能; Zhào Rǔnéng; 趙汝能

1929-2008 **First publication: 1987**

• Employment: Department of Pharmacy, Lanzhou Medical College; Institute of Medicinal Plants, Lanzhou Medical College (兰州医学院药学系; 兰州医学院药用植物研究所)
• Research interest: Asparagaceae, Caprifoliaceae, Melanthiaceae [S]
• Published taxa: *Asparagus, Paris, Patrinia, Ypsilandra*
• Region: CHINA (Gansu)

S. J. Zhao

Zhao, Sheng Jie; 赵胜杰 ; Zhào Shèngjié

1952- **First publication: 2006**

- Employment: Landscape Administration of Huaguoshan, Lianyungang, Jiangsu（江苏省连云港市花果山风景区管理处）
- Research interest: Poaceae [S]
- Published taxa: *Phyllostachys*
- Region: CHINA (Jiangsu)

S. D. Zhao

Zhao, Shi Dong; 赵士洞 ; Zhào Shìdòng; 趙士洞

1941- **First publication: 1980**

- Employment: Institute of Forestry and Soil Sciences, Chinese Academy of Sciences; Institute of Applied Ecology, Chinese Academy of Sciences（中国科学院林业土壤研究所；中国科学院沈阳应用生态研究所）
- Research interest: Boraginaceae, Ericaceae, Malvaceae, Oleaceae, Plumbaginaceae, Poaceae, Polemoniaceae, Salicaceae, Ulmaceae [S]
- Published taxa: *Hordeum, Limonium, Myosotis, Polemonium, Pyrola, Salix, Syringa, Tilia, Ulmus*
- Affiliation: IFP
- Location of specimens: IFP
- Region: CHINA

S. W. Zhao

Zhao, Shi Wang; 赵世望 ; Zhào Shìwàng; 趙世望

1934- **First publication: 1979**

- Employment: Kunming Institute of Botany, Chinese Academy of Sciences（中国科学院昆明植物研究所）
- Research interest: Zingiberaceae; Plants of Yunnan [S]
- Published taxa: *Amomum*
- Affiliation: KUN
- Location of specimens: KUN
- Region: CHINA

Shu Y. Zhao

Zhao, Shu Yuan; 赵书元 ; Zhào Shūyuán; 趙書元

1934-2018 **First publication: 1991**

- Employment: Inner Mongolia University（内蒙古大学）
- Research interest: Amaranthaceae [S]
- Published taxa: *Ceratoides*
- Region: CHINA (Nei Mongol)

Chaw

Chaw, Shu Miaw; Zhao, Shu Miao; 趙淑妙 ; Zhào Shūmiào; 赵淑妙

1954- **First publication: 1991**

- Employment: Herbarium, Institute of Botany, "Academia Sinica"（中研院植物研究所标本馆）
- Research interest: Euphorbiaceae, Lamiaceae, Rubiaceae [S]
- Published taxa: *Antirhea, Callicarpa, Chamaesyce*
- Affiliation: HAST
- Location of specimens: HAST
- Region: CHINA (Taiwan)

S. Y. Zhao

Zhao, Su Yun; 赵素云 ; Zhào Sùyún; 趙素雲

1941- **First publication: 1985**

- Employment: Sichuan Institute of Chinese Materia Medica（四川省中药研究所）
- Research interest: Asteraceae, Menispermaceae [S]
- Published taxa: *Artemisia, Cyclea, Stephania*
- Affiliation: SM
- Location of specimens: SM
- Region: CHINA

T. B. Chao

Chao, Tien Bang; Chao, Tien Bung; Zhao, Tien Bang; Zhao, Tian Bang; 赵天榜 ; Zhào Tiānbǎng; 趙天榜

1935- **First publication: 1978**

- Employment: Henan Agricultural College; Henan Agricultural University（河南农学院；河南农业大学）
- Research interest: Calycanthaceae, Euphorbiaceae, Fabaceae, Fagaceae, Ginkgoaceae, Magnoliaceae, Orchidaceae, Rosaceae, Salicaceae, Simaroubaceae, Staphyleaceae [S]
- Published taxa: *Ailanthus, Cercis, Chimonanthus, Dendrobium, Ginkgo, Magnolia, Populus, Pyracantha, Quercus, Salix, Sapium, Staphylea, Yulania*
- Location of specimens: HEAC
- Region: CHINA (Henan)

W. Y. Zhao

Zhao, Wan Yi; 赵万义 ; Zhào Wànyì

1991- **First publication: 2017**

- Employment: School of Life Sciences, Sun Yat-sen University（中山大学生命科学学院）
- Research interest: Begoniaceae, Melastomataceae, Saxifragaceae, Styracaceae [S]
- Published taxa: *Begonia, Bredia, Rehderodendron, Saxifraga*
- Region: CHINA (Guangdong, Guangxi)

W. L. Zhao

Zhao, Wei Liang; 赵维良 ; Zhào Wéiliáng

1959- **First publication: 1987**

- Employment: Department of Pharmacy, Zhejiang Medical University（浙江医科大学药学系）
- Research interest: Dioscoreaceae [S]
- Published taxa: *Dioscorea*
- Region: CHINA (Zhejiang)

W. Z. Zhao

Zhao, Wen Zhong; 赵文忠 ; Zhào Wénzhōng; 趙文忠

1940- First publication: 1992
- Employment: Jishan County Nationalized Forest Farm, Shanxi（山西省稷山县国营林场）
- Research interest: Paeoniaceae [S]
- Published taxa: *Paeonia*
- Region: CHINA (Shanxi)

X. F. Zhao

Zhao, Xiao Feng; 赵晓峰；Zhào Xiǎofēng
1957-2009 First publication: 1998
- Employment: Hinggan League Institute for Drug Control, Inner Mongolia（内蒙古兴安盟药品检验所）
- Research interest: Campanulaceae, Ranunculaceae [S]
- Published taxa: *Adenophora, Pulsatilla*
- Region: CHINA (Nei Mongol)

H. C. Chao

Chao, Hsiu Chien; Chao, Hsiu Ch'ien; Zhao, Xiu Qian; 赵修谦；Zhào Xiūqiān; 趙修謙
1911-2001 First publication: 1948
- Employment: Department of Biology, Xiamen University（厦门大学生物系）
- Research interest: Podostemaceae; Bryophyte [S]
- Published taxa: *Cladopus, Lawiella, Terniopsis*
- Affiliation: AU
- Location of specimens: AU
- Region: CHINA (Fujian)

X. W. Zhao

Zhao, Xuan Wu; 赵宣武；Zhào Xuānwǔ
1991- First publication: 2018
- Employment: College of Forestry, Southwest Forestry University（西南林业大学林学院）
- Research interest: Ebenaceae [S]
- Published taxa: *Diospyros*
- Region: CHINA (Yunnan)

X. L. Zhao

Zhao, Xue Li; 赵雪利；Zhào Xuělì
1987- First publication: 2015
- Employment: Chengdu Institute of Biology, Chinese Academy of Sciences（中国科学院成都生物研究所）
- Research interest: Fabaceae [S]
- Published taxa: *Indigofera*
- Region: CHINA (Sichuan)
- IPNI as: Xue Li Zhao

Y. Z. Zhao

Zhao, Yi Zhi; 赵一之；Zhào Yīzhī; 趙一之
1940-2016 First publication: 1979
- Employment: Department of Biology, Inner Mongolia University; School of Life Sciences, Inner Mongolia University（内蒙古大学生物系；内蒙古大学生命科学学院）
- Research interest: Amaranthaceae, Amaryllidaceae, Apiaceae, Asteraceae, Brassicaceae, Campanulaceae, Caryophyllaceae, Cistaceae, Ericaceae, Fabaceae, Gentianaceae, Lamiaceae, Liliaceae, Orobanchaceae, Plantaginaceae, Poaceae, Ranunculaceae, Rhamnaceae, Rosaceae [S]
- Published taxa: *Aconitum, Adenophora, Allium, Anagallidium, Astragalus, Atriplex, Caragana, Clematis, Delphinium, Dianthus, Gagea, Hedysarum, Helianthemum, Lilium, Limnophila, Lomatogonium, Melandrium, Oxytropis, Panzerina, Pedicularis, Pulsatilla, Pyrola, Ranunculus, Rhamnus, Rosa, Seseli, Silene, Spiraea, Stellaria, Stipa, Synstemon, Tugarinovia, Tulipa, Veronica, Yinshania, Youngia*
- Affiliation: HIMC
- Location of specimens: IMDC, HIMC
- Region: CHINA (Nei Mongol)

Y. S. Chao

Chao, Yi Shan; 趙怡姍；Zhào Yíshān; 赵怡姗
1976- First publication: 2015
- Employment: Department of Biomedical Science and Environment Biology, Kaohsiung Medical University（高雄医学大学生物医学暨环境生物学系）
- Research interest: Dryopteridaceae, Hymenophyllaceae, Pteridaceae [P]
- Published taxa: *Bolbitis, Hymenophyllum, Pteris*
- Region: CHINA

Y. J. Zhao

Zhao, Yin Jia; 赵银佳；Zhào Yínjiā
1987- First publication: 2011
- Employment: College of Life and Environmental Sciences, Hangzhou Normal University（杭州师范大学生命与环境科学学院）
- Research interest: Cyperaceae [S]
- Published taxa: *Carex*
- Region: CHINA (Zhejiang)

Y. H. Zhao

Zhao, Yu Hou; 赵裕后；Zhào Yùhòu; 趙裕後
1937- First publication: 1995
- Employment: Henan Institute of Forestry Science（河南省林业科学研究所）
- Research interest: Paulowniaceae [S]
- Published taxa: *Paulownia*
- Region: CHINA (Henan)

Y. H. Chao

Chao, Yü Huang; Chao, Yu Huang; 赵燏黄；Zhào Yùhuáng; 趙燏黃
First publication: 1957
- Employment: Department of Pharmacy, Beijing

Medical College (北京医学院药学系)
• Research interest: Orobanchaceae [S]
• Published taxa: *Rehmannia*
• Region: CHINA

Y. T. Zhao

Zhao, Yu Tang; 赵毓棠; Zhào Yùtáng; 趙毓棠
1932-2010 **First publication: 1980**
• Employment: Department of Biology, Northeast Normal University (东北师范大学生物系)
• Research interest: Amaryllidaceae, Fabaceae, Hydrangeaceae, Iridaceae, Pinaceae, Polygonaceae, Ranunculaceae, Rosaceae, Typhaceae; Plants of Changbai Mountain [S]
• Published taxa: *Allium, Caragana, Iris, Philadelphus, Pinus, Polygonum, Pulsatilla, Rosa, Typha*
• Affiliation: NENU
• Location of specimens: NENU
• Region: CHINA

Y. L. Zhao

Zhao, Yun Lin; 赵运林; Zhào Yùnlín
1959- **First publication: 1996**
• Employment: Department of Biology, Sun Yat-sen University (中山大学生物系)
• Research interest: Melastomataceae, Primulaceae [S]
• Published taxa: *Lysimachia, Phyllagathis*
• Location of specimens: HUST
• Region: CHINA (Hunan)

J. M. Chao

Chao, Jew Ming; Zhao, Zhe Ming; 趙哲明; Zhào Zhémíng; 赵哲明
First publication: 1964
• Employment: Department of Biology, Taiwan Normal University; State Bureau of identification, West Trenton, New Jersey, U.S.A. (台湾师范大学生物系；美国新泽西州西特伦顿国家鉴定局)
• Research interest: Hamamelidaceae, Loranthaceae, Rubiaceae [S]
• Published taxa: *Corylopsis, Hyphear, Lasianthus, Rubia*
• Location of specimens: TNU
• Region: CHINA (Taiwan)
• IPNI as: L. M. Chao

Z. J. Zhao

Zhao, Zhen Ju; 赵振鐻; Zhào Zhènjù; 趙振鐻
1940- **First publication: 1982**
• Employment: Department of Biology, Sichuan University; College of Life Sciences, Sichuan University (四川大学生物系；四川大学生命科学学院)
• Research interest: Ericaceae [S]
• Published taxa: *Rhododendron*
• Region: CHINA (Sichuan)

Z. L. Zhao

Zhao, Zhi Li; 赵志礼; Zhào Zhìlǐ
1956- **First publication: 1998**
• Employment: China Pharmaceutical University (中国药科大学)
• Research interest: Zingiberaceae [S]
• Published taxa: *Alpinia*
• Region: CHINA

Zhi L. Zhao

Zhao, Zhi Long; 赵志龙; Zhào Zhìlóng
1963- **First publication: 2003**
• Employment: West China Subalpine Botanical Garden, Institute of Botany, Chinese Academy of Sciences (中国科学院植物研究所华西亚高山植物园)
• Research interest: Ericaceae [S]
• Published taxa: *Rhododendron*
• Location of specimens: WCSBG
• Region: CHINA (Sichuan)
• IPNI as: Z. L. Zhao

Z. Z. Zhao

Zhao, Zhong Zhen; 赵中振; Zhào Zhōngzhèn
1957- **First publication: 1987**
• Employment: Institute of Chinese Materia Medica, China Academy of Chinese Medical Sciences (中国中医研究院中药研究所)
• Research interest: Magnoliaceae [S]
• Published taxa: *Magnolia*
• Affiliation: CMMI
• Location of specimens: CMMI
• Region: CHINA (Hubei)

Z. F. Zhao

Zhao, Zhu Fa; 赵柱发; Zhào Zhùfā
First publication: 2007
• Employment: Amateur (业余爱好者)
• Research interest: Orchidaceae [S]
• Published taxa: *Paphiopedilum*
• Region: CHINA (Guangxi)

Z. E. Chao

Chao, Zi En; Zhao, Zi En; 赵子恩; Zhào Zǐ'ēn; 趙子恩
1938- **First publication: 1982**
• Employment: Wuhan Institute of Botany, Chinese Academy of Sciences (中国科学院武汉植物研究所)
• Research interest: Apocynaceae, Brassicaceae, Caryophyllaceae, Juglandaceae, Plantaginaceae, Polygonaceae, Primulaceae; Plants of Hubei [S]
• Published taxa: *Arenaria, Lysimachia, Marsdenia, Neomartinella, Orychophragmus, Plantago, Polygonum, Pseudostellaria, Pterocarya*

- Affiliation: HIB
- Location of specimens: HIB
- Region: CHINA (Hubei)
- Also as: Z. E. Zhao

Z. C. Zhao

Zhao, Zuo Cheng; 赵佐成 ; Zhào Zuǒchéng; 趙佐成

1941- **First publication: 1987**

- Employment: Department of Biology, Wuhan University（武汉大学生物系）
- Research interest: Hydrocharitaceae; Aquatic Plants [S]
- Published taxa: *Ottelia*
- Affiliation: CDBI
- Location of specimens: CDBI
- Region: CHINA (Guangxi)

B. Q. Zheng

Zheng, Bao Qiang; 郑宝强 ; Zhèng Bǎoqiáng

1981- **First publication: 2020**

- Employment: Research Institute of Forestry, Chinese Academy of Forestry（中国林业科学研究院林业研究所）
- Research interest: Orchidaceae [S]
- Published taxa: *Dendrobium*
- Region: CHINA (Yunnan)

C. H. Zheng

Zheng, Chao Han; 郑朝汉 ; Zhèng Cháohàn

1982- **First publication: 2013**

- Employment: South China Botanical Garden, Chinese Academy of Sciences（中国科学院华南植物园）
- Research interest: Poaceae [S]
- Published taxa: *Ampelocalamus, Bambusa, Schizostachyum*
- Region: CHINA (Fujian, Guangdong)

C. Z. Zheng

Zheng, Chao Zong; Cheng, Chao Tsung; Cheng, Chao Zong; 郑朝宗 ; Zhèng Cháozōng; 鄭朝宗

1934- **First publication: 1979**

- Employment: Department of Biology, Hangzhou University; College of Life Sciences, Zhejiang University（杭州大学生物系；浙江大学生命科学学院）
- Research interest: Acanthaceae, Aquifoliaceae, Cucurbitaceae, Cyperaceae, Fabaceae, Polygonaceae, Primulaceae [S]
- Published taxa: *Carex, Fimbristylis, Hemsleya, Ilex, Indigofera, Lysimachia, Polygonum, Scleria, Strobilanthes*
- Affiliation: HZU
- Location of specimens: HZU
- Region: CHINA (Zhejiang)

C. J. Zheng

Zheng, Cheng Jin; 郑承金 ; Zhèng Chéngjīn

1953- **First publication: 1982**

- Employment: Yichang Institute of Forestry Science, Hubei（湖北省宜昌地区林科所）
- Research interest: Juglandaceae [S]
- Published taxa: *Pterocarya*
- Region: CHINA (Hubei)

G. R. Zheng

Zheng, Guang Rong; 郑光荣 ; Zhèng Guāngróng

First publication: 1996

- Employment: Beishan Forest Farm of Huzhu Tu Autonomous County, Qinghai（青海省互助土族自治县北山林场）
- Research interest: Boraginaceae [S]
- Published taxa: *Eritrichium*
- Region: CHINA (Qinghai)

H. L. Zheng

Zheng, Hai Lei; 郑海磊 ; Zhèng Hǎilěi

1990- **First publication: 2019**

- Employment: Wild Dali Nature Education and Research Center, Dali, Yunnan（野性大理自然教育与研究中心）
- Research interest: Aristolochiaceae [S]
- Published taxa: *Isotrema*
- Region: CHINA (Yunnan)

H. C. Zheng

Zheng, Han Chen; 郑汉臣 ; Zhèng Hànchén; 鄭漢臣

1939-2012 **First publication: 1994**

- Employment: College of Pharmacy, Second Military Medical University（第二军医大学药学院）
- Research interest: Araliaceae; Medicinal Plants [S]
- Published taxa: *Aralia*
- Affiliation: SMMU-BH
- Location of specimens: SMMU-BH
- Region: CHINA (Gansu, Ningxia, Shaanxi)

Hong C. Zheng

Zheng, Hong Chun; 郑宏春 ; Zhèng Hóngchūn

1964- **First publication: 1992**

- Employment: Department of Biology, Yan' an University（延安大学生物系）
- Research interest: Paeoniaceae [S]
- Published taxa: *Paeonia*
- Region: CHINA (Shaanxi)

H. Zheng

Zheng, Hui; 郑晖 ; Zhèng Huī

1957- **First publication: 1991**

- Employment: Wuyishan Nature Reserve Management Office, Jiangxi; Yingtan Forestry Bureau, Jiangxi（江

西省武夷山自然保护区管理处；江西省鹰潭市林业局）
- Research interest: Rosaceae [S]
- Published taxa: *Rubus*
- Region: CHINA (Jiangxi)

H. X. Zheng

Zheng, Hui Xian; 郑惠贤；Zhèng Huìxián; 鄭惠賢
1945- **First publication: 1998**
- Employment: Nanning Arboretum, Guangxi Zhuang Autonomous Region（广西壮族自治区南宁树木园）
- Research interest: Cycadaceae [S]
- Published taxa: *Cycas*
- Region: CHINA (Guangxi)

J. Q. Zheng

Zheng, Ji Qing; 郑纪庆；Zhèng Jìqìng
1976- **First publication: 2006**
- Employment: Shandong Normal University（山东师范大学）
- Research interest: Brassicaceae [S]
- Published taxa: *Lepidium*
- Region: CHINA (Shandong)

J. G. Zheng

Zheng, Jian Guan; 郑建官；Zhèng Jiànguān; 鄭建官
1945- **First publication: 2006**
- Employment: Gutian County Forestry Bureau, Fujian（福建省古田县林业局）
- Research interest: Poaceae [S]
- Published taxa: *Pseudosasa*
- Region: CHINA (Fujian)

J. H. Zheng

Zheng, Jie Hua; 郑洁华；Zhèng Jiéhuá; 鄭洁華
1931-2009 **First publication: 2002**
- Employment: Wuhan Institute of Botany, Chinese Academy of Sciences（中国科学院武汉植物研究所）
- Research interest: Lamiaceae [S]
- Published taxa: *Phlomis, Teucrium*
- Region: CHINA (Hubei)

L. Zheng

Zheng, Lin; 郑林；Zhèng Lín
First publication: 2014
- Employment: Forestry College, Fujian Agriculture and Forestry University（福建农林大学林学院）
- Research interest: Fagaceae [S]
- Published taxa: *Cyclobalanopsis*
- Region: CHINA (Fujian)

M. Cheng

Cheng, Mien; Chêng, Mien; Zheng, Mian; 郑勉；Zhèng Miǎn; 鄭勉
1899-1987 **First publication: 1974**
- Employment: Department of Biology, Shanghai Normal University; Department of Biology, East China Normal University（上海师范大学生物系；华东师范大学生物系）
- Research interest: Apocynaceae, Berberidaceae, Buxaceae, Lamiaceae, Plantaginaceae; Plants of E. China [S]
- Published taxa: *Biondia, Buxus, Callicarpa, Cynanchum, Dysosma, Pachysandra, Sarcococca, Veronicastrum, Vincetoxicum*
- Affiliation: HSNU
- Location of specimens: HSNU
- Region: CHINA

Q. F. Zheng

Zheng, Qing Fang; 郑清芳；Zhèng Qīngfāng; 鄭清芳
1934- **First publication: 1979**
- Employment: Fujian Forestry College（福建林学院）
- Research interest: Fagaceae, Lauraceae, Magnoliaceae, Myrtaceae, Poaceae [S]
- Published taxa: *Bambusa, Castanopsis, Cyclobalanopsis, Dendrocalamopsis, Lithocarpus, Machilus, Michelia, Oligostachyum, Phyllostachys, Pleioblastus, Pseudosasa, Shibataea, Syzygium, Yushania*
- Affiliation: FJFC
- Location of specimens: FJFC
- Region: CHINA (Fujian)

Q. Y. Zheng

Zheng, Quin Yan; Zheng, Qing Yan; 郑庆衍；Zhèng Qìngyǎn; 鄭慶衍
1939- **First publication: 1994**
- Employment: Yichun Institute of Forestry Science, Jiangxi（江西宜春市林业科学研究所）
- Research interest: Magnoliaceae [S]
- Published taxa: *Manglietia, Sinomanglietia*
- Region: CHINA (Jiangxi)

R. X. Zheng

Zheng, Ruo Xian; 郑若仙；Zhèng Ruòxiān; 鄭若仙
1935- **First publication: 1986**
- Employment: Kunming Institute of Botany, Chinese Academy of Sciences（中国科学院昆明植物研究所）
- Research interest: Begoniaceae [S]
- Published taxa: *Begonia*
- Region: CHINA (Yunnan)

S. Q. Zheng

Zheng, Shi Qun; 郑世群；Zhèng Shìqún
1971- **First publication: 2005**
- Employment: Forestry College, Fujian Agriculture and Forestry University（福建农林大学林学院）
- Research interest: Lauraceae; Woody Plants [S]

- Published taxa: *Machilus*
- Affiliation: FJFC
- Location of specimens: FJFC
- Region: CHINA (Fujian)
- IPNI as: Sh. Q. Zheng

S. H. Cheng

Cheng, Sze Hsu; Zheng, Si Xu; Cheng, f.; 郑斯绪 ; Zhèng Sīxù; 鄭斯緒

1931-1967 **First publication: 1959**

- Employment: Institute of Botany, Chinese Academy of Sciences（中国科学院植物研究所）
- Research interest: Betulaceae, Fabaceae, Scrophulariaceae [S]
- Published taxa: *Astragalus, Ammopiptanthus, Chesneya, Chesniella, Glycyrrhiza, Oxytropis, Pedicularis*
- Affiliation: PE
- Region: CHINA
- Also as: Cheng f.

T. K. Zheng

Zheng, Tai Kun; 郑太坤 ; Zhèng Tàikūn; 鄭太坤

1940- **First publication: 1992**

- Employment: Department of Traditional Chinese Pharmacy, Liaoning College of Traditional Chinese Medicine（辽宁中医学院中药系）
- Research interest: Plantaginaceae [S]
- Published taxa: *Plantago*
- Location of specimens: LNCM
- Region: CHINA (Liaoning)

W. C. Cheng

Cheng, Wan Chun; Zheng, Wan Jun; Cheng, Wan Chün; 郑万钧 ; Zhèng Wànjūn; 鄭萬鈞

1904-1983 **First publication: 1931**

- Employment: Department of Botany, Biological Laboratory of Science Society of China; Department of Biology, National Central University; Nanjing Forestry College（中国科学社生物研究所植物部 ; 国立中央大学生物系 ; 南京林学院）
- Research interest: Altingiaceae, Betulaceae, Calycanthaceae, Cannabaceae, Celastraceae, Cupressaceae, Cycadaceae, Ebenaceae, Fabaceae, Fagaceae, Gnetaceae, Hamamelidaceae, Hydrangeaceae, Lauraceae, Lythraceae, Magnoliaceae, Malvaceae, Phyllanthaceae, Pinaceae, Rhamnaceae, Rosaceae, Salicaceae, Sapindaceae, Schisandraceae, Styracaceae, Taxaceae, Theaceae, Thymelaeaceae, Ulmaceae, Vitaceae; Woody Plants [PS]
- Published taxa: *Abies, Acer, Altingia, Beilschmiedia, Bischofia, Calocedrus, Carpinus, Castanopsis, Celtis, Cephalotaxus, Corylopsis, Cryptocarya, Cupressus, Cycas, Cyclobalanopsis, Deutzia, Diospyros, Distylium, Euonymus, Fagus, Gnetum, Hovenia, Illicium, Juniperus, Keteleeria, Lagerstroemia, Larix, Lindera, Liquidambar, Lithocarpus, Litsea, Machilus, Magnolia, Manglietia, Metasequoia, Michelia, Neolitsea, Ormosia, Parakmeria, Paramanglietia, Pasania, Phoebe, Picea, Pinus, Pleiarina, Populus, Pseudotaxus, Pseudotsuga, Quercus, Rehderodendron, Rhamnus, Rubus, Sabina, Salix, Schima, Schisandra, Sinocalycanthus, Sorbus, Stewartia, Styrax, Taxus, Tilia, Torreya, Tsuga, Ulmus, Vitis, Wikstroemia*
- Affiliation: CAF, NF
- Location of specimens: CAF, CQNM, NF, PE
- Region: CHINA
- Also as: Cheng

W. Zheng

Zheng, Wei; 郑伟 ; Zhèng Wěi

First publication: 2018

- Employment: Faculty of Architecture and City Planning, Kunming University of Science and Technology（昆明理工大学建筑与城市规划学院）
- Research interest: Asteraceae [S]
- Published taxa: *Oreoseris*
- Region: [WORLD]

W. L. Cheng

Cheng, Wei Lie; Zheng, Wei Lie; 郑维列 ; Zhèng Wéiliè

1963- **First publication: 1997**

- Employment: Xizang Plateau Ecology Institute（西藏高原生态研究所）
- Research interest: Campanulaceae, Gentianaceae, Loranthaceae, Ranunculaceae, Rosaceae; Plant Ecology [S]
- Published taxa: *Cerasus, Crawfurdia, Lobelia, Oxygraphis, Ranunculus, Taxillus*
- Affiliation: XZE
- Location of specimens: XZE
- Region: CHINA (Xizang)

X. L. Zheng

Zheng, Xi Long; 郑希龙 ; Zhèng Xīlóng

1983- **First publication: 2010**

- Employment: South China Botanical Garden, Chinese Academy of Sciences（中国科学院华南植物园）
- Research interest: Cucurbitaceae, Pteridaceae [P]
- Published taxa: *Gomphogyne, Pteris*
- Region: CHINA (Hainan)

X. R. Zheng

Zheng, Xi Rong; 郑锡荣 ; Zhèng Xīróng

1993- **First publication: 2019**

- Employment: South China Botanical Garden, Chinese Academy of Sciences（中国科学院华南植物园）

- Research interest: Poaceae [S]
- Published taxa: *Khoonmengia, Phyllostachys*
- Region: [ASIA]

X. Q. Zheng

Zheng, Xin Qiang; 郑新强 ; Zhèng Xīnqiáng

1974- **First publication: 2001**

- Employment: Department of Biology, Sun Yat-sen University（中山大学生物系）
- Research interest: Theaceae [S]
- Published taxa: *Camellia*
- Region: CHINA (Guangdong)

X. J. Zheng

Zheng, Xiu Ju; 郑秀菊 ; Zhèng Xiùjú

First publication: 1987

- Employment: Yumin County Fritillaria Test Station, Xinjiang（新疆裕民县贝母试验站）
- Research interest: Liliaceae [S]
- Published taxa: *Fritillaria*
- Region: CHINA (Xinjiang)

Y. Zheng

Zheng, Yan; 郑艳 ; Zhèng Yàn

1967- **First publication: 2000**

- Employment: Department of Biology, Anhui Normal University（安徽师范大学生物系）
- Research interest: Crassulaceae [S]
- Published taxa: *Sedum*
- Region: CHINA (Anhui)

Y. L. Zheng

Zheng, Yong Li; 郑永利 ; Zhèng Yǒnglì

1976- **First publication: 2002**

- Employment: South China Institute of Botany, Chinese Academy of Sciences（中国科学院华南植物研究所）
- Research interest: Gesneriaceae, Melastomataceae [S]
- Published taxa: *Blastus, Oreocharis, Primulina*
- Region: CHINA (Guangdong)

Y. Y. Zheng

Zheng, Yu Yun; 郑宇云 ; Zhèng Yǔyún

1970- **First publication: 2012**

- Employment: The Orchid Conservation & Research Center of Shenzhen, Guangdong（广东省深圳市兰科植物保护研究中心）
- Research interest: Orchidaceae [S]
- Published taxa: *Cypripedium*
- Region: CHINA (Sichuan)

Z. Zheng

Zheng, Zhong; Cheng, Chung; Chêng, Chung; 郑重 ; Zhèng Zhòng; 鄭重

1934-2020 **First publication: 1987**

- Employment: Wuhan Institute of Botany, Chinese Academy of Sciences; Wuhan Botanical Garden, Chinese Academy of Sciences（中国科学院武汉植物研究所；中国科学院武汉植物园）
- Research interest: Berberidaceae, Cornaceae, Liliaceae; Plants of Hubei [S]
- Published taxa: *Alangium, Dysosma, Fritillaria*
- Affiliation: HIB
- Location of specimens: HIB
- Region: CHINA (Hubei)
- Also as: Z. Cheng

L. Zhi

Zhi, Li; 智丽 ; Zhì Lì

1973- **First publication: 2006**

- Employment: College of Horticulture and Landscape Architecture, Southwest Agricultural University（西南农业大学园艺园林学院）
- Research interest: Poaceae [S]
- Published taxa: *Leymus*
- Region: CHINA (Qinghai)

P. C. Tsoong

Tsoong, Pu Chiu; Tsoong, Pu Ch'iu; Chung, Pu Ch'iu; Zhong, Bu Qiu; 钟补求 ; Zhōng Bǔqiú; 鐘補求

1906-1981 **First publication: 1935**

- Employment: Institute of Botany, National Academy of Peiping; Institute of Systematic Botany, Academia Sinica; Institute of Botany, Chinese Academy of Sciences（国立北平研究院植物学研究所；中国科学院植物分类研究所；中国科学院植物研究所）
- Research interest: Campanulaceae, Celastraceae, Fabaceae, Juglandaceae, Linderniaceae, Mazaceae, Orobanchaceae, Phrymaceae, Plantaginaceae, Sapindaceae, Scrophulariaceae [S]
- Published taxa: *Acer, Adenophora, Adenosma, Brandisia, Celastrus, Centranthera, Codonopsis, Lagotis, Lindernia, Mazus, Mimulicalyx, Mimulus, Pedicularis, Pterocarya, Pterygiella, Rehmannia, Scrophularia, Sophora, Sopubia, Veronica, Veronicastrum*
- Affiliation: PE
- Location of specimens: PE
- Region: CHINA
- Also as: Tsoong

K. F. Chung

Chung, Kuo Fang; Zhong, Guo Fang; 鍾國芳 ; Zhōng Guófāng; 钟国芳

First publication: 2007

- Employment: School of Forestry and Resources Conservation, Taiwan University（台湾大学森林环境暨资源学系）

- Research interest: Apiaceae, Begoniaceae, Berberidaceae, Gesneriaceae; Plant Systematics [S]
- Published taxa: *Alloberberis, Begonia, Berberis, Chaerophyllum, Mahonia, Moranothamnus, Petrocodon, Primulina,*
- Affiliation: HAST, NTUF
- Location of specimens: HAST, NTUF
- Region: CHINA

G. R. Zhong

Zhong, Guo Rong; 钟国荣 ; Zhōng Guóróng

1963- **First publication: 1988**

- Employment: Hangzhou Botanical Garden（杭州植物园）
- Research interest: Malvaceae, Staphyleaceae, Theaceae; Woody Plants [S]
- Published taxa: *Corchoropsis, Euscaphis, Stewartia*
- Affiliation: HHBG
- Location of specimens: HHBG
- Region: CHINA (Zhejiang)

G. Y. Zhong

Zhong, Guo Yue; 钟国跃 ; Zhōng Guóyuè

1958- **First publication: 2007**

- Employment: Chongqing Academy of Chinese Material Medica（重庆市中药研究院）
- Research interest: Berberidaceae [S]
- Published taxa: *Epimedium*
- Affiliation: SM
- Location of specimens: SM
- Region: CHINA (Chongqing, Sichuan)

C. H. Tsoong

Tsoong, Chi Hsin; Chung, Chi Hsing; Zhong, Ji Xin; 钟济新 ; Zhōng Jìxīn; 鐘濟新

1909-1993 **First publication: 1963**

- Employment: National Kwangsi Univertsity; Guangxi Institute of Botany, Chinese Academy of Sciences（国立广西大学；广西壮族自治区中国科学院广西植物研究所）
- Research interest: Magnoliaceae [S]
- Published taxa: *Magnolia*
- Location of specimens: GAC, IBK
- Region: CHINA
- Also as: C. H. Chung

J. P. Zhong

Zhong, Jian Ping; 钟建平 ; Zhōng Jiànpíng

1974- **First publication: 2020**

- Employment: Amateur（业余爱好者）
- Research interest: Boraginaceae [S]
- Published taxa: *Omphalotrigonotis*
- Region: CHINA (Zhejiang)

J. S. Zhong

Zhong, Jin Shun; 钟晋顺 ; Zhōng Jìnshùn

1982- **First publication: 2010**

- Employment: Xishuangbanna Tropical Botanical Garden, Chinese Academy of Sciences（中国科学院西双版纳热带植物园）
- Research interest: Lamiaceae [S]
- Published taxa: *Isodon, Siphocranion*
- Region: CHINA

M. C. Chung

Chung, Mei Chu; 鍾美珠 ; Zhōng Měizhū; 钟美珠

First publication: 2017

- Employment: Institute of Plant and Microbial Biology, "Academia Sinica"（中研院植物暨微生物学研究所）
- Research interest: Orchidaceae [S]
- Published taxa: *Paphiopedilum*
- Region: CHINA (Taiwan)

M. J. Jung

Jung, Ming Jer; 鍾明哲 ; Zhōng Míngzhé; 钟明哲

First publication: 2013

- Employment: Department of Life Science, Taiwan Normal University（台湾师范大学生命科学系）
- Research interest: Caprifoliaceae, Juncaceae [S]
- Published taxa: *Juncus, Valeriana*
- Region: CHINA (Taiwan)

N. J. Chung

Chung, Nian June; Zhong, Nian jun; 鐘年鈞 ; Zhōng Niánjūn; 钟年钧

First publication: 1977

- Employment: Taiwan University（台湾大学）
- Research interest: Begoniaceae, Crassulaceae, Orchidaceae [S]
- Published taxa: *Begonia, Gastrodia, Sedum*
- Region: CHINA (Taiwan)

P. S. Zhong

Zhong, Ping Sheng; 钟平生 ; Zhōng Píngshēng

1971?- **First publication: 2016**

- Employment: Nanxiong City Forestry Bureau, Guangdong（广东省南雄市林业局）
- Research interest: Orchidaceae [S]
- Published taxa: *Apostasia*
- Region: CHINA (Guangdong)

S. W. Chung

Chung, Shih Wen; Zhong, Shi Wen; 鐘詩文 ; Zhōng Shīwén; 钟诗文

First publication: 1998

- Employment: Forest Biology Division, Taiwan Forestry Research Institute, Council of Agriculture,

"Executive Yuan"（"行政院"农业委员会林业试验所森林生物组）
- Research interest: Asteraceae, Gentianaceae, Melastomataceae, Orchidaceae, Polygonaceae, Urticaceae, Zingiberaceae [S]
- Published taxa: *Bredia, Bulbophyllum, Eupatorium, Gastrodia, Hayata, Ixeridium, Koenigia, Kuhlhasseltia, Lecanorchis, Luisia, Neottia, Nervilia, Oberonia, Parasenecio, Peristylus, Persicaria, Pouzolzia, Senecio, Tripterospermum, Zingiber*
- Affiliation: TAIF
- Location of specimens: TAIF
- Region: CHINA (Taiwan)

S. L. Zhong

Zhong, Shi Li; 钟世理；Zhōng Shìlǐ; 鍾世理
1926- **First publication: 1982**
- Employment: Southwest Agricultural University（西南农业大学）
- Research interest: Poaceae; Pteridophytes [S]
- Published taxa: *Arthraxon, Cenchrus, Diandranthus, Microstegium, Miscanthus, Pennisetum, Phacelurus, Spodiopogon*
- Affiliation: HWA
- Location of specimens: HWA
- Region: CHINA

S. Q. Zhong

Zhong, Shi Qiang; 钟仕强；Zhōng Shìqiáng; 鍾仕強
1944-2010 **First publication: 1984**
- Employment: Guangxi Botanical Garden of Medicinal Plants（广西药用植物园）
- Research interest: Cucurbitaceae [S]
- Published taxa: *Siraitia*
- Region: CHINA

S. H. Zhong

Zhong, Shu Hua; 钟树华；Zhōng Shùhuá
1958- **First publication: 2000**
- Employment: Guangxi Institute of Botany, Chinese Academy of Sciences（广西壮族自治区中国科学院广西植物研究所）
- Research interest: Gesneriaceae; Plants of Guangxi [S]
- Published taxa: *Allocheilos, Chirita*
- Affiliation: IBK
- Region: CHINA (Guangxi)

H. H. Chung

Chung, Hsin Hsuan; Chung, Hsin Hsüan; Zhong, Xin Xuan; 钟心煊；Zhōng Xīnxuān; 鍾心煊
1893-1961 **First publication: 1924**
- Employment: Department of Biology, National Wuhan University; Department of Botany, Institute of Biology, The Science Institute of West China; Department of Biology, Wuhan University（国立武汉大学生物系；中国西部科学院生物研究所植物部；武汉大学生物系）
- Research interest: Berberidaceae [S]
- Published taxa: *Mahonia*
- Affiliation: AU, WH
- Location of specimens: AU, WH
- Region: CHINA (Chongqing, Sichuan)

X. W. Zhong

Zhong, Xiong Wen; 钟雄文；Zhōng Xióngwén; 鍾雄文
1935?- **First publication: 1992**
- Employment: Department of Biology, Wuhan University（武汉大学生物系）
- Research interest: Acoraceae, Pandanaceae, Triuridaceae [S]
- Published taxa: *Pandanus*
- Affiliation: WH
- Location of specimens: WH
- Region: CHINA (Hainan)

Y. C. Zhong

Zhong, Ye Cong; 钟业聪；Zhōng Yècōng; 鍾業聰
1935- **First publication: 1981**
- Employment: Guangxi Forest Inventory & Planning Institute（广西壮族自治区林业勘测设计院）
- Research interest: Cycadaceae, Ericaceae, Oleandraceae, Pinaceae, Theaceae [S]
- Published taxa: *Camellia, Cycas, Oleandra, Pinus*
- Affiliation: GXF
- Location of specimens: GXF
- Region: CHINA (Guangxi)

Yuan C. Zhong

Zhong, Yuan Chun; 钟远春；Zhōng Yuǎnchūn; 鍾遠春
1940-2014 **First publication: 1997**
- Employment: Guizhou Academy of Forestry（贵州省林业科学研究院）
- Research interest: Poaceae [S]
- Published taxa: *Drepanostachyum*
- Affiliation: GF
- Location of specimens: GF
- Region: CHINA (Guizhou)

Z. J. Zhong

Zhong, Zhan Jiang; 钟占江；Zhōng Zhànjiāng
First publication: 1997
- Employment: Changbai Mountain National Nature Reserve Administration, Jilin（吉林长白山国家级自然保护区管理局）
- Research interest: Amaryllidaceae [S]
- Published taxa: *Allium*
- Region: CHINA (Jilin)

Z. M. Zhong

Zhong, Zhi Ming; 钟智明 ; Zhōng Zhìmíng

First publication: 2018

- Employment: Zijin Baixi Provincial Nature Reserve Management Office, Guangdong（广东紫金白溪省级自然保护区管理处）
- Research interest: Orchidaceae [S]
- Published taxa: *Platanthera*
- Region: CHINA (Guangdong)

M. J. Zhong

Zhong, Ming Jin; 仲铭锦 ; Zhòng Míngjǐn

1960- **First publication: 1985**

- Employment: Department of Biology, Northwest University（西北大学生物系）
- Research interest: Cyperaceae, Tamaricaceae [S]
- Published taxa: *Kobresia, Reaumuria*
- Location of specimens: HIMC
- Region: CHINA (Ningxia, Shaanxi)

P. K. Chou

Chou, Pan Kai; Zhou, Bang Kai; **周邦楷 ; Zhōu Bāngkǎi**

1927- **First publication: 1979**

- Employment: Chengdu Institute of Biology, Chinese Academy of Sciences（中国科学院成都生物研究所）
- Research interest: Caprifoliaceae, Rhamnaceae [S]
- Published taxa: *Berchemia, Hovenia, Lonicera, Rhamnus, Sageretia, Ventilago, Ziziphus*
- Affiliation: CDBI
- Location of specimens: CDBI
- Region: CHINA

C. S. Zhou

Zhou, Chang Shan; 周长山 ; Zhōu Chángshān; 周長山

1945-1990 **First publication: 1987**

- Employment: Henan Institute of Biology（河南生物研究所）
- Research interest: Liliaceae [S]
- Published taxa: *Fritillaria*
- Region: CHINA (Henan)

D. S. Zhou

Zhou, Da Song; 周大松 ; Zhōu Dàsōng

1990- **First publication: 2016**

- Employment: College of Forestry, Central South University of Forestry and Technology（中南林业科技大学林学院）
- Research interest: Saxifragaceae [S]
- Published taxa: *Chrysosplenium*
- Region: CHINA (Hunan)

D. W. Zhou

Zhou, Dao Wei; 周道玮 ; Zhōu Dàowěi

1963- **First publication: 1990**

- Employment: Department of Biology, Inner Mongolia University（内蒙古大学生物系）
- Research interest: Fabaceae [S]
- Published taxa: *Caragana*
- Region: CHINA (Nei Mongol)

D. X. Zhou

Zhou, Duon Xuon; Zhou, Dong Xiong; **周东雄 ; Zhōu Dōngxióng**

1955- **First publication: 1991**

- Employment: Sha County Institute of Forestry, Fujian（福建沙县林业科学研究所）
- Research interest: Pinaceae [S]
- Published taxa: *Pinus*
- Region: CHINA (Fujian)

F. Q. Zhou

Zhou, Feng Qin; 周凤琴 ; Zhōu Fèngqín

1951- **First publication: 2001**

- Employment: Shandong University of Traditional Chinese Medicine（山东中医药大学）
- Research interest: Caryophyllaceae, Dryopteridaceae, Equisetaceae, Hypodematiaceae [PS]
- Published taxa: *Cyrtomium, Dianthus, Hippochaete, Hypodematium*
- Location of specimens: SDCM
- Region: CHINA (Shandong)

F. S. Chou

Chou, Fu Shan; 周富三 ; Zhōu Fùsān

First publication: 2008

- Employment: Lioukuei Research Center, Taiwan Forestry Research Institute, Council of Agriculture, "Executive Yuan"（"行政院"农业委员会林业试验所六龟研究中心）
- Research interest: Plantaginaceae [S]
- Published taxa: *Veronicastrum*
- Region: CHINA (Taiwan)

G. L. Zhou

Zhou, Gui Ling; Zhou, Gui Lin; **周桂玲 ; Zhōu Guìlíng**

1956- **First publication: 1990**

- Employment: Xinjiang Bayi Agricultural College（新疆八一农学院）
- Research interest: Brassicaceae; Plants of Xinjiang [S]
- Published taxa: *Hedinia, Lepidium*
- Affiliation: XJA
- Location of specimens: XJA
- Region: CHINA (Xinjiang)

H. F. Chow

Chow, Hang Fan; Chou, Han Fan; Zhou, Han Fan; **周汉藩 ; Zhōu Hànfān; 周漢藩**

1877-1944 **First publication: 1934**

- Employment: Fan Memorial Institute of Biology（静生生物调查所）
- Research interest: Salicaceae [S]
- Published taxa: *Populus*
- Location of specimens: PE
- Region: CHINA (Hebei)

H. H. Zhou

Zhou, Han Hua; 周汉华 ; Zhōu Hànhuá

First publication: 1991

- Employment: Guiyang College of Traditional Chinese Medicine（贵阳中医学院）
- Research interest: Trilliaceae [S]
- Published taxa: *Paris*
- Region: CHINA (Guizhou)

Hang Zhou

Zhou, Hang; 周行 ; Zhōu Háng

First publication: 2010

- Employment: Amateur（业余爱好者）
- Research interest: Araceae [S]
- Published taxa: *Cryptocoryne*
- Region: CHINA (Guangxi)

Hao Zhou

Zhou, Hao; 周浩 ; Zhōu Hào

1982- **First publication: 2016**

- Employment: Guangxi Institute of Botany（广西植物研究所）
- Research interest: Asparagaceae [S]
- Published taxa: *Aspidistra*
- Region: CHINA (Chongqing)

H. Zhou

Zhou, Hong; 周红 ; Zhōu Hóng

1959- **First publication: 1985**

- Employment: Guizhou Research Institute of Forestry（贵州省林业科学研究所）
- Research interest: Theaceae [S]
- Published taxa: *Camellia*
- Region: CHINA (Guizhou)

Hong B. Zhou

Zhou, Hong Bo; 周宏博 ; Zhōu Hóngbó

First publication: 2020

- Employment: University of Science and Technology of China（中国科学技术大学）
- Research interest: Orchidaceae [S]
- Published taxa: *Cymbidium*
- Region: CHINA (Yunnan)

H. F. Zhou

Zhou, Hong Fu; Chow, Hung Fu; Chow, Hong Fu; 周洪富 ; Zhōu Hóngfù

First publication: 1980

- Employment: Sichuan Academy of Forestry（四川省林业科学研究院）
- Research interest: Elaeagnaceae, Thymelaeaceae [S]
- Published taxa: *Daphne, Elaeagnus, Wikstroemia*
- Location of specimens: SCFI
- Region: CHINA (Sichuan)
- Also as: H. F. Chow

H. G. Zhou

Zhou, Hou Gao; 周厚高 ; Zhōu Hòugāo

1962- **First publication: 1991**

- Employment: Guangxi Agricultural College（广西农学院）
- Research interest: Dennstaedtiaceae, Dipteridaceae, Dryopteridaceae, Hymenophyllaceae, Ophioglossaceae, Polypodiaceae, Pteridaceae, Thelypteridaceae; Pteridophytes [P]
- Published taxa: *Aleuritopteris, Ataxipteris, Colysis, Coniogramme, Ctenitis, Hypolepis, Mecodium, Metathelypteris, Ophioglossum, Parathelypteris, Phymatodes, Polystichum*
- Affiliation: GAUA
- Location of specimens: GAUA
- Region: CHINA (Guangxi)

Hui Zhou

Zhou, Hui; 周辉 ; Zhōu Huī

First publication: 2016

- Employment: Nanjing Institute of Environmental Sciences, Ministry of Environmental Protection（环境保护部南京环境科学研究所）
- Research interest: Saxifragaceae [S]
- Published taxa: *Chrysosplenium*
- Location of specimens: CSFI
- Region: CHINA (Hunan)

J. J. Zhou

Zhou, Jian Jun; 周建军 ; Zhōu Jiànjūn

1988- **First publication: 2015**

- Employment: College of Forestry, Central South University of Forestry and Technology; Hunan Prospectiong Designing & Research Institute for Agriculture Forestry & Industry（中南林业科技大学林学院；湖南省农林工业勘察设计研究院）
- Research interest: Gesneriaceae, Lauraceae, Primulaceae, Ranunculaceae [S]
- Published taxa: *Litsea, Lysimachia, Primulina, Semiaquilegia*
- Location of specimens: CSFI
- Region: CHINA (Hunan)

J. Zhou

Zhou, Jie; 周杰 ; Zhōu Jié

1978- First publication: 2010

- Employment: School of Landscape Architecture, Beijing Forestry University（北京林业大学园林学院）
- Research interest: Asteraceae [S]
- Published taxa: *Chrysanthemum*
- Region: CHINA (Henan, Hubei)

J. S. Zhou

Zhou, Jin Song; 周劲松；Zhōu Jìnsōng

1981- First publication: 2008

- Employment: College of Pharmacy, Guangzhou University of Chinese Medicine（广州中医药大学中药学院）
- Research interest: Violaceae [S]
- Published taxa: *Viola*
- Region: CHINA (Guangdong)

Jing Zhou

Zhou, Jing; 周静；Zhōu Jìng

1981- First publication: 2020

- Employment: School of Pharmaceutical Science, Kunming Medical University（昆明医科大学药学院）
- Research interest: Apiaceae [S]
- Published taxa: *Angelica*
- Region: CHINA (Yunnan)

K. F. Zhou

Zhou, Ke Fan; 周可范；Zhōu Kěfàn; 周可範

1934- First publication: 1981

- Employment: Henan Institute of Drug Control（河南省药品检验所）
- Research interest: Ranunculaceae [S]
- Published taxa: *Delphinium*
- Region: CHINA (Henan)

L. D. Zhou

Zhou, Li Duan; 周立端；Zhōu Lìduān

First publication: 1985

- Employment: Horticultural Research Institute, Yunnan Academy of Agricultural Sciences（云南省农业科学院园艺作物研究所）
- Research interest: Solanaceae [S]
- Published taxa: *Capsicum, Solanum*
- Region: CHINA (Yunnan)

L. H. Zhou

Zhou, Li Hua; Chou, L. H.; **周立华；Zhōu Lìhuá; 周立華**

1934-2013 First publication: 1979

- Employment: Northwest Plateau Institute of Biology, Chinese Academy of Sciences（中国科学院西北高原生物研究所）
- Research interest: Caryophyllaceae, Papaveraceae, Poaceae, Ranunculaceae [S]
- Published taxa: *Arenaria, Cerastium, Corydalis, Cucubalus, Halerpestes, Meconopsis, Melandrium, Panicum, Silene, Stellaria*
- Affiliation: HNWP
- Location of specimens: HNWP
- Region: CHINA (Gansu, Qinghai, Sichuan, Xizang, Yunnan)

L. J. Zhou

Zhou, Li Jiang; 周立江；Zhōu Lìjiāng

1956- First publication: 1983

- Employment: Sichuan Forestry Inventory and Planning Institute（四川省林业调查规划院）
- Research interest: Pinaceae [S]
- Published taxa: *Picea, Pseudotsuga*
- Region: CHINA (Sichuan)

Li H. Zhou

Zhou, Li Hua; 周丽华；Zhōu Lìhuá

1963- First publication: 2000

- Employment: Kunming Institute of Botany, Chinese Academy of Sciences; Department of Botany, California Academy of Sciences, U.S.A.（中国科学院昆明植物研究所；美国加利福尼亚州科学院植物部）
- Research interest: Ericaceae, Rosaceae [S]
- Published taxa: *Cotoneaster, Dichotomanthes, Gaultheria, Pleiosorbus*
- Region: CHINA (Yunnan)

L. S. Zhou

Zhou, Li Shuang; 周丽双；Zhōu Lìshuāng

1958- First publication: 1995

- Employment: Guangxi Institute of Traditional Medical and Pharmaceutical Sciences（广西中医药研究所）
- Research interest: Loganiaceae; Plants of Guangxi [S]
- Published taxa: *Mitreola*
- Affiliation: GXNM
- Location of specimens: GXNM
- Region: CHINA (Guangxi)

L. X. Zhou

Zhou, Lian Xuan; 周联选；Zhōu Liánxuǎn

1965- First publication: 2018

- Employment: South China Botanical Garden, Chinese Academy of Sciences（中国科学院华南植物园）
- Research interest: Gesneriaceae; Plants of S. China [S]
- Published taxa: *Oreocharis*
- Affiliation: IBSC
- Location of specimens: IBSC
- Region: CHINA (Guangdong)

L. Zhou

Zhou, Lin; 周林 ; Zhōu Lín

1931- **First publication: 1981**

- Employment: Landscape Office, Urban Construction Bureau of Dukou Municipal, Sichuan（四川省渡口市城建局园林处）
- Research interest: Cycadaceae [S]
- Published taxa: *Cycas*
- Region: CHINA (Sichuan)

L. L. Zhou

Zhou, Lin Lin; Zhou, Linlin; **周琳琳 ; Zhōu Línlín**

1983- **First publication: 2009**

- Employment: School of Biological Sciences, The University of Hong Kong（香港大学生物科学学院）
- Research interest: Annonaceae [S]
- Published taxa: *Uvaria*
- Region: [ASIA]

L. Y. Zhou

Zhou, Ling Yun; 周凌云 ; Zhōu Língyún; 周淩雲

1918- **First publication: 1988**

- Employment: Department of Biology, Wuhan University（武汉大学生物系）
- Research interest: Acoraceae, Hydrocharitaceae, Pandanaceae, Potamogetonaceae, Triuridaceae [S]
- Published taxa: *Najas, Pandanus, Potamogeton*
- Affiliation: WH
- Location of specimens: WH
- Region: CHINA

M. L. Zhou

Zhou, Mei Liang; 周美亮 ; Zhōu Měiliàng

1985- **First publication: 2015**

- Employment: Biotechnology Research Institute, Chinese Academy of Agricultural Sciences; College of Life Sciences, Sichuan Agricultural University（中国农业科学院生物技术研究所；四川农业大学生命科学学院）
- Research interest: Polygonaceae [S]
- Published taxa: *Fagopyrum*
- Region: CHINA (Sichuan)

M. Y. Zhou

Zhou, Meng Yuan; 周梦媛 ; Zhōu Mèngyuàn

1989- **First publication: 2017**

- Employment: Kunming Institute of Botany, Chinese Academy of Sciences（中国科学院昆明植物研究所）
- Research interest: Poaceae [S]
- Published taxa: *Holttumochloa, Melocalamus*
- Region: CHINA

Q. J. Zhou

Zhou, Qiu Jie; 周秋杰 ; Zhōu Qiūjié

1993- **First publication: 2018**

- Employment: School of Life Sciences, Sun Yat-sen University（中山大学生命科学学院）
- Research interest: Melastomataceae [S]
- Published taxa: *Bredia, Tashiroea*
- Region: CHINA (Guangxi, Hunan)

R. Zhou

Zhou, Ren Chao; 周仁超 ; Zhōu Rénchāo

1976- **First publication: 2019**

- Employment: School of Life Sciences, Sun Yat-sen University（中山大学生命科学学院）
- Research interest: Melastomataceae [S]
- Published taxa: *Bredia, Tashiroea*
- Location of specimens: HUST
- Region: CHINA
- Also as: Ren C. Zhou

R. Z. Zhou

Zhou, Ren Zhang; 周仁章 ; Zhōu Rénzhāng

1938- **First publication: 1986**

- Employment: South China Institute of Botany, Chinese Academy of Sciences（中国科学院华南植物研究所）
- Research interest: Magnoliaceae [S]
- Published taxa: *Magnolia, Manglietia, Michelia*
- Location of specimens: IBSC
- Region: CHINA

R. B. Zhou

Zhou, Ri Bao; 周日宝 ; Zhōu Rìbǎo

1962- **First publication: 1988**

- Employment: Hunan College of Traditional Chinese Medicine（湖南省中医学院）
- Research interest: Fabaceae [S]
- Published taxa: *Gleditsia*
- Affiliation: HNCM
- Location of specimens: HNCM
- Region: CHINA (Hunan)

Y. H. Chou

Chou, Yong Han; Zhou, Rong Han; **周荣汉 ; Zhōu Rónghàn**

1953- **First publication: 1980**

- Employment: Shenyang Pharmaceutical College; China Pharmaceutical University（沈阳药学院；中国药科大学）
- Research interest: Papaveraceae [S]
- Published taxa: *Corydalis*
- Location of specimens: SYPC
- Region: CHINA (Liaoning)

R. C. Zhou

Zhou, Rui Chang; Chou, R. C.; **周瑞昌 ; Zhōu**

Ruìchāng
1938- First publication: 1981
- Employment: Plant Resources Laboratory, Heilongjiang Institute of Natural Resources（黑龙江省自然资源研究所）
- Research interest: Ericaceae. [BMS]
- Published taxa: *Pyrola*
- Affiliation: HNR
- Location of specimens: HNR
- Region: CHINA

S. Q. Zhou

Zhou, Si Quang; Zhou, Shi Quan; 周世权；Zhōu Shìquán; 周世權
1937-2010 First publication: 1979
- Employment: Inner Mongolia Forestry College（内蒙古林学院）
- Research interest: Berberidaceae, Euphorbiaceae, Lamiaceae, Oleaceae, Salicaceae, Tamaricaceae [S]
- Published taxa: *Berberis, Euphorbia, Salix, Syringa, Tamarix, Vitex*
- Affiliation: NMAC, NMFC
- Location of specimens: NMAC, NMFC
- Region: CHINA (Nei Mongol, Shanxi)

S. C. Zhou

Zhou, Shi Chun; 周仕春；Zhōu Shìchūn
First publication: 1996
- Employment: Leshan Teachers School, Sichuan（乐山师范高等专科学校）
- Research interest: Brassicaceae [S]
- Published taxa: *Cardamine, Draba*
- Region: CHINA (Sichuan)

S. S. Zhou

Zhou, Shi Shun; 周仕顺； Zhōu Shìshùn
1979- First publication: 2017
- Employment: Xishuangbanna Tropical Botanical Garden, Chinese Academy of Sciences（中国科学院西双版纳热带植物园）
- Research interest: Annonaceae, Araceae, Balsaminaceae, Ericaceae, Linaceae, Magnoliaceae, Orchidaceae, Rubiaceae, Zingiberaceae; Plants of Yunnan [S]
- Published taxa: *Agapetes, Canthium, Coelogyne, Colocasia, Impatiens, Magnolia, Ophiorrhiza, Reinwardtia, Trivalvaria, Zingiber*
- Affiliation: HITBC
- Location of specimens: HITBC
- Region: CHINA (Yunnan)

S. B. Zhou

Zhou, Shou Biao; 周守标；Zhōu Shǒubiāo
1964- First publication: 1991
- Employment: Anhui Normal University（安徽师范大学）
- Research interest: Crassulaceae, Gesneriaceae, Lamiaceae, Lythraceae, Magnoliaceae, Orobanchaceae, Polypodiaceae, Primulaceae, Ranunculaceae, Santalaceae, Solanaceae; Plants of Anhui [PS]
- Published taxa: *Boea, Buckleya, Clematis, Hemiboea, Lagerstroemia, Lysimachia, Melampyrum, Michelia, Paraphlomis, Petrocodon, Physaliastrum, Primulina, Pyrrosia, Scutellaria, Sedum*
- Affiliation: ANUB
- Location of specimens: ANUB
- Region: CHINA

S. J. Zhou

Zhou, Shu Jun; 周树军；Zhōu Shùjūn
1964- First publication: 1996
- Employment: Forestry College, Shandong Agricultural University（山东农业大学林学院）
- Research interest: Asteraceae [S]
- Published taxa: *Dendranthema*
- Region: CHINA (Hubei)

T. J. Zhou

Zhou, Tai Jiu; 周太久；Zhōu Tàijiǔ
1971- First publication: 2009
- Employment: Guangxi Institute of Botany, Chinese Academy of Sciences（广西壮族自治区中国科学院广西植物研究所）
- Research interest: Gesneriaceae [S]
- Published taxa: *Chirita*
- Region: CHINA (Guangxi)

T. Y. Cheo

Cheo, Tai Yien; Chou, Tai Yen; Ch'ou, Tai Yen; Zhou, Tai Yan; 周太炎；Zhōu Tàiyán
1912-2003 First publication: 1948
- Employment: Institute of Botany, Jiangsu Province（江苏省植物研究所）
- Research interest: Brassicaceae [S]
- Published taxa: *Arabis, Brassica, Cardamine, Chorispora, Dimorphostemon, Draba, Eutrema, Isatis, Loxostemon, Pegaeophyton, Platycraspedum, Solms-laubachia, Synstemon, Yinshania*
- Affiliation: NAS
- Location of specimens: CPU, NAS
- Region: CHINA
- Also as: T. Y. Chou

Wei Zhou

Zhou, Wei; 周伟；Zhōu Wěi
1982- First publication: 2015
- Employment: Institute of Botany, Jiangsu Province

and Chinese Academy of Sciences（江苏省中国科学院植物研究所）
- Research interest: Apiaceae [S]
- Published taxa: *Libanotis*
- Region: CHINA (Jiangsu)
- IPNI as: W. Zhou

W. C. Chou

Chou, Wei Chuen; 周伟权；Zhōu Wěiquán
1963- **First publication: 2019**
- Employment: Guangxi Institute of Botany, Chinese Academy of Sciences（广西壮族自治区中国科学院广西植物研究所）
- Research interest: Gesneriaceae [S]
- Published taxa: *Primulina*
- Region: CHINA (Guangxi)

Wen Zhou

Zhou, Wen; 周闻；Zhōu Wén
First publication: 2020
- Employment: College of Life Sciences, Nanjing Agricultural University（南京农业大学生命科学学院）
- Research interest: Phytolaccaceae [S]
- Published taxa: *Phytolacca*
- Region: CHINA (Yunnan)

X. J. Zhou

Zhou, Xiao Jun; 周晓君；Zhōu Xiǎojūn
First publication: 2020
- Employment: Life Science College, Luoyang Normal University（洛阳师范学院生命科学学院）
- Research interest: Ericaceae [S]
- Published taxa: *Rhododendron*
- Region: CHINA (Henan)

X. X. Zhou

Zhou, Xin Xin; 周欣欣；Zhōu Xīnxīn
1980- **First publication: 2019**
- Employment: South China Botanical Garden, Chinese Academy of Sciences（中国科学院华南植物园）
- Research interest: Aristolochiaceae [S]
- Published taxa: *Isotrema*
- Region: CHINA (Guangdong)

Xin M. Zhou

Zhou, Xin Mao; 周新茂；Zhōu Xīnmào
1987- **First publication: 2013**
- Employment: Chengdu Institute of Biology, Chinese Academy of Sciences; Missouri Botanical Garden, U.S.A.; School of Ecology and Environmental Science, Yunnan University（中国科学院成都生物研究所；美国密苏里植物园；云南大学生态学与环境学院）
- Research interest: Apiaceae, Dryopteridaceae, Lycopodiaceae, Polypodiaceae, Pteridryaceae, Selaginellaceae [P]
- Published taxa: *Acronema, Arachniodes, Dendrolycopodium, Hovenkampia, Huperzia, Pteridrys, Pyrrosia, Selaginella*
- Region: [WORLD]
- IPNI as: X. M. Zhou

X. M. Zhou

Zhou, Xin Min; 周新民；Zhōu Xīnmín
First publication: 1996
- Employment: Ji' an Forestry Bureau, Jiangxi（江西吉安地区林业局）
- Research interest: Poaceae [S]
- Published taxa: *Pseudosasa*
- Region: CHINA (Jiangxi)

X. P. Zhou

Zhou, Xu Ping; 周旭平；Zhōu Xùpíng
1972- **First publication: 2007**
- Employment: Bureau of Urban Landscape Management, Shenzhen（深圳市城市绿化管理处）
- Research interest: Orchidaceae [S]
- Published taxa: *Cymbidium*
- Region: CHINA (Yunnan)

S. Y. Cheo

Cheo, Shuh Yuen; Cheo, Shu Yuen; Chou, Hsu Yuan; Chou, Hsü Yüan; Zhou, Xu Yuan; 周蓄源；Zhōu Xùyuán
1901-2000 **First publication: 1951**
- Employment: University of Nanking; Nanjing University; Arnold Arboretum, Harvard University, U.S.A.; Fudan University; Jiangxi Agricultural University（金陵大学；南京大学；美国哈佛大学阿诺德树木园；复旦大学；江西农业大学）
- Research interest: Fagaceae, Rutaceae; Plants of Jiangxi [S]
- Published taxa: *Castanea, Fagara, Zanthoxylum*
- Affiliation: JXAU
- Location of specimens: JXAU
- Region: CHINA
- Also as: C. Y. Cheo; X. Y. Zhou

S. Chow

Chow, Shuan; Zhou, Xuan; 周铉；Zhōu Xuàn; 周鉉
1926- **First publication: 1962**
- Employment: Kunming Institute of Botany, Chinese Academy of Sciences（中国科学院昆明植物研究所）
- Research interest: Lamiaceae, Orchidaceae [S]
- Published taxa: *Ajuga, Elsholtzia, Gastrodia, Holocheila, Kinostemon, Scutellaria, Teucrium, Wenchengia*
- Affiliation: KUN
- Location of specimens: KUN

• Region: CHINA

Y. D. Zhou

Zhou, Ya Dong; 周亚东 ; Zhōu Yàdōng

1987- **First publication: 2014**

• Employment: Wuhan Botanical Garden, Chinese Academy of Sciences（中国科学院武汉植物园）

• Research interest: Crassulaceae, Cucurbitaceae, Menispermaceae, Menyanthaceae; Plants of E. Africa [S]

• Published taxa: *Cissampelos, Nymphoides, Sedum, Zehneria*

• Affiliation: HIB

• Location of specimens: HIB

• Region: [WORLD]

Y. L. Chou

Chou, Yi Liang; Chou, Yu Liang; Chou, I Liang; Zhou, Yi Liang; 周以良 ; Zhōu Yǐliáng

1922-2005 **First publication: 1958**

• Employment: Department of Forestry, Northeast Forestry Institute; Herbarium, Department of Forestry, Northeast Forestry University（东北林学院林学系；东北林业大学林学系植物标本室）

• Research interest: Cyperaceae, Ericaceae, Grossulariaceae, Oleaceae, Pinaceae, Rosaceae, Salicaceae. [AS]

• Published taxa: *Carex, Cheilotheca, Eremotropa, Larix, Ledum, Orthilia, Picea, Prunus, Pyrola, Ribes, Salix, Sorbus, Syringa*

• Affiliation: NEFI

• Location of specimens: NEAU, NEFI

• Region: CHINA (Heilongjiang)

Y. F. Zhou

Zhou, Yi Feng; 周义峰 ; Zhōu Yìfēng

1973- **First publication: 2008**

• Employment: Institute of Botany, Jiangsu Province and Chinese Academy of Sciences（江苏省中国科学院植物研究所）

• Research interest: Dioscoreaceae [S]

• Published taxa: *Dioscorea*

• Region: CHINA (Yunnan)

Y. S. Zhou

Zhou, Yin Sou; 周印锁 ; Zhōu Yìnsuǒ; 周印鎖

1935- **First publication: 1985**

• Employment: Department of Pharmacy, Lanzhou Medical College（兰州医学院药学系）

• Research interest: Campanulaceae, Liliaceae, Polygalaceae [S]

• Published taxa: *Adenophora, Adenophora, Fritillaria , Polygala*

• Region: CHINA (Gansu)

Y. Y. Zhou

Zhou, Ying Ying; 周莹莹 ; Zhōu Yíngyíng

1992- **First publication: 2013**

• Employment: College of Life and Environmental Sciences, Hangzhou Normal University（杭州师范大学生命与环境科学学院）

• Research interest: Brassicaceae, Cyperaceae, Rubiaceae [S]

• Published taxa: *Carex, Rubia, Sinalliaria*

• Region: CHINA (Zhejiang)

Y. H. Zhou

Zhou, Yong Hong; 周永红 ; Zhōu Yǒnghóng

1962- **First publication: 1997**

• Employment: Triticeae Research Institute, Sichuan Agricultural University（四川农业大学小麦研究所）

• Research interest: Poaceae [S]

• Published taxa: *Asperella, Leymus, Roegneria, Trichopyrum*

• Affiliation: SAU, SAUT

• Location of specimens: SAU, SAUT

• Region: CHINA

Z. K. Zhou

Zhou, Zhe Kun; 周浙昆 ; Zhōu Zhèkūn

1956- **First publication: 1996**

• Employment: Kunming Institute of Botany, Chinese Academy of Sciences; Xishuangbanna Tropical Botanical Garden, Chinese Academy of Sciences（中国科学院昆明植物研究所；中国科学院西双版纳热带植物园）

• Research interest: Bignoniaceae, Boraginaceae, Ericaceae, Fagaceae, Melanthiaceae, Moraceae, Sapindaceae; Fossil plants [S]

• Published taxa: *Acer, Agapetes, Cyclobalanopsis, Ficus, Incarvillea, Lithocarpus, Maclura, Microula, Paris, Quercus*

• Affiliation: KUN

• Location of specimens: KUN

• Region: CHINA

Z. C. Zhou

Zhou, Zhen Cheng; 周珍诚 ; Zhōu Zhēnchéng; 周珍誠

1939- **First publication: 1984**

• Employment: Guangxi Institute for Drug Control（广西药品检验所）

• Research interest: Fabaceae; Medicinal Plants [S]

• Published taxa: *Sophora*

• Affiliation: GXDC

• Region: CHINA (Guangxi)

• IPNI as: Z. C. Chou

C. Chow

Chow, Chen; Chow, Cheng; Zhou, Zhen; 周鎮 ; Zhōu

Zhèn; 周镇

First publication: 1970

- Employment: The Orchid Society of Taiwan Province（台湾省兰艺协会）
- Research interest: Orchidaceae [S]
- Published taxa: *Cymbidium*
- Region: CHINA (Taiwan)

Z. D. Zhou

Zhou, Zhi De; 周芝德 ; Zhōu Zhīdé

1935- **First publication: 1982**

- Employment: Jiangxi Agricultural University（江西农业大学）
- Research interest: Fagaceae [S]
- Published taxa: *Castanea*
- Region: CHINA (Jiangxi)

Z. Z. Zhou

Zhou, Zhong Ze; 周忠泽 ; Zhōu Zhōngzé

1967- **First publication: 2001**

- Employment: School of Life Sciences, Anhui University（安徽大学生命科学学院）
- Research interest: Polygonaceae [S]
- Published taxa: *Koenigia, Polygonum*
- Affiliation: ANU
- Location of specimens: ANU
- Region: CHINA (Anhui, Sichuan, Xizang)

Zhuang Zhou

Zhou, Zhuang; 周庄 ; Zhōu Zhuāng

1978- **First publication: 2020**

- Employment: Institute of Subtropical Crops, Zhejiang Academy of Agricultural Sciences; College of Landscape Architecture, Fujian Agriculture and Forestry University（浙江省农业科学院亚热带作物研究所；福建农林大学园林学院）
- Research interest: Orchidaceae [S]
- Published taxa: *Cymbidium, Dendrobium*
- Region: CHINA

Z. Zhou

Zhou, Zhuo; 周卓 ; Zhōu Zhuó

1986- **First publication: 2017**

- Employment: Kunming Institute of Botany, Chinese Academy of Sciences（中国科学院昆明植物研究所）
- Research interest: Euphorbiaceae [S]
- Published taxa: *Tsaiodendron*
- Region: CHINA (Yunnan)

C. S. Zhu

Zhu, Chang Shan; 朱长山 ; Zhū Chángshān; 朱長山

1945- **First publication: 1994**

- Employment: Henan Agricultural University（河南农业大学）
- Research interest: Amaranthaceae, Balsaminaceae, Caryophyllaceae, Fabaceae, Lamiaceae, Lauraceae, Rosaceae, Scrophulariaceae, Vitaceae; Plants of Henan [S]
- Published taxa: *Chenopodium, Exochorda, Glycine, Impatiens, Lindera, Nepeta, Scrophularia, Stellaria, Vitis*
- Affiliation: HEAC
- Location of specimens: HEAC
- Region: CHINA (Henan)

G. P. Zhu

Zhu, Gan Pei; 朱甘培 ; Zhū Gānpéi

1936- **First publication: 1995**

- Employment: Department of Chinese Materia Medica, Beijing University of Chinese Medicine（北京中医药大学中药系）
- Research interest: Lamiaceae, Orchidaceae [S]
- Published taxa: *Mosla*
- Affiliation: BCMM
- Location of specimens: BCMM
- Region: CHINA (Jiangxi)

G. L. Chu

Chu, Ge Ling; Chu, Ge Lin; Zhu, Ge Lin; Zhu, Ge Ling; 朱格麟 ; Zhū Gélín

1934- **First publication: 1978**

- Employment: Institute of Botany, Northwest Normal College（西北师范学院植物研究所）
- Research interest: Amaranthaceae, Boraginaceae, Chenopodiaceae [S]
- Published taxa: *Acroglochin, Archiatriplex, Arnebia, Atriplex, Baolia, Bienertia, Borszczowia, Carocarpidium*
- Affiliation: NWTC
- Location of specimens: NWTC
- Region: CHINA

G. H. Zhu

Zhu, Guang Hua; 朱光华 ; Zhū Guānghuá

1964-2005 **First publication: 1995**

- Employment: Institute of Botany, Chinese Academy of Sciences（中国科学院植物研究所）
- Research interest: Amaryllidaceae, Araceae, Ephedraceae, Fabaceae, Orchidaceae, Poaceae, Ranunculaceae, Salicaceae [S]
- Published taxa: *Allium, Caragana, Cephalanthera, Cypripedium, Dracontium, Elymus, Ephedra, Epipactis, Leymus, Listera, Pinellia, Pleione, Poa, Populus, Salix, Thalictrum*
- Region: CHINA

G. Q. Zhu

Zhu, Guang Quan; 朱光权 ; Zhū Guāngquán

First publication: 2020

- Employment: Zhejiang Academy of Forestry（浙江省林业科学研究院）
- Research interest: Cucurbitaceae [S]
- Published taxa: *Trichosanthes*
- Region: CHINA (Zhejiang)

Hua Zhu

Zhu, Hua; Chu, Hua; 朱华 ; Zhū Huá
1960- **First publication: 1989**
- Employment: Xishuangbanna Tropical Botanical Garden, Chinese Academy of Sciences（中国科学院西双版纳热带植物园）
- Research interest: Acanthaceae, Ebenaceae, Euphorbiaceae, Rubiaceae, Solanaceae; Plants of Yunnan [S]
- Published taxa: *Andrographis, Baphicacanthus, Diospyros, Duperrea, Lasianthus, Paralasianthus, Solanum, Tsaiodendron*
- Affiliation: HITBC
- Location of specimens: HITBC
- Region: CHINA
- IPNI as: H. Zhu

L. T. Zhu

Zhu, Li Tao; 朱立涛 ; Zhū Lìtāo
1978- **First publication: 2007**
- Employment: College of Life Science, Shandong Normal University（山东师范大学生命科学学院）
- Research interest: Polygonaceae [S]
- Published taxa: *Polygonum*
- Region: CHINA

M. R. Zhu

Zhu, Meng Ru; 朱梦如 ; Zhū Mèngrú
1997- **First publication: 2018**
- Employment: College of Life and Environmental Sciences, Hangzhou Normal University（杭州师范大学生命与环境科学学院）
- Research interest: Potamogetonaceae [S]
- Published taxa: *Potamogeton*
- Region: CHINA (Zhejiang)

P. C. Zhu

Zhu, Pei Zhi; 朱培智 ; Zhū Péizhì
First publication: 1979
- Employment: Yunnan Institute of Tropical Botany, Chinese Academy of Sciences（中国科学院云南热带植物研究所）
- Research interest: Piperaceae [S]
- Published taxa: *Peperomia, Piper*
- Affiliation: HITBC
- Location of specimens: HITBC
- Region: CHINA (Yunnan)

Q. Zhu

Zhu, Qiang; 朱强 ; Zhū Qiáng
1980- **First publication: 2009**
- Employment: College of Life Sciences, Ningxia University（宁夏大学生命科学学院）
- Research interest: Asteraceae, Gentianaceae, Geraniaceae [S]
- Published taxa: *Gentiana, Geranium, Mulgedium*
- Region: CHINA (Ningxia)

R. B. Zhu

Zhu, Ren Bin; 朱仁斌 ; Zhū Rénbīn
1988- **First publication: 2014**
- Employment: College of Natural Resources and Environment, Northwest A&F University; Xishuangbanna Tropical Botanical Garden, Chinese Academy of Sciences（西北农林科技大学资源环境学院；中国科学院西双版纳热带植物园）
- Research interest: Scrophulariaceae [S]
- Published taxa: *Buddleja*
- Region: CHINA (Shaanxi)

S. X. Zhu

Zhu, Shi Xin; 朱世新 ; Zhū Shìxīn
1975- **First publication: 2008**
- Employment: Department of Biological Engineering, Zhengzhou University（郑州大学生物工程系）
- Research interest: Asteraceae, Fabaceae, Gesneriaceae [S]
- Published taxa: *Anaphalis, Chirita, Glycine*
- Region: CHINA (Henan)

S. Zhu

Zhu, Shu; 朱姝 ; Zhū Shū
1973- **First publication: 2003**
- Employment: Department of natural medicines, School of Pharmaceutical Sciences, Peking University（北京大学药学院天然药物学系）
- Research interest: Araliaceae [S]
- Published taxa: *Panax*
- Region: CHINA (Yunnan)

W. Zhu

Zhu, Wei; 朱炜 ; Zhū Wěi
First publication: 2020
- Employment: Huzhou Bureau of Natural Resources and Planning, Zhejiang（湖州市自然资源和规划局）
- Research interest: Rutaceae [S]
- Published taxa: *Zanthoxylum*
- Region: CHINA (Zhejiang)

W. M. Chu

Chu, Wei Ming; Zhu, Wei Ming; 朱维明 ; Zhū Wéimíng; 朱維明

1930- **First publication: 1978**

- Employment: Yunnan University（云南大学）
- Research interest: Athyriaceae, Dennstaedtiaceae, Diplaziopsidaceae, Dryopteridaceae, Gleicheniaceae, Hymenophyllaceae, Lycopodiaceae, Marattiaceae, Ophioglossaceae, Osmundaceae, Plagiogyriaceae, Polypodiaceae, Pteridaceae, Selaginellaceae, Thelypteridaceae; Pteridophytes [PS]
- Published taxa: *Aleuritopteris, Allantodia, Allantodia, Angiopteris, Arthromeris, Athyriopsis, Athyrium, Bolbitis, Cornopteris, Craspedosorus, Ctenitis, Cyclosorus, Diplaziopsis, Diplazium, Diplopterygium, Dryoathyrium, Dryopteris, Glaphyropteridopsis, Huperzia, Hypolepis, Lastreopsis, Lepidomicrosorium, Lepisorus, Lunathyrium, Mecodium, Metapolypodium, Metathelypteris, Microsorum, Monomelangium, Onychium, Ophioglossum, Osmundastrum, Palhinhaea, Phlegmariurus, Phymatopteris, Plagiogyria, Polypodiodes, Polystichum, Pseudocyclosorus, Pteris, Selaginella*
- Affiliation: PYU, YUKU
- Location of specimens: PYU, YUKU
- Region: CHINA

X. Y. Zhu

Zhu, Xiang Yun; 朱相云 ; Zhū Xiāngyún

1964- **First publication: 1994**

- Employment: Institute of Botany, Chinese Academy of Sciences（中国科学院植物研究所）
- Research interest: Araliaceae, Fabaceae [S]
- Published taxa: *Abarema, Adenanthera, Archidendron, Astragalus, Butea, Caesalpinia, Callerya, Chesneya, Codariocalyx, Corethrodendron, Crotalaria, Derris, Dumasia, Eleutherococcus, Glycine, Hylodesmum, Indigofera, Lathyrus, Lespedeza, Medicago, Oxytropis, Phanera, Phyllolobium, Piptanthus, Senegalia, Senna, Thermopsis, Tibetia*
- Affiliation: PE
- Location of specimens: PE
- Region: CHINA

X. X. Zhu

Zhu, Xin Xin; 朱鑫鑫 ; Zhū Xīnxīn

1986- **First publication: 2014**

- Employment: Kunming Institute of Botany, Chinese Academy of Sciences; Shanghai Chenshan Botanical Garden; Xinyang Normal University（中国科学院昆明植物研究所；上海辰山植物园；信阳师范学院）
- Research interest: Aristolochiaceae, Colchicaceae, Gesneriaceae, Orchidaceae [S]
- Published taxa: *Aristolochia, Disporum, Hemipilia, Isotrema, Primulina*
- Region: CHINA

Y. Q. Zhu

Zhu, Ying Qun; 朱英群 ; Zhū Yīngqún

1957- **First publication: 1993**

- Employment: Shandong Forestry School（山东省林业学校）
- Research interest: Adoxaceae, Cannabaceae, Fabaceae, Fagaceae, Rhamnaceae, Rosaceae, Salicaceae [S]
- Published taxa: *Celtis, Quercus, Rhamnus, Salix, Spiraea, Viburnum, Vicia*
- Region: CHINA (Shandong)

Y. P. Zhu

Zhu, You Ping; 朱友平 ; Zhū Yǒupíng

1963- **First publication: 1993**

- Employment: College of Pharmacy, Second Military Medical University（第二军医大学药学院）
- Research interest: Rosaceae [S]
- Published taxa: *Armeniaca*
- Region: CHINA

Y. C. Chu

Chu, You Chang; Zhu, You Chang; Chu, Yu Chang; 朱有昌 ; Zhū Yǒuchāng

1924- **First publication: 1959**

- Employment: Plant Resources Laboratory, Heilongjiang Institute of Natural Resources（黑龙江省自然资源研究所植物资源研究室）
- Research interest: Apiaceae, Araceae, Araliaceae, Asparagaceae, Asteraceae, Caprifoliaceae, Caryophyllaceae, Crassulaceae, Cupressaceae, Ericaceae, Euphorbiaceae, Geraniaceae, Lamiaceae, Malvaceae, Nymphaeaceae, Orobanchaceae, Papaveraceae, Polemoniaceae, Ranunculaceae, Rosaceae, Rutaceae; Medicinal Plants [S]
- Published taxa: *Aralia, Arisaema, Armeniaca, Atractylodes, Bupleurum, Cerastium, Cicuta, Convallaria, Corydalis, Dasiphora, Dianthus, Elsholtzia, Euphorbia, Geranium, Juniperus, Leonurus, Melandrium, Mentha, Monotropastrum, Nymphaea, Ostericum, Phellodendron, Polemonium, Polygonatum, Ranunculus, Rehmannia, Rhododendron, Sanguisorba, Sedum, Silene, Sorbus, Stellaria, Tilia, Weigela*
- Affiliation: HNR
- Location of specimens: HNR
- Region: CHINA (Liaoning)

Y. T. Zhu

Zhu, Yu Tong; 朱宇同 ; Zhū Yǔtóng

1929- **First publication: 1996**

- Employment: Guangzhou University of Chinese Medicine（广州中医药大学）
- Research interest: Phyllanthaceae [S]

• Published taxa: *Phyllanthus*
• Region: CHINA (Hainan)

Y. J. Zhu

Zhu, Yu Jian; 朱玉简 ; Zhū Yùjiǎn; 朱玉簡
1934- **First publication: 1986**
• Employment: Southern Anhui Agricultural University（安徽皖南农学院）
• Research interest: Fabaceae [S]
• Published taxa: *Lathyrus*
• Region: CHINA (Anhui)

Yu P. Zhu

Zhu, Yu Ping; 朱昱苹 ; Zhū Yùpíng; 朱昱萍
1981- **First publication: 2004**
• Employment: Institute of Botany, Chinese Academy of Sciences（中国科学院植物研究所）
• Research interest: Stachyuraceae [S]
• Published taxa: *Stachyurus*
• Region: [ASIA]
• IPNI as: Y. P. Zhu

C. Y. Chu

Chu, Chao Yi; Chu, Chao I; Zhu, Zhao Yi; 朱兆仪 ; Zhū Zhàoyí; 朱兆儀
1934- **First publication: 1962**
• Employment: Institute of Medicinal Plant Development, Chinese Academy of Medical Sciences（中国医学科学院药用植物资源开发研究所）
• Research interest: Araliaceae, Lamiaceae, Menispermaceae [S]
• Published taxa: *Panax*
• Affiliation: IMD
• Location of specimens: IMD
• Region: CHINA

C. D. Chu

Chu, Cheng De; Zhu, Zheng De; 朱政德 ; Zhū Zhèngdé
1928- **First publication: 1975**
• Employment: Nanjing Forestry University（南京林业大学）
• Research interest: Phyllanthaceae, Pinaceae, Poaceae, Sapindaceae; Gymnospermae [S]
• Published taxa: *Acer, Acidosasa, Ampelocalamus, Arundinaria, Bischofia, Chimonobambusa, Gelidocalamus, Indocalamus, Indosasa, Phyllostachys, Pinus, Pleioblastus, Pseudosasa, Sasa, Sinarundinaria, Sinobambusa, Thamnocalamus*
• Affiliation: NF
• Location of specimens: NF
• Region: CHINA
• Also as: Z. D. Chu

Z. Y. Chu

Chu, Zong Yuan; Zhu, Zong Yuan; 朱宗元 ; Zhū Zōngyuán
1940- **First publication: 1978**
• Employment: Ulanqab Science and Technology Commission, Inner Mongolia; School of Life Sciences, Inner Mongolia University（内蒙古乌兰察布盟科委；内蒙古大学生命科学学院）
• Research interest: Amaranthaceae, Asteraceae, Brassicaceae, Cistaceae, Fabaceae, Gentianaceae, Orobanchaceae [S]
• Published taxa: *Anagallidium, Astragalus, Atriplex, Caragana, Corethrodendron, Corispermum, Elachanthemum, Hedysarum, Helianthemum, Kalidium, Microsisymbrium, Oxytropis, Pedicularis, Salsola, Suaeda*
• Affiliation: HIMC
• Location of specimens: HIMC
• Region: CHINA (Nei Mongol)
• Also as: Zong Y. Zhu

R. Zhuge

Zhuge, Ren; 诸葛仁 ; Zhūgě Rén
1956- **First publication: 1990**
• Employment: Southwest Forestry College（西南林学院）
• Research interest: Malvaceae [S]
• Published taxa: *Burretiodendron, Grewia*
• Affiliation: SWFC
• Location of specimens: SWFC
• Region: CHINA (Yunnan)

S. J. Zhu

Zhu, Shi Jie; 祝世杰 ; Zhù Shìjié
1971- **First publication: 2008**
• Employment: Sichuan School of Chinese Materia Medica（四川省中药学校）
• Research interest: Araceae, Orchidaceae, Rubiaceae; Medicinal Plants [S]
• Published taxa: *Arisaema, Dendrobium, Mussaenda, Paederia*
• Affiliation: EMA
• Location of specimens: EMA
• Region: CHINA (Sichuan)

Z. Y. Zhu

Zhu, Zheng Yin; 祝正银 ; Zhù Zhèngyín; 祝正銀
1944- **First publication: 1981**
• Employment: Sichuan School of Chinese Materia Medica（四川省中药学校）
• Research interest: Acoraceae, Amaryllidaceae, Apocynaceae, Araceae, Araliaceae, Asparagaceae, Asteraceae, Campanulaceae, Convolvulaceae, Cornaceae, Gentianaceae, Lamiaceae, Liliaceae,

Orchidaceae, Primulaceae, Rhamnaceae, Rubiaceae, Saururaceae, Zingiberaceae; Medicinal Plants [S]
- Published taxa: *Acorus, Adenophora, Allium, Alpinia, Ardisia, Arisaema, Aspidistra, Aster, Biondia, Blumea, Changruicaoia, Dendrobium, Euaraliopsis, Gentiana, Globba, Gynura, Hedychium, Houttuynia, Ipomoea, Lilium, Lomatogonium, Mussaenda, Myrsine, Ophiopogon, Paederia, Panzhuyuia, Polygonatum, Reineckea, Rhamnus, Roscoea, Salvia, Swertia, Tupistra, Tylophora, Typhonium, Yinquania, Zingiber*
- Affiliation: EMA
- Location of specimens: EMA
- Region: CHINA (Sichuan)

T. I. Chuang

Chuang, Tsan Iang; Chuang, Tsan Yang; Chuang, Ts'an Yang; Zhuang, Can Yang; 莊燦煬；Zhuāng Cànyáng; 庄灿炀；莊燦暘；庄灿旸

1933-1994 **First publication: 1969**
- Employment: Illinois State University, U.S.A.（美国伊利诺伊州立大学）
- Research interest: Apiaceae, Orobanchaceae [S]
- Published taxa: *Castilleja, Cordylanthus, Orthocarpus, Perideridia, Triphysaria*
- Location of specimens: HAST
- Region: UNITED STATES

K. C. Chuang

Chuang, Kuei Chun; 莊貴竣；Zhuāng Guìjùn; 庄贵竣

First publication: 2020
- Employment: Department of Life Science, Taiwan Normal University（台湾师范大学生命科学系）
- Research interest: Asparagaceae [S]
- Published taxa: *Aspidistra*
- Region: CHINA (Taiwan)

P. Zhuang

Zhuang, Ping; 庄平；Zhuāng Píng

1957- **First publication: 1999**
- Employment: West China Subalpine Botanical Garden, Institute of Botany, Chinese Academy of Sciences; Sichuan Nature Resource Institute（中国科学院植物研究所华西亚高山植物园；四川省自然资源研究所）
- Research interest: Berberidaceae [S]
- Published taxa: *Dysosma, Podophyllum*
- Affiliation: WCSBG, SR
- Location of specimens: WCSBG, SR
- Region: CHINA (Sichuan)

T. D. Zhuang

Zhuang, Ti De; 庄体德；Zhuāng Tǐdé; 莊體德

1935- **First publication: 1982**
- Employment: Institute of Botany, Jiangsu Province（江苏省植物研究所）
- Research interest: Apiaceae, Lamiaceae, Poaceae [S]
- Published taxa: *Angelica, Clerodendrum, Panicum, Pseudanthistiria, Sacciolepis, Themeda*
- Affiliation: NAS
- Location of specimens: NAS
- Region: CHINA

H. Chuang

Chuang, Hsuan; Zhuang, Xuan; 庄璇；Zhuāng Xuán; 莊璇

1938- **First publication: 1979**
- Employment: Kunming Institute of Botany, Chinese Academy of Sciences（中国科学院昆明植物研究所）
- Research interest: Asteraceae, Boraginaceae, Caryophyllaceae, Celastraceae, Crassulaceae, Grossulariaceae, Papaveraceae, Sapotaceae, Saxifragaceae [S]
- Published taxa: *Ainsliaea, Arenaria, Bergenia, Corydalis, Dicranostigma, Heliotropium, Meconopsis, Papaver, Parnassia, Pertya, Rhodiola, Ribes, Saxifraga, Silene, Sinocrassula, Sinosideroxylon, Stellaria, Tillaea, Trigonotis, Wedelia*
- Affiliation: KUN
- Location of specimens: KUN
- Region: CHINA (Sichuan, Xizang, Yunnan)

X. Y. Zhuang

Zhuang, Xue Ying; 庄雪影；Zhuāng Xuěyǐng

1961-2016 **First publication: 1986**
- Employment: College of Forestry and Landscape Architecture, South China Agricultural University（华南农业大学林学与风景园林学院）
- Research interest: Gesneriaceae, Melastomataceae, Orchidaceae, Sapotaceae [S]
- Published taxa: *Cestichis, Donella, Fordiophyton, Hemiboea, Mostichodendron, Platystyliparis, Primulina*
- Affiliation: CANT
- Location of specimens: CANT
- Region: CHINA
- Also as: X. Y. Chuang

L. H. Zhuo

Zhuo, Li Huan; 卓丽环；Zhuō Lìhuán

1955- **First publication: 1983**
- Employment: Northeast Forestry Institute; Northeast Forestry University（东北林学院；东北林业大学）
- Research interest: Fabaceae, Primulaceae, Rosaceae, Schisandraceae, Ulmaceae [S]
- Published taxa: *Geum, Oxytropis, Primula, Schisandra, Ulmus*
- Affiliation: NEFI
- Location of specimens: NEFI

• Region: CHINA

Z. J. Zong

Zong, Zhan Jiang; 宗占江 ; Zōng Zhànjiāng
1950- **First publication: 1993**
• Employment: Administrative Bureau of Nature Reserve of Changbai Mountain, Jilin（吉林省长白山自然保护区管理局）
• Research interest: Amaranthaceae, Caryophyllaceae, Fabaceae, Liliaceae [S]
• Published taxa: *Oxytropis*
• Affiliation: ANTU
• Region: CHINA (Jilin)

C. Y. Zou

Zou, Chun Yu; 邹春玉 ; Zōu Chūnyù
1992- **First publication: 2017**
• Employment: Guangxi Institute of Botany, Chinese Academy of Sciences; College of Life Sciences, Guangxi Normal University（广西壮族自治区中国科学院广西植物研究所；广西师范大学生命科学学院）
• Research interest: Asparagaceae [S]
• Published taxa: *Aspidistra*
• Region: CHINA (Guangxi)

H. Y. Chou

Chou, Hui Yu; Zou, Hui Yu; Zhou, Hui Yu; **邹惠渝** ; Zōu Huìyú; **鄒惠渝**
1945-2001 **First publication: 1976**
• Employment: Key Laboratory of Forest Genetics and Gene Engineering, Nanjing Forstry University; Department of Forestry, Nanjing Forestry College（南京林业大学林木遗传和基因工程重点实验室；南京林学院林学系）
• Research interest: Aquifoliaceae, Poaceae; Woody Plants [S]
• Published taxa: *Arundinaria, Ilex, Phyllostachys, Shibataea*
• Affiliation: NF
• Location of specimens: NF
• Region: CHINA (Fujian, Zhejiang)
• Also as: H. Y. Zou; H. Y. Zhou

L. H. Zou

Zou, Long Hai; 邹龙海 ; Zōu Lónghǎi
1988- **First publication: 2014**
• Employment: College of Forestry, South China Agricultural University（华南农业大学林学院）
• Research interest: Orchidaceae [S]
• Published taxa: *Vanda*
• Region: CHINA (Yunnan)

P. Zou

Zou, Pu; 邹璞 ; Zōu Pú
1978- **First publication: 2015**
• Employment: South China Botanical Garden, Chinese Academy of Sciences（中国科学院华南植物园）
• Research interest: Lowiaceae, Zingiberaceae [S]
• Published taxa: *Alpinia, Amomum, Orchidantha*
• Region: CHINA (Guangdong, Hainan)

R. F. Zou

Zou, Rong Fu; 邹荣福 ; Zōu Róngfú
First publication: 1983
• Employment: Majiang County Forestry Bureau, Guizhou（贵州省麻江县林业局）
• Research interest: Cycadaceae [S]
• Published taxa: *Cycas*
• Region: CHINA (Guizhou)

S. Q. Zou

Zou, Shou Qing; 邹寿青 ; Zōu Shòuqīng; **鄒壽青**
1943- **First publication: 1984**
• Employment: Yunnan Institute of Tropical Botany, Chinese Academy of Sciences（中国科学院云南热带植物研究所）
• Research interest: Fabaceae, Rubiaceae [S]
• Published taxa: *Dalbergia, Neonauclea*
• Region: CHINA (Yunnan)

Y. Zou

Zou, Yuan; 邹垣 ; Zōu Yuán
?-2018 **First publication: 1991**
• Employment: Jiujiang Institute of Forestry Science, Jiangxi（江西省九江市林业科学研究所）
• Research interest: Poaceae [S]
• Published taxa: *Indocalamus, Indosasa*
• Location of specimens: IBSC
• Region: CHINA (Jiangxi)

C. H. Tsou

Tsou, Chih Hua; Zou, Zhi Hua; **鄒稚華** ; Zōu Zhìhuá; **邹稚华**
1957- **First publication: 1994**
• Employment: National Institute of Botany, "Academia Sinica"（中研院植物研究所）
• Research interest: Cycadaceae, Pentaphylacaceae, Theaceae [S]
• Published taxa: *Camellia, Cycas, Eurya*
• Affiliation: HAST
• Location of specimens: HAST
• Region: CHINA (Taiwan)

J. F. Zuo

Zuo, Jia Fu; 左家哺 ; Zuǒ Jiābǔ
1960- **First publication: 1995**
• Employment: Hunan Forestry School（湖南林业专科学校）

• Research interest: Lauraceae, Poaceae [S]
• Published taxa: *Machilus, Neosinocalamus*
• Region: CHINA (Hunan)

Tso

Tso, Ching Lieh; Zuo, Jing Lie; 左景烈 ; Zuǒ Jǐngliè
First publication: 1933

• Employment: Botanical Institute, College of Agriculture, National Sun Yat-sen University; South China Institute of Botany, Chinese Academy of Sciences (国立中山大学农林植物研究所 ; 中国科学院华南植物研究所)
• Research interest: Orchidaceae [S]
• Published taxa: *Cremastra, Dendrobium, Epipogium, Eria, Goodyera, Liparis, Oberonia, Pleione, Tainia*
• Location of specimens: IBSC
• Region: CHINA (Guangdong, Hainan)
• Also as: C. L. Tso

Y. W. Zuo

Zuo, You Wei; 左有为 ; Zu Yǒuwéi
First publication: 2020

• Employment: College of Life Sciences, Southwest University (西南大学生命科学学院)
• Research interest: Apocynaceae [S]
• Published taxa: *Hoya*
• Region: CHINA (Xizang)

Z. Y. Zuo

Zuo, Zheng Yu; 左政裕 ; Zu Zhèngyù
First publication: 2020

• Employment: Kunming Institute of Botany, Chinese Academy of Sciences; School of Life Sciences, Yun nan University (中国科学院昆明植物研究所 ; 云南大学生命科学学院)
• Research interest: Cyatheaceae [P]
• Published taxa: *Gymnosphaera*
• Region: [ASIA]

Unclear

L. S. Chen

Chen, L. S. **First publication: 2004**

• Research interest: Ericaceae [S]
• Published taxa: *Rhododendron*
• Region: CHINA (Sichuan)

in *J. Sichuan Univ., Nat. Sci. Ed.* 41(6): 1298 (2004)
No details!

J. Han

Han, J. **First publication: 1988**

• Research interest: Hydrangeaceae [S]
• Published taxa: *Deutzia*
• Region: CHINA (Zhejiang)

in *Bull. Bot. Res., Harbin* 8(2): 141 (1988)
No details!

S. D. Zhang

Zhang, S. D. **First publication: 1985**

• Research interest: Schisandraceae [S]
• Published taxa: *Illicium*
• Region: CHINA (Fujian, Jiangxi)

in *Guihaia* 5(3): 175 (1985)
No details!

Part II

Chinese
Plant Collectors

and

Herbarium
Staff

第二部分

中国的植物采集者和标本馆工作人员

236-6 Exped.; 236-6 队 ; 236-6 Duì
- Location of specimens: PE. Collection Team

75 Exped.; 75 考察队 ; 75 Kǎocháduì
- Location of specimens: ATCH. Collection Team

FLPH Xizang Exped.; FLPH 西藏采集队 ; FLPH Xīzàng Cǎijíduì
- Location of specimens: PE. Collection Team

A

Abudula, Abas; 阿布都拉 • 阿巴斯 ; Ābùdūlā Ābāsī (1951-)
- Research interest: Fungi
- Affiliation: XJU
- Location of specimens: XJU

Altay Exped.; 阿勒泰队 ; Ālètài Duì
- Location of specimens: XTNM. Collection Team

Ai, Xi Zhi; 艾喜芝 ; Ài Xǐzhī (1948-)
- Research interest: Medicinal Plants
- Affiliation: ECM

An, Ding Guo; 安定国 ; Ān Dìngguó; 安定國 (1932-)
- Research interest: Plants of Gansu
- Affiliation: MJS
- Location of specimens: MJS

An, Fang Zhou; 安放舟 ; Ān Fàngzhōu (1960-)
- Research interest: Plumbaginaceae
- Affiliation: XJUG
- Location of specimens: XJUG

An, Jia Cheng; 安家成 ; Ān Jiāchéng (1961-)
- Affiliation: GXFS
- Location of specimens: GXFS

An, Zuo Jun; 安作军 ; Ān Zuòjūn
- Location of specimens: HEBI

Anshun Exped.; 安顺队 ; Ānshùn Duì
- Location of specimens: PE. Collection Team

Aur

Aur, Chih Wen; 敖志文 ; Áo Zhìwén (1932-2014)
- Employment: Northeast Forestry Institute（东北林学院）
- Research interest: Bryophyte
- Affiliation: NEFI
- Location of specimens: NEFI

B (P)

Bahargül; 巴哈尔古丽 ; Bāhā'ěrgǔlì (1970-)
- Research interest: Woody Plants
- Affiliation: XJFA
- Location of specimens: XJFA

Pasang Tenzin; 巴桑丹增 ; Bāsāng Dānzēng (1963-)
- Research interest: Medicinal Plants
- Affiliation: XZDC

Bayingolin Exped.; 巴州队 ; Bāzhōu Duì
- Location of specimens: XTNM. Collection Team

Bai, Cai; Pai, Tsai; 白埰 ; Bái Cài; 白采
- Location of specimens: BJFC

Bai, Jie; 白洁 ; Bái Jié (1970-)
- Research interest: Economic Plants
- Affiliation: SZ

Bai, Ke Zhi; 白克智 ; Bái Kèzhì (1934-)
- Location of specimens: PE

Bai, Ping; 白平 ; Bái Píng (1971-)
- Research interest: Magnoliceae
- Affiliation: YAF

Park, S. K.; 白思九 ; Bái Sījiǔ
- Location of specimens: IBSC

Bai, Tuo Qin; 白拖琴 ; Bái Tuōqín (1964-)
- Research interest: Medicinal Plants
- Affiliation: SSMM

Bai, Xin Sheng; 白新生 ; Bái Xīnshēng (1938-)
- Research interest: Plants of Shanxi
- Affiliation: LINF

• Location of specimens: LINF

X. L. Bai

Bai, Xue Liang; 白学良 ; Bái Xuéliáng (1950-)
• Employment: School of Life Sciences, Inner Mongolia University（内蒙古大学生命科学学院）
• Research interest: Bryophyte
• Affiliation: HIMC
• Location of specimens: HIMC

Y. P. Bai

Bai, Yun Peng; 白云鹏 ; Bái Yúnpéng (1963-)
• Employment: Jilin Academy of Traditional Chinese Medicine and Medica（吉林省中医中药研究院）
• Research interest: Fungi
• Affiliation: JLMP
• Location of specimens: JLMP

Baise Exped.; Bose Exped.; 百色队 ; Bǎisè Duì
• Location of specimens: PE, IBK, IBSC. Collection Team

Ban, Ji De; 班继德 ; Bān Jìdé; 班繼德 (1926-)
• Research interest: Plant Ecology
• Affiliation: CCNU
• Location of specimens: CCNU

Bao, Hua Yin; 包华音 ; Bāo Huáyīn
• Location of specimens: SDCM

Bao, Wen Mei; 包文美 ; Bāo Wénměi (1930-)
• Research interest: Algae
• Affiliation: HANU
• Location of specimens: HANU

Bao, Xue Sheng; 包雪声 ; Bāo Xuěshēng; 包雪聲 (1927-)
• Research interest: Medicinal Plants
• Affiliation: SHDC
• Location of specimens: SHDC

Bao, Ying; 包颖 ; Bāo Yǐng (1970-)
• Research interest: Poaceae
• Affiliation: QFNU

Beijing Exped.; 北京队 ; Běijīng Duì
• Location of specimens: PE. Collection Team

Beijing Youth Team; 北京青年队 ; Běijīng Qīngnián Duì
• Location of specimens: PE. Collection Team

PE Hengduanshan Exped.; 北京所横断山队 Běijīngsuǒ Héngduànshān Duì
• Location of specimens: PE. Collection Team

Bi, Guo Chang; 毕国昌 ; Bì Guóchāng
• Location of specimens: CAF

L. J. Bi

Bi, Lie Jue; Bi, Lie Jiu; 毕列爵 ; Bì Lièjué; 畢列爵 (1917-2004)
• Employment: Department of Biology, Hubei University（湖北大学生物系）
• Research interest: Algae
• Affiliation: EU
• Location of specimens: EU

Bi, Run Cheng; 毕润成 ; Bì Rùnchéng (1955-)
• Research interest: Plant Ecology
• Affiliation: LINF
• Location of specimens: LINF

Bijie Exped.; 毕节队 ; Bìjié Duì
• Location of specimens: PE. Collection Team

Bi, Zu Zhao; 闭祖昭 ; Bì Zǔzhāo
• Location of specimens: GXSP

Bian, Yun Yun; 卞云云 ; Biàn Yúnyún (1973-)
• Research interest: Medicinal Plants
• Affiliation: CPU

Bortala Exped.; 博州队 ; Bózhōu Duì
• Affiliation: XTNM. Collection Team

Bo, Ying Sheng; 卜颖生 ; Bǔ Yǐngshēng
• Location of specimens: YL

C (T)

Tsemo; 才毛 ; Cáimáo (1968-)
• Research interest: Medicinal Plants
• Affiliation: QDC

Tsai, T. S.; 蔡灿星 ; Cài Cànxīng; 蔡燦星 (1914-2000)
• Affiliation: IBSC
• Location of specimens: IBK

Cai, Guo Liang; Tsai, Kwo Liang; 蔡国梁 ; Cài Guóliáng; 蔡國樑

• Location of specimens: IBSC, FJSI, PE

Choi, Pung Sun; Cai, Pan Sheng; Choy, Pun Sang; 蔡磐生; Cài Pánshēng; 蔡盘生 (1951-)
• Research interest: Plants of Hong Kong
• Affiliation: HK
• Location of specimens: HK

Cai, Pei Ying; 蔡佩英; Cài Pèiyīng (1938-)
• Research interest: Typhaceae
• Affiliation: CDCM
• Location of specimens: CDCM

Cai, Ping Cheng; 蔡平成; Cài Píngchéng
• Location of specimens: CSFI

Cai, Qi Ying; 蔡奇英; Cài Qíyīng (1973-)
• Research interest: Bryophyte
• Affiliation: JXU

Cai, jing; 蔡箐; Cài Qìng (1984-)
• Research interest: Fungi
• Affiliation: KUN

Cai, Ru Wu; 蔡如武; Cài Rúwǔ
• Location of specimens: YF

Tsai, Jui Hsiung; 蔡瑞熊; Cài Ruìxióng
• Location of specimens: HAST

Tsai, Y. P.; 蔡延平; Cài Yánpíng
• Location of specimens: HAST

Cai, Yong Li; 蔡永立; Cài Yǒnglì
• Affiliation: AAUB
• Location of specimens: AAUB

Cai, Yue Wen; 蔡岳文;
Cài Yuèwén (1951-)
• Research interest: Medicinal Plants
• Affiliation: GDMM

Cao, Jian Guo; 曹建国;
Cáo Jiànguó (1968-)
• Research interest: Pteridophytes
• Affiliation: SHTU
• Location of specimens: SHTU

Cao, Ming; 曹明; Cáo Míng (1963-)
• Research interest: Rutaceae
• Affiliation: IBK

T. Cao

Cao, Tong; 曹同; Cáo Tóng (1945-)
• Employment: Institute of Forestry and Soil Sciences, Chinese Academy of Sciences; Institute of Applied Ecology, Chinese Academy of Sciences; College of Life and Environmental Science, Shanghai Normal University（中国科学院林业土壤研究所；中国科学院沈阳应用生态研究所；上海师范大学生命科学与环境科学学院）
• Research interest: Bryophyte
• Affiliation: IFP, SHTU
• Location of specimens: IFP, SHTU

Cao, Wen Xuan; 曹文宣; Cáo Wénxuān
• Location of specimens: HBI

Cao, Wen Gen; 曹稳根; Cáo Wěngēn (1964-)
• Research interest: Plants of Anhui
• Affiliation: ST
• Location of specimens: ST

Y. H. Cao

Cao, Yu Hui; 曹玉惠; Cáo Yùhuì (1938-)
• Employment: Herbarium, Chengdu Institute for Drug Control, Sichuan（四川省成都市药品检验所植物标本室）
• Research interest: Bombacaceae, Nyctaginaceae, Portulacaceae
• Affiliation: CDC
• Location of specimens: CDC. *Flora sichuanica*

Cao, Zhan Bo; 曹展波; Cáo Zhǎnbō
• Affiliation: JXF

Chai, Yong; 柴勇; Chái Yǒng (1976-)
• Research interest: Oleaceae
• Affiliation: YCP

Changji Exped.; 昌吉队; Chāngjí Duì
• Location of specimens: XTNM. Collection Team

Chang, Zhe Xin; 长哲新; Cháng Zhéxīn; 萇哲新 (1918-)
• Research interest: Plants of Henan
• Affiliation: HEAC
• Location of specimens: HEAC

Chang, Hong Xiu; 常红秀; Cháng Hóngxiù (1931-)
• Research interest: Bryophyte
• Affiliation: JXU

Chang, Ying; 常缨; Cháng Yīng (1970-)
• Research interest: Pteridophytes
• Affiliation: NEAU

Chang, Yung Ching; 常永祯; Cháng Yǒngzhēn; 常永禎 (1916-?)

• Location of specimens: PE

Chang, Zi Li; 常自力 ; Cháng Zìlì (1940-)
• Research interest: Medicinal Plants
• Affiliation: HNCM
• Location of specimens: HNCM

Chenshan Pl. Coll. Team; 辰山引种采集小组 ; Chénshān Yǐnzhǒng Cǎijí Xiǎozǔ
• Location of specimens: CSH. Collection Team

P. C. Chen

Chen, Pang Chieh; Chen, Pan Chieh; Ch'ên, Pang Chieh; 陈邦杰 ; Chén Bāngjié; 陳邦傑 (1907-1970)
• Employment: National Central University; Biological Laboratory of Science Society of China; Nanjing Normal College（国立中央大学；中国科学社生物研究所；南京师范学院）
• Research interest: Bryophyte
• Affiliation: PE
• Location of specimens: PE

Chen, Bao Sheng; 陈宝生 ; Chén Bǎoshēng (1960-)
• Affiliation: ABDC

Chen, Pi Hua; 陳碧華 ; Chén Bìhuá; 陈碧华
• Location of specimens: HAST

Chen, Bing Hui; 陈炳辉 ; Chén Bǐnghuī
• Location of specimens: IBSC

Chen, Bo; 陈波 ; Chén Bō (1966-)
• Research interest: Pteridophytes
• Affiliation: HTC

Chen, Tsai Hung; 陳才鴻 ; Chén Cáihóng; 陈才鸿
• Location of specimens: HAST

Chen, Ce; 陈策 ; Chén Cè
• Location of specimens: SHM

Chen, Chang Bin; 陈昌斌 ; Chén Chāngbīn (1967-)
• Affiliation: HSNU

Chen, Chang Jun; 陈昌俊 ; Chén Chāngjùn; 陳昌俊 (1937-)
• Research interest: Plants of Qinghai
• Affiliation: QUA
• Location of specimens: QUA

Chen, Chang Nien; Chen, Chang Nian; 陈长年 ; Chén Chángnián; 陳長年
• Location of specimens: IBSC, LBG, NAS, PE

Chen, Chaur Tzuhn; 陳朝圳 ; Chén Cháozhèn; 陈朝圳 (1953-)
• Research interest: Plant Ecology
• Affiliation: PPI

Chen, Chen; 陈辰 ; Chén Chén; 陳辰 (1933-)
• Research interest: Plants of Liaoning
• Affiliation: LNNU
• Location of specimens: LNNU

Chen, Chong Ming; Chen, Chung Ming; 陈重明 ; Chén Chóngmíng; 陳重明 (1938-)
• Location of specimens: NAS, PE

Chen, Chuan Chieh; 陳傳杰 ; Chén Chuánjié; 陈传杰
• Location of specimens: HAST

Chen, Chuan; 陈椽 ; Chén Chuán (1963-)
• Research interest: Algae
• Affiliation: GNUB
• Location of specimens: GNUB

Chen, De Rong; 陈德荣 ; Chén Déróng (1964-)
• Research interest: Medicinal Plants
• Affiliation: GXMG

Chen, Ding Ru; 陈定如 ; Chén Dìngrú; 陳定如 (1935-)
• Affiliation: IBSD, SN
• Location of specimens: IBSC, IBSD, SN

Chen, Fa Sheng; 陈发生; Chén Fāshēng; 陳發生 (1935-)
• Research interest: Fungi
• Affiliation: HANU

Chen, Feng; 陈锋 ; Chén Fēng
• Location of specimens: SWCTU

Chen, Fu Dong; 陈阜东 ; Chén Fùdōng; 陳阜東 (1930-)
• Research interest: Plant Systematics
• Affiliation: BJTC
• Location of specimens: BJTC

Chen, Ge Xin; 陈革新 ; Chén Géxīn
• Research interest: Scientific Illustrator
• Affiliation: HIB

Chen, Ku Chi; 陳谷季 ; Chén Gǔjì; 陈谷季
• Location of specimens: HAST

Chen, Guan Bin; 陳觀斌 ; Chén Guānbīn; 陈观斌
• Location of specimens: HAST

Chen, Kuang Lu; 陈光禄 ; Chén Guānglù; 陳光祿
• Location of specimens: IBSC, N, NAS, PE

Chen, Guang Yao; 陈广耀 ; Chén Guǎngyào
• Location of specimens: BCMM

Chan, Kwai Shang; 陈桂生 ; Chén Guìshēng; 陳桂生
• Location of specimens: SYS

Chun, Kuo Fu; 陈国富 ; Chén Guófù; 陳國富
• Location of specimens: IBSC

Chen, Guo Yang; 陈国扬 ; Chén Guóyáng; 陳國揚 (1925-2005)
• Research interest: Plants of Fujian
• Affiliation: FFVTC
• Location of specimens: FFVTC

Chen, Kuoh chang; 陳國章 ; Chén Guózhāng; 陈国章
• Location of specimens: HAST

Chen, Han Bang; 陈汉邦 ; Chén Hànbāng
• Location of specimens: HFB

Chen, Han Bin; 陈汉斌 ; Chén Hànbīn; 陳漢斌 (1931-)
• Research interest: Plants of Shandong
• Affiliation: SDNU
• Location of specimens: SDNU

Chen, Hao; 陈昊 ; Chén Hào (1974-)
• Location of specimens: XBGH

Chen, Heng Chun; 陈亨春 ; Chén Hēngchūn
• Location of specimens: IBK, IBSC

Chen, Hong Xun; 陈虹勋 ; Chén Hóngxūn
• Location of specimens: SCSG

Chen, Huan yu; 陳奐宇 ; Chén Huànyǔ; 陈奂宇
• Location of specimens: HAST

Chen, Hui Yang; 陳卉陽 ; Chén Huìyáng; 陈卉阳
• Location of specimens: HAST

Chen, Jia Ming; 陈家明 ; Chén Jiāmíng; 陳家明 (1937-)
• Location of specimens: GZTM

J. Y. Chen

Chen, Jia You; 陈嘉佑 ; Chén Jiāyòu; 陳嘉佑 (1936-1990)
• Employment: Institute of Hydrobiology, Chinese Academy of Sciences（中国科学院水生生物研究所）
• Research interest: Algae
• Affiliation: HBI
• Location of specimens: HBI

Chen, Jian Guo; 陈建国 ; Chén Jiànguó (1983-)
• Research interest: Caryophyllaceae
• Affiliation: KUN

Chen, Jian Hua; 陈建华 ; Chén Jiànhuá (1967-)
• Research interest: Economic Plants
• Affiliation: ZNU
• Location of specimens: ZNU

Chen, C. N.; Chen, J. N.; 陳建男 ; Chén Jiànnán; 陈建男
• Location of specimens: HAST

Chen, Jian Ping; 陈建平 ; Chén Jiànpíng (1962-)
• Affiliation: EU

Chen, Jian Ping; 陈建平 ; Chén Jiànpíng (1974-)
• Affiliation: CSH

Chen, Chien Wen; 陳建文 ; Chén Jiànwén; 陈建文
• Research interest: Rubiaceae
• Affiliation: TAIF

Chen, Chien Chih; 陳建志 ; Chén Jiànzhì; 陈建志
• Location of specimens: HAST

Chen, Jian Bin; 陈健斌 ; Chén Jiànbīn; 陳健斌 (1940-)
• Location of specimens: HMAS

Chen, Jin Xiang; 陈锦祥 ; Chén Jǐnxiáng
• Location of specimens: XMBG

Chen, Jing Fang; 陈景方 ; Chén Jǐngfāng
• Research interest: Cactaceae; Plants of Shenzhen
• Affiliation: SZG
• Location of specimens: SZG

Chen, Jun Fu; 陈俊福; Chén Jùnfú; 陳俊福 (1928-2013)
• Location of specimens: NJNU

Chen, Chun Ming; 陳俊銘 ; Chén Jùnmíng; 陈俊铭
• Location of specimens: HAST

Chen, Jiun Ching; 陳俊清 ; Chén Jùnqīng; 陈俊清
• Location of specimens: HAST

Chen, Kai Ji; 陈开基 ; Chén Kāijī; 陳開基 (1928-)
• Research interest: Herbaceous Plants
• Affiliation: HZU, ZAU
• Location of specimens: HZU, ZAU

Chen, Ke Gui; 陈可贵 ; Chén Kěguì; 陳可貴 (1936-)
• Research interest: Plants of Jilin
• Affiliation: JLFC

Chen, Ke Ke; 陈可可 ; Chén Kěkě (1957-)
• Research interest: Fungi

• Affiliation: KUN

Chen, Kun Hao; 陈坤浩 ; Chén Kūnhào (1969-)
• Research interest: Plant Ecology
• Affiliation: BJ
• Location of specimens: BJ

Chen, Lei; 陈磊 ; Chén Lěi (1981-)
• Research interest: Plant Ecology
• Affiliation: NKU
• Location of specimens: XJNU

Chun, Li Hing; Chen, Li Ching; Ch'ên, Li Ch'ing; 陈立卿 ; Chén Lìqīng; 陳立卿
• Location of specimens: IBK

Chen, Liang; 陈亮 ; Chén Liàng (1967-)
• Research interest: Theaceae
• Affiliation: TEA

Chen, Lin Hai; 陈林海 ; Chén Línhǎi
• Location of specimens: HMAS

Chen, Lin Bin; 陈临彬 ; Chén Línbīn; 陳臨彬 (1932-)
• Affiliation: SR

Chen, Lin; 陈琳 ; Chén Lín
• Location of specimens: HON

Chen, Ling Zhi; 陈灵芝 ; Chén LíngZhī; 陳靈芝 (1933-)
• Location of specimens: PE

Chen, Ling Jing; 陈令静 ; Chén Lìngjìng (1953-)
• Research interest: Plant Embryology
• Affiliation: BNU
• Location of specimens: BNU

Chen, Long Qing; 陈龙清 ; Chén Lóngqīng (1964-)
• Research interest: Calycanthaceae
• Affiliation: CCAU
• Location of specimens: CCAU

Chen, Long Zhu; 陈龙珠 ; Chén Lóngzhū
• Location of specimens: GZTM

Chun, Lucy; 陈露斯 ; Chén Lùsī; 陳露斯
• Location of specimens: IBSC

Chen, Lun Xiang; 陈伦祥 ; Chén Lúnxiáng
• Location of specimens: GXF

Chen, Luo Bi; 陈罗比 ; Chén Luóbǐ
• Location of specimens: ZHAN

Chen, Mei Sheng; 陈梅生 ; Chén Méishēng
• Location of specimens: JXU

Chen, Mei Lan; 陈美兰 ; Chén Měilán (1975-)
• Research interest: Medicinal Plants
• Affiliation: CMMI

Chen, Meng Shi; 陈梦士 ; Chén Mèngshì
• Location of specimens: IBSC

Chen, Min; 陈敏 ; Chén Mǐn (1961-)
• Research interest: Medicinal Plants
• Affiliation: CMMI

Chen, Ming Hong; 陈明洪 ; Chén Mínghóng; 陳明洪 (1937-2002)
• Location of specimens: WCSBG

Chen, Ming Hua; 陈明华 ; Chén Mínghuá (1963-)
• Affiliation: SHMU

Chen, Ming Lin; 陈明林 ; Chén Mínglín (1972-)
• Research interest: Plants of Anhui
• Affiliation: ANUB

Chen, Ming Yih; 陳明義 ; Chén Míngyì; 陈明义
• Affiliation: TCB
• Location of specimens: TCB

M. C. Chen

Chen, Ming Che; Chen, Ming Zhe; 陳明哲 ; Chén Míngzhé; 陈明哲 (1950-)
• Employment: Institute of Forestry, Taiwan University （台湾大学森林学研究所）
• Research interest: Plants of Taiwan. Flora of Taiwan

Chen, Mou; 陈谋 ; Chén Móu; 陳謀 (1903-1935)
• Location of specimens: IBSC, KUN, N, NAS, NF, PE, QNUN, SZ

Chun, Nim Keoi; 陈念劬 ; Chén Niànqú; 陳念劬
• Location of specimens: IBSC

Chen, Peng Ju; 陈鹏举 ; Chén Péngjǔ; 陳鵬舉
• Location of specimens: HUTM

Chen, Qi; 陈齐 ; Chén Qí (1959-)
• Research interest: Medicinal Plants
• Affiliation: CPU

Chen, Qi Chang; 陈启瑺 ; Chén Qǐcháng; 陈启嫦
• Location of specimens: HZU

Chen, Qi Tai; 陈起泰 ; Chén Qǐtài
• Location of specimens: IMDC

Chen, Qing; 陈清 ; Chén Qīng (1992-)
• Affiliation: SABG

Chen, Qing Kui; 陈清奎 ; Chén Qīngkuí
• Location of specimens: ANUB

C. H. Chen

Chen, Ching Hsia; Chen, Qing Xia; 陳擎霞 ;
Chén Qíngxiá; 陈擎霞 (1942-)
• Employment: Chung Hsing University (中兴大学)
• Research interest: Plants of Taiwan.
Flora of Taiwan

Chen, Qing Cheng; 陈庆诚 ; Chén Qìngchéng
• Location of specimens: NAS, PE, WUK

Chen, Ren Jun; Chun, Ren Jun; 陈仁钧 ;
Chén Rénjūn; 陳仁鈞 (1935-)
• Research interest: Pteridophytes
• Affiliation: ANUG
• Location of specimens: ANUG

Y. Chen

Chen, Yung; Ch'ên, Yung; Chen, Rong; 陈嵘 ;
Chén Róng; 陳嶸 (1888-1971)
• Employment: Department of Forestry, University of Nanking; Forestry Research Institute, Department of Forestry (金陵大学森林系 ; 林业部林业科学研究所)
• Research interest: Woody Plants
• Affiliation: NF
• Location of specimens: N, NF.
Illustrated Manual of Chinese Trees and Shrubs

Chen, Y. N.; 陈汝爱 ; Chén Rǔ'ài; 陳汝愛
• Location of specimens: CAF, IBSC

Chen, Y. F.; 陈汝芬 ; Chén Rǔfēn; 陳汝芬
• Location of specimens: IBK, IBSC, PE

Chen, Ru Ming; 陈汝明 ; Chén Rǔmíng
• Affiliation: SN

Zuei C. Chen

Chen, Zuei Ching; Chen, Zui Ching; 陳瑞青 ;
Chén Ruìqīng; 陈瑞青 (1930-)
• Employment: Taiwan University (台湾大学)
• Research interest: Fungi
• Affiliation: TAI

Chen, Rui Xue; 陈瑞雪 ; Chén Ruìxuě; 陳瑞雪
(1933-2013)
• Research interest: Plants of N. China
• Affiliation: TIE
• Location of specimens: TIE

Chen, San Mao; 陈三茂 ; Chén Sānmào (1956-)
• Research interest: Pteridophytes
• Affiliation: HUE
• Location of specimens: HUE

Chen, Shao Cheng; 陈绍成 ; Chén Shàochéng (1966-)
• Research interest: Medicinal Plants
• Affiliation: WXDC
• Location of specimens: WXDC

Chen, Shao Rong; 陈绍荣 ; Chén Shàoróng (1957-)
• Research interest: Woody Plants
• Affiliation: HUE
• Location of specimens: HUE

Chen, Shao Xing; Chen, Shao Yu; 陈绍煋 ;
Chén Shàoxīng; 陳紹煋，陈绍煜 (1923-2016)
• Research interest: Plants of N. China
• Affiliation: BJM
• Location of specimens: BJFC, BJM, PE

Chen, Shi; 陈诗 ; Chén Shī; 陳詩
• Location of specimens: IBSC, NAS, PE, SZ, WUK

Chen, Shi Feng; 陈世锋 ; Chén Shìfēng (1964-)
• Research interest: Plants of Henan
• Affiliation: XYTC
• Location of specimens: XYTC

Cheng, Sh Chung; 陳世棕 ; Chén Shìzōng; 陈世棕
• Location of specimens: HAST

Chen, Su Hwa; Chen, Shu Hua; 陳淑華 ;
Chén Shūhuá; 陈淑华 (1948-)
• Research interest: Palynology
• Affiliation: TAI

Chen, Shu Yuan; 陳淑媛 ; Chén Shūyuàn; 陈淑媛
• Location of specimens: HAST

Chen, Shu Si; 陈树思 ; Chén Shùsī (1963-)
• Affiliation: HGTC

Chen, Shu Yao; 陈树尧 ; Chén Shùyáo (1965-)
• Research interest: Theaceae
• Affiliation: TEA

Chen, Shun Li; 陈舜礼 ; Chén Shùnlǐ; 陳舜禮
• Location of specimens: CAF, PE, PEY.

Chen, Tan Qing; 陈潭清 ; Chén Tánqīng; 陳潭清 (1941-)
• Research interest: Plants of Hubei
• Affiliation: SZG
• Location of specimens: SZG

Chen, Tong Chun; 陈同春 ; Chén Tóngchūn
• Location of specimens: IBSC

Cheng, Tong An; 陈桐庵 ; Chén Tóng'ān; 陳桐庵 (1930-)
• Research interest: Plants of Hebei
• Affiliation: CHA
• Location of specimens: CHA

Chen, Wei Pei; 陈维培 ; Chén Wéipéi; 陳維培 (1931-)
• Research interest: Nymphaeaceae
• Affiliation: NJNU
• Location of specimens: NJNU

Chen, Wei Lie; 陈伟烈 ; Chén Wěiliè; 陳偉烈 (1939-)
• Location of specimens: PE

Chen, Wei Hui; 陈蔚辉 ; Chén Wèihuī (1963-)
• Research interest: Plants of Guangdong
• Affiliation: CZH
• Location of specimens: CZH

Chen, Wen Ming; 陳文明 ; Chén Wénmíng; 陈文明
• Location of specimens: HAST

Chen, Xi Ling; 陈锡龄 ; Chén Xīlíng; 陳錫齡 (1934-)
• Research interest: Fungi
• Affiliation: IFP
• Location of specimens: IFP

Chen, Xi Xin; 陈锡欣 ; Chén Xīxīn; 陳錫欣 (1935-)
• Affiliation: TIE

Chen, Xiao Hong; 陈小红 ; Chén Xiǎohóng (1977-)
• Research interest: Lauraceae; Woody Plants
• Affiliation: SAUF

Chen, Xiao Ling; 陈晓玲 ; Chén Xiǎolíng (1978-)
• Research interest: Cultivated Plants
• Affiliation: HHBG

X. Q. Chen

Chen, Xing Qiu; 陈星球 ; Chén Xīngqiú; 陳星球 (1931-)
• Employment: Department of Biology, Central China Normal University（华中师范大学生物系）
• Research interest: Algae
• Affiliation: CCNU

Chen, Hsiu Ti; 陈修棣 ; Chén Xiūdì; 陳修棣
• Affiliation: PE

Chen, Hsiu Sheng; 陳秀生 ; Chén Xiùshēng; 陈秀生
• Location of specimens: HAST

Chen, Xu Hui; 陈旭辉 ; Chén Xùhuī (1970-)
• Research interest: Orchidaceae
• Affiliation: NOCC
• Location of specimens: NOCC

Chen, Xu Hui; 陈旭辉 ; Chén Xùhuī (1981-)
• Research interest: Orchidaceae
• Affiliation: SYAU
• Location of specimens: SYAU

Chen, Shyuan wu; 陳玄武 ; Chén Xuánwǔ; 陈玄武
• Location of specimens: HAST

Y. J. Chen

Chen, Ya Jun; 陈雅君 ; Chén Yǎjūn (1964-)
• Employment: College of Horticulture and Landscape Architecture, Northeast Agricultural University（东北农业大学园艺园林学院）
• Research interest: Plants of Heilongjiang. *Flora Heilongjiangensis*

Chen, Yan Song; 陈延松 ; Chén Yánsōng (1979-)
• Research interest: Plant Ecology
• Affiliation: ACE
• Location of specimens: ACE

Chen, Yan Sheng; 陈彦生 ; Chén Yànshēng (1952-2013)
• Research interest: Campanulaceae, Lamiaceae
• Affiliation: WUK
• Location of specimens: WUK

Chen, Yan; 陈燕 ; Chén Yàn (1958-)
• Affiliation: ZHAN

Chen, Ye; 陈晔 ; Chén Yè (1965-)
• Research interest: Fungi
• Affiliation: JJT
• Location of specimens: JJT

Chen, Yi Yu; 陈宜瑜 ; Chén Yíyú; 陳宜瑜 (1944-)
• Location of specimens: HBI

Chen, Yi Ru; 陳奕如 ; Chén Yìrú; 陈奕如
• Location of specimens: HAST

Chen, I Ming; Chen, Yih Ming; 陳益明 ; Chén Yìmíng; 陈益明 (?-2010)
• Research interest: Plant Physiology
• Affiliation: TAI

Chen, Yi Chung; 陳逸忠 ; Chén Yìzhōng; 陈逸忠

• Location of specimens: HAST

Chen, Yeng yi; 陳穎宜 ; Chén Yǐngyí; 陈颖宜
• Location of specimens: HAST

Chen, Yong Chang; 陈永昌 ; Chén Yǒngchāng; 陳永昌 (1926-)
• Research interest: Actinidiaceae, Annonaceae, Olacaceae, Santalaceae
• Affiliation: IBK, YBDC
• Location of specimens: YBDC

Chen, Yong Qin; 陈永勤 ; Chén Yǒngqín (1963-)
• Research interest: Medicinal Plants
• Affiliation: EU

Chen, Yong Sheng; 陈永生 ; Chén Yǒngshēng (1987-)
• Research interest: Rhamnaceae
• Affiliation: NEAU

Chen, Yong; 陈勇 ; Chén Yǒng (1954-)
• Research interest: Plants of Fujian
• Affiliation: NDTC
• Location of specimens: NDTC

Chen, You Qing; 陈有卿 ; Chén Yǒuqīng (1958-)
• Affiliation: IBSC
• Location of specimens: IBSC

Chen, Yu; 陈禹 ; Chén Yǔ (1967-)
• Affiliation: HLNM

Chen, Yu Feng; 陳玉峰 ; Chén Yùfēng; 陈玉峰
• Location of specimens: HAST

Chen, Yu Xuan; 陈玉璇 ; Chén Yùxuán; 陳玉璇 (1939-)
• Research interest: Plants of Heilongjiang
• Affiliation: HLNM

Chen, Yu Jie; 陈钰洁 ; Chén Yùjié
• Research interest: Scientific Illustrator
• Affiliation: HHBG

Chen, Yue Rong; 陈岳蓉 ; Chén Yuèróng
• Research interest: Medicinal Plants
• Affiliation: QDC

Chen, Yun Xia; 陈云霞 ; Chén Yúnxiá (1982-)
• Affiliation: NFP

Chen, Yun Xiu; 陈云岫 ; Chén Yúnxiù; 陳雲岫 (1917-?)
• Location of specimens: SY

Chen, Yun Fa; 陈运发 ; Chén Yùnfā
• Affiliation: GXNM

Chen, Ze Lian; 陈泽濂 ; Chén Zélián; 陳澤濂 (1933-)
• Location of specimens: IBSC

Ze Y. Chen

Chen, Ze Ying; 陈泽映 ; Chén Zéyìng; 陳澤映 (1936-)
• Employment: Department of Biology, Sichuan University（四川大学生物系）
• Research interest: Plants of Sichuan. *Flora sichuanica*

Chen, Zhan Shou; 陈占寿 ; Chén Zhànshòu
• Location of specimens: FNU

Chen, Zhang He; 陈章和 ; Chén Zhānghé (1954-)
• Affiliation: SN
• Location of specimens: SN

Chen, Zhang; 陳仉 ; Chén Zhǎng; 陈仉
• Location of specimens: HAST

Chen, Zhen Chuan; 陈珍传 ; Chén Zhēnchuán (1970-)
• Research interest: Pteridophytes
• Affiliation: SZG
• Location of specimens: SZG

Chen, Chen Tung; 陈振东 ; Chén Zhèndōng
• Location of specimens: IBSC

Chen, Zheng Rong; 陈正蓉 ; Chén Zhèngróng; 陳正蓉 (1940-)
• Research interest: Stachyuraceae
• Affiliation: CQNM
• Location of specimens: CQNM

Chen, Zhi Yuan; 陈志远 ; Chén Zhìyuǎn; 陳志遠 (1927-)
• Research interest: Palynology
• Affiliation: CCAU
• Location of specimens: CCAU

Chen, Chung Hsien; 陳仲賢 ; Chén Zhòngxián; 陈仲贤
• Location of specimens: HAST

Chen, Zhu Sheng; 陈竹生 ; Chén Zhúshēng; 陳竹生 (1943-)
• Research interest: Rutaceae
• Affiliation: CIT

Chen, Zhuo; Chen, Cho; Ch'ên, Cho; 陈倬 ; Chén Zhuō; 陳倬 (1926-1967)

• Affiliation: JSPC
• Location of specimens: JSPC

Chen, Tzu dwan; 陳子端 ; Chén Zǐduān; 陈子端
• Location of specimens: HAST

Chen, Zi Niu; 陈子牛 ; Chén Zǐniú
• Location of specimens: YFS

Cheng, Fang Yun; 成仿云 ; Chéng Fǎngyún
• Location of specimens: BJFC

Chen, Xia Lan; 成夏岚 ; Chéng Xiàlán (1982-)
• Affiliation: ZHAN

Cheng, Guan Ying; 程冠英 ; Chéng Guānyīng (1926-)
• Research interest: Apiaceae
• Affiliation: SYPC
• Location of specimens: SYPC

Cheng, Rui Mei; 程瑞梅 ; Chéng Ruìméi (1967-)
• Research interest: Biodiversity
• Affiliation: CAF

Cheng, Xia Fang; 程夏芳 ; Chéng Xiàfāng (1984-)
• Research interest: Bryophyte
• Affiliation: HSNU

Cheng, Yun Fei; 程云飞 ; Chéng Yúnfēi
• Location of specimens: NEFI

Chen, Zhi Ming; 程志铭 ; Chéng Zhìmíng
• Location of specimens: CMMI

Cheng, Zi Jun; 程子俊 ; Chéng Zijùn (1924-)
• Research interest: Algae
• Affiliation: NWTC, NWUB
• Location of specimens: NWTC, NWUB

Chu, Qing Gang; 初庆刚 ; Chū Qìnggāng (1963-)
• Research interest: Poaceae
• Affiliation: LYAC

Chu, Xiao Fang; 褚晓芳 ; Chǔ Xiǎofāng (1982-)
• Research interest: Apiaceae
• Affiliation: NAS

Sichuan-Guizhou Exped.; 川黔队 ; Chuānqián Duì
• Location of specimens: PE

Tsoden Dorjee; 次旦多吉 ; Cìdàn Duōjí (1985-)
• Research interest: Medicinal Plants
• Affiliation: XZDC
• Location of specimens: XZDC

Tsetop; 次多 ; Cìduō
• Location of specimens: XZ

Cui, Bo; 崔波 ; Cuī Bō (1961-)
• Affiliation: HEBI
• Location of specimens: HEBI

Cui, Guang Hong; 崔光红 ; Cuī Guānghóng (1976-)
• Research interest: Medicinal Plants
• Affiliation: CMMI

Cui, Jian Li; 崔建丽 ; Cuī Jiànlì (1950-)
• Research interest: Poaceae
• Affiliation: PEM

Cui, Ming Kun; 崔明昆 ; Cuī Míngkūn (1963-)
• Research interest: Bryophyte
• Affiliation: YNUB
• Location of specimens: YCE

D(T)

Dawa Tsering; 达娃次仁 ; Dáwá Cìrén (1950-)
• Research interest: Medicinal Plants
• Affiliation: XZDC

Dayaoshan Exped.; 大瑶山队 ; Dàyáoshān Duì
• Affiliation: GXMI, IBK, IBSC, PE. Collection Team

Dai, Bao He; 戴宝合 ; Dài Bǎohé
• Location of specimens: JLAU

F. T. Tai

Tai, Fan Tsien; Tai, Fan Chin; Dai, Fan Jin; 戴蕃瑨 ; Dài Fānjìn; 戴蕃晋 (1900-2001)
• Employment: Department of Biology, Southwest Normal University（西南师范大学生物系）
• Research interest: Styracaceae, Symplocaceae; Plants of Sichuan
• Affiliation: SWCTU.
Flora sichuanica

Tai, Kuo Huei; 戴國輝 ; Dài Guóhuī; 戴国辉
• Affiliation: TAIF

Dai, Hui Ping; 戴惠平 ; Dài Huìpíng (1964-)

• Research interest: Algae
• Affiliation: SHM

Dai, Lun Ying; 戴伦膺 ; Dài Lúnyīng; 戴倫膺 (1917-?)
• Location of specimens: WH

Dai, Qi Jin; 戴启金 ; Dài Qǐjīn (1966-)
• Research interest: Rosaceae
• Affiliation: XYTC
• Location of specimens: XYTC

T. L. Dai

Dai, Tian Lun; Dai, Tien Lun; 戴天伦 ; Dài Tiānlún; 戴天倫 (1922-2012)
• Employment: Sichuan Institute of Chinese Materia Medica（四川省中药研究所）
• Research interest: Meliaceae, Saururaceae
• Affiliation: SM
• Location of specimens: SM, SZ, PE. *Flora sichuanica*

Dai, Wei Min; 戴伟民 ; Dài Wěimín (1976-)
• Research interest: Weeds
• Affiliation: NAU

Tai, Wen Kai; 戴文凯 ; Dài Wénkǎi
• Location of specimens: HAST

Dai, Xiu Zhang; 戴秀章 ; Dài Xiùzhāng
• Location of specimens: NXF

De, Ying; 德英 ; Dé Yīng (1978-)
• Research interest: Poaceae
• Affiliation: FGC

Teng, P. L.; 邓柏林 ; Dèng Bǎilín; 鄧柏林
• Location of specimens: IBSC

Deng, Chun Kuang; 邓春匡 ; Dèng Chūnkuāng; 鄧春匡 (1931-)
• Research interest: Algae
• Affiliation: GUN
• Location of specimens: GUN

Teng, C. M.; 邓纯眉 ; Dèng Chúnméi; 鄧純眉
• Location of specimens: SZ

Deng, De Ying; 邓德英 ; Dèng Déyīng (1968-)
• Research interest: Medicinal Plants
• Affiliation: HECM
• Location of specimens: HECM

Deng, Hui Sheng; 邓辉胜 ; Dèng Huīshèng (1971-)
• Research interest: Gymnospermae; Plants of Jiangxi
• Affiliation: JJT
• Location of specimens: JJT

Deng, Jing Fa; 邓晶发 ; Dèng Jīngfā; 鄧晶發 (1936-1994)
• Research interest: Scientific Illustrator
• Affiliation: IBSC

Teng, Liang; 邓良 ; Dèng Liáng; 鄧良
• Location of specimens: IBSC, PE

Deng, Lun Xiu; 邓伦秀 ; Dèng Lúnxiù (1977-)
• Research interest: Garden Plants
• Affiliation: GF
• Location of specimens: GF

Deng, Ming Lu; 邓明鲁 ; Dèng Mínglǔ; 鄧明魯 (1936-)
• Research interest: Medicinal Plants
• Affiliation: CCM
• Location of specimens: CCM

Deng, G. Y.; 邓期颖 ; Dèng Qīyǐng; 鄧期穎
• Affiliation: IBSC

Deng, Rong Yan; 邓荣艳 ; Dèng Róngyàn (1980-)
• Research interest: Woody Plants
• Affiliation: GAC

Teng, Shi Wei; 邓世纬 ; Dèng Shìwěi; 鄧世緯 (191?-1936)
• Location of specimens: IBK, IBSC, PE, SZ

Deng, Shu Lin; 鄧書麟 ; Dèng Shūlín; 邓书麟
• Location of specimens: HAST

Teng

Teng, Shu Chün; 鄧叔群 ; Dèng Shūqún; 鄧叔群 (1902-1970)
• Employment: Biological Laboratory of Science Society of China; Institute of Microbiology, Chinese Academy of Sciences（中国科学社生物研究所；中国科学院微生物研究所）
• Research interest: Fungi
• Affiliation: HMAS
• Location of specimens: HMAS

Ten, Simeon; Ten, Pere Simeon; Ten, Siméon; Ten, Semon; 邓西蒙 ; Dèng Xīméng; 邓培根，鄧西蒙，邓西门，鄧培根
• Location of specimens: A, KUN, P

Teng, Sian Fok; 邓先福 ; Dèng Xiānfú; 鄧先福
• Location of specimens: IBK

Deng, Xian Lan; 邓贤兰 ; Dèng Xiánlán (1969-)
• Research interest: Plant Ecology

• Affiliation: JGSU
• Location of specimens: JGSU

Teng, Hsiang Kun; 邓祥坤 ; Dèng Xiángkūn; 鄧祥坤 (1915-)
• Location of specimens: IBSC, KUN, PE

H. C. Tang

Tang, Hune Cheung; 鄧萱祥 ; Dèng Xuānxiáng; 邓萱祥 (1917-1971)
• Employment: Department of Biology, The Chinese University of Hong Kong（香港中文大学生物学系）
• Research interest: Plants of Hong Kong
• Location of specimens: HK. *Herbs and Vines of Hong Kong; Trees of Hong Kong*

Deng, Ying Feng; 邓盈丰 ; Dèng Yíngfēng; 鄧盈豐 (1933-2009)
• Research interest: Scientific Illustrator
• Affiliation: IBSC

Deng, Zhao Qun; 邓兆群 ; Dèng Zhàoqún
• Location of specimens: FTS

Tang, C. N.; 邓志农 ; Dèng Zhìnóng; 鄧志農
• Location of specimens: IBK, IBSC

Deng, Zhong Wu; 邓仲吾 ; Dèng Zhòngwú; 鄧仲吾 (1929-)
• Research interest: Plants of Guilin
• Affiliation: GUN
• Location of specimens: GUN

Di, Zhao Zhuang; 翟肇庄 ; Dí Zhàozhuāng; 翟肇莊 (1907-2012)
• Research interest: Medicinal Plants
• Affiliation: CZH
• Location of specimens: CZH

Di, Chun Ji; 邸春吉 ; Dǐ Chūnjí
• Research interest: Fagaceae
• Affiliation: LEF
• Location of specimens: LEF

Dilber; 地里拜尔 ; Dìlǐbài'ěr (1958-)
• Research interest: Moraceae, Primulaceae
• Affiliation: XJDC
• Location of specimens: XJDC

Ding, Chun Bang; 丁春邦 ; Dīng Chūnbāng (1966-)
• Research interest: Economic Plants
• Affiliation: SAU
• Location of specimens: SAU

Ding, Hou Yong; 丁厚勇 ; Dīng Hòuyǒng
• Research interest: Woody Plants
• Affiliation: HUF

Ding, Hua Jiao; 丁华娇 ; Dīng Huájiāo (1971-)
• Research interest: Herbaceous Plants
• Affiliation: HHBG
• Location of specimens: HHBG

Ding, Jing Ye; 丁经业 ; Dīng Jīngyè; 丁經業 (1933-)
• Location of specimens: HNWP, PE, WUK

Ding, Jing He; 丁景和 ; Dīng Jǐnghé (1915-)
• Location of specimens: JXCM

Ding, Kai Yu; 丁开宇 ; Dīng Kāiyǔ (1963-)
• Research interest: Liliaceae
• Affiliation: LNNU

Ding, Ling Xiao; 丁凌霄 ; Dīng Língxiāo (1954-)
• Research interest: Plants of Jiulianshan
• Affiliation: JNR
• Location of specimens: JNR

Ding, Shen Yan; 丁慎言 ; Dīng Shènyán (1928-)
• Research interest: Orchidaceae
• Affiliation: ATCH
• Location of specimens: ATCH

Ding, Sheng Yan; 丁圣彦 ; Dīng Shèngyàn
• Location of specimens: KAI

Ding, Shou Qin; 丁守琴 ; Dīng Shǒuqín (1935-)
• Location of specimens: IGA

Ting, Su; Ting, Su, William; 丁骕 ; Dīng Sù; 丁驌 (1912-?)
• Location of specimens: N, NF, PE

W. J. Ding

Ding, Wen Jiang; 丁文江 ; Dīng Wénjiāng (1939-)
• Employment: Institute of Grassland Research, Chinese Academy of Agricultural Sciences（中国农业科学院草原研究所）
• Research interest: Plants of Nei Mongol
• Location of specimens: FGC. *Flora Innermongolica*

Ding, Xiao Yu; 丁小余 ; Dīng Xiǎoyú (1965-)
• Research interest: Orchidaceae
• Affiliation: NJNU

Ting, Y. S.; 丁衍畴 ; Dīng Yǎnchóu; 丁衍疇
• Location of specimens: IBSC, KUN, PE, PEM

Dong, An Miao; 董安淼 ; Dǒng Ānmiǎo
• Location of specimens: JJF

Tong, Chang Chun; Tung, Chang Chun; Tung, Ch'ang Ch'un; 董长椿 ; Dǒng Chángchūn; 董長椿
• Location of specimens: IBSC

Dong, Chuan Hong; 董川宏 ; Dǒng Chuānhóng (1968-)
• Affiliation: SN

Dong, De Fen; 董德芬 ; Dǒng Défēn
• Affiliation: LEF

Dong, Gang; 董刚 ; Dǒng Gāng (1983-)
• Research interest: Plants of Shanxi
• Affiliation: SXU

Tung, Hui Min; Tung, Hwei Nin; Dong, Hui Min; 董惠民 ; Dǒng Huìmín (1931-)
• Location of specimens: PE

Tung, C. S.; 董景生 ; Dǒng Jǐngshēng
• Location of specimens: HAST

Dong, Lin Ge; 董林阁 ; Dǒng Língé
• Affiliation: DQTC

Dong, Mei Fang; 董美芳 ; Dǒng Měifāng (1969-)
• Research interest: Plants of N. China
• Affiliation: KAI

M. L. Dong

Dong, Mei Ling; 董美龄 ; Dǒng Měilíng; 董美齡 (1928-2011)
• Employment: Institute of Oceanology, Chinese Academy of Sciences（中国科学院海洋研究所）
• Research interest: Algae
• Affiliation: MBMCAS

Dong, Tian Ying; 董天英 ; Dǒng Tiānyīng (1932-)
• Research interest: Plants of Hebei
• Affiliation: CHA
• Location of specimens: CHA

Tung, Hsiao Weei; 董晓瑋 ; Dǒng Xiǎowěi; 董晓玮
• Location of specimens: HAST

Dong, Xiao Yu; 董晓宇 ; Dǒng Xiǎoyǔ (1984-)
• Research interest: Schisandraceae
• Affiliation: NAS

Tung, Yi You; 董以有 ; Dǒng Yǐyǒu
• Location of specimens: PE

Dou, Ping Zhen; 窦萍珍 ; Dòu Píngzhēn (1957-)
• Research interest: Plants of Guangdong
• Affiliation: ZHAN
• Location of specimens: ZHAN

Dulongjiang Exped.; 独龙江考察队 ; Dúlóngjiāng Kǎochádùi
• Location of specimens: KUN. Collection Team

Tu, Tsung Ming; 杜聰明 ; Dù Cōngmíng; 杜聪明
• Location of specimens: HAST

Tu, Ta Hua; Du, Da Hua; 杜大华 ; Dù Dàhuá; 杜大華
• Location of specimens: CQNM, SZ

Du, Fan Zhang; 杜凡章 ; Dù Fánzhāng (1949-)
• Affiliation: HHNNR

Du, Feng Guo; 杜凤国 ; Dù Fèngguó (1960-)
• Research interest: Plants of Jilin
• Affiliation: JLFC
• Location of specimens: JLFC

Du

Du, Fu; Tu, Fu; 杜复 ; Dù Fù; 杜複 (1937-)
• Employment: Shanxi University（山西大学）
• Research interest: Fungi
• Affiliation: SXU
• Location of specimens: SXU

To, Kang Peng; 杜庚平 ; Dù Gēngpíng
• Affiliation: IBSC, NAS, PE, SYS

Du, Gui Sen; 杜桂森 ; Dù Guìsēn (1948-)
• Research interest: Bryophyte; Pteridophytes
• Affiliation: BJTC
• Location of specimens: BJTC

Du, Juan; 杜娟 ; Dù Juān
• Affiliation: JMSMC

Du, Tie Ying; 杜铁英 ; Dù Tiěyīng; 杜鐵英 (1946-)
• Affiliation: QG

Du, Wu Feng; 杜武峰 ; Dù Wǔfēng (1936-)
• Research interest: Amaryllidaceae
• Affiliation: IVF
• Location of specimens: IVF

Du, Yi Bin; 杜怡斌 ; Dù Yíbīn (1929-)
• Research interest: Plants of Hebei
• Affiliation: HBAU
• Location of specimens: HBAU

Du, Zhen Zhu; 杜珍珠 ; Dù Zhēnzhū (1987-)
- Research interest: Plants of Xinjiang
- Affiliation: SHI
- Location of specimens: SHI

Du, Zu Yu; 杜祖玉 ; Dù Zǔyù (1938-)
- Location of specimens: LINF

Duan, Cheng Yun; 段澄云 ; Duàn Chéngyún; 段澄雲 (1937-)
- Research interest: Euphorbiaceae, Gymnospermae, Malvaceae
- Affiliation: TIE
- Location of specimens: TIE

Duan, Hua; 段华 ; Duàn Huá
- Location of specimens: IMDY

Duan, Li Sheng; 段立胜 ; Duàn Lìshèng
- Location of specimens: IMDY

Duan, Shi Min; 段士民 ; Duàn Shìmín (1962-)
- Research interest: Plants of Xinjiang
- Affiliation: TURP
- Location of specimens: TURP

Duan, Xi Hua; 段喜华 ; Duàn Xǐhuá (1961-)
- Research interest: Salicaceae
- Affiliation: NEFI

F

Fan, Xing; 凡星 ; Fán Xīng (1979-)
- Research interest: Poaceae
- Affiliation: SAUT
- Location of specimens: SAUT

Fan, Zhong Liang; 凡忠良 ; Fán Zhōngliáng (1945-)
- Affiliation: HGTC

Fan, Cong Zhao; 樊从照 ; Fán Cóngzhào (1984-)
- Research interest: Medicinal Plants
- Affiliation: XTNM
- Location of specimens: XTNM

Fan, Jie; 樊杰 ; Fán Jié (1972-)
- Research interest: Medicinal Plants
- Affiliation: SXTCM
- Location of specimens: SXTCM

Fan, Jing Min; 樊京敏 ; Fán Jīngmǐn (1949-)
- Location of specimens: XBGH

Fan, Jing; 樊晶 ; Fán Jīng
- Location of specimens: XJNU

Fan, Ching Sheng; Fan, Ching Seng; Fan, Ch'ing Sêng; Fan, Ch'ing Shêng; Fan, Qing Sheng; 樊庆笙 ; Fán Qìngshēng; 樊慶笙 ; 樊庆生 (1911-1998)
- Location of specimens: N

Fan, Fa Hui; 范發輝 ; Fàn Fāhuī; 范发辉 ;
- Location of specimens: HAST

L. Fan

Fan, Li; 范黎 ; Fàn Lí (1964-)
- Employment: Shanxi University（山西大学）
- Research interest: Fungi
- Affiliation: SXU

Fan, Li Xiang; 范莉香 ; Fàn Lìxiāng
- Location of specimens: PEM

Fan, Lian Qin; 范连琴 ; Fàn Liánqín; 範連琴 (1944-2015)
- Research interest: Plants of Shanghai
- Affiliation: SG
- Location of specimens: SG

Fan, Long Qing; 范隆庆 ; Fàn Lóngqìng (1964-)
- Research interest: Woody Plants
- Affiliation: SIFS

Fan, Qing Ci; 范青慈 ; Fàn Qīngcí (1962-)
- Affiliation: QG

Fan, Ya Wen; 范亚文 ; Fàn Yàwén (1965-)
- Research interest: Algae
- Affiliation: HANU
- Location of specimens: HANU

Fan, Ying Ying; 范莹莹 ; Fàn Yíngyíng (1985-)
- Research interest: Medicinal Plants
- Affiliation: QDC

Y. G. Fan

Fan, Yu Guang; 范宇光 ; Fàn Yǔguāng (1982-)
- Employment: Jilin Agricultural University（吉林农业大学）
- Research interest: Fungi

• Affiliation: ANTU

Fan, Zong Zhong; 范宗忠 ; Fàn Zōngzhōng (1960-)
• Research interest: Apiaceae, Asteraceae
• Affiliation: JSPC

Fang, Beng De; 方琫德 ; Fāng Běngdé (1930-2004)
• Research interest: Plants of Shanxi
• Affiliation: SXAU

Fang, Bo; 方波 ; Fāng Bō (1972-)
• Research interest: Betulaceae
• Affiliation: YCP

Fang, Cheng Wu; 方成武 ; Fāng Chéngwǔ (1961-)
• Research interest: Medicinal Plants
• Affiliation: BZCM
• Location of specimens: BZCM

Fang, Fang; 方芳 ; Fāng Fāng (1969-)
• Research interest: Economic Plants
• Affiliation: ZNU
• Location of specimens: ZNU

Fang, Jue Shu; 方觉曙 ; Fāng Juéshǔ
• Affiliation: ANUG

Fang, Li Gen; 方利根 ; Fāng Lìgēn (1945-)
• Location of specimens: SG

Fang, Liang; 方亮 ; Fāng Liàng (1964-)
• Research interest: Balsaminaceae, Ranunculaceae
• Affiliation: JJT
• Location of specimens: JJT

Fang, Jui Nan; 方瑞男 ; Fāng Ruìnán
• Location of specimens: HAST

Fang, Sheng; 方胜 ; Fāng Shèng; 方勝 (1943-)
• Affiliation: ZJFI

Fang, Xiang Liang; 方响亮 ; Fāng Xiǎngliàng (1981-)
• Affiliation: ENS
• Location of specimens: ENS

Fang, Xiao Ping; 方小平 ; Fāng Xiǎopíng
• Research interest: Gymnospermae
• Affiliation: GF
• Location of specimens: GF

Fang, Yan; 方彦 ; Fāng Yàn (1960-)
• Affiliation: NFP

Fang, Ye; 方晔 ; Fāng Yè (1990-)
• Affiliation: SABG
• Location of specimens: SABG

Fang, Ying Cai; 方英才 ; Fāng Yīngcái
• Location of specimens: NYA

Fang, Yong Sing; Fang, Yong Xin; 方永鑫 ; Fāng Yǒngxīn (1935-)
• Affiliation: SHTU

Fan, Jui Yung; 芳瑞勇 ; Fāng Ruìyǒng
• Location of specimens: HAST

B. Feng

Feng, Bang; 冯邦 ; Féng Bāng (1983-)
• Employment: Kunming Institute of Botany, Chinese Academy of Sciences（中国科学院昆明植物研究所）
• Research interest: Fungi
• Affiliation: KUN

C. Feng

Feng, Chao; 冯超 ; Féng Chāo (1985-)
• Employment: School of Life Sciences, Inner Mongolia University（内蒙古大学生命科学学院）
• Research interest: Bryophyte
• Affiliation: NMAC

Feung, C. S.; 馮朝勳 ; Féng Cháoxūn; 冯朝勋
• Location of specimens: HAST

Feng, Jeng Ru; 冯澄如 ; Féng Chéngrú; 馮澄如 (1896-1968)
• Research interest: Scientific Illustrator
• Affiliation: PE

J. Feng

Feng, Jia; 冯佳 ; Féng Jiā (1980-)
• Employment: Shanxi University（山西大学）
• Research interest: Algae
• Affiliation: SXU
• Location of specimens: SXU

Feng, Jin Huan; 冯金环 ; Féng Jīnhuán; 馮金環 (1941-)
• Research interest: Scientific Illustrator
• Affiliation: IFP

Feng, Jin Yong; 冯晋庸 ; Féng Jìnyōng; 馮晉庸 (1925-2019)
• Research interest: Scientific Illustrator
• Affiliation: PE

Feng, Li; 冯丽 ; Féng Lì (1982-)
• Research interest: Plant Ecology
• Affiliation: LZD

Feng, Lu Tian; 冯鲁田 ; Féng Lǔtián; 馮魯田 (1948-)
• Research interest: Medicinal Plants
• Affiliation: SXDC
• Location of specimens: SXDC

Feng, Ming; 冯明 ; Féng Míng
• Location of specimens: GXF

Feng, Ming Kai; 冯明开 ; Féng Míngkāi; 馮明開 (1937-)
• Research interest: Medicinal Plants
• Affiliation: GDMM

Feng, Qi Li; 冯启理 ; Féng Qǐlǐ
• Affiliation: SN

Feng, Qian; 冯倩 ; Féng Qiàn (1975-)
• Research interest: Meliaceae
• Affiliation: YAF

Fung, Hom; 冯钦 ; Féng Qīn; 馮欽
• Location of specimens: PE, SYS

Feng, Tu; 冯图 ; Féng Tú (1982-)
• Research interest: Bryophyte
• Affiliation: BJ
• Location of specimens: BJ

Feng, Xian Kui; 冯显逵 ; Féng Xiǎnkuí; 馮顯逵 (1935-)
• Research interest: Plants of Ningxia
• Affiliation: NXF
• Location of specimens: NXF

Feng, Zheng Bo; 冯正波 ; Féng Zhèngbō (1975-2008)
• Location of specimens: WCSBG

Feng, Zhong Yuan; Phoon, Zhong Yuan; 冯钟元 ; Féng Zhōngyuán; 馮鍾元 (1916-2011)
• Research interest: Scientific Illustrator
• Affiliation: IBSC

Feng, Zu Xiang; 冯祖祥 ; Féng Zǔxiáng
• Location of specimens: EBF

Feng, Kuei Li; 奉貴禮 ; Fèng Guìlǐ; 奉贵礼 ;
• Location of specimens: HAST

Feng, Shu Cheng; 奉树成 ; Fèng Shùchéng (1966-)
• Research interest: Plants of Shanghai
• Affiliation: SG

Fu, Ya Ru; 符亚儒 ; Fú Yàrú (1955-)
• Research interest: Plant Physiology
• Affiliation: YLD

Fu, Yu Pin; 付玉嫔 ; Fù Yùpín (1974-)
• Research interest: Schisandraceae
• Affiliation: YCP

Fu, C. S.; 傅家瑞 ; Fù Jiāruì
• Location of specimens: SYS

Fu, Lian Zhong; 傅连中 ; Fù Liánzhòng (1962-)
• Affiliation: PE

Fu, Long Geng; 傅龙庚 ; Fù Lónggēng (1950-)
• Research interest: Medicinal Plants
• Affiliation: SHDC
• Location of specimens: SHDC

Fu, Pei Xing; 傅培兴 ; Fù Péixìng
• Location of specimens: JAS

Fu, Peng; 傅鹏 ; Fù Péng (1978-)
• Research interest: Medicinal Plants
• Affiliation: GXCM
• Location of specimens: GXCM

P. D. Fu

Fu, Ping Du; 傅平都 ; Fù Píngdū (1937-)
• Employment: Chengdu Bureau of Gardening and Greening（成都市园林管理局）
• Research interest: Plants of Sichuan
• Flora sichuanica

Fu, Qiang; 傅强 ; Fù Qiáng (1967-)
• Research interest: Plants of Hubei
• Affiliation: CCAU

Fu, Qing; 傅青 ; Fù Qīng (1959-)
• Research interest: Araceae
• Affiliation: WUK

Fu, Shun Mo; 傅舜谟 ; Fù Shùnmó
• Location of specimens: IBSC

X. Fu

Fu, Xing; 傅星 ; Fù Xīng (1963-)
• Employment: Institute of Applied Ecology, Chinese Academy of Sciences（中国科学院沈阳应用生态研究所）
• Research interest: Bryophyte
• Affiliation: IFP
• Location of specimens: IFP

Fu, Yi Zheng; 傅以政 ; Fù Yǐzhèng
• Location of specimens: SAUF

G(K)

Garody; 嘎日迪 ; Gārìdí (1962-)
• Research interest: Herbaceous Plants
• Affiliation: NMAC

Gan, Qing Mei; 甘青梅 ; Gān Qīngméi
• Research interest: Medicinal Plants
• Affiliation: QDC

Gan, Xiao Hong; 甘小洪 ; Gān Xiǎohóng
• Research interest: Economic Plants
• Affiliation: SITC
• Location of specimens: SITC

C. H. Gao

Gao, Cai Hua; 高彩华 ; Gāo Cǎihuá; 高彩華 (1946-)
• Employment: Shanghai Natural History Museum (Branch of Shanghai Science & Technology Museum) (上海自然博物馆(上海科技馆分馆))
• Research interest: Bryophyte
• Affiliation: SHM
• Location of specimens: SHM

Gao, Chang Lan; 高昌兰 ; Gāo Chānglán; 高昌蘭 (1947-)
• Research interest: Medicinal Plants
• Affiliation: SSMM
• Location of specimens: SSMM

Gao, Chi; 高迟 ; Gāo Chí; 高遲 (1948-)
• Research interest: Woody Plants
• Affiliation: HUF

Gao, De En; 高德恩 ; Gāo Dé'ēn (1940-)
• Location of specimens: IFP

Gao, De Min; 高德民 ; Gāo Démín (1973-)
• Research interest: Medicinal Plants
• Affiliation: SDCM
• Location of specimens: SDCM

Gao, Gui Zhen; 高贵珍 ; Gāo Guìzhēn (1962-)
• Research interest: Plants of Anhui
• Affiliation: ST
• Location of specimens: ST

Gao, Hai Ning; 高海宁 ; Gāo Hǎiníng (1973-)
• Research interest: Plants of Qilianshan
• Affiliation: ZYTC
• Location of specimens: ZYTC

Gao, Ji Guang; 高继光 ; Gāo Jìguāng
• Location of specimens: XTNM

Gao, Jin Nan; 高瑾南 ; Gāo Jǐnnán
• Location of specimens: SHTU

Gao, Ju Lin; 高举林 ; Gāo Jǔlín
• Location of specimens: WCSBG

Gao, Kai; 高凯 ; Gāo Kǎi (1971-)
• Research interest: Plant Systematics
• Affiliation: TIE

Gao, Kan; 高侃 ; Gāo Kǎn (1935-)
• Research interest: Plants of Dalian
• Affiliation: LNNU
• Location of specimens: LNNU

Gao, Li An; 高礼安 ; Gāo Lǐ'ān
• Affiliation: QNUN
• Location of specimens: QNUN

Kao, Mei Fang; 高美芳 ; Gāo Měifāng
• Location of specimens: HAST

C. Gao

Gao, Chien; Ko, Chien; Gao, Qian; 高谦 ; Gāo Qiān; 高謙 (1929-2016)
• Employment: Institute of Applied Ecology, Chinese Academy of Sciences (中国科学院沈阳应用生态研究所)
• Research interest: Bryophyte
• Affiliation: IFP
• Location of specimens: IFP

Gao, Qing Bo; 高庆波 ; Gāo Qìngbō (1980-)
• Research interest: Saxifragaceae
• Affiliation: HNWP

Kao, Yui Ching; 高瑞卿 ; Gāo Ruìqīng
• Location of specimens: HAST

Gao, RunMei; 高润梅 ; Gāo Rùnméi (1974-)
• Research interest: Plants of Shanxi
• Affiliation: SXAU

Gao, Shi Xian; 高士贤 ; Gāo Shìxián; 高士賢 (1933-)

• Research interest: Medicinal Plants
• Affiliation: CCM
• Location of specimens: CCM

Gao, Shu Zhen; 高淑贞 ; Gāo Shūzhēn; 高淑貞 (1930-2010)
• Research interest: Fabaceae
• Affiliation: SANU
• Location of specimens: SANU

Gao, Wen Bo; 高文博 ; Gāo Wénbó
• Location of specimens: SYPC

Ko, Sik Pang; Ko, Hsi Peng; Ko, Sik Peng; 高锡朋 ; Gāo Xīpéng; 高錫朋
• Location of specimens: IBK, IBSC

Gao, Ya Hong; 高亚红 ; Gāo Yàhóng (1980-)
• Affiliation: HHBG
• Location of specimens: HHBG

Gao, Yuan Tai; 高元泰 ; Gāo Yuántài (1945-)
• Location of specimens: TJDC

Kao, Yuan Hsiang; 高源祥 ; Gāo Yuánxiáng
• Location of specimens: HAST

Gao, Zuo Hua; 高作华 ; Gāo Zuòhuá; 高作華 (1926-)
• Location of specimens: CCM

Kelsang; Gesang; 格桑 ; Gésāng (1958-)
• Research interest: Economic Plants
• Affiliation: XZ
• Location of specimens: XZ

Ge, Bin Jie; 葛斌杰 ; Gě Bīnjié (1983-)
• Research interest: Plant Anatomy
• Affiliation: CSH
• Location of specimens: CSH

Ge, Chuan Ji; 葛传吉 ; Gě Chuánjí; 葛傳吉 (1932-)
• Research interest: Medicinal Plants
• Affiliation: SDCM
• Location of specimens: SDCM

Ge, Fei; 葛菲 ; Gě Fēi (1965-)
• Research interest: Verbenaceae
• Affiliation: JXCM

Ge, Gang; 葛刚 ; Gě Gāng (1968-)
• Research interest: Plant Ecology
• Affiliation: JXU

Ge, Ji Xian; 葛继贤 ; Gě Jìxián
• Location of specimens: HBFC

Ge, Li Ping; 葛丽萍 ; Gě Lìpíng (1969-)
• Research interest: Woody Plants
• Affiliation: SXAU

Z. W. Ge

Ge, Zai Wei; 葛再伟 ; Gě Zàiwěi (1975-)
• Employment: Kunming Institute of Botany, Chinese Academy of Sciences（中国科学院昆明植物研究所）
• Research interest: Fungi
• Affiliation: KUN

Gong, Ming Xuan; 龚明暄 ; Gōng Míngxuān; 龔明暄 (1923-1975)
• Location of specimens: JXU

Gong, Wei; 龚维 ; Gōng Wéi (1979-)
• Research interest: Plant Geography
• Affiliation: SCAUB

Gong, Zhu Nan; 龚祝南 ; Gōng Zhùnán (1963-)
• Research interest: Medicinal Plants
• Affiliation: CPU

Gu, Zhong Cun; 谷中村 ; Gǔ Zhōngcūn (1943-)
• Research interest: Plants of W. Hunan
• Affiliation: JIU
• Location of specimens: JIU

Gu, Jian; 顾健 ; Gù Jiàn
• Location of specimens: CDBI

Gu, Yue Ping; 顾月萍 ; Gù Yuèpíng; 顧月萍 (1936-)
• Research interest: Plants of Shaanxi
• Affiliation: WUK
• Location of specimens: WUK

Gu, Zhi Jian; 顾志建 ; Gù Zhìjiàn (1949-2009)
• Research interest: Plant Cytology
• Affiliation: KUN
• Location of specimens: KUN

Gu, Zhong Hua; 顾钟骅 ; Gù Zhōnghuá
• Location of specimens: NJNU

Gu, Zi Xia; 顾子霞 ; Gù Zixiá (1985-)
• Research interest: Scientific Illustrator
• Affiliation: NAS

Kan, Toh; Gan, Duo; 干铎 ; Gān duó; 干鐸 (1903-1961)
• Research interest: Woody Plants
• Affiliation: NF

Guan, Fang Ling; 关芳玲 ; Guān Fānglíng (1956-)
• Affiliation: HSIB

Guan, Guang Qing; 关广清 ; Guān Guǎngqīng; 關廣清 (1938-)
• Research interest: Weeds
• Affiliation: SYAU
• Location of specimens: NAU, SYAU

Kuan, Chung Hsiung; 關忠雄 ; Guān Zhōngxióng; 关忠雄 ;
• Location of specimens: HAST

Guan, Zhong Ming; 关钟鸣 ; Guān Zhōngmíng
• Location of specimens: HGAS

Guan, Bi Cai; 管毕财 ; Guǎn Bìcái (1976-)
• Research interest: Pteridophytes
• Affiliation: JXU

Guan, Yan Hong; 管燕红 ; Guǎn Yànhóng
• Affiliation: IMDY
• Location of specimens: IMDY

Guangdong Med. Pl. Exped.; 广东省中药资源普查队 ; Guǎngdōngshěng; Zhōngyào Zīyuán Pǔchádui
• Location of specimens: GDMM. Collection Team

Kwangfu Exped.; 广福林区调查队 ; Guǎngfú Línqū Diàocháduì
• Location of specimens: IBK, IBSC, KUN, PE. Collection Team

Kwangsi Prov. Mus.; 广西省立博物馆 ; Guǎngxī Shěnglì Bówùguǎn
• Location of specimens: IBSC. Collection Team

Guizhou Exped.; 贵州队 ; Guìzhōu Duì
• Location of specimens: PE. Collection Team

Gui, Ming Zhu; 桂明珠 ; Guì Míngzhū (1946-)
• Location of specimens: NEAU

Guo, Cheng Yong; Guo, C. U.; 郭成勇 ; Guō Chéngyǒng
• Location of specimens: PE, QFNU

Guo, Chun Yan; 郭春燕 ; Guō Chūnyàn (1980-)
• Research interest: Plants of Shanxi
• Affiliation: HSIB
• Location of specimens: HSIB

Kuo, Fu Lin; 郭福麟 ; Guō Fúlín
• Location of specimens: HAST

Guo, Gui Lin; 郭贵林 ; Guō Guìlín; 郭貴林 (1937-)
• Location of specimens: NEAU

Kwok, Wah Shau; 郭华秀 ; Guō Huáxiù; 郭華秀
• Location of specimens: SYS

Guo, Lan Ping; 郭兰萍 ; Guō Lánpíng (1969-)
• Research interest: Asteraceae
• Affiliation: CMMI

Kuo, Li Hua; 郭黎華 ; Guō Líhuá; 郭黎华
• Location of specimens: HAST

Guo, Li Qun; 郭立群 ; Guō Lìqún (1937-)
• Research interest: Pinaceae, Taxodiaceae
• Affiliation: YCP

Guo, Mu Sen; 郭木森 ; Guō Mùsēn (1940-)
• Research interest: Scientific Illustrator
• Affiliation: PE

Guo, Peng Ju; 郭鹏举 ; Guō Péngjǔ
• Research interest: Medicinal Plants
• Affiliation: QDC

Guo, Qing Mei; 郭庆梅 ; Guō Qìngméi
• Location of specimens: SDCM

Kwok, Kin Fong; 郭琼芳 ; Guō Qióngfāng; 郭瓊芳
• Location of specimens: IBSC

Guo, Quan Shui; 郭泉水 ; Guō Quánshuǐ (1954-)
• Research interest: Forest Ecology
• Affiliation: CAF

Guo, Shao Rong; 郭绍荣 ; Guō Shàoróng
• Research interest: Medicinal Plants
• Affiliation: IMDY
• Location of specimens: IMDY

Guo, Shou Xi; 郭守锡 ; Guō Shǒuxī
• Affiliation: CQBG

Guo, Shu Xian; 郭书贤 ; Guō Shūxián (1963-)
• Research interest: Salicaceae
• Affiliation: QUA
• Location of specimens: QUA

Kuo, Shu Miao; 郭淑妙 ; Guō Shūmiào
• Location of specimens: HAST

S. L. Guo

Guo, Shui Liang; 郭水良 ; Guō Shuǐliáng (1964-)
• Employment: College of Life and Environmental

Science, Shanghai Normal University（上海师范大学生命科学与环境科学学院）
• **Research interest: Bryophyte; Plants of Zhejiang**
• **Affiliation: SHTU, ZNU**
• Location of specimens: NAU, SHTU, ZNU

Kuo, S. P.; Kwok, S. P.; 郭素白 ; Guō Sùbái
• Location of specimens: IBSC

Guo, Wei Na; 郭伟娜 ; Guō Wěinà (1983-)
• Research interest: Gentianaceae
• Affiliation: BZCM

Kuo, Wen Hsi; 郭聞喜 ; Guō Wénxǐ; 郭闻喜
• Location of specimens: HAST

Guo, Xi Chang; 郭锡昌 ; Guō Xīchāng; 郭錫昌 (1926-)
• Research interest: Fagaceae, Magnoliceae
• Affiliation: SYAUF
• Location of specimens: SYAUF

Guo, Xiao Qiang; 郭小强 ; Guō Xiǎoqiáng (1965-)
• Research interest: Plants of Gansu
• Affiliation: QYTC
• Location of specimens: QYTC

X. Q. Guo

Guo, Xin Qing; 郭新清 ; Guō Xīnqīng (1920-)
• Employment: Inner Mongolia Institute of Forestry Science（内蒙古林业研究所）
• Research interest: Plants of Nei Mongol. *Flora Innermongolica*

Guo, Yi Min; 郭一敏 ; Guō Yīmǐn (1986-)
• Research interest: Plants of Xinjiang
• Affiliation: SHI

Guo, Yi Song; 郭艺松 ; Guō Yìsōng
• Location of specimens: XMBG

Guo, Yin Qing; 郭荫卿 ; Guō Yīnqīng
• Location of specimens: SWFC

Guo, Yun Zhen; 郭允珍 ; Guō Yǔnzhēn (1924-)
• Location of specimens: SYPC

Guo, Quan Sheng; 过全生 ; Guò Quánshēng; 過全生 (1937-)
• Affiliation: ZAU

H(K,W)

Khasbagan; 哈斯巴根 ; Hāsībāgēn (1963-)
• Research interest: Lamiaceae
• Affiliation: NMTC
• Location of specimens: NMTC

Hami Exped.; 哈密队 ; Hāmì Duì
• Location of specimens: XTNM. Collection Team

Hai, Ping; 海平 ; Hǎi Píng (1964-)
• Affiliation: QDC

Hai, Xian; 海仙 ; Hǎi Xiān (1984-)
• Affiliation: SABG
• Location of specimens: SABG

Hai, Ying; 海鹰 ; Hǎi Yīng (1952-)
• Location of specimens: XJUG

Hai, Yu Sheng; 海昱生 ; Hǎi Yùshēng (1941-)
• Affiliation: DFEC
• Location of specimens: DFEC

Han, Chu Xue; 韩初雪 ; Hán Chūxuě
• Location of specimens: SYAUF

Han, Duo Hong; 韩多宏 ; Hán Duōhóng (1978-)
• Research interest: Plants of Gansu
• Affiliation: ZYTC
• Location of specimens: ZYTC

Han, Fang; 韩芳 ; Hán Fāng (1954-)
• Research interest: Fungi
• Affiliation: TIE

Han, Feng Chun; 韩凤春 ; Hán Fèngchūn
• Affiliation: HLCM

Han, Gui Zhen; 韩贵珍 ; Hán Guìzhēn; 韓貴珍 (1936-)
• Research interest: Woody Plants
• Affiliation: SCFI

Han, Gui Jun; 韩桂军 ; Hán Guìjūn (1982-)
• Location of specimens: XBGH

Han, Guo Ying; 韩国营 ; Hán Guóyíng (1982-)
- **Research interest: Bryophyte; Fungi**
- **Affiliation: GYBG**
- Location of specimens: GYBG

Han, Jian Lin; 韩建林 ; Hán Jiànlín
- Affiliation: YNUB

L. F. Han

Han, Liu Fu; 韩留福 ; Hán Liúfú (1965-)
- Employment: College of Life Sciences, Hebei Normal University（河北师范大学生命科学学院）
- **Research interest: Bryophyte; Fungi**
- **Affiliation: HBNU**
- Location of specimens: HBNU

Han, Mei; 韩梅 ; Hán Méi (1964-)
- Research interest: Medicinal Plants
- Affiliation: JLAU

Han, Ting; 韩婷 ; Hán Tíng
- Research interest: Medicinal Plants
- Affiliation: SMMU-BH

Han, Xing Jie; 韩兴杰 ; Hán Xìngjié (1976-)
- Research interest: Lardizablaceae
- Affiliation: JJT
- Location of specimens: JJT

Han, Ya Guang; 韩亚光 ; Hán Yàguāng; 韓亞光 ; (1942-)
- Research interest: Fabaceae
- Affiliation: SYAU
- Location of specimens: SYAU

Han, Yan Ting; 韩艳婷 ; Hán Yàntíng (1981-)
- Research interest: Vitaceae
- Affiliation: XYTC

Han, Yi Fong; 韩裕丰 ; Hán Yùfēng; 韓裕豐
- Location of specimens: CIS

Han, Yuan Ji; 韩远记 ; Hán Yuǎnjì (1982-)
- Research interest: Plants of N. China
- Affiliation: KAI

Han, Yun; 韩云 ; Hán Yún (1965-)
- Affiliation: CIS

Han, Zhong Ming; 韩忠明 ; Hán Zhōngmíng (1978-)
- Research interest: Medicinal Plants
- Affiliation: JLAU

Han, Pao Teh; 漢寶德 ; Hàn Bǎodé; 汉宝德 (1934-)
- Affiliation: TNM

Hang, Jin Xin; 杭金欣 ; Háng Jīnxīn (1939-)
- Research interest: Algae
- Affiliation: SHM
- Location of specimens: SHM

Hao, Jia Bo; 郝佳波 ; Hǎo Jiābō (1981-)
- Research interest: Magnoliceae
- Affiliation: YAF

Hao, Jian Hua; 郝建华 ; Hǎo Jiànhuá (1963-)
- Research interest: Plants of Gansu
- Affiliation: QYTC
- Location of specimens: QYTC

Hao, Shu Fang; 郝淑芳 ; Hǎo Shūfāng (1936-)
- Research interest: Brassicaceae
- Affiliation: HWA

Hao, Si Ping; 郝四平 ; Hǎo Sìpíng (1969-)
- Research interest: Plants of Shanxi
- Affiliation: SXU

Hao, Xiao Jiang; 郝小江 ; Hǎo Xiǎojiāng (1952-)
- Affiliation: KUN
- Location of specimens: KUN

He, Bin; 何斌 ; Hé Bīn
- Location of specimens: BJ

He, Dong Quan; 何冬泉 ; Hé Dōngquán
- Research interest: Scientific Illustrator
- Affiliation: ZJMA

Ho, K. C.; 何观洲 ; Hé Guānzhōu; 何觀洲
- Location of specimens: IBSC, PE, WUK

He, Han Tao; 何汉滔 ; Hé Hàntāo
- Location of specimens: IBSC

H. T. Ho

Ho, Huei Tin; 何汇珍 ; Hé Huìzhēn; 何彙珍 ; (1932-)
- Employment: Fujian Institute of Subtropical Botany（福建省亚热带植物研究所）
- Research interest: Plants of Fujian
- Affiliation: FJSI

Flora Fujianica

He, Hui Zhen; 何惠珍 ; Hé Huìzhēn (1951-1999)
- Affiliation: IBSC

He, Jin; 何今 ; Hé Jīn
- Location of specimens: CDBI

He, Jin Ling; 何金铃 ; Hé Jīnlíng (1962-)

• Research interest: Aquatic Plants
• Affiliation: AAUB

He, Jin; 何进 ; Hé Jìn (1970-)
• Affiliation: GNUG

He, Lin; 何林 ; Hé Lín (1980-)
• Research interest: Bryophyte
• Affiliation: ZY
• Location of specimens: ZY

He, Ping; 何平 ; Hé Píng
• Location of specimens: TJDC

Qiang He

He, Qiang; 何强 ; Hé Qiáng (1973-)
• Employment: Institute of Botany, Chinese Academy of Sciences（中国科学院植物研究所）
• Research interest: Bryophyte
• Affiliation: PE

He, Quan Hua; 何全华 ; Hé Quánhuá
• Location of specimens: NWFC

He, Ren Yuan; 何仁远 ; Hé Rényuǎn
• Location of specimens: PE, YDC

He, Ru Bao; 何汝保 ; Hé Rǔbǎo (1934-)
• Research interest: Plants of Henan
• Affiliation: HENU
• Location of specimens: HENU

S. C. He

He, Shao Chang; 何绍昌 ; Hé Shàochāng; 何紹昌 (1940-)
• Employment: Institute of Biology, Guizhou Academy of Sciences（贵州省科学院生物研究所）
• Research interest: Fungi
• Affiliation: HGAS
• Location of specimens: HGAS

He, Shao Yi; 何绍颐 ; Hé Shàoyí
• Location of specimens: IBSC

He, Shu Chun; 何树春 ; Hé Shùchūn
• Location of specimens: YFS

S. He

He, Si; 何思 ; Hé Sī (1959-)
• Employment: Institute of Botany, Chinese Academy of Sciences（中国科学院植物研究所）
• Research interest: Bryophyte
• Location of specimens: PE

Ho, Tien Hsiang; Ho, T'ien Hsiang; He, Tian Xiang; 何天相 ; Hé Tiānxiāng (1916- ？)
• Location of specimens: IBSC

Ho, Wen feng; 何文豐 ; Hé Wénfēng; 何文丰
• Location of specimens: HAST

X. He

He, Xian; 何显 ; Hé Xiǎn; (1951-)
• Employment: Department of Biology, Northeast Normal University（东北师范大学生物系）
• Research interest: Fungi
• Affiliation: NENU

Ho, Hsien Chang; Hoh, Hin Cheung; He, Xian Zhang; 何宪章 ; Hé Xiànzhāng; 何憲章
• Location of specimens: IBSC

X. L. He

He, Xiao Lan; 何小兰 ; Hé Xiǎolán (1965-)
• Employment: Herbarium, Department of Forestry, Northeast Forestry University（东北林业大学林学系植物标本室）
• Research interest: Bryophyte
• Affiliation: PE

He, Xiao Ling; 何晓玲 ; Hé Xiǎolíng
• Location of specimens: ZJFI

He, Xing Yuan; 何兴元 ; Hé Xīngyuán (1962-)
• Location of specimens: IFP

Ho, Hsiu Lan; 何秀蘭 ; Hé Xiùlán; 何秀兰
• Location of specimens: HAST

He, Yan Xia; 何艳霞 ; Hé Yànxiá (1978-)
• Research interest: Plants of N. China
• Affiliation: KAI

He, Yi Kun; 何奕騉 ; Hé Yìkūn (1957-)
• Affiliation: BJTC

He, Yong Hua; 何永华 ; Hé Yǒnghuá (1964-)
• Research interest: Plant Anatomy
• Affiliation: CDBI
• Location of specimens: CDBI

He, You Qian; 何有乾 ; Hé Yǒuqián
• Location of specimens: IBK

He, Yun Song; 何云松 ; Hé Yúnsōng (1976-)
• Affiliation: HGAS

Ho, Cheng Min; 何正民 ; Hé Zhèngmín

• Location of specimens: HAST

He, Zhong Sheng; 何中声 ; Hé Zhōngshēng (1984-)
• Research interest: Fagaceae
• Affiliation: FJFC

Z. Z. He

He, Zong Zhi; 何宗智 ; Hé Zōngzhì (1932-)
• Employment: School of Life Science and Food Engineering, Nanchang University（南昌大学生命科学与食品工程学院）
• Research interest: Fungi
• Affiliation: JXU

He, Zu Xia; 何祖霞 ; Hé Zǔxiá (1975-)
• Location of specimens: HUST

Ho, Hung Chang; 和鸿昌 ; Hé Hóngchāng; 和鴻昌
• Location of specimens: IBSC, KUN, PE, PEM

He, Tai Ping; 和太平 ; Hé Tàipíng (1963-)
• Research interest: Woody Plants
• Affiliation: GAC

Khotan Exped.; 和田队 ; Hétián Duì
• Location of specimens: XTNM. Collection Team

Hebei Exped.; 河北队 ; Héběi Duì
• Location of specimens: PE. Collection Team

Hebei Med. Pl. Exped.; 河北中药资源普查队 ; Héběi Zhōngyào Zīyuán Pǔcháduì
• Location of specimens: HBDC. Collection Team

Henan Plant Res. Exped.; 河南植物资源考察队 ; Hénán Zhíwù Zīyuán Kǎocháduì
• Location of specimens: HEBI. Collection Team

He, Jun Hui; 贺军辉 ; Hè Jūnhuī (1963-)
• Research interest: Plants of Hunan
• Affiliation: HUIF
• Location of specimens: HUIF

He, Jun Ying; 贺俊英 ; Hè Jùnyīng (1976-)
• Research interest: Invasive Plants
• Affiliation: NMTC
• Location of specimens: NMTC

He, Run Li; 贺润丽 ; Hè Rùnlì (1971-)
• Research interest: Medicinal Plants
• Affiliation: SXTCM
• Location of specimens: SXTCM

Ho, Yien Yoh; He, Xian Yu; 贺贤育 ; Hè Xiányù; 賀賢育
• Affiliation: HHBG
• Location of specimens: HHBG, HIB, IBSC, NAS, NF, PE, SYS, WUK, ZJFC

He, Xin Qiang; 贺新强 ; Hè Xīnqiáng
• Affiliation: PEY, SDNU
• Location of specimens: SDNU

Hengduanshan Exped.; 横断山考察队 Héngduànshān Kǎocháduì
• Location of specimens: CIS, KUN, PE. Collection Team

Hong, Bi Gong; 洪必恭 ; Hóng Bìgōng (1932-)
• Research interest: Plant Geography
• Affiliation: N

Hung, Kuei chih; 洪桂治 ; Hóng Guìzhì
• Location of specimens: HAST

Hong, Li Xing; 洪利兴 ; Hóng Lìxīng (1955-)
• Research interest: Plants of Zhejiang
• Affiliation: ZJFI
• Location of specimens: ZJFI

Hong, Lin; 洪林 ; Hóng Lín
• Location of specimens: HHBG

Hueng, Shu Hua; 洪淑華 ; Hóng Shūhuá; 洪淑华
• Location of specimens: HAST

Hou, Hui Tsung; Hou, Hui Zong; 侯惠宗 ; Hóu Huìzōng
• Affiliation: BJFC

Hou, Jia Long; 侯家龙 ; Hóu Jiālóng
• Location of specimens: IFP

Hou, Xi Xiang; 侯喜祥 ; Hóu Xǐxiáng
• Location of specimens: FJSI, IBSC, WUK

Hou, Xiao Qi; 侯小琪 ; Hóu Xiǎoqí (1983-)
• Research interest: Orchidaceae
• Affiliation: GYBG
• Location of specimens: GYBG

Hou, Hsue Yu; 侯学煜 ; Hóu Xuéyù; 侯學煜 (1912-1991)
• Location of specimens: PE

Hu, Bao Zhong; 胡宝忠 ; Hú Bǎozhōng (1962-)
• Research interest: Fabaceae, Rosaceae
• Affiliation: NEAU
• Location of specimens: NEAU

Hu, Chang Xu; 胡昌序 ; Hú Chāngxù (1934-)
• Location of specimens: PE

Hu, Chao; 胡超 ; Hú Chāo (1988-)
• Research interest: Orchidaceae
• Affiliation: CSH

Hu, Chao; 胡超 ; Hú Chāo (1963-)
• Research interest: Poaceae
• Affiliation: SAU
• Location of specimens: SAU

Hu, Cheng Gang; 胡成刚 ; Hú Chénggāng (1969-)
• Research interest: Medicinal Plants
• Affiliation: GZTM
• Location of specimens: GZTM

Hu, Dong; 胡东 ; Hú Dōng (1952-)
• Research interest: Economic Plants
• Affiliation: BJTC
• Location of specimens: BJTC

Hu, Feng Yu; 胡凤玉 ; Hú Fèngyù
• Research interest: Plants of Fujian
• Affiliation: FFVTC

Hu, Gao Sheng; 胡高升 ; Hú Gāoshēng (1982-)
• Research interest: Dioscoreaceae, Solanaceae
• Affiliation: SYPC
• Location of specimens: SYPC

Hu, Gen Yong; 胡根勇 ; Hú Gēnyǒng
• Location of specimens: TIPR

Hu, Hong Jun; 胡鸿钧 ; Hú Hóngjūn; 胡鴻鈞 (1934-)
• Location of specimens: HBI

Hu, Jiang Qin; 胡江琴 ; Hú Jiāngqín (1967-)
• Research interest: Valerianaceae; Medicinal Plants
• Affiliation: HTC

Hu, Jin Liang; 胡金良 ; Hú Jīnliáng (1961-)
• Research interest: Plants of E. China
• Affiliation: NAU

Hu, Ning Zuo; 胡宁拙 ; Hú Níngzhuō; 胡寧拙 (1933-)
• Research interest: Fungi
• Affiliation: HGAS
• Location of specimens: HGAS

R. L. Hu

Hu, Ren Liang; 胡人亮 ; Hú Rénliàng (1932-2009)
• Employment: Department of Biology, East China Normal University (华东师范大学生物系)
• Research interest: Bryophyte
• Affiliation: HSNU
• Location of specimens: HSNU

Hu, Ruo Ying; 胡若瑛 ; Hú Ruòyīng (1941-)
• Research interest: Medicinal Plants
• Affiliation: LSDC

Hu, Sheng Fu; 胡生福 ; Hú Shēngfú (1978-)
• Research interest: Piperaceae
• Affiliation: JXCM

Hu, Shi Zhi; 胡式之 ; Hú Shìzhī
• Location of specimens: LZD, PE, XJBI

Hu, Shi Lin; 胡是林 ; Hú Shìlín (1933-)
• Research interest: Solanaceae
• Affiliation: IVF

Hu, Shih Yi; Hu, Shih I; Hu, Shi Yi; 胡适宜 ; Hú Shìyí; 胡適宜 ;
• Location of specimens: SN

Hu, Ting Song; 胡廷松 ; Hú Tíngsōng (1935-)
• Research interest: Medicinal Plants
• Affiliation: GXMG

Hu, Wei Hsin; 胡維新 ; Hú Wéixīn; 胡维新
• Location of specimens: HAST

Hu, Wen Feng; 胡文凤 ; Hú Wénfèng
• Location of specimens: NFP

Hu, Xi You; 胡希优 ; Hú Xīyōu (1978-)
• Research interest: Fungi
• Affiliation: TIE

Hu, Xu Jia; 胡旭佳 ; Hú Xùjiā (1968-)
• Research interest: Medicinal Plants
• Affiliation: YDC

Hu, Xue Hua; 胡雪华 ; Hú Xuěhuá (1977-)
• Research interest: Economic Plants
• Affiliation: JGSU
• Location of specimens: JGSU

Hu, Ying; 胡莹 ; Hú Yíng (1982-)
• Research interest: Medicinal Plants
• Affiliation: SM

Y. C. Hu

Hu, Yu Chen; 胡玉琛 ; Hú Yùchēn (1939-)
• Employment: Administrative Bureau of Nature Reserve of Changbai Mountain, Jilin (吉林长白山自

然保护局）
• Research interest: Fungi
• Affiliation: ANTU
• Location of specimens: ANTU

Hu, Yu Shi; Hu, Yu Xi; 胡玉熹；Hú Yùxī (1936-)
• Affiliation: PE
• Location of specimens: PE

Hu, Yue Ying; 胡月英；Hú Yuèyīng (1922-)
• Research interest: Plants of Yunnan
• Affiliation: YIM
• Location of specimens: YIM

Hu, Yun Chuan; 胡云川；Hú Yúnchuān
• Location of specimens: SHDC

Hu, Zheng Yu; 胡征宇；Hú Zhēngyǔ (1957-)
• Research interest: Algae
• Affiliation: HBI
• Location of specimens: HBI

Hu, Zhi Xin; 胡志新；Hú Zhìxīn (1953-)
• Research interest: Medicinal Plants
• Affiliation: SXMP

Hu, Zu Kun; 胡祖坤；Hú Zǔkūn (1932-)
• Location of specimens: SDAU

Hupingshan Exped.; 壶瓶山考察队；Húpíngshān Kǎocháduì
• Location of specimens: HHNNR, PE. Collection Team

Hunan Museum; 湖南博物馆；Húnán Bówùguǎn
• Location of specimens: PE. Collection Team

Statio Orientali-Sinensis; 华东工作站；Huádōng Gōngzuòzhàn
• Location of specimens: PE. Collection Team

Hua, Dong; 华栋；Huà Dòng; 華棟 (1944-)
• Research interest: Plants of E. China
• Affiliation: XZTC
• Location of specimens: XZTC

Hwa, Ching Tsan; 华敬灿；Huà Jìngcàn; 華敬燦 (1921-2012)
• Location of specimens: HIB, NAS, PE

Huang, Bo Wen; 黄柏雯；Huáng Bǎiwén; 黄柏雯
• Location of specimens: HAST

Huang, Bang Quan; 黄帮全；Huáng Bāngquán (1969-)
• Research interest: Economic Plants
• Affiliation: EU

Huang, Bao Kang; 黄宝康；Huáng Bǎokāng (1969-)
• Research interest: Medicinal Plants
• Affiliation: SMMU-BH

Huang, Bao Xian; 黄宝贤；Huáng Bǎoxián
• Research interest: Geraniaceae
• Affiliation: IBSC

Huang, Bao You; 黄宝优；Huáng Bǎoyōu
• Location of specimens: GXMG

Huang, Bo Hui; 黄伯惠；Huáng Bóhuì (1954-)
• Research interest: Plants of Zhejiang
• Affiliation: ZJFI

Huang, Cai Jiang; 黄才江；Huáng Cáijiāng; 黄才江 (1935-)
• Research interest: Cactaceae, Potamogetonaceae, Trapaceae
• Affiliation: GNUB
• Location of specimens: GNUB

Wang, Sing; 黄成；Huáng Chéng; 黄成
• Location of specimens: IBSC

Huang, Dao Nian; 黄道年；Huáng Dàonián
• Location of specimens: IBK

Huang, De Ai; Huang, Te Ai; 黄德爱；Huáng Dé'ài; 黄德愛 (1934-)
• Research interest: Convolvulaceae, Fabaceae
• Affiliation: IBK

Huang, Gang; 黄刚；Huáng Gāng (1983-)
• Research interest: Plants of Xinjiang
• Affiliation: SHI
• Location of specimens: SHI

Huang, Guang Bin; 黄广宾；Huáng Guǎngbīn (1962-)
• Research interest: Daphniphyllaceae, Buxaceae
• Affiliation: IBK

Huang, Gui Rong; 黄桂荣；Huáng Guìróng; 黄桂榮 (1936-)
• Research interest: Medicinal Plants
• Affiliation: LNCM
• Location of specimens: LNCM

Huang, Han Yau; 黄瀚嶢；Huáng Hànyáo; 黄瀚峣
• Location of specimens: HAST

Huang, Hua Ze; 黄华泽 ; Huáng Huázé
• Location of specimens: IBSC

Huang, Huan Chang; 黄焕章 ; Huáng Huànzhāng; 黄焕章 ;
• Location of specimens: HAST

Huang, Jean; 黄惠君 ; Huáng Huìjūn; 黄惠君
• Location of specimens: HAST

Wang, Chi Chuang; Huang, Ji Zhuang; 黄季庄 ; Huáng Jìzhuāng
• Location of specimens: IBSC

Huang, Jia Min; 黄佳民 ; Huáng Jiāmín; 黄佳民 (1938-)
• Affiliation: GXCM

Huang, Chia long; 黄嘉隆 ; Huáng Jiālóng; 黄嘉隆
• Location of specimens: HAST

Huang, Chien I; 黄建益 ; Huáng Jiànyì; 黄建益
• Location of specimens: HAST

Huang, Jian Zhong; 黄建中 ; Huáng Jiànzhōng (1956-)
• Location of specimens: NAU

Huang, Jian; 黄健 ; Huáng Jiàn (1963-)
• Research interest: Plant Ecology
• Affiliation: XZ
• Location of specimens: XZ

Huang, Chieh Lin; 黄捷琳 ; Huáng Jiélín; 黄捷琳
• Location of specimens: HAST

Huang, Jing Song; 黄劲松 ; Huáng Jìngsōng (1965-)
• Research interest: Plants of Zhongtiaoshan
• Affiliation: BJM

Huang, Jing Hua; 黄京华 ; Huáng Jīnghuá
• Location of specimens: N

Huang, K.; 黄景 ; Huáng Jǐng
• Location of specimens: PE

Huang, Ching win; 黄静雯 ; Huáng Jìngwén; 黄静雯
• Location of specimens: HAST

Huang, Juan; 黄娟 ; Huáng Juān (1968-)
• Research interest: Medicinal Plants
• Affiliation: SMN

Huang, Chun Lin; 黄俊霖 ; Huáng Jùnlín; 黄俊霖 (1972-)
• Research interest: Moraceae
• Affiliation: TNM

Huang, Ke; 黄可 ; Huáng Kě; 黄可 ; (1934-2010)
• Research interest: Plants of Shaanxi
• Affiliation: SANU

Huang, Lan Jie; 黄岚杰 ; Huáng Lánjié (1985-)
• Research interest: Ericaceae, Magnoliceae, Menispermaceae
• Affiliation: EU

Huang, Li; 黄立 ; Huáng Lì
• Location of specimens: IBSC

Huang, Man Rong; 黄满荣 ; Huáng Mǎnróng (1975-)
• Research interest: Fungi
• Affiliation: BJM
• Location of specimens: BJM

Huang, Mei Chi; 黄美琪 ; Huáng Měiqí; 黄美琪
• Location of specimens: HAST

Huang, Peng Fei; 黄鹏飛 ; Huáng Péngfēi; 黄鹏飞
• Location of specimens: HAST

Huang, Qi Bin; 黄启斌 ; Huáng Qǐbīn
• Location of specimens: IBK

Huang, Chi Chun; 黄啟俊 ; Huáng Qǐjùn; 黄启俊
• Location of specimens: HAST

Huang, Qing Quan; 黄清泉 ; Huáng Qīngquán (1979-)
• Research interest: Medicinal Plants
• Affiliation: GXDC

Huang, Qing Yang; 黄庆阳 ; Huáng Qìngyáng (1981-)
• Research interest: Plants of N. E. China
• Affiliation: HNR

Huang, Chiu Chu; 黄秋菊 ; Huáng Qiūjú; 黄秋菊
• Location of specimens: HAST

Huang, Qun; 黄群 ; Huáng Qún (1955-)
• Affiliation: NFP

Huang, Chiun Jr; 黄群智 ; Huáng Qúnzhì; 黄群智
• Location of specimens: HAST

Huang, Jung Kuang; 黄榮光 ; Huáng Róngguāng; 黄荣光
• Location of specimens: HAST

Huang, Rong; 黄蓉 ; Huáng Róng (1965-)
• Research interest: Plants of Hubei

• Affiliation: HIB

Huang, Rong Hui; 黄榕辉 ; Huáng Rónghuī (1963-)
• Affiliation: FJFC

Huang, Ru Bo; 黄如波 ; Huáng Rúbō (1963-)
• Affiliation: WXDC

Huang, Shan Tao; 黄山涛 ; Huáng Shāntāo
• Location of specimens: IBK, IBSC

Huang, Shao Hua; 黄少华 ; Huáng Shàohuá
• Research interest: Economic Plants
• Affiliation: ATCH
• Location of specimens: ATCH

Huang, Shong; Huang, Sheng; 黄生 ; Huáng Shēng; 黄生 (1941-)
• Research interest: Plant Systematics
• Affiliation: TNU

Huang, Sheng Pai; 黄胜白 Huáng Shèngbái (1889-1982)
• Location of specimens: NAS

Huang, Shi Man; 黄世满 Huáng Shìmǎn; 黄世滿 ; (1946-)
• Research interest: Plants of Hainan
• Affiliation: HUTB
• Location of specimens: HUTB

Huang, Shih hsun; 黄世勳 ; Huáng Shìxūn; 黄世勋
• Location of specimens: HAST

Huang, Shu Fen; 黄淑芬 ; Huáng Shūfēn; 黄淑芬
• Location of specimens: HAST

Huang, Song Dian; 黄松殿 ; Huáng Sōngdiàn (1966-)
• Affiliation: NNA

Huang, Tao; 黄韬 ; Huáng Tāo; 黄韜 (1938-)
• Affiliation: ZHAN

Huang, Wei Chia; 黄韋嘉 ; Huáng Wéijiā; 黄韦嘉
• Location of specimens: HAST

Wang, Wei Yan; 黄维炎 ; Huáng Wéiyán
• Location of specimens: IBSC

W. D. Huang

Huang, Wen Da; 黄文達 ; Huáng Wéndá; 黄文达
• Employment: Institute of Forestry, Taiwan University（台湾大学森林学研究所）
• Research interest: Plants of Taiwan. *Flora of Taiwan*

Huang, Wen Xiu; 黄文秀 ; Huáng Wénxiù
• Affiliation: CIS

Wang, Si Tchen; 黄锡珍 ; Huáng Xīzhēn; 黄錫珍
• Location of specimens: PE

Huang, Xi Xiong; 黄羲雄 ; Huáng Xīxióng; 黄羲雄 (1957-)
• Research interest: Casuarinaceae
• Affiliation: TNM

Huang, Xian De; 黄先德 ; Huáng Xiāndé; 黄先德 (1933-)
• Affiliation: ABDC

Huang, Xiang Xu; 黄向旭 ; Huáng Xiàngxù (1960-)
• Research interest: Zingiberaceae
• Location of specimens: IBSC

Huang, Xiao Qiang; 黄小强 ; Huáng Xiǎoqiáng (1956-)
• Affiliation: JXAU

Huang, Xin Bi; 黄欣碧 ; Huáng Xīnbì
• Affiliation: GXSP

Huang, Ya Yi; 黄雅怡 ; Huáng Yǎyí; 黄雅怡
• Location of specimens: HAST

Huang, Yan Chuan; 黄衍串 ; Huáng Yǎnchuàn
• Affiliation: JXF

Huang, Yan Nan; 黄燕南 ; Huáng Yànnán (1955-)
• Affiliation: GNUG

Huang, Yao Moan; 黄曜謀 ; Huáng Yàomóu; 黄曜谋
• Research interest: Pteridophytes
• Affiliation: TAIF

Huang, Yi Ping; 黄一平 ; Huáng Yīpíng; 黄一平
• Location of specimens: HAST

Hwang, Yih Jen; 黄以仁 ; Huáng Yǐrén; 黄以仁 (1874-1944)
• Location of specimens: PE

Huang, Yi Zhi; 黄以之 ; Huáng Yǐzhī; 黄以之 (1931-)
• Research interest: Fabaceae
• Affiliation: ZM

Hwang, Yee hsiung; 黄義雄 ; Huáng Yìxióng; 黄义雄
• Location of specimens: HAST

Huang, Ying Feng; 黄颖锋 ; Huáng Yǐngfēng (1965-)
• Research interest: Medicinal Plants

• Affiliation: GXMG

Huang, Yung Shun; 黄永顺 ; Huáng Yǒngshùn; 黄永顺
• Location of specimens: HAST

Hwang, Yu Ju; Hwang, You Ru; Huang, You Ru; 黄友儒 ; Huáng Yǒurú; 黄友儒 (1928-)
• Research interest: Plants of Fujian
• Affiliation: FNU
• Location of specimens: FNU

Huang, Yu Jia; 黄玉佳 ; Huáng Yùjiā (1953-)
• Research interest: Plants of Dinghushan
• Affiliation: IBSD

Huang, Yu Min; 黄玉民 ; Huáng Yùmín; 黄玉民 (1936-)
• Affiliation: SY
• Location of specimens: SY

Huang, Yu Lan; 黄郁嵐 ; Huáng Yùlán; 黄郁岚
• Location of specimens: HAST

Huang, Yue Long; 黄跃龙 ; Huáng Yuèlóng
• Location of specimens: XMBG

Huang, Zhao; 黄钊 ; Huáng Zhāo; 黄釗 (1939-)
• Affiliation: NNA

Huang, Zhao Hua; 黄兆华 ; Huáng Zhàohuá
• Location of specimens: LZD

Huang, Zheng Zhang; 黄正璋 ; Huáng Zhèngzhāng
• Location of specimens: HZU

Wang, Chi; Huang, Zhi; Wang, Yung Kun; 黄志 ; Huáng Zhì; 黄荣琨 , 黄志 , 黃榮琨 ;
• Location of specimens: IBSC, PE

Huang, Zhi Hui; 黄志辉 ; Huáng Zhìhuī (1954-)
• Research interest: Woody Plants
• Affiliation: GAC
• Location of specimens: GAC

Huang, Zhi Ming; 黄志明 ; Huáng Zhìmíng
• Location of specimens: CQBG

Huang, Zhong Liang; 黄忠良 ; Huáng Zhōngliáng (1957-)
• Affiliation: IBSD

Huang, Zi Liang; 黄梓良 ; Huáng Zǐliáng (1965-)
• Research interest: Poaceae
• Affiliation: FFVTC
• Location of specimens: FFVTC

Huang, Tso Chieh; Hwang, Tso Chie; Huang, Zuo Jie; 黄作杰 ; Huáng Zuòjié; 黃作傑
• Location of specimens: IBK, IBSC, PE

Yellow River Exped.; 黄河调查队 ; Huánghé Diàochádùi
• Location of specimens: CAF, KUN. Collection Team

Loess Plateaus Exped.; 黄土高原调查队 ; Huángtǔ Gāoyuán Diàochádùi
• Location of specimens: WUK. Collection Team

J (C,K)

Ji, Tao; 吉涛 ; Jí Tāo
• Research interest: Medicinal Plants
• Affiliation: GXMG

Jirumtoo; 纪茹穆图 ; Jìrúmùtú (1920-)
• Location of specimens: NMTC

Ji, Hua; 季华 ; Jì Huá (1974-)
• Research interest: Woody Plants
• Affiliation: CCAU

Ji, Shen; 季申 ; Jì Shēn (1963-)
• Research interest: Medicinal Plants
• Affiliation: SHDC

Ji, Shu Yi; 暨淑仪 ; Jì Shūyí (1955-)
• Location of specimens: SCAUB

Ji, Chao Zhen; 冀朝祯 ; Jì Cháozhēn; 冀朝禎 (1936-)
• Research interest: Scientific Illustrator
• Affiliation: PE

Jia, Hou Li; 贾厚礼 ; Jiǎ Hòulǐ; 賈厚禮 (1933-)
• Location of specimens: YLD

Jia, Jing Ming; 贾景明 ; Jiǎ Jǐngmíng
• Affiliation: SYPC
• Location of specimens: SYPC

Jia, Ling Yun; 贾凌云 ; Jiǎ Língyún (1974-)
• Research interest: Asclepiadoideae, Fabaceae, Orchidaceae
• Affiliation: SYPC

• Location of specimens: SYPC

Jia, Min; 贾敏 ; Jiǎ Mǐn (1981-)
• Research interest: Medicinal Plants
• Affiliation: SMMU-BH

Chia, Shen Hsiu; Jia, Shen Xiu; 贾慎修 ; Jiǎ Shènxiū; 賈慎修 (1912-1988)
• Location of specimens: KUN, PE, XJBI

Jia, Xin Lan; 贾新兰 ; Jiǎ Xīnlán; 賈新蘭 (1935-)
• Research interest: Plants of Hebei
• Affiliation: HBAU
• Location of specimens: HBAU

X. Y. Jia

Jia, Xue Yi; 贾学乙 ; Jiǎ Xuéyǐ (1959-)
• Employment: Dalian Natural History Museum（大连自然博物馆）
• Research interest: Bryophyte
• Affiliation: DNHM
• Location of specimens: DNHM

Y. Jia

Jia, Yu; 贾渝 ; Jiǎ Yú (1965-)
• Employment: Institute of Botany, Chinese Academy of Sciences（中国科学院植物研究所）
• Research interest: Bryophyte
• Affiliation: PE
• Location of specimens: PE

T. C. Chia

Chia, Tsu Chang; Kia, Tchou Tsang; Jia, Zhu Zhang; 贾祖璋 ; Jiǎ Zǔzhāng; 賈祖璋 (1901-1988)
• Employment: Enlightened Bookstore（开明书店）
• Research interest: Plants of China
中国植物图鉴(Illustrated Dictionary of Chinese Flora)

Jian, Ming Wei; 簡名瑋 ; Jiǎn Míngwěi; 简名玮
• Location of specimens: HAST

C. Y. Chien

Chien, Chiu Yuan; 簡秋源 ; Jiǎn Qiūyuán; 简秋源 (1933-)
• Employment: School of Life Science, Taiwan Normal University（台湾师范大学生命科学专业学院）
• Research interest: Fungi
• Affiliation: TNU

Jane, Wann Neng; 簡萬能 ; Jiǎn Wànnéng; 简万能
• Location of specimens: HAST

Chien, Chang Jen; 簡章仁 ; Jiǎn Zhāngrén; 简章仁
• Location of specimens: HAST

Chiang, Her Long; 江合隆 ; Jiāng Hélóng
• Location of specimens: HAST

Jiang, Hong; 江洪 ; Jiāng Hóng (1980-)
• Research interest: Bryophyte
• Affiliation: BJ
• Location of specimens: BJ

Jiang, Ming Xi; 江明喜 ; Jiāng Míngxǐ (1965-)
• Research interest: Plants of C. China
• Affiliation: HIB

Chiang, J. S.; 江日昇 ; Jiāng Rìshēng; 江日升
• Location of specimens: HAST

Jiang, Ying Zhi; 江英志 ; Jiāng Yīngzhì (1938-)
• Research interest: Medicinal Plants
• Affiliation: FMP
• Location of specimens: FMP

Chiang, Yu Chung; 江友中 ; Jiāng Yǒuzhōng
• Location of specimens: HAST

Jiang, Ze Rong; 江泽荣 ; Jiāng Zéróng; 江澤榮 (1933-)
• Location of specimens: SYPC

Chiang, Tsen Pin; 江增彬 ; Jiāng Zēngbīn
• Location of specimens: HAST

Jiangxi Exped.; 江西队 ; Jiāngxī Duì
• Location of specimens: PE. Collection Team

Jiang, Chun Ning; 姜春宁 ; Jiāng Chūnníng (1980-)
• Research interest: Magnoliceae
• Affiliation: CANT

Jiang, Hai Lou; 姜海楼 ; Jiāng Hǎilóu
• Location of specimens: ZCA

Jiang, Hao; 姜昊 ; Jiāng Hào
• Affiliation: CCAU

Jiang, Ming; 姜明 ; Jiāng Míng (1971-)
• Research interest: Economic Plants
• Affiliation: IGA

Jiang, Ru Bi; 姜如碧 ; Jiāng Rúbì (1937-)
• Affiliation: GF
• Location of specimens: GF

Jiang, Run Xiao; 姜润潇 ; Jiāng Rùnxiāo (1956-)
• Affiliation: XAG

S. Z. Jiang

Jiang, Shou Zhong; 姜守忠 ; Jiāng Shǒuzhōng (1928-)
- Employment: Department of Biology, Guizhou Normal College（贵州师范学院生物系）
- Research interest: Fungi
- Affiliation: GNUB
- Location of specimens: GNUB

Jiang, Shu; 姜恕 ; Jiāng Shù (1925-2019)
- Location of specimens: PE

Jiang, Shun Shan; 姜顺善 ; Jiāng Shùnshàn
- Location of specimens: TIPR

Jiang, Yan Jing; 姜彦景 ; Jiāng Yànjǐng (1980-)
- Research interest: Biodiversity
- Affiliation: IGA

Jiang, Zai Min; 姜在民 ; Jiāng Zàimín (1963-)
- Research interest: Plants of Shaanxi
- Affiliation: WUK
- Location of specimens: WUK

Jiang, Cheng Zeng; 蒋承曾 ; Jiǎng Chéngzēng
- Location of specimens: IBK, IBSC

Jiang, Gui Hua; 蒋桂华 ; Jiǎng Guìhuá (1970-)
- Research interest: Apiaceae
- Affiliation: CDCM

Jiang, Jie Yun; 蒋洁云 ; Jiǎng Jiéyún (1973-)
- Research interest: Bryophyte
- Affiliation: BJ
- Location of specimens: BJ

Jiang, Li Ming; 蒋黎明 ; Jiǎng Límíng (1958-)
- Affiliation: GUN

Jiang, Mu Qing; 蒋木青 ; Jiǎng Mùqīng; 蔣木青 (1930-)
- Research interest: Pteridophytes
- Affiliation: ANUG
- Location of specimens: ANUG

X. L. Jiang

Jiang, Xing Lin; Tsiang, Hsing Lin; 蒋兴麐 ; Jiǎng Xìnglín; 蔣兴麟 (1927-)
- Employment: Department of Biology, Sichuan University（四川大学生物系）
- Research interest: Plants of Sichuan
- Affiliation: SCFI
- Location of specimens: HWA, PE, SCFI, SZ. *Flora sichuanica*

Jiang, You Xu; 蒋有绪 ; Jiǎng Yǒuxù; 蔣有緒 (1932-)
- Research interest: Forest Ecology
- Affiliation: CAF

Jiang, Zhao Lan; 蒋兆兰 ; Jiǎng Zhàolán; 蔣兆蘭 (1932-)
- Research interest: Scientific Illustrator
- Affiliation: LZD

T. Y. Chiang

Chiang, Tzen Yuh; Chiang, Tseng Yu; Jiang, Zhen Yu; 蔣鎮宇 ; Jiǎng Zhènyǔ ; 蒋镇宇 (1960-)
- Employment: Department of Life Sciences, "National" Cheng Kung University（"國立"成功大學生命科學系）
- Research interest: Bryophyte
- Affiliation: NCKU

Jiang, Zu De; 蒋祖德 ; Jiǎng Zǔdé; 蔣祖德 (1926-2001)
- Research interest: Scientific Illustrator
- Affiliation: HIB

Jiao, Hua Fu; 焦华富 ; Jiāo Huáfù (1962-)
- Affiliation: ANUG

Jiao, Xing Ping; 焦兴萍 ; Jiāo Xīngpíng (1989-)
- Research interest: Medicinal Plants
- Affiliation: QDC

Jie, Zheng Ping; 揭正平 ; Jiē Zhèngpíng
- Location of specimens: JXAU

Jin, Bo; 金波 ; Jīn Bō (1938-)
- Affiliation: GZTM

Jin, De Xun; 金德逊 ; Jīn Déxùn; 金德遜 (1927-)
- Research interest: Magnoliceae
- Affiliation: ANU

King, Duo Han; 金多翰 ; Jīn Duōhàn
- Location of specimens: IBSC

Jin, Feng; 金凤 ; Jīn Fèng (1979-)
- Research interest: Poaceae
- Affiliation: NMTC
- Location of specimens: NMTC

Jin, Ji Qiang; 金基强 ; Jīn Jīqiáng (1983-)
- Research interest: Theaceae
- Affiliation: TEA

Jin, Lian Cheng; 金联城; Jīn Liánchéng; 金聯城 (1938-)
- Research interest: Medicinal Plants
- Affiliation: ZJMA

Jin, Liang; 金樑 ; Jīn Liáng (1974-)

• Research interest: Plant Ecology
• Affiliation: SHM

Jin, Ling; 金玲 ; Jīn Líng
• Affiliation: NEFI

Jin, Mu Hua; 金睦华 ; Jīn Mùhuá; 金睦華 (1925-)
• Research interest: Plants of Henan
• Affiliation: HENU
• Location of specimens: HENU, KAI

Jin, Ren; 金仁 ; Jīn Rén (1940-)
• Research interest: Woody Plants
• Affiliation: GAFS
• Location of specimens: GAFS

Jin, Sha; 金沙 ; Jīn Shā
• Location of specimens: ZJFI

Jin, Shan; 金山 ; Jīn Shān (1972-)
• Research interest: Plant Systematics
• Affiliation: SES
• Location of specimens: SES

Jin, Wei Jian; Chin, Wei Chien; King, Wei Jean; 金维坚 ; Jīn Wéijiān; 金維堅 (1902-1986)
• Location of specimens: SDAU

Jin, Xin Jie; 金鑫杰 ; Jīn Xīnjié (1990-)
• Research interest: Smilacaceae; Bryophyte; Scientific Illustrator
• Affiliation: HSNU, HZU

Jin, Yan; 金艳 ; Jīn Yàn (1978-)
• Research interest: Medicinal Plants
• Affiliation: CMMI

Jin, Yi Xing; 金义兴 ; Jīn Yìxīng; 金義興 (1937-)
• Research interest: Plant Ecology
• Affiliation: HIB

Jinfoshan Exped.; 金佛山考察队 ; Jīnfóshān Kǎochádùi
• Location of specimens: PE. Collection Team

Jin, Wan Jun; 靳万军 ; Jìn Wànjūn
• Location of specimens: XTNM

Chin, Hsiao Pai; 靳晓白 ; Jìn Xiǎobái; 靳晓白 (1946-)
• Location of specimens: HAST

Jing, Wang Chun; 景望春 ; Jǐng Wàngchūn (1968-)
• Affiliation: SITC
• Location of specimens: SITC

Jiuwanshan Exped.; 九万山考察队 ; Jiǔwànshān Kǎochádùì
• Location of specimens: PE. Collection Team

Ju, Ai Xia; 鞠爱霞 ; Jū Àixiá
• Location of specimens: HLCM

K

Kang, Hong Mei; 康洪梅 ; Kāng Hóngméi (1987-)
• Research interest: Nyssaceae
• Affiliation: YCP

Kang, Shuang Long; 康双龙 ; Kāng Shuānglóng (1950-)
• Research interest: Medicinal Plants
• Affiliation: IMDC
• Location of specimens: IMDC

Kang, Ting Guo; 康廷国 ; Kāng Tíngguó (1955-)
• Research interest: Medicinal Plants
• Affiliation: LNCM
• Location of specimens: LNCM

Kang, Yong Xiang; 康永祥 ; Kāng Yǒngxiáng (1963-)
• Research interest: Woody Plants
• Affiliation: NWFC

Ke, Wen Shan; 柯文山 ; Kē Wénshān (1965-)
• Research interest: Araceae, Lamiaceae, Theaceae
• Affiliation: EU

Ko, Yung Nan; 柯勇男 ; Kē Yǒngnán
• Location of specimens: HAST

Krym; 克里木 ; Kèlǐmù (1938-)
• Location of specimens: XJBI

Kong, Dong Mei; 孔冬梅 ; Kǒng Dōngméi (1973-)
• Research interest: Plants of Shanxi
• Affiliation: SXU
• Location of specimens: SXU

Kong, Hong Zhi; 孔宏智 ; Kǒng Hóngzhì (1973-)
• Research interest: Chloranthaceae
• Affiliation: PE

Kung, Shi Pei; Kong, Shi Pei; 孔世培 ; Kǒng Shìpéi
• Location of specimens: PEY

J. Kou

Kou, Jin; 寇瑾 ; Kòu Jǐn (1985-)
• Employment: School of Life Sciences, Inner Mongolia University（内蒙古大学生命科学学院）
• Research interest: Bryophyte
• Affiliation: HIMC
• Location of specimens: HIMC

Kurban; 库尔班 ; Kù'ěrbān (1960-)
• Research interest: Primulaceae
• Affiliation: XJUG
• Location of specimens: XJUG

Kuang, Li Gang; 邝立刚 ; Kuàng Lìgāng
• Research interest: Pinaceae
• Affiliation: TYF

Kuang, Sheng Shun; 邝生舜 ; Kuàng Shēngshùn; 鄺生舜 (1933-)
• Research interest: Plants of Henan
• Affiliation: HENU
• Location of specimens: HENU

Kuang, Ren Ping; 旷仁平 ; Kuàng Rénpíng (1976-)
• Research interest: Balsaminaceae
• Affiliation: HNNU
• Location of specimens: HNNU

L

Lai, Shou Guo; 赖守国 ; Lài Shǒuguó; 賴守國 (1932-)
• Research interest: Bryophyte
• Affiliation: CTS
• Location of specimens: CTS

Lai, Shu Huei; 賴書輝 ; Lài Shūhuī; 赖书辉
• Location of specimens: HAST

Lai, Xue Wen; 赖学文 ; Lài Xuéwén; 賴學文 (1949-)
• Research interest: Polygonaceae
• Affiliation: JXCM
• Location of specimens: JXCM

Lai, Yen Ju; 賴嬿如 ; Lài Yànrú; 赖嬿如
• Location of specimens: HAST

Lai, Yi Hsiu; 賴易秀 ; Lài Yìxiù; 赖易秀
• Location of specimens: HAST

Lan, Deng Ming; 兰登明 ; Lán Dēngmíng (1961-)
• Research interest: Elaeagnaceae, Tamaricaceae
• Affiliation: NMAC, NMFC
• Location of specimens: NMAC, NMFC

Lan, Ling; 兰玲 ; Lán Líng
• Location of specimens: GXFS

Lan, Zhi Qiong; 兰志琼 ; Lán Zhìqióng (1979-)
• Research interest: Polygonaceae
• Affiliation: CDCM

Lan, Ding Cheng; 蓝鼎城 ; Lán Dǐngchéng
• Location of specimens: IBK

Lang, Kui Chang; 郎奎昌 ; Láng Kuíchāng (1927-1996)
• Research interest: Bryophyte
• Affiliation: NENU

Lei, Da Mei; Rei, Ta Mei; 雷达美 ; Léi Dáměi
• Location of specimens: GXF

Lei, Kuei Hsiang; 雷貴香 ; Léi Guìxiāng; 雷贵香 (1933-)
• Location of specimens: HAST

Lei, Jun; 雷俊 ; Léi Jùn
• Location of specimens: GXFS

Lei, Ling Su; 雷令蘇 ; Léi Lìngsū; 雷令苏
• Location of specimens: HAST

Lei, Xi Ting; 雷喜亭 ; Léi Xǐtíng
• Location of specimens: HIMC

Lei, Yun; 雷耘 ; Léi Yún
• Research interest: Plant Ecology
• Affiliation: CCNU

Leng, Qiao Zhen; 冷巧珍 ; Lěng Qiǎozhēn (1932-)
• Research interest: Fabaceae
• Affiliation: XJBI
• Location of specimens: XJBI

Li, Huan Ji; 黎焕琦 ; Lí Huànqí; 黎煥琦 (1926-)
• Location of specimens: FJSI, HITBC, IBK, IBSC, KUN

Li, Nian Lin; 黎念林 ; Lí Niànlín (1960-)
• Research interest: Rosaceae
• Affiliation: HHBG
• Location of specimens: HHBG

S. H. Li

Li, Shang Hao; Ley, Shang Hao; 黎尚豪 ; Lí Shàngháo (1917-1993)
• Employment: Institute of Hydrobiology, Chinese Academy of Sciences（中国科学院水生生物研究所）
• Research interest: Algae
• Affiliation: HBI
• Location of specimens: HBI, IBSC, NAS, PE

Li, Su Ping; 黎素萍 ; Lí Sùpíng
• Location of specimens: GXFS

Li, Tong Shou; 黎同寿 ; Lí Tóngshòu
• Research interest: Seagrass
• Affiliation: SCSG
• Location of specimens: SCSG

Li, Xi Rong; 黎系荣 ; Lí Xìróng; 黎系榮 (1935-)
• Research interest: Poaceae; Woody Plants
• Affiliation: SR
• Location of specimens: SR

Li, Xiang Dong; 黎向东 ; Lí Xiàngdōng; 黎向東 (1933-)
• Research interest: Forest Ecology
• Affiliation: GAC
• Location of specimens: GAC

Shin C. Lee

Lee, Shin Chiang; Li, Hsin Kiang; Li, Shin Chiang; Li, Xing Jiang; 黎兴江 ; Lí Xīngjiāng; 黎興江 (1932-2020)
• Employment: Kunming Institute of Botany, Chinese Academy of Sciences（中国科学院昆明植物研究所）
• Research interest: Bryophyte
• Affiliation: KUN
• Location of specimens: IFP, KUN

Li, Y. C.; 黎旭祥 ; Lí Xùxiáng
• Location of specimens: IBSC

Li, Ai De; 李爱德 ; Lǐ Àidé; 李愛德
• Location of specimens: MQ

Li, Ai Li; 李爱莉 ; Lǐ Àilì (1973-)
• Research interest: Scientific Illustrator
• Affiliation: PE

Li, An Min; 李安民 ; Lǐ Ānmín (1921-)
• Research interest: Plant Anatomy
• Affiliation: SAU
• Location of specimens: SAU

Li, Bao Xia; 李宝霞 ; Lǐ Bǎoxiá (1984-)
• Research interest: Medicinal Plants
• Affiliation: SSMM

Li, Bao Gui; 李保贵 ; Lǐ Bǎoguì (1958-)
• Research interest: Pteridophytes
• Affiliation: HITBC

Li, Bao Guo; 李保国 ; Lǐ Bǎoguó
• Affiliation: WNU

Li, Bao Li; 李葆莉 ; Lǐ Bǎolì (1963-)
• Affiliation: IMD

Li, Bing Song; 李秉宋 ; Lǐ Bǐngsòng (1925-)
• Research interest: Rosaceae
• Affiliation: MJS

Li, Bing Luan; 李炳銮 ; Lǐ Bǐngluán; 李炳鑾 (1924-1966)
• Research interest: Seed Plants
• Affiliation: BJTC
• Location of specimens: BJTC

Li, Bo; 李博 ; Lǐ Bó (1929-1998)
• Research interest: Plant Ecology
• Affiliation: HIMC
• Location of specimens: HIMC

Li, Bo; 李博 ; Lǐ Bó; (1963-)
• Research interest: Plant Ecology
• Affiliation: CCNU
• Location of specimens: CCNU

B. S. Li

Li, Bo Sheng; 李勃生 ; Lǐ Bóshēng; 李渤生 (1946-)
• Employment: Institute of Botany, Chinese Academy of Sciences（中国科学院植物研究所）
• Research interest: Collector
• Location of specimens: PE

Li, Cai Wang; 李才旺 ; Lǐ Cáiwàng (1951-)
• Research interest: Economic Plants
• Affiliation: HON

Lee, Tsai Chi; Lee, Ts'ai Ch'i; Le, Ts'ae Ch'i; Li, Chai Qi; 李彩祺 ; Lǐ Cǎiqí; 李彩琪
• Location of specimens: IBK, IBSC, PE, PEY, SHM, SZ, TIE

Li, Chang Long; 李昌龙 ; Lǐ Chānglóng (1974-)
• Research interest: Chenopodiaceae, Fabaceae
• Affiliation: MQ

• Location of specimens: MQ

Li, Chang Hai; 李长海 ; Lǐ Chánghǎi (1960-)
• Affiliation: HFBG

Li, Chang Bao; 李常宝 ; Lǐ Chángbǎo
• Location of specimens: ZYTC

Li, Chao Dou; 李朝斗 ; Lǐ Cháodǒu (1938-)
• Location of specimens: GZTM

Li, Chao Li; 李朝利 ; Lǐ Cháolì
• Location of specimens: IMC

Lei, C. I.; 李朝贤 ; Lǐ Cháoxián; 李朝賢
• Location of specimens: IBSC

Li, Chong Hao; 李崇皓 ; Lǐ Chónghào
• Location of specimens: IGA

Li, Cun Hua; 李存华 ; Lǐ Cúnhuá
• Affiliation: SDFS
• Location of specimens: SDFS

Li, Da Zhou; 李大周 ; Lǐ Dàzhōu (1951-)
• Research interest: Woody Plants
• Affiliation: HAF

Li, De Lu; 李得禄 ; Lǐ Délù
• Location of specimens: MQ

Li, De Xiao; 李德孝 ; Lǐ Déxiào (1950-)
• Research interest: Medicinal Plants
• Affiliation: HNCM
• Location of specimens: HNCM

D. K. Li

Li, Deng Ke; 李登科 ; Lǐ Dēngkē (1937-2012)
• Employment: Shanghai Natural History Museum (Branch of Shanghai Science & Technology Museum) (上海自然博物馆(上海科技馆分馆))
• Research interest: Bryophyte
• Affiliation: SHM
• Location of specimens: SHM

Li, Di Qiang; 李迪强 ; Lǐ Díqiáng (1966-)
• Research interest: Biodiversity
• Affiliation: CAF

Li, Dong Hai; 李东海 ; Lǐ Dōnghǎi (1971-)
• Research interest: Plants of Hainan
• Affiliation: HUTB
• Location of specimens: HUTB

Lee, Tung Sheng; Li, Tung Sheng; Li, Tung Shêng; 李东生 ; Lǐ Dōngshēng; 李東生 (1920-)
• Location of specimens: CAF, IBSC

Li, En Xiang; 李恩香 ; Lǐ Ēnxiāng (1969-)
• Research interest: Smilacacea, Stemonaceae
• Affiliation: JXU

Li, Fang Rao; 李仿尧 ; Lǐ Fǎngyáo; 李仿堯 (1934-)
• Research interest: Lamiaceae
• Affiliation: CDCM
• Location of specimens: CDCM

Li, Feng; 李峰 ; Lǐ Fēng (1963-)
• Research interest: Medicinal Plants
• Affiliation: LNCM

Li, Feng Hua; 李凤华 ; Lǐ Fènghuá
• Location of specimens: ZY

Li, Feng Lan; 李凤兰 ; Lǐ Fènglán (1973-)
• Research interest: Lamiaceae
• Affiliation: NEAU

Li, Feng Qin; 李凤琴 ; Lǐ Fèngqín
• Affiliation: LZD

Li, Qian Zhen; 李乾振 ; Lǐ Qiánzhèn (1946-)
• Research interest: Economic Plants
• Affiliation: XZ

Li, Guang Xin; 李光信 ; Lǐ Guāngxìn
• Location of specimens: IBK

Li, Gui He; 李贵和 ; Lǐ Guìhé; 李貴和 (1934-)
• Affiliation: LNAF

Li, Gui Lan; 李桂兰 ; Lǐ Guìlán (1963-)
• Research interest: Plants of Hebei
• Affiliation: CHA
• Location of specimens: CHA

Li, Gui Qin; 李桂琴 ; Lǐ Guìqín (1954-)
• Research interest: Asteraceae
• Affiliation: NEAU
• Location of specimens: NEAU

Li, Guo Chen; 李国臣 ; Lǐ Guóchén (1962-)
• Research interest: Woody Plants
• Affiliation: YAK

Li, Guo Feng; 李国凤 ; Lǐ Guófèng; 李國鳳 (1936-)
• Location of specimens: PE, SCFI, SZ

Li, Guo Qiu; 李国酋 ; Lǐ Guóqiú
• Location of specimens: CAF

Li, Hai Ning; 李海宁 ; Lǐ Hǎiníng
• Research interest: Fabaceae, Ranunculaceae, Rosaceae
• Affiliation: YNTCM

Li, Hai Tao; 李海涛 ; Lǐ Hǎitāo (1974-)
• Research interest: Medicinal Plants
• Affiliation: IMDY
• Location of specimens: IMDY

Li, He Li; 李和利 ; Lǐ Hélì (1955-)
• Location of specimens: JXM

Li, He; 李鹤 ; Lǐ Hè (1989-)
• Affiliation: GF
• Location of specimens: GF

Li, Hong; 李红 ; Lǐ Hóng (1963-)
• Research interest: Herbaceous Plants
• Affiliation: NMAC
• Location of specimens: NMAC

Li, Hong; 李红 ; Lǐ Hóng (1977-)
• Affiliation: SABG
• Location of specimens: SABG

Li, Hong Fang; 李红方 ; Lǐ Hóngfāng
• Location of specimens: SMMU-BH

Li, Hong Bin; 李宏斌 ; Lǐ Hóngbīn (1969-)
• Research interest: Medicinal Plants
• Affiliation: EMA
• Location of specimens: EMA

Li, Hong Jun; 李洪钧 ; Lǐ Hóngjūn; 李洪鈞 (1931-)
• Location of specimens: HIB, PE

Li, Hui; 李晖 ; Lǐ Huī (1966-)
• Research interest: Plant Ecology
• Affiliation: XZ
• Location of specimens: XZ

Li, Hui Ru; 李惠茹 ; Lǐ Huìrú (1985-)
• Research interest: Invasive Plants
• Affiliation: CSH
• Location of specimens: CSH

Li, Hui Yu; 李惠玉 ; Lǐ Huìyù (1937-)
• Research interest: Caprifoliaceae, Ulmaceae
• Affiliation: GZAC

Li, Tsi Tung; Li, Ji Dong; 李继侗 ; Lǐ Jìdòng; 李繼侗 (1897-1961)
• Research interest: Plant Physiology
• Affiliation: HIMC
• Location of specimens: PE, PEY

Li, Jian Dong; 李建东 ; Lǐ Jiàndōng; 李建東 (1936-)
• Research interest: Grassland Plants
• Affiliation: NENU
• Location of specimens: NENU

Li, Chian Fan; Li, Jian Fan; 李建藩 ; Lǐ Jiànfān
• Location of specimens: NY, PE

Li, Jian Tang; 李建堂 ; Lǐ Jiàntáng (1933-)
• Affiliation: GAUA
• Location of specimens: GAUA

Li, Jian Wei; 李建伟 ; Lǐ Jiànwěi (1956-)
• Research interest: Pteridophytes
• Affiliation: PYU

Li, Jian Wen; 李建文 ; Lǐ Jiànwén
• Research interest: Economic Plants
• Affiliation: CAF
• Location of specimens: CAF

Jian Z. Li

Li, Jian Zong; 李建宗 ; Lǐ Jiànzōng (1949-)
• Employment: College of Life Sciences, Hunan Normal University（湖南师范大学生命科学学院）
• **Research interest: Algae; Fungi**
• **Affiliation: HNNU**
• Location of specimens: HNNU

Li, Jiang; 李江 ; Lǐ Jiāng (1966-)
• Research interest: Bryophyte
• Affiliation: FTS
• Location of specimens: FTS

Li, Jiang Ling; 李江陵 ; Lǐ Jiānglíng (1966-)
• Research interest: Solanaceae
• Affiliation: SM

Li, Jiao Lan; 李娇兰 ; Lǐ Jiāolán; 李嬌蘭 (1932-)
• Research interest: Plant Bibliography
• Affiliation: PE

Lee, Chin Mei; 李金梅 ; Lǐ Jīnméi
• Research interest: Woody Plants
• Affiliation: TAIF

Li, Jing; 李晶 ; Lǐ Jīng (1970-)
• Research interest: Brassicaceae

• Affiliation: NEAU

Li, Jing Xiang; 李景侠 ; Lǐ Jǐngxiá (1960-)
• Research interest: Oleaceae
• Affiliation: NWFC

Li, Jing Xin; 李景信 ; Lǐ Jǐngxìn (1935-)
• Research interest: Poaceae, Valerianaceae
• Affiliation: HANU
• Location of specimens: HANU

Li, Jing Yuan; 李景原 ; Lǐ Jǐngyuán (1963-)
• Affiliation: HENU
• Location of specimens: HENU

Li, Jing Li; 李静丽 ; Lǐ Jìnglì; 李靜麗 (1937-)
• Research interest: Fungi
• Affiliation: WNU
• Location of specimens: WNU

Li, Juan; 李娟 ; Lǐ Juān (1984-)
• Research interest: Biodiversity
• Affiliation: GXFI

Lee, C. C.; 李钧祥 ; Lǐ Jūnxiáng; 李鈞祥
• Location of specimens: IBSC

Li, Ke Gang; 李克纲 ; Lǐ Kègāng (1958-)
• Research interest: Amaranthaceae
• Affiliation: JIU
• Location of specimens: JIU

Lee, Ke Yu; 李克愉 ; Lǐ Kèyú
• Location of specimens: HAST

Li, Li Jia; 李丽嘉 ; Lǐ Lìjiā; 李麗嘉 (1946-)
• Research interest: Fungi
• Affiliation: BJM
• Location of specimens: BJM

Li, Lian Fang; 李连方 ; Lǐ Liánfāng (1963-)
• Research interest: Violaceae
• Affiliation: BAU

Li, Liang Guan; 李良官 ; Lǐ Liángguān (1924-)
• Research interest: Medicinal Plants
• Affiliation: FMP
• Location of specimens: FMP

L. Ching Li

Li, Liang Ching; 李良庆 ; Lǐ Liángqìng (1900-1952)
• Employment: Fan Memorial Institute of Biology; Institute of Systematic Botany, Academia Sinica; Institute of Botany, Chinese Academy of Sciences（静生生物调查所 ; 中国科 ; 学院植物分类研究所 ; 中国科 ; 学院植物研究所）
• Research interest: Algae
• Affiliation: PE
• Location of specimens: PE

Lin Li

Li, Lin; 李琳 ; Lǐ Lín (1978-)
• Employment: College of Life Sciences, Hebei Normal University（河北师范大学生命科学学院）
• Research interest: Bryophyte
• Affiliation: HBNU
• Location of specimens: HBNU

Li, Mao; 李茂 ; Lǐ Mào (1971-)
• Research interest: Garden Plants
• Affiliation: GF

Li, Meng Yang; 李孟扬 ; Lǐ Mèngyáng; 李孟揚 (1931-)
• Research interest: Plants of Shandong
• Affiliation: QFNU

Min Li

Li, Min; 李敏 ; Lǐ Mǐn (1973-)
• Employment: College of life Sciences, Hebei Normal University（河北师范大学生命科学学院）
• Research interest: Bryophyte
• Affiliation: HBNU
• Location of specimens: HBNU

Li, Min; 李敏 ; Lǐ Mǐn (1977-)
• Research interest: Plant Database
• Affiliation: PE

Li, Ming Hong; 李明红 ; Lǐ Mínghóng
• Location of specimens: NYA

Li, Ming Kang; 李鸣冈 ; Lǐ Mínggāng; 李鳴崗 (1899-1983)
• Location of specimens: KUN, NF

Li, Ming Hong; 李铭红 ; Lǐ Mínghóng (1963-)
• Research interest: Biodiversity
• Affiliation: ZNU
• Location of specimens: ZNU

Li, Na; 李娜 ; Lǐ Nà (1980-)
• Research interest: Papaveraceae, Rosaceae
• Affiliation: SYPC
• Location of specimens: SYPC

Li, Nian Yi; 李念易 ; Lǐ Niànyì
• Location of specimens: PE

Lee, Pei hsuan; 李沛軒 ; Lǐ Pèixuān; 李沛轩
• Location of specimens: HAST

Li, Peng Fu; 李朋富 ; Lǐ Péngfù (1969-)
• Research interest: Algae
• Affiliation: N

Li, Peng; 李鹏 ; Lǐ Péng (1965-)
• Research interest: Plants of Gansu
• Affiliation: ZYTC
• Location of specimens: ZYTC

Li, Pu Yan; 李普衍 ; Lǐ Pǔyǎn
• Research interest: Medicinal Plants
• Affiliation: QDC

Li, Qi Yun; 李其允 ; Lǐ Qíyǔn (1927-2002)
• Research interest: Brassicaceae, Bretschneideraceae, Solanaceae
• Affiliation: HWA
• Location of specimens: HWA

Li, Qi; 李琪 ; Lǐ Qí (1928-)
• Research interest: Grass
• Affiliation: LZAH
• Location of specimens: LZAH

Li, Qi He; 李启和 ; Lǐ Qǐhé
• Location of specimens: PE

Li, Qi Min; 李启敏 ; Lǐ Qǐmǐn; 李啟敏 (1927-2013)
• Research interest: Algae
• Affiliation: SANU
• Location of specimens: SANU

Li, Qiang; 李强 ; Lǐ Qiáng (1962-)
• Research interest: Forest Ecology
• Affiliation: YLD
• Location of specimens: YLD

Li, Qiao Ming; 李巧明 ; Lǐ Qiǎomíng
• Research interest: Dipterocarpaceae
• Affiliation: HITBC

Li, Qin Qin; 李琴琴 ; Lǐ Qínqín (1983-)
• Research interest: Liliaceae
• Affiliation: NMTC
• Location of specimens: NMTC

Li, Qing; 李青 ; Lǐ Qīng (1967-)
• Research interest: Medicinal Plants
• Affiliation: SDCM

Li, Qing Yun; 李青云 ; Lǐ Qīngyún; 李青雲 (1932-)
• Research interest: Fabaceae, Tamaricaceae
• Affiliation: MQ
• Location of specimens: MQ

Li, Qing Hua; 李庆华 ; Lǐ Qìnghuá
• Location of specimens: CQNM

Li, C. Y.; 李慶堯 ; Lǐ Qìngyáo; 李庆尧
• Location of specimens: HAST

Li, C. C.; 李慶鐘 ; Lǐ Qìngzhōng; 李庆钟
• Location of specimens: HAST

Lee, Chung Ni; 李瓊妮 ; Lǐ Qióngnī; 李琼妮
• Location of specimens: HAST

Li, Chiu Fang; 李秋芳 ; Lǐ Qiūfāng
• Location of specimens: HAST

Li, Ren Hui; 李仁辉 ; Lǐ Rénhuī (1965-)
• Research interest: Algae
• Affiliation: HBI
• Location of specimens: HBI

Li, Ren Wei; 李仁伟 ; Lǐ Rénwěi (1959-)
• Research interest: Bryophyte
• Affiliation: CTS

Li, Ren Yu; 李仁郁 ; Lǐ Rényù (1931-)
• Location of specimens: HLCM

Lee, Y. K.; 李日光 ; Lǐ Rìguāng
• Location of specimens: IBSC

Li, Ri Ming; 李日明 ; Lǐ Rìmíng
• Location of specimens: YF

Li, Rong Tong; 李荣同 ; Lǐ Róngtóng (1965-)
• Research interest: Pteridophytes
• Affiliation: FTS
• Location of specimens: FTS

Li, Rong Ying; 李荣英 ; Lǐ Róngyīng
• Location of specimens: IMDY

Li, Ru Guang; 李茹光 ; Lǐ Rúguāng (1910-2003)
• Research interest: Fungi
• Affiliation: NENU
• Location of specimens: NENU

Li, Rui Jun; 李瑞军 ; Lǐ Ruìjūn
• Research interest: Campanulaceae, Fabaceae
• Affiliation: HANU
• Location of specimens: HANU

Li, Run Zhi; 李润植 ; Lǐ Rùnzhí (1959-)
• Research interest: Oleaceae
• Affiliation: SXAU

Li, San Qing; 李三青 ; Lǐ Sānqīng (1985-)
• Research interest: Plants of N. China
• Affiliation: TIE

Li, Sheng Bao; 李生宝 ; Lǐ Shēngbǎo
• Affiliation: NXF

Li, Shi Yang; 李士諹 ; Lǐ Shìyáng (1933-)
• Research interest: Woody Plants
• Affiliation: GAC
• Location of specimens: GAC

Li, Shi Ying; 李世英 ; Lǐ Shìyīng (1921-1985)
• Location of specimens: PE

Li, Shou Qiao; 李寿乔 ; Lǐ Shòuqiáo; 李壽喬 (1930-)
• Research interest: Weeds
• Affiliation: BAU
• Location of specimens: BAU

Li, Shu Yu; 李淑玉 ; Lǐ Shūyù
• Location of specimens: IBSC

Li, Shu Ying; 李树英 ; Lǐ Shùyīng; 李樹英 (1928-)
• Research interest: Violaceae
• Affiliation: HANU

Li, Shuang Zhi; 李双智 ; Lǐ Shuāngzhì (1980-)
• Research interest: Plants of Yunnan
• Affiliation: SWFC
• Location of specimens: SWFC

Li, Su Ying; 李素英 ; Lǐ Sùyīng
• Location of specimens: IBSC

Li, Ti Jun; 李体俊 ; Lǐ Tǐjùn; 李體俊 (1937-)
• Research interest: Actinidiaceae, Berberidaceae
• Affiliation: SR
• Location of specimens: SR

Li, Tian Yu; 李天煜 ; Lǐ Tiānyù (1964-)
• Research interest: Plants of Henan
• Affiliation: XYTC
• Location of specimens: XYTC

Li, Tong Jian; 李同建 ; Lǐ Tóngjiàn (1982-)
• Research interest: Lardizablaceae, Ranunculaceae, Urticaceae
• Affiliation: JJT
• Location of specimens: JJT

Li, Wei Min; 李为民 ; Lǐ Wèimín (1982-)
• Location of specimens: XBGH

Li, Wen Bin; 李文斌 ; Lǐ Wénbīn
• Location of specimens: PE

Li, Wen Qing; 李文清 ; Lǐ Wénqīng (1962-)
• Research interest: Woody Plants
• Affiliation: SDFGR

Li, Wen Ting; 李文亭 ; Lǐ Wéntíng (1942-)
• Location of specimens: CCM

Li, Xi Chou; 李锡畴 ; Lǐ Xīchóu; 李錫疇 (1940-)
• Research interest: Scientific Illustrator
• Affiliation: KUN

Li, Xi Quan; 李锡泉 ; Lǐ Xīquán (1960-)
• Research interest: Liliaceae
• Affiliation: HUIF

Lee, Hay Yue, Lawrence; 李熙瑜 ; Lǐ Xīyú
• Affiliation: HK

Li, Xian Geng; 李宪庚 ; Lǐ Xiàngēng; 李憲庚 (1938-)
• Research interest: Plants of Hebei
• Affiliation: CHA
• Location of specimens: CHA

Li, Xiang Hong; 李向红 ; Lǐ Xiànghóng
• Location of specimens: ACM

Li, Xiao Jun; 李小军 ; Lǐ Xiǎojūn
• Location of specimens: LZD

Li, Xiao Ping; 李小平 ; Lǐ Xiǎopíng
• Affiliation: WNU

Li, Xiao Chen; 李晓晨 ; Lǐ Xiǎochén (1991-)
• Research interest: Plants of Zhejiang
• Affiliation: CSH
• Location of specimens: CSH, ZJFC

Li, Xiao Jin; 李晓瑾 ; Lǐ Xiǎojǐn (1962-)
• Research interest: Medicinal Plants
• Affiliation: XTNM
• Location of specimens: XTNM

Li, Xin; 李欣 ; Lǐ Xīn (1994-)
• Affiliation: HHNNR

Li, Xin Guo; 李新国 ; Lǐ Xīnguó (1956-)
• Research interest: Plants of Zhejiang
• Affiliation: SHCT

Li, Xin Ping; 李新平 ; Lǐ Xīnpíng (1958-)
- Research interest: Betulaceae, Fagaceae
- Affiliation: TYF

Li, Xin; 李馨 ; Lǐ Xīn
- Location of specimens: PE, SCFI, SZ

Li, Shing San; 李省三 ; Lǐ Xǐngsān
- Location of specimens: HAST

Xiu Q. Li

Li, Xiu Qin; 李秀芹 ; Lǐ Xiùqín (1971-)
- Employment: College of Life Sciences, Hebei Normal University（河北师范大学生命科学学院）
- Research interest: Bryophyte
- Affiliation: HBNU
- Location of specimens: HBNU

Li, Xue Dong; 李学东 ; Lǐ Xuédōng (1961-)
- Research interest: Bryophyte
- Affiliation: BJTC
- Location of specimens: BJTC

Lee, Hsue Ken; Li, H. K.; 李学根 ; Lǐ Xuégēn; 李學根 (1929-)
- Location of specimens: IBSC

Li, Xue Lan; 李学兰 ; Lǐ Xuélán
- Affiliation: IMDY
- Location of specimens: IMDY

Li, Xue Xia; 李雪霞 ; Lǐ Xuěxiá (1981-)
- Research interest: Orchidaceae, Ulmaceae
- Affiliation: NF

Li, Yan Sheng; 李延生 ; Lǐ Yánshēng (1924-)
- Research interest: Woody Plants
- Affiliation: LNAF
- Location of specimens: LNAF

Li, Yan Nan; 李研南 ; Lǐ Yánnán
- Location of specimens: BJFC

Y. C. Li

Li, Yan Chun; 李艳春 ; Lǐ Yànchūn (1980-)
- Employment: Kunming Institute of Botany, Chinese Academy of Sciences（中国科学院昆明植物研究所）
- Research interest: Fungi
- Affiliation: KUN

Li, Yan Hui; 李艳晖 ; Lǐ Yànhuī (1977-)
- Research interest: Algae
- Affiliation: TYNUB

Li, Yang; 李扬 ; Lǐ Yáng (1978-)
- Research interest: Algae
- Affiliation: SN

Li, Yang Han; 李扬汉 ; Lǐ Yánghàn; 李揚漢 (1913-2004)
- Research interest: Weeds
- Affiliation: NAU
- Location of specimens: NAU

Y. Y. Lee

Lee, Yao Yin; Li, Rao Ying; Li, Yao Ying; 李尧英 ; Lǐ Yáoyīng; 李堯英 ; (1930-)
- Employment: Institute of Hydrobiology, Chinese Academy of Sciences（中国科学院水生生物研究所）
- Research interest: Algae
- Affiliation: HBI
- Location of specimens: HBI

Li, Yao; 李耀 ; Lǐ Yào
- Location of specimens: IBK

Li, Yi; 李仪 ; Lǐ Yí; 李儀 (1930-)
- Research interest: Medicinal Plants
- Affiliation: YAF

Li, I Chen; 李宜臻 ; Lǐ Yízhēn
- Location of specimens: HAST

Li, Yi Bing; 李以镔 ; Lǐ Yǐbīn; 李以鑌 (1941-)
- Research interest: Onagraceae; Plants of Jiangxi
- Affiliation: JCE, JXU
- Location of specimens: JCE

Li, Yi Jiu; 李义久 ; Lǐ Yìjiǔ
- Location of specimens: LNAF

Li, Yi; 李奕 ; Lǐ Yì (1969-)
- Research interest: Plant Database
- Affiliation: PE

Li, Ying Jun; 李应军 ; Lǐ Yìngjūn (1975-)
- Research interest: Medicinal Plants
- Affiliation: EMA
- Location of specimens: EMA

Li, Yong Biao; 李永彪 ; Lǐ Yǒngbiāo
- Location of specimens: NKU

Li, Yong He; 李永和 ; Lǐ Yǒnghé (1955-)
- Research interest: Medicinal Plants
- Affiliation: XM
- Location of specimens: XM

Li, Yong Jiang; 李永江 ; Lǐ Yǒngjiāng

• Location of specimens: CDBI

Li, Yong; 李勇 ; Lǐ Yǒng (1967-)
• Location of specimens: SZG

Li, Yong; 李勇 ; Lǐ Yǒng (1977-)
• Research interest: Plant Systematics
• Affiliation: TIE

Li, You Zhu; 李有竹 ; Lǐ Yǒuzhú (1929-)
• Location of specimens: RE

Li, Yu Mei; 李榆梅 ; Lǐ Yúméi
• Location of specimens: SXU

Li, Yu Jia; 李庾嘉 ; Lǐ Yǔjiā (1937-)
• Affiliation: HUTM
• Location of specimens: HUTM

Li, Yu Nong; 李育农 ; Lǐ Yùnóng; 李育農 (1921-)
• Research interest: Rosaceae
• Affiliation: SWAU
• Location of specimens: SWAU

Li, Yu Jiu; 李裕久 ; Lǐ Yùjiǔ (1939-1993)
• Research interest: Woody Plants
• Affiliation: BJFC

Li, Yun Ping; 李云萍 ; Lǐ Yúnpíng (1958-)
• Research interest: Woody Plants
• Affiliation: TYF

Li, Yun Ting; 李运婷 ; Lǐ Yùntíng
• Location of specimens: SWCTU

Lee, C. T.; 李泽堂 ; Lǐ Zétáng; 李澤堂
• Location of specimens: IBSC

Li, Zeng Li; 李增礼 ; Lǐ Zēnglǐ; 李增禮
• Research interest: Scientific Illustrator
• Affiliation: IMM

Li, Zhao Lan; 李兆兰 ; Lǐ Zhàolán; 李兆蘭 (1935-)
• Research interest: Fungi
• Affiliation: N
• Location of specimens: N

Li, Zhen; 李砧 ; Lǐ Zhēn (1963-)
• Research interest: Algae
• Affiliation: TYNUB
• Location of specimens: TYNUB

Li, Zhen Qin; 李振琴 ; Lǐ Zhènqín
• Location of specimens: FJFC

Li, Zhen Kui; 李镇魁 ; Lǐ Zhènkuí (1968-)
• Research interest: Medicinal Plants
• Affiliation: CANT

Z. H. Li

Li, Zhi Hua; 李植华 ; Lǐ Zhíhuá; 李植華 (1935-)
• Employment: Department of Biology, Sun Yat-sen University（中山大学生物系）
• Research interest: Bryophyte
• Affiliation: SYS

Li, Zhi Hao; 李志浩 ; Lǐ Zhìhào (1975-)
• Research interest: Medicinal Plants
• Affiliation: EMA
• Location of specimens: EMA

Li, Zhi Ji; 李治基 ; Lǐ Zhìjī (1917-1995)
• Research interest: Woody Plants
• Affiliation: GAC
• Location of specimens: GAC

Li, Zhi Hui; 李智辉 ; Lǐ Zhìhuī (1975-)
• Research interest: Woody Plants
• Affiliation: SYAUF

Li, Zhi Xuan; 李智选 ; Lǐ Zhìxuǎn (1959-)
• Research interest: Plants of Shaanxi
• Affiliation: WNU
• Location of specimens: WNU

Li, Chung Ti; 李中提 ; Lǐ Zhōngtí
• Location of specimens: IBK

Li, Zhong Tao; 李忠涛 ; Lǐ Zhōngtāo
• Location of specimens: YAK

Li, Zhong Xiao; 李忠孝 ; Lǐ Zhōngxiào (1961-)
• Research interest: Plant Ecology
• Affiliation: YAK
• Location of specimens: YAK

Li, Zhuo Yu; 李卓玉 ; Lǐ Zhuōyù (1964-)
• Research interest: Plants of Shanxi
• Affiliation: SXU

Li, Zi Wei; 李紫微 ; Lǐ Zǐwēi (1980-)
• Research interest: Medicinal Plants
• Affiliation: SM

Z. X. Li

Li, Zong Xiu; 李宗秀 ; Lǐ Zōngxiù (1937-)
• Employment: Chengdu Institute of Biology, Chinese Academy of Sciences（中国科学院成都生物研究所）
• Research interest: Ulmaceae

• Affiliation: CDBI
• Location of specimens: CDBI
Flora sichuanica

Li, Zong Ying; Li, Tsung Ying; 李宗英 ; Lǐ Zōngyīng (1935-)
• Research interest: Fungi
• Affiliation: SXU
• Location of specimens: SXU

Lee, Zu Wen; 李祖文 ; Lǐ Zǔwén
• Location of specimens: HAST

Li, Er; 里二 ; Lǐ Èr
• Location of specimens: IMDY

Libo Exped.; 荔波队 ; Lìbō Duì
• Location of specimens: PE. Collection Team

Liang, Jun Wen; 连俊文 ; Lián Jùnwén
• Location of specimens: YAK

Lian, Yan; 连艳 ; Lián Yàn (1990-)
• Research interest: Ranunculaceae
• Affiliation: CDCM

Liang, K. W.; 梁光伟 ; Liáng Guāngwěi
• Location of specimens: IBSC

Liang, Guo Lu; 梁国鲁 ; Liáng Guólǔ (1963-)
• Research interest: Rosaceae
• Affiliation: SWAU

Liang, Kuo Hsien; 梁国贤 ; Liáng Guóxián; 梁國賢 (1941-)
• Location of specimens: IBSC, KUN

Liang, Han Xing; 梁汉兴 ; Liáng Hànxīng; 梁漢興 (1938-)
• Location of specimens: KUN

Liang, He Yin; 梁和印 ; Liáng Héyìn (1937-)
• Location of specimens: TYF

Liang, Heng; 梁恒 ; Liáng Héng
• Location of specimens: IBK, IBSC

Liang, Hong Zhu; 梁红柱 ; Liáng Hóngzhù (1975-)
• Research interest: Biodiversity
• Affiliation: HBNU
• Location of specimens: HBNU

Liang, Jian Ping; 梁建平 ; Liáng Jiànpíng (1958-)
• Affiliation: NNA

Liang, Rui Long; 梁瑞龙 ; Liáng Ruìlóng (1962-)
• Research interest: Biodiversity
• Affiliation: GXFI

Liang, Y. T.; 梁润德 ; Liáng Rùndé; 梁潤德
• Location of specimens: IBK, IBSC

Liang, She Jian; 梁社坚 ; Liáng Shèjiān (1978-)
• Research interest: Medicinal Plants
• Affiliation: SCAUB

Liang, Shi Yan; 梁诗炎 ; Liáng Shīyán; 梁詩炎 (1923-)
• Research interest: Algae
• Affiliation: GUN
• Location of specimens: GUN

Liang, Shi Chu; 梁士楚 ; Liáng Shìchǔ (1965-)
• Research interest: Plant Ecology
• Affiliation: GUN
• Location of specimens: GUN

Liang, W. C.; 梁维祥 ; Liáng Wéixiáng; 梁維祥
• Location of specimens: IBSC

Liang, Hoeng Yip; Liang, Xiang Ri; Liang, Kuei; Liang, K'uei; Liang, Kui; 梁向日 ; Liáng Xiàngrì; 梁葵 (1907-1986)
• Research interest: Plants of S. China
• Affiliation: CANT
• Location of specimens: CANT, IBK, IBSC, PE

Leong, Hsiang Yueh; 梁向月 ; Liáng Xiàngyuè
• Location of specimens: HAST

Liang, Xue Zhong; 梁学忠 ; Liáng Xuézhōng; 梁學忠 (1940-)
• Research interest: Woody Plants
• Affiliation: HBFC

Liang, Yin Fan; 梁寅芳 ; Liáng Yínfāng (1938-)
• Affiliation: QG
• Location of specimens: QG

Liao, Pen Yu; 廖本裕 ; Liào Běnyù
• Location of specimens: HAST

Liao, Chuan Wan; 廖传万 ; Liào Chuánwàn
• Location of specimens: GNA

Liao, Tung Yu; 廖東裕 ; Liào Dōngyù; 廖东裕
• Location of specimens: HAST

Liao, Gwo Ing; Liao, Guo Ying; 廖國瑛 ; Liào Guóyīng; 廖国瑛
• Research interest: Convolvulaceae

• Affiliation: NCKU
• Location of specimens: NCKU

Liao, Heng Song; 廖衡松 ; Liào Héngsōng
• Location of specimens: CSFI

Liao, Kuo; 廖廓 ; Liào Kuò (1977-)
• Research interest: Aquatic Plants
• Affiliation: HIB

Liao, Min An; 廖民安 ; Liào Mín'ān (1931-)
• Location of specimens: IBK

Liao, Chi Cheng; 廖啟政 ; Liào Qǐzhèng; 廖启政
• Location of specimens: HAST

Liao, Chiu Cheng; 廖秋成 ; Liào Qiūchéng
• Research interest: Plants of Taiwan
• Affiliation: CHIA

Liao, Jen chang; 廖仁滄 ; Liào Réncāng; 廖仁沧
• Location of specimens: HAST

Liao, Wei Zhang; 廖伟章 ; Liào Wěizhāng; 廖偉章 (1938-)
• Research interest: Plants of Shangrao
• Affiliation: SRF
• Location of specimens: NF

Liao, Xiao Shan; 廖小珊 ; Liào Xiǎoshān
• Affiliation: SCSG
• Location of specimens: SCSG

Liao, Ying Han; 廖英汉 ; Liào Yīnghàn
• Affiliation: GXFS
• Location of specimens: GXFS

Liao, Yu; 廖瑜 ; Liào Yú (1965-)
• Affiliation: ABDC

Liao, Yuan Neng; 廖远能 ; Liào Yuǎnnéng; 廖遠能 (1930-)
• Research interest: Poaceae
• Affiliation: GACP
• Location of specimens: GACP

P.J. Lin

Lin, Pang Juan; Lin, Pang Jun; Lin, Bang Juan; 林邦娟 ; Lín Bāngjuān (1936-)
• Employment: South China Institute of Botany, Chinese Academy of Sciences（中国科学院华南植物研究所）
• Research interest: Bryophyte
• Affiliation: IBSC

Lin, Choun Sea; 林崇熙 ; Lín Chóngxī
• Location of specimens: HAST

Lin, Chun Song; 林春松 ; Lín Chūnsōng
• Location of specimens: CSFI

Lin, Feng; 林峰 ; Lín Fēng
• Location of specimens: IBSC

Ling, Kang; Lin, Gang; 林刚 ; Lín Gāng; 林剛 (1891-1979)
• Location of specimens: CAF, IBSC, N, NAS, NF, PE

Lin, Gui Bing; 林贵兵 ; Lín Guìbīng (1981-)
• Research interest: Verbenaceae
• Affiliation: JXCM

Lin, Guo Yu; 林国宇 ; Lín Guóyǔ (1961-)
• Location of specimens: FNU

Lin, Hann Song; 林漢松 ; Lín Hànsōng; 林汉松
• Location of specimens: HAST

Lin, Hong; 林红 ; Lín Hóng
• Affiliation: GXFS
• Location of specimens: GXFS

Lin, Hong Mei; 林红梅 ; Lín Hóngméi (1980-)
• Research interest: Medicinal Plants
• Affiliation: JLAU

Lin, H. M.; 林慧美 ; Lín Huìměi
• Location of specimens: HAST

Lin, Chia Hua; 林佳樺 ; Lín Jiāhuà; 林佳桦
• Location of specimens: HAST

Lin, Chia yu; 林家瑜 ; Lín Jiāyú
• Location of specimens: HAST

Lin, Jian Liang; 林建梁 ; Lín Jiànliáng
• Location of specimens: FJSI

Lin, Jian Yong; 林建勇 ; Lín Jiànyǒng (1985-)
• Research interest: Biodiversity
• Affiliation: GXFI

Lin, Chin Lung; 林金龍 ; Lín Jīnlóng; 林金龙
• Location of specimens: HAST

Lin, Ling Yuan; 林玲遠 ; Lín Língyuǎn; 林玲远
• Location of specimens: HAST

Lin, Mao Xiang; 林茂祥 ; Lín Màoxiáng (1977-)

• Research interest: Medicinal Plants
• Affiliation: IMC
• Location of specimens: IMC

Lin, Min; 林敏 ; Lín Mǐn (1991-)
• Affiliation: NOCC

Lin, Pei Jung; 林佩蓉 ; Lín Pèiróng
• Location of specimens: HAST

Lin, Peng; 林鹏 ; Lín Péng; 林鵬 (1931-2007)
• Location of specimens: AU

Qi W. Lin

Lin, Qi Wei; 林齐维 ; Lín Qíwéi; 林齊維 (1943-)
• Employment: Guizhou Provincial Museum（贵州省博物馆）
• Research interest: Bryophyte

Lin, Chi Hsien; 林绮仙 ; Lín Qǐxiān; 林綺仙
• Location of specimens: HAST

Lin, Ching Ping; 林青平 ; Lín Qīngpíng
• Location of specimens: HAST

Lam, S.; 林全 ; Lín Quán
• Location of specimens: IBSC

Lin, Ru Chang; Lim, Ju Chang; 林汝昌 ; Lín Rǔchāng
• Location of specimens: AU

S. H. Lin

Lin, Shan Hsiung; Lin, Shan Xiong; 林善雄 ; Lín Shànxióng (1942-)
• Employment: Department of Life Science, Tunghai University（東海大學生命科學系）
• Research interest: Bryophyte
• Affiliation: TUNG
• Location of specimens: TUNG

Lin, Shih Yung; Lin, Shi Rong; 林仕榕 ; Lín Shìróng (1936-)
• Research interest: Medicinal Plants
• Affiliation: FMP
• Location of specimens: CSFI

Lin, Shou Quan; 林寿全; Lín Shòuquán; 林壽全 (1930-2013)
• Research interest: Aristolochiaceae, Fabaceae
• Affiliation: IMD
• Location of specimens: IMD

Lin, Shu Huan; 林淑環 ; Lín Shūhuán; 林淑环
• Location of specimens: HAST

Lin, Su ching; 林素淨 ; Lín Sùjìng; 林素净
• Location of specimens: HAST

Lin, Wan Hao; 林万豪 ; Lín Wànháo
• Location of specimens: HAF

Lin, Wen Bao; 林文豹 ; Lín Wénbào
• Location of specimens: EBF

Lin, Wen Chih; 林文智 ; Lín Wénzhì
• Location of specimens: HAST

Ling, Hsieh; Lin, Hsieh; Lin, Xie; 林协 ; Lín Xié; 林協 (1933-)
• Research interest: Woody Plants
• Affiliation: ZJFI
• Location of specimens: ZJFI

Lam, H. C.; 林熊祥 ; Lín Xióngxiáng
• Location of specimens: IBSC

Lin, Xue Min; 林学岷 ; Lín Xuémín; 林學岷 (1937-)
• Affiliation: CHA

Lin, Yan Xing; 林炎兴 ; Lín Yánxīng; 林炎興 (1936-)
• Research interest: Anacardiaceae
• Affiliation: LAC
• Location of specimens: LAC

Lin, Yih Ren; 林益仁 ; Lín Yìrén
• Location of specimens: HAST

Lin, Ying; Lam, Y.; 林英 ; Lín Yīng (1914-2003)
• Research interest: Plants of Jiangxi
• Affiliation: HUTB
• Location of specimens: FJFC, FNU, JN, JXU

Lam, Ying Wai; 林英偉 ; Lín Yīngwěi; 林英伟 (1948-)
• Research interest: Plants of Hong Kong
• Affiliation: HK

Lin, Yung Che; 林永哲 ; Lín Yǒngzhé
• Location of specimens: HAST

Lin, Yu Lin; 林余霖 ; Lín Yúlín (1965-)
• Research interest: Medicinal Plants
• Affiliation: IMD

Lin, Yu Mei; 林玉梅 ; Lín Yùméi
• Location of specimens: HAST

Lin, Zheng Mei; 林正眉 ; Lín Zhèngméi (1969-)
• Affiliation: SN

Lin, Jyh Chin; 林志欽 ; Lín Zhìqīn; 林志钦
• Location of specimens: HAST

Lin, Jr Jan; 林志展 ; Lín Zhìzhǎn
• Location of specimens: HAST

Lin, Zhong Wen; 林忠文 ; Lín Zhōngwén
• Affiliation: GXSP

Lin, Tsung Kan; Lin, Tsung Kang; Lin, Chung Kang; Lin, Zhong Gang; 林仲剛 ; Lín Zhònggāng; 林仲刚 (1959-)
• Research interest: Bryophyte
• Affiliation: TNM
• Location of specimens: TNM

Lin, Tsu Min; 林祖民 ; Lín Zǔmín
• Location of specimens: HAST

Ling, Yuan Jie; Ling, Yuan Chi; Ling, Yuan Jue; 凌元洁 ; Líng Yuánjié; 凌元潔 (1930-)
• Research interest: Algae
• Affiliation: SXU
• Location of specimens: SXU

Liu, Ai Hong; 刘爱红 ; Liú Àihóng
• Affiliation: CSFI

Liu, Bai Ling; 刘柏玲 ; Liú Bǎilíng (1978-)
• Research interest: Gesneriaceae, Lamiaceae
• Affiliation: QFNU

Liu, Bao; 刘宝 ; Liú Bǎo (1980-)
• Research interest: Lauraceae; Woody Plants
• Affiliation: FJFC

Liu, Bao Dong; 刘保东 ; Liú Bǎodōng (1962-)
• Research interest: Pteridophytes
• Affiliation: HANU
• Location of specimens: HANU

Liu, Bing Quan; 刘冰泉 ; Liú Bīngquán; 劉冰泉 (1940-)
• Affiliation: YLD

Liu, Bing Rong; 刘炳荣 ; Liú Bǐngróng (1957-)
• Research interest: Pteridophytes
• Affiliation: HUST
• Location of specimens: HUST

Liu, Po; Liu, Bo; 刘波 ; Liú Bō; 劉波 (1927-2017)
• Research interest: Fungi
• Affiliation: SXU

Liu, Bo; 刘波 ; Liú Bō (1982-)
• Affiliation: IGA
• Location of specimens: IGA
• Location of specimens: SXU

Liu, Cheng Yun; 刘成运 ; Liú Chéngyùn
• Location of specimens: KUN

Liu, Cheng Ze; 刘承泽 ; Liú Chéngzé; 劉承澤 (1935-)
• Location of specimens: CTC

Liu, Chun Chao; 刘春朝 ; Liú Chūncháo (1977-)
• Research interest: Medicinal Plants
• Affiliation: HECM
• Location of specimens: HECM

Liu, Chun Rong; 刘春荣 ; Liú Chūnróng; 劉春榮 (1910-1992)
• Research interest: Scientific Illustrator
• Affiliation: PE

Liu, Cui Jing; 刘翠晶 ; Liú Cuìjīng (1977-)
• Research interest: Medicinal Plants
• Affiliation: JLAU

Liu, Tsui Ya; 劉翠雅 ; Liú Cuìyǎ; 刘翠雅
• Location of specimens: HAST

Liu, Da Chang; 刘大昌 ; Liú Dàchāng (1951-)
• Research interest: Fagaceae
• Affiliation: SWFC
• Location of specimens: SWFC

Liu, Da wei; 劉大維 ; Liú Dàwéi; 刘大维
• Location of specimens: HAST

Liu, Ta Yi; 劉大義 ; Liú Dàyì; 刘大义
• Location of specimens: HAST

Liu, De Yi; 刘德仪 ; Liú Déyí; 劉德儀 (1916-1981)
• Location of specimens: JSPC, KUN, NKU

Liu, Dong Yun; 刘东云 ; Liú Dōngyún (1963-)
• Research interest: Orchidaceae
• Affiliation: SXAU

Liu, Fang Sun; Liu, Fang Hsün; Liu, Fang Xun; 刘昉勋 ; Liú Fǎngxūn; 劉昉勳
• Location of specimens: IBSC, NAS, PE, WUK

Liu, Feng Qin; 刘凤琴 ; Liú Fèngqín; 劉鳳琴 (1943-)
• Research interest: Plants of Qinghai
• Affiliation: QUA
• Location of specimens: QUA

Liu, Gang; 刘钢 ; Liú Gāng (1960-)

• Affiliation: SG

Lau, Kwun Ming, David; **劉觀明 ; Liú Guānmíng;**
刘观明
• Research interest: Medicinal Plants
• Affiliation: CUHK

Liu, Kuo Sheng; 刘国声 ; Liú Guóshēng
• Location of specimens: PEM

Liu, Guo Xiang; 刘国祥 ; Liú Guóxiáng (1970-)
• Research interest: Algae
• Affiliation: HBI
• Location of specimens: EU, HBI

Liu, Hai Sang; 刘海桑 ; Liú Hǎisāng (1971-)
• Research interest: Araucariaceae, Arecaceae
• Affiliation: FJSI

Liu, He Ling; 刘鹤龄 ; Liú Hèlíng (1957-)
• Research interest: Medicinal Plants
• Affiliation: ACM
• Location of specimens: ACM

Liu, Hong Yan; 刘红燕 ; Liú Hóngyàn (1980-)
• Research interest: Medicinal Plants
• Affiliation: SDCM

Liu, Hua Jie; 刘华杰 ; Liú Huájié (1966-)
• Location of specimens: HBU, PE

Liu, Hui Qing; 刘惠卿 ; Liú Huìqīng; 劉惠卿 (1936-)
• Research interest: Lardizablaceae
• Affiliation: CDBI

Liu, Hui Yuan; 刘慧圆 ; Liú Huìyuán (1982-)
• Research interest: Digitization
• Affiliation: PE

Lau, C. H.; 刘集汉 ; Liú Jíhàn; 劉集漢 (1930-)
• Location of specimens: IBK, IBSC

Liu, Ji Quan; 刘计权 ; Liú Jìquán (1972-)
• Research interest: Medicinal Plants
• Affiliation: SXTCM
• Location of specimens: SXTCM

Liou, Ki Mon; Liu, Ji Meng; Liu, Ki Meng; Liu, Chi Mon;
刘继孟 ; Liú Jìmèng; 劉繼孟 (1909-1993)
• Location of specimens: PE

Liu, Jia Xi; 刘家熙 ; Liú Jiāxī (1963-)
• Research interest: Pteridophytes
• Affiliation: BJTC
• Location of specimens: BJTC

Liu, Jia Yi; 刘家宜 ; Liú Jiāyí; 劉家宜 (1928-2008)
• Research interest: Typhaceae; Aquatic Plants
• Affiliation: TIE
• Location of specimens: TIE

J. Q. Liu

Liu, Jian Qiu; 刘剑秋 ; Liú Jiànqiū (1956-)
• Employment: College of Life Sciences, Fujian Normal University（福建师范大学生命科学学院）
• Research interest: Plants of Fujian
• Affiliation: FNU
• Location of specimens: FNU

Liu, Jie; 刘杰 ; Liú Jié (1982-)
• Research interest: Taxaceae
• Affiliation: KUN

Liu, Jie Ping; 刘捷平 ; Liú Jiépíng; 劉捷平 (1932-)
• Affiliation: BJTC

C. H. Liu

Liu, Chin Hui; Liu, Jin Hui; **劉錦惠 ; Liú Jǐnhuì; 刘锦惠**
• Employment: Taiwan University（台湾大学）
• Research interest: Fungi
• Affiliation: TAI

Liou, Ching kuoh; 劉景國 ; Liú Jǐngguó; 刘景国
• Location of specimens: HAST

Liu, Jing; 刘静 ; Liú Jìng (1978-)
• Research interest: Plant Systematics
• Affiliation: SAU
• Location of specimens: SAU

Liu, Juan; 刘娟 ; Liú Juān; 劉娟 (1949-)
• Research interest: Geraniaceae
• Affiliation: JMSMC
• Location of specimens: JMSMC

Liu, Lei; 刘磊 ; Liú Lěi (1981-)
• Research interest: Fabaceae, Poaceae
• Affiliation: FGC

Liu, Li Cheng; 刘立成 ; Liú Lìchéng (1982-)
• Location of specimens: XBGH

Liu, Li Jie; 刘丽杰 ; Liú Lìjié
• Affiliation: ANTU

Liu, Li Xian; 刘丽仙 ; Liú Lìxiān; 劉麗仙 (1937-)
• Research interest: Medicinal Plants
• Affiliation: HNCM

• Location of specimens: HNCM

Liu, Li Yan; 刘丽燕 ; Liú Lìyàn
• Research interest: Woody Plants
• Affiliation: XJFA
• Location of specimens: XJFA

Liu, Li; Liu, Lee; 刘利 ; Liú Lì; 劉利
• Research interest: Pteridophytes
• Affiliation: ANTU
• Location of specimens: ANTU

Liu, Lian; 刘涟 ; Liú Lián; 劉漣 (1917-)
• Research interest: Algae
• Affiliation: CCNU
• Location of specimens: CCNU

Liu, Lin; 刘林 ; Liú Lín
• Location of specimens: DFEC

Liu, Lin Li; 刘琳莉 ; Liú Línlì (1977-)
• Research interest: Weeds
• Affiliation: NAU

Liu, Lu Xian; 刘路贤 ; Liú Lùxián (1985-)
• Research interest: Plants of N. China
• Affiliation: KAI

Liu, Lun Hui; 刘伦辉 ; Liú Lúnhuī; 劉倫輝 (1934-)
• Research interest: Plant Ecology
• Affiliation: HITBC, KUNE
• Location of specimens: KUNE

Liu, Mei; 刘玫 ; Liú Méi (1957-)
• Research interest: Apiaceae
• Affiliation: HANU

Liu, Mei Si; 刘美斯 ; Liú Měisī (1989-)
• Affiliation: HHNNR

Liu, Ming Zhuang; 刘明壮 ; Liú Míngzhuàng
• Location of specimens: HSNU

Liu, Ning; 刘宁 ; Liú Níng (1962-)
• Research interest: Plant Anatomy
• Affiliation: BNU
• Location of specimens: GNUB

P. G. Liu

Liu, Pei Gui; 刘培贵 ; Liú Péiguì (1953-)
• Employment: Kunming Institute of Botany, Chinese Academy of Sciences（中国科学院昆明植物研究所）
• Research interest: Fungi
• Affiliation: KUN
• Location of specimens: KUN

Liu, Peng; 刘鹏 ; Liú Péng (1965-)
• Research interest: Plants of Dabieshan
• Affiliation: ZNU
• Location of specimens: ZNU

Liu, Pin Hui; 刘品辉 ; Liú Pǐnhuī; 劉品輝 (1938-)
• Research interest: Styracaceae
• Affiliation: GAFS
• Location of specimens: GAFS

Liu, Qi Xie; 刘其燮 ; Liú Qíxiè
• Location of specimens: JXU

Liu, Chi Jung; 劉啟榮 ; Liú Qǐróng; 刘启荣
• Location of specimens: HAST

Liu, Qi Heng; 刘起衡 ; Liú Qǐhéng; 劉起衡 (1930-)
• Research interest: Woody Plants
• Affiliation: HUIF

Liu, Qian Xin; 刘倩心 ; Liú Qiànxīn
• Location of specimens: IBSC

Liu, Qing; 刘青 ; Liú Qīng (1974-)
• Research interest: Poaceae
• Affiliation: IBSC

Liu, Qing Hua; 刘庆华 ; Liú Qìnghuá; 劉慶華 (1948-)
• Research interest: Medicinal Plants
• Affiliation: JXCM
• Location of specimens: JXCM

Liu, Qing Hua; 刘庆华 ; Liú Qìnghuá (1962-)
• Affiliation: LYAC

Lau, Yung Sum; 劉榕森 ; Liú Róngsēn; 刘榕森
• Location of specimens: HK

Liu, Rui Xiang; 刘瑞祥 ; Liú Ruìxiáng
• Location of specimens: MJS

Liu, Ruo Yong; 刘若庸 ; Liú Ruòyōng; 劉若庸 (1945-)
• Research interest: Medicinal Plants
• Affiliation: HECM
• Location of specimens: HECM

Liu, Shao Ying; 刘少英 ; Liú Shàoyīng
• Affiliation: SCFI

Liu, Shao Wen; 刘绍文 ; Liú Shàowén; 劉紹文 (1939-)
• Affiliation: YAK

Liu, Sheng Long; 刘生龙 ; Liú Shēnglóng
• Location of specimens: MQ

Liu, S. Y.; 劉聖譽 ; Liú Shèngyù; 刘圣誉
• Location of specimens: HAST

Liu, Shi Xin; 刘诗馨 ; Liú Shīxīn
• Location of specimens: IGA

Liu, Shih Hui; 劉世慧 ; Liú Shìhuì; 刘世慧
• Location of specimens: HAST

Liu, Shi Qiao; 刘式乔 ; Liú Shìqiáo; 劉式喬 (1912-1972)
• Research interest: Medicinal Plants
• Affiliation: IMC
• Location of specimens: IMC

Liu, Shou Jin; 刘守金 ; Liú Shǒujīn (1968-)
• Research interest: Medicinal Plants
• Affiliation: ACM
• Location of specimens: ACM

Lau, Shau Yan; Liu, Sheo Jên; Liu, Shou Ren; 刘守仁 ; Liú Shǒurén; 劉守仁
• Location of specimens: IBSC

Liu, Shu Huai; 刘书淮 ; Liú Shūhuái
• Location of specimens: HIMC

Liu, Shu Lan; 刘淑兰 ; Liú Shūlán
• Research interest: Plants of Ningxia
• Affiliation: NXAC

Liu, Shu Mei; 劉淑美 ; Liú Shūměi; 刘淑美
• Location of specimens: HAST

Liu, Shu; 刘树 ; Liú Shù (1954-)
• Research interest: Poaceae
• Affiliation: RE
• Location of specimens: RE

Liu, Shun; 刘顺 ; Liú Shùn
• Location of specimens: IFP

Liu, Shun Zhi; 刘顺治 ; Liú Shùnzhì
• Location of specimens: XMBG

Liu, Si Yi; 刘思益 ; Liú Sīyì (1962-)
• Research interest: Medicinal Plants
• Affiliation: CPU

Liu, Tian Wei; 刘天慰 ; Liú Tiānwèi; 劉天慰 (1936-)
• Research interest: Plants of Shanxi
• Affiliation: HSIB
• Location of specimens: HSIB

Liu, Wan Sheng; 刘万生 ; Liú Wànshēng
• Research interest: Juglandaceae
• Affiliation: LEF
• Location of specimens: LEF

Liou, W. S.; 刘伟心 ; Liú Wěixīn; 劉偉心
• Location of specimens: WUK

Liu, Wei Rong; 刘卫荣 ; Liú Wèiróng (1972-)
• Research interest: Orchidaceae
• Affiliation: NOCC
• Location of specimens: NOCC

Liu, Wen Liang; 刘文亮 ; Liú Wénliàng
• Location of specimens: JSPC

Liu, Xia; 刘霞 ; Liú Xiá (1965-)
• Research interest: Medicinal Plants
• Affiliation: JLAU

Liu, Xian Zhi; 刘显芝 ; Liú Xiǎnzhī; 劉顯芝 (1946-)
• Location of specimens: ZCA

Liu, Xiang Shan; 刘祥山 ; Liú Xiángshān; 劉祥山 (1949-)
• Research interest: Medicinal Plants
• Affiliation: SHDC
• Location of specimens: SHDC

Liu, Xiang; 刘翔 ; Liú Xiáng (1981-)
• Research interest: Economic Plants
• Affiliation: SM
• Location of specimens: SM

Liu, Xiao Li; 刘小莉 ; Liú Xiǎolì
• Location of specimens: YNTCM

Liu, Xiao Yang; 刘小阳 ; Liú Xiǎoyáng
• Location of specimens: ST

Liu, Xiao Juan; 刘晓娟 ; Liú Xiǎojuān (1980-)
• Research interest: Plants of Gansu
• Affiliation: GAUF
• Location of specimens: GAUF

Liu, Xiao Li; 刘晓丽 ; Liú Xiǎolì (1974-)
• Research interest: Wood Identification
• Affiliation: BJM

Lau, Sin Ki; Liu, Hsin Chi; 刘心祈 ; Liú Xīnqí; 劉心祈
• Location of specimens: IBK, IBSC, SYS

Liu, Xin Yuan; 刘心源 ; Liú Xīnyuán
• Location of specimens: HSIB

Liu, Xiu Qun; 刘秀群 ; Liú Xiùqún (1975-)
• Research interest: Woody Plants
• Affiliation: CCAU

Liu, Xue Yi; 刘学医 ; Liú Xuéyī
• Location of specimens: BZCM

Liu, Xue Ming; 刘雪明 ; Liú Xuěmíng
• Location of specimens: TJMP

Liu, Xue Xian; 刘雪娴 ; Liú Xuěxián; 劉雪嫻 (1936-)
• Research interest: Algae
• Affiliation: N
• Location of specimens: N

Liu, Ya Tian; 刘亚田 ; Liú Yàtián; 劉亞田 (1935-)
• Research interest: Fabaceae
• Affiliation: ZCA
• Location of specimens: ZCA

Liu, Yan; 刘妍 ; Liú Yán (1982-)
• Research interest: Algae
• Affiliation: HANU

Liu, Yang; 刘鸯 ; Liú Yāng (1981-)
• Research interest: Plants of Xinjiang
• Affiliation: SHI

Liu, Yang; 刘杨 ; Liú Yáng (1981-)
• Research interest: Medicinal Plants
• Affiliation: SDCM

Liu, Yang; 刘洋 ; Liú Yáng (1977-)
• Research interest: Medicinal Plants
• Affiliation: LNCM
• Location of specimens: LNCM

Yang Liu bis

Liu, Yang; 刘阳 ; Liú Yáng (1978-)
• Employment: Institute of Botany, Chinese Academy of Sciences（中国科学院植物研究所）
• Research interest: Bryophyte
• Affiliation: PE
• Location of specimens: PE

Liu, Yao Wu; 刘耀武 ; Liú Yàowǔ (1975-)
• Research interest: Medicinal Plants
• Affiliation: BZCM

Liu, Yi Qiao; 刘一樵 ; Liú Yīqiáo; 劉一樵 (1931-1989)
• Research interest: Woody Plants
• Affiliation: BJFC
• Location of specimens: BJFC

Liu, Yi Zhen; 刘以珍 ; Liú Yǐzhēn (1984-)
• Research interest: Plants of Jiangxi
• Affiliation: JXU

Lau, Y. S.; 刘瑛光 ; Liú Yīngguāng; 劉瑛光
• Location of specimens: IBSC

Liu, Ying Nan; 刘赢男 ; Liú Yíngnán
• Location of specimens: HNR

Liu, Ying Di; 刘应迪 ; Liú Yīngdí (1958-)
• Research interest: Apiaceae; Algae; Bryophyte
• Affiliation: HNNU, JIU
• Location of specimens: HNNU, JIU

Liu, Yong; 刘勇 ; Liú Yǒng (1962-)
• Research interest: Lardizablaceae, Rutaceae
• Affiliation: JXCM

Y. Y. Liu

Liu, Yong Ying; 刘永英 ; Liú Yǒngyīng (1969-)
• Employment: Jiaozuo Teachers' College, Henan（焦作师范高等专科学校）
• Research interest: Bryophyte

Liu, You Na; 刘幼娜 ; Liú Yòunà (1953-)
• Research interest: Medicinal Plants
• Affiliation: HECM

Liu, Yu Qing; 刘玉青 ; Liú Yùqīng
• Location of specimens: KUN

Liu, Yu Heng; 刘育衡 ; Liú Yùhéng; 劉育衡 (1947-)
• Research interest: Medicinal Plants
• Affiliation: HUTM

Liu, Yun Xiao; 刘运笑 ; Liú Yùnxiào (1975-)
• Research interest: Scientific Illustrator
• Affiliation: IBSC

Liu, Zhen Qing; 刘振清 ; Liú Zhènqīng
• Research interest: Medicinal Plants
• Affiliation: HBDC

Liou, C. S.; 刘振书 ; Liú Zhènshū; 劉振書 ; 刘式民 (1902-1949)
• Location of specimens: PE

Liu, Zheng Hua; 刘正华 ; Liú Zhènghuá
• Affiliation: GNA

Liu, Zheng; 刘政 ; Liú Zhèng
• Location of specimens: GXFI

Liu, Chih chen; 劉芝辰 ; Liú Zhīchén; 刘芝辰
• Location of specimens: HAST

Lau, T. C.; 刘执中 ; Liú Zhízhōng; 劉執中
• Location of specimens: IBSC

Liu, Zhi Li; 刘志礼 ; Liú Zhìlǐ; 劉志禮 (1934-)
• Research interest: Algae
• Affiliation: N
• Location of specimens: N

Liu, Zhong Fu; 刘忠福 ; Liú Zhōngfú
• Location of specimens: KUN

Z. L. Liu

Liu, Zhong Ling; 刘仲苓 ; Liú Zhònglíng (1953-)
• Employment: Shanghai Natural History Museum (Branch of Shanghai Science & Technology Museum)（上海自然博物馆(上海科技馆分馆)）
• Research interest: Bryophyte
• Affiliation: SHM
• Location of specimens: SHM

Zhong L. Liu

Liu, Zhong Ling; 刘钟龄 ; Liú Zhōnglíng; 劉鍾齡 (1930-)
• Employment: School of Ecology and Environment, Inner Mongolia University（内蒙古大学生态与环境学院）
• Research interest: Plants of Nei Mongol
• Affiliation: HIMC
• Location of specimens: HIMC. IPNI as: Z. L. Liu; *Flora Innermongolica*

Lau, C. P.; 刘卓斌 ; Liú Zhuōbīn; 劉卓斌
• Location of specimens: IBK

Liu, Tsing; 柳楷 ; Liǔ Jiàn
• Location of specimens: HAST, TAIF

Liu, Yan Yang; 柳延杨 ; Liǔ Yányáng; 柳延楊 (1933-)
• Research interest: Plants of Nantong
• Affiliation: NAN
• Location of specimens: NAN

Long, Cheng Liang; 龙成良 ; Lóng Chéngliáng
• Location of specimens: CSFI

Long, Cui Ling; 龙翠玲 ; Lóng Cuìlíng (1973-)
• Research interest: Plant Ecology
• Affiliation: GNUG
• Location of specimens: GNUG

Long, Fei Yun; 龙飞云 ; Lóng Fēiyún; 龍飛雲 (1941-)
• Research interest: Plants of Guilin
• Affiliation: GUN
• Location of specimens: GUN

Long, Feng Li; 龙凤丽 ; Lóng Fènglì
• Location of specimens: DQTC

Long, Hong; 龙鸿 ; Lóng Hóng (1964-)
• Research interest: Poaceae
• Affiliation: SYAU
• Location of specimens: SYAU

Long, Ru; 龙茹 ; Lóng Rú (1973-)
• Research interest: Plants of Hebei
• Affiliation: CHA
• Location of specimens: BJFC, CHA

Long, Wen Xing; 龙文兴 ; Lóng Wénxìng (1974-)
• Research interest: Plants of Hainan
• Affiliation: HUTB
• Location of specimens: HUTB

Longxishan Exped.; 龙栖山考察队 ; Lóngqīshān Kǎochádui
• Location of specimens: IBSC, PE. Collection Team

Long, Wei Ge; 隆卫革 ; Lóng Wèigé
• Affiliation: GXFS
• Location of specimens: GXFS

Lou, Yu Xia; 娄玉霞 ; Lóu Yùxiá (1970-)
• Research interest: Bryophyte
• Affiliation: SHTU

Loa, Mei fung; 樓梅芳 ; Lóu Méifāng; 楼梅芳
• Location of specimens: HAST

Lu, Cheng Ying; 卢成英 ; Lú Chéngyīng (1952-)
• Research interest: Fungi
• Affiliation: JIU
• Location of specimens: JIU

Lu, De Bing; 卢德炳 ; Lú Débǐng; 盧德炳 (1931-)
• Research interest: Algae
• Affiliation: EU
• Location of specimens: EU

Lu, Dong Sheng; 卢东升 ; Lú Dōngshēng (1962-)
• Research interest: Plants of Henan
• Affiliation: XYTC
• Location of specimens: XYTC

Lu, Jin Mei; 卢金梅 ; Lú Jīnméi (1977-)
• Research interest: Pteridophytes
• Affiliation: KUN

Lu, Liang Cheng; 卢良成 ; Lú Liángchéng
• Location of specimens: EBF

Lu, Ning; 卢宁 ; Lú Níng (1984-)
• Research interest: Plant Physiology
• Affiliation: HSIB

Lu, Shen te; 盧盛德 ; Lú Shèngdé; 卢盛德
• Location of specimens: HAST

Lu, Xian Ming; 卢先明 ; Lú Xiānmíng (1950-)
• Research interest: Fabaceae
• Affiliation: CDCM
• Location of specimens: CDCM

Lu, Xin Gu; 卢心固 ; Lú Xīngù; 盧心固 (1935-)
• Research interest: Rutaceae
• Affiliation: AAUB
• Location of specimens: AAUB

Lu, Ying; 卢颖 ; Lú Yǐng (1964-)
• Research interest: Medicinal Plants
• Affiliation: BCMM

Lu, Yuan; 卢元 ; Lú Yuán (1985-)
• Research interest: Plants of Qinling
• Affiliation: XBGH
• Location of specimens: XBGH

Lu, Zhe; 卢喆 ; Lú Zhé; 盧喆 (1934-)
• Location of specimens: HNR

B. Ren Lu

Lu, Bao Ren; 陆保仁 ; Lù Bǎorén; 陸保仁 (1937-2004)
• Employment: Institute of Oceanology, Chinese Academy of Sciences（中国科学院海洋研究所）
• Research interest: Algae
• Affiliation: MBMCAS
• Location of specimens: MBMCAS

Lu, Ding An; 陆定安 ; Lù Dìng'ān; 陸定安 (1925-1964)
• Research interest: Bryophyte; Fungi
• Affiliation: N

Lu, Hui Xian; 陆惠娴 ; Lù Huìxián (1951-)
• Affiliation: GXSP

Lu, Ming Zhen; 陆明珍 ; Lù Míngzhēn; 陸明珍 (1945-)
• Affiliation: SG

Lu, Ting Qi; Lu, Ting Chi; 陆廷琦 ; Lù Tíngqí; 陸廷琦 (1925-1990)
• Research interest: Actinidiaceae
• Affiliation: HZU, ZAU
• Location of specimens: HZU, ZAU

Luk, W. K.; 陆文光 ; Lù Wénguāng; 陸文光
• Location of specimens: IBSC

Lu, Bin Ju; 鹿滨菊 ; Lù Bīnjú
• Location of specimens: HFBG

Lu, Zhan Xiang; 鹿占详 ; Lù Zhànxiáng
• Affiliation: YAK

Lu, Yong Man; 逯永满 ; Lù Yǒngmǎn
• Location of specimens: XJU

Lu, Jin Cai; 路金才 ; Lù Jīncái (1971-)
• Research interest: Asteraceae, Rosaceae
• Affiliation: SYPC
• Location of specimens: SYPC

Lu, Yuan Xin; 路元新 ; Lù Yuánxīn
• Location of specimens: QG

Luan, Ri Xiao; 栾日孝 ; Luán Rìxiào; 欒日孝 (1938-)
• Research interest: Algae
• Affiliation: DNHM
• Location of specimens: DNHM

Luan, Shu Jun; 栾淑君 ; Luán Shūjūn (1953-)
• Research interest: Algae
• Affiliation: DNHM
• Location of specimens: DNHM

Lo, P. Y.; 罗柏友 ; Luó Bǎiyǒu; 羅柏友
• Location of specimens: IBSC

Luo, Chang Hai; 罗昌海; Luó Chānghǎi; 羅昌海 (1940-)
• Research interest: Poaceae; Pteridophytes
• Affiliation: SWCTU

Luo, Da Shang; 罗达尚 ; Luó Dáshàng
• Location of specimens: QDC

Luo, Feng Xia; 罗凤霞 ; Luó Fēngxiá (1958-)
• Research interest: Woody Plants
• Affiliation: SYAUF
• Location of specimens: SYAUF

Lo, Kuang Meu; 罗光茂 ; Luó Guāngmào; 羅光茂
• Location of specimens: IBSC

Luo, He Yun; 罗鹤云 ; Luó Hèyún
• Affiliation: KUNE

Lo, Hung Chan; 羅鴻展 ; Luó Hóngzhǎn; 罗鸿展
• Location of specimens: HAST

J. X. Luo

Luo, Jian Xin; Luo, Chien Hsing; Luo, Jian Shing; 罗健馨 ; Luó Jiànxīn; 羅健馨 (1935-2020)
• Research interest: Bryophyte
• Location of specimens: PE

Lo, K. F.; 罗开富 ; Luó Kāifù; 羅開富
• Location of specimens: PE

Luo, Kai Jun; 罗开钧 ; Luó Kāijūn; 羅開鈞 (1938-)
• Location of specimens: YIM

Luo, Lin Bo; 罗林波 ; Luó Línbō
• Location of specimens: HITBC, HUST, IBK, PE

Luo, Lin Yuan; 罗林元 ; Luó Línyuán
• Location of specimens: EBF

Luo, Ming Cheng; 罗明城 ; Luó Míngchéng (1962-)
• Research interest: Poaceae
• Affiliation: SAUT
• Location of specimens: SAUT

Luo, Qun; 罗群 ; Luó Qún (1975-)
• Research interest: Theaceae
• Affiliation: YAF

Lo, S. H.; 罗生辉 ; Luó Shēnghuī; 羅生輝
• Location of specimens: IBSC, WUK

Luo, Shi Jia; 罗世家 ; Luó Shìjiā (1966-)
• Affiliation: ENS
• Location of specimens: ENS

Law, D. K.; 罗彤监 ; Luó Tóngjiān; 羅彤監
• Location of specimens: IBSC

Luo, Wei Xiang; 罗伟祥 ; Luó Wěixiáng
• Affiliation: YL

Luo, Xiao Peng; 罗霄鹏 ; Luó Xiāopéng
• Research interest: Plant Ecology
• Location of specimens: YAK

Luo, Ying Hua; 罗应华 ; Luó Yīnghuá (1978-)
• Research interest: Forest Ecology
• Affiliation: GAC

Luo, Zhi Jing; 罗志静 ; Luó Zhìjìng; 羅志靜 (1938-)
• Affiliation: CDC
• Location of specimens: CDC

Luo, Zhong Chun; 罗仲春 ; Luó Zhòngchūn
• Location of specimens: CSFI, HITBC, HUST, IBK, PE

Luo, Zu Jun; 罗祖均 ; Luó Zǔjūn; 羅祖均 (1936-)
• Location of specimens: GF

Lu, Chun Chao; 吕春潮 ; Lǚ Chūncháo; 呂春潮 (1939-)
• Location of specimens: KUN

Lui, Fa Qiang; 吕发强 ; Lǚ Fāqiáng
• Location of specimens: CDBI

Lu, Gui Bao; 吕归宝 ; Lǚ Guībǎo; 呂歸寶 (1941-)
• Research interest: Medicinal Plants
• Affiliation: TJDC

Lv, Hong Fei; 吕洪飞 ; Lǚ Hóngfēi (1963-)
• Research interest: Theaceae, Hypericaceae, Orchidaceae
• Affiliation: ZNU
• Location of specimens: ZNU

Lui, C. H.; 吕清华 ; Lǚ Qīnghuá; 呂清華 (1929-)
• Location of specimens: HITBC, IBK, IBSC, KUN, LBG, NAS, PE, SHM

Lu, Ching Min; 呂清敏 ; Lǚ Qīngmǐn; 呂清敏
• Location of specimens: HAST

Lu, Rong Sen; 吕荣森 ; Lǚ Róngsēn
• Location of specimens: CDBI

Lv, Xian Guo; 吕宪国 ; Lǚ Xiànguó
• Affiliation: IGA

Lu, Yi Ru; 呂怡儒 ; Lǚ Yírú; 呂怡儒
• Location of specimens: HAST

Lu, Yu Chuan; 吕玉娟 ; Lǚ Yùjuān; 呂玉娟
• Location of specimens: HAST

Lu, Zheng Wei; 吕正伟 ; Lǚ Zhèngwěi; 呂正偉
• Location of specimens: BJM, KUN, PE

Lu, C. S.; 吕志松 ; Lǚ Zhìsōng; 呂志松 (1936-)
• Location of specimens: HIB

M

Ma, Chun Lei; 马春雷 ; Mǎ Chūnléi (1982-)
• Research interest: Theaceae
• Affiliation: TEA

Ma, De Zhong; 马德钟 ; Mǎ Dézhōng
• Location of specimens: HLNM

Ma, Feng Shan; 马丰山 ; Mǎ Fēngshān (1963-)
• Location of specimens: SDCM

Ma, Hai Ying; 马海英 ; Mǎ Hǎiyīng (1971-)
• Research interest: Poaceae
• Affiliation: YUKU

Ma, Jian Qiang; 马建强 ; Mǎ Jiànqiáng (1985-)
• Research interest: Theaceae
• Affiliation: TEA

Ma, Ke; 马可 ; Mǎ Kě; 馬可 (1928-)
• Research interest: Fungi
• Affiliation: HENU
• Location of specimens: HENU

Ma, Ke Yuan; 马克元 ; Mǎ Kèyuán
• Affiliation: HBAUD
• Location of specimens: HBAUD

Ma, Li Fei; 馬利飛 ; Mǎ Lìfēi; 马利飞
• Location of specimens: HAST

Ma, Lin; 马林 ; Mǎ Lín (1962-)
• Research interest: Medicinal Plants
• Affiliation: IMM

Ma, Lin Ting; 马林庭 ; Mǎ Líntíng
• Affiliation: SES

Ma, Lin; 马琳 ; Mǎ Lín (1963-)
• Affiliation: TJMP
• Location of specimens: TJMP

Ma, Miao; 马淼 ; Mǎ Miǎo (1970-)
• Research interest: Fabaceae, Iridaceae, Orchidaceae
• Affiliation: SHI

Ma, Qing Qing; 马青青 ; Mǎ Qīngqīng (1985-)
• Research interest: Medicinal Plants
• Affiliation: QDC

Ma, Qing Wen; 马清温 ; Mǎ Qīngwēn (1969-)
• Research interest: Taxodiaceae
• Affiliation: BJM
• Location of specimens: BJM

Ma, Sai; 马赛 ; Mǎ Sài
• Location of specimens: HSIB

Ma, Shao Bin; 马绍斌 ; Mǎ Shàobīn
• Location of specimens: IMDY

Ma, Shi Rong; 马世荣 ; Mǎ Shìróng (1980-)
• Research interest: Plants of Gansu
• Affiliation: QYTC
• Location of specimens: QYTC

Ma, Wan Li; 马万里 ; Mǎ Wànlǐ (1963-)
• Research interest: Cyperaceae
• Affiliation: NMTC
• Location of specimens: NMTC

W. Z. Ma

Ma, Wen Zhang; 马文章 ; Mǎ Wénzhāng (1981-)
• Employment: Kunming Institute of Botany, Chinese Academy of Sciences（中国科学院昆明植物研究所）
• Research interest: Bryophyte
• Affiliation: KUN

Ma, Xiao Jie; 马小杰 ; Mǎ Xiǎojié (1968-)
• Research interest: Apiaceae, Asteraceae
• Affiliation: SDAU

Ma, Xiao Qiang; 马晓强 ; Mǎ Xiǎoqiáng (1965-)
• Research interest: Medicinal Plants
• Affiliation: XM
• Location of specimens: XM

Ma, Xin Yu; 马新玉 ; Mǎ Xīnyù (1963-)
• Research interest: Boraginaceae, Ephedraceae, Fabaceae, Lamiaceae
• Affiliation: XJDC
• Location of specimens: XJDC

Ma, Xing Hua; 马兴华 ; Mǎ Xīnghuá; 馬興華 (1931-)
• Location of specimens: XM

Ma, Yang Jun; 马养俊 ; Mǎ Yǎngjùn
• Location of specimens: JLFC

Ma, Yi Lun; 马义伦 ; Mǎ Yìlún
• Location of specimens: PE

Ma, Yong Hong; 马永红 ; Mǎ Yǒnghóng (1977-)
• Research interest: Plant Ecology
• Affiliation: SITC
• Location of specimens: SITC

Ma, Yu Ying; 马逾英 ; Mǎ Yúyīng (1958-)
• Research interest: Apiaceae
• Affiliation: CDCM

Ma, Ze Xin; 马泽新 ; Mǎ Zéxīn
• Location of specimens: BCMM

Ma, Zhen Feng; 马振凤 ; Mǎ Zhènfèng (1957-)
• Affiliation: YLD
• Location of specimens: YLD

Ma, Zhen Yu; 马振宇 ; Mǎ Zhènyǔ
• Research interest: Grass
• Affiliation: LZAH
• Location of specimens: LZAH

Ma, Zheng Ping; 马正平 ; Mǎ Zhèngpíng
• Location of specimens: XJFA

Ma, Zhi An; 马治安 ; Mǎ Zhì'ān
• Location of specimens: IMDY

Mohammat, Yiti; 买买提 · 依提 ; Mǎimǎití·Yītí
• Location of specimens: TURP

Mamatjan, Tursun; 买买提江 · 吐尔逊 ; Mǎimǎitíjiāng·Tǔ'ěrxùn (1958-)
• Research interest: Rosaceae, Salicaceae
• Affiliation: XJA
• Location of specimens: XJA

Mamtimin

Mamtimin, Sulayman; 买买提明 · 苏莱曼 ; Mǎimǎitímíng·Sūláimàn (1964-)
• Employment: College of Life Science and Technology, Xinjiang University（新疆大学生命科学技术学院）
• Research interest: Bryophyte
• Affiliation: XJU
• Location of specimens: XJU

Mai, He Yun; 麦鹤云 ; Mài Hèyún; 麥鶴雲 (1915-?)
• Location of specimens: SN

Mark, H. P.; 麦学榜 ; Mài Xuébǎng; 麥學榜
• Location of specimens: IBSC

Mark, Y. F.; 麦一飞 ; Mài Yīfēi; 麥一飛
• Location of specimens: IBSC

Mao, Hua Xun; 毛花训 ; Máo Huāxùn
• Location of specimens: CMMI

Mao, Zi Jun; 毛子军 ; Máo Zǐjūn (1958-)
• Research interest: Ericaceae
• Affiliation: NEFI

Mao, Zong Guo; 毛宗国 ; Máo Zōngguó
• Affiliation: HHBG
• Location of specimens: HHBG, NAS, PE

Mao, Zong Zheng; 毛宗铮 ; Máo Zōngzhēng; 毛宗錚 (1931-)
• Research interest: Gymnospermae, Ulmaceae
• Affiliation: IBK

Mei, Li Juan; 梅丽娟 ; Méi Lìjuān (1964-)
• Research interest: Gymnospermae
• Affiliation: HNWP

Mei, Qi Chun; 梅其春 ; Méi Qíchūn (1963-)
• Affiliation: FUS

Mei, Zai Mei; 梅再美 ; Méi Zàiměi (1961-)
• Research interest: Plant Ecology
• Affiliation: GNUG
• Location of specimens: GNUG

Meng, Kao Fei; 蒙高飛 ; Méng Gāofēi; 蒙高飞
• Location of specimens: HAST

Meng, Hao; 蒙浩 ; Méng Hào
• Location of specimens: IBK

Meng, Chao; 孟超 ; Mèng Chāo (1960-)
• Affiliation: IMM

Meng, Xian Dong; 孟宪东 ; Mèng Xiàndōng (1955-)
• Research interest: Plants of Hebei
• Affiliation: CHA
• Location of specimens: CHA

Meng, Zhen Nong; 孟振农 ; Mèng Zhènnóng (1962-)
• Affiliation: JSPC
• Location of specimens: JSPC

Mi, Tai Kang; 米太康 ; Mǐ Tàikāng
• Location of specimens: IMD

Mi, Tai Yan; 米太岩 ; Mǐ Tàiyán (1929-)
• Research interest: Economic Plants; Medicinal Plants

• Affiliation: AAUB
• Location of specimens: AAUB

Mijit; 米吉提 ; Mǐ jítí (1938-2009)
• Research interest: Ericaceae, Pyrolaceae; Gymnospermae
• Affiliation: XJU, XJUG
• Location of specimens: XJU, XJUG

Myanmar Exped.; 缅甸考察队 Miǎndiàn Kǎochádui
• Location of specimens: PE. Collection Team

Miao, Chen; 苗琛 ; Miáo Chēn (1964-)
• Research interest: Plants of N. China
• Affiliation: KAI
• Location of specimens: KAI

Miao, Yan Ming; 苗艳明 ; Miáo Yànmíng (1982-)
• Research interest: Plant Ecology
• Affiliation: LINF

Min, Xiang Peng; 闵祥鹏 ; Mǐn Xiángpéng; 閔祥鵬 (1935-)
• Research interest: Plants of Shandong
• Affiliation: QFNU
• Location of specimens: QFNU

Miao, Yi Qing; 缪以清 ; Miào Yǐqīng
• Location of specimens: JJF

Mo, Tao; 莫道 ; Mò Dào
• Location of specimens: HAST

Mo, Ji Ping; 莫季平 ; Mò Jìpíng
• Research interest: Plant Ecology
• Affiliation: HTC
• Location of specimens: HTC

Mo, Jian Bin; 莫健彬 ; Mò Jiànbīn (1964-)
• Research interest: Plants of Shanghai
• Affiliation: SG

Mo, Xi Mu; 莫熙穆 ; Mò Xīmù
• Location of specimens: JXU

Mo, Ya Ying; 莫亚鹰 ; Mò Yàyīng (1982-)
• Research interest: Magnoliceae
• Affiliation: HHBG
• Location of specimens: HHBG

Mo, Chen Heng; 莫槙恒 ; Mò Zhēnhéng; 莫桢恒
• Location of specimens: HAST

Medog Exped.; 墨脱队 ; Mòtuō Duì
• Location of specimens: KUN. Collection Team

N

Nanshuibeidiao Exped.; 南水北调队 ; Nánshuǐběidiào Duì
• Location of specimens: KUN. Collection Team

Nyima Pandor; 尼玛潘多 ; Nímǎpānduō (1975-)
• Research interest: Medicinal Plants
• Affiliation: XZDC

Ni, Zhi Yu; 倪芝瑜 ; Ní Zhīyú
• Location of specimens: GXMG

Ni, Zhuo Chi; 倪灼炽 ; Ní Zhuóchì
• Location of specimens: HON

Nie, Rui Lin; 聂瑞麟 ; Niè Ruìlín; 聶瑞麟 (1939-)
• Location of specimens: KUN

Ning, Bu; 宁布 ; Níng Bù
• Location of specimens: FGC

Ning, Xi Ping; 宁熙平 ; Níng Xīpíng (1965-)
• Research interest: Medicinal Plants
• Affiliation: SCAUB

Ning, Yu; 宁宇 ; Níng Yǔ (1941-)
• Location of specimens: BJFC

Niu, Qian; 牛倩 ; Niú Qiàn (1983-)
• Research interest: Medicinal Plants
• Affiliation: BZCM

Niu, Yang; 牛洋 ; Niú Yáng (1984-)
• Research interest: Campanulaceae
• Affiliation: KUN

Y. L. Niu

Niu, Yu Lu; 牛玉璐 ; Niú Yùlù
• Employment: College of Life Sciences, Hebei Normal University（河北师范大学生命科学学院）
• Research interest: Bryophyte
• Affiliation: HBNU
• Location of specimens: HBNU

Nong, Shao Feng; 农少丰 ; Nóng Shàofēng (1955-2004)
• Affiliation: NNA

Nurbay; 努尔巴衣 ; Nǔ'ěrbāyī
• Affiliation: XJUG
• Location of specimens: XJUG

Nurken; 努尔跟 ; Nǔ'ěrgēn (1959-)
• Research interest: Apocynaceae, Gentianaceae, Oleaceae
• Affiliation: XJUG

O

Ou, Lien Ling; 歐怜伶 ; Ōu Liánlíng; 欧怜伶
• Location of specimens: HAST

Ouyang, Bei; 欧阳蓓 ; Ōuyáng Bèi; 歐陽蓓 (1938-)
• Research interest: Medicinal Plants
• Affiliation: WCU

Ouyang, Hai Bo; 欧阳海波 ; Ōuyáng Hǎibō (1979-)
• Research interest: Cycadaceae
• Affiliation: FJSI

Ouyang, Hui; 欧阳辉 ; Ōuyáng Huī (1964-)
• Affiliation: CQNM

Ou, Zu Lan; 欧祖兰 ; Ōu Zǔlán (1973-)
• Research interest: Plant Ecology
• Affiliation: ACE
• Location of specimens: ACE

P

Pan, Gang; 潘刚 ; Pān Gāng (1968-)
• Research interest: Plant Ecology
• Affiliation: XZE
• Location of specimens: XZE

Pan, Guo Ying; Pan, Kwo Ying; 潘国瑛 ; Pān Guóyīng; 潘國瑛 (1939-)
• Research interest: Algae
• Affiliation: SCSG
• Location of specimens: SCSG

Pan, Hong; 潘鸿 ; Pān Hóng
• Location of specimens: GNUB

Pan, Jian Bin; 潘建斌 ; Pān Jiànbīn (1985-)
• Affiliation: LZU

Pan, Jie; 潘洁 ; Pān Jié (1964-)
• Affiliation: CQNM

Pan, Ming Qing; 潘明清 ; Pān Míngqīng
• Location of specimens: WH

T. C. Pan

Pan, Ti Chang; 潘体常 ; Pān Tǐcháng; 潘體常 (1937-)
• Employment: Southwest Normal College（西南师范学院）
• Research interest: Apocynaceae, Ebenaceae, Oxalidaceae, Styracaceae
• Affiliation: SWCTU
• Location of specimens: SWCTU. *Flora sichuanica*

Pan, Yang Dong; 潘仰东 ; Pān Yǎngdōng (1961-)
• Research interest: Algae
• Affiliation: HTC

Pan, Yi Min; 潘以敏 ; Pān Yǐmǐn (1934-)
• Research interest: Asteraceae, Ranunculaceae
• Affiliation: LZU

Pan, Yu Mei; 潘玉梅 ; Pān Yùméi (1981-)
• Research interest: Invasive Plants
• Affiliation: IBK

Pan, Yan Ming; 盘延明 ; Pán Yánmíng
• Affiliation: GXFS

Pang, Hou Xin; 庞厚新 ; Páng Hòuxīn (1965-)
• Affiliation: GZAC

Pei, Li Xin; 裴莉昕 ; Péi Lìxīn (1980-)
• Research interest: Medicinal Plants
• Affiliation: HECM
• Location of specimens: HECM

Pei, Yuan Rong; 裴元蓉 ; Péi Yuánróng (1926-)
• Research interest: Plants of Henan

• Affiliation: HENU
• Location of specimens: HENU

Peng, Chao Zhong; 彭朝忠 ; Péng Cháozhōng
• Location of specimens: IMDY

Peng, Chuan Cheng; 彭传诚 ; Péng Chuánchéng; 彭傳誠 (1936-)
• Research interest: Woody Plants
• Affiliation: SAUF
• Location of specimens: SAUF

Peng, De Chun; 彭德纯 ; Péng Déchún
• Location of specimens: HUF

Peng, Ding Ren; 彭定人 ; Péng Dìngrén (1979-)
• Research interest: Woody Plants
• Affiliation: GXF
• Location of specimens: GXF

Peng, Ding Yi; 彭定一 ; Péng Dìngyī
• Location of specimens: CDBI

Peng, Guang Tian; 彭光天 ; Péng Guāngtiān
• Location of specimens: JGSU

Peng, Shi Qi; 彭士琪 ; Péng Shìqí (1940-)
• Affiliation: JUJ

Peng, Shi Kui; 彭仕葵 ; Péng Shìkuí (1986-)
• Affiliation: HITBC

T. Peng

Peng, Tao; 彭涛 ; Péng Tāo (1977-)
• Employment: School of Life Science, Guizhou Normal University（贵州师范大学生命科学学院）
• Research interest: Bryophyte
• Affiliation: GNUB
• Location of specimens: GNUB

Peng, Xi Xu; 彭喜旭 ; Péng Xǐxù (1977-)
• Research interest: Plant Ecology
• Affiliation: HUST

Peng, Yan Song; 彭焱松 ; Péng Yànsōng (1975-)
• Research interest: Plants of Jiangxi
• Affiliation: LBG
• Location of specimens: LBG

Peng, Yin Bin; 彭寅斌 ; Péng Yínbīn (1922-)
• Research interest: Polygonaceae; Fungi
• Affiliation: HNNU
• Location of specimens: HNNU

Peng, Yu; 彭宇 ; Péng Yǔ (1967-)
• Research interest: Invasive Plants
• Affiliation: EU

Ping, Li Li; 平莉莉 ; Píng Lìlì (1977-)
• Research interest: Medicinal Plants
• Affiliation: SXTCM
• Location of specimens: SXTCM

Pu, Xun; 蒲训 ; Pú Xùn (1953-)
• Research interest: Apiaceae, Boraginaceae, Lamiaceae, Salicaceae
• Affiliation: LZU
• Location of specimens: LZU

Q(C)

Qi, Ji Zhong; 戚继忠 ; Qī Jìzhōng (1964-)
• Research interest: Plants of Jilin
• Affiliation: JLFC
• Location of specimens: JLFC

Qi, Yu Fang; 戚育芳 ; Qī Yùfāng (1937-)
• Research interest: Medicinal Plants
• Affiliation: YIM
• Location of specimens: YIM

Qi, Jian Zhong; 漆建忠 ; Qī Jiànzhōng (1936-)
• Research interest: Plant Ecology
• Affiliation: YLD

Qi, Wei Chen; 齐伟辰 ; Qí Wěichén (1979-)
• Research interest: Medicinal Plants
• Affiliation: CCM
• Location of specimens: CCM

Qian, Bi Xuan; 钱碧萱 ; Qián Bìxuān (1965-)
• Affiliation: SHMI

Qian, Chong Hai; Chien, Chung Hai; 钱重海 ; Qián Chónghǎi
• Location of specimens: WH

Qian, Qing; 钱青 ; Qián Qīng; 錢青 (1938-)
• Research interest: Medicinal Plants
• Affiliation: GDMP

Z. G. Qian

Qian, Zhi Guang; 钱之广; Qián Zhīguǎng (1953-)
- Employment: Shanghai Natural History Museum (Branch of Shanghai Science & Technology Museum) （上海自然博物馆(上海科技馆分馆)）
- Research interest: Fungi
- Affiliation: SHM
- Location of specimens: SHM

N. Guizhou Exped.; 黔北队；Qiánběi Duì
- Location of specimens: PE. Collection Team

S. Guizhou Exped.; 黔南队；Qiánnán Duì
- Location of specimens: PE. Collection Team

Qiang, Sheng; 强胜；Qiáng Shèng (1960-)
- Research interest: Apiaceae; Invasive Plants
- Affiliation: NAU
- Location of specimens: NAU

Qiao, Cen Jian; Chiao, Tseng Chien; Chiao, Tsêng Chien; 乔曾鉴；Qiáo Céngjiàn; 喬曾鑒 (1911-1970)
- Research interest: Plants of N. China
- Affiliation: BNU

Qiao, Ji; 乔继；Qiáo Jì
- Research interest: Economic Plants
- Affiliation: YAK

Qin, Guo Wei; 秦国伟；Qín Guówěi; 秦國偉 (1941-)
- Affiliation: SHMI

Chin, Hui Chen; Chin, Hui Zhen; Qin, Hui Zhen; 秦慧贞；Qín Huìzhēn; 秦慧貞 (1933-)
- Affiliation: NAS

Qin, Jun Yong; 秦俊用；Qín Jùnyòng
- Location of specimens: IBK

Qin, Lu Ping; 秦路平；Qín Lùpíng (1966-)
- Research interest: Medicinal Plants
- Affiliation: SMMU-BH

Qin, Rui Ming; 秦瑞明；Qín Ruìmíng (1937-)
- Affiliation: HFBG

Qin, Sheng Hong; 秦胜红；Qín Shènghóng (1966-)
- Research interest: Medicinal Plants
- Affiliation: EMA
- Location of specimens: EMA

Qin, Song Yun; 秦松云；Qín Sōngyún
- Research interest: Economic Plants
- Affiliation: SM
- Location of specimens: SM

Qin, Yun Cheng; 秦云程；Qín Yúnchéng; 秦雲程 (1934-)
- Research interest: Dioscoreaceae
- Affiliation: CDCM

Z. S. Qin

Qin, Zi Sheng; 秦自生；Qín Zìshēng (1932-)
- Employment: Nanchong Normal School, Sichuan（四川省南充师范学院）
- Research interest: Plants of Sichuan
- Location of specimens: SITC. Flora sichuanica

Qin, Zong De; 秦宗德；Qín Zōngdé
- Location of specimens: IBK

Qinling Pl. Exped.; 秦岭植物调查队；Qínlǐng Zhíwù Diàochádùì
- Location of specimens: WUK. Collection Team

Chin, Hao Fu; 覃灏富；Qín Hàofù; 覃灝富
- Location of specimens: IBK

Qin, Jia Li; 覃家理；Qín Jiālǐ
- Research interest: Medicinal Plants
- Affiliation: SWFC
- Location of specimens: SWFC

Qinghai-Xizang Exped.; 青藏考察队；Qīngzàng Kǎochádùì
- Location of specimens: CDBI, CIS, HNWP, KUN, KUNE, PE. Collection Team

Qinghai-Gansu Exped.; 青甘调查队；Qīnggān Diàochádùì
- Location of specimens: PE. Collection Team

Chiu, Ping Yun; Qiu, Bing Yun; 邱炳云；Qiū Bǐngyún (1906-1989)
- Location of specimens: KUN, PE

Chiu, Hui Ching; 邱輝清；Qiū Huīqīng; 邱辉清
- Location of specimens: HAST

Chiou, Nian Yung; 邱年永；Qiū Niányǒng
- Location of specimens: HAST

Chiu, Ching An; 邱清安；Qiū Qīng'ān
- Location of specimens: HAST

Chiou, Yi Ying; 邱奕穎；Qiū Yìyǐng; 邱奕颖
- Location of specimens: HAST

Qiu, Ying Xiong; 邱英雄 ; Qiū Yīngxióng (1969-)
• Research interest: Berberidaceae
• Affiliation: HZU

Qiu, Yong Wei; 邱咏薇 ; Qiū Yǒngwēi (1969-)
• Research interest: Medicinal Plants
• Affiliation: JXCM

Qiu, Min He; 裘敏和 ; Qiú Mǐnhé (1956-)
• Affiliation: JAS
• Location of specimens: JAS

Qiu, Shu Ping; 裘树平 ; Qiú Shùpíng (1954-)
• Research interest: Pteridophytes
• Affiliation: SHM
• Location of specimens: SHM

Qiu, Xiao Wen; 裘晓雯 ; Qiú Xiǎowén (1965-)
• Research interest: Plants of Fujian
• Affiliation: FFVTC

Qu, Bo; 曲波 ; Qū Bō (1972-)
• Research interest: Invasive Plants
• Affiliation: SYAU
• Location of specimens: SYAU

Quan, Yi Shu; 权宜淑 ; Quán Yíshū; 權宜淑 (1939-)
• Research interest: Medicinal Plants
• Affiliation: SXMP

The Fourth National Survey on Chinese Materia Medica Resources; 全国第四次中药资源普查大队 ; (2011-2015) Quánguó Dìsìcì Zhōngyào Zīyuán Pǔ chá Dàduì (2011-2015)
• Location of specimens: CMMI. Collection Team

The National Survey on Chinese Materia Medica Resources; 全国中药资源普查队 ; Quánguó Zhōngyào Zīyuán Pǔchádùi
• Location of specimens: IMDY, SM. Collection Team

R(J)

Ran, Jian Hua; 冉建华 ; Rǎn Jiànhuá (1954-)
• Research interest: Plants of Jiangxi
• Affiliation: JCE
• Location of specimens: JCE

Rao, Jun; 饶军 ; Ráo Jūn (1964-)
• Research interest: Fungi
• Affiliation: FTS
• Location of specimens: FTS

C. C. Jao

Jao, Chin Chih; Jao, Ch'in Chih; Rao, Qin Zhi; 饶钦止 ; Ráo Qīnzhǐ; 饒欽止 (1900-1998)
• Employment: Institute of Hydrobiology, Chinese Academy of Sciences（中国科学院水生生物研究所）
• Research interest: Algae
• Affiliation: HBI
• Location of specimens: HBI

Ren, De Lan; 任德兰 ; Rèn Délán; 任德蘭 (1931-)
• Location of specimens: LNNU

Ren, Ming Bo; 任明波 ; Rèn Míngbō (1973-)
• Research interest: Medicinal Plants
• Affiliation: IMC
• Location of specimens: IMC

Q. Ren

Ren, Qiang; 任强 ; Rèn Qiáng (1976-)
• Employment: College of Life Science, Shandong Normal University（山东师范大学生命科学学院）
• Research interest: Fungi
• Affiliation: SDNU
• Location of specimens: SDNU

Rong, Li; 容丽 ; Róng Lì (1973-)
• Research interest: Plant Ecology
• Affiliation: GNUG
• Location of specimens: GNUG

Ru, Wen Ming; 茹文明 ; Rú Wénmíng (1961-)
• Research interest: Plant Ecology
• Affiliation: SES
• Location of specimens: SES

Ru, Xin; 茹欣 ; Rú Xīn (1968-)
• Research interest: Bryophyte
• Affiliation: TIE

Ruan, Jia Peng; 阮嘉蓬 ; Ruǎn Jiāpéng (1964-)
• Research interest: Poaceae
• Affiliation: N

Juan, Lu Jane; 阮吕真 ; Ruǎn Lǚzhēn; 阮吕真
• Location of specimens: HAST

S

Sang, Yu Wen; 桑于雯 ; Sāng Yúwén
• Location of specimens: HAST

Sangye Chodron; 桑杰曲珍 ; Sāngjié Qūzhēn (1947-)
• Research interest: Medicinal Plants
• Affiliation: XZDC

Sha, Li Na; 沙莉娜 ; Shā Lìnà (1978-)
• Research interest: Poaceae
• Affiliation: SAUT
• Location of specimens: SAUT

S. G. Sha

Sha, Shi Gui; 沙世贵 ; Shā Shìguì; 沙世貴 (1932-)
• Employment: Nanchong Normal School, Sichuan（四川省南充师范学院）
• Research interest: Bromeliaceae, Eriocaulaceae, Pontederiaceae
• Affiliation: SITC
• Location of specimens: SITC
Flora sichuanica

Sha, Wei; 沙伟 ; Shā Wěi (1963-)
• Research interest: Plants of Qiqihar
• Affiliation: QTC

Sha, Ren; 莎仁 ; Shā Rén (1941-)
• Research interest: Woody Plants
• Affiliation: IMFA
• Location of specimens: IMFA

Shanxi Exped.; 山西队 ; Shānxī Duì
• Location of specimens: PE. Collection Team

Shan, Han Rong; 单汉荣 ; Shàn Hànróng; 單漢榮 (1934-2008)
• Research interest: Stachyuraceae; Plants of Jiangxi
• Affiliation: LBG

Shan, Zhen Guang; 单振光 ; Shàn Zhènguāng (1963-)
• Research interest: Plants of Yunnan
• Affiliation: YNUB

Shangguan, Tie Liang; 上官铁梁 ; Shàngguān Tiěliáng (1956-)
• Research interest: Plant Ecology
• Affiliation: SXU
• Location of specimens: SXU

Shang, Fu De; 尚富德 ; Shàng Fùdé (1963-)
• Research interest: Weeds
• Affiliation: KAI
• Location of specimens: KAI

Shao, Hui Min; 邵慧敏 ; Shào Huìmǐn (1979-)
• Affiliation: WCSBG

Shao, Jin Ping; 邵金平 ; Shào Jīnpíng (1973-)
• Research interest: Lauraceae
• Affiliation: YAF

Shao, Mei Ni; 邵美妮 ; Shào Měinī (1975-)
• Research interest: Smilacacea
• Affiliation: SYAU
• Location of specimens: SYAU

X. M. Shao

Shao, Xiao Ming; 邵小明 ; Shào Xiǎomíng (1962-)
• Employment: College of Biological Sciences, China Agricultural University（中国农业大学生物学院）
• Research interest: Bryophyte
• Affiliation: BAU
• Location of specimens: BAU

Shao, Yu; 邵郁 ; Shào Yù
• Location of specimens: IBSC

Shen, Cong Xiang; 申聪香 ; Shēn Cōngxiāng (1983-)
• Affiliation: SN

Shen, Shi Kun; 申世坤 ; Shēn Shìkūn (1969-)
• Affiliation: XTNM
• Location of specimens: XTNM

Shen, Ye Gen; 申业 ; Shēn Yè (1972-)
• Research interest: Medicinal Plants
• Affiliation: CMMI

Shennongjia Pl. Exped.; 神农架植物考察队 ; Shénnóngjià Zhíwù Kǎochádùi
• Location of specimens: EDC, HIB. Collection Team

Shen, Ai Ru; 沈霭如 ; Shěn Ǎirú; 沈靄如 (1915-)
• Affiliation: HTC

Shen, Bin; 沈彬 ; Shěn Bīn (1990-)
• Affiliation: CSH

Shen, Di Yu; 沈迪玉 ; Shěn Díyù (1958-)
• Research interest: Woody Plants
• Affiliation: SAUF

Shen, Jin Gui; 沈金贵 ; Shěn Jīnguì
• Location of specimens: XTNM

Shen, Tsun; Shen, Tsuin; Chen, C.; 沈儁 ; Shěn Jùn; 沈隽 (1913-1994)
• Location of specimens: HIB, IBSC, NAS, PE, SYS

Shen, Lian Sheng; 沈连生 ; Shěn Liánshēng; 沈連生 (1933-)
• Research interest: Medicinal Plants
• Affiliation: BCMM
• Location of specimens: BCMM

Shen, Ming Hui; 沈明輝 ; Shěn Mínghuī; 沈明辉
• Location of specimens: HAST

Shen, Shao Jin; 沈绍金 ; Shěn Shàojīn; 沈紹金 (1930-2008)
• Research interest: Poaceae
• Affiliation: SG

Shen, Hsiao Ying; 沈曉瑩 ; Shěn Xiǎoyíng; 沈晓莹
• Location of specimens: HAST

Shen, Zhang Jun; 沈章军 ; Shěn Zhāngjūn (1977-)
• Research interest: Plant Ecology
• Affiliation: ACE

Sheng, Su Jun; 盛束军 ; Shèng Shùjūn (1964-)
• Affiliation: NMPG
• Location of specimens: HZU, NMPG

Sheng, Yuan Bin; 盛元斌 ; Shèng Yuánbīn (1926-)
• Research interest: Scrophulariaceae
• Affiliation: LEF

Shi, Hong Bin; 师红斌 ; Shī Hóngbīn (1960-)
• Affiliation: KUN

Shi, Rui Ping; 师瑞萍 ; Shī Ruìpíng (1982-)
• Research interest: Bryophyte
• Affiliation: SHM

X. Q. Shi

Shi, Xue Qin; 师雪芹 ; Shī Xuěqín (1980-)
• Employment: College of Life Sciences, Anhui Normal University（安徽师范大学生命科学学院）
• Research interest: Bryophyte
• Affiliation: ANUB

Shi, Da Wen; 施大文 ; Shī Dàwén (1931-)
• Research interest: Berberidaceae
• Affiliation: SHMU
• Location of specimens: SHMU

Shi, Ding Ji; 施定基 ; Shī Dìngjī (1939-)
• Location of specimens: BNU

Shi, Guo Xin; 施国新 ; Shī Guóxīn (1950-)
• Research interest: Nymphaeaceae
• Affiliation: NJNU

Shi, Xing Hua; Shih, Hsing Hua; 施兴华 ; Shī Xīnghuá; 施興華 (1932-)
• Research interest: Tiliaceae; Gymnospermae
• Affiliation: JXAU
• Location of specimens: JXAU

Z. X. Shi

Shi, Zhi Xin; 施之新 ; Shī Zhīxīn (1941-2011)
• Employment: Institute of Hydrobiology, Chinese Academy of Sciences（中国科学院水生生物研究所）
• Research interest: Algae
• Affiliation: HBI
• Location of specimens: HBI

Shi, Guang Yu; 石光裕 ; Shí Guāngyù (1935-)
• Research interest: Plants of Heilongjiang
• Affiliation: QTC
• Location of specimens: QTC

Shi, Guo Liang; 石国梁 ; Shí Guóliáng; 石國樑 (1937-)
• Research interest: Plants of S. China
• Affiliation: IBSD
• Location of specimens: IBSC, IBSD

Shi, Ming; 石明 ; Shí Míng (1980-)
• Research interest: Poaceae
• Affiliation: SWFC

Shi, Shuo; 石硕 ; Shí Shuò (1980-)
• Location of specimens: HBNU, HBU

Shih, H. T.; 石憲宗 ; Shí Xiànzōng; 石宪宗
• Location of specimens: HAST

Shi, Xing Shan; 石兴山 ; Shí Xīngshān; 石興山 (1937-)
• Research interest: Cyperaceae
• Affiliation: LNNU
• Location of specimens: LNNU

Shi, Ya Ya; 石亚亚 ; Shí Yàyà (1982-)
• Research interest: Plant Systematics
• Affiliation: SHM

Shi, Ying; 石瑛 ; Shí Yīng (1974-)
• Research interest: Algae
• Affiliation: TYNUB
• Location of specimens: TYNUB

Shi, Hua Min; 时华民 ; Shí Huámín; 時華民 (1910-)
• Research interest: Plants of Henan
• Affiliation: HEAC
• Location of specimens: HEAC

Shi, Mei Zhong; 史美中 ; Shǐ Měizhōng (1965-)
• Research interest: Economic Plants
• Affiliation: HZU
• Location of specimens: HZU

Shih, Ching Hua; 史清華 ; Shǐ Qīnghuá; 史清华
• Location of specimens: HAST

Shi, Quan Fen; 史全芬 ; Shǐ Quánfēn (1978-)
• Research interest: Aristolochiaceae
• Affiliation: AAUF

Shi, Wei Guo; 史伟国 ; Shǐ Wěiguó
• Location of specimens: JMSMC

Shi, Yu Qin; 史玉琴 ; Shǐ Yùqín (1932-)
• Location of specimens: KAI

Shi, Zuo Min; 史作民 ; Shǐ Zuòmín (1968-)
• Research interest: Biodiversity
• Affiliation: CAF

Shou, Hai Yang; 寿海洋 ; Shòu Hǎiyáng (1983-)
• Location of specimens: CSH

Shou, Hui Zhong; 寿惠中 ; Shòu Huìzhōng (1955-)
• Affiliation: QUA

Shu, Guang Ming; 舒光明 ; Shū Guāngmíng (1954-)
• Affiliation: SM

L. Shu

Shu, Lei; 舒蕾 ; Shū Lěi (1988-)
• Employment: School of Life Sciences, East China Normal University（华东师范大学生命科学学院）
• Research interest: Bryophyte
• Affiliation: HSNU
• Location of specimens: HSNU

Shu, Shu; 舒抒 ; Shū Shū (1977-)
• Research interest: Medicinal Plants
• Affiliation: SM

Shu, Yu Min; 舒渝民 ; Shū Yúmín
• Location of specimens: BJFC

Sichuan Econ. Pl. Exped.; 四川经济植物考察队 ; Sìchuān Jīngjìzhíwù Kǎochádùì
• Location of specimens: CDBI, PE, SM. Collection Team

Sichuan Med. Pl. Exped.; 四川药用植物考察队 ; Sìchuān Yàoyòngzhíwù Kǎochádùì
• Location of specimens: ABDC, PE, YBDC. Collection Team

Sichuan Veget. Pl. Exped.; 四川植被考察队 ; Sìchuān Zhíbèi Kǎochádùì
• Location of specimens: CDBI, PE. Collection Team

Song, Bai Zhong; 宋百忠 ; Sòng Bǎizhōng
• Location of specimens: YAK

Song, Bao Yu; 宋宝玉 ; Sòng Bǎoyù; 宋寶玉 (1941-)
• Research interest: Woody Plants
• Affiliation: SXAU

Song, Bo; 宋波 ; Sòng Bō (1982-)
• Research interest: Alpine Plants
• Affiliation: KUN

Song, Chao Shu; 宋朝枢 ; Sòng Cháoshū; 宋朝樞 (1930-?)
• Research interest: Woody Plants
• Affiliation: CAF

Song, Guo Yuan; 宋国元 ; Sòng Guóyuán (1956-)
• Affiliation: SHTU

Song, Jian Zhong; 宋建中 ; Sòng Jiànzhōng (1953-)
• Research interest: Plants of Hubei
• Affiliation: CCNU
• Location of specimens: CCNU

Song, Jin Bin; 宋金斌 ; Sòng Jīnbīn
• Location of specimens: SHDC

Song, Min Li; 宋敏丽 ; Sòng Mǐnlì (1972-)
• Research interest: Biodiversity
• Affiliation: TYNUB
• Location of specimens: TYNUB

Song, Pei Lang; 宋培浪 ; Sòng Péilàng
• Affiliation: GYBG
• Location of specimens: GYBG

Song, Shi Liang; 宋世良 ; Sòng Shìliáng (1928-)
• Location of specimens: JLAU

Song, Tai Wei; 宋太伟 ; Sòng Tàiwěi; 宋太偉 (1941-)
• Affiliation: ENS

Song, Xiao Ling; 宋小玲 ; Sòng Xiǎolíng (1969-)
• Research interest: Weeds
• Affiliation: NAU

Song, Xue Cheng; 宋学成 ; Sòng Xuéchéng
• Location of specimens: SAUF

Song, Yan Mei; 宋艳梅 ; Sòng Yànméi
• Location of specimens: SDCM

Song, Yu Huan; 宋宇环 ; Sòng Yǔhuán; 宋宇環 (1935-)
• Research interest: Caprifoliaceae
• Affiliation: CCM
• Location of specimens: CCM

Song, Yu Xia; 宋玉霞 ; Sòng Yùxiá (1962-)
• Affiliation: NXF

Su, Hong Han; 苏宏汉 ; Sū Hónghàn; 蘇宏漢 (1911-)
• Research interest: Plants of Hubei
• Affiliation: CCNU
• Location of specimens: CCNU

Su, Hui Ru; 苏惠茹 ; Sū Huìrú
• Affiliation: IBSC

Su, Ke Min; 蘇克敏 ; Sū Kèmǐn; 苏克敏
• Location of specimens: HAST

M. L. So

So, May Ling; 蘇美靈 ; Sū Měilíng; 苏美灵 (1944-)
• Employment: Hong Kong Baptist University（香港浸会大学）
• Research interest: Bryophyte
• Affiliation: HKBU
• Location of specimens: HKBU

Sue, Chian Yi; 蘇倩儀 ; Sū Qiànyí; 苏倩仪
• Location of specimens: HAST

Su, Sheng Hsin; 蘇聲欣 ; Sū Shēngxīn; 苏声欣
• Location of specimens: HAST

Su, Xue; 苏雪 ; Sū Xuě (1974-)
• Research interest: Plant Ecology
• Affiliation: NWTC

Suyalatu; 苏亚拉图 ; Sūyàlātú (1968-)
• Research interest: Fabaceae
• Affiliation: NMTC
• Location of specimens: NMTC

Su, Yan Qiu; 苏燕秋 ; Sū Yànqiū (1956-)
• Research interest: Medicinal Plants
• Affiliation: GXMG

Su, Yong Ge; 苏永革 ; Sū Yǒnggé (1958-)
• Research interest: Bryophyte
• Affiliation: KUN

Su, Yong Xin; 苏永欣 ; Sū Yǒngxīn (1989-)
• Affiliation: CSH

Su, Yu Te; 蘇祐德 ; Sū Yòudé; 苏佑德
• Location of specimens: HAST

Su, Zhen Zhi; 苏珍枝 ; Sū Zhēnzhī (1975-)
• Research interest: Medicinal Plants
• Affiliation: SSMM

Su, Zhi Hong; 苏志红 ; Sū Zhìhóng
• Location of specimens: TJDC

Sun, Bao Hui; 孙宝惠 ; Sūn Bǎohuì
• Research interest: Medicinal Plants
• Affiliation: HBDC

Sun, Chang Gao; 孙昌高 ; Sūn Chānggāo (1951-)
• Research interest: Plant Physiology
• Affiliation: NMPG
• Location of specimens: NMPG

Sun, Chang Qing; **孙长庆 ; Sūn Chángqìng; 孫長慶 (1948-)**
• Research interest: Plants of Heilongjiang
• Affiliation: HLNM

Sun, Da Li; 孙大力 ; Sūn Dàlì (1962-)
• Research interest: Woody Plants
• Affiliation: HBFC

Sun, De Wu; 孙德武 ; Sūn Déwǔ (1963-)
• Research interest: Plants of N. E. China
• Affiliation: HANU
• Location of specimens: HANU

Sun, Dong Xue; 孙冬雪 ; Sūn Dōngxuě (1973-)
• Research interest: Brassicaceae, Polygonaceae
• Affiliation: SYPC
• Location of specimens: SYPC

Sun, Dun Yuan; 孙敦渊 ; Sūn Dūnyuān
• Research interest: Plants of Fanjingshan
• Affiliation: FAN
• Location of specimens: FAN

Sun, Gen Lou; 孙根楼 ; Sūn Gēnlóu (1962-)
- Research interest: Poaceae
- Affiliation: SAUT
- Location of specimens: SAUT

Sun, Hong Fan; 孙洪范; Sūn Hóngfàn; 孫洪範 (?-1979)
- Location of specimens: PE

Sun, Hong Jun; 孙鸿骏 ; Sūn Hóngjùn (1954-)
- Research interest: Medicinal Plants
- Affiliation: SHDC
- Location of specimens: SHDC

Sun, Hong Liang; 孙鸿良 ; Sūn Hóngliáng
- Location of specimens: HIMC

Sun, Huo Yu; 孙火玉 ; Sūn Huǒyù
- Location of specimens: WUH

Sun, Jian Xing; 孙建兴 ; Sūn Jiànxìng
- Affiliation: MJS
- Location of specimens: MJS

Sun, Chieh Shan; 孫介山 ; Sūn Jièshān; 孙介山
- Location of specimens: HAST

J. Sun

Sun, Jun; 孙军 ; Sūn Jūn
- Employment: College of Life Science, Liaoning University（辽宁大学生命科学学院）
- Research interest: Bryophyte
- Location of specimens: IFP

Sun, Min; 孙敏 ; Sūn Mǐn
- Location of specimens: SWCTU

Sun, Ming Zhou; 孙明洲 ; Sūn Míngzhōu (1977-)
- Research interest: Iridaceae; Plants of Changbai Mountain
- Affiliation: NENU

Sun, Pei Fang; 孫珮芳 ; Sūn Pèifāng; 孙珮芳
- Location of specimens: HAST

Sun, Pei Chan; 孙丕燀 ; Sūn Pīchǎn
- Research interest: Plants of Shandong
- Affiliation: SDFI
- Location of specimens: SDFI

Sun, Quan; 孙权 ; Sūn Quán (1976-)
- Research interest: Rosaceae
- Affiliation: SYAU
- Location of specimens: SYAU

Sun, Tong Xing; 孙统兴 ; Sūn Tǒngxīng (1962-)
- Research interest: Medicinal Plants
- Affiliation: LYAC

Sun, C. L.; 孙祥麟 ; Sūn Xiánglín; 孫祥麟
- Location of specimens: TIE, SZ

Sun, Ye Gen; 孙叶根 ; Sūn Yègēn (1963-)
- Research interest: Plants of Anhui
- Affiliation: ANUG
- Location of specimens: ANUG

Sun, Ying Bao; 孙英宝 ; Sūn Yīngbǎo (1976-)
- Research interest: Scientific Illustrator
- Affiliation: PE
- Location of specimens: PE

Sun, Ying De; 孙应德 ; Sūn Yìngdé; 孫應德 (1925-)
- Research interest: Asteraceae, Fabaceae, Tamaricaceae
- Affiliation: QF
- Location of specimens: QF

Sun, Yong Hui; 孙永辉 ; Sūn Yǒnghuī (1966-)
- Research interest: Scrophulariaceae
- Affiliation: MJS

Sun, Yu Zheng; 孙煜铮 ; Sūn Yùzhēng (1985-)
- Research interest: Pteridophytes
- Affiliation: BZCM

Sun, Zhong Min; 孙忠民 ; Sūn Zhōngmín (1977-)
- Research interest: Algae
- Affiliation: MBMCAS
- Location of specimens: MBMCAS

Sun, C. K.; 孙仲光 ; Sūn Zhòngguāng; 孫仲光
- Location of specimens: PE

Sophia; 索菲亚 ; Suǒ fēiyà
- Location of specimens: XJU

T

Tarbaghatay Exped.; 塔城队 ; Tǎ chéng Duì
- Location of specimens: XTNM. Collection Team

Tan, Ce Ming; 谭策铭 ; Tán Cèmíng (1952-)
- Research interest: Plants of Jiangxi
- Affiliation: JJF
- Location of specimens: JJF, SMMU-BH

H. C. Tan

Tan, Hui Ci; 谭惠慈 ; Tán Huìcí; 譚惠慈 (1932-)
- Employment: Shanghai Natural History Museum (Branch of Shanghai Science & Technology Museum) (上海自然博物馆(上海科技馆分馆))
- Research interest: Fungi
- Affiliation: SHM

Tan, Jing Zheng; 谭经正 ; Tán Jīngzhèng (1956-2012)
- Research interest: Woody Plants
- Affiliation: SIFS

Tan, Jing Xin; Tarn, J. S.; 谭景燊 ; Tán Jǐngshēn; 譚景燊 (1918-2011)
- Research interest: Plants of Hubei
- Affiliation: CCNU
- Location of specimens: CCNU

Tan, Qiu Ping; 谭秋平 ; Tán Qiūpíng
- Location of specimens: IMC

Tan, Wen Hong; 谭文红 ; Tán Wénhóng (1967-)
- Affiliation: YNTCM
- Location of specimens: YNTCM

Tan, Yan Bang; 谭彦邦 ; Tán Yànbāng; 譚彥邦 (1941-)
- Affiliation: HUE

Tan, Yang Mei; 谭杨梅 ; Tán Yángméi (1950-)
- Research interest: Bryophyte
- Affiliation: IMC
- Location of specimens: IMC

Tan, Ye Hui; 谭烨辉 ; Tán Yèhuī
- Research interest: Seagrass
- Affiliation: SCSG

Tam, Y. W.; 谭英华 ; Tán Yīnghuá; 譚英華
- Location of specimens: IBSC

Tang, Xing Chun; 汤行春 ; Tāng Xíngchūn (1969-)
- Research interest: Economic Plants
- Affiliation: EU

Tang, Xiao Xin; 汤晓辛 ; Tāng Xiǎoxīn (1984-)
- Affiliation: GNUB

Tang, Yi Feng; 汤艺峰 ; Tāng Yìfēng (1963-)
- Affiliation: HSNU

Tang, Yin Zhu; 汤银珠 ; Tāng Yínzhū
- Affiliation: IBSC

Tang, An Ke; 唐安科 ; Táng Ānkē
- Location of specimens: CTC

Tang, De Ying; 唐德英 ; Táng Déyīng
- Location of specimens: IMDY

Tang, Hong Liang; 唐宏亮 ; Táng Hóngliàng
- Research interest: Fabaceae; Plants of Hebei
- Affiliation: HBU
- Location of specimens: HBU

Tang, Hui Huang; 唐輝煌 ; Táng Huīhuáng; 唐辉煌
- Location of specimens: HAST

Tang, Kai Ying; 唐开盈 ; Táng Kāiyíng
- Location of specimens: WXDC

Tang, Li Jun; 唐立俊 ; Táng Lìjùn
- Location of specimens: ZY

Tang, Ming Kun; 唐明坤 ; Táng Míngkūn (1981-)
- Research interest: Woody Plants
- Affiliation: SCFI

Tang, Pan Chang; 唐盘昌 ; Táng Pánchāng; 唐盤昌 (1936-)
- Affiliation: JSPC
- Location of specimens: JSPC

Tang, Shao Qing; 唐绍清 ; Táng Shàoqīng (1964-)
- Affiliation: GUN
- Location of specimens: GUN

Tang, Shu Ben; 唐树本 ; Táng Shùběn
- Location of specimens: IGA

Tang, Ting Gui; 唐廷贵 ; Táng Tíngguì; 唐廷貴 (1935-)
- Research interest: Plant Ecology
- Affiliation: NKU

Tang, Yao; T'ang, Yao; 唐耀 ; Táng Yào (1905-2011)
- Research interest: Woody Plants
- Affiliation: KUN

Tong, Y. H.; 唐有恒 ; Táng Yǒuhéng; 唐有恆
- Location of specimens: IBSC

Tang, Zhong Hua; 唐中华 ; Táng Zhōnghuá (1977-)
- Research interest: Araliaceae
- Affiliation: NEFI

Tang, Chung Chang; 唐仲璋 ; Táng Zhòngzhāng
• Location of specimens: AU

K. Tao

Tao, Kai; 陶恺 ; Táo Kǎi (1963-)
• Employment: Shanxi University (山西大学)
• Research interest: Fungi
• Affiliation: SXU

Tao, Ming Qin; 陶明琴 ; Táo Míngqín (1956-)
• Research interest: Scientific Illustrator
• Affiliation: LZD

Tao, Yi Peng; 陶一鹏 ; Táo Yīpéng
• Location of specimens: GXMI

Tau, Y. H.; 陶玉辉 ; Táo Yùhuī; 陶玉輝
• Location of specimens: SZ

Tian, De Chang; 田德昌 ; Tián Déchāng (1935-)
• Location of specimens: NEAU

Tian, Duo Xian; 田多贤; Tián Duōxián; 田多賢 (1935-)
• Research interest: Aristolochiaceae
• Affiliation: PEM

Tian, Jin Wei; 田谨为 ; Tián Jǐnwèi; 田謹為 (1929-1991)
• Research interest: Medicinal Plants
• Affiliation: IMC
• Location of specimens: IMC

Tian, Lin; 田琳 ; Tián Lín (1985-)
• Research interest: Plants of Xinjiang
• Affiliation: SHI

Tian, Qing; 田青 ; Tián Qīng (1974-)
• Research interest: Plants of Gansu
• Affiliation: GAUF
• Location of specimens: GAUF

Tian, Sheng Ni; 田胜尼 ; Tián Shèngní (1971-)
• Research interest: Plants of Anhui
• Affiliation: AAUB
• Location of specimens: AAUB

Tian, Shu Rong; 田书荣 ; Tián Shūróng (1973-)
• Affiliation: HHNNR

Tian, Shu Ge; 田树革 ; Tián Shùgé (1968-)
• Research interest: Medicinal Plants
• Affiliation: XM
• Location of specimens: XM

H. Tian

Tian, Hong; 田虹 ; Tián Hóng
• Employment: School of Life Sciences, Inner Mongolia University (内蒙古大学生命科学学院)
• Research interest: Plants of Nei Mongol
• Flora Innermongolica

Tian, Xian Hua; 田先华 ; Tián Xiānhuá (1952-)
• Research interest: Plants of Shaanxi
• Affiliation: SANU
• Location of specimens: SANU

Tian, Xiao Wen; 田效文 ; Tián Xiàowén
• Location of specimens: CIS

Tie, Jun; 铁军 ; Tiě Jūn (1974-)
• Research interest: Plant Ecology
• Affiliation: SES
• Location of specimens: BJFC, SES

Tong, Bo Qiang; 仝伯强 ; Tóng Bóqiáng
• Affiliation: SDFGR

Tong, Zhi Guo; Tung, Chi Guo; 仝治国 ; Tóng Zhìguó; 仝治國 ; (1925-1979)
• Location of specimens: HIMC

Tong, Jiang Hai; 佟江海 ; Tóng Jiānghǎi (1936-)
• Research interest: Medicinal Plants
• Affiliation: IMDC

Tong, Xi Da; 佟希达 ; Tóng Xīdá; 佟希達 (1938-)
• Research interest: Plants of Heilongjiang
• Affiliation: HLNM
• Location of specimens: HLNM

Tong, Ben Qun; 童本群 ; Tóng Běnqún
• Affiliation: LEF

C. R. Tong

Tong, Cheng Ren; 童成仁 ; Tóng Chéngrén (1953-)
• Employment: Inner Mongolia Institute of Forestry Science (内蒙古林业研究所)
• Research interest: Woody Plants
• Affiliation: IMFA
• Location of specimens: IMFA
• Flora Innermongolica

Tong, Jiang Bo; 童江波 ; Tóng Jiāngbō
• Affiliation: CQNM

Tong, Jun Ping; 童军平 ; Tóng Jūnpíng (1959-)
• Research interest: Scientific Illustrator
• Affiliation: HHBG

• Location of specimens: HHBG

Tong, Xiao Ping; 童效平；Tóng Xiàopíng
• Location of specimens: AAUF

Tu, Xiao Ning; 土小宁；Tǔ Xiǎoníng (1964-)
• Research interest: Woody Plants
• Affiliation: YL

Tu, Yan Li; 土艳丽；Tǔ Yànlì (1972-)
• Location of specimens: XZ

W

Wan, De Guang; 万德光；Wàn Déguāng; 萬德光 (1935-)
• Research interest: Polygalaceae
• Affiliation: CDCM
• Location of specimens: CDCM

Wan, Ding Rong; 万定荣；Wàn Dìngróng (1958-)
• Research interest: Medicinal Plants
• Affiliation: EDC

Wan, Peng; 万鹏；Wàn Péng (1961-)
• Research interest: Medicinal Plants
• Affiliation: SDCM
• Location of specimens: SDCM

Wan, Tao; 万涛；Wàn Tāo (1983-)
• Research interest: Gnetaceae; Plants of E. Africa
• Affiliation: SZG
• Location of specimens: SZG

Wan, Zi Jun; 万子俊；Wàn Zijùn (1952-)
• Research interest: Woody Plants
• Affiliation: YLD

T. L. Wan

Wan, Thung Ling; Wan, Tsung Ling; Wan, Zong Ling; 万宗玲；Wàn Zōnglíng; 萬宗玲 (1907-2006)
• Employment: Institute of Botany, Chinese Academy of Sciences（中国科学院植物研究所）
• Research interest: Bryophyte
• Affiliation: PE

Wan, Zuo Xi; 万佐玺；Wàn Zuǒxǐ (1968-)
• Research interest: Plant Ecology
• Affiliation: ENS
• Location of specimens: ENS

Wanxian Herb. Med. Exped.; 万县中草药普查队；Wànxiàn Zhōngcǎoyào Pǔcháduì
• Location of specimens: WXDC. Collection Team

Wang, Jie; 汪杰；Wāng Jié
• Research interest: Algae
• Affiliation: HBI

M. Z. Wang

Wang, Mei Zhi; 汪楣芝；Wāng Méizhī (1947-)
• Employment: Institute of Botany, Chinese Academy of Sciences（中国科学院植物研究所）
• Research interest: Bryophyte
• Affiliation: PE
• Location of specimens: PE

Wang, Min Xue; 汪敏学；Wāng Mǐnxué; 汪敏學 (1932-)
• Location of specimens: CDBI, NAS, PE, SHM, SITC, SM, SZ, TIE

Wang, Qing; 汪庆；Wāng Qìng (1965-)
• Research interest: Bryophyte
• Affiliation: NAS

Wang, Yu Xiang; 汪玉祥；Wāng Yùxiáng
• Research interest: Fagaceae
• Affiliation: LEF

Wang, Yuan; 汪远；Wāng Yuǎn (1987-)
• Research interest: Cultivated Plants
• Affiliation: CSH
• Location of specimens: CSH

Chen J. Wang

Wang, Chen Ju; Wang, Jan Ru; Wang, Yen Chieh; Wang, Yan Jie; 汪振儒；Wāng Zhènrú; 汪燕杰 (1908-2008)
• Employment: College of Agriculture, National University of Peking; Department of Forestry, Beijing Agricultural University; Beijing Forestry College（国立北京大学农学院；北京农业大学森林系；北京林学院）
• Research interest: Forest Scientist
• Affiliation: BJFC

Wang, Zheng Li; 汪正利；Wāng Zhènglì (1965-)
• Research interest: Economic Plants
• Affiliation: XZ
• Location of specimens: XZ

Wang, Zheng Xiang; 汪正祥 ;
Wāng Zhèngxiáng (1966-)
• Research interest: Fagaceae; Bryophyte
• Affiliation: EU

Wang, Zhi Jun; 汪志军 ; Wāng Zhìjūn
• Research interest: Woody Plants
• Affiliation: XJFA
• Location of specimens: XJFA

Wang, Ai Min; 王爱民 ; Wáng Àimín
• Research interest: Plants of Shangrao
• Affiliation: SRF

Wang, Bo Qing; 王柏青 ; Wáng Bǎiqīng (1961-)
• Research interest: Plants of Jilin
• Affiliation: JLFC
• Location of specimens: JLFC

Wang, Bi Jao; 王弼昭 ; Wáng Bìzhāo (1953-1992)
• Location of specimens: HAST, NCKU

Wang, Bi Qin; 王碧琴 ; Wáng Bìqín (1957-)
• Research interest: Plants of Jiangxi
• Affiliation: JAS
• Location of specimens: JAS

Wang, Bing; 王冰 ; Wáng Bīng (1952-)
• Location of specimens: LNCM

Bo Wang

Wang, Bo; 王伯 ; Wáng Bó
• Employment: Changbai Mountain National Nature Reserve Administration, Jilin（吉林长白山国家级自然保护区管理局）
• Research interest: Fungi
• Affiliation: ANTU
• Location of specimens: ANTU

Wang, Cai Ling; 王彩玲 ; Wáng Cǎilíng (1937-)
• Research interest: Caryophyllaceae
• Affiliation: TIE
• Location of specimens: TIE

Wang, Chang An; 王昌安 ; Wáng Chāng'ān
• Location of specimens: NJNU

Wang, Chang Hua; 王昌华 ; Wáng Chānghuá
• Research interest: Medicinal Plants
• Affiliation: SM
• Location of specimens: SM

Wang, Chang Gui; 王常贵 ; Wáng Chángguì
• Location of specimens: XJBI

Wang, Chang Qing; 王长清 ; Wáng Chángqīng
• Location of specimens: CCAU

Wang, Chao Hui; 王朝辉 ; Wáng Cháohuī
• Location of specimens: IMC

Wang, Chao Chien; 王朝鍵 ; Wáng Cháojiàn; 王朝键
• Location of specimens: HAST

Wang, Cheng Xin; 王成信 ; Wáng Chéngxìn (1952-)
• Research interest: Medicinal Plants
• Affiliation: MQ
• Location of specimens: MQ

Wang, Cheng Lu; 王承录 ; Wáng Chénglù; 王承錄 (1949-2011)
• Research interest: Aquatic Plants
• Affiliation: GNUB
• Location of specimens: GNUB

Wang, Cheng Ming; 王承明 ; Wáng Chéng Míng
• Location of specimens: JLFC

Wang, Chong Shu; 王崇书 ; Wáng Chóng Shū
• Location of specimens: IFP

Wang, Chun Bo; 王春波 ; Wáng Chūnbō (1987-)
• Research interest: Gymnospermae
• Affiliation: QNUN
• Location of specimens: QNUN

Wang, Chun Lan; 王春兰 ; Wáng Chūnlán;
王春蘭 (1943-)
• Research interest: Betulaceae, Salicaceae
• Affiliation: YAF

Wang, Chun Lei; 王春雷 ; Wáng Chūnléi (1966-)
• Research interest: Medicinal Plants
• Affiliation: HECM
• Location of specimens: HECM

Wang, Cong Yang; 王从阳 ; Wáng Cóngyáng
• Location of specimens: YNUB

Wang, T. S.; 王大顺 ; Wáng Dàshùn; 王大順
• Location of specimens: PE

Wang, Da Xuan; 王大萱 ; Wáng Dàxuān
• Location of specimens: HUTM

Wang, Dai Xing; 王代兴 ; Wáng Dàixìng (1969-)
• Research interest: Woody Plants
• Affiliation: GFS

Wang, Dao Mo; 王道模 ; **Wáng Dàomó (1964-)**
• Research interest: Woody Plants
• Affiliation: SIFS

Wang, De Chang; 王德昌 ; **Wáng Déchāng (1963-)**
• Research interest: Fungi
• Affiliation: GNUB
• Location of specimens: GNUB

Wang, Te Hui; 王德辉 ; **Wáng Déhuī**; 王德輝
• Location of specimens: PE, W

Wang, T. C.; 王德祯 ; **Wáng Dézhēn**; 王德禎
• Location of specimens: PE

Wang, Teng Wen; 王登文 ; **Wáng Dēngwén**
• Location of specimens: HAST

Wang, Di; 王迪 ; **Wáng Dí (1938-)**
• Location of specimens: HLCM

F. L. Wang

Wang, Fan Lung; Wang, Fan Long; 王繁隆 ;
Wáng Fánlóng
• Employment: Institute of Forestry, Taiwan University（台湾大学森林学研究所）
• Research interest: Plants of Taiwan
Revision of Piperales in Taiwan

Wang, Fang Li; 王芳礼 ; **Wáng Fānglǐ (1920-)**
• Location of specimens: SAUF

Wang, Feng; 王丰 ; **Wáng Fēng**; 王豐 **(1935-)**
• Research interest: Juncaceae
• Affiliation: ZNU
• Location of specimens: ZNU

Wang, Feng; 王峰 ; **Wáng Fēng (1964-)**
• Research interest: Pteridophytes
• Affiliation: GFS
• Location of specimens: GFS

Wang, Feng Chun; 王凤春 ; **Wáng Fèngchūn (1957-)**
• Research interest: Fabaceae, Plantaginaceae
• Affiliation: HANU
• Location of specimens: HANU

Wang, Feng Zhi; 王凤芝 ; **Wáng Fèngzhī**
• Affiliation: HLCM

Wang, Fu Bao; 王富葆 ; **Wáng Fùbǎo**
• Location of specimens: N

Wang, Ge Rong; 王戈戎 ; **Wáng Gēróng (1974-)**
• Research interest: Plants of Jilin
• Affiliation: JLFC
• Location of specimens: JLFC

Wang, Kuang Yuh; 王光玉 ; **Wáng Guāngyù**
• Location of specimens: HAST

Wang, Guang Zheng; 王光正 ; **Wáng Guāngzhèng**
• Location of specimens: IFP

Wang, Gui; 王贵 ; **Wáng Guì (1955-)**
• Research interest: Juglandaceae
• Affiliation: TYF

Wang, Gui Hua; 王桂花 ; **Wáng Guìhuā (1968-)**
• Research interest: Bryophyte
• Affiliation: SXU

Wang, Gui Yun; 王桂云 ; **Wáng Guìyún**
• Location of specimens: HLCM

Wang, Guo Dong; 王国栋 ; **Wáng Guódòng (1987-)**
• Research interest: Biodiversity
• Affiliation: IGA
• Location of specimens: SZG

Wang, Guo Ping; 王果平 ; **Wáng Guǒpíng (1979-)**
• Research interest: Medicinal Plants
• Affiliation: XTNM
• Location of specimens: XTNM

H. Y. Wang

Wang, Hai Ying; 王海英 ; **Wáng Hǎiyīng (1976-)**
• Employment: College of Life Science, Shandong Normal University（山东师范大学生命科学学院）
• Research interest: Fungi
• Affiliation: SDNU
• Location of specimens: SDNU

Wang, Han Chen; 王汉臣 ; **Wáng Hànchén**; 王漢臣
• Location of specimens: KUN, PE

Wang, Heng; 王恒 ; **Wáng Héng**; 王恆 **(1934-)**
• Research interest: Plants of Hebei
• Affiliation: IMM

Wang, Hong Bing; 王红兵 ; **Wáng Hóngbīng (1951-)**
• Research interest: Scientific Illustrator
• Affiliation: SWFC
• Location of specimens: SWFC

Wang, Hong Qing; 王宏庆 ; **Wáng Hóngqìng**
• Location of specimens: GXFI

H. W. Wang

Wang, Hong Wei; 王宏伟 ; Wáng Hóngwěi (1963-)
• Employment: School of Life Science, Liaoning Normal University（辽宁师范大学生命科学学院）
• Research interest: Algae
• Affiliation: LNNU
• Location of specimens: LNNU

Wang, Hong; 王虹 ; Wáng Hóng (1962-)
• Research interest: Plant Anatomy
• Affiliation: XJU
• Location of specimens: XJU

Wang, Hong Ye; 王洪业 ; Wáng Hóngyè
• Location of specimens: CCNU

Wang, Hong Bin; 王鸿斌 ; Wáng Hóngbīn
• Affiliation: CAF

Wang, Huan; 王欢 ; Wáng Huān (1978-)
• Research interest: Plants of Changbai Mountain
• Affiliation: JLFC
• Location of specimens: JLFC

Wang, Huan; 王桓 ; Wáng Huán
• Location of specimens: IMD

Wang, Huan Xing; 王焕星 ; Wáng Huànxīng; 王煥星 (1935-)
• Research interest: Medicinal Plants
• Affiliation: GDMP

Wang, Hui; 王晖 ; Wáng Huī (1974-)
• Research interest: Plants of Anhui
• Affiliation: ANUB

Wang, Hui Ling; 王惠玲 ; Wáng Huìlíng (1962-)
• Research interest: Biodiversity
• Affiliation: TYNUB
• Location of specimens: TYNUB

Wang, Ji Feng; 王继丰 ; Wáng Jìfēng (1980-)
• Research interest: Plants of N. E. China
• Affiliation: HNR
• Location of specimens: HNR

Wang, Jia Sheng; 王佳胜 ; Wáng Jiāshèng
• Location of specimens: NAU

Wang, Jian Shu; 王建书 ; Wáng Jiànshū (1962-)
• Affiliation: HBAUD
• Location of specimens: HBAUD

Jian Wang bis

Wang, Jian; 王健 ; Wáng Jiàn (1980-)
• Employment: School of Life Sciences, East China Normal University（华东师范大学生命科学学院）
• Research interest: Bryophyte
• Affiliation: HSNU

Wang, Jian Jun; 王鉴钧 ; Wáng Jiànjūn
• Location of specimens: GXMI

Wang, Jiang Lin; 王江林 ; Wáng Jiānglín (1938-)
• Location of specimens: LBG

Wang, Jin Ao; 王金鳌 ; Wáng Jīn'áo
• Location of specimens: CDBI

Wang, Jin Feng; 王金凤 ; Wáng Jīnfèng; 王金鳳 (1940-)
• Research interest: Scientific Illustrator
• Affiliation: PE

Wang, Jin Ping; 王金平 ; Wáng Jīnpíng (1962-)
• Research interest: Ranunculaceae
• Affiliation: XYTC
• Location of specimens: XYTC

Wang, Jin Sheng; 王金生 ; Wáng Jīnshēng (1935-)
• Affiliation: QF
• Location of specimens: QF

Wang, Chin Ting; Wang, Jin Ting; Wang, Chin T'ing; **王金亭 ; Wáng Jīntíng (1932-)**
• Location of specimens: PE

Wang, Jin Wei; 王金维 ; Wáng Jīnwéi
• Location of specimens: HBNU

Wang, Jin Xiu; 王锦秀 ; Wáng Jǐnxiù (1975-)
• Research interest: Ethnobotany
• Affiliation: PE

Wang, Jing; 王晶 ; Wáng Jīng (1977-)
• Research interest: Campanulaceae, Ranunculaceae
• Affiliation: SYPC
• Location of specimens: SYPC

Wang, Jing Yi; 王景义 ; Wáng Jǐngyì; 王景義 (1936-)
• Research interest: Brassicaceae
• Affiliation: IVF

Wang, Jing; 王静 ; Wáng Jìng
• Location of specimens: HLCM

Wang, Jing; 王静 ; Wáng Jìng (1978-)
• Research interest: Plant Systematics

• Affiliation: HENU
• Location of specimens: HENU

Wang, Jun Hao; 王俊浩 ; **Wáng Jùnhào (1963-)**
• Research interest: Plants of Dinghushan
• Affiliation: IBSD

Wang, Jun Hua; 王俊华 ; **Wáng Jùnhuá**
• Location of specimens: IMC

Wang, Chun Neng; 王俊能 ; **Wáng Jùnnéng (1968-)**
• Research interest: Plant Systematics
• Affiliation: TAI

Wang, Kang Man; 王康满 ; **Wáng Kāngmǎn**
• Affiliation: QFNU
• Location of specimens: QFNU

Wang, Ke Lie; 王可烈 ; **Wáng Kěliè**
• Location of specimens: DNHM

Wang, Ke Qin; 王克勤 ; **Wáng Kèqín (1942-)**
• Research interest: Crassulaceae
• Affiliation: XJNU
• Location of specimens: XJNU

Wang, Kuan; 王宽 ; **Wáng Kuān**
• Location of specimens: IBK

Wang, Kun Yu; 王昆玉 ; **Wáng Kūnyù**
• Location of specimens: ANTU

Wang, Lei; 王磊 ; **Wáng Lěi (1985-)**
• Research interest: Woody Plants
• Affiliation: GAC, NNA

Wang, Li; 王力 ; **Wáng Lì (1979-)**
• Research interest: Poaceae
• Affiliation: HITBC

Wang, Li Hui; 王立辉 ; **Wáng Lìhuī (1984-)**
• Research interest: Plant Ecology
• Affiliation: XZ

Wang, Li Ming; 王立明 ; **Wáng Lìmíng**
• Location of specimens: MBMCAS

Li S. Wang

Wang, Li Song; 王立松 ; **Wáng Lìsōng (1963-)**
• Employment: Kunming Institute of Botany, Chinese Academy of Sciences（中国科学院昆明植物研究所）
• Research interest: Fungi
• Affiliation: KUN
• Location of specimens: KUN

Wang, Lih Jih; 王立志 ; **Wáng Lìzhì**
• Location of specimens: HAST

Wang, Li; 王丽 ; **Wáng Lì (1963-)**
• Research interest: Plant Anatomy
• Affiliation: BAU

Wang, Li; 王丽 ; **Wáng Lì (1971-)**
• Research interest: Plant Systematics
• Affiliation: SZ

Wang, Li Hong; 王丽红 ; **Wáng Lìhóng (1968-)**
• Affiliation: JMSMC
• Location of specimens: JMSMC

Wang, Li Juan; 王丽娟 ; **Wáng Lìjuān (1967-)**
• Research interest: Araceae
• Affiliation: NEAU

Wang, Liang Xin; 王良信 ; **Wáng Liángxìn (1937-)**
• Research interest: Geraniaceae
• Affiliation: JMSMC
• Location of specimens: JMSMC

Wang, Ling; 王凌 ; **Wáng Líng (1976-)**
• Research interest: Scientific Illustrator
• Affiliation: KUN

L. Y. Wang

Wang, Liu Ying; 王六英 ; **Wáng Liùyīng (1947-)**
• Employment: Inner Mongolia Agricultural University（内蒙古农业大学）
• Research interest: Chenopodiaceae, Cyperaceae
• Affiliation: NMAC. *Flora Innermongolica*

Wang, Man Si; 王满思 ; **Wáng Mǎnsī (1951-)**
• Research interest: Medicinal Plants
• Affiliation: SSMM
• Location of specimens: SSMM

Wang, Mei Hua; 王美华 ; **Wáng Měihuá (1950-)**
• Research interest: Medicinal Plants
• Affiliation: HNCM
• Location of specimens: HNCM

Wang, Meng; 王萌 ; **Wáng Méng (1983-)**
• Research interest: Algae
• Location of specimens: DNHM

Wang, Ming Chuan; 王明川 ; **Wáng Míngchuān (1989-)**
• Research interest: Medicinal Plants
• Affiliation: GYBG
• Location of specimens: GYBG

Wang, Ming Shu; 王明书 ; Wáng Míngshū (1953-)
• Location of specimens: SWCTU

Wang, Ming Zhong; 王明忠 ; Wáng Míngzhōng (1941-)
• Research interest: Actinidiaceae
• Affiliation: SR
• Location of specimens: SR

Wang, Pan Ji; 王磐基 ; Wáng Pánjī (1936-)
• Affiliation: KAI
• Location of specimens: KAI

Wang, Qi; 王琦 ; Wáng Qí
• Research interest: Medicinal Plants
• Affiliation: SDMP

Wang, Qi De; 王启德 ; Wáng Qǐdé
• Affiliation: YNUB

Wang, Qiang; 王强 ; Wáng Qiáng (1973-)
• Research interest: Bryophyte; Pteridophytes
• Affiliation: ZM

Wang, Qing Quan; 王清泉 ; Wáng Qīngquán
• Location of specimens: CDBI

Qing H. Wang

Wang, Qing Hua; 王庆华 ; Wáng Qìnghuá (1982-)
• Employment: Institute of Botany, Chinese Academy of Sciences（中国科学院植物研究所）
• Research interest: Bryophyte
• Affiliation: PE

Wang, Qing Ya; 王庆亚 ; Wáng Qìngyà (1959-)
• Research interest: Plants of E. China
• Affiliation: NAU

Wang, Quan Xi; 王全喜 ; Wáng Quánxǐ (1956-)
• Research interest: Algae
• Affiliation: HANU, SHTU

Wang, Quan Xiu; 王全秀 ; Wáng Quánxiù
• Location of specimens: SHM

Wang, Ren Qing; 王仁卿 ; Wáng Rénqīng (1955-)
• Research interest: Plant Ecology
• Affiliation: JSPC
• Location of specimens: JSPC

Wang, Rong Xiang; 王荣祥 ; Wáng Róngxiáng (1951-)
• Research interest: Medicinal Plants
• Affiliation: LNCM
• Location of specimens: LNCM

Wang, Ruo Gu; 王若谷 ; Wáng Ruògǔ
• Location of specimens: HTC, PE

Wang, San Chi; 王三吉 ; Wáng Sānjí
• Location of specimens: HAST

Wang, Shan Ling; 王善龄 ; Wáng Shànlíng
• Location of specimens: IBK

Wang, Shao Qing; 王少青 ; Wáng Shàoqīng (1963-)
• Affiliation: MBMCAS

Wang, Shi Jin; 王世金 ; Wáng Shìjīn (1927-2015)
• Research interest: Poaceae
• Affiliation: HNWP

Wang, Shou Cheng; 王守正 ; Wáng Shǒuzhèng
• Location of specimens: HAST

Wang, Shou Chuan; 王首川 ; Wáng Shǒuchuān
• Location of specimens: HUIF

Wang, Shu Zhi; 王淑芝 ; Wáng Shūzhī (1965-)
• Research interest: Bryophyte
• Affiliation: SYAU
• Location of specimens: SYAU

Wang, Shu Bo; 王树渤 ; Wáng Shùbó; 王樹渤 (1919-)
• Research interest: Algae
• Affiliation: LNNU
• Location of specimens: LNNU

Wang, S. C.; 王树嘉 ; Wáng Shùjiā; 王樹嘉
• Location of specimens: NAS

Wang, Su; 王素 ; Wáng Sù (1938-)
• Research interest: Fabaceae
• Affiliation: IVF

Wang, Tai Xia; 王太霞 ; Wáng Tàixiá (1964-)
• Affiliation: HENU
• Location of specimens: HENU

Wang, Tian Min; 王添敏 ; Wáng Tiānmǐn (1980-)
• Research interest: Medicinal Plants
• Affiliation: LNCM

Wang, Wei; 王伟 ; Wáng Wěi (1956-)
• Research interest: Plant Systematics
• Affiliation: HIMC

Wong, W. W.; 王伟华 ; Wáng Wěihuá; 王偉華
• Location of specimens: SZ

Wang, Wei Dong; 王卫东 ; **Wáng Wèidōng (1966-)**
• Research interest: Plants of Zhejiang
• Affiliation: ZDC
• Location of specimens: ZDC

Wang, Wei Feng; 王卫锋 ; **Wáng Wèifēng (1985-)**
• Research interest: Plants of Shanxi
• Affiliation: SXAU

W. H. Wang

Wang, Wen He; 王文和 ; **Wáng Wénhé**
• Employment: Shenyang Agricultural University（沈阳农业大学）
• Research interest: Bryophyte
• Affiliation: SYAU
• Location of specimens: SYAU

Wang, Wen Jie; 王文杰 ; **Wáng Wénjié (1974-)**
• Research interest: Woody Plants
• Affiliation: NEFI

Wang, Xi Ping; 王希平 ; **Wáng Xīpíng**
• Location of specimens: ACM

Wang, Xi Yong; 王喜勇 ; **Wáng Xǐyǒng (1978-)**
• Research interest: Chenopodiaceae
• Affiliation: TURP
• Location of specimens: TURP

H. C. Wang

Wang, Hsien Chih; Wang, Xian Zhi; 王先志 ; **Wáng Xiānzhì**
• Employment: Institute of Forestry, Taiwan University（台湾大学森林学研究所）
• Research interest: *Plants of Taiwan. Biosystematical Studies on the Cyatheaceae of Taiwan*

Wang, H. P.; 王献溥 ; **Wáng Xiànpǔ**; 王獻溥 **(1929-2015)**
• Location of specimens: PE

Wang, Hsing Hua; 王相華 ; **Wáng Xiānghuá**; 王相华
• Location of specimens: HAST

Wang, Xiang; 王翔 ; **Wáng Xiáng (1985-)**
• Affiliation: HSIB

X. H. Wang

Wang, Xiang Hua; 王向华 ; **Wáng Xiànghuá (1972-)**
• Employment: Kunming Institute of Botany, Chinese Academy of Sciences（中国科学院昆明植物研究所）
• Research interest: Fungi
• Affiliation: KUN

Wang, Xiao Mei; 王小梅 ; **Wáng Xiǎoméi**
• Affiliation: N

Wang, Xiao Ping; 王小平 ; **Wáng Xiǎopíng**
• Location of specimens: MJS

Wang, Xiao Juan; 王晓娟 ; **Wáng Xiǎojuān (1972-)**
• Research interest: Plant Systematics
• Affiliation: SHM

Wang, Hsiao; Wang, Siao; 王孝 ; **Wáng Xiào**
• Location of specimens: IBSC

Xin Yu Wang

Wang, Xin Yu; 王欣宇 ; **Wáng Xīnyǔ (1984-)**
• Employment: Kunming Institute of Botany, Chinese Academy of Sciences（中国科学院昆明植物研究所）
• Research interest: Fungi
• Affiliation: KUN

Wang, Xin; 王馨 ; **Wáng Xīn (1984-)**
• Research interest: Economic Plants
• Affiliation: CQNM
• Location of specimens: SWCTU

Wang, Xin; 王鑫 ; **Wáng Xīn**
• Location of specimens: SWCTU

Wang, Xing Xing; 王星星 ; **Wáng Xīngxīng (1991-)**
• Research interest: Orchidaceae, Ranunculaceae
• Affiliation: BZCM

Wang, Xing Hua; 王兴华 ; **Wáng Xìnghuá**; 王興華 **(1934-)**
• Research interest: Algae
• Affiliation: HENU
• Location of specimens: HENU

Wang, Xu Hong; 王旭红 ; **Wáng Xùhóng (1964-)**
• Research interest: Medicinal Plants
• Affiliation: CPU

Wang, Xue Hong; 王雪宏 ; **Wáng Xuěhóng (1983-)**
• Research interest: Plant Ecology
• Affiliation: IGA

Wang, Ya Jun; 王亚俊 ; **Wáng Yàjùn**; 王亞俊 **(1936-)**
• Location of specimens: BJM

Wang, Ya Zhou; 王亚洲 ; **Wáng Yàzhōu**
• Location of specimens: WNU

Wang, Yan; 王彦 ; **Wáng Yàn**; 王彥 **(1942-)**
• Affiliation: SDFI

Wang, Yen Jen; 王彦仁 ; Wáng Yànrén; 王彥仁
• Location of specimens: HAST

Wang, Yei Zeing; Wang, Ye Zhen; 王也珍 ; Wáng Yězhēn (1956-)
• Research interest: Fungi
• Affiliation: TNM
• Location of specimens: TNM

Wang, Yi Feng; 王义凤 ; Wáng Yìfèng; 王義鳳 (1930-)
• Location of specimens: PE

Wang, Yong Chuan; 王永川 ; Wáng Yǒngchuān (1936-)
• Affiliation: SCSG
• Location of specimens: SCSG

Wang, Yong Qiang; 王永强 ; Wáng Yǒngqiáng (1972-)
• Research interest: Algae
• Affiliation: MBMCAS
• Location of specimens: MBMCAS

Wang, Yong Jin; 王勇进 ; Wáng Yǒngjìn (1968-)
• Research interest: Plants of S. China
• Affiliation: SZG
• Location of specimens: SZG

Y. F. Wang

Wang, You Fang; 王幼芳 ; Wáng Yòufāng (1953-)
• Employment: School of Life Sciences, East China Normal University（华东师范大学生命科学学院）
• Research interest: Bryophyte
• Affiliation: HSNU
• Location of specimens: HSNU

Wang, Yu Chao; 王宇超 ; Wáng Yǔchāo (1978-)
• Location of specimens: XBGH

Wang, Yu Min; 王育民 ; Wáng Yùmín (1930-)
• Research interest: Pteridophytes
• Affiliation: GFS
• Location of specimens: GFS

Wang, Yu Guo; 王裕国 ; Wáng Yùguó; 王裕國 (1935-)
• Location of specimens: XBGH

Wang, Yue Wei; 王曰玮 ; Wáng Yuēwěi; 王曰瑋 (1907-1988)
• Location of specimens: HZU

Y. Wang

Wang, Yun; 王云 ; Wáng Yún; 王雲 (1941-)
• Employment: Institute of Applied Ecology, Chinese Academy of Sciences（中国科学院沈阳应用生态研究所）
• Research interest: Fungi
• Affiliation: IFP
• Location of specimens: IFP

Wang, Yun Qiang; 王云强 ; Wáng Yúnqiáng (1974-)
• Research interest: Orchidaceae
• Affiliation: IMDY
• Location of specimens: IMDY

Wang, Yun Xing; 王允兴 ; Wáng Yǔnxìng; 王允興 (1935-)
• Affiliation: SHDC

Wang, Zao An; 王灶安 ; Wáng Zàoān (1930-)
• Research interest: Plant Anatomy
• Affiliation: CCAU
• Location of specimens: CCAU

Wong, T. Y.; 王泽荣 ; Wáng Zéróng; 王澤榮
• Location of specimens: IBSC, PE

Wang, Zhang Huai; 王章淮 ; Wáng Zhānghuái (1935-)
• Research interest: Araliaceae
• Affiliation: HFBG
• Location of specimens: HFBG

Wang, Zheng Wei; 王正伟 ; Wáng Zhèngwěi (1986-)
• Research interest: Biodiversity
• Affiliation: CSH
• Location of specimens: CSH

Wang, Chih Chia; 王志嘉 ; Wáng Zhìjiā
• Location of specimens: HAST

Z. M. Wang

Wang, Zhi Min; 王智敏 ; Wáng Zhìmǐn
• Employment: Baotou Medical College（包头医学院）
• Research interest: Plants of Nei Mongol. *Flora Innermongolica*

Wang, Zhi Min; 王智敏 ; Wáng Zhìmǐn (1936-)
• Research interest: Algae
• Affiliation: HTC
• Location of specimens: HTC

Wang, Zhi Xue; 王志学 ; Wáng Zhìxué (1954-)
• Research interest: Algae
• Affiliation: BJM

Wang, Zhong Hui; 王中会 ; Wáng Zhōnghuì; 王中會 (1936-)
• Research interest: Medicinal Plants
• Affiliation: HECM
• Location of specimens: HECM

Wang, Jong Yuan; 王中原 ; Wáng Zhōngyuán
• Location of specimens: HAST

C. K. Wang

Wang, Chung Kuei; Wang, Chung K'uei; Wang, Zhong Kui; 王忠魁 ; Wáng Zhōngkuí (1922-2016)
• Employment: Department of Life Science, Tunghai University（东海大学生命科学系）
• Research interest: Bryophyte
• Affiliation: TUNG

Wang, Zhong Ming; 王忠明 ; Wáng Zhōngmíng
• Location of specimens: SCSG

Wang, Zhong Tao; 王忠涛 ; Wáng Zhōngtāo (1962-)
• Affiliation: PE

Wang, Zi He; 王子和 ; Wáng Zǐhé
• Location of specimens: SDAU

Wang, Zong Zheng; 王宗正 ; Wáng Zōngzhèng (1937-)
• Research interest: Plants of Shandong
• Affiliation: SDAU
• Location of specimens: SDAU

Wei, Li; 危莉 ; Wēi Lì (1964-)
• Affiliation: GZTM

Wei, Sheng Ying; 巍圣瑛 ; Wēi Shèngyīng
• Location of specimens: WUH

Wei, Chun Qiang; 韦春强 ; Wéi Chūnqiáng (1982-)
• Research interest: Invasive Plants
• Affiliation: IBK

Wei, Jia Fu; 韦家福 ; Wéi Jiāfú (1952-)
• Research interest: Medicinal Plants
• Affiliation: GXDC
• Location of specimens: GXDC

Wei, Li Hui; 韦立辉 ; Wéi Lìhuī
• Location of specimens: IBK

Wei, Mei Qin; 韦梅芹 ; Wéi Méiqín (1963-)
• Research interest: Plants of Qinghai
• Affiliation: QUA

Wei, Ming Qin; 韦明勤 ; Wéi Míngqín
• Location of specimens: GZTM

Wei, Ming Si; 韦明思 ; Wéi Míngsī
• Location of specimens: GXMG

Wei, Qun Hui; 韦群辉 ; Wéi Qúnhuī
• Location of specimens: YNTCM

Wei, Wei; 韦威 ; Wéi Wēi (1981-)
• Research interest: Medicinal Plants
• Affiliation: GXCM
• Location of specimens: GXCM

Y. M. Wei

Wei, Yu Mei; 韦玉梅 ; Wéi Yùméi (1982-)
• Employment: Guangxi Institute of Botany, Chinese Academy of Sciences（广西壮族自治区中国科学院广西植物研究所）
• Research interest: Bryophyte
• Affiliation: IBK

Wei, Zhong Xin; 韦仲新 ; Wéi Zhòngxīn; 韋仲新 (1941-)
• Research interest: Palynology
• Affiliation: KUN

Wei, Ying Fang; 卫莹芳 ; Wèi Yíngfāng; 衛瑩芳 (1945-)
• Research interest: Loranthaceae
• Affiliation: CDCM

Wei, Cheng Lu; 魏成录 ; Wèi Chénglù
• Location of specimens: ANTU

Wei, D. S.; 魏道行 ; Wèi DàoXíng
• Location of specimens: HAST

Wei, Fu Lun; 魏福伦 ; Wèi Fúlún
• Location of specimens: ZY

Wei, Lin Yuan; 魏林源 ; Wèi Línyuán
• Location of specimens: MQ

Wei, Sheng Hua; 魏升华 ; Wèi Shēnghuá (1964-)
• Research interest: Medicinal Plants
• Affiliation: GZTM

Wei, Xue Zhi; 魏学智 ; Wèi Xuézhì
• Research interest: Plants of Shanxi
• Affiliation: LINF
• Location of specimens: LINF

Y. X. Wei

Wei, Yin Xin; Wei, Yin Shin; 魏印心 ; Wèi Yìnxīn (1939-)
• Employment: Institute of Hydrobiology, Chinese Academy of Sciences（中国科学院水生生物研究所）
• Research interest: Algae
• Affiliation: HBI
• Location of specimens: HBI

Y. L. Wei

Wei, Yu Lian; 魏玉莲 ; Wèi Yùlián (1975-)
• Employment: Institute of Applied Ecology, Chinese Academy of Sciences（中国科学院沈阳应用生态研究所）
• Research interest: Fungi
• Affiliation: IFP
• Location of specimens: IFP

Wen, Jie; 温洁 ; Wēn Jié
• Location of specimens: PE

Wen, Jun Da; 温俊达 ; Wēn Jùndá (1950-)
• Research interest: Medicinal Plants
• Affiliation: HUTM
• Location of specimens: HUTM

Wen, H. P.; 温歇平 ; Wēn Xiēpíng; 溫歇平

Wen, Yuan Guang; 温远光 ; Wēn Yuǎnguāng (1957-)
• Research interest: Forest Ecology
• Affiliation: GAC
• Location of specimens: IBSC

Wen, Zhi Guo; 温志国 ; Wēn Zhìguó
• Research interest: Forest Ecology
• Affiliation: YAK
• Location of specimens: YAK

Wen, Shao Kang; 文绍康 ; Wén Shàokāng
• Location of specimens: KUN

Wen, Xue Mei; 文雪梅 ; Wén Xuěméi (1982-)
• Research interest: Fungi
• Affiliation: XZ
• Location of specimens: XZ

Wen, Zhi Bin; 闻志彬 ; Wén Zhìbīn (1982-)
• Research interest: Plant Systematics
• Affiliation: XJBI

Weng, Mao Lun; 翁茂倫 ; Wēng Màolún; 翁茂伦
• Location of specimens: HAST

Weng, Ruo Fen; 翁若芬 ; Wēng Ruòfēn
• Location of specimens: SHM

Weng, Yu Fang; 翁玉芳 ; Wēng Yùfāng (1934-)
• Research interest: Geraniaceae
• Affiliation: GLMC
• Location of specimens: GLMC

Wolong Exped.; 卧龙自然保护区考察队 ; Wòlóng Zìránbǎohùqū Kǎocháduì
• Location of specimens: WL. Collection Team

Wuyun; 乌云 ; Wūyún; 烏雲 (1941-)
• Affiliation: FGC

Wu, Wen Xiang; Wu, Wen Hsiang; 邬文祥 ; Wū Wénxiáng; 鄔文祥 ; (?-2010)
• Location of specimens: NAS

Wu, Hui Min; 巫惠民 ; Wū Huìmín (1935-)
• Affiliation: GXNM

Wu, King Cheng; 巫金城 ; Wū Jīnchéng
• Location of specimens: HAST

Wu, Bao Cheng; 吳宝成 ; Wú Bǎochéng; 吴宝成
• Location of specimens: HAST

Wu, Da Cheng; 吴大诚 ; Wú Dàchéng; 吳大誠 (1940-)
• Research interest: Annonaceae, Combretaceae
• Affiliation: GNA
• Location of specimens: GNA

Wu, Feng; 吴丰 ; Wú Fēng (1963-)
• Research interest: Medicinal Plants
• Affiliation: IMM

G. Wu

Wu, Gang; 吴刚 ; Wú Gāng (1987-)
• Employment: Kunming Institute of Botany, Chinese Academy of Sciences（中国科学院昆明植物研究所）
• Research interest: Fungi
• Affiliation: KUN

Wu, Guang Biao; 吴广彪 ; Wú Guǎngbiāo (1962-)
• Affiliation: YF
• Location of specimens: YF

Wu, Gui Hua; 吴贵华 ; Wú Guìhuá (1955-)
• Research interest: Medicinal Plants
• Affiliation: TJDC
• Location of specimens: TJDC

Wu, Hai Long; 吴海龙 ; Wú Hǎilóng
• Affiliation: ANUB

Wu, Hai Peng; 吴海鹏 ; Wú Hǎipéng; 吳海鵬 (1938-)
• Research interest: Medicinal Plants
• Affiliation: CPB

J. N. Wu

Wu, Ji Nong; 吴继农 ; Wú Jìnóng; 吳繼農 (1922-1999)
• Employment: Department of Biology, Nanjing Normal University（南京师范大学生物系）

• Research interest: Fungi
• Affiliation: NJNU
• Location of specimens: NJNU

Wu, C. C.; 吳家進 ; Wú Jiājìn; 吴家进
• Location of specimens: HAST

Wu, Jia Qi; 吴家其 ; Wú Jiāqí; 吳家其 (1932-)
• Location of specimens: GZTM

Wu, Jian Fu; 吴建福 ; Wú Jiànfú (1963-)
• Affiliation: GAFS
• Location of specimens: GAFS

Wu, Jin Ling; 吴金陵 ; Wú Jīnlíng; 吳金陵 (1937-)
• Research interest: Fungi
• Affiliation: WUK
• Location of specimens: WUK

Wu, Chin Hsiung; 吳錦雄 ; Wú Jǐnxióng; 吴锦雄
• Location of specimens: HAST

Wu, Jing Min; 吴京民 ; Wú Jīngmín
• Affiliation: HBFC

Wu, Jing Ni; 吴静妮 ; Wú Jìngnī (1962-)
• Research interest: Plants of Jiangxi
• Affiliation: JCE
• Location of specimens: JCE

Wu, Chun Chi; 吳俊奇 ; Wú Jùnqí; 吴俊奇
• Location of specimens: HAST

Wu, Kai; 吴凯 ; Wú Kǎi (1980-)
• Research interest: Rosaceae
• Affiliation: YNTCM

Wu, Ke Min; 吴克民 ; Wú Kèmín
• Location of specimens: IBSC

Wu, Ke Ru; 吴克儒 ; Wú Kèrú
• Location of specimens: FJFC

Wu, Liang Hung; 吳亮宏 ; Wú Liànghóng; 吴亮宏
• Location of specimens: HAST

Wu, Lu Zhong; 吴履中 ; Wú Lǚzhōng; 吳履中 (1925-)
• Research interest: Medicinal Plants
• Affiliation: SDMP

Wu, Ming Yu; 吴明煜 ; Wú Míngyù (1977-)
• Research interest: Grassland Plants
• Affiliation: EU

P. C. Wu

Wu, Pan Cheng; Wu, Pang Cheng; Wu, Peng Cheng; 吴鹏程 ; Wú Péngchéng; 吳鵬程 (1935-)
• Employment: Institute of Botany, Chinese Academy of Sciences（中国科学院植物研究所）
• Research interest: Bryophyte
• Affiliation: PE
• Location of specimens: PE

Wu, Ki; 吴岐 ; Wú Qí
• Location of specimens: IBSC

Wu, Qi; 吴琪 ; Wú Qí (1987-)
• Research interest: Medicinal Plants
• Affiliation: CPU

Wu, Qing Yu; 吴庆余 ; Wú Qìngyú (1955-)
• Research interest: Algae
• Affiliation: N

Wu, Chiu Yen; 吳秋燕 ; Wú Qiūyàn; 吴秋燕
• Location of specimens: HAST

Wu, Ren Run; 吴仁润 ; Wú Rénrùn; 吳仁潤 (1915-2000)
• Research interest: Grass
• Affiliation: LZAH
• Location of specimens: LZAH

Wu, S. T.; Ng, S. T.; 吴瑞庭 ; Wú Ruìtíng; 吳瑞庭
• Location of specimens: IBSC

Wu, Shan Huah; 吳姍樺 ; Wú Shānhuà; 吴姗桦
• Location of specimens: HAST

Sheng H. Wu

Wu, Sheng Hua; 吳聲華 ; Wú Shēnghuá; 吴声华 (1961-)
• Employment: "National" Museum of Natural Science（"國立"自然科学博物馆）
• Research interest: Bryophyte, Fungi
• Affiliation: TNM
• Location of specimens: TNM

Wu, Sheng Chieh; 吳聖傑 ; Wú Shèngjié; 吴圣杰
• Location of specimens: HAST

Ng, Chung Lam; 吴松林 ; Wú Sōnglín; 吳松林
• Location of specimens: SYS

Wu, Tao; 吴涛 ; Wú Tāo
• Location of specimens: HLCM

Wu, Tian Xiang; 吴天香 ; Wú Tiānxiāng; 吳天香 (1941-)
• Affiliation: YF

Wu, Ting Jun; 吴廷俊 ; **Wú Tíngjùn**; 吳廷俊 **(1938-)**
- Research interest: Stemonaceae
- Affiliation: WCU
- Location of specimens: WCU

Wu, Wei Chun; 吴维春 ; **Wú Wéichūn**; 吳維春 **(1940-2013)**
- Research interest: Crassulaceae
- Affiliation: SYPC

Wu, Wei Hsiu; 吳維修 ; **Wú Wéixiū**; 吴维修
- Research interest: Plants of Taiwan
- Affiliation: TAIF

Wu, Wen Juan; 吴文娟 ; **Wú Wénjuān (1948-)**
- Location of specimens: TJMP

Wu, Xi Ling; 吴锡麟 ; **Wú Xīlín (1955-)**
- Research interest: Scientific Illustrator
- Affiliation: KUN

Wu, Xian Kun; 吴显坤 ; **Wú Xiǎnkūn (1981-)**
- Affiliation: NFP

Wu, Hsin Kan; 吳信淦 ; **Wú Xìngàn**; 吴信淦
- Location of specimens: HAST

Wu, Xiu Ren; 吴修仁 ; **Wú Xiūrén**; 吳修仁 **(1932-1996)**
- Research interest: Medicinal Plants
- Affiliation: CZH
- Location of specimens: CZH

Wu, Xiu Ju; 吴秀菊 ; **Wú Xiùjú (1972-)**
- Research interest: Brassicaceae
- Affiliation: NEAU

Wu, Xue Liang; 吴学良 ; **Wú Xuéliáng**
- Location of specimens: NFP

Wu, Ying; 吴莹 ; **Wú Yíng (1987-)**
- Research interest: Medicinal Plants
- Affiliation: LNCM

Wu, Yong Bin; 吴永彬 ; **Wú Yǒngbīn (1972-)**
- Research interest: Plants of Guangdong
- Affiliation: CANT
- Location of specimens: CANT

Wu, Yong Zhong; 吴永忠 ; **Wú Yǒngzhōng (1964-)**
- Research interest: Medicinal Plants
- Affiliation: JXM
- Location of specimens: JXM

Wu, You Chang; 吴有昌 ; **Wú Yǒuchāng**
- Affiliation: HFB

Y. Huan Wu

Wu, Yu Huan; 吴玉环 ; **Wú Yùhuán (1972-)**
- Employment: College of Life and Environmental Sciences, Hangzhou Normal University（杭州师范大学生命与环境科学学院）
- Research interest: Bryophyte
- Affiliation: HTC

Wu, Yu Hua; 吴育华 ; **Wú Yùhuá (1953-)**
- Research interest: Pteridophytes
- Affiliation: JCE
- Location of specimens: JCE

Wu, Zhang Hua; 吴彰桦 ; **Wú Zhānghuà**; 吳彰樺 **(1933-)**
- Research interest: Scientific Illustrator
- Affiliation: PE

Wu, J. S.; 吴志昇 ; **Wú Zhìshēng**; 吴志升
- Location of specimens: HAST

Wu, Zhong Fa; 吴忠发 ; **Wú Zhōngfā (1963-)**
- Research interest: Medicinal Plants
- Affiliation: GXMG

C. L. Wu

Wu, Chung Luen; Wu, Chung Lwen; Wu, Chung Lun; Wu, Zhong Lun; 吴中伦 ; **Wú Zhōnglún**; 吳中倫 **(1913-1995)**
- Employment: Chinese Academy of Forestry（中国林业科学研究院）
- Research interest: Gymnospermae
- Affiliation: CAF
- Location of specimens: CAF, NF

Wu, Zu Fa; 吴祖发 ; **Wú Zǔfā**; 吳祖發 **(1938-)**
- Research interest: Magnoliceae
- Affiliation: ACM
- Location of specimens: ACM

Wu, Pei Huang; 伍培煌 ; **Wǔ Péihuáng**
- Location of specimens: HAST

Wu, Shu Hui; 伍淑惠 ; **Wǔ Shūhuì**
- Research interest: Plant Ecology
- Affiliation: TAIF

Wu, Bao Cheng; 武宝成 ; **Wǔ Bǎochéng (1955-)**
- Research interest: Fabaceae, Poaceae
- Affiliation: FGC
- Location of specimens: FGC

Wu, Jia Geng; 武嘉庚 ; Wǔ Jiāgēng (1980-)
• Research interest: Medicinal Plants
• Affiliation: QDC

Wulingshan Exped.; 武陵山考察队 ; Wǔ língshān Kǎochádui
• Location of specimens: HIB, PE. Collection Team

Wu, Chuan An; Wu, Quan An; 武全安 ; Wǔ Quán'ān (1934-)
• Location of specimens: KUN

Wu, Hsiao Kung; 武孝功 ; Wǔ Xiàogōng
• Location of specimens: HAST

Wu, Yun; 武芸 ; Wǔ Yún
• Location of specimens: ENS

X (H,S,T)

Xizang Exped.; 西藏队 ; Xīzàng Duì
• Location of specimens: PE. Collection Team

XZ Pl. Res. Exped.; 西藏生物所植物资源队 ; Xīzàng Shēngwùsuǒ Zhíwù Zīyuán Duì
• Location of specimens: XZ. Collection Team

Xizang Herb. Med. Exped.; 西藏中草药普查队 ; Xīzàng Zhōngcǎoyào Pǔchádui
• Location of specimens: PE. Collection Team

Lianda Exped.; 西南联大队 ; Xīnán Liándà Duì
• Location of specimens: KUN. Collection Team

Xishuangbanna Med. Pl. Exped.; 西双版纳中药资源普查队 ; Xīshuāngbǎnnà Zhōngyào Zīyuán Pǔ cháduì
• Location of specimens: IMDY. Collection Team

Xishuangbanna Nat. Res. Exped.; 西双版纳自然保护区采集队 ; Xīshuāngbǎnnà Zìrán Bǎohùqū Cǎijíduì
• Location of specimens: HITBC. Collection Team

WUK Xinjiang Exped.; 西植新疆队 ; Xīzhí Xīnjiāng Duì
• Location of specimens: WUK. Collection Team

Xi, Xiang Ai; 席湘媛 ; Xí Xiāng'ài; 席湘嫒 (1930-)
• Location of specimens: SDAU

Xi, Yi Zhe; 席以珍 ; Xí Yǐzhēn (1935-)
• Location of specimens: PE

Xia, Bang Mei; 夏邦美 ; Xià Bāngměi (1934-)
• Research interest: Algae
• Affiliation: MBMCAS
• Location of specimens: MBMCAS

E. Z. Xia

Xia, En Zhan; 夏恩湛 ; Xià Ēnzhàn (1930-2012)
• Employment: Institute of Oceanology, Chinese Academy of Sciences (中国科学院海洋研究所)
• Research interest: Algae
• Affiliation: MBMCAS
• Location of specimens: MBMCAS

Xia, Fu Cai; 夏富才 ; Xià Fùcái (1973-)
• Research interest: Plants of Jilin
• Affiliation: JLFC
• Location of specimens: JLFC

Xia, Jiang Lin; 夏江林 ; Xià Jiānglín (1968-)
• Research interest: Plants of Nanyue
• Affiliation: NYA
• Location of specimens: NYA

Xia, Min Sheng; 夏民生 ; Xià Mínshēng (1929-)
• Research interest: Weeds
• Affiliation: GAUA
• Location of specimens: GAUA

Xia, Xiao Fei; 夏晓飞 ; Xià Xiǎofēi (1983-)
• Research interest: Asteraceae
• Affiliation: BJM

Xia, Zhi Jun; 夏志俊 ; Xià Zhìjùn (1963-)
• Research interest: Medicinal Plants
• Affiliation: ZJMA

Xia, Zun Cheng; 夏尊成 ; Xià Zūnchéng (1932-)
• Research interest: Medicinal Plants
• Affiliation: GXDC

Xiang, Gui Quan; 相桂权 ; Xiāng Guìquán (1960-)
• Affiliation: NENU

Xiang, Gang; 向刚 ; Xiàng Gāng (1976-)
• Research interest: Plant Ecology
• Affiliation: GNUG
• Location of specimens: GNUG

Xiang, Yan Ci; 向言词 ; Xiàng Yáncí (1969-)
• Research interest: Plant Ecology
• Affiliation: HUST

Xiao, Bang Sen; 肖邦森 ; Xiāo Bāngsēn
• Location of specimens: ATCH

Xiao, Du Zhi; 肖笃志 ; Xiào Dǔzhì; 蕭篤志 (1936-)
• Location of specimens: XJBI

Xiao, Guo Ping; 肖国平 ; Xiào Guópíng (1961-)
• Research interest: Fungi
• Affiliation: KUN

Xiao, Hong Bin; 肖洪彬 ; Xiào Hóngbīn
• Affiliation: HLCM

Xiao, Jia; 肖加 ; Xiào Jiā
• Location of specimens: HAF

Xiao, Jia Geng; 肖家庚 ; Xiào Jiāgēng
• Location of specimens: CSFI

Xiao, Ming; 肖鸣 ; Xiào Míng (1963-)
• Research interest: Medicinal Plants
• Affiliation: JXM
• Location of specimens: JXM

Xiao, Sa; 肖洒 ; Xiào Sǎ (1985-)
• Affiliation: HNWP

S. C. Xiao

Xiao, Shun Chung; 肖顺昌 ; Xiào Shùnchāng
• Employment: Chengdu Institute of Biology, Chinese Academy of Sciences（中国科学院成都生物研究所）
• Research interest: Plants of Sichuan
• Affiliation: CDBI
Flora sichuanica

Xiao, Wen Fa; 肖文发 ; Xiào Wénfā (1964-)
• Research interest: Forest Ecology
• Affiliation: CAF

Xiao, Xin Nan; 肖心楠 ; Xiào Xīnnán (1930-)
• Research interest: Caryophyllaceae, Fabaceae
• Affiliation: GACP
• Location of specimens: GACP

Xiao, Ya Ping; 肖娅萍 ; Xiào Yàpíng (1956-)
• Research interest: Bryophyte; Pteridophytes
• Affiliation: SANU

Xiao, Yu Tan; 肖育檀 ; Xiào Yùtán; 蕭育檀 (1938-)
• Research interest: Plants of Hunan
• Affiliation: CSFI
• Location of specimens: CSFI

Xiao, Yun Feng; 肖运峰 ; Xiào Yùnfēng; 肖云峰 , 萧运峰 ; 蕭運峰 (1938-)
• Location of specimens: AIB, IBSC, PE

Xiao, Bai Zhong; 蕭百中 ; Xiāo Bǎizhòng; 萧百中
• Location of specimens: HAST

Hsiao, C. B.; 蕭成炳 ; Xiāo Chéngbǐng; 萧成炳
• Location of specimens: HAST

Shiau, Hwei Jun; 蕭慧君 ; Xiāo Huìjūn; 萧慧君
• Location of specimens: HAST

J. Y. Hsiao

Hsiao, Ju Ying; Xiao, Ru Ying; 蕭如英 ; Xiāo Rúyīng; 萧如英 ; 肖如英
• Employment: Herbarium, Department of Botany, Chung Hsing University（中兴大学植物系标本室）
• Research interest: Plants of Taiwan
• Affiliation: TCB

Hsiao, Shu Pi; 蕭淑碧 ; Xiāo Shūbì; 萧淑碧
• Location of specimens: HAST

Hsiao, Shu Chan; 蕭淑娟 ; Xiāo Shūjuān; 萧淑娟
• Location of specimens: NCKU

A. T. Hsieh

Hsieh, A.Tsai; 謝阿才 ; Xiè Ācái; 谢阿才
• Employment: Taiwan Forestry Research Institute, Taiwan Provincial Administrative Office（台湾省政府农林厅林业试验所）
• Research interest: Plants of Taiwan. 台湾兰科植物目录 ; 台湾府志录植物名汇

Xie, Ai Fang; 谢爱芳 ; Xiè Àifāng (1981-)
• Affiliation: SABG

B. G. Xie

Xie, Bao Gui; 谢宝贵 ; Xiè Bǎoguì; 謝寶貴 (1934-)
• Employment: College of Agriculture, Guangxi University（广西大学农学院）
• Research interest: Algae
• Affiliation: GAUA
• Location of specimens: GAUA

Xie, Chao Jun; 谢朝俊 ; Xiè Cháojùn
• Location of specimens: SCFI

Xie, Cheng Zhang; Hsieh, Cheng Chang; 谢成章 ; Xiè Chéngzhāng; 謝成章 (1916-)

• Research interest: Poaceae
• Affiliation: CCAU
• Location of specimens: CCAU

Xie, Da Jun; 谢大军 ; Xiè Dàjūn (1978-)
• Research interest: Woody Plants
• Affiliation: SCFI

Xie, De Ci; 谢德慈 ; Xiè Décí; 謝德慈 (1932-)
• Research interest: Fungi
• Affiliation: SITC
• Location of specimens: SITC

Xie, De Rong; 谢德镕 ; Xiè Déróng; 謝德鎔 (1932-)
• Research interest: Plants of Hanzhong
• Affiliation: HZTC
• Location of specimens: HZTC

Xie, De Wen; 谢德文 ; Xiè Déwén; 謝德文 (1935-)
• Research interest: Ebenaceae, Fabaceae
• Affiliation: GACP
• Location of specimens: GACP

Hsieh, F. H.; 谢福惠 ; Xiè Fúhuì; 謝福惠 (1915-)
• Location of specimens: IBK

Hsieh, Guang Pu; 謝光普 ; Xiè Guāngpǔ; 谢光普
• Location of specimens: HAST

Xie, Hua; 谢华 ; Xiè Huá (1954-)
• Research interest: Moraceae
• Affiliation: HGAS

Xie, Huan Song; 谢焕松 ; Xiè Huànsōng
• Research interest: Plants of Nantong
• Affiliation: NAN
• Location of specimens: NAN

Xie, Hui; 谢晖 ; Xiè Huī (1976-)
• Research interest: Apiaceae
• Affiliation: SHMU

Xie, Hui An; 谢惠安 ; Xiè Huì'ān
• Location of specimens: ANU

Xie, Ming; 谢明 ; Xiè Míng (1962-)
• Research interest: Medicinal Plants
• Affiliation: LNCM
• Location of specimens: LNCM

Xie, Pei De; 谢培德 ; Xiè Péidé (1963-)
• Research interest: Medicinal Plants
• Affiliation: GXDC

Tsa, K. P.; 谢其炳 ; Xiè Qíbǐng; 謝其炳
• Location of specimens: IBSC

Xie, Qiang; 谢强 ; Xiè Qiáng
• Affiliation: GUN
• Location of specimens: GUN

Xie, Qing Hong; 谢庆红 ; Xiè Qìnghóng (1966-)
• Research interest: Plants of Jiulianshan
• Affiliation: JNR
• Location of specimens: JNR

Xie, Qing Shu; 谢庆书 ; Xiè Qìngshū
• Location of specimens: ZY

Hsieh, Shang Hui; 謝尚慧 ; Xiè Shànghuì; 谢尚慧
• Location of specimens: HAST

S. L. Xie

Xie, Shu Lian; 谢树莲 ; Xiè Shùlián (1962-)
• Employment: School of Life Science, Shanxi University（山西大学生命科学学院）
• **Research interest: Algae; Bryophyte; Pteridophytes**
• **Affiliation: SXU**
• Location of specimens: SXU

Xie, Shuang Xi; 谢双喜 ; Xiè Shuāngxǐ
• Location of specimens: GZAC

Hsieh, Wan Lun; 謝宛倫 ; Xiè Wǎnlún; 谢宛伦
• Location of specimens: CHIA

Xie, Yi Lin; 谢义林 ; Xiè Yìlín (1963-)
• Research interest: Plants of Guangxi
• Affiliation: GAUA
• Location of specimens: GAUA

Xie, Zao Yun; 谢早云 ; Xiè Zǎoyún
• Location of specimens: NYA

Xie, Zhao Ming; 谢昭明 ; Xiè Zhāomíng (1962-)
• Research interest: Medicinal Plants
• Affiliation: HUTM

Xie, Zheng Kuan; 谢正宽 ; Xiè Zhèngkuān (1965-)
• Research interest: Algae
• Affiliation: N

Xie, Zhi Xi; 谢支锡 ; Xiè Zhīxī; 謝支錫 (1939-)
• Location of specimens: IFP

Xie, Zhi Jun; 谢志钧 ; Xiè Zhìjūn; 謝志鈞 (1926-)
• Research interest: Plants of Yunnan
• Affiliation: YNUB

• Location of specimens: YNUB

Xie, Chuan Jie; 解传杰 ; Xiè Chuánjié (1968-)
• Affiliation: YBDC

Xie, Dong; 解冬 ; Xiè Dōng (1961-)
• Research interest: Bryophyte
• Affiliation: SCNU
• Location of specimens: SCNU

Xie, Xin Ming; 解新明 ; Xiè Xīnmíng (1963-)
• Research interest: Poaceae
• Affiliation: NMTC
• Location of specimens: NMTC

Xin, Hai Liang; 辛海量 ; Xīn Hǎiliàng
• Research interest: Medicinal Plants
• Affiliation: SMMU-BH

Hsin, Shu Chih; Hsin, Shu Ch'ih; Sin, S. S.; Xin, Shu Zhi; 辛树帜 ; Xīn Shùzhì; 辛樹幟 (1894-1977)
• Location of specimens: IBSC

Xin, Xiao Gui; 辛孝贵 ; Xīn Xiàoguì; 辛孝貴 (1940-)
• Research interest: Economic Plants
• Affiliation: SYAU
• Location of specimens: SYAU

Xing, Yi Qun; 辛益群 ; Xīn Yìqún (1954-)
• Research interest: Ulmaceae
• Affiliation: JSPC

Xin, You Jun; 辛有俊 ; Xīn Yǒujùn
• Location of specimens: QG

Xinjiang Exped.; 新疆综合考察队 ; Xīnjiāng Zònghé Kǎochádùi
• Location of specimens: PE, XJBI. Collection Team

Xing, Jian Guo; 邢建国 ; Xíng Jiànguó
• Location of specimens: XM

Xing, Qi Hua; 邢其华 ; Xíng Qíhuá; 邢其華 (1921-1995)
• Research interest: Plant Geography
• Affiliation: BNU

Xing, Qi Yan; 邢启妍 ; Xíng Qǐyán; 邢啟妍 (1926-)
• Location of specimens: NEAU

Xiong, Jie; 熊杰 ; Xióng Jié; 熊傑 (1923-)
• Location of specimens: JN, JXF, LBG

Xiong, Jin Qiao; 熊金桥 ; Xióng Jīnqiáo
• Location of specimens: CCAU

Xiong, Rong Xian; 熊荣先 ; Xióng Róngxiān
• Location of specimens: WCU

R. L. Xiong

Xiong, Ruo Li; 熊若莉 ; Xióng Ruòlì (1928-1985)
• Employment: Department of Biology, Yunnan University（云南大学生物系）
• Research interest: Bryophyte
• Affiliation: YUKU
• Location of specimens: YIM

Xiong, Shu Xiang; 熊述祥 ; Xióng Shùxiáng
• Affiliation: ECM

Xiong, Xing; 熊星 ; Xióng Xīng (1967-)
• Research interest: Asteraceae, Melastomataceae
• Affiliation: IBSC

Hsiung, Yao Kuo; Xiong, Yao Guo; 熊耀国 ; Xióng Yàoguó; 熊耀國 (1910-2004)
• Location of specimens: LBG, NAS, PE

Xiong, Yu Ning; 熊豫宁 ; Xióng Yùníng (1961-)
• Research interest: Plants of E. China
• Affiliation: NAS
• Location of specimens: NAS

Xiong, Zi Xian; 熊子仙 ; Xióng Zixiān (1945-)
• Research interest: Ericaceae
• Affiliation: YNUB

A S. Xu

Xu, A Sheng; 徐阿生 ; Xú Āshēng (1967-)
• Employment: Xizang Agriculture and Animal Husbandry College（西藏农牧学院）
• Research interest: Fungi
• Affiliation: XZE
• Location of specimens: XZE

Xu, Ai Ju; 徐爱菊 ; Xú Àijú; 徐愛菊 (1935-)
• Affiliation: LNNU

Hsu, Tsang Yuan; 徐滄源 ; Xú Cāngyuán; 徐沧源
• Location of specimens: HAST

C. Xu

Xu, Chang; 徐嫦 ; Xú Cháng (1931-)
• Employment: Inner Mongolia Institute for Drug Control（内蒙古药品检验所）
• Research interest: Plants of Nei Mongol
Flora Innermongolica

Xu, Cun Bo; 徐春波 ; Xú Chūnbō (1979-)
• Research interest: Fabaceae

• Affiliation: FGC

Xu, Cui Xin; 徐粹新 ; Xú Cuìxīn (1932-)
• Research interest: Plants of Henan
• Affiliation: HENU
• Location of specimens: KAI, HENU

Tsui, T. M.; 徐德明 ; Xú Démíng
• Location of specimens: KUN

Hsu, D. S.; 徐德生 ; Xú Déshēng
• Location of specimens: HAST

Xu, Fa Li; 徐法礼 ; Xú Fǎlǐ
• Location of specimens: MBMCAS

Xu, Guang Yuan; 徐光远 ; Xú Guāngyuǎn; 徐光遠 (1934-)
• Location of specimens: YL

Xu, Guo Jing; 徐国经 ; Xú Guójīng (1952-)
• Research interest: Medicinal Plants
• Affiliation: JLMP
• Location of specimens: JLMP

Xu, Hai Yan; 徐海燕 ; Xú Hǎiyàn (1980-)
• Research interest: Medicinal Plants
• Affiliation: XM
• Location of specimens: XM

Xu, Han Qing; 徐汉卿 ; Xú Hànqīng; 徐漢卿 (1928-1998)
• Research interest: Plants of E. China
• Affiliation: NAU
• Location of specimens: NAU

Xu, Ji Min; 徐纪民 ; Xú Jìmín
• Research interest: Medicinal Plants
• Affiliation: CPB
• Location of specimens: CPB

Hsu, Chia Chun; 徐嘉君 ; Xú Jiājūn
• Location of specimens: HAST

Xu, Jie; 徐杰 ; Xú Jié (1969-)
• Research interest: Bryophyte
• Affiliation: NMTC
• Location of specimens: NMTC

Xu, Jing Xian; 徐景先 ; Xú Jǐngxiān (1974-)
• Research interest: Palynology
• Affiliation: BJM

Xu, Ke Xue; 徐克学 ; Xú Kèxué; 徐克學 (1937-)
• Research interest: Plant Systematics
• Affiliation: PE

Lei Xu

Xu, Lei; 徐蕾 ; Xú Lěi (1970-)
• Employment: Shanghai Natural History Museum (Branch of Shanghai Science & Technology Museum) (上海自然博物馆(上海科技馆分馆))
• Research interest: Fungi
• Affiliation: SHM

Xu, Li Xia; 徐丽霞 ; Xú Lìxiá (1980-)
• Research interest: Medicinal Plants
• Affiliation: SSMM
• Location of specimens: SSMM

Xu, Ling Ling; 徐玲玲 ; Xú Línglíng (1963-)
• Research interest: Lardizablaceae, Ranunculaceae, Urticaceae
• Affiliation: JJT
• Location of specimens: JJT

Xu, Qi Hu; 徐期瑚 ; Xú Qīhú
• Location of specimens: CSFI

Xu, Qing; 徐庆 ; Xú Qìng (1964-)
• Research interest: Forest Ecology
• Affiliation: CAF

Shiu, Chieng Yuen; 徐慶雲 ; Xú Qìngyún; 徐庆云
• Location of specimens: HAST

Xu, Qiu Hua; 徐秋华 ; Xú Qiūhuá
• Research interest: Herbaceous Plants
• Affiliation: ANTU

Hsu, Jen; Hsu, Jên; Xu, Ren; 徐仁 ; Xú Rén (1910-1992)
• Location of specimens: N, PE

Xu, Sheng Xiu; 徐声修 ; Xú Shēngxiū; 徐聲修 (1939-)
• Research interest: Pteridophytes
• Affiliation: JXU
• Location of specimens: JXU

Xu, Shi Xiu; 徐士秀 ; Xú Shìxiù
• Location of specimens: PE

Xu, Shi Song; 徐世松 ; Xú Shìsōng
• Research interest: Woody Plants
• Affiliation: ATCH
• Location of specimens: ATCH

Xu, Wan Rong; 徐琬荣 ; Xú Wǎnróng; 徐琬榮 (1943-)
• Affiliation: LNAF

• Location of specimens: LNAF

Xu, Wen Bin; 徐文斌 ; Xú Wénbīn (1983-)
• Research interest: Plants of Xinjiang
• Affiliation: SHI
• Location of specimens: SHI

W. X. Xu

Xu, Wen Xuan; 徐文宣 ; Xú Wénxuān (1919-1985)
• Employment: Department of Biology, Yunnan University（云南大学生物系）
• Research interest: Bryophyte
• Affiliation: YUKU
• Location of specimens: YUKU

Xu, Xing You; 徐兴友 ; Xú Xīngyǒu (1964-)
• Research interest: Plants of Hebei
• Affiliation: CHA
• Location of specimens: CHA

Xu, Yan Qin; 徐艳琴 ; Xú Yànqín (1980-)
• Research interest: Berberidaceae, Polygalaceae
• Affiliation: JXCM

Xu, Yan Hong; 徐燕红 ; Xú Yànhóng
• Affiliation: NFP

Xu, Ying; 徐莹 ; Xú Yíng
• Location of specimens: SHMI

Xu, Yong Fu; 徐永福 ; Xú Yǒngfú (1979-)
• Research interest: Plants of Hunan
• Affiliation: CSFI
• Location of specimens: CSFI

Xu, Yong Qing; 徐永清 ; Xú Yǒngqīng (1977-)
• Research interest: Violaceae
• Affiliation: NEAU

Xu, You Yuan; 徐友源 ; Xú Yǒuyuán (1937-1987)
• Research interest: Aquifoliaceae, Rhamnaceae
• Affiliation: GZAC
• Location of specimens: FAN, GZAC

Hsu, Yu Fong; 徐堉峰 ; Xú Yùfēng
• Location of specimens: HAST

Hsu, Yueh Pan; 徐月帮 ; Xú Yuèbāng; 徐月幫
• Location of specimens: PE

Xu, Chao Peng; Hsu, Chao Peng; Xu, Zhao Peng; 徐兆鹏 ; Xú Zhàopéng; 徐兆鵬 (1937-)
• Affiliation: HBAUD
• Location of specimens: HBAUD

Xu, Zhi Jie; 徐志杰 ; Xú Zhìjié; 徐志傑 (1935-)
• Research interest: Amaranthaceae
• Affiliation: JXCM
• Location of specimens: JXCM

Xu, Zhi Yuan; 徐志远 ; Xú Zhìyuǎn; 徐志遠 (1932-)
• Research interest: Medicinal Plants
• Affiliation: CCM, JLMP
• Location of specimens: CCM, JLMP

Z. Xu

Xu, Zhu; 徐柱 ; Xú Zhù (1952-2012)
• Employment: Institute of Grassland Research, Chinese Academy of Agricultural Sciences（中国农业科学院草原研究所）
• Research interest: Fabaceae, Poaceae
• Affiliation: FGC
• Location of specimens: FGC. *Flora Innermongolica*

Xu, Chong Jiu; 许重九 ; Xǔ Chóngjiǔ; 許重九 (1936-)
• Research interest: Caprifoliaceae, Ephedraceae, Ericaceae
• Affiliation: QF
• Location of specimens: QF

Xu, Fang; 许方 ; Xǔ Fāng; 許方 (1928-)
• Location of specimens: LYAC

Hsu, H. Y.; 許涵雅 ; Xǔ Hányǎ; 许涵雅
• Location of specimens: HAST

Xu, Hong Fa; 许鸿发 ; Xǔ Hóngfā; 許鴻發 (1937-)
• Affiliation: AIB

Xu, Hong Yuan; 许鸿鹓 ; Xǔ Hóngyuān; 許鴻鵷 (1933-2007)
• Research interest: Poaceae; Pteridophytes
• Affiliation: SWCTU
• Location of specimens: SWCTU

Hsu, Chia chien; 許家謙 ; Xǔ Jiāqiān; 许家谦
• Location of specimens: HAST

Xu, Liang; 许亮 ; Xǔ Liàng (1978-)
• Research interest: Medicinal Plants
• Affiliation: LNCM

Xu, Ning; 许宁 ; Xǔ Níng (1963-)
• Research interest: Theaceae
• Affiliation: TEA

Xu, Ren Xin; 许仁鑫 ; Xǔ Rénxīn (1968-)
• Research interest: Aquatic Plants
• Affiliation: ANU

• Location of specimens: ANU

Xu, Shao Nan; 许绍南 ; Xǔ Shàonán
• Location of specimens: SZ

Hsu, S. K.; 许溯桂 ; Xǔ Sùguì
• Location of specimens: WUK

Hsu, W. T.; 许纬东 ; Xǔ Wěidōng; 許緯東
• Location of specimens: IBSC

Xu, Wen Wei; 许文蔚 ; Xǔ Wénwèi
• Affiliation: CQBG
• Location of specimens: CQBG

Shing, WeiTsung; 許文宗 ; Xǔ Wénzōng; 许文宗
• Location of specimens: HAST

Xu, Xuan Yu; 许炫玉 ; Xǔ Xuànyù; 許炫玉 (1939-)
• Affiliation: NMPG

Xu, Yu Feng; 许玉凤 ; Xǔ Yùfèng (1970-)
• Research interest: Iridaceae
• Affiliation: SYAU
• Location of specimens: SYAU

Xue, Da Yuan; 薛达元 ; Xuē Dáyuán (1955-)
• Location of specimens: NAU

Shien, F. S.; 薛敷三 ; Xuē Fūsān
• Location of specimens: PE

Xue, Gui Shan; 薛贵山 ; Xuē Guìshān; 薛貴山 (1934-)
• Research interest: Poaceae
• Affiliation: ZJFI
• Location of specimens: ZJFI

Xue, Jin Ding; 薛金鼎 ; Xuē Jīndǐng (1938-)
• Location of specimens: HEBI

Hsieh, W. P.; 薛万鹏 ; Xuē Wànpéng; 薛萬鵬
• Location of specimens: PE

Xue, Yue Gui; 薛跃规 ; Xuē Yuèguī (1964-)
• Affiliation: GUN
• Location of specimens: GUN

Xun, Lu Lu; 寻路路 ; Xún Lùlù (1988-)
• Research interest: Cyperaceae, Poaceae
• Affiliation: XBGH
• Location of specimens: XBGH

Y (I)

Yarmemeti; 牙尔买买提 ; Yá'ěrmǎimǎití
• Location of specimens: XJU

Yarlung Zangbo Big Bend Exped.; Yarlung Zangbo Great Turn Exped.; 雅鲁藏布大拐弯队 ; Yǎlǔzàngbù Dàguǎiwān Duì
• Affiliation: XZE. Collection Team

Yan, Zhi Yuan; 焉志远 ; Yān Zhìyuǎn
• Location of specimens: HNR

Yan, Yu Huai; 鄢玉怀 ; Yān Yùhuái (1951-)
• Research interest: Fungi
• Affiliation: IFP
• Location of specimens: IFP

Yan, Dao Liang; 闫道良 ; Yán Dàoliáng (1973-)
• Research interest: Plants of Zhejiang
• Affiliation: ZJFC

Yan, Lai Ji; 闫来基 ; Yán Láijī (1948-)
• Affiliation: MQ

Yan, Xiao Ling; 闫小玲 ; Yán Xiǎolíng (1981-)
• Research interest: Invasive Plants
• Affiliation: CSH
• Location of specimens: CSH

X. L. Yan

Yan, Xiao Li; 闫晓丽 ; Yán Xiǎolì
• Employment: Chengdu Institute of Biology, Chinese Academy of Sciences（中国科学院成都生物研究所）
• Research interest: Bryophyte
• Affiliation: CDBI
• Location of specimens: CDBI

J. P. Yan

Yan, Jian Ping; 阎建平 ; Yán Jiànpíng (1963-)
• Employment: Institute of Botany, Chinese Academy of Sciences（中国科学院植物研究所）
• Research interest: Collector
• Affiliation: PE
• Location of specimens: PE

Yan, Fa Chun; 严发春 ; Yán Fāchūn; 嚴發春
• Location of specimens: YUYU

Yan, Hong Ming; 严洪明 ; Yán Hóngmíng
• Affiliation: ZM

Yan, Jing; 严靖 ; Yán Jìng (1989-)
• Research interest: Invasive Plants
• Affiliation: CSH
• Location of specimens: CSH

Yan, Sheng Jun; 严生俊 ; Yán Shēngjùn
• Location of specimens: HSIB

Yen, Hsin Fu; 嚴新富 ; Yán Xīnfù; 严新富 (1959-)
• Research interest: Begoniaceae, Convolvulaceae
• Affiliation: TNM

Yan, Ying; 严英 ; Yán Yīng; 嚴英 (1935-)
• Research interest: Bryophyte
• Affiliation: TIE
• Location of specimens: TIE

Yan, Zeng Nan; 严增南 ; Yán Zēngnán; 嚴增南 (1927-2010)
• Affiliation: FUS
• Location of specimens: FUS

Yan, Zhi Hui; 严智慧 ; Yán Zhìhuì; 嚴智慧 (1941-)
• Affiliation: SXDC

Yan, Zhong Kai; 严仲铠 ; Yán Zhòngkǎi; 嚴仲鎧 (1938-)
• Research interest: Medicinal Plants
• Affiliation: JLMP
• Location of specimens: ANTU, JLMP

Yan, Zi Zhu; 严子柱 ; Yán Zǐzhù
• Research interest: Herbaceous Plants
• Affiliation: MQ

Yen, Chao Lin; 顔兆麟 ; Yán Zhàolín; 颜兆麟
• Location of specimens: HAST

Yan, Yi Xiang; 晏一祥 ; Yàn Yīxiáng (1937-)
• Research interest: Amaryllidaceae
• Affiliation: YCE

Yan, Ling; 燕玲 ; Yàn Líng (1959-)
• Research interest: Biodiversity
• Affiliation: NMAC
• Location of specimens: NMAC

Yangjen Drolkar; 央金卓嘎 ; Yāngjīn Zhuōgā (1971-)
• Research interest: Plant Ecology
• Affiliation: XZ
• Location of specimens: XZ

B. Y. Yang

Yang, Bao Yu; 楊寶瑜 ; Yáng Bǎoyú; 杨宝瑜
• Employment: Taiwan University（台湾大学）
• Research interest: Bryophytes
• Affiliation: TAI
• Location of specimens: TAI

Yang, Bin Sheng; 杨斌生 ; Yáng Bīnshēng; 楊斌生 (1930-)
• Affiliation: SHTU
• Location of specimens: SHTU

Yang, Tsang Hsiung; 楊藏雄 ; Yáng Cángxióng; 杨藏雄
• Location of specimens: HAST

Yang, Chang Xu; 杨昌煦 ; Yáng Chāngxù; 楊昌煦 (1940-)
• Research interest: Asteraceae
• Affiliation: HWA
• Location of specimens: HWA

Yang, Cheng Yuan; Yang, Ch'êng Yüan; 杨承元 ; Yáng Chéngyuán; 楊承元 (1912-1941?)
• Location of specimens: PEY

Yang, Tsung Ren; Yang, Chong Ren; 杨崇仁 ; Yáng Chóngrén; 楊崇仁 (1943-)
• Location of specimens: KUN

Yang, Chun Hua; 杨春华 ; Yáng Chūnhuá (1954-)
• Affiliation: BJFC

Yang, Ci Fu; Yang, Tsi Fuk; 杨赐福 ; Yáng Cìfú
• Location of specimens: FJFC

Yang, Cun Cun; 杨存存 ; Yáng Cúncún (1992-)
• Affiliation: HHNNR

Yang, Da Rong; 杨大荣 ; Yáng Dàróng
• Research interest: Moraceae
• Affiliation: HITBC

Yang, Di Qing; 杨涤清 ; Yáng Díqīng; 楊滌清 (1939-)
• Research interest: Liliaceae, Orchidaceae
• Affiliation: LBG

Yang, Tung Cheng; 楊東政 ; Yáng Dōngzhèng; 杨东政
• Location of specimens: HAST

Yang, Dong Sheng; 杨冬生 ; Yáng Dōngshēng
• Affiliation: SAUF

Yang, Fa Hao; 杨发浩 ; Yáng Fāhào; 楊發浩
• Location of specimens: IBSC

Yang, Feng Jian; 杨逢建 ; Yáng Féngjiàn (1971-)
• Research interest: Gymnospermae
• Affiliation: NEFI

Yang, Feng Mei; 杨凤梅 ; Yáng Fèngméi (1966-)
• Research interest: Medicinal Plants
• Affiliation: QDC

Yaun, H. C.; 杨宏清 ; Yáng Hóngqīng; 楊宏清
• Location of specimens: SZ

Yang, Huei Ru; 楊惠如 ; Yáng Huìrú; 杨惠如
• Location of specimens: HAST

Yang, Chi shou; 楊吉壽 ; Yáng Jíshòu; 杨吉寿
• Location of specimens: HAST

Yang, Ji Zhong; 杨济中 ; Yáng Jìzhōng; 楊濟中 (1913-)
• Location of specimens: GZTM

Yang, Jin Shu; 杨金书 ; Yáng Jīnshū; 楊金書 (1902-1978)
• Research interest: Medicinal Plants
• Affiliation: CZH
• Location of specimens: CZH

Yang, Jin Gang; 杨锦刚 ; Yáng Jǐngāng; 楊錦剛 (1944-)
• Location of specimens: GZTM

Yang, Jing Sheng; 杨竞生 ; Yáng Jìngshēng; 楊競生 (1921-2002?)
• Location of specimens: IBSC, KUN, PE, WUK

Yang, Lei Lei; 杨蕾蕾 ; Yáng Lěilěi (1988-)
• Research interest: Gentianaceae
• Affiliation: SZG
• Location of specimens: SZG

Yang, Li Pan; 杨礼攀 ; Yáng Lǐpān (1974-)
• Research interest: Taxaceae
• Affiliation: YNTCM

Yang, Li Min; 杨利民 ; Yáng Lìmín (1963-)
• Research interest: Economic Plants
• Affiliation: JLAU
• Location of specimens: JLAU

L. Yang

Yang, Long; 杨龙 ; Yáng Lóng; 楊龍 (1942-)
• Employment: Department of Geography, Guizhou Normal College（贵阳师范学院地理系）
• Research interest: Commelinaceae, Oxalidaceae, Styracaceae
• Affiliation: GNUG
• Location of specimens: GNUG

M. J. Yang

Yang, Ming Jin; 杨明今 ; Yáng Míngjīn; 楊明今 (1920-2003)
• Employment: Sichuan Forestry School（四川省林业学校）
• Research interest: Juglandaceae, Staphyleaceae
• Affiliation: SIFS
• Location of specimens: SIFS. *Flora sichuanica*

M. Q. Yang

Yang, Ming Quan; 杨明权 ; Yáng Míngquán
• Employment: Daqingshan Forest Farm, Inner Mongolia（内蒙古大青山林场）
• Research interest: Plants of Nei Mongol
• Location of specimens: SY. *Flora Innermongolica*

Yang, Peng; 杨鹏 ; Yáng Péng (1962-)
• Research interest: Woody Plants
• Affiliation: SXAU

Yang, Qi Quan; 杨奇全 ; Yáng Qíquán
• Location of specimens: JLFC

Yang, Qi Xiu; 杨启修 ; Yáng Qǐxiū; 楊啟修 (1940-)
• Location of specimens: CDBI

Yang, Qi Yin; 杨启银 ; Yáng Qǐyín (1950-)
• Research interest: Plants of Jiangsu
• Affiliation: NJNU

Q. Yang

Yang, Qian; 杨茜 ; Yáng Qiàn
• Employment: Inner Mongolia Medical College（内蒙古医学院）
• Research interest: Plants of Nei Mongol. *Flora Innermongolica*

Yang, Chiaw Fu; 楊喬富 ; Yáng Qiáofù; 杨乔富
• Location of specimens: HAST

Yang, Qing Shan; 杨青山 ; Yáng Qīngshān
• Location of specimens: ACM

Yang, Qiu Rong; 杨秋容 ; Yáng Qiūróng (1975-)
• Research interest: Medicinal Plants
• Affiliation: EMA
• Location of specimens: EMA

Yang, Rui Wu; 杨瑞武 ; Yáng Ruìwǔ (1969-)
• Research interest: Poaceae

• Affiliation: SAU
• Location of specimens: SAU

Yang, Shan Yun; 杨善云 ; Yáng Shànyún
• Location of specimens: GXFS

Yang, Shi Ji; 杨世基 ; Yáng Shìjī
• Location of specimens: N, NAS, PE, SHM, WUK

Yang, Shu Ping; 杨淑萍 ; Yáng Shūpíng (1976-)
• Research interest: Plants of Xinjiang
• Affiliation: SHI
• Location of specimens: SHI

Yang, Shu De; 杨树德 ; Yáng Shùdé (1956-)
• Research interest: Medicinal Plants
• Affiliation: YNTCM
• Location of specimens: YNTCM

Yang, Wang Wei; 杨王伟 ; Yáng Wángwěi
• Location of specimens: HTC

Yang, Wen Chin; 楊文欽 ; Yáng Wénqīn; 杨文钦
• Location of specimens: HAST

Yang, Wen Sheng; 杨文胜 ; Yáng Wénshèng (1959-)
• Location of specimens: HIMC

Yang, Xian Chen; 杨仙臣 ; Yáng Xiānchén; 楊仙臣 (1930-)
• Location of specimens: LINF

Yang, Xiang Fu; 杨相甫 ; Yáng Xiāngfǔ (1963-)
• Research interest: Plant Systematics
• Affiliation: HENU

Yang, Xiang Xue; 杨祥学 ; Yáng Xiángxué; 楊祥學 (1917-)
• Affiliation: JXU
• Location of specimens: JXU

Yang, Xiao Bo; 杨小波 ; Yáng Xiǎobō (1962-)
• Research interest: Plants of Hainan
• Affiliation: HUTB
• Location of specimens: HUTB

Yang, Xiao Jie; 杨晓杰 ; Yáng Xiǎojié (1962-)
• Research interest: Plants of Qiqihar
• Affiliation: QTC

Yang, Xiu Jian; 杨秀坚 ; Yáng Xiùjiān (1955-)
• Research interest: Plants of Guangdong
• Affiliation: ZHAN
• Location of specimens: ZHAN

Yang, Ya Bin; 杨亚滨 ; Yáng Yàbīn
• Location of specimens: CDBI

Yang, Yang; 杨扬 ; Yáng Yáng (1979-)
• Research interest: Alpine Plants
• Affiliation: KUN

Yang, Yao Wen; 杨耀文 ; Yáng Yàowén (1967-)
• Research interest: Zingiberaceae
• Affiliation: YNTCM
• Location of specimens: YNTCM

Yang, Ye; 杨野 ; Yáng Yě; 楊野 (1935-)
• Research interest: Fabaceae, Ranunculaceae, Salicaceae
• Affiliation: ANTU
• Location of specimens: ANTU

Yang, Ye Qin; 杨业勤 ; Yáng Yèqín
• Location of specimens: FAN

Yang, Yi Chuan; 杨一川 ; Yáng Yīchuān (1960-)
• Research interest: Economic Plants
• Affiliation: SR
• Location of specimens: SR

Yang, Yong Lan; 杨永兰 ; Yáng Yǒnglán
• Location of specimens: CQBG

Yang, Yong Qing; 杨永清 ; Yáng Yǒngqīng (1976-)
• Research interest: Aquatic Plants
• Affiliation: CTC
• Location of specimens: CTC

Yang, Yu Geng; 杨玉庚 ; Yáng Yùgēng
• Location of specimens: GXMG

Yu P. Yang

Yang, Yu Pei; 杨玉培 ; Yáng Yùpéi
• Employment: Chengdu Bureau of Gardening and Greening (成都市园林管理局)
• Research interest: Plants of Sichuan. *Flora sichuanica*

Yang, Yu Yu; 楊玉虞 ; Yáng Yùyú; 杨玉虞
• Location of specimens: HAST

Yang, Yue; 杨悦 ; Yáng Yuè 楊悅 (1931-)
• Research interest: Seed Plants
• Affiliation: BJTC
• Location of specimens: BJTC

Yang, Zai Xin; 杨再新 ; Yáng Zàixīn; 楊再新 (1946-)
• Research interest: Woody Plants
• Affiliation: SCFI

Yang, Zeng Chuann; 楊正釧 ; Yáng Zhèngchuàn; 杨正钏
• Location of specimens: HAST

Yang, Chi Bin; 杨志斌 ; Yáng Zhìbīn; 楊志斌 (1934-)
• Location of specimens: IBSC, NAS, PE

Yang, Chih Kai; 楊智凱 ; Yáng Zhìkǎi; 杨智凯
• Location of specimens: HAST

Zhu L. Yang

Yang, Zhu Liang; 杨祝良 ; Yáng Zhùliáng (1963-)
• Employment: Kunming Institute of Botany, Chinese Academy of Sciences（中国科学院昆明植物研究所）
• Research interest: Fungi
• Affiliation: KUN
• Location of specimens: KUN

Yang, Zong Dai; 杨宗岱 ; Yáng Zōngdài; 楊宗岱 (1932-1993)
• Research interest: Seagrass
• Affiliation: MBMCAS

Yang, Zong Han; 杨宗汉 ; Yáng Zōnghàn; 楊宗漢
• Research interest: Actinidiaceae
• Affiliation: YFS
• Location of specimens: IBSC, YFS

Yao, Cai Hong; 姚才洪 ; Yáo Cáihóng
• Location of specimens: ANUB

Yao, Chong Huai; 姚崇怀 ; Yáo Chónghuái (1962-)
• Research interest: Oleaceae
• Affiliation: CCAU
• Location of specimens: CCAU

Yao, Kai Yuan; 姚开元 ; Yáo Kāiyuán
• Location of specimens: NF

Yao, Rong; 姚榕 ; Yáo Róng
• Affiliation: NFP
• Location of specimens: NFP

Yao, Yong; 姚勇 ; Yáo Yǒng
• Location of specimens: HBI

Yao, Zhen Sheng; 姚振生 ; Yáo Zhènshēng (1946-)
• Research interest: Chloranthaceae
• Affiliation: JXCM
• Location of specimens: JXCM

Yao, Zheng Xiang; 姚正祥 ; Yáo Zhèngxiáng
• Location of specimens: HUIF

Yao, C. W.; Yao, H. W.; 姚仲吾 ; Yáo Zhòngwú
• Location of specimens: KUN, NAS, PE, SZ

Ye, Ai Hua; 叶爱华 ; Yè Àihuá (1968-)
• Research interest: Plants of Anhui
• Affiliation: AAUB

Ye, Da Jin; 叶大进 ; Yè Dàjìn (1958-)
• Affiliation: SWCTU
• Location of specimens: SWCTU

Yeh, Ta Yu; 葉大裕 ; Yè Dàyù; 叶大裕
• Location of specimens: HAST

Ye, De Xian; 叶德娴 ; Yè Déxián; 葉德嫻 (1929-)
• Research interest: Algae
• Affiliation: N
• Location of specimens: IBSC, N, PE, SZ

Ye, Guo Dong; 叶国栋 ; Yè Guódòng; 葉國棟 (1948-)
• Research interest: Plants of Fujian
• Affiliation: FJSI
• Location of specimens: FJSI

Yeh, Chin Fang; 葉錦芳 ; Yè Jǐnfāng; 叶锦芳
• Location of specimens: HAST

Ye, Ju Xin; 叶居新 ; Yè Jūxīn
• Location of specimens: IGA

Ye, Sheng Ming; 叶胜明 ; Yè Shèngmíng (1972-)
• Research interest: Rosaceae
• Affiliation: BZCM
• Location of specimens: BZCM

W. Ye

Ye, Wen; 叶文 ; Yè Wén (1982-)
• Employment: School of Life Sciences, East China Normal University; South China Botanical Garden, Chinese Academy of Sciences（华东师范大学生命科学学院 ;; 中国科 ; 学院华南植物园）
• Research interest: Bryophyte
• Affiliation: HSNU, IBSC
• Location of specimens: HSNU, IBSC

Ye, Xin Nian; 叶新年 ; Yè Xīnnián; 葉新年 (1935-)
• Research interest: Plants of Shangrao
• Affiliation: SRF

Yeh, H. J.; 葉修珍 ; Yè Xiūzhēn; 叶修珍
• Location of specimens: TCF

Yeh, Hsiu Yun; 葉秀芸 ; Yè Xiùyún; 叶秀芸
• Location of specimens: HAST

Ip, H. K.; 叶雅各 ; Yè Yǎgè; 葉雅各 , 叶雅谷 , 葉雅谷 ; (1894-1967)
• Location of specimens: IBSC, N

Ye, Yong Zhong; 叶永忠 ; Yè Yǒngzhōng (1957-)
• Research interest: Plants of Henan
• Affiliation: HEAC
• Location of specimens: HEAC

Z. Y. Yeh

Yeh, Zeng Yung; 葉增勇 ; Yè Zēngyǒng; 叶增勇 (1950-)
• Employment: School of Life Science, Taiwan Normal University（台湾师范大学生命科学专业学院）
• Research interest: Fungi
• Affiliation: TNU

Y. J. Yi

Yi, Yan Jun; 衣艳君 ; Yī Yànjūn
• Employment: Department of Biology, Qufu Normal University（曲阜师范大学生物系）
• Research interest: Bryophyte

Ili Exped.; 伊犁队 ; Yīlí Duì
• Location of specimens: XTNM. Collection Team

Yi, Fa Bin; 易发彬 ; Yì Fābīn
• Location of specimens: JJF

Yi, Fu Ke; 易富科 ; Yì Fùkē (1937-)
• Location of specimens: ANTU, IGA

Yi, Gui Hua; 易桂花 ; Yì Guìhuā (1954-)
• Location of specimens: JJF

Yi, Su; 易俗 ; Yì Sú (1965-)
• Research interest: Plant Systematics
• Affiliation: HUST

Yi, Yong Mei; 易咏梅 ; Yì Yǒngméi (1967-)
• Affiliation: ENS
• Location of specimens: ENS

Imzab; 音扎布 ; Yīnzhābù (1937-)
• Research interest: Fabaceae, Geraniaceae
• Affiliation: NMTC
• Location of specimens: NMTC

Yin, Rong Hua; 殷荣华 ; Yīn Rónghuá; 殷榮華 (1938-)
• Research interest: Plant Ecology
• Affiliation: CCNU
• Location of specimens: CCNU

Yin, Xue Bo; 殷学波 ; Yīn Xuébō (1970-)
• Research interest: Seed Plants
• Affiliation: BJM
• Location of specimens: BJM

Yin, Fu Jun; 银福军 ; Yín Fújūn
• Research interest: Economic Plants
• Affiliation: SM
• Location of specimens: SM

Yin, Guo Ping; 尹国萍 ; Yǐn Guópíng (1952-)
• Research interest: Plants of Sichuan
• Affiliation: SM

Yin, Hai Bo; 尹海波 ; Yǐn Hǎibō (1973-)
• Research interest: Medicinal Plants
• Affiliation: LNCM

Yin, Hang; 尹航 ; Yǐn Háng
• Research interest: Aceraceae, Celastraceae, Rutaceae
• Affiliation: ANTU

Yin, Lin Ke; 尹林克 ; Yǐn Línkè (1957-)
• Research interest: Plants of Xinjiang
• Affiliation: TURP, XJBI
• Location of specimens: TURP

Yin, Zi Li; 尹子丽 ; Yǐn Zilì
• Location of specimens: YNTCM

Yin, Kai Pu; 印开蒲 ; Yìn Kāipú; 印開蒲 (1943-)
• Location of specimens: CDBI

Yong, Ji Bing; 雍际炳 ; Yōng Jìbǐng; 雍際炳 (1929-)
• Research interest: Grass
• Affiliation: LZAH
• Location of specimens: LZAH

S. P. Yong

Yong, Shi Peng; 雍世鹏 ; Yōng Shìpéng; 雍世鵬 (1931-2013)
• Employment: Department of Biology, Inner Mongolia University（内蒙古大学生物系）
• Research interest: Plants of Nei Mongol
• Location of specimens: HIMC. *Flora Innermongolica*

You, Rui Lin; 尤瑞麟 ; Yóu Ruìlín; 尤瑞麟 (1935-)
• Affiliation: PEY

You, Chun; 游春 ; Yóu Chūn
• Location of specimens: YNTCM

You, Jun; 游浚 ; Yóu Jùn (1958-)
• Research interest: Hydrocharitaceae
• Affiliation: WH

You, Guang Lin; 游光琳 ; Yóu Guānglín (1942-)
- Research interest: Scientific Illustrator
- Affiliation: PE

Yui, P. L.; 于伯鲁 ; Yú Bólǔ; 於伯魯
- Location of specimens: IBSC

Yu, Ti Hua; 于棣華 ; Yú Dìhuá; 于棣华
- Location of specimens: HAST

Yu, Feng Ge; 于风阁 ; Yú Fēnggé
- Location of specimens: HLNM

Yu, Jia Bin; 于加宾 ; Yú Jiābīn; 於加賓 (1946-)
- Location of specimens: HLCM

Yu, Jing; 于晶 ; Yú Jīng (1972-)
- Research interest: Bryophyte
- Affiliation: SHTU
- Location of specimens: SHTU

Yu, Ming; 于明 ; Yú Míng (1966-)
- Research interest: Algae; Bryophyte
- Affiliation: BNU

N. N. Yu

Yu, Ning Ning; 于宁宁 ; Yú Níngníng (1981-)
- Employment: Institute of Botany, Chinese Academy of Sciences（中国科学院植物研究所）
- Research interest: Bryophyte
- Affiliation: PE

Yu, Shu Hua; 于树华 ; Yú Shùhuá (1964-)
- Research interest: Saxifragaceae
- Affiliation: SCNU

Yu, Xing Hua; 于兴华 ; Yú Xìnghuá (1960-)
- Location of specimens: IFP

Yu, Xue Ren; 于学仁 ; Yú Xuérén; 于學仁 (1935-)
- Location of specimens: NEAU

Yu, Xue Ying; 于雪莹 ; Yú Xuěyíng (1971-)
- Research interest: Asteraceae, Rutaceae
- Affiliation: NEFI

Yu, Ying Ru; 于英茹 ; Yú Yīngrú
- Affiliation: CAF
- Location of specimens: CAF

Yu, Yong Li; 于永莉 ; Yú Yǒnglì (1955-)
- Research interest: Plants of N. China
- Affiliation: TIE

Yu, Yow shin; 于幼新 ; Yú Yòuxīn
- Location of specimens: HAST

Yu, Zhao Lu; 于兆璐 ; Yú Zhàolù; 於兆璐 (1934-)
- Affiliation: DFEC
- Location of specimens: DFEC

Yu, Zi Wen; 于子文 ; Yú Zǐwén
- Location of specimens: GYBG

Yu, Feng; 余峰 ; Yú Fēng (1946-)
- Research interest: Scientific Illustrator
- Affiliation: IBSC

Yu, Hui Jun; 余慧君 ; Yú Huìjūn (1931-)
- Research interest: Bryophyte; Pteridophytes
- Affiliation: HENU
- Location of specimens: HENU

Yu, Chien Hsun; 余建勳 ; Yú Jiànxūn; 余建勋
- Location of specimens: HAST

Yu, Shao Lin; 余少林 ; Yú Shàolín
- Location of specimens: IBK, IBSC, KUN, PE, WUK

Yu, Xiao Ping; 余小平 ; Yú Xiǎopíng
- Location of specimens: CTC

Yu, Yan; 余岩 ; Yú Yán (1986-)
- Affiliation: SZ

Yu, Yan Hua; 余燕华 ; Yú Yànhuá (1985-)
- Research interest: Plants of Fujian
- Affiliation: FFVTC

Yu, You De; 余有德 ; Yú Yǒudé (1939-)
- Location of specimens: KUN

Yu, Zai Bai; 余再柏 ; Yú Zàibǎi
- Location of specimens: SM

Yu, Zhi Man; 余志满 ; Yú Zhìmǎn (1954-)
- Location of specimens: IBSC

Yu, Hong Yuan; 俞宏渊 ; Yú Hóngyuān (1963-)
- Location of specimens: KUN

Yu, Min Juan; 俞敏娟 ; Yú Mǐnjuān (1930-)
- Location of specimens: HBI

Yu, Xi Zhang; 俞锡章 ; Yú Xīzhāng; 俞錫章 (1935-)
- Location of specimens: QG

Yu, Xiao Ya; 俞筱押 ; Yú Xiǎoyā (1980-)

• Research interest: Plants of Guizhou
• Affiliation: QNUN
• Location of specimens: QNUN

Yu, Xu Ping; 俞旭平 ; Yú Xùpíng
• Location of specimens: NMPG

Yu, Yi Fu; 俞义甫 ; Yú Yìfǔ
• Research interest: Woody Plants
• Affiliation: SIFS

Yu, Ce Sun; 虞策荪 ; Yú Cèsūn; 虞策蓀 (1934-)
• Location of specimens: SITC

Yu, Ping Hua; 禹平华 ; Yǔ Pínghuá; 禹平華 (1927-)
• Location of specimens: HIB, HITBC, IBSC, KUN, LBG, PE, WUK

Yuxi Exped.; 玉溪队 ; Yùxī Duì
• Location of specimens: KUN. Collection Team

Yuan, Chang Chun; 袁长春 ; Yuán Chángchūn (1964-)
• Location of specimens: HUST

Yuan, Fa Yin; 袁发银 ; Yuán Fāyín (1959-)
• Affiliation: NF

Yuan, Hai Sheng; 袁海生 ; Yuán Hǎishēng
• Location of specimens: IFP

Yuan, Jia Mo; 袁家漠 ; Yuán Jiāmò (1936-)
• Research interest: Economic Plants
• Affiliation: HGAS
• Location of specimens: HGAS

Yuan, Ke Kai; 袁克侃 ; Yuán Kèkǎn (1940-)
• Affiliation: EBF

Yuan, Ming; 袁明 ; Yuán Míng (1975-)
• Research interest: Economic Plants
• Affiliation: SAU
• Location of specimens: SAU

Yuan, Mo Jun; 袁模军 ; Yuán Mójūn
• Location of specimens: GLMC

Yuan, Qiang; 袁强 ; Yuán Qiáng (1977-)
• Research interest: Liliaceae
• Affiliation: NEAU

Yuan, Qing Jun; 袁庆军 ; Yuán Qìngjūn (1964-)
• Research interest: Apiaceae, Ranunculaceae
• Affiliation: CMMI

Yuen, S. F.; 袁淑芬 ; Yuán Shūfēn
• Location of specimens: IBK, IBSC, NAS, SYS

Yuen, Y. S.; 袁义生 ; Yuán Yìshēng; 袁義生
• Location of specimens: IBSC

Yuan, Yong Ge; 袁永革 ; Yuán Yǒnggé (1987-)
• Research interest: Plant Ecology
• Affiliation: SHM

Yuan, Yuan; 袁媛 ; Yuán Yuàn (1978-)
• Research interest: Medicinal Plants
• Affiliation: CMMI

Yuan, Zhi Liang; 袁志良 ; Yuán Zhìliáng (1976-)
• Research interest: Bryophyte
• Location of specimens: HEAC

Yuan, Shu Xiu; 苑淑秀 ; Yuàn Shūxiù (1936-)
• Affiliation: KUN

Yue, Jian Ying; 岳建英 ; Yuè Jiànyīng (1962-)
• Research interest: Plants of Shanxi
• Affiliation: HSIB
• Location of specimens: HSIB

Yok, Chin Shan; Yue, Jun San; Yue, Jun Shan; 岳俊三 ; Yuè Jùnsān (1934-)
• Affiliation: NAS, PE
• Location of specimens: NAS, PE

Yue, Ming; 岳明 ; Yuè Míng (1967-)
• Research interest: Plant Ecology
• Affiliation: WNU
• Location of specimens: WNU

Yue, Cheng San; 乐承三 ; Yuè Chéngsān
• Location of specimens: NF

Yunnan Key Cons. Wild Pl. Exped.; 云南重点保护野生植物调查队 ; Yúnnán Zhòngdiǎnbǎohù Yěshēngzhíwù Diàochá Duì
• Affiliation: YCP. Collection Team

Z (C,J,T)

M. Zang

Zang, Mu; 臧穆 ; Zāng Mù (1928-2011)
- Employment: Kunming Institute of Botany, Chinese Academy of Sciences（中国科学院昆明植物研究所）
- Research interest: Bryophytes; Fungi
- Affiliation: KUN
- Location of specimens: IFP, KUN

Zang, Run Guo; 臧润国 ; Zàng Rùnguó (1963-)
- Research interest: Forest Ecology
- Affiliation: CAF

Zeng, Chao Hui; 曾朝辉 ; Zēng Cháohuī (1977-)
- Affiliation: BJM

Tseng, Cheng Kuei; Tsêng, Ch'eng K'uei; Tsêng, Chêng K'uei; Tseng, Cheng Kwei; Zeng, Cheng Kui; 曾呈奎 ; Zēng Chéngkuí (1909-2005)
- Research interest: Algae
- Location of specimens: AU, MBMCAS

Zeng, Fei Yan; 曾飞燕 ; Zēng Fēiyàn (1967-)
- Affiliation: IBSC
- Location of specimens: IBSC

Tsang, Wai Tak; Zeng, Huai De; 曾怀德 ; Zēng Huáidé; 曾懷德
- Location of specimens: IBSC

Zeng, Jue Min; 曾觉民 ; Zēng Juémín; 曾覺民 (1940-)
- Research interest: Plant Geography
- Affiliation: SWFC

Tseng, Jing Liang; 曾景亮 ; Zēng Jǐngliàng
- Location of specimens: NCKU

Zeng, Jun Chao; 曾俊超 ; Zēng Jùnchāo (1940-)
- Affiliation: CDCM

L. C. Tseng

Tseng, Ling Chang; 曾令畅 ; Zēng Lìngchàng
- Employment: Sichuan Daily Chemical Industry Research Institute（四川省日用化学工业研究所）
- Research interest: Plants of Sichuan Flora sichuanica

Zeng, Pei; 曾沛 ; Zēng Pèi
- Location of specimens: SYS

S. Y. Zeng

Zeng, Shu Ying; Tseng, Shu Ying; 曾淑英 ; Zēng Shūyīng (1936-)
- Employment: Kunming Institute of Botany, Chinese Academy of Sciences（中国科学院昆明植物研究所）
- Research interest: Bryophyte
- Affiliation: KUN

Zeng, Tai Long; 曾太龙 ; Zēng Tàilóng
- Location of specimens: GAFS

Zeng, Wen Bin; 曾文彬 ; Zēng Wénbīn (1932-)
- Research interest: Plant Geography
- Affiliation: AU
- Location of specimens: AU

Zeng, Xian Feng; Cheng, Xian Feng; 曾宪锋 ; Zēng Xiànfēng (1962-)
- Research interest: Plants of Hebei, Plants of Guangdong
- Affiliation: CHA, CZH
- Location of specimens: CHA, CZH

Zeng, You De; 曾有德 ; Zēng Yǒudé
- Location of specimens: KUNE

Tsang, Uen Kin; 曾远见 ; Zēng Yuǎnjiàn; 曾遠見
- Location of specimens: SYS

Zeng, Zhao Ling; 曾昭玲 ; Zēng Zhāolíng
- Location of specimens: HSIB

Zeng, Zhao Qi; 曾昭琪 ; Zēng Zhāoqí (1932-)
- Research interest: Algae
- Affiliation: N
- Location of specimens: N

Tashi Tseten; 扎西次旦 ; Zhāxī Cìdàn
- Location of specimens: XZ

Tashi Tsering; 扎西次仁 ; Zhāxī Cìrén (1964-)
- Research interest: Economic Plants
- Affiliation: XZ

Zhai, Ping; 翟苹 ; Zhái Píng
- Location of specimens: KUN

Zhai, Yan Jun; 翟延君 ; Zhái Yánjūn (1956-)

• Research interest: Medicinal Plants
• Affiliation: LNCM
• Location of specimens: LNCM

Zhang, Ai Juan; 张爱娟 ; Zhāng Àijuān; 張愛娟 (1934-)
• Location of specimens: TJMP

Zhang, Bai Yu; 张百誉 ; Zhāng Bǎiyù; 張百譽 (1936-2005)
• Research interest: Pteridophytes
• Affiliation: CTC
• Location of specimens: CTC

Zhang, Bi Yu; 张碧玉 ; Zhāng Bìyù
• Location of specimens: IBK

Chang, P. M.; 张冰明 ; Zhāng Bīngmíng; 張冰明
• Location of specimens: IBSC

Zhang, Bo; 张博 ; Zhāng Bó (1974-)
• Research interest: Plants of Gansu
• Affiliation: QYTC
• Location of specimens: QYTC

Zhang, Chao; 张超 ; Zhāng Chāo (1972-)
• Location of specimens: WCSBG

Zhang, Chao Liang; 张超良 ; Zhāng Chāoliáng
• Location of specimens: GXMI, IBK, PE

Zhang, Chao; 张潮 ; Zhāng Cháo
• Affiliation: GNUB
• Location of specimens: GNUB

Zhang, Chun; 张春 ; Zhāng Chūn
• Location of specimens: BJ

Zhang, Chun Fang; 张春芳 ; Zhāng Chūnfāng (1951-)
• Research interest: Scientific Illustrator
• Affiliation: PE

Zhang, Chun He; 张春禾 ; Zhāng Chūnhé (1957-)
• Research interest: Poaceae
• Affiliation: ZCA
• Location of specimens: ZCA

Zhang, Chun Yu; 张春宇 ; Zhāng Chūnyǔ (1972-)
• Research interest: Violaceae
• Affiliation: SYAU
• Location of specimens: SYAU

Da C. Zhang

Zhang, Da Cheng; 张大成 ; Zhāng Dàchéng
• Employment: Kunming Institute of Botany, Chinese Academy of Sciences（中国科学院昆明植物研究所）
• Research interest: Bryophyte
• Affiliation: KUN

Zhang, Dao Yuan; 张道远 ; Zhāng Dàoyuǎn (1973-)
• Research interest: Fabaceae, Tamaricaceae
• Affiliation: TURP

Zhang, De Ming; 张德明 ; Zhāng Démíng; 張德明 (1935-)
• Affiliation: SN
• Location of specimens: SN

D. R. Zhang

Zhang, De Rui; Chang, Tê Shui; 张德瑞 ; Zhāng Déruì; 張德瑞 (1916-2001)
• Employment: Institute of Oceanology, Chinese Academy of Sciences（中国科学院海洋研究所）
• Research interest: Algae
• Affiliation: MBMCAS

Zhang, De Shan; 张德山 ; Zhāng Déshān; 張德山 (1937-)
• Location of specimens: JSPC

Zhang, De Yin; 张德银 ; Zhāng Déyín
• Location of specimens: LZAH

Zhang, Ding Yu; 张定宇 ; Zhāng Dìngyǔ (1957-)
• Research interest: Saxifragaceae
• Affiliation: SXAU

Chang, T. H.; 张东旭 ; Zhāng Dōngxù; 張東旭
• Location of specimens: LBG, NAS, PE, ZM

Zhang, En Hou; 张恩厚 ; Zhāng Ēnhòu (1960-)
• Research interest: Amaranthaceae
• Affiliation: NMAC

Zhang, Fa Qi; 张发起 ; Zhāng Fāqǐ (1983-)
• Research interest: Plants of Qinghai-Xizang Plateau
• Affiliation: HNWP
• Location of specimens: HNWP

Zhang, Feng; 张峰 ; Zhāng Fēng (1955-)
• Research interest: Plants of Shanxi
• Affiliation: SXU
• Location of specimens: SXU

Zhang, Fu San; 张福三 ; Zhāng Fúsān; 張福三 (1937-)
• Affiliation: TONG

Chang, Fu Yan; Chang, H. Q.; Zhang, Fu Yan; Zhang, Hai Qiu; 张福延 ; Zhāng Fúyán; 张海秋，

張福延，張海秋 (1891-1972)
• Location of specimens: NF

K. C. Chang

Chang, Kuang Chu; Chang, Kwang Chu; Zhang, Guang Chu; 张光初；Zhāng Guāngchū; 張光初 (1940-)
• Employment: Institute of Applied Ecology, Chinese Academy of Sciences（中国科学院沈阳应用生态研究所）
• Research interest: Bryophyte
• Affiliation: IFP
• Location of specimens: IFP

Zhang, Guang Fei; 张光飞；Zhāng Guāngfēi (1966-)
• Research interest: Pteridophytes
• Affiliation: PYU, YUKU

Zhang, Guang Fu; 张光富；Zhāng Guāngfù (1970-)
• Research interest: Magnoliceae, Papaveraceae
• Affiliation: NJNU

Zhang, Guang Ping; 张广平；Zhāng Guǎngpíng (1956-)
• Research interest: Medicinal Plants
• Affiliation: SSMM
• Location of specimens: SSMM

Zhang, Guang Qiang; 张广强；Zhāng Guǎngqiáng; 張廣強 (1937-)
• Research interest: Medicinal Plants
• Affiliation: HECM

Zhang, Gui Bin; 张桂宾；Zhāng Guìbīn
• Location of specimens: KAI

Zhang, Gui Ping; 张桂萍；Zhāng Guìpíng (1964-)
• Research interest: Economic Plants
• Affiliation: SES
• Location of specimens: SES

Zhang, Gui Zhi; 张桂芝；Zhāng Guìzhī; 張桂芝 (1938-)
• Research interest: Scientific Illustrator
• Affiliation: IFP

Zhang, Guo Qing; 张国庆；Zhāng Guóqìng (1953-)
• Research interest: Medicinal Plants
• Affiliation: HECM

Zhang, Guo Wei; Chang, Kuo Wei; 张国维；Zhāng Guówéi; 張國維 (1939-)
• Research interest: Plants of Jilin
• Affiliation: JLFC
• Location of specimens: JLFC

Cheung, Kwok Wai; 張國偉；Zhāng Guówěi; 张国伟 (1959-)
• Affiliation: HK

Zhang, Han Ming; 张汉明；Zhāng Hànmíng
• Location of specimens: SMMU-BH

H. T. Chang

Chang, Ho Tseng; 张和岑；Zhāng Hécén; 張和岑 (1898-1985)
• Employment: Department of Biology, Soochow University（东吴大学生物系）
• Research interest: Medicinal Plants
• Location of specimens: N, PE, SYS

H. S. Chang

Chang, Ho Shii; Chang, Ho His; 張和喜；Zhāng Héxǐ; 张和喜 (1938-)
• Employment: Institute of Botany, "Academia Sinica"（中央研究院植物研究所）
• Research interest: Fungi
• Affiliation: HAST

Zhang, He Ling; 张鹤龄；Zhāng Hèlíng; 張鶴齡 (1932-)
• Affiliation: KAI
• Location of specimens: KAI

Zhang, Hong; 张虹；Zhāng Hóng (1963-)
• Research interest: Medicinal Plants
• Affiliation: CQNM
• Location of specimens: CQNM, SSMM

Zhang, Hong Chang; 张鸿昌；Zhāng Hóngchāng; 張鴻昌 (1934-)
• Research interest: Berberidaceae, Pinaceae, Zygophyllaceae
• Affiliation: QF
• Location of specimens: QF

Zhang, Hua Yu; 张华雨；Zhāng Huáyǔ
• Location of specimens: SWCTU

Zhang, Hui; 张慧；Zhāng Huì (1970-)
• Research interest: Medicinal Plants
• Affiliation: LNCM

Zhang, Huo Zhong; 张豁中；Zhāng Huōzhōng
• Location of specimens: SYPC

Zhang, Ji Hua; 张吉华；Zhāng Jíhuá
• Location of specimens: JJF

Zhang, Ji Xiang; 张吉祥；Zhāng Jíxiáng; 張吉祥 (1937-)
• Affiliation: HZTC

Zhang, Ji; 张继 ; Zhāng Jì
- Research interest: Medicinal Plants
- Affiliation: CPB
- Location of specimens: CPB

Zhang, Jia Hui; 张家辉 ; Zhāng Jiāhuī (1979-)
- Research interest: Fungi
- Affiliation: SWCTU
- Location of specimens: SWCTU

Zhang, Jian Chen; 张建琛 ; Zhāng Jiànchēn (1954-)
- Research interest: Plants of Sichuan
- Affiliation: HON

Zhang, Jian Kui; 张建奎 ; Zhāng Jiànkuí (1980-)
- Research interest: Medicinal Plants
- Affiliation: LNCM

Zhang, Jian Xin; 张建新 ; Zhāng Jiànxīn (1965-)
- Affiliation: ENS
- Location of specimens: ENS

Zhang, Jian Min; 张健民 ; Zhāng Jiànmín; 張健民 (1930-)
- Research interest: Medicinal Plants
- Affiliation: WXDC

Zhang, Jie; 张洁 ; Zhāng Jié
- Research interest: Medicinal Plants
- Affiliation: YNTCM
- Location of specimens: YNTCM

Zhang, Jin Yu; 张晋豫 ; Zhāng Jìnyù (1962-)
- Research interest: Plants of Henan
- Affiliation: HENU
- Location of specimens: HENU

Chang, C. W.; 张经纬 ; Zhāng Jīngwěi; 張經緯
- Location of specimens: PE

Zhang, Jing Long; 张景龙 ; Zhāng Jǐnglóng (1959-)
- Research interest: Medicinal Plants
- Affiliation: CCM
- Location of specimens: CCM

Chang, Ching Sung; 張景淞 ; Zhāng Jǐngsōng; 张景淞
- Location of specimens: HAST

Zhang, Jing Xiang; 张景祥 ; Zhāng Jǐngxiáng; 張景祥 (1934-)
- Research interest: Liliaceae; Plants of Hebei
- Affiliation: HBNU
- Location of specimens: HBNU

Zhang, Jing Wen; 张静文 ; Zhāng Jìngwén
- Location of specimens: NFP

Chang, C. C.; 张镜澄 ; Zhāng Jìngchéng; 張鏡澄
- Location of specimens: PE

Chang, K. C.; 张镜清 ; Zhāng Jìngqīng; 張鏡清
- Location of specimens: IBSC

J. F. Zhang

Zhang, Jun Fu; Chang, Tsun Fu; 张峻甫 ; Zhāng Jùnfǔ ; 張峻甫 (1918-1996)
- Employment: Institute of Oceanology, Chinese Academy of Sciences（中国科学院海洋研究所）
- Research interest: Algae
- Affiliation: MBMCAS
- Location of specimens: MBMCAS

Zhang, Ke Wen; 张科文 ; Zhāng Kēwén
- Affiliation: WL

Zhang, Le Hua; 张乐华 ; Zhāng Lèhuá (1966-)
- Research interest: Ericaceae
- Affiliation: LBG

Li Zhang

Zhang, Li; 张力 ; Zhāng Lì (1967-)
- Employment: South China Institute of Botany, Chinese Academy of Sciences; South China Botanical Garden, Chinese Academy of Sciences; Fairy Lake Botanical Garden, Shenzhen & Chinese Academy of Sciences（中国科学院华南植物研究所；中国科学院华南植物园；深圳市中国科学院仙湖植物园）
- Research interest: Bryophyte
- Affiliation: IBSC, SZG
- Location of specimens: SZG

Zhang, Li Rong; 张立荣 ; Zhāng Lìróng
- Location of specimens: YLD

Chang, Li Wan; 張勵婉 ; Zhāng Lìwǎn; 张励婉
- Location of specimens: HAST

M. H. Chang

Chang, Man Hsiang; Chang, Man Siang; Zhang, Man Xiang; 张满祥 ; Zhāng Mǎnxiáng; 張滿祥 (1934-)
- Employment: Northwest China Institute of Botany, Chinese Academy of Sciences and Shaanxi Province; Xi' an Botanical Garden, Shaanxi（陕西省中国科学院西北植物研究所；陕西省；西安植物园）
- Research interest: Bryophyte
- Affiliation: XBGH, WUK
- Location of specimens: XBGH, WUK

Zhang, Ming Zhe; 张铭哲 ; Zhāng Míngzhé; 張銘哲 (1926-)
• Research interest: Plants of Henan
• Affiliation: HENU
• Location of specimens: HENU

Zhang, Ping; 张苹 ; Zhāng Píng
• Location of specimens: SDFGR

Zhang, Qi Hua; 张启华 ; Zhāng Qǐhuá; 張啟華 (1947-)
• Affiliation: DQTC
• Location of specimens: DQTC

Zhang, Qiang; 张强 ; Zhāng Qiáng (1968-)
• Research interest: Medicinal Plants
• Affiliation: CCM
• Location of specimens: CCM

Zhang, Qiao Yan; 张巧艳 ; Zhāng Qiǎoyàn
• Research interest: Medicinal Plants
• Affiliation: SMMU-BH

Zhang, Qing Lin; 张青林 ; Zhāng Qīnglín (1989-)
• Research interest: Medicinal Plants
• Affiliation: GYBG
• Location of specimens: GYBG

Zhang, Qing Song; 张青松 ; Zhāng Qīngsōng (1965-)
• Affiliation: LBG

Zhang, Qing Lu; 张庆禄 ; Zhāng Qìnglù
• Location of specimens: GXFI

Zhang, Rong Hou; 张荣厚 ; Zhāng Rónghòu; 張榮厚 (1910-1975)
• Research interest: Scientific Illustrator
• Affiliation: PE

Chang, S. L.; 张瑞麟 ; Zhāng Ruìlín; 張瑞麟
• Location of specimens: IBSC

Zhang, Shao Chun; 张少春 ; Zhāng Shàochūn
• Location of specimens: LBG

Cheung, Shai Hung; 张世雄 ; Zhāng Shìxióng; 張世雄
• Location of specimens: KUN

Zhang, Song Hua; 张松华 ; Zhāng Sōnghuá
• Location of specimens: CQNM

Zhang, Su Ju; 张素菊 ; Zhāng Sùjú; 張素菊 (1936-)
• Location of specimens: HBFC

Zhang, Su Ru; 张素茹 ; Zhāng Sùrú (1963-)
• Research interest: Plants of Hubei
• Affiliation: HIB

Zhang, Sui Shen; 张遂申 ; Zhāng Suìshēn; 張遂申 (1935-2002)
• Research interest: Plant Anatomy
• Affiliation: WUK

Zhang, Tai Li; 张泰利 ; Zhāng Tàilì; 張泰利 (1938-)
• Research interest: Scientific Illustrator
• Affiliation: PE

Zhang, Tian Zhu; 张天柱 ; Zhāng Tiānzhù (1977-)
• Research interest: Medicinal Plants
• Affiliation: CCM
• Location of specimens: CCM

Zhang, Ting Hua; 张廷华 ; Zhāng Tínghuá; 張廷華 (1945-)
• Research interest: Plants of Yunnan
• Affiliation: YNUB
• Location of specimens: YNUB

Zhang, Wei; 张炜 ; Zhāng Wěi (1984-)
• Research interest: Medicinal Plants
• Affiliation: QDC

Chang, Wen Yu; 張文宇 ; Zhāng Wényǔ; 张文宇
• Location of specimens: HAST

Zhang, Wen Zhong; 张文仲 ; Zhāng Wénzhòng; 張文仲 (1934-)
• Location of specimens: ANTU, NENU

Zhang, Xi Ting; 张锡亭; Zhāng Xītíng; 張錫亭 (1935-)
• Location of specimens: HUST

Chang, S. M.; 张相明 ; Zhāng Xiāngmíng; 張相明
• Location of specimens: IBSC

Zhang, Xiang Wen; 张相文 ; Zhāng Xiāngwén
• Location of specimens: ZY

Zhang, Xiang Bin; 张向彬 ; Zhāng Xiàngbīn (1967-)
• Research interest: Zingiberaceae
• Affiliation: HNNU

Zhang, Xiao Bing; 张小冰 ; Zhāng Xiǎobīng (1958-)
• Research interest: Plant Physiology
• Affiliation: TYNUB
• Location of specimens: TYNUB

Zhang, Xiao Bo; 张小波 ; Zhāng Xiǎobō (1980-)
• Research interest: Medicinal Plants

• Affiliation: CMMI

Zhang, Xiao Hang; 张小杭 ; Zhāng Xiǎoháng (1963-)
• Affiliation: FJSI

Zhang, Xiao Ling; 张晓玲 ; Zhāng Xiǎolíng (1966-)
• Affiliation: TYF

Zhang, Xiao Xiao; 张晓晓 ; Zhāng Xiǎoxiǎo (1985-)
• Research interest: Plants of N. China
• Affiliation: TIE

Zhang, Xin Xin; 张欣欣 ; Zhāng Xīnxīn (1982-)
• Research interest: Plants of N. E. China
• Affiliation: HANU
• Location of specimens: HANU

Zhang, Xin Hou; 张新厚 ; Zhāng Xīnhòu (1985-)
• Research interest: Plant Ecology
• Affiliation: IGA

Zhang, Xin Yue; 张信岳 ; Zhāng Xìnyuè (1968-)
• Research interest: Medicinal Plants
• Affiliation: ZDC

Chang, H. F.; 张雄飞 ; Zhāng Xióngfēi; 張雄飛
• Location of specimens: IBSC

Zhang, Xue Jie; 张学杰 ; Zhāng Xuéjié (1976-)
• Research interest: Plants of Shandong
• Affiliation: SDNU
• Location of specimens: SDNU

Zhang, Xue Xing; 张学星 ; Zhāng Xuéxīng (1966-)
• Research interest: Aceraceae, Magnoliceae
• Affiliation: YAF

Zhang, Xue Mei; 张雪梅 ; Zhāng Xuěméi (1982-)
• Affiliation: SITC
• Location of specimens: SITC

Zhang, Xun; 张训 ; Zhāng Xùn (1971-)
• Research interest: Medicinal Plants
• Affiliation: WCU

Zhang, Ya Zhi; 张亚芝 ; Zhāng Yàzhī (1957-)
• Location of specimens: CCM

Zhang, Yan Zhen; 张衍箴 ; Zhāng Yǎnzhēn
• Location of specimens: CMMI

Zhang, Yan; 张燕 ; Zhāng Yàn (1960-)
• Affiliation: KUN

Zhang, Yang; 张阳 ; Zhāng Yáng (1986-)
• Research interest: Plant Ecology
• Affiliation: SHM

Zhang, Yang; 张洋 ; Zhāng Yáng (1983-)
• Research interest: Plant Ecology
• Affiliation: ZM

Zhang, Yi Fan; 张一帆 ; Zhāng Yīfān
• Research interest: Plant Anatomy
• Affiliation: YNUB

Zhang, Yi; 张怡 ; Zhāng Yí; 張怡 (1936-)
• Location of specimens: GZTM

Zhang, Yin Qiao; 张荫桥 ; Zhāng Yīnqiáo
• Location of specimens: JLAU

Chang, Ying Pai; Chang, Ying Bai; 张英伯 ;
Zhāng Yīngbó; 張英伯 (1913-1985)
• Location of specimens: HITBC, IBK, IBSC, KUN, PE, WUK

Zhang, Ying Tao; 张英涛 ; Zhāng Yīngtāo (1970-)
• Research interest: Medicinal Plants
• Affiliation: PEM

Chang, Ying Wen; 張嚶文 ; Zhāng Yīngwén; 张嘤文
• Location of specimens: HAST

Zhang, Ying; 张莹 ; Zhāng Yíng (1972-)
• Research interest: Plants of Qinling
• Affiliation: XBGH

Zhang, Yong Gang; 张永刚 ; Zhāng Yǒnggāng (1978-)
• Research interest: Economic Plants
• Affiliation: JLAU

Zhang, Yong Hua; 张永华 ; Zhāng Yǒnghuá;
張永華 (1934-)
• Research interest: Poaceae
• Affiliation: XBGH

Zhang, Yong Sheng; 张永昇 ; Zhāng Yǒngshēng;
張永昇 (1934-)
• Location of specimens: TJMP, QDC

Zhang, Yong Mei; 张咏梅 ; Zhāng Yǒngméi (1970-)
• Affiliation: CDBI

Zhang, You De; 张友德 ; Zhāng Yǒudé; 張友德 (1936-)
• Research interest: Poaceae
• Affiliation: CCAU
• Location of specimens: CCAU

Zhang, You Lin; 张友林 ; Zhāng Yǒulín; 張友林 (1942-)
• Affiliation: HGTC

Chang, Yu Hai; 張有海 ; Zhāng Yǒuhǎi; 张有海
• Location of specimens: HAST

Zhang, Yu; 张妤 ; Zhāng Yú
• Location of specimens: SSMM

Zhang, Yu Long; Chang, Yu Lung; Chang, Yu Long; 张玉龙 ; Zhāng Yùlóng
• Location of specimens: HEAC

Zhang, Yu Zhi; 张玉芝 ; Zhāng Yùzhī
• Research interest: Juglandaceae
• Affiliation: LEF

Zhang, Yue; 张越 ; Zhāng Yuè (1990-)
• Affiliation: SAUT

Zhang, Yun Fei; 张云飞 ; Zhāng Yúnfēi (1969-)
• Research interest: Plant Ecology
• Affiliation: SHM

Zhang, Zhao Jie; 张昭洁 ; Zhāng Zhāojié (1963-)
• Research interest: Ulmaceae
• Affiliation: JSPC
• Location of specimens: JSPC

Z. H. Zhang

Zhang, Zhao Hui; 张朝晖 ; Zhāng Zhāohuī (1963-)
• Employment: Department of Biology, Guizhou Normal University; School of Life Science, Guizhou Normal University（贵州师范大学生物系；贵州师范大学生命科学学院）
• Research interest: Bryophyte
• Affiliation: GNUB
• Location of specimens: GNUB

Zhang, Zheng; 张峥 ; Zhāng Zhēng (1985-)
• Research interest: Weeds
• Affiliation: NAU

Chang, Chi Ming; 张之铭 ; Zhāng Zhī Míng; 張之銘 (1872-1947?)
• Location of specimens: TI

Zhang, Zhi Wei; 张植玮 ; Zhāng Zhíwěi (1983-)
• Research interest: Economic Plants
• Affiliation: SM

Chang, Chi-Shan; 張至善 ; Zhāng Zhìshàn; 张至善
• Location of specimens: HAST

Zhang, Zhi Nong; 张志农 ; Zhāng Zhìnóng (1963-)
• Affiliation: BAU

Zhang, Zhi Song; Chang, Che Sung; 张志松 ; Zhāng Zhìsōng; 張志松 (1930-)
• Location of specimens: SHM

Zhang, Zhi Min; 张智敏 ; Zhāng Zhìmǐn
• Location of specimens: SYAUF

Zhang, Zhong Lian; 张忠廉 ; Zhāng Zhōnglián
• Research interest: Asparagaceae
• Affiliation: IMDY

Zhang, Chong Ling; 张重岭 ; Zhāng Chónglǐng (1964-)
• Research interest: Plants of Nei Mongol
• Affiliation: YAK
• Location of specimens: YAK

Chang, C. S.; 张祝三 ; Zhāng Zhùsān; 張祝三
• Location of specimens: GXMI

Zhang, Zi Gang; 张紫刚 ; Zhāng Zǐgāng (1983-)
• Research interest: Menispermaceae
• Affiliation: NAU

Chang, Tsung Sü; Chang, Shwang Shü; 张宗绪 ; Zhāng Zōngxù; 張宗緒 (1879-1945)
• Location of specimens: NAS, PE

Zhang, Jing Hua; 章菁华 ; Zhāng Jīnghuá; 章菁華 (1929-)
• Location of specimens: SDFS

Chang, Lo Min; 章樂民 ; Zhāng Lèmín; 章乐民
• Location of specimens: HAST, TAIF

Zhang, Shu; 章菽 ; Zhāng Shū (1961-)
• Research interest: Cephalotaxaceae
• Affiliation: IMM

Chang, Shu Fêng; Zhang, Shu Feng; 章树枫 ; Zhāng Shùfēng
• Location of specimens: IBSC, PE

Zhang, Yu Ying; 章毓英 ; Zhāng Yùyīng (1913-)
• Research interest: Weeds
• Affiliation: NAU
• Location of specimens: NAU

Zhao, Bao Hui; 赵宝惠 ; Zhào Bǎohuì; 趙寶惠 (1930-)
• Research interest: Plants of Hubei
• Affiliation: CCNU
• Location of specimens: CCNU

Zhao, Bing Zhu; 赵炳柱 ; Zhào Bǐngzhù (1965-)
• Affiliation: YAK
• Location of specimens: YAK

Zhao, Bo; 赵博 ; Zhào Bó (1961-)
• Affiliation: DNHM

Chao, Chung Wen; 赵重蕴 ; Zhào Chóngyùn; 趙重蘊
• Location of specimens: IBSC, KUN, PE

Zhao, Cong Fu; 赵从福 ; Zhào Cóngfú
• Location of specimens: IFP

Zhao, Da Wen; 赵达文 ; Zhào Dáwèn; 趙達文 (1931-)
• Research interest: Medicinal Plants
• Affiliation: CPB

Zhao, De Lin; 赵德林 ; Zhào Délín
• Location of specimens: BJM

Zhao, Hong Quan; 赵洪全 ; Zhào Hóngquán
• Research interest: Araliaceae, Asteraceae, Gymnospermae
• Affiliation: ANTU
• Location of specimens: ANTU

Hung C. Chao

Chao, Hung Chi; 赵洪志 ; Zhào Hóngzhì; 趙洪志 (1932-)
• Employment: Sichuan Daily Chemical Industry Research Institute（四川省日用化学工业研究所）
• Research interest: Plants of Sichuan

Flora sichuanica

Zhao, Hua; 赵桦 ; Zhào Huà (1957-)
• Affiliation: HZTC

Zhao, Ji Feng; 赵纪峰 ; Zhào Jìfēng (1981-)
• Research interest: Medicinal Plants
• Affiliation: SM
• Location of specimens: SM

J. C. Zhao

Zhao, Jian Cheng; 赵建成 ; Zhào Jiànchéng (1956-)
• Employment: College of Life Sciences, Hebei Normal University（河北师范大学生命科学学院）
• Research interest: Bryophyte
• Affiliation: HBNU, XJU
• Location of specimens: HBNU, XJU

Zhao, Kai Ge; 赵凯歌 ; Zhào Kǎigē (1975-)
• Research interest: Woody Plants
• Affiliation: CCAU

Zhao, Kui Yi; 赵魁义 ; Zhào Kuíyì; 趙魁義 (1937-)
• Location of specimens: IGA

Zhao, li Fen; 赵丽芬 ; Zhào Lìfēn
• Location of specimens: HLCM

Zhao, Liang Cheng; 赵良成 ; Zhào Liángchéng (1973-)
• Affiliation: BJFC
• Location of specimens: BJFC

Zhao, Ling; 赵玲 ; Zhào Líng (1965-)
• Research interest: Plants of Anhui
• Affiliation: AIB

Zhao, Min; 赵敏 ; Zhào Mǐn (1973-)
• Research interest: Pinaceae
• Affiliation: YAF

Zhao, Ming; 赵明 ; Zhào Míng
• Affiliation: MQ

Chao, Jung Kuang; 趙榮光 ; Zhào Róngguāng; 赵荣光
• Location of specimens: HAST

Chao, Ru Lin; Chao, Zi Siao; Chao, Tsi Siao; Zhao, Ru Lin; Zhao, Zi Xiao; **赵儒林 ; Zhào Rúlín; 赵子孝 , 趙儒林 , 趙子孝 (1915-)**
• Research interest: Fagaceae
• Affiliation: N
• Location of specimens: N, SWFC

Zhao, Rui Feng; 赵瑞峰; Zhào Ruìfēng; 趙瑞峰 (1940-)
• Location of specimens: IBK

Chiao, S. W.; 赵善欢 ; Zhào Shànhuān; 趙善歡
• Location of specimens: IBSC

Zhao, Shu Chun; 赵淑春 ; Zhào Shūchūn; 趙淑春 (1945-)
• Location of specimens: JLAU

Zhao, Shu Wen; 赵淑文 ; Zhào Shūwén (1981-)
• Research interest: Plants of Nei Mongol
• Affiliation: NMAC
• Location of specimens: NMAC

Zhao, Ting; 赵挺 ; Zhào Tǐng
• Research interest: Anacardiaceae
• Affiliation: LAC

Zhao, Wen Shu; 赵文书 ; Zhào Wénshū; 趙文書 (1941-)
• Research interest: Dipterocarpaceae, Fagaceae
• Affiliation: YCP
• Location of specimens: YCP

Zhao, Xin Lei; 赵鑫磊 ; Zhào Xīnlěi (1991-)
- Research interest: Orchidaceae, Ranunculaceae
- Affiliation: BZCM
- Location of specimens: BZCM

Zhao, Xing Cun; 赵兴存 ; Zhào Xìngcún
- Location of specimens: GAUF

Zhai, Xiu Zhen; 赵秀贞; Zhào Xiùzhēn; 趙秀貞 (1936-)
- Research interest: Medicinal Plants
- Affiliation: FMP
- Location of specimens: FMP

Zhao, Xue Yuan; 赵学源 ; Zhào Xuéyuán
- Location of specimens: CIT

Zhao, Yan Min; 赵彦民 ; Zhào Yànmín
- Location of specimens: HBNU

Zhao, Yi Qing; 赵一庆 ; Zhào Yīqìng (1964-)
- Research interest: Woody Plants
- Affiliation: YL
- Location of specimens: YL

Zhao, Ying Hua; 赵英华 ; Zhào Yīnghuá; 趙英華 (1929-2011)
- Research interest: Algae
- Affiliation: N

Zhao, Yu; 赵禹 ; Zhào Yǔ; 趙禹 (1932-)
- Location of specimens: KUN

Chao, Yü Chang; 赵裕章 ; Zhào Yùzhāng; 趙裕章
- Location of specimens: IBSC, KUN, PE

Zhao, Yue; 赵玥 ; Zhào Yuè (1982-)
- Research interest: Apiaceae, Araliaceae
- Affiliation: SYPC
- Location of specimens: SYPC

Zhao, Yun Peng; 赵云鹏 ; Zhào Yúnpéng (1978-)
- Research interest: Actinidiaceae, Smilacacae, Theaceae
- Affiliation: HZU
- Location of specimens: HZU

Chao, Chu Kuang; 赵治光 ; Zhào Zhìguāng; 趙治光
- Location of specimens: KUN

Z. T. Zhao

Zhao, Zun Tian; 赵遵田 ; Zhào Zūntián (1952-)
- Employment: College of Life Science, Shandong Normal University（山东师范大学生命科学学院）
- Research interest: Bryophyte; Fungi
- Affiliation: SDNU
- Location of specimens: SDNU

Zhejiang Plant Res. Exped.; 浙江植物资源调查队 ; Zhèjiāng Zhíwùzīyuán Diàochádùi
- Location of specimens: HHBG. Collection Team

Zheng, Bo Ren; 郑博仁 ; Zhèng Bórén; 鄭博仁 (1932-)
- Research interest: Medicinal Plants
- Affiliation: YIM

Zheng, Cheng Jian; 郑承剑 ; Zhèng Chéngjiàn
- Research interest: Medicinal Plants
- Affiliation: SMMU-BH

Jen, Kuo Hen; 鄭國亨 ; Zhèng Guóhēng; 郑国亨
- Location of specimens: HAST

Cheng, Chun Li; 鄭君理 ; Zhèng Jūnlǐ; 郑君理
- Location of specimens: HAST

Cheng, Chun Jen; 鄭君仁 ; Zhèng Jūnrén; 郑君仁
- Location of specimens: HAST

Zheng, Ming Xuan; 郑明轩 ; Zhèng Míngxuān (1981-)
- Location of specimens: CANT

Cheng, Ming Yi; 鄭明宜 ; Zhèng Míngyí; 郑明宜
- Location of specimens: HAST

Zheng, Shi Zhang; 郑师章 ; Zhèng Shīzhāng; 鄭師章 (1936-)
- Research interest: Fabaceae
- Affiliation: FUS

Zheng, Shi Chuan; 郑士川 ; Zhèng Shìchuān; 鄭士川 (1936-)
- Research interest: Liliaceae, Poaceae, Solanaceae
- Affiliation: TIE

Zheng, Shu Dong; 郑树栋 ; Zhèng Shùdòng
- Location of specimens: MBMCAS

Zheng, Wei Fa; 郑维发 ; Zhèng Wéifā (1963-)
- Research interest: Bryophyte
- Affiliation: XZTC
- Location of specimens: XZTC

W. T. Cheng

Cheng, Wu Tsang; Zheng, Wu Can; 鄭武燦 ; Zhèng Wǔcàn; 郑武灿 (1940-)
- Employment: Taiwan University（台湾大学）
- Research interest: Plant Systematics
- Affiliation: TAI

• Location of specimens: TAI

Zheng, Xiao Jiang; 郑小江 ; Zhèng Xiǎojiāng (1958-)
• Research interest: Plant Systematics
• Affiliation: ENS
• Location of specimens: ENS

Zheng, Xiao Ming; 郑小明 ; Zhèng Xiǎomíng (1992-)
• Location of specimens: HZU

Zheng, Xiao Hong; 郑晓虹 ; Zhèng Xiǎohóng (1957-)
• Affiliation: XAG

Zheng, Xuan Feng; 郑萱凤 ; Zhèng Xuānfèng; 鄭萱鳳 (1935-)
• Location of specimens: IGA

Zheng, Yi Jin; 郑亦津 ; Zhèng Yìjīn; 鄭亦津 (1931-)
• Research interest: Poaceae, Ulmaceae
• Affiliation: JSPC
• Location of specimens: JSPC

Cheng, Yu pin; 鄭育斌 ; Zhèng Yùbīn; 郑育斌
• Location of specimens: HAST

Cheng, Yuan Chun; Jeng, Y. C.; 鄭元春 ; Zhèng Yuánchūn; 郑元春
• Location of specimens: HAST

Zheng, Yuan Run; 郑元润 ; Zhèng Yuánrùn (1968-)
• Affiliation: WCSBG

Zhi, Qi; 支琦 ; Zhī Qí (1962-)
• Research interest: Medicinal Plants
• Affiliation: SHDC

Plant Res. Exped.; 植物资源考察队 ; Zhíwùzīyuán Kǎochāduì
• Location of specimens: PE. Collection Team

Sino-Germany Shaanxi Exped.; 中德陕西队 ; Zhōngdé Shǎnxī Duì
• Location of specimens: PE. Collection Team

Sino-Africa Joint Investigation Team; 中 - 非联合考察队 ; Zhōngfēi Liánhé Kǎochāduì
• Location of specimens: HIB. Collection Team

Sino-American W. Hubei Pl. Exped.; 中美联合鄂西植物考察队 ; Zhōngměi Liánhé Èxī Zhíwù Kǎochāduì
• Location of specimens: WH. Collection Team

Sino-American Shennongjia Pl. Exped.; 中美神农架队 ; Zhōngměi Shénnóngjià Duì
• Location of specimens: HIB, PE. Collection Team

Sino-Russia Yunnan Exped.; 中苏云南考察团 ; Zhōngsū Yúnnán Kǎochátuán
• Location of specimens: KUN, PE. Collection Team

Zhong, Ben Gu; 钟本固 ; Zhōng Běngù; 鐘本固 (1929-)
• Research interest: Bryophyte
• Affiliation: GNUB
• Location of specimens: GNUB

Tsoong, Pu Chin; Tsoong, Pu Ch'in; Chung, Pu Chin; Chung, Pu Ch'in; Zhong, Bu Qin; 钟补勤 ; Zhōng Bǔ qín; 鐘補勤 (1896-?)
• Location of specimens: FNU, GFS, PE

Chung, Ting Chuan; 鍾錠全 ; Zhōng Dìngquán; 钟锭全
• Location of specimens: HAST

K. K. Tsoong

Tsoong, Kuan Kwang; Tsoong, Kuan Kuang; Zhong, Guan Guang; 钟观光 ; Zhōng Guānguāng; 鐘觀光 (1868-1940)
• Employment: National University of Peking; National Third Sun Yat-sen University; National Chekiang University（国立北京大学；国立第三中山大学；国立浙江大学）
• Research interest: Collector
• Location of specimens: BNU, PE, PEY

Zhong, Hua Ping; 钟华平 ; Zhōng Huápíng (1964-)
• Research interest: Economic Plants
• Affiliation: CIS

Tsoong, Chia Chin; Zhong, Jia Qin; 钟稼勤 ; Zhōng Jiàqín; 鐘稼勤 (1898-?)
• Location of specimens: PE

Zhong, Jian; 钟坚 ; Zhōng Jiān
• Location of specimens: IBK, SYS

Zhong, Jun Di; 钟军弟 ; Zhōng Jūndì (1980-)
• Affiliation: ZHAN
• Location of specimens: ZHAN

Zhong, Ming Fang; 钟明芳 ; Zhōng Míngfāng; 鐘明芳 (1927-)
• Location of specimens: SM

Chung, Jung Ching; 鍾榮青 ; Zhōng Róngqīng; 钟荣青
• Location of specimens: HAST

Zhong, Shu Quan; 钟树权 ; Zhōng Shùquán; 鍾樹權 (1929-)

• Location of specimens: IBK

Zhong, Shu Ying; 钟树英 ; Zhōng Shùyīng (1971-)
• Affiliation: HITBC

Chung, To; 钟桃 ; Zhōng Táo
• Location of specimens: IBSC

Zhong, Xia Jun; 钟霞军 ; Zhōng Xiájūn (1964-)
• Research interest: Medicinal Plants
• Affiliation: GXCM
• Location of specimens: GXCM

Zhong, Xin; 钟鑫 ; Zhōng Xīn (1989-)
• Research interest: Biodiversity
• Affiliation: CSH
• Location of specimens: CSH

I Chung

Chung, I; Chung, Yih; Zhong, Yi; 钟义 ; Zhōng Yì; 鐘義 ; (1922-)
• Employment: South China Institute of Botany, Chinese Academy of Sciences（中国科学院华南植物研究所）
• Research interest: Collector
• Affiliation: IBSC
• Location of specimens: HITBC, IBSC, PE

Zhong, Ying Ying; 种影影 ; Zhǒng Yǐngyǐng
• Location of specimens: TJMP

Chung, Chung Hsin; Zhong, Chong Xin; 仲崇信 ; Zhòng Chóngxìn (1908-2008)
• Research interest: Plant Ecology
• Affiliation: N
• Location of specimens: N

Zhou, Bang Di; 周榜第 ; Zhōu Bǎngdì
• Location of specimens: XZ

Zhou, Bing; 周兵 ; Zhōu Bīng (1978-)
• Research interest: Invasive Plants
• Affiliation: JGSU
• Location of specimens: JGSU

Zhou, Bing Zhen; 周秉珍 ; Zhōu Bǐngzhēn (1936-)
• Research interest: Weeds
• Affiliation: GAUA
• Location of specimens: GAUA

Chou, Chang Hung; 周昌弘 ; Zhōu Chānghóng (1942-)
• Research interest: Plant Ecology
• Affiliation: HAST

Zhou, Cheng Wei; 周呈维 ; Zhōu Chéngwéi (1951-)
• Location of specimens: CTC

Chow, C. L.; 周承烈 ; Zhōu Chénglìe
• Location of specimens: SZ

Zhou, De; 周德 ; Zhōu Dé (1972-)
• Affiliation: ABDC

Zhou, De Ben; 周德本 ; Zhōu Déběn (1938-)
• Affiliation: HNR

Chow, Kew Sheng; Zhou, Gen Sheng; 周根生 ; Zhōu Gēnshēng (1917-)
• Research interest: Plants of N. China
• Affiliation: PE
• Location of specimens: IBSC, PE

Zhou, Guang Yu; Chou, Kuang Yu; Chou, Kuang Yü; 周光裕 ; Zhōu Guāngyù (1924-)
• Location of specimens: JSPC

Zhou, Guang Zhu; 周广柱 ; Zhōu Guǎngzhù (1964-)
• Research interest: Woody Plants
• Affiliation: SYAUF

Zhou, Guo Qi; 周国齐 ; Zhōu Guóqí; 周國齊 (1930-)
• Research interest: Plants of Hubei
• Affiliation: ENS
• Location of specimens: ENS

Zhou, Han Quan; 周汉泉 ; Zhōu Hànquán; 周漢泉 (1920-)
• Affiliation: IBSC

Zhou, He Chang; Chow, Ho Chang; 周鹤昌 ; Zhōu Hèchāng; 周鶴昌
• Location of specimens: WH, N

Zhou, Hong Bin; 周鸿彬 ; Zhōu Hóngbīn
• Location of specimens: IBSC

Zhou, Hua Rong; 周华蓉 ; Zhōu Huáróng (1958-)
• Research interest: Medicinal Plants
• Affiliation: SM

Zhou, Hui Xin; 周惠鑫 ; Zhōu Huìxīn
• Location of specimens: HHBG, HTC, NAS, PE

Zhou, Jian Liang; 周建良 ; Zhōu Jiànliáng (1955-)
• Research interest: Plant Systematics
• Affiliation: HUST

J. Zhong

Zhong, Jian; Zhou, Jian; 周俭 ; Zhōu Jiǎn
• Employment: Chengdu Bureau of Gardening and Greening（成都市园林管理局）
• Research interest: Plants of Sichuan. *Flora sichuanica*

Zhou, Jin Hua; 周锦华 ; Zhōu Jǐnhuá; 周錦華 (1939-1990)
• Research interest: Algae
• Affiliation: MBMCAS

Chow, Jun; 周俊 ; Zhōu Jùn (1932-2020)
• Location of specimens: PE

Zhou, Jun Yi; 周俊义 ; Zhōu Jùnyì (1963-)
• Affiliation: JUJ

Zhou, Kai Long; 周开隆; Zhōu Kāilóng; 周開隆 (1916-)
• Research interest: Rutaceae
• Affiliation: CIT

Zhou, Li Xia; 周丽霞 ; Zhōu Lìxiá (1963-)
• Research interest: Poaceae
• Affiliation: LZAH

Zhou, Li Jun; 周莉君 ; Zhōu Lìjūn
• Location of specimens: SAU

Zhou, Liang Cai; 周良才 ; Zhōu Liángcái
• Affiliation: IBK
• Location of specimens: IBK

Zhou, Lin Bin; 周林滨 ; Zhōu Línbīn
• Location of specimens: SCSG

Zhou, Mou Qin; 周卯勤 ; Zhōu Mǎoqín (1956-)
• Research interest: Medicinal Plants
• Affiliation: IMC
• Location of specimens: IMC

Zhou, Ming Kang; 周明康 ; Zhōu Míngkāng (1944-)
• Research interest: Medicinal Plants
• Affiliation: YXDC

Zhou, Pei Chun; 周沛椿 ; Zhōu Pèichūn
• Location of specimens: IBSC

Zhou, Qiong; 周琼 ; Zhōu Qióng (1967-)
• Research interest: Fabaceae
• Affiliation: GAUA
• Location of specimens: GAUA

Zhou, Shao Li; 周绍莉 ; Zhōu Shàolì; 周紹莉 (1938-)
• Research interest: Plant Anatomy
• Affiliation: SAU

Zhou, Shi Liang; 周世良 ; Zhōu Shìliáng (1961-)
• Research interest: Paeoniaceae, Rosaceae
• Affiliation: PE

Zhou, Shi Qiang; 周世强 ; Zhōu Shìqiáng (1966-)
• Research interest: Plants of Wolong
• Affiliation: WL

Zhou, Shu De; 周树德 ; Zhōu Shùdé
• Affiliation: ANUB
• Location of specimens: ANUB

Zhou, Song Dong; 周颂东 ; Zhōu Sòngdōng (1972-)
• Research interest: Liliaceae
• Affiliation: SZ

Zhou, Tong; 周彤 ; Zhōu Tóng (1987-)
• Research interest: Medicinal Plants
• Affiliation: JMSMC
• Location of specimens: JMSMC

Zhou, Tong Shui; 周铜水 ; Zhōu Tóngshuǐ
• Location of specimens: ACM

Chow, W. C.; 周蔚成 ; Zhōu Wèichéng
• Location of specimens: IBSC, PE

Chou, W. H.; 周文豪 ; Zhōu Wénháo
• Location of specimens: HAST

W. N. Chou

Chou, Wen Neng; 周文能 ; Zhōu Wénnéng (1958-)
• Employment: Museum of Natural Science（自然科学博物馆）
• Research interest: Fungi
• Affiliation: TNM

Zhou, Wen Wei; 周文伟 ; Zhōu Wénwěi
• Research interest: Poaceae
• Affiliation: ZJFI
• Location of specimens: ZJFI

Zhou, Xi Le; 周喜乐 ; Zhōu Xǐlè
• Location of specimens: CSH

Zhou, Ya Fu; 周亚福 ; Zhōu Yàfú (1982-)
• Location of specimens: XBGH

Zhou, Yin; Chou, Yin; 周崟 ; Zhōu Yín
• Location of specimens: CAF

Cheo, Y. C.; Zhou, Ying Chang; 周映昌 ; Zhōu

Yìngchāng
• Location of specimens: NAF, NF, PE

Zhou, You Yuan; 周有元 ; Zhōu Yǒuyuán (1937-)
• Affiliation: EDC

Thow, Y. S.; 周远瑞 ; Zhōu Yuǎnruì; 周遠瑞 (1921-)
• Location of specimens: IBK, IBSC

Zhou, Yun Long; 周云龙 ; Zhōu Yúnlóng; 周雲龍 (1937-)
• Research interest: Algae; Bryophyte
• Affiliation: BNU

Zhou, Yun Long; 周云龙 ; Zhōu Yúnlóng (1955-)
• Affiliation: SN
• Location of specimens: SN

Zhou, Yun De; 周芸德 ; Zhōu Yúndé (1936-)
• Location of specimens: JXAU

Zhou, Zhong Kai; 周仲凯 ; Zhōu Zhòngkǎi (1943-)
• Research interest: Plants of Nanyue
• Affiliation: NYA

Zhou, Zi Lin; 周子林 ; Zhōu Zilín
• Location of specimens: HWA

Zhu, Cai Xia; 朱彩霞 ; Zhū Cǎixiá (1962-)
• Affiliation: IFP

Zhu, Da Hai; 朱大海 ; Zhū Dàhǎi (1977-)
• Location of specimens: HITBC, JJF, PE, WCSBG

Zhu, Dao Guang; 朱道光 ; Zhū Dàoguāng (1972-)
• Research interest: Plants of N. E. China
• Affiliation: HNR
• Location of specimens: HNR

Zhu, De Wei; 朱德蔚 ; Zhū Déwèi (1938-)
• Affiliation: IVF

Chu, Ti Pin; 朱棣彬 ; Zhū Dìbīn
• Location of specimens: HAST

Zhu, Guo Fang; 朱国芳 ; Zhū Guófāng
• Location of specimens: LBG

Chu, K. H.; 朱国兴 ; Zhū Guóxīng; 朱國興
• Location of specimens: IBK, IBSC

H. J. Chu

Chu, Hao Jan; Zhu, Hao Ran; 朱浩然 ; Zhū Hàorán (1904-1999)
• Employment: Department of Biology, Nanjing University（南京大学生物系）
• Research interest: Algae
• Affiliation: N
• Location of specimens: N

Zhu, Huan; 朱欢 ; Zhū Huān (1988-)
• Research interest: Algae
• Affiliation: HBI
• Location of specimens: HBI

H. Z. Zhu

Zhu, Hui Zhong; 朱蕙忠 ; Zhū Huìzhōng (1928-2014)
• Employment: Institute of Hydrobiology, Chinese Academy of Sciences（中国科学院水生生物研究所）
• Research interest: Algae
• Location of specimens: HBI

Zhu, Jun; 朱军 ; Zhū Jūn (1982-)
• Research interest: Medicinal Plants
• Affiliation: XTNM
• Location of specimens: XTNM

Zhu, Jun Yi; 朱俊义 ; Zhū Jùnyì (1966-)
• Affiliation: TONG

Zhu, Li Juan; 朱丽娟 ; Zhū Lìjuān (1962-)
• Research interest: Asparagaceae
• Affiliation: YCE
• Location of specimens: YCE

R. L. Zhu

Zhu, Rui Liang; 朱瑞良 ; Zhū Ruìliáng (1963-)
• Employment: School of Life Sciences, East China Normal University（华东师范大学生命科学学院）
• Research interest: Bryophyte
• Affiliation: HSNU
• Location of specimens: HSNU

Chu, Shih hsiang; 朱石象 ; Zhū Shíxiàng
• Location of specimens: HAST

Chu, S. F.; 朱水法 ; Zhū Shuǐfǎ
• Location of specimens: PE, IBSC

Chu, Tai Ping; Zhu, Tai Ping; 朱太平 ; Zhū Tàipíng (1930-)
• Location of specimens: CDBI, HITBC, IBK, IBSC, KUN, NAS, PE, WUK

Zhu, Xiang Fu; 朱祥福 ; Zhū Xiángfú (1962-)
• Affiliation: JNR

Zhu, Xiao Yun; 朱孝云 ; Zhū Xiàoyún; 朱孝雲 (1937-)

- Research interest: Medicinal Plants
- Affiliation: SHDC

Y. M. Ju

Ju, Yu Ming; 朱宇敏 ; Zhū Yǔmǐn
- Employment: Institute of Plant and Microbial Biology, "Academia Sinica"（中央研究院植物暨微生物学研究所）
- Research interest: Fungi
- Affiliation: HAST

Zhu, Yu Shan; 朱玉善 ; Zhū Yùshàn (1960-)
- Research interest: Scientific Illustrator
- Affiliation: LBG

Zhu, Yuan Fang; 朱元方 ; Zhū Yuánfāng
- Location of specimens: NAS

Chu, C. H.; 朱哲輝 ; Zhū Zhéhuī; 朱哲辉
- Location of specimens: HAST

Chu, Tze Sung; 朱志淞 ; Zhū Zhìsōng (1910-1989)
- Location of specimens: IBSC

Zhu, Dong Li; 祝东立 ; Zhù Dōnglì
- Location of specimens: HBU

Zhu, Ting Cheng; Chu, Ting Cheng; Chu, T'ing Chêng; 祝廷成 ; Zhù Tíngchéng (1926-2011)
- Location of specimens: NENU, PE

Zhuang, Mao Chang; 庄茂长 ; Zhuāng Màozhǎng; 莊茂長 (1916-)
- Research interest: Woody Plants
- Affiliation: SG
- Location of specimens: SG

Chuang, Shiaw Kuang; 莊效光 ; Zhuāng Xiàoguāng; 庄效光
- Location of specimens: HAST

Zong, Xi Ming; 宗希明 ; Zōng Xīmíng
- Location of specimens: JMSMC

Zong, Xiu Hong; 宗秀虹 ; Zōng Xiùhóng
- Location of specimens: SWCTU

Zou, Qi Li; 邹琦丽 ; Zōu Qílì; 鄒琦麗 (1946-)
- Research interest: Plant Anatomy
- Affiliation: IBK

Zu, Yuan Gang; 祖元刚 ; Zǔ Yuángāng (1954-)
- Research interest: Cyperaceae, Fabaceae, Rosaceae
- Affiliation: NEFI

Zuo, Da Xun; Tso, Ta Hsun; 左大勋 ; Zuǒ Dàxūn; 左大勳 (1923-2013)
- Research interest: Rutaceae
- Affiliation: NAS
- Location of specimens: NAS

Q. Zuo

Zuo, Qin; 左勤 ; Zuǒ Qín (1984-)
- Employment: Fairy Lake Botanical Garden, Shenzhen & Chinese Academy of Sciences（深圳市中国科学院仙湖植物园）
- Research interest: Bryophyte
- Affiliation: SZG
- Location of specimens: SZG

Zuo, Xian Dong; 左显东 ; Zuǒ Xiǎndōng; 左顯東 (1940-)
- Research interest: Cupressaceae
- Affiliation: YCP

Zuo, Yun Juan; 左云娟 ; Zuǒ Yúnjuān (1982-)
- Research interest: Celastraceae
- Affiliation: CSH, HITBC
- Location of specimens: CSH

Zuo, Zhen Chang; 左振常 ; Zuǒ Zhèncháng (1933-)
- Research interest: Medicinal Plants
- Affiliation: QDC
- Location of specimens: QDC

Appendix

附 录

Appendix I
Chinese Plant Institutions

Appendix II
Chinese Herbaria

Appendix III
Index of Chinese Plant Taxonomists by Standard Spelling

Appendix IV
Index of Chinese Plant Taxonomists by Romanized Spelling

附录一
中国的植物学研究机构及其名称沿革

附录二
中国的植物标本馆

附录三
中国植物分类学者名称标准拼写索引

附录四
中国植物分类学者名称罗马拼写索引

图字：01-2022-1078号

策划编辑 孟 丽 田 红
责任编辑 孟 丽
装帧设计 姜 磊
责任印制 赵义民
出版发行 高等教育出版社
社 址 北京市西城区德外大街4号
邮政编码 100120
印 刷 北京盛通印刷股份有限公司
开 本 787mm×1092mm 1/16
印 张 28.5
字 数 600千字
购书热线 010-58581118
咨询电话 400-810-0598
网 址 http://www.hep.edu.cn
http://www.hep.com.cn
网上订购 http://www.hepmall.com.cn
http://www.hepmall.com
http://www.hepmall.cn
版 次 2022年5月第1版
印 次 2022年5月第1次印刷
定 价 128.00元

图书在版编目（CIP）数据

中国植物分类学者/杜诚，马金双主编. --北京：高等教育出版社，2022.5
ISBN 978-7-04-056571-3

Ⅰ. ①中… Ⅱ. ①杜… ②马… Ⅲ. ①植物分类学-科学工作者-生平事迹-中国 Ⅳ. ①K826.15

中国版本图书馆CIP数据核字（2021）第153935号

Chinese Plant Taxonomists

中国植物分类学者

ZHONGGUO
ZHIWU FENLEI
XUEZHE

郑重声明

高等教育出版社依法对本书享有专有出版权。任何未经许可的复制、销售行为均违反《中华人民共和国著作权法》，其行为人将承担相应的民事责任和行政责任；构成犯罪的，将被依法追究刑事责任。为了维护市场秩序，保护读者的合法权益，避免读者误用盗版书造成不良后果，我社将配合行政执法部门和司法机关对违法犯罪的单位和个人进行严厉打击。社会各界人士如发现上述侵权行为，希望及时举报，本社将奖励举报有功人员。

反盗版举报电话 （010）58581999 58582371 58582488
反盗版举报传真 （010）82086060
反盗版举报邮箱 dd@hep.com.cn
通信地址 北京市西城区德外大街4号
高等教育出版社法律事务与版权管理部
邮政编码 100120

防伪查询说明

用户购书后刮开封底防伪涂层，利用手机微信等软件扫描二维码，会跳转至防伪查询网页，获得所购图书详细信息。也可将防伪二维码下的20位密码按从左到右、从上到下的顺序发送短信至106695881280，免费查询所购图书真伪。

反盗版短信举报
编辑短信“JB，图书名称，出版社，购买地点”发送至10669588128
防伪客服电话（010）58582300

本书如有缺页、倒页、脱页等质量问题，请到所购图书销售部门联系调换
版权所有，侵权必究
物料号 56571-00